A-Z WEST YOR

C000182918

REFERENCE

Motorway	**M1**
Primary Route	**A61**
A Road	A58
B Road	B6157
Dual Carriageway	
One-way Street Traffic flow on A Roads is indicated by a heavy line on the driver's left.	→
Road Under Construction Opening dates are correct at the time of publication.	
Proposed Road	
Restricted Access	
Pedestrianized Road	
Leeds City Centre Loop Junctions are shown on Large Scale Pages only.	①
Track / Footpath	
Residential Walkway	
Railway	Heritage Station / Station / Level Crossing / Tunnel
Built-up Area	ALMA ST.
Local Authority Boundary	
National Park Boundary	
Posttown Boundary	
Postcode Boundary (within Posttown)	
Map Continuation	80 / Large Scale Centres / 8

Airport	✈
Car Park (selected)	P
Church or Chapel	†
Cycleway (selected)	⬮⬮⬮
Fire Station	■
Hospital	Ⓗ
House Numbers (A & B Roads only)	13 8
Information Centre	🅸
National Grid Reference	430
Park & Ride	King Lane P+R
Police Station	▲
Post Office	★
Toilet: without facilities for the Disabled with facilities for the Disabled Disabled use only	▽ ▽ ▼
Safety Camera with Speed Limit Fixed cameras and long term road works cameras. Symbols do not indicate camera direction.	(40)
Viewpoint	⁂ ✳
Educational Establishment	▭
Hospital or Healthcare Building	▭
Industrial Building	▭
Leisure or Recreational Facility	▭
Place of Interest	▭
Public Building	▭
Shopping Centre or Market	▭
Other Selected Buildings	▭

SCALE

Map Pages 4-9   1:9,051

0	⅛	¼ Mile
0 100 200 300		400 Metres

7 inches (17.78 cm) to 1 mile   11.05 cm to 1 kilometre

Map Pages 10-175   1:19,000

0	¼	½ Mile
0 250 500		750 Metres

3⅓ Inches (8.47 cm) to 1 mile   5.26 cm to 1 kilometre

A-Z AZ AtoZ
registered trade marks of
Geographers' A-Z Map Company Ltd

www./az.co.uk

EDITION 4 2014
Copyright © Geographers' A-Z Map Co. Ltd.
Telephone: 01732 781000 (Enquiries & Trade Sales)
           01732 783422 (Retail Sales)

© Crown copyright and database rights 2013 Ordnance Survey 100017302.

Safety camera information supplied by www.PocketGPSWorld.com.
Speed Camera Location Database Copyright 2013 © PocketGPSWorld.com

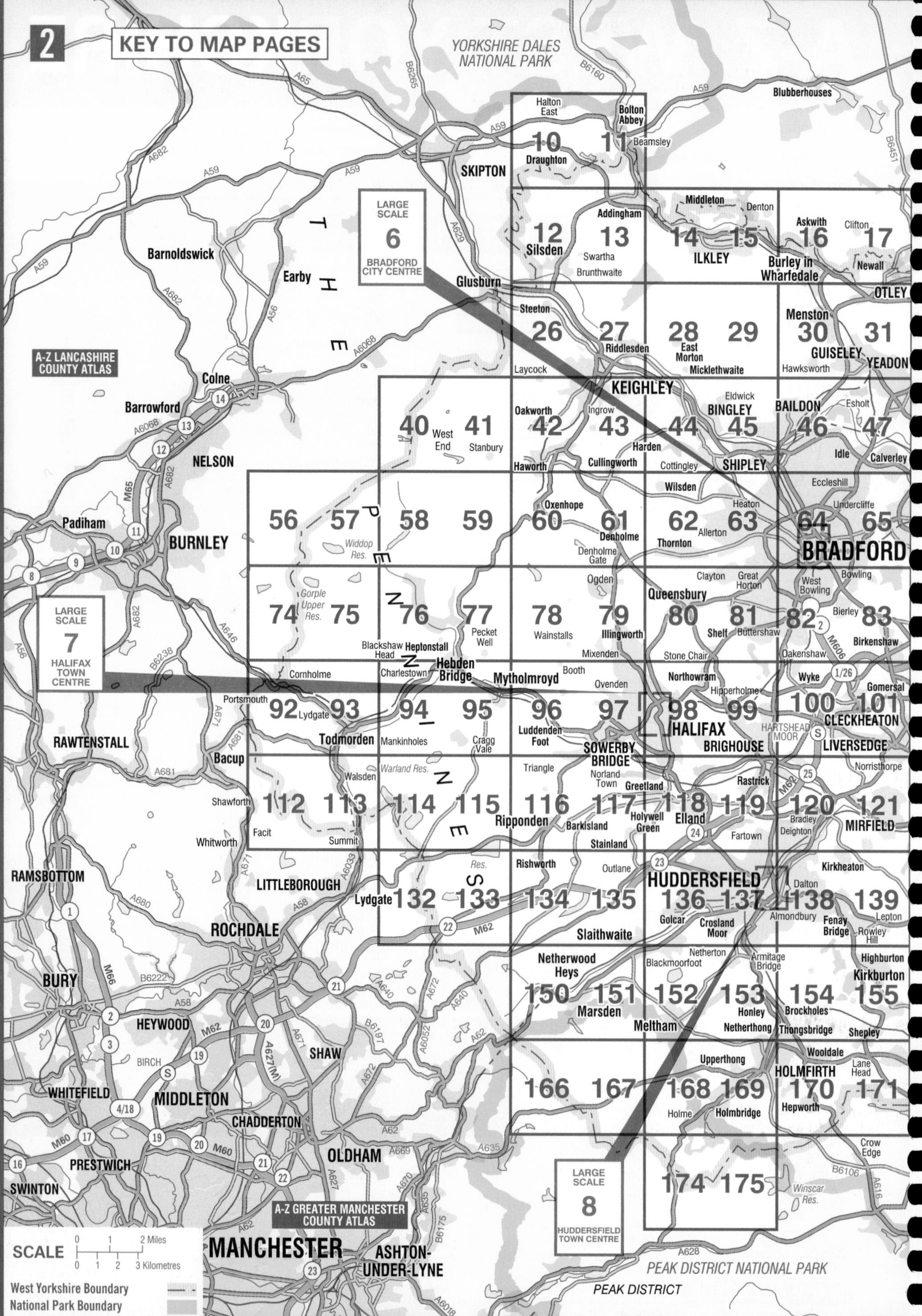

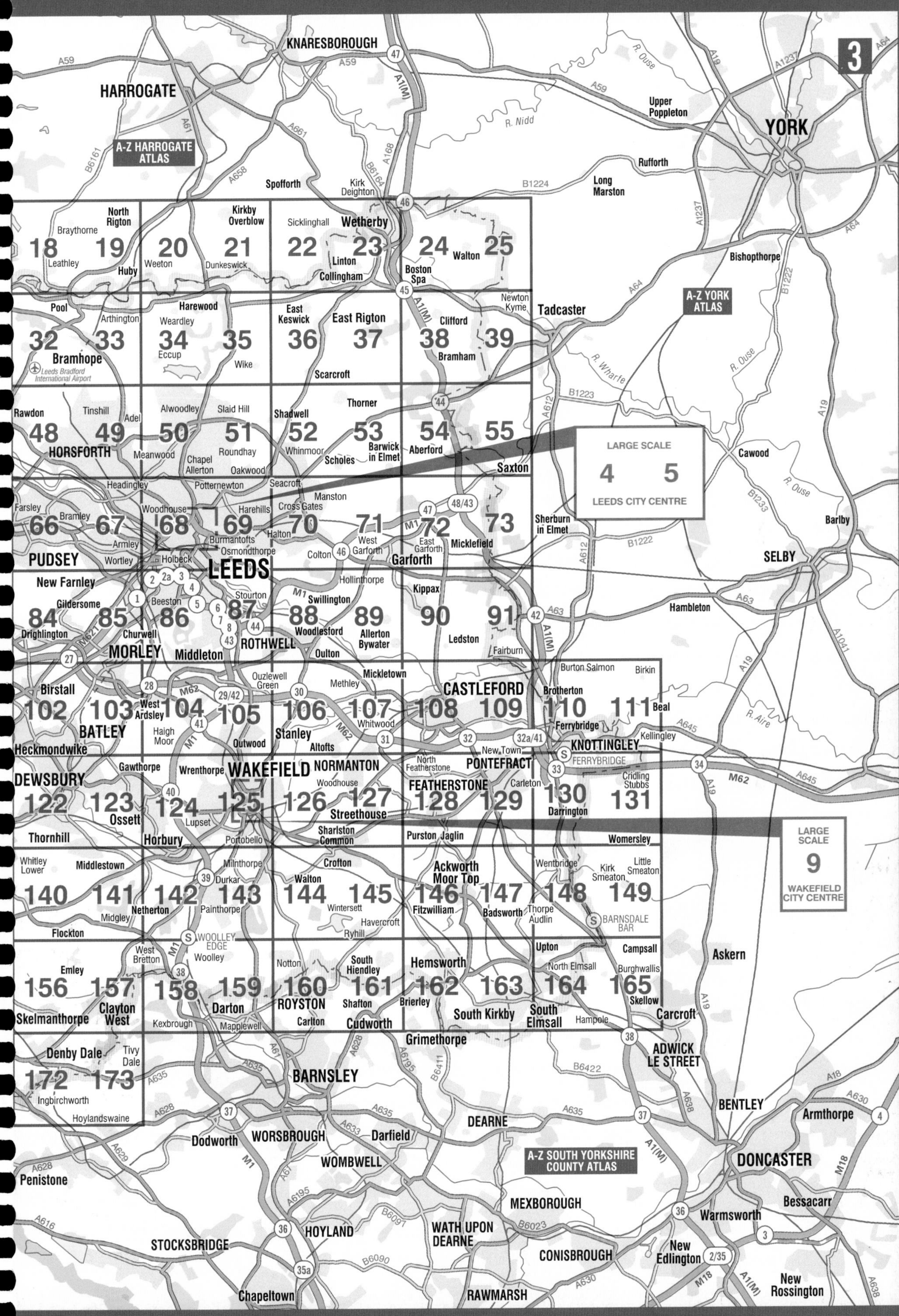
KNARESBOROUGH
HARROGATE
A-Z HARROGATE ATLAS
YORK
Upper Poppleton
Rufforth
Long Marston
Spofforth
Kirk Deighton
Wetherby
Tadcaster
A-Z YORK ATLAS
Bishopthorpe
LARGE SCALE
4 5
LEEDS CITY CENTRE
Cawood
Sherburn in Elmet
Barlby
SELBY
Hambleton
LEEDS
HORSFORTH
PUDSEY
MORLEY
ROTHWELL
CASTLEFORD
KNOTTINGLEY
WAKEFIELD
NORMANTON
PONTEFRACT
FEATHERSTONE
DEWSBURY
BATLEY
Heckmondwike
LARGE SCALE
9
WAKEFIELD CITY CENTRE
Askern
Carcroft
ADWICK LE STREET
BARNSLEY
BENTLEY
Armthorpe
DONCASTER
DEARNE
A-Z SOUTH YORKSHIRE COUNTY ATLAS
Penistone
WORSBROUGH
WOMBWELL
MEXBOROUGH
Bessacarr
Warmsworth
STOCKSBRIDGE
HOYLAND
WATH UPON DEARNE
CONISBROUGH
New Edlington
Chapeltown
RAWMARSH
New Rossington
18 19 20 21 22 23 24 25
32 33 34 35 36 37 38 39
48 49 50 51 52 53 54 55
66 67 68 69 70 71 72 73
84 85 86 87 88 89 90 91
102 103 104 105 106 107 108 109 110 111
122 123 124 125 126 127 128 129 130 131
140 141 142 143 144 145 146 147 148 149
156 157 158 159 160 161 162 163 164 165
172 173

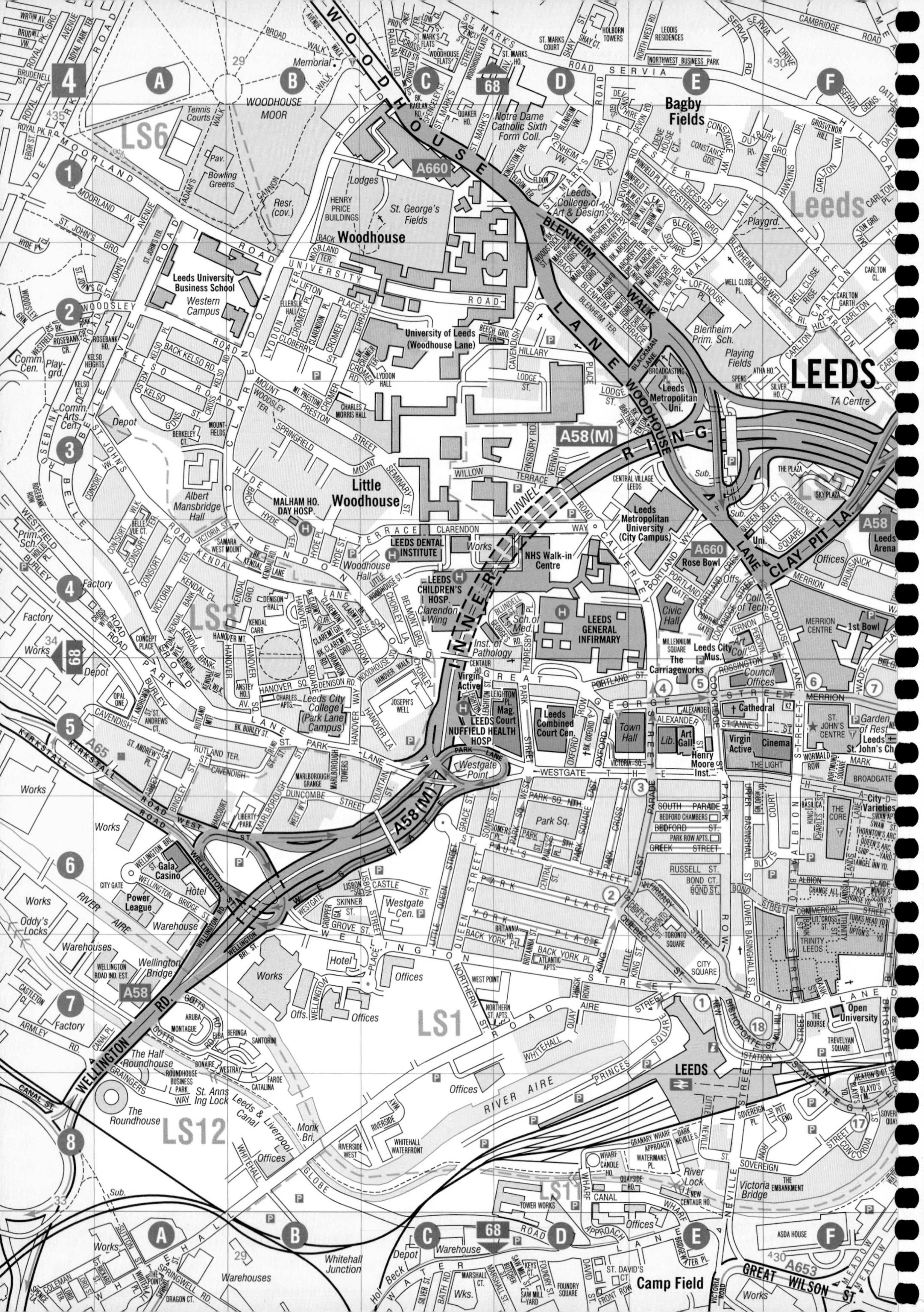

4
A
B
C
D
E
F
1
2
3
4
5
6
7
8
WOODHOUSE LANE
WOODHOUSE MOOR
LS6
LS3
LS1
LS12
LS11
LS2
Leeds
LEEDS
Woodhouse
Little Woodhouse
Bagby Fields
Camp Field
A660
A58(M)
A58
A65
A653
68
INNER RING ROAD
CLAY PIT LA.
CAMBRIDGE ROAD
SERVIA ROAD
MOORLAND ROAD
UNIVERSITY ROAD
CLARENDON ROAD
PARK LANE
KIRKSTALL ROAD
WELLINGTON ROAD
WELLINGTON STREET
WESTGATE
THE HEADROW
BOAR LANE
PARK ROW
CALVERLEY ST.
GREAT GEORGE STREET
BURLEY ROAD
BELLE VUE ROAD
HYDE PARK ROAD
BLENHEIM WALK
BLACKMAN LANE
GREAT WILSON ST.
WATER LANE
Notre Dame Catholic Sixth Form Coll.
Leeds College of Art & Design
Leeds University Business School
Western Campus
University of Leeds (Woodhouse Lane)
St. George's Fields
HENRY PRICE BUILDINGS
Leeds Metropolitan Uni.
Leeds Metropolitan University (City Campus)
Blenheim Prim. Sch.
Playing Fields
TA Centre
Leeds Arena
LEEDS DENTAL INSTITUTE
LEEDS CHILDREN'S HOSP.
NHS Walk-in Centre
LEEDS GENERAL INFIRMARY
Inst. of Pathology
NUFFIELD HEALTH HOSP.
Virgin Active
Mag. Court
Leeds Combined Court Cen.
Town Hall
Lib.
Art Gall.
Henry Moore Inst.
Civic Hall
Rose Bowl
Millennium Square
The Carriageworks
Leeds City Mus.
Cathedral
MERRION CENTRE
1st Bowl
Cinema
THE LIGHT
City Varieties
TRINITY LEEDS
Open University
Leeds City College (Park Lane Campus)
Albert Mansbridge Hall
MALHAM HO. DAY HOSP.
Westgate Point
Park Sq.
CITY SQUARE
LEEDS
Gala Casino
Power League
River Aire
Wellington Bridge
The Half Roundhouse
The Roundhouse
St. Anns Ing Lock
Leeds & Liverpool Canal
Monk Bri.
Whitehall Junction
Victoria Bridge
River Lock
ASDA HOUSE
Works
Factory
Depot
Offices
Warehouses
Oddy's Locks

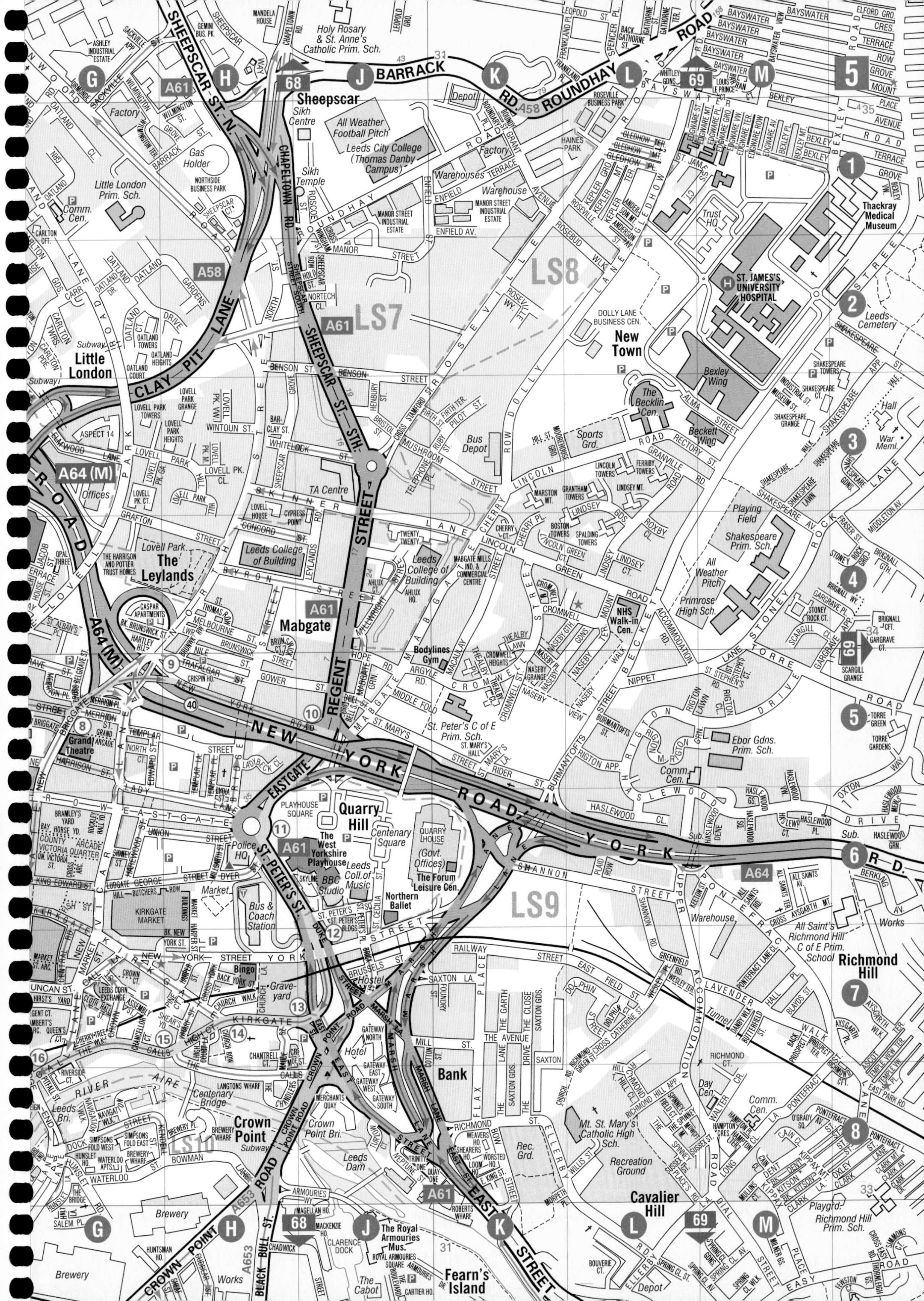
Holy Rosary & St. Anne's Catholic Prim. Sch.
Sheepscar
BARRACK
ROUNDHAY ROAD
BAYSWATER
68
69
A61
A58
A64 (M)
A64
A653
Factory
Sikh Centre
All Weather Football Pitch
Leeds City College (Thomas Danby Campus)
Gas Holder
Sikh Temple
Warehouses
Warehouse
Little London Prim. Sch.
Comm. Cen.
NORTHSIDE BUSINESS PARK
MANOR STREET INDUSTRIAL ESTATE
ENFIELD AV.
Trust HQ
Thackray Medical Museum
ST. JAMES'S UNIVERSITY HOSPITAL
LS8
LS7
LS9
Leeds Cemetery
DOLLY LANE BUSINESS CEN.
New Town
Bexley Wing
The Becklin Cen.
Beckett Wing
Little London
CLAY PIT LANE
SHEEPSCAR ST. STH.
Bus Depot
Sports Grd.
Hall
War Meml.
Playing Field
Shakespeare Prim. Sch.
All Weather Pitch
Primrose High Sch.
Offices
TA Centre
Lovell Park
The Leylands
Leeds College of Building
Mabgate
REGENT STREET
Bodylines Gym
NHS Walk-in Cen.
St. Peter's C of E Prim. Sch.
NEW YORK ROAD
Grand Theatre
Ebor Gdns. Prim. Sch.
Comm. Cen.
Quarry Hill
Centenary Square
QUARRY HOUSE (Govt. Offices)
The West Yorkshire Playhouse
Leeds Coll. of Music
BBC Studio
The Forum Leisure Cen.
Northern Ballet
Police HQ
Market
KIRKGATE MARKET
Bus & Coach Station
Bingo
Graveyard
Hostel
Hotel
Bank
Warehouse
All Saint's Richmond Hill C of E Prim. School
Works
Richmond Hill
Tunnel
Day Cen.
Comm. Cen.
Mt. St. Mary's Catholic High Sch.
Rec. Grd.
Recreation Ground
Centenary Bridge
RIVER AIRE
Crown Point
Crown Point Bri.
Leeds Dam
LS10
Brewery
Cavalier Hill
The Royal Armouries Mus.
Fearn's Island
The Cabot
Depot
Playgrd.
Richmond Hill Prim. Sch.
Works
EAST STREET
CROWN POINT ROAD
BLACK BULL ST.
G
H
J
K
L
M
1
2
3
4
5
6
7
8

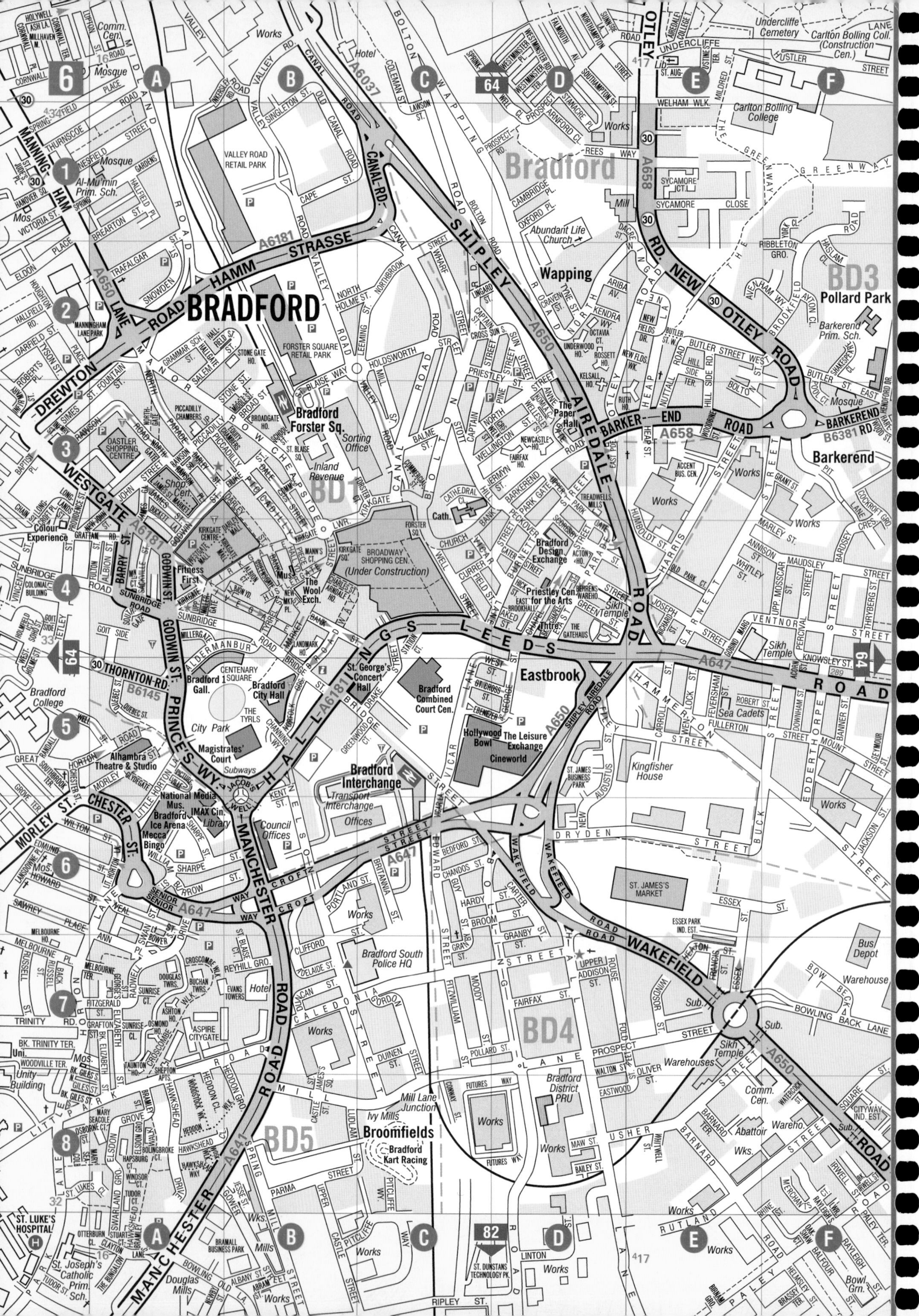

6
A
B
C
D
E
F
1
2
3
4
5
6
7
8
64
82
BRADFORD
Bradford
BD1
BD3
BD4
BD5
Wapping
Barkerend
Pollard Park
Eastbrook
Broomfields
Undercliffe Cemetery
Carlton Bolling Coll. (Construction Cen.)
Carlton Bolling College
VALLEY ROAD RETAIL PARK
FORSTER SQUARE RETAIL PARK
Bradford Forster Sq.
Sorting Office
Inland Revenue
Cath.
OASTLER SHOPPING CENTRE
KIRKGATE CENTRE
BROADWAY SHOPPING CEN. (Under Construction)
The Wool Exch.
Fitness First
Bradford Design Exchange
Priestley Cen. for the Arts
Sikh Temple
Bradford 1 Gall.
CENTENARY SQUARE
Bradford City Hall
City Park
Magistrates' Court
St. George's Concert Hall
Bradford Combined Court Cen.
Hollywood Bowl
The Leisure Exchange
Cineworld
Bradford Interchange
Transport Interchange Offices
Council Offices
Alhambra Theatre & Studio
National Media Mus.
IMAX Cin.
Bradford Ice Arena
Library
Mecca Bingo
Bradford College
Colour Experience
Kingfisher House
ST. JAMES'S MARKET
Sea Cadets
Bus Depot
Warehouse
Bradford South Police HQ
Bradford District PRU
Bradford Kart Racing
Ivy Mills
Mill Lane Junction
ST. LUKE'S HOSPITAL
St. Joseph's Catholic Prim. Sch.
Douglas Mills
ST. DUNSTANS TECHNOLOGY PK.
Abundant Life Church
Al-Mu'min Prim. Sch.
Barkerend Prim. Sch.
Abattoir
Comm. Cen.
Mosque
Works
Mill
Hotel
A650
A6181
A6037
A658
A647
A641
B6145
B6381
MANNINGHAM LANE
HAMM STRASSE
CANAL RD.
SHIPLEY AIREDALE ROAD
OTLEY ROAD
NEW OTLEY RD.
BARKEREND ROAD
LEEDS ROAD
WAKEFIELD ROAD
MANCHESTER ROAD
PRINCE'S WAY
GODWIN ST.
WESTGATE
DREWTON ROAD
THORNTON RD.
MORLEY ST.
CHESTER ST.
HALL INGS
CHEAPSIDE
KIRKGATE
BOLTON ROAD
VALLEY ROAD
WAPPING ROAD
HARRIS STREET
CROFT STREET
BOWLING BACK LANE
PARK LANE
MILL LANE
RIPLEY ST.

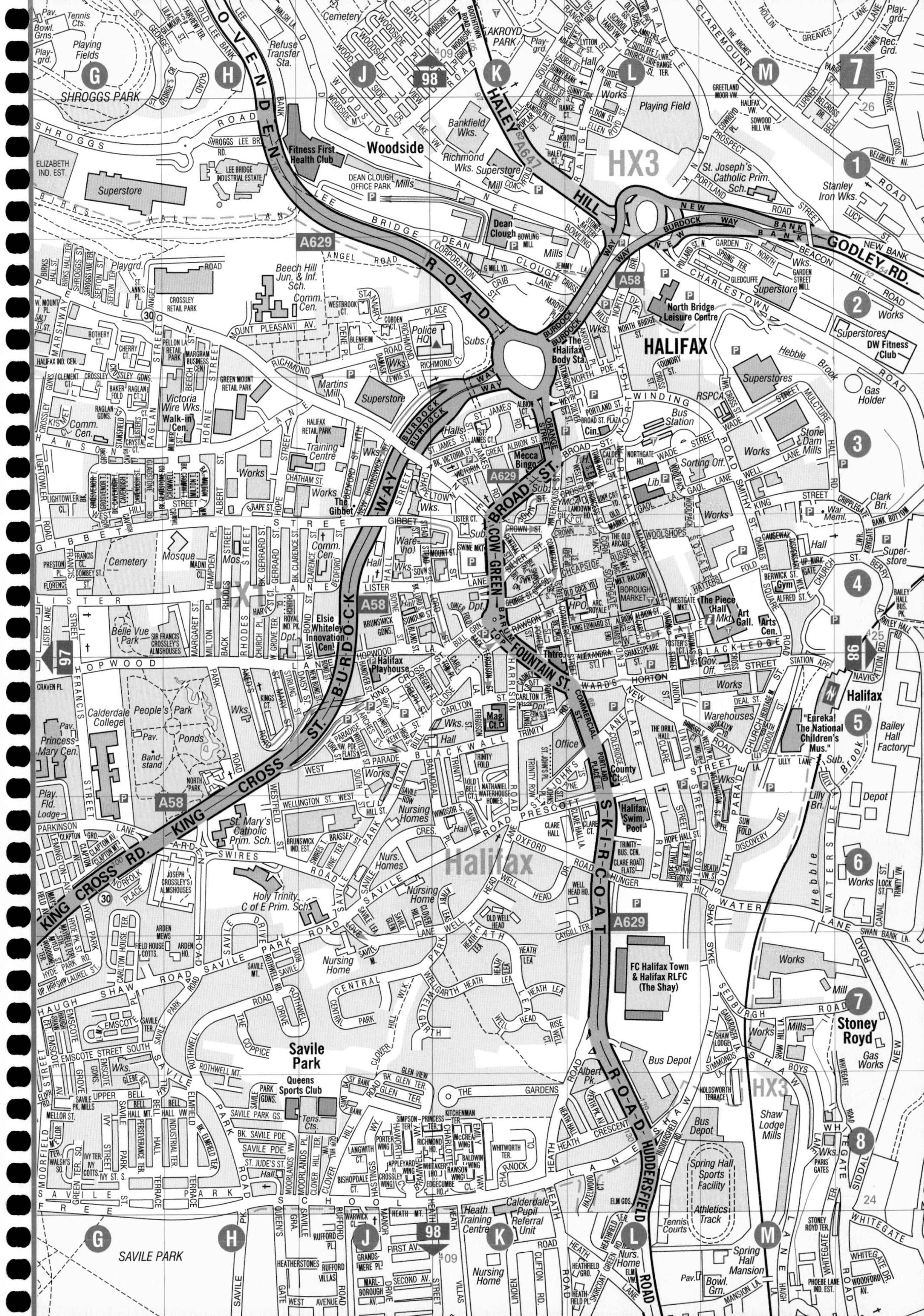

HALIFAX
Halifax
HX1
HX3
Woodside
Savile Park
Stoney Royd
SHROGGS PARK
SAVILE PARK
G
H
J
K
L
M
1
2
3
4
5
6
7
8
98
97
99
A629
A58
A647
OVENDEN
BURDOCK WAY
BURDOCK
KING CROSS RD.
KING CROSS
BROAD ST.
COW GREEN
FOUNTAIN ST.
SKIRCOAT ROAD
HUDDERSFIELD ROAD
GODLEY RD.
GIBBET STREET
LEE BRIDGE
DEAN CLOUGH
HALEY HILL
NEW ROAD
CHARLESTOWN ROAD
HOPWOOD LANE
LISTER LANE
BLACKWALL
PRESCOTT ST.
WARD'S END
HORTON ST.
WATER LANE
SHAW HILL
SAVILE ROAD
SAVILE PARK ROAD
HEATH ROAD
FREE SCHOOL LANE
Fitness First Health Club
Superstore
Superstores
Dean Clough
Mecca Bingo
North Bridge Leisure Centre
The Halifax Body Sta.
Police HQ
Halifax Playhouse
Elsie Whiteley Innovation Cen.
The Piece Hall
Art Gall.
Arts Cen.
Borough Market
Bus Station
"Eureka! The National Children's Mus."
Halifax
Calderdale College
People's Park
Princess Mary Cen.
St. Mary's Catholic Prim. Sch.
Holy Trinity C of E Prim. Sch.
Halifax Swim. Pool
County Ct.
FC Halifax Town & Halifax RLFC (The Shay)
Bus Depot
Queens Sports Club
Spring Hall Sports Facility
Athletics Track
Spring Hall Mansion
Calderdale Pupil Referral Unit
Heath Training Centre
Shaw Lodge Mills
Gas Works
Bailey Hall Factory
DW Fitness Club
Stone Dam Mills
St. Joseph's Catholic Prim. Sch.
Beech Hill Jun. & Inf. Sch.
Victoria Wire Wks.
Cemetery
Mosque
Belle Vue Park
Nursing Home

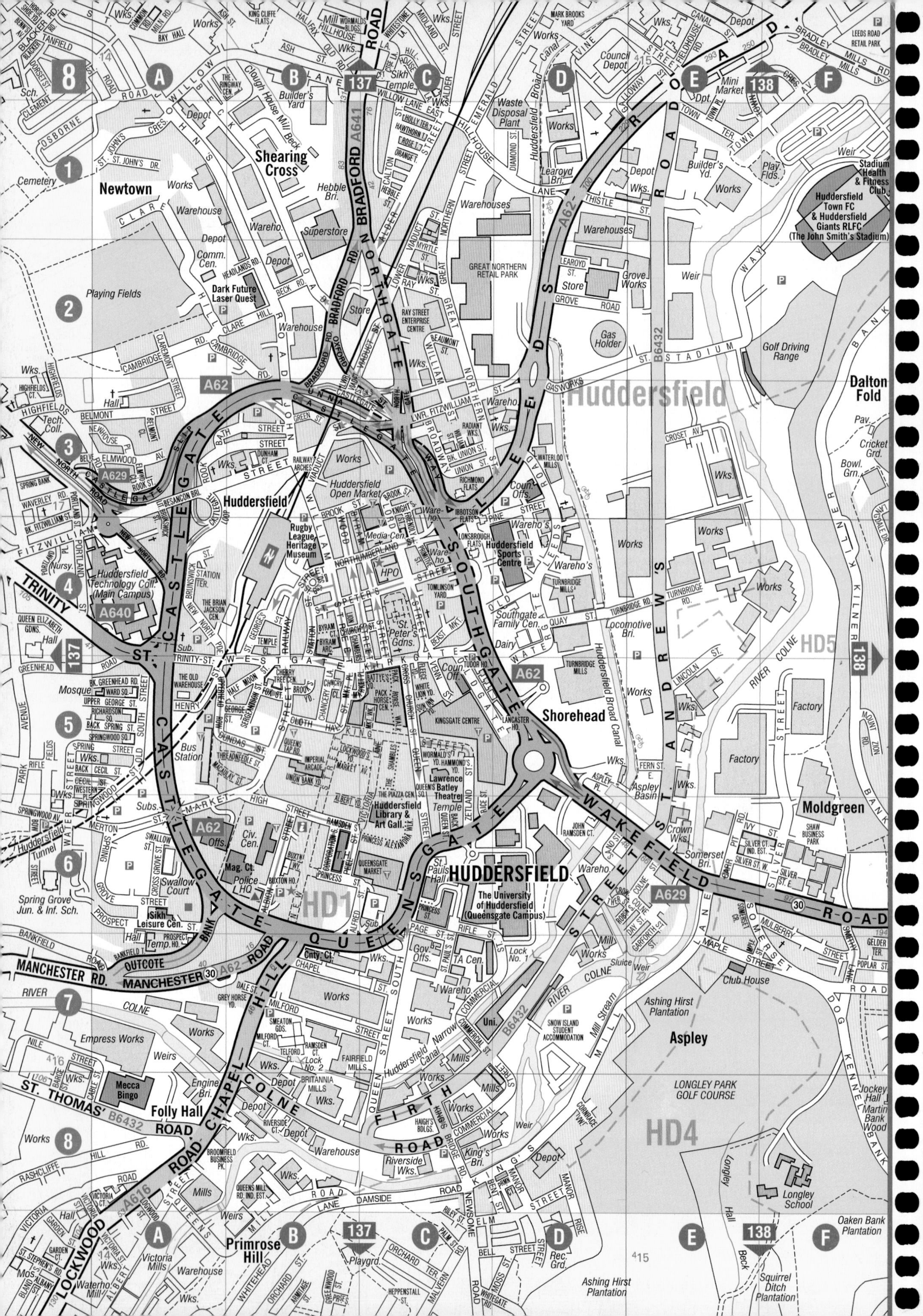
8
A
B
C
D
E
F
137
138
1
2
3
4
5
6
7
8
HD1
HD4
HD5
Newtown
Shearing Cross
Huddersfield
HUDDERSFIELD
Shorehead
Dalton Fold
Moldgreen
Aspley
Folly Hall
Primrose Hill
Lockwood
Cemetery
Playing Fields
Dark Future Laser Quest
Comm. Cen.
Superstore
GREAT NORTHERN RETAIL PARK
RAY STREET ENTERPRISE CENTRE
Waste Disposal Plant
Council Depot
Gas Holder
Golf Driving Range
Huddersfield Town FC & Huddersfield Giants RLFC (The John Smith's Stadium)
Stadium Health & Fitness Club
Cricket Grd.
Bowl. Grn.
Huddersfield Open Market
Rugby League Heritage Museum
Media Cen.
HPO
Huddersfield Sports Centre
Huddersfield Technology Coll. (Main Campus)
Tech. Coll.
Southgate Family Cen.
Locomotive Bri.
St. Peter's Gdns.
KINGSGATE CENTRE
Lawrence Batley Theatre
Huddersfield Library & Art Gall.
QUEENSGATE MARKET
St. Pauls Hall
The University of Huddersfield (Queensgate Campus)
Civ. Cen.
Mag. Ct.
Police HQ
Swallow Court
Spring Grove Jun. & Inf. Sch.
Sikh Leisure Cen.
Bus Station
Mosque
Empress Works
Mecca Bingo
SNOW ISLAND STUDENT ACCOMMODATION
Ashing Hirst Plantation
LONGLEY PARK GOLF COURSE
Longley School
Oaken Bank Plantation
Squirrel Ditch Plantation
Club House
SHAW BUSINESS PARK
Huddersfield Broad Canal
Huddersfield Narrow Canal
RIVER COLNE
Aspley Basin
Lock No. 1
Lock No. 2
Victoria Mills
Waterho. Mill
Jockey Hall
Martin Bank Wood
A62
A629
A640
A641
A616
B6432
CASTLEGATE
SOUTHGATE
QUEENSGATE
NORTHGATE
LEEDS ROAD
WAKEFIELD ROAD
BRADFORD ROAD
MANCHESTER RD.
TRINITY ST.
WESTGATE
KIRKGATE
ST. ANDREW'S ROAD
CHAPEL HILL
FIRTH ROAD
ST. THOMAS' ROAD
STADIUM WAY
KILNER BANK
DOG KENNEL BANK
415
416

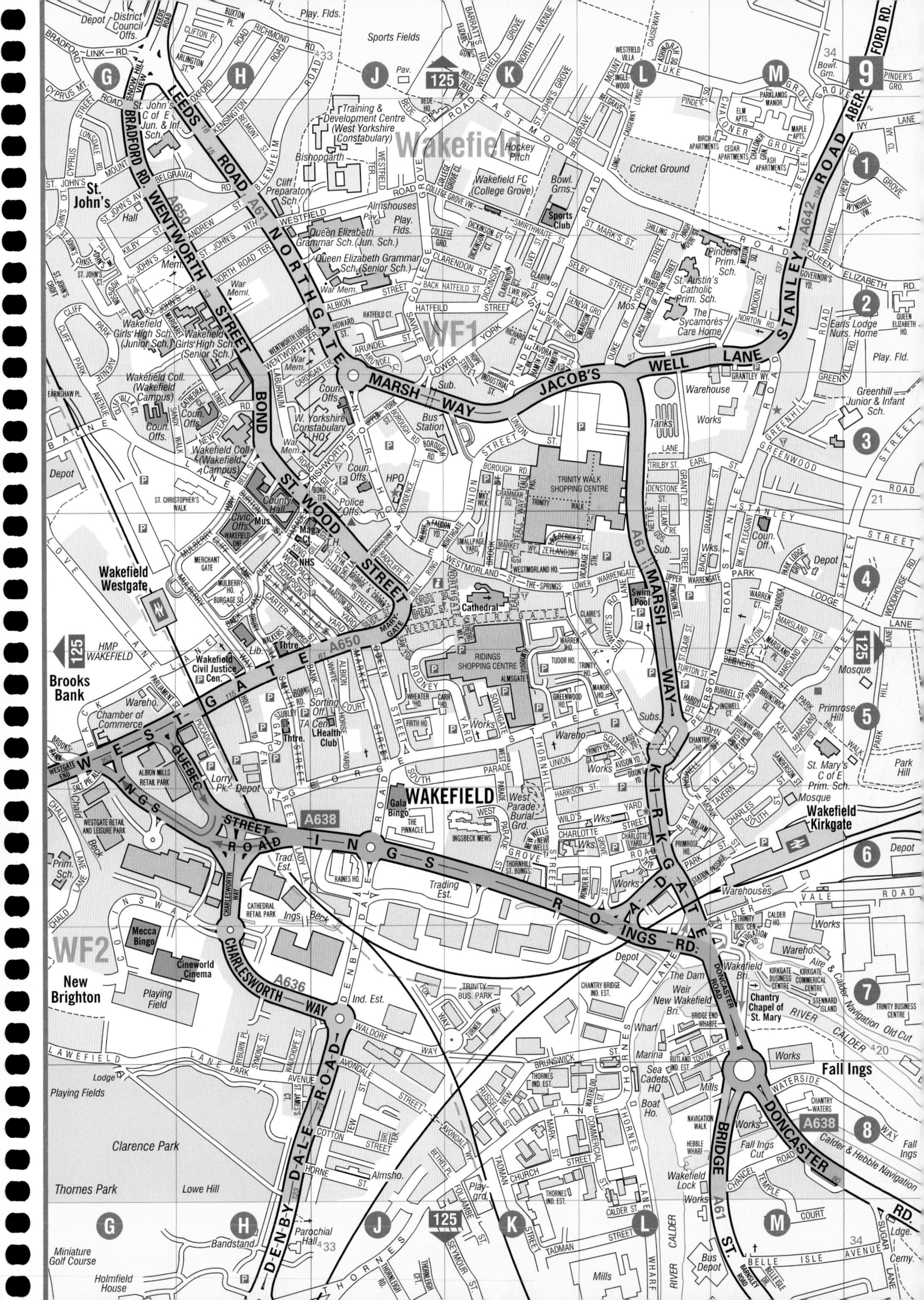

Wakefield
WAKEFIELD
WF1
WF2
St. John's
Wakefield Westgate
Wakefield Kirkgate
Brooks Bank
New Brighton
Fall Ings
Clarence Park
Thornes Park
Lowe Hill
Playing Fields
Sports Fields
Cricket Ground
Trinity Walk Shopping Centre
Ridings Shopping Centre
Cathedral
Queen Elizabeth Grammar Sch. (Jun. Sch.)
Queen Elizabeth Grammar Sch. (Senior Sch.)
Wakefield Girls' High Sch. (Junior Sch.)
Wakefield Girls' High Sch. (Senior Sch.)
Wakefield Coll. (Wakefield Campus)
Wakefield FC (College Grove)
Training & Development Centre (West Yorkshire Constabulary)
W. Yorkshire Constabulary HQ
Wakefield Civil Justice Cen.
Chamber of Commerce
Mecca Bingo
Cineworld Cinema
Gala Bingo
Chantry Chapel of St. Mary
St. Mary's C of E Prim. Sch.
Greenhill Junior & Infant Sch.
Earls Lodge Nurs. Home
St. Austin's Catholic Prim. Sch.
The Sycamores Care Home
Pinders Prim. Sch.
Aire & Calder Navigation
Calder & Hebble Navigation
River Calder
Fall Ings Cut
Wakefield Lock
HMP Wakefield
Primrose Hill
Park Hill
Miniature Golf Course
Holmfield House
WESTGATE
KIRKGATE
NORTHGATE
MARSH WAY
JACOB'S WELL LANE
INGS ROAD
DONCASTER ROAD
DENBY DALE ROAD
CHARLESWORTH WAY
LEEDS ROAD
BRADFORD RD.
WENTWORTH STREET
BOND STREET
ST. JOHN'S SQ.
STANLEY ROAD
ABERFORD RD.
QUEEN ELIZABETH ROAD
A61
A638
A636
A642
A650
125
9

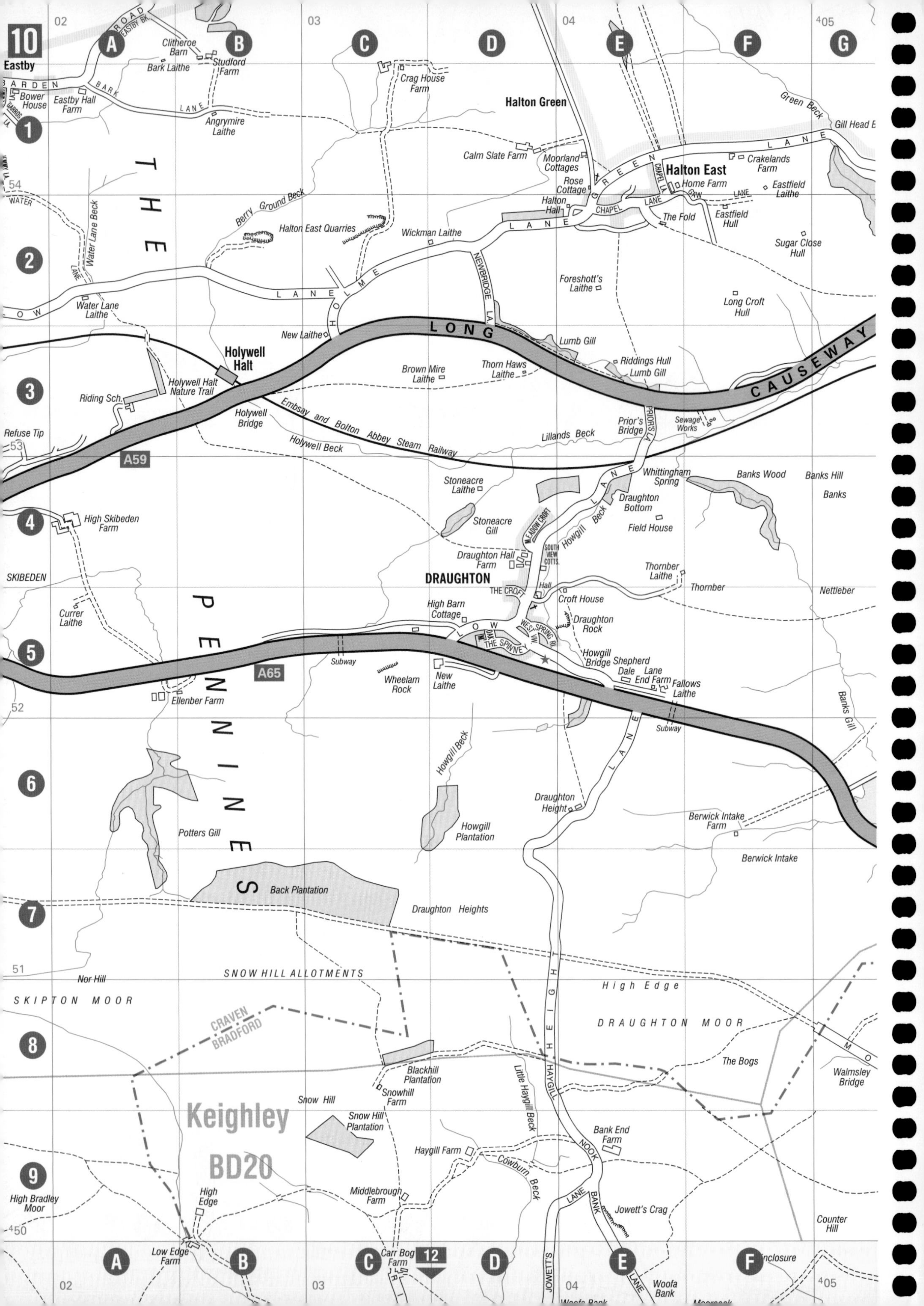
Eastby
Clitheroe Barn
Studford Farm
Bark Laithe
Bower House
Eastby Hall Farm
Angrymire Laithe
Crag House Farm
Halton Green
Calm Slate Farm
Moorland Cottages
Rose Cottage
Halton Hall
Halton East
Home Farm
Crakelands Farm
Eastfield Laithe
Eastfield Hull
The Fold
Sugar Close Hull
Green Beck
Gill Head
THE PENNINES
Berry Ground Beck
Halton East Quarries
Wickman Laithe
Water Lane Beck
Water Lane Laithe
Foreshott's Laithe
Long Croft Hull
New Laithe
LONG CAUSEWAY
Holywell Halt
Holywell Halt Nature Trail
Riding Sch.
Brown Mire Laithe
Thorn Haws Laithe
Lumb Gill
Riddings Hull
Refuse Tip
Holywell Bridge
Embsay and Bolton Abbey Steam Railway
Holywell Beck
A59
Lillands Beck
Prior's Bridge
Sewage Works
Stoneacre Laithe
Stoneacre Gill
Whittingham Spring
Banks Wood
Banks Hill
Banks
High Skibeden Farm
Draughton Bottom
Field House
SKIBEDEN
Draughton Hall Farm
DRAUGHTON
Thornber Laithe
Thornber
Nettleber
Currer Laithe
High Barn Cottage
Croft House
Draughton Rock
Howgill Bridge
Shepherd Dale Lane End Farm
Fallows Laithe
Subway
Wheelam Rock
New Laithe
A65
Ellenber Farm
Banks Gill
Howgill Beck
Draughton Height
Berwick Intake Farm
Howgill Plantation
Potters Gill
Berwick Intake
Back Plantation
Draughton Heights
SNOW HILL ALLOTMENTS
Nor Hill
SKIPTON MOOR
High Edge
DRAUGHTON MOOR
CRAVEN
BRADFORD
Blackhill Plantation
Snowhill Farm
The Bogs
Walmsley Bridge
Snow Hill
Snow Hill Plantation
Keighley
BD20
Little Haygill Beck
Bank End Farm
Haygill Farm
Cowburn Beck
High Bradley Moor
High Edge
Middlebrough Farm
Jowett's Crag
Counter Hill
Low Edge Farm
Carr Bog Farm
12
Inclosure
Woofa Bank

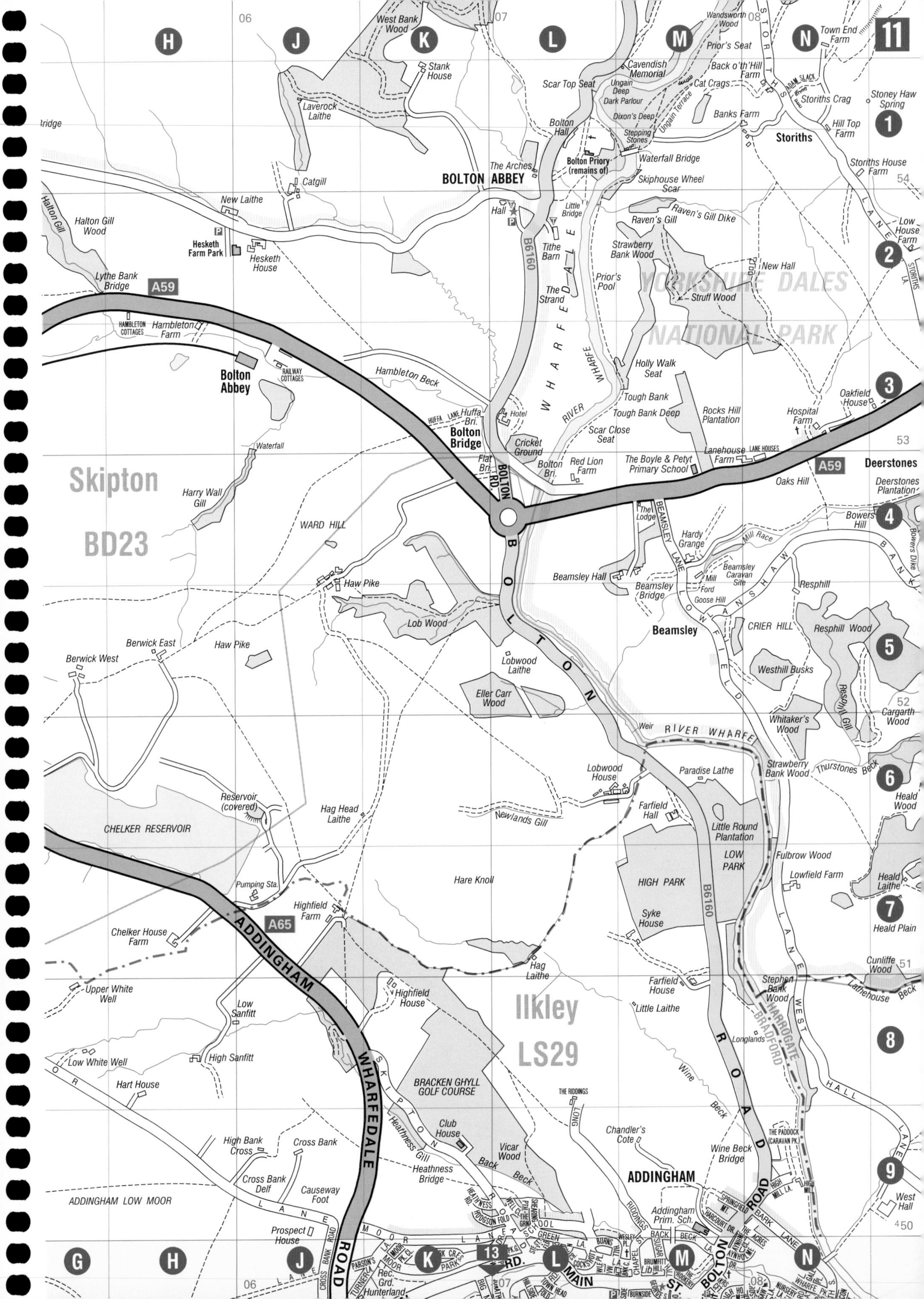

11
H
J
K
L
M
N
06
07
08
West Bank Wood
Stank House
Wandsworth Wood
Prior's Seat
Town End Farm
Cavendish Memorial
Back o'th'Hill Farm
Scar Top Seat
Ungain Deep
Dark Parlour
Cat Crags
Storiths Crag
Stoney Haw Spring
Laverock Laithe
Dixon's Deep
Ungain Terrace
Banks Farm
Hill Top Farm
Bridge
Bolton Hall
Stepping Stones
Storiths
Bolton Priory (remains of)
Waterfall Bridge
The Arches
BOLTON ABBEY
Catgill
Skiphouse Wheel Scar
Storiths House Farm
New Laithe
Little Bridge
Halton Gill
Halton Gill Wood
Hall
Raven's Gill
Raven's Gill Dike
Low House Farm
Hesketh Farm Park
Hesketh House
Tithe Barn
B6160
Strawberry Bank Wood
New Hall
Lythe Bank Bridge
A59
Prior's Pool
The Strand
YORKSHIRE DALES
NATIONAL PARK
Stuff Wood
HAMBLETON COTTAGES
Hambleton Farm
Bolton Abbey
RAILWAY COTTAGES
Hambleton Beck
WHARFEDALE
RIVER WHARFE
Holly Walk Seat
Tough Bank
Tough Bank Deep
Rocks Hill Plantation
Oakfield House
Hospital Farm
HUFFA LANE
Huffa Bri.
Bolton Bridge
Hotel
Cricket Ground
Scar Close Seat
Waterfall
Lanehouse Farm
LANE HOUSES
Skipton
Flat Bri.
BOLTON RD.
Bolton Bri.
Red Lion Farm
The Boyle & Petyt Primary School
Deerstones
Deerstones Plantation
Oaks Hill
Harry Wall Gill
The Lodge
Bowers Hill
WARD HILL
BD23
BEAMSLEY LANE
Hardy Grange
Mill Race
Bowers Dike
BANK
Beamsley Hall
Beamsley Caravan Site
Mill
Ford
Goose Hill
Beamsley Bridge
LANSHAW
Resphill
Haw Pike
Lob Wood
BOLTON
LOWFIELD
Beamsley
CRIER HILL
Resphill Wood
Berwick East
Berwick West
Lobwood Laithe
Westhill Busks
Resphill Gill
Eller Carr Wood
Cargarth Wood
Weir
RIVER WHARFE
Whitaker's Wood
Strawberry Bank Wood
Thurstones Beck
Lobwood House
Paradise Lathe
Heald Wood
Reservoir (covered)
Hag Head Laithe
Newlands Gill
Farfield Hall
CHELKER RESERVOIR
Little Round Plantation
LOW PARK
Fulbrow Wood
Hare Knoll
HIGH PARK
Lowfield Farm
Heald Laithe
Pumping Sta.
Highfield Farm
Syke House
Heald Plain
Chelker House Farm
A65
ADDINGHAM
Hag Laithe
Cunliffe Wood
Farfield House
Stephen Bank Wood
Lathehouse Beck
Upper White Well
Highfield House
Ilkley
Low Sanfitt
Little Laithe
HARROGATE
BRADFORD
WEST LANE
Longlands
LS29
High Sanfitt
ROAD
Low White Well
Wine Beck
Hart House
BRACKEN GHYLL GOLF COURSE
THE RIDDINGS
HALL
SKIPTON
Heathness Gill
Club House
LONG
Chandler's Cote
THE PADDOCK CARAVAN PK.
High Bank Cross
Cross Bank
Vicar Wood
Wine Beck Bridge
Cross Bank Delf
Causeway Foot
Heathness Bridge
Back Beck
ADDINGHAM
ADDINGHAM LOW MOOR
LANE
WHARFEDALE ROAD
SPRINGFIELD MT.
BARK LANE
HIGH MILL
West Hall
Addingham Prim. Sch.
HARCOURT DR.
THE ACRES
Prospect House
MOOR LANE
SCHOOL
G
13
MAIN ST.
Rec. Grd.
Hunterland
CROSS BANK ROAD
PARSON'S LA.
MOOR PK. CL.
TURNER'S LA.
HILLSIDE
TOWN HEAD
BURNSIDE
WHARFE PK.
NURSERY
1
2
3
4
5
6
7
8
9
54
53
52
51
4150

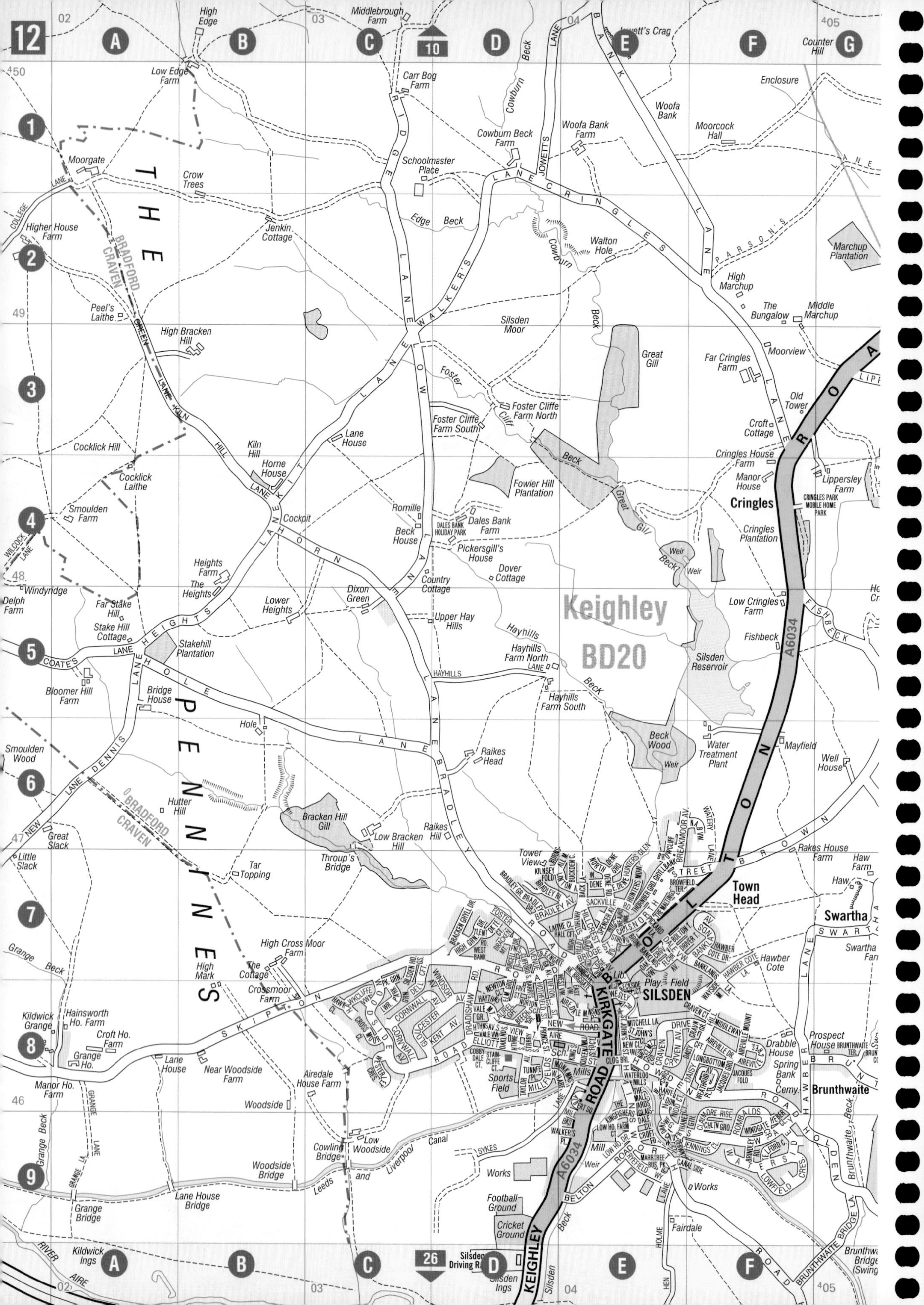

Keighley
BD20
THE PENNINES
SILSDEN
Cringles
Town Head
Swartha
Brunthwaite
Silsden Moor
Silsden Reservoir
Great Gill
Beck Wood
Water Treatment Plant
Moorgate
Crow Trees
Higher House Farm
Jenkin Cottage
Peel's Laithe
High Bracken Hill
Cocklick Hill
Cocklick Laithe
Smoulden Farm
Kiln Hill
Horne House
Cockpit
Heights Farm
The Heights
Windyridge
Delph Farm
Far Stake Hill
Stake Hill Cottage
Stakehill Plantation
Bloomer Hill Farm
Bridge House
Hole
Smoulden Wood
Hutter Hill
Great Slack
Little Slack
Tar Topping
Bracken Hill Gill
Low Bracken Hill
Throup's Bridge
Raikes Hill
Raikes Head
High Cross Moor Farm
High Mark
The Cottage
Crossmoor Farm
Kildwick Grange
Hainsworth Ho. Farm
Croft Ho. Farm
Grange Ho.
Lane House
Near Woodside Farm
Manor Ho. Farm
Woodside
Airedale House Farm
Low Woodside
Cowling Bridge
Woodside Bridge
Lane House Bridge
Grange Bridge
Kildwick Ings
Leeds and Liverpool Canal
River Aire
Silsden Driving Range
Silsden Ings
Works
Football Ground
Cricket Ground
Fairdale
Sports Field
Mills
Mill
Weir
High Edge
Low Edge Farm
Middlebrough Farm
Carr Bog Farm
Schoolmaster Place
Edge Beck
Cowburn Beck Farm
Woofa Bank Farm
Jowett's Crag
Woofa Bank
Moorcock Hall
Enclosure
Counter Hill
Walton Hole
Marchup Plantation
High Marchup
The Bungalow
Middle Marchup
Moorview
Far Cringles Farm
Old Tower
Croft Cottage
Cringles House Farm
Manor House
Lippersley Farm
Cringles Park Mobile Home Park
Cringles Plantation
Low Cringles Farm
Fishbeck
Mayfield
Well House
Rakes House Farm
Haw Farm
Haw
Hawber Cote
Swartha Farm
Prospect House
Drabble House
Spring Bank Cemy.
Foster Cliffe Farm North
Foster Cliffe Farm South
Fowler Hill Plantation
Lane House
Romille
Beck House
Dales Bank Holiday Park
Dales Bank Farm
Pickersgill's House
Dover Cottage
Country Cottage
Dixon Green
Lower Heights
Upper Hay Hills
Hayhills Farm North
Hayhills Farm South
Tower View
Play Field
Lib.
Sch.
RIDGE LANE
WALKER'S LANE
CRINGLES LANE
JOWETT'S LANE
BANK LANE
PARSON'S LANE
KILN HILL LANE
KIT LANE
HORN LANE
LOW LANE
BRADLEY LANE
HOLE LANE
HAYHILLS LANE
HEIGHTS LANE
COATE'S LANE
DENNIS LANE
NEW LANE
SKIPTON ROAD
GRANGE LANE
KEIGHLEY ROAD
KIRKGATE
BOLTON ROAD
BROWN STREET
HOLDEN ROAD
BELTON ROAD
HOLME LANE
BRUNTHWAITE LANE
BRUNTHWAITE BRIDGE LA.
SWARTHA LANE
HAWBER LANE
FISHBECK LANE
A6034
BRADFORD
CRAVEN
10
26

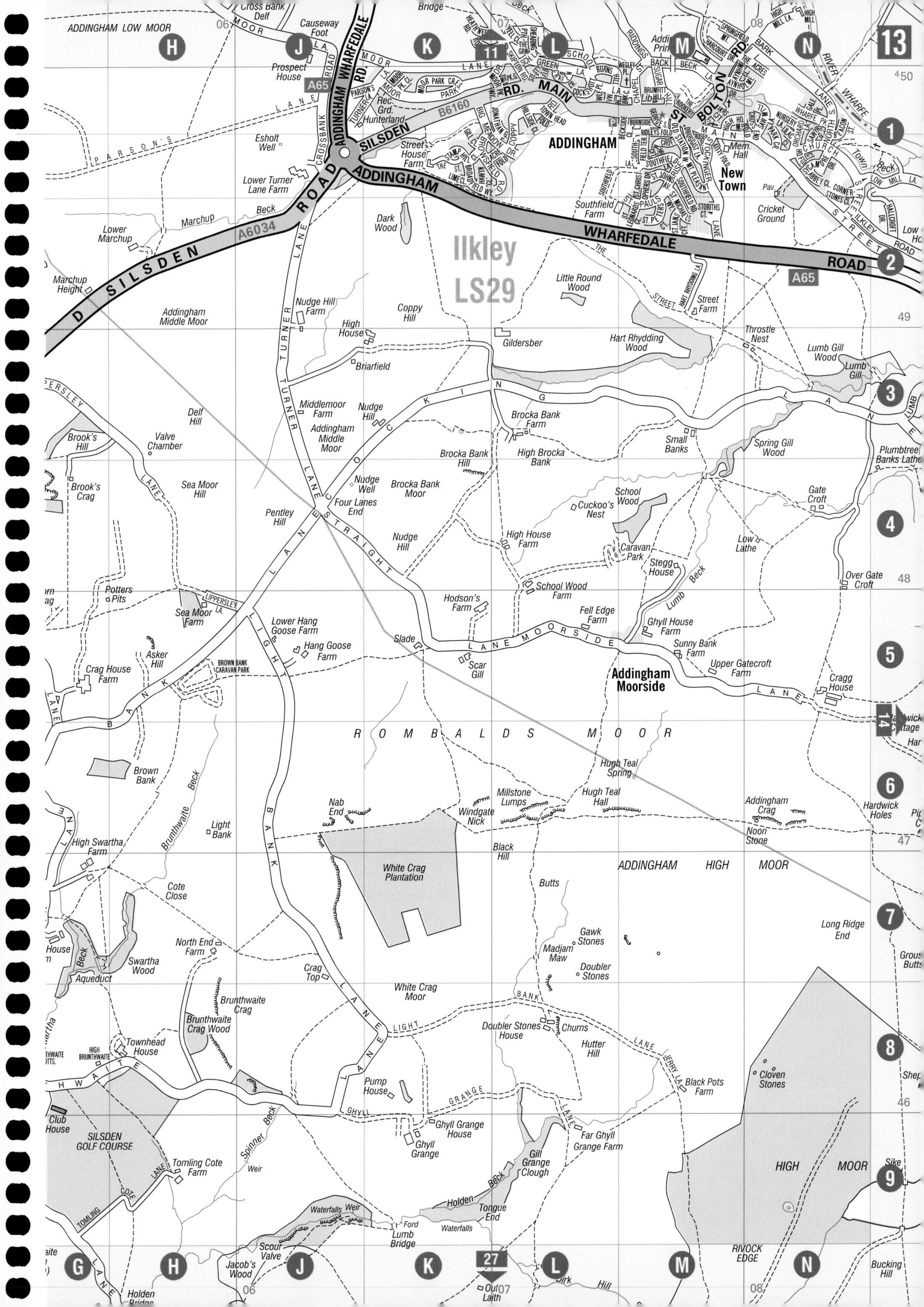

13
ADDINGHAM LOW MOOR
Cross Bank Delf
Causeway Foot
Prospect House
A65
Esholt Well
Lower Turner Lane Farm
Lower Marchup
Marchup Beck
Marchup Height
A6034
SILSDEN ROAD
ADDINGHAM WHARFEDALE RD.
CROSSBANK ROAD
TURNER LANE
MOOR LANE
PARSON'S LANE
Rec. Grd.
Hunterland
B6160
SILSDEN RD.
MAIN
ADDINGHAM
Street House Farm
ADDINGHAM WHARFEDALE ROAD
Dark Wood
Ilkley LS29
Little Round Wood
Street Farm
THE STREET
Southfield Farm
New Town
Mem. Hall
Cricket Ground
BOLTON RD.
RIVER WHARFE
ILKLEY ROAD
Addingham Middle Moor
Nudge Hill Farm
Coppy Hill
High House
Briarfield
Gildersber
Hart Rhydding Wood
Throstle Nest
Lumb Gill Wood
Lumb Gill
COCKING LANE
Middlemoor Farm
Nudge Hill
Addingham Middle Moor
Delf Hill
Brook's Hill
Valve Chamber
Brook's Crag
Sea Moor Hill
Brocka Bank Farm
High Brocka Bank
Brocka Bank Hill
Brocka Bank Moor
Small Banks
Spring Gill Wood
Plumbtree Banks Lathe
Nudge Well
Four Lanes End
Pentley Hill
STRAIGHT LANE
School Wood
Cuckoo's Nest
Gate Croft
High House Farm
Nudge Hill
Caravan Park
Low Lathe
Stegg House
Lumb Beck
Over Gate Croft
Potters Pits
LIPPERSLEY LA.
Sea Moor Farm
School Wood Farm
Hodson's Farm
Fell Edge Farm
Ghyll House Farm
Lower Hang Goose Farm
Hang Goose Farm
Slade
MOORSIDE LANE
Sunny Bank Farm
Upper Gatecroft Farm
Asker Hill
Crag House Farm
BROWN BANK CARAVAN PARK
Scar Gill
Addingham Moorside
Cragg House
BANK LANE
LIGHT BANK
R O M B A L D S M O O R
Brown Bank
Hugh Teal Spring
Millstone Lumps
Hugh Teal Hall
Addingham Crag
Hardwick Holes
Nab End
Windgate Nick
Noon Stone
Light Bank
High Swartha Farm
Bruntwaite Beck
Black Hill
White Crag Plantation
ADDINGHAM HIGH MOOR
Cote Close
Butts
Long Ridge End
North End Farm
Gawk Stones
Madjam Maw
Doubler Stones
Swartha Wood
Aqueduct
Crag Top
White Crag Moor
Brunthwaite Crag
Brunthwaite Crag Wood
Doubler Stones House
Churns
Hutter Hill
JERRY LA.
Townhead House
HIGH BRUNTHWAITE
Pump House
Black Pots Farm
Cloven Stones
GHYLL GRANGE LANE
Club House
SILSDEN GOLF COURSE
Ghyll Grange House
Ghyll Grange
Far Ghyll Grange Farm
Spinner Beck
Weir
Tomling Cote Farm
TOMLING COTE LANE
Gill Grange Clough
Holden Beck
Tongue End
HIGH MOOR
Waterfalls
Scour Valve
Ford
Lumb Bridge
RIVOCK EDGE
Jacob's Wood
Bucking Hill
Holden Bridge
Out Laith
G H J K L M N
11
14
27
06 07 08
450 49 48 47 46
1 2 3 4 5 6 7 8 9

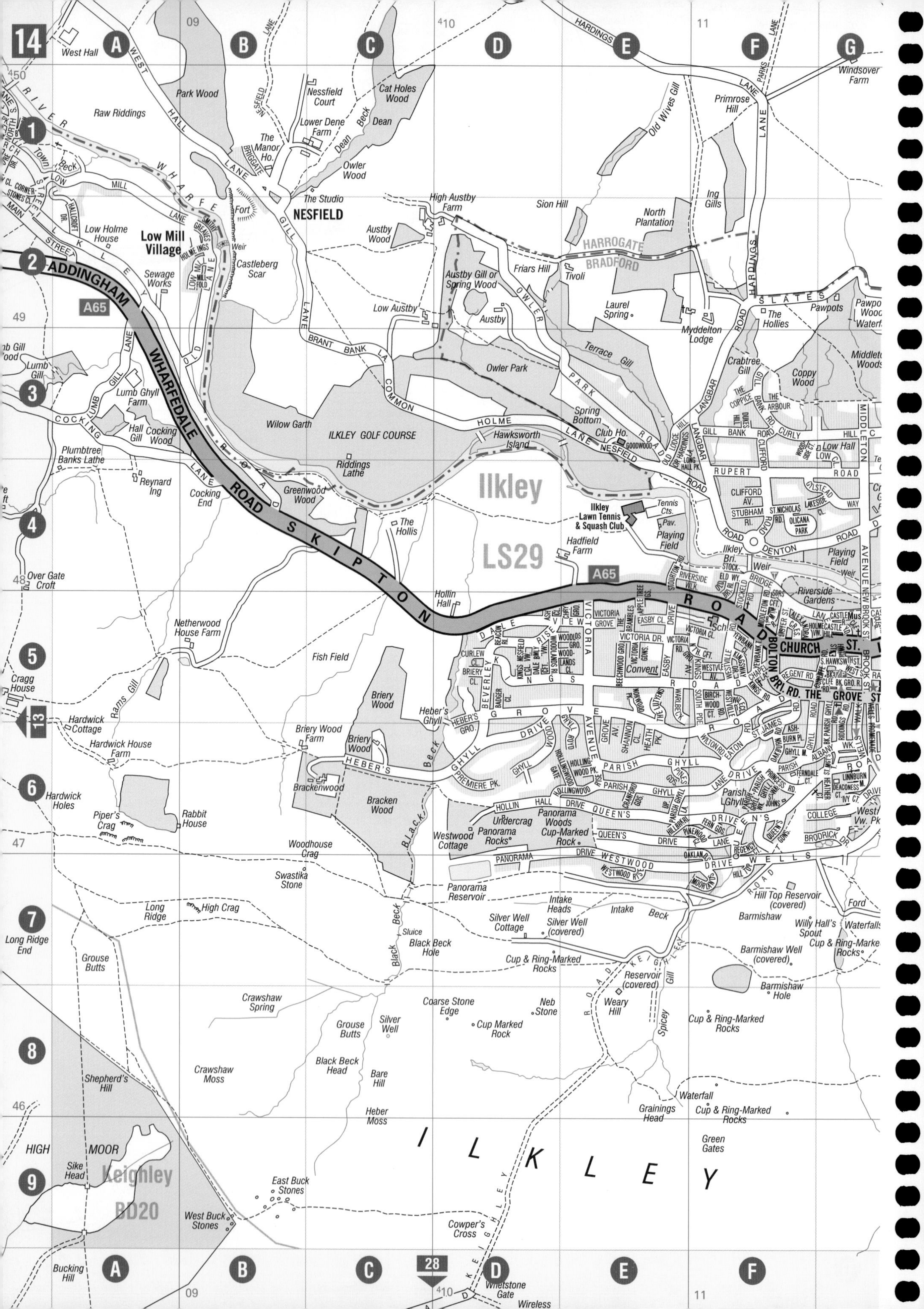

West Hall
Park Wood
Raw Riddings
Nessfield Court
Cat Holes Wood
Lower Dene Farm
Dean
The Manor Ho.
Owler Wood
The Studio
NESFIELD
Low Mill Village
Low Holme House
Castleberg Scar
Sewage Works
High Austby Farm
Austby Wood
Sion Hill
Old Wives Gill
Primrose Hill
Windsover Farm
Ing Gills
North Plantation
HARROGATE
BRADFORD
Friars Hill
Tivoli
Austby Gill or Spring Wood
Laurel Spring
Myddelton Lodge
The Hollies
Pawpots
Low Austby
Austby
Terrace Gill
Owler Park
Crabtree Gill
Coppy Wood
Lumb Ghyll Farm
Hall Gill
Cocking Wood
Wilow Garth
ILKLEY GOLF COURSE
Spring Bottom
Club Ho.
Hawksworth Island
Plumbtree Banks Lathe
Reynard Ing
Riddings Lathe
Cocking End
Greenwood Wood
Ilkley
Ilkley Lawn Tennis & Squash Club
Playing Field
The Hollis
LS29
Hadfield Farm
A65
ADDINGHAM
WHARFEDALE ROAD
SKIPTON ROAD
Over Gate Croft
Hollin Hall
Netherwood House Farm
Fish Field
Riverside Gardens
CHURCH ST.
Convent
Cragg House
Briery Wood
Heber's Ghyll
Hardwick Cottage
Hardwick House Farm
Briery Wood Farm
Brackenwood
Bracken Wood
Hardwick Holes
Piper's Crag
Rabbit House
Undercrag
Panorama Rocks
Panorama Woods
Cup-Marked Rock
Westwood Cottage
Woodhouse Crag
Swastika Stone
Panorama Reservoir
Hill Top Reservoir (covered)
Barmishaw
Long Ridge
High Crag
Silver Well Cottage
Silver Well (covered)
Intake Heads
Black Beck Hole
Cup & Ring-Marked Rocks
Long Ridge End
Grouse Butts
Crawshaw Spring
Coarse Stone Edge
Neb Stone
Weary Hill
Cup Marked Rock
Silver Well
Barmishaw Well (covered)
Barmishaw Hole
Crawshaw Moss
Black Beck Head
Bare Hill
Shepherd's Hill
Heber Moss
Waterfall
Grainings Head
Green Gates
ILKLEY
HIGH MOOR
Sike Head
Keighley
BD20
East Buck Stones
West Buck Stones
Cowper's Cross
Bucking Hill
Whetstone Gate
Wireless
13
28

MIDDLETON
ILKLEY
Ben Rhydding
Denton
Hunger Hill
Andrew's Plantation
Hill Top Farm
The Cottage
Lane End Farm
Home Farm
Westville Ho. Sch.
Grange Farm
Pomona
Nell Bank Wood
Stubham Wood
Hudson Wood
Nell Bank Centre
Hudson's Wood
Stubbs' Wood
Whinthorn Farm
Bore Hill
Worm Beck
Bunyip Lodge
Lane End Farm
Yarnett House Farm
Carrow Bank
Willow Hill Farm
Lady's Walk Plantation
High Park
Wellhouse Plantation
Church Farm
Denton Hall
DENTON PARK
West Park Wood
Cinder Gill
Beckfoot House
Beck Foot Farm
Brentwood
Hepper Carr
Chapel Plantation
Sawmill Plantation
Ilkley Pool & Lido
Cricket Grd.
Cromwheel
Beanlands Island
Sewage Works
Cemetery
Middleton Sports Ground
Denton Bri.
Sports Ground
Wheatley Grange
Crook
Low Park Plantation
Low Park
A65
LEEDS ROAD
COUTANCES WAY
WHARFE
Playing Fields
Cock Busk
Sewage Works
Spring Wood
BOLLING ROAD
SPRINGS LANE
B6382
CORONATION HOSP.
Moorfield School
Rowley House
Five Oaks
Wheatley Chase
Saxon Lodge
Riversdale
Langwith
Uplands
Club Ho.
BEN RHYDDING GOLF COURSE
Gib Farm
Reservoir (covered)
The Tarn
Simons Ridding
White Wells Spa Cott.
Cow Close Gill
Hanging Stones
Cup & Ring-Marked Rock
Cow & Calf Rocks
Res. (cov.)
Highfield Farm
Highfield House
Low House Farm
West Rock
Ilkley Crags
Rocky Valley
Lady Stones
Waterfall
Pancake Stone Cup-Marked Rock
Pancake Ridge
Cup-Marked Rock
Cranshaw Thorn Hill
Cup & Ring-Marked Rocks
Gill Head Reservoir (covered)
Mount Stead
High Stead
Reservoir
Stead
Low Stead Farm
Stead Hall Farm
Kennels Farm
Stead Hall Wood
Rushy Beck
Gill Head
Backstone Beck
Green Crag
Idol Stone
Green Crag Slack
MOOR
Low Cragg Farm
High Cragg Farm
Rose Farm
Garden Centre
Stead Crag
Robin Hole
Lanshaw Lass Stone
DANGER AREA
Lanshaw Delves
Coldstone House (Rock)
White Crag Moss
House Butts
29
16

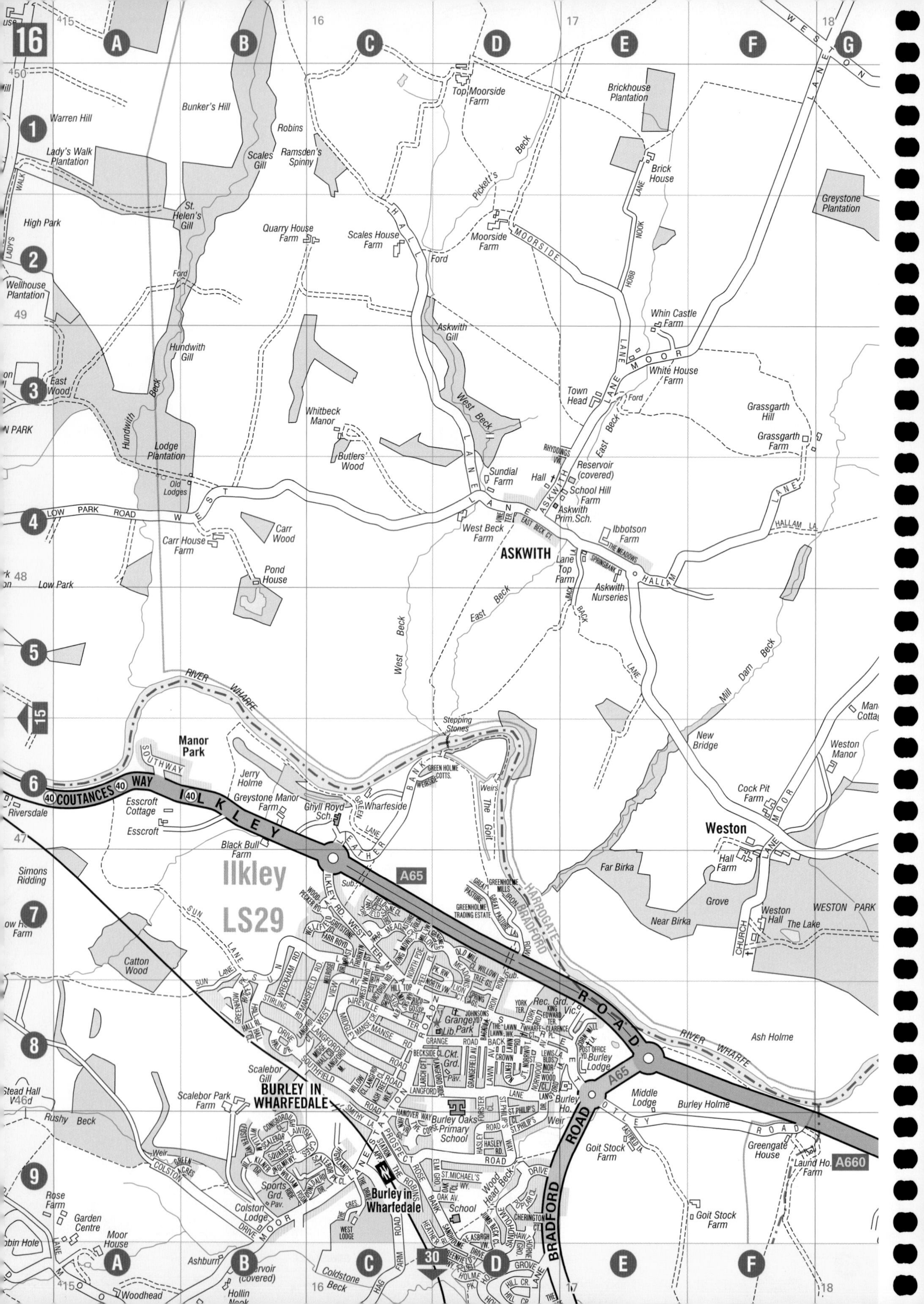

Bunker's Hill
Warren Hill
Lady's Walk Plantation
Robins
Scales Gill
Ramsden's Spinny
Top Moorside Farm
Brickhouse Plantation
Brick House
Greystone Plantation
High Park
St. Helen's Gill
Quarry House Farm
Scales House Farm
Moorside Farm
Pickett's Beck
Wellhouse Plantation
Hundwith Gill
Askwith Gill
Whin Castle Farm
White House Farm
East Wood
Whitbeck Manor
Town Head
West Beck
Grassgarth Hill
Grassgarth Farm
Hundwith Beck
Lodge Plantation
Butlers' Wood
Sundial Farm
Reservoir (covered)
School Hill Farm
Askwith Prim.Sch.
Old Lodges
LOW PARK ROAD
Carr Wood
Carr House Farm
West Beck Farm
ASKWITH
Ibbotson Farm
Lane Top Farm
Askwith Nurseries
Pond House
Low Park
East Beck
Mill Dam Beck
RIVER WHARFE
Stepping Stones
Manor Park
Jerry Holme
New Bridge
Weston Manor
COUTANCES WAY
ILKLEY ROAD
Esscroft Cottage
Riversdale
Greystone Manor Farm
Ghyll Royd Sch.
Wharfeside
Cock Pit Farm
Esscroft
Weston
Black Bull Farm
Hall Farm
Ilkley LS29
A65
Far Birka
Simons Ridding
Grove
Near Birka
Weston Hall
WESTON PARK
The Lake
Catton Wood
HARROGATE BRADFORD ROAD
Grange Park
Ash Holme
Burley Lodge
Scalebor Gill
Scalebor Park Farm
BURLEY IN WHARFEDALE
Middle Lodge
Burley Holme
Burley Oaks Primary School
Rushy Beck
Goit Stock Farm
Greengate House
Laund Ho. Farm
A660
Sports Grd.
Colston Lodge
Burley in Wharfedale
Rose Farm
Garden Centre
School
Moor House
BRADFORD ROAD
Goit Stock Farm
Ashburn
Reservoir (covered)
Coldstone Beck
Woodhead
Hollin Nook
30
15

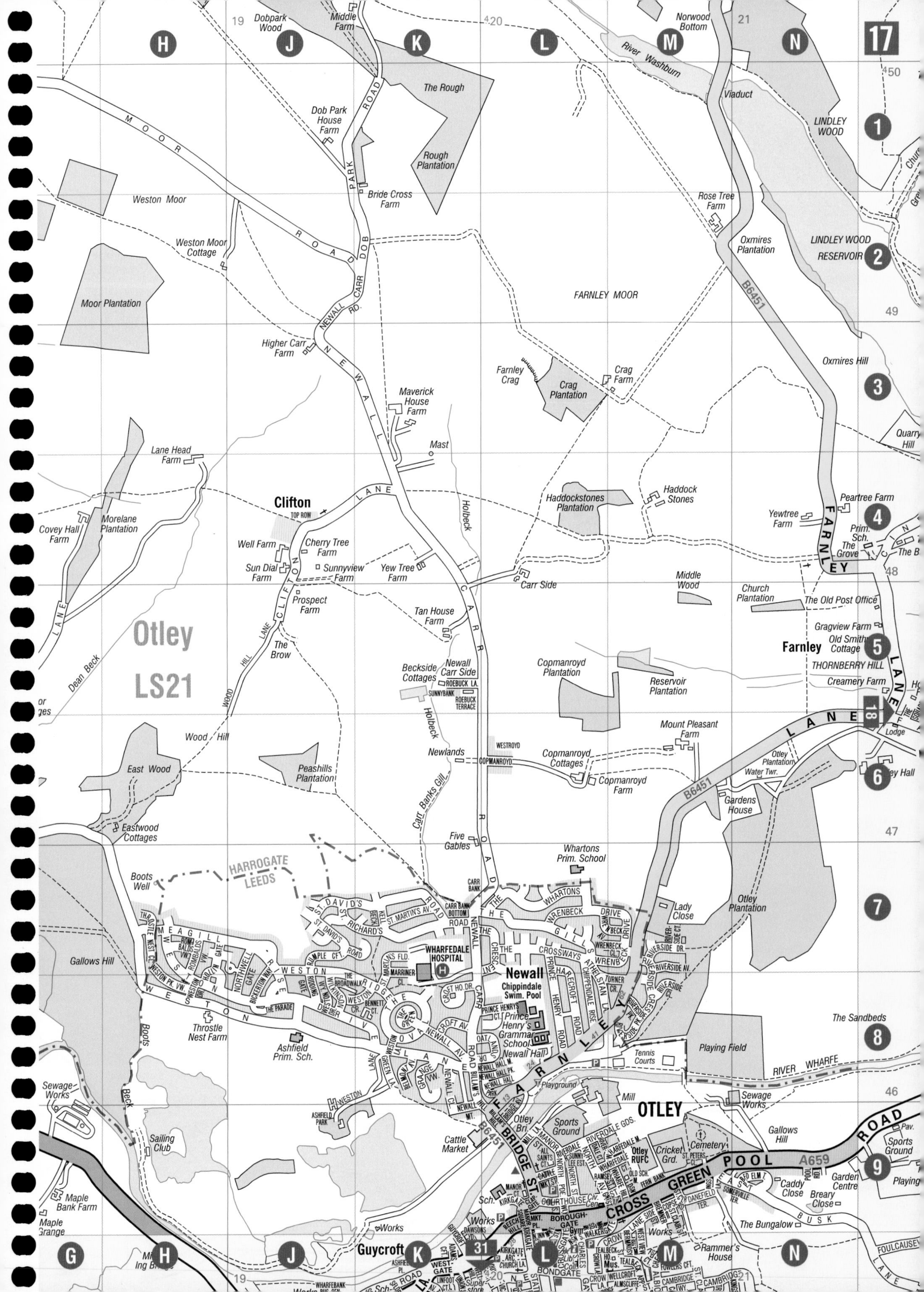
Dobpark Wood
Middle Farm
Norwood Bottom
River Washburn
The Rough
Dob Park House Farm
Rough Plantation
Viaduct
LINDLEY WOOD
MOOR ROAD
PARK ROAD
DOB
Bride Cross Farm
Weston Moor
Weston Moor Cottage
Rose Tree Farm
Oxmires Plantation
LINDLEY WOOD RESERVOIR
Moor Plantation
FARNLEY MOOR
B6451
NEWALL CARR RD.
Higher Carr Farm
Oxmires Hill
Farnley Crag
Crag Plantation
Crag Farm
Maverick House Farm
Mast
Lane Head Farm
Quarry Hill
Clifton
TOP ROW
LANE
Haddockstones Plantation
Haddock Stones
Peartree Farm
Yewtree Farm
Covey Hall Farm
Morelane Plantation
Holbeck
Prim. Sch.
The Grove
Well Farm
Cherry Tree Farm
Sun Dial Farm
Sunnyview Farm
Yew Tree Farm
Carr Side
Middle Wood
FARNLEY
Church Plantation
The Old Post Office
Prospect Farm
Tan House Farm
Gragview Farm
Old Smith Cottage
Farnley
THORNBERRY HILL
Otley LS21
The Brow
Dean Beck
CLIFTON LANE
WOOD HILL LANE
Beckside Cottages
Newall Carr Side
ROEBUCK LA.
SUNNYBANK
ROEBUCK TERRACE
Copmanroyd Plantation
Reservoir Plantation
Creamery Farm
LANE
Wood Hill
Mount Pleasant Farm
WESTROYD
Newlands
COPMANROYD
Copmanroyd Cottages
Lodge
Otley Plantation
Water Twr.
East Wood
Peashills Plantation
Copmanroyd Farm
Carr Banks Gill
B6451
Gardens House
Eastwood Cottages
Five Gables
47
Whartons Prim. School
HARROGATE
LEEDS
Boots Well
CARR BANK
CARR BANK BOTTOM
WHARTONS
Lady Close
Otley Plantation
Gallows Hill
WHARFEDALE HOSPITAL
Newall
Chippindale Swim. Pool
Prince Henry's Grammar School
Newall Hall
Throstle Nest Farm
Ashfield Prim. Sch.
The Sandbeds
Playing Field
Tennis Courts
RIVER WHARFE
Boots Beck
Sewage Works
Playground
Mill
OTLEY
Sewage Works
Sailing Club
Cattle Market
Otley Br.
Sports Ground
Otley RUFC
Cricket Grd.
Cemetery
Gallows Hill
Sports Ground
BRIDGE ST
CROSS GREEN
POOL ROAD
A659
Garden Centre
Caddy Close
Breary Close
Playing
Maple Bank Farm
Maple Grange
Works
Sch.
Works
BOROUGHGATE
The Bungalow
BUSK LANE
Guycroft
Rammer's House
FOULCAUSEY
BONDGATE
WESTGATE
31
18
G H J K L M N
1 2 3 4 5 6 7 8 9
19 20 21
46 47 48 49 50

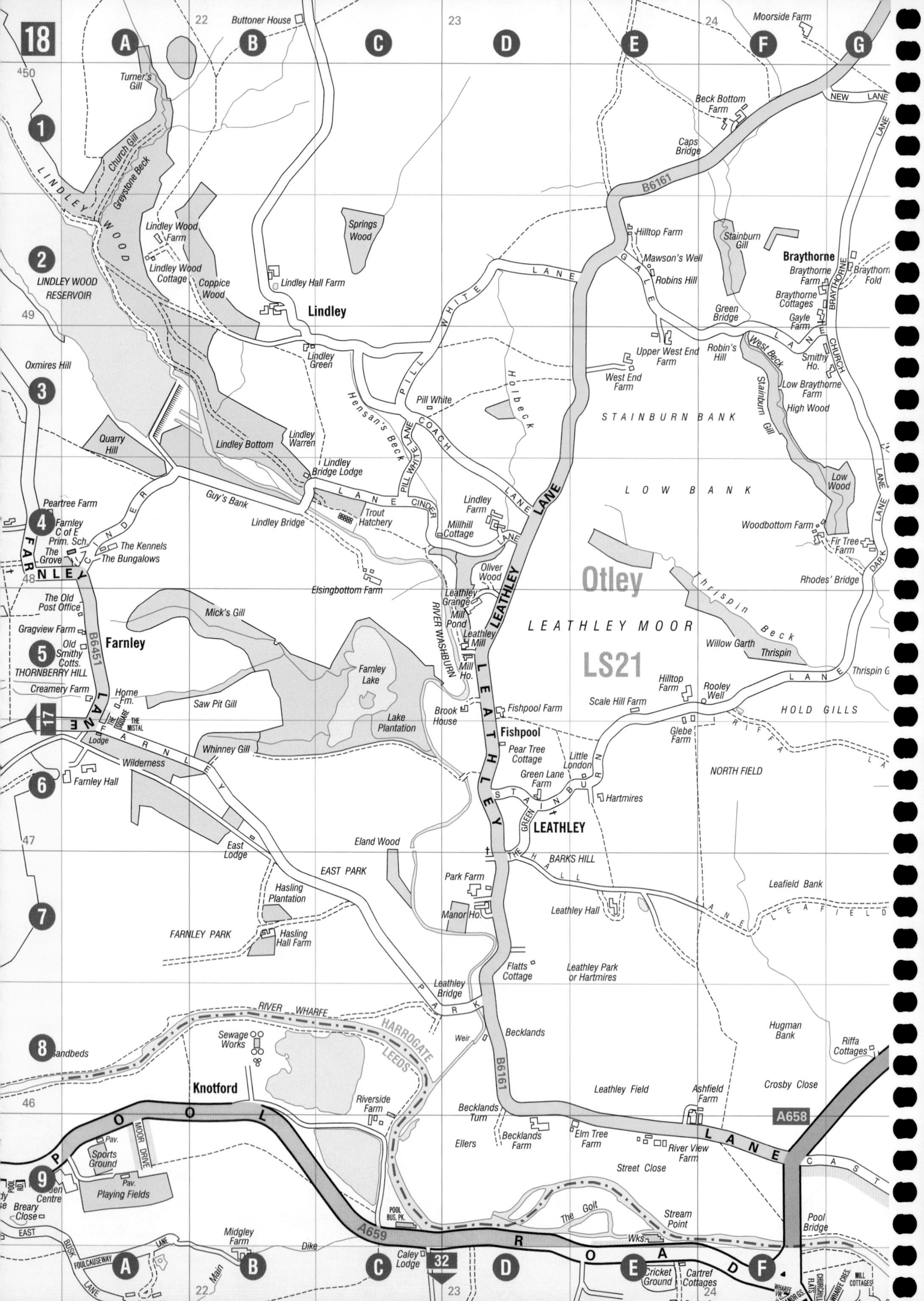
Buttoner House
Moorside Farm
Turner's Gill
Beck Bottom Farm
Caps Bridge
NEW LANE
Church Gill
Greystone Beck
LINDLEY WOOD
B6161
Springs Wood
Lindley Wood Farm
Hilltop Farm
Stainburn Gill
Braythorne
LINDLEY WOOD RESERVOIR
Lindley Wood Cottage
Coppice Wood
Lindley Hall Farm
Mawson's Well
Robins Hill
Braythorne Farm
Braythorne Fold
Braythorne Cottages
Lindley
Green Bridge
Gayle Farm
Oxmires Hill
Lindley Green
Upper West End Farm
Robin's Hill
West Beck
Smithy Ho.
West End Farm
Low Braythorne Farm
Pill White
Hensan's Beck
Holbeck
High Wood
STAINBURN BANK
Quarry Hill
Lindley Bottom
Lindley Warren
Lindley Bridge Lodge
COACH
Guy's Bank
CINDER LANE
LOW BANK
Low Wood
Peartree Farm
Lindley Bridge
Trout Hatchery
Lindley Farm
Millhill Cottage
Woodbottom Farm
Fir Tree Farm
Farnley C of E Prim. Sch.
The Kennels
The Grove
The Bungalows
Oliver Wood
Otley
Rhodes' Bridge
FARNLEY LANE
Elsingbottom Farm
Leathley Grange
Thrispin Beck
The Old Post Office
Mick's Gill
RIVER WASHBURN
Mill Pond
LEATHLEY MOOR
Gragview Farm
B6451
Farnley
Leathley Mill
Willow Garth
Thrispin
Old Smithy Cotts.
Farnley Lake
Mill Ho.
LS21
THORNBERRY HILL
Thrispin G
Creamery Farm
Home Fm.
Saw Pit Gill
Brook House
Fishpool Farm
Hilltop Farm
Rooley Well
Scale Hill Farm
HOLD GILLS
17
THE SQUARE
THE MISTAL
Lake Plantation
Fishpool
Glebe Farm
RIFFA LANE
Lodge
Whinney Gill
Pear Tree Cottage
Little London
Wilderness
NORTH FIELD
Farnley Hall
Green Lane Farm
STAINBURN
Hartmires
GREEN
LEATHLEY
Eland Wood
East Lodge
BARKS HILL
THE HALL LANE
EAST PARK
Park Farm
Leafield Bank
Hasling Plantation
Leathley Hall
Manor Ho.
LEAFIELD
FARNLEY PARK
Hasling Hall Farm
Flatts Cottage
Leathley Park or Hartmires
Leathley Bridge
PARK
RIVER WHARFE
HARROGATE
LEEDS
Sewage Works
Weir
Becklands
Hugman Bank
Riffa Cottages
Sandbeds
Crosby Close
Knotford
Leathley Field
Ashfield Farm
Riverside Farm
Becklands Turn
A658
POOL ROAD
MOOR DRIVE
Becklands Farm
Elm Tree Farm
Ellers
River View Farm
Pav.
Sports Ground
LANE
CAST
Street Close
Playing Fields
Garden Centre
Breary Close
The Goit
Stream Point
Pool Bridge
POOL BUS. PK.
EAST
A659
Wks.
Midgley Farm
Dike
FOULCAUSEWAY LANE
BUSK
Main
Caley Lodge
32
Cricket Ground
Cartref Cottages
MILL COTTAGES
WHARFE CRES.
CHURCHILL FLATS
A B C D E F G
1 2 3 4 5 6 7 8 9
22 23 24
450 49 48 47 46

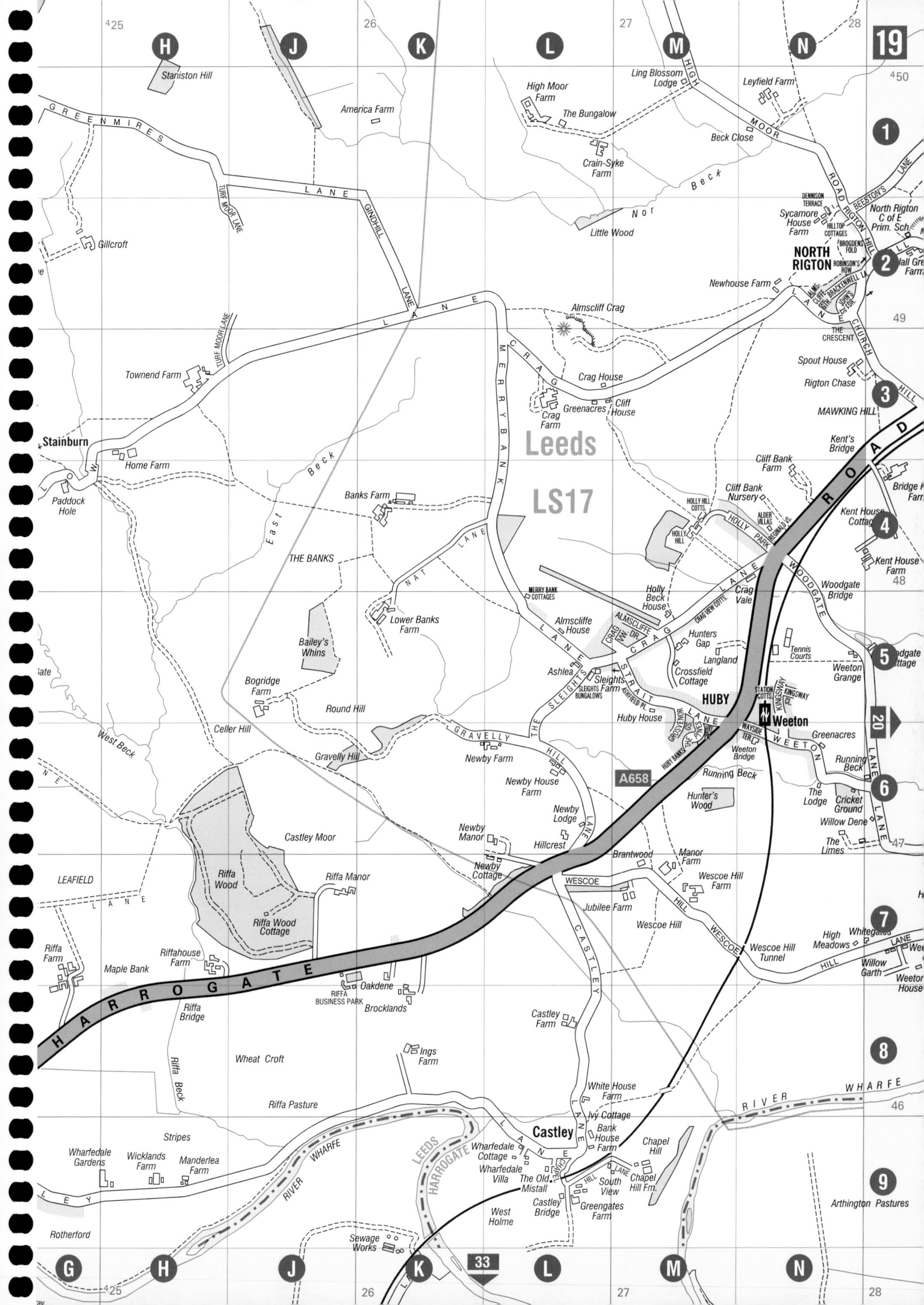
19
H
J
K
L
M
N
1
2
3
4
5
6
7
8
9
G
425
26
27
28
450
49
48
47
46
Staniston Hill
America Farm
High Moor Farm
The Bungalow
Ling Blossom Lodge
Leyfield Farm
Beck Close
Crain-Syke Farm
Nor Beck
Little Wood
GREENMIRES LANE
TURF MOOR LANE
GINDHILL LANE
HIGH MOOR ROAD
RIGTON HILL
BEESTON'S LANE
DENNISON TERRACE
Sycamore House Farm
HILLTOP COTTAGES
BROGDENS FOLD
ROBINSON'S ROW
North Rigton C of E Prim. Sch.
NORTH RIGTON
Hall Green Farm
Newhouse Farm
BRACKENWELL LA.
JOHN'S CROFT
THE CRESCENT
CHURCH HILL
Gillcroft
Almscliff Crag
CRAG LANE
Crag House
Townend Farm
Spout House
Rigton Chase
MAWKING HILL
Greenacres
Cliff House
Crag Farm
Stainburn
Home Farm
Paddock Hole
Leeds
LS17
East Beck
MERRY BANK
Banks Farm
Kent's Bridge
Cliff Bank Farm
Cliff Bank Nursery
HOLLY HILL COTTS.
ALDER VILLAS
HOLLY PARK
REGINALD VS.
Bridge Farm
Kent House Cottage
Kent House Farm
THE BANKS
NAT LANE
HOLLY HILL
MERRY BANK COTTAGES
Holly Beck House
Crag Vale
WOODGATE LANE
Woodgate Bridge
Lower Banks Farm
Bailey's Whins
Almscliffe House
ALMSCLIFFE CRAG VW. DR.
CRAG VIEW COTTS.
Hunters Gap
Langland
Tennis Courts
Woodgate Cottage
Weeton Grange
Bogridge Farm
Ashlea
Sleights Farm
SLEIGHTS BUNGALOWS
ASHFIELD PL.
STRAIT LANE
Crossfield Cottage
HUBY
STATION COTTS.
KINGSWAY
KINGSWAY CL.
Round Hill
Huby House
Weeton
20
Celler Hill
West Beck
THE SLEIGHTS
GRAVELLY HILL
Gravelly Hill
Newby Farm
GROSVENOR
THE GY
PINES
WAYSIDE TER.
Weeton Bridge
WEETON LANE
Greenacres
Running Beck
A658
HUBY BANKS
Running Beck
Newby House Farm
Hunter's Wood
The Lodge
Cricket Ground
Willow Dene
The Limes
Newby Lodge
Newby Manor
Hillcrest
Castley Moor
Brantwood
Manor Farm
Newby Cottage
Wescoe Hill Farm
WESCOE HILL
Riffa Wood
Riffa Manor
LEAFIELD LANE
Jubilee Farm
Wescoe Hill
Riffa Wood Cottage
Wescoe Hill Tunnel
High Meadows
Whitegates
Weeton
Willow Garth
Weeton House
Riffa Farm
Maple Bank
Riffahouse Farm
HARROGATE ROAD
Oakdene
RIFFA BUSINESS PARK
Brocklands
CASTLEY LANE
Riffa Bridge
Castley Farm
Wheat Croft
Ings Farm
Riffa Beck
White House Farm
RIVER WHARFE
Riffa Pasture
Ivy Cottage
Castley
Bank House Farm
Chapel Hill
Stripes
Wharfedale Gardens
Wicklands Farm
Manderlea Farm
LEEDS HARROGATE
Wharfedale Cottage
Wharfedale Villa
The Old Mistall
South View
Chapel Hill Fm.
CHAPEL HILL LANE
Arthington Pastures
Castley Bridge
Greengates Farm
West Holme
Rotherford
Sewage Works
33

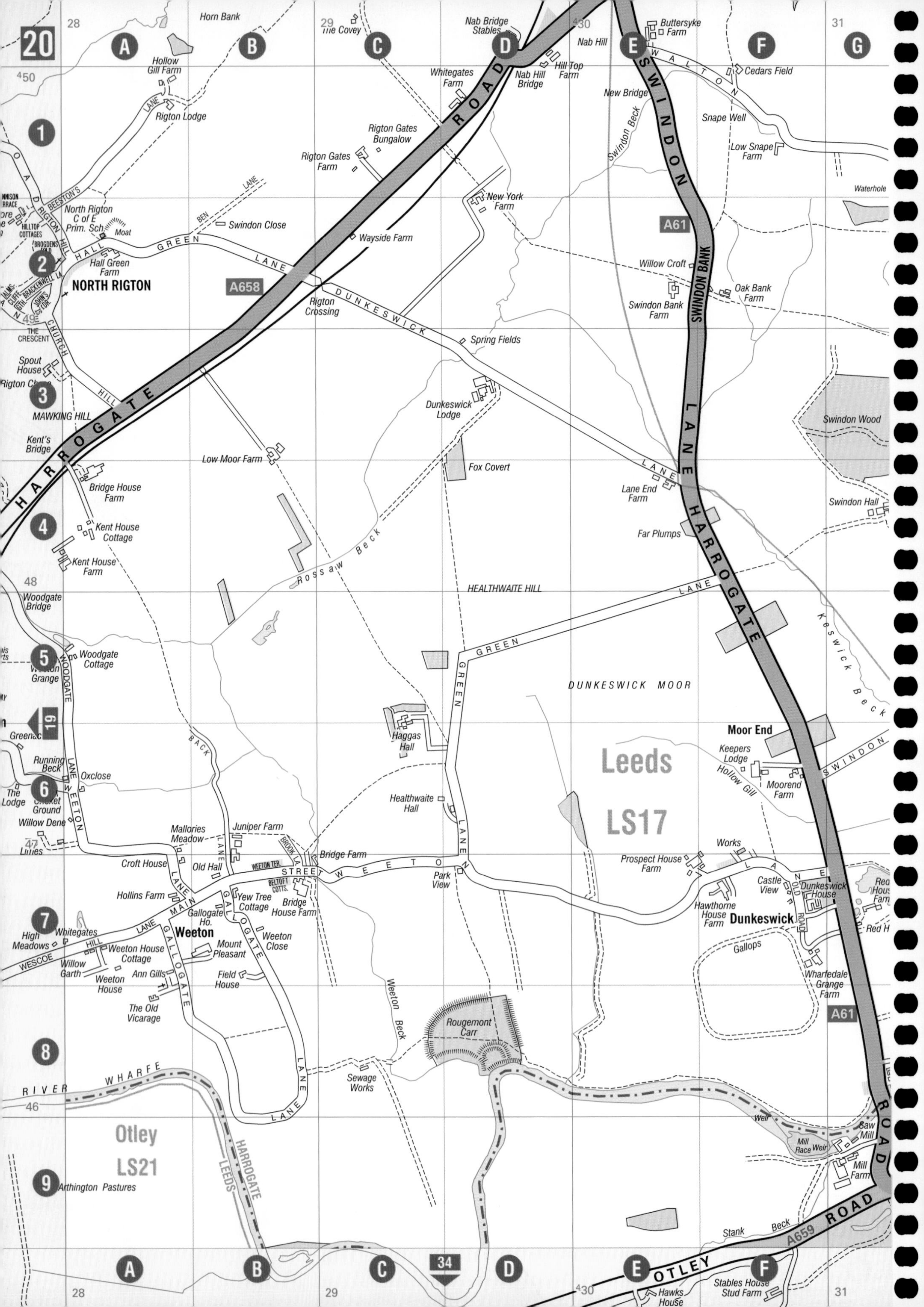

Horn Bank
The Covey
Nab Bridge Stables
Buttersyke Farm
Nab Hill
Hollow Gill Farm
Whitegates Farm
Nab Hill Bridge
Hill Top Farm
Cedars Field
WALTON
New Bridge
Rigton Lodge
Snape Well
Rigton Gates Bungalow
Rigton Gates Farm
Low Snape Farm
Swindon Beck
Waterhole
New York Farm
North Rigton C of E Prim. Sch
Moat
Swindon Close
A61
Wayside Farm
GREEN LANE
Hall Green Farm
Willow Croft
NORTH RIGTON
A658
Rigton Crossing
DUNKESWICK
Oak Bank Farm
Swindon Bank Farm
SWINDON BANK
THE CRESCENT
Spring Fields
Spout House
MAWKING HILL
Dunkeswick Lodge
Swindon Wood
Kent's Bridge
HARROGATE ROAD
Low Moor Farm
Fox Covert
Bridge House Farm
Lane End Farm
Swindon Hall
Kent House Cottage
Far Plumps
Rossaw Beck
Kent House Farm
HEALTHWAITE HILL
Woodgate Bridge
Keswick Beck
Woodgate Cottage
Weeton Grange
DUNKESWICK MOOR
Haggas Hall
Moor End
Greenacre
Running Beck
Keepers Lodge
Leeds
LS17
Oxclose
Hollow Gill
Moorend Farm
The Lodge
Cricket Ground
Healthwaite Hall
Willow Dene
Juniper Farm
Mallories Meadow
Works
Croft House
Old Hall
Bridge Farm
Prospect House Farm
WEETON TER.
BELTOFT COTTS.
Park View
Castle View
Dunkeswick House
Hollins Farm
Yew Tree Cottage
Bridge House Farm
Hawthorne House Farm
Dunkeswick
Gallogate Ho.
Red House Farm
Whitegates
High Meadows
Weeton
Weeton Close
Red H
Mount Pleasant
Weeton House Cottage
Gallops
Willow Garth
Ann Gills
Weeton House
Field House
Wharfedale Grange Farm
The Old Vicarage
Weeton Beck
Rougemont Carr
A61
RIVER WHARFE
Sewage Works
Weir
Saw Mill
Mill Race Weir
Otley
LS21
LEEDS HARROGATE
Mill Farm
Arthington Pastures
Stank Beck
OTLEY ROAD
A659
Stables House Stud Farm
Hawks House
19
34

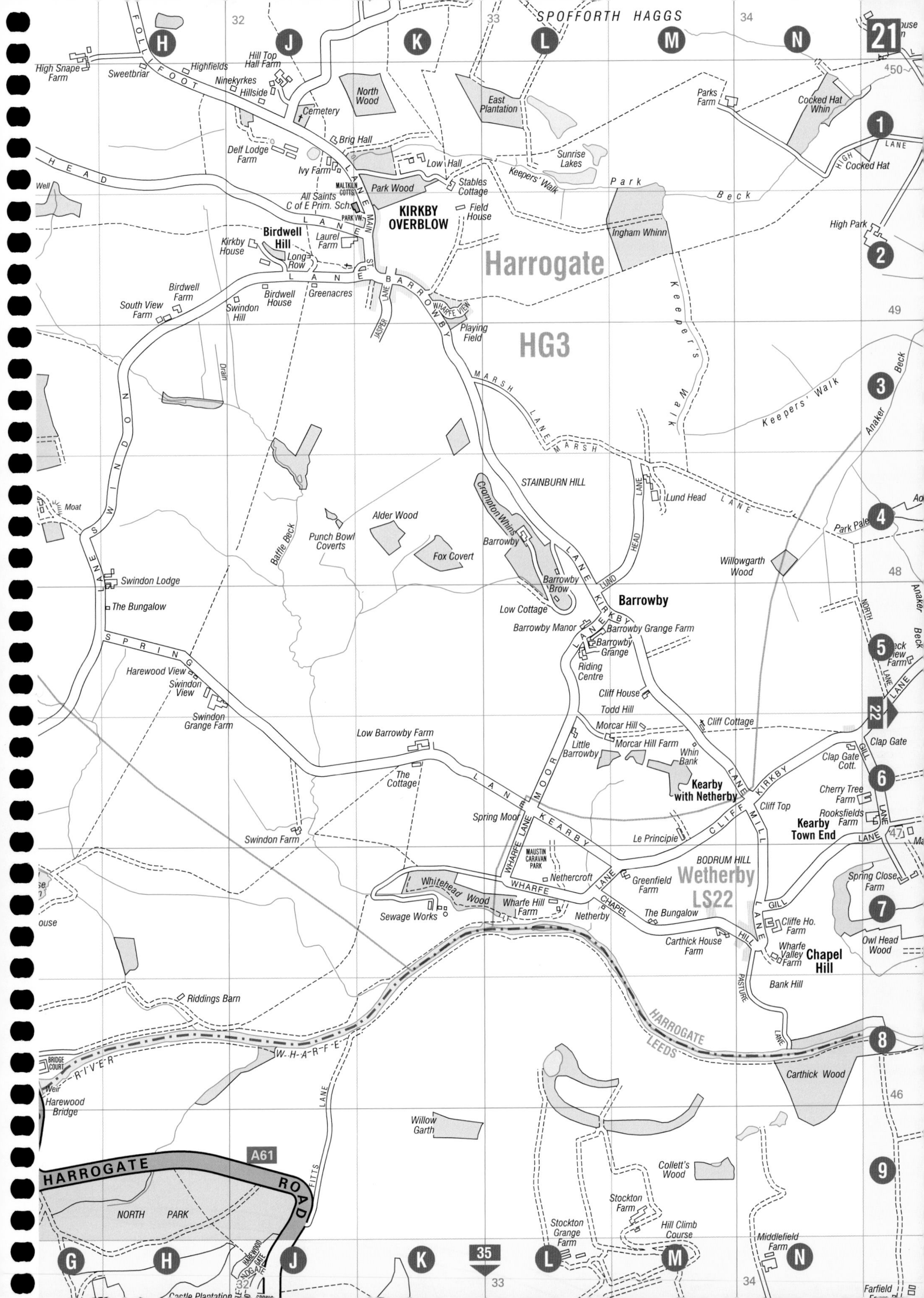
SPOFFORTH HAGGS
FOLLIFOOT LANE
High Snape Farm
Sweetbriar
Highfields
Ninekyrkes
Hillside
Hill Top Hall Farm
Cemetery
North Wood
East Plantation
Parks Farm
Cocked Hat Whin
Brig Hall
Delf Lodge Farm
Ivy Farm
Low Hall
Sunrise Lakes
Keepers' Walk
HEAD LANE
Park Wood
Stables Cottage
Park Beck
HIGH LANE
Cocked Hat
All Saints C of E Prim. Sch.
KIRKBY OVERBLOW
Field House
Ingham Whinn
High Park
Birdwell Hill
Kirkby House
Laurel Farm
Long Row
Harrogate
Birdwell Farm
South View Farm
Swindon Hill
Birdwell House
Greenacres
BARROWBY LANE
WHARFE VIEW
Playing Field
HG3
Keeper's Walk
MARSH LANE
Drain
SWINDON LANE
Anaker Beck
Moat
STAINBURN HILL
Crompton Whins
Lund Head
Alder Wood
Punch Bowl Coverts
Fox Covert
Barrowby
Battle Beck
Park Pale
Willowgarth Wood
Swindon Lodge
The Bungalow
Barrowby Brow
Low Cottage
Barrowby
Barrowby Manor
Barrowby Grange Farm
Barrowby Grange
Riding Centre
SPRING LANE
Harewood View
Swindon View
Beck View Farm
Cliff House
Todd Hill
Swindon Grange Farm
Morcar Hill
Cliff Cottage
Little Barrowby
Morcar Hill Farm
Whin Bank
Clap Gate
Clap Gate Cott.
Low Barrowby Farm
The Cottage
Kearby with Netherby
Cherry Tree Farm
Cliff Top
Rooksfields Farm
Spring Moor
Kearby Town End
Swindon Farm
Le Principie
KEARBY LANE
CLIFF LANE
MILL LANE
MAUSTIN CARAVAN PARK
BODRUM HILL
Wetherby LS22
Spring Close Farm
Nethercroft
Greenfield Farm
Whitehead Wood
WHARFE LANE
Wharfe Hill Farm
Sewage Works
Netherby
CHAPEL HILL
The Bungalow
Cliffe Ho. Farm
Carthick House Farm
Wharfe Valley Farm
Chapel Hill
Owl Head Wood
PASTURE LANE
Bank Hill
Riddings Barn
HARROGATE LEEDS
RIVER WHARFE
BRIDGE COURT
Carthick Wood
Weir
Harewood Bridge
Willow Garth
A61
HARROGATE ROAD
Collett's Wood
FITTS LANE
NORTH PARK
Stockton Farm
Stockton Grange Farm
Hill Climb Course
Middlefield Farm
Castle Plantation
Farfield
32
33
34
46
47
48
49
450

22
35

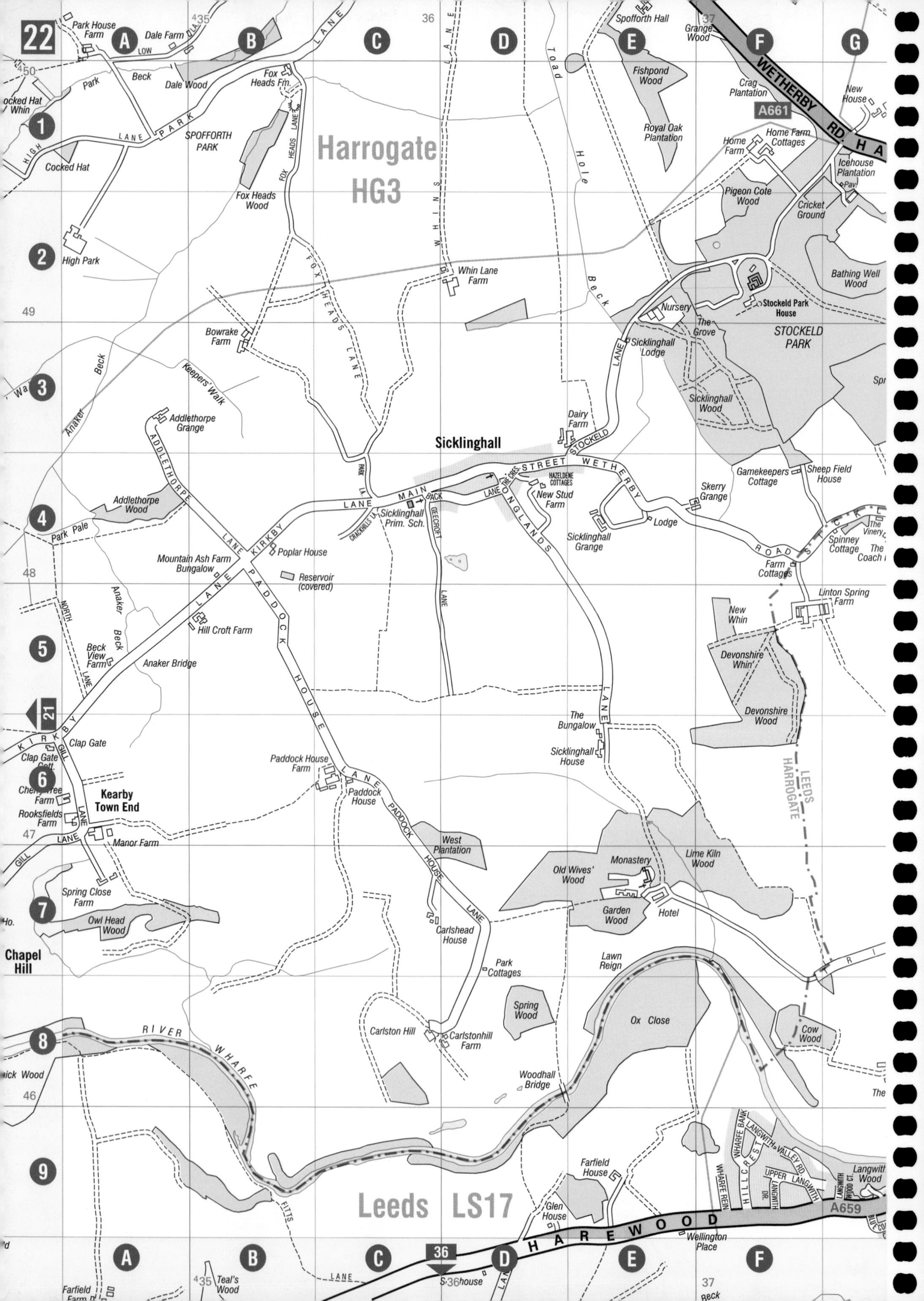
A
B
C
D
E
F
G
Park House Farm
Dale Farm
Low Dale Lane
Spofforth Hall
Grange Wood
Beck
Dale Wood
Fox Heads Fm.
Fishpond Wood
Crag Plantation
Wetherby Rd.
A661
New House
Park
Park Lane
Spofforth Park
Royal Oak Plantation
Home Farm Cottages
Home Farm
High Lane
Cocked Hat
Fox Heads Lane
Harrogate HG3
Whins Lane
Toad Hole Beck
Icehouse Plantation
Pav.
Pigeon Cote Wood
Cricket Ground
Fox Heads Wood
High Park
Whin Lane Farm
Bathing Well Wood
Stockeld Park House
Nursery
The Grove
Stockeld Park
Bowrake Farm
Fox Heads Lane
Sicklinghall Lodge
Anaker Beck
Keepers' Walk
Sicklinghall Wood
Addlethorpe Grange
Dairy Farm
Sicklinghall
Stockeld Lane
Wetherby Street
The Cres.
Hazeldene Cottages
Gamekeepers Cottage
Sheep Field House
Addlethorpe Lane
Park La.
Main Lane
Back Lane
New Stud Farm
Skerry Grange
Addlethorpe Wood
Park Pale
Crackhills La.
Sicklinghall Prim. Sch.
Geecroft Lane
Longlands Lane
Sicklinghall Grange
Lodge
Kirkby Lane
Poplar House
Road
Spinney Cottage
Mountain Ash Farm Bungalow
Reservoir (covered)
Farm Cottages
Linton Spring Farm
Paddock House Lane
New Whin
North Lane
Hill Croft Farm
Devonshire Whin
Beck View Farm
Anaker Bridge
Devonshire Wood
21
The Bungalow
Clap Gate
Clap Gate Cott.
Sicklinghall House
Paddock House Farm
Leeds
Harrogate
Cherry Tree Farm
Kearby Town End
Paddock House
Rooksfields Farm
Gill Lane
Manor Farm
West Plantation
Lime Kiln Wood
Monastery
Old Wives' Wood
Spring Close Farm
Hotel
Garden Wood
Owl Head Wood
Carlshead House
Chapel Hill
Lawn Reign
Park Cottages
Spring Wood
Ox Close
River Wharfe
Carlston Hill
Carlstonhill Farm
Cow Wood
Woodhall Bridge
Farfield House
Wharfe Bank
Langwith Valley Rd.
Hillcrest
Upper Langwith
Wharfe Rein
Langwith Dr.
Langwith Wood
Leeds LS17
Glen House
A659
Harewood Road
Fitts Lane
Wellington Place
36
Teal's Wood
Farfield Farm
Beck
49
48
47
46
1
2
3
4
5
6
7
8
9
435
36
37

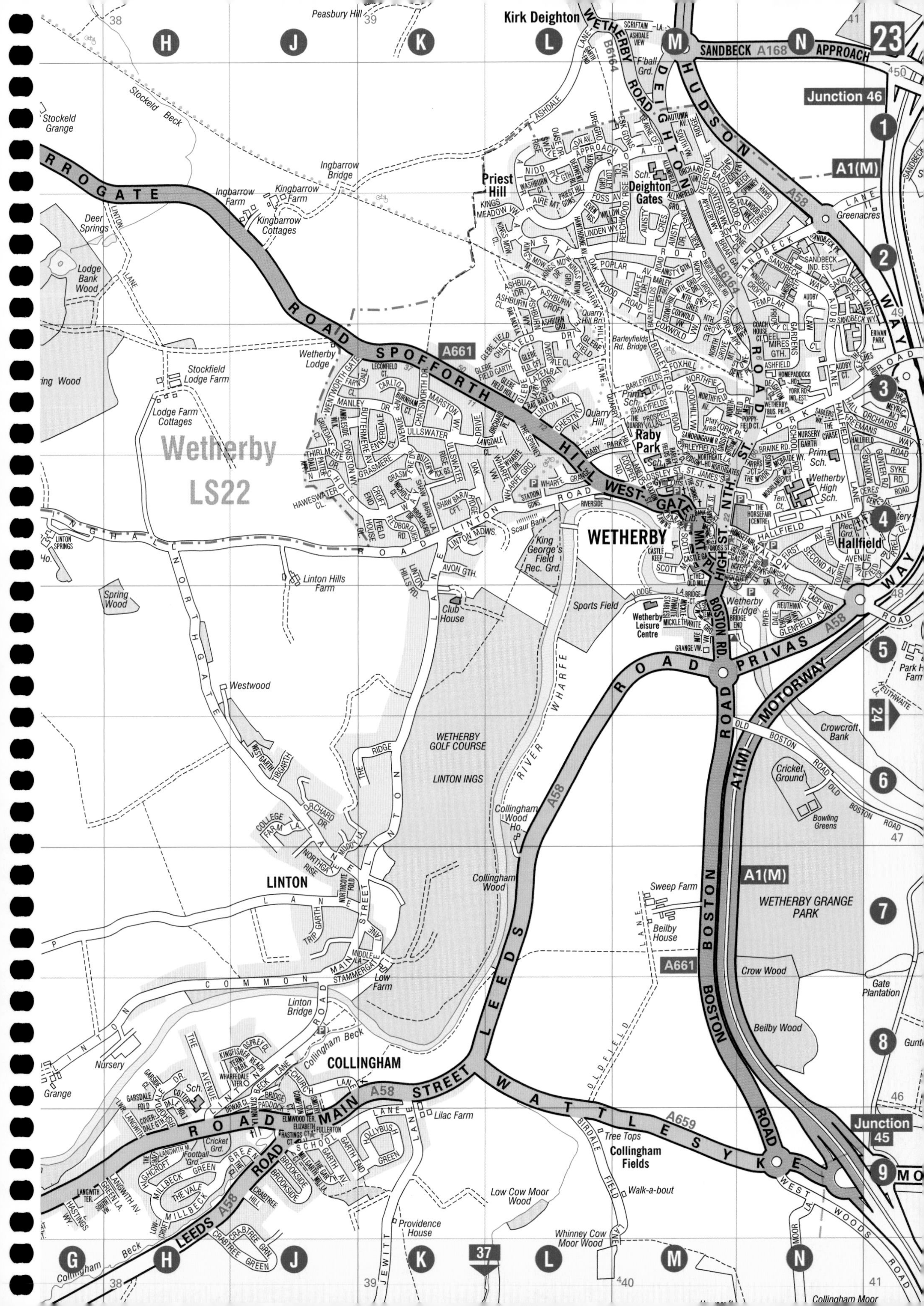

Kirk Deighton
Peasbury Hill
WETHERBY ROAD
DEIGHTON ROAD
HUDSON WAY
SANDBECK A168 APPROACH
Junction 46
A1(M)
A58
Greenacres
Stockeld Grange
Stockeld Beck
HARROGATE ROAD
Ingbarrow Bridge
Ingbarrow Farm
Kingbarrow Farm
Kingbarrow Cottages
Deer Springs
Lodge Bank Wood
Priest Hill
Deighton Gates
SPOFFORTH HILL
A661
Wetherby Lodge
Stockfield Lodge Farm
Lodge Farm Cottages
Wetherby
LS22
Raby Park
Quarry Hill
WEST GATE
WETHERBY
HIGH ST.
NTH. ST.
YORK RD.
Hallfield
Wetherby High Sch.
Sandbeck Ind. Est.
LINTON ROAD
Linton Hills Farm
Spring Wood
King George's Field Rec. Grd.
Sports Field
Wetherby Leisure Centre
Wetherby Bridge
Club House
PRIVAS ROAD
BOSTON RD.
MOTORWAY
Crowcroft Bank
Cricket Ground
Bowling Greens
OLD BOSTON ROAD
Park Farm
Westwood
NORTHGATE
WETHERBY GOLF COURSE
LINTON INGS
RIVER WHARFE
Collingham Wood Ho.
Collingham Wood
LINTON
LINTON LANE
COMMON LANE
Linton Bridge
Low Farm
Sweep Farm
Beilby House
WETHERBY GRANGE PARK
Crow Wood
Beilby Wood
Gate Plantation
COLLINGHAM
Collingham Beck
MAIN STREET
LEEDS ROAD
WATTLESYKE
A659
Junction 45
Lilac Farm
Tree Tops
Collingham Fields
Nursery
Grange
Walk-a-bout
Low Cow Moor Wood
Providence House
Whinney Cow Moor Wood
WEST WOODS ROAD
Collingham Moor
24
37

A1(M)
Wetherby Service Area
Junction 46
SANDBECK APPROACH
A168
INGMANTHORPE PARK
Hall
Duckpond Plantation
RACECOURSE
SANDBECK LANE
Sandbeck Ho.
Sandbeck Bridge
Sandbeck Wood
Sand Beck
Swinnow Hill
Moss Carrs Farm
B1224
Noble Wood
Greenacres
Cockshot Wood
APPROACH
SWINNOW PARK
Timber Yard
SPRINGS LANE
HUDSON WAY
CARR LANE
HMYOI WETHERBY
THE ROWANS
Sand Bri.
YORK ROAD
Lodge
Nova Scotia
Champagne Whin
Warehouses
Moor Plantation
The Rampart
WETHERBY RACECOURSE
Grand Stands
Caravan Site
Parade Ring
Hornshaw Plantation
Sykes House Farm
Stables
LS22
Wetherby
Springs Wood
Spring Wood
SPRING LANE
Jackson Wood
MOOR LANE
Hallfield
Cemetery
Wetherby High Sch.
Rose Dene Farm
PRIVAS WAY
WALTON ROAD
A1(M) MOTORWAY
A58
WATERSOLE LANE
60
Park Hill Farm
HEUTHWAITE LANE
WALTON GATES
WETHERBY ROAD
30
WALTON
Walton Old Hall
SCHOOL LA.
MAIN STREET
Fox C
Hall Ir
23
Crow Bank
West Field
FLINT MILL LANE
Flint Mill Farm
The Flint Mill
Weir
Flint Mill Grange
Snowden Garden
WOOD LANE
LS23
Horn Bank
Sewage Works
Wray Wood Farm
Wray Wood
The Bank
Leeds United FC Training Grd.
WALTON CHASE
THORP ARCH GRANGE
Sports Ground
Pav.
HMP WEALSTUN
Bowling Greens
BOSTON ROAD
WETHERBY GRANGE
Hatfield Bank
WETHERBY GRANGE PARK
Whin Covert
New Springs
Middle Field
Spoilbank Plantation
Long Nursery
Gate Plantation
The Leys
Hall Farm
RIVER WHARFE
Hall Wood
Jackdaw Crag
Robin Hood's Cave
West Park
DEEPDALE
Deepdale Lodge
Thorparch Hall
Thorparch Park
THORP ARCH
DOWKELL LANE
Lady Elizabeth Hastings C of E Prim. Sch.
Cricket Grd.
The Firs
Whitegates
Playing Field
WALTON CAUSEWAY
Gunter Wood
Front Wood
WHINS LANE
CHURCH CAUSEWAY
Grange Moor
Moor End Farm
Cherry Tree Cottages
Comm. Cen.
BOSTON SPA
Weir
Bridge Farm
Thorparch Bridge
CHURCH FIELD
MOOR END
HIGH STREET
A659
Grove Farm
Junction 45
LEYS LANE
CLARENDON RD.
Prim. Sch.
West Oaks
Spa Baths
TOWN INGS
Playing Field
38
A1(M) MOTORWAY
A B C D E F G
1 2 3 4 5 6 7 8 9
41 42 43 44
450 49 48 47 46
Collingham Moor

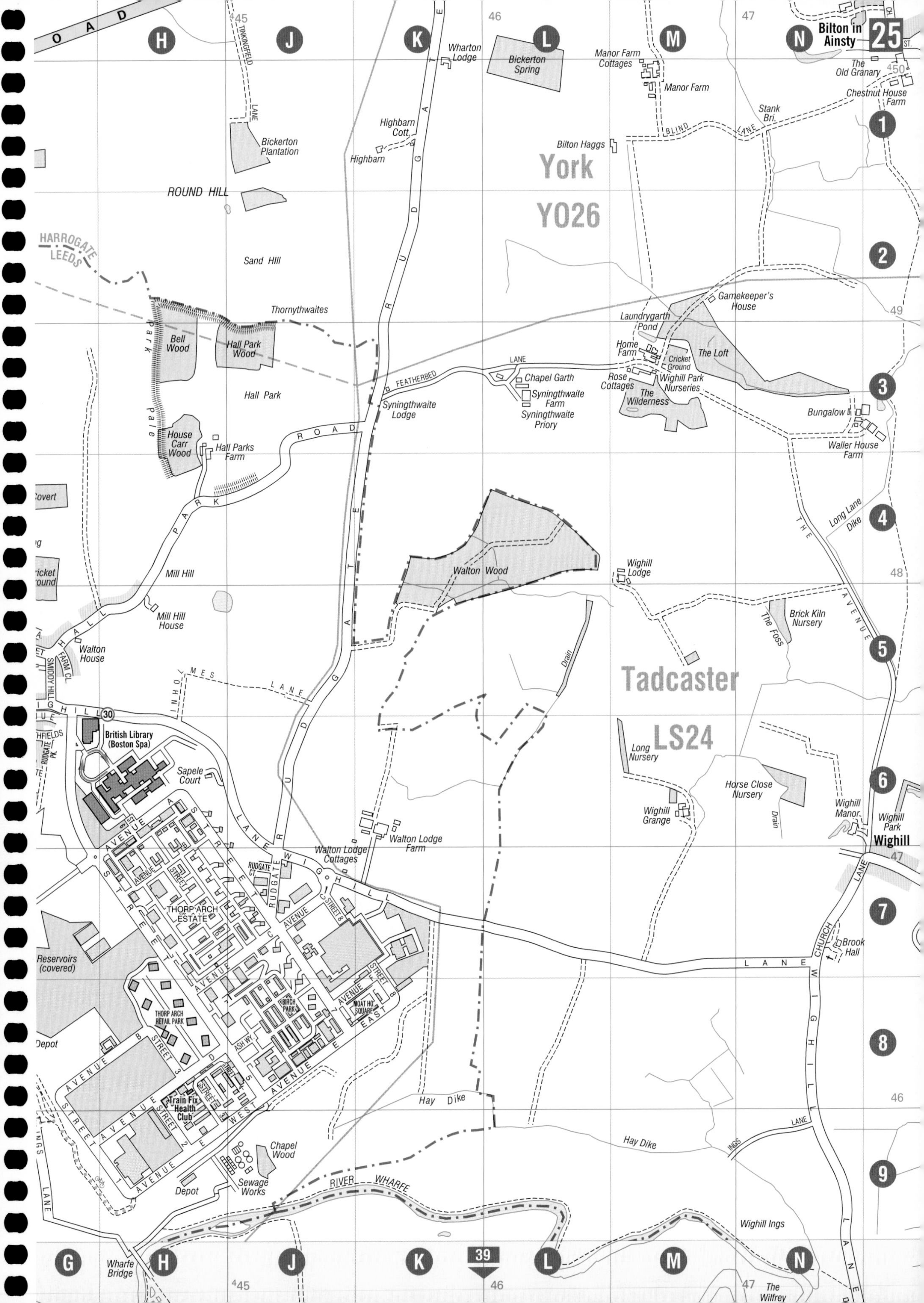
Bilton in Ainsty
York
YO26
Tadcaster
LS24
Wighill
Walton Wood
British Library (Boston Spa)
Thorp Arch Estate
Hall Park
Bickerton Spring
Bickerton Plantation
Round Hill
Sand Hill
Thornythwaites
Bell Wood
Hall Park Wood
House Carr Wood
Hall Parks Farm
Mill Hill
Mill Hill House
Walton House
Walton Lodge Farm
Walton Lodge Cottages
Syningthwaite Lodge
Chapel Garth
Syningthwaite Farm
Syningthwaite Priory
Wighill Park Nurseries
The Wilderness
The Loft
Gamekeeper's House
Laundrygarth Pond
Home Farm
Rose Cottages
Wighill Lodge
Brick Kiln Nursery
Long Nursery
Horse Close Nursery
Wighill Grange
Wighill Manor
Wighill Park
Brook Hall
Manor Farm
Manor Farm Cottages
Bilton Haggs
Wharton Lodge
Highbarn
Highbarn Cott.
Stank Bri.
Chestnut House Farm
The Old Granary
Waller House Farm
Bungalow
Hay Dike
Wighill Ings
River Wharfe
Chapel Wood
Sewage Works
Depot
Reservoirs (covered)
Wharfe Bridge
The Wilfrey
Sapele Court
Thorp Arch Retail Park
Train Fix Health Club
Moat Ho. Square
Birch Park
Rudgate
Featherbed Lane
Wighill Lane
Church Lane
The Avenue
Long Lane Dike
The Foss
Drain
Harrogate
Leeds
39

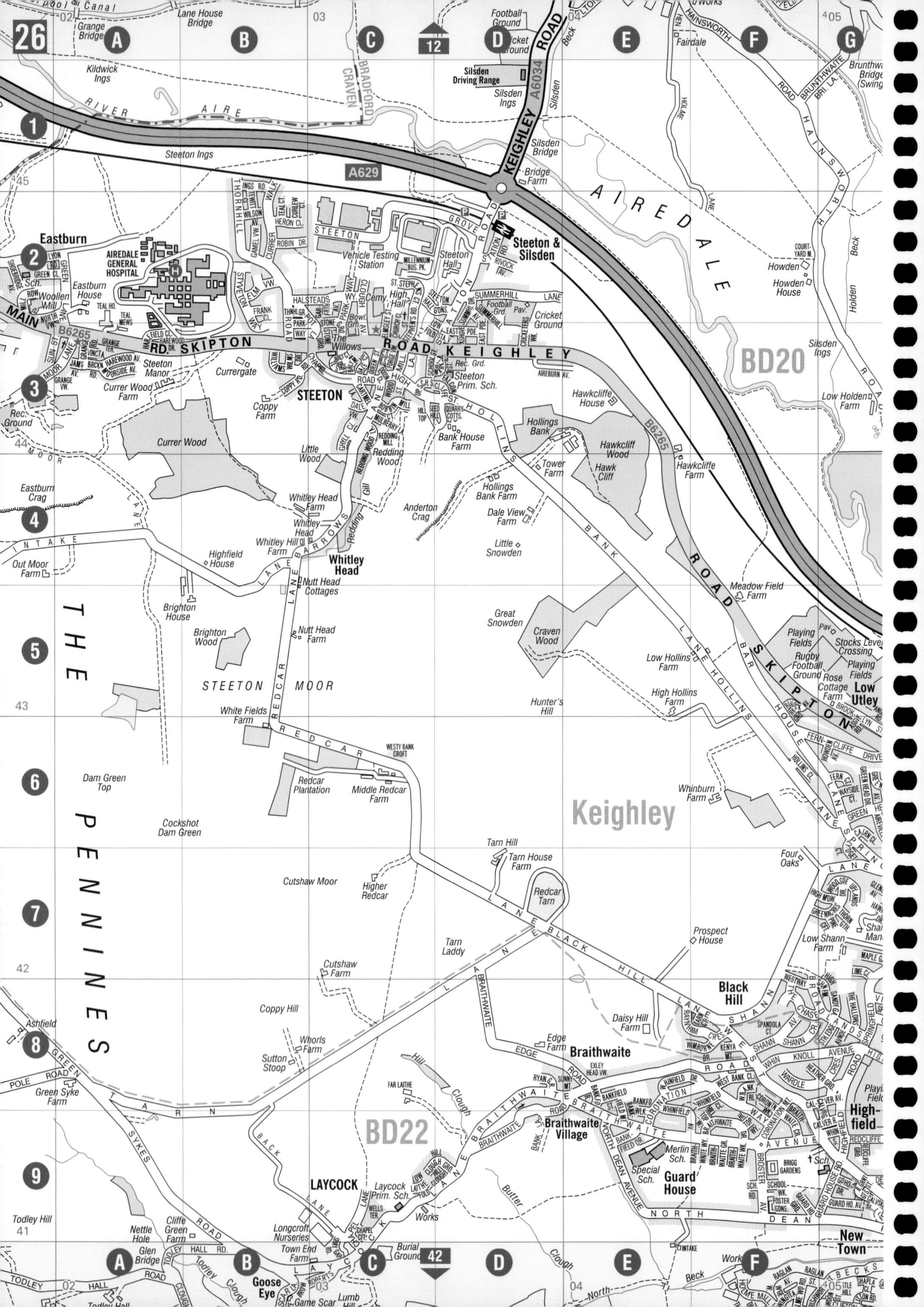

A
B
C
D
E
F
G
12
42
1
2
3
4
5
6
7
8
9
02
03
04
405
45
44
43
42
41
Grange Bridge
Lane House Bridge
Football Ground
Cricket Ground
Silsden Driving Range
Silsden Ings
KEIGHLEY ROAD
A6034
Silsden
Beck
Fairdale
HAINSWORTH
Brunthwaite Bridge (Swing)
BRUNTHWAITE BRI. LA.
Kildwick Ings
RIVER AIRE
CRAVEN
BRADFORD
Steeton Ings
A629
Silsden Bridge
Bridge Farm
AIREDALE
HOLME
LANE
Eastburn
AIREDALE GENERAL HOSPITAL
Eastburn House
Woollen Mill
Sch.
TEAL HO.
TEAL MEWS
MAIN
B6265
RD. SKIPTON
ROAD KEIGHLEY
Steeton Manor
Currergate
Currer Wood Farm
Rec. Ground
STEETON
Coppy Farm
STEETON
Vehicle Testing Station
MILLENNIUM BUS. PK.
Steeton Hall
Steeton & Silsden
GROVE
STATION ROAD
RIVOCK AV.
SUMMERHILL LANE
Football Grd.
Pav.
Cricket Ground
CRICKETERS WK.
AIREBURN AV.
Cemy.
High Hall
Bowl. Grn.
The Willows
HALSTEADS
Rec. Grd.
Steeton Prim. Sch.
HOLLINS
Hawkcliffe House
Hollings Bank
Hawkcliff Wood
Hawk Cliff
Hawkcliffe Farm
Tower Farm
Bank House Farm
Redding Wood
Little Wood
Currer Wood
MOOR
Eastburn Crag
LANE
INTAKE
Out Moor Farm
Highfield House
Whitley Head Farm
Whitley Head
Whitley Hill Farm
Whitley Head
BARROWS LANE
Redding
Gill
Anderton Crag
Hollings Bank Farm
Dale View Farm
Little Snowden
BANK
Nutt Head Cottages
Brighton House
Brighton Wood
Nutt Head Farm
Great Snowden
Craven Wood
ROAD
Meadow Field Farm
Playing Fields
Rugby Football Ground
Rose Cottage Farm
Stocks Lever Crossing
Playing Fields
Low Utley
SKIPTON
BAR HOUSE LANE
LANE HOLLINS
Low Hollins Farm
High Hollins Farm
Hunter's Hill
STEETON MOOR
THE PENNINES
White Fields Farm
REDCAR ROAD
REDCAR
WESTY BANK CROFT
Redcar Plantation
Middle Redcar Farm
Dam Green Top
Cockshot Dam Green
Whinburn Farm
Keighley
FERNCLIFFE DRIVE
Tarn Hill
Tarn House Farm
Redcar Tarn
Four Oaks
Cutshaw Moor
Higher Redcar
LANE
Tarn Laddy
BLACK HILL LANE
Prospect House
Low Shann Farm
Cutshaw Farm
Black Hill
Coppy Hill
BRAITHWAITE
Daisy Hill Farm
Ashfield
Whorls Farm
Sutton Stoop
Edge Farm
EDGE ROAD
Braithwaite
SHANN
WEST LANE
SHANN
KNOLL
AVENUE
POLE ROAD
GREEN
Green Syke Farm
TARN
Hill
Clough
FAR LAITHE
BRAITHWAITE ROAD
BRAITHWAITE
Braithwaite Village
CORONATION WAY
WHINFIELD
BRAITHWAITE AVENUE
Highfield
REDCLIFFE
BD22
SYKES
BACK LANE
LAYCOCK
Laycock Prim. Sch.
Works
Butter
Special Sch.
Merlin Sch.
Guard House
NORTH DEAN AVENUE
BROSTER AV.
BRIGG GARDENS
Sch.
GUARD HOUSE RD.
Todley Hill
Nettle Hole
Cliffe Green Farm
ROAD
Longcroft Nurseries
Town End Farm
Burial Ground
Clough
INTAKE
New Town
NORTH DEAN
Glen Bridge
TODLEY HALL RD.
Todley Clough
LAYCOCK
Goose Eye
Game Scar
Lumb
Beck
North
Works
TODLEY HALL ROAD
BD20

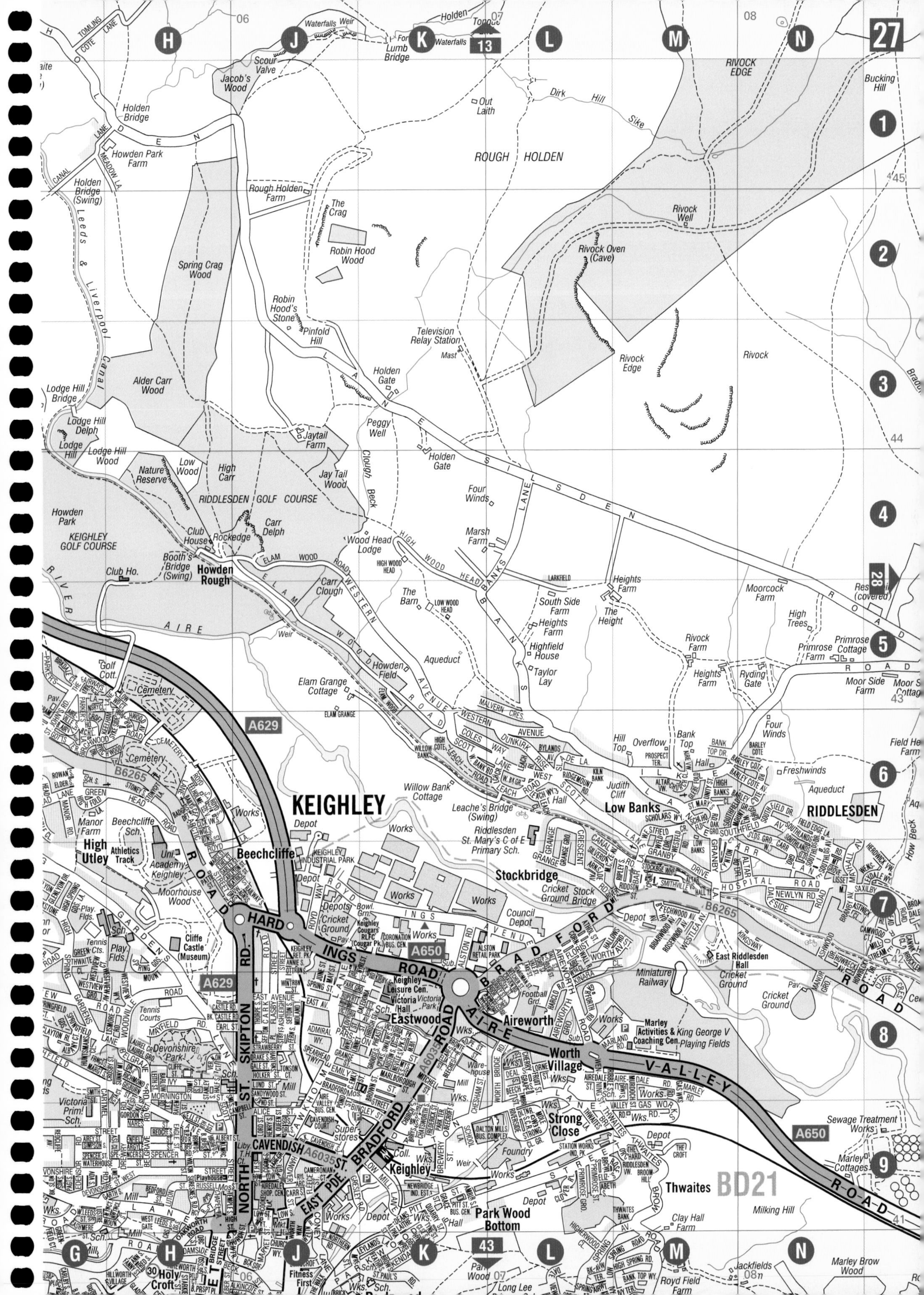
KEIGHLEY
RIDDLESDEN
Low Banks
Stockbridge
Beechcliffe
High Utley
Eastwood
Aireworth
Worth Village
Strong Close
Thwaites
BD21
Howden Rough
Park Wood Bottom
Holy Croft
Keighley
ROUGH HOLDEN
RIVOCK EDGE
Rivock Edge
Rivock Oven (Cave)
Rivock Well
Rivock
Bucking Hill
Robin Hood Wood
The Crag
Robin Hood's Stone
Pinfold Hill
Television Relay Station
Spring Crag Wood
Alder Carr Wood
Jacob's Wood
Holden Bridge
Howden Park Farm
Holden Bridge (Swing)
Rough Holden Farm
Lumb Bridge
Waterfalls
Weir
Scour Valve
Out Laith
Dirk Hill Sike
Lodge Hill Bridge
Lodge Hill Delph
Lodge Hill Wood
Nature Reserve
Low Wood
High Carr
Jaytail Farm
Jay Tail Wood
RIDDLESDEN GOLF COURSE
KEIGHLEY GOLF COURSE
Howden Park
Club House
Rockedge
Carr Delph
Booth's Bridge (Swing)
Club Ho.
Peggy Well
Holden Gate
Clough Beck
Four Winds
Marsh Farm
Wood Head Lodge
Carr Clough
The Barn
Heights Farm
The Height
South Side Farm
Highfield House
Taylor Lay
Moorcock Farm
High Trees
Primrose Farm
Primrose Cottage
Moor Side Farm
Rivock Farm
Ryding Gate
Aqueduct
Howden Field
Elam Grange Cottage
Willow Bank Cottage
Leache's Bridge (Swing)
Riddlesden St. Mary's C of E Primary Sch.
Judith Cliff
Hill Top
Overflow
Bank Top
Freshwinds
East Riddlesden Hall
Miniature Railway
Cricket Ground
King George V Playing Fields
Marley Activities & Coaching Cen.
Sewage Treatment Works
Marley Cottages
Milking Hill
Clay Hall Farm
Jackfields
Royd Field Farm
Marley Brow Wood
Long Lee
Cliffe Castle (Museum)
Devonshire Park
Victoria Prim. Sch.
Keighley Leisure Cen.
Victoria Hall
Victoria Park
Keighley Cougars RLFC (Cougar Pk.)
KEIGHLEY INDUSTRIAL PARK
Works
Depot
Council Depot
Foundry
Stock Bridge
Uni. Academy Keighley
Moorhouse Wood
Athletics Track
Beechcliffe Sch.
Manor Farm
Cemetery
Golf Cott.
SILSDEN ROAD
HOLDEN LANE
HIGH WOOD HEAD
BANKS LANE
WESTERN AVENUE
ELAM WOOD ROAD
SKIPTON RD.
NORTH ST.
HARD INGS ROAD
BRADFORD RD.
AIRE VALLEY ROAD
CAVENDISH ST.
EAST PDE.
LEEDS & LIVERPOOL CANAL
RIVER AIRE
A629
A650
A6035
B6265
13
28
43
H J K L M N
G H J K L M N
06 07 08
1 2 3 4 5 6 7 8 9
45 44 43 42 41

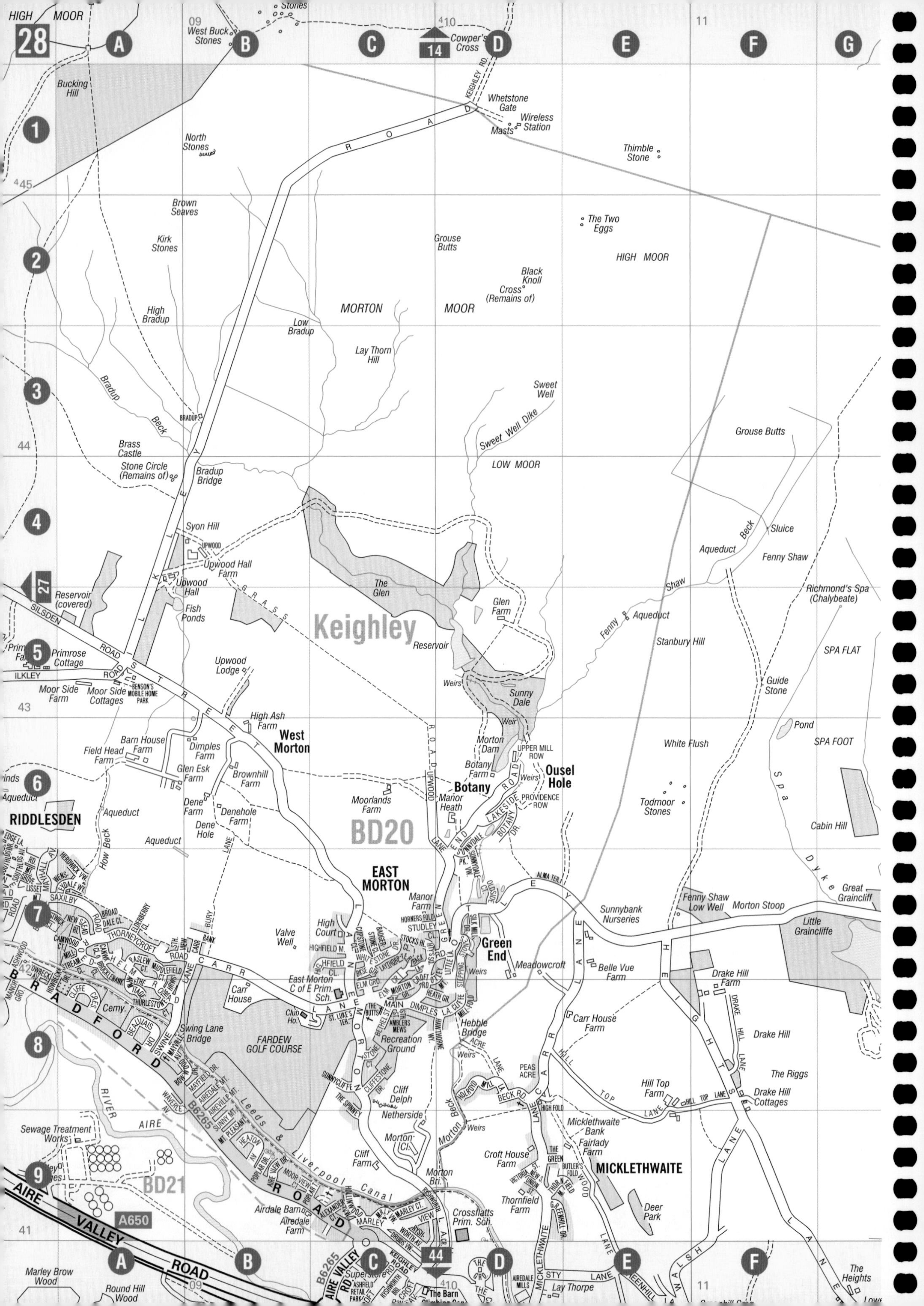
28
HIGH MOOR
West Buck Stones
Stones
Cowper's Cross
14
Bucking Hill
KEIGHLEY RD.
ROAD
Whetstone Gate
Wireless Station
Masts
North Stones
Thimble Stone
Brown Seaves
Kirk Stones
The Two Eggs
Grouse Butts
HIGH MOOR
Black Knoll
Cross (Remains of)
High Bradup
MORTON
MOOR
Low Bradup
Lay Thorn Hill
Bradup
Beck
BRADUP
Sweet Well
Sweet Well Dike
Grouse Butts
Brass Castle
Stone Circle (Remains of)
Bradup Bridge
LOW MOOR
Syon Hill
UPWOOD
Upwood Hall Farm
Upwood Hall
Sluice
Beck
Aqueduct
Fenny Shaw
27
Reservoir (covered)
GRASS
The Glen
Glen Farm
Shaw
Richmond's Spa (Chalybeate)
Fish Ponds
Keighley
Fenny
Aqueduct
SILSDEN
ROAD
Primrose Cottage
Reservoir
Stanbury Hill
SPA FLAT
ILKLEY
Upwood Lodge
Weirs
Sunny Dale
Guide Stone
Moor Side Farm
Moor Side Cottages
BENSON'S MOBILE HOME PARK
STREET
High Ash Farm
Weir
Pond
West Morton
Morton Dam
UPPER MILL ROW
White Flush
SPA FOOT
Barn House Farm
Dimples Farm
Field Head Farm
Glen Esk Farm
Brownhill Farm
Botany Farm
Weirs
Ousel Hole
Spa
RIDDLESDEN
Aqueduct
Dene Farm
Denehole Farm
Dene Hole
Moorlands Farm
Botany
Manor Heath
UPWOOD ROAD
PROVIDENCE ROW
LAKESIDE
BOTANY DR.
Todmoor Stones
Cabin Hill
BD20
How Beck
Aqueduct
LANE
EAST MORTON
ALMA TER.
Dyke
Great Graincliff
Fenny Shaw Low Well
Morton Stoop
Manor Farm
Sunnybank Nurseries
Little Graincliffe
High Court
Valve Well
STUDLEY
Green End
Meadowcroft
Belle Vue Farm
Drake Hill Farm
East Morton C of E Prim. Sch.
Carr House
BRADFORD
CARR LANE
Cemy.
Club Ho.
ST. LUKE'S TER.
MAIN
DIMPLES
Recreation Ground
Hebble Bridge
Carr House Farm
Drake Hill
Swing Lane Bridge
FARDEW GOLF COURSE
PEAS ACRE
The Riggs
Cliff Delph
Netherside
Hill Top Farm
HILL TOP LANE
Drake Hill Cottages
RIVER
AIRE
B6265
Leeds & Liverpool Canal
Morton Beck
Weirs
Micklethwaite Bank
Fairlady Farm
Sewage Treatment Works
Morton Cl.
Croft House Farm
Cliff Farm
MICKLETHWAITE
BD21
Morton Bri.
Thornfield Farm
Deer Park
AIRE VALLEY ROAD
A650
Airdale Barn
Airedale Farm
Crossflatts Prim. Sch.
41
42
43
44
45
09
410
11
A
B
C
D
E
F
G
1
2
3
4
5
6
7
8
9
44
Marley Brow Wood
Round Hill Wood
Superstore
ASHFIELD RETAIL PARK
The Barn
Lay Thorpe
AIREDALE MILLS
The Heights
LANE
WALSH LANE

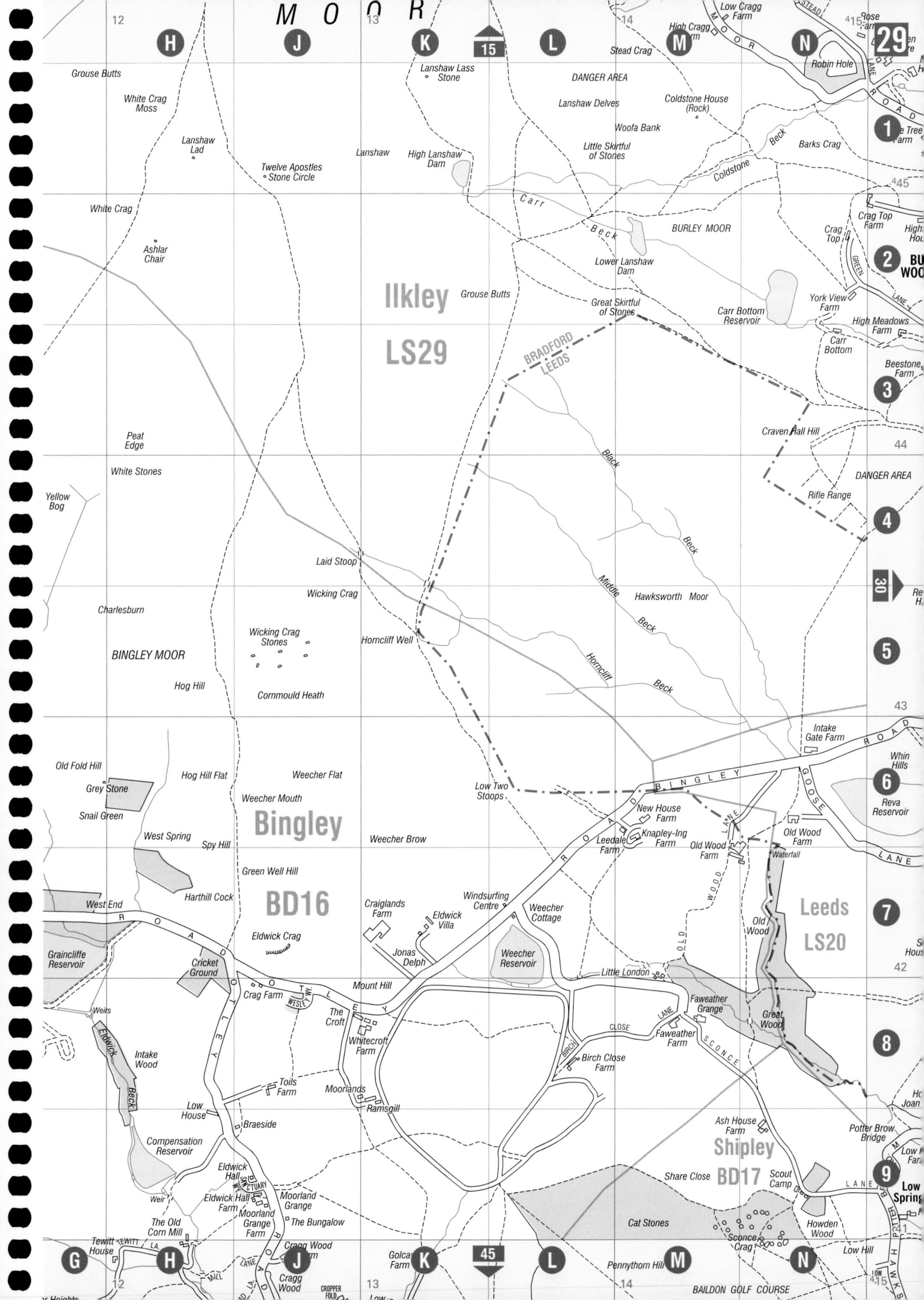

29
MOOR
Ilkley
LS29
Bingley
BD16
Leeds
LS20
Shipley
BD17
BRADFORD
LEEDS
Grouse Butts
White Crag Moss
Lanshaw Lad
Twelve Apostles Stone Circle
Lanshaw Lass Stone
Lanshaw
High Lanshaw Dam
DANGER AREA
Lanshaw Delves
Coldstone House (Rock)
Woofa Bank
Little Skirtful of Stones
Stead Crag
Low Cragg Farm
Robin Hole
Barks Crag
Coldstone Beck
Carr Beck
BURLEY MOOR
White Crag
Ashlar Chair
Lower Lanshaw Dam
Crag Top Farm
Crag Top
Great Skirtful of Stones
Carr Bottom Reservoir
York View Farm
High Meadows Farm
Carr Bottom
Beestone Farm
Craven Hall Hill
Rifle Range
Peat Edge
White Stones
Yellow Bog
Black Beck
Laid Stoop
Wicking Crag
Charlesburn
Middle Beck
Hawksworth Moor
Wicking Crag Stones
Horncliff Well
BINGLEY MOOR
Hog Hill
Cornmould Heath
Horncliff Beck
Intake Gate Farm
Old Fold Hill
Hog Hill Flat
Weecher Flat
Grey Stone
Weecher Mouth
Low Two Stoops
BINGLEY ROAD
New House Farm
Knapley-Ing Farm
Leedale Farm
Old Wood Farm
Waterfall
Whin Hills
Reva Reservoir
GOOSE LANE
Snail Green
West Spring
Spy Hill
Weecher Brow
Green Well Hill
Harthill Cock
West End
Craiglands Farm
Eldwick Villa
Windsurfing Centre
Weecher Cottage
OLD WOOD LANE
Old Wood
Graincliffe Reservoir
Cricket Ground
Eldwick Crag
Jonas Delph
Weecher Reservoir
Little London
Crag Farm
WESLEY WY.
Mount Hill
OTLEY ROAD
The Croft
Whitecroft Farm
Faweather Grange
Great Wood
CLOSE LANE
BIRCH
Faweather Farm
SCONCE
Birch Close Farm
Weirs
Eldwick Beck
Intake Wood
Toils Farm
Moorlands
Ramsgill
Low House
Braeside
Ash House Farm
Potter Brow Bridge
Compensation Reservoir
Eldwick Hall
SANCTUARY
Eldwick Hall Farm
Moorland Grange
Moorland Grange Farm
The Bungalow
Share Close
Scout Camp
LANE
Weir
The Old Corn Mill
Cat Stones
Sconce Crag
Howden Wood
Tewitt House
TEWITT LA
MILL LANE
Cragg Wood Farm
Cragg Wood
Golcar Farm
Pennythorn Hill
Low Hill
BAILDON GOLF COURSE
CROPPER FOLD
Low Spring
POTTER HAWKS
12
13
14
415
445
44
43
42
441
H
J
K
L
M
N
G
1
2
3
4
5
6
7
8
9
15
30
45

Burley in Wharfedale
16
Garden Centre
Moor House
Robin Hole
Ashburn
Reservoir (covered)
Hollin Nook
Woodhead
Moorlands
Coldstone Beck
Plane Tree Farm
Jubilee Trees
Ghylmoor
Spring Acres
Far Bron
Hillside
Crag Top Farm
Highfield House
Prospect Row
Redwalls
Rough Hole
Carr Beck
BURLEY WOODHEAD
Hag Farm
Ilkley
LS29
Bleach Mill
York View Farm
High Meadows Farm
Field Head Farm
Jumb Beck Farm
Carr Bottom
Beestone Farm
Turnpike Farm
Bracken Hill
Stock Gate Farm
Southpiece Cottage
Almscliffe View
Stocks Hill
Reservoir (covered)
Heather Bank
Gynesta
DANGER AREA
Rifle Range
Highfield House
Low Toft
Hilltop Farm
Wayside
Matthew Dike
Reva Hill
29
Sunny Mead
Hawthorne Villas
Hillcrest
Derry Hill Farm
Thorn Bank
Hillside
The Coach House
MENSTON
BRADFORD
LEEDS
Haggwood Farm
Albury
Cotton Field
Reevadale
The Rhyddings
Cemy.
Brookleigh Farm
Menston
Recreation Ground
Home Farm
High Royds Hall
Intake Gate Farm
Whin Hills
Sailing Club
Reva Reservoir
Hawksworth Equestrian Centre
Wrose View
Meadowcroft Farm
New Dam
Storth House Farm
Jum Bridge
Moor View
Hawksworth Quarry
Odda Hill
Jum Dam
Four Lane Ends
Jum Wood
Sunnyside Farm
Intake Side Farm
HAWKSWORTH
Hawksworth Hall
Hawksworth C of E Primary School
Alders Well
Corn Mill Farm
Round Hill
Honey Joan Wood
Honey Joan Hill
Potter Brow Bridge
Low Mill Farm
Roundabout Wood
Birkin Hill
BRADFORD GOLF COURSE
Hall Croft
Greenhouse Hill
Club House
Hawksworth Rec. Grd.
LS20
Low Springs
Hollings Farm
Low Spring Farm
Hawksworth Spring
Low Hill
Birks Wood
46
Goit Stock Farm
OTLEY GOLF COURSE
Mickle Ing
Club House
Milner Wood
Acre Cliffe Farm
Recycle Cen.
Works
Oaks Farm
Gill Beck
Brooklands
Chevin Grange
Delph Cottage
Chevin Grange Farm
Cemetery
St. Marys Cath. Comp. Sch.
Playing Fields
Superstore
White Cross
Mire Beck
Tran Mire Beck
The Grange
Tranmere Park
Tranmere Park Prim. Sch.
Lane Side Farm
Four Lane Ends
Hawkstone Farm
Hawkstone Wood
Hawks Stone
Elm Wood
BRADFORD ROAD
OTLEY ROAD
BINGLEY ROAD
GOOSE LANE
HOLLINS

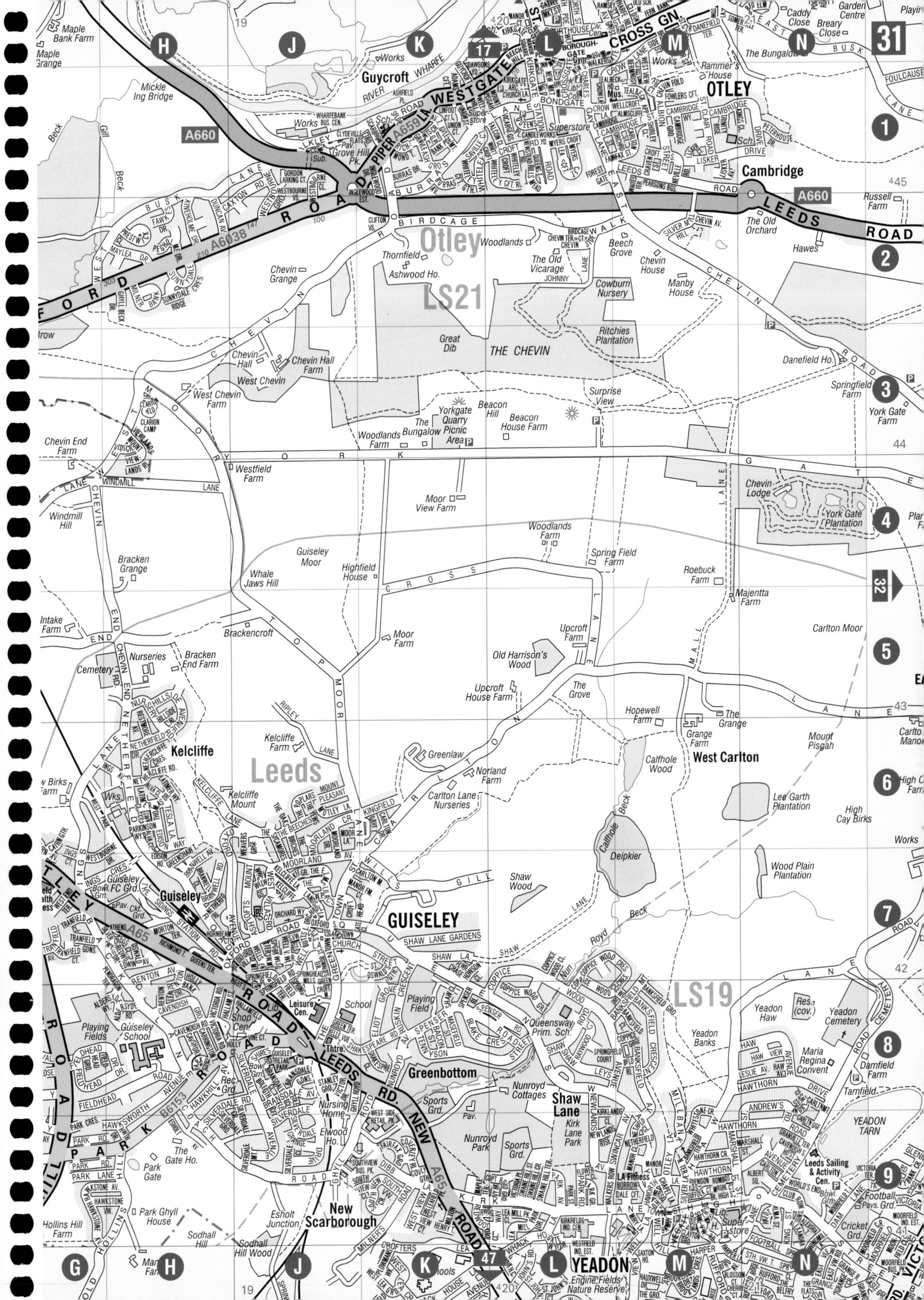

31
OTLEY
Otley
LS21
Guycroft
Cambridge
THE CHEVIN
Guiseley
GUISELEY
Kelcliffe
Leeds
West Carlton
LS19
YEADON
New Scarborough
Greenbottom
Shaw Lane
A660
A6038
A65
B6153
LEEDS ROAD
YORK GATE
CHEVIN END
CARLTON LANE
MALL LANE
Calfhole Wood
Deipkier
Yeadon Cemetery
YEADON TARN
32
17
47

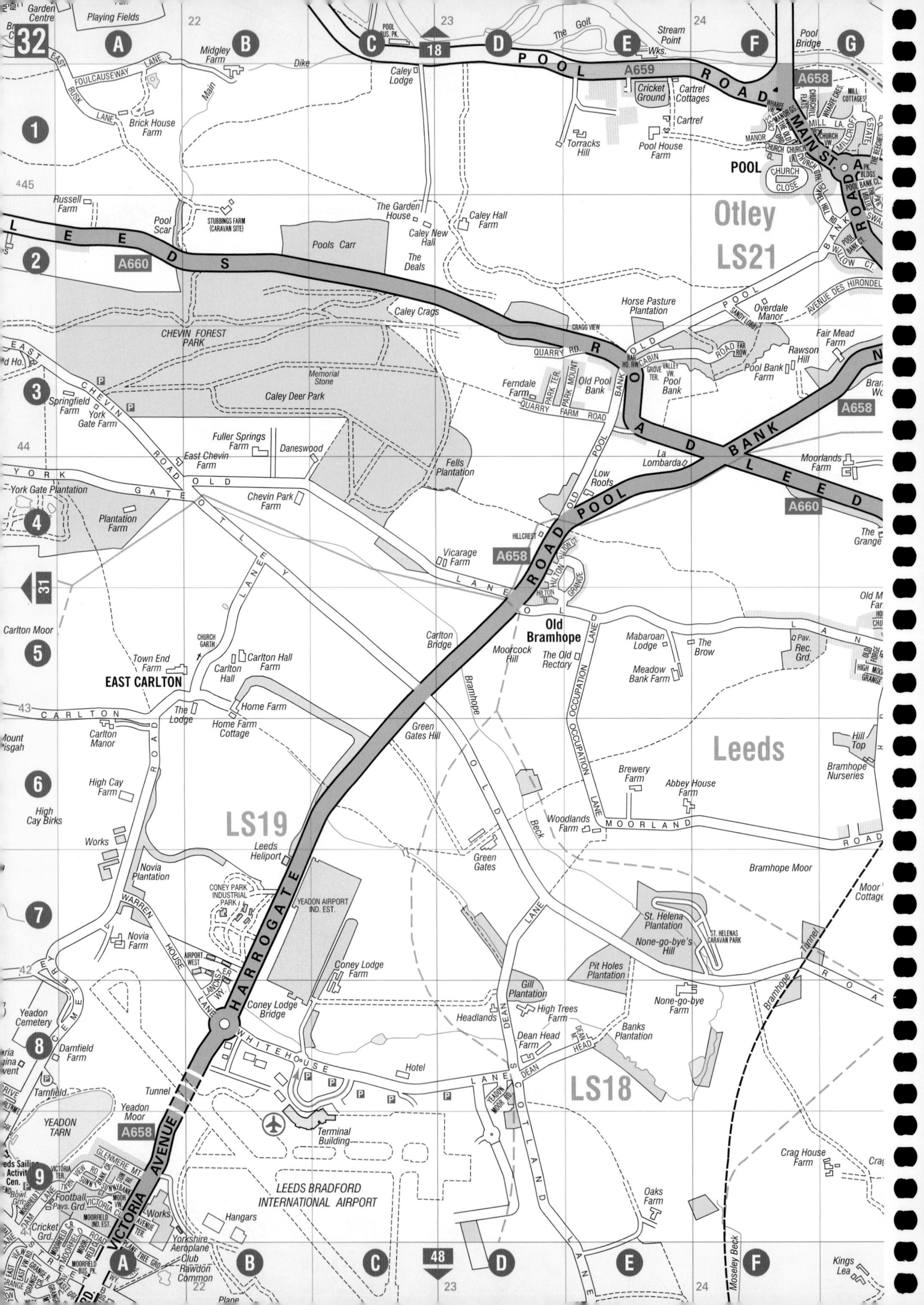

Otley
LS21
Leeds
LS19
LS18
POOL
Old Bramhope
EAST CARLTON
LEEDS BRADFORD INTERNATIONAL AIRPORT
POOL ROAD
A659
A658
A660
LEEDS ROAD
HARROGATE ROAD
VICTORIA AVENUE
OLD POOL BANK
POOL BANK
CHEVIN FOREST PARK
Caley Deer Park
Pools Carr
Caley Crags
Memorial Stone
Fells Plantation
Midgley Farm
Brick House Farm
Russell Farm
Pool Scar
STUBBINGS FARM (CARAVAN SITE)
Caley Lodge
The Garden House
Caley New Hall
Caley Hall Farm
The Deals
Cricket Ground
Cartref Cottages
Cartref
Torracks Hill
Pool House Farm
Stream Point
The Goit
Pool Bridge
Horse Pasture Plantation
Overdale Manor
Fair Mead Farm
Rawson Hill
Pool Bank Farm
Ferndale Farm
Old Pool Bank
La Lombarda
Moorlands Farm
Low Roofs
The Grange
Springfield Farm
York Gate Farm
York Gate Plantation
Plantation Farm
East Chevin Farm
Fuller Springs Farm
Daneswood
Chevin Park Farm
Vicarage Farm
Carlton Moor
Town End Farm
Carlton Hall
Carlton Hall Farm
Home Farm
Home Farm Cottage
The Lodge
Carlton Manor
High Cay Farm
High Cay Birks
Works
Novia Plantation
Novia Farm
Leeds Heliport
CONEY PARK INDUSTRIAL PARK
YEADON AIRPORT IND. EST.
Coney Lodge Farm
Coney Lodge Bridge
Carlton Bridge
Moorcock Hill
The Old Rectory
Green Gates Hill
Green Gates
Mabaroan Lodge
The Brow
Meadow Bank Farm
Rec. Grd.
Brewery Farm
Abbey House Farm
Woodlands Farm
Hill Top
Bramhope Nurseries
Bramhope Moor
Moor Cottage
St. Helena Plantation
None-go-bye's Hill
ST. HELENAS CARAVAN PARK
Pit Holes Plantation
None-go-bye Farm
Gill Plantation
High Trees Farm
Headlands
Dean Head Farm
Banks Plantation
Hotel
Terminal Building
Hangars
Oaks Farm
Crag House Farm
Kings Lea
Moseley Beck
Yeadon Moor
YEADON TARN
Tunnel
Yeadon Cemetery
Damfield Farm
Tarnfield
Football Pavs. Grd.
Cricket Grd.
Yorkshire Aeroplane Club
Rawdon Common
MOORLAND ROAD
OCCUPATION LANE
CARLTON ROAD
WARREN HOUSE LANE
WHITEHOUSE LANE
SCOTLAND LANE
DEAN LANE
YORK GATE
OLD LANE
OTLEY LANE
EAST CHEVIN ROAD
QUARRY FARM ROAD
MAIN ST.
Playing Fields
Garden Centre

18
31
48

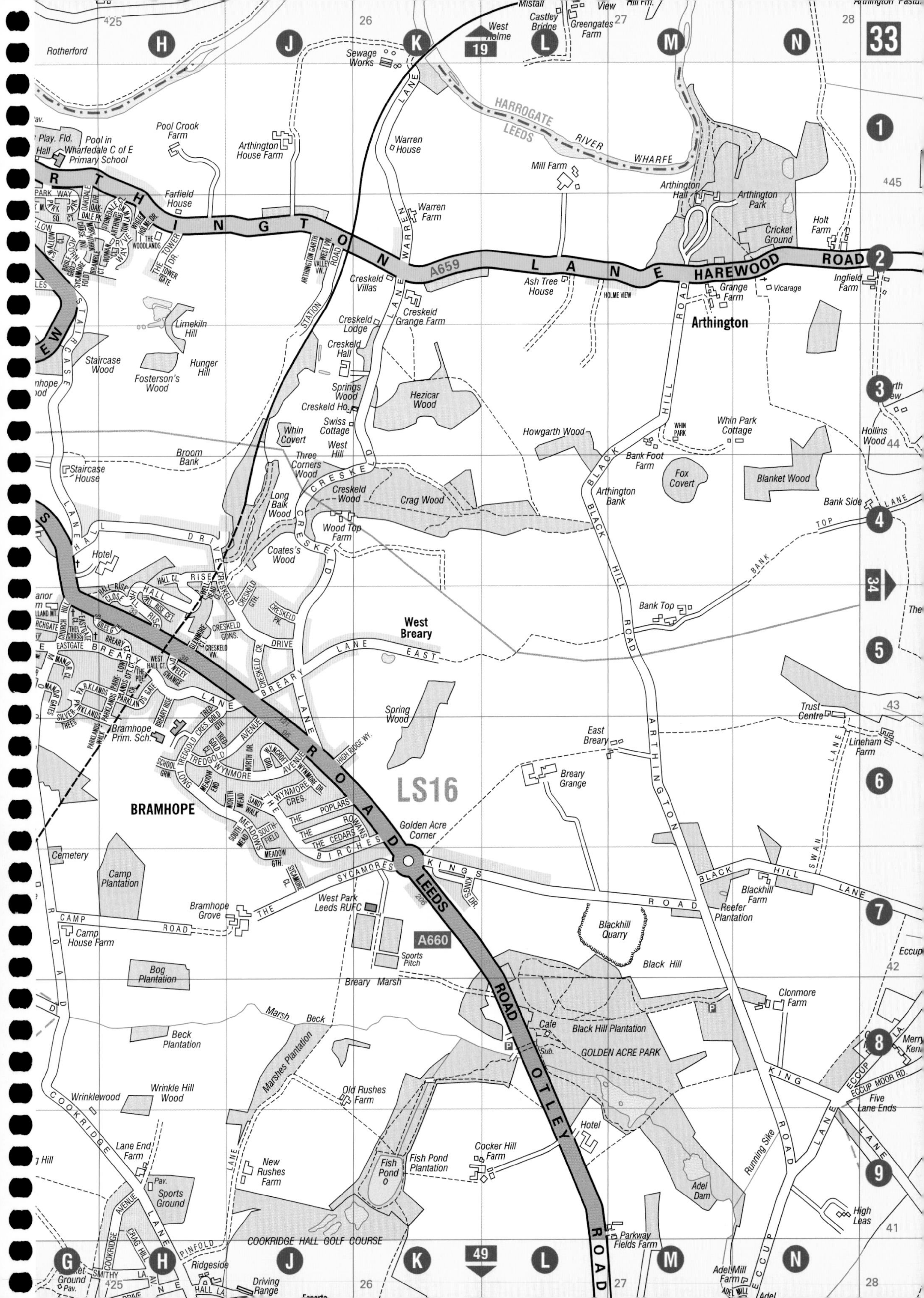
H
J
K
L
M
N
19
Rotherford
Sewage Works
West Holme
Castley Bridge
Greengates Farm
HARROGATE
LEEDS
RIVER WHARFE
Pool Crook Farm
Play. Fld.
Pool in Wharfedale C of E Primary School
Arthington House Farm
Warren House
Mill Farm
Arthington Hall
Arthington Park
Farfield House
Warren Farm
Holt Farm
Cricket Ground
ARTHINGTON LANE
A659
HAREWOOD ROAD
Creskeld Villas
Ash Tree House
HOLME VIEW
Grange Farm
Vicarage
Ingfield Farm
Creskeld Lodge
Creskeld Grange Farm
Arthington
Limekiln Hill
Creskeld Hall
Staircase Wood
Hunger Hill
Fosterson's Wood
Springs Wood
Hezicar Wood
Creskeld Ho.
Swiss Cottage
Whin Covert
West Hill
Howgarth Wood
WHIN PARK
Whin Park Cottage
Hollins Wood
Broom Bank
Three Corners Wood
Bank Foot Farm
Staircase House
Fox Covert
Blanket Wood
Creskeld Wood
Crag Wood
Arthington Bank
Long Balk Wood
Bank Side
Wood Top Farm
TOP BANK
Hotel
Coates's Wood
34
Bank Top
West Breary
BREARY LANE EAST
BRAMHOPE
Bramhope Prim. Sch.
Spring Wood
East Breary
Trust Centre
Lineham Farm
LS16
Breary Grange
Golden Acre Corner
Cemetery
Camp Plantation
Blackhill Farm
BLACK HILL LANE
KINGS ROAD
West Park Leeds RUFC
Reefer Plantation
Bramhope Grove
CAMP ROAD
Camp House Farm
A660
Blackhill Quarry
Sports Pitch
Black Hill
Bog Plantation
Breary Marsh
Clonmore Farm
Marsh Beck
Cafe
Black Hill Plantation
Beck Plantation
GOLDEN ACRE PARK
Marshes Plantation
Wrinklewood
Wrinkle Hill Wood
Old Rushes Farm
Five Lane Ends
ECCUP MOOR RD.
Hotel
Lane End Farm
New Rushes Farm
Fish Pond
Fish Pond Plantation
Cocker Hill Farm
Running Sike
Adel Dam
Sports Ground
High Leas
COOKRIDGE HALL GOLF COURSE
Parkway Fields Farm
OTLEY ROAD
LEEDS ROAD
Ridgeside
Driving Range
Adel Mill Farm
G
49
1
2
3
4
5
6
7
8
9
26
27
28
425
445
44
43
42
41

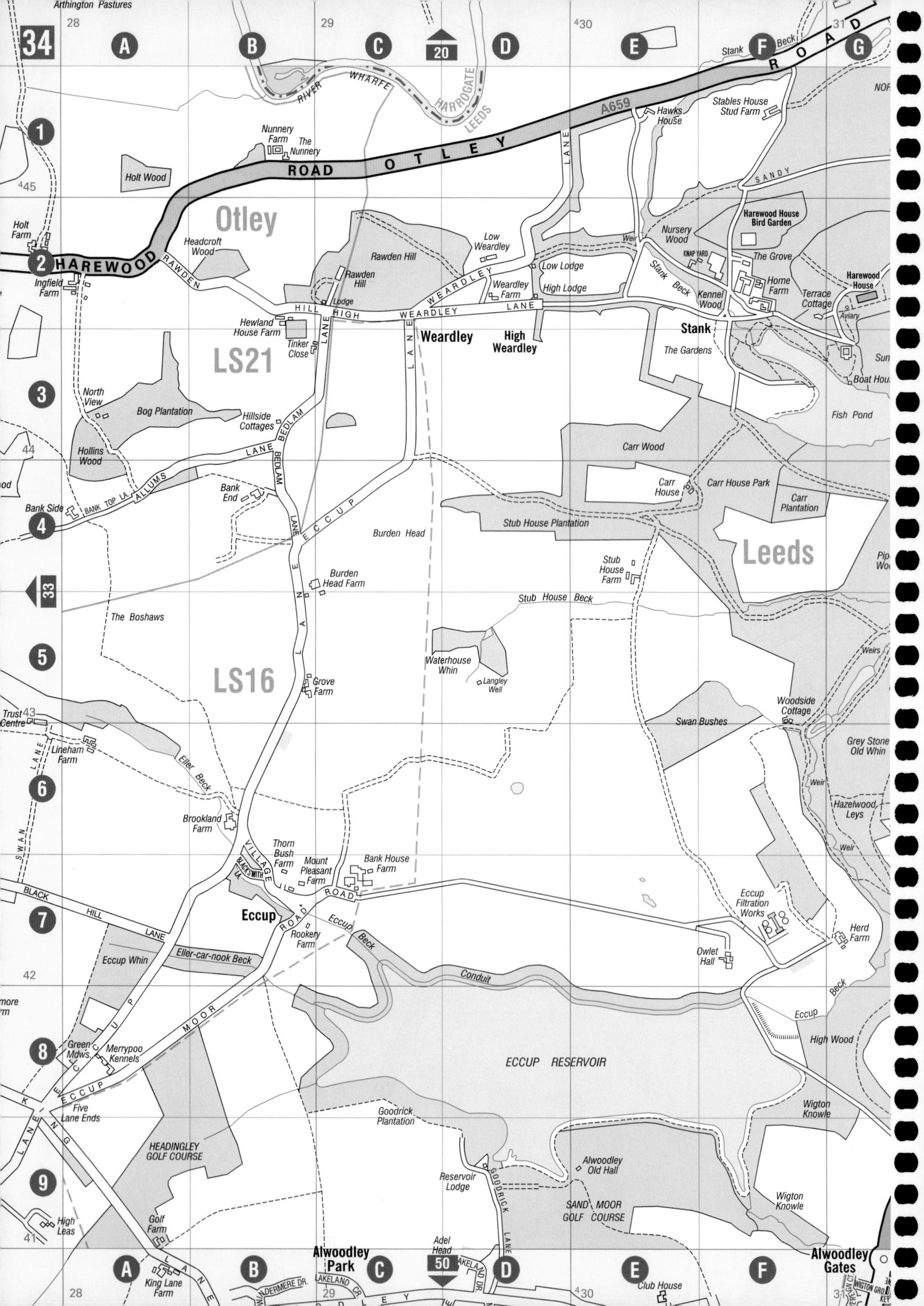
Arthington Pastures
A
B
C
D
E
F
G
20
33
50
1
2
3
4
5
6
7
8
9
28
29
430
31
445
44
43
42
41
RIVER WHARFE
HARROGATE
LEEDS
A659
OTLEY ROAD
HAREWOOD ROAD
Nunnery Farm
The Nunnery
Holt Wood
Holt Farm
Ingfield Farm
RAWDEN HILL
Headcroft Wood
Otley
Rawden Hill
Lodge
HIGH WEARDLEY LANE
Low Weardley
Weardley Farm
Low Lodge
High Lodge
Hewland House Farm
Tinker Close
LS21
Weardley
High Weardley
North View
Bog Plantation
Hillside Cottages
Hollins Wood
BEDLAM LANE
ALLUMS LANE
BANK TOP LA.
Bank Side
Bank End
ECCUP LANE
Burden Head
Burden Head Farm
The Boshaws
LS16
Grove Farm
Trust Centre
Lineham Farm
Eller Beck
SWAN LANE
Brookland Farm
Thorn Bush Farm
Mount Pleasant Farm
Bank House Farm
VILLAGE
BLACKSMITH LA.
BLACK HILL LANE
Eccup
ROAD
Rookery Farm
Eccup Beck
Eccup Whin
Eller-car-nook Beck
MOOR
ECCUP
Green Mdws.
Merrypoo Kennels
Five Lane Ends
KING LANE
HEADINGLEY GOLF COURSE
Golf Farm
High Leas
King Lane Farm
Alwoodley Park
WINDERMERE DR.
LAKELAND CR.
LAKELAND DR.
Adel Head
Goodrick Plantation
Reservoir Lodge
GOODRICK LANE
Conduit
ECCUP RESERVOIR
Alwoodley Old Hall
SAND MOOR GOLF COURSE
Club House
Wigton Knowle
Alwoodley Gates
WIGTON GRO.
Stank Beck
ROAD
Hawks House
Stables House Stud Farm
SANDY
LANE
Weir
Nursery Wood
KNAP YARD
Harewood House Bird Garden
The Grove
Home Farm
Kennel Wood
Terrace Cottage
Harewood House
Aviary
Stank
The Gardens
Boat House
Fish Pond
Carr Wood
Carr House
Carr House Park
Carr Plantation
Stub House Plantation
Leeds
Stub House Farm
Stub House Beck
Waterhouse Whin
Langley Well
Swan Bushes
Woodside Cottage
Weirs
Grey Stone Old Whin
Hazelwood Leys
Eccup Filtration Works
Owlet Hall
Herd Farm
Eccup Beck
High Wood

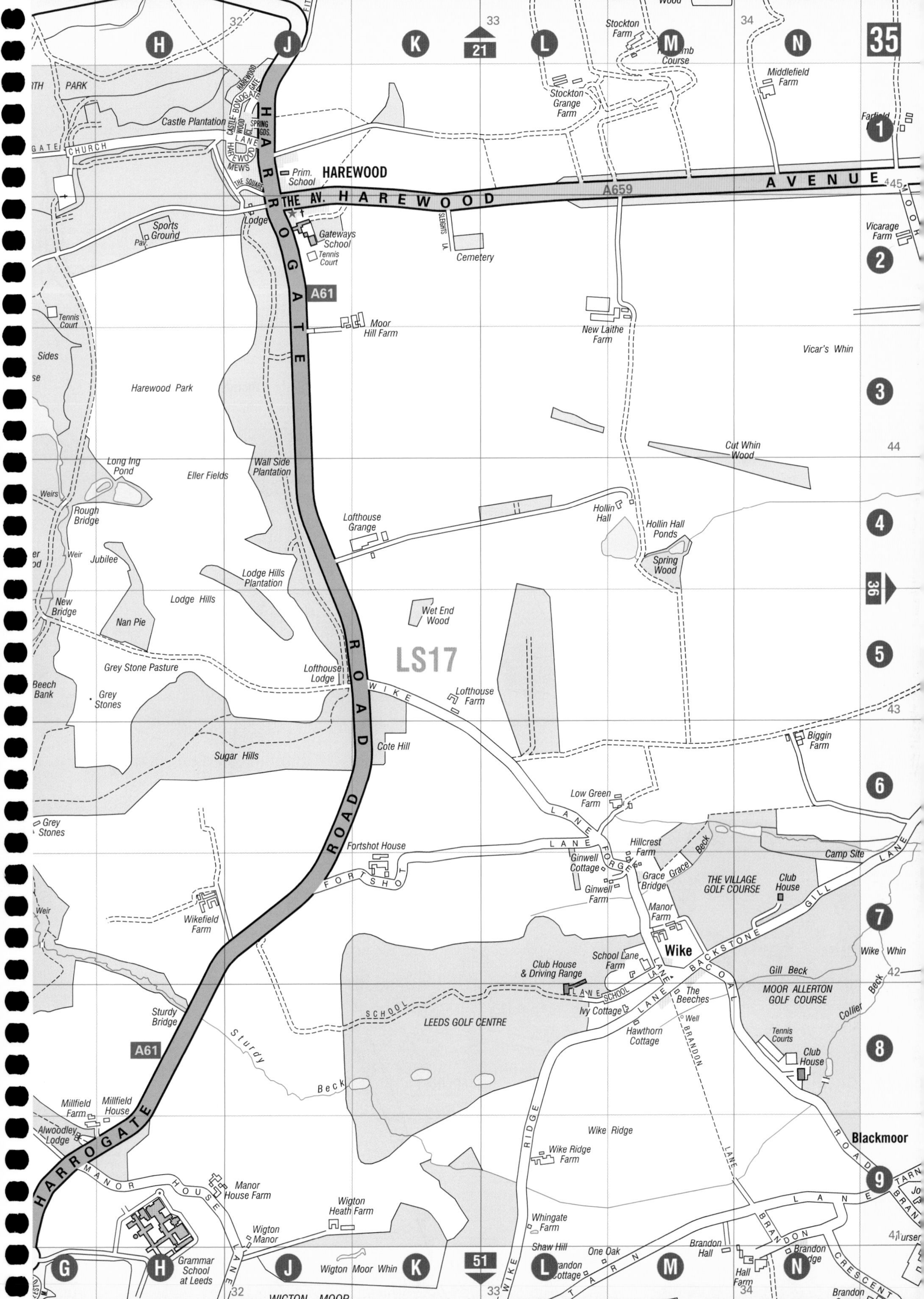
HAREWOOD
HARROGATE ROAD
A61
HAREWOOD AVENUE
A659
THE AV.
Castle Plantation
Prim. School
Gateways School
Sports Ground
Lodge
Cemetery
Moor Hill Farm
New Laithe Farm
Stockton Farm
Stockton Grange Farm
Middlefield Farm
Vicarage Farm
Vicar's Whin
Harewood Park
Cut Whin Wood
Long Ing Pond
Eller Fields
Wall Side Plantation
Rough Bridge
Jubilee
Lofthouse Grange
Hollin Hall
Hollin Hall Ponds
Spring Wood
Lodge Hills Plantation
Lodge Hills
New Bridge
Nan Pie
Wet End Wood
LS17
Grey Stone Pasture
Lofthouse Lodge
Lofthouse Farm
Beech Bank
Grey Stones
Cote Hill
Sugar Hills
Biggin Farm
Low Green Farm
WIKE LANE
FORGE LANE
Fortshot House
FORTSHOT LANE
Hillcrest Farm
Ginwell Cottage
Ginwell Farm
Grace Bridge
Grace Beck
THE VILLAGE GOLF COURSE
Club House
Camp Site
GILL LANE
BACKSTONE
Manor Farm
Wikefield Farm
Wike
School Lane Farm
Club House & Driving Range
SCHOOL LANE
The Beeches
Ivy Cottage
Well
Hawthorn Cottage
MOOR ALLERTON GOLF COURSE
Wike Whin
Gill Beck
Collier Beck
Tennis Courts
Sturdy Bridge
Sturdy Beck
LEEDS GOLF CENTRE
BRANDON LANE
COAL ROAD
Millfield Farm
Millfield House
Alwoodley Lodge
HARROGATE
MANOR HOUSE LANE
Manor House Farm
Wike Ridge
WIKE RIDGE
Wike Ridge Farm
Blackmoor
Wigton Heath Farm
Whingate Farm
Wigton Manor
Shaw Hill
One Oak
Brandon Hall
Grammar School at Leeds
Wigton Moor Whin
Brandon Cottage
Hall Farm
Brandon Lodge
TARN LANE
BRANDON CRESCENT
WIGTON MOOR
21
36
51

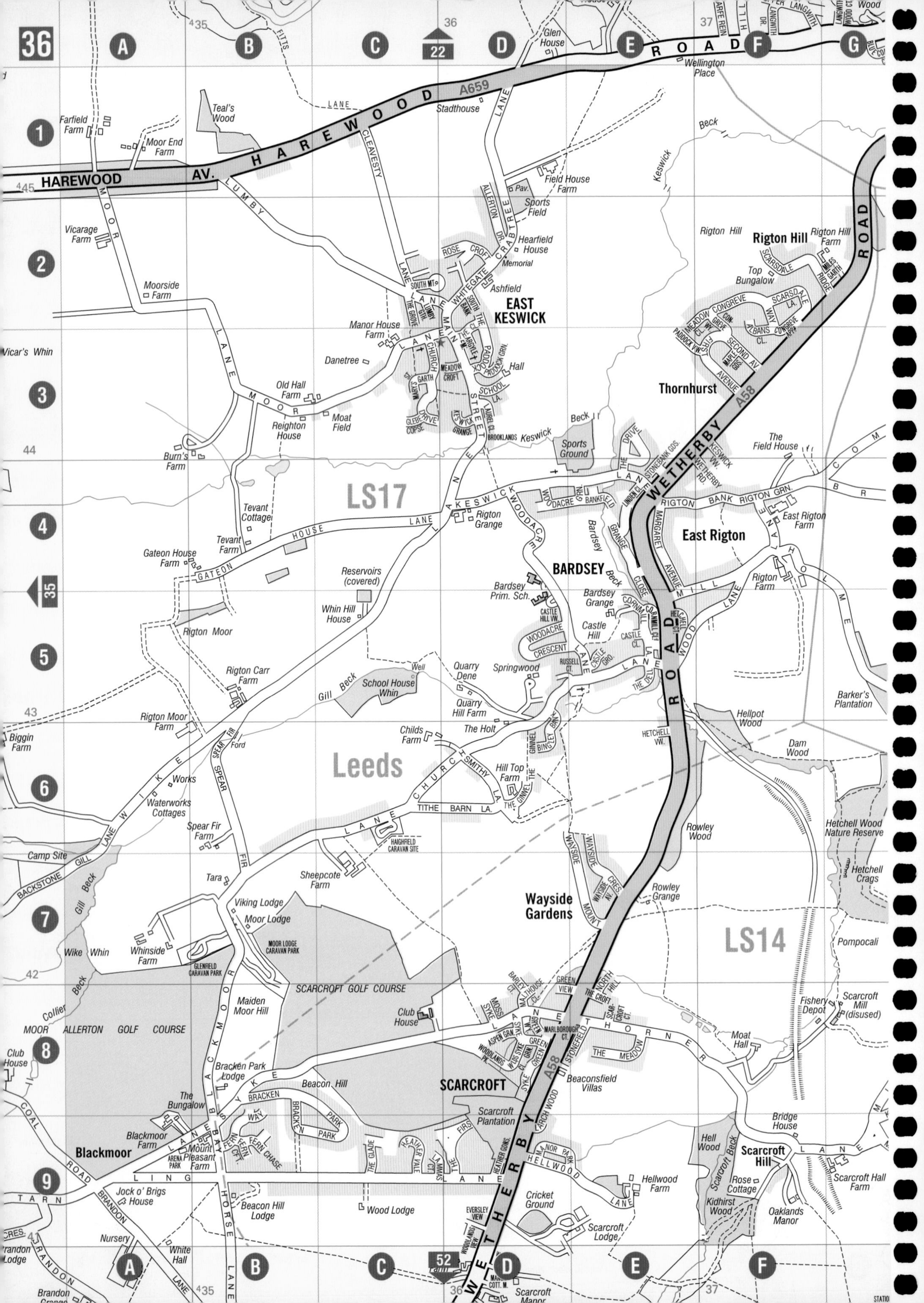
A
B
C
D
E
F
G
22
36
37
1
2
3
4
5
6
7
8
9
HAREWOOD
AV.
HAREWOOD
ROAD
A659
Glen House
Wellington Place
Teal's Wood
Farfield Farm
Moor End Farm
Stadthouse
LANE
CLEAVESTY
LUMBY
MOOR
Field House Farm
Pav.
Sports Field
ALLERTON DR.
CRABTREE
Hearfield House
Memorial
Vicarage Farm
Rigton Hill
Rigton Hill Farm
Top Bungalow
Keswick
Beck
ROAD
Moorside Farm
ROSE CROFT
WHITEGATE
SOUTH MT.
Ashfield
EAST KESWICK
Manor House Farm
MAIN
CHURCH
Danetree
Hall
SCHOOL LA.
MEADOW CROFT
GARTH
GLEBE COPSE
DRIVE
Vicar's Whin
Old Hall Farm
Moat Field
Reighton House
STREET
BROOKLANDS
Keswick
Beck
Sports Ground
THE DRIVE
Thornhurst
A58
WETHERBY
CONGREVE
SCARSDALE
MEADOW CL.
SECOND AV.
AVENUE
The Field House
Burn's Farm
44
LS17
KESWICK
LANE
RIGTON BANK
RIGTON GRN.
East Rigton Farm
East Rigton
Tevant Cottage
Rigton Grange
HOUSE
Tevant Farm
Gateon House Farm
GATEON
Reservoirs (covered)
WOODACRE
BARDSEY
Bardsey Beck
Bardsey Prim. Sch.
Bardsey Grange
GRANGE
MARGARET AVENUE
MILL
LANE
Rigton Farm
HOLME
35
Whin Hill House
Rigton Moor
Castle Hill
CASTLE HILL VW.
WOODACRE CRESCENT
RUSSELL CT.
CASTLE GRO.
THE DELL
ROAD
WOOD
Quarry Dene
Springwood
Well
Gill Beck
School House Whin
Rigton Carr Farm
Quarry Hill Farm
Barker's Plantation
43
Rigton Moor Farm
Biggin Farm
Childs Farm
The Holt
HETCHELL VW.
Hellpot Wood
Dam Wood
Leeds
SPEAR FIR
Ford
CHURCH
SMITHY LA.
Hill Top Farm
THE GINNEL
BINGLEY BANK
Works
WIKE LANE
Waterworks Cottages
TITHE BARN LA.
LANE
Rowley Wood
Hetchell Wood Nature Reserve
Spear Fir Farm
HAIGHFIELD CARAVAN SITE
WAYSIDE
WAYSIDE CRES.
Camp Site
GILL
BACKSTONE
Gill Beck
Tara
Sheepcote Farm
Rowley Grange
Hetchell Crags
Viking Lodge
Moor Lodge
Wayside Gardens
MOUNT
LS14
Wike Whin
Whinside Farm
MOOR LODGE CARAVAN PARK
GLENFIELD CARAVAN PARK
Pompocali
42
SCARCROFT GOLF COURSE
Collier Beck
Maiden Moor Hill
Club House
BARLEY CT.
MALTHOUSE CL.
GREEN VIEW
NORTH HILL
THE CROFT
Fishery Depot
Scarcroft Mill (disused)
MOOR ALLERTON GOLF COURSE
MOSS SYKE
THORNER
LANE
Moat Hall
Club House
ASPEN GRN.
MARLBOROUGH CT.
STONEFIELD
THE MEADOW
WOODLANDS PK.
Bracken Park Lodge
SYKE
Beacon Hill
SCARCROFT
A58
Beaconsfield Villas
COAL
The Bungalow
BRACKEN
BRACKEN PARK
Scarcroft Plantation
LARCH WOOD
Hell Wood
Scarcroft Beck
Bridge House
Blackmoor Farm
Blackmoor
Mount Pleasant Farm
ARENA PARK
FERN CHASE
THE GLADE
HEATHER VALE
THE FIRS
HEATHER GDNS.
MANOR PARK
HELLWOOD
Scarcroft Hill
Scarcroft Hall Farm
Rose Cottage
ROAD
LING
LANE
Hellwood Farm
TARN
BRANDON
Jock o' Brigs House
HORSE
Beacon Hill Lodge
Wood Lodge
EVERSLEY VIEW
Cricket Ground
Kidhirst Wood
Oaklands Manor
Scarcroft Lodge
Nursery
Brandon Lodge
White Hall
41
LANE
52
Scarcroft Manor
Brandon Grange
435
36
37

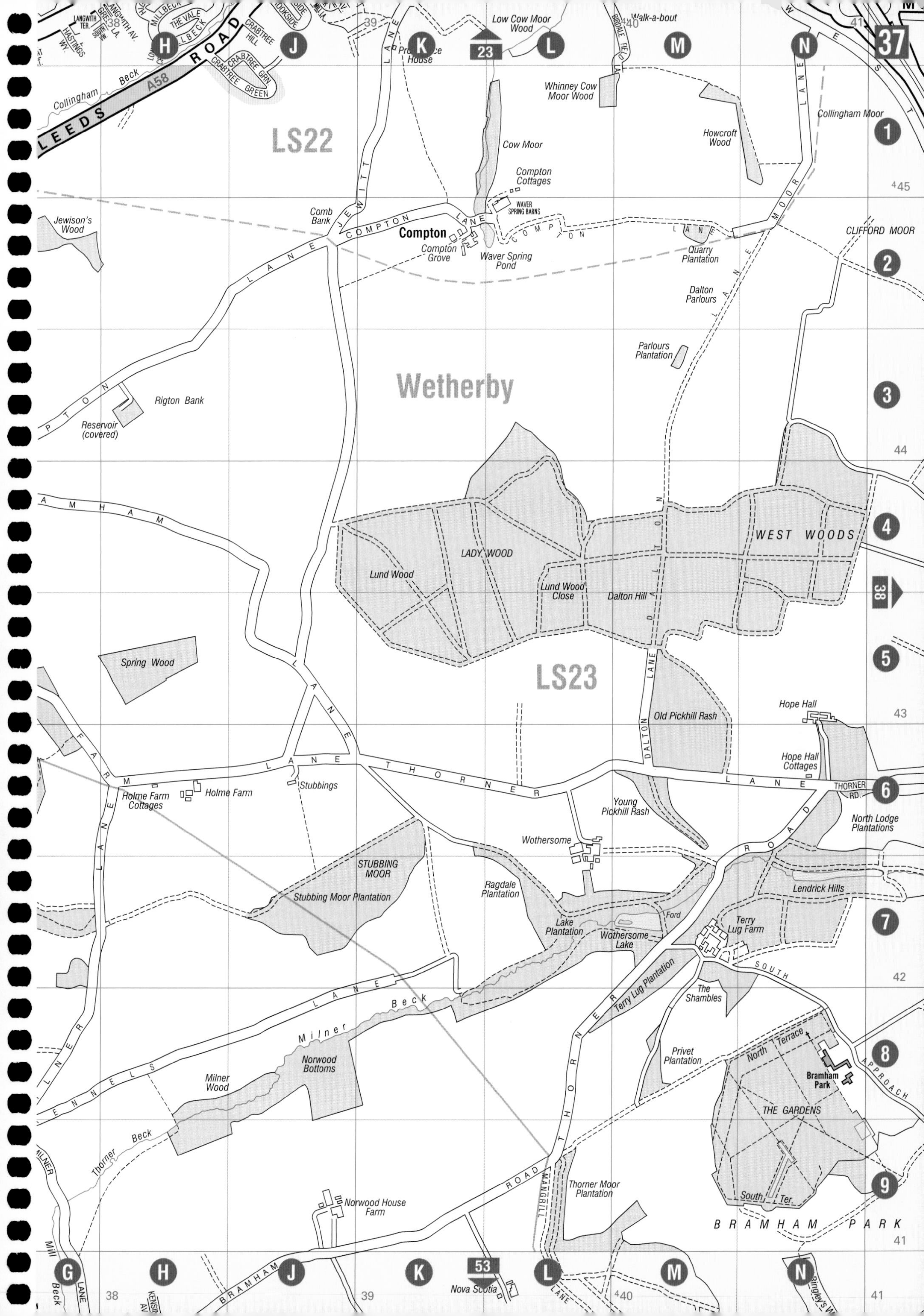
LS22
LS23
Wetherby
Compton
Compton Lane
Jewitt Lane
Comb Bank
Compton Grove
Waver Spring Pond
Waver Spring Barns
Compton Cottages
Cow Moor
Low Cow Moor Wood
Walk-a-bout
Whinney Cow Moor Wood
Howcroft Wood
Collingham Moor
Collingham Beck
Leeds Road
A58
Crabtree Hill
Crabtree Grn.
Crabtree Green
Jewison's Wood
Rigton Bank
Reservoir (covered)
Quarry Plantation
Dalton Parlours
Parlours Plantation
Moor Lane
Clifford Moor
Lady Wood
Lund Wood
Lund Wood Close
Dalton Hill
West Woods
Dalton Lane
Spring Wood
Old Pickhill Rash
Hope Hall
Hope Hall Cottages
Thorner Lane
Thorner Rd.
Farm Lane
Holme Farm Cottages
Holme Farm
Stubbings
Young Pickhill Rash
Wothersome
North Lodge Plantations
Stubbing Moor
Stubbing Moor Plantation
Ragdale Plantation
Lake Plantation
Wothersome Lake
Ford
Terry Lug Farm
Lendrick Hills
Terry Lug Plantation
The Shambles
South
Privet Plantation
North Terrace
Bramham Park
The Gardens
Approach
South Ter.
Bramham Park
Milner Beck
Milner Wood
Norwood Bottoms
Kennels Lane
Thorner Beck
Thorner Road
Mangrill
Thorner Moor Plantation
Norwood House Farm
Bramham Road
Nova Scotia
Mill Beck Lane
Milner Lane
23
38
53
1
2
3
4
5
6
7
8
9
G
H
J
K
L
M
N
38
39
440
41
445
44
43
42
41

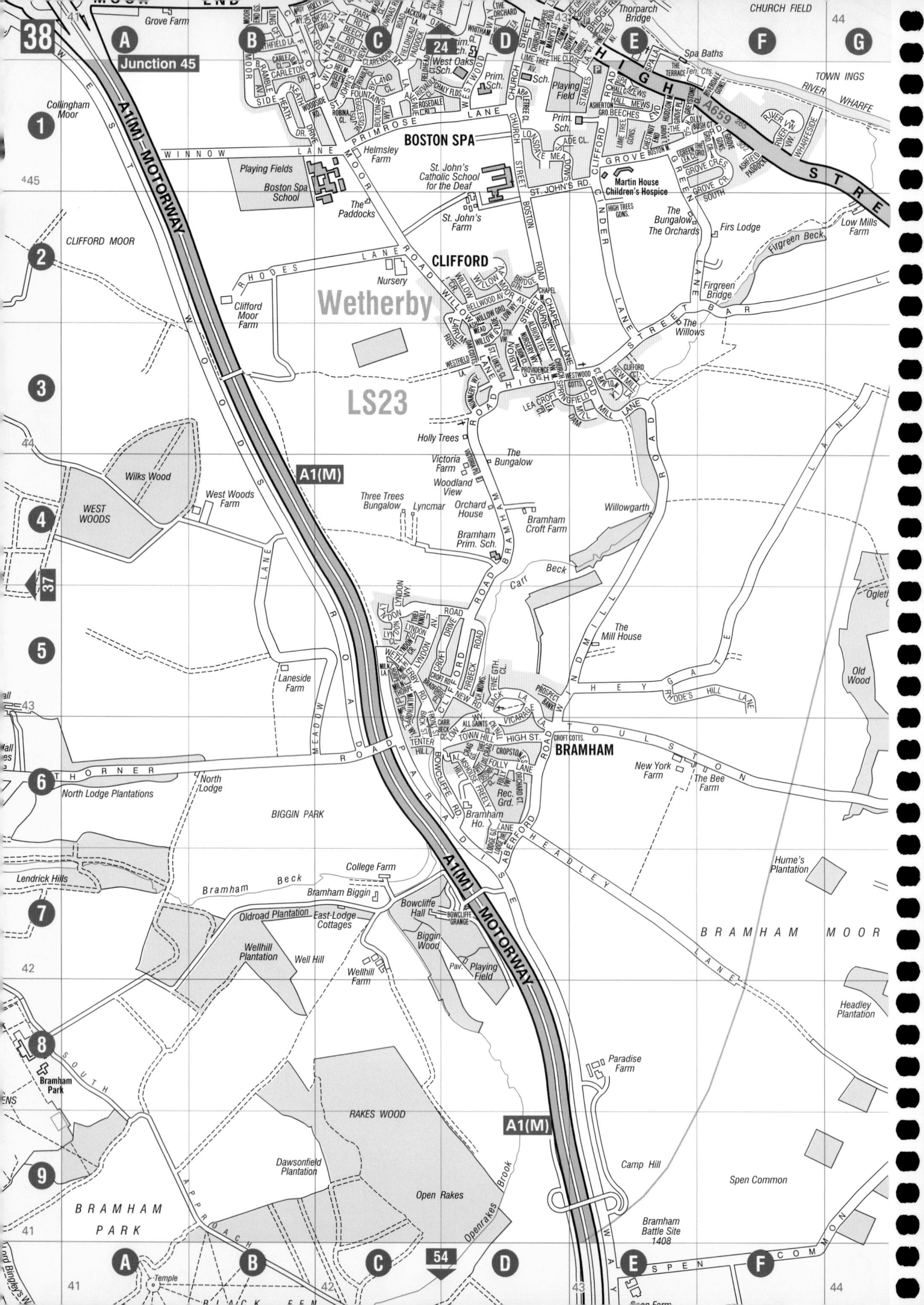
Junction 45
A1(M) MOTORWAY
BOSTON SPA
CLIFFORD
Wetherby
LS23
BRAMHAM
CLIFFORD MOOR
Collingham Moor
Grove Farm
Playing Fields
Boston Spa School
Helmsley Farm
St. John's Catholic School for the Deaf
Martin House Children's Hospice
The Paddocks
St. John's Farm
Nursery
Clifford Moor Farm
Thorparch Bridge
CHURCH FIELD
Spa Baths
TOWN INGS
RIVER WHARFE
A659
HIGH STREET
Low Mills Farm
Firs Lodge
The Bungalow
The Orchards
Firgreen Beck
Firgreen Bridge
The Willows
Wilks Wood
WEST WOODS
West Woods Farm
Holly Trees
Victoria Farm
The Bungalow
Woodland View
Three Trees Bungalow
Lyncmar
Orchard House
Bramham Croft Farm
Bramham Prim. Sch.
Willowgarth
Carr Beck
The Mill House
Old Wood
Laneside Farm
New York Farm
The Bee Farm
North Lodge
North Lodge Plantations
BIGGIN PARK
Lendrick Hills
Bramham Beck
College Farm
Bramham Biggin
Oldroad Plantation
East-Lodge Cottages
Bowcliffe Hall
Biggin Wood
Playing Field
Wellhill Plantation
Well Hill
Wellhill Farm
Hume's Plantation
BRAMHAM MOOR
Headley Plantation
Paradise Farm
Bramham Park
RAKES WOOD
Dawsonfield Plantation
Open Rakes
Openrakes Brook
Camp Hill
Spen Common
Bramham Battle Site 1408
BRAMHAM PARK
Temple
WINNOW LANE
PRIMROSE LANE
RHODES LANE
WOODS ROAD
THORNER ROAD
MEADOW LANE
PARADISE WAY
BRAMHAM ROAD
HEYGATE LANE
TOULSTON LANE
HEADLEY LANE
APPROACH
SOUTH
SPEN COMMON
BAR LANE
MILL LANE
WINDMILL LANE

24
37
54

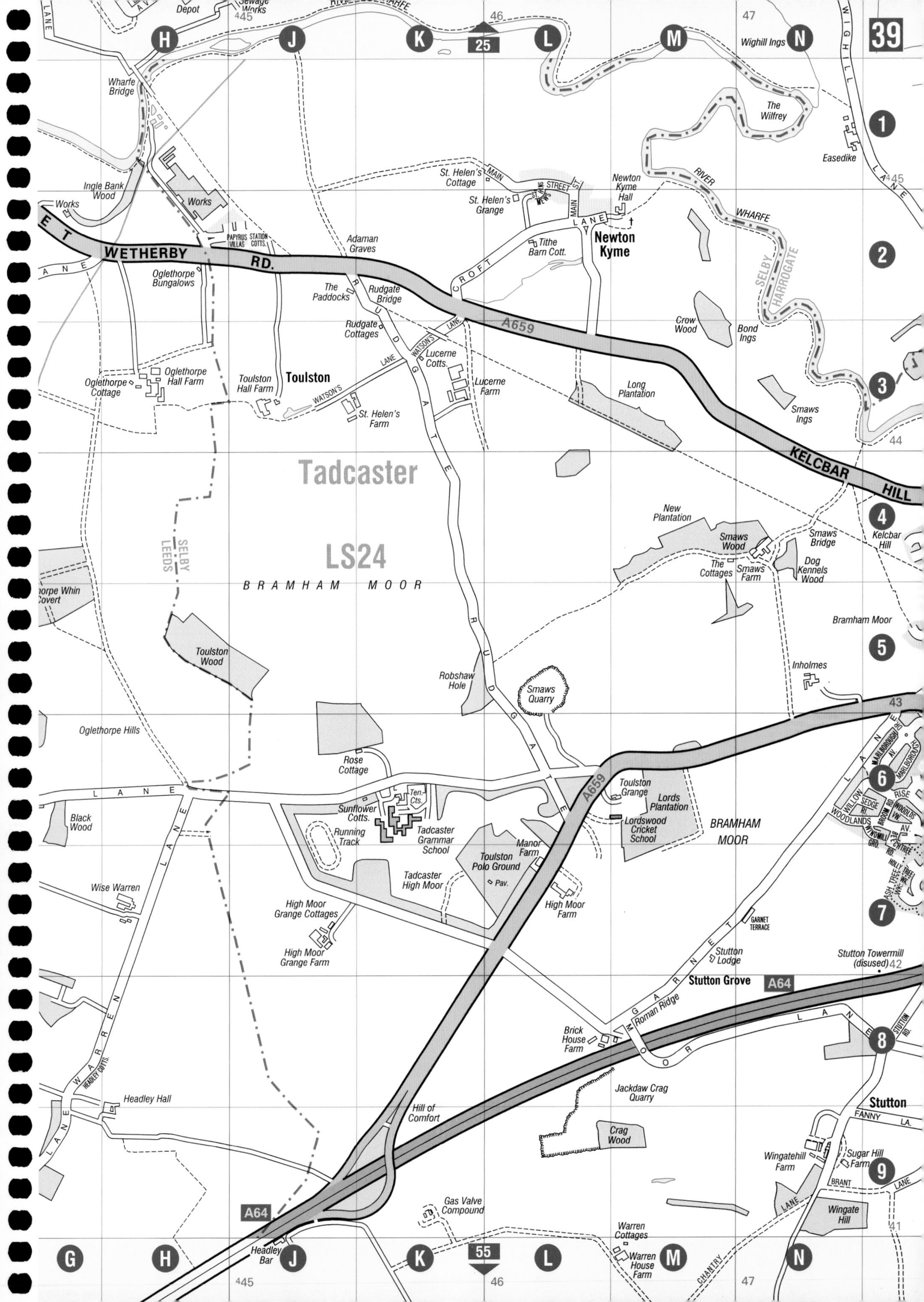

Depot
Sewage Works
445
46
47
H
J
K
L
M
N
25
Wighill Ings
Wharfe Bridge
The Wilfrey
Easedike
WIGHILL LANE
St. Helen's Cottage
MAIN STREET
St. Helen's Grange
Newton Kyme Hall
RIVER WHARFE
Ingle Bank Wood
Works
Works
PAPYRUS VILLAS
STATION COTTS.
WETHERBY RD.
Adaman Graves
Tithe Barn Cott.
Newton Kyme
CROFT LANE
SELBY HARROGATE
Oglethorpe Bungalows
The Paddocks
Rudgate Bridge
Rudgate Cottages
A659
Crow Wood
Bond Ings
WATSON'S LANE
Lucerne Cotts.
Oglethorpe Cottage
Oglethorpe Hall Farm
Toulston Hall Farm
Toulston
Lucerne Farm
Long Plantation
Smaws Ings
St. Helen's Farm
44
KELCBAR HILL
Tadcaster
RUDGATE
New Plantation
SELBY LEEDS
LS24
Smaws Wood
Smaws Bridge
Kelcbar Hill
The Cottages
Smaws Farm
Dog Kennels Wood
BRAMHAM MOOR
Thorpe Whin Covert
Bramham Moor
Toulston Wood
Robshaw Hole
Inholmes
Smaws Quarry
43
Oglethorpe Hills
Rose Cottage
MARLBOROUGH AV.
LANE
Toulston Grange
Lords Plantation
Black Wood
Sunflower Cotts.
Ten. Cts.
Lordswood Cricket School
BRAMHAM MOOR
WILLOW
SEDGE RI.
BROOM RD.
WOODLANDS
Running Track
Tadcaster Grammar School
Manor Farm
Toulston Polo Ground
Pav.
Tadcaster High Moor
Wise Warren
High Moor Grange Cottages
High Moor Farm
GARNET TERRACE
High Moor Grange Farm
GARNET
Stutton Lodge
Stutton Towermill (disused)
42
Stutton Grove
A64
Roman Ridge
MOOR LANE
Brick House Farm
STUTTON RD.
WARREN LANE
HEADLEY COTTS.
Headley Hall
Jackdaw Crag Quarry
Hill of Comfort
Stutton
FANNY LA.
Crag Wood
Wingatehill Farm
Sugar Hill Farm
BRANT LANE
A64
Gas Valve Compound
Wingate Hill
41
Warren Cottages
Headley Bar
Warren House Farm
CHANTRY
G
H
J
K
55
L
M
N
445
46
47
1
2
3
4
5
6
7
8
9

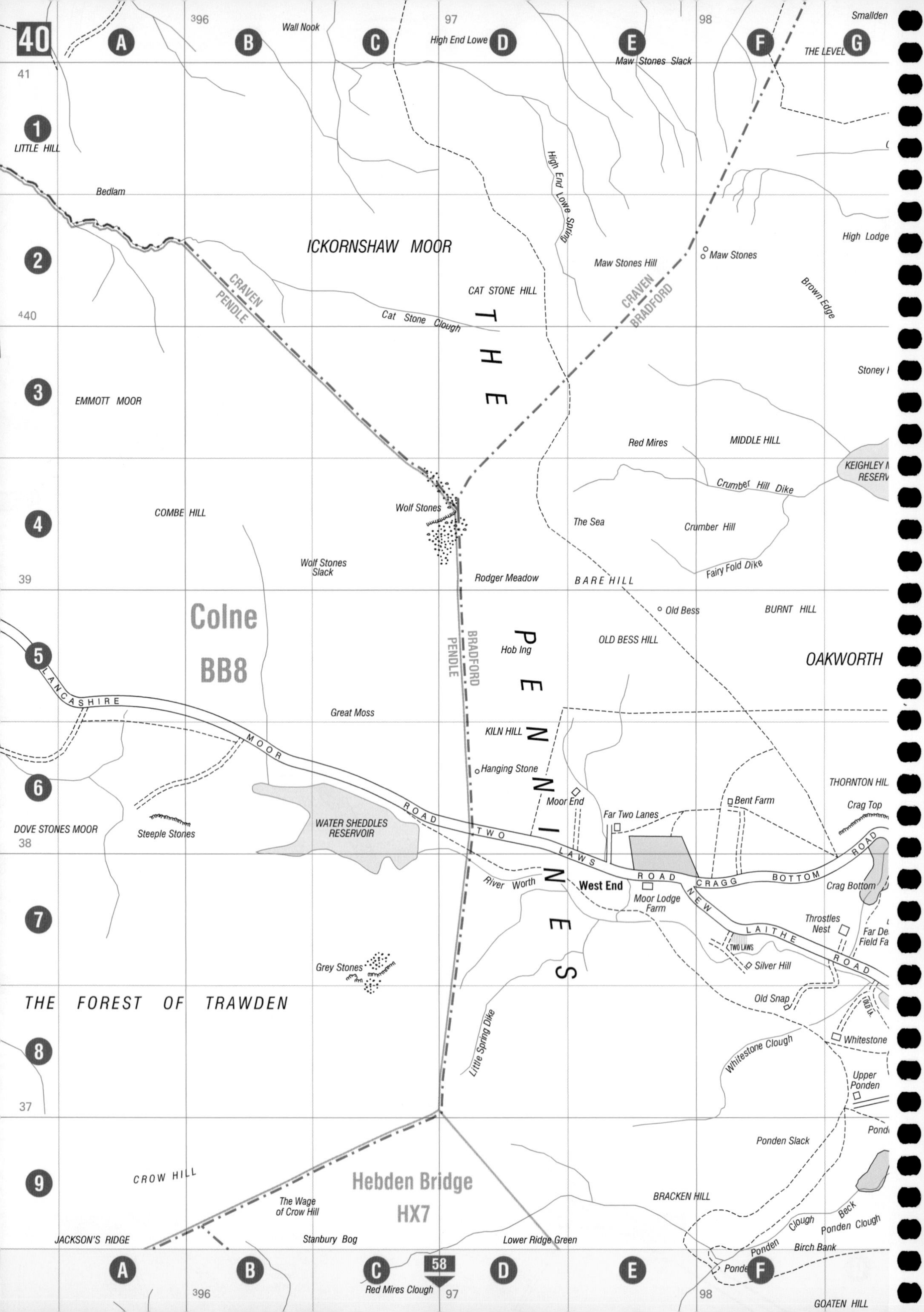

ICKORNSHAW MOOR
THE PENNINES
Wall Nook
High End Lowe
Maw Stones Slack
Smallden
THE LEVEL
LITTLE HILL
Bedlam
High End Lowe Spring
Maw Stones
Maw Stones Hill
High Lodge
CAT STONE HILL
Cat Stone Clough
CRAVEN
PENDLE
BRADFORD
Brown Edge
EMMOTT MOOR
Stoney
Red Mires
MIDDLE HILL
KEIGHLEY
Crumber Hill Dike
COMBE HILL
Wolf Stones
The Sea
Crumber Hill
Wolf Stones Slack
Rodger Meadow
BARE HILL
Fairy Fold Dike
Old Bess
BURNT HILL
Colne
BB8
OLD BESS HILL
Hob Ing
OAKWORTH
LANCASHIRE MOOR ROAD
Great Moss
KILN HILL
Hanging Stone
THORNTON HILL
Moor End
Bent Farm
Far Two Lanes
Crag Top
DOVE STONES MOOR
Steeple Stones
WATER SHEDDLES RESERVOIR
TWO LAWS ROAD
River Worth
West End
CRAGG BOTTOM ROAD
Moor Lodge Farm
Crag Bottom
NEW LAITHE ROAD
Throstles Nest
Far Dean Field Farm
TWO LAWS
Silver Hill
Grey Stones
THE FOREST OF TRAWDEN
Old Snap
Whitestone
Little Spring Dike
Whitestone Clough
Upper Ponden
Ponden Slack
CROW HILL
Hebden Bridge
HX7
The Wage of Crow Hill
BRACKEN HILL
JACKSON'S RIDGE
Stanbury Bog
Lower Ridge Green
Ponden Beck
Ponden Clough
Birch Bank
Red Mires Clough
58
GOATEN HILL
396
97
98
41
440
39
38
37

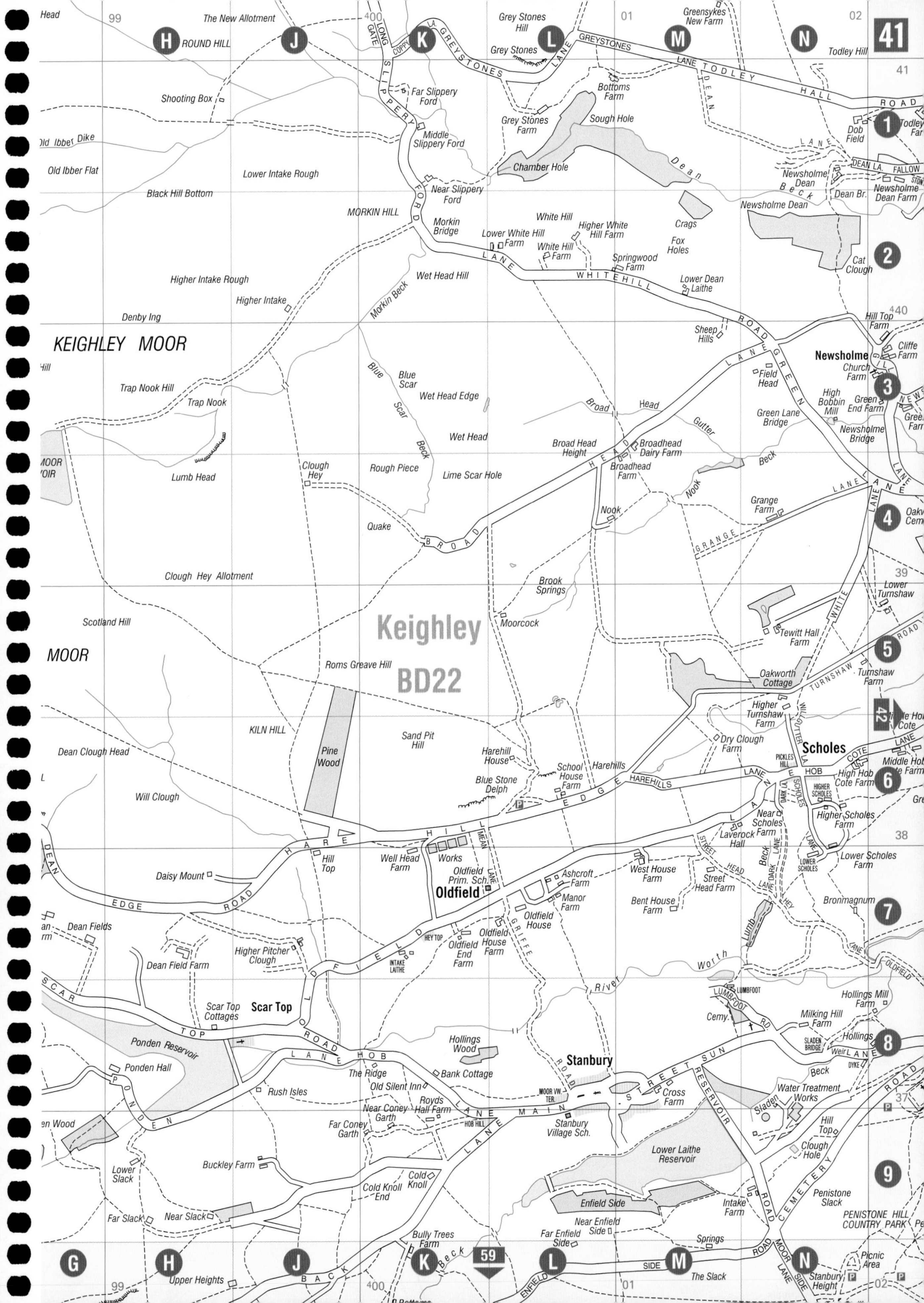

Keighley
BD22
KEIGHLEY MOOR
MOOR
Newsholme
Scholes
Oldfield
Scar Top
Stanbury
ROUND HILL
The New Allotment
Shooting Box
Old Ibber Dike
Old Ibber Flat
Lower Intake Rough
Black Hill Bottom
MORKIN HILL
Higher Intake Rough
Higher Intake
Denby Ing
Trap Nook Hill
Trap Nook
Lumb Head
Clough Hey
Rough Piece
Quake
Clough Hey Allotment
Scotland Hill
Roms Greave Hill
KILN HILL
Dean Clough Head
Will Clough
Pine Wood
Sand Pit Hill
Daisy Mount
Hill Top
Dean Fields
Dean Field Farm
Higher Pitcher Clough
Scar Top Cottages
Ponden Reservoir
Ponden Hall
Rush Isles
Lower Slack
Far Slack
Near Slack
Buckley Farm
Upper Heights
Grey Stones Hill
Grey Stones
Greensykes New Farm
Todley Hill
Far Slippery Ford
Middle Slippery Ford
Near Slippery Ford
Bottoms Farm
Grey Stones Farm
Sough Hole
Chamber Hole
Dean
Newsholme Dean
Dean Br.
Newsholme Dean Farm
Dob Field
Crags
Fox Holes
Morkin Bridge
Lower White Hill Farm
White Hill
White Hill Farm
Higher White Hill Farm
Springwood Farm
Lower Dean Laithe
Cat Clough
Wet Head Hill
Morkin Beck
Sheep Hills
Hill Top Farm
Cliffe Farm
Church Farm
Field Head
Blue Scar
Blue Scar Beck
Wet Head Edge
Wet Head
Lime Scar Hole
Broad Head
Broad Head Height
Broadhead Dairy Farm
Broadhead Farm
Gutter
Green Lane Bridge
High Bobbin Mill
Green End Farm
Newsholme Bridge
Nook
Nook Beck
Grange Farm
Brook Springs
Moorcock
Tewitt Hall Farm
Lower Turnshaw
Oakworth Cottage
Turnshaw Farm
Higher Turnshaw Farm
Dry Clough Farm
Harehill House
School House Farm
Harehills
Blue Stone Delph
Middle Hob Cote Farm
High Hob Cote Farm
Higher Scholes Farm
Near Scholes Farm
Laverock Hall
Lower Scholes Farm
Well Head Farm
Works
Oldfield Prim. Sch.
Ashcroft Farm
Manor Farm
West House Farm
Street Head Farm
Bent House Farm
Bronmagnum
Oldfield House
Oldfield House Farm
Oldfield End Farm
HEY TOP
INTAKE LAITHE
River Worth
Lumb
LUMBFOOT
Cemy.
Hollings Mill Farm
Milking Hill Farm
Hollings
SLADEN BRIDGE
Weir
DYKE
Beck
Water Treatment Works
Sladen
Hill Top
Clough Hole
Hollings Wood
The Ridge
Old Silent Inn
Bank Cottage
Near Coney Garth
Royds Hall Farm
Far Coney Garth
MOOR VW. TER.
Stanbury Village Sch.
Cross Farm
HOB HILL
Lower Laithe Reservoir
Cold Knoll
Cold Knoll End
Enfield Side
Near Enfield Side
Far Enfield Side
Intake Farm
Springs
Penistone Slack
PENISTONE HILL COUNTRY PARK
Picnic Area
Stanbury Height
Bully Trees Farm
The Slack
Beck
GREYSTONES LANE
TODLEY HALL ROAD
LONG GATE
SLIPPERY FORD
DEAN LA.
FALLOW
WHITEHILL ROAD
GREEN LANE
BROAD HEAD LANE
GRANGE LANE
WHITE LANE
TURNSHAW ROAD
HAREHILLS LANE
HILL EDGE
HARE HILL EDGE ROAD
DEAN EDGE ROAD
OLDFIELD LANE
GRIFFE
MEAN LANE
PICKLES HILL
HOB COTE LANE
HIGHER SCHOLES
DARK LANE
STREET HEAD LANE
SCHOLES LANE
LOWER SCHOLES
WILLGUTTER LA.
SCAR TOP ROAD
HOB LANE
PONDEN LANE
MAIN STREET
SUN STREET
RESERVOIR ROAD
LUMBFOOT RD.
CEMETERY ROAD
MOOR SIDE LANE
ENFIELD SIDE ROAD
BACK LANE
H J K L M N G
1 2 3 4 5 6 7 8 9
99 400 01 02
41 440 39 38 37
42
59

A
B
C
D
E
F
G
1
2
3
4
5
6
7
8
9
02
03
04
405
41
40
39
38
37
26
41
Scholes
60
LAYCOCK
Laycock Prim. Sch.
Longcroft Nurseries
Burial Ground
Town End Farm
Nettle Hole
Cliffe Green Farm
Glen Bridge
TODLEY HALL RD.
GREEN SYKES ROAD
Todley Hall Farm
Todley Clough
Goose Eye
Clough Bank Farm
Game Scar Farm
Lumb Hill
Higher Holme House Wood
Lower Holme House Wood
Brow End Farm
DEAN LA.
FALLOW
Newsholme Dean Farm
Dean Bri.
Owl Hill
Goose Eye Wood
Lower Holme House
STELL HILL
HOUSE LANE
Park House
Carr Laithe
True Well Hall Farm
Holme House
Green Top Farm
Hill Top Farm
Brown Hill
Cliffe Farm
Church Farm
Newsholme
NEW ROAD
Lower Laithe
Green End Farm
Green Bottom Farm
Newsholme Bridge
Higher Bobbin Mill
MACKINGSTONE LANE
Cemetery
Newsholme Manor
Slack Lane Farm
New Laithe Farm
SLAYMAKER LANE
SLACK LANE
Oakworth Cemetery
Oakworth Crematorium
Cricket Grd.
Griff Wood
Low Bank
Cure Laithe Farm
Gill Clough Farm
BRANSHAW GOLF COURSE
Branshaw Plantation
BRANSHAW MOOR
OCCUPATION LANE
Sykes Head
Club House
Greyscar Farm
Goodley
OAKWORTH
Holden Park
Lidget Hill
Lower Turnshaw
GREY SCAR ROAD
Honey Hole
Lane Ends
COLNE RD.
B6143
Withens
KEIGHLEY LANE
Lidget
Rec. Grd.
Turnshaw Farm
Denby Hill
Church Street
Hill Top Farm
Clough Houses
PROVIDENCE LANE
Dockroyd Farm
Cackleshaw
New House
Cackleshaw Farm
Harewood Hill Farm
Keighley
Hoyle House Barn
Middle Hob Cote
HOB COTE LANE
Denby Hill Fm.
White Gates Farm
Chapel Lane
Oakworth Farm
Wildfell
Middle Hob Cote Farm
Providence Farm
Lower Hoyle House
Oakworth
Keighley and Worth Valley Railway
Green Well Farm
Higher Scholes Farm
Lodge Farm
Low Wood
Vale Mills
Low Laithe Farm
BD22
West Field
Lower Scholes Farm
Lord Bridge
The Spinning Mill
Tunnel
Murgatroyd Wood
Youth Hostel
LEES
Bronmagnum
River Worth
SPRING HEAD ROAD
Mytholmes
Cook Gate
Mill Ebor Farm
Lower Oldfield Farm
Cook Gate Farm
Hollings Mill Farm
Hollings
Ckt. Grd.
NORTH STREET
RAWDON RD.
MILL HEY
LEES LANE
HAWORTH ROAD
Cliffe Hill
Green Head Farm
Cross Roads
Sugden Reservoir
Haworth Prim. Sch.
Haworth
WEST LANE
SUN LANE
DIMPLES LANE
Rectory
Brontë Parsonage Museum
Haworth Cemetery
Reservoir (covered)
Rec. Grd.
Mill Hill
Central Park
BRIDGEHOUSE LA.
STATION ROAD
Middle Brow Farm
Brow Top
Lower Brow Farm
A6033
HEBDEN BRIDGE ROAD
TOP ROAD
B6144
HAWORTH RD.
Sugden Brow
Stump Cross
Stump Cross Farm
Sowdens Farm
PENISTONE HILL COUNTRY PARK
Penistone Hill
Penistone Slack
Picnic Area
Upper
HAWORTH
Mills
Brow Moor
Brow Moor Edge
Naylor Hill Quarry
Naylor Hill
Laveroc Hall Farm
CULLINGWORTH
MOOR
Flappit Springs
Bleak House Farm
Castle Stead Ring
A629
HALIFAX ROAD
Springfield Farm
Wicking Crag
Saw Mills
Refuse Tip
Barcroft
Bocking
Myrtle Farm
Lower Pierce Close Farm
Upper Pierce Close Farm
Reservoir
Lees Moor Farm
BRONTE CARAVAN PK.
Damems
Worth Valley Prim. Sch
Bracken Bank
Greystones Farm
Harewood Hill
Sports Field
Play. Fld.
Bogthorn
Higher Spring Head Farm
Low Spring Head Farm
OAKWORTH ROAD
Cricket Ground
Playing Fields
Oakbank School
Exley Head
Low Fold Farm
High Wheat Head
Bunker's House
Bunker's Hill Farm
Beltrees
WHEATHEAD LANE
Nessfield Prim. Sch.
High Fm.
Woodlands Farm
Works
New Town
NORTH DEAN
House
Intake
North Beck
Butter Clough

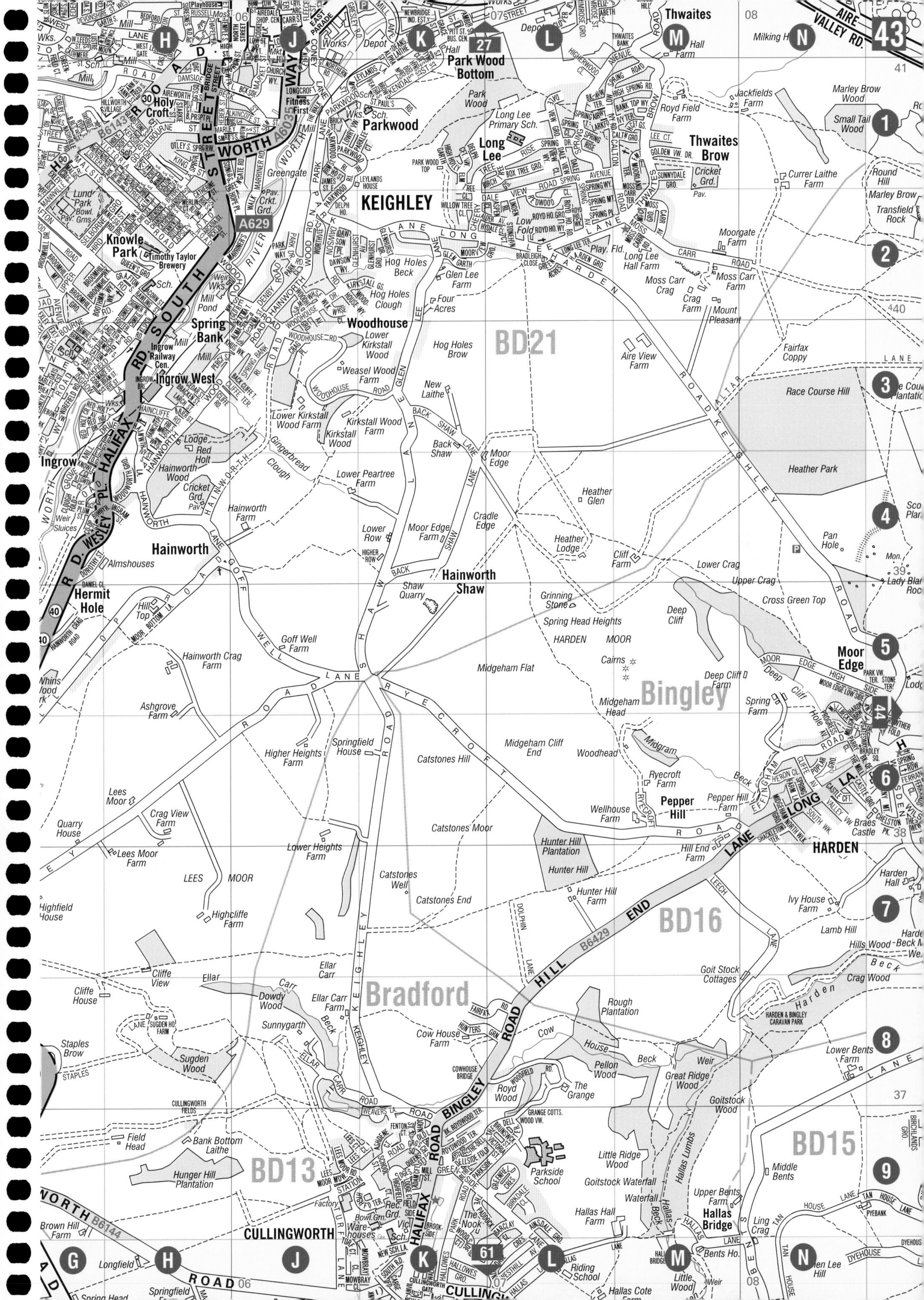

KEIGHLEY
Thwaites
Park Wood Bottom
Park Wood
Parkwood
Long Lee
Long Lee Primary Sch.
Thwaites Brow
Holy Croft
Knowle Park
Timothy Taylor Brewery
Spring Bank
Ingrow Railway Cen.
Ingrow West
Ingrow
Hainworth
Hermit Hole
Woodhouse
Hog Holes Beck
Hog Holes Clough
Glen Lee Farm
Four Acres
Lower Kirkstall Wood
Weasel Wood Farm
Hog Holes Brow
BD21
Aire View Farm
Moss Carr Crag
Crag Farm
Mount Pleasant
Moorgate Farm
Long Lee Hall Farm
Fairfax Coppy
Race Course Hill
Heather Park
Royd Field Farm
Jackfields Farm
Marley Brow Wood
Small Tail Wood
Currer Laithe Farm
Round Hill
Marley Brow
Transfield Rock
New Laithe
Lower Kirkstall Wood Farm
Kirkstall Wood Farm
Kirkstall Wood
Back Shaw
Moor Edge
Lower Peartree Farm
Gingerbread Clough
Hainworth Wood
Cricket Grd.
Hainworth Farm
Lower Row
Moor Edge Farm
Cradle Edge
Heather Glen
Heather Lodge
Cliff Farm
Lower Crag
Upper Crag
Cross Green Top
Pan Hole
Hainworth Shaw
Shaw Quarry
Almshouses
Grinning Stone
Spring Head Heights
HARDEN MOOR
Cairns
Deep Cliff
Moor Edge
Goff Well Farm
Hainworth Crag Farm
Midgeham Flat
Deep Cliff Farm
Bingley
Midgeham Head
Spring Farm
Ashgrove Farm
Higher Heights Farm
Springfield House
Catstones Hill
Midgeham Cliff End
Woodhead
Midgram
Ryecroft Farm
Pepper Hill
Pepper Hill Farm
Wellhouse Farm
Lees Moor
Crag View Farm
Quarry House
Lees Moor Farm
Catstones Moor
Hunter Hill Plantation
Hunter Hill
Hill End Farm
HARDEN
Braes Castle
Lower Heights Farm
LEES MOOR
Catstones Well
Catstones End
Hunter Hill Farm
BD16
Harden Hall
Ivy House Farm
Highfield House
Highcliffe Farm
Lamb Hill
Hills Wood
Cliffe View
Ellar Carr
Goit Stock Cottages
Crag Wood
Cliffe House
Dowdy Carr Wood
Ellar Carr Farm
Bradford
Rough Plantation
HARDEN & BINGLEY CARAVAN PARK
Staples Brow
Sugden Wood
Sunnygarth
Cow House Farm
Pellon Wood
Great Ridge Wood
Lower Bents Farm
Royd Wood
The Grange
Goitstock Wood
Field Head
Bank Bottom Laithe
BD13
Parkside School
Little Ridge Wood
BD15
Middle Bents
Hunger Hill Plantation
Goitstock Waterfall
Hallas Lumbs
Upper Bents Farm
Hallas Bridge
Ling Crag
Brown Hill Farm
CULLINGWORTH
Hallas Hall Farm
Longfield
Riding School
Bents Ho.
Little Wood
Springfield
Hallas Cote
B6143
A6035
A629
B6429
B6144
HILL END ROAD
BINGLEY ROAD
HALIFAX ROAD
KEIGHLEY ROAD
RYECROFT ROAD
GOFF WELL LANE
SHAW LANE
LONG LEE LANE
HARDEN ROAD
KEIGHLEY ROAD
LONG LA.
AIRE VALLEY RD.
27
44
61
06
07
08
H
J
K
L
M
N
G
1
2
3
4
5
6
7
8
9
41
40
39
38
37

A B C D E F G
1 2 3 4 5 6 7 8 9
09
410
11
41
440
39
38
37
AIRE VALLEY ROAD
A650
BD21
Keighley
Marley Brow Wood
Round Hill Wood
Small Tail Wood
Marley
Marley Hall Farm
Round Hill
Marley Brow
Transfield Rock
Transfield Wood
Upper Transfield Farm
Transfield Top
Hutler Hill
Settling Ponds
Blakey Wood
Cop Hirst Wood
Altar Farm
Altar Wood
Druid's Altar
Altar Crag
Altar Well
ALTAR LANE
Race Course Plantation
HOLLIN PLANTATION
CROSS GATES LANE
White Cote
Ewe Hills
Square Plantation
Cross Gates
BINGLEY ST. IVES GOLF COURSE
Scotch Fir Plantation
Golf Cotts.
Pan Hole
Fairfax Entrenchment
Lady Blantyre's Rock
The Coppice
Round Plantation
Home Farm
The Sports Turf Research Institute
Club Ho.
Betty's Lodge
Milner Spring
Bell Bank Wood
Holme House Wood
Coppice Pond
Cuckoo Nest Wood
Low Park
Goose Wing
B6429
Moor Edge
HARDEN
Lodge
Cricket Ground
Football Grd.
Woodbank Nurseries
Harden Grange Farm
Harden Grange
Woodbank
Bingley
BD16
HARDEN ROAD
Birkey Bank Wood
Carr Wood
Beckfoot House
Harden Beck
Weir
Beck Foot
Beckfoot Farm
SHIPLEY GOLF COURSE
Park Rocks
North Wood
Mytholme Beck
Ruin Bank Wood
Black Hills
Harden Hall
Harden Beck Bridge
Mytholme
Mytholme Bridge
Lamb Hill
Hills Wood
Harden Beck Mill
Crag Wood
Bank Top
Bank Top Quarry
Bilberry Bank
Wilsden Beck
Bradford
Lee Farm
Copy House
Ridge Holes
COTTINGLEY WOOD ESTATE
Deepstone
Deep Stone
NURSERY GARDENS
Park Rocks
BD15
Coplowe Hall
Coplowe Hill
Birket Hill
Stockagate
Farview Fishing Lakes
Cottingley Moor
Cottingley Beck Bridge
COTTINGLEY
Norr
Claremont Farm
Norr Fold Farm
Norr Hill Farm
Norr Farm
Norr Hill
Wilsden Prim. School
WILSDEN
Wilsden Hill
62
43
28
Crossflatts
Crossflatts Prim. Sch.
Thornfield Farm
Deer Park
Lay Thorpe
Micklethwaite Bridge (Swing)
Green Hill Wood
Greenhill Farm
Greenhill Crag Farm
Higher Heights Farm
The Heights
Leeds & Liverpool Canal
Lady Park Nursing Home
Dunnock Farm
Prince of Wales Park
Superstore
The Barn Climbing Cen.
Play. Fld.
Rec. Grd.
Spts. Grd.
Offices
Castlefields Ind. Est.
Castlefields Trading Est.
Mill Race
Mill Stream
Morton Beck
Raven Royd Farm
Bingley Grammar Sch.
Playing Field
Bingley Cemetery
RIVER AIRE
B6265
Swing Bri.
Bingley Five-Rise Locks
Five Rise Farm
Three Rise Lock
Bowling Green
Priestthorpe
Crow Nest
MAIN STREET
BINGLEY
MYRTLE PARK
Bingley Pool
Town Hall
Arts Cen. & Theatre
Resr. (covered)
Clay Gates
Hesp Hills
Sports Grd.
Cricket Grd.
Tennis Cts.
Ford
Club House
Hazelbeck Special Sch.
Play. Fld.
Cottingley Bri.
Cricket Grd.
Rugby Grd.
Gill Wood
BRADFORD ROAD
B6146
COTTINGLEY MOOR
Cottingley Moor Bridge

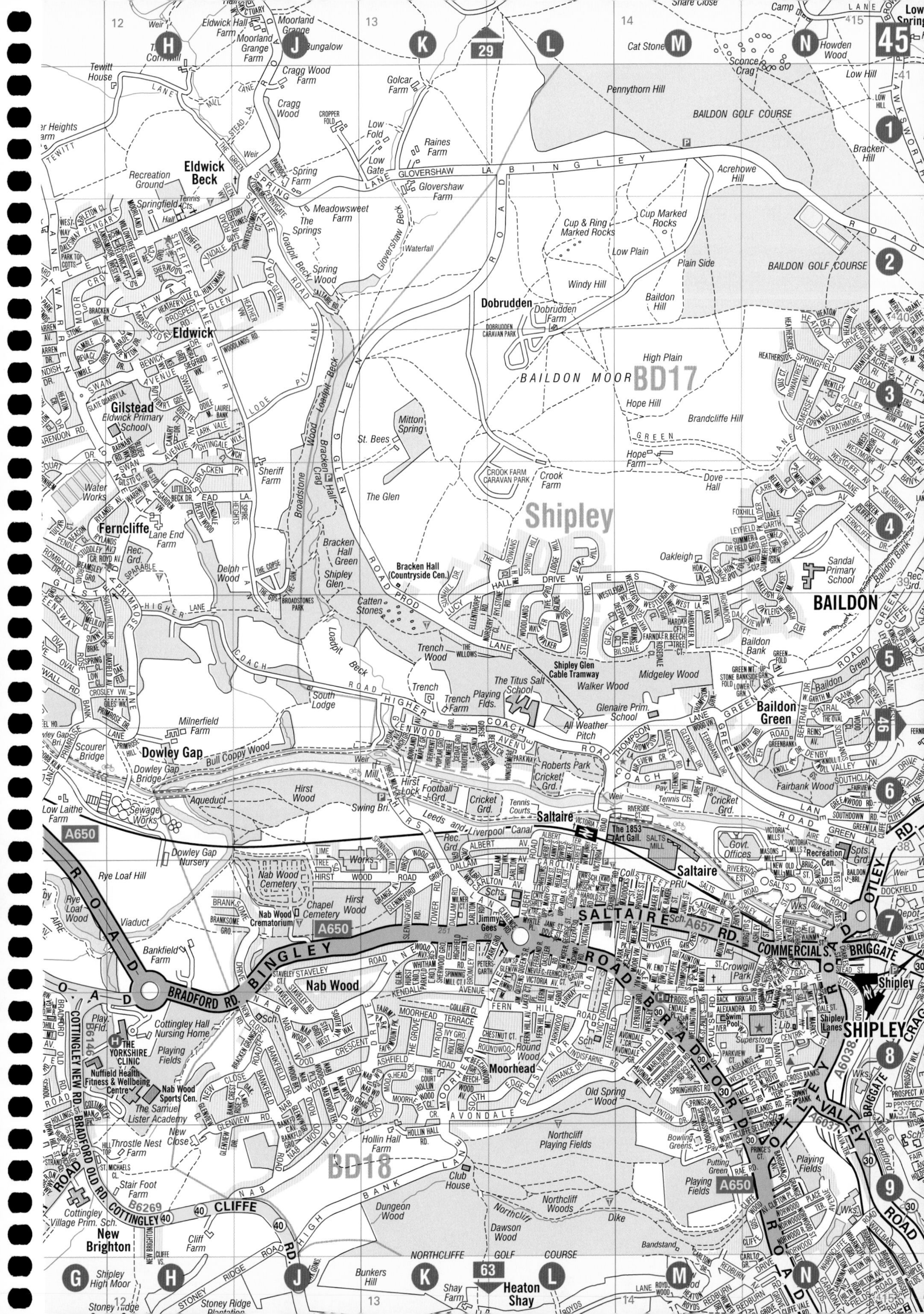
45
29
63
46
Eldwick Beck
Eldwick
Gilstead
Eldwick Primary School
Ferncliffe
Dowley Gap
Dobrudden
BAILDON MOOR
BD17
Shipley
BAILDON
Baildon Green
Saltaire
SHIPLEY
Nab Wood
Moorhead
BD18
New Brighton
Heaton Shay
Tewitt House
Moorland Grange Farm
Cragg Wood Farm
Golcar Farm
Cat Stone
Howden Wood
Low Hill
Pennythorn Hill
BAILDON GOLF COURSE
Raines Farm
Low Fold
Low Gate
Gloversham Farm
Acrehowe Hill
Bracken Hill
Recreation Ground
Meadowsweet Farm
The Springs
Spring Farm
Spring Wood
Cup & Ring Marked Rocks
Cup Marked Rocks
Low Plain
Plain Side
Windy Hill
Baildon Hill
Dobrudden Farm
High Plain
Hope Hill
Brandcliffe Hill
Mitton Spring
St. Bees
The Glen
Crook Farm
Dove Hall
Hope Farm
Water Works
Sheriff Farm
Lane End Farm
Delph Wood
Bracken Hall Green
Shipley Glen
Bracken Hall (Countryside Cen.)
Catten Stones
Sandal Primary School
Oakleigh
Trench Wood
Shipley Glen Cable Tramway
Walker Wood
Midgeley Wood
Baildon Bank
The Titus Salt School
Playing Flds.
Glenaire Prim. School
All Weather Pitch
Milnerfield Farm
South Lodge
Bull Coppy Wood
Scourer Bridge
Dowley Gap Bridge
Hirst Wood
Hirst Lock
Roberts Park
Cricket Grd.
Fairbank Wood
Low Laithe Farm
Sewage Works
Aqueduct
Swing Bri.
Leeds and Liverpool Canal
The 1853 Art Gall.
SALTS MILL
Govt. Offices
Recreation Cen.
Dowley Gap Nursery
Rye Loaf Hill
Rye Loaf Wood
Nab Wood Cemetery
Chapel Cemetery
Hirst Wood
Nab Wood Crematorium
Viaduct
Bankfield Farm
Jimmy Gees
A650
A657
A6038
A6037
B6146
B6269
SALTAIRE RD.
BINGLEY RD.
BRADFORD RD.
COMMERCIAL ST.
BRIGGATE
OTLEY RD.
Crowgill Park
Swim. Pool
Superstore
Shipley Lanes
Cottingley Hall Nursing Home
THE YORKSHIRE CLINIC
Nuffield Health Fitness & Wellbeing Centre
Nab Wood Sports Cen.
The Samuel Lister Academy
Throstle Nest Farm
Stair Foot Farm
Cottingley Village Prim. Sch.
Round Wood
Old Spring Wood
Northcliff Playing Fields
Hollin Hall Farm
Club House
Dungeon Wood
Northcliff Woods
Dawson Wood
NORTHCLIFFE GOLF COURSE
Bunkers Hill
Cliff Farm
Shipley High Moor
Stoney Ridge Farm
Shay Farm
Bowling Greens
Putting Green
Playing Fields
Bandstand
Dike

Low Springs
Low Spring Farm
Hawksworth Spring
Greenhouse Hill
Elm Wood
Hawks Stone
LS20
Birks Wood
Lunds Farm
Moor Valley Park
Bracken Hill
Club Ho.
Hollins Hall
Hawkswood
High Lawn
The Manor
HOLLINS HALL GOLF COURSE
Sunny Brow
Moorside Equestrian Centre
Willy Wood
Lamb Springs
ESHOLT
St. Leonard's Farm Park
Bunkers Hill
BAILDON GOLF COURSE
Hazel Head Wood
Mill Pond
BD17
Tong Park
Baildon C of E Primary School
Gill Beck Farm
Caravan Site
Field Wood
Low Baildon
Bean House
Aqueduct
Buck Wood
Poggy Wood
Brook Hill
Baildon
Round Wood
Ford House Farm
Buck Mill Bridge
Swing-bridge
Leeds & Liverpool Canal
Thackley FC (Dennyfield)
The Nosegay
Shipley
BAILDON
Sandal Primary School
Charlestown
Low Ash Farm
Birk Hill
Thackley Tunnels
Burnwells
Thackley
Baildon Wood
Thackley West Wood
Park Hill Farm
Community College
Baildon Wood Bottom
Thackley End
Health & Fitness Cen.
Dockfield Industrial Park
Bradford
Baildon Holmes
Saltaire Brewery
Guiseley Junct.
Swing Bridge
Carcase End
Cemetery
Idle Rec. Grd.
IDLE
West Royd
Catstones Wood
Shipley
SHIPLEY
Windmill C of E Prim. Sch.
Idle Hill Reservoir (covered)
Idle Hill
Cricket Ground
Woodend
Windhill
Wrose Brow Plantation
Idle Moor
Thorpe
BD18
Wrose Hill
Eccleshill Utd. FC
Springfield
Wrose
Gaisby Hill
Moor End
BD2
Playing Field
Five Lane Ends
Bank Top
Gaisby
A6038
A657
A6037
B6151
B6149
30
64

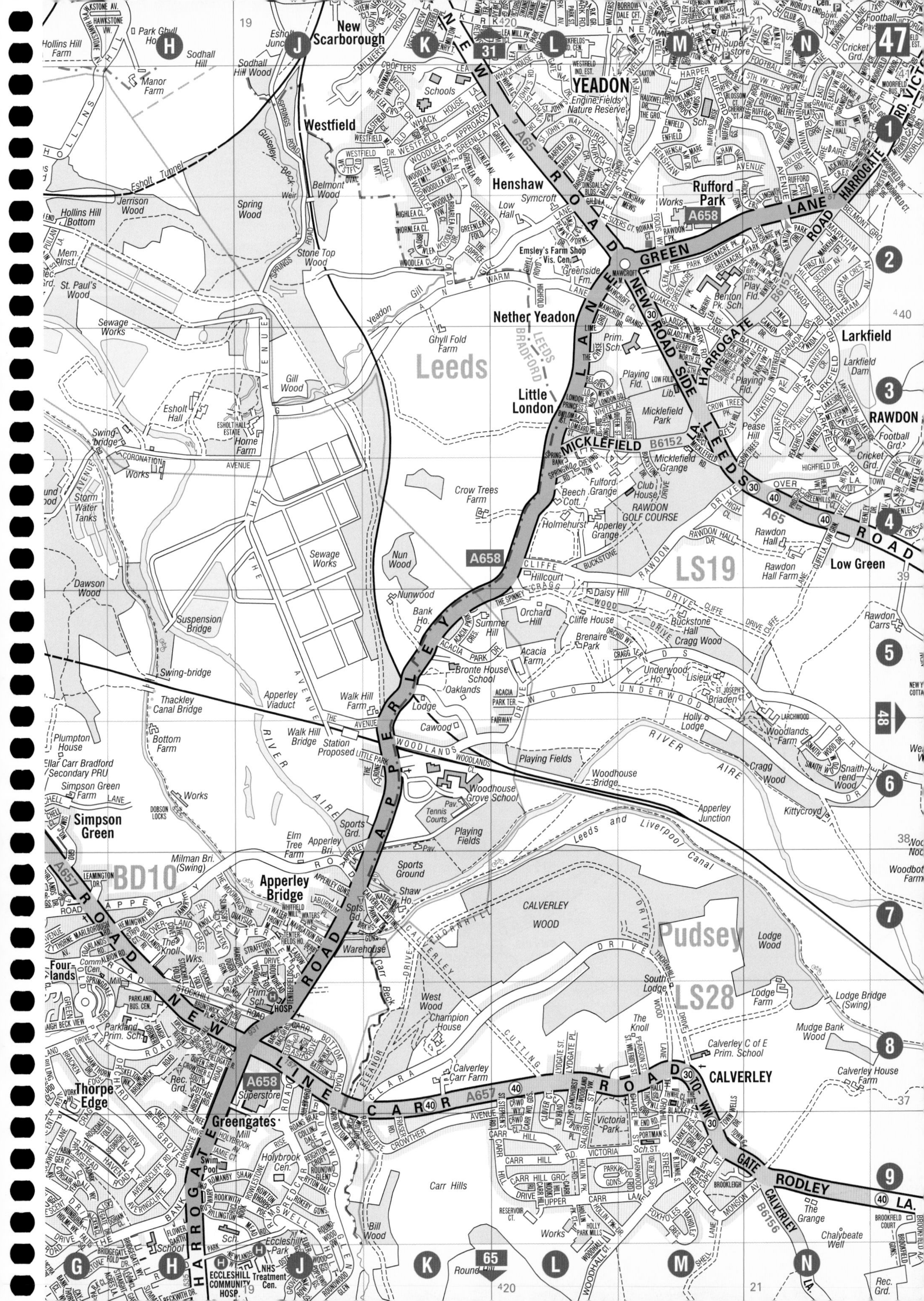
YEADON
Henshaw
Rufford Park
Nether Yeadon
Leeds
Little London
Larkfield
RAWDON
Low Green
LS19
Westfield
New Scarborough
Esholt Hall
Apperley Bridge
BD10
Simpson Green
Pudsey
LS28
CALVERLEY
Thorpe Edge
Greengates
Four-lands
Calverley Wood
Carr Hills
Rawdon Golf Course
Woodhouse Grove School
Leeds and Liverpool Canal
River Aire
A658
A65
A657
B6152
B6156

LEEDS BRADFORD INTERNATIONAL AIRPORT
YEADON
HORSFORTH GOLF COURSE
Scotland
Cookridge
Larkfield
RAWDON
LS19
Leeds
Lane Ends
Beechwood
Horsforth
Troy
Low Green
LS18
West End
HORSFORTH
Woodbottom
Low Fold
Calverley Bridge
Newlay
LS13
Leeds City College (Horsforth Campus)
Leeds Trinity University Coll.
Rawdon Crematorium
Horsforth School
Horsforth Cemetery
32
47
66

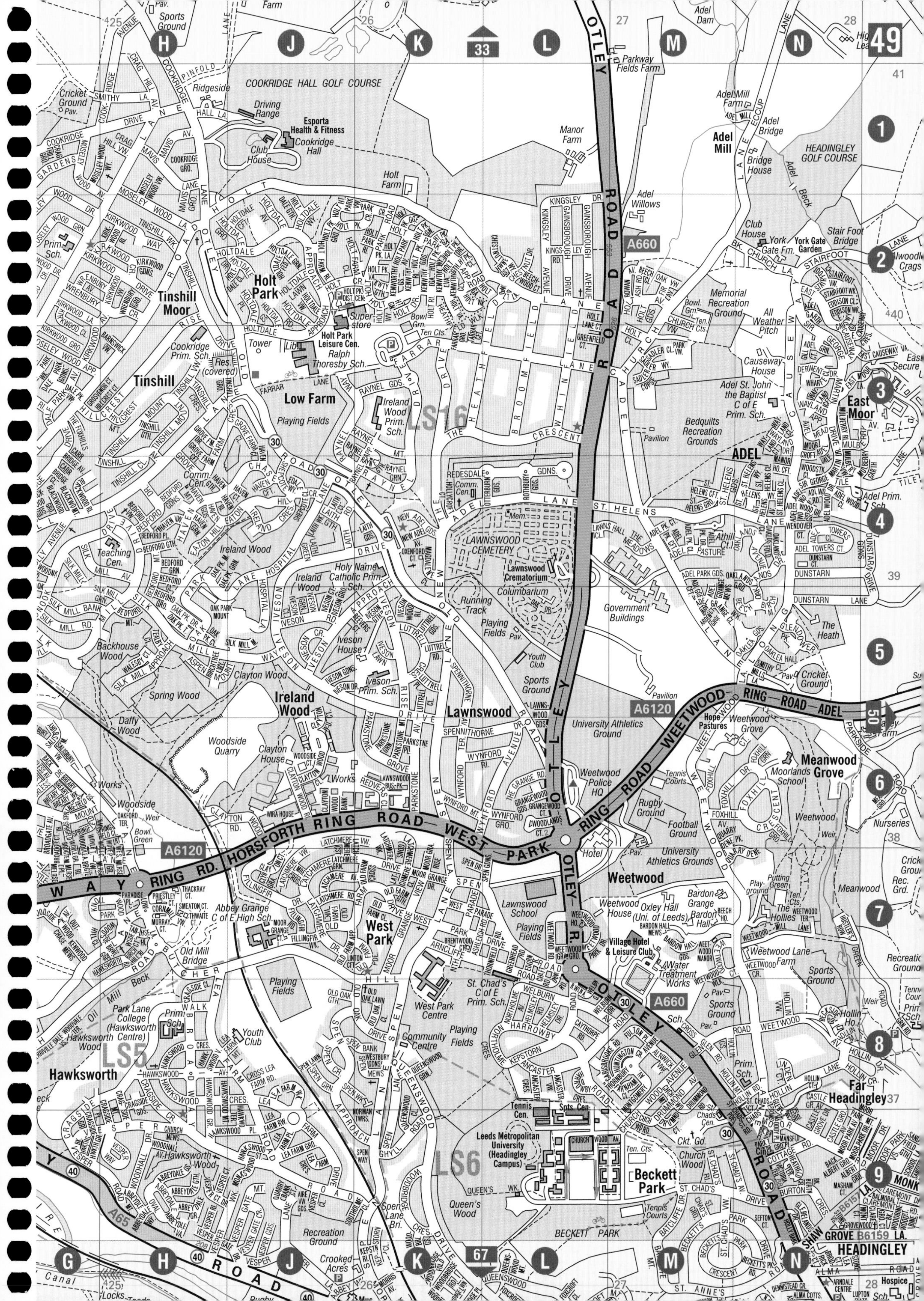

COOKRIDGE HALL GOLF COURSE
Driving Range
Esporta Health & Fitness
Cookridge Hall
Club House
Holt Farm
Manor Farm
Parkway Fields Farm
Adel Dam
Adel Mill Farm
Adel Mill
Adel Bridge
Bridge House
HEADINGLEY GOLF COURSE
Adel Willows
York Gate Garden
Stair Foot Bridge
Memorial Recreation Ground
All Weather Pitch
Causeway House
Adel St. John the Baptist C of E Prim. Sch.
Bedquilts Recreation Grounds
East Moor
ADEL
Adel Prim. Sch.
Holt Park
Holt Park Leisure Cen.
Ralph Thoresby Sch.
Tinshill Moor
Tinshill
Cookridge Prim. Sch.
Low Farm
Playing Fields
Ireland Wood Prim. Sch.
LS16
LAWNSWOOD CEMETERY
Lawnswood Crematorium
Columbarium
Government Buildings
The Heath
Cricket Ground
Teaching Cen.
Ireland Wood
Holy Name Catholic Prim. Sch.
Iveson House
Iveson Prim. Sch.
Running Track
Youth Club
Sports Ground
Backhouse Wood
Clayton Wood
Spring Wood
Daffy Wood
Woodside Quarry
Clayton House
Lawnswood
University Athletics Ground
Hope Pastures
Weetwood Grove
Meanwood Grove
Moorlands School
Weetwood Police HQ
Rugby Ground
Football Ground
University Athletics Grounds
Hotel
Weetwood
Nurseries
HORSFORTH RING ROAD
RING RD.
WEST PARK RING ROAD
WEETWOOD RING ROAD
RING ROAD ADEL
OTLEY ROAD
A660
A6120
A65
Abbey Grange C of E High Sch.
West Park
Lawnswood School
Weetwood House
Oxley Hall (Uni. of Leeds)
Bardon Grange
Bardon Hall
The Hollies
Weetwood Lane Farm
Village Hotel & Leisure Club
Water Treatment Works
Sports Ground
Old Mill Bridge
Park Lane College (Hawksworth Centre)
Hawksworth Wood
LS5
Hawksworth
Youth Club
West Park Centre
Community Centre
St. Chad's C of E Prim. Sch.
Far Headingley
Leeds Metropolitan University (Headingley Campus)
Tennis Cen.
Beckett Park
Church Wood
Queen's Wood
LS6
Recreation Ground
Crooked Acres
Spen Lane Bri.
BECKETT PARK
HEADINGLEY
Hospice
Canal
G H J K L M N
1 2 3 4 5 6 7 8 9
25 26 27 28
37 38 39 40 41
33 50 67

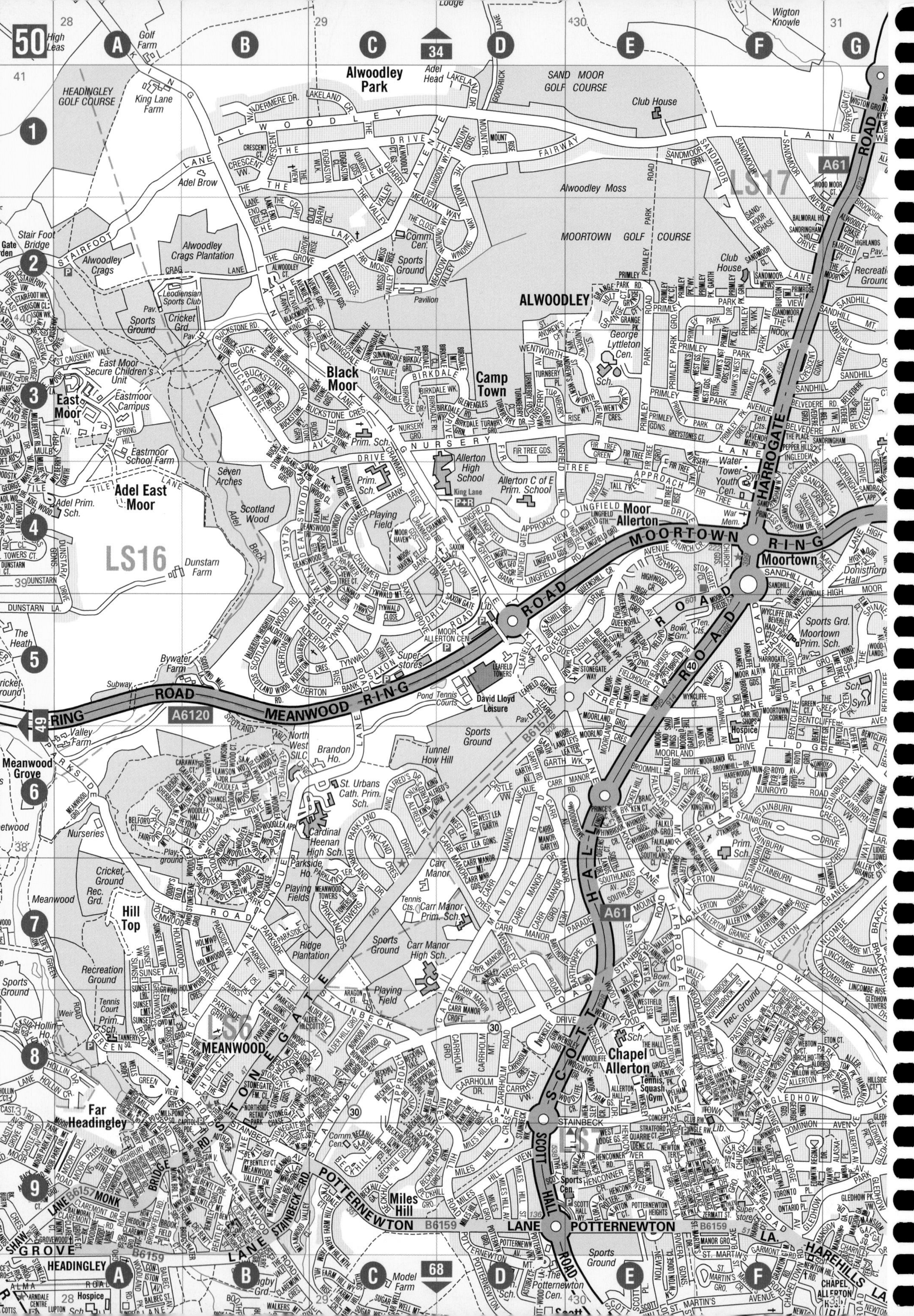
Alwoodley Park
SAND MOOR GOLF COURSE
HEADINGLEY GOLF COURSE
LS17
Alwoodley Moss
MOORTOWN GOLF COURSE
ALWOODLEY
Black Moor
Camp Town
East Moor
Adel East Moor
LS16
Moor Allerton
Moortown
MOORTOWN RING ROAD
MEANWOOD RING ROAD
HARROGATE ROAD
Meanwood Grove
Hill Top
LS6
MEANWOOD
Chapel Allerton
LS7
Far Headingley
HEADINGLEY
Miles Hill
POTTERNEWTON LANE
HAREHILLS LA.
34
49
68

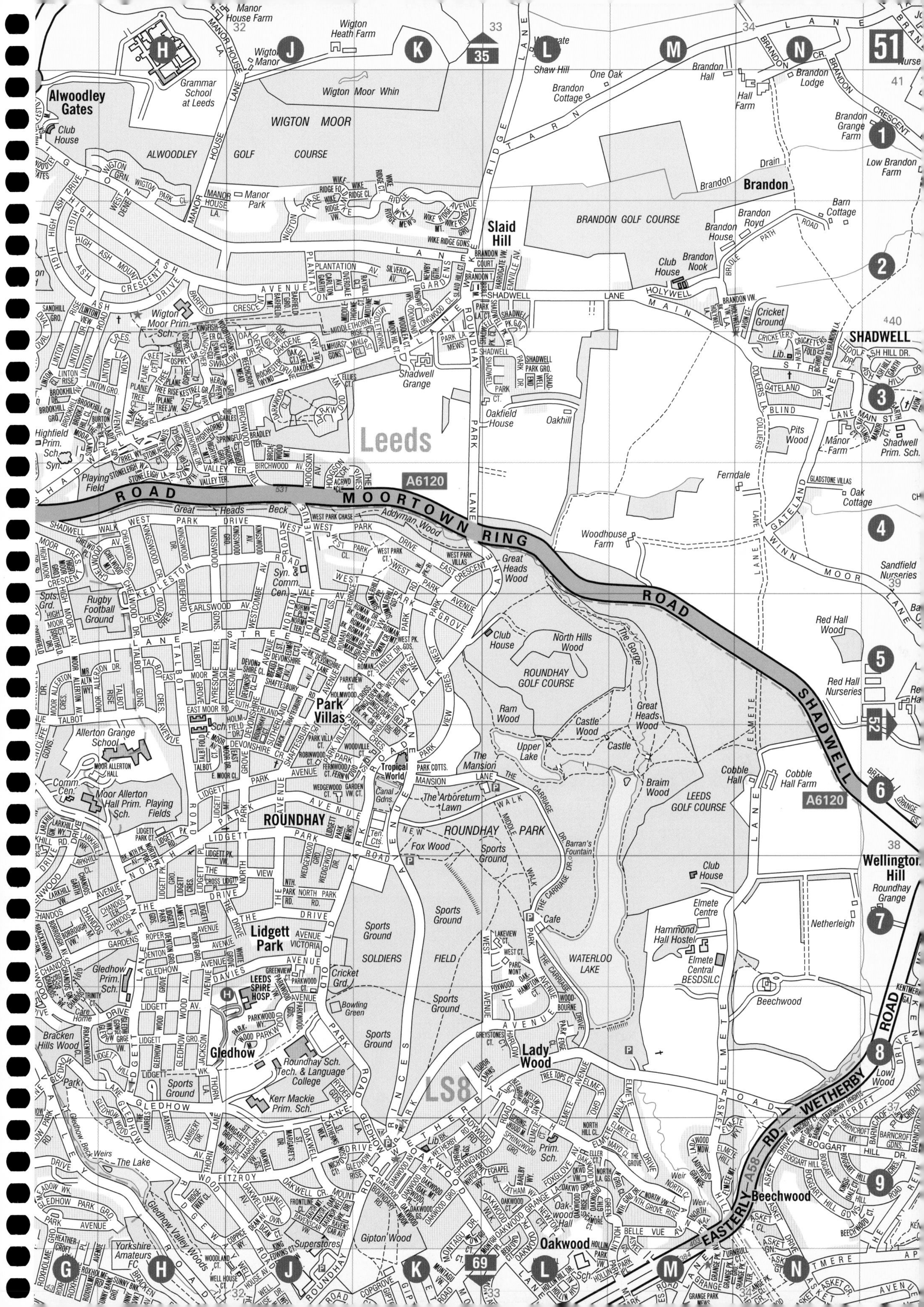

Alwoodley Gates
Club House
Grammar School at Leeds
Manor House Farm
Wigton Heath Farm
Wigton Manor
Wigton Moor Whin
WIGTON MOOR
ALWOODLEY GOLF COURSE
Manor Park
35
Shaw Hill
One Oak
Brandon Cottage
Brandon Hall
Hall Farm
Brandon Lodge
Brandon Grange Farm
Low Brandon Farm
Brandon
Brandon Drain
BRANDON GOLF COURSE
Barn Cottage
Brandon Royd
Brandon House
Brandon Nook
Club House
Slaid Hill
Cricket Ground
SHADWELL
Wigton Moor Prim. Sch.
Shadwell Grange
Oakfield House
Oakhill
Leeds
Pits Wood
Manor Farm
Shadwell Prim. Sch.
Highfield Prim. Sch.
Syn.
Playing Field
A6120
Ferndale
Oak Cottage
MOORTOWN RING ROAD
Great Heads Beck
Addyman Wood
Woodhouse Farm
Great Heads Wood
Sandfield Nurseries
Red Hall Wood
Red Hall Nurseries
Syn. & Comm. Cen.
Rugby Football Ground
Spts. Grd.
Club House
North Hills Wood
The Gorge
ROUNDHAY GOLF COURSE
Ram Wood
Castle Wood
Great Heads Wood
Castle
Upper Lake
Braim Wood
Park Villas
Allerton Grange School
Moor Allerton Hall
Comm. Cen.
Moor Allerton Hall Prim. Sch.
Playing Fields
Tropical World
The Mansion
Canal Gdns.
The Arboretum Lawn
ROUNDHAY PARK
Cobble Hall
Cobble Hall Farm
LEEDS GOLF COURSE
SHADWELL
52
A6120
ROUNDHAY
Fox Wood
Sports Ground
Barran's Fountain
Ten. Cts.
Club House
Wellington Hill
Roundhay Grange
Netherleigh
Elmete Centre
Hammond Hall Hostel
Elmete Central BESDSILC
Beechwood
Cafe
Lidgett Park
Sports Ground
SOLDIERS FIELD
WATERLOO LAKE
Cricket Grd.
Gledhow Prim. Sch.
LEEDS SPIRE HOSP.
Bowling Green
Care Home
Bracken Hills Wood
Gledhow
Roundhay Sch. Tech. & Language College
Sports Ground
Lady Wood
Low Wood
LS8
Kerr Mackie Prim. Sch.
Lib.
Prim. Sch.
The Lake
Weirs
Gledhow Beck
Gledhow Valley Woods
Beechwood
Oakwood Hall
Superstores
Gipton Wood
Yorkshire Amateurs FC
Oakwood
Sch.
69
WETHERBY ROAD
EASTERLY RD. A58

LS17
SHADWELL
LS14
Sandhills
Leeds
Whinmoor
Wellington Hill
Beechwood
Seacroft
WETHERBY ROAD
WELLINGTON HILL
RING ROAD SHADWELL
RING ROAD
SEACROFT
YORK ROAD
A58
A6120
A64
Scarcroft Manor
Scarcroft Grange
Scarcroft Lodge
Wood Farm
Beech Grove
Grange Cottages
Bay Horse Farm
Brandon Grange Farm
Low Brandon Farm
Barn Cottage
Jock o' Brigs House
White Hall
Nursery
Eltofts Farm
Eltofts House
Beech View Barn
Riding School
The Homestead
Carr Farm
Bog Plantation
Birkby Grange Farm
Birkby Hall Farm
Birkby Hill
Bank House
Shadwell Prim. Sch.
Manor Farm
Oak Cottage
Sandfield Nurseries
Barnaby Cotts.
Hill Top Farm
Hobberley House
Red Hall Wood
Red Hall Nurseries
Red Hall
Red Hall Playing Fields
Roundhay Grange
Intake Farm
Intake Grange
The Grove
Holly Croft
Miry Carr Farm
Field Head
Thorner Lane Farm
Bramley Grange College
Bramley Grange Farm
Skelton Hall Farm
Sandhills Farm
Sandhills House
Thorner Grange
Thorner Bottoms Wood
Hillcrest
Sports Ground
Cricket Grd.
Brookeside
Whinmoor Grange
Home Farm
Glebe Farm
Morwick Hall
Morwick Farm
Willow Garth Farm
Grimes Dyke Prim. Sch.
Scholes Prim. Sch.
Scholes Park
White Laith Prim. Sch.
Seacroft Industrial Estate
Warehouses
Works
Lime Pits Wood
Low Wood
Oak Tree Business Park
Powerleague (North)
Ramshead Wood
Training Cen.
Grange Farm Prim. Sch.
Our Lady Catholic Prim. Sch.
Play. Field
Comm. Cen.
Prim. Sch.

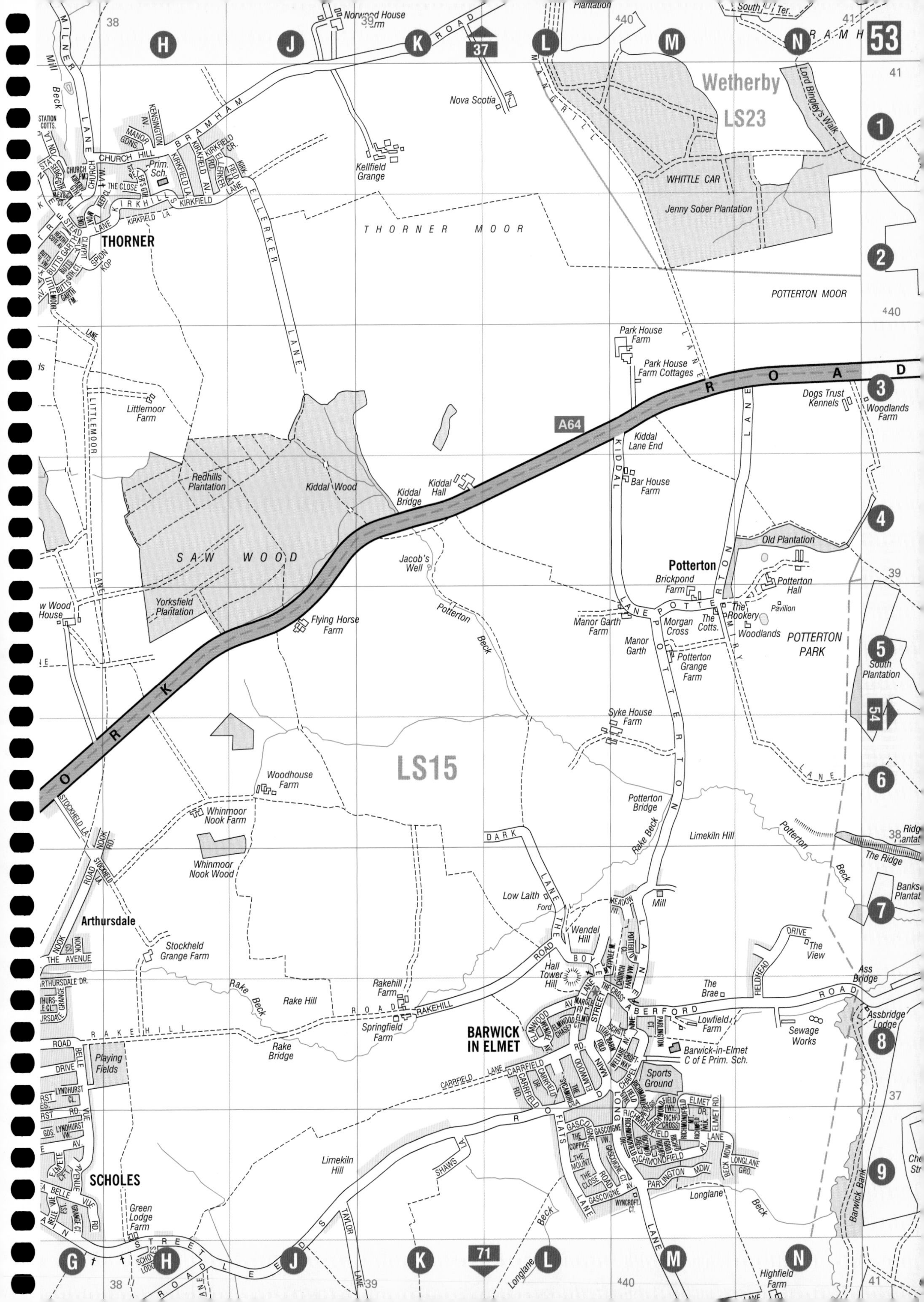

Wetherby
LS23
WHITTLE CAR
Jenny Sober Plantation
Lord Bingley's Walk
POTTERTON MOOR
THORNER MOOR
THORNER
Kellfield Grange
Nova Scotia
Norwood House Farm
Littlemoor Farm
Redhills Plantation
Kiddal Wood
SAW WOOD
Yorksfield Plantation
Kiddal Bridge
Kiddal Hall
A64
YORK ROAD
Jacob's Well
Flying Horse Farm
Park House Farm
Park House Farm Cottages
Dogs Trust Kennels
Woodlands Farm
Kiddal Lane End
Bar House Farm
Old Plantation
Potterton
Brickpond Farm
Potterton Hall
Manor Garth Farm
Morgan Cross
The Cotts.
The Rookery
Woodlands
Pavilion
POTTERTON PARK
Manor Garth
Potterton Grange Farm
South Plantation
Potterton Beck
Syke House Farm
LS15
Woodhouse Farm
Whinmoor Nook Farm
Whinmoor Nook Wood
Potterton Bridge
Limekiln Hill
The Ridge
Rake Beck
Low Laith
Ford
Mill
Arthursdale
Stockheld Grange Farm
Wendel Hill
Hall Tower Hill
The View
The Brae
Ass Bridge
Assbridge Lodge
Rake Hill
Rakehill Farm
Springfield Farm
Lowfield Farm
Sewage Works
BARWICK IN ELMET
Barwick-in-Elmet C of E Prim. Sch.
Sports Ground
Rake Bridge
Playing Fields
SCHOLES
Limekiln Hill
Green Lodge Farm
Longlane Beck
Barwick Bank
Highfield Farm
37
54
71

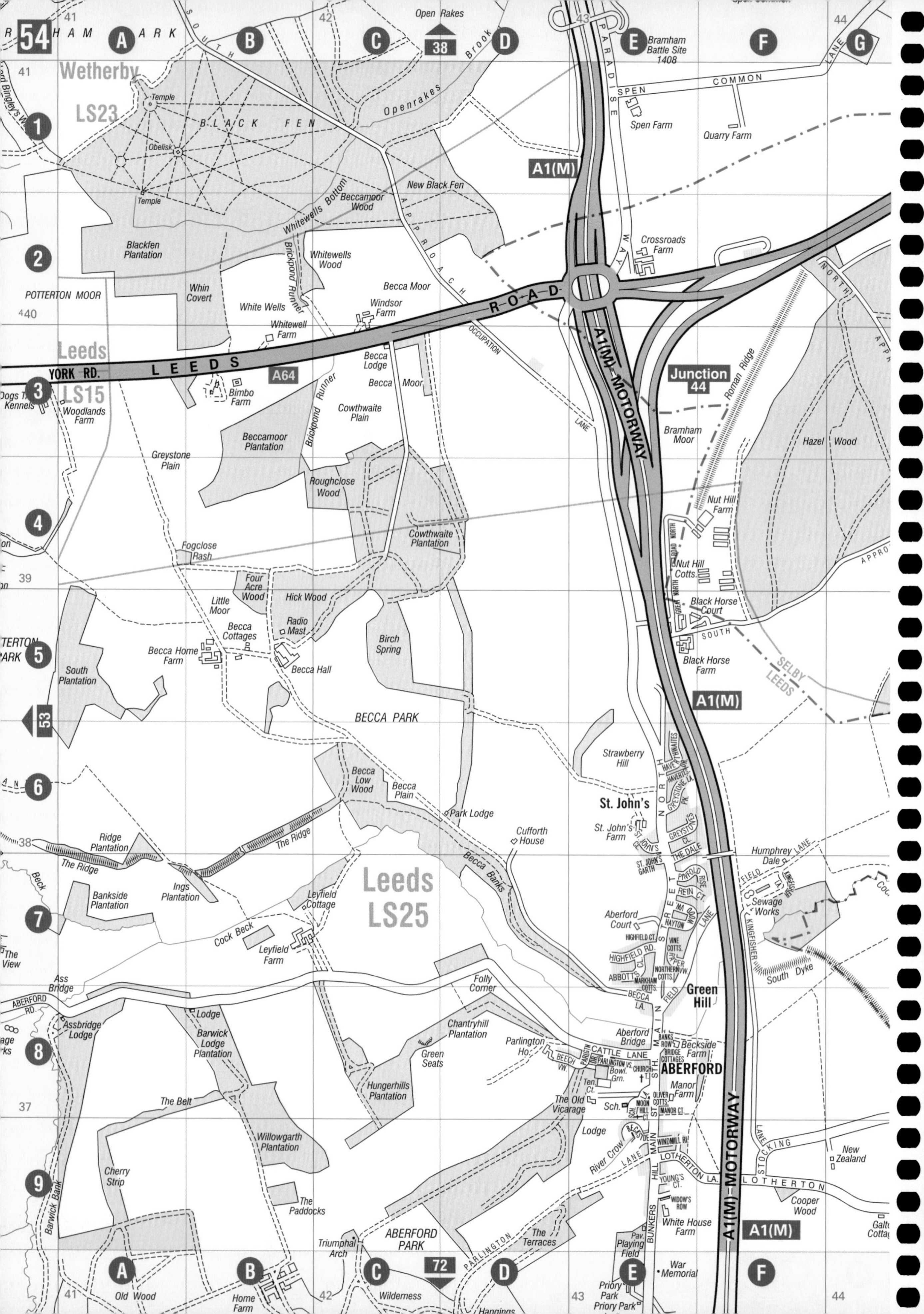
Wetherby
LS23
Black Fen
Temple
Obelisk
Open Rakes
38
Openrakes
Brook
Bramham Battle Site 1408
Spen Common
Spen Farm
Quarry Farm
Paradise Way
A1(M)
New Black Fen
Beccamoor Wood
Whitewells Bottom
Blackfen Plantation
Whitewells Wood
Brickpond Runner
Crossroads Farm
Becca Moor
Windsor Farm
Potterton Moor
Whin Covert
White Wells
Whitewell Farm
Leeds
LS15
York Rd.
Leeds Road
A64
Becca Lodge
Occupation Lane
Junction 44
Roman Ridge
Dogs Kennels
Woodlands Farm
Bimbo Farm
Cowthwaite Plain
Bramham Moor
Beccamoor Plantation
Greystone Plain
Hazel Wood
Roughclose Wood
A1(M) Motorway
Nut Hill Farm
Cowthwaite Plantation
Fogclose Rash
Nut Hill Cotts.
Great North Road
Four Acre Wood
Hick Wood
Little Moor
Black Horse Court
Radio Mast
Becca Cottages
Becca Home Farm
Birch Spring
South Plantation
Becca Hall
Black Horse Farm
Selby
Leeds
53
Becca Park
Strawberry Hill
Thwaites
Haverthwaites
Greystone Pk.
Becca Low Wood
Becca Plain
St. John's
Park Lodge
St. John's Farm
Cufforth House
Greystones Cl.
The Dale
Ridge Plantation
The Ridge
Humphrey Lane
Dale
Becca Banks
St. John's Garth
Pinfold Rise
Rein Ct.
Leeds LS25
Ings Plantation
Bankside Plantation
Leyfield Cottage
Sewage Works
Kingfisher
Aberford Court
Hayton
Cock Beck
Highfield Ct.
Vine Cotts.
Leyfield Farm
Highfield Rd.
Northern Vw.
Ass Bridge
Abbotts Cl.
Markham Cotts.
South Dyke
Folly Corner
Becca La.
Green Hill
Aberford Rd.
Lodge
Assbridge Lodge
Chantryhill Plantation
Barwick Lodge Plantation
Aberford Bridge
Banks Row
Beckside Farm
Parlington Ho.
Cattle Lane
Green Seats
Bridge Cottages
Beech Vw.
Bowl. Grn.
Church
Aberford
Manor Farm
Hungerhills Plantation
Ten. Ct.
The Belt
The Old Vicarage
Sch.
Oliver Cotts.
Moon Hill Ct.
Manor Ct.
Lodge
Becksyde
Windmill Ri.
Stocking Lane
New Zealand
Willowgarth Plantation
River Crow
Lotherton La.
Lotherton
Cherry Strip
Young's Ct.
Widow's Row
Cooper Wood
The Paddocks
Barwick Bank
White House Farm
Bunkers Hill
Aberford Park
The Terraces
Triumphal Arch
Parlington
Pav.
Playing Field
War Memorial
72
Old Wood
Home Farm
Wilderness
Hangings
Priory Park
Priory Park
Main St.
North St.

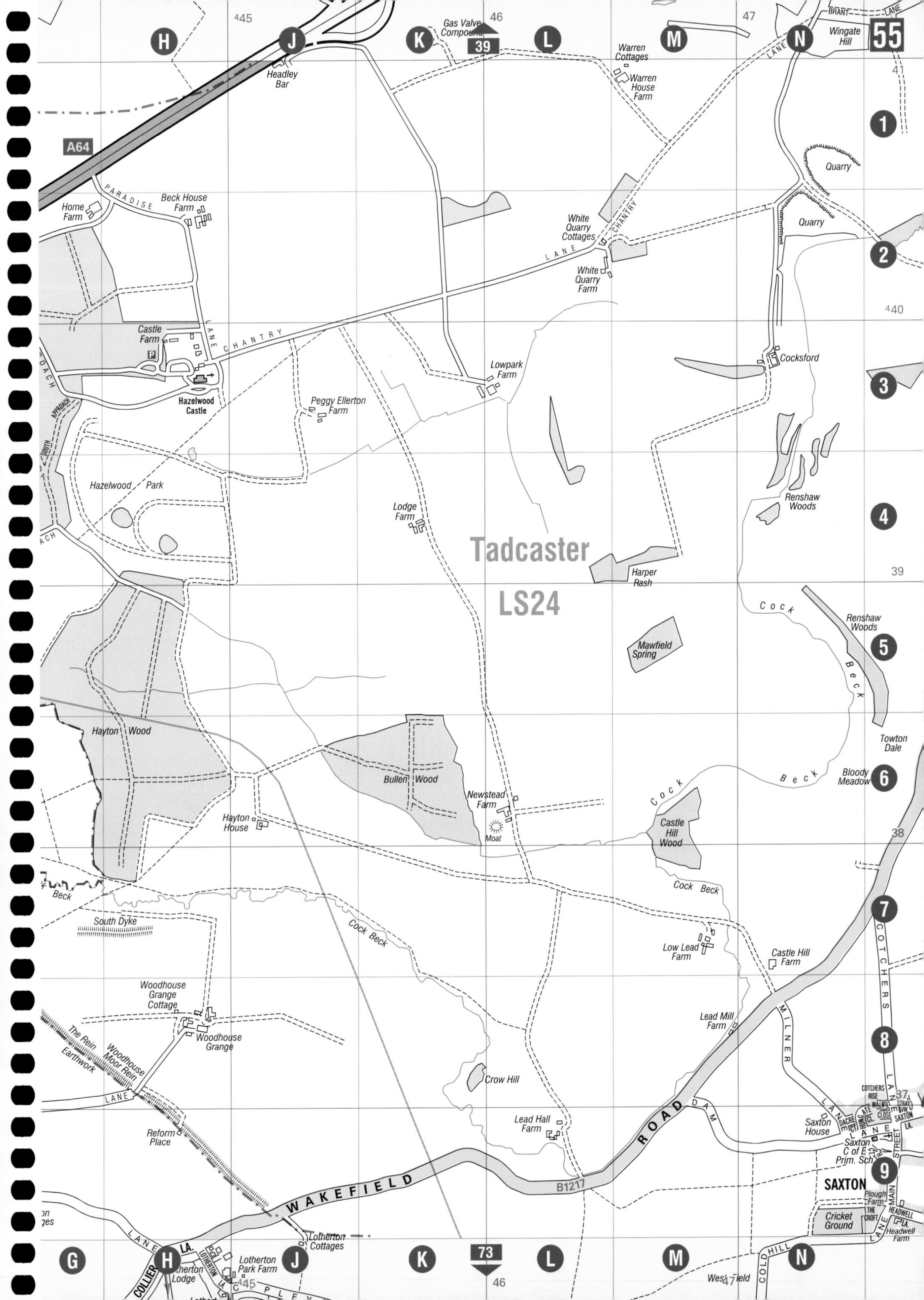
Tadcaster
LS24
Headley Bar
Gas Valve Compound
39
Warren Cottages
Warren House Farm
Wingate Hill
BRANT LANE
A64
Paradise
Home Farm
Beck House Farm
Quarry
Quarry
White Quarry Cottages
White Quarry Farm
Chantry Lane
Castle Farm
Hazelwood Castle
Lowpark Farm
Cocksford
Peggy Ellerton Farm
Hazelwood Park
Lodge Farm
Renshaw Woods
Harper Rash
Mawfield Spring
Renshaw Woods
Cock Beck
Towton Dale
Hayton Wood
Bullen Wood
Newstead Farm
Moat
Hayton House
Castle Hill Wood
Bloody Meadow
Cock Beck
South Dyke
Low Lead Farm
Castle Hill Farm
Cotchers Lane
Woodhouse Grange Cottage
Woodhouse Grange
Lead Mill Farm
Milner Lane
The Rein Earthwork
Woodhouse Moor Rein
Crow Hill
Dam Lane
Reform Place
Lead Hall Farm
Saxton House
Saxton C of E Prim. Sch.
Wakefield Road
B1217
SAXTON
Plough Farm
Cricket Ground
The Croft
Headwell La.
Headwell Farm
Main Street
Lotherton Cottages
Lotherton Park Farm
Lotherton Lodge
Collier La.
Cold Hill
West Field
73

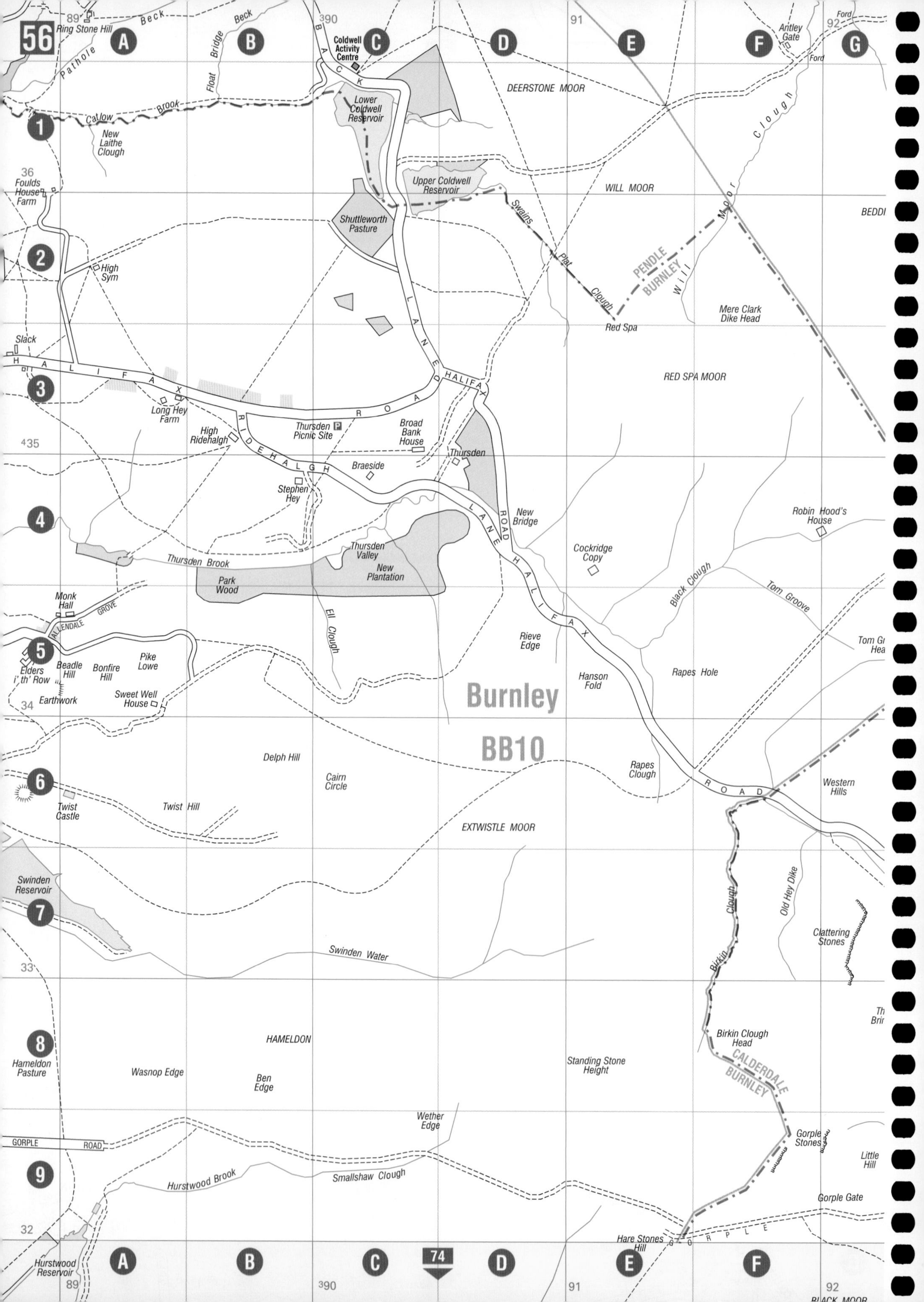

56

Ring Stone Hill

A   B   C   D   E   F   G

Pathole Beck

Float Bridge Beck

Coldwell Activity Centre

Ford
Antley Gate
Ford

Callow Brook

New Laithe Clough

Lower Coldwell Reservoir

DEERSTONE MOOR

Upper Coldwell Reservoir

WILL MOOR

BEDDI

36
Foulds House Farm

Shuttleworth Pasture

Swains

Plat Clough

PENDLE

BURNLEY

Will Moor

Clough

High Sym

Red Spa

Mere Clark Dike Head

Slack

HALIFAX ROAD

HALIFAX

RED SPA MOOR

Long Hey Farm

High Ridehalgh

RIDEHALGH

Thursden Picnic Site

Broad Bank House

Thursden

435

Braeside

Stephen Hey

New Bridge

Robin Hood's House

LANE ROAD HALIFAX

Cockridge Copy

Thursden Brook

Thursden Valley

New Plantation

Black Clough

Tom Groove

Park Wood

Ell Clough

Rieve Edge

Tom Gr Hea

Monk Hall

GROVE

Hanson Fold

Rapes Hole

PENDALE

Beadle Hill

Pike Lowe

Elders i' th' Row

Bonfire Hill

Earthwork

Sweet Well House

Burnley

BB10

Rapes Clough

ROAD

Western Hills

34

Delph Hill

Cairn Circle

Twist Castle

Twist Hill

EXTWISTLE MOOR

Birkin Clough

Old Hey Dike

Clattering Stones

Swinden Reservoir

Swinden Water

Th Brir

33

HAMELDON

Standing Stone Height

Birkin Clough Head

CALDERDALE

BURNLEY

Hameldon Pasture

Wasnop Edge

Ben Edge

Wether Edge

Gorple Stones

Little Hill

GORPLE ROAD

Hurstwood Brook

Smallshaw Clough

Gorple Gate

32

Hurstwood Reservoir

A   B   C   74   D   E   F

Hare Stones Hill

GORPLE

BLACK MOOR

89   390   91   92

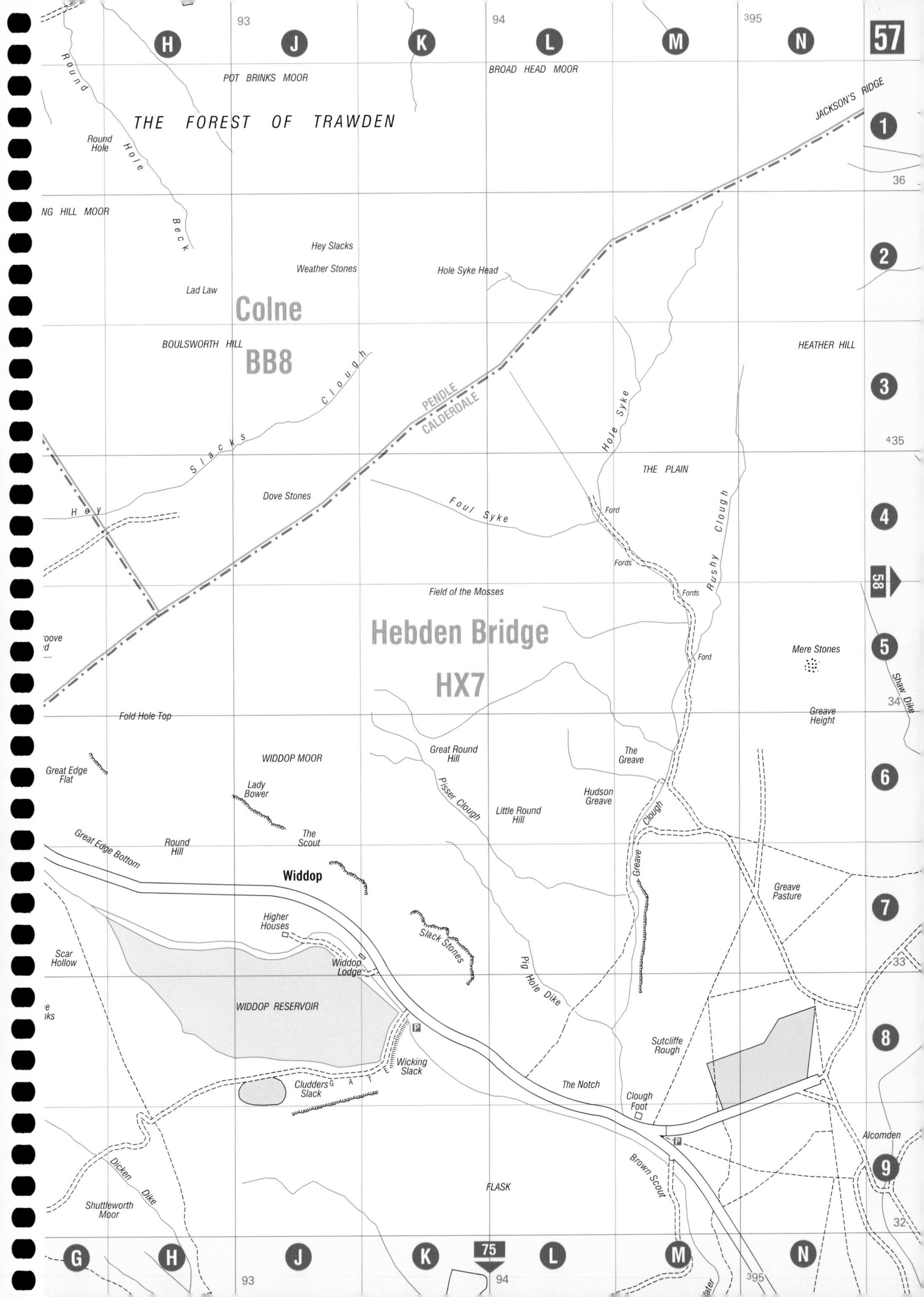
93
94
395
H
J
K
L
M
N
POT BRINKS MOOR
BROAD HEAD MOOR
THE FOREST OF TRAWDEN
JACKSON'S RIDGE
Round Hole
Round Hole Beck
NG HILL MOOR
Hey Slacks
Weather Stones
Hole Syke Head
Lad Law
Colne
BB8
BOULSWORTH HILL
HEATHER HILL
Slacks Clough
PENDLE
CALDERDALE
Hole Syke
THE PLAIN
Dove Stones
Foul Syke
Hey
Ford
Fords
Rushy Clough
Field of the Mosses
Hebden Bridge
HX7
Mere Stones
Shaw Dike
Fold Hole Top
Greave Height
Great Round Hill
The Greave
WIDDOP MOOR
Great Edge Flat
Pisser Clough
Hudson Greave
Lady Bower
Little Round Hill
Greave Clough
Great Edge Bottom
Round Hill
The Scout
Widdop
Greave Pasture
Higher Houses
Slack Stones
Scar Hollow
Widdop Lodge
Pig Hole Dike
WIDDOP RESERVOIR
Sutcliffe Rough
Wicking Slack
Cludders Slack
GATE
The Notch
Clough Foot
Alcomden
Brown Scout
Dicken Dike
Shuttleworth Moor
FLASK
1
2
3
4
5
6
7
8
9
36
435
34
33
32
58
75
G

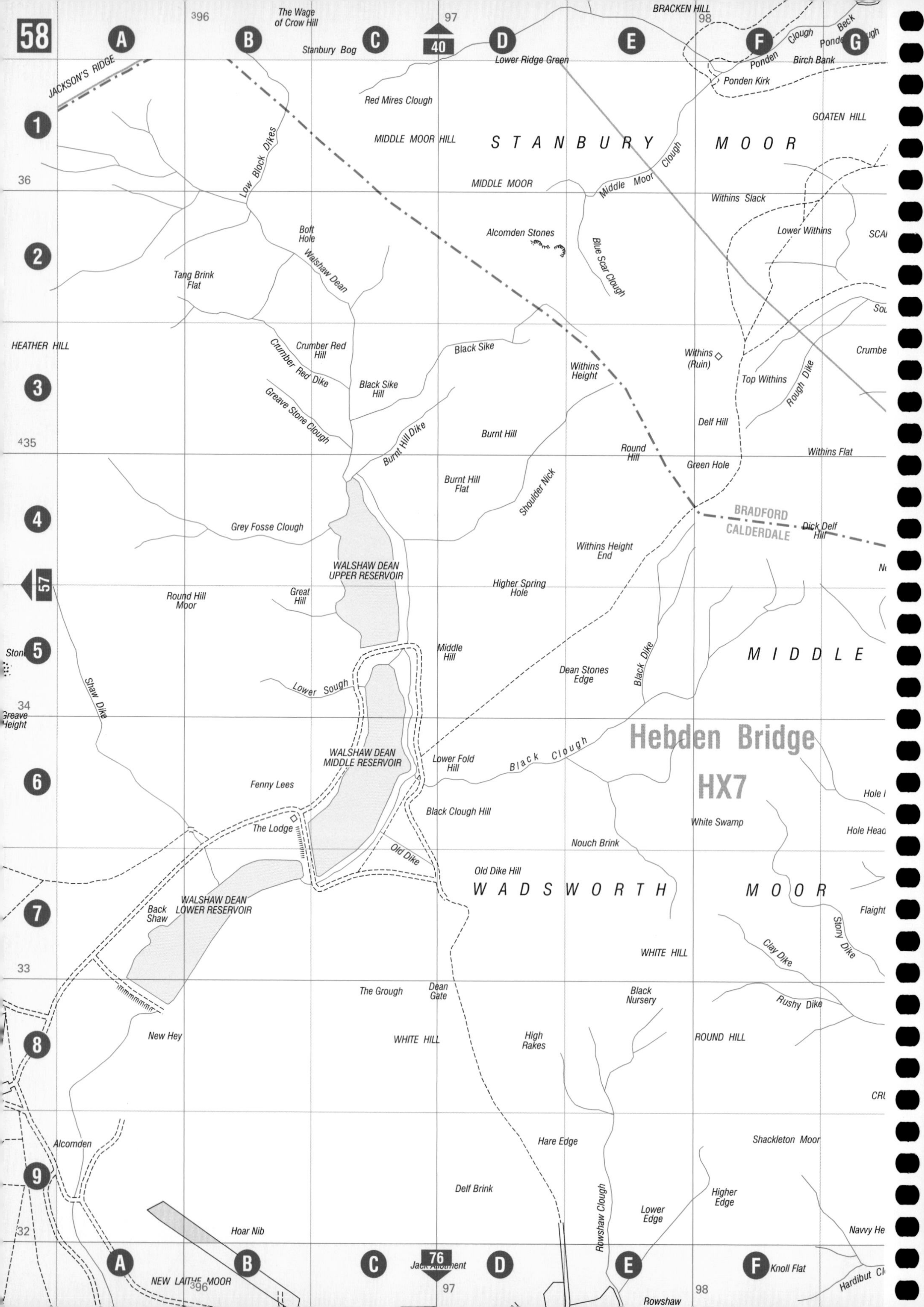

JACKSON'S RIDGE

The Wage of Crow Hill

BRACKEN HILL

Stanbury Bog

Lower Ridge Green

Ponden Clough

Beck

Ponden

Birch Bank

Ponden Kirk

Red Mires Clough

GOATEN HILL

MIDDLE MOOR HILL

S T A N B U R Y   M O O R

Low Biock Dikes

MIDDLE MOOR

Middle Moor Clough

Withins Slack

Boft Hole

Walshaw Dean

Alcomden Stones

Blue Scar Clough

Lower Withins

SCA

Tang Brink Flat

HEATHER HILL

Crumber Red Hill

Black Sike

Withins Height

Withins (Ruin)

Top Withins

Rough Dike

Crumbe

Crumber Red Dike

Black Sike Hill

Sou

Greave Stone Clough

Burnt Hill Dike

Burnt Hill

Delf Hill

435

Burnt Hill Flat

Shoulder Nick

Round Hill

Green Hole

Withins Flat

Grey Fosse Clough

Withins Height End

BRADFORD CALDERDALE

Dick Delf Hill

N

57

WALSHAW DEAN UPPER RESERVOIR

Great Hill

Higher Spring Hole

M I D D L E

Round Hill Moor

Middle Hill

Dean Stones Edge

Black Dike

Ston

Lower Sough

Greave Height

WALSHAW DEAN MIDDLE RESERVOIR

Lower Fold Hill

Black Clough

Hebden Bridge

Hole

Fenny Lees

Black Clough Hill

White Swamp

HX7

Hole Head

The Lodge

Old Dike

Nouch Brink

WALSHAW DEAN LOWER RESERVOIR

Back Shaw

Old Dike Hill

W A D S W O R T H

M O O R

Flaight

WHITE HILL

Clay Dike

Stony Dike

New Hey

The Grough

Dean Gate

Black Nursery

ROUND HILL

Rushy Dike

CRU

WHITE HILL

High Rakes

Alcomden

Hare Edge

Shackleton Moor

Delf Brink

Rowshaw Clough

Higher Edge

Lower Edge

Navvy He

Hoar Nib

NEW LAITHE MOOR

Jack Montment

Knoll Flat

Hardibut Cl

Rowshaw

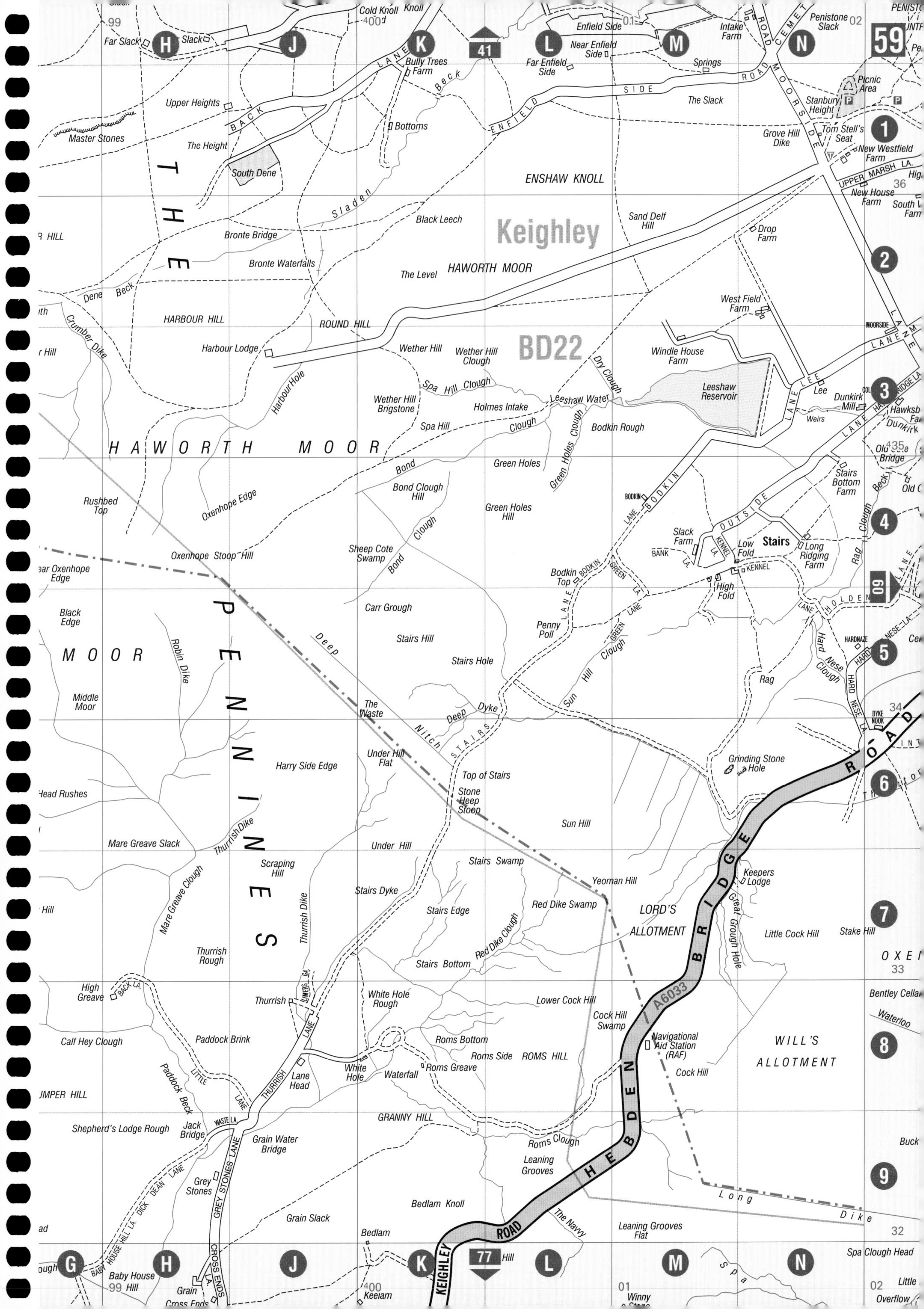
41
Keighley
BD22
HAWORTH MOOR
H A W O R T H   M O O R
THE
PENNINES
ENSHAW KNOLL
Far Slack
Slack
Cold Knoll
Bully Trees Farm
Enfield Side
Near Enfield Side
Far Enfield Side
Intake Farm
Penistone Slack
Springs
The Slack
Stanbury Height
Picnic Area
Tom Stell's Seat
New Westfield Farm
Grove Hill Dike
UPPER MARSH LA.
New House Farm
Upper Heights
Master Stones
The Height
Bottoms
South Dene
Black Leech
Sladen
Bronte Bridge
Bronte Waterfalls
Sand Delf Hill
Drop Farm
The Level
Dene Beck
HARBOUR HILL
ROUND HILL
Crumber Dike
West Field Farm
Harbour Lodge
Wether Hill
Wether Hill Clough
Windle House Farm
Dry Clough
Spa Hill Clough
Leeshaw Water
Leeshaw Reservoir
Lee
Dunkirk Mill
Weirs
Harbour Hole
Wether Hill Brigstone
Holmes Intake
Spa Hill
Clough
Green Holes Clough
Bodkin Rough
Bond
Green Holes
Bond Clough Hill
Rushbed Top
Oxenhope Edge
Green Holes Hill
BODKIN LANE
OUTSIDE
Stairs Bottom Farm
Slack Farm
Low Fold
Stairs
Long Ridging Farm
BANK LA.
KENNEL LA.
Sheep Cote Swamp
Oxenhope Stoop Hill
Bodkin Top
GREEN LA.
High Fold
Black Edge
Carr Grough
Penny Poll
HOLDEN LANE
MOOR
Robin Dike
Deep
Stairs Hill
Stairs Hole
Green Clough
Sun Hill
Hard Nese Clough
HARD NESE LA.
Middle Moor
The Waste
Deep Dyke
Nitch
STAIRS
Rag
Harry Side Edge
Under Hill Flat
Top of Stairs
Grinding Stone Hole
Head Rushes
Stone Heep Stoop
Sun Hill
Mare Greave Slack
Thurrish Dike
Under Hill
Scraping Hill
Stairs Swamp
Yeoman Hill
Keepers Lodge
Mare Greave Clough
Stairs Dyke
Stairs Edge
Red Dike Swamp
LORD'S ALLOTMENT
Great Grough Hole
Little Cock Hill
Stake Hill
Thurrish Dike
Red Dike Clough
Thurrish Rough
Stairs Bottom
High Greave
BACK LA.
Thurrish
White Hole Rough
Lower Cock Hill
Cock Hill Swamp
A6033
Bentley Cellar
Waterloo
Navigational Aid Station (RAF)
WILL'S ALLOTMENT
Calf Hey Clough
Paddock Brink
Roms Bottom
Roms Side
ROMS HILL
Paddock Beck
LITTLE LANE
THURRISH LANE
Lane Head
White Hole
Waterfall
Roms Greave
Cock Hill
JUMPER HILL
WASTE LA.
GRANNY HILL
Shepherd's Lodge Rough
Jack Bridge
Grain Water Bridge
Roms Clough
Buck
Leaning Grooves
Grey Stones
DICK DEAN LANE
GREY STONES LANE
Grain Slack
Bedlam Knoll
The Navvy
Long Dike
Leaning Grooves Flat
HEBDEN BRIDGE ROAD
KEIGHLEY ROAD
Bedlam
Hill
BABY HOUSE HILL LA.
Baby House Hill
CROSS ENDS LA.
Grain
Keelam
Spa
Spa Clough Head
Little Overflow
Winny
77
60

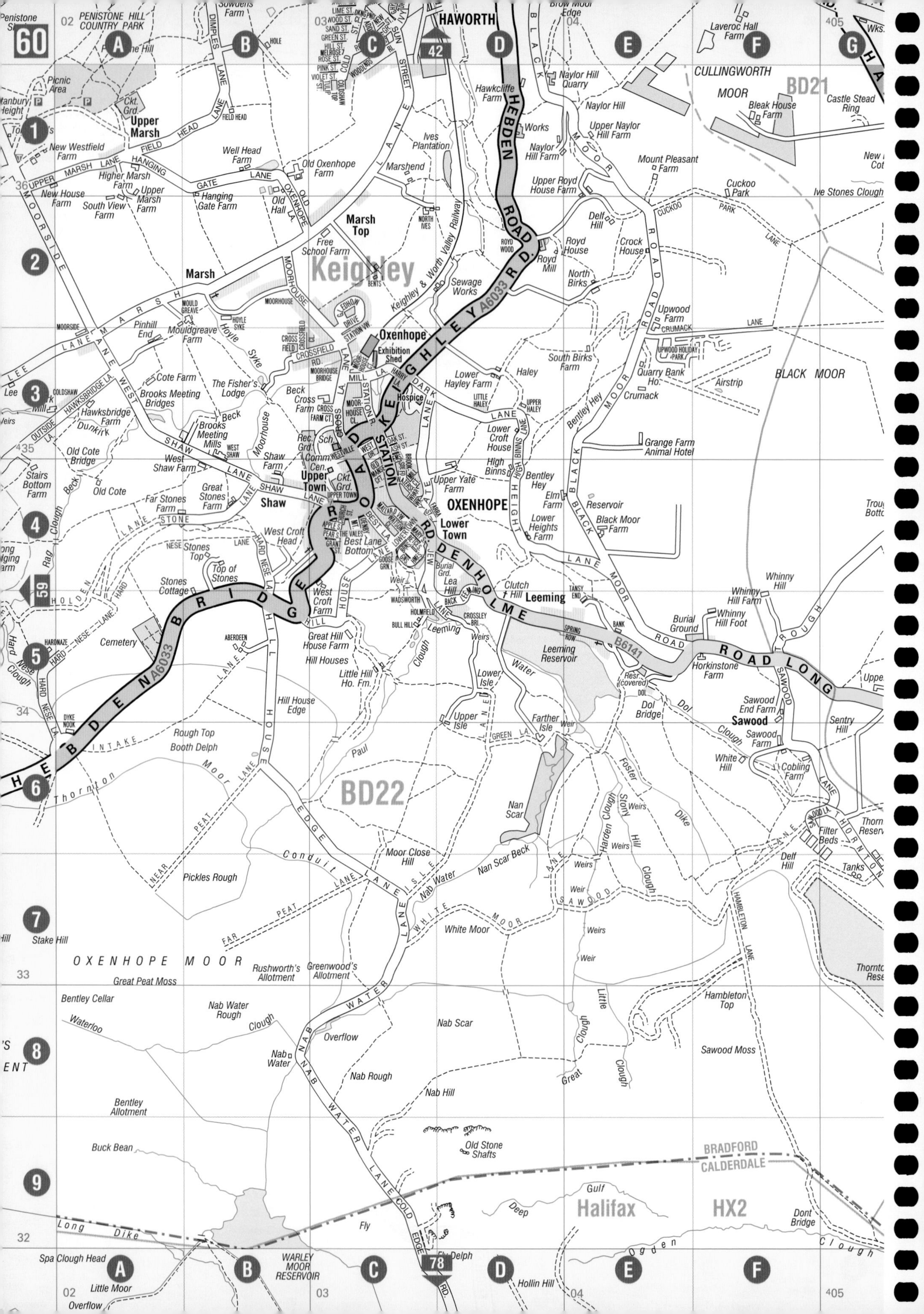
HAWORTH
42
Penistone Hill Country Park
Upper Marsh
Marsh Top
Keighley
Marsh
Oxenhope
OXENHOPE
Upper Town
Lower Town
Shaw
Leeming
Leeming Reservoir
Sawood
Cullingworth Moor
BD21
BD22
BLACK MOOR
HEBDEN ROAD
KEIGHLEY ROAD
HEBDEN BRIDGE ROAD
DENHOLME ROAD
LONG ROAD
A6033
B6141
59
Oxenhope Moor
Great Peat Moss
Nab Water
Nab Scar
Nab Hill
Old Stone Shafts
Sawood Moss
Hambleton Top
Warley Moor Reservoir
BRADFORD
CALDERDALE
Halifax
HX2
78

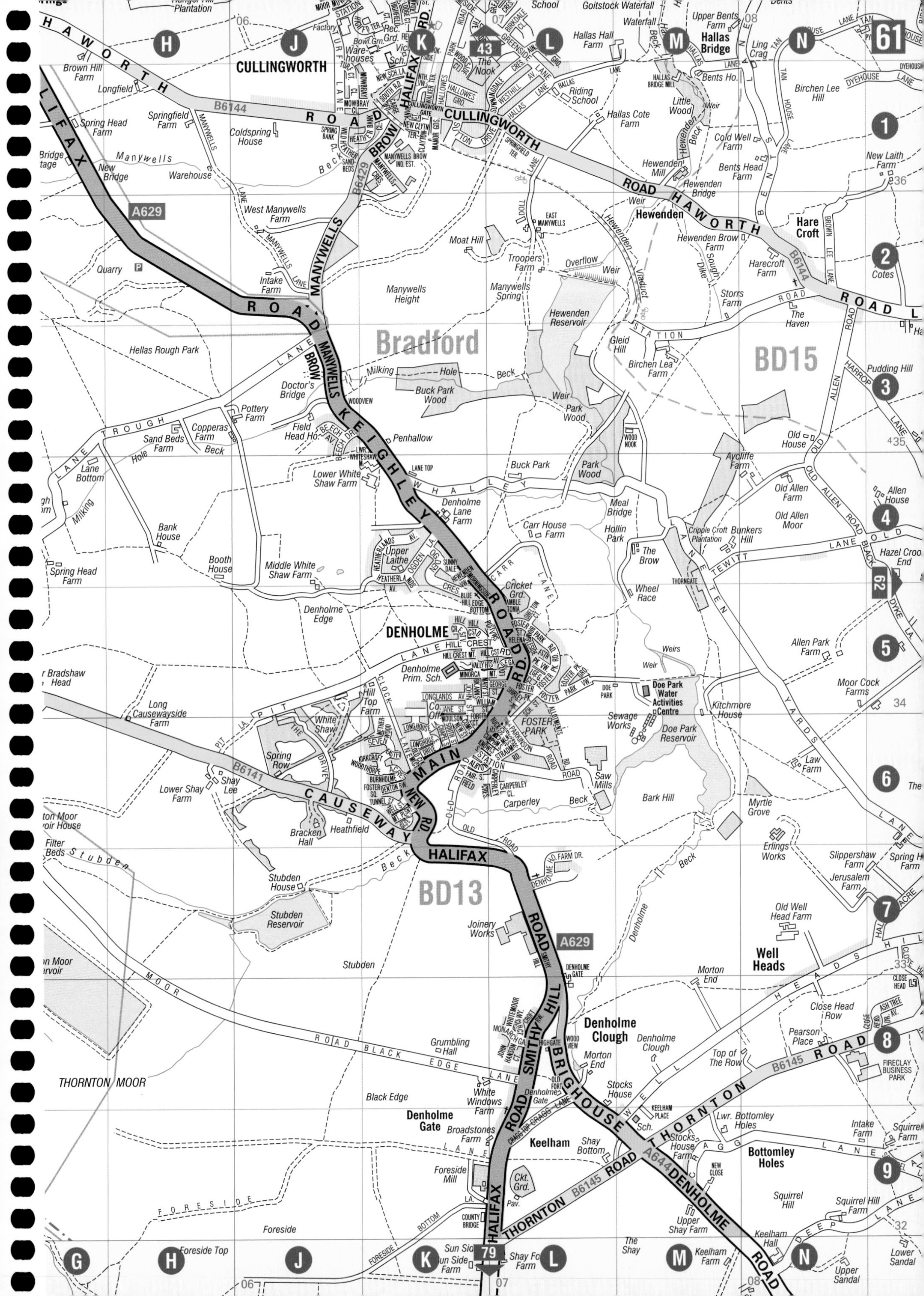
CULLINGWORTH
Bradford
BD15
BD13
DENHOLME
Hewenden
Hare Croft
Hallas Bridge
Denholme Gate
Keelham
Well Heads
Bottomley Holes
Denholme Clough
THORNTON MOOR
Hewenden Reservoir
Doe Park Reservoir
Stubden Reservoir
Doe Park Water Activities Centre
Denholme Prim. Sch.
Manywells Height
Hellas Rough Park
Buck Park Wood
Park Wood
Foster Park
Cricket Grd.
Sewage Works
Saw Mills
Joinery Works
Erlings Works
Bark Hill
Stubden
Foreside
Black Edge
Grumbling Hall
Squirrel Hill
The Shay
FIRECLAY BUSINESS PARK
A629
A644
B6144
B6141
B6145
B6429
HAWORTH ROAD
HALIFAX ROAD
KEIGHLEY ROAD
MANYWELLS BROW
CAUSEWAY
MAIN
SMITHY HILL
BRIGHOUSE DENHOLME ROAD
THORNTON ROAD
WHALLEY
STATION ROAD
TROUGH LANE
BLACK EDGE LANE
FORESIDE BOTTOM
HEADS LANE
TEWITT LANE
OLD ALLEN ROAD
YARDS LANE
43
62
79
G H J K L M N
1 2 3 4 5 6 7 8 9
06 07 08
32 33 34 35 36

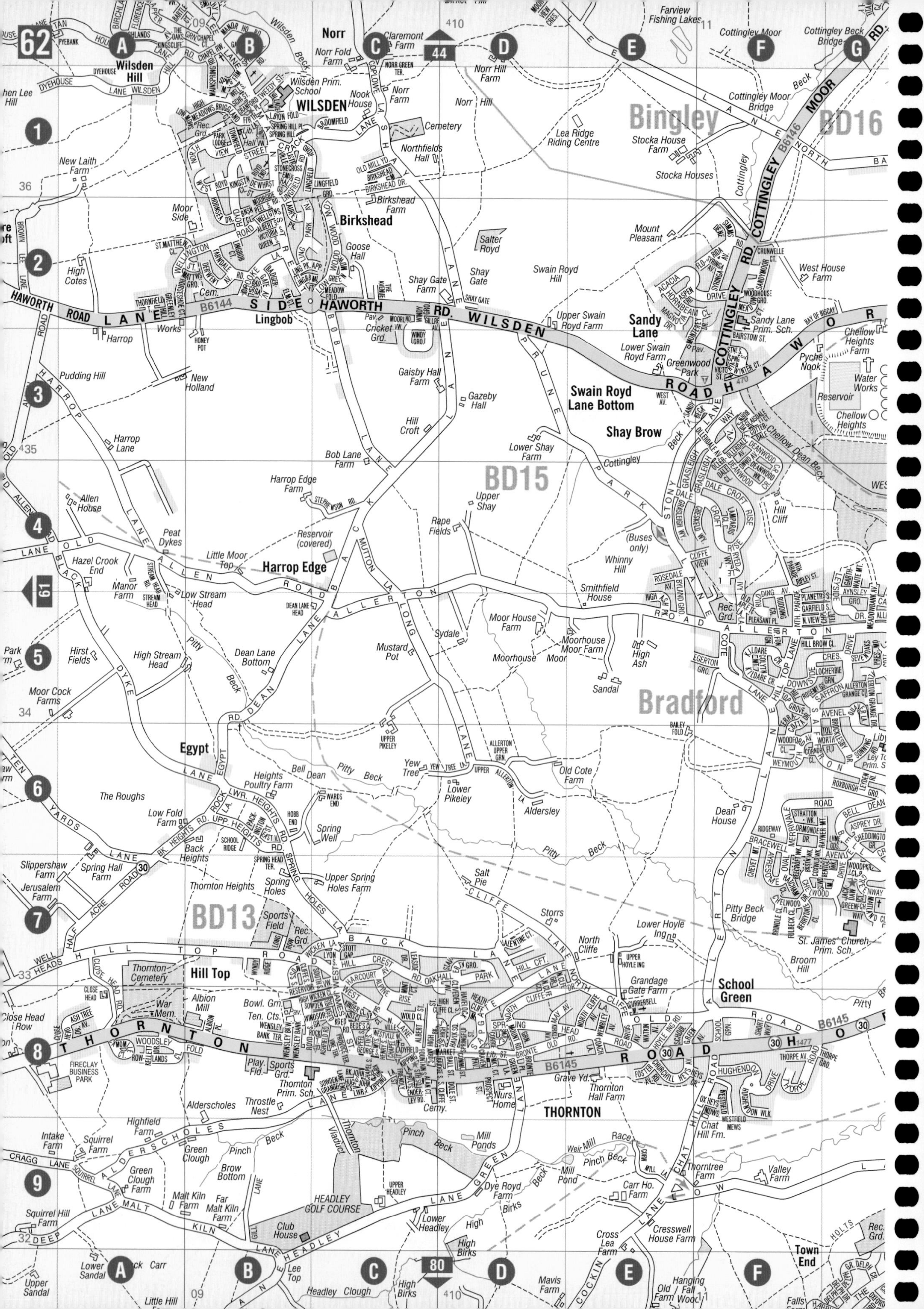

Wilsden Hill
WILSDEN
Norr
Birkshead
Lingbob
Bingley
BD16
Sandy Lane
Swain Royd Lane Bottom
Shay Brow
BD15
Harrop Edge
Egypt
Bradford
Hill Top
BD13
THORNTON
School Green
Town End
HAWORTH ROAD
WILSDEN RD.
THORNTON ROAD
ALLERTON ROAD
COTTINGLEY RD.
HEADLEY GOLF COURSE
Thornton Cemetery
Fireclay Business Park
44
61
80

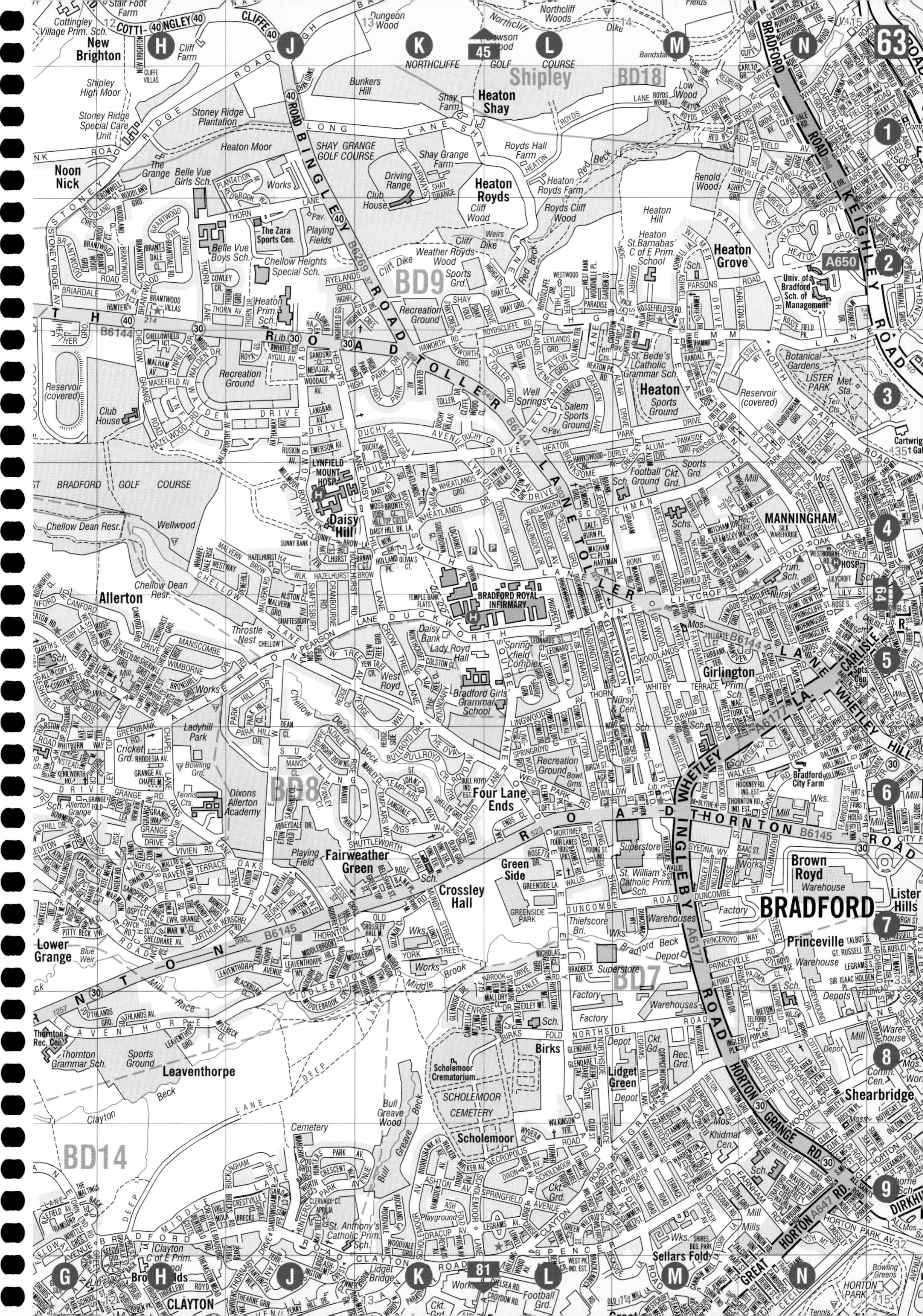

Stair Foot Farm
Cottingley Village Prim. Sch.
COTTINGLEY CLIFFE
New Brighton
Cliff Farm
Dungeon Wood
Northcliff
Northcliff Woods
Dawson Wood
45
NORTHCLIFFE GOLF COURSE
Shipley
BD18
Bandstand
Shipley High Moor
Stoney Ridge Special Care Unit
Stoney Ridge Plantation
Bunkers Hill
Shay Farm
Heaton Shay
Low Wood
Heaton Moor
SHAY GRANGE GOLF COURSE
Shay Grange Farm
Royds Hall Farm
Noon Nick
The Grange
Belle Vue Girls Sch.
Works
Driving Range
Club House
Heaton Royds
Heaton Royds Farm
Renold Wood
Cliff Wood
Royds Cliff Wood
Heaton Hill
The Zara Sports Cen.
Playing Fields
Belle Vue Boys Sch.
Chellow Heights Special Sch.
Cliff Dike
Weirs
Red Beck
Heaton St.Barnabas' C of E Prim. School
Heaton Grove
Weather Royds Wood
BD9
Sports Grd.
A650
Univ. of Bradford Sch. of Management
Heaton Prim. Sch.
Recreation Ground
TOLLER ROAD
B6144
B6269
BINGLEY ROAD
KEIGHLEY ROAD
BRADFORD ROAD
Reservoir (covered)
Club House
Recreation Ground
St. Bede's Catholic Grammar Sch.
Heaton
Botanical Gardens
LISTER PARK
Met. Sta.
Well Springs
Salem Sports Ground
Heaton Sports Ground
Reservoir (covered)
Cartwright Gal.
BRADFORD GOLF COURSE
LYNFIELD MOUNT HOSP.
Daisy Hill
Football Ground
Sports Grd.
Mill
MANNINGHAM
SILK WAREHOUSE
Chellow Dean Resr.
Wellwood
Schs.
Prim. Sch.
HOSP.
64
Chellow Dean Resr.
Allerton
BRADFORD ROYAL INFIRMARY
TEMPLE BANK FLATS
Throstle Nest
Daisy Bank
Lady Royd Hall
Springfield Complex
Girlington
Bradford Girls Grammar School
West Royd
Chellow Dean Beck
Ladyhill Park
Cricket Grd.
Bowling Green
Tennis Cts.
Dixons Allerton Academy
BD8
Four Lane Ends
Recreation Ground
Bradford City Farm
WHETLEY LANE
WHETLEY HILL
A6177
THORNTON ROAD
B6145
Superstore
St. William's Catholic Prim. Sch.
Brown Royd Warehouse
BRADFORD
Lister Hills
Playing Field
Fairweather Green
Green Side
Crossley Hall
GREENSIDE PARK
Thiefscore Bri.
Warehouses
Factory
Princeville
Warehouse
Lower Grange
Blue Weir
Works
Middle Brook
Bradford Beck
Depot
Superstore
BD7
INGLEBY ROAD
Mill Race
Factory
Warehouses
Depots
Thornton Rec. Cen.
Thornton Grammar Sch.
Sports Ground
Leaventhorpe
Scholemoor Crematorium
SCHOLEMOOR CEMETERY
Birks
Lidget Green
Depot
Rec. Grd.
Mill
Warehouse
Comm. Cen.
Shearbridge
Clayton
Bull Greave Wood
Cemetery
Scholemoor
Khidmat Cen.
HORTON GRANGE RD.
BD14
Playground
St. Anthony's Catholic Prim. Sch.
Ckt. Grd.
Wks.
Mills
Sellars Fold
A647
HORTON PARK AV.
Clayton C of E Prim. School
Broadfields
Lidget Bridge
81
Football Grd.
CLAYTON
GREAT HORTON RD.
Bowling Greens
HORTON PARK
G
H
J
K
L
M
N
1
2
3
4
5
6
7
8
9

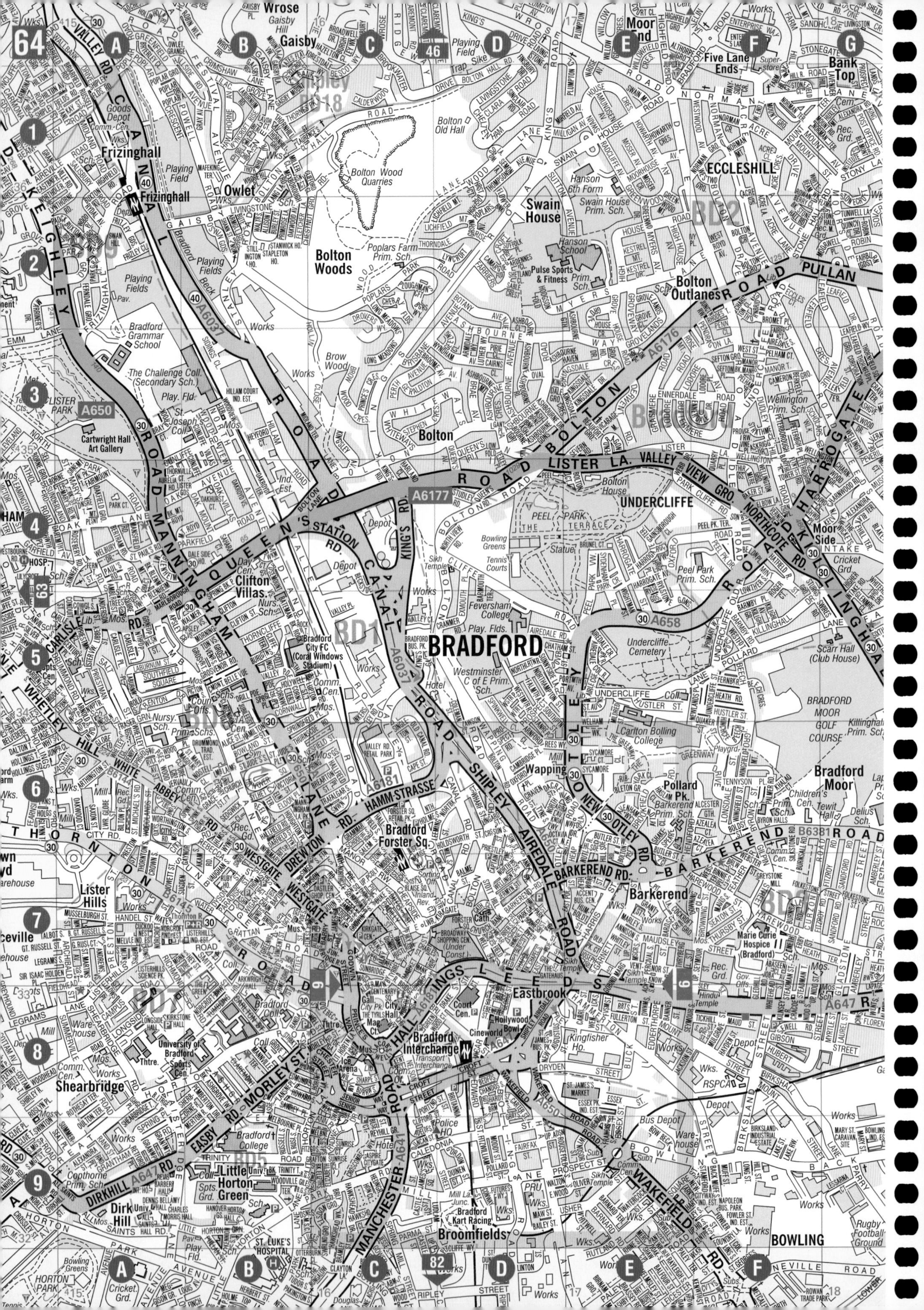

BRADFORD
Frizinghall
Owlet
Gaisby
Wrose
Bolton Woods
Swain House
ECCLESHILL
Bolton Outlanes
Bolton
UNDERCLIFFE
Moor Side
Clifton Villas
Lister Hills
Shearbridge
Little Horton Green
Dirk Hill
Broomfields
Barkerend
Eastbrook
Wapping
Bradford Moor
BOWLING
Bradford Interchange
Bradford Forster Sq.
BD1
BD2
BD3
BD4
BD5
BD7
BD8

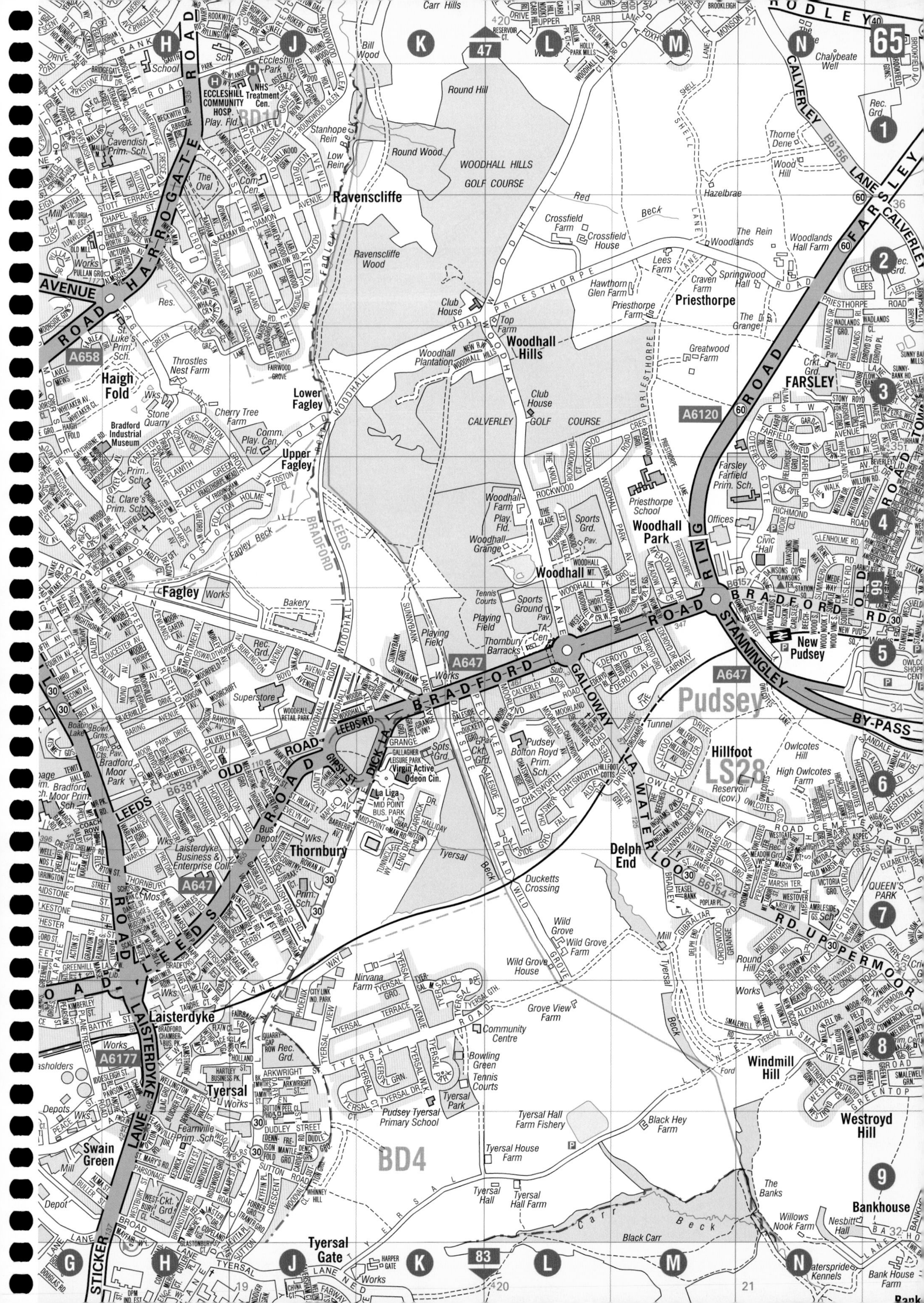

Carr Hills
47
Bill Wood
Round Hill
Round Wood
WOODHALL HILLS GOLF COURSE
Ravenscliffe
Ravenscliffe Wood
Stanhope Rein
Low Rein
ECCLESHILL COMMUNITY HOSP.
NHS Treatment Cen.
Eccleshill Park
BD10
Cavendish Prim. Sch.
The Oval
STOTT TERRACE
HARROGATE ROAD
AVENUE ROAD
A658
Haigh Fold
Throstles Nest Farm
Stone Quarry
Bradford Industrial Museum
Cherry Tree Farm
Lower Fagley
Upper Fagley
St. Luke's Prim. Sch.
St. Clare's Prim. Sch.
Fagley
Fagley Beck
Bakery
BRADFORD
LEEDS
Woodhall Plantation
Woodhall Hills
Club House
Top Farm
PRIESTHORPE ROAD
CALVERLEY GOLF COURSE
Crossfield Farm
Crossfield House
Red Beck
Lees Farm
Hawthorn Glen Farm
Priesthorpe Farm
Priesthorpe
Craven Farm
Springwood Hall
The Grange
Greatwood Farm
Hazelbrae
The Rein
Woodlands
Woodlands Hall Farm
Thorne Dene
Wood Hill
Chalybeate Well
Rec. Grd.
RODLEY
CALVERLEY LANE
B6156
FARSLEY
CALVERLEY
A6120
RING ROAD
FARSLEY
Farsley Farfield Prim. Sch.
Priesthorpe School
Woodhall Park
Woodhall
Woodhall Farm
Woodhall Grange
Sports Grd.
Sports Ground
Playing Field
Thornbury Barracks
TA Cen.
Offices
Civic Hall
New Pudsey
B6157
BRADFORD ROAD
STANNINGLEY BY-PASS
A647
Pudsey
Hillfoot
LS28
Owlcotes Hill
High Owlcotes Farm
Reservoir (cov.)
GALLOWAY LA.
WATERLOO ROAD
Delph End
B6154
UPPERMOOR
QUEEN'S PARK
Tunnel
Pudsey Bolton Royd Prim. Sch.
Superstore
Woodhall Retail Park
LEEDS OLD ROAD
B6381
Bradford Moor Park
Boating Lake
GIPSY ST.
DICK LA.
Virgin Active Odeon Cin.
La Liga
MID POINT BUS. PARK
Thornbury
Bus Depot
Laisterdyke Business & Enterprise Coll.
LEEDS ROAD
A647
Tyersal Beck
Ducketts Crossing
Wild Grove
Wild Grove Farm
Wild Grove House
Grove View Farm
Community Centre
Bowling Green
Tennis Courts
Tyersal Park
Pudsey Tyersal Primary School
Nirvana Farm
CITY LINK IND. PARK
Laisterdyke
Works
A6177
LAISTERDYKE
Tyersal
Fearnville Prim. Sch.
Swain Green
Depot
Depots
Mill
Tyersal Hall Farm Fishery
Black Hey Farm
Tyersal House Farm
Tyersal Hall
Tyersal Hall Farm
BD4
Carr Beck
Black Carr
Windmill Hill
Westroyd Hill
Round Hill
The Banks
Bankhouse
Willows Nook Farm
Nesbitt Hall
Waterspride Kennels
Bank House Farm
Tyersal Gate
HARPER GATE
STICKER LANE
83
G H J K L M N
1 2 3 4 5 6 7 8 9
19 420 21

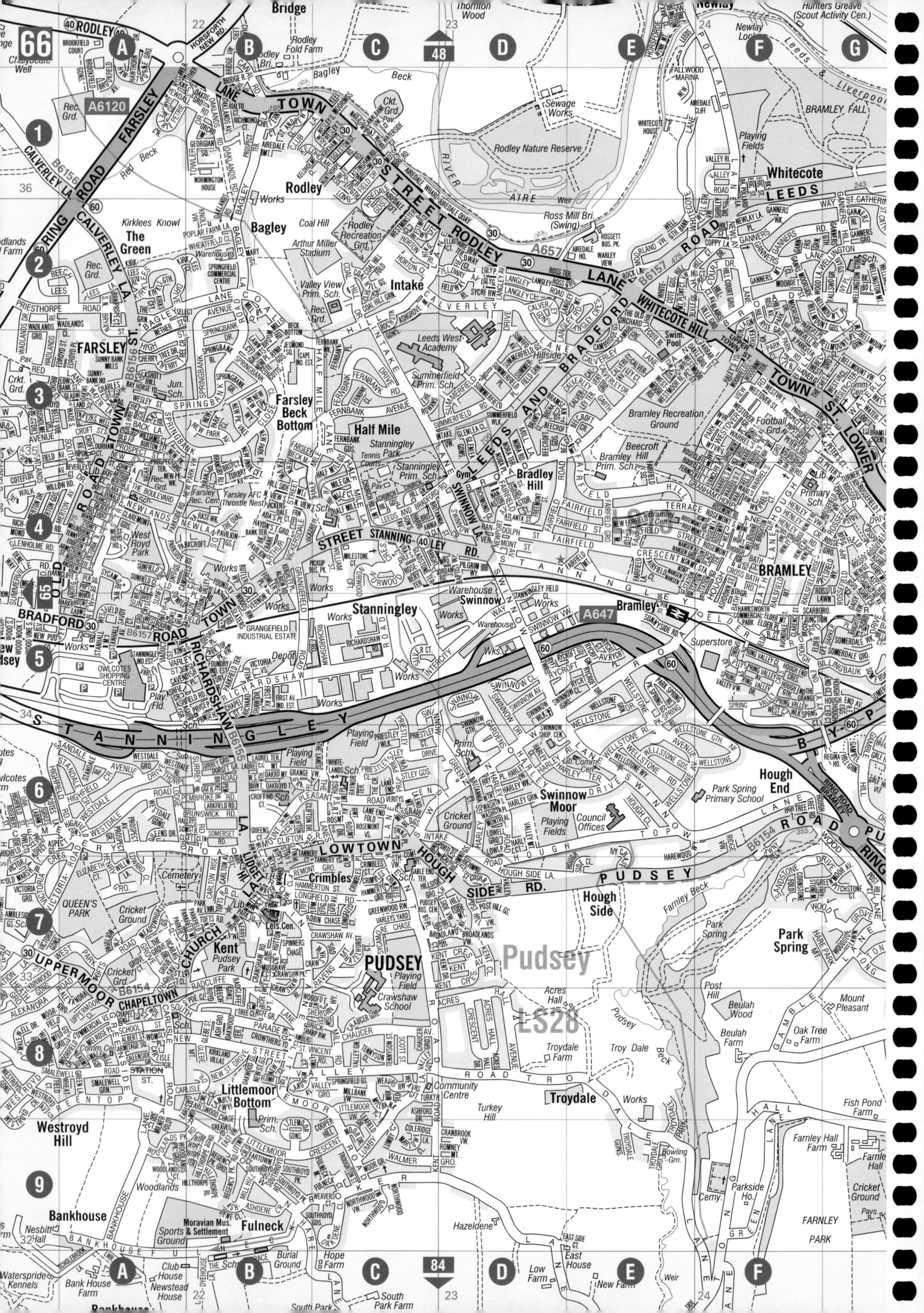
66
48
84
65
RODLEY
FARSLEY
Rodley
Bagley
The Green
Farsley Beck Bottom
Half Mile
Stanningley
Bramley
BRAMLEY
Whitecote
Rodley Nature Reserve
Swinnow Moor
Hough End
Pudsey
PUDSEY
LS28
Littlemoor Bottom
Fulneck
Westroyd Hill
Bankhouse
Troydale
Park Spring
STANNINGLEY
A657
A647
A6120
B6155
B6154
B6157
B6156

67
49
68
85
H
J
K
L
M
N
G
1
2
3
4
5
6
7
8
9
HEADINGLEY
LS6
LS5
LS4
LS12
Sandford
Moorside
Leeds
Kirkstall
Headingley
Burley
Burley Pk.
Upper Armley
Armley
Hill Top
Gamble Hill
Hill End
Far Fold
Moor Top
Moor End
Swallow Hill
Carr Crofts
Wiring Field
Town End
New Scarborough
Cabbage Hill
Upper Wortley
Silver Royd Hill
Low Fold
Bawn
WORTLEY
Lower Wortley
New Blackpool
Farnley
Beckett Park
Queen's Wood
Kirkstall Abbey (rems.)
Abbey Gardens
Kirkstall Lock
Forge Locks
Toads Hole Wood
Rugby Football Grd.
Public Park
Recreation Ground
Crooked Acres
Batcliffe Wood
Yorkshire Co. Cricket Club (Headingley)
Leeds Rhinos RLFC & Leeds Carnegie RUFC
Abbey Light Railway
Leeds Rugby Academy
Kirkstall Valley Nature Reserve
CITY GOLF COURSE
GOTTS PARK GOLF COURSE
The Mansion (Club House)
GOTTS PARK
Redcote Bridge
Ridge Wood
Armley Tennis Club
Armley Cemetery
ST. MARY'S HOSPITAL
Goals Soccer Centre
Fitness First
AIRE VALLEY MARINA
Armley Mills Leeds Ind. Mus.
Armley Pk. Centre
Sports Ground
Burley Rec. Ground
HMP LEEDS
New Wortley Cemetery
Castleton Prim. Sch.
Wortley Recreation Ground
Wortley South Junction
Upper & Lower Wortley Cemy.
Bowling Greens
The Leeds Wall
Reservoir
Playing Fields
Fish Pond
Lawns Farm
Holly Farm
The Farnley Academy
West SILC (Victoria Park Site)
Cobden Prim. Sch.
Little Wood
Western Flatts Park
Cliff Park
Recreation Grd.
Leeds and Liverpool Canal
RIVER AIRE
ABBEY ROAD
BRADFORD ROAD
KIRKSTALL ROAD
COMMERCIAL RD.
BRIDGE RD.
KIRKSTALL LANE
KIRKSTONE RD.
STANNINGLEY ROAD
ARMLEY ROAD
TOWN ST.
ROAD TO WORTLEY
FARNLEY RING ROAD
LOWER WORTLEY ROAD
WHITEHALL ROAD
GELDERD ROAD
OTLEY ROAD
CARDIGAN ROAD
BURLEY ROAD
A65
A660
A647
A657
A6110
A58
A62
B6157
B6154

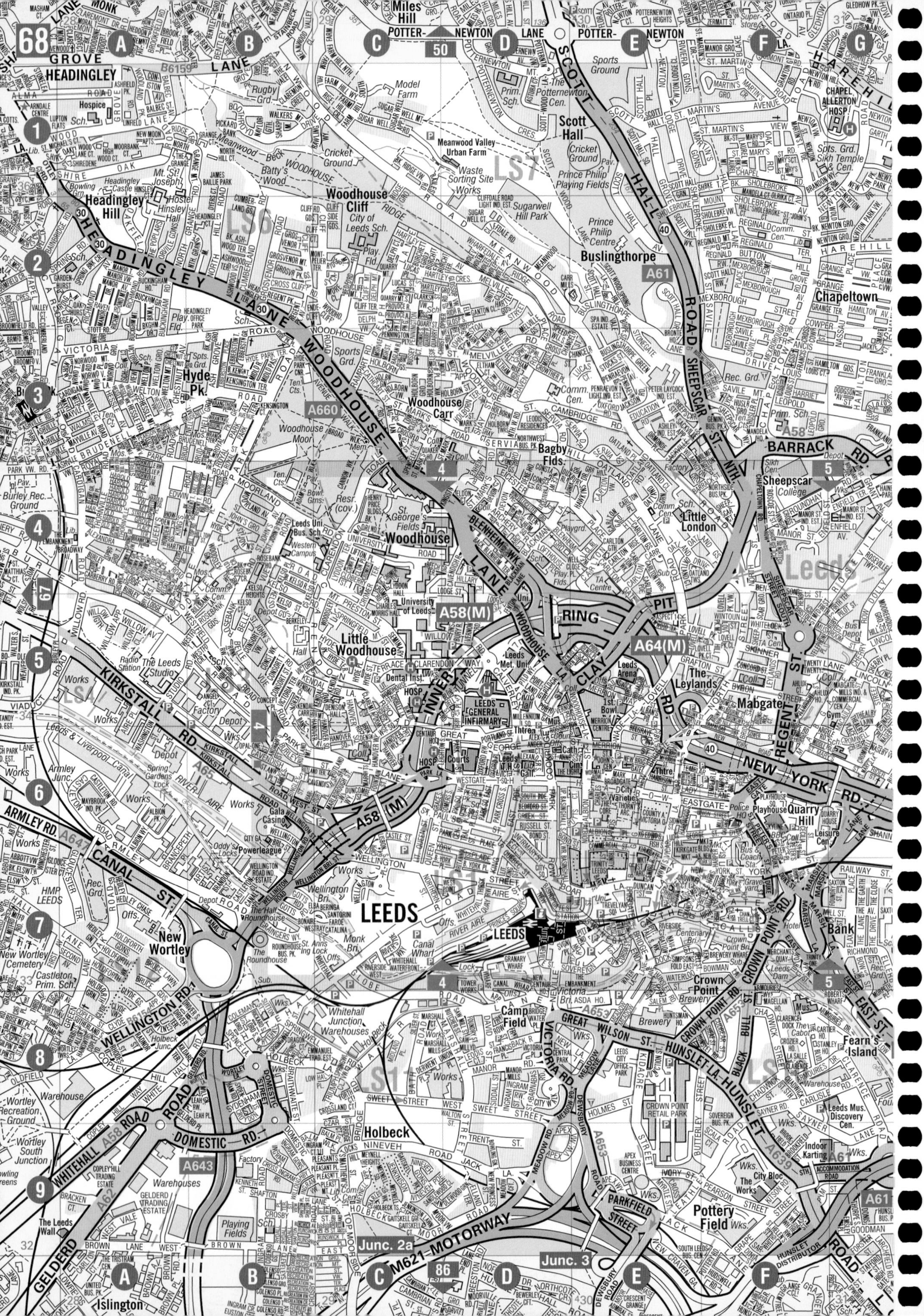
A
B
C
D
E
F
G
1
2
3
4
5
6
7
8
9
50
4
5
67
86
LEEDS
Headingley
Headingley Hill
Hyde Pk.
Woodhouse
Little Woodhouse
Woodhouse Cliff
Woodhouse Carr
Woodhouse Moor
Scott Hall
Buslingthorpe
Chapeltown
Chapel Allerton Hosp.
Little London
Sheepscar
The Leylands
Mabgate
Quarry Hill
Bank
Fearn's Island
Crown Point
Pottery Field
Holbeck
Camp Field
New Wortley
Islington
Burley Rec. Ground
Armley Junc.
HMP Leeds
Wortley Recreation Ground
Wortley South Junction
New Wortley Cemetery
Castleton Prim. Sch.
The Leeds Wall
Playing Fields
Warehouses
Gelderd Trading Estate
Whitehall Junction Warehouses
University of Leeds
Leeds General Infirmary
Leeds Met. Uni
Leeds Arena
Leeds Uni Bus. Sch.
Leeds Mus. Discovery Cen.
Indoor Karting
City Bloc
Crown Point Retail Park
Apex Business Centre
Leeds City Office Park
Prince Philip Playing Fields
Prince Philip Centre
Sugarwell Hill Park
Meanwood Valley Urban Farm
Model Farm
Rugby Grd.
Cricket Ground
Sports Ground
Potternewton Cen.
Batty's Wood
Waste Sorting Site Works
City of Leeds Sch.
Bagby Flds.
Hospice
Powerleague
Gala Casino
The Roundhouse
Monk Bri.
Canal Wharf
Granary Wharf
Leeds Dam
Brewery
Leisure Cen.
Sheepscar College
The Leeds Studio
Radio Station
Leeds & Liverpool Canal
River Aire
LS1
LS6
LS7
LS11
HEADINGLEY LANE
WOODHOUSE LANE
SCOTT HALL ROAD
SHEEPSCAR ST. NTH.
BARRACK RD.
REGENT ST.
NEW YORK RD.
KIRKSTALL RD.
ARMLEY RD.
CANAL ST.
WELLINGTON RD.
WHITEHALL ROAD
GELDERD ROAD
DOMESTIC RD.
VICTORIA RD.
GREAT WILSON ST.
HUNSLET LA.
HUNSLET ROAD
CROWN POINT RD.
BLACK BULL ST.
EAST ST.
M621 MOTORWAY
Junc. 2a
Junc. 3
PARKFIELD STREET
DEWSBURY ROAD
INNER RING
CLAY PIT LA.
BLENHEIM WK.
POTTER-NEWTON LANE
MEANWOOD RIDGE
WOODHOUSE RIDGE
A58(M)
A64(M)
A660
A61
A58
A65
A647
A643
A62
A653
A639
40
30
Sugar Well Rd.
Moorland Rd.
Hyde Park Rd.
Westgate
Wellington St.
Eastgate
Merrion Centre
City Varieties
Leeds Station
Courts

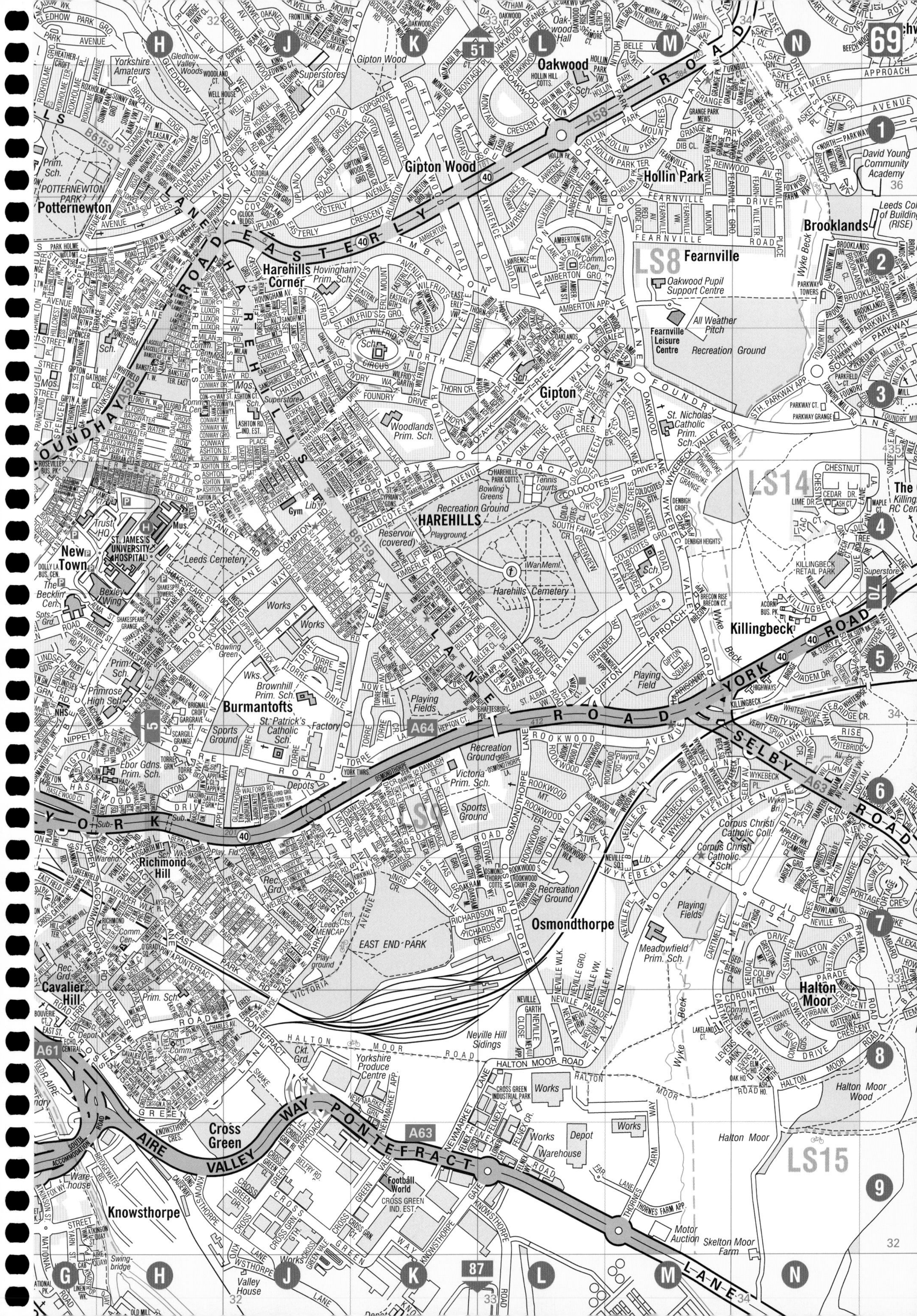
H
J
K
51
L
M
N
Yorkshire Amateurs FC
Gledhow Valley Woods
Gipton Wood
Superstores
Oakwood
Oakwood Hall
Sch.
A58
Potternewton
Prim. Sch.
Gipton Wood
Hollin Park
David Young Community Academy
Leeds Coll of Building (RISE)
Brooklands
Harehills Corner
Hovingham Prim. Sch.
LS8
Fearnville
Oakwood Pupil Support Centre
All Weather Pitch
Fearnville Leisure Centre
Recreation Ground
EASTERLY ROAD
HAREHILLS LANE
ROUNDHAY ROAD
Gipton
St. Nicholas Catholic Prim. Sch.
Woodlands Prim. Sch.
LS14
Superstore
Mus.
St. James's University Hospital
Leeds Cemetery
New Town
Bexley Wing
The Becklin Cen.
Recreation Ground
HAREHILLS
Reservoir (covered)
Playground
Harehills Cemetery
Killingbeck Retail Park
Killingbeck
70
Works
Bowling Green
Primrose High Sch.
Brownhill Prim. Sch.
Burmantofts
Playing Fields
Playing Field
YORK ROAD
SELBY ROAD
Sports Ground
St. Patrick's Catholic Sch.
Factory
A64
Recreation Ground
Ebor Gdns. Prim. Sch.
Depots
Victoria Prim. Sch.
Sports Ground
A63
Corpus Christi Catholic Coll.
Corpus Christi Catholic Sch.
Richmond Hill
Rec. Grd.
Leeds MENCAP
EAST END PARK
Recreation Ground
Osmondthorpe
Playing Fields
Meadowfield Prim. Sch.
Halton Moor
Cavalier Hill
Prim. Sch.
Neville Hill Sidings
HALTON MOOR ROAD
A61
Ckt. Grd.
Yorkshire Produce Centre
Cross Green Industrial Park
Works
Halton Moor Wood
Cross Green
AIRE VALLEY WAY
PONTEFRACT LANE
Works
Depot
Warehouse
Halton Moor
LS15
Football World
Cross Green Ind. Est.
Knowsthorpe
Motor Auction
Skelton Moor Farm
Swing-bridge
Valley House
87
1
2
3
4
5
6
7
8
9
G
H
J
K
L
M
N
32
33
34
35
36

70
Beechwood
Seacroft
Mill Green
A6120
52
Scholes Park
Stanks
Swarcliffe
Swarcliffe Prim. Sch.
David Young Community Academy
Brooklands
Leeds Coll. of Building (RISE)
Beechwood Prim. Sch.
Library
The Green
Super-store
E-ACT Leeds Academy
Parklands
Superstore
Parklands Primary School
Playing Fields
Tennis Courts
St. Theresa's Catholic Prim. Sch.
Manston
Manston Prim. Sch.
John Smeaton Community College
John Smeaton Leisure Cen.
LS14
Comm. Cen.
Seacroft Gardens
Brianside
A6120
The Oval
Killingbeck RC Cemetery
A64
CROSS GATES
Cross-Gates
Crossgates Shopping Centre
Rec. Grd.
Playgrd.
Works
LS15
Superstore
Seacroft Hospital
Newsam Unit
Cross Gates Prim. Sch.
Parish Cen.
Graveleythorpe
Whitkirk
Austhorpe Hall
Whitkirk Lane End
Austhorpe Prim. Sch.
Austhorpe
Halton Deans
Sports Ground
Tennis Courts
Bowling Green
Halton
SELBY ROAD
A63
HALTON ROAD
RING ROAD
SEACROFT
CROSS GATES
STATION
YORK ROAD
Temple Moor High Sch. Science Coll.
Playing Flds.
Cricket Ground
Football Ground
Whitkirk Prim. Sch.
Superstore
Colton Retail Park
Colton Common
Colton
Holly Tree Farm
Halton Moor
Club House
Halton Moor Wood
North Plantation
Whitehead Wood
Lodges
Sports Arena
Pavilion
Grange Farm
Sycamore House
Beech Ho.
Rose Garden
Colton Farm
Menagerie Wood
Damingdike Wood
Menagerie Ponds
Elm & Oak Wood
Mather Wood
Temple Newsam Home Farm (Rare Breeds)
Pump Wood
The Sycamore Walk
TEMPLE NEWSAM GOLF COURSE
Park Wood
Jacob's Well
Temple Newsam House
Little Temple
TEMPLE NEWSAM PARK
Stork Pond
Dog Kennel
88
Charcoal Wood
Wilderness Wood
Hertford Springs
A B C D E F G
1 2 3 4 5 6 7 8 9

SCHOLES
Green Lodge Farm
Leeds
Pendas Fields
Barnbow Wood
Barnbow Carr
Honesty Farm
Lower Barnbow Farm
Upper Barnbow Farm
Hillside Farm
Highfield Farm
Throstle Nest Farm
Throstlenest Bridge
Club House
GARFORTH GOLF COURSE
Laverack Cottage
The Lake
Lake Cottage
Willow Park Farm
Cock Beck
Shippen Plantation
Lazencroft Farm
Manston Ho.
Manston Gate
Shippen House Farm
Sports Ground
Shippen Cottages
Barnbow Common
Manor Farm Cottage
Manor House
M1
M1 MOTORWAY
Pear Trees
Lowside Cott.
Rose Cott.
The Elms
White House Farm
Crawshaw Wood
Brown Moor
Barrowby Hall
Barrowby Carr
Barrowby
Carr Wood
LS25
GARFORTH
Moor Garforth
Garforth
Clear View Farm
Moorhouse Farm
Bradbury Grange
Barrowby Cottage
BARROWBY PARK
Warren House
Spring Wood
Ormesby House
Swillington Common Farm
Junction 46
A63
Swillington Common
Nurseries
Waterloo Manor
Brookfield Ho.
Brookfield Farm
Garforth Bridge
Hotel
West Garforth
Lidgett Playing Fields
Garforth Community College
Church Garforth
Grave Yard
Sewage Works
LS26
A642
B6137
Hollinthorpe Farm
Hollinthorpe
Field House
Southfield Bungalow
53
72
89

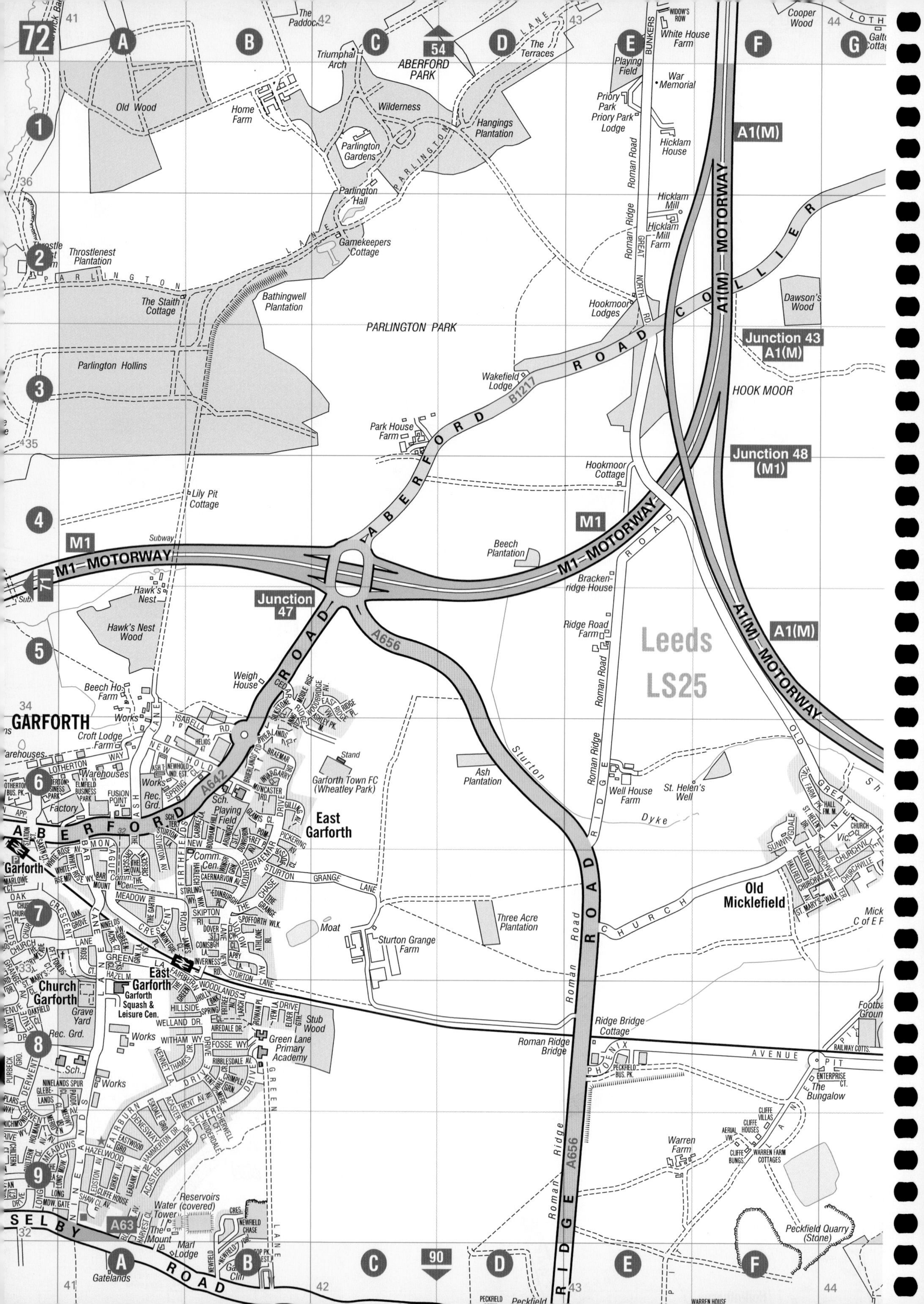

ABERFORD PARK
Old Wood
Home Farm
Wilderness
Hangings Plantation
Parlington Gardens
Parlington Hall
Gamekeepers Cottage
Throstlenest Plantation
The Staith Cottage
Bathingwell Plantation
PARLINGTON PARK
Parlington Hollins
Triumphal Arch
The Paddocks
The Terraces
White House Farm
Playing Field
War Memorial
Priory Park
Priory Park Lodge
Hicklam House
Hicklam Mill
Hicklam Mill Farm
Hookmoor Lodges
Dawson's Wood
Cooper Wood
Junction 43 A1(M)
HOOK MOOR
Junction 48 (M1)
Hookmoor Cottage
Wakefield Lodge
Park House Farm
Lily Pit Cottage
M1 MOTORWAY
A1(M) MOTORWAY
Junction 47
Beech Plantation
Bracken-ridge House
Ridge Road Farm
Hawk's Nest
Hawk's Nest Wood
Leeds LS25
GARFORTH
Croft Lodge Farm
Beech Ho. Farm
Weigh House
Garforth Town FC (Wheatley Park)
East Garforth
Ash Plantation
Well House Farm
St. Helen's Well
Old Micklefield
Three Acre Plantation
Sturton Grange Farm
Moat
Church Garforth
Garforth Squash & Leisure Cen.
Green Lane Primary Academy
Stub Wood
Ridge Bridge Cottage
Roman Ridge Bridge
Warren Farm
The Bungalow
Peckfield Quarry (Stone)
Reservoirs
Water (covered) Tower
The Mount
Marl Lodge
Gatelands
SELBY ROAD
ABERFORD ROAD
RIDGE ROAD
CHURCH LANE
PIT LANE
PARLINGTON LANE
54
90
71

SAXTON
Plough Farm
Cricket Ground
Headwell Farm
Tadcaster
LS24
WAKEFIELD RD.
LOTHERTON LANE
COPLEY LANE
B1217
Lotherton Cottages
Lotherton Park Farm
Lotherton Lodge
Lotherton Cott.
Lotherton Hall Estate
Bird Garden
Captain Wood
Lotherton Hall
Deer Park
Vevers Bushes
West Field
COLDHILL LANE
Garlic Flats
Rose Cottage
Coldhill Pond
Coldhill Cottage
Lower Cold Hill Farm
OLDGATE LANE
Stream Dike
Cold Hill
Coldhill Farm
Prospect Hill
The Avenue
Ringhay Wood
Bragdale
RANGERS WALK
Coburnhill Wood
Scott's Wood
Near Fox Covert
Far Fox Covert
Middle Fox Covert
SELBY
LEEDS
Weet Wood
The Marsh
Longroyd Wood
Daniel Hartly's Wood
LAITH STAID LANE
Huddleston Hall
Huddleston Grange Riding School
Huddleston
Huddleston Grange
HARTLEY WOOD COTTAGES
Huddleston Old Wood
Hartly Wood
Gunner Hill
Sheep Dike
Keepers Cottage
Grange Fm.
Manor House Fm.
MICKLEFIELD
A1(M)
Newthorpe Farm
Micklefield
Brookfield House
Newthorpe Barrack
Newthorpe Beck
Highroyds Wood
New Micklefield
Newthorpe
Newthorpe Grange
Hill House Farm
B1222
Gorse Cottage
Ash Grove
GORSE LANE
Beckfield
HALL LANE
NEWTHORPE LANE
Castle Hills
Highfield
Newthorpe Quarry
Castle Plains
Micklefield Plantation
HIGHFIELD LANE
NORTH ROAD
Peckfield Plantation
55
91
445
46
47
36
435
34
33
32
H J K L M N G
1 2 3 4 5 6 7 8 9

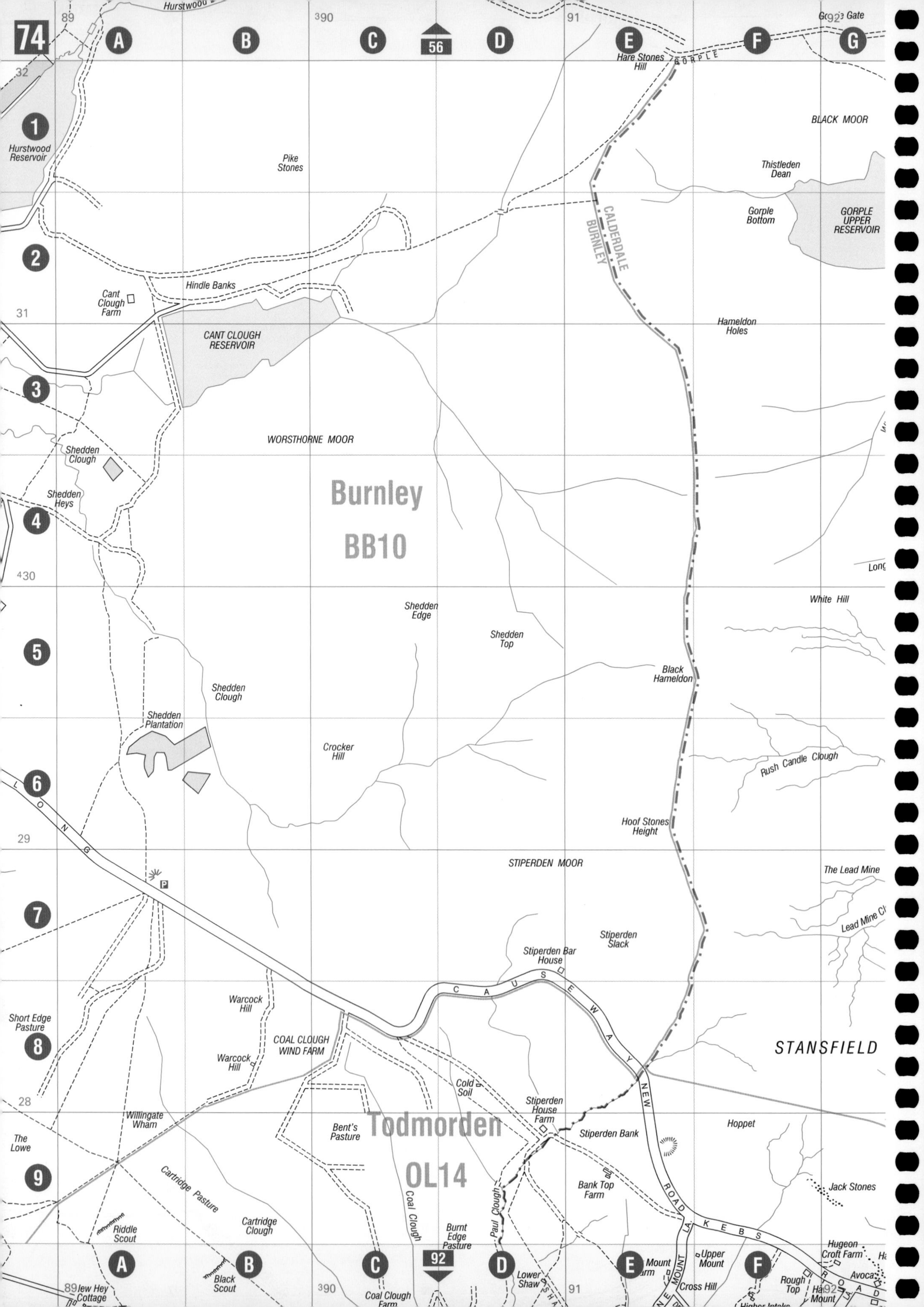
56
Hurstwood Reservoir
Pike Stones
Hare Stones Hill
GORPLE
BLACK MOOR
Thistleden Dean
Gorple Bottom
GORPLE UPPER RESERVOIR
CALDERDALE
BURNLEY
Cant Clough Farm
Hindle Banks
CANT CLOUGH RESERVOIR
Hameldon Holes
WORSTHORNE MOOR
Shedden Clough
Shedden Heys
Burnley
BB10
White Hill
Shedden Edge
Shedden Top
Black Hameldon
Shedden Clough
Shedden Plantation
Crocker Hill
Rush Candle Clough
LONG
Hoof Stones Height
STIPERDEN MOOR
The Lead Mine
Lead Mine Cl
Stiperden Slack
Stiperden Bar House
CAUSEWAY
Warcock Hill
Short Edge Pasture
COAL CLOUGH WIND FARM
Warcock Hill
STANSFIELD
Cold Soil
NEW
Stiperden House Farm
Stiperden Bank
Willingate Wham
Bent's Pasture
Todmorden
OL14
Hoppet
The Lowe
Cartridge Pasture
Coal Clough
Paul Clough
Bank Top Farm
Jack Stones
KEBS ROAD
Riddle Scout
Cartridge Clough
Burnt Edge Pasture
Hugeon Croft Farm
Upper Mount
92
Jew Hey Cottage
Black Scout
Coal Clough Farm
Lower Shaw
Cross Hill
Rough Top
Avoca
89
390
91
92
32
31
430
29
28

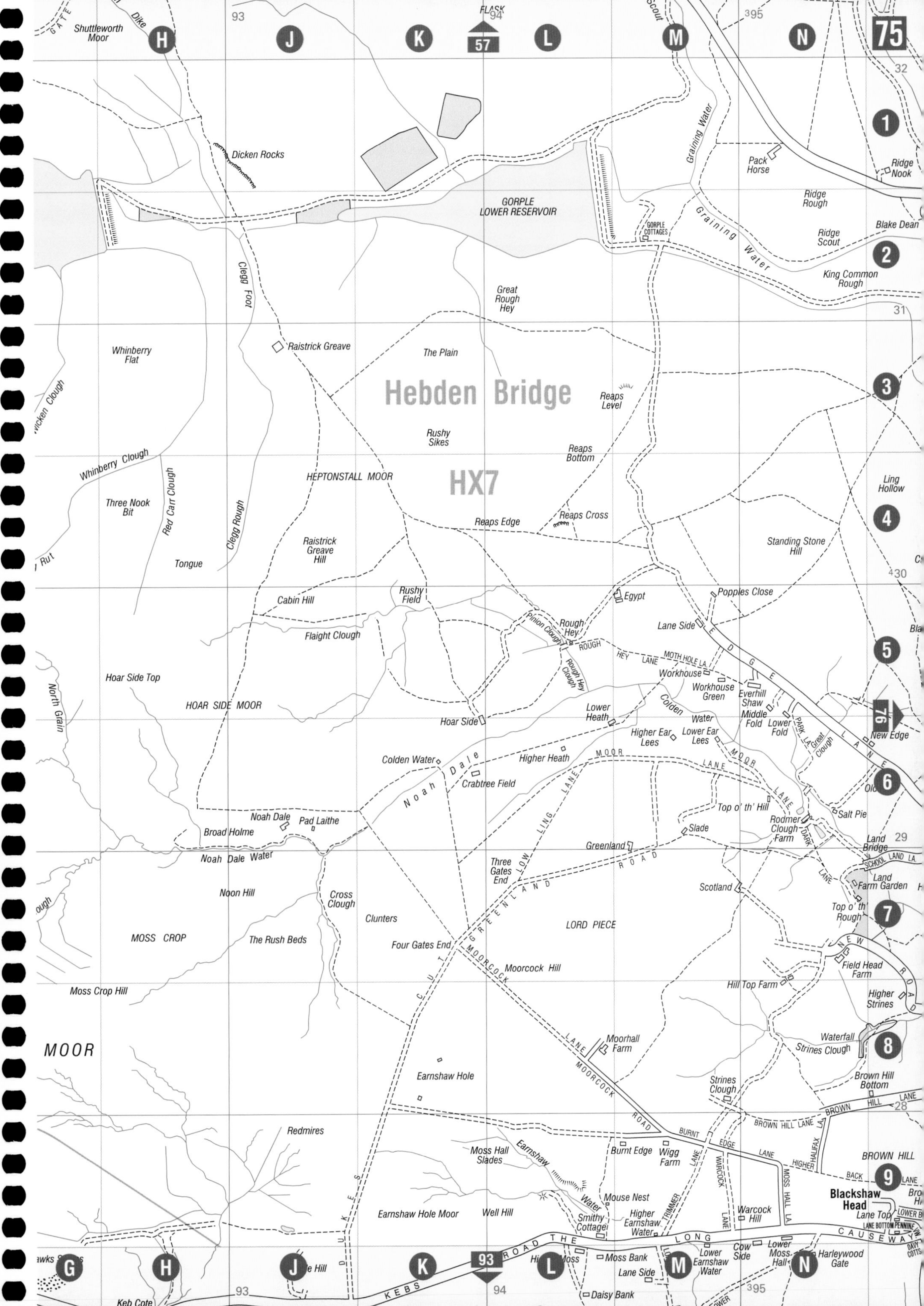
Hebden Bridge
HX7
GORPLE LOWER RESERVOIR
Shuttleworth Moor
Dicken Rocks
Clegg Foot
Raistrick Greave
The Plain
Great Rough Hey
Whinberry Flat
Whinberry Clough
Three Nook Bit
Red Carr Clough
Clegg Rough
Tongue
HEPTONSTALL MOOR
Rushy Sikes
Reaps Level
Reaps Bottom
Reaps Edge
Reaps Cross
Raistrick Greave Hill
Cabin Hill
Rushy Field
Flaight Clough
Egypt
Popples Close
Lane Side
Rough Hey
Pinion Clough
Rough Hey Clough
Hoar Side Top
North Grain
HOAR SIDE MOOR
Hoar Side
Lower Heath
Workhouse
Workhouse Green
Everhill Shaw
Middle Fold
Lower Fold
Colden Water
Higher Ear Lees
Lower Ear Lees
Higher Heath
Crabtree Field
Noah Dale
Pad Laithe
Broad Holme
Noah Dale Water
Top o' th' Hill
Rodmer Clough Farm
Slade
Greenland
Three Gates End
Salt Pie
Land Bridge
Land Farm Garden
Scotland
Noon Hill
Cross Clough
Clunters
MOSS CROP
The Rush Beds
Four Gates End
LORD PIECE
Moorcock Hill
Top o' th' Rough
Field Head Farm
Hill Top Farm
Higher Strines
Moss Crop Hill
MOOR
Moorhall Farm
Waterfall
Strines Clough
Earnshaw Hole
Strines Clough
Brown Hill Bottom
Redmires
Moss Hall Slades
Burnt Edge
Wigg Farm
BROWN HILL
Blackshaw Head
Earnshaw Hole Moor
Well Hill
Mouse Nest
Smithy Cottage
Higher Earnshaw Water
Warcock Hill
Lane Top
Moss Bank
Lower Earnshaw Water
Cow Side
Lower Moss Hall
Harleywood Gate
Lane Side
Daisy Bank
Keb Cote
Pack Horse
Ridge Nook
Ridge Rough
Ridge Scout
Blake Dean
King Common Rough
Ling Hollow
Standing Stone Hill
New Edge
Graining Water
GORPLE COTTAGES
EDGE LANE
MOTH HOLE LA
ROUGH HEY LANE
MOOR LANE
LING LANE
LOW GREENLAND ROAD
CUT
MOORCOCK LANE
MOORCOCK ROAD
BURNT EDGE LANE
BROWN HILL LANE
HIGHER BACK LANE
HALIFAX LA
MOSS HALL LA
WARCOCK LANE
TRIMMER LANE
DUKES CUT
KEBS ROAD
THE LONG CAUSEWAY
NEW ROAD
SCHOOL LAND LA.
DARK LANE
PARK LA
Great Clough
FLASK
57
76
93
H J K L M N G
1 2 3 4 5 6 7 8 9
93 94 395
32 31 30 29 28

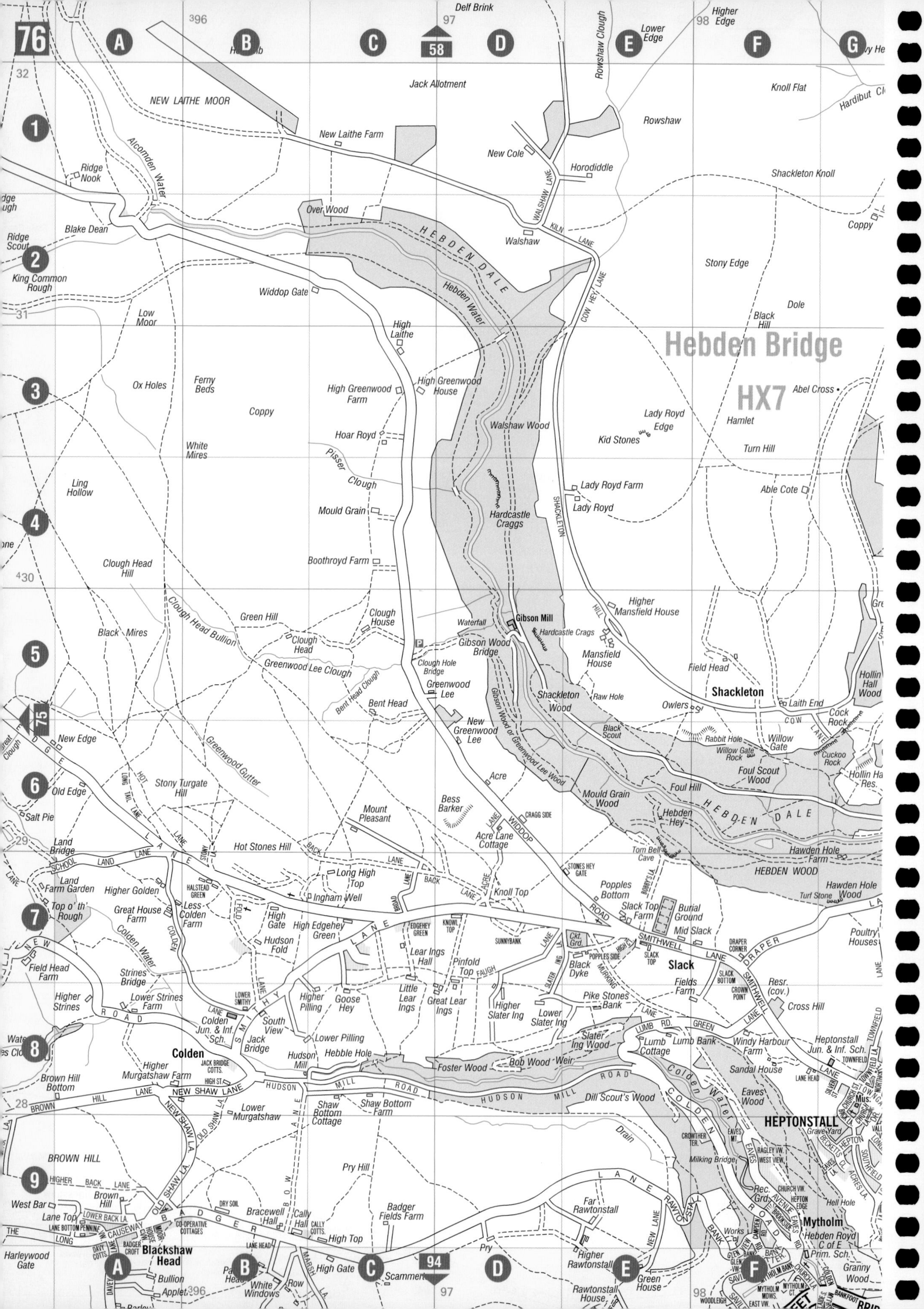
76
A
B
C
D
E
F
G
58
97
98
396
Delf Brink
Higher Edge
Lower Edge
Rowshaw Clough
32
31
30
29
28
1
2
3
4
5
6
7
8
9
Jack Allotment
NEW LAITHE MOOR
New Laithe Farm
Knoll Flat
Hardibut Clough
Rowshaw
New Cole
Horodiddle
Alcomden Water
Ridge Nook
Shackleton Knoll
Coppy
Over Wood
HEBDEN DALE
Blake Dean
Ridge Scout
King Common Rough
Walshaw
WALSHAW LANE
KILN LANE
Stony Edge
Widdop Gate
Hebden Water
COW HEY LANE
Low Moor
High Laithe
Black Hill
Dole
Hebden Bridge
HX7
Abel Cross
Ox Holes
Ferny Beds
High Greenwood Farm
High Greenwood House
Coppy
Lady Royd Edge
Hamlet
Kid Stones
Walshaw Wood
White Mires
Hoar Royd
Turn Hill
Pisser Clough
Ling Hollow
Lady Royd Farm
Able Cote
Lady Royd
Mould Grain
Hardcastle Craggs
SHACKLETON
Boothroyd Farm
Clough Head Hill
Higher Mansfield House
HILL
Green Hill
Clough House
Gibson Mill
Waterfall
Hardcastle Crags
Black Mires
Clough Head Bullion
Clough Head
Gibson Wood Bridge
Mansfield House
Greenwood Lee Clough
Clough Hole Bridge
Field Head
Hollin Hall Wood
Greenwood Lee
Shackleton Wood
Raw Hole
Shackleton
Bent Head Clough
Bent Head
Owlers
Laith End
75
New Edge
New Greenwood Lee
Black Scout
COW LANE
Cock Rock
Rabbit Hole
Willow Gate
Willow Gate Rock
Cuckoo Rock
Greenwood Gutter
Foul Scout Wood
Hollin Hall Res.
Old Edge
Stony Turgate Hill
Acre
Mould Grain Wood
Foul Hill
Salt Pie
Bess Barker
Mount Pleasant
Hebden Hey
HEBDEN DALE
CRAGG SIDE
Acre Lane Cottage
WIDDOP
Land Bridge
SCHOOL LAND LANE
Hot Stones Hill
BACK LANE
Tom Bell Cave
Hawden Hole Farm
HEBDEN WOOD
Land Farm Garden
Higher Golden
HALSTEAD GREEN
Long High Top
STONES HEY GATE
Popples Bottom
Hawden Hole Wood
Turf Stone
Top o' th' Rough
Great House Farm
Less Colden Farm
Ingham Well
Knoll Top
Slack Top Farm
Burial Ground
Mid Slack
High Gate
High Edgehey Green
EDGEHEY GREEN
KNOWL TOP
Ckt. Grd.
SMITHWELL LANE
DRAPER CORNER
DRAPER
Poultry Houses
Hudson Fold
SUNNYBANK
POPPLES SIDE
SLACK TOP
Slack
Field Head Farm
Colden Water
Lear Ings Hall
Pinfold Top
FAUGH
Black Dyke
Fields Farm
SLACK BOTTOM
CROWN POINT
Resr. (cov.)
Strines Bridge
Little Lear Ings
Great Lear Ings
Higher Strines
Lower Strines Farm
LOWER SMITHY
Higher Pilling
Goose Hey
Higher Slater Ing
Lower Slater Ing
Pike Stones Bank
Cross Hill
ROAD
Colden Jun. & Inf. Sch.
South View
Slater Ing Wood
LUMB RD.
GREEN LANE
Lumb Cottage
Lumb Bank
Windy Harbour Farm
Heptonstall Jun. & Inf. Sch.
Jack Bridge
Lower Pilling
Hudson Mill
Hebble Hole
Foster Wood
Bob Wood
Weir
Colden
JACK BRIDGE COTTS.
HIGH ST.
Higher Murgatshaw Farm
Sandal House
LANE HEAD
TOWNFIELD
Brown Hill Bottom
BROWN HILL LANE
NEW SHAW LANE
HUDSON MILL ROAD
Dill Scout's Wood
Eaves Wood
Mus.
Lower Murgatshaw
Shaw Bottom Cottage
Shaw Bottom Farm
HEPTONSTALL
Grave Yard
Drain
CROWTHER TER.
EAVES MT.
RAGLEY VW.
WEST VIEW
BROWN HILL
Pry Hill
Milking Bridge
HIGHER BACK LANE
Rec. Grd.
CHURCH VW.
HEPTON EDGE
Hell Hole
West Bar
Brown Hill
DRY SOIL
Far Rawtonstall
RAWTONSTALL BANK
Lane Top
LOWER BACK LA.
LANE BOTTOM
PENNINE
CO-OPERATIVE COTTAGES
Bracewell Hall
Cally Hall
CALLY COTTS.
Badger Fields Farm
Mytholm
THE LONG CAUSEWAY
BADGER LANE
High Top
Works
Hebden Royd C of E Prim. Sch.
Harleywood Gate
DAVEY COTTS.
BADGER CROFT
Blackshaw Head
LANE HEAD
Pry
Higher Rawtonstall
Granny Wood
Bullion
White Windows
Row
High Gate
Scammer
94
Green House
Rawtonstall House
MYTHOLM MDWS.
EAST VW.
WOODLEIGH

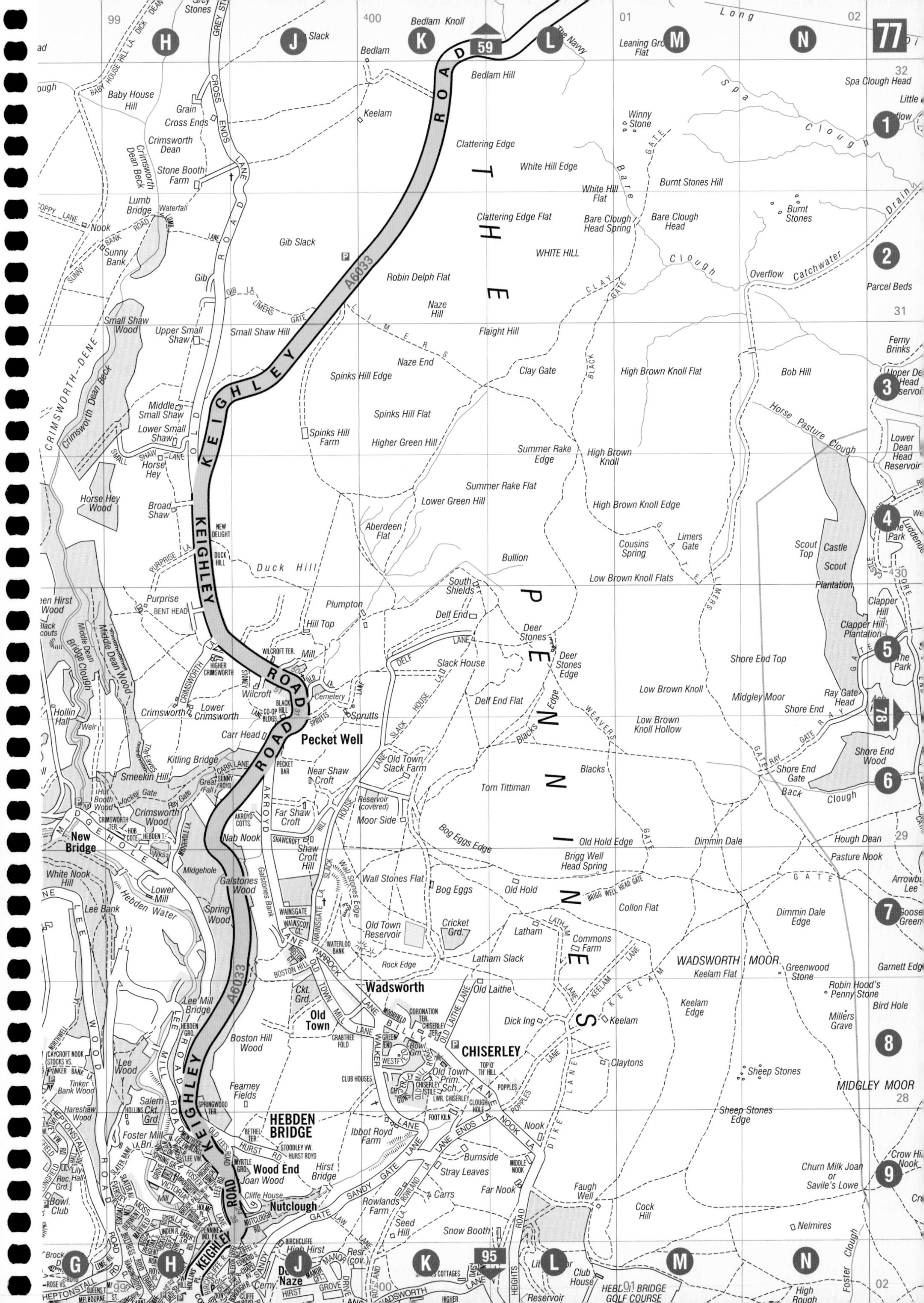

Bedlam Knoll
59
Bedlam
Slack
Leaning Grove Flat
Long
Bedlam Hill
Keelam
Baby House Hill
Grain Cross Ends
Crimsworth Dean
Stone Booth Farm
Lumb Bridge
Nook
Sunny Bank
Gib
Gib Slack
Winny Stone
Clattering Edge
White Hill Edge
White Hill Flat
Burnt Stones Hill
Spa Clough Head
Clattering Edge Flat
Bare Clough Head Spring
Bare Clough Head
Burnt Stones
WHITE HILL
Robin Delph Flat
Overflow
Catchwater
Parcel Beds
Naze Hill
Small Shaw Wood
Upper Small Shaw
Small Shaw Hill
Flaight Hill
Naze End
Clay Gate
High Brown Knoll Flat
Bob Hill
Spinks Hill Edge
Spinks Hill Flat
Spinks Hill Farm
Higher Green Hill
Middle Small Shaw
Lower Small Shaw
Horse Hey
Horse Hey Wood
Broad Shaw
Summer Rake Edge
High Brown Knoll
Summer Rake Flat
Lower Green Hill
High Brown Knoll Edge
Lower Dean Head Reservoir
Horse Pasture Clough
Aberdeen Flat
Cousins Spring
Limers Gate
Scout Top
Castle Scout Plantation
Duck Hill
Bullion
Low Brown Knoll Flats
Purprise
Plumpton
South Shields
Hill Top
Delf End
Deer Stones
Deer Stones Edge
Clapper Hill
Clapper Hill Plantation
Mill
Slack House
Shore End Top
Wilcroft
Crimsworth
Lower Crimsworth
Cemetery
Sprutts
Delf End Flat
Low Brown Knoll
Midgley Moor
Shore End
Ray Gate Head
Low Brown Knoll Hollow
Hollin Hall
Weir
Carr Head
Pecket Well
Blacks Edge
Kitling Bridge
Old Town Slack Farm
Near Shaw Croft
Blacks
Shore End Wood
Shore End Gate
Smeekin Hill
Tom Tittiman
Crimsworth Wood
Jockey Gate
Ray Gate
Reservoir (covered)
Moor Side
Far Shaw Croft
New Bridge
Nab Nook
Shaw Croft Hill
Bog Eggs Edge
Old Hold Edge
Dimmin Dale
Hough Dean
Pasture Nook
Brigg Well Head Spring
Midgehole
White Nook Hill
Lower Mill
Galstones Wood
Wall Stones Flat
Bog Eggs
Old Hold
Hebden Water
Spring Wood
Collon Flat
Dimmin Dale Edge
Lee Bank
Old Town Reservoir
Cricket Grd.
Latham
Commons Farm
Rock Edge
Latham Slack
WADSWORTH MOOR
Keelam Flat
Greenwood Stone
Garnett Edge
Wadsworth
Old Laithe
Robin Hood's Penny Stone
Keelam Edge
Bird Hole
Lee Mill Bridge
Old Town
Dick Ing
Keelam
Millers Grave
Boston Hill Wood
CHISERLEY
Claytons
Sheep Stones
Lee Wood
Old Town Prim. Sch.
MIDGLEY MOOR
Tinker Bank Wood
Fearney Fields
Hareshaw Wood
Salem Ckt. Grd.
HEBDEN BRIDGE
Sheep Stones Edge
Foster Mill
Nook
Ibbot Royd Farm
Burnside
Wood End
Joan Wood
Hirst Bridge
Stray Leaves
Churn Milk Joan or Savile's Lowe
Crow Hill Nook
Lily Hall
Rec. Grd.
Cliffe House
Nutclough
Carrs
Far Nook
Faugh Well
Bowl. Club
Rowlands Farm
Seed Hill
Cock Hill
Nelmires
Snow Booth
High Hirst
Resr. (cov.)
95
Club House
Naze
Reservoir
HEBDEN BRIDGE GOLF COURSE
High Rough
Foster Clough
KEIGHLEY ROAD
A6033
THE PENNINES

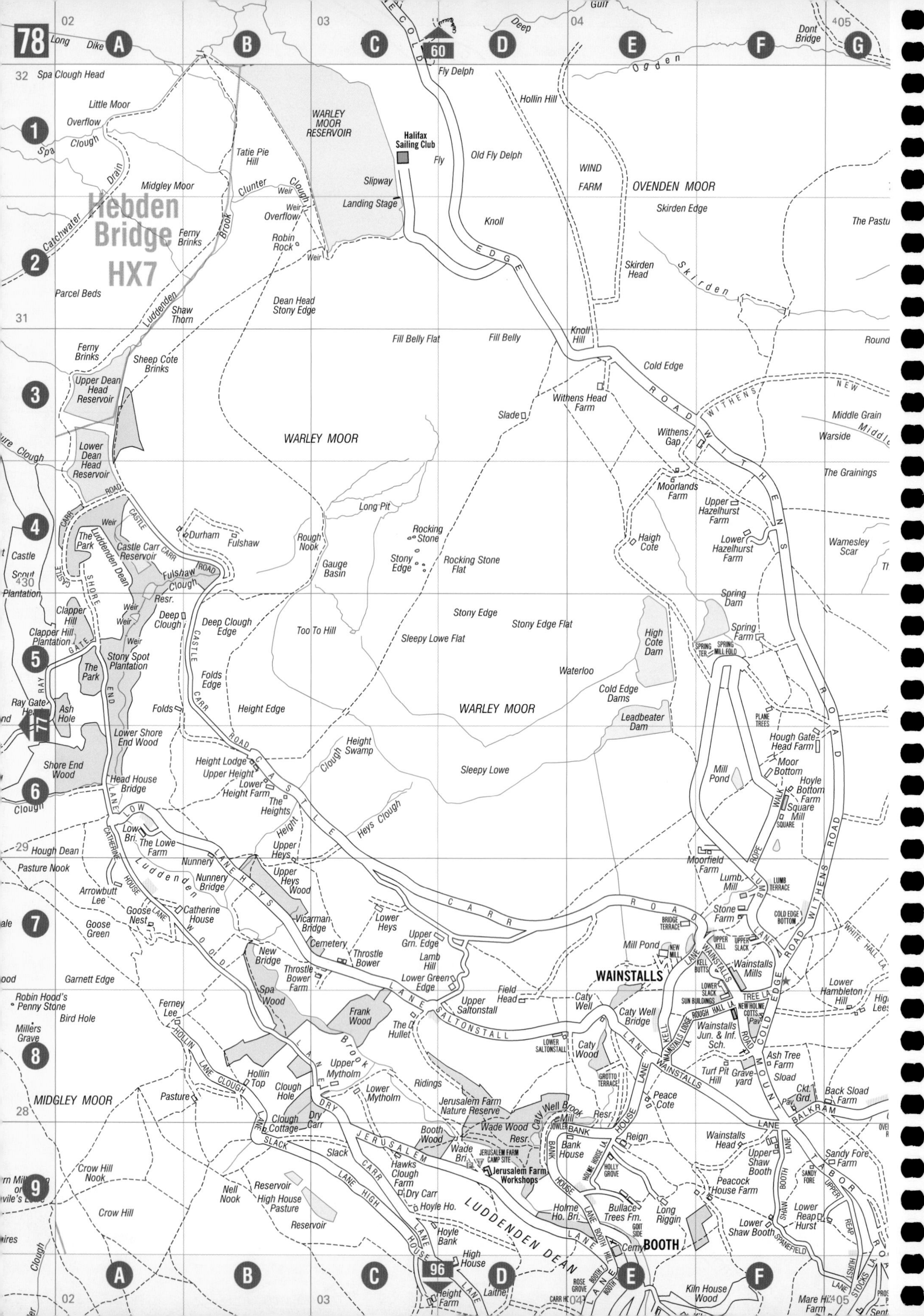
Hebden Bridge HX7
WARLEY MOOR RESERVOIR
Halifax Sailing Club
Slipway
Landing Stage
Fly Delph
Hollin Hill
Old Fly Delph
WIND FARM
OVENDEN MOOR
Skirden Edge
Knoll
Skirden Head
Spa Clough Head
Little Moor
Overflow
Tatie Pie Hill
Midgley Moor
Clunter
Robin Rock
Ferny Brinks
Parcel Beds
Shaw Thorn
Dean Head Stony Edge
Fill Belly Flat
Fill Belly
Knoll Hill
Cold Edge
Withens Head Farm
Slade
Sheep Cote Brinks
Upper Dean Head Reservoir
Lower Dean Head Reservoir
WARLEY MOOR
Withens Gap
Moorlands Farm
Upper Hazelhurst Farm
Lower Hazelhurst Farm
Middle Grain
Warside
The Grainings
Wamesley Scar
Long Pit
Rocking Stone
Rough Nook
Durham
Fulshaw
Castle Carr Reservoir
Stony Edge
Rocking Stone Flat
Gauge Basin
Haigh Cote
Spring Dam
Spring Farm
Deep Clough Edge
Too To Hill
Sleepy Lowe Flat
Stony Edge Flat
High Cote Dam
Clapper Hill
Clapper Hill Plantation
The Park
Stony Spot Plantation
Folds Edge
Waterloo
Cold Edge Dams
Leadbeater Dam
Ray Gate Head
Ash Hole
Folds
Height Edge
Lower Shore End Wood
Shore End Wood
Head House Bridge
Height Swamp
Sleepy Lowe
Hough Gate Head Farm
Moor Bottom
Hoyle Bottom Farm
Square Mill
Mill Pond
Height Lodge
Upper Height
Lower Height Farm
The Heights
Heys Clough
Low Bri.
The Lowe Farm
Hough Dean
Pasture Nook
Nunnery
Nunnery Bridge
Upper Heys
Upper Heys Wood
Moorfield Farm
Lumb Mill
Arrowbutt Lee
Goose Nest
Catherine House
Goose Green
Vicarman Bridge
Lower Heys
Upper Grn. Edge
Stone Farm
Mill Pond
Cemetery
Throstle Bower
New Bridge
Throstle Bower Farm
Lamb Hill
Lower Green Edge
WAINSTALLS
Wainstalls Mills
Garnett Edge
Robin Hood's Penny Stone
Millers Grave
Bird Hole
Ferney Lee
Spa Wood
Frank Wood
Upper Saltonstall
Field Head
Caty Well
Caty Well Bridge
Wainstalls Jun. & Inf. Sch.
Lower Hambleton Hill
The Hullet
Caty Wood
Ash Tree Farm
Sload
Turf Pit Hill
Grave-yard
Upper Mytholm
Hollin Top
Clough Hole
Ridings
MIDGLEY MOOR
Pasture
Lower Mytholm
Jerusalem Farm Nature Reserve
Peace Cote
Back Sload Farm
Clough Cottage
Dry Carr
Booth Wood
Wade Wood
Resr.
Mill
Reign
Wainstalls Head
Upper Shaw Booth
Sandy Fore Farm
Crow Hill Nook
Slack
Hawks Clough Farm
Wade Bri.
Jerusalem Farm Workshops
Bank House
Peacock House Farm
Nell Nook
Reservoir
High House Pasture
Dry Carr
Hoyle Ho.
Crow Hill
Reservoir
Hoyle Bank
Holme Ho. Bri.
Bullace Trees Fm.
Long Riggin
Lower Shaw Booth
Lower Reap Hurst
LUDDENDEN DEAN
High House
BOOTH
Cemy
Kiln House Wood
Height Farm
Laithe
Mare Hill Farm
Ogden
Dont Bridge
Deep
Gulf
60
96
77

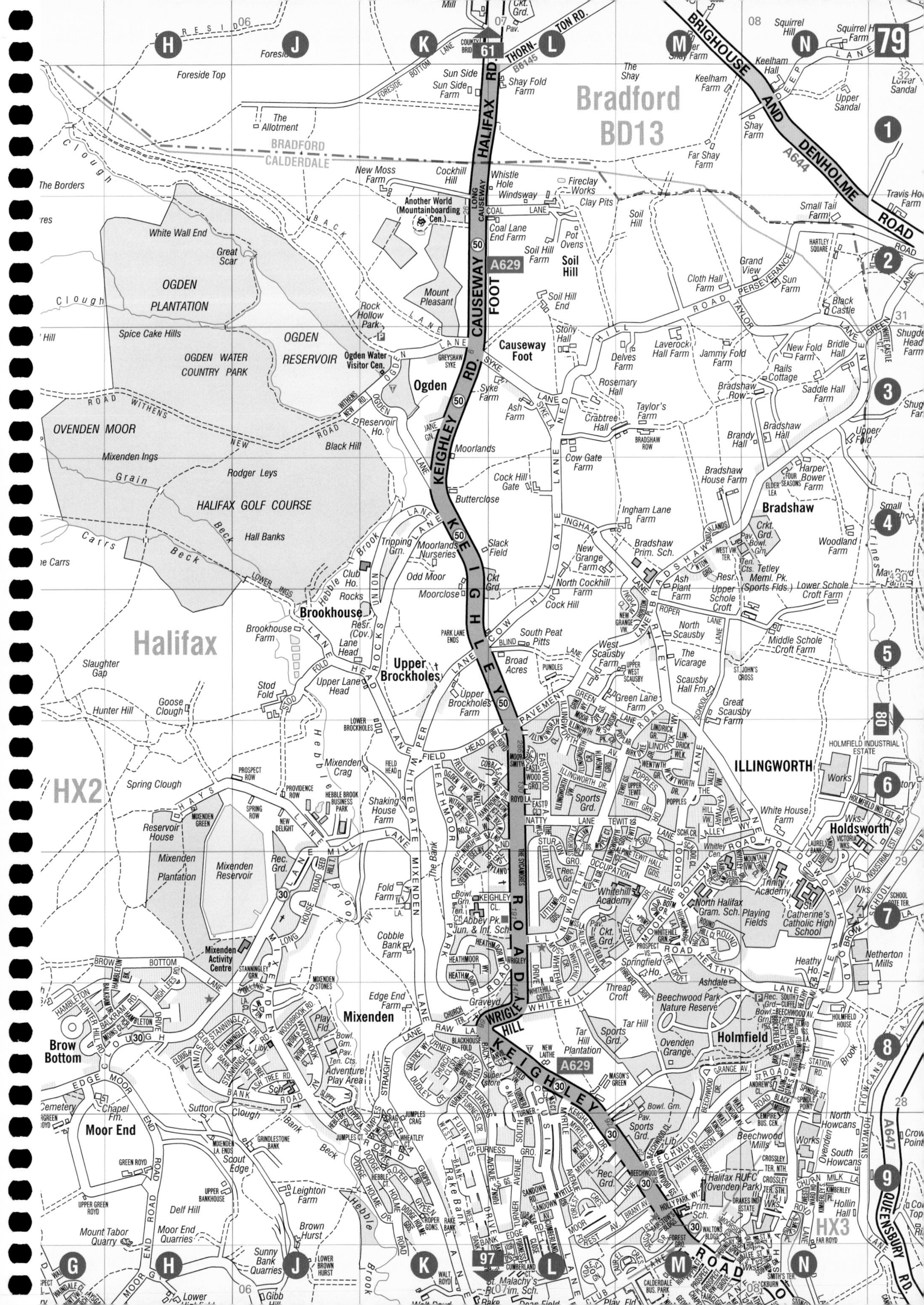
Bradford
BD13
BRADFORD
CALDERDALE
Halifax
HX2
HX3
OGDEN PLANTATION
OGDEN RESERVOIR
OGDEN WATER COUNTRY PARK
Ogden Water Visitor Cen.
OVENDEN MOOR
HALIFAX GOLF COURSE
Mixenden Reservoir
Mixenden Plantation
Ogden
Causeway Foot
Soil Hill
Brookhouse
Upper Brockholes
Mixenden
ILLINGWORTH
Bradshaw
Holdsworth
Holmfield
Brow Bottom
Moor End
HALIFAX RD.
CAUSEWAY FOOT
KEIGHLEY RD.
KEIGHLEY ROAD
WRIGLEY HILL
A629
A644
A647
B6145
BRIGHOUSE AND DENHOLME ROAD
QUEENSBURY RD.
THORNTON RD.
Another World (Mountainboarding Cen.)
Beechwood Park Nature Reserve
Ovenden Grange
North Halifax Gram. Sch.
Trinity Academy
St. Catherine's Catholic High School
Whitehill Academy
Halifax RUFC (Ovenden Park)
Holmfield Industrial Estate
Tetley Meml. Pk. (Sports Flds.)
Mixenden Activity Centre
Adventure Play Area
61
80
97

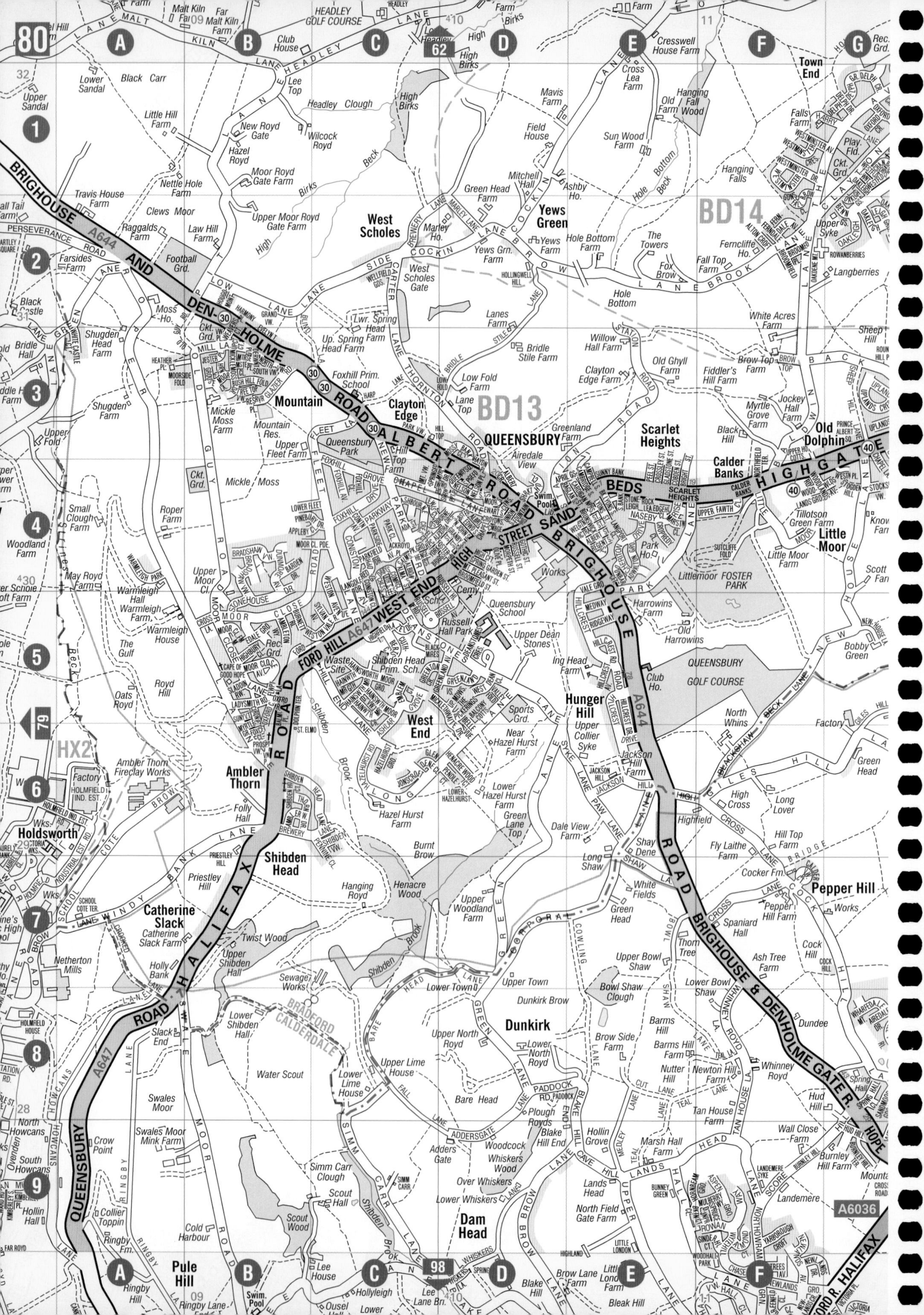
Malt Kiln
Far Malt Kiln Farm
HEADLEY GOLF COURSE
Club House
Headley
62
High Birks
Cresswell House Farm
Town End
Black Carr
Lower Sandal
Upper Sandal
Lee Top
Headley Clough
High Birks
Cross Lea Farm
Mavis Farm
Old Farm
Hanging Fall Wood
Little Hill Farm
New Royd Gate
Wilcock Royd
Field House
Sun Wood Farm
Hazel Royd
Moor Royd Gate Farm
Nettle Hole Farm
Mitchell Hall
Ashby Ho.
Hanging Falls
Travis House Farm
Green Head Farm
Yews Green
Clews Moor
West Scholes
Marley Ho.
Raggalds Farm
Law Hill Farm
Upper Moor Royd Gate Farm
Yews Farm
Hole Bottom Farm
The Towers
BD14
Football Grd.
Yews Grn. Farm
Fernccliffe Ho.
Upper Syke
Farsides Farm
West Scholes Gate
Fox Brow
Fall Top Farm
Langberries
Black Castle
BRIGHOUSE AND DENHOLME ROAD
Moss Ho.
Hole Bottom
White Acres Farm
Shugden Head Farm
Lwr. Spring Head Farm
Up. Spring Head Farm
Lanes Farm
Willow Hall Farm
Bridle Stile Farm
Sheep Hill
Bridle Hall
Foxhill Prim. School
Clayton Edge Farm
Old Ghyll Farm
Fiddler's Hill Farm
Brow Top Farm
Shugden Farm
Mickle Moss Farm
Mountain
Low Fold Farm
Lane Top
BD13
Jockey Hall Farm
Myrtle Grove Farm
Upper Fold
Mountain Res.
Clayton Edge
Greenland Farm
Scarlet Heights
Black Hill
Old Dolphin
Upper Fleet Farm
Queensbury Park
QUEENSBURY
Airedale View
Calder Banks
HIGHGATE
Ckt. Grd.
Mickle Moss
Hill Top Farm
Swim. Pool
BEDS
Small Clough Farm
Roper Farm
ALBERT ROAD
SAND STREET
BRIGHOUSE ROAD
Tillotson Green Farm
Little Moor
Woodland Farm
Park Ho.
Little Moor Farm
Works
Scott Farm
May Royd Farm
Upper Moor Cl.
Littlemoor FOSTER PARK
Warmleigh Hall
Warmleigh Farm
Warmleigh House
Queensbury School
Harrowins Farm
Old Harrowins
WEST END
HIGH STREET
A647
Cemy.
Russell Hall Park
Upper Dean Stones
Bobby Green
The Gulf
FORD HILL
Waste Site
Shibden Head Prim. Sch.
Ing Head Farm
Club Ho.
QUEENSBURY GOLF COURSE
Royd Hill
Oats Royd
Hunger Hill
Upper Collier Syke
North Whins
Factory
79
West End
Sports Grd.
Near Hazel Hurst Farm
A644
HX2
Ambler Thorn Fireclay Works
Ambler Thorn
Jackson Hill Farm
Green Head
Factory
HOLMFIELD IND. EST.
Lower Hazel Hurst Farm
High Cross
Long Lover
Holdsworth
Folly Hall
Hazel Hurst Farm
Green Lane Top
Dale View Farm
Highfield
Hill Top Farm
Burnt Brow
Shay Dene
Fly Laithe Farm
Shibden Head
Priestley Hill
Long Shaw
Cocker Fm.
Hanging Royd
Henacre Wood
White Fields
Pepper Hill
Catherine Slack
Catherine Slack Farm
Upper Woodland Farm
Green Head
Pepper Hill Farm
Works
Spaniard Hall
Twist Wood
Thorn Tree
Cock Hill
Netherton Mills
Upper Shibden Hall
Upper Bowl Shaw
Ash Tree Farm
Holly Bank
Shibden
Sewage Works
Lower Town
Upper Town
Bowl Shaw Clough
Lower Bowl Shaw
Dundee
HALIFAX ROAD
Dunkirk Brow
Lower Shibden Hall
BRADFORD
CALDERDALE
Dunkirk
Slack End
Upper North Royd
Lower North Royd
Brow Side Farm
Barms Hill
Barms Hill Farm
Nutter Hill
Newton Hill Farm
Whinney Royd
Water Scout
Upper Lime House
Lower Lime House
Spring Hall
BRIGHOUSE & DENHOLME GATE R.
Swales Moor
Bare Head
Plough Royds
Hud Hill
Tan House Farm
North Howcans
Swales Moor Mink Farm
Crow Point
Adders Gate
Blake Hill End
Hollin Grove
Marsh Hall Farm
Wall Close Farm
Burnley Hill Farm
Woodcock Whiskers Wood
South Howcans
Ovenden
Simm Carr Clough
Over Whiskers
Lands Head
Landemere
Scout Hall
Lower Whiskers
A6036
Hollin Hall
Collier Toppin
North Field Gate Farm
Scout Wood
Dam Head
Cold Harbour
QUEENSBURY
Ringby Fm.
Pule Hill
Lee House
98
Brow Lane Farm
Little London Farm
Ringby Hill
Swim. Pool
Hollyleigh
Lee Lane Bri.
Blake Hill
Bleak Hill
Rigby Lane
Ousel
Lower
09
410
11
32
31
430
29
28

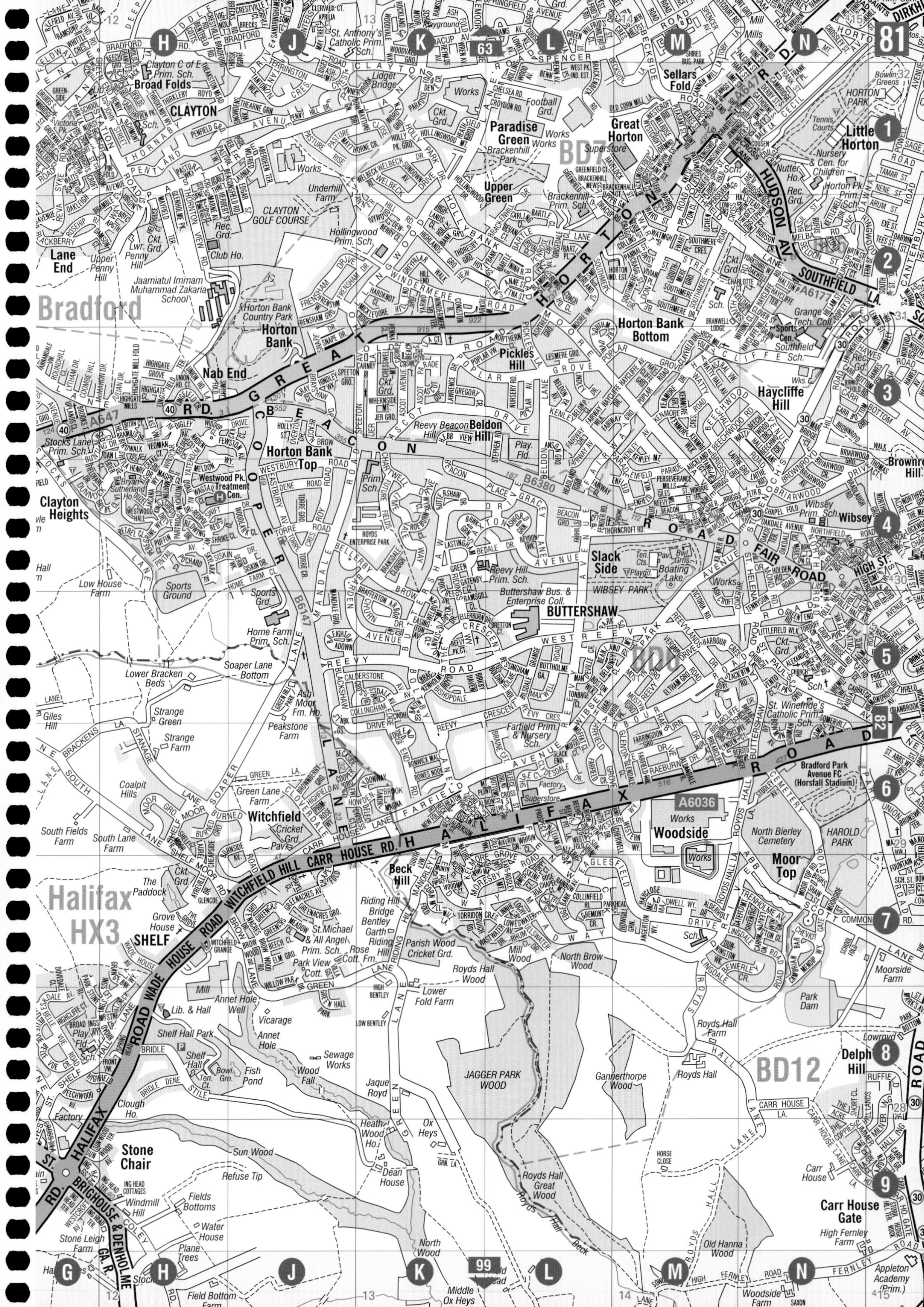

81
63
99
82
Bradford
Halifax
HX3
BD7
BD6
BD12
Broad Folds
CLAYTON
Clayton C of E Prim. Sch.
Lidget Bridge
Paradise Green
Great Horton
Sellars Fold
Little Horton
Upper Green
Brackenhill Park
CLAYTON GOLF COURSE
Underhill Farm
Hollingwood Prim. Sch.
Lane End
Upper Penny Hill
Jaamiatul Imaam Muhammad Zakaria School
Horton Bank Country Park
Horton Bank
Nab End
Pickles Hill
Horton Bank Bottom
Haycliffe Hill
Grange Tech. Coll.
Horton Bank Top
Beldon Hill
Clayton Heights
Westwood Pk. Treatment Cen.
Wibsey
Slack Side
WIBSEY PARK
BUTTERSHAW
Buttershaw Bus. & Enterprise Coll.
Reevy Hill Prim. Sch.
Home Farm Prim. Sch.
Low House Farm
Sports Ground
Lower Bracken Beds
Soaper Lane Bottom
Strange Green
Strange Farm
Giles Hill
Coalpit Hills
Peakstone Farm
Ash Moor Fm. Ho.
Green Lane Farm
Witchfield
South Fields Farm
South Lane Farm
The Paddock
Grove House
SHELF
Farfield Prim. & Nursery Sch.
St. Winefride's Catholic Prim. Sch.
Bradford Park Avenue FC (Horsfall Stadium)
North Bierley Cemetery
HAROLD PARK
Woodside
Moor Top
Beck Hill
Riding Hill
Bentley Garth
St.Michael & All Angel Prim. Sch.
Rose Cott. Fm.
Park View Cott.
Parish Wood Cricket Grd.
Royds Hall Wood
North Brow Wood
Mill Wood
Lower Fold Farm
Annet Hole Well
Vicarage
Annet Hole
Shelf Hall Park
Fish Pond
Wood Fall
Sewage Works
JAGGER PARK WOOD
Gannerthorpe Wood
Royds Hall
Royds Hall Farm
Park Dam
Moorside Farm
Delph Hill
Jaque Royd
Heath Wood Ho.
Ox Heys
Dean House
Clough Ho.
Stone Chair
Sun Wood
Refuse Tip
Windmill Hill
Fields Bottoms
Water House
Stone Leigh Farm
Plane Trees
North Wood
Royds Hall Great Wood
Old Hanna Wood
Carr House
Carr House Gate
High Fernley Farm
Appleton Academy (Prim.)
Woodside Farm
Field Bottom Farm
Middle Ox Heys
GREAT HORTON RD.
HALIFAX ROAD
BEACON RD.
FAIR ROAD
HUDSON AV.
SOUTHFIELD LA.
WITCHFIELD HILL CARR HOUSE RD.
WADE HOUSE ROAD
BRIGHOUSE & DENHOLME GA. R.
A647
A6036
A6177
B6380
B6147

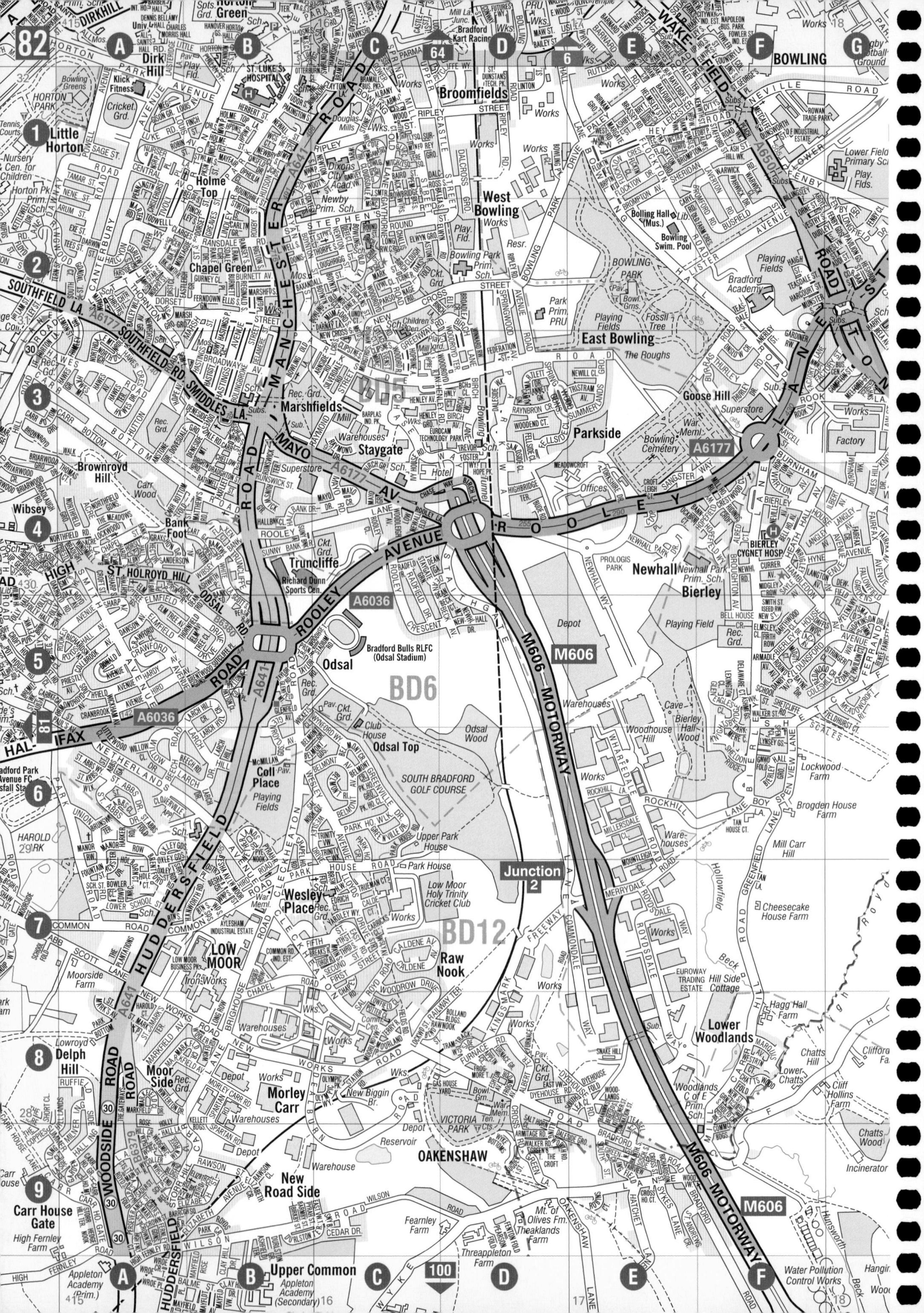

Dirk Hill
Horton Green
Broomfields
BOWLING
Little Horton
St. Luke's Hospital
Klick Fitness
Cricket Grd.
Holme Top
West Bowling
Chapel Green
Bolling Hall (Mus.)
Bowling Swim. Pool
Bradford Academy
Bowling Park
East Bowling
The Roughs
Goose Hill
Marshfields
Staygate
Parkside
BD5
Brownroyd Hill
Wibsey
Bank Foot
Truncliffe
Richard Dunn Sports Cen.
ROOLEY AVENUE
ROOLEY LANE
MAYO AV.
MANCHESTER ROAD
SOUTHFIELD LA.
SMIDDLES LA.
Newhall
Bierley
Bierley Cygnet Hosp.
Prologis Park
HIGH ST.
HOLROYD HILL
ODSAL
Odsal
Bradford Bulls RLFC (Odsal Stadium)
BD6
M606 MOTORWAY
A6036
A6177
A641
A650
A6379
Coll Place
Odsal Top
Odsal Wood
South Bradford Golf Course
Bierley Hall Wood
Woodhouse Hill
Lockwood Farm
Brogden House Farm
Mill Carr Hill
Cheesecake House Farm
Upper Park House
Park House
Low Moor Holy Trinity Cricket Club
Junction 2
Wesley Place
BD12
LOW MOOR
Raw Nook
HUDDERSFIELD ROAD
Moorside Farm
Euroway Trading Estate
Hill Side Cottage
Hagg Hall Farm
Lower Woodlands
Delph Hill
Moor Side
Morley Carr
Chatts Hill
Lower Chatts
Cliff Hollins Farm
Chatts Wood
Victoria Park
OAKENSHAW
New Road Side
Woodlands C of E Prim. Sch.
Incinerator
Carr House Gate
High Fernley Farm
WOODSIDE ROAD
Fearnley Farm
Mt. of Olives Fm.
Theaklands Farm
Threappleton Farm
Upper Common
Appleton Academy
Appleton Academy (Secondary)
Water Pollution Control Works
HAL-IFAX
81
64
6
100

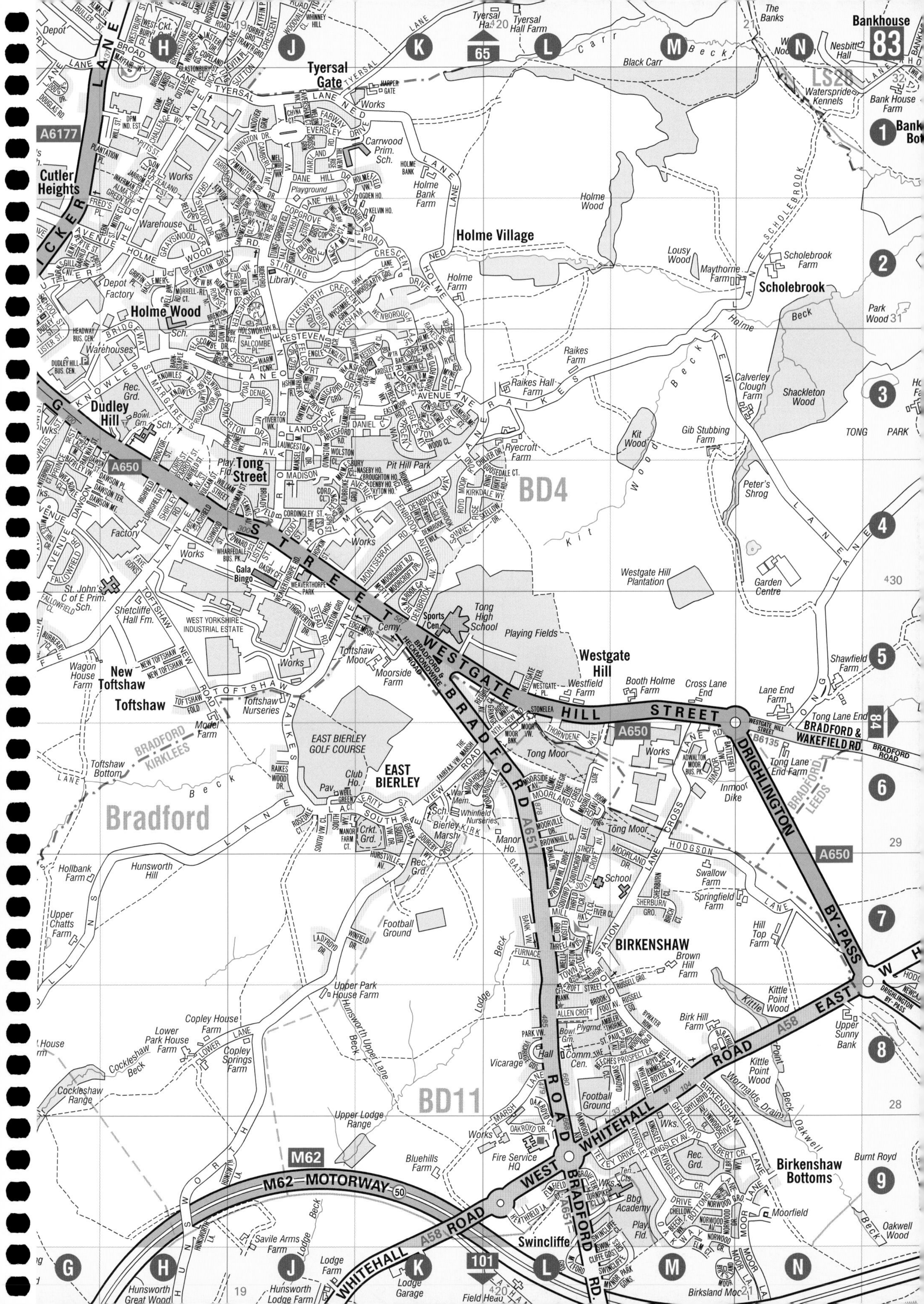

Bankhouse
83
Tyersal Gate
Cutler Heights
Holme Village
Holme Wood
Dudley Hill
Tong Street
BD4
Scholebrook
Westgate Hill
New Toftshaw
Toftshaw
EAST BIERLEY
Bradford
BIRKENSHAW
BD11
Birkenshaw Bottoms
Swincliffe
M62 MOTORWAY
WESTGATE HILL STREET
DRIGHLINGTON BY-PASS
WHITEHALL ROAD
BRADFORD ROAD
A650
A651
A58
A6177
65
84
101

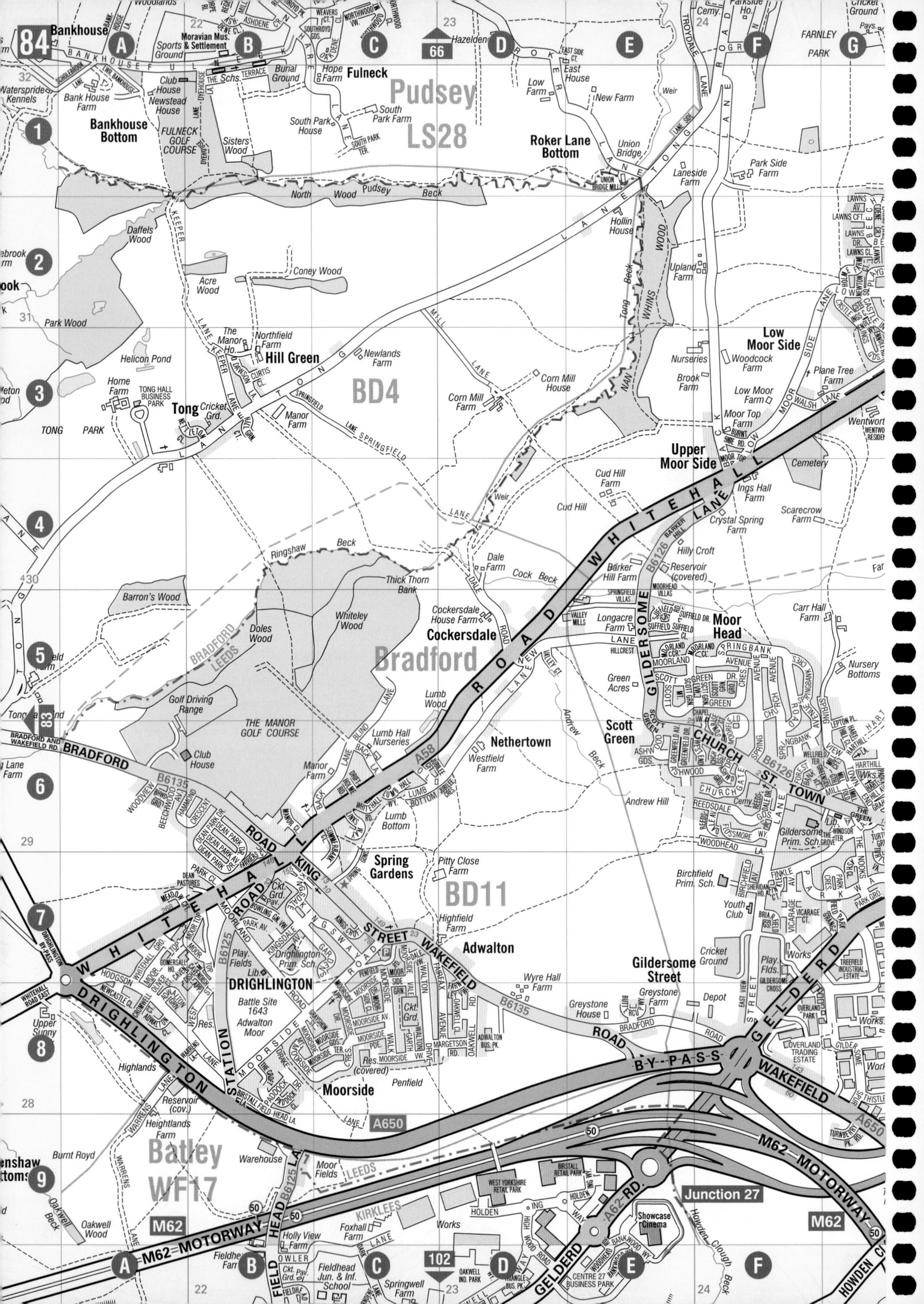
Bankhouse
Fulneck
Pudsey
LS28
Hazelden
Moravian Mus. & Settlement
Sports & Settlement Ground
Bankhouse Bottom
Bank House Farm
Fulneck Golf Course
Sisters Wood
Burial Ground
Hope Farm
South Park House
South Park Farm
Low Farm
East House
New Farm
Roker Lane Bottom
Union Bridge
Laneside Farm
Park Side Farm
Farnley Park
Pudsey Beck
North Wood
Daffels Wood
Hollin House
Coney Wood
Acre Wood
Upland Farm
Park Wood
Helicon Pond
Home Farm
Tong Hall Business Park
Tong
Tong Park
Hill Green
Northfield Farm
The Manor Ho.
Newlands Farm
BD4
Corn Mill House
Corn Mill Farm
Manor Farm
Nurseries
Woodcock Farm
Low Moor Side
Brook Farm
Low Moor Farm
Plane Tree Farm
Moor Top Farm
Upper Moor Side
Cemetery
Cud Hill Farm
Cud Hill
Ings Hall Farm
Scarecrow Farm
Crystal Spring Farm
Hilly Croft
Ringshaw Beck
Thick Thorn Bank
Dale Farm
Cock Beck
Barker Hill Farm
Reservoir (covered)
Barron's Wood
Whiteley Wood
Doles Wood
Cockersdale House Farm
Cockersdale
Longacre Farm
Moor Head
Carr Hall Farm
Bradford
Green Acres
Scott Green
Nursery Bottoms
Golf Driving Range
The Manor Golf Course
Club House
Lumb Wood
Lumb Hall Nurseries
Nethertown
Westfield Farm
Manor Farm
Andrew Beck
Andrew Hill
Gildersome Prim. Sch.
Lumb Bottom
Spring Gardens
Pitty Close Farm
BD11
Birchfield Prim. Sch.
Youth Club
Highfield Farm
Adwalton
Drighlington
Drighlington Prim. Sch.
Play. Fields
Battle Site 1643
Adwalton Moor
Wyre Hall Farm
Gildersome Street
Cricket Ground
Greystone House
Greystone Farm
Depot
Gildersome Cross
Treefield Industrial Estate
Overland Park
Overland Trading Estate
Upper Sunny
Highlands
Reservoir (cov.)
Moorside
Res. (covered)
Penfield
Heightlands Farm
Burnt Royd
Batley
WF17
Warehouse
Moor Fields
West Yorkshire Retail Park
Birstall Retail Park
Junction 27
Showcase Cinema
Oakwell Wood
Holly View Farm
Foxhall Farm
Works
Fieldhead Jun. & Inf. School
Springwell Farm
Oakwell Ind. Park
Triangle Bus. Pk.
Centre 27 Business Park
Howden Clough Beck
Whitehall Road
Wakefield Road
Bradford Road
Gelderd Road
Drighlington By-Pass
M62 Motorway
A650
A58
B6135
B6125
B6126
Tong Lane
King Street
Station Road
Church St.
Town
Springbank
66
83
102

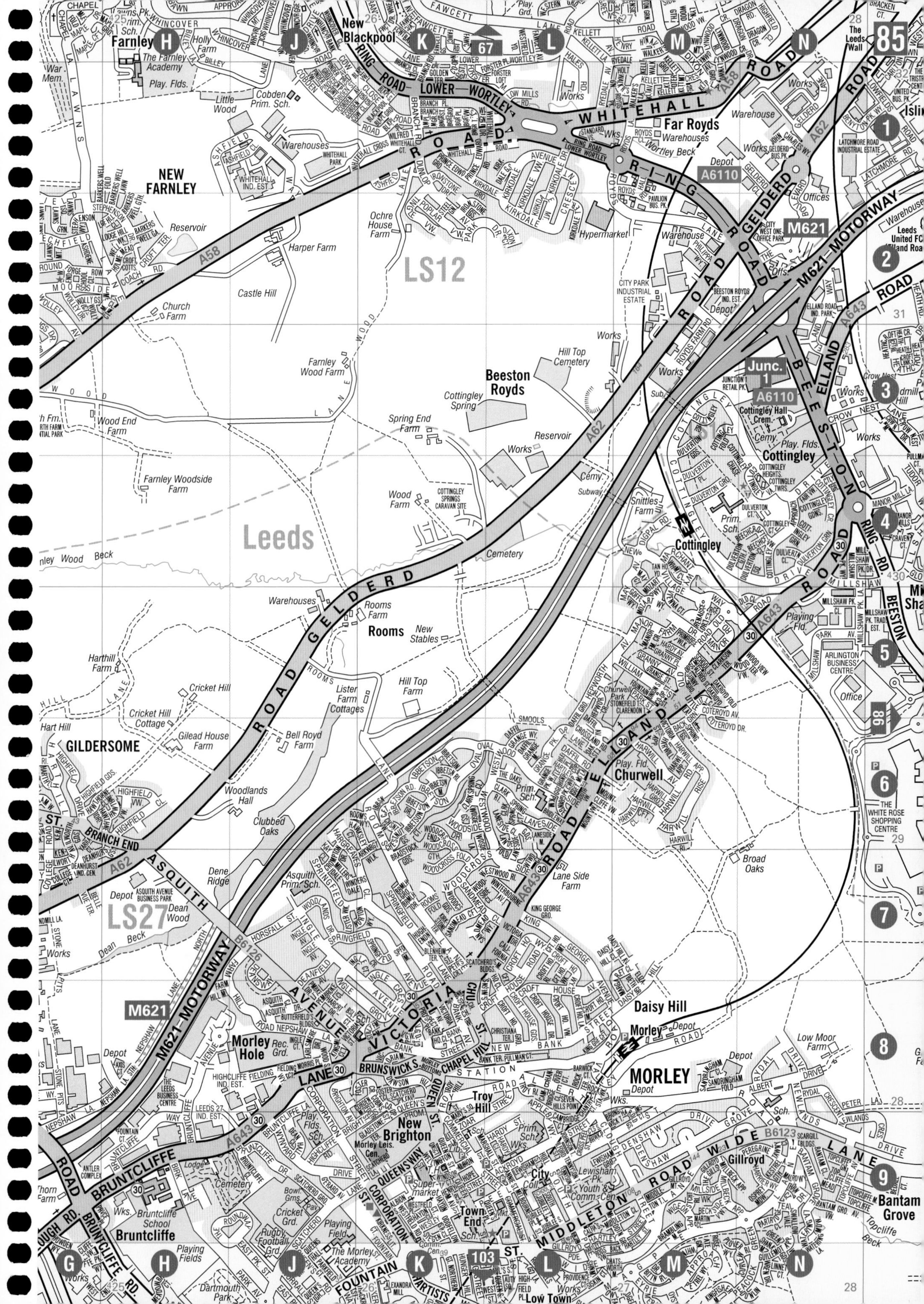
Farnley
New Blackpool
NEW FARNLEY
Far Royds
LS12
Beeston Royds
Leeds
Cottingley
Rooms
GILDERSOME
Churwell
LS27
Daisy Hill
Morley Hole
MORLEY
New Brighton
Troy Hill
Gillroyd
Bantam Grove
Bruntcliffe
Town End
Low Town
RING ROAD LOWER WORTLEY
WHITEHALL ROAD
GELDERD ROAD
M621 MOTORWAY
ELLAND ROAD
BEESTON RING ROAD
ASQUITH AVENUE
VICTORIA ROAD
BRUNTCLIFFE ROAD
MIDDLETON ROAD
WIDE LANE
A58
A62
A643
A6110
M621
B6126
B6123
Junc. 1
The White Rose Shopping Centre
Leeds United FC Elland Road
The Farnley Academy
The Morley Academy
Bruntcliffe School
Hill Top Cemetery
Cottingley Hall Crem.
67
103
86

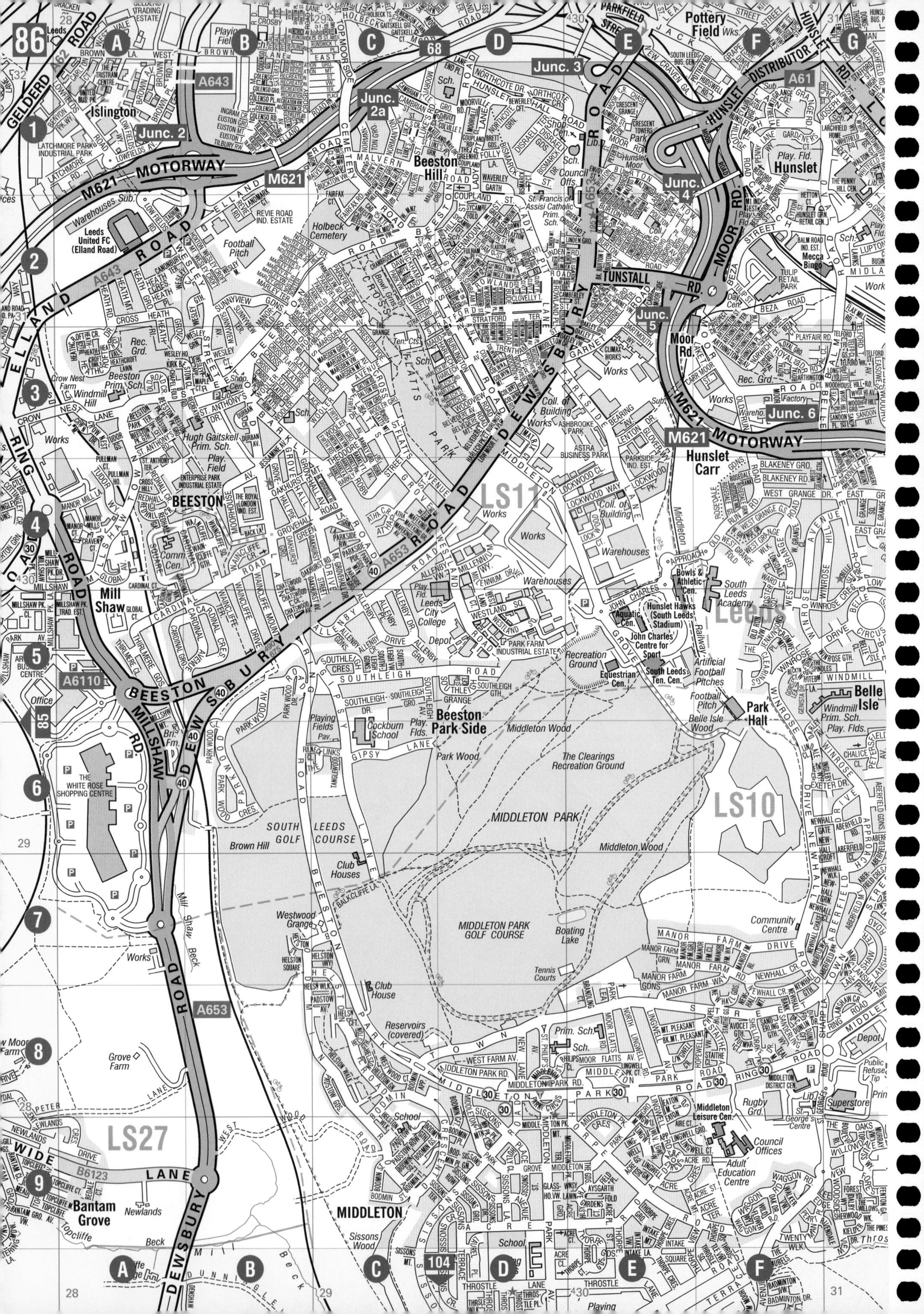

86
A
B
C
D
E
F
G
1
2
3
4
5
6
7
8
9
Islington
Junc. 2
Junc. 2a
Junc. 3
Junc. 4
Junc. 5
Junc. 6
M621 MOTORWAY
M621
A643
A653
A61
A6110
B6123
68
85
104
Leeds United FC (Elland Road)
Revie Road Ind. Estate
Football Pitch
Holbeck Cemetery
Beeston Hill
Pottery Field
Hunslet
Tunstall
Moor Rd.
Hunslet Carr
Hunslet Moor
Crescent Towers Park
Tulip Retail Park
Mecca Bingo
Beeston
Beeston Prim. Sch.
Windmill Hill
Crow Nest Farm
Hugh Gaitskell Prim. Sch.
Enterprise Park Industrial Estate
The Royal London Ind. Est.
Comm. Cen.
Mill Shaw
Millshaw Pk. Trad. Est.
LS11
LS10
LS27
Leeds City College
Park Farm Industrial Estate
Astra Business Park
Parkside Ind. Est.
Coll. of Building
Warehouses
Works
Hunslet Hawks (South Leeds Stadium)
John Charles Centre for Sport
South Leeds Ten. Cen.
Equestrian Cen.
Recreation Ground
Aquatic Cen.
Bowls & Athletic Cen.
South Leeds Academy
Artificial Football Pitches
Park Halt
Belle Isle
Belle Isle Wood
Windmill Prim. Sch.
Beeston Park Side
Cockburn School
Middleton Wood
Park Wood
The Clearings Recreation Ground
Middleton Park
South Leeds Golf Course
Brown Hill
Club Houses
Westwood Grange
Middleton Park Golf Course
Boating Lake
Tennis Courts
Club House
Reservoirs (covered)
The White Rose Shopping Centre
Office
Grove Farm
Bantam Grove
Newlands
Middleton
Sissons Wood
Middleton Leisure Cen.
Council Offices
Adult Education Centre
Community Centre
Rugby Grd.
Superstore
Public Refuse Tip
Depot
DEWSBURY ROAD
ELLAND ROAD
RING ROAD
BEESTON RING ROAD
MILLSHAW RD.
MIDDLETON PARK ROAD
MIDDLETON RING ROAD
WIDE LANE
HUNSLET DISTRIBUTOR
MOOR RD.
GELDERD ROAD
28
29
30
31
430

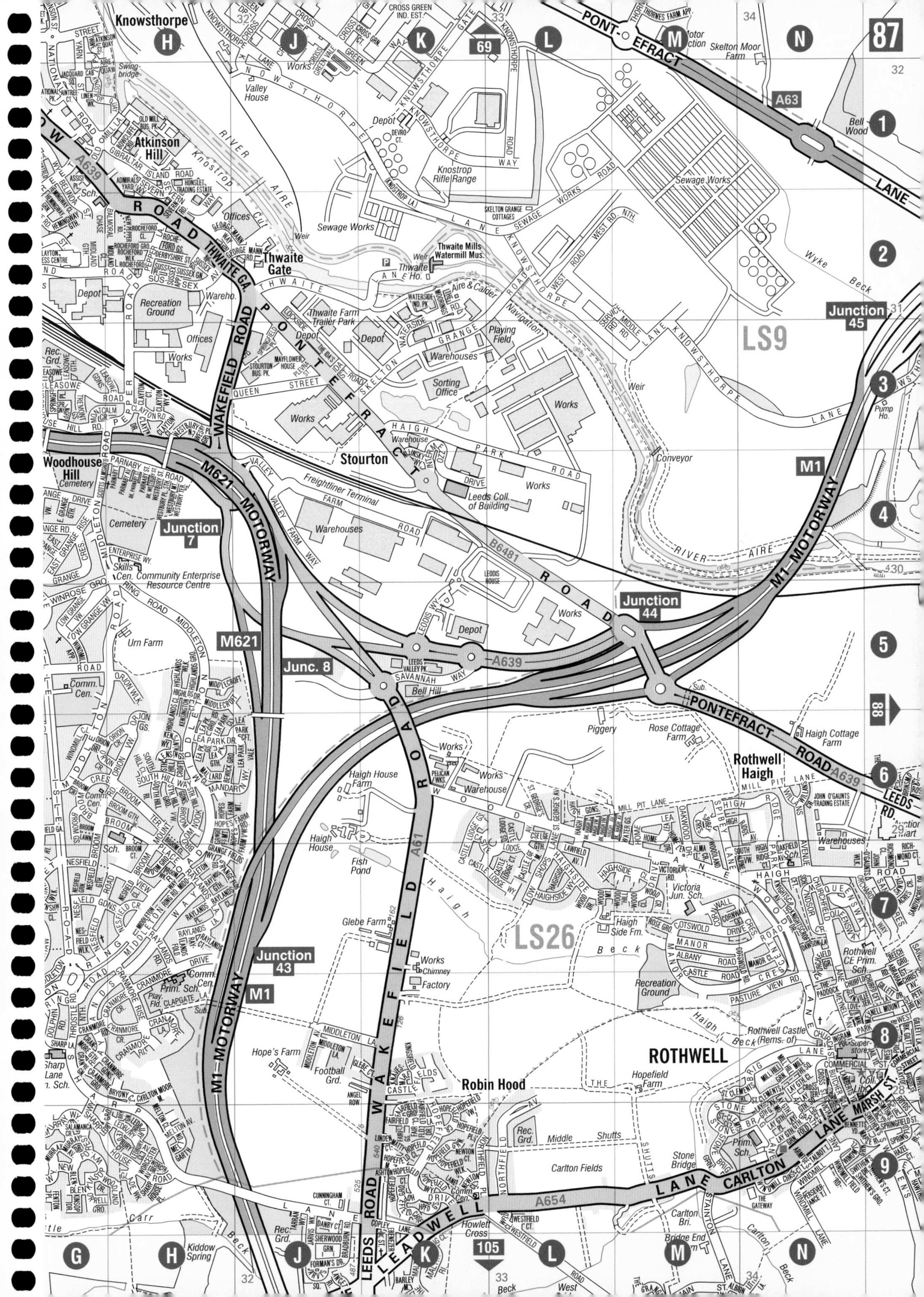
Knowsthorpe
Atkinson Hill
Thwaite Gate
Stourton
Woodhouse Hill
Rothwell Haigh
ROTHWELL
Robin Hood
LS9
LS26
Junction 7
Junction 43
Junction 44
Junction 45
Junc. 8
M621
M1
A63
A639
A61
A654
B6481
69
88
105
PONTEFRACT LANE
PONTEFRACT ROAD
WAKEFIELD ROAD
M621 MOTORWAY
M1 MOTORWAY
RIVER AIRE
Aire & Calder Navigation
Knostrop Cut
Sewage Works
Skelton Moor Farm
Bell Wood
Wyke Beck
Thwaite Mills Watermill Mus.
Knostrop Rifle Range
Valley House
Recreation Ground
Thwaite Farm Trailer Park
Freightliner Terminal
Leeds Coll. of Building
Sorting Office
Playing Field
Conveyor
Pump Ho.
Cemetery
Skills Cen. Community Enterprise Resource Centre
Urn Farm
Haigh House Farm
Haigh House
Fish Pond
Glebe Farm
Hope's Farm
Football Grd.
Piggery
Rose Cottage Farm
Haigh Cottage Farm
Victoria Jun. Sch.
Haigh Side Fm.
Rothwell CE Prim. Sch.
Rothwell Castle (Rems. of)
Hopefield Farm
Carlton Fields
Middle Shutts
Stone Bridge
Carlton Bri.
Bridge End
Howlett Cross
Kiddow Spring
Sharp Lane Sch.
Carr Beck
LEADWELL LANE
CARLTON LANE
MARSH ST.
LEEDS RD.
WOOD LANE
MIDDLETON RING ROAD
G
H
J
K
L
M
N
1
2
3
4
5
6
7
8
9
32
33
34

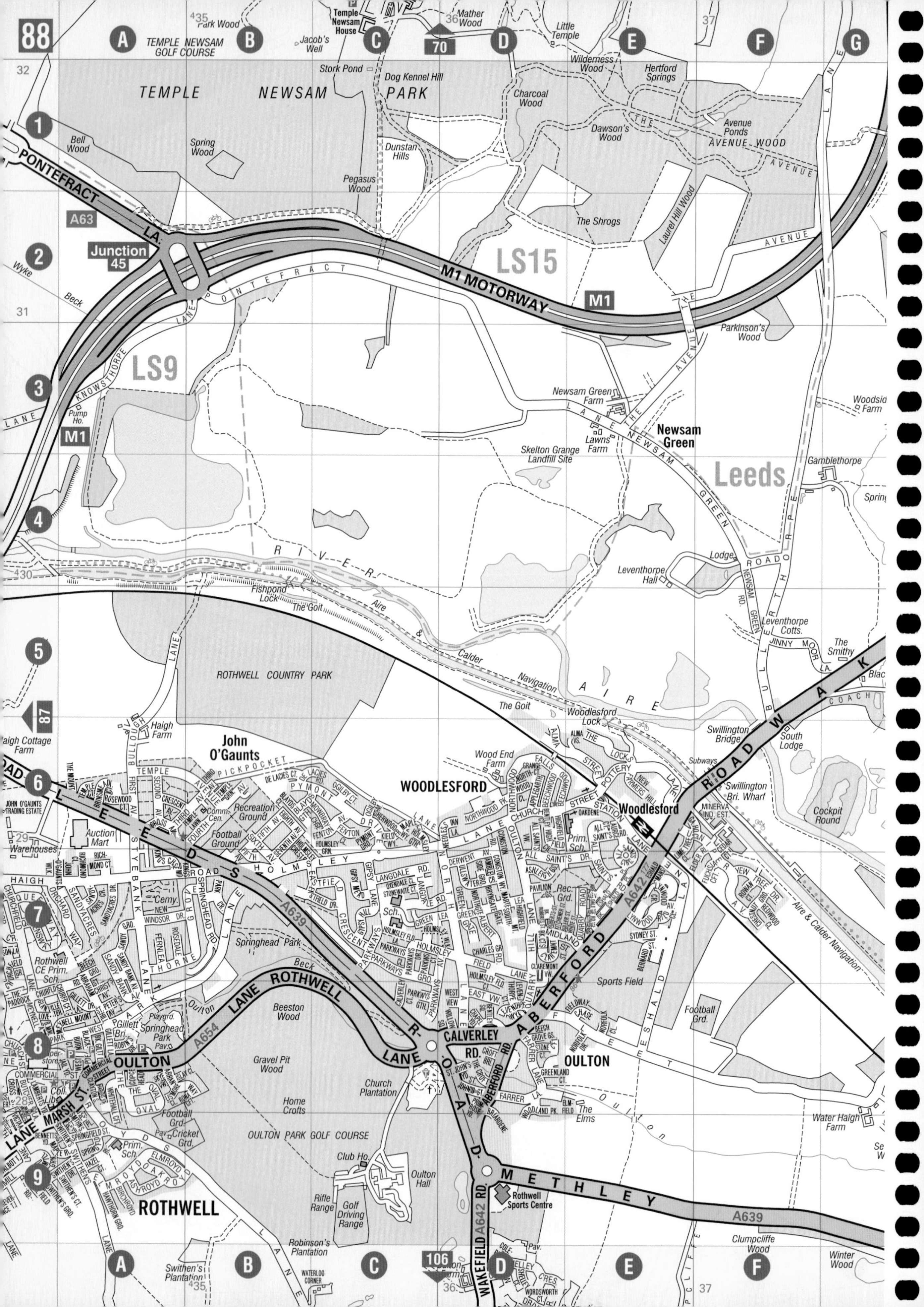
TEMPLE NEWSAM GOLF COURSE
TEMPLE NEWSAM PARK
Temple Newsam House
Jacob's Well
Stork Pond
Dog Kennel Hill
Mather Wood
Little Temple
Wilderness Wood
Hertford Springs
Charcoal Wood
Dawson's Wood
Avenue Ponds
AVENUE WOOD
Bell Wood
Spring Wood
Dunstan Hills
Pegasus Wood
The Shrogs
Laurel Hill Wood
PONTEFRACT LA.
A63
Junction 45
M1 MOTORWAY
M1
LS15
LS9
Parkinson's Wood
Newsam Green Farm
Newsam Green
Lawns Farm
Skelton Grange Landfill Site
Leeds
Gamblethorpe
Woodside Farm
Pump Ho.
Leventhorpe Hall
Lodge
Leventhorpe Cotts.
The Smithy
JINNY MOOR LA.
RIVER AIRE
Fishpond Lock
The Goit
Aire & Calder Navigation
ROTHWELL COUNTRY PARK
Woodlesford Lock
Swillington Bridge
South Lodge
Swillington Bri. Wharf
Cockpit Round
Haigh Farm
Haigh Cottage Farm
John O'Gaunts
JOHN O'GAUNTS TRADING ESTATE
Auction Mart
Warehouses
WOODLESFORD
Woodlesford
Wood End Farm
Recreation Ground
Football Ground
Rothwell CE Prim. Sch.
Springhead Park
Beeston Wood
Gravel Pit Wood
Church Plantation
Home Crofts
OULTON PARK GOLF COURSE
Club Ho.
Oulton Hall
Rifle Range
Golf Driving Range
Robinson's Plantation
Swithen's Plantation
ROTHWELL
OULTON
CALVERLEY RD.
ABERFORD RD.
WAKEFIELD RD.
METHLEY LANE
A639
A654
A642
Rothwell Sports Centre
Sports Field
Football Grd.
The Elms
Water Haigh Farm
Clumpcliffe Wood
Winter Wood
Cricket Grd.
70
87
106

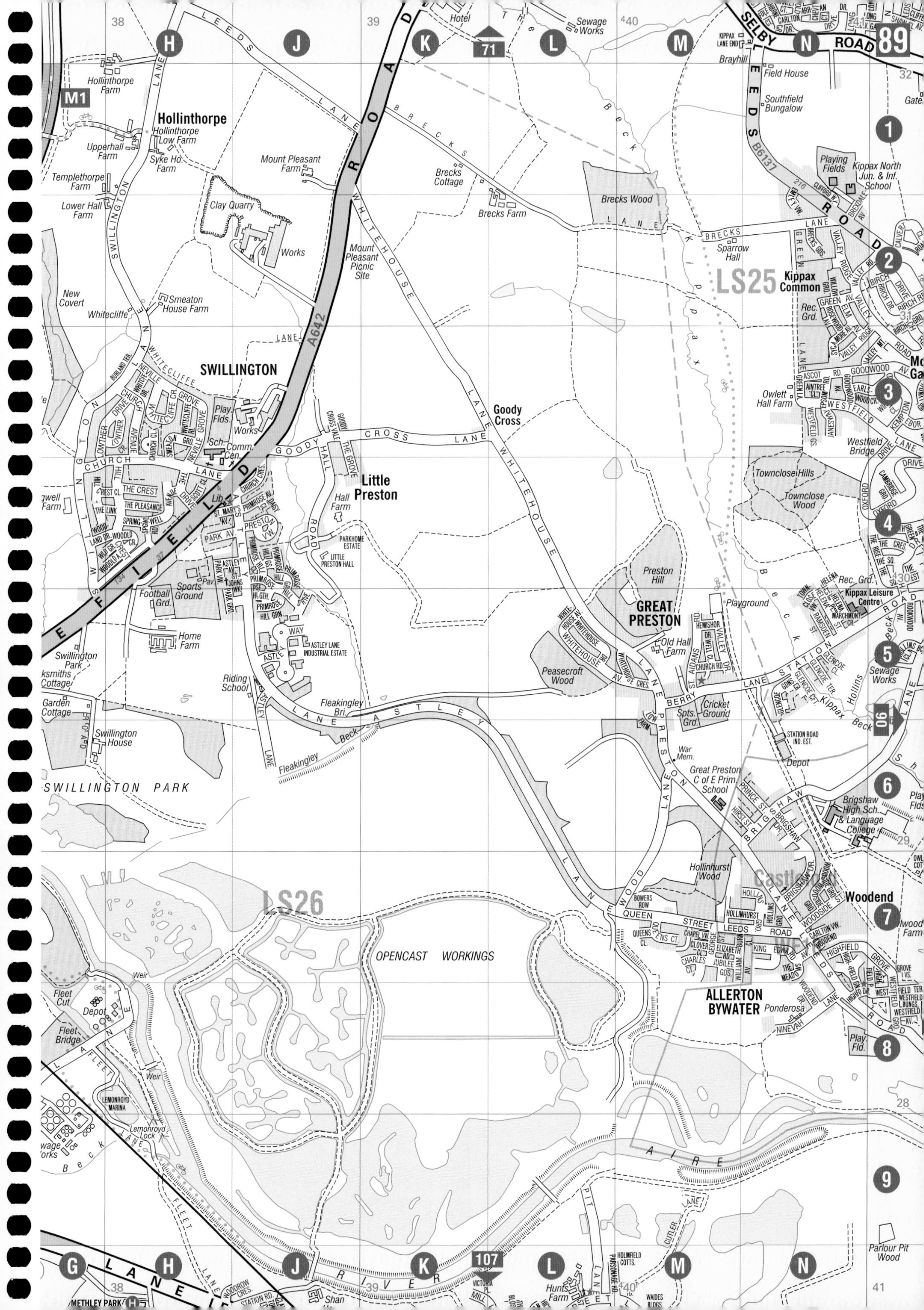
Hollinthorpe
Hollinthorpe Farm
Hollinthorpe Low Farm
Upperhall Farm
Syke Ho. Farm
Templethorpe Farm
Lower Hall Farm
Clay Quarry
Works
Mount Pleasant Farm
Mount Pleasant Picnic Site
Brecks Cottage
Brecks Farm
Brecks Wood
Sewage Works
Hotel
Brayhill
Field House
Southfield Bungalow
Playing Fields
Kippax North Jun. & Inf. School
Sparrow Hall
LS25
Kippax Common
New Covert
Whitecliffe
Smeaton House Farm
SWILLINGTON
Goody Cross
Little Preston
Hall Farm
Owlett Hall Farm
Westfield Bridge
Townclose Hills
Townclose Wood
Preston Hill
GREAT PRESTON
Kippax Leisure Centre
Playground
Old Hall Farm
Peasecroft Wood
Cricket Ground
Football Grd.
Sports Ground
Home Farm
Swillington Park
Riding School
Astley Lane Industrial Estate
Fleakingley Bri.
Garden Cottage
Swillington House
SWILLINGTON PARK
Fleakingley Beck
War Mem.
Great Preston C of E Prim. School
Station Road Ind. Est.
Depot
Brigshaw High Sch. & Language College
Hollinhurst Wood
Woodend
LS26
OPENCAST WORKINGS
ALLERTON BYWATER
Ponderosa
Fleet Cut
Depot
Fleet Bridge
Weir
Lemonroyd Marina
Lemonroyd Lock
River Aire
Parlour Pit Wood
Holmfield Cotts.
Hunts Farm
A642
M1
B6137
71
90
107

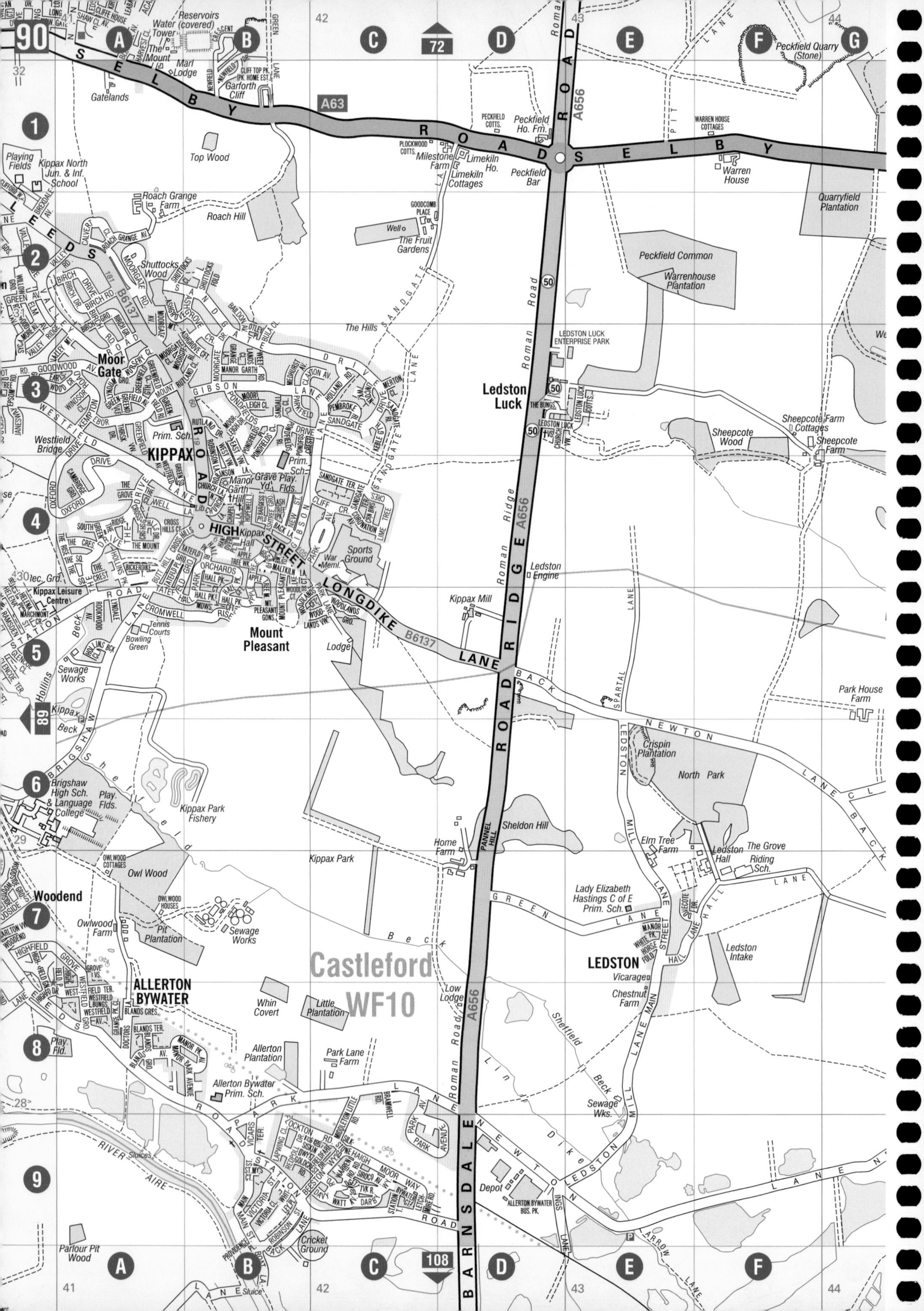
72
108
89
Castleford
WF10
KIPPAX
ALLERTON
BYWATER
LEDSTON
Ledston
Luck
Moor
Gate
Mount
Pleasant
Woodend
Kippax Park
Peckfield Common
North Park
SELBY ROAD
ROMAN RIDGE ROAD
BARNSDALE ROAD
LONGDIKE LANE
HIGH STREET
A63
A656
B6137

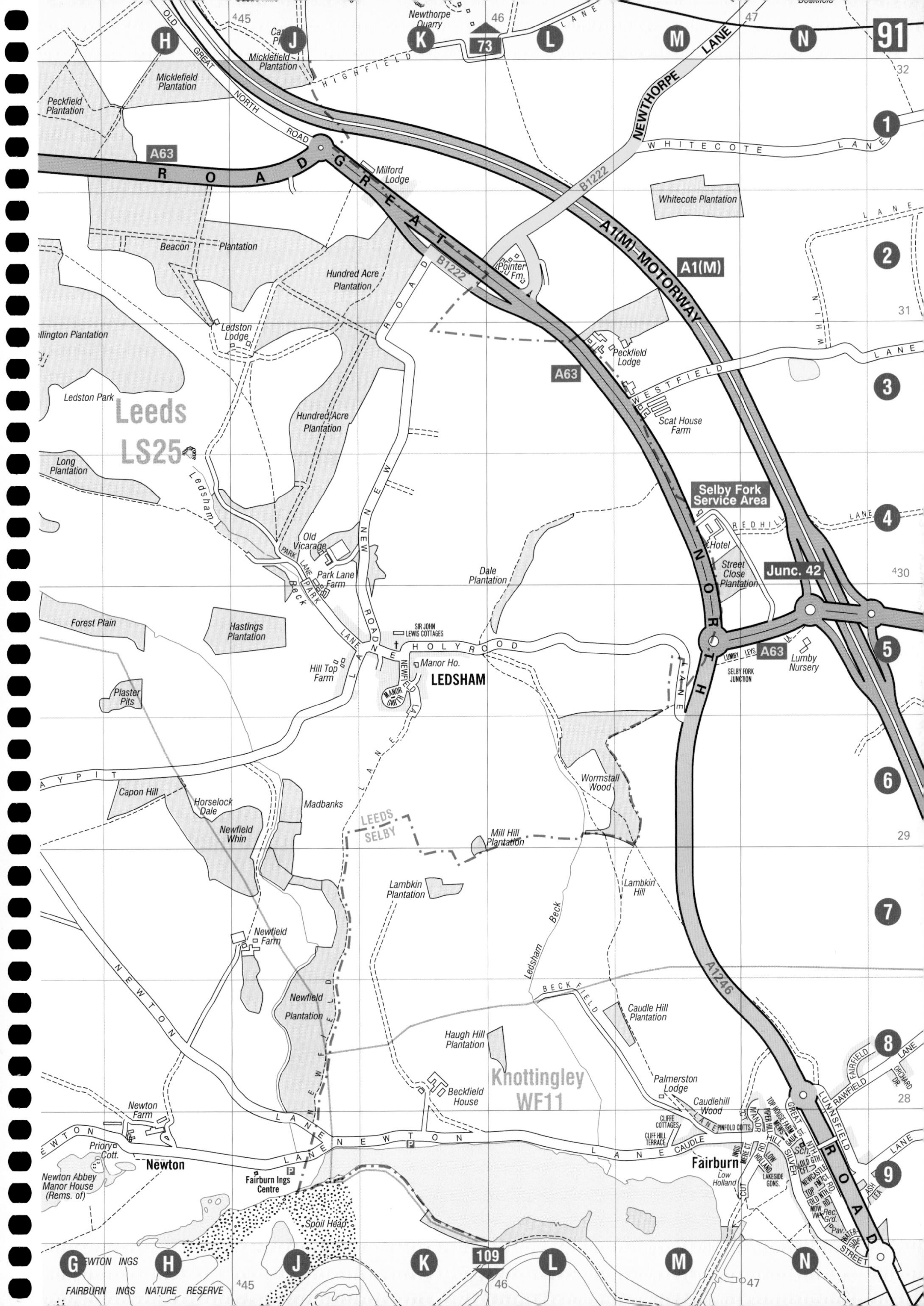
Newthorpe Quarry
Micklefield Plantation
Peckfield Plantation
GREAT NORTH ROAD
HIGHFIELD LANE
NEWTHORPE LANE
WHITECOTE LANE
A63
ROAD
GREAT
Milford Lodge
B1222
Whitecote Plantation
Beacon Plantation
Hundred Acre Plantation
Pointer Fm.
A1(M) MOTORWAY
A1(M)
Ledston Lodge
Peckfield Lodge
WESTFIELD LANE
Ledston Park
Leeds LS25
Hundred Acre Plantation
Scat House Farm
Long Plantation
Ledsham Beck
Selby Fork Service Area
REDHILL LANE
Old Vicarage
Park Lane Farm
Dale Plantation
Street Close Plantation
Junc. 42
Forest Plain
Hastings Plantation
SIR JOHN LEWIS COTTAGES
HOLYROOD
Hill Top Farm
Manor Ho.
LEDSHAM
MANOR GARTH
NEWFIELD LANE
LUMBY LEYS LA
SELBY FORK JUNCTION
Lumby Nursery
NORTH
Plaster Pits
HAYPIT
Capon Hill
Horselock Dale
Newfield Whin
Madbanks
LEEDS
SELBY
Wormstall Wood
Mill Hill Plantation
Lambkin Plantation
Lambkin Hill
Newfield Farm
NEWTON
Ledsham Beck
A1246
BECKFIELD
Caudle Hill Plantation
Newfield Plantation
Haugh Hill Plantation
Knottingley WF11
Beckfield House
Palmerston Lodge
Caudlehill Wood
Newton Farm
CLIFFE COTTAGES
CLIFF HILL TERRACE
PINFOLD COTTS
LANE
NEWTON LANE
CAUDLE LANE
Priory Cott.
Newton
Fairburn
Newton Abbey Manor House (Rems. of)
Fairburn Ings Centre
Low Holland
Spoil Heap
LAKESIDE GDNS.
GREAT NORTH ROAD
LUNNSFIELD
RAWFIELD
ORCHARD DR.
FAIRFIELD LANE
WATERSIDE
STREET
NEWTON INGS
FAIRBURN INGS NATURE RESERVE
G H J K L M N
73
109
445 46 47
32 31 430 29 28
1 2 3 4 5 6 7 8 9

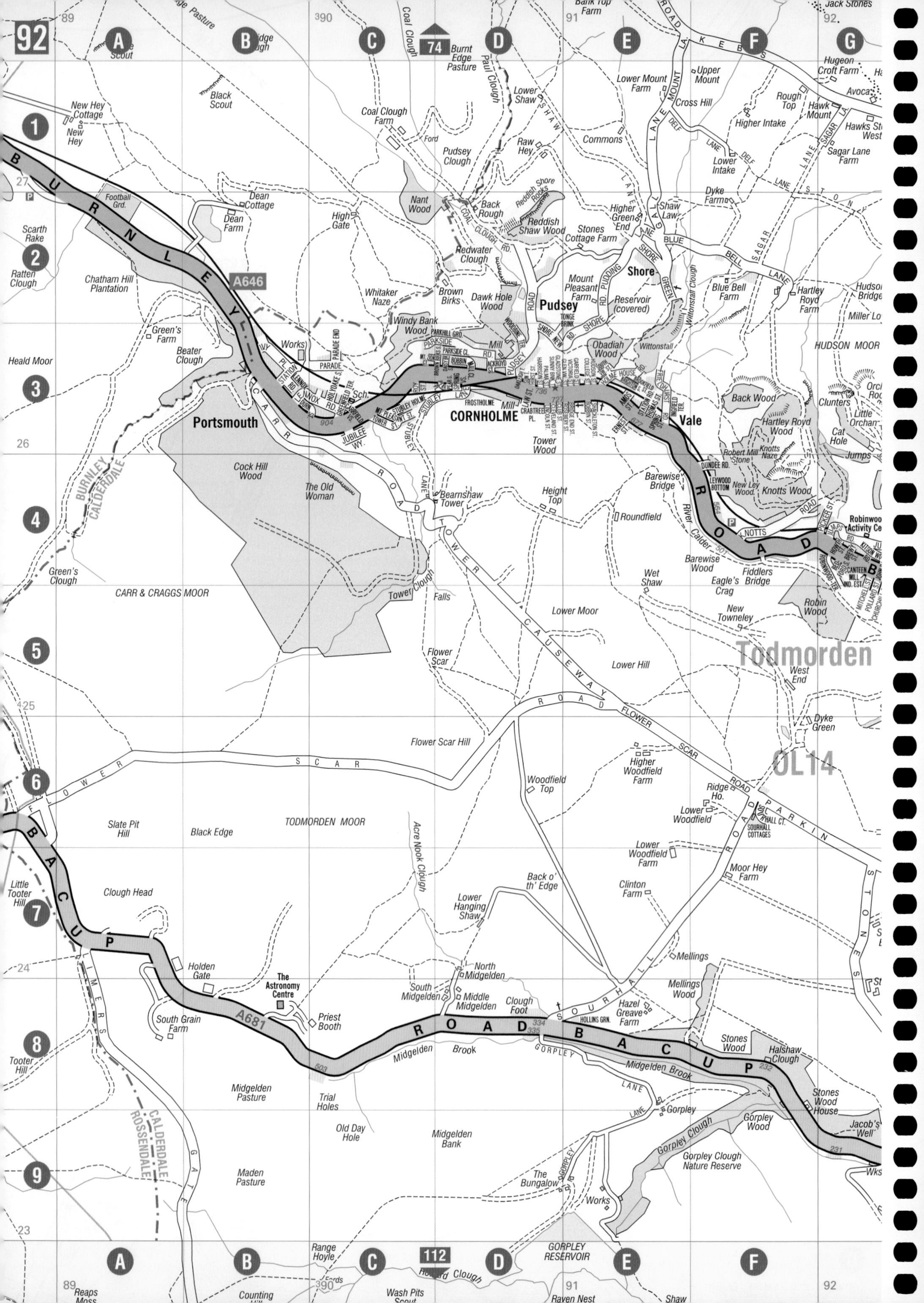

Portsmouth
CORNHOLME
Pudsey
Shore
Vale
Todmorden
OL14
BURNLEY ROAD
A646
BACUP ROAD
A681
TOWER CAUSEWAY
FLOWER SCAR ROAD
CARR & CRAGGS MOOR
TODMORDEN MOOR
HUDSON MOOR
Heald Moor
Cock Hill Wood
The Old Woman
Flower Scar Hill
Slate Pit Hill
Black Edge
Clough Head
The Astronomy Centre
Holden Gate
South Grain Farm
Priest Booth
Midgelden Pasture
Trial Holes
Old Day Hole
Midgelden Bank
Maden Pasture
Gorpley Clough Nature Reserve
GORPLEY RESERVOIR
Lower Moor
Lower Hill
Woodfield Top
Higher Woodfield Farm
Lower Woodfield
Lower Woodfield Farm
Clinton Farm
Moor Hey Farm
Back Wood
Hartley Royd Wood
Knotts Wood
Robinwood Activity Ce
Barewise Bridge
Barewise Wood
Fiddlers Bridge
Eagle's Crag
New Towneley
Robin Wood
West End
Dyke Green
Ridge Ho.
Stones Wood
Halshaw Clough
Stones Wood House
Jacob's Well
Gorpley Wood
Mellings Wood
Hazel Greave Farm
Clough Foot
North Midgelden
Middle Midgelden
South Midgelden
Lower Hanging Shaw
Back o' th' Edge
Flower Scar
Falls
Tower Clough
Bearnshaw Tower
Height Top
Roundfield
Wet Shaw
Tower Wood
Obadiah Wood
Mount Pleasant Farm
Reservoir (covered)
Stones Cottage Farm
Reddish Shaw Wood
Back Rough
Nant Wood
Pudsey Clough
Coal Clough Farm
Burnt Edge Pasture
Black Scout
New Hey Cottage
Dean Cottage
Dean Farm
Scarth Rake
Ratten Clough
Chatham Hill Plantation
Green's Farm
Beater Clough
Green's Clough
Lower Mount Farm
Upper Mount
Cross Hill
Higher Intake
Lower Intake
Rough Top
Hawk Mount
Sagar Lane Farm
Blue Bell Farm
Hartley Royd Farm
Hugeon Croft Farm
Jack Stones
Little Tooter Hill
Tooter Hill
The Bungalow
Range Hoyle
Reaps Moss
Counting Hill
Wash Pits Scout
Raven Nest

74
112

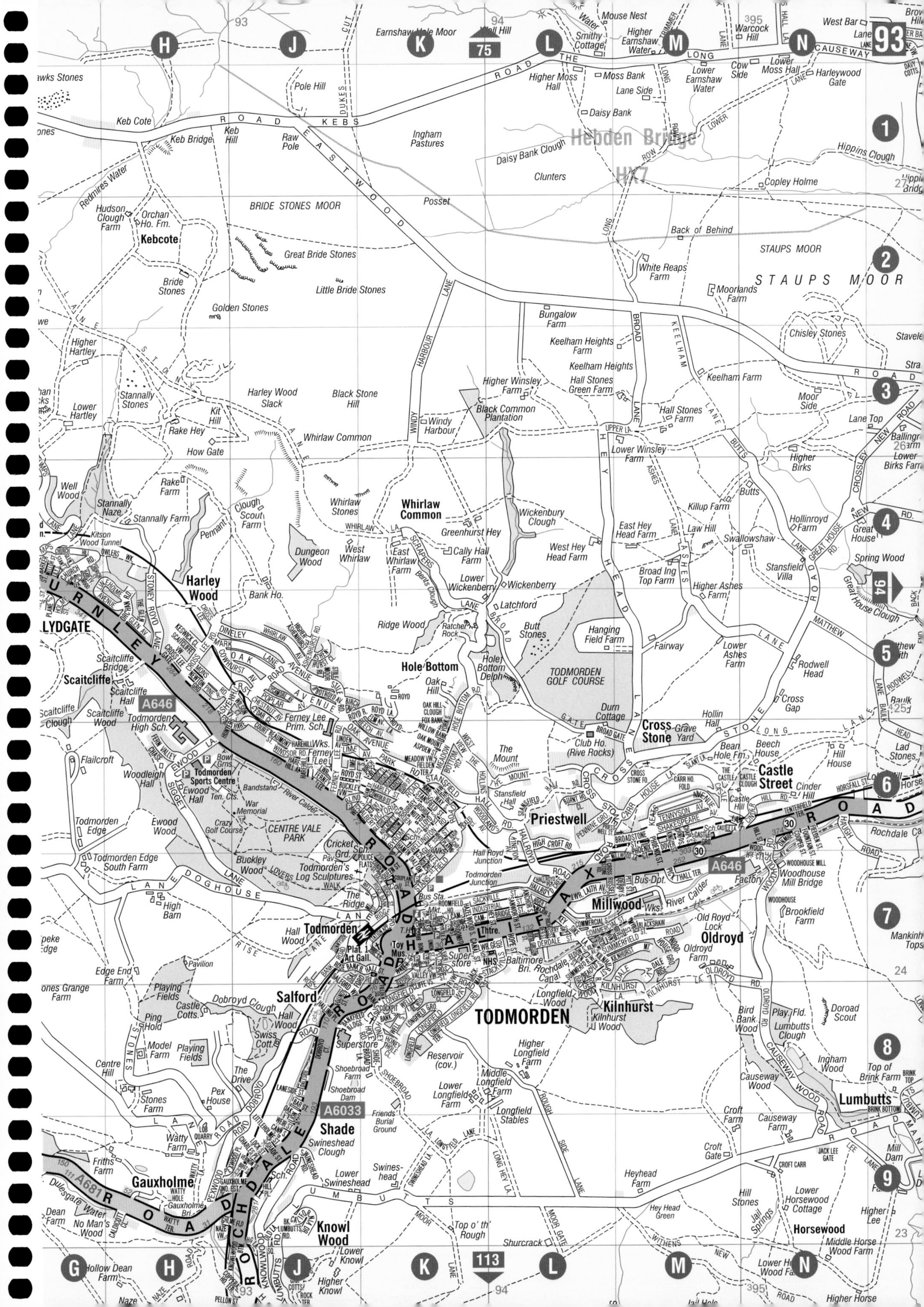

H
J
K
L
M
N
75
Earnshaw Hole Moor
Mouse Nest
Higher Earnshaw Water
Smithy Cottage
Warcock Hill
West Bar
THE LONG CAUSEWAY
Higher Moss Hall
Moss Bank
Lane Side
Lower Earnshaw Water
Cow Side
Lower Moss Hall
Harleywood Gate
Hawks Stones
Pole Hill
Keb Cote
KEBS ROAD
Keb Bridge
Keb Hill
Raw Pole
Daisy Bank
Ingham Pastures
Hebden Bridge
HX7
Daisy Bank Clough
Clunters
Hippins Clough
Copley Holme
Redmires Water
Hudson Clough Farm
Orchan Ho. Fm.
Kebcote
BRIDE STONES MOOR
EASTWOOD ROAD
Posset
Back of Behind
STAUPS MOOR
Great Bride Stones
White Reaps Farm
Moorlands Farm
Bride Stones
Little Bride Stones
Golden Stones
Bungalow Farm
Keelham Heights Farm
Keelham Heights
Chisley Stones
Higher Hartley
Stannally Stones
Harley Wood Slack
Black Stone Hill
HARBOUR LANE
Higher Winsley Farm
Hall Stones Green Farm
Keelham Farm
Moor Side
Lower Hartley
Kit Hill
Rake Hey
Windy Harbour
Black Common Plantation
Hall Stones Farm
Lane Top
How Gate
Whirlaw Common
Lower Winsley Farm
Higher Birks
Lower Birks Farm
Well Wood
Rake Farm
Stannally Naze
Stannally Farm
Clough Scout Farm
Whirlaw Stones
Whirlaw Common
Wickenbury Clough
Killup Farm
Butts
Hollinroyd Farm
Great House
Kitson Wood Tunnel
Pennant
Greenhurst Hey
East Hey Head Farm
Law Hill
Swallowshaw
Dungeon Wood
West Whirlaw
East Whirlaw Farm
Cally Hall Farm
West Hey Head Farm
Spring Wood
Stansfield Villa
Harley Wood
Bank Ho.
Lower Wickenberry
Wickenberry
Broad Ing Top Farm
Higher Ashes Farm
Great House Clough
BURNLEY ROAD
LYDGATE
Latchford
Ridge Wood
Ratcher Rock
Butt Stones
Hanging Field Farm
Fairway
Lower Ashes Farm
Rodwell Head
Scaitcliffe Bridge
Scaitcliffe
Hole Bottom
Hole Bottom Delph
TODMORDEN GOLF COURSE
Scaitcliffe Hall
A646
Oak Hill
Cross Gap
Scaitcliffe Clough
Scaitcliffe Wood
Todmorden High Sch.
Ferney Lee Prim. Sch.
Durn Cottage
Cross Stone
Grave Yard
Hollin Hall
Flailcroft
Club Ho. (Rive Rocks)
The Mount
Bean Hole Fm.
Beech House
Hill House
Lad Stones
Woodleigh Hall
Todmorden Sports Centre
Castle Street
Cinder Hill
Ewood Hall
Bandstand
Stansfield Hall
Priestwell
Castle Hill
River Calder
War Memorial
Todmorden Edge
Ewood Wood
Crazy Golf Course
CENTRE VALE PARK
HALIFAX ROAD
30
ROAD
Rochdale Canal
Cricket Grd.
Hall Royd Junction
A646
Factory
Woodhouse Mill Bridge
Todmorden Edge South Farm
Buckley Wood
Todmorden's Log Sculptures
Todmorden Junction
Bus Dpt.
Millwood
DOGHOUSE LANE
High Barn
The Ridge
Bus Sta.
Brookfield Farm
Old Royd Lock
Oldroyd
Hall Wood
Todmorden
Toy Mus.
Art Gall.
Thtre.
Oldroyd Farm
Mankinholes Tops
Super store
Baltimore Bri.
Edge End Farm
Pavilion
Playing Fields
Jones Grange Farm
Castle Cotts.
Dobroyd Clough
Salford
Longfield Wood
Kilnhurst
Kilnhurst Wood
Bird Bank Wood
Play. Fld.
Lumbutts Clough
Doroad Scout
Ping Hold
Hall Wood
TODMORDEN
Swiss Cott.
Higher Longfield Farm
Model Farm
Playing Fields
Superstore
Reservoir (cov.)
Ingham Wood
Top of Brink Farm
Centre Hill
The Drive
Shoebroad Farm
Middle Longfield Farm
Causeway Wood
Stones Farm
Pex House
Shoebroad Dam
Lower Longfield Farm
Lumbutts
A6033
Friends' Burial Ground
Longfield Stables
Croft Farm
Causeway Farm
Watty Farm
Shade
Swineshead Clough
Friths Farm
Croft Gate
Mill Dam
A681
Gauxholme
ROCHDALE ROAD
Lower Swineshead
Swines-head
Heyhead Farm
Croft Carr
Jack Lee Gate
Dulesgate Water
Dean Farm
No Man's Wood
LUMBUTTS ROAD
Hill Stones
Lower Horsewood Cottage
Hey Head Green
Higher Lee
Knowl Wood
Top o' th' Rough
Jail Springs
Horsewood
Shurcrack
Middle Horse Wood Farm
G
H
J
K
113
L
M
N
Hollow Dean Farm
Lower Knowl
Higher Knowl
Lower Horsewood Farm
Naze
Higher Horse
94

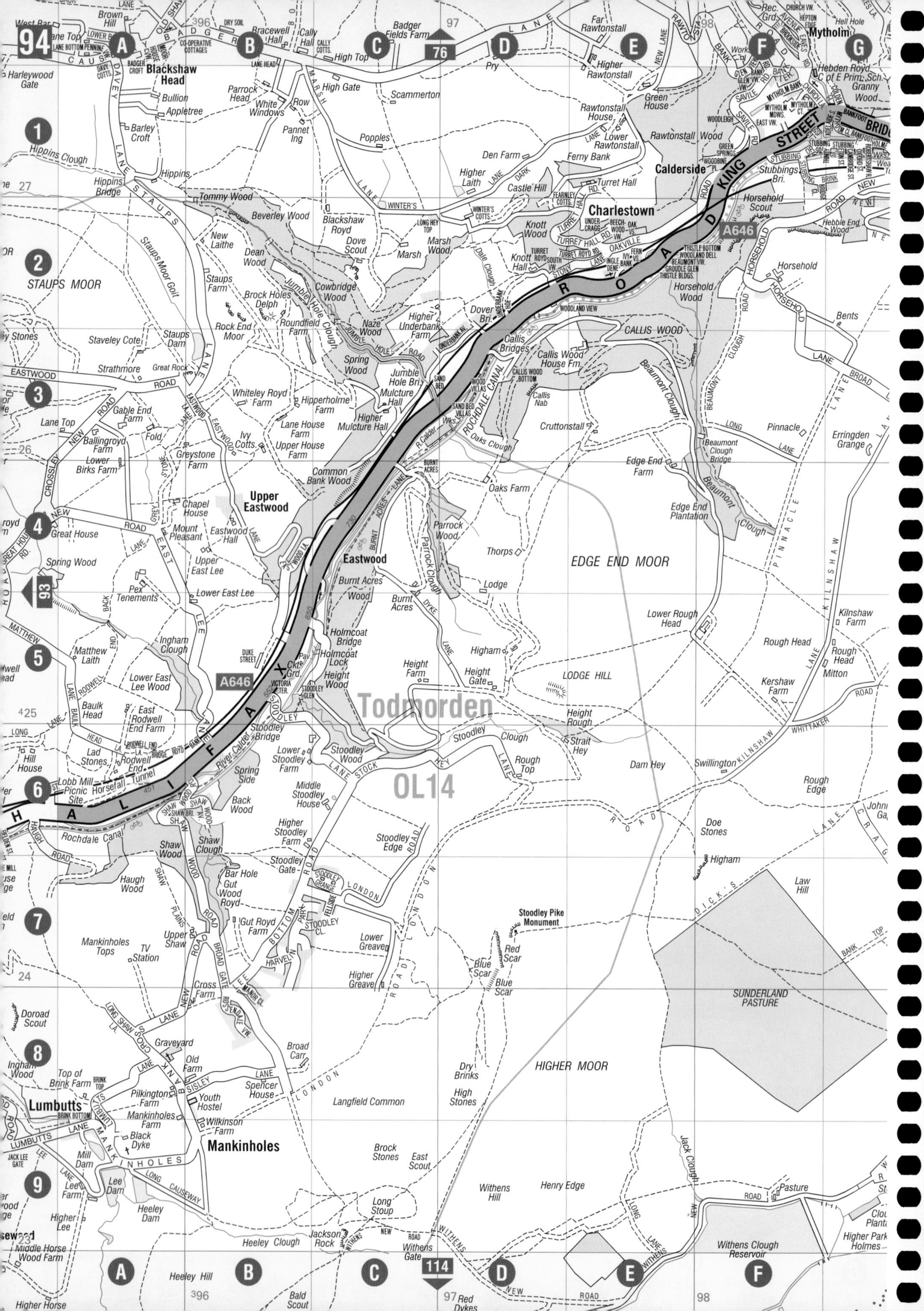
94
Blackshaw Head
Mytholm
Calderside
Charlestown
Todmorden
OL14
Eastwood
Upper Eastwood
Lumbutts
Mankinholes
STAUPS MOOR
EDGE END MOOR
LODGE HILL
HIGHER MOOR
SUNDERLAND PASTURE
Stoodley Pike Monument
Langfield Common
Withens Clough Reservoir
Rochdale Canal
River Calder
A646
HALIFAX ROAD
KING STREET
76
93
114
Callis Wood
Horsehold
Hebden Royd C of E Prim. Sch.
Youth Hostel
TV Station
Higher Rawtonstall
Rawtonstall Wood
Beverley Wood
Jumble Hole Clough
Beaumont Clough
Kilnshaw Farm
Rough Head
Mitton
Erringden Grange
Pinnacle
Stoodley Edge
Lower Greave
Higher Greave
Blue Scar
Red Scar
Henry Edge
Withens Hill
Jack Clough
Heeley Dam
Lee Dam
Heeley Clough
Jackson Rock
Withens Gate
Long Stoup
Doe Stones
Law Hill
Dam Hey
Swillington
Rough Edge
Higham
Thorps
Lodge
Edge End Farm
Edge End Plantation
Cruttonstall
Oaks Farm
Holmcoat Bridge
Spring Wood
Great House
Staups Dam
Staveley Cote
Strathmore
Hippins Bridge
Hippins Clough
Tommy Wood
Harleywood Gate
Doroad Scout
Ingham Wood
Black Dyke
Mill Dam
Higher Lee
Middle Horse Wood Farm
Higher Horse
Heeley Hill
Bald Scout
Red Dykes

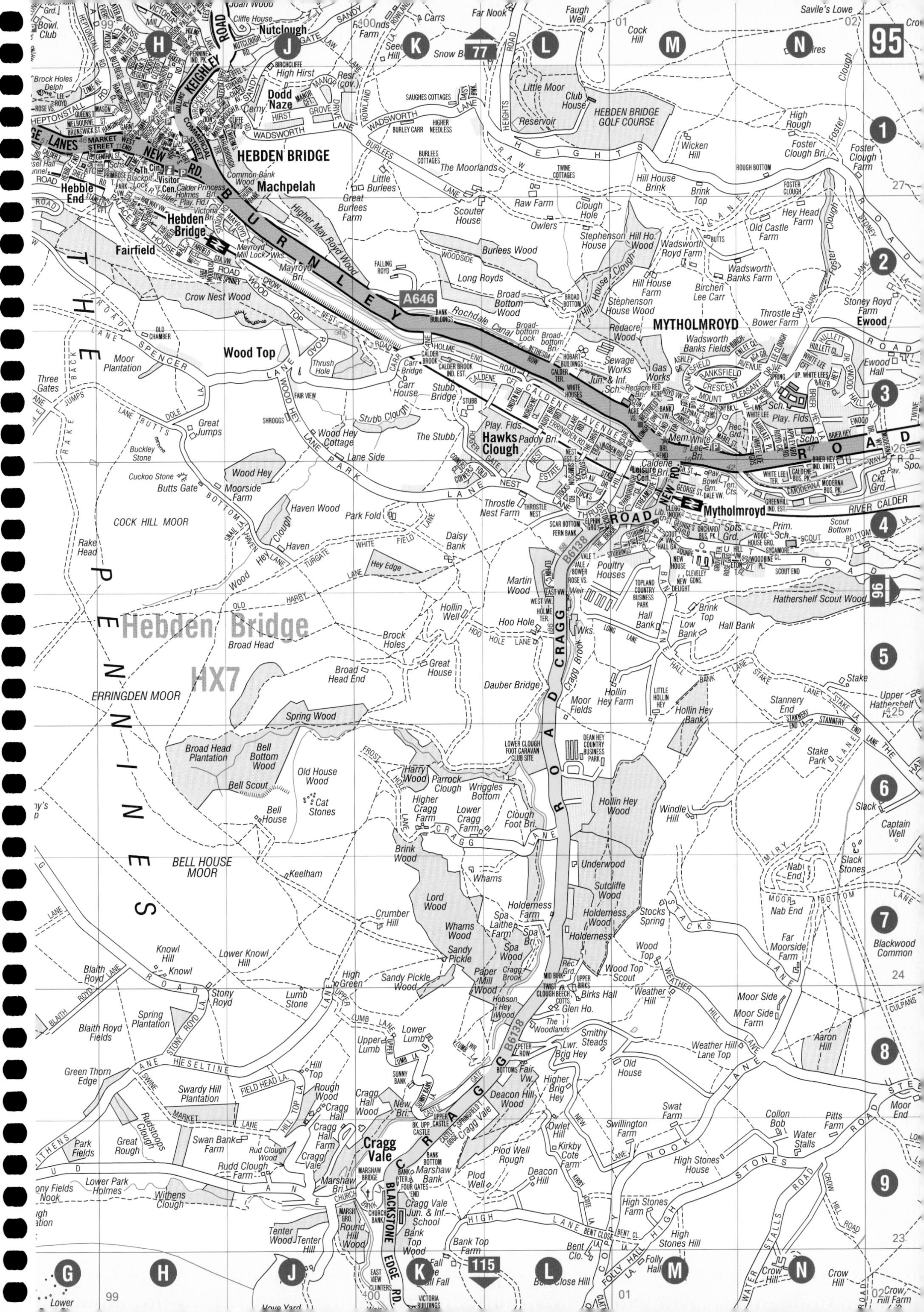

HEBDEN BRIDGE
Hebden Bridge
HX7
MYTHOLMROYD
Mytholmroyd
Machpelah
Nutclough
Dodd Naze
Hebble End
Fairfield
Wood Top
Cragg Vale
Hawks Clough
Ewood
THE PENNINES
A646
B6138
BURNLEY ROAD
CRAGG ROAD
KEIGHLEY ROAD
NEW RD.
Rochdale Canal
RIVER CALDER
HEBDEN BRIDGE GOLF COURSE
Crow Nest Wood
COCK HILL MOOR
ERRINGDEN MOOR
BELL HOUSE MOOR
Broad Head
Spring Wood
Broad Head Plantation
Bell Bottom Wood
Bell Scout
Cat Stones
Old House Wood
Hathershelf Scout Wood
Hollin Hey Wood
Underwood
Sutcliffe Wood
Holderness Wood
Lord Wood
Whams Wood
Sandy Pickle
Paper Mill Wood
Deacon Hill Wood
Little Moor
Reservoir
Club House
High Rough
Foster Clough Bri.
Wicken Hill
Hill House Brink
Brink Top
Raw Farm
Clough Hole
Owlers
Scouter House
Burlees Wood
Long Royds
Broad Bottom Wood
Stephenson House Wood
Redacre Wood
Wadsworth Royd Farm
Wadsworth Banks Farm
Birchen Lee Carr
Throstle Bower Farm
Stoney Royd Farm
Ewood Hall
Moor Plantation
Three Gates
Great Jumps
Buckley Stone
Cuckoo Stone
Butts Gate
Wood Hey
Moorside Farm
Haven Wood
Haven
Rake Head
Park Fold
Daisy Bank
Hey Edge
Martin Wood
Hollin Well
Hoo Hole
Brock Holes
Great House
Broad Head End
Dauber Bridge
Moor Fields
Hollin Hey Farm
Hall Bank
Low Bank
Poultry Houses
Stake
Upper Hathershelf
Stannery End
Stake Park
Slack
Captain Well
Slack Stones
Nab End
Far Moorside Farm
Blackwood Common
Stocks Spring
Wood Top Scout
Weather Hill
Moor Side Farm
Aaron Hill
Weather Hill Lane Top
Old House
Swat Farm
Collon Bob
Pitts Farm
Water Stalls
Moor End
Swillington Farm
High Stones House
High Stones Farm
High Stones Hill
Folly Hall
Crow Hill
Crow Hill Farm
Bent Clo.
Bent Close Hill
Kirkby Cote Farm
Owlet Hill
Higher Brig Hey
Lwr. Brig Hey
Smithy Steads
Glen Ho.
Birks Hall
Plod Well Rough
Plod Well
Deacon Hill
Marshaw Bank
Bank Top Wood
Bank Top Farm
Round Hill Wood
Tenter Wood
Tenter Hill
Cragg Vale Jun. & Inf. School
Marshaw Bri.
Cragg Hall Farm
Cragg Hall
Rough Wood
Hill Top
Lower Lumb
Upper Lumb
Lumb Stone
High Green
Sandy Pickle Wood
Crumber Hill
Keelham
Knowl Hill
Knowl
Lower Knowl Hill
Stony Royd
Blaith Royd
Blaith Royd Fields
Spring Plantation
Green Thorn Edge
Swardy Hill Plantation
Rudstops Clough
Park Fields
Great Rough
Swan Bank Farm
Rudd Clough Farm
Lower Park Holmes
Withens Clough
Harry Wood
Parrock Clough
Wriggles Bottom
Higher Cragg Farm
Lower Cragg Farm
Clough Foot Bri.
Brink Wood
Whams
Holderness Farm
Spa Laithe Farm
Spa Wood
Spa Bri.
Hobson Hey Wood
The Woodlands
Lane Side
Wood Hey Cottage
Stubb Clough
The Stubb
Stubb Bridge
Carr House
Carr Bridge
Thrush Hole
Sewage Works
Gas Works
Throstle Nest Farm
Leisure Cen.
Sch.
Play. Flds.
Far Nook
Faugh Well
Cock Hill
Savile's Lowe
Carrs
Snow B
Seed Hill
High Hirst
Little Burlees
Great Burlees Farm
The Moorlands
Mayroyd Bri.
Mayroyd Mill Lock
Calder Princess Bri.
Visitor Cen.
Lower
Hove Yard
Fall
Fall Fall
Bank
Knowl
G
H
J
K
L
M
N
1
2
3
4
5
6
7
8
9
77
96
115
99
400
01
02
27
26
24
23
425

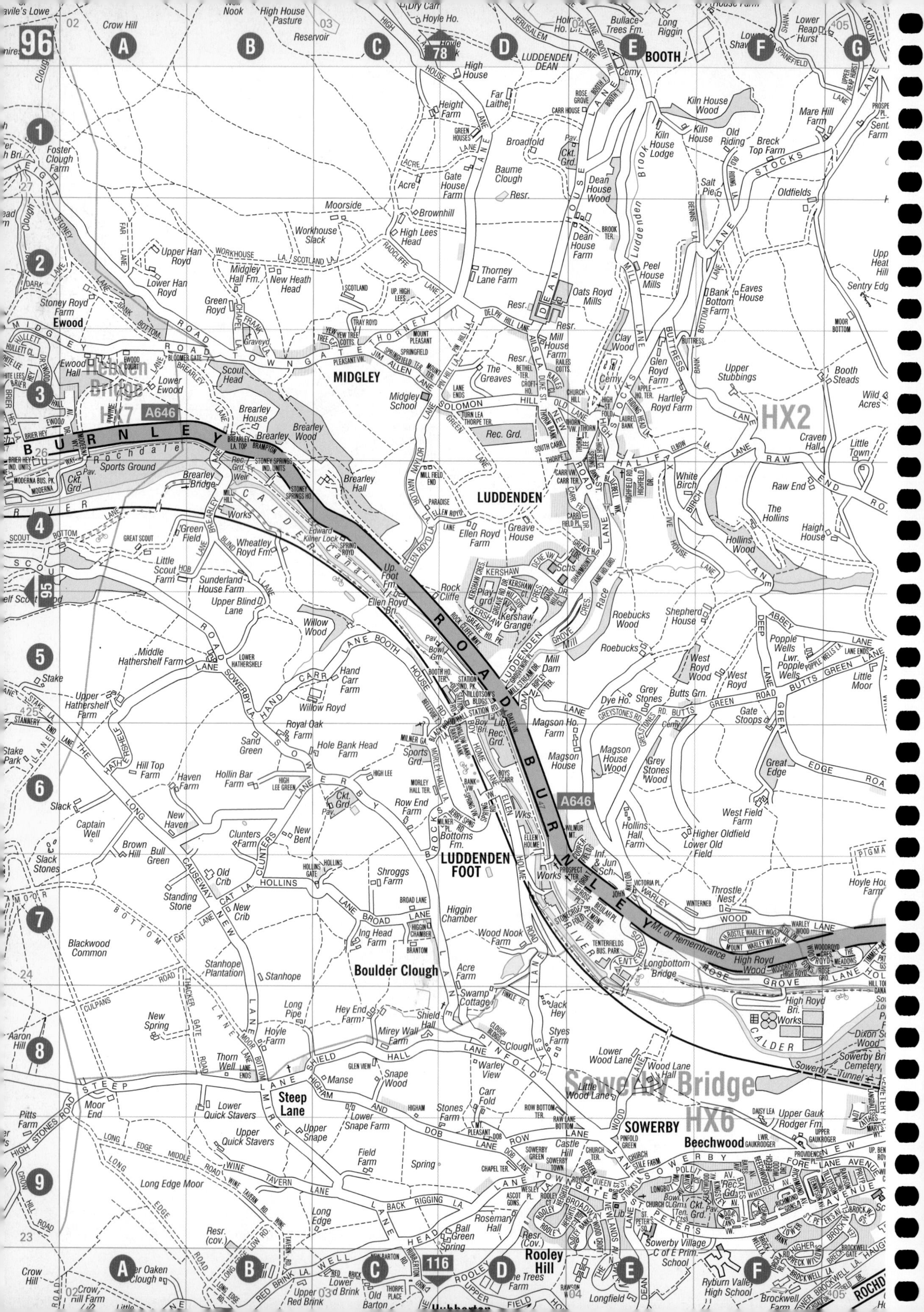

Crow Hill
High House Pasture
Reservoir
Dry Carr
Hoyle Ho.
78
Holme Ho.
Bullace Trees Fm.
Long Riggin
Lower Reap Hurst
Lower Shaw
LUDDENDEN DEAN
BOOTH
Foster Clough Farm
High House
Far Laithe
Height Farm
Kiln House Wood
Kiln House
Kiln House Lodge
Mare Hill Farm
Old Riding
Breck Top Farm
Broadfold
Ckt. Grd.
Baume Clough
Resr.
Acre
Gate House Farm
Dean House Wood
Salt Pie
Oldfields
Moorside
Brownhill
Workhouse Slack
High Lees Head
Dean House Farm
Upper Han Royd
Lower Han Royd
Midgley Hall Fm.
New Heath Head
Thorney Lane Farm
Peel House Mills
Bank Bottom Farm
Eaves House
Sentry Edge
Stoney Royd Farm
Ewood
Green Royd
Oats Royd Mills
Resr.
Clay Wood
Mill House Farm
Glen Royd Farm
Upper Stubbings
Booth Steads
Ewood Hall
Hebden Bridge
HX7
A646
Scout Head
Lower Ewood
MIDGLEY
Midgley School
The Greaves
Cemy.
Hartley Royd Farm
HX2
Wild Acres
Brearley House
Brearley Wood
Rec. Grd.
Craven Hall
Little Town
BURNLEY ROAD
Rochdale
Sports Ground
Brearley Bridge
Brearley Hall
LUDDENDEN
White Birch
Raw End
The Hollins
Haigh House
Hollins Wood
Works
Green Field
Wheatley Royd Fm.
Edward Kilner Lock
Up. Foot Fm.
Ellen Royd Farm
Greave House
Little Scout Farm
Sunderland House Farm
Upper Blind Lane
95
Rock Cliffe
Ellen Royd Bri.
Play grd.
Kershaw Grange
Roebucks Wood
Shepherd House
Willow Wood
Middle Hathershelf Farm
Hand Carr Farm
Mill Dam
Roebucks
Popple Wells
Lwr. Popple Wells
West Royd Wood
West Royd
Little Moor
Stake
Upper Hathershelf Farm
Willow Royd
Grey Stones
Butts Grn.
Dye Ho.
Gate Stoops
Royal Oak Farm
Sand Green
Hole Bank Head Farm
Sports Grd.
Rec. Grd.
Magson Ho. Farm
Magson House
Magson House Wood
Grey Stones Wood
Great Edge
Stake Park
Hill Top Farm
Haven Farm
Hollin Bar Farm
Ckt. Grd.
Row End Farm
A646
West Field Farm
Slack
New Haven
Captain Well
Clunters Farm
New Bent
Bottoms Fm.
Wks.
Hollins Hall Farm
Higher Oldfield
Lower Old Field
Brown Hill
Bull Green
Slack Stones
Old Crib
Shroggs Farm
LUDDENDEN FOOT
Inf. & Jun Sch.
Works
Hoyle House Farm
Standing Stone
New Crib
Higgin Chamber
Throstle Nest
Ing Head Farm
Wood Nook Farm
Mt. of Remembrance
High Royd Wood
Blackwood Common
Longbottom Bridge
Stanhope Plantation
Stanhope
Boulder Clough
Acre Farm
Swamp Cottage
High Royd Bri.
Works
New Spring
Long Pipe
Hey End Farm
Shield Hall
Jack Hey
Aaron Hill
Hoyle Farm
Mirey Wall Farm
Clough
Styes Farm
Dixon Scar Wood
Thorn Well
Warley View
Lower Wood Lane
Wood Lane Hall
Sowerby Bridge Cemetery
Sowerby Tunnel
Moor End
Lower Quick Stavers
Manse
Snape Wood
Steep Lane
Carr Fold
Little Wood Lane
Sowerby Bridge
Pitts Farm
Stones Farm
SOWERBY
HX6
Upper Gauk Rodger Fm.
Upper Quick Stavers
Upper Snape
Lower Snape Farm
Beechwood
Field Farm
Castle Hill
Spring
Long Edge Moor
Ckt. Grd.
Long Edge
Rosemary Hall
Resr. (cov.)
Ball Green
Spring
Sowerby Village C of E Prim. School
Resr. (Cov.)
Rooley Hill
Ryburn Valley High School
Crow Hill
Lower Oaken Clough
Crow Hill Farm
Upper Red Brink
Lower Brink
Old Barton
116
Pine Trees Farm
Longfield
Brockwell
RIVER CALDER
Calder and Hebble Canal

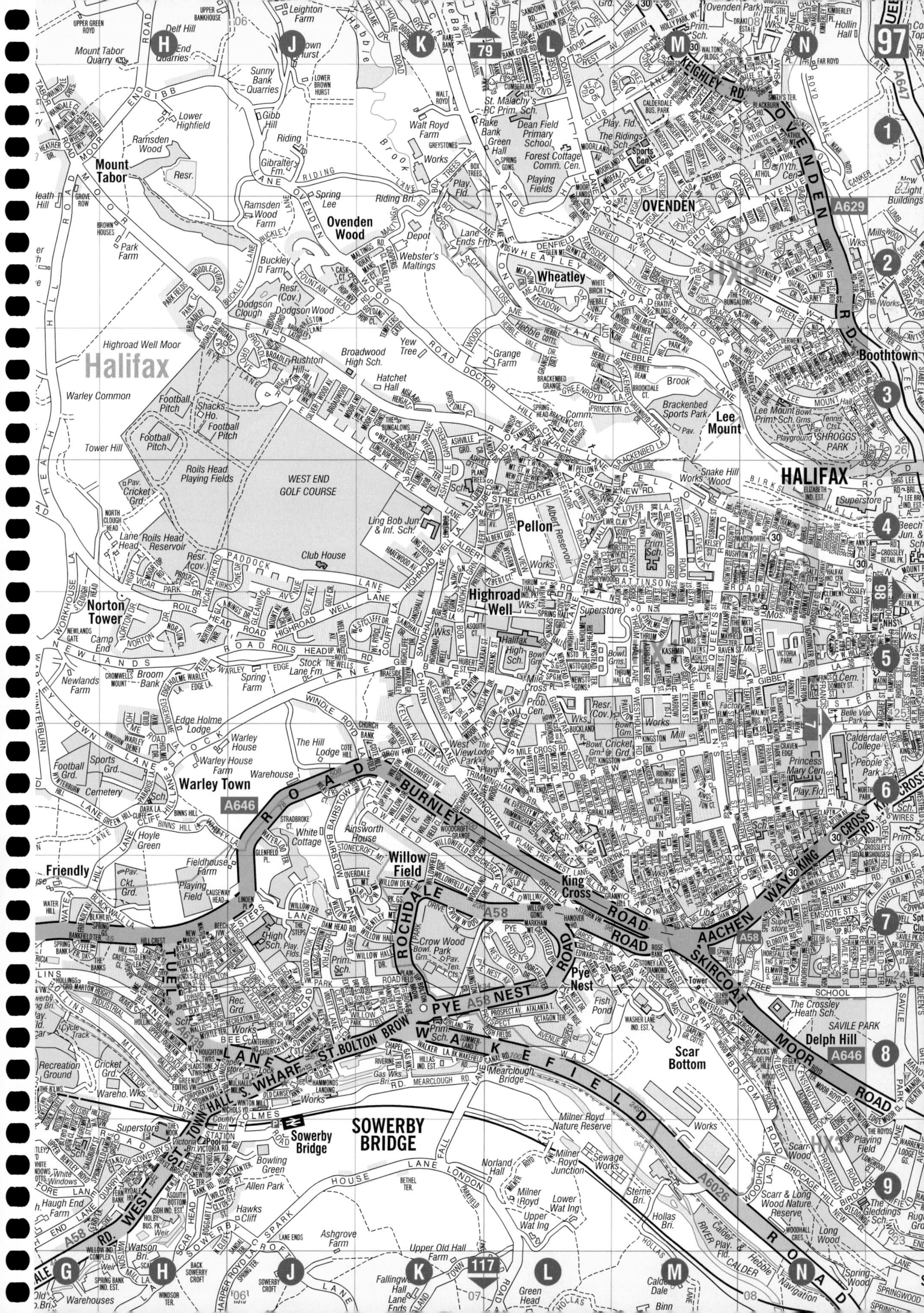

Mount Tabor
Halifax
Highroad Well Moor
Warley Common
Ovenden Wood
Ovenden
Wheatley
Boothtown
Lee Mount
HALIFAX
Pellon
Highroad Well
West End Golf Course
Norton Tower
Warley Town
Friendly
Willow Field
King Cross
Pye Nest
Scar Bottom
Delph Hill
Sowerby Bridge
SOWERBY BRIDGE
Halifax High Sch.
Calderdale College
People's Park
Albert Reservoir
Roils Head Reservoir
Brackenbed Sports Park
Shroggs Park
Savile Park
The Crossley Heath Sch.
Milner Royd Nature Reserve
Scarr & Long Wood Nature Reserve
Norland Hall
Milner Royd Junction
Allen Park
Hawks Cliff
Ashgrove Farm
Upper Old Hall Farm
Green Head
Calder Dale
A629
A646
A58
A6026
A647
79
117
96
7

Pule Hill
Woodlands
Boothtown
Akroydon
HALIFAX
Wood-side
Dean Clough
NORTHOWRAM
Stump Cross
Claremount
Shibden Park
Shibden Hall
Halifax
HX3
Bank Top
Caddy Field
Stoney Royd
Savile Pk.
Delph Hill
SOUTHOWRAM
Siddal
Skircoat Green
Salterhebble
Dam Head
Calderdale Royal Hospital
The Halifax Ski & Snowboarding Centre
Eureka! (Children's Mus.)
FC Halifax Town & Halifax RLFC (The Shay)
Manor Heath Park & Jungle Experience
A629
A647
A58
A6036
A646
BOOTHTOWN ROAD
GODLEY LANE
LEEDS BRADFORD ROAD
SKIRCOAT MOOR ROAD
HUDDERSFIELD ROAD
SKIRCOAT ROAD
BURDOCK WAY
HALEY HILL
NEW BANK

80
97
118

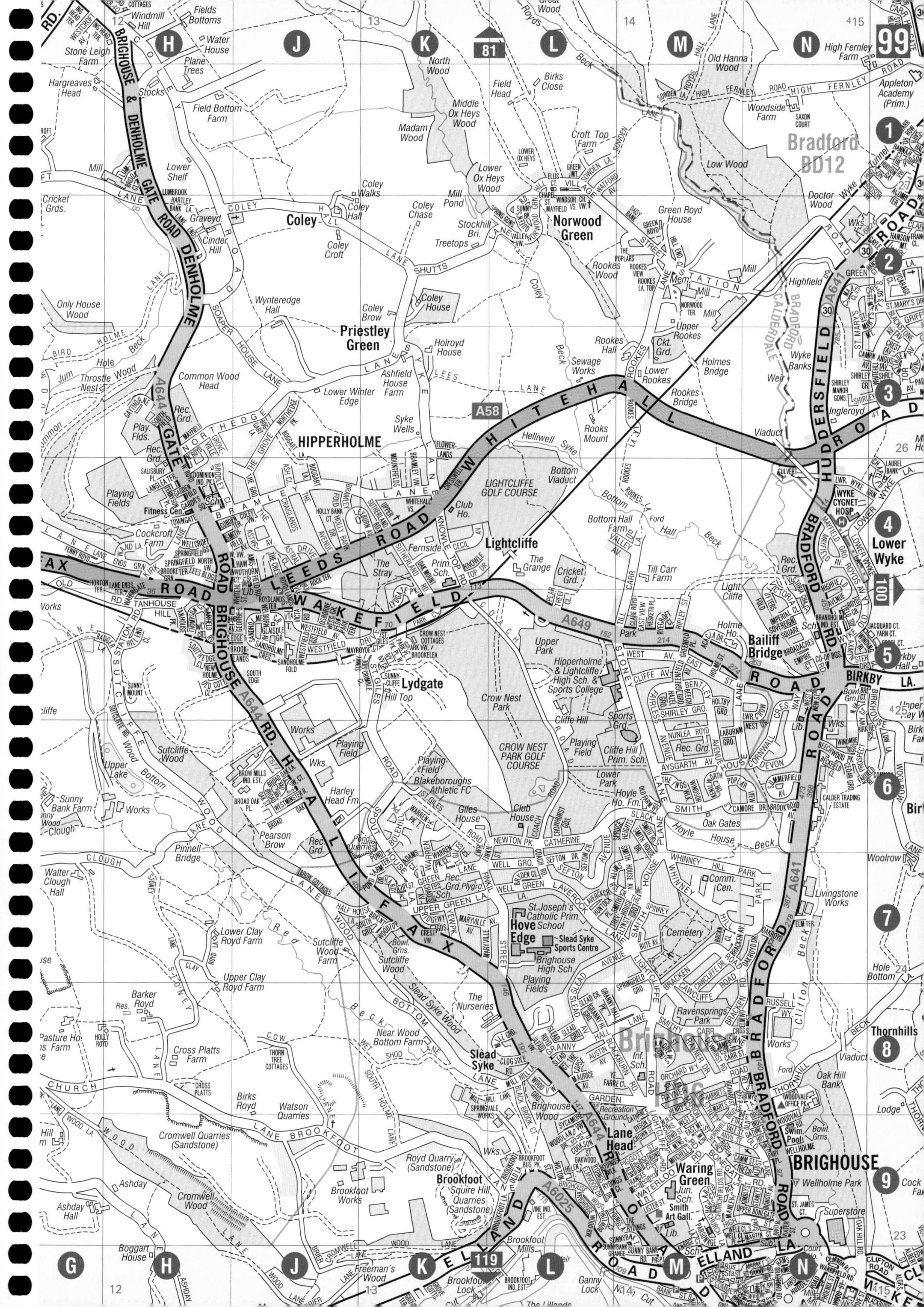

81
100
119
Coley
Priestley Green
HIPPERHOLME
Norwood Green
Lightcliffe
Lydgate
Bailiff Bridge
Lower Wyke
Hove Edge
Slead Syke
Lane Head
Waring Green
Brookfoot
BRIGHOUSE
Bradford BD12
Stone Leigh Farm
Hargreaves Head
Windmill Hill
Fields Bottoms
Water House
Plane Trees
Stocks
Field Bottom Farm
Lower Shelf
Graveyd.
Cinder Hill
Coley Walks
Coley Hall
Coley Chase
Coley Croft
North Wood
Middle Ox Heys Wood
Madam Wood
Lower Ox Heys Wood
Mill Pond
Stockhill Bri.
Treetops
Field Head
Birks Close
Croft Top Farm
Old Hanna Wood
High Fernley Farm
Appleton Academy (Prim.)
Woodside Farm
Low Wood
Doctor Wood
Green Royd House
Rookes Wood
Highfield
Wynteredge Hall
Coley Brow
Coley House
Holroyd House
Only House Wood
Common Wood Head
Ashfield House Farm
Lower Winter Edge
Syke Wells
Upper Rookes
Rookes Hall
Sewage Works
Lower Rookes
Holmes Bridge
Rookes Bridge
Wyke Banks
Ingleroyd
Rooks Mount
Helliwell Syke
Bottom Viaduct
LIGHTCLIFFE GOLF COURSE
Bottom Hall Farm
Till Carr Farm
Playing Fields
Fitness Cen.
Cockcroft Farm
Tanhouse Hill
The Stray
The Grange
Upper Park
Hipperholme & Lightcliffe High Sch. & Sports College
Crow Nest Park
CROW NEST PARK GOLF COURSE
Cliffe Hill
Cliffe Hill Prim. Sch.
Lower Park
Hoyle Ho. Fm.
Oak Gates
Holme Ho.
Light Cliffe
Sutcliffe Wood
Upper Lake
Sunny Bank Farm
Pinnell Bridge
Walter Clough Hall
Harley Head Fm.
Blakeboroughs Athletic FC
Giles House
Club House
Pearson Brow
Lower Clay Royd Farm
Upper Clay Royd Farm
Sutcliffe Wood Farm
St.Joseph's Catholic Prim. School
Slead Syke Sports Centre
Brighouse High Sch.
Cemetery
Ravensprings Park
Livingstone Works
Barker Royd
Cross Platts Farm
Near Wood Bottom Farm
The Nurseries
Birks Royd
Watson Quarries
Cromwell Quarries (Sandstone)
Royd Quarry (Sandstone)
Squire Hill Quarries (Sandstone)
Brookfoot Works
Brookfoot Mills
Cromwell Wood
Ashday Hall
Boggart House
Freeman's Wood
Brookfoot Lock
Ganny Lock
Brighouse Wood
Recreation Ground
Smith Art Gall.
Wellholme Park
Superstore
Oak Hill Bank
Thornhills
Hole Bottom
Woolrow
Calder Trading Estate
WHITEHALL ROAD
LEEDS ROAD
WAKEFIELD ROAD
HALIFAX ROAD
BRIGHOUSE & DENHOLME GATE ROAD
HUDDERSFIELD ROAD
BRADFORD ROAD
ELLAND ROAD
BIRKBY LA.
A58
A644
A649
A641
A6025

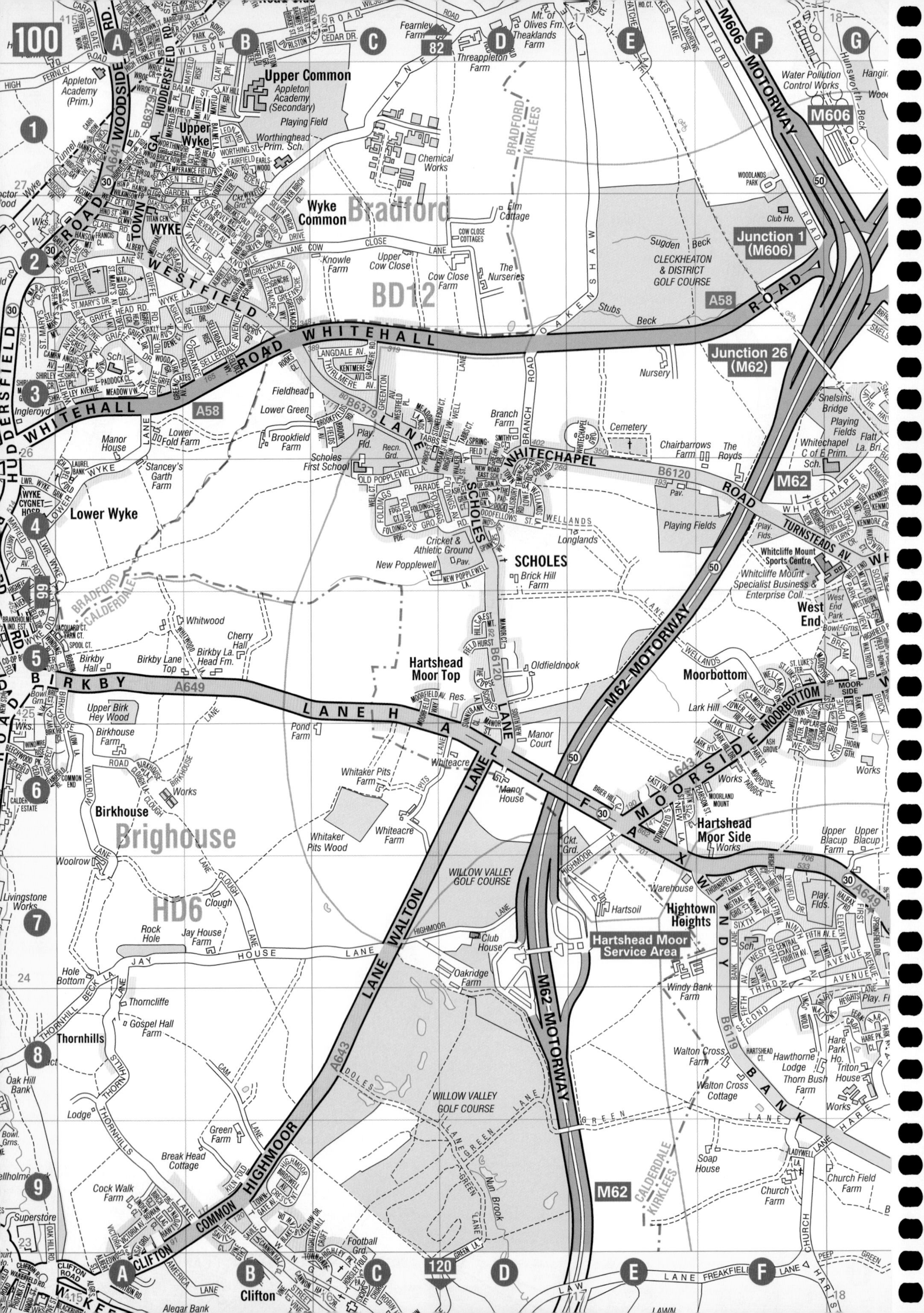
A
B
C
D
E
F
G
82
Upper Common
Appleton Academy (Prim.)
Appleton Academy (Secondary)
Playing Field
Worthinghead Prim. Sch.
Upper Wyke
Fearnley Farm
Threappleton Farm
Mt. of Olives Fm.
Theaklands Farm
Chemical Works
Water Pollution Control Works
M606
MOTORWAY
Hunsworth Beck
BRADFORD
KIRKLEES
WOODLANDS PARK
Club Ho.
Wyke Common
Bradford
Elm Cottage
WYKE
COW CLOSE COTTAGES
Junction 1 (M606)
Sugden Beck
CLECKHEATON & DISTRICT GOLF COURSE
Knowle Farm
Upper Cow Close
Cow Close Farm
The Nurseries
BD12
A58
Stubs Beck
WESTFIELD
WHITEHALL ROAD
Junction 26 (M62)
Nursery
Snelsins Bridge
Playing Fields
Flatt La. Bri.
Whitechapel C of E Prim. Sch.
HUDDERSFIELD
Ingleroyd
Fieldhead
Lower Green
Branch Farm
Cemetery
Chairbarrows Farm
The Royds
Manor House
Lower Fold Farm
Brookfield Farm
Play. Fld.
Recn. Grd.
Scholes First School
WHITECHAPEL
B6120
ROAD
M62
Stancey's Garth Farm
Pav.
Playing Fields
TURNSTEADS AV.
Lower Wyke
SCHOLES
Longlands
Cricket & Athletic Ground
New Popplewell
Brick Hill Farm
Whitcliffe Mount Sports Centre
Whitcliffe Mount Specialist Business & Enterprise Coll.
West End
BRADFORD
CALDERDALE
Whitwood
Cherry Hall
Birkby Hall
Birkby Lane Top
Birkby La. Head Fm.
Hartshead Moor Top
Oldfieldnook
Moorbottom
BIRKBY LANE
A649
HALIFAX
Upper Birk Hey Wood
Birkhouse Farm
Pond Farm
Res.
Manor Court
Lark Hill
MOORBOTTOM
Whiteacre
Whitaker Pits Farm
Manor House
Works
MOORSIDE
Birkhouse
Brighouse
Whitaker Pits Wood
Whiteacre Farm
Hartshead Moor Side
Upper Blacup Farm
Upper Blacup
Woolrow
WILLOW VALLEY GOLF COURSE
Ckt. Grd.
Warehouse
Livingstone Works
HD6
Clough
Hartsoil
Hightown Heights
Play. Flds.
Rock Hole
Jay House Farm
JAY HOUSE LANE
Club House
Hartshead Moor Service Area
Hole Bottom
Oakridge Farm
Windy Bank Farm
Thorncliffe
Gospel Hall Farm
Thornhills
Oak Hill Bank
Walton Cross Farm
Hartshead Ct.
Hawthorne Lodge
Hare Park Ho.
Triton House
Thorn Bush Farm
Walton Cross Cottage
Lodge
WILLOW VALLEY GOLF COURSE
WALTON LANE
A643
M62 MOTORWAY
WINDY BANK
B6119
Green Farm
Break Head Cottage
Soap House
Cock Walk Farm
HIGHMOOR LANE
CLIFTON COMMON
Mun Brook
M62
CALDERDALE
KIRKLEES
Church Farm
Church Field Farm
Superstore
Football Grd.
120
Clifton
Alegar Bank
FREAKFIELD LANE
1
2
3
4
5
6
7
8
9
99

M62 MOTORWAY
WEST ROAD
WHITEHALL RD.
HUNSWORTH
Hunsworth Great Wood
Hunsworth Little Wood
Hunsworth Lodge Farm
Savile Arms Farm
Lodge Farm
Lodge Garage
Lower Lodge Range
Canary Hall
Field Head Farm
Swincliffe
Bbg Academy
BD11
Birksland Moor
Wheatleys Farm
The Wheatleys
Brecks Farm
Oakwell Hall Country Park
Sewage Works
Holme House
Thorn Hill Knowls
West House
Drub
Primrose Hill
Owlett Hall Farm
Mazebrook
Cleckheaton
BD19
Merchant Fields
Merchant Fields Farm
Scandinavia Mills
Hunsworth Bri.
Lands Farm
Upper Brook House
Round Hill
Lanes Wood
Latham Farm
Nursery
Bawson Cliffe
Gomersal Hall
Gomersal Prim. School
Birdacre
Pollard Hall
Gomersal C of E Middle School
Church Wood
Church Farm
MONK INGS
WF17
Moorend
CLECKHEATON
Egypt
Roundhill Mills
Firdene
Fusden Wood
Tannery
Gomersal Hill Top
CHURCH LANE
MUFFIT LA.
GOMERSAL
Popeley Farm
POPELEY FIELDS
102
WHITCLIFFE RD.
SPEN LA.
Spen Hall
Spen Lower
Royds Hill
Royds Farm
Rec. Ground
Moorgate
Moorfields
St. Peg Bridge
Mount Pleasant Farm
WESTGATE
DEWSBURY RD.
BRADFORD RD.
Howard Park Sch.
Gomersal House
Listing Mill Cottages
Stubley Farm
Castle House
Castle Hill
Marsh
Lower Blacup
Royds Park
Football Grd.
Spen Pyenot Hall Bridge
Rawfolds
Primrose Hill Farm
Princess Mary Stadium
Spenborough Pool
Littletown
Hightown
Lawnbank
Springfield Farm
King George V Play. Fld.
Rugby Football Grd.
Miniature Golf Course
Primrose Lane Bridge
Knowler Hill
Mill Bridge
Lower Popeley
Westfield
HECKMONDWIKE
Clough Beck
Croft Farm
Upper House Farm
Headlands C of E Jun. & Inf. Sch.
Liversedge
WF15
LIVERSEDGE
Spa Pump Beck
Triangle Farm
Bullace Trees Farm
Playing Fields
Spen Valley Sports College
Algernon Firth Park
Flush
HUDDERSFIELD ROAD
Cemetery
Moorside
Old Hall Farm
Pogg Myres
Smithy Hill
Hartshead Jun.& Inf.
121
83
G H J K L M N

M62 MOTORWAY
Oakwell
Oakwell Hall
Oakwell Hall Country Park
Sewage Works
Oakwell House
Fieldhead Farm
Fieldhead Jun. & Inf. School
Holly View Farm
Foxhall Farm
Springwell Farm
OAKWELL INDUSTRIAL PARK
Showcase Cinema
CENTRE 27 BUSINESS PARK
HOWDEN CLOUGH INDUSTRIAL ESTATE
OAKWELL INDUSTRIAL ESTATE
Howden Clough
HOWDEN CLOUGH ROAD
Howden Clough Farm
Birkby Brow Wood
Boggard Fields
Rods Wood
Cliff Wood
Still House
St. Patrick's Catholic Prim. Sch.
FAIRWAY INDUSTRIAL PARK
Copley Hill
BIRSTALL
Old Hall
DW Fitness Club
Batley Sports & Ten. Cen.
Batley Girls High School
Brownhill Inf. Sch. & St. Saviour's C of E Jun. Sch.
Nook
Brownhill End
Sugar Hill
Brown Hill
Brookroyd
Little Wood
Bagshaw Museum
Wilton Park
Observatory
Conservation Greenhouse
Reservoir (covered)
Upper Batley
Batley
Batley Hall
Elmwood House
Croft House Farm
Playing Fields
Batley Grammar Sch.
Boating Park
WF17
BD19
Birstall Smithies
Smithies Moor
Cricket Ground
Ridings Wood
Park Mills
Depot
Popeley Farm
Woodside Farm
POPELEY FIELDS
Church Wood
Church Farm
War. Meml.
HUDDERSFIELD ROAD
LEEDS ROAD
BRADFORD ROAD
CHURCH LANE
White Lee
Football Grd.
Carlinghow
Carlinghow Princess Royal Jun. & Inf. Sch.
Fairfield Sch.
Leeside Prim. Sch.
Batley Business & Enterprise College
Lamplands
Stubley Farm
Cross Bank
Field Head Farm
Batley Cemetery
Clerk Green
Healey
Dryfield House (Hostle)
Nunroyd
Westfield
Forrest Hall
Heckmondwyke Sports. Cen.
HEALEY LANE
WEST PARK RD.
Jessop Pk.
Batley Baths
BATLEY
Bank Foot
Staincliffe
Manorfield Inf. Sch.
HALIFAX ROAD
HIGH STREET
Batley Bulldogs RLFC (Mt. Pleasant)
Mount Pleasant
HECKMONDWIKE
Football Ground
Hyrstlands Park
Batley Carr
LONGLANDS CLASSIC
Chapel Fold
DEWSBURY & DISTRICT HOSPITAL
St. Joseph's Catholic Prim. Sch.
SYCAMORE INDUSTRIAL ESTATE
WALKLEY LANE
101
84
122

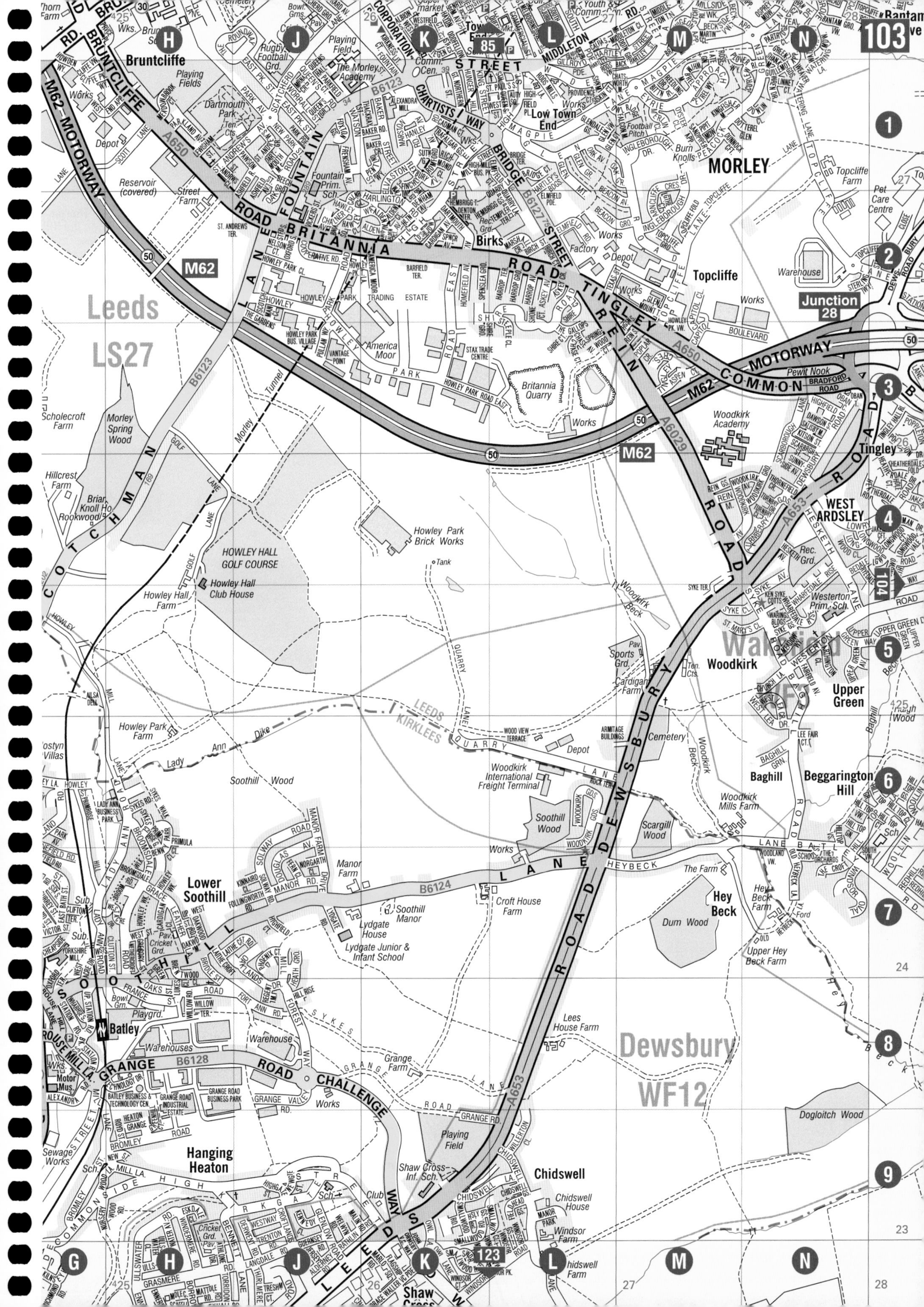
Bruntcliffe
Playing Fields
Dartmouth Park
Reservoir (covered)
Street Farm
M62 MOTORWAY
M62
Leeds
LS27
Rugby Football Grd.
Playing Field
The Morley Academy
Fountain Prim. Sch.
BRITANNIA ROAD
FOUNTAIN
CORPORATION
Comm. Cen.
STREET
CHARTISTS WAY
BRIDGE
Birks
MIDDLETON
Low Town End
MORLEY
Topcliffe Farm
Pet Care Centre
Topcliffe
Warehouse
Junction 28
TINGLEY
COMMON
Pewit Nook
HOWLEY PARK TRADING ESTATE
America Moor
STAX TRADE CENTRE
Britannia Quarry
Woodkirk Academy
Tingley
WEST ARDSLEY
Rec. Grd.
Westerton Prim. Sch.
Scholecroft Farm
Morley Spring Wood
Hillcrest Farm
Briar Knoll Ho.
Rookwood
COTCHMAN
Morley Tunnel
Howley Park Brick Works
HOWLEY HALL GOLF COURSE
Howley Hall Club House
Howley Hall Farm
Howley Park Farm
Lady Ann Dike
Soothill Wood
LEEDS
KIRKLEES
QUARRY
Woodkirk International Freight Terminal
Depot
Cemetery
Sports Grd.
Cardigan Farm
Woodkirk
Wakefield
WF3
Upper Green
Baghill
Beggarington Hill
Woodkirk Mills Farm
Soothill Wood
Scargill Wood
Manor Farm
Lower Soothill
Croft House Farm
Soothill Manor
Lydgate House
Lydgate Junior & Infant School
Hey Beck
Hey Beck Farm
Dum Wood
Upper Hey Beck Farm
Lees House Farm
Dewsbury
WF12
Batley
Warehouse
Warehouses
GRANGE ROAD
CHALLENGE WAY
Grange Farm
Motor Mus.
BATLEY BUSINESS & TECHNOLOGY CEN.
GRANGE ROAD INDUSTRIAL ESTATE
Sewage Works
Hanging Heaton
Playing Field
Shaw Cross Inf. Sch.
Chidswell
Chidswell House
Windsor Farm
Chidswell Farm
Dogloitch Wood
DEWSBURY ROAD
LEEDS ROAD
Shaw Cross
A650
A6029
A653
B6123
B6124
B6127
B6128
85
104
123

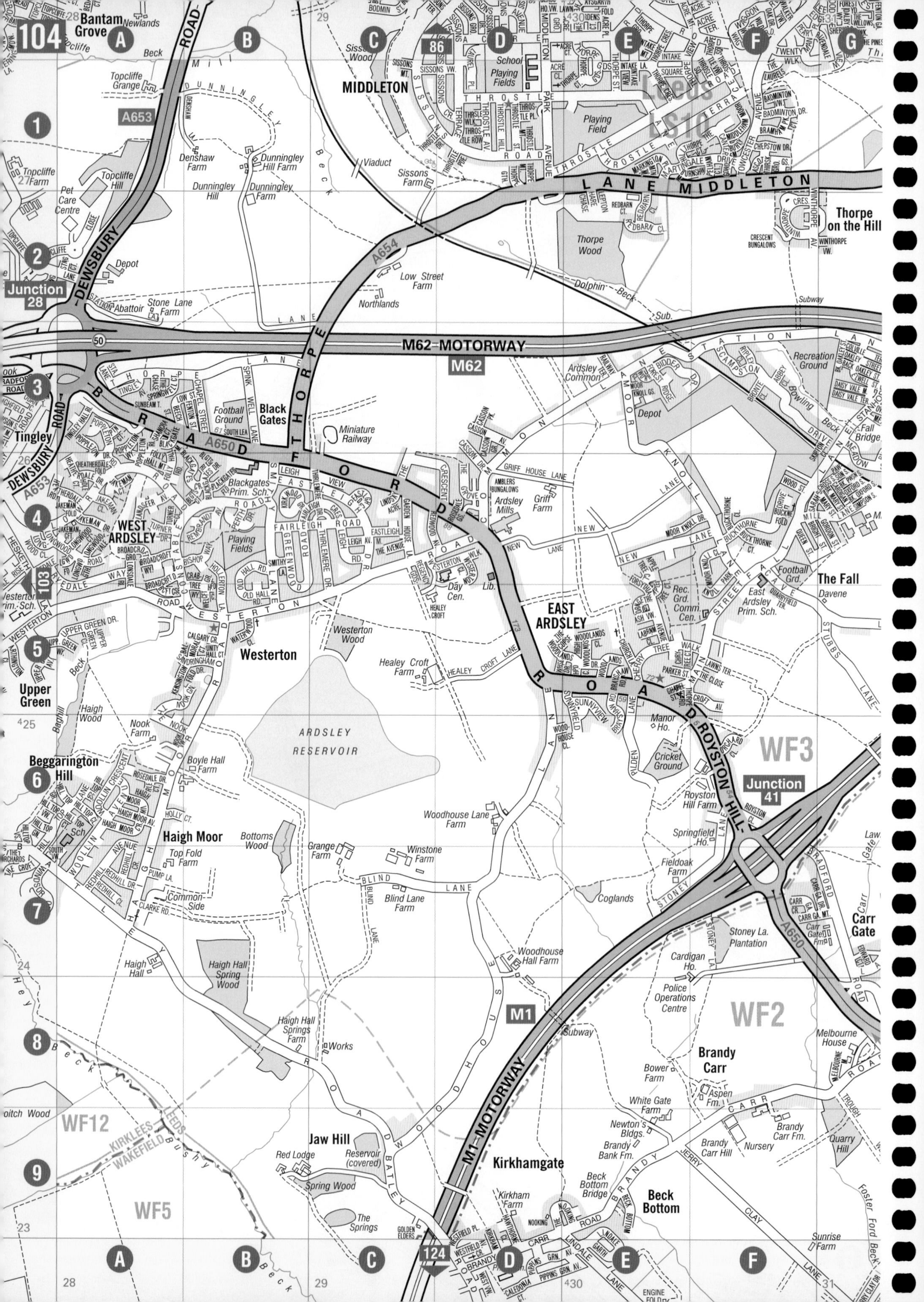

Bantam Grove
Newlands
Topcliffe Grange
MIDDLETON
Sissons Wood
School Playing Fields
Playing Field
Leeds LS10
DEWSBURY ROAD
A653
Denshaw Farm
Dunningley Hill Farm
Dunningley Hill
Dunningley Farm
Viaduct
Sissons Farm
THROSTLE ROAD
LANE MIDDLETON
Thorpe on the Hill
Topcliffe Farm
Topcliffe Hill
Pet Care Centre
Depot
Junction 28
Stone Lane Farm
Abattoir
A654
Low Street Farm
Northlands
Thorpe Wood
Dolphin Beck
Subway
M62 MOTORWAY
M62
Recreation Ground
Ardsley Common
Tingley
Football Ground
Black Gates
Miniature Railway
BRADFORD ROAD
A650
Blackgates Prim. Sch.
WEST ARDSLEY
Playing Fields
Ardsley Mills
Griff Farm
Fall Bridge
Football Grd.
The Fall
East Ardsley Prim. Sch.
Day Cen.
Lib.
EAST ARDSLEY
Rec. Grd. Comm. Cen.
Westerton Wood
Westerton
Healey Croft Farm
Upper Green
Haigh Wood
Nook Farm
ARDSLEY RESERVOIR
Manor Ho.
Cricket Ground
WF3
Junction 41
Beggarington Hill
Boyle Hall Farm
Royston Hill Farm
ROYSTON HILL
Springfield Ho.
Woodhouse Lane Farm
Haigh Moor
Bottoms Wood
Grange Farm
Winstone Farm
Top Fold Farm
Fieldoak Farm
Common Side
Blind Lane Farm
Coglands
Carr Gate
Stoney La. Plantation
Woodhouse Hall Farm
Haigh Hall
Haigh Hall Spring Wood
Cardigan Ho.
Police Operations Centre
M1
WF2
Melbourne House
Haigh Hall Springs Farm
Works
Subway
Brandy Carr
Bower Farm
Aspen Fm.
White Gate Farm
WF12
Jaw Hill
Newton's Bldgs.
Brandy Bank Fm.
Brandy Carr Fm.
Brandy Carr Hill
Nursery
Quarry Hill
KIRKLEES LEEDS WAKEFIELD
Red Lodge
Reservoir (covered)
Kirkhamgate
M1 MOTORWAY
Spring Wood
Kirkham Farm
Beck Bottom Bridge
Beck Bottom
WF5
The Springs
Sunrise Farm
Foster Ford Beck
Golden Elders
124
86
103

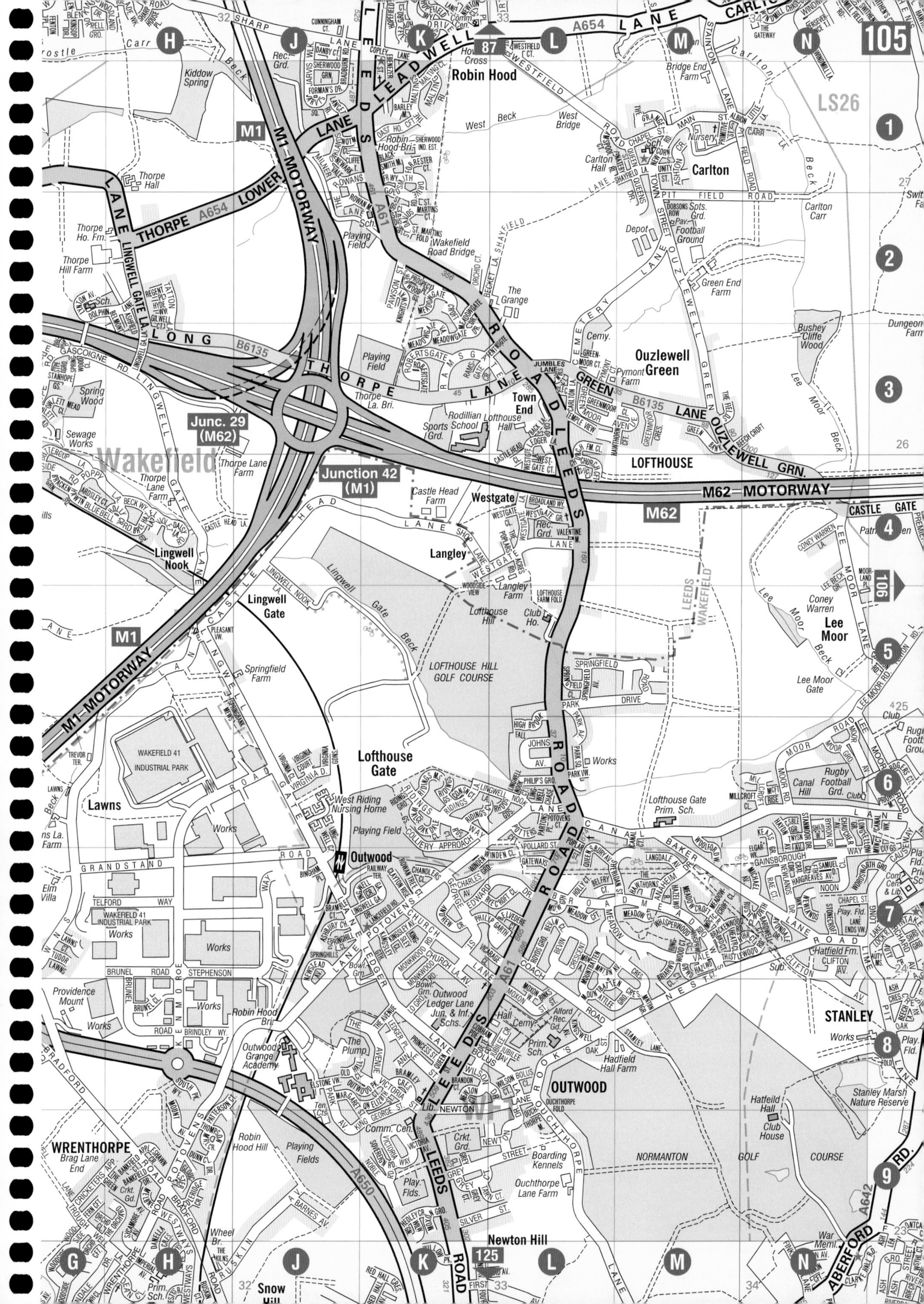

Robin Hood
Carlton
LS26
Ouzlewell Green
LOFTHOUSE
Town End
Westgate
Langley
Lingwell Gate
Lofthouse Gate
Wakefield
Lingwell Nook
Lawns
WAKEFIELD 41 INDUSTRIAL PARK
Outwood
OUTWOOD
WRENTHORPE
STANLEY
Lee Moor
Coney Warren
Newton Hill
M1 MOTORWAY
M62 MOTORWAY
Junc. 29 (M62)
Junction 42 (M1)
LOFTHOUSE HILL GOLF COURSE
NORMANTON GOLF COURSE
Stanley Marsh Nature Reserve
Outwood Grange Academy
Robin Hood Hill
Springfield Farm
Thorpe Hall
Thorpe Hill Farm
Kiddow Spring
Spring Wood
Bushey Cliffe Wood
Hatfeild Hall
LEEDS ROAD
A61
A654
A650
A642
B6135
87
106
125

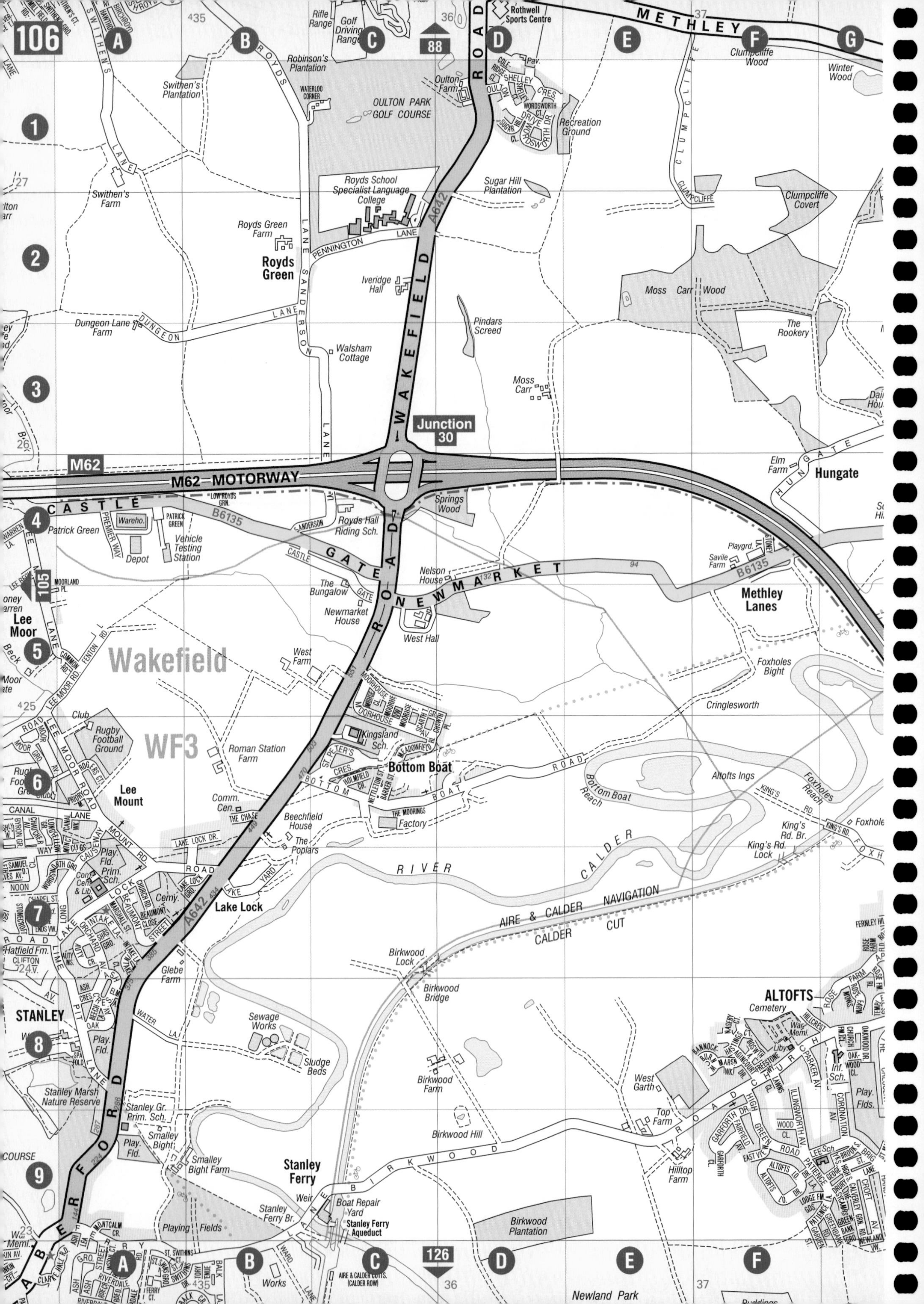
88
126
105
Rothwell Sports Centre
METHLEY
Clumpcliffe Wood
Winter Wood
Rifle Range
Golf Driving Range
Robinson's Plantation
Swithen's Plantation
OULTON PARK GOLF COURSE
Oulton Farm
Recreation Ground
Royds School Specialist Language College
Sugar Hill Plantation
Clumpcliffe Covert
Swithen's Farm
Royds Green Farm
Royds Green
PENNINGTON LANE
Iveridge Hall
WAKEFIELD ROAD
A642
Moss Carr Wood
Dungeon Lane Farm
DUNGEON LANE
SANDERSON LANE
Walsham Cottage
Pindars Screed
The Rookery
Moss Carr
Junction 30
M62
M62 MOTORWAY
Elm Farm
Hungate
CASTLE GATE
B6135
Patrick Green
Wareho.
Depot
Vehicle Testing Station
Royds Hall Riding Sch.
Springs Wood
NEWMARKET
Nelson House
Savile Farm
Methley Lanes
The Bungalow
Newmarket House
West Hall
Lee Moor
Wakefield
West Farm
Foxholes Bight
Cringlesworth
WF3
Club
Rugby Football Ground
Roman Station Farm
Kingsland Sch.
Bottom Boat
BOTTOM BOAT ROAD
Altofts Ings
Bottom Boat Reach
Foxholes Reach
Lee Mount
Comm. Cen.
Factory
Beechfield House
The Poplars
KING'S RD.
King's Rd. Br.
King's Rd. Lock
RIVER CALDER
Cemy.
Lake Lock
AIRE & CALDER NAVIGATION
CALDER CUT
Glebe Farm
Birkwood Lock
Birkwood Bridge
ALTOFTS
Cemetery
STANLEY
Sewage Works
Sludge Beds
War Meml.
Stanley Marsh Nature Reserve
Birkwood Farm
West Garth
Stanley Gr. Prim. Sch.
Smalley Bight
Top Farm
Birkwood Hill
Hilltop Farm
Play. Fld.
Smalley Bight Farm
Stanley Ferry
BIRKWOOD ROAD
Boat Repair Yard
Stanley Ferry Aqueduct
Stanley Ferry Br.
Playing Fields
Birkwood Plantation
ABERFORD ROAD
Works
Newland Park
AIRE & CALDER COTTS. (CALDER ROW)

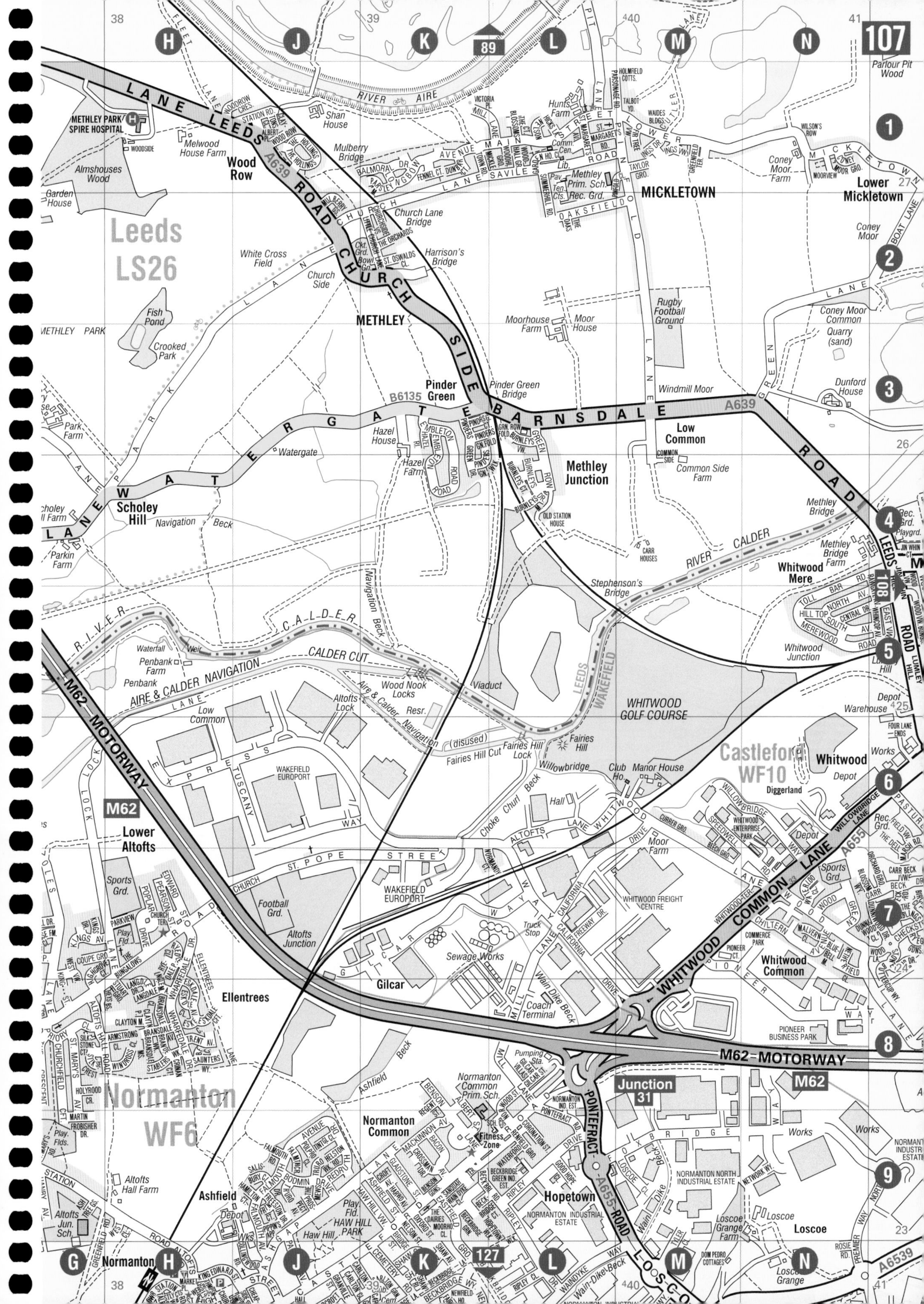
38
39
440
41
H
J
K
L
M
N
89
Parlour Pit Wood
RIVER AIRE
LEEDS LANE
METHLEY PARK SPIRE HOSPITAL
Melwood House Farm
Wood Row
Shan House
Mulberry Bridge
Hunts Farm
Comm. Cen.
Lib.
Methley Prim. Sch.
Rec. Grd.
MICKLETOWN
Coney Moor Farm
Lower Mickletown
Coney Moor
Almshouses Wood
Garden House
Leeds LS26
Church Lane Bridge
White Cross Field
Harrison's Bridge
Church Side
CHURCH SIDE
METHLEY
Fish Pond
Crooked Park
METHLEY PARK
Moorhouse Farm
Moor House
Rugby Football Ground
Coney Moor Common
Quarry (sand)
Dunford House
Pinder Green
Pinder Green Bridge
Windmill Moor
BARNSDALE ROAD
A639
B6135
WATERGATE
Hazel House
Hazel Farm
Low Common
Common Side Farm
Methley Junction
Park Farm
Watergate
Scholey Hill
Scholey Hill Farm
Navigation Beck
Parkin Farm
OLD STATION HOUSE
CARR HOUSES
Methley Bridge
Methley Bridge Farm
Whitwood Mere
RIVER CALDER
Stephenson's Bridge
Navigation Beck
Whitwood Junction
Lumley Hill
Waterfall
Weir
Penbank Farm
Penbank
CALDER CUT
AIRE & CALDER NAVIGATION
Wood Nook Locks
Altofts Lock
Aire & Calder Navigation
Resr.
Viaduct
LEEDS
WAKEFIELD
WHITWOOD GOLF COURSE
Depot
Warehouse
M62 MOTORWAY
Low Common
EXPRESS WAY
WAKEFIELD EUROPORT
TUSCANY WAY
(disused)
Fairies Hill Cut
Fairies Hill Lock
Fairies Hill
Willowbridge
Club Ho.
Manor House
Castleford WF10
Whitwood
Works
Diggerland
Choke Churl Beck
Hall
WHITWOOD LANE
M62
Lower Altofts
ST. POPE STREET
Moor Farm
Sports Grd.
Football Grd.
WAKEFIELD EUROPORT
WHITWOOD FREIGHT CENTRE
Altofts Junction
Truck Stop
Sewage Works
WHITWOOD COMMON LANE
A655
Whitwood Common
Gilcar
Ellentrees
Wain Dike Beck
Coach Terminal
PIONEER BUSINESS PARK
M62 MOTORWAY
Pumping Sta.
Ashfield Beck
Normanton Common Prim. Sch.
Junction 31
Normanton WF6
Normanton Common
Fitness Zone
NORMANTON IND. EST.
Works
NORMANTON NORTH INDUSTRIAL ESTATE
Altofts Hall Farm
Ashfield
Play Fld.
HAW HILL PARK
Haw Hill
Depot
Hopetown
NORMANTON INDUSTRIAL ESTATE
PONTEFRACT ROAD
A655
Loscoe Grange Farm
Loscoe
Altofts Jun. Sch.
Normanton
127
DOM PEDRO COTTAGES
Loscoe Grange
A6539
G
1
2
3
4
5
6
7
8
9
27
26
25
24
23
108

Leeds
LS26
Lower Mickletown
Coney Moor
Willow Grove Farm
THE OXBOW LAKES
River Calder (Old Course)
The Island
RIVER CALDER
Allerton Ings
Ledston Ings
Bulholme Clough
Bulholme Lock
Castleford Cut
Aire & Calder Navigation
Castleford Ings
Spoil Heap
Castleford Tigers RLFC (The PROBIZ Coliseum)
Whitwood Mere
METHLEY RD.
SAVILE RD
AIRE ST.
BRIDGE ST.
PONTEFRACT ROAD
LEEDS ROAD
LUMLEY STREET
Hightown
CASTLEFORD NORMANTON & DISTRICT HOSP.
Castleford Swimming Pool
CASTLEFORD
Castleford
Round Hill
Half Acres
King George's Field
Whitwood
Whitwood Common
Ackton Pasture
Cutsyke
Glass Houghton
JUNCTION 32 OUTLET VILLAGE
Xscape
Glasshoughton
Castleford Tigers RLFC Stadium Proposed
Wakefield College Skills Xchange
Mickle Hill
Rose Bungalow
M62 MOTORWAY
ACKTON PASTURE WOOD
Wood House Farm
NORMANTON INDUSTRIAL ESTATE
WF7
Low Laithe Farm
PONTEFRACT PARK (RACECOURSE)
90
107
128

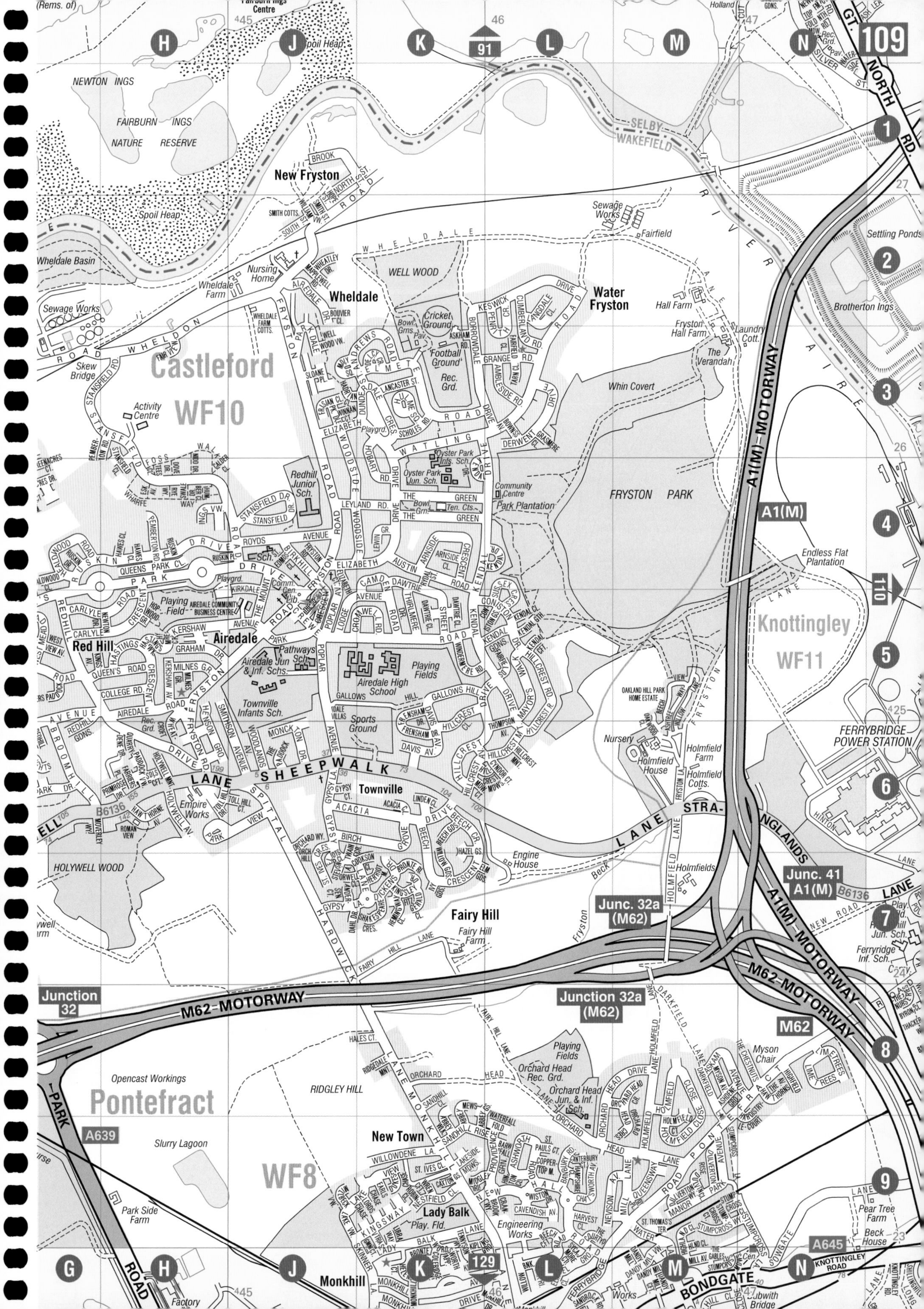
Castleford
WF10
Knottingley
WF11
Pontefract
WF8
New Fryston
Wheldale
Water Fryston
Airedale
Red Hill
Townville
Fairy Hill
New Town
Lady Balk
Monkhill
NEWTON INGS
FAIRBURN INGS NATURE RESERVE
FRYSTON PARK
FERRYBRIDGE POWER STATION
Brotherton Ings
Settling Ponds
Whin Covert
WELL WOOD
HOLYWELL WOOD
RIDGLEY HILL
Opencast Workings
Slurry Lagoon
SHEEPWALK
M62-MOTORWAY
A1(M)-MOTORWAY
Junction 32
Junc. 32a (M62)
Junction 32a (M62)
Junc. 41 A1(M)
A639
A645
B6136
Airedale High School
Redhill Junior Sch.
Oyster Park Jun. Sch.
Oyster Park Infs. Sch.
Airedale Jun & Inf. Schs.
Townville Infants Sch.
Orchard Head Jun. & Inf. Sch.
Engineering Works
Empire Works
Sewage Works
Park Side Farm
Holmfield House
Engine House
Fairy Hill Farm
Fryston Hall Farm
Hall Farm
Endless Flat Plantation
Park Plantation

91
110
129

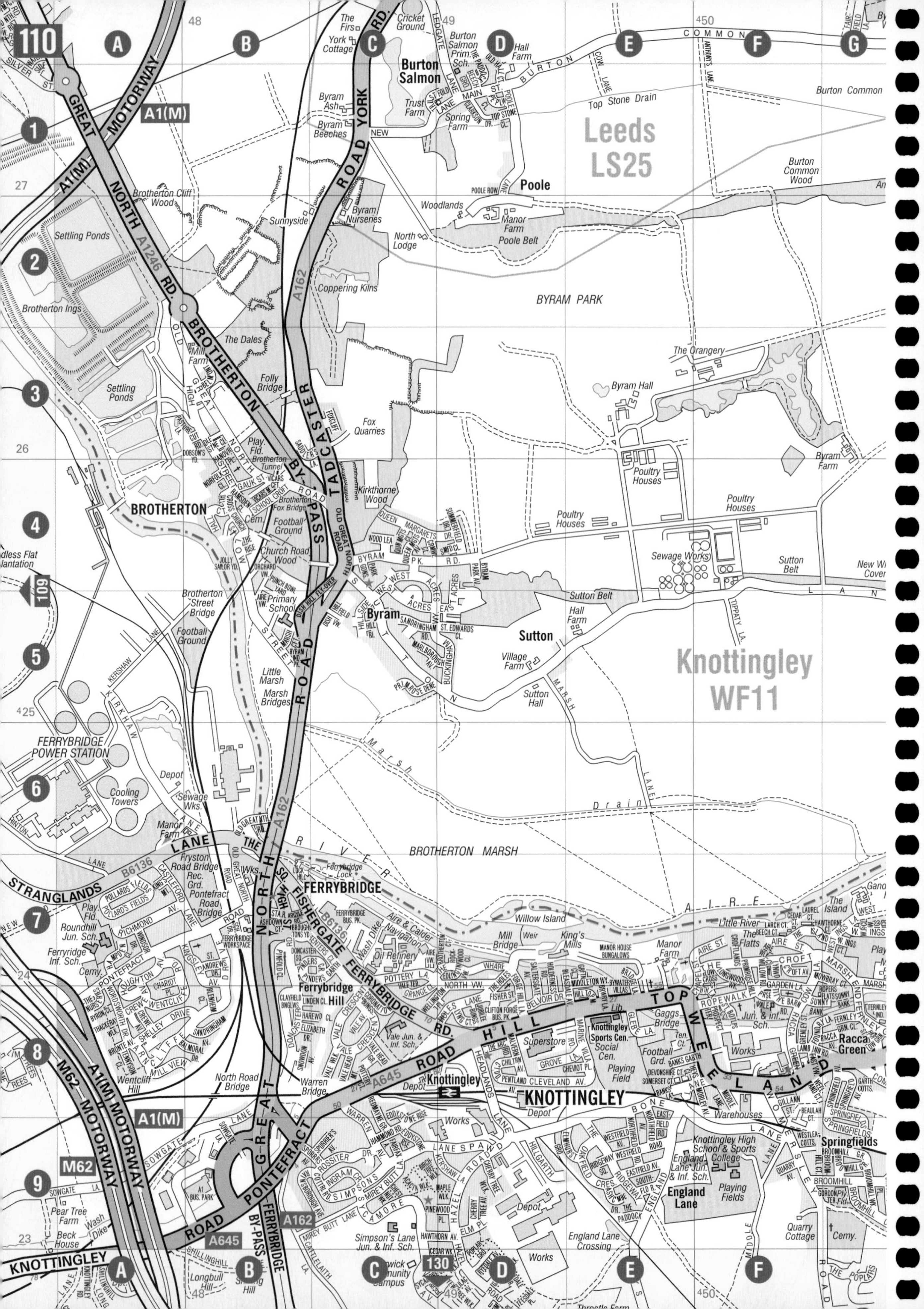
Leeds LS25
Knottingley WF11
Burton Salmon
Poole
BYRAM PARK
BROTHERTON
Byram
Sutton
FERRYBRIDGE
KNOTTINGLEY
Knottingley
BROTHERTON MARSH
RIVER AIRE
Ferrybridge Hill
Springfields
Racca Green
England Lane
FERRYBRIDGE POWER STATION
Cooling Towers
Settling Ponds
Brotherton Ings
Brotherton Cliff Wood
Sewage Works
Poultry Houses
Byram Hall
The Orangery
Burton Common
Burton Common Wood
Top Stone Drain
Sutton Belt
Hall Farm
Village Farm
Sutton Hall
Manor Farm
Poole Belt
Coppering Kilns
Fox Quarries
Kirkthorne Wood
Byram Nurseries
North Lodge
Woodlands
The Dales
Folly Bridge
Mill Farm
Brotherton Tunnel
Football Ground
Church Road Wood
Primary School
Brotherton Street Bridge
Little Marsh
Marsh Bridges
Willow Island
Mill Bridge
King's Mills
Oil Refinery
Aire & Calder Navigation
Ferrybridge Lock
Superstore
Knottingley Sports Cen.
Playing Field
Gaggs Bridge
Knottingley High School & Sports College
England Lane Jun. & Inf. Sch.
Simpson's Lane Jun. & Inf. Sch.
Vale Jun. & Inf. Sch.
Roundhill Jun. Sch.
Ferryridge Inf. Sch.
Warren Bridge
North Road Bridge
Wentcliff Hill
Pear Tree Farm
Beck House
Quarry Cottage
Warehouses
Works
Depot
A1(M)
M62
A162
A645
B6136
A1246
GREAT NORTH RD.
TADCASTER ROAD
YORK RD.
BROTHERTON BY-PASS
FERRYBRIDGE BY-PASS
PONTEFRACT ROAD
FERRYBRIDGE RD.
HILL TOP
WEELAND RD.
STRANGLANDS LANE
KNOTTINGLEY
130
109

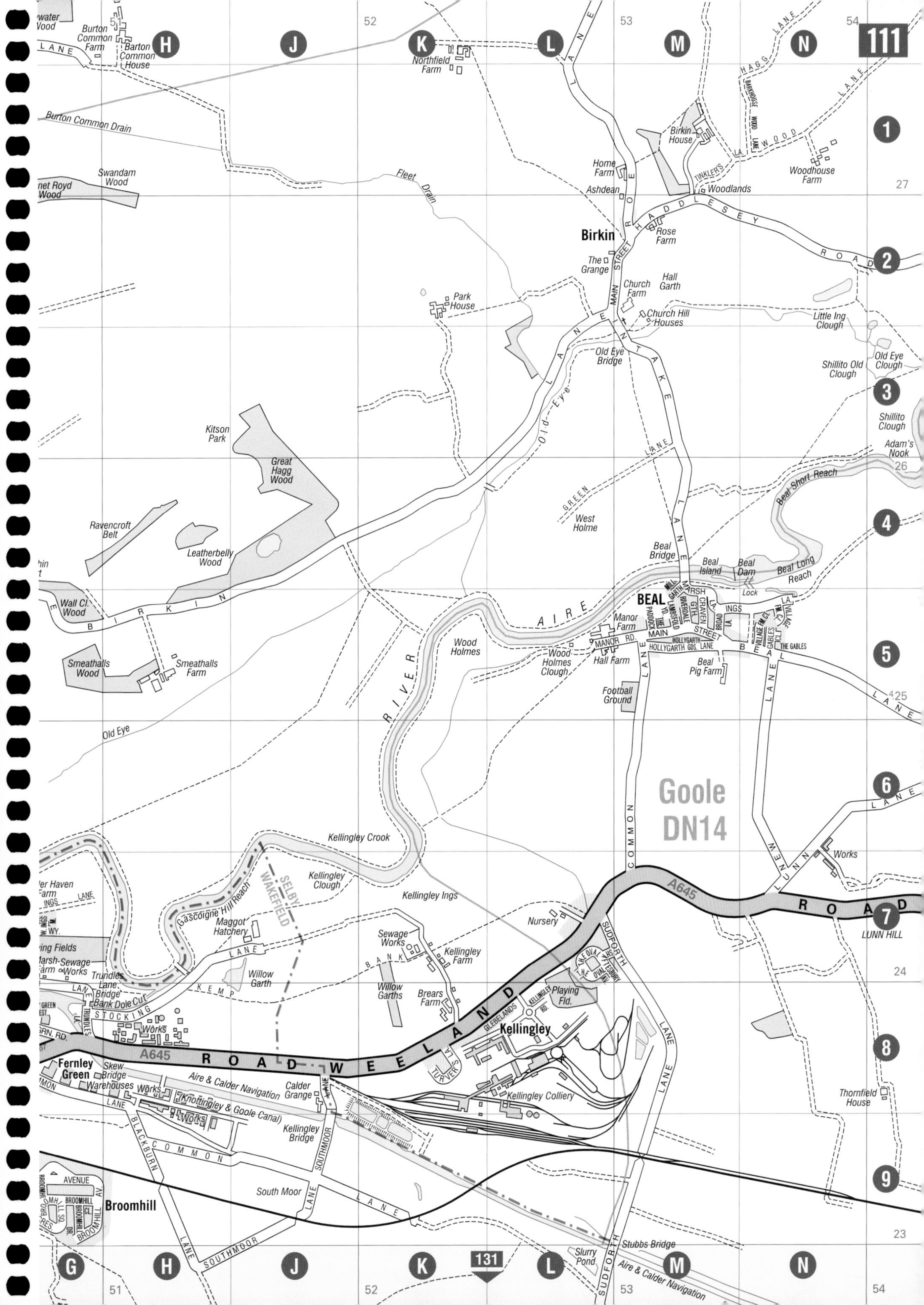
Burton Common Farm
Barton Common House
Northfield Farm
Burton Common Drain
Swandam Wood
Fleet Drain
Home Farm
Ashdean
Birkin House
Woodhouse Farm
Woodlands
Birkin
Rose Farm
HADDLESEY ROAD
The Grange
Church Farm
Hall Garth
Park House
Church Hill Houses
Little Ing Clough
Old Eye Bridge
Old Eye Clough
Shillito Old Clough
Shillito Clough
Adam's Nook
Kitson Park
Great Hagg Wood
Beal Short Reach
Ravencroft Belt
Leatherbelly Wood
West Holme
Beal Bridge
Beal Island
Beal Dam
Beal Long Reach
Lock
BEAL
Wall Cl. Wood
BIRKIN LANE
RIVER AIRE
Manor Farm
Wood Holmes
Wood Holmes Clough
Hall Farm
Beal Pig Farm
Smeathalls Wood
Smeathalls Farm
Football Ground
Old Eye
Goole DN14
Kellingley Crook
Works
Kellingley Clough
Kellingley Ings
Gascoigne Hill Reach
Maggot Hatchery
SELBY
WAKEFIELD
Nursery
A645 ROAD
LUNN HILL
Sewage Works
Kellingley Farm
Willow Garth
Willow Garths
Playing Fld.
Trundles Lane Bridge
Bank Dole Cut
Brears Farm
Kellingley
Works
A645 ROAD WEELAND
Fernley Green
Skew Bridge
Warehouses
Aire & Calder Navigation
Calder Grange
Kellingley Colliery
Thornfield House
(Knottingley & Goole Canal)
Kellingley Bridge
Broomhill
South Moor
Slurry Pond
Stubbs Bridge
Aire & Calder Navigation
COMMON LANE
SUDFORTH LANE
LUNN LANE
SOUTHMOOR LANE
BLACKBURN LANE
G H J K L M N
1 2 3 4 5 6 7 8 9
51 52 53 54
27 26 25 24 23

131

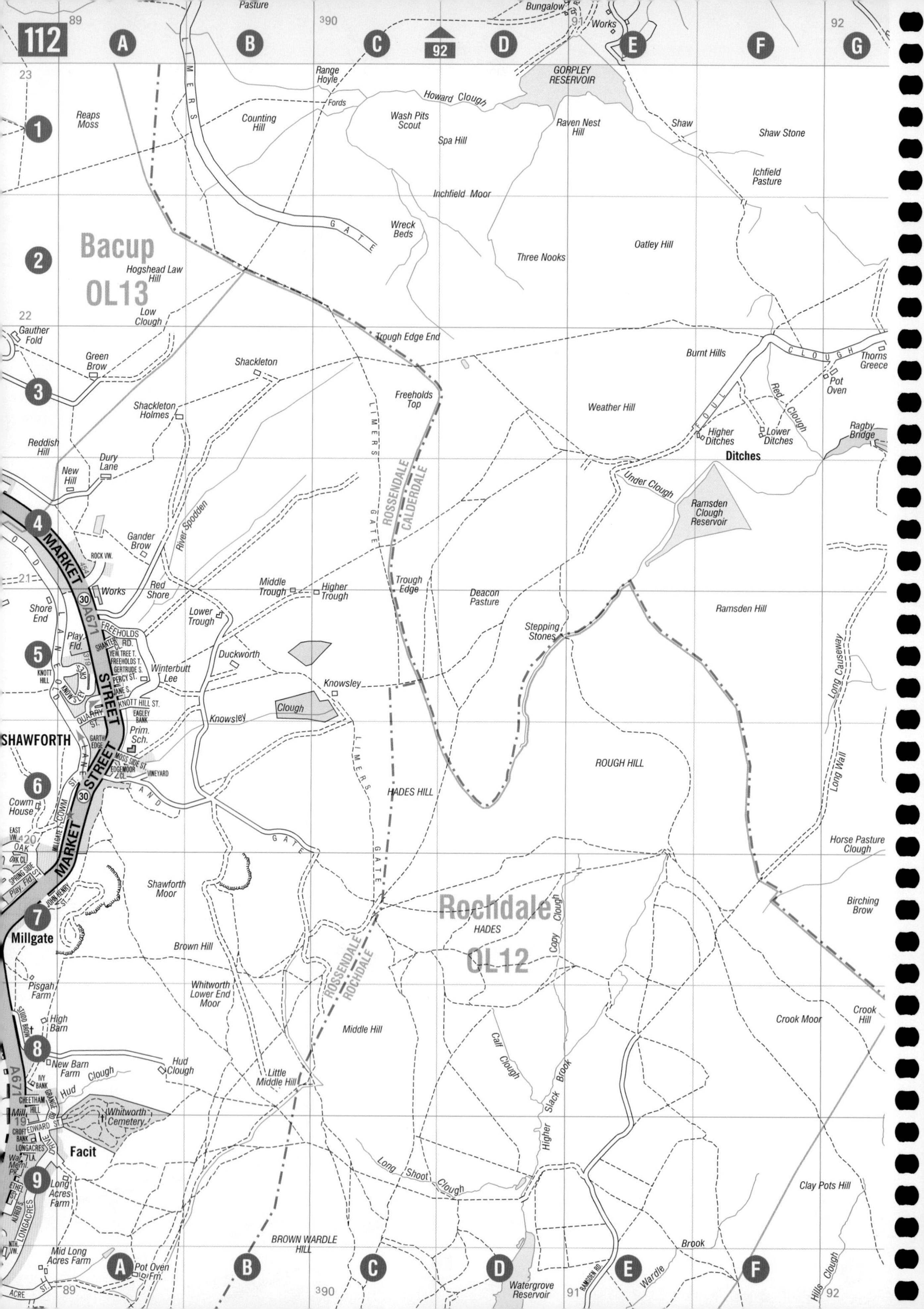

92
A
B
C
D
E
F
G
89
390
91
Pasture
Bungalow
Works
23
22
21
20
19
Range Hoyle
Fords
Howard Clough
GORPLEY RESERVOIR
Reaps Moss
Counting Hill
Wash Pits Scout
Spa Hill
Raven Nest Hill
Shaw
Shaw Stone
Ichfield Pasture
Inchfield Moor
Wreck Beds
LIMERS GATE
Bacup
OL13
Hogshead Law Hill
Three Nooks
Oatley Hill
Low Clough
Gauther Fold
Trough Edge End
Green Brow
Shackleton
Burnt Hills
Thorns Greece
Pot Oven
FOUL CLOUGH
Freeholds Top
Shackleton Holmes
Weather Hill
Red Clough
Higher Ditches
Lower Ditches
Ragby Bridge
Reddish Hill
Ditches
Dury Lane
New Hill
Under Clough
Ramsden Clough Reservoir
ROSSENDALE
CALDERDALE
River Spodden
Gander Brow
MARKET STREET
OLD LANE
ROCK VW.
A671
Red Shore
Works
Middle Trough
Higher Trough
Trough Edge
Deacon Pasture
Ramsden Hill
Shore End
Lower Trough
FREEHOLDS RD.
Stepping Stones
Play. Fld.
SHANTER
YEW TREE T.
FREEHOLDS T.
GERTRUDE S.
PERCY ST.
JANE S.
Winterbutt Lee
Duckworth
KNOTT HILL
KNOTT HILL ST.
Knowsley
Long Causeway
QUARRY ST.
EAGLEY BANK
Clough
Knowsley
Prim. Sch.
SHAWFORTH
GARTH EDGE
MOSS SIDE ST.
EDGEMOOR CL.
VINEYARD
LAND GATE
ROUGH HILL
Long Wall
COWM ST.
Cowm House
HADES HILL
EAST VW.
OAK CL.
MILLGATE
SPRING SIDE
Play. Fld.
Horse Pasture Clough
JOHN HENRY ST.
Shawforth Moor
Birching Brow
Millgate
Rochdale
HADES
OL12
Copy Clough
ROSSENDALE
ROCHDALE
Brown Hill
Pisgah Farm
Whitworth Lower End Moor
Crook Moor
Crook Hill
STUDD BROW
High Barn
Middle Hill
Calf Clough
Slack Brook
New Barn Farm
Hud Clough
Hud Clough
IVY BANK
Little Middle Hill
CHEETHAM HILL
GRANGE RD.
Whitworth Cemetery
Mill
EDWARD ST.
CROFT BANK
LONGACRES
Facit
Higher Slack Brook
War Meml. Pk.
Long Shoot Clough
Clay Pots Hill
ETHEL ST.
Long Acres Farm
LONGACRES
ALFRED S.
BROWN WARDLE HILL
NTH. VW.
Brook
Mid Long Acres Farm
Pot Oven Fm.
RAMSDEN RD.
Wardle
Hills Clough
ACRE ST.
Watergrove Reservoir

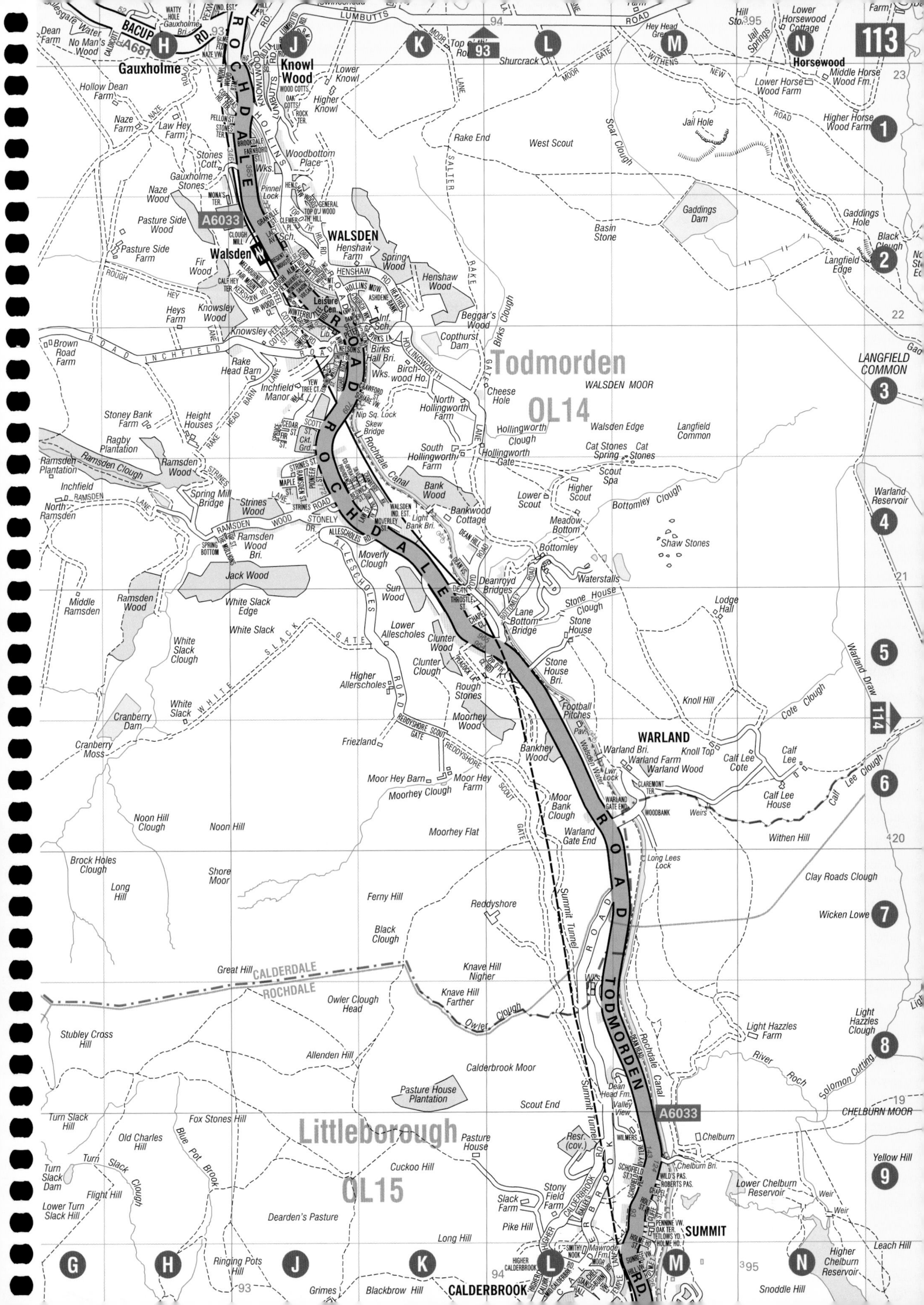
Gauxholme
Knowl Wood
Walsden
WALSDEN
Todmorden
OL14
WALSDEN MOOR
Walsden Edge
Langfield Common
LANGFIELD COMMON
Horsewood
Jail Hole
West Scout
Rake End
Gaddings Dam
Basin Stone
Shurcrack
Warland Reservoir
Shaw Stones
Waterstalls
Lodge Hall
Knoll Hill
WARLAND
Warland Farm
Warland Wood
Calf Lee House
Withen Hill
Clay Roads Clough
Wicken Lowe
Light Hazzles Farm
River Roch
Solomon Cutting
CHELBURN MOOR
Chelburn
Lower Chelburn Reservoir
Higher Chelburn Reservoir
SUMMIT
Yellow Hill
Leach Hill
Snoddle Hill
CALDERDALE
ROCHDALE
Great Hill
Littleborough
OL15
Calderbrook Moor
Pasture House Plantation
Knave Hill Nigher
Knave Hill Farther
Owler Clough Head
Allenden Hill
Reddyshore
Moorhey Flat
Ferny Hill
Black Clough
Noon Hill
Noon Hill Clough
Shore Moor
Long Hill
Brock Holes Clough
Stubley Cross Hill
Turn Slack Hill
Turn Slack Dam
Old Charles Hill
Fox Stones Hill
Blue Pot Brook
Flight Hill
Lower Turn Slack Hill
Dearden's Pasture
Cuckoo Hill
Long Hill
Pike Hill
Slack Farm
Stony Field Farm
Ringing Pots Hill
Grimes
Blackbrow Hill
CALDERBROOK
Jack Wood
White Slack Edge
White Slack
Cranberry Dam
Cranberry Moss
Middle Ramsden
Ramsden Wood
Ramsden Clough
Inchfield
North Ramsden
Brown Road Farm
Rake Head Barn
Inchfield Manor
Stoney Bank Farm
Height Houses
Ragby Plantation
Strines Wood
Spring Mill Bridge
Moverly Clough
Sun Wood
Lower Allescholes
Higher Allerscholes
Friezland
Moor Hey Barn
Moor Hey Farm
Moorhey Clough
Rough Stones
Moorhey Wood
Clunter Wood
Deanroyd Bridges
Lane Bottom Bridge
Stone House Bri.
Football Pitches
Bankhey Wood
Warland Gate End
Summit Tunnel
Rochdale Canal
A6033
A681
ROCHDALE ROAD
TODMORDEN ROAD
G H J K L M N
1 2 3 4 5 6 7 8 9
93 94 95
19 20 21 22 23
114

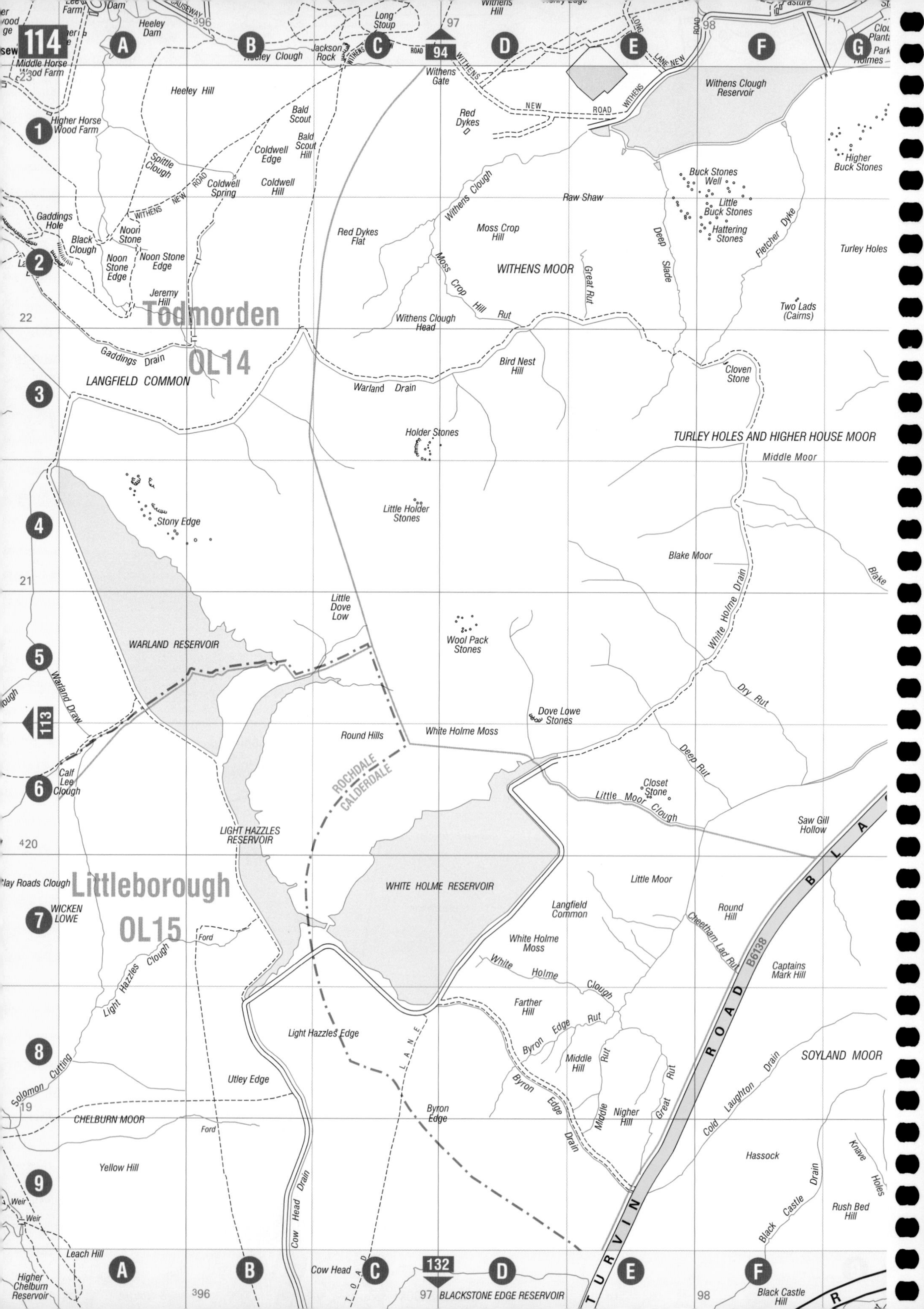
Heeley Dam
Middle Horse Wood Farm
Heeley Hill
Higher Horse Wood Farm
Heeley Clough
Jackson Rock
Long Stoup
Withens Gate
Bald Scout
Bald Scout Hill
Coldwell Edge
Coldwell Spring
Coldwell Hill
Spittle Clough
Gaddings Hole
Black Clough
Noon Stone
Noon Stone Edge
Jeremy Hill
Todmorden
OL14
Gaddings Drain
LANGFIELD COMMON
Red Dykes
Red Dykes Flat
Withens Clough
Moss Crop Hill
Moss Crop Hill Rut
Withens Clough Head
WITHENS MOOR
Raw Shaw
Great Rut
Withens Clough Reservoir
Buck Stones Well
Little Buck Stones
Hattering Stones
Higher Buck Stones
Deep Slade
Fletcher Dyke
Turley Holes
Two Lads (Cairns)
Bird Nest Hill
Warland Drain
Cloven Stone
Holder Stones
TURLEY HOLES AND HIGHER HOUSE MOOR
Middle Moor
Little Holder Stones
Stony Edge
Blake Moor
White Holme Drain
Little Dove Low
Wool Pack Stones
WARLAND RESERVOIR
Warland Drain
Dry Rut
Dove Lowe Stones
Round Hills
White Holme Moss
Deep Rut
Calf Lee Clough
ROCHDALE
CALDERDALE
Closet Stone
Little Moor Clough
Saw Gill Hollow
LIGHT HAZZLES RESERVOIR
WHITE HOLME RESERVOIR
Little Moor
Littleborough
OL15
WICKEN LOWE
Langfield Common
Round Hill
Cheetham Lad Rut
White Holme Moss
White Holme Clough
Captains Mark Hill
Light Hazzles Clough
Ford
Farther Hill
Byron Edge Rut
Light Hazzles Edge
Middle Hill
Middle Rut
Great Rut
SOYLAND MOOR
Cold Laughton Drain
Solomon Cutting
Utley Edge
Byron Edge
Byron Edge Drain
Nigher Hill
CHELBURN MOOR
Ford
Yellow Hill
Hassock
Knave Holes
Cow Head Drain
Black Castle Drain
Rush Bed Hill
Weir
Leach Hill
Higher Chelburn Reservoir
Cow Head
BLACKSTONE EDGE RESERVOIR
Black Castle Hill
TURVIN ROAD
B6138
WITHENS NEW ROAD
LONG LANE
CAUSEWAY
LANE
ROAD
94
113
132
396
97
98
22
21
420
19

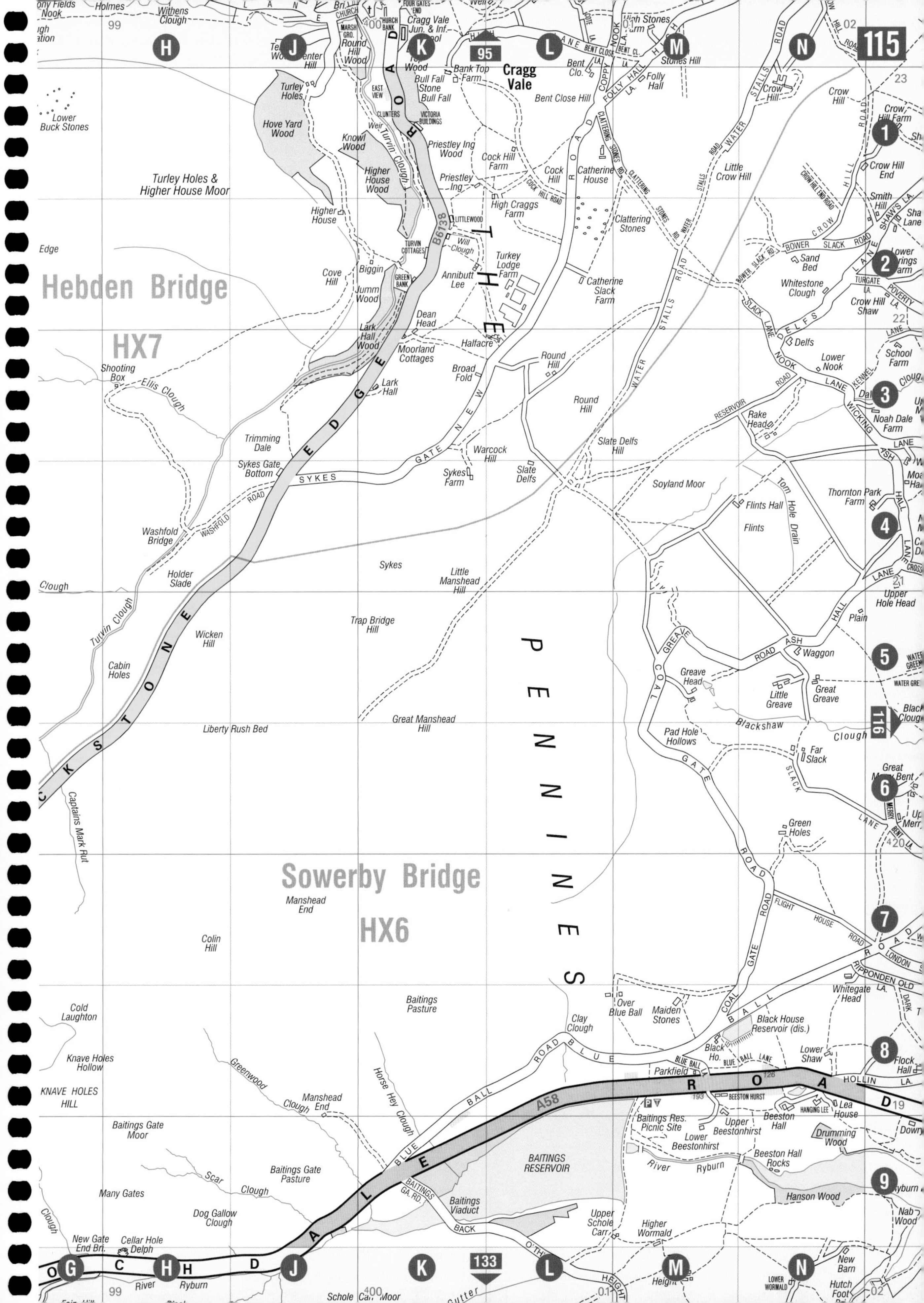
Hebden Bridge
HX7
Sowerby Bridge
HX6
THE PENNINES
Cragg Vale
BLACKSTONE EDGE ROAD
BAITINGS RESERVOIR
Soyland Moor
Turley Holes & Higher House Moor
95
116
133

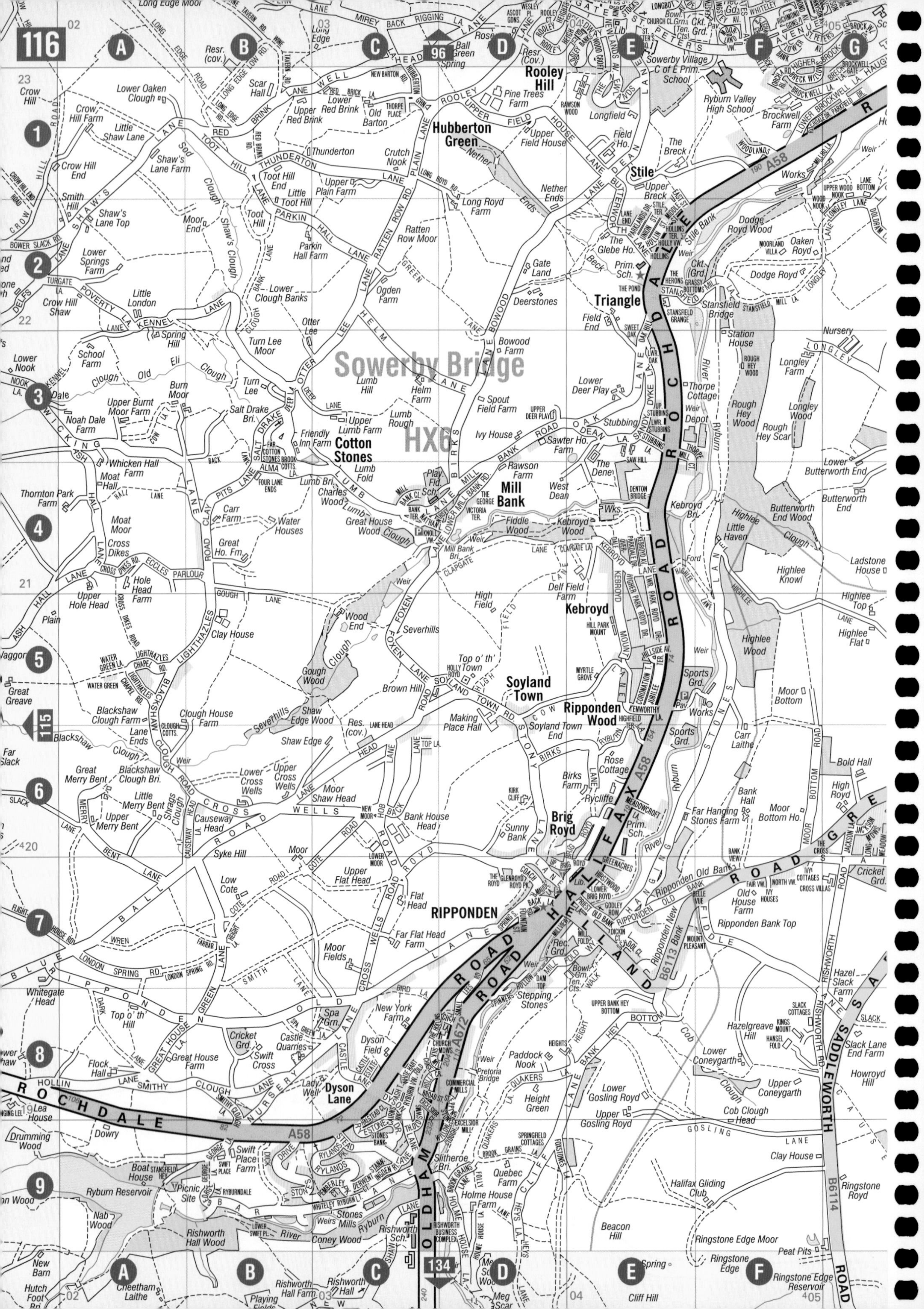
Sowerby Bridge
HX6
Rooley Hill
Hubberton Green
Stile
Triangle
Cotton Stones
Mill Bank
Kebroyd
Soyland Town
Ripponden Wood
Brig Royd
RIPPONDEN
Dyson Lane
Ryburn Reservoir
Ryburn Valley High School
Sowerby Village C of E Prim. School
Rishworth Hall Wood
Halifax Gliding Club
Ringstone Edge Moor
Ringstone Edge Reservoir
Beacon Hill
ROCHDALE ROAD
HALIFAX ROAD
OLDHAM ROAD
SADDLEWORTH ROAD
A58
A672
B6113
B6114
96
115
134

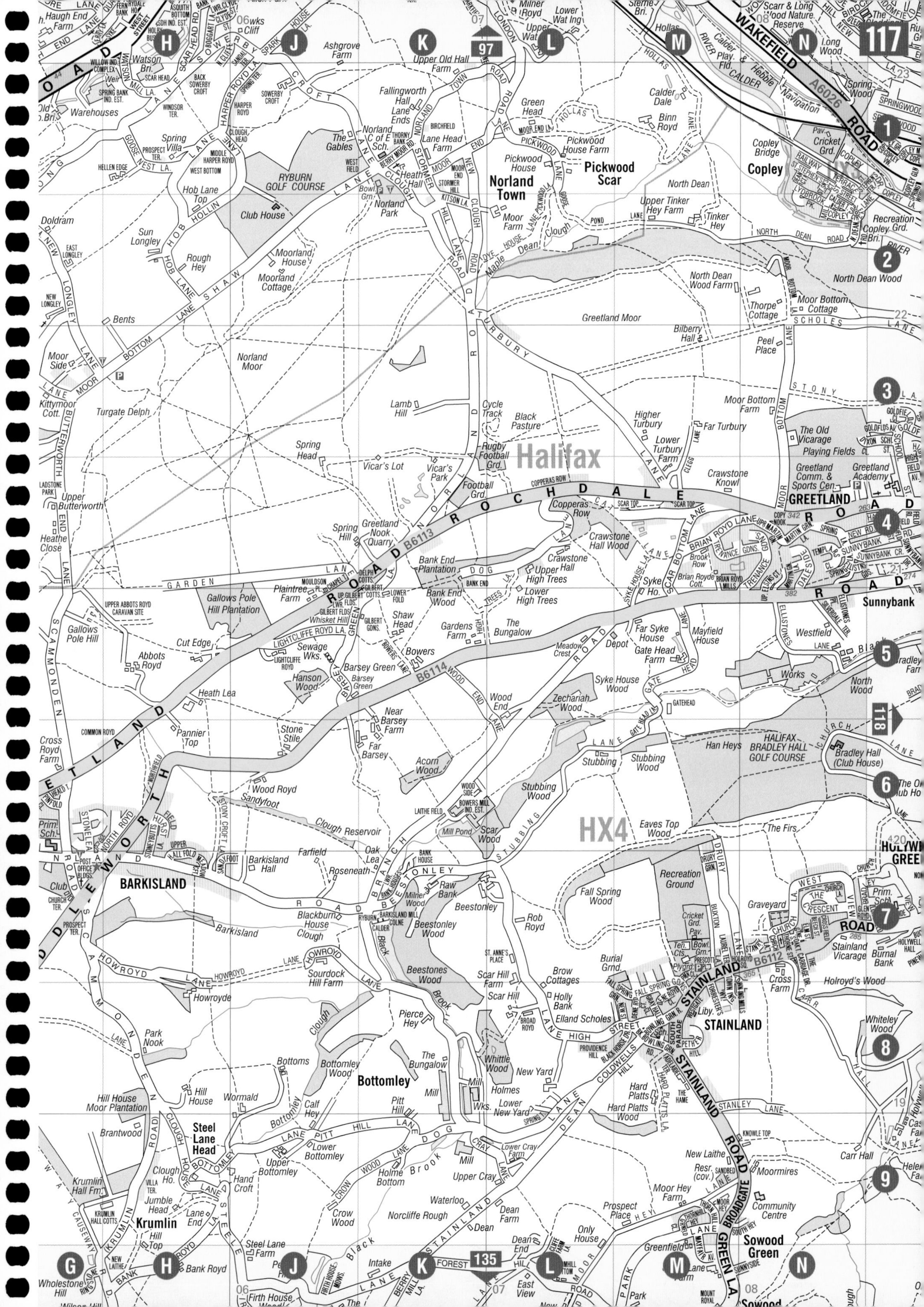
Halifax
HX4
Norland Town
Pickwood Scar
Copley
GREETLAND
Sunnybank
BARKISLAND
Bottomley
STAINLAND
Krumlin
Steel Lane Head
Sowood Green
Ryburn Golf Course
Halifax Bradley Hall Golf Course
Norland Moor
Greetland Moor
North Dean Wood
Clough Reservoir
Rochdale Road
B6113
B6114
B6112
A6026
Wakefield Road
Stainland Road
Greetland Road
Barkisland Hall
Bank End Plantation
Gallows Pole Hill Plantation
Beestonley Wood
Stubbing Wood
Fall Spring Wood
Recreation Ground
Halifax Rugby Football Grd.
Greetland Academy
Greetland Comm. & Sports Cen.
Moor Bottom Farm
Sowerby Croft
Upper Butterworth
Cross Royd Farm
Howroyde
Holroyd's Wood
Whiteley Wood
Hill House Moor Plantation
Norcliffe Rough
Dean Farm
Upper Cray
Lower Cray Farm
Community Centre
Moormires
Wholestone Hill
Firth House
97
135
118

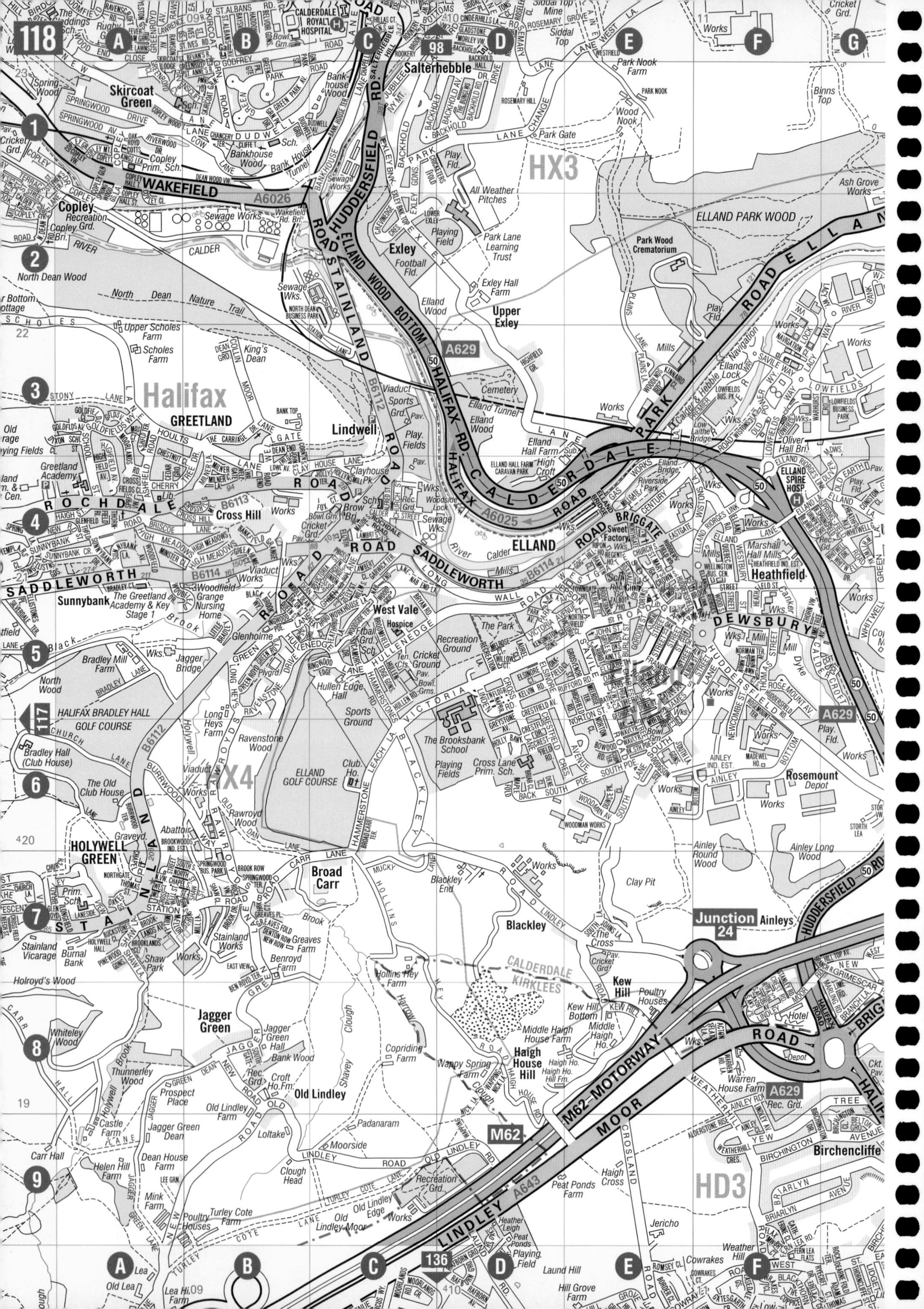

Skircoat Green
Salterhebble
Copley
Exley
HX3
ELLAND PARK WOOD
Park Wood Crematorium
Upper Exley
Halifax
GREETLAND
Lindwell
Cross Hill
ELLAND
West Vale
Heathfield
Sunnybank
HX4
ELLAND GOLF COURSE
HALIFAX BRADLEY HALL GOLF COURSE
HOLYWELL GREEN
Broad Carr
Blackley
Junction 24
Ainleys
Kew Hill
Jagger Green
Haigh House Hill
Old Lindley
M62 MOTORWAY
HD3
Birchencliffe
WAKEFIELD
A6026
HUDDERSFIELD RD.
ELLAND WOOD BOTTOM
A629
HALIFAX RD.
CALDERDALE
A6025
ROCHDALE ROAD
B6113
SADDLEWORTH ROAD
B6114
B6112
STAINLAND ROAD
DEWSBURY
A643
LINDLEY MOOR
CALDERDALE
KIRKLEES

98
117
136

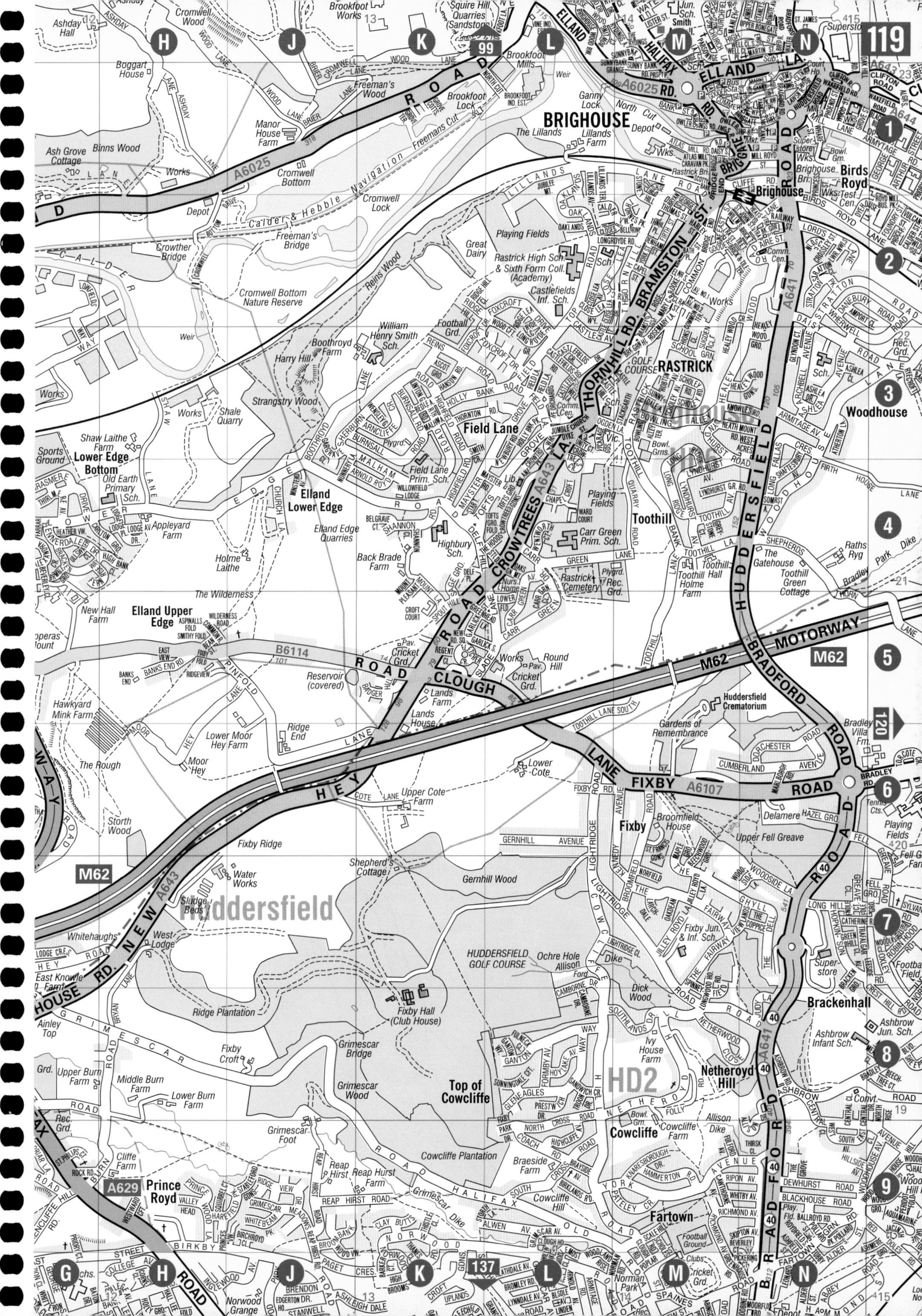

BRIGHOUSE
RASTRICK
Brighouse
Field Lane
Elland Lower Edge
Elland Upper Edge
Lower Edge Bottom
Toothill
Woodhouse
Birds Royd
Fixby
Huddersfield
Top of Cowcliffe
Cowcliffe
Fartown
Netheroyd Hill
Brackenhall
Prince Royd
HD2
A6025
A643
A641
A6107
A629
B6114
M62
MOTORWAY
HUDDERSFIELD ROAD
BRADFORD ROAD
ELLAND RD.
CROWTREES ROAD
THORNHILL RD.
BRAMSTON ST.
CLOUGH LANE
FIXBY ROAD
HEY LANE
NEW HOUSE RD.
HALIFAX OLD ROAD
GRIMESCAR ROAD
Calder & Hebble Navigation
Cromwell Bottom Nature Reserve
Rastrick High Sch. & Sixth Form Coll. (Academy)
Castlefields Inf. Sch.
William Henry Smith Sch.
Field Lane Prim. Sch.
Highbury Sch.
Carr Green Prim. Sch.
Rastrick Cemetery
Huddersfield Crematorium
Gardens of Remembrance
HUDDERSFIELD GOLF COURSE
Fixby Hall (Club House)
Fixby Jun. & Inf. Sch.
Ashbrow Jun. Sch.
Ashbrow Infant Sch.
Gernhill Wood
Grimescar Wood
Cowcliffe Plantation
Ridge Plantation
Reins Wood
Strangstry Wood
Binns Wood
Shale Quarry
Elland Edge Quarries
Fixby Ridge
Upper Fell Greave
Bradley Villa Fm.
H J K L M N
1 2 3 4 5 6 7 8 9
99
120
137

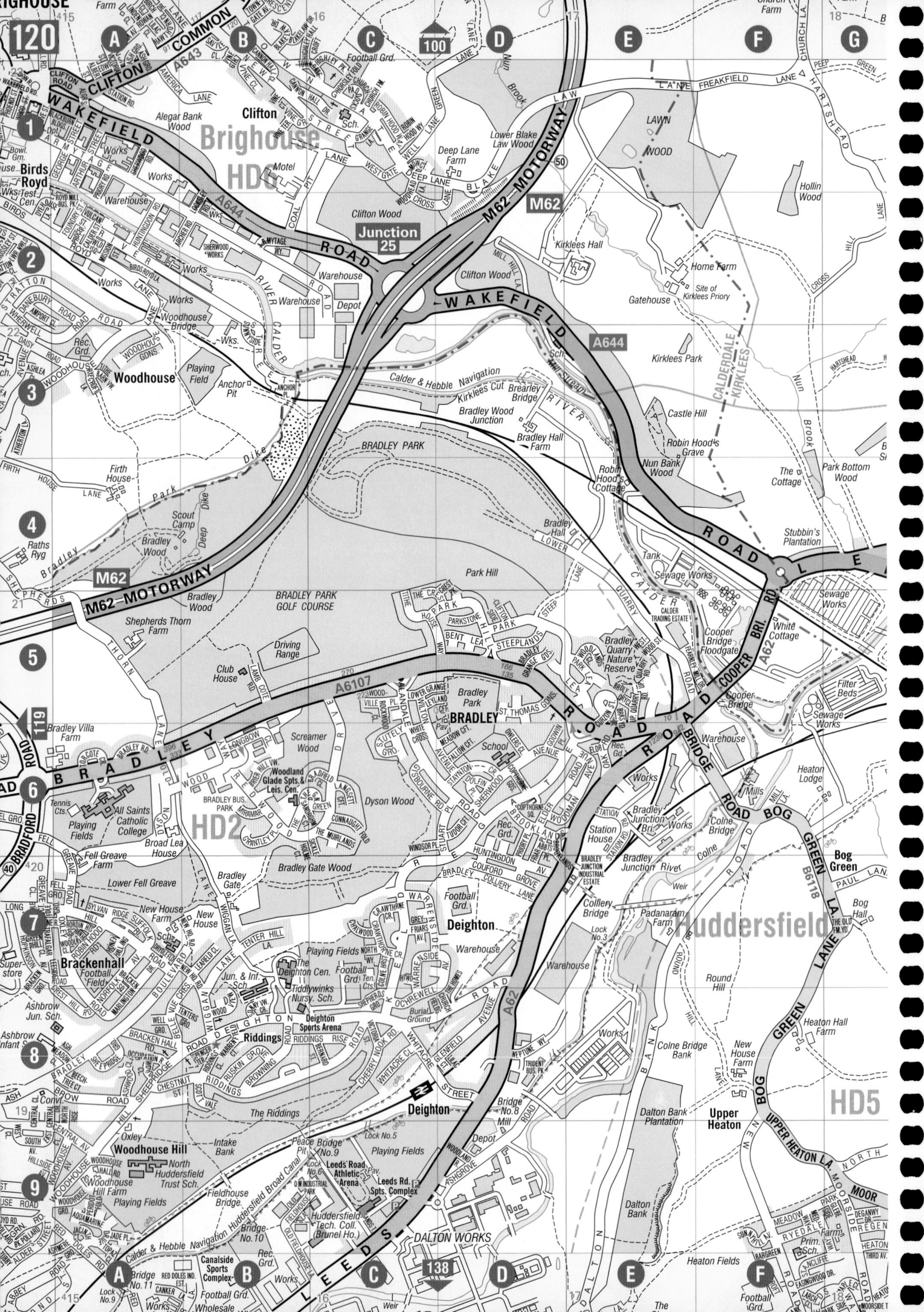
A
B
C
D
E
F
G
100
Brighouse
HD6
Clifton
Clifton Common
A643
Wakefield Road
A644
Birds Royd
Woodhouse
M62 Motorway
Junction 25
Lawn Wood
Kirklees Hall
Home Farm
Site of Kirklees Priory
Kirklees Park
Calder & Hebble Navigation
Kirklees Cut
River Calder
Bradley Park
Bradley Wood
Shepherds Thorn Farm
Bradley Park Golf Course
Park Hill
A6107
Bradley Road
Bradley
HD2
Cooper Bridge
A62
Leeds Road
Deighton
Huddersfield
Brackenhall
Riddings
Woodhouse Hill
Upper Heaton
HD5
Bog Green
Colne Bridge
Dalton Bank
Dalton Works
119
138
1
2
3
4
5
6
7
8
9

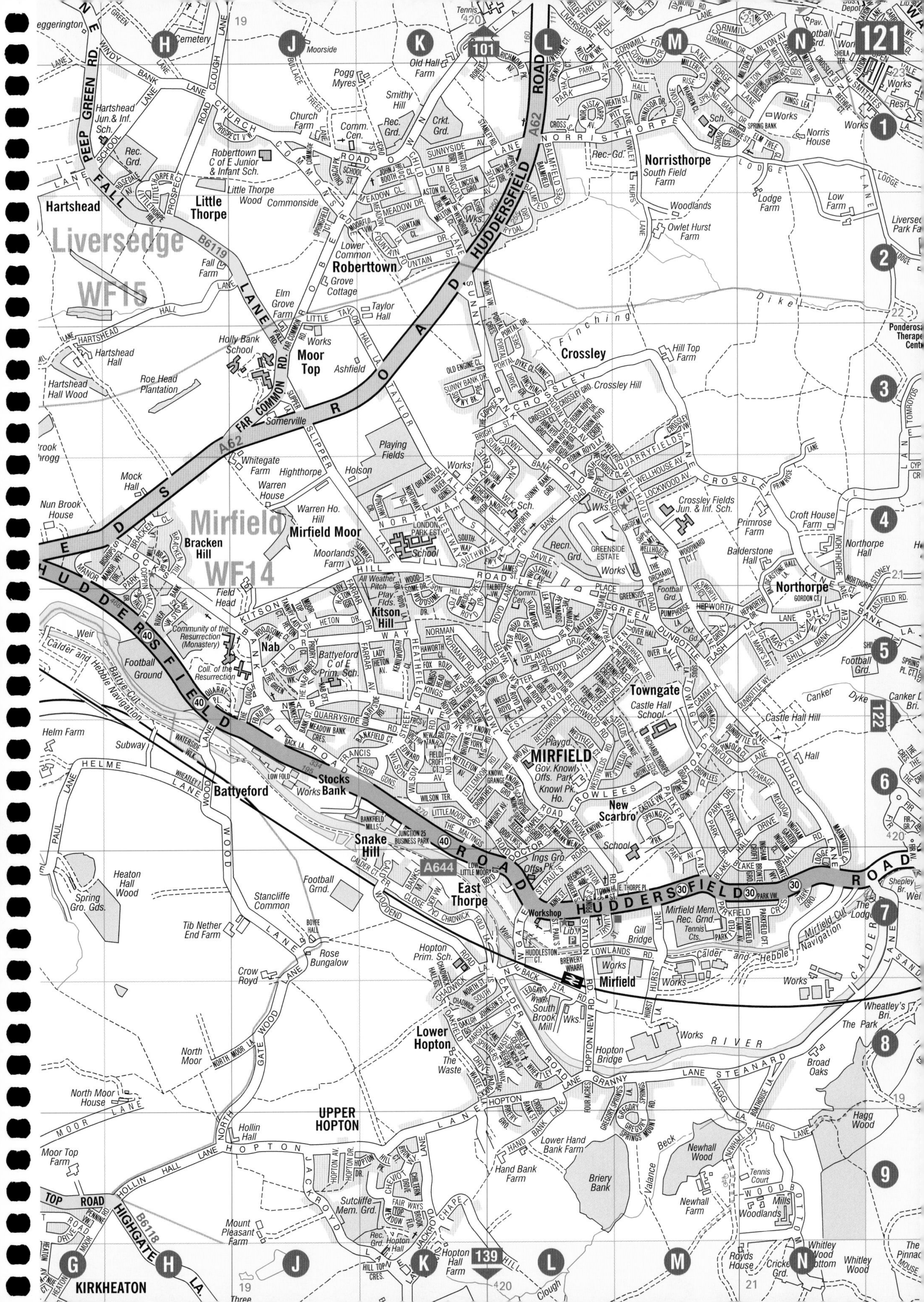
Liversedge
WF15
Mirfield
WF14
Hartshead
Little Thorpe
Roberttown
Norristhorpe
Crossley
Moor Top
Mirfield Moor
Bracken Hill
Kitson Hill
Nab
Battyeford
Stocks Bank
Snake Hill
East Thorpe
MIRFIELD
Towngate
Northorpe
New Scarbro'
Lower Hopton
UPPER HOPTON
KIRKHEATON
HUDDERSFIELD ROAD
A62
A644
B6119
B6118
Calder and Hebble Navigation
River Calder
101
122
139

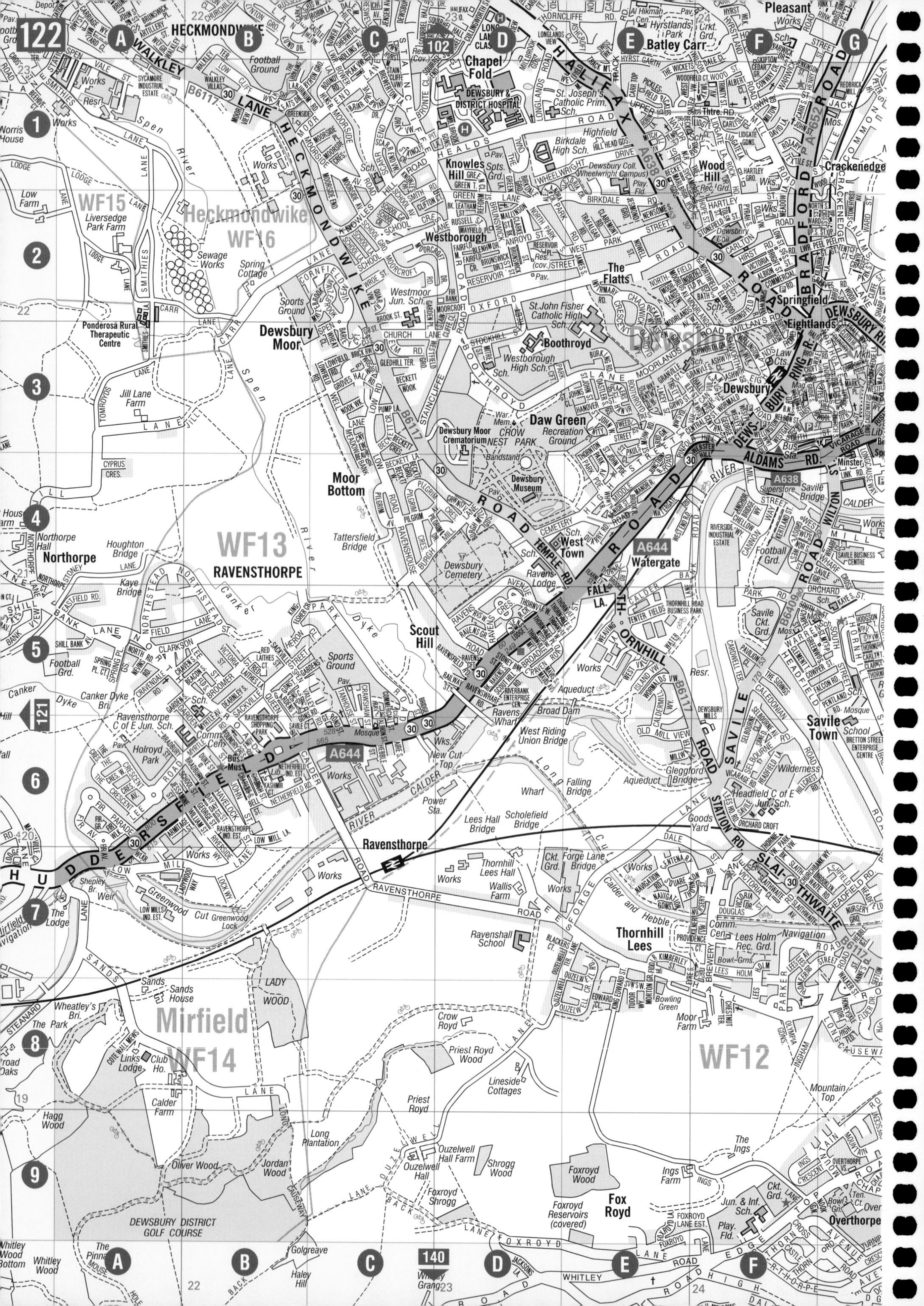
HECKMONDWIKE
Chapel Fold
Batley Carr
Pleasant
WALKLEY LANE
HECKMONDWIKE
Dewsbury & District Hospital
Knowles Hill
Westborough
Wood Hill
Crackenedge
Heckmondwike WF16
WF15
Liversedge Park Farm
Sewage Works
The Flatts
Springfield
Eightlands
Dewsbury Moor
Boothroyd
Dewsbury
Daw Green
Dewsbury Moor Crematorium
Dewsbury Museum
Moor Bottom
West Town
Watergate
Northorpe
WF13
RAVENSTHORPE
Scout Hill
Savile Town
Ravensthorpe
Thornhill Lees
Mirfield
WF14
WF12
Dewsbury District Golf Course
Fox Royd
Overthorpe
A638
A644
A652
B6117
B6409
HALIFAX ROAD
BRADFORD ROAD
ALDAMS RD.
SAVILE ROAD
HUDDERSFIELD
THORNHILL
SLAITHWAITE
River Calder
Ravenshall School
Lady Wood
Priest Royd Wood
Foxroyd Wood
Mountain Top
121
140
102

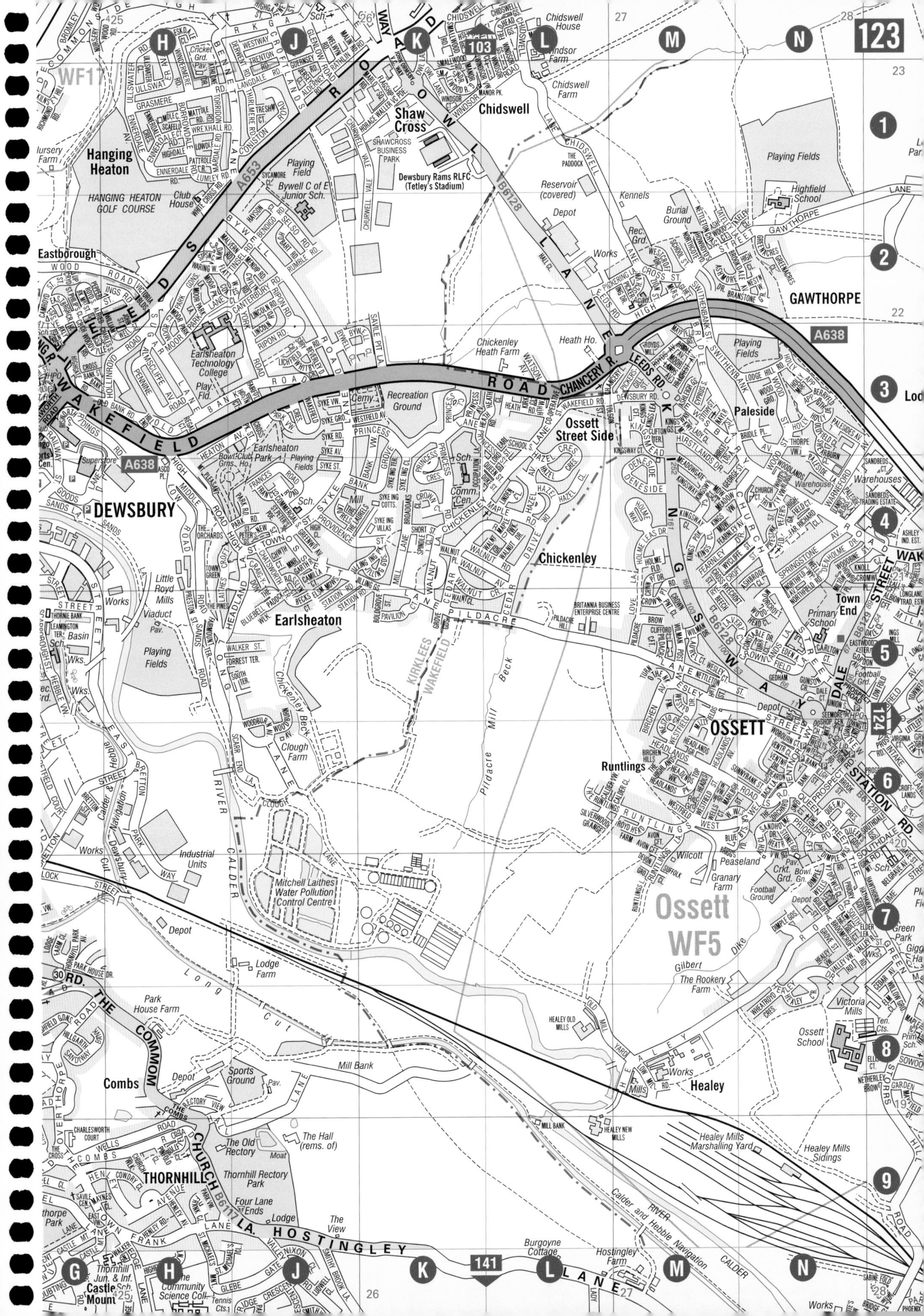

WF17
Hanging Heaton
HANGING HEATON GOLF COURSE
Club House
Playing Field
Bywell C of E Junior Sch.
Shaw Cross
SHAWCROSS BUSINESS PARK
Dewsbury Rams RLFC (Tetley's Stadium)
Chidswell
Chidswell House
Windsor Farm
Chidswell Farm
THE PADDOCK
Reservoir (covered)
Kennels
Depot
Burial Ground
Highfield School
Playing Fields
Works
GAWTHORPE
A638
A653
B6128
103
Eastborough
Earlsheaton Technology College
Play. Fld.
Chickenley Heath Farm
Heath Ho.
Recreation Ground
Cemy.
Ossett Street Side
Paleside
Warehouses
SANDBEDS TRADING ESTATE
ASHLEY IND. EST.
Superstore
Earlsheaton Park
Playing Fields
DEWSBURY
Comm. Cen.
Chickenley
BRITANNIA BUSINESS ENTERPRISE CENTRE
Little Royd Mills
Works
Viaduct
Basin
Earlsheaton
Town End
Primary School
Football Grd.
Playing Fields
KIRKLEES
WAKEFIELD
Clough Farm
OSSETT
Runtlings
Depot
Mitchell Laithes Water Pollution Control Centre
Industrial Units
Works
Wilcott
Peaseland
Granary Farm
Football Ground
Crkt. Grd.
Ossett WF5
Depot
Lodge Farm
Park House Farm
Gilbert Dike
The Rookery Farm
HEALEY OLD MILLS
Victoria Mills
Ossett School
Mill Bank
Combs
Sports Ground
Depot
Healey
Works
HEALEY NEW MILLS
The Old Rectory
The Hall (rems. of)
Healey Mills Marshalling Yard
Healey Mills Sidings
THORNHILL
Thornhill Rectory Park
Four Lane Ends
Lodge
The View
Burgoyne Cottage
Hostingley Farm
Calder and Hebble Navigation
RIVER CALDER
HOSTINGLEY LANE
141
124
Thornhill Jun. & Inf. Sch.
Castle Mount
The Community Science Coll.
Tennis Cts.
Works
WAKEFIELD ROAD
LEEDS ROAD
CHANCERY RD.
STATION RD.
THE COMMON
CHURCH LA.

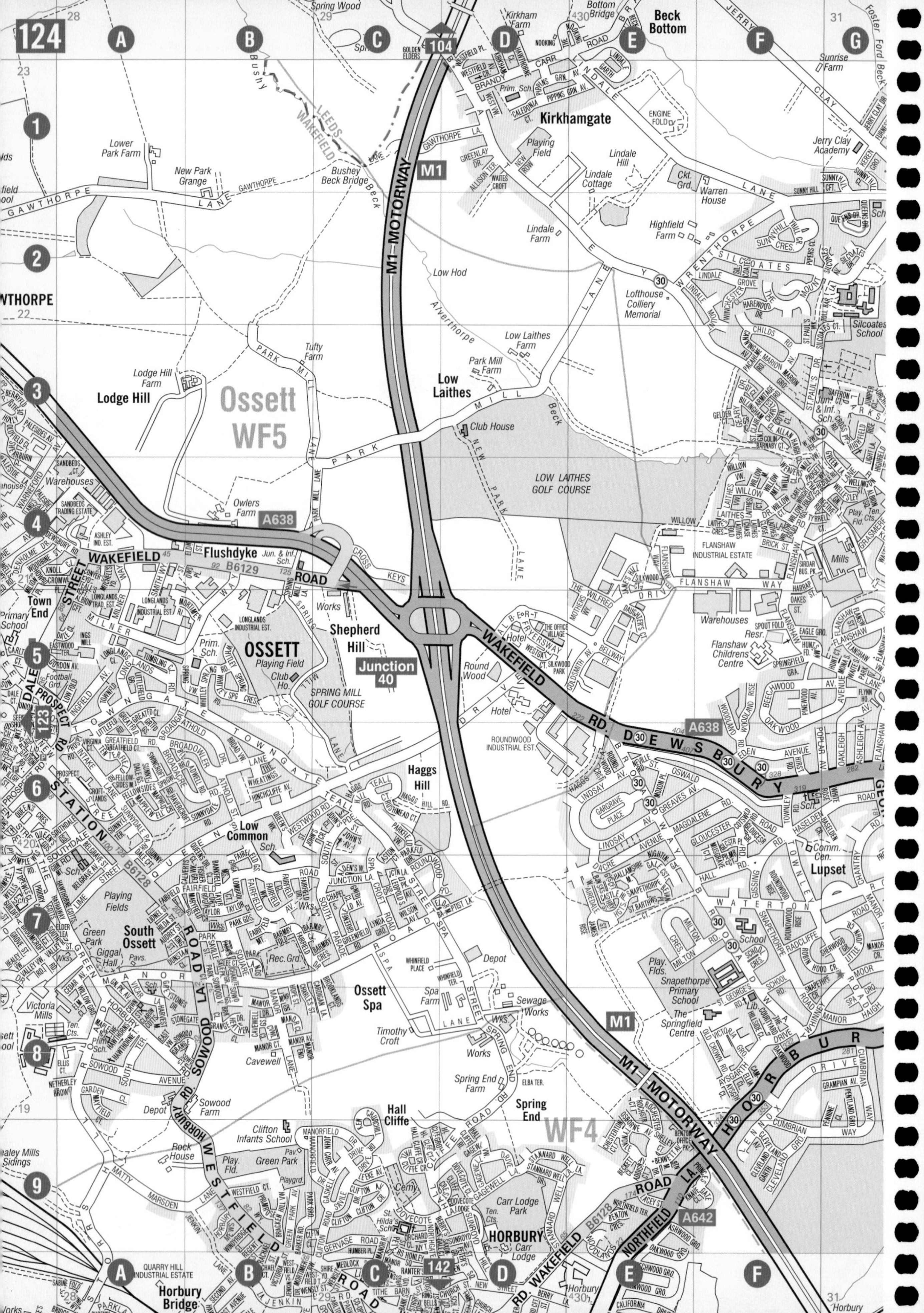

A
B
C
D
E
F
G
1
2
3
4
5
6
7
8
9
104
123
142
Spring Wood
Kirkham Farm
Beck Bottom Bridge
Beck Bottom
Sunrise Farm
Foster Ford Beck
JERRY
CLAY
Bushy
LEEDS
WAKEFIELD
Lower Park Farm
New Park Grange
GAWTHORPE
LANE
Bushey Beck Bridge
Beck
GAWTHORPE LA.
M1
M1–MOTORWAY
BRANDY
CARR
ROAD
Prim. Sch.
Kirkhamgate
ENGINE FOLD
Playing Field
Lindale Hill
Lindale Cottage
Ckt. Grd.
Warren House
Jerry Clay Academy
Highfield Farm
Lindale Farm
WRENTHORPE
SILCOATES
Silcoates School
Low Hod
Alverthorpe
Lofthouse Colliery Memorial
Low Laithes Farm
Park Mill Farm
Tufty Farm
Lodge Hill Farm
Lodge Hill
Ossett WF5
Low Laithes
PARK MILL LANE
Club House
NEW PARK LANE
LOW LAITHES GOLF COURSE
Owlers Farm
Warehouses
SANDBEDS TRADING ESTATE
A638
WAKEFIELD ROAD
Flushdyke
Jun. & Inf. Sch.
B6129
CROSS KEYS
Town End
Primary School
LONGLANDS INDUSTRIAL EST.
Works
Shepherd Hill
OSSETT
Playing Field
Junction 40
Round Wood
Hotel
SPRING MILL GOLF COURSE
FLANSHAW INDUSTRIAL ESTATE
FLANSHAW WAY
Warehouses
Flanshaw Childrens Centre
Mills
ROUNDWOOD INDUSTRIAL EST.
DEWSBURY RD.
Haggs Hill
TOWNGATE
STATION RD.
Low Common
Sch.
Lupset
Playing Fields
South Ossett
Green Park
Giggal Hall
Rec. Grd.
Depot
Ossett Spa
Spa Farm
Victoria Mills
Sewage Works
Timothy Croft
Cavewell
Works
Snapethorpe Primary School
The Springfield Centre
School
HORBURY ROAD
SOWOOD LA.
Sowood Farm
Depot
Spring End Farm
Hall Cliffe
Spring End
WF4
Clifton Infants School
Rock House
Green Park
WESTFIELD ROAD
Carr Lodge Park
HORBURY
WAKEFIELD RD.
B6128
NORTHFIELD LA.
A642
M1 MOTORWAY
CUMBRIAN WAY
QUARRY HILL INDUSTRIAL ESTATE
Horbury Bridge
Horbury

Newton Hill
Snow Hill
Wrenthorpe
Wakefield
Alverthorpe
Flanshaw
WF2
WF3
WF1
Field Head
Fieldhead Hospital
Pinderfields General Hospital
Stanley Grange
Wakefield Hospice
Stanley Hall (Nurses Home)
Clark Hall Educational Mus. & Visitor Cen.
East Moor
King George's Field
Heath Vw. Primary School
St. John's
Wakefield Westgate
Westgate Common
HMP Wakefield
Brooks Bank
Borough Corner
New Brighton
Thornes Park Athletics Stadium
Wakefield College (Thornes Park Campus)
Clarence Park
Thornes Park
Lowe Hill
Miniature Golf Course
Thornes
Cathedral School
The Mount
The Mount Jun. & Inf. School
City of Wakefield Golf Course
Club House
Playing Fields
Boat House Farm
Calder Bridge
River Calder
Nuffield Health Fitness & Wellbeing Centre
Moncton Rd. Industrial Estate
Trading Estate
Belle Isle
Portobello
Sandal
Castle Grove Park
Manygates Adult Educ. Cen.
Sandal Magna Jun. & Inf. Sch.
Agbrigg
St. Thomas a Becket Catholic College
Sports Ground
Calder Vale
Fall Ings
Sewage Works
Kirkgate
WAKEFIELD
Chantry Chapel of St. Mary
Wakefield Trinity Hlth. Club
Wildcats Bowl. RLFC
Cath.
Mus.
Trinity Walk Shop. Cen.
Ridings Shop. Cen.
Jacob's Well La.
Marsh Wy.
Westgate
Ings Road
Kirkgate
Doncaster Road
Barnsley Road
Denby Dale Road
Leeds Road
Aberford Road
Stanley Rd.
Northgate
Thornes Road
George-a-Green Road
Bar Lane
Hatfield Vw.
A61
A650
A642
A636
A638
B6475
B6389
105
143
126
9
32
33
34
G
H
J
K
L
M
N
1
2
3
4
5
6
7
8
9

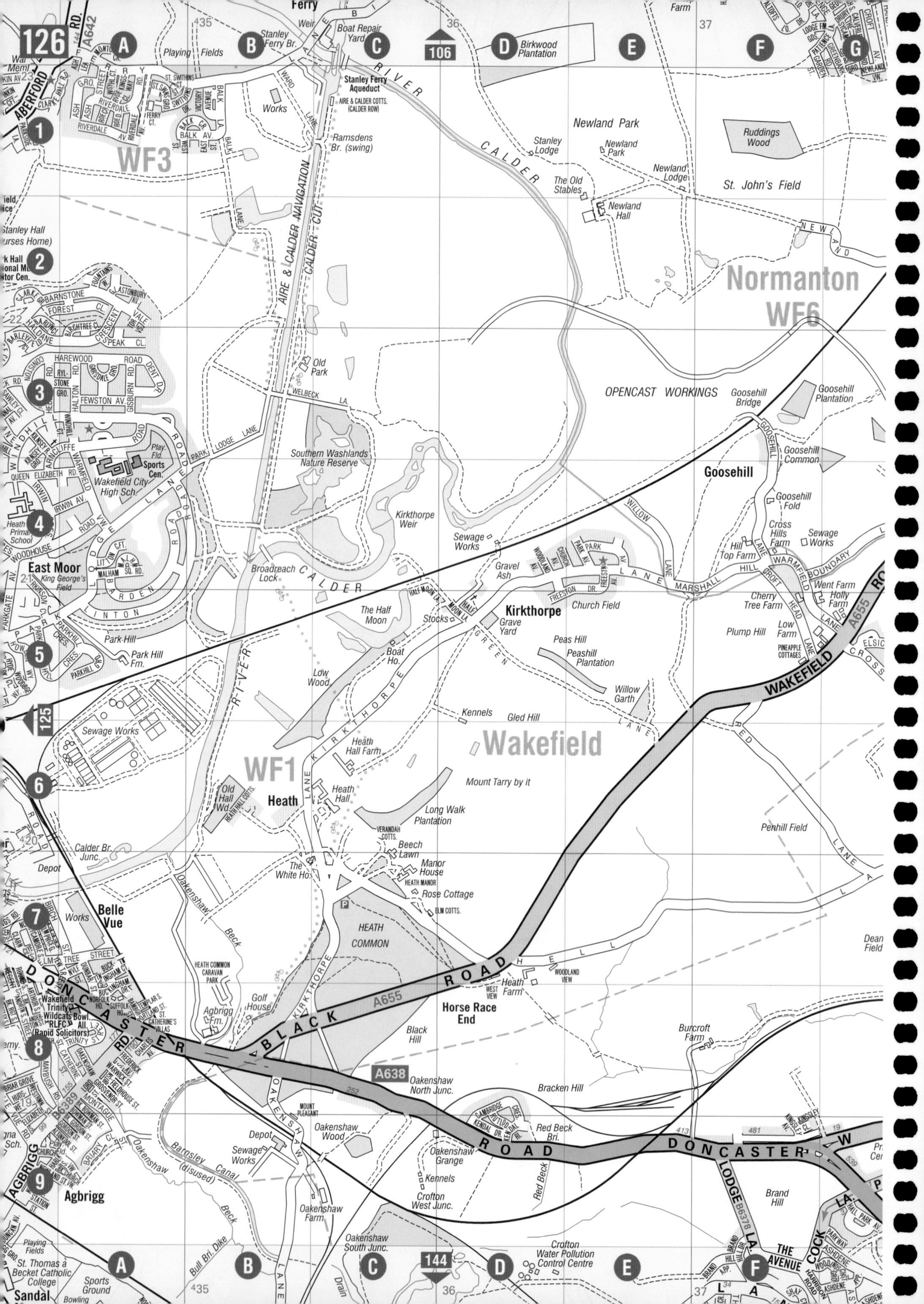
A
B
C
D
E
F
G
1
2
3
4
5
6
7
8
9
106
125
144
WF3
WF1
Normanton
WF6
Wakefield
Stanley Ferry Br.
Playing Fields
Boat Repair Yard
Birkwood Plantation
Stanley Ferry Aqueduct
AIRE & CALDER COTTS. (CALDER ROW)
Works
Ramsdens Br. (swing)
RIVER CALDER
Newland Park
Stanley Lodge
Ruddings Wood
Newland Lodge
St. John's Field
The Old Stables
Newland Hall
AIRE & CALDER NAVIGATION
CALDER CUT
Stanley Hall (Nurses Home)
Old Park
WELBECK LA.
OPENCAST WORKINGS
Goosehill Bridge
Goosehill Plantation
Goosehill Common
Goosehill
Goosehill Fold
Southern Washlands Nature Reserve
Wakefield City High Sch.
Sports Cen.
Kirkthorpe Weir
Sewage Works
Cross Hills Farm
Hill Top Farm
Gravel Ash
MARSHALL HILL LANE
WARMFIELD LANE
Went Farm
Holly Farm
Cherry Tree Farm
Broadreach Lock
East Moor
King George's Field
The Half Moon
Stocks
Kirkthorpe
Grave Yard
Church Field
Peas Hill
Peashill Plantation
Plump Hill
Low Farm
PINEAPPLE COTTAGES
Park Hill
Park Hill Fm.
Boat Ho.
Low Wood
Willow Garth
WAKEFIELD ROAD
A655
Sewage Works
Kennels
Gled Hill
Heath Hall Farm
Mount Tarry by it
Heath
Heath Hall
Old Hall Wd.
Long Walk Plantation
Penhill Field
Calder Br. Junc.
Depot
VERANDAH COTTS.
Beech Lawn
Manor House
HEATH MANOR
Rose Cottage
ELM COTTS.
The White Ho.
Belle Vue
Works
HEATH COMMON
Oakenshaw Beck
Dean Field
HEATH COMMON CARAVAN PARK
Golf House
Agbrigg Fm.
Heath Farm
WOODLAND VIEW
Horse Race End
BLACK ROAD
Wakefield Trinity Wildcats Bowl. RLFC (Rapid Solicitors)
Black Hill
Burcroft Farm
DONCASTER RD.
A638
Oakenshaw North Junc.
Bracken Hill
MOUNT PLEASANT
Oakenshaw Wood
Red Beck Bri.
DONCASTER ROAD
Depot
Sewage Works
Oakenshaw Grange
Kennels
Crofton West Junc.
Barnsley Canal (disused)
Oakenshaw Farm
Brand Hill
LODGE LA.
B6378
THE AVENUE
Agbrigg
Oakenshaw South Junc.
Crofton Water Pollution Control Centre
Bull Bri. Dike
St. Thomas a Becket Catholic College
Sports Ground
Sandal
Playing Fields
Bowling

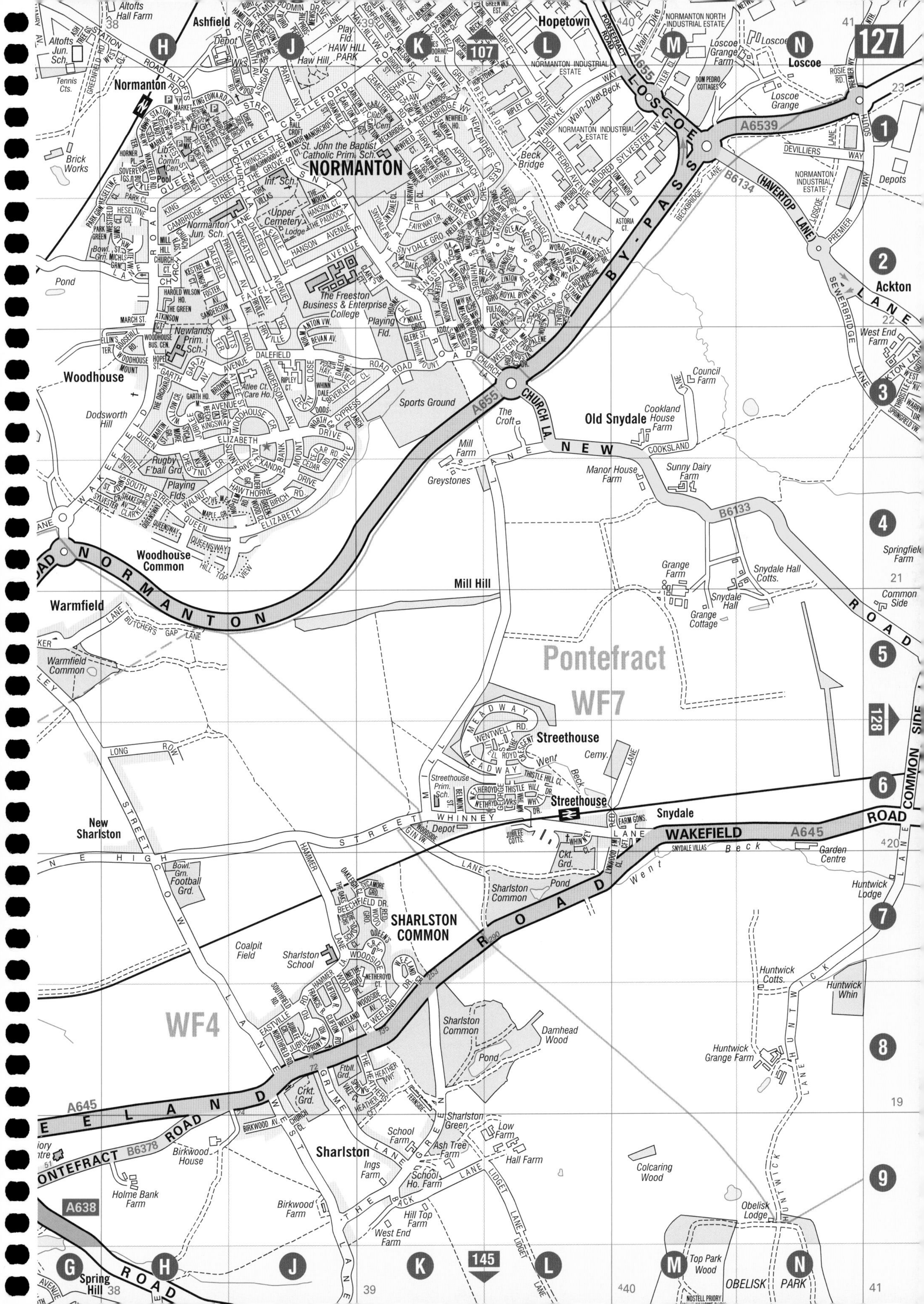

NORMANTON
Normanton
Ashfield
Hopetown
Loscoe
Ackton
Woodhouse
Woodhouse Common
Warmfield
Warmfield Common
Old Snydale
Mill Hill
Pontefract
WF7
Streethouse
Snydale
New Sharlston
SHARLSTON COMMON
Sharlston
Sharlston Common
WF4
Spring Hill
NORMANTON
LOSCOE BY-PASS
A655
A6539
B6134
B6133
A645
A638
B6378
WAKEFIELD ROAD
PONTEFRACT ROAD
COMMON SIDE
The Freeston Business & Enterprise College
Sharlston School
Streethouse Prim. Sch.
Normanton Jun. Sch.
Newlands Prim. Sch.
Sports Ground
Rugby F'ball Grd.
Damhead Wood
Colcaring Wood
Huntwick Grange Farm
Obelisk Lodge
Top Park Wood
OBELISK PARK
107
128
145

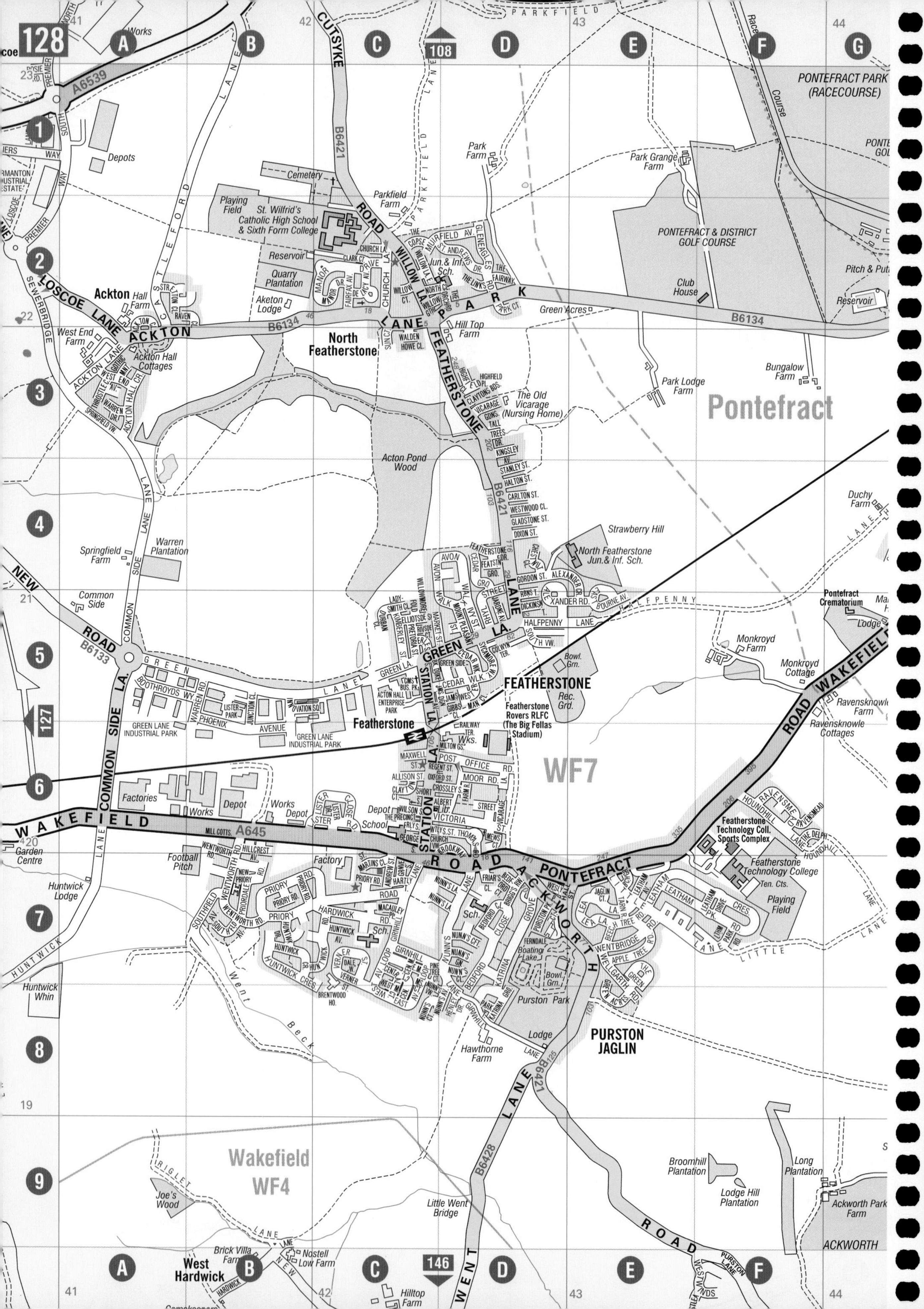

Pontefract
PONTEFRACT PARK (RACECOURSE)
PONTEFRACT & DISTRICT GOLF COURSE
Club House
Reservoir
Pitch & Putt
B6134
Park Grange Farm
Park Farm
Parkfield Farm
Cemetery
Playing Field
St. Wilfrid's Catholic High School & Sixth Form College
Reservoir
Quarry Plantation
Akeion Lodge
Ackton
Hall Farm
LOSCOE LANE
ACKTON
West End Farm
Ackton Hall Cottages
North Featherstone
Hill Top Farm
Green Acres
Park Lodge Farm
Bungalow Farm
The Old Vicarage (Nursing Home)
Acton Pond Wood
Warren Plantation
Springfield Farm
Common Side
Strawberry Hill
North Featherstone Jun.& Inf. Sch.
Pontefract Crematorium
Duchy Farm
Monkroyd Farm
Monkroyd Cottage
Ravensknowle Farm
Ravensknowle Cottages
FEATHERSTONE
Featherstone Rovers RLFC (The Big Fellas Stadium)
Featherstone
GREEN LANE INDUSTRIAL PARK
WF7
Factories
Works
Depot
WAKEFIELD ROAD
A645
Garden Centre
Football Pitch
Huntwick Lodge
Huntwick Whin
Featherstone Technology Coll. Sports Complex
Featherstone Technology College
Playing Field
PONTEFRACT ROAD
ACKWORTH
Boating Lake
Purston Park
Hawthorne Farm
PURSTON JAGLIN
Lodge
Wakefield WF4
Joe's Wood
Little Went Bridge
Broomhill Plantation
Lodge Hill Plantation
Long Plantation
Ackworth Park Farm
ACKWORTH
West Hardwick
Brick Villa Farm
Nostell Low Farm
Hilltop Farm
B6428
B6421
Went Beck
108
127
146

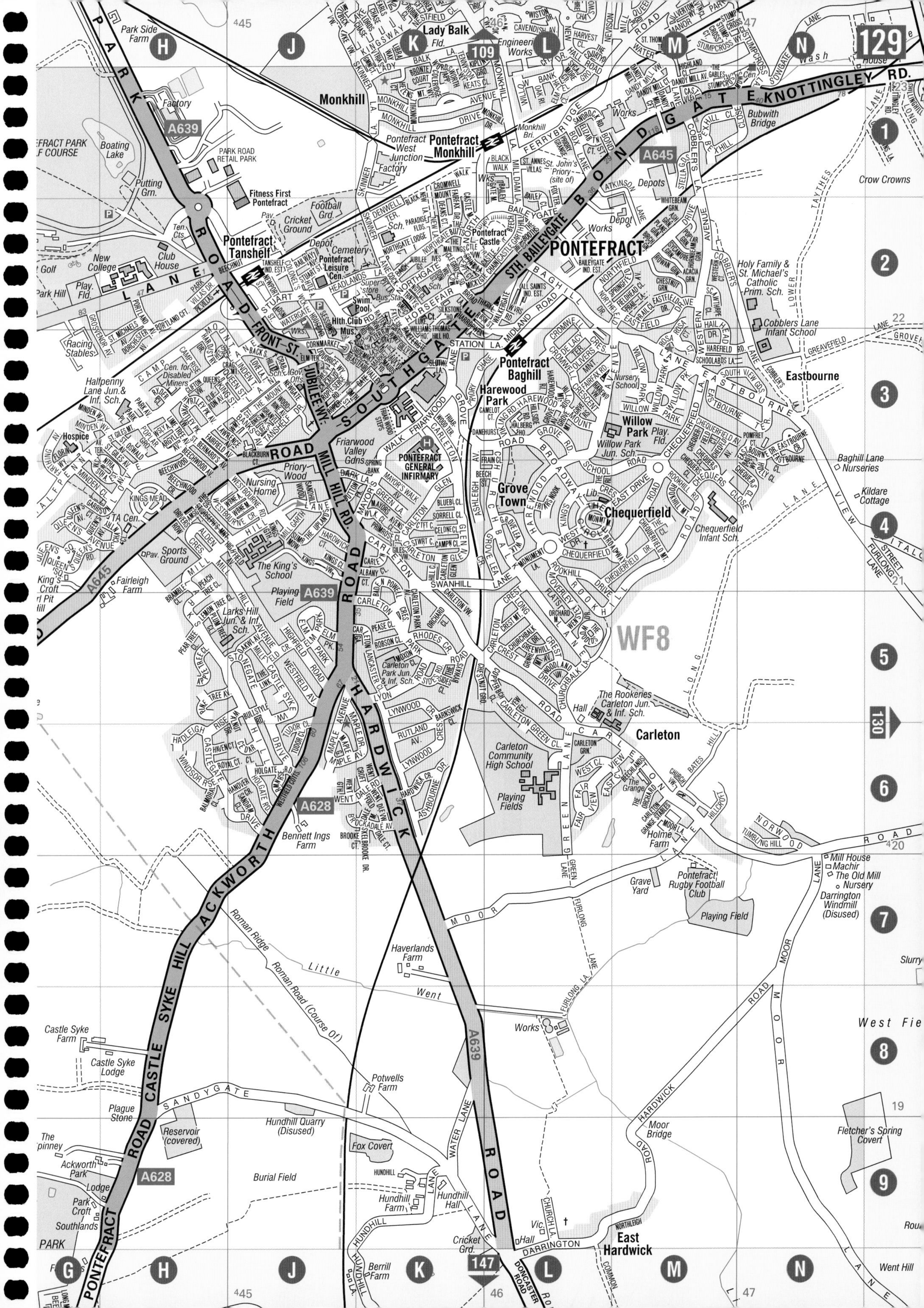

129
109
147
130
H
J
K
L
M
N
G
1
2
3
4
5
6
7
8
9
445
46
47
22
21
20
19
23
WF8
PONTEFRACT
Park Side Farm
Lady Balk Fld.
Engineering Works
Monkhill
Factory
A639
A645
A628
PARK ROAD
KNOTTINGLEY RD.
BONDGATE
Bubwith Bridge
Crow Crowns
Pontefract West Junction
Pontefract Monkhill
Monkhill Bri.
PARK ROAD RETAIL PARK
Fitness First Pontefract
Boating Lake
Putting Grn.
Football Grd.
Cricket Ground
Pontefract Tanshelf
Club House
New College
Play. Fld.
Park Hill
LANE
Cemetery
Pontefract Leisure Cen.
Pontefract Castle
St. John's Priory (site of)
Depots
Works
Depot
STH. BAILEYGATE
BAILEYGATE IND. EST.
ALL SAINTS IND. EST.
MIDLAND ROAD
Holy Family & St. Michael's Catholic Prim. Sch.
Cobblers Lane Infant School
Eastbourne
Swim. Pool
Hlth Club
Mus.
Super store
Bus Sta.
STATION LA.
Pontefract Baghill
FRONT ST.
JUBILEE WY.
SOUTHGATE
Racing Stables
Cen. for Disabled Miners
Halfpenny Lane Jun. & Inf. Sch.
Hospice
ROAD
MILL HILL RD.
Friarwood Valley Gdns.
PONTEFRACT GENERAL INFIRMARY
Harewood Park
Nursery School
Willow Park
Play. Fld.
Willow Park Jun. Sch.
Baghill Lane Nurseries
Kildare Cottage
Priory Wood
Nursing Home
TA Cen.
Sports Ground
The King's School
Grove Town
Chequerfield
Lib.
Chequerfield Infant Sch.
Fairleigh Farm
King's Croft
Playing Field
A639
Larks Hill Jun. & Inf. Sch.
SWANHILL LANE
Carleton Park Jun. & Inf. Sch.
The Rookeries Carleton Jun. & Inf. Sch.
Hall
Carleton
Carleton Community High School
Playing Fields
HARDWICK
Bennett Ings Farm
Holme Farm
NORWOOD ROAD
TUMBLING HILL
Mill House
Machir
The Old Mill
Nursery
Darrington Windmill (Disused)
Grave Yard
Pontefract Rugby Football Club
Playing Field
ACKWORTH
SYKE HILL
CASTLE
MOOR
Roman Ridge
Roman Road (Course Of)
Little
Went
Haverlands Farm
Works
FURLONG LA.
West Fie
Castle Syke Farm
Castle Syke Lodge
Potwells Farm
SANDYGATE
Plague Stone
Reservoir (covered)
Hundhill Quarry (Disused)
Fox Covert
WATER LANE
Moor Bridge
HARDWICK ROAD
Fletcher's Spring Covert
The Spinney
Ackworth Park
Lodge
Burial Field
Park Croft
Southlands
PARK
Hundhill Farm
Hundhill Hall
HUNDHILL
Cricket Grd.
Berrill Farm
Vic.
Hall
CHURCH LA.
DARRINGTON
East Hardwick
DONCASTER ROAD
COMMON
PONTEFRACT ROAD
Went Hill
LANE

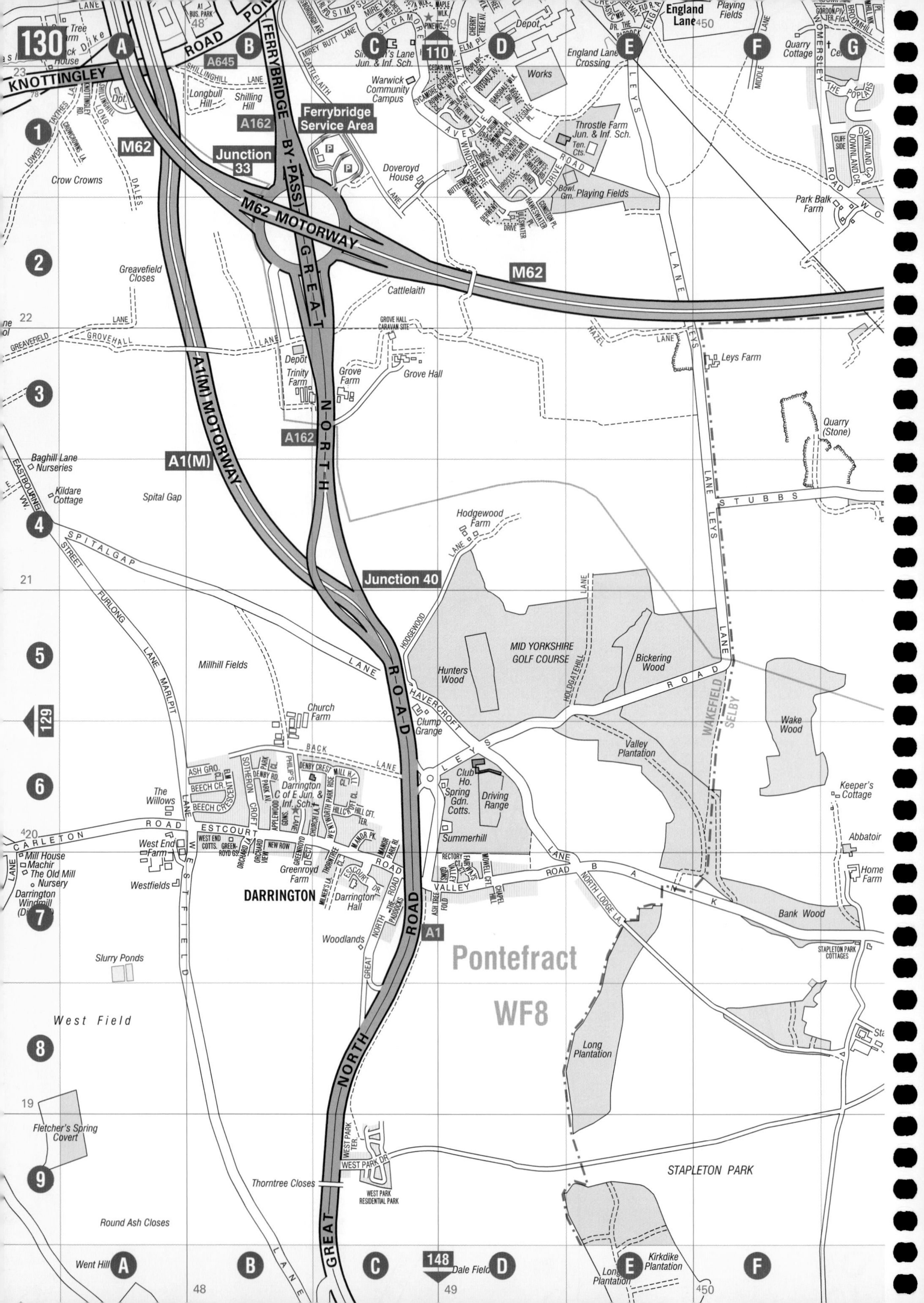
KNOTTINGLEY
Ferrybridge Service Area
Junction 33
M62 MOTORWAY
M62
A1(M) MOTORWAY
A1(M)
A162
A645
A1
Junction 40
GREAT NORTH ROAD
FERRYBRIDGE BY-PASS
Crow Crowns
Longbull Hill
Shilling Hill
Warwick Community Campus
Doveroyd House
Works
Throstle Farm Jun. & Inf. Sch.
England Lane
England Lane Crossing
Playing Fields
Quarry Cottage
Park Balk Farm
Greavefield Closes
Cattlelaith
Grove Hall
Grove Farm
Trinity Farm
Depot
Leys Farm
Quarry (Stone)
Baghill Lane Nurseries
Kildare Cottage
Spital Gap
Hodgewood Farm
MID YORKSHIRE GOLF COURSE
Hunters Wood
Bickering Wood
Millhill Fields
Church Farm
Clump Grange
Valley Plantation
Wake Wood
WAKEFIELD
SELBY
Club Ho.
Spring Gdn. Cotts.
Driving Range
Summerhill
The Willows
West End Farm
Westfields
Mill House
Machir
The Old Mill Nursery
Darrington Windmill
DARRINGTON
Darrington C of E Jun. & Inf. Sch.
Greenroyd Farm
Darrington Hall
Woodlands
Keeper's Cottage
Abbatoir
Home Farm
Bank Wood
STAPLETON PARK COTTAGES
Pontefract
WF8
Slurry Ponds
West Field
Long Plantation
Fletcher's Spring Covert
STAPLETON PARK
Thorntree Closes
WEST PARK RESIDENTIAL PARK
Round Ash Closes
Went Hill
Dale Field
Kirkdike Plantation
Long Plantation

110
129
148

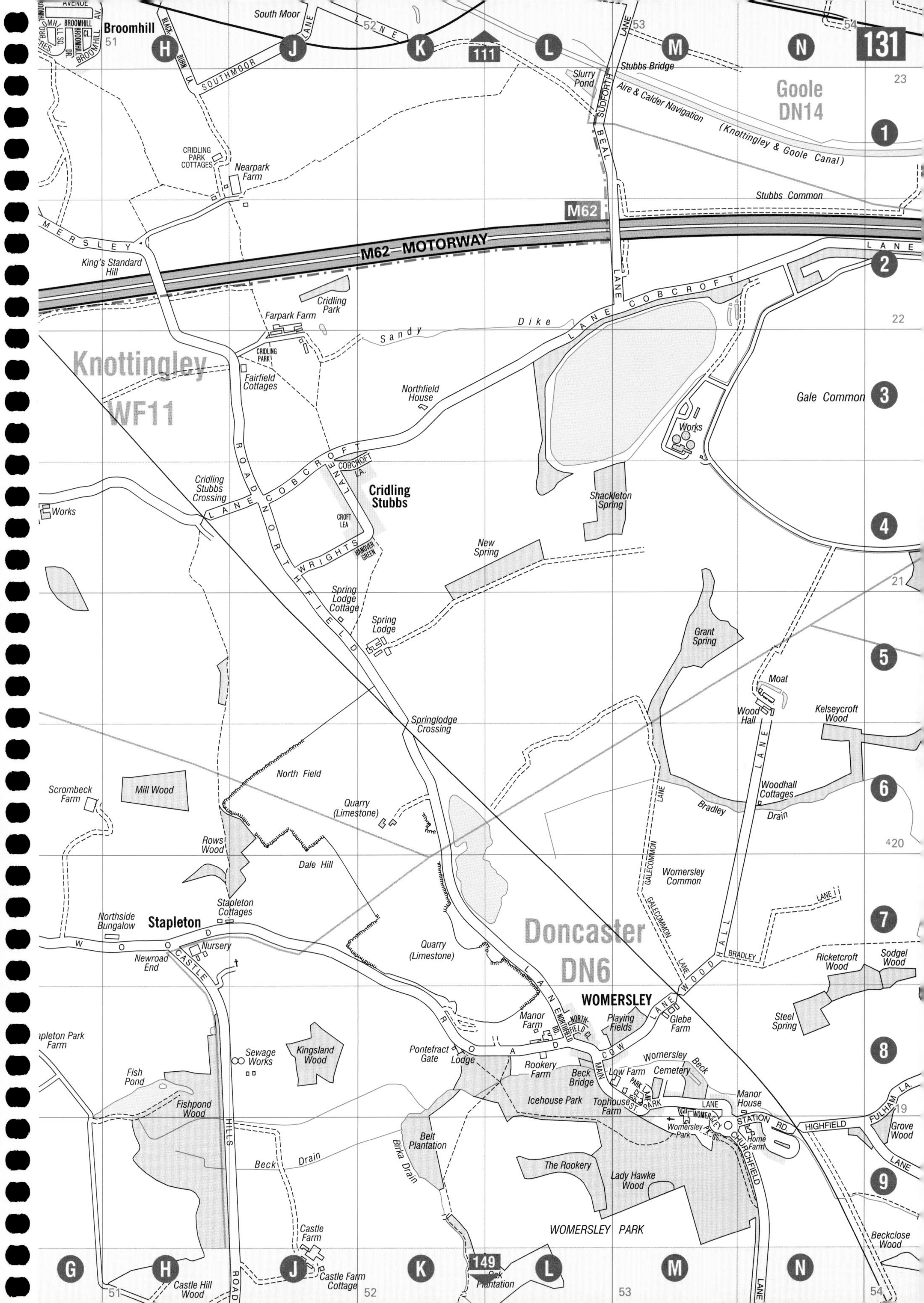

Broomhill
South Moor
Southmoor
Stubbs Bridge
Slurry Pond
Aire & Calder Navigation
(Knottingley & Goole Canal)
Goole DN14
Cridling Park Cottages
Nearpark Farm
Stubbs Common
M62 MOTORWAY
King's Standard Hill
Cridling Park
Farpark Farm
Sandy Dike
Cobcroft Lane
Knottingley WF11
Fairfield Cottages
Northfield House
Gale Common
Works
Cridling Stubbs Crossing
Cridling Stubbs
Shackleton Spring
New Spring
Spring Lodge Cottage
Spring Lodge
Grant Spring
Moat
Wood Hall
Kelseycroft Wood
Springlodge Crossing
North Field
Scrombeck Farm
Mill Wood
Quarry (Limestone)
Woodhall Cottages
Bradley Drain
Rows Wood
Dale Hill
Womersley Common
Northside Bungalow
Stapleton
Stapleton Cottages
Doncaster DN6
Nursery
Newroad End
Ricketcroft Wood
Sodgel Wood
WOMERSLEY
Manor Farm
Playing Fields
Glebe Farm
Steel Spring
Stapleton Park Farm
Sewage Works
Kingsland Wood
Pontefract Gate
Lodge
Rookery Farm
Beck Bridge
Low Farm
Womersley Beck
Cemetery
Fish Pond
Fishpond Wood
Icehouse Park
Tophouse Farm
Manor House
Womersley Park
Home Farm
Station Rd.
Highfield
Fulham La.
Grove Wood
Belt Plantation
Birka Drain
Beck Drain
The Rookery
Lady Hawke Wood
WOMERSLEY PARK
Castle Farm
Castle Farm Cottage
Beckclose Wood
Castle Hill Wood
Oak Plantation
111
149

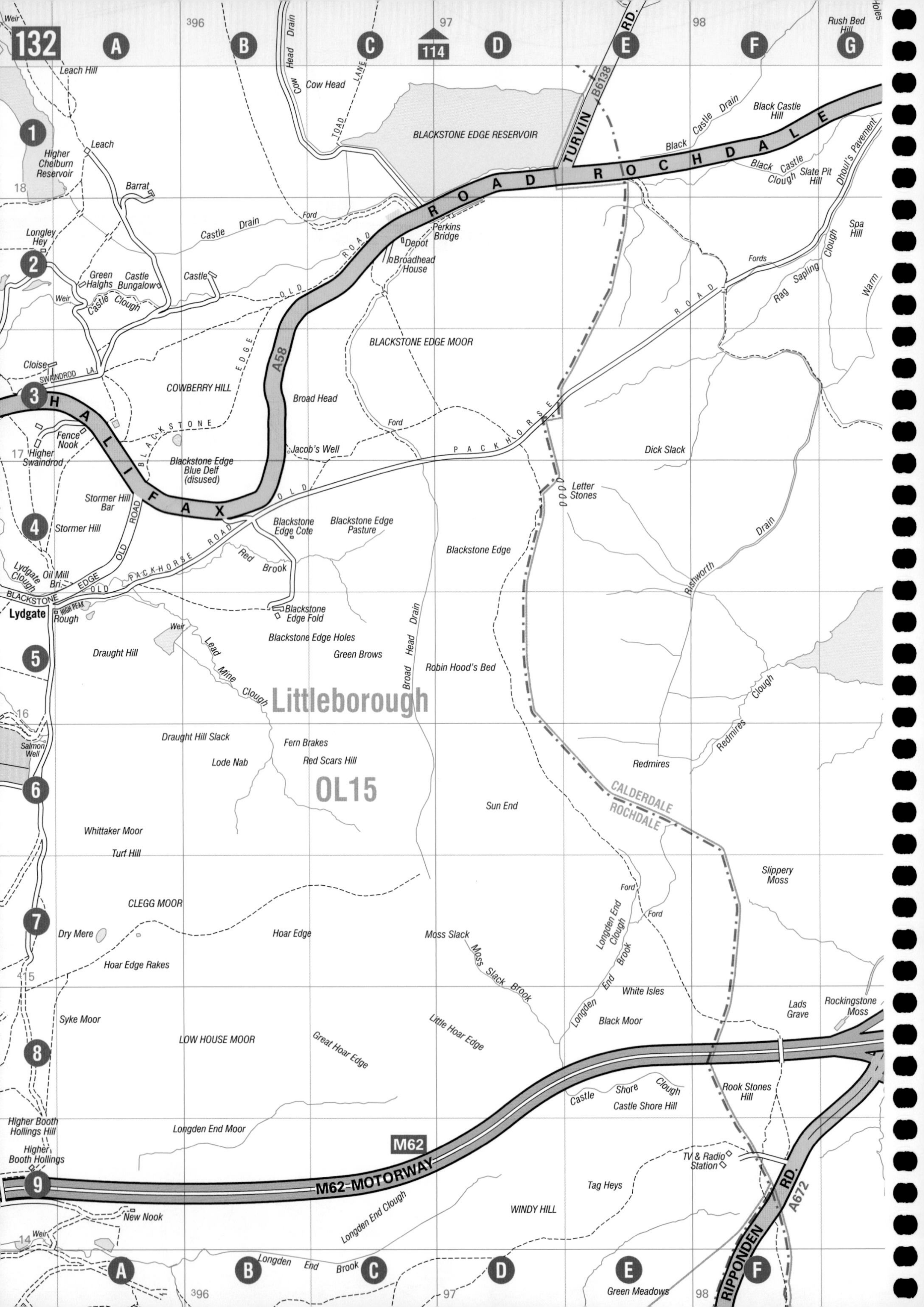

A
B
C
D
E
F
G
396
97
114
98
Rush Bed Hill
Leach Hill
Cow Head
Cow Head Drain
TOAD LANE
BLACKSTONE EDGE RESERVOIR
TURVIN RD. B6138
Black Castle Hill
Black Castle Drain
Black Castle Clough
Slate Pit Hill
Dhoul's Pavement
ROCHDALE ROAD
Leach
Higher Chelburn Reservoir
Barrat
Longley Hey
Castle Drain
Ford
Perkins Bridge
Depot
Broadhead House
Spa Hill
Fords
Sapling Clough
Rag Sapling
Warm
Green Halghs
Castle Bungalow
Castle
Weir
Castle Clough
OLD ROAD
ROAD
BLACKSTONE EDGE MOOR
Cloise
SWAINDROD LA.
COWBERRY HILL
EDGE
A58
Broad Head
HALIFAX ROAD
BLACKSTONE
Fence Nook
Higher Swaindrod
Ford
PACKHORSE
Dick Slack
Jacob's Well
Blackstone Edge Blue Delf (disused)
Letter Stones
Stormer Hill Bar
Stormer Hill
Blackstone Edge Cote
Blackstone Edge Pasture
OLD ROAD
PACKHORSE ROAD
Drain
Red Brook
Blackstone Edge
Lydgate Clough
Oil Mill Bri.
EDGE
OLD
BLACKSTONE
Lydgate
HIGH PEAK
Rough
Blackstone Edge Fold
Rishworth
Weir
Blackstone Edge Holes
Draught Hill
Lead Mine Clough
Green Brows
Broad Head Drain
Robin Hood's Bed
Littleborough
Clough
Salmon Well
Draught Hill Slack
Fern Brakes
Redmires
Lode Nab
Red Scars Hill
Redmires
OL15
Sun End
CALDERDALE
ROCHDALE
Whittaker Moor
Turf Hill
Slippery Moss
Ford
CLEGG MOOR
Ford
Longden End Clough
Dry Mere
Hoar Edge
Moss Slack
Moss Slack Brook
Longden End Brook
Hoar Edge Rakes
White Isles
Syke Moor
Little Hoar Edge
Lads Grave
Rockingstone Moss
LOW HOUSE MOOR
Black Moor
Great Hoar Edge
Castle Shore Clough
Rook Stones Hill
Castle Shore Hill
Higher Booth Hollings Hill
Longden End Moor
M62
Higher Booth Hollings
TV & Radio Station
M62-MOTORWAY
Tag Heys
RIPPONDEN RD. A672
Longden End Clough
WINDY HILL
New Nook
Weir
Longden End Brook
Green Meadows
1
2
3
4
5
6
7
8
9
18
17
16
415
14

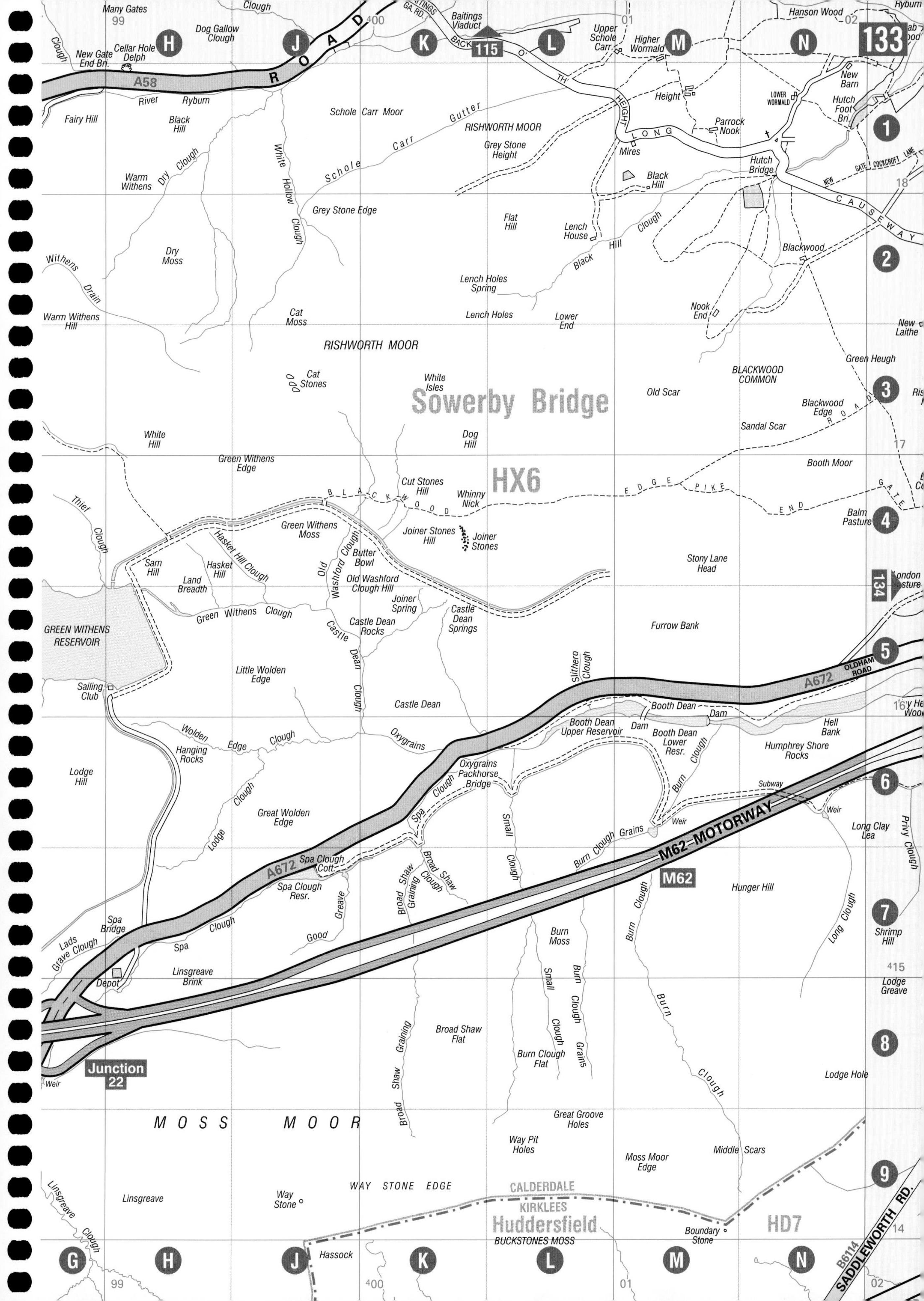
Many Gates
Clough
Dog Gallow Clough
New Gate End Bri.
Cellar Hole Delph
A58
ROAD
Baitings Viaduct
115
BACK O' TH' HEIGHT
Upper Schole Carr
Higher Wormald
Hanson Wood
Ryburn
River Ryburn
Fairy Hill
Black Hill
Schole Carr Moor
Schole Carr Gutter
RISHWORTH MOOR
Grey Stone Height
Height
Lower Wormald
Parrock Nook
New Barn
Hutch Foot Bri.
LONG
Mires
Hutch Bridge
NEW GATE
COCKCROFT LANE
CAUSEWAY
Warm Withens
Dry Clough
White Hollow Clough
Grey Stone Edge
Black Hill
Flat Hill
Lench House
Black Hill Clough
Blackwood
Withens Drain
Dry Moss
Lench Holes Spring
Lench Holes
Lower End
Nook End
Warm Withens Hill
Cat Moss
RISHWORTH MOOR
New Laithe
Green Heugh
Cat Stones
White Isles
Sowerby Bridge
BLACKWOOD COMMON
Old Scar
Blackwood Edge
ROAD
Sandal Scar
White Hill
Dog Hill
Green Withens Edge
Booth Moor
Cut Stones Hill
HX6
Whinny Nick
BLACKWOOD
EDGE PIKE END GATE
Balm Pasture
Thief Clough
Green Withens Moss
Joiner Stones Hill
Joiner Stones
Sam Hill
Hasket Hill Clough
Hasket Hill
Land Breadth
Old Washford Clough
Butter Bowl
Old Washford Clough Hill
Stony Lane Head
134
Joiner Spring
Green Withens Clough
Castle Dean Rocks
Castle Dean Springs
GREEN WITHENS RESERVOIR
Castle Dean Clough
Furrow Bank
Little Wolden Edge
Slithero Clough
A672
OLDHAM ROAD
Sailing Club
Castle Dean
Booth Dean
Dam
Booth Dean Upper Reservoir
Booth Dean Lower Resr.
Hell Bank
Humphrey Shore Rocks
Wolden Edge Clough
Hanging Rocks
Oxygrains
Oxygrains Packhorse Bridge
Lodge Hill
Burn Clough
Subway
Weir
Great Wolden Edge
Spa Clough
Small Clough
Long Clay Lea
Privy Clough
Lodge Clough
Burn Clough Grains
M62 MOTORWAY
A672
Spa Clough Cott.
Broad Shaw Clough
Broad Shaw Graining
M62
Spa Clough Resr.
Greave
Hunger Hill
Spa Bridge
Good
Burn Moss
Long Clough
Shrimp Hill
Lads Grave Clough
Spa
Linsgreave Brink
Depot
Lodge Greave
Broad Shaw Flat
Burn Clough Flat
Small Clough Grains
Burn Clough
Junction 22
Weir
Lodge Hole
Broad Shaw Graining
MOSS MOOR
Great Groove Holes
Way Pit Holes
Moss Moor Edge
Middle Scars
Linsgreave
Linsgreave Clough
Way Stone
WAY STONE EDGE
CALDERDALE
KIRKLEES
Huddersfield
BUCKSTONES MOSS
HD7
Boundary Stone
B6114 SADDLEWORTH RD.
Hassock
G H J K L M N

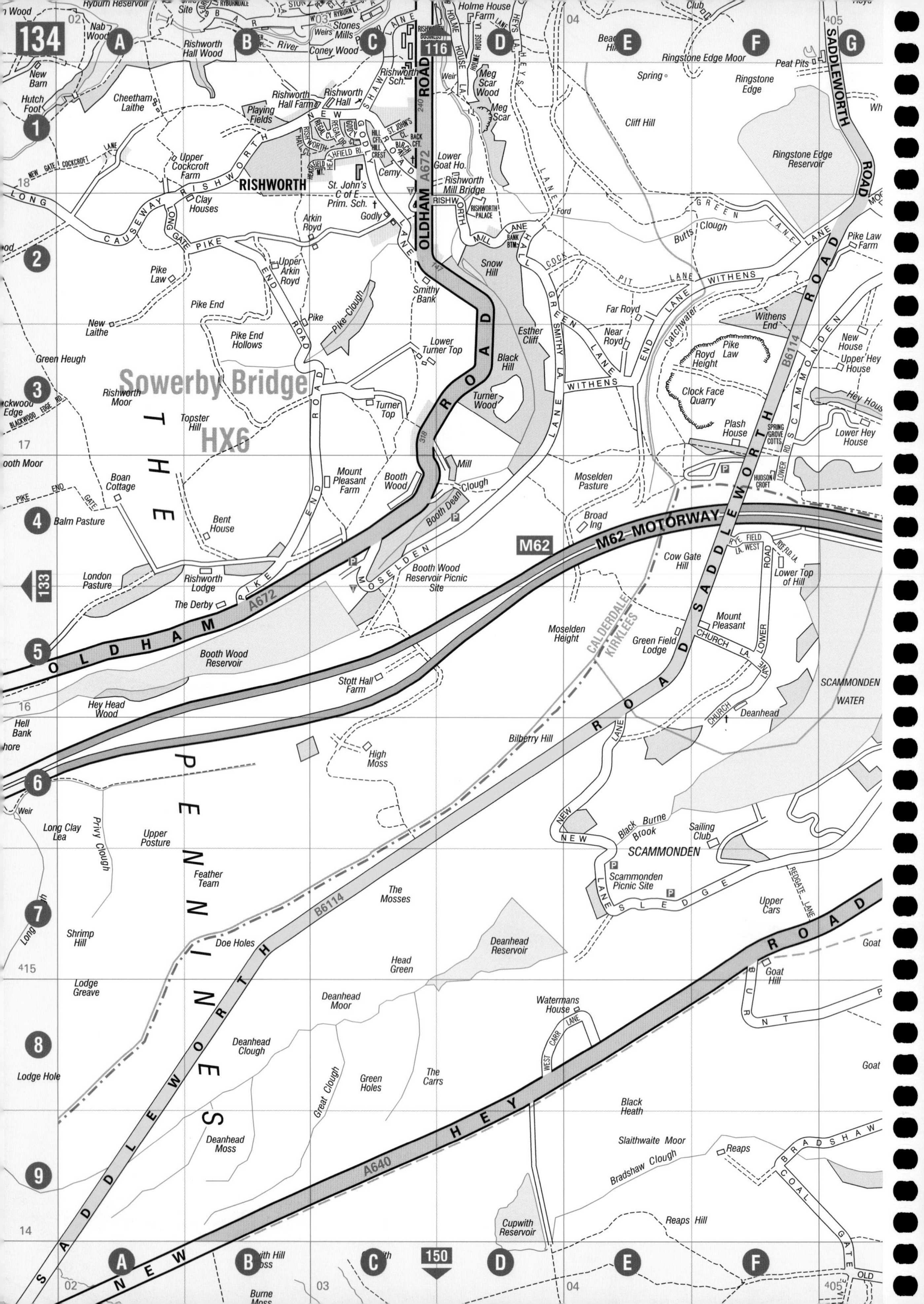
A
B
C
D
E
F
G
116
Rishworth Hall Wood
Coney Wood
Stones Mills
Holme House Farm
Ringstone Edge Moor
Peat Pits
SADDLEWORTH ROAD
Ringstone Edge
Spring
Cliff Hill
Ringstone Edge Reservoir
Meg Scar Wood
Meg Scar
Rishworth Sch.
Rishworth Hall Farm
Rishworth Hall
Playing Fields
Cheetham Laithe
Hutch Foot
New Barn
Nab Wood
Upper Cockcroft Farm
RISHWORTH
Lower Goat Ho.
Rishworth Mill Bridge
Cemy.
St. John's C of E. Prim. Sch.
Godly
Arkin Royd
Clay Houses
LONG CAUSEWAY
PIKE
OLDHAM ROAD
A672
Snow Hill
Butts Clough
GREEN LANE
Pike Law Farm
WITHENS
Far Royd
Near Royd
Withens End
Catchwater
Royd Height
Pike Law
Clock Face Quarry
Plash House
New House
Upper Hey House
Lower Hey House
Hey House
Upper Arkin Royd
Pike Law
Pike End
New Laithe
Pike End Hollows
Pike Clough
Smithy Bank
Lower Turner Top
Esther Cliff
Black Hill
Turner Wood
Turner Top
Green Heugh
Sowerby Bridge
HX6
Rishworth Moor
Topster Hill
Blackwood Edge
Booth Moor
Boan Cottage
Mount Pleasant Farm
Booth Wood
Mill
Clough
Moselden Pasture
Balm Pasture
Bent House
Booth Dean
Broad Ing
M62
M62 MOTORWAY
Cow Gate Hill
Lower Top of Hill
London Pasture
Rishworth Lodge
The Derby
Booth Wood Reservoir Picnic Site
Moselden Height
CALDERDALE KIRKLEES
Mount Pleasant
Green Field Lodge
CHURCH LA.
Booth Wood Reservoir
Stott Hall Farm
SCAMMONDEN WATER
Deanhead
Hey Head Wood
Hell Bank
Bilberry Hill
High Moss
THE PENNINES
Long Clay Lea
Privy Clough
Upper Posture
Sailing Club
Black Burne Brook
SCAMMONDEN
Scammonden Picnic Site
SLEDGE LANE
Feather Team
The Mosses
B6114
Upper Cars
REDGATE LANE
Shrimp Hill
Doe Holes
Deanhead Reservoir
Head Green
Goat Hill
Lodge Greave
Deanhead Moor
Watermans House
WEST CARR LANE
Deanhead Clough
Lodge Hole
Green Holes
The Carrs
Great Clough
Black Heath
Slaithwaite Moor
Reaps
Bradshaw Clough
BRADSHAW
COAL GATE
Deanhead Moss
A640
NEW HEY ROAD
Cupwith Reservoir
Reaps Hill
133
150

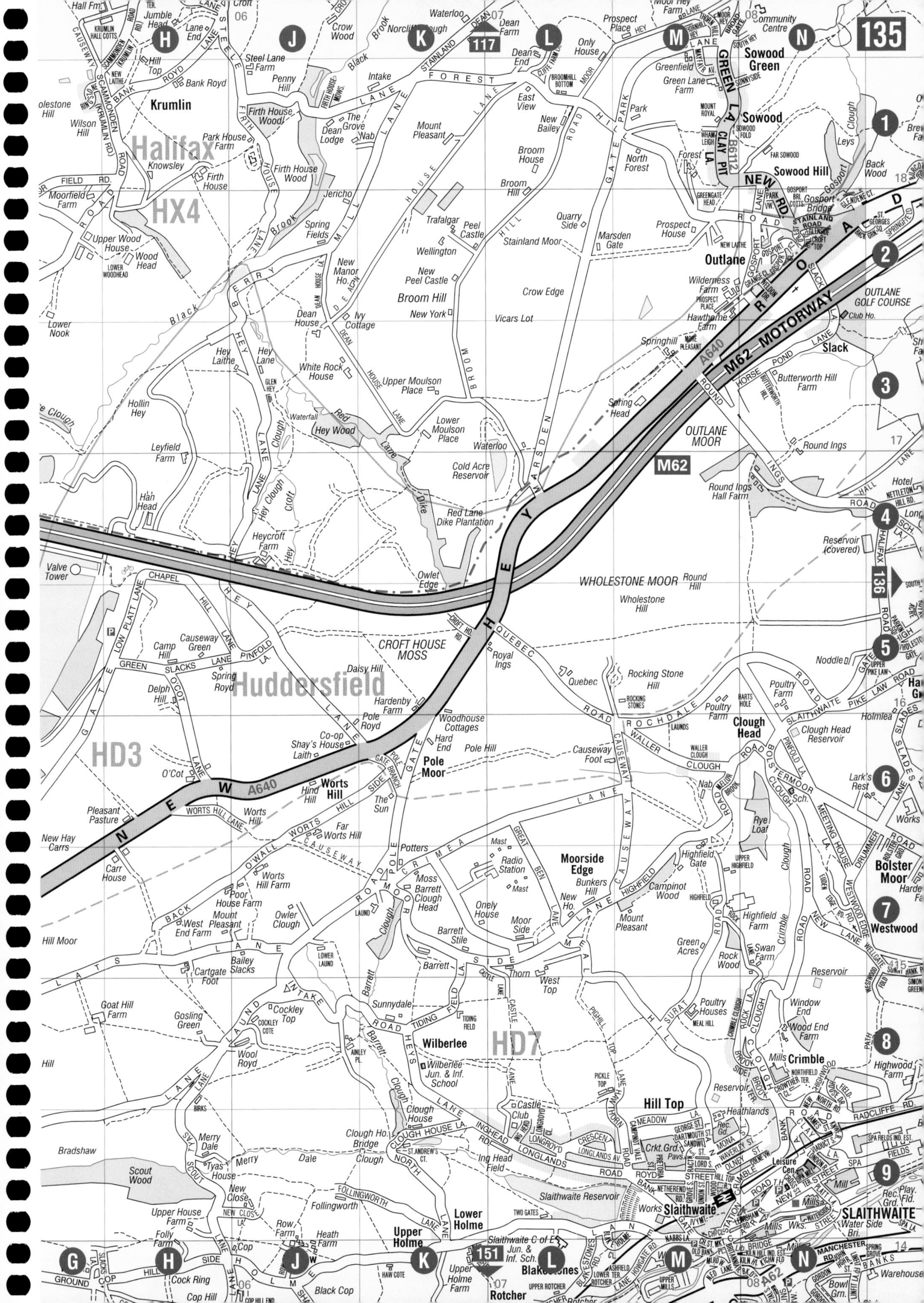

HX4
HD3
HD7
Huddersfield
M62 MOTORWAY
M62
Junction 23
118
135
152
CALDERDALE
KIRKLEES
NEW HEY ROAD
A640
LINDLEY MOOR RD.
A643
MANCHESTER ROAD
A62
B6111
Mink Farm
Poultry Houses
Turley Cote Farm
Old Lindley
Old Lindley Moor
Peat Ponds Farm
Peat Ponds
Jericho
Weather Hill
Cowrakes
New Lea
Old Lea
Lea Hill Farm
Brewery Farm
Leys
Back Wood
Mount
YMCA Sports Centre
Moorlands Prim. Sch.
YMCA
Laund Hill
Hill Grove Farm
Lindley
Leeches Hill
Lower Hurst Farm
Snow Lea
Shaw Wood
OUTLANE GOLF COURSE
Hirst Wood
Longwood Brook
Slack
Shaw Farm
Pendle Hill
Pighill Wood
Compensation Reservoir
Salendine Nook
Huddersfield New College
Salendine Nook High Sch.
Playing Fields
Tennis Courts
Longwood Edge
Holly Bank Farm
Oakes
Whin Gate
Poultry Houses
Nettleton Hill
Longwood Reservoirs
Holmefield
Dodlee
Royles Head Farm
Mole's Head
Works
Hotel
Longwood Common
Scapegoat Hill Jun. & Inf. Sch.
Reservoir (covered)
Scapegoat Hill
Milking Clough
Bonny Clough Wood
Clay Wood Brook
Longwood
Quarmby
Quarmby Cliff
Nab End
Vicarage
Greenroyd Farm
Hollin Hall
Whitwam Bank
Hill Side
Hall Ings
Beech Jun. & Inf. Sch.
Leymoor Recreation Ground
Playing Field
Newhaven Business Park
Noddlebury
Haughs Green
Wood Bank
Upper Fields
St.John's C of E Jun. & Inf. Sch.
GOLCAR
Golcar Jun. & Inf. Sch.
Cricket Grd.
Town End
Museum
Holmlea
Duke Ings
Heath House Wood
Lark's Rest
Works
Sharehill
Scar Wood
Milnsbridge
Bolster Moor
Harden Road Farm
Headwall Green
Westwood
Wellhouse
The Gables
High Beeches
Rob Royd
Scarwood Bridge
Folly Wks.
Guy Edge
Cowlersley Primary School
Cowlersley
Woodside Cottage
Coronation Park
Golcar Brook Bridge
Westwood House
Lowestwood
Low Westwood Bridge
Highwood Farm
Hill Top
Hazel Grove
Factory
Crosland Hill
Cock's Crossing
Huddersfield Narrow Canal (Disused)
Bank Bottom Fm.
Lees Mill Bridge
Lees Mill Farm
Linthwaite
Lane End
Rye Croft Edge
Felks Stile Cottage
CROSLAND HEATH GOLF COURSE
Club House
Shaw Green
Linthwaite Ardron C of E Jun. & Inf. School
Colne Valley Specialist Arts College
Sports Centre
Linthwaite Jun. & Inf. Sch.
Lower Clough
Water Side Bridge
SLAITHWAITE
Warehouse
Black Rock Mills
Hill Tree Park
Waterholes Quarry (Sandstone)
AIRFIELD

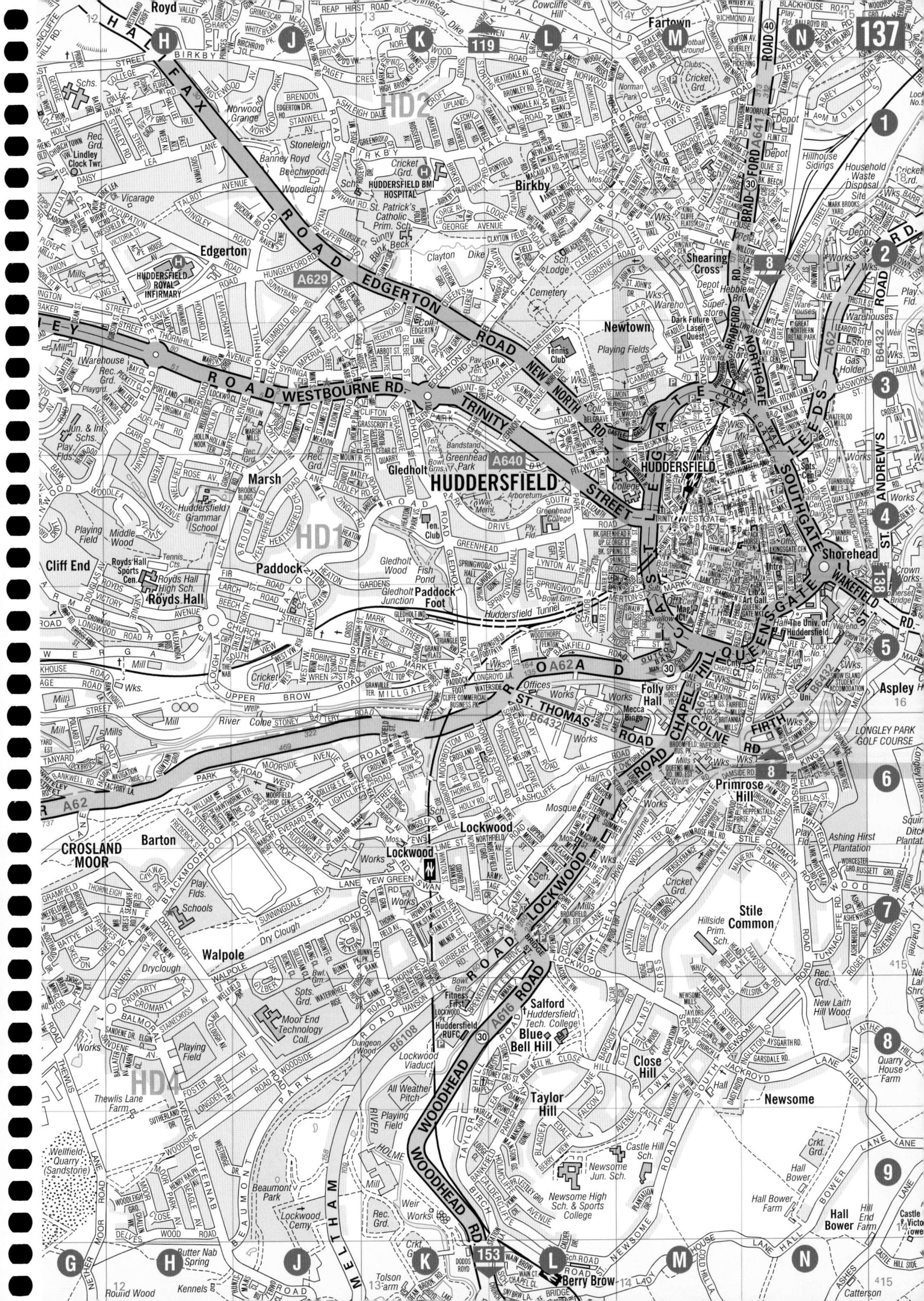
137
119
153
138
8
HD1
HD2
HD4
HUDDERSFIELD
Fartown
Birkby
Edgerton
Newtown
Marsh
Paddock
Cliff End
Royds Hall
Paddock Foot
Lockwood
Barton
CROSLAND MOOR
Walpole
Drycluogh
Salford
Blue Bell Hill
Taylor Hill
Close Hill
Newsome
Primrose Hill
Stile Common
Folly Hall
Shorehead
Aspley
Hall Bower
Berry Brow
Shearing Cross
Royd
HALIFAX ROAD
EDGERTON ROAD
NEW NORTH RD.
TRINITY STREET
WESTBOURNE RD.
A629
A640
A62
A616
A641
B6432
B6108
WOODHEAD ROAD
LOCKWOOD ROAD
CHAPEL HILL
QUEENSGATE
SOUTHGATE
NORTHGATE
LEEDS ROAD
WAKEFIELD RD.
ST. THOMAS ROAD
COLNE RD.
FIRTH RD.
MELTHAM RD.
HUDDERSFIELD ROYAL INFIRMARY
HUDDERSFIELD BMI HOSPITAL
Huddersfield Grammar School
Royds Hall High Sch.
Greenhead Park
Greenhead College
Huddersfield Tunnel
River Colne
Lockwood Viaduct
Huddersfield RUFC
Moor End Technology Coll.
Newsome High Sch. & Sports College
Huddersfield Tech. College
Household Waste Disposal Site
Hillhouse Sidings
Gas Holder
The Univ. of Huddersfield
Mecca Bingo
Dark Future Laser Quest
Wellfield Quarry (Sandstone)
LONGLEY PARK GOLF COURSE
Thewlis Lane Farm
Butter Nab Spring
Lockwood Cemy.
Beaumont Park
Dungeon Wood
Tolson Farm
Round Wood
Kennels
Catterson
Quarry House Farm
Hall Bower Farm
Ashing Hirst Plantation
New Laith Hill Wood
Dry Clough
Clayton Dike
Cemetery
Gledholt Wood
Fish Pond
Gledholt Junction
Lindley Clock Twr.
Norwood Grange
Stoneleigh
Banney Royd
Beechwood
Woodleigh
G H J K L M N
1 2 3 4 5 6 7 8 9
12 13 14 15 16 17 18
415

A
B
C
D
E
F
G
1
2
3
4
5
6
7
8
9
120
137
154
8
Playing Fields
Huddersfield Tech. Coll. (Brunel Ho.)
DALTON WORKS
Dalton Bank
Calder & Hebble Navigation
Huddersfield Broad Canal
Canalside Sports Complex
Football Grd.
Wholesale Market
HD2
UK Superbowl
Household Waste Disposal Site
Cricket Grd.
Depot
Works
Briery Bank
Dalton Grange
Reservoir
Heaton Fields
The Close
Nab Hill
Wellhouse Farm
Prim. Sch.
Cricket Ground
Playing Fields
Jagger Hill
Rawthorpe
Nether Hall Barn
Bradley Mills
Rawthorpe High Sch.
Comm. Cen.
Rawthorpe St. James C of E Inf. Sch.
Stadium Health & Fitness Club
Odeon Cinema
Huddersfield Town FC & Huddersfield Giants RLFC (The John Smith's Stadium)
HD1
Golf Driving Range
Dalton Fold
Rawthorpe Jun. Sch.
Recreation Ground
Briggate Bridge
Cold Royd Wood
Hill Top Farm
Hill Side
Round Wood Bridge
Hospice
HD5
Dalton
Playing Fields
Schools
Dalton Green
Waterloo
Round Wood
Tandem
Tandem Industrial Estate
Gallagher Retail Park
Lwr. Hall
Lower Hall
Shorehead
Crown Works
Moldgreen
Tolson Mus.
Ravensknowle Park
A629
WAKEFIELD ROAD
PENISTONE ROAD
Soccer City
Total Fitness
Superstore
Greenside
Aspley
Club House
LONGLEY PARK GOLF COURSE
Martin Bank Wood
Jockey Hall
Gosling Hall Farm
Greenside Inf. Sch.
Almondbury Sports Cen.
Almondbury High Sch. & Language Coll.
Fernside Park
Paddling Pool
Longley School
Benomley
Almondbury
Almondbury Jun. Sch.
Fenay Bridge
Ashing Hirst Plantation
Squirrel Ditch Plantation
Oaken Bank Plantation
Lowerhouse C of E Jun. & Inf. Sch.
Lower Houses
Penny Spring Wood
Benholmley Banks
Cemetery
Nurseries
Fenay Cottage
Fenay Hall
Fenay Grange
Ashenhurst
Longley Old Hall
Hay Farm Nurseries
Longley
Longley Hill Plantation
Almondbury C of E Inf. Sch.
Broken Cross
King James's School
Birks
New Laith Hill Wood
Gledhill Hill
Quarry House Farm
Ashes Common
Reservoir (covered)
Wheat Royd Wood
Wheat Royd Lodge
Littlecroft
Sunninghill
Greylands
Almondbury Common
WOODSOME HALL GOLF COURSE
Birks Wood
Ashes Common Farm
Clough Hall
Mellor Wood
HD4
Three Oaks
Bottoms Farm
Rushfield Bridge
Woodsome Hall (Club House)
Castle Hill Bottom
Clough Ings
Yew Croft
Low Common
Farnley Wood
Spring Wood
Hall Bower
Castle Hill Fort
Castle Hill & Victoria Tower
Lower Castle Hill
Lower Castle Hill Farm
Shrogg Wood
Anchor Wood
Castle Hill Side
Clay Hall
Bank Foot Bridge
Bankfoot
Fletcher House
Royd House
Park Cottage
Lumb
The Lumb
Ogley
Catterson
415
16
17
18
14

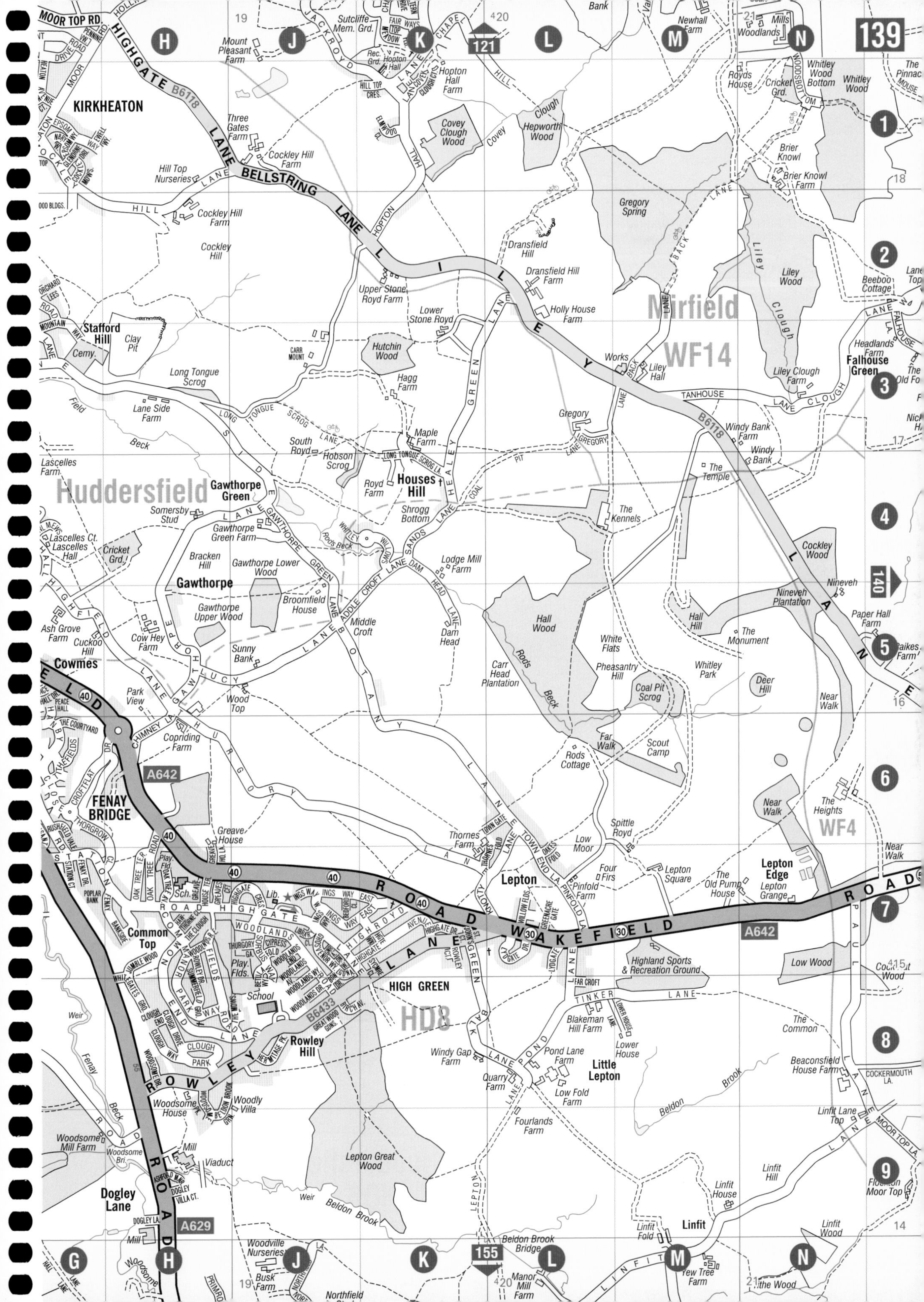
KIRKHEATON
Highgate Lane
B6118
Bellstring Lane
Lilley Lane
Three Gates Farm
Cockley Hill Farm
Hill Top Nurseries
Cockley Hill
Mount Pleasant Farm
Sutcliffe Mem. Grd.
Hopton Hall Farm
Covey Clough Wood
Hepworth Wood
Clough
Gregory Spring
Liley Wood
Liley Clough
Mirfield
WF14
Whitley Wood Bottom
Whitley Wood
Royds House
Cricket Grd.
Brier Knowl
Brier Knowl Farm
Beeboo Cottage
Headlands Farm
Falhouse Green
Liley Clough Farm
Tanhouse Lane
Windy Bank Farm
Windy Bank
The Temple
Dransfield Hill
Dransfield Hill Farm
Holly House Farm
Upper Stone Royd Farm
Lower Stone Royd
Hutchin Wood
Works
Liley Hall
Gregory
Hagg Farm
Maple Farm
Stafford Hill
Clay Pit
Cemy.
Long Tongue Scrog
Lane Side Farm
Lascelles Farm
Huddersfield
Gawthorpe Green
South Royd
Hobson Scrog
Royd Farm
Houses Hill
Shrogg Bottom
Somersby Stud
Gawthorpe Green Farm
Lascelles Ct.
Lascelles Hall
Cricket Grd.
Bracken Hill
Gawthorpe Lower Wood
Lodge Mill Farm
The Kennels
Cockley Wood
Nineveh
Nineveh Plantation
Gawthorpe
Gawthorpe Upper Wood
Broomfield House
Middle Croft
Dam Head
Hall Wood
Hall Hill
The Monument
Paper Hall Farm
Ash Grove Farm
Cuckoo Hill
Cow Hey Farm
Sunny Bank
Carr Head Plantation
White Flats
Pheasantry Hill
Whitley Park
Deer Hill
Cowmes
Park View
Wood Top
Coal Pit Scrog
Near Walk
Copriding Farm
Far Walk
Scout Camp
Rods Cottage
A642
FENAY BRIDGE
Greave House
Thornes Farm
Spittle Royd
Low Moor
Four Firs
Lepton Square
The Old Pump House
Lepton Edge
Lepton Grange
The Heights
WF4
Lepton
Pinfold Farm
Wakefield Road
Common Top
School
High Green
HD8
Highland Sports & Recreation Ground
Low Wood
Cockersmouth Wood
Blakeman Hill Farm
Lower House
The Common
Rowley Hill
Windy Gap Farm
Pond Lane Farm
Little Lepton
Quarry Farm
Low Fold Farm
Beaconsfield House Farm
Woodsome House
Woodly Villa
Fourlands Farm
Beldon Brook
Linfit Lane Top
Woodsome Mill Farm
Woodsome Bri.
Mill
Viaduct
Lepton Great Wood
Linfit Hill
Dogley Lane
Linfit House
Flockton Moor Top
A629
Linfit
Linfit Fold
Linfit Wood
Woodville Nurseries
Beldon Brook Bridge
Busk Farm
Manor Mill Farm
Yew Tree Farm
Northfield
The Wood
121
140
155

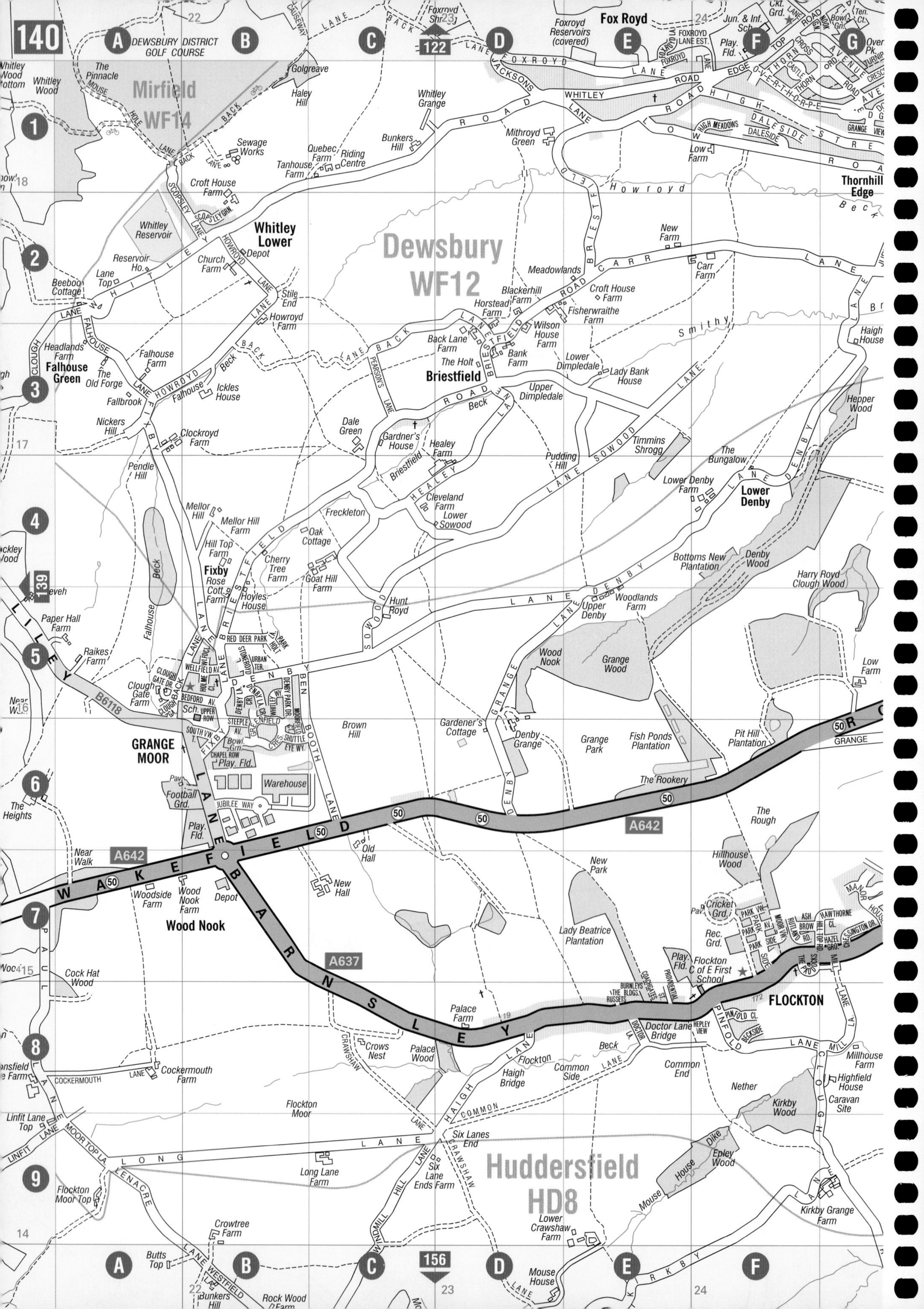

Mirfield WF14
Dewsbury WF12
Huddersfield HD8
DEWSBURY DISTRICT GOLF COURSE
Whitley Lower
Falhouse Green
Briestfield
Fixby
GRANGE MOOR
Wood Nook
Lower Denby
FLOCKTON
Fox Royd
Thornhill Edge
Whitley Reservoir
Denby Wood
Grange Wood
Kirkby Wood
Epley Wood
Lady Beatrice Plantation
Flockton Moor
Six Lanes End
A642
A637
B6118
WAKEFIELD ROAD
BARNSLEY ROAD
LONG LANE
DENBY LANE
SOWOOD LANE
CARR LANE
122
139
156

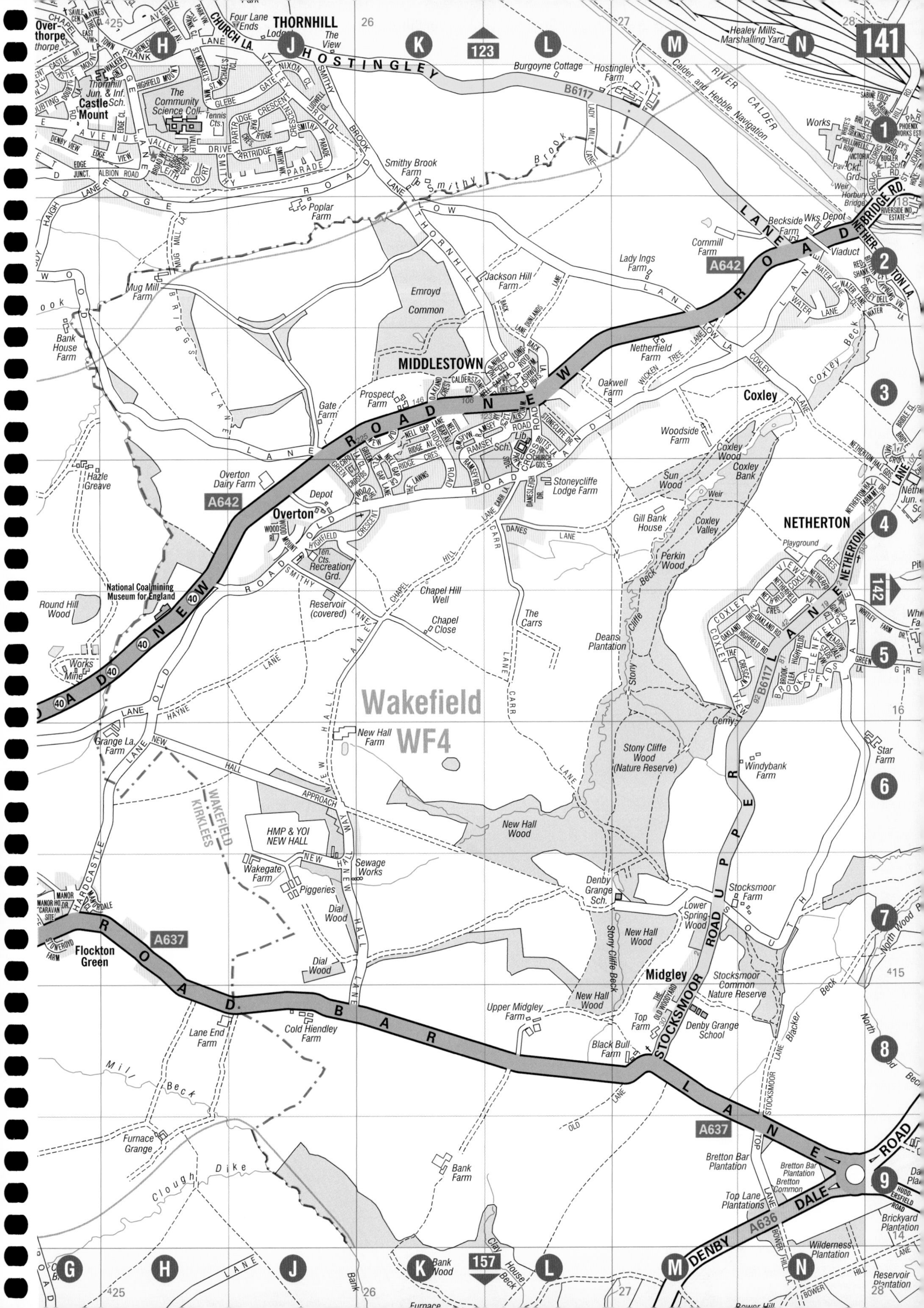
141
123
157
142
THORNHILL
Over-thorpe
Castle Mount
Thornhill Jun. & Inf. Sch.
The Community Science Coll.
Four Lane Ends
Lodge
The View
HOSTINGLEY
B6117
Burgoyne Cottage
Hostingley Farm
Healey Mills Marshalling Yard
Calder and Hebble Navigation
RIVER CALDER
Works
Smithy Brook Farm
Poplar Farm
EDGE LANE
EDGE JUNCT.
ALBION ROAD
HAIGH
Mug Mill Farm
Bank House Farm
Jackson Hill Farm
Emroyd Common
MIDDLESTOWN
Lady Ings Farm
Cornmill Farm
Beckside Farm
Wks.
Depot
Viaduct
NETHERTON LA.
BRIDGE RD.
Horbury Bridge
Weir
RIVERSIDE IND. ESTATE
A642
NEW ROAD
Netherfield Farm
Oakwell Farm
Coxley
WATER LANE
Coxley Beck
Prospect Farm
Gate Farm
Woodside Farm
Coxley Wood
Coxley Bank
Sun Wood
Hazle Greave
Overton Dairy Farm
Overton
Depot
Stoneycliffe Lodge Farm
Gill Bank House
Coxley Valley
NETHERTON
Playground
Ten. Cts.
Recreation Grd.
DANES LANE
Perkin Wood
National Coalmining Museum for England
Round Hill Wood
Reservoir (covered)
Chapel Hill Well
Chapel Close
The Carrs
Deans Plantation
Stony Cliffe Beck
Works
Mine
Wakefield WF4
New Hall Farm
Grange La. Farm
Stony Cliffe Wood (Nature Reserve)
Windybank Farm
Star Farm
WAKEFIELD
KIRKLEES
HMP & YOI NEW HALL
New Hall Wood
Wakegate Farm
Piggeries
Sewage Works
Dial Wood
Denby Grange Sch.
Stocksmoor Farm
Lower Spring Wood
UPPER ROAD
SOUTH LANE
MANOR HO CARAVAN SITE
Flockton Green
A637
BAR ROAD
Midgley
Stocksmoor Common Nature Reserve
Upper Midgley Farm
Top Farm
Black Bull Farm
Denby Grange School
Lane End Farm
Cold Hiendley Farm
Mill Beck
North Wood
STOCKSMOOR LANE
Furnace Grange
Clough Dike
Bank Farm
Bretton Bar Plantation
Bretton Common
Top Lane Plantations
DENBY DALE ROAD
A636
Brickyard Plantation
Wilderness Plantation
Bank Wood
Clay House Beck
Reservoir Plantation
G
H
J
K
L
M
N
1
2
3
4
5
6
7
8
9
425
26
27
28
14
15
16
17
18

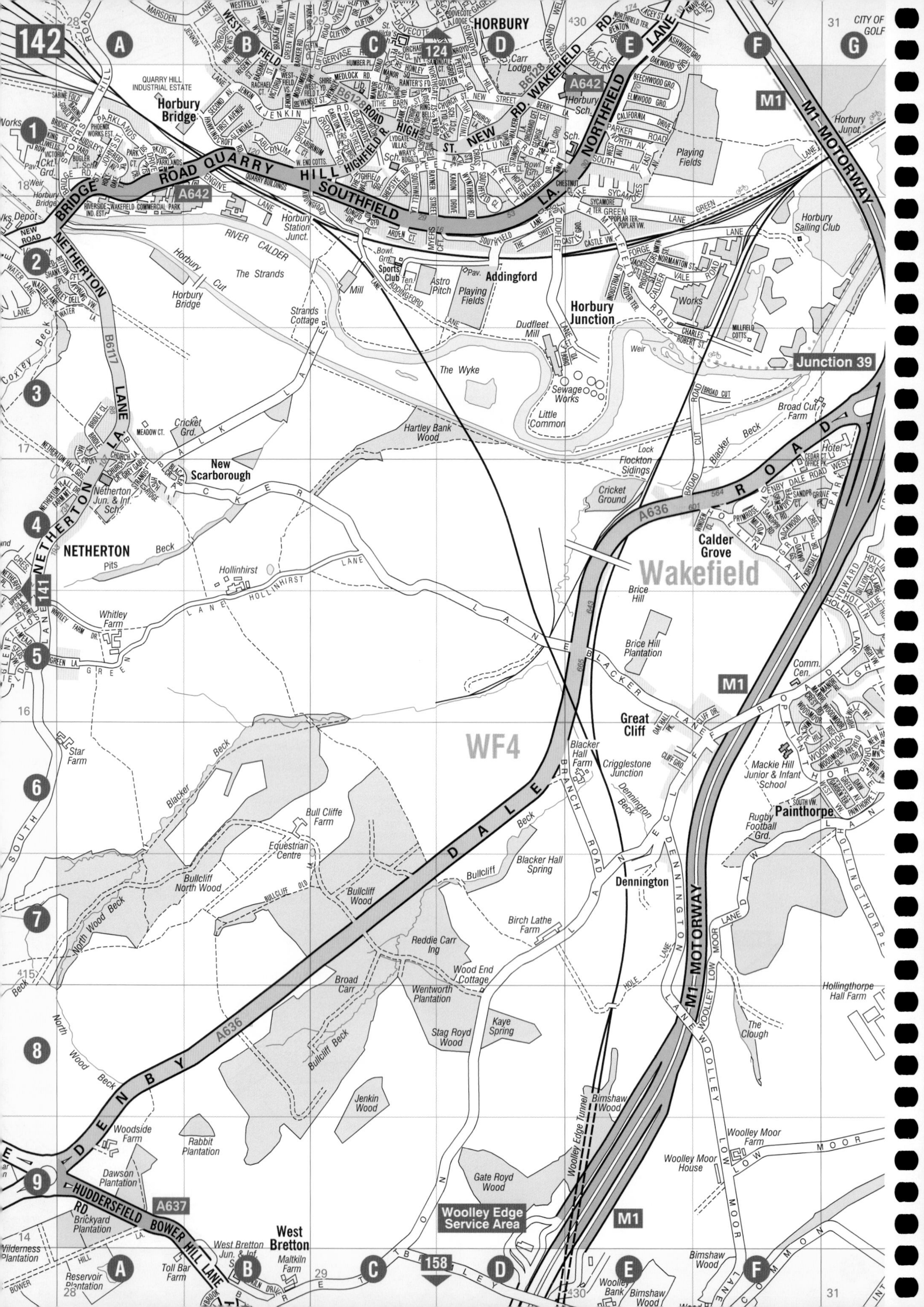
HORBURY
Horbury Bridge
QUARRY HILL INDUSTRIAL ESTATE
QUARRY HILL
SOUTHFIELD LA.
NORTHFIELD LANE
WAKEFIELD RD.
NEW ST.
HIGH ST.
B6128
A642
124
M1
M1 MOTORWAY
Horbury Junct.
Playing Fields
Horbury Sailing Club
CITY OF GOLF
Carr Lodge
Horbury Sch.
BRIDGE ROAD
NEW ROAD
NETHERTON LANE
B6117
RIVER CALDER
Horbury Cut
The Strands
Horbury Station Junct.
Sports Club
Astro Pitch
Addingford
Mill
Strands Cottage
Horbury Junction
Dudfleet Mill
Sewage Works
Little Common
The Wyke
Junction 39
Broad Cut Farm
BROAD CUT
Blacker Beck
Hartley Bank Wood
Cricket Grd.
New Scarborough
Netherton Jun. & Inf. Sch.
NETHERTON
Pits
Beck
Hollinhirst
HOLLINHIRST LANE
Whitley Farm
GREEN LA.
141
Coxley Beck
Flockton Sidings
Lock
Cricket Ground
A636
DENBY DALE ROAD
Calder Grove
Wakefield
Brice Hill
Brice Hill Plantation
BLACKER LANE
Great Cliff
WF4
Blacker Hall Farm
Crigglestone Junction
Dennington Beck
Mackie Hill Junior & Infant School
Painthorpe
Rugby Football Grd.
Comm. Cen.
Hotel
Star Farm
SOUTH LANE
Blacker Beck
Bull Cliffe Farm
Equestrian Centre
Bullcliff North Wood
Bullcliff Wood
North Wood Beck
Blacker Hall Spring
Bullcliff
Dennington
Birch Lathe Farm
Reddie Carr Ing
Wood End Cottage
Broad Carr
Wentworth Plantation
Stag Royd Wood
Kaye Spring
Bullcliff Beck
Jenkin Wood
Hollingthorpe Hall Farm
The Clough
HOLLINGTHORPE
WOOLLEY LOW MOOR LANE
DENNINGTON LANE
HOLE LANE
North Wood Beck
Woodside Farm
Rabbit Plantation
Dawson Plantation
Gate Royd Wood
Woolley Edge Tunnel
Bimshaw Wood
Woolley Moor Farm
Woolley Moor House
MOOR
Woolley Edge Service Area
HUDDERSFIELD RD.
BOWER HILL LANE
A637
Brickyard Plantation
West Bretton
West Bretton Jun. & Inf. Sch.
Maltkiln Farm
Toll Bar Farm
Reservoir Plantation
Wilderness Plantation
158
Bimshaw Wood
Woolley Bank
COMMON
A B C D E F G
1 2 3 4 5 6 7 8 9
28 29 430 31
18 17 16 415 14

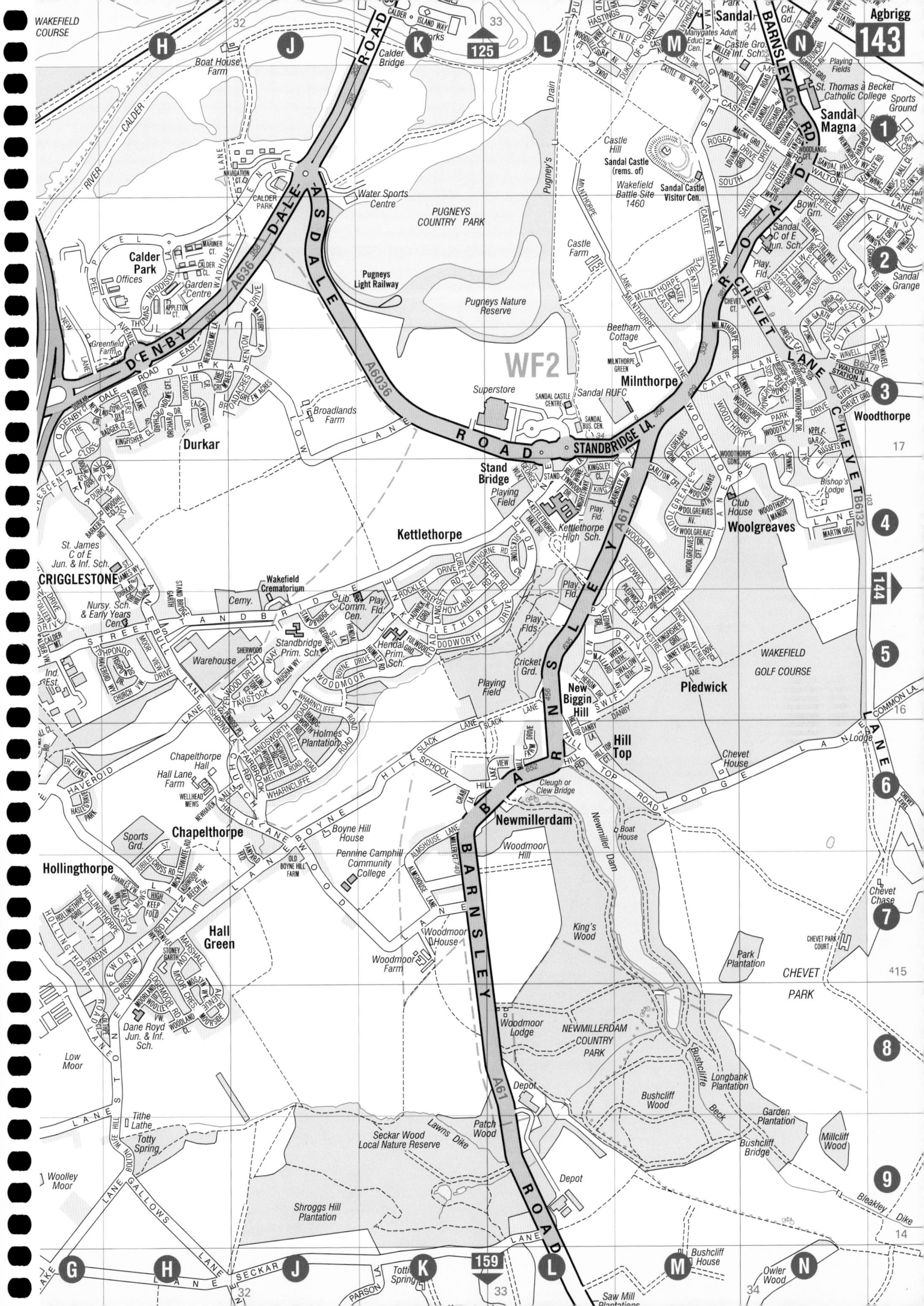

WAKEFIELD COURSE
Agbrigg
Sandal
Sandal Magna
St. Thomas à Becket Catholic College
Sports Ground
Calder Bridge
Boat House Farm
Castle Hill
Sandal Castle (rems. of)
Wakefield Battle Site 1460
Sandal Castle Visitor Cen.
Water Sports Centre
PUGNEYS COUNTRY PARK
Pugneys Light Railway
Pugneys Nature Reserve
Calder Park
Castle Farm
Beetham Cottage
Sandal Grange
WF2
Milnthorpe
Superstore
Sandal RUFC
Woodthorpe
Durkar
Broadlands Farm
Stand Bridge
Playing Field
Kettlethorpe
Kettlethorpe High Sch.
Woolgreaves
Bishop's Lodge
St. James C of E Jun. & Inf. Sch.
CRIGGLESTONE
Wakefield Crematorium
Standbridge Prim. Sch.
Hendal Prim. Sch.
Warehouse
WAKEFIELD GOLF COURSE
Pledwick
New Biggin Hill
Hill Top
Chevet House
Holmes Plantation
Chapelthorpe Hall
Hall Lane Farm
Chapelthorpe
Newmillerdam
Boyne Hill House
Pennine Camphill Community College
Woodmoor Hill
Hollingthorpe
Hall Green
King's Wood
Woodmoor House
Woodmoor Farm
Chevet Chase
Park Plantation
CHEVET PARK
Dane Royd Jun. & Inf. Sch.
Woodmoor Lodge
NEWMILLERDAM COUNTRY PARK
Low Moor
Longbank Plantation
Bushcliff Wood
Garden Plantation
Millcliff Wood
Tithe Lathe
Totty Spring
Seckar Wood Local Nature Reserve
Patch Wood
Bushcliff Bridge
Woolley Moor
Shroggs Hill Plantation
Depot
Bushcliff House
Owler Wood
Saw Mill Plantations
BARNSLEY ROAD
A61
ASDALE ROAD
A6036
DENBY DALE ROAD
A636
CHEVET LANE
B6132
STANDBRIDGE LA.
125
144
159

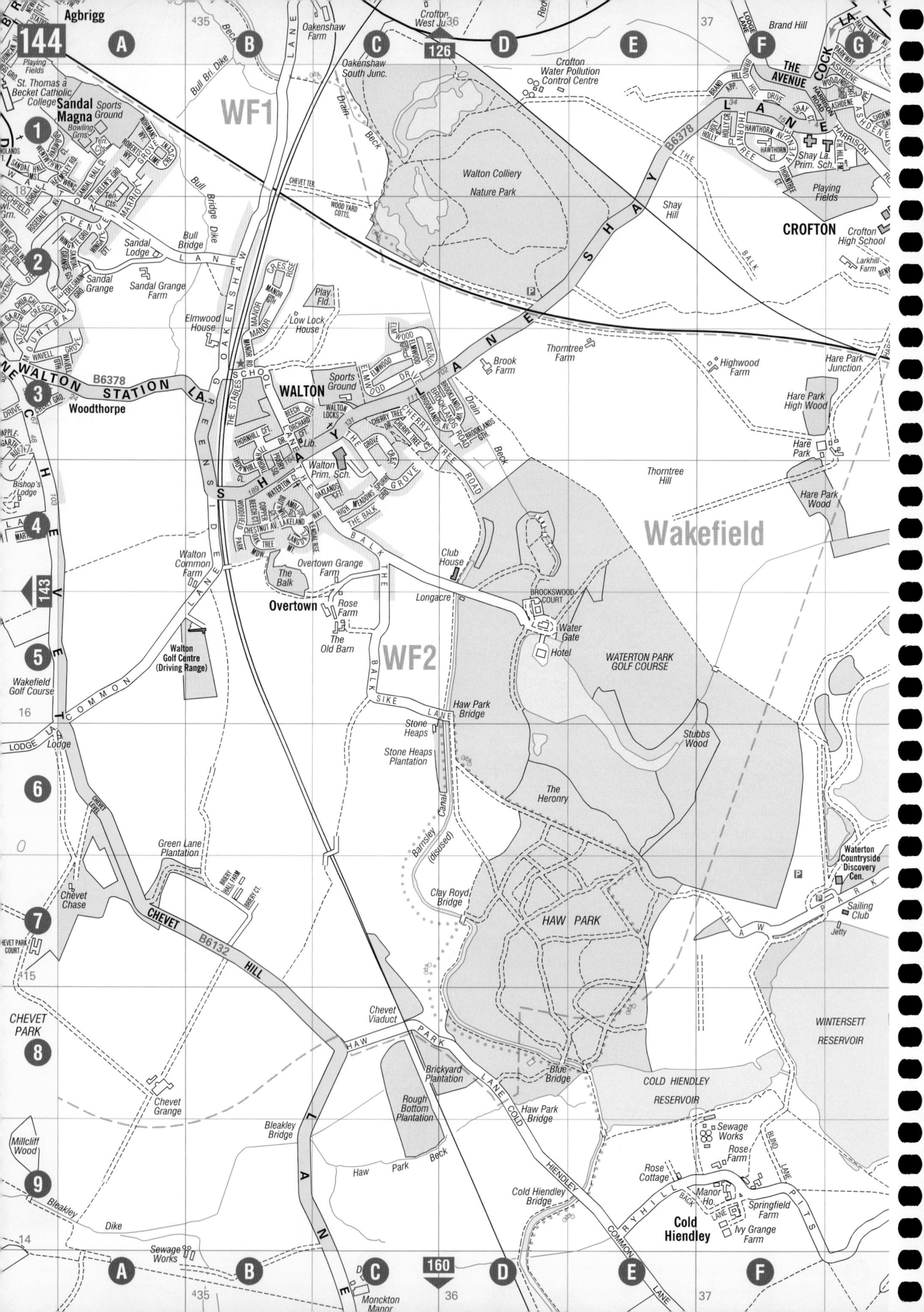

Agbrigg
Sandal Magna
St. Thomas à Becket Catholic College
Sports Ground
Woodthorpe
WALTON STATION LA.
B6378
WF1
WF2
Oakenshaw Farm
Oakenshaw South Junc.
Crofton West Jn.
Crofton Water Pollution Control Centre
Walton Colliery Nature Park
Brand Hill
THE AVENUE
CROFTON
Crofton High School
Shay La. Prim. Sch.
Playing Fields
Shay Hill
SHAY LANE
Sandal Lodge
Sandal Grange
Sandal Grange Farm
Bull Bridge
Elmwood House
Low Lock House
Play. Fld.
WALTON
Walton Prim. Sch.
Thorntree Farm
Brook Farm
Highwood Farm
Hare Park Junction
Hare Park High Wood
Hare Park
Thorntree Hill
Hare Park Wood
Wakefield
Bishop's Lodge
Walton Common Farm
Overtown Grange Farm
The Balk
Overtown
Rose Farm
The Old Barn
Club House
Longacre
Brockswood Court
Water Gate
Hotel
WATERTON PARK GOLF COURSE
Walton Golf Centre (Driving Range)
Wakefield Golf Course
Haw Park Bridge
Stone Heaps
Stone Heaps Plantation
Stubbs Wood
The Heronry
Barnsley Canal (disused)
Green Lane Plantation
Chevet Chase
Clay Royd Bridge
HAW PARK
Waterton Countryside Discovery Cen.
Sailing Club
Jetty
CHEVET HILL
B6132
CHEVET PARK
Chevet Viaduct
Brickyard Plantation
Rough Bottom Plantation
WINTERSETT RESERVOIR
Blue Bridge
COLD HIENDLEY RESERVOIR
Chevet Grange
Haw Park Bridge
Bleakley Bridge
Sewage Works
Rose Farm
Rose Cottage
Millcliff Wood
Haw Park Beck
Cold Hiendley Bridge
Manor Ho.
Springfield Farm
Ivy Grange Farm
Cold Hiendley
Bleakley Dike
Sewage Works
Monckton Manor
COLD HIENDLEY COMMON LANE

126
143
160

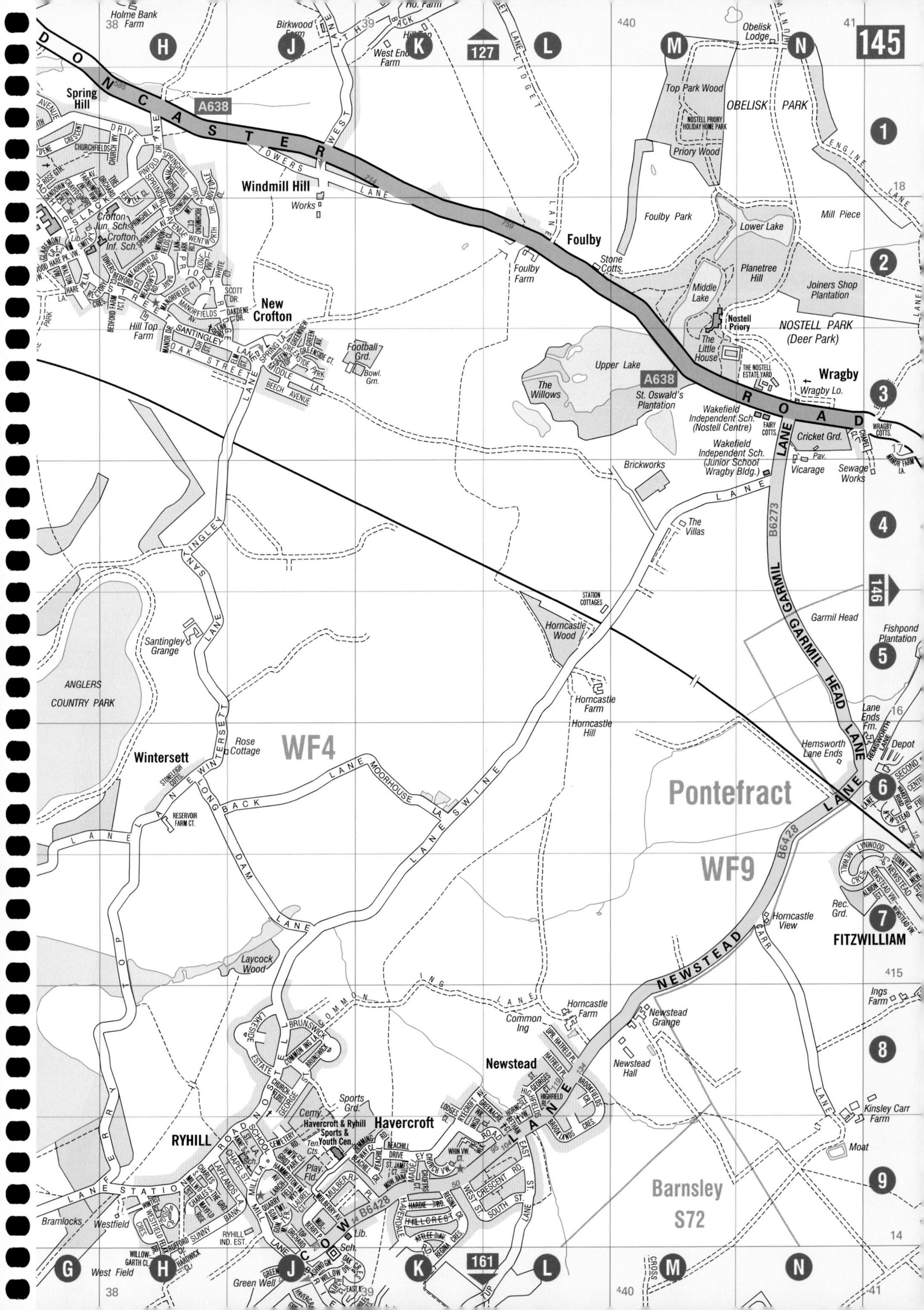

DONCASTER ROAD
A638
Spring Hill
Windmill Hill
Works
Crofton Jun. Sch.
Crofton Inf. Sch.
New Crofton
Hill Top Farm
SANTINGLEY LANE
OAK STREET
MIDDLE LA.
BEECH AVENUE
Football Grd.
Bowl. Grn.
Foulby
Foulby Farm
Stone Cotts.
Top Park Wood
OBELISK PARK
NOSTELL PRIORY HOLIDAY HOME PARK
Priory Wood
Foulby Park
Lower Lake
Mill Piece
Planetree Hill
Middle Lake
Joiners Shop Plantation
Nostell Priory
The Little House
NOSTELL PARK (Deer Park)
Upper Lake
The Willows
St. Oswald's Plantation
Wragby
Wragby Lo.
Wakefield Independent Sch. (Nostell Centre)
Cricket Grd.
Wakefield Independent Sch. (Junior School Wragby Bldg.)
Vicarage
Sewage Works
Brickworks
The Villas
B6273
GARMIL LANE
GARMIL HEAD LANE
Garmil Head
Fishpond Plantation
STATION COTTAGES
Horncastle Wood
Horncastle Farm
Horncastle Hill
Santingley Grange
ANGLERS COUNTRY PARK
Wintersett
Rose Cottage
WF4
MOORHOUSE LA.
LONG BACK LANE
SWINE LANE
DAM LANE
RESERVOIR FARM CT.
STONELEIGH COTTS.
Lane Ends Fm.
Hemsworth Lane Ends
Depot
Pontefract
WF9
B6428
NEWSTEAD LANE
Horncastle View
Rec. Grd.
FITZWILLIAM
Ings Farm
Laycock Wood
COMMON ING LANE
Common Ing
Horncastle Farm
Newstead Grange
Newstead Hall
Kinsley Carr Farm
Moat
CARR LANE
Newstead
Havercroft
Havercroft & Ryhill Sports & Youth Cen.
Sports Grd.
Cemy.
RYHILL
STATION LANE
TOP FERRY LANE
Bramlocks
Westfield
West Field
Green Well
RYHILL IND. EST.
Lib.
Sch.
Barnsley S72
Holme Bank Farm
Birkwood Farm
West End Farm
Obelisk Lodge
ENGINE LANE
127
146
161

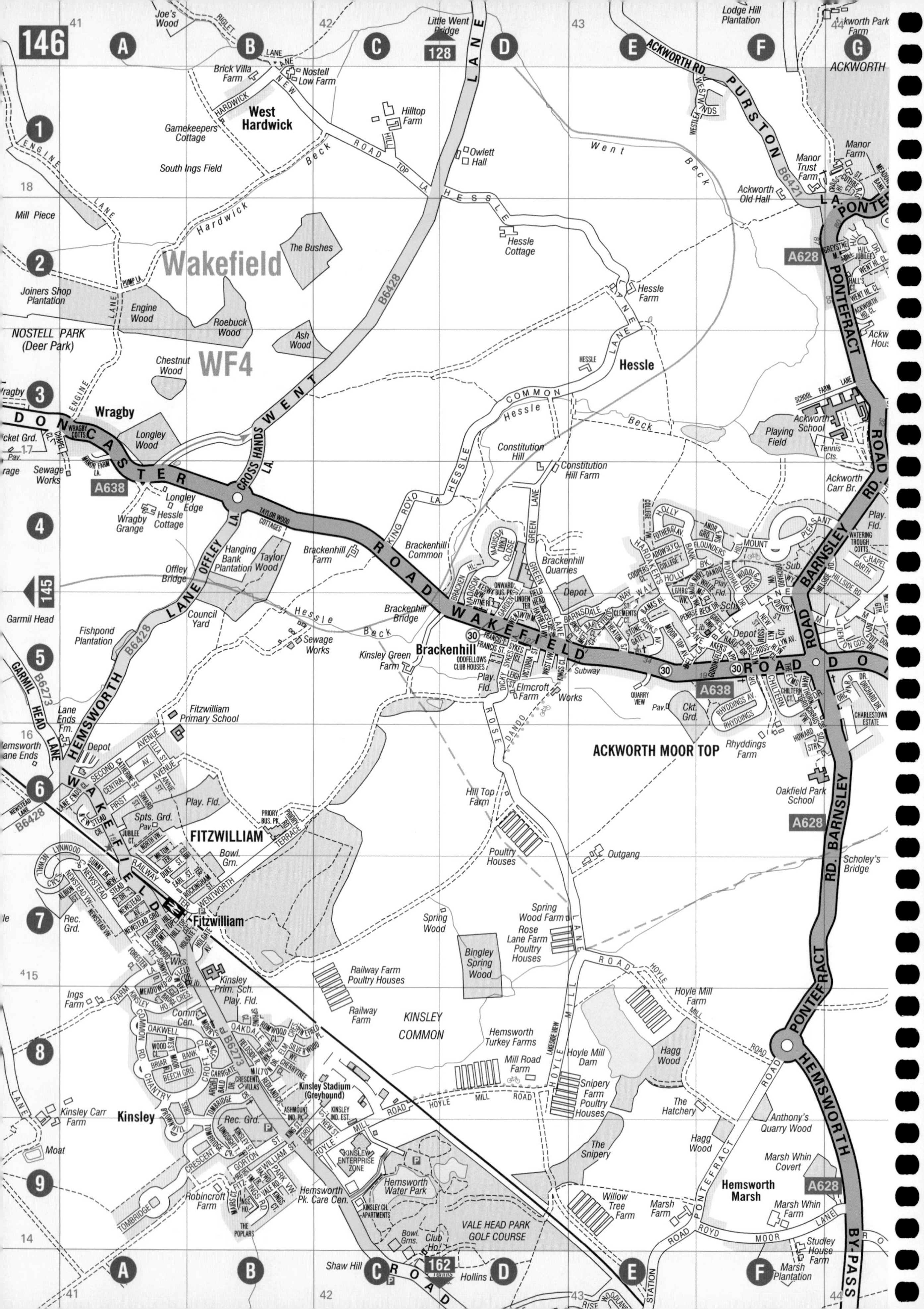
146
Wakefield
WF4
West Hardwick
Wragby
Hessle
Brackenhill
ACKWORTH MOOR TOP
ACKWORTH
FITZWILLIAM
Fitzwilliam
Kinsley
KINSLEY COMMON
Hemsworth Marsh
NOSTELL PARK (Deer Park)
DONCASTER ROAD
WAKEFIELD ROAD
A638
A628
B6428
B6273
B6421
PONTEFRACT ROAD
BARNSLEY ROAD
HEMSWORTH BY-PASS
HEMSWORTH LANE
WENT LANE
CROSS HANDS LA.
OFFLEY LANE
HESSLE LANE
HESSLE COMMON
PURSTON LA.
ACKWORTH RD.
HOYLE MILL ROAD
Joe's Wood
Brick Villa Farm
Nostell Low Farm
Gamekeepers Cottage
South Ings Field
Mill Piece
Hilltop Farm
Owlett Hall
Hessle Cottage
Hessle Farm
The Bushes
Engine Wood
Roebuck Wood
Ash Wood
Chestnut Wood
Joiners Shop Plantation
Longley Wood
Wragby Grange
Hessle Cottage
Hanging Bank Plantation
Taylor Wood
Offley Bridge
Garmil Head
Fishpond Plantation
Council Yard
Sewage Works
Brackenhill Farm
Brackenhill Common
Brackenhill Bridge
Brackenhill Quarries
Kinsley Green Farm
Constitution Hill
Constitution Hill Farm
Elmcroft Farm
Ackworth School
Playing Field
Ackworth Carr Br.
Ackworth Old Hall
Manor Trust Farm
Manor Farm
Lodge Hill Plantation
Little Went Bridge
128
145
162
Went Beck
Hessle Beck
Hardwick Beck
Rhyddings Farm
Oakfield Park School
Scholey's Bridge
Hill Top Farm
Poultry Houses
Outgang
Spring Wood Farm
Rose Lane Farm Poultry Houses
Spring Wood
Bingley Spring Wood
Railway Farm Poultry Houses
Railway Farm
Hemsworth Turkey Farms
Mill Road Farm
Hoyle Mill Dam
Snipery Farm Poultry Houses
The Snipery
Hoyle Mill Farm
Hagg Wood
The Hatchery
Anthony's Quarry Wood
Marsh Whin Covert
Marsh Whin Farm
Willow Tree Farm
Marsh Farm
Studley House Farm
Marsh Plantation
Kinsley Stadium (Greyhound)
Kinsley Enterprise Zone
Hemsworth Water Park
Hemsworth Pk. Care Cen.
VALE HEAD PARK GOLF COURSE
Shaw Hill
Hollins
Fitzwilliam Primary School
Kinsley Prim. Sch.
Ings Farm
Kinsley Carr Farm
Moat
Robincroft Farm
Lane Ends Fm.
Hemsworth Lane Ends
Priory Bus. Pk.
ROYD MOOR LANE
STATION ROAD
CHARLESTOWN ESTATE

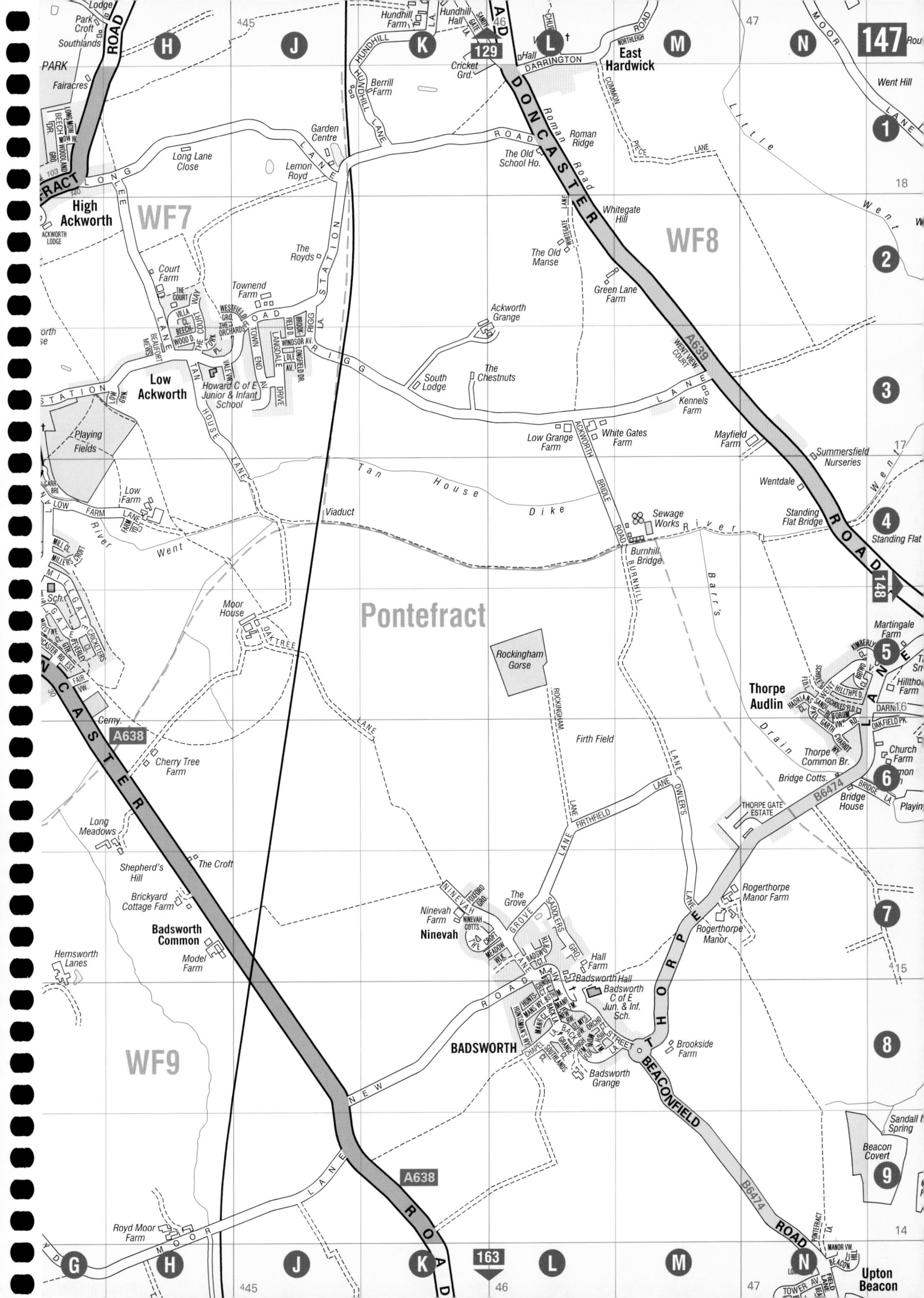
Pontefract
WF7
WF8
WF9
High Ackworth
Low Ackworth
East Hardwick
Thorpe Audlin
Ninevah
BADSWORTH
Badsworth Common
Upton Beacon
DONCASTER ROAD
A639
A638
B6474
Rockingham Gorse
Playing Fields
Sewage Works
Burnhill Bridge
Viaduct
Tan House Dike
River Went
Ackworth Grange
Badsworth Hall
Howard C of E Junior & Infant School
Badsworth C of E Jun. & Inf. Sch.
Beacon Covert
Firth Field
Royd Moor Farm
Cherry Tree Farm
Long Meadows
Shepherd's Hill
Brickyard Cottage Farm
Model Farm
Hemsworth Lanes
Rogerthorpe Manor Farm
Rogerthorpe Manor
Brookside Farm
Badsworth Grange
Hall Farm
Kennels Farm
Mayfield Farm
White Gates Farm
Low Grange Farm
Summersfield Nurseries
Wentdale
Standing Flat Bridge
Martingale Farm
Church Farm
Bridge Cotts.
Bridge House
Thorpe Common Br.
Thorpe Gate Estate
Green Lane Farm
Whitegate Hill
The Old Manse
The Old School Ho.
Roman Ridge
Berrill Farm
Hundhill Farm
Hundhill Hall
Cricket Grd.
Garden Centre
Lemon Royd
Long Lane Close
The Royds
Townend Farm
Court Farm
South Lodge
The Chestnuts
Low Farm
Moor House
Fairacres
Park Croft
Southlands
Went Hill
Sandall Spring
129
148
163

Went Hill
Dale Field
Kirkdike Plantation
Long Plantation
STAPLETON PARK
Horse Race Closes
Jackson's Hill
Brockadale Plantation
Sod Wall Plantation
Wenthill Plantation
Wentbridge Ings
Timbertops Equestrian Centre
Brockadale Crags
Brockadale Houses
Swiss Cottage
Jackson's Hill Pantation
Brockadale House
Dale Field
Brockadale Oaks Farm
BROCKADALE PLANTATION
Hotel
Rectory Farm
Went Bridge
Castle Hill Enclosure
Brockadale Bridge
BROCKADALE
Smeaton Crags
Wentbridge
Wentbridge Viaduct
Thorp Marsh
Little Plantation
Sayle's Plantation
SMEATON INDUSTRIAL PARK
Summersfield Nurseries
Ings House
Manor House
WENT EDGE ROAD
WF8
Standing Flat Bridge
Standing Flat
Went Edge Field
Broom Hill
Sunnydale Bungalow
Thorpe Audlin
Martingale Farm
Thorp Plantation
Peartree Field
Pontefract
A1
Little Bottom Plantation
The Smithy
Hillthorpe
Hillthorpe Ho.
Pear Tree Farm
Hillthorpe Farm
Hillthorpe Cotts.
Gingerbread Plantation
The Bungalow
Went Farm
Thorpe Manor
Church Farm
Common Farm
Far Thorpe Farm
Manor Farm
Hepworth Farm
Shooters Hill Farm
Middle Field
Upper Wells Lair
Bridge House
Playing Fld.
Morning Field Farm
Thorpe Grange Farm
Salliwell Field
Long Close Plantation
Rose Cottage
Poultry Farm
Barnsdale
Mutton Hall Farm
Walton Wood Cottage
Burnshaw
Packsaddle Plantation
Sewage Works
Barnsdale Bar Services
Bullcarmires
Walton Wood Ho.
Motel
Walton Wood
Sandall Ing Spring
Glebe Farm
Beacon Covert
WF9
Coal Pit Plantation
Tower
Upton Beacon
Barnsdale Bar
DONCASTER ROAD
A639
GREAT NORTH ROAD
B6474
WENTBRIDGE LANE
130
147
164

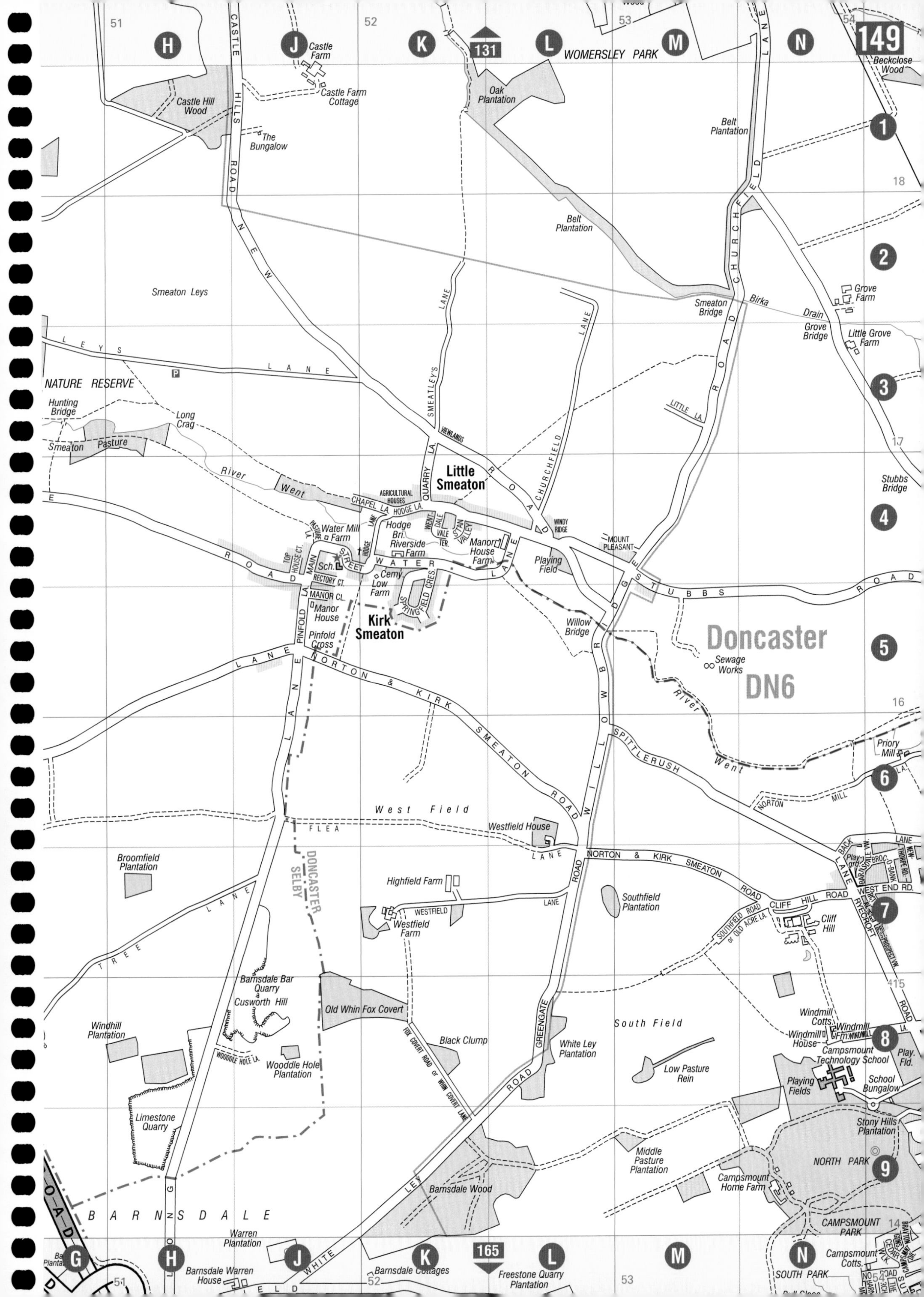

131
WOMERSLEY PARK
Beckclose Wood
Castle Farm
Castle Farm Cottage
Castle Hill Wood
CASTLE HILLS ROAD
The Bungalow
Oak Plantation
Belt Plantation
Belt Plantation
NEW ROAD
Smeaton Leys
LEYS LANE
NATURE RESERVE
Hunting Bridge
Long Crag
Smeaton Pasture
River Went
SMEATLEY'S LANE
LANE
CHURCHFIELD ROAD
Smeaton Bridge
Birka Drain
Grove Farm
Grove Bridge
Little Grove Farm
LITTLE LA.
VIEWLANDS
QUARRY LA.
Little Smeaton
CHURCHFIELD
AGRICULTURAL HOUSES
CHAPEL LA.
HODGE LA.
Water Mill Farm
Hodge Bri.
Riverside Farm
Manor House Farm
WINDY RIDGE
MOUNT PLEASANT
Stubbs Bridge
Playing Field
STUBBS ROAD
WATER LANE
Sch.
Cemy.
Low Farm
SPRINGFIELD CRES.
RECTORY CT.
MANOR CL.
Manor House
Pinfold Cross
Kirk Smeaton
Willow Bridge
Doncaster
DN6
Sewage Works
River Went
PINFOLD LA.
NORTON & KIRK SMEATON ROAD
WILLOWBRIDGE
SPITTLERUSH
Priory Mill
NORTON MILL LA.
West Field
FLEA LANE
Westfield House
Broomfield Plantation
DONCASTER
SELBY
Highfield Farm
WESTFIELD LANE
Westfield Farm
Southfield Plantation
CLIFF HILL ROAD
WEST END RD.
RYECROFT ROAD
Cliff Hill
SOUTHFIELD ROAD or OLD ACRE LA.
TREE LANE
Barnsdale Bar Quarry
Cusworth Hill
Old Whin Fox Covert
GREENGATE
South Field
Windhill Plantation
Black Clump
White Ley Plantation
Windmill Cotts.
Windmill House
Campsmount Technology School
Play. Fld.
WOODDLE HOLE LA.
Wooddle Hole Plantation
FOX COVERT ROAD or WHIN COVERT LANE
Low Pasture Rein
Playing Fields
School Bungalow
Limestone Quarry
Stony Hills Plantation
Middle Pasture Plantation
NORTH PARK
WHITE LEY ROAD
Barnsdale Wood
Campsmount Home Farm
BARNSDALE
LONG LANE
CAMPSMOUNT PARK
Warren Plantation
Barnsdale Warren House
Barnsdale Cottages
Freestone Quarry Plantation
165
Campsmount Cotts.
SOUTH PARK

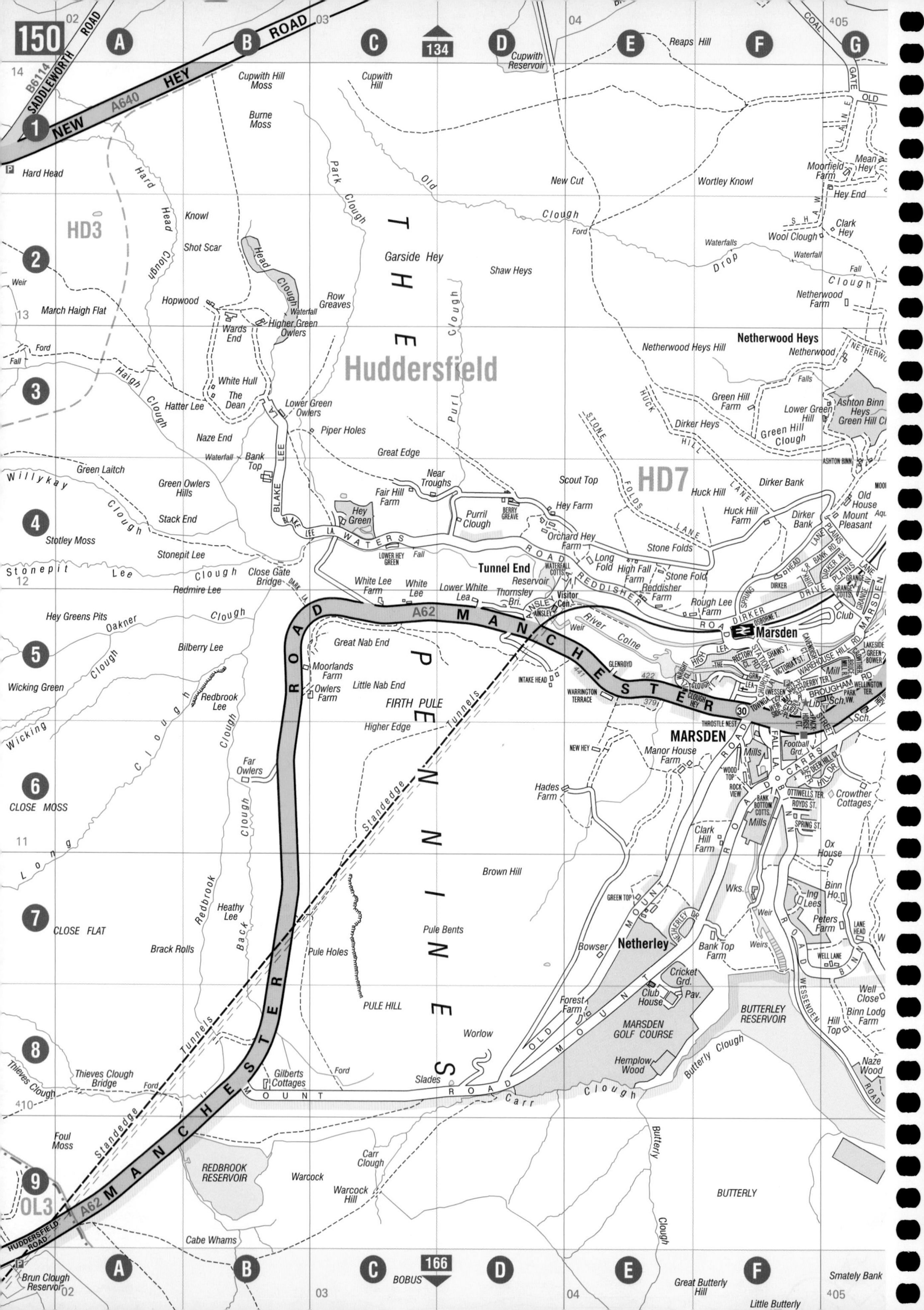
134
166
Huddersfield
THE PENNINES
MARSDEN
Marsden
Netherley
Tunnel End
HD3
HD7
OL3
NEW HEY ROAD A640
SADDLEWORTH ROAD B6114
MANCHESTER ROAD A62
HUDDERSFIELD ROAD
Hard Head
Cupwith Hill Moss
Cupwith Hill
Cupwith Reservoir
Burne Moss
Reaps Hill
New Cut
Wortley Knowl
Moorfield Farm
Mean Hey
Hey End
Clark Hey
Wool Clough
Knowl
Shot Scar
Garside Hey
Shaw Heys
Hopwood
March Haigh Flat
Row Greaves
Wards End
Higher Green Owlers
Netherwood Farm
Netherwood Heys
Netherwood Heys Hill
White Hull
The Dean
Hatter Lee
Lower Green Owlers
Piper Holes
Naze End
Green Hill Farm
Dirker Heys
Ashton Binn Heys
Green Laitch
Green Owlers Hills
Stack End
Great Edge
Near Troughs
Fair Hill Farm
Scout Top
Huck Hill
Dirker Bank
Stotley Moss
Stonepit Lee
Hey Green
Purril Clough
Hey Farm
Orchard Hey Farm
Stone Folds
Redmire Lee
Close Gate Bridge
White Lee Farm
Lower White Lee
Thornsley Bri.
Reservoir
Visitor Cen.
Hey Greens Pits
Bilberry Lee
Great Nab End
Moorlands Farm
Owlers Farm
Little Nab End
FIRTH PULE
Higher Edge
Wicking Green
Redbrook Lee
CLOSE MOSS
Far Owlers
New Hey
Manor House Farm
Hades Farm
Clark Hill Farm
Brown Hill
CLOSE FLAT
Heathy Lee
Brack Rolls
Pule Holes
Pule Bents
PULE HILL
Bowser
Bank Top Farm
Forest Farm
Cricket Grd.
Club House
MARSDEN GOLF COURSE
Hemplow Wood
BUTTERLEY RESERVOIR
Worlow
Slades
Gilberts Cottages
Thieves Clough Bridge
Foul Moss
REDBROOK RESERVOIR
Warcock
Carr Clough
Warcock Hill
BUTTERLY
Cabe Whams
Brun Clough Reservoir
BOBUS
Great Butterly Hill
Little Butterly
Smately Bank
Ox House
Ing Lees
Peters Farm
Binn Lodge Farm
Hill Top
Naze Wood
Crowther Cottages
Standedge Tunnels

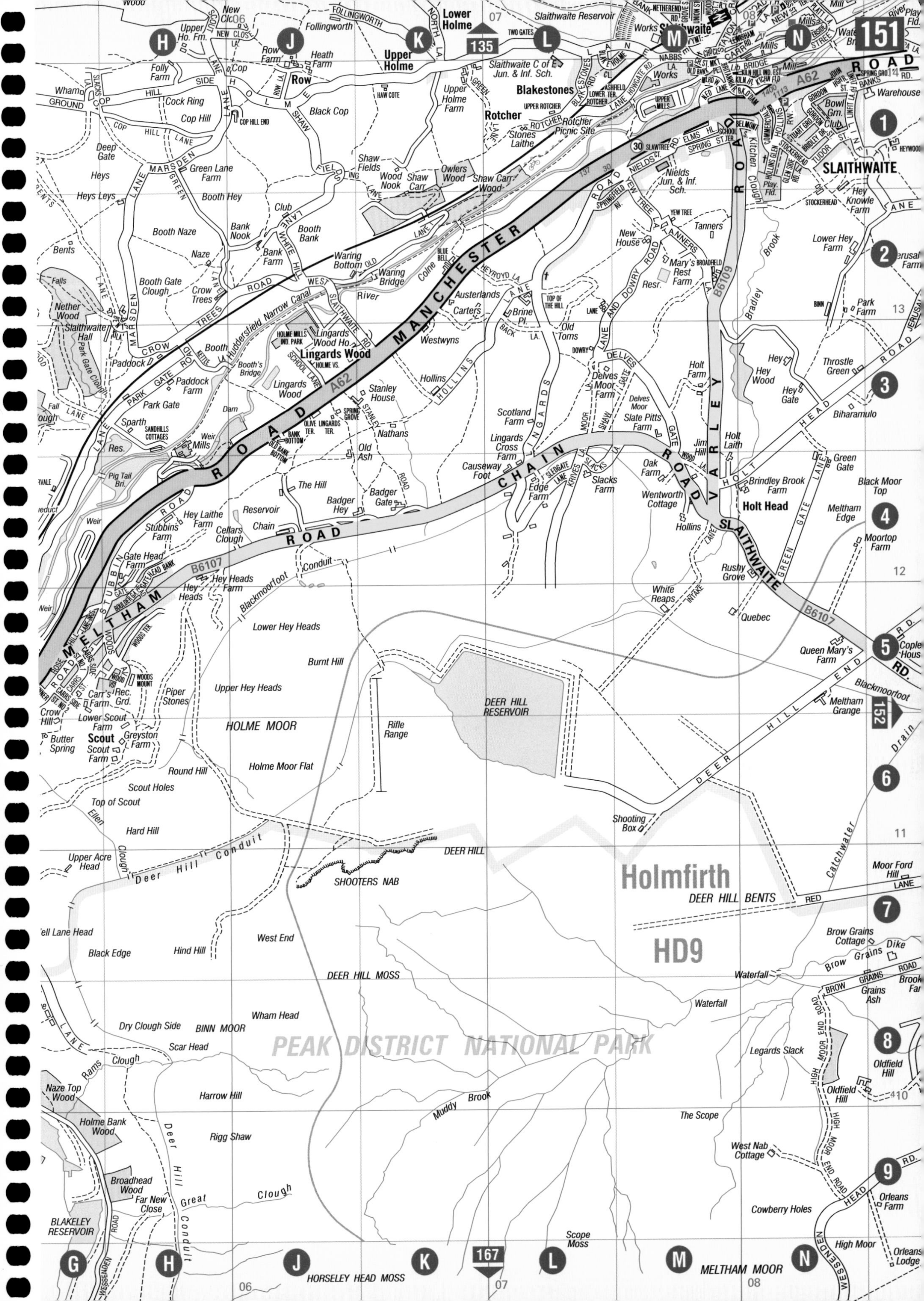

Slaithwaite Reservoir
Slaithwaite
Lower Holme
Upper Holme
Row
Blakestones
Rotcher
SLAITHWAITE
Lingards Wood
Holt Head
Scout
MANCHESTER ROAD
CHAIN ROAD
MELTHAM ROAD
SLAITHWAITE ROAD
VARLEY ROAD
Huddersfield Narrow Canal
DEER HILL RESERVOIR
HOLME MOOR
Holme Moor Flat
Rifle Range
DEER HILL
SHOOTERS NAB
Holmfirth
DEER HILL BENTS
HD9
DEER HILL MOSS
BINN MOOR
PEAK DISTRICT NATIONAL PARK
BLAKELEY RESERVOIR
HORSELEY HEAD MOSS
MELTHAM MOOR
Scope Moss
Cowberry Holes
Meltham Grange
Shooting Box
Deer Hill Conduit

135
152
167

152
A
B
C
D
E
F
G
1
2
3
4
5
6
7
8
9
136
151
168
MANCHESTER ROAD
A62
SLAITHWAITE
Warehouse
Club
Linthwaite Jun. & Inf. Sch.
C of E Jun. & Inf. School
Colne Valley Specialist Arts College
Sports Centre
CROSLAND HEATH GOLF COURSE
Hill Tree Park
AIRFIELD
Bate's Square
Huddersfield
Black Rock Mills
Black Rock Farm
Lower Clough
Playing Fields
Height
Pack Fold
High House
Pog Hall Farm
Pog Hall
Upper Clough
Hey Knowle Farm
HIGH HOUSE LANE
Ftbl. Grd.
Wild Brow Farm
Green House
Hadden Farm
Walker Syke
Moor End Farm
Nether Moor
Jerusalem Farm
Bethany Wood
Bethany Farm
HD7
BLACKMOOR FOOT ROAD
BLACK LANE
INTAKE LANE
SCHOOL LANE
Stony Better
Sunny Bank
Park Farm
HEAD ROAD
Windsor
Pioneer Farm
Blackmoorfoot
Water Works
Lake House
Top of Hill
South Crosland
Throstle Green
HOLT
Biharamulo
BLACKMOORFOOT RESERVOIR
WHITEHEAD LANE
MADGIN LA.
CHURCH LANE
BLACK MOOR
Green Gate
Black Moor Top
Edge End
Edge Moor
Works
Orange Wood
Bank Wood
Crosland Hall
Picnic Area
Depot
CROSLAND FACTORY LA.
Cote
Factory
Cottage Home Farm
Cop End Farm
Helme Wood
Moortop Farm
Woodlands Farm
Helme
Helme Edge
Meltham Cop
Hall Heys Wood
Laund Farm
Laund
Copley House
Helme C of E Jun. & Inf. School
The Heys
Far Fields
Conduit
Blackmoorfoot
SLAITHWAITE ROAD
HUDDERSFIELD ROAD
Helme Hall
Lower Edge
Well Heads
Weirs
Sewage Works
Wood Bottom Farm
Riding School
Upper Hey
Lower Hey Farm
Lane Side
High Brow
Bent Ley Farm
Drain
HASSOCKS ROAD
HONLEY WOOD
Quarry (Sandstone)
Rec. Grd.
Mill
Harewood Br.
Meltham Moor Prim. School
B6107
B6108
Works
MELTHAM
Catchwater
Moor Ford Hill
Britain
New Bridge
Rough Nook Farm
Meltham Dike
Meltham Hall Park
Greasy Slack Wood
Knowl Top
Knowl Top Farm
Quarry (Disused)
Knowl Top Poultry Farm
Upper Cote Fm.
Slate Pits Wood
Brow Grains Cottage
Brow Grains Dike
Golcar Brow
Gledholt Farm
Brookfield Farm
Grains Ash
Halfroods Farm
Town Gate
School
The Pleasure Grds.
Round Ing
Thick Hollins
Club Ho.
MELTHAM GOLF COURSE
Meltham Mills Reservoir
Windy Bank Wood
Oldfield Hill
Oldfield Hill
Wentworth Farm
Upper Colders
Sunfield
Calmlands
Catchwater Drain
Royd Edge
Mills
Meal Hill
Heady Fields
Gill Birks
WILSHAW
Greave Dike
High Moor
Royd Edge
PEAK DISTRICT NATIONAL PARK
Orleans Farm
Banister Edge
Waithe Close
Wet Hill
Lower Royd
Fox Royd
Old Mill Farm
High Moor
Orleans Lodge
Sun Royd
Upper Royd
Royd Farm
Burned Hill
THICK HOLLINS
WESSENDEN HEAD ROAD

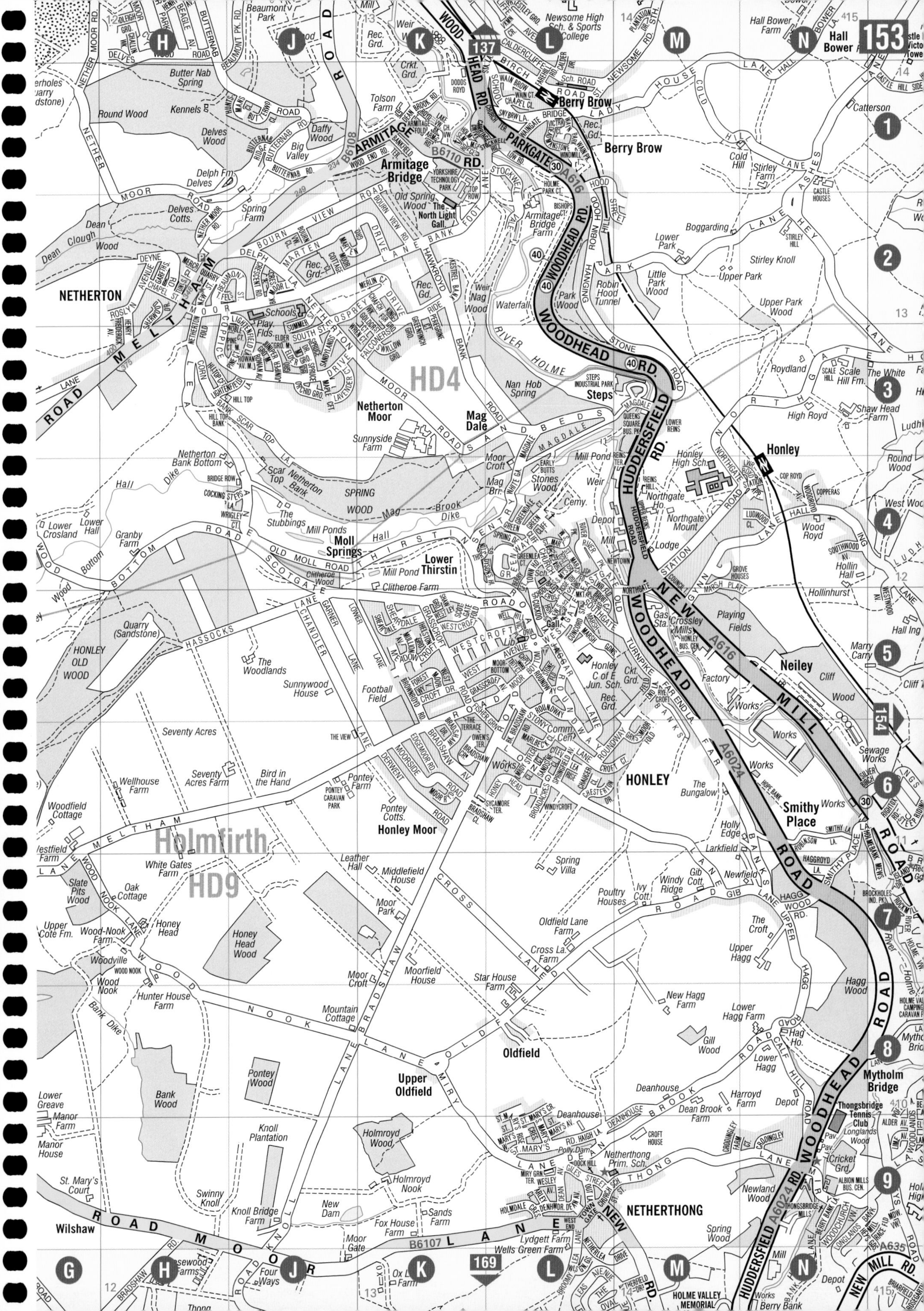
Netherton
Armitage Bridge
Berry Brow
Honley
Netherton Moor
Mag Dale
Moll Springs
Lower Thirstin
Steps
Neiley
Smithy Place
Honley Moor
Oldfield
Upper Oldfield
Netherthong
Mytholm Bridge
Wilshaw
Holmfirth
HD4
HD9
Woodhead Rd.
New Mill Road
Huddersfield Rd.
Moor Lane
Meltham Road
Scotgate Road
Thirstin Road
Oldfield Road
Miry Lane
Butter Nab Spring
Round Wood
Delves Wood
Daffy Wood
Big Valley
Old Spring Wood
Dean Clough Wood
Honley Old Wood
Quarry (Sandstone)
Spring Wood
Hagg Wood
Gill Wood
Pontey Wood
Bank Wood
Holmroyd Wood
Honey Head Wood
Knoll Plantation
Newland Wood
Spring Wood
Wood Royd
Park Wood
Robin Hood Tunnel
River Holme
Nan Hob Spring
Lower Park
Little Park Wood
Upper Park
Stirley Knoll
Upper Park Wood
Roydland
Scale Hill Fm.
High Royd
Shaw Head Farm
Honley High Sch.
Northgate Mount
Playing Fields
Crossley Mills
Factory
Works
Sewage Works
The Bungalow
Holly Edge
Larkfield
Newfield
Gib Cott.
Windy Ridge
Ivy Cott.
Poultry Houses
Spring Villa
Oldfield Lane Farm
Cross La. Farm
Star House Farm
New Hagg Farm
Lower Hagg Farm
Upper Hagg
The Croft
Lower Hagg
Hag Ho.
Deanhouse
Dean Brook Farm
Harroyd Farm
Thongsbridge Tennis Club
Longlands Wood
Netherthong Prim. Sch.
Holmroyd Nook
Sands Farm
Fox House Farm
Lydgett Farm
Wells Green Farm
Moor Gate
Four Ways
Ox Lee Farm
Holme Valley Memorial
Berry Bank
Swinny Knoll
Knoll Bridge Farm
New Dam
St. Mary's Court
Manor Farm
Manor House
Lower Greave
Hunter House Farm
Woodville
Wood Nook
Wood-Nook Farm
Upper Cote Fm.
Honey Head
Slate Pits Wood
Oak Cottage
White Gates Farm
Westfield Farm
Woodfield Cottage
Wellhouse Farm
Seventy Acres
Seventy Acres Farm
Bird in the Hand
Pontey Farm
Pontey Cotts.
Leather Hall
Middlefield House
Moor Park
Moorfield House
Moor Croft
Mountain Cottage
Football Field
Sunnywood House
The Woodlands
Clitheroe Farm
Clitheroe Wood
Mill Pond
Mill Ponds
The Stubbings
Lower Crosland
Lower Hall
Granby Farm
Netherton Bank Bottom
Scar Top
Netherton Bank
Spring Wood
Sunnyside Farm
Moor Croft
Mag Brook
Stones Wood
Cemy.
Depot
Mill Pond
Weir
Honley C of E Jun. Sch.
Rec. Grd.
Ckt. Grd.
Comm. Cen.
Tolson Farm
Yorkshire Technology Park
The North Light Gall.
Armitage Bridge Farm
Delph Fm
Delves
Delves Cotts.
Spring Farm
Kennels
Beaumont Park
Newsome High Sch. & Sports College
Hall Bower Farm
Hall Bower
Catterson
Cold Hill
Stirley Farm
Boggarding
Catterson
Hollinhurst
Hollin Hall
Marry Carry
Cliff Wood
154
137
169

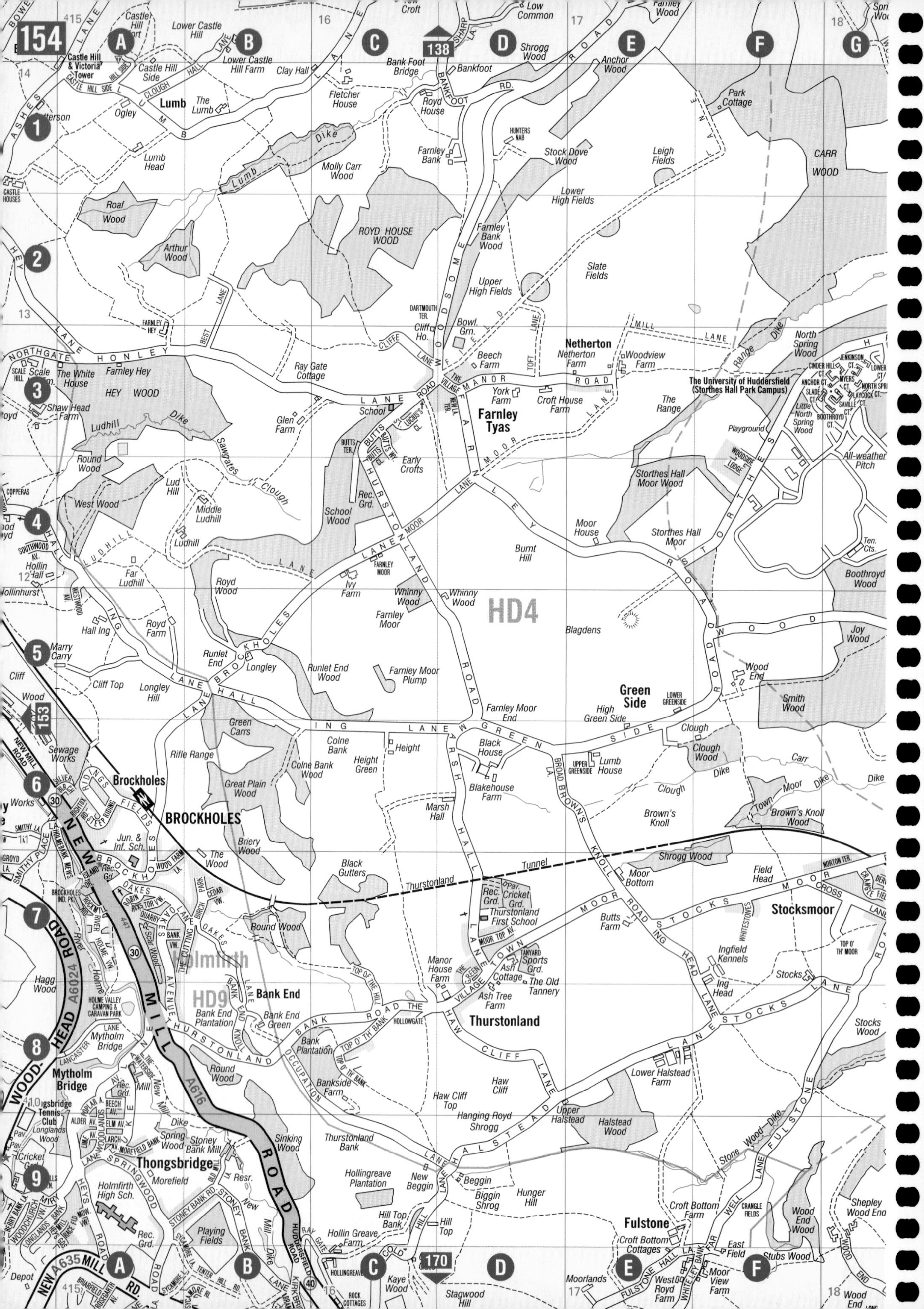

A
B
C
D
E
F
G
138
153
170
1
2
3
4
5
6
7
8
9
Castle Hill & Victoria Tower
Lower Castle Hill
Lower Castle Hill Farm
Castle Hill Side
Lumb
The Lumb
Ogley
Lumb Head
Clay Hall
Bank Foot Bridge
Bankfoot
Fletcher House
Royd House
Shrogg Wood
Anchor Wood
Park Cottage
Low Common
Farnley Bank
Molly Carr Wood
Roaf Wood
Arthur Wood
ROYD HOUSE WOOD
Stock Dove Wood
Leigh Fields
Lower High Fields
CARR WOOD
Farnley Bank Wood
Upper High Fields
Slate Fields
Farnley Hey
Cliff Ho.
Bowl. Grn.
Beech Farm
Netherton
Netherton Farm
Woodview Farm
North Spring Wood
The University of Huddersfield (Storthes Hall Park Campus)
Ray Gate Cottage
The White House
HEY WOOD
Shaw Head Farm
Ludhill
Glen Farm
School
York Farm
Croft House Farm
Farnley Tyas
The Range
Little North Spring Wood
Playground
All-weather Pitch
Round Wood
Early Crofts
Storthes Hall Moor Wood
Lud Hill
West Wood
Middle Ludhill
Rec. Grd.
School Wood
Moor House
Storthes Hall Moor
Burnt Hill
Hollin Hall
Far Ludhill
Royd Wood
Ivy Farm
Whinny Wood
Farnley Moor
Boothroyd Wood
HD4
Blagdens
Hall Ing
Royd Farm
Marry Carry
Joy Wood
Runlet End
Longley
Runlet End Wood
Farnley Moor Plump
Wood End
Cliff Top
Longley Hill
Green Side
High Green Side
Farnley Moor End
Smith Wood
Green Carrs
Colne Bank
Height
Height Green
Black House
Clough Wood
Sewage Works
Rifle Range
Colne Bank Wood
Lumb House
Brockholes
BROCKHOLES
Great Plain Wood
Blakehouse Farm
Brown's Knoll
Brown's Knoll Wood
Marsh Hall
Jun. & Inf. Sch.
Briery Wood
The Wood
Shrogg Wood
Moor Bottom
Field Head
Black Gutters
Thurstonland
Tunnel
Rec. Grd.
Pav. Cricket Grd.
Thurstonland First School
Stocksmoor
Butts Farm
Round Wood
Holmfirth
Hagg Wood
Manor House Farm
Ash Cottage
Sports Grd.
The Old Tannery
Ingfield Kennels
Ing Head
Stocks
HD9
Bank End
Bank End Plantation
Bank End Green
Ash Tree Farm
Thurstonland
Stocks Wood
Mytholm Bridge
Bank Plantation
Round Wood
Lower Halstead Farm
Bankside Farm
Haw Cliff
Haw Cliff Top
Hanging Royd Shrogg
Upper Halstead
Halstead Wood
Thongsbridge Tennis Club
Spring Wood
Stoney Bank Mill
Sinking Wood
Thurstonland Bank
Thongsbridge
Morefield
Hollingreave Plantation
New Beggin
Beggin
Biggin Shrog
Hunger Hill
Holmfirth High Sch.
Croft Bottom Farm
Shepley Wood End
Wood End Wood
Rec. Grd.
Playing Fields
Hill Top Bank
Hill Top
Hollin Greave Farm
Fulstone
Croft Bottom Cottages
East Field
Stubs Wood
Depot
Kaye Wood
Stagwood Hill
Moorlands
West Royd Farm
Moor View Farm
Wood End
HONLEY LANE
NEW MILL ROAD
WOODHEAD ROAD
A6024
A616
A635
MOOR LANE
HALL ING LANE
THURSTONLAND BANK ROAD
HALSTEAD LANE
STOCKS LANE
STOCKS MOOR ROAD
FULSTONE LANE
BROWN'S KNOLL ROAD
STORTHES ROAD
WOOD ROAD

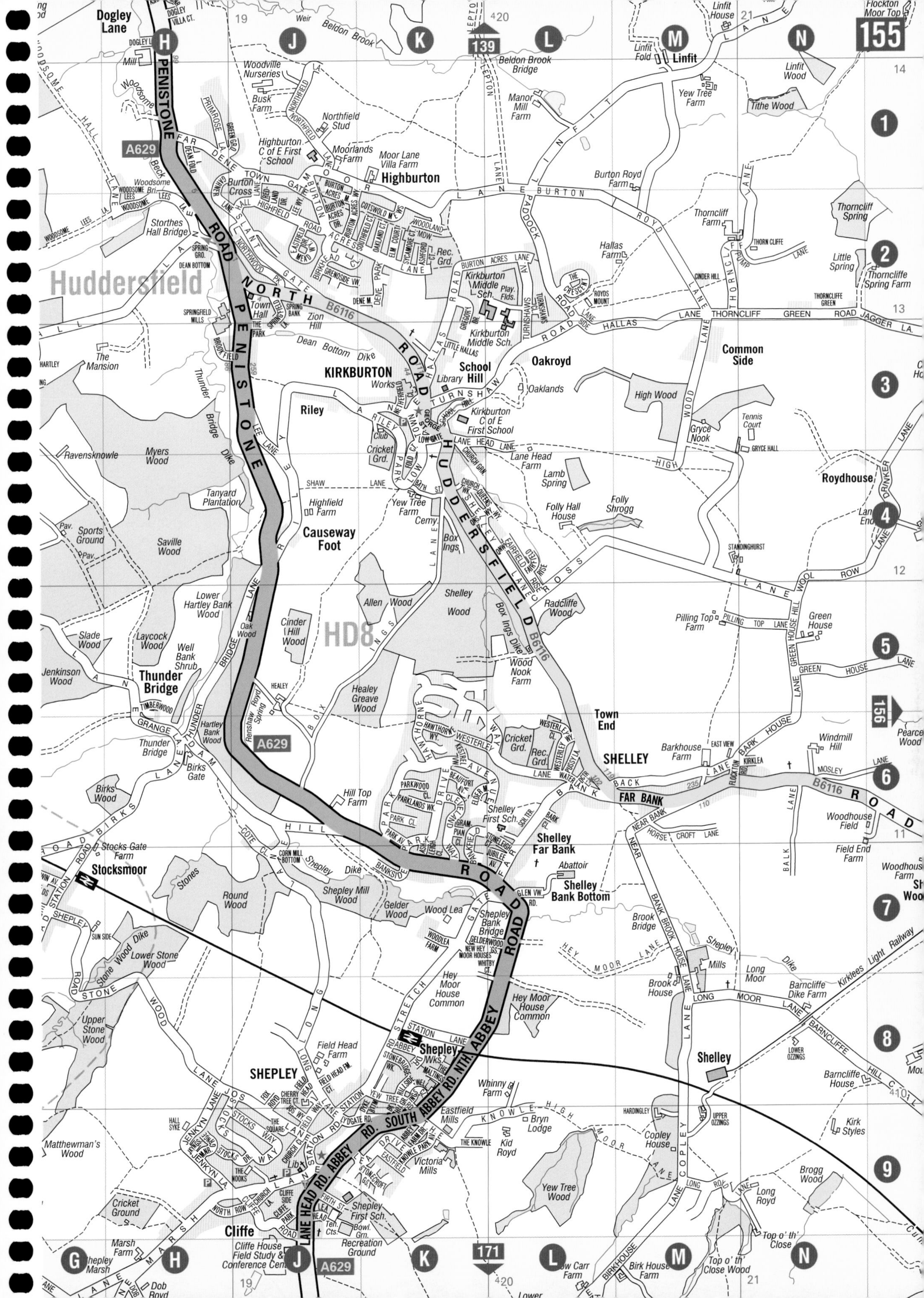
Dogley Lane
Linfit
Highburton
Huddersfield
KIRKBURTON
Riley
School Hill
Oakroyd
Common Side
Roydhouse
Causeway Foot
HD8
Thunder Bridge
Town End
SHELLEY
Shelley Far Bank
Stocksmoor
SHEPLEY
Shepley
Shelley
Cliffe
PENISTONE ROAD
NORTH ROAD
HUDDERSFIELD ROAD
A629
B6116
FAR BANK
ABBEY ROAD
Highburton C of E First School
Kirkburton Middle Sch.
Kirkburton C of E First School
Shelley First Sch.
Shepley First Sch.
Cliffe House Field Study & Conference Cen.
Kirklees Light Railway
139
171
156
Shelley Wood
Saville Wood
Myers Wood
Round Wood
Yew Tree Wood

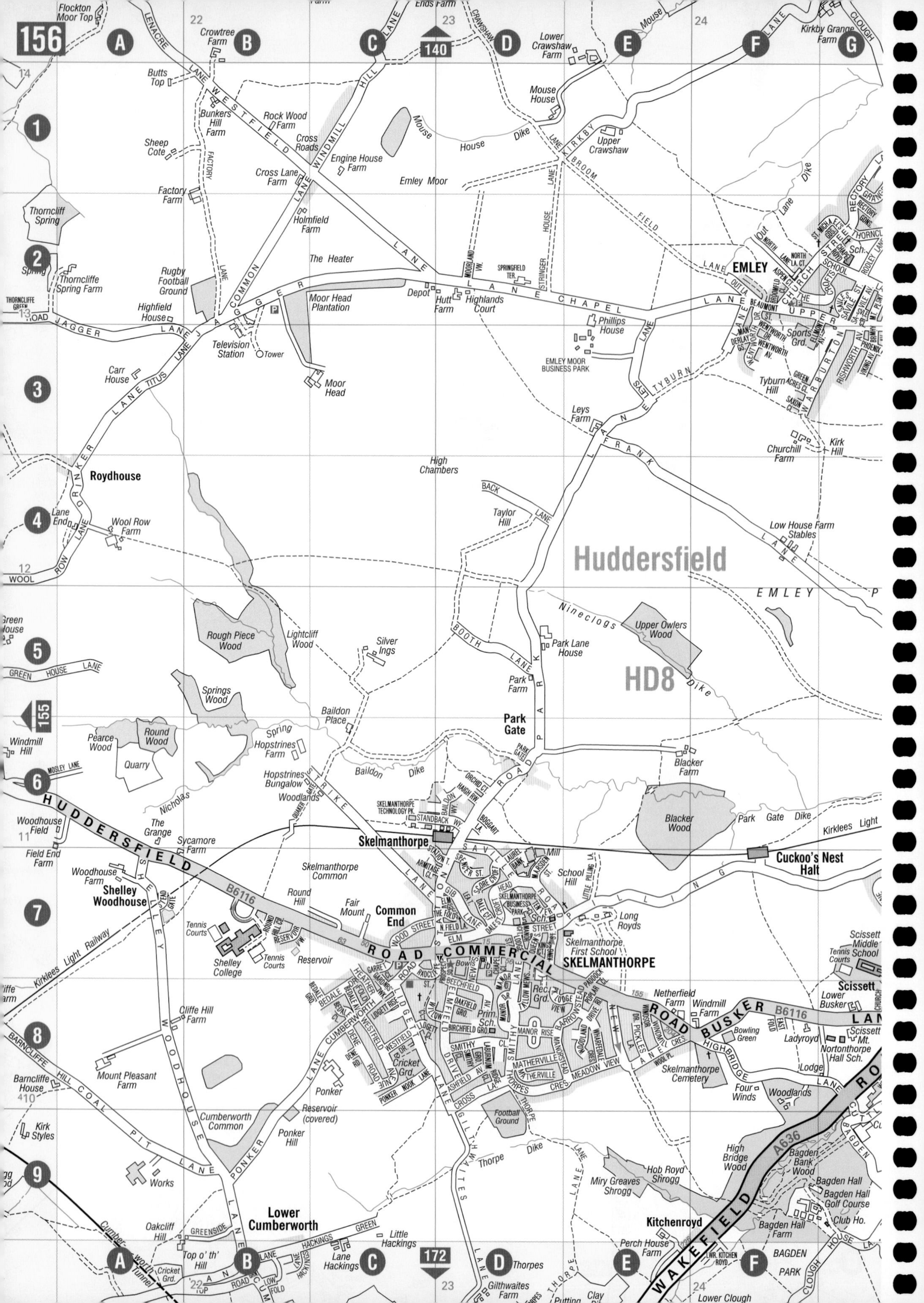

Flockton Moor Top
Crowtree Farm
Lower Crawshaw Farm
Kirkby Grange Farm
140
Butts Top
Bunkers Hill Farm
Rock Wood Farm
Cross Roads
Mouse House
Upper Crawshaw
Sheep Cote
Engine House Farm
Cross Lane Farm
Emley Moor
Factory Farm
Thorncliff Spring
Holmfield Farm
The Heater
Thorncliffe Spring Farm
Rugby Football Ground
EMLEY
Moor Head Plantation
Depot
Hutt Farm
Highlands Court
Phillips House
Highfield House
Television Station
Tower
EMLEY MOOR BUSINESS PARK
Sports Grd.
Carr House
Moor Head
Tyburn Hill
Leys Farm
Churchill Farm
Kirk Hill
Roydhouse
High Chambers
Taylor Hill
Lane End
Wool Row Farm
Low House Farm Stables
Huddersfield
Rough Piece Wood
Lightcliff Wood
Silver Ings
Upper Owlers Wood
Park Lane House
Park Farm
HD8
Springs Wood
Baildon Place
Park Gate
155
Round Wood
Pearce Wood
Quarry
Windmill Hill
Hopstrines Farm
Blacker Farm
Hopstrines Bungalow
Woodlands
SKELMANTHORPE TECHNOLOGY PK.
Blacker Wood
Woodhouse Field
The Grange
Sycamore Farm
Skelmanthorpe
Cuckoo's Nest Halt
Field End Farm
Woodhouse Farm
Skelmanthorpe Common
School Hill
Shelley Woodhouse
Round Hill
Fair Mount
Common End
Long Royds
Tennis Courts
Skelmanthorpe First School
Scissett Middle School
Shelley College
Reservoir
SKELMANTHORPE
Scissett
Lower Busker
Netherfield Farm
Windmill Farm
Cliffe Hill Farm
Prim. Sch.
Bowling Green
Ladyroyd
Scissett Mt.
Nortonthorpe Hall Sch.
Mount Pleasant Farm
Cricket Grd.
Skelmanthorpe Cemetery
Barncliffe House
Ponker
Four Winds
Woodlands
Kirk Styles
Cumberworth Common
Reservoir (covered)
Football Ground
Ponker Hill
High Bridge Wood
Bagden Bank Wood
Works
Miry Greaves Shrogg
Hob Royd Shrogg
Bagden Hall
Bagden Hall Golf Course
Oakcliff Hill
Lower Cumberworth
Kitchenroyd
Club Ho.
Little Hackings
Bagden Hall Farm
Top o' th' Hill
Lane Hackings
172
Thorpes
Perch House Farm
Cumberworth Tunnel
Cricket Grd.
Gilthwaites Farm
Lower Clough
HUDDERSFIELD ROAD
COMMERCIAL ROAD
BUSKER LANE
WAKEFIELD ROAD
B6116
A636
Kirklees Light Railway

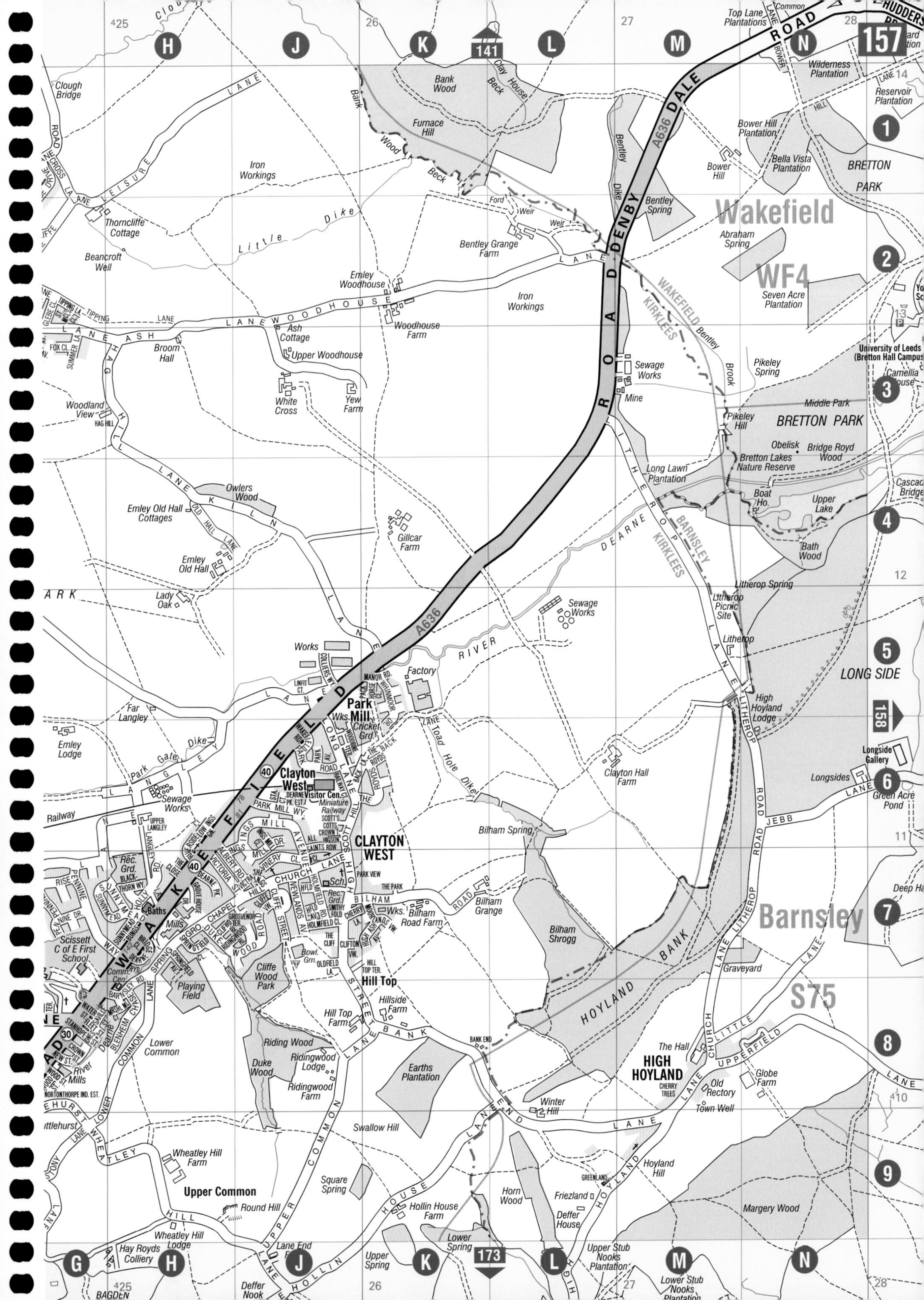
Clough Bridge
Bank Wood
Furnace Hill
Iron Workings
Thorncliffe Cottage
Beancroft Well
Little Dike
Bentley Grange Farm
Emley Woodhouse
Woodhouse Farm
Iron Workings
Ash Cottage
Upper Woodhouse
Broom Hall
White Cross
Yew Farm
Woodland View
Owlers Wood
Emley Old Hall Cottages
Emley Old Hall
Lady Oak
Gillcar Farm
Works
Park Mill
Cricket Grd.
Factory
Far Langley
Emley Lodge
Sewage Works
Railway
Clayton West
Visitor Cen.
Miniature Railway
CLAYTON WEST
Baths
Scissett C of E First School
Playing Field
Cliffe Wood Park
Hill Top
Hillside Farm
Hill Top Farm
Riding Wood
Ridingwood Lodge
Duke Wood
Ridingwood Farm
Earths Plantation
Swallow Hill
Wheatley Hill Farm
Upper Common
Round Hill
Square Spring
Hollin House Farm
Wheatley Hill Lodge
Hay Royds Colliery
Lane End Farm
Upper Spring
Lower Spring
Deffer Nook
Horn Wood
Friezland
Deffer House
Winter Hill
Hoyland Hill
Upper Stub Nooks Plantation
Lower Stub Nooks Plantation
Margery Wood
HIGH HOYLAND
The Hall
Old Rectory
Town Well
Globe Farm
Graveyard
S75
Barnsley
Bilham Shrogg
Bilham Grange
Bilham Road Farm
Bilham Spring
Clayton Hall Farm
Sewage Works
RIVER DEARNE
Litherop Spring
Litherop Picnic Site
High Hoyland Lodge
LONG SIDE
Longside Gallery
Longsides
Green Acre Pond
Bath Wood
Upper Lake
Boat Ho.
Bretton Lakes Nature Reserve
Bridge Royd Wood
Obelisk
BRETTON PARK
Middle Park
Pikeley Hill
Pikeley Spring
Long Lawn Plantation
Sewage Works
Mine
University of Leeds (Bretton Hall Campus)
Seven Acre Plantation
WF4
Wakefield
Abraham Spring
Bentley Spring
Bentley Dike
Bower Hill
Bella Vista Plantation
Bower Hill Plantation
BRETTON PARK
Reservoir Plantation
Wilderness Plantation
Top Lane Plantations
DENBY DALE ROAD
A636
WAKEFIELD FIELD LANE
HOYLAND BANK
LITHEROP LANE
JEBB LANE
WOODHOUSE LANE
KILN LANE
WAKEFIELD
KIRKLEES
BARNSLEY
141
173
158

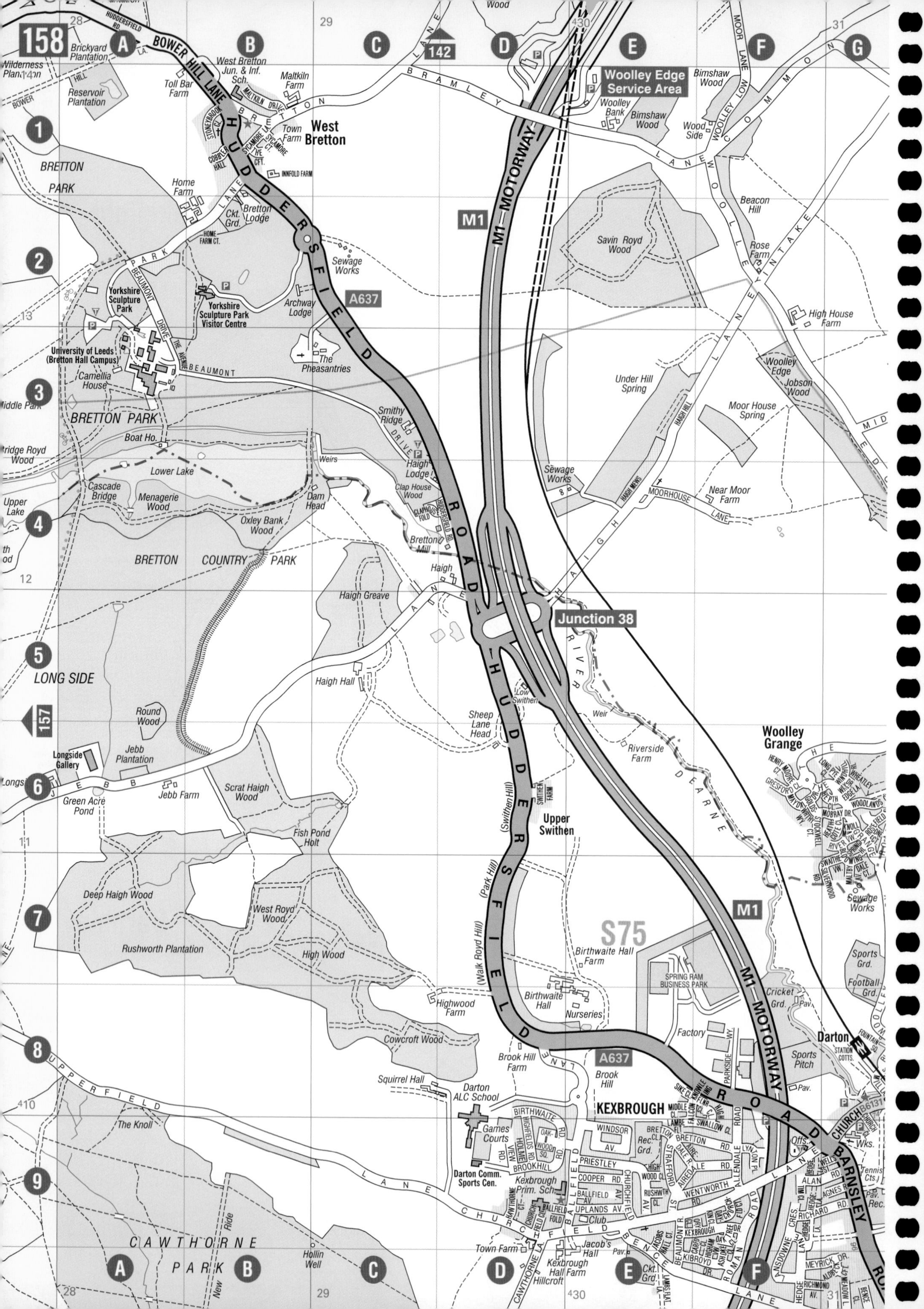
West Bretton
Woolley Edge Service Area
M1 MOTORWAY
HUDDERSFIELD ROAD
A637
BRETTON PARK
Yorkshire Sculpture Park
Yorkshire Sculpture Park Visitor Centre
University of Leeds (Bretton Hall Campus)
BRETTON COUNTRY PARK
Lower Lake
Upper Lake
Junction 38
RIVER DEARNE
LONG SIDE
Longside Gallery
Woolley Grange
Upper Swithen
S75
SPRING RAM BUSINESS PARK
KEXBROUGH
Darton
CAWTHORNE PARK
BARNSLEY ROAD
Deep Haigh Wood
Rushworth Plantation
West Royd Wood
High Wood
Cowcroft Wood
Savin Royd Wood
Haigh Hall
Haigh Greave
Darton ALC School
Kexbrough Prim. Sch.

142
157

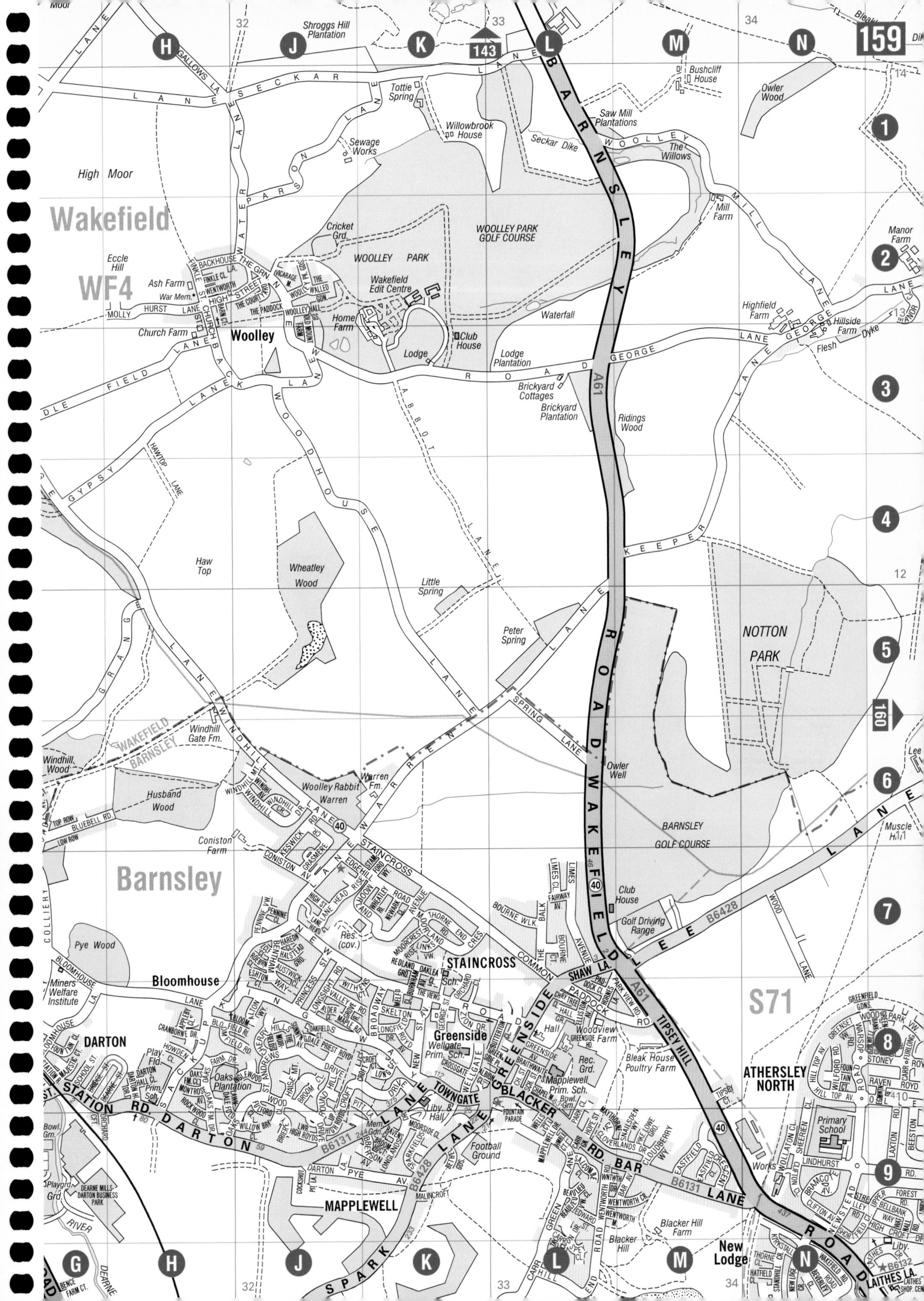

Wakefield
WF4
Woolley
WOOLLEY PARK
WOOLLEY PARK GOLF COURSE
Wakefield Edit Centre
High Moor
Eccle Hill
Ash Farm
Church Farm
Home Farm
Club House
Lodge
Lodge Plantation
Waterfall
Cricket Grd.
Sewage Works
Willowbrook House
Tottie Spring
Shroggs Hill Plantation
Saw Mill Plantations
Seckar Dike
The Willows
Bushcliff House
Owler Wood
Mill Farm
Manor Farm
Highfield Farm
Hillside Farm
Flesh Dyke
Brickyard Cottages
Brickyard Plantation
Ridings Wood
Haw Top
Wheatley Wood
Little Spring
Peter Spring
NOTTON PARK
Owler Well
BARNSLEY GOLF COURSE
Club House
Golf Driving Range
Windhill Gate Fm.
Windhill Wood
Husband Wood
Woolley Rabbit Warren
Warren Fm.
Coniston Farm
Barnsley
Pye Wood
Bloomhouse
Miners Welfare Institute
STAINCROSS
DARTON
Greenside
Oaks Plantation
MAPPLEWELL
Football Ground
Bleak House Poultry Farm
Blacker Hill Farm
Blacker Hill
New Lodge
ATHERSLEY NORTH
S71
Muscle Hill
BARNSLEY ROAD
WAKEFIELD ROAD
A61
B6428
B6131
B6132
STATION RD.
DARTON LANE
TOWNGATE
BLACKER RD.
BAR LANE
TIPSEY HILL
SPARK LANE
LEE LANE
GEORGE ROAD
SECKAR LANE
WOOLLEY EDGE LANE

143
160

Cold Hiendley
Wakefield
WF4
Notton
Royston
S71
Carlton
Athersley North
Carlton Green
Notton Park
Cold Hiendley Common
Notton Bridge Plantation
Barnsley Canal (disused)
Applehaigh Wood
Applehaigh Clough
Monckton Manor
Notton Grange
Grange Cottages
Manor Farm
Hillside Farm
Common Lane Farm
Playing Fields
Low Common
Active Workings
Leisure Centre
Civic Hall
Royston Welfare Park
Chapel Hill
Church Hill
Royston Bridge
Scot Bridge
Pools Lane Bridge
Pools Ings
Cronk Hill
Pools Bridge
Boulder Bridge
Sports Ground
Lund Hill
Carlton Community College
Games Courts
Recreation Ground
Shaw Bridge
Shaw Viaduct
Sewage Wks.
Warehouse
Bakery
Athersley Memorial Park
Sports Ground
Wharncliffe Business Park
Carlton Industrial Estate
Carlton Prim. Sch.
Muscle Hill
Lee Lane Farm
Ellis Laithe
Ivy Grange Farm
Springfield Farm
Cold Hiendley Bridge
Notton Bridge
High Bridge
Cold Hiendley Hill
Windmill Hill
Primary School
Playing Field

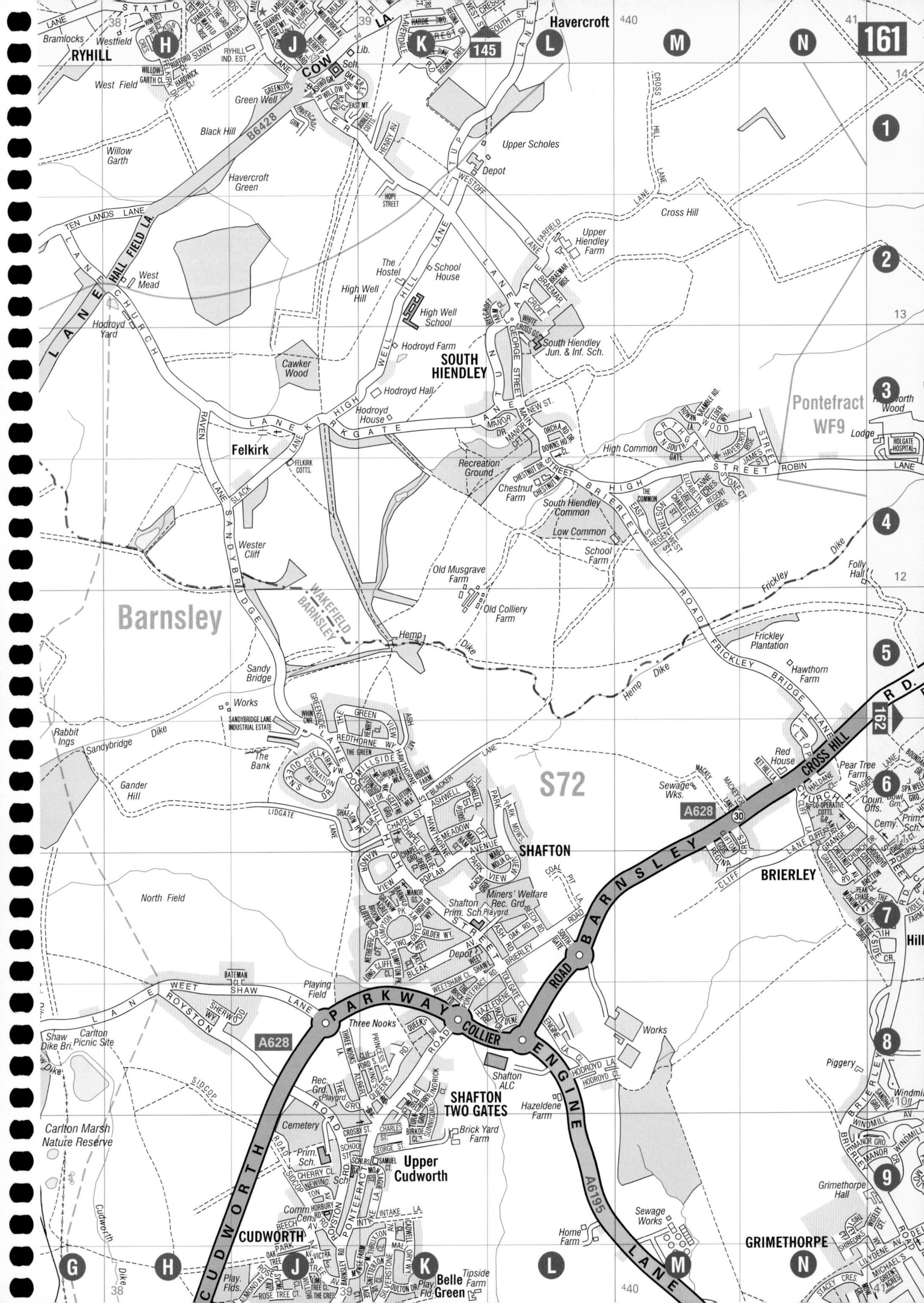

Havercroft
RYHILL
Bramlocks
Westfield
West Field
Green Well
Black Hill
Willow Garth
Havercroft Green
Upper Scholes
Depot
Cross Hill
Upper Hiendley Farm
West Mead
Hodroyd Yard
The Hostel
School House
High Well Hill
High Well School
Hodroyd Farm
Cawker Wood
SOUTH HIENDLEY
South Hiendley Jun. & Inf. Sch.
Hodroyd Hall
Hodroyd House
Felkirk
Recreation Ground
Chestnut Farm
South Hiendley Common
Low Common
School Farm
High Common
Pontefract WF9
Lodge
Wester Cliff
Old Musgrave Farm
Old Colliery Farm
Barnsley
WAKEFIELD
BARNSLEY
Hemp Dike
Frickley Dike
Folly Hall
Frickley Plantation
Hawthorn Farm
Sandy Bridge
Works
SANDYBRIDGE LANE INDUSTRIAL ESTATE
Rabbit Ings
Sandybridge Dike
The Bank
Gander Hill
S72
Red House
Sewage Wks.
Pear Tree Farm
A628
SHAFTON
BRIERLEY
North Field
Shafton Prim. Sch.
Miners' Welfare Rec. Grd.
Depot
Playing Field
Three Nooks
PARKWAY
COLLIER
ENGINE
A628
Shaw Dike Bri.
Carlton Picnic Site
Works
Shafton ALC
Hazeldene Farm
SHAFTON TWO GATES
Cemetery
Rec. Grd.
Brick Yard Farm
Piggery
Carlton Marsh Nature Reserve
Upper Cudworth
Prim. Sch.
A6195
Grimethorpe Hall
Sewage Works
Home Farm
CUDWORTH
GRIMETHORPE
Belle Green
Tipside Farm
Play. Flds.
CUDWORTH
LANE
Hill

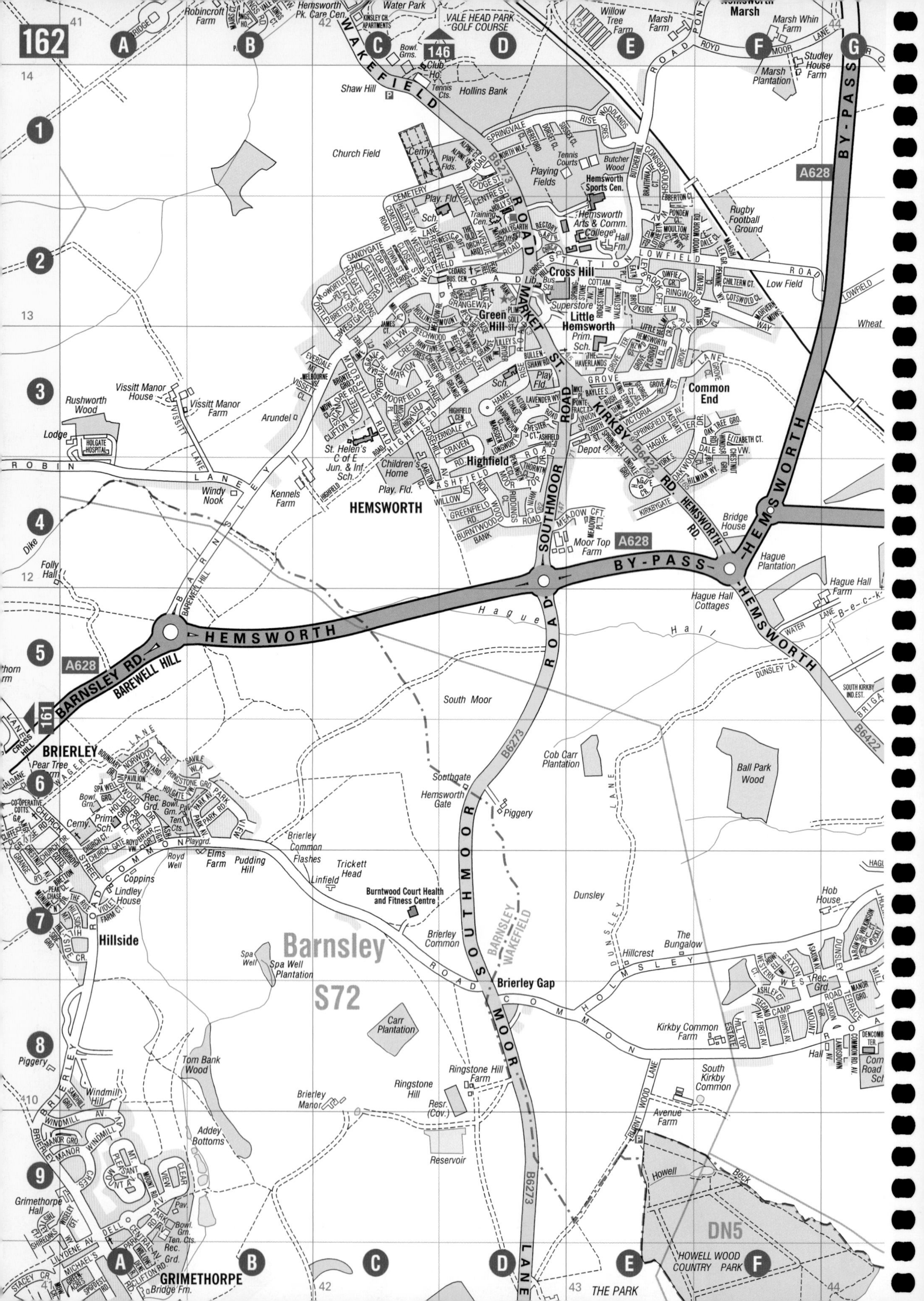

HEMSWORTH
Hemsworth
Cross Hill
Little Hemsworth
Green Hill
Highfield
Common End
BRIERLEY
Hillside
GRIMETHORPE
Barnsley
S72
DN5
Hemsworth Marsh
Vale Head Park Golf Course
Water Park
Hemsworth Pk. Care Cen.
Robincroft Farm
Willow Tree Farm
Marsh Farm
Marsh Whin Farm
Studley House Farm
Marsh Plantation
Shaw Hill
Hollins Bank
Church Field
Playing Fields
Hemsworth Sports Cen.
Hemsworth Arts & Comm. College
Butcher Wood
Rugby Football Ground
Low Field
Wheat
Vissitt Manor House
Vissitt Manor Farm
Rushworth Wood
Lodge
Holgate Hospital
Arundel
St. Helen's C of E Jun. & Inf. Sch.
Children's Home
Kennels Farm
Windy Nook
Folly Hall
Dike
Moor Top Farm
Bridge House
Hague Plantation
Hague Hall Farm
Hague Hall Cottages
South Moor
Cob Carr Plantation
Ball Park Wood
Southgate
Hemsworth Gate
Piggery
Brierley Common Flashes
Trickett Head
Linfield
Burntwood Court Health and Fitness Centre
Elms Farm
Pudding Hill
Royd Well
Coppins
Lindley House
Spa Well
Spa Well Plantation
Brierley Common
Brierley Gap
Dunsley
Hillcrest
The Bungalow
Hob House
Kirkby Common Farm
South Kirkby Common
Avenue Farm
Carr Plantation
Ringstone Hill Farm
Ringstone Hill
Brierley Manor
Resr. (Cov.)
Reservoir
Tom Bank Wood
Addey Bottoms
Windmill Hill
Piggery
Grimethorpe Hall
Bridge Fm.
Howell Wood Country Park
Howell Beck
The Park
HEMSWORTH BY-PASS
A628
B6273
B6422
WAKEFIELD ROAD
MARKET ST.
SOUTHMOOR ROAD
SOUTHMOOR LANE
KIRKBY ROAD
HEMSWORTH RD.
BARNSLEY RD.
BAREWELL HILL
BARNSLEY ROAD
ROBIN LANE
VISSITT LANE
STATION ROAD
LOWFIELD ROAD
HOLMSLEY LANE
COMMON ROAD
BRIERLEY ROAD
BURNT WOOD LANE
DUNSLEY LANE
WATER LANE
CHURCH STREET
BARNSLEY WAKEFIELD
146
161

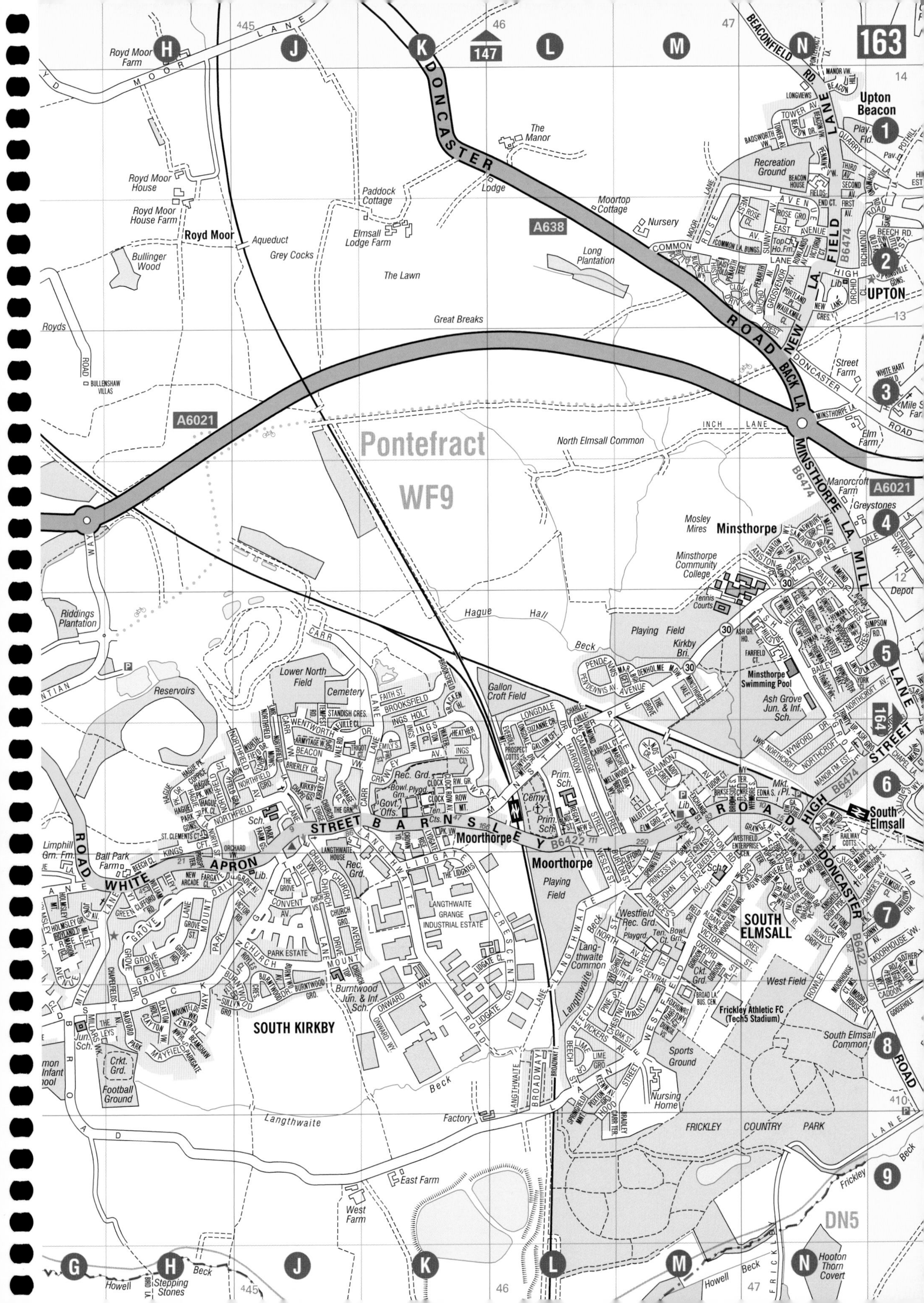
Pontefract
WF9
DN5
Upton Beacon
UPTON
Minsthorpe
Moorthorpe
SOUTH ELMSALL
SOUTH KIRKBY
Royd Moor
DONCASTER ROAD
A638
A6021
B6474
B6422
BARNSLEY STREET
WHITE APRON
HIGH STREET
MINSTHORPE LA.
MILL LANE
FRICKLEY COUNTRY PARK
Frickley Athletic FC (Tech5 Stadium)
Minsthorpe Community College
Minsthorpe Swimming Pool
Langthwaite Grange Industrial Estate
North Elmsall Common
South Elmsall Common
Hague Hall Beck
Howell Beck
Hooton Thorn Covert
147
164

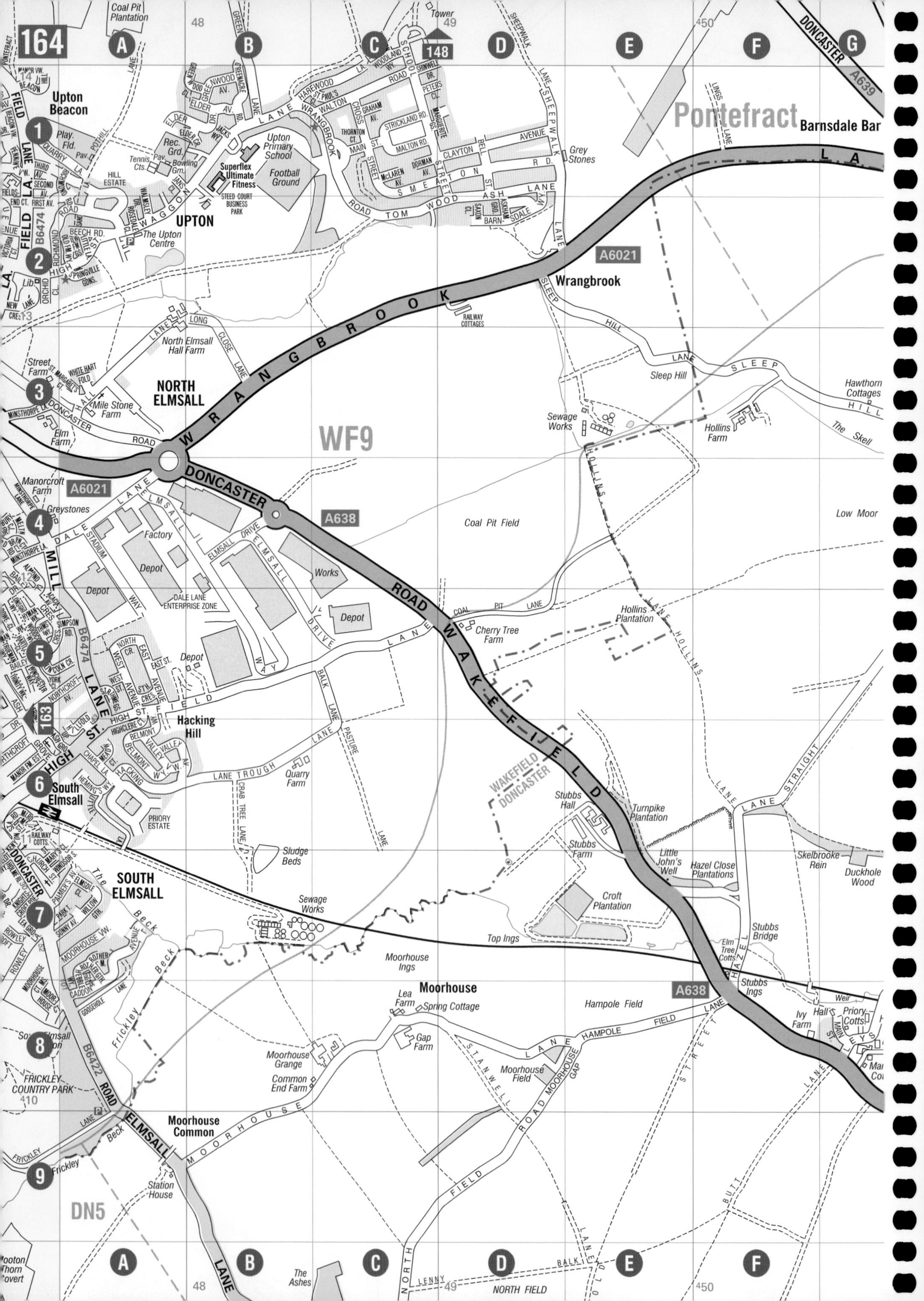
Upton Beacon
UPTON
Upton Primary School
Football Ground
Superflex Ultimate Fitness
The Upton Centre
Pontefract
Barnsdale Bar
Wrangbrook
WRANGBROOK
A6021
NORTH ELMSALL
North Elmsall Hall Farm
Mile Stone Farm
WF9
DONCASTER
A638
Sleep Hill
Sewage Works
Hollins Farm
Coal Pit Field
Low Moor
DALE LANE ENTERPRISE ZONE
Factory
Depot
Works
Cherry Tree Farm
Hollins Plantation
Hacking Hill
Quarry Farm
WAKEFIELD
DONCASTER
Stubbs Hall
Turnpike Plantation
Stubbs Farm
Little John's Well
Hazel Close Plantations
Skelbrooke Rein
Duckhole Wood
SOUTH ELMSALL
South Elmsall
PRIORY ESTATE
Sludge Beds
Croft Plantation
Top Ings
Moorhouse Ings
Moorhouse
Lea Farm
Spring Cottage
Hampole Field
Stubbs Bridge
Stubbs Ings
Gap Farm
Moorhouse Grange
Common End Farm
Moorhouse Field
FRICKLEY COUNTRY PARK
Moorhouse Common
Frickley
Station House
DN5
The Ashes
NORTH FIELD

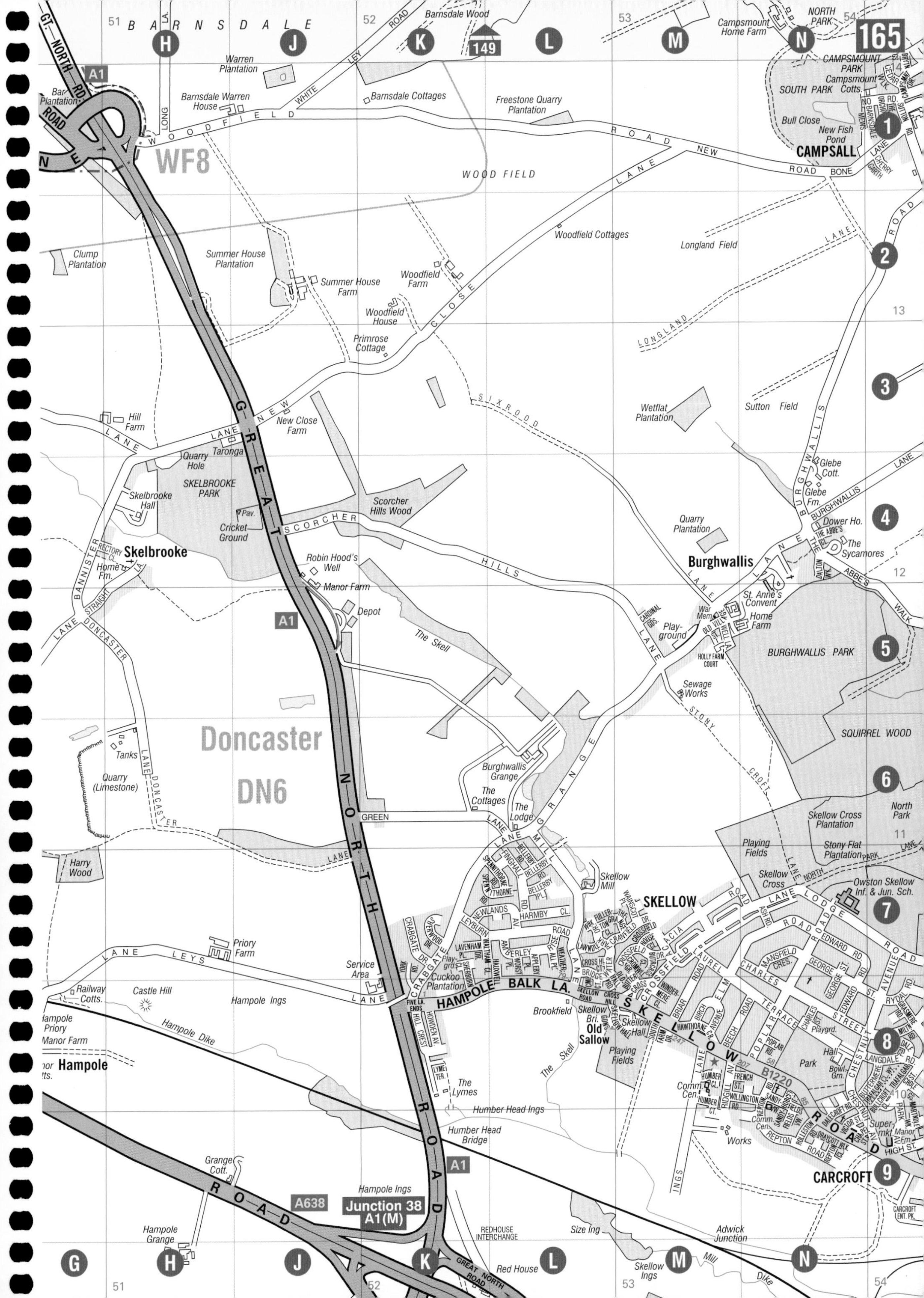
BARNSDALE
Barnsdale Wood
149
Warren Plantation
Barnsdale Cottages
Barnsdale Warren House
Bar Plantation
A1
WF8
WOODFIELD ROAD
Freestone Quarry Plantation
WOOD FIELD
NEW ROAD
BONE LANE
Campsmount Home Farm
NORTH PARK
CAMPSMOUNT PARK
Campsmount Cotts.
SOUTH PARK
Bull Close
New Fish Pond
CAMPSALL
Clump Plantation
Summer House Plantation
Summer House Farm
Woodfield Farm
Woodfield House
Woodfield Cottages
Longland Field
LONGLAND LANE
Primrose Cottage
CLOSE LANE
SIXROOD
Wetflat Plantation
Sutton Field
Hill Farm
NEW LANE
New Close Farm
Taronga
Quarry Hole
SKELBROOKE PARK
Skelbrooke Hall
Scorcher Hills Wood
SCORCHER HILLS
Cricket Ground
Skelbrooke
Robin Hood's Well
Manor Farm
Depot
A1
The Skell
Quarry Plantation
Burghwallis
BURGHWALLIS LANE
Glebe Cott.
Glebe Fm.
Dower Ho.
The Sycamores
ABBE'S WALK
St. Anne's Convent
Home Farm
Playground
BURGHWALLIS PARK
Sewage Works
SQUIRREL WOOD
STONY CROFT
Doncaster
DN6
Tanks
Quarry (Limestone)
DONCASTER LANE
Burghwallis Grange
The Cottages
The Lodge
GRANGE LANE
GREEN LANE
MILL LANE
GREAT NORTH ROAD
Harry Wood
Skellow Cross Plantation
North Park
Playing Fields
Stony Flat Plantation
Skellow Cross
Owston Skellow Inf. & Jun. Sch.
SKELLOW
Skellow Mill
Priory Farm
LEYS LANE
Service Area
Railway Cotts.
Castle Hill
Hampole Ings
Hampole Dike
Hampole Priory
Manor Farm
Hampole
Cuckoo Plantation
HAMPOLE BALK LA.
Brookfield
Skellow Bri.
Old Sallow
Skellow Hall
Playing Fields
SKELLOW ROAD
B1220
Park
Comm. Cen.
Works
The Lymes
Humber Head Ings
Humber Head Bridge
Grange Cott.
ROAD
A638
A1
Hampole Ings
Junction 38 A1(M)
Hampole Grange
REDHOUSE INTERCHANGE
Size Ing
Adwick Junction
Red House
Skellow Ings
Mill Dike
CARCROFT
CARCROFT ENT. PK.

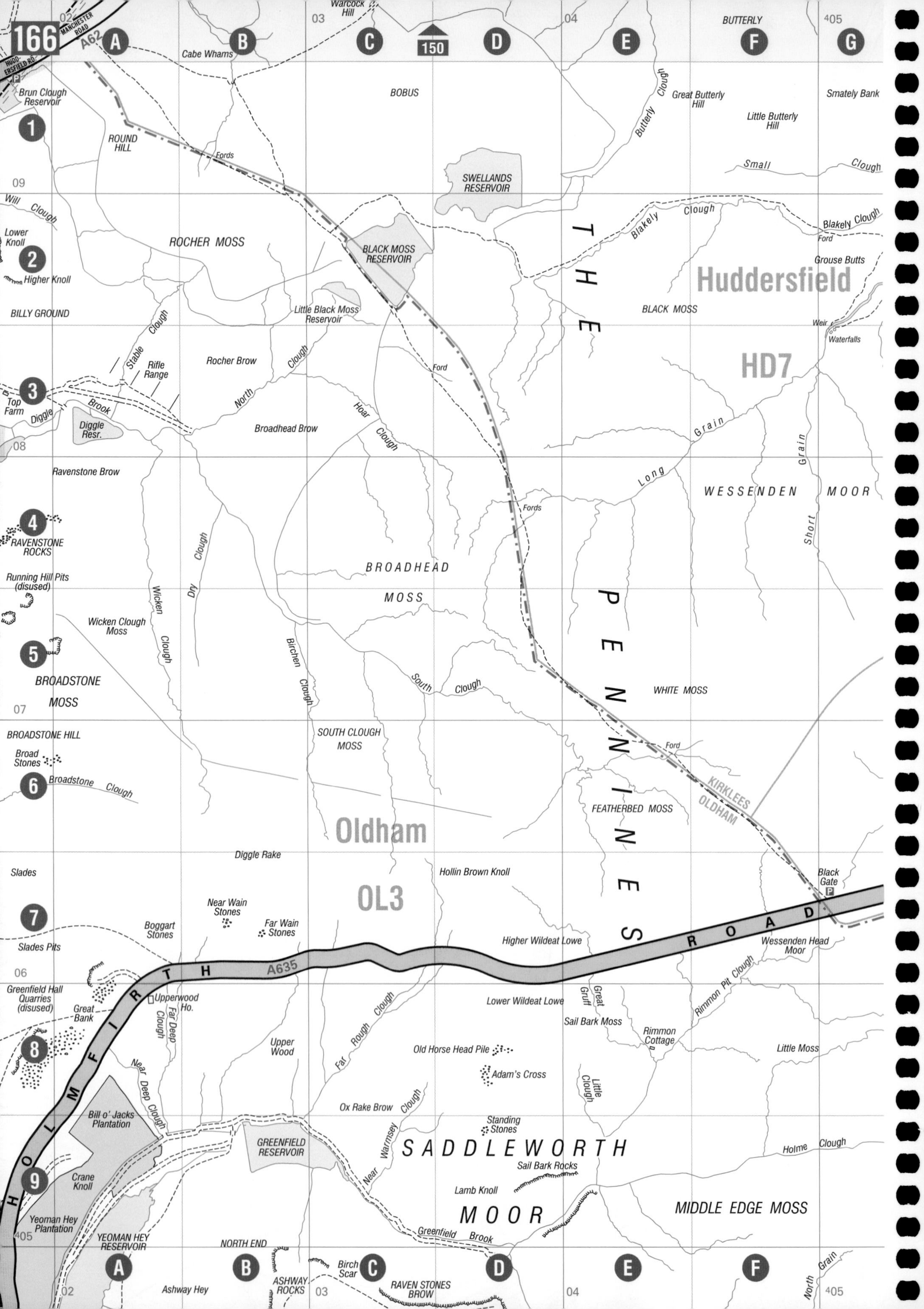

A62
MANCHESTER ROAD
HUDDERSFIELD RD

A B C 150 D E F G

Brun Clough Reservoir
ROUND HILL
Fords
BOBUS
Cabe Whams
Warcock Hill
BUTTERLY
Great Butterly Hill
Little Butterly Hill
Smately Bank
Butterly Clough
Small Clough

Will Clough
Lower Knoll
Higher Knoll
BILLY GROUND
ROCHER MOSS
SWELLANDS RESERVOIR
Blakely Clough
Blakely Clough
Ford
Grouse Butts
Huddersfield
BLACK MOSS
Weir
Waterfalls

Stable Clough
Rifle Range
Rocher Brow
Brook
Diggle
Top Farm
Diggle Resr.
North Clough
Little Black Moss Reservoir
BLACK MOSS RESERVOIR
Ford
HD7
Long Grain
Short Grain
WESSENDEN MOOR

Ravenstone Brow
Broadhead Brow
Hoar Clough
Fords

Wicken Clough
Dry Clough
RAVENSTONE ROCKS
Running Hill Pits (disused)
Wicken Clough Moss
BROADSTONE MOSS
Birchen Clough
BROADHEAD MOSS
T H E   P E N N I N E

South Clough
WHITE MOSS

BROADSTONE HILL
Broad Stones
Broadstone Clough
SOUTH CLOUGH MOSS
FEATHERBED MOSS
KIRKLEES
OLDHAM
Ford
Black Gate P

Slades
Diggle Rake
Oldham
Hollin Brown Knoll
OL3
Near Wain Stones
Far Wain Stones
Boggart Stones
Slades Pits
Greenfield Hall Quarries (disused)
Great Bank
H O L M F I R T H
A635
Upperwood Ho.
Far Deep Clough
Upper Wood
Near Deep Clough
Higher Wildeat Lowe
Lower Wildeat Lowe
Far Rough Clough
Old Horse Head Pile
Adam's Cross
Ox Rake Brow
Near Warnsey Clough
Standing Stones
S A D D L E W O R T H
Sail Bark Rocks
Lamb Knoll
M O O R
Sail Bark Moss
Great Gruff
Little Clough
R O A D
S
Rimmon Pit Clough
Wessenden Head Moor
Rimmon Cottage
Little Moss
Holme Clough
MIDDLE EDGE MOSS

Bill o' Jacks Plantation
Crane Knoll
Yeoman Hey Plantation
YEOMAN HEY RESERVOIR
GREENFIELD RESERVOIR
NORTH END
Ashway Hey
Birch Scar
ASHWAY ROCKS
RAVEN STONES BROW
Greenfield Brook
North Grain

405
02 03 04 405

1 2 3 4 5 6 7 8 9

A B C D E F

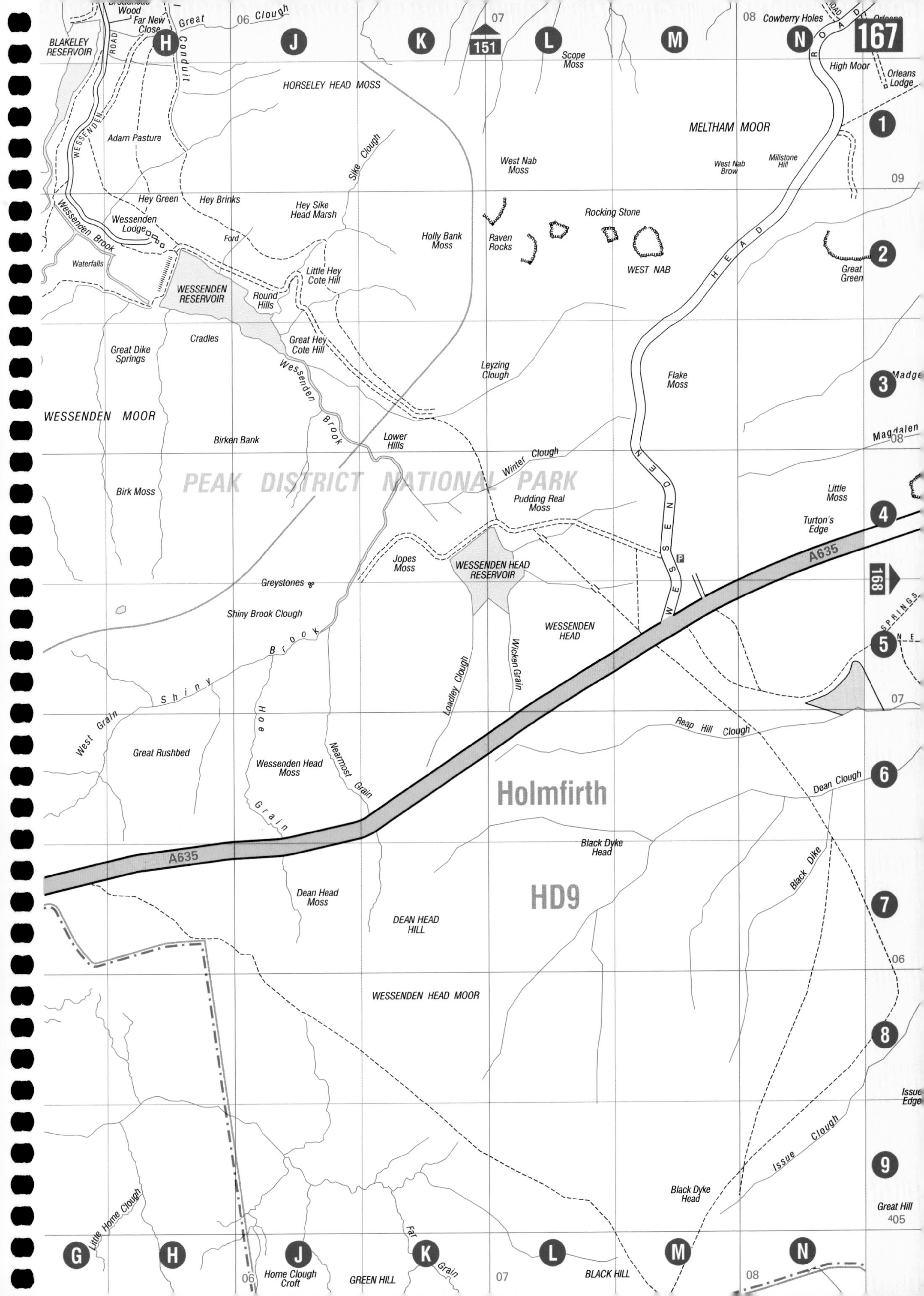

BLAKELEY RESERVOIR
Far New Close
Great Clough
Conduit
HORSELEY HEAD MOSS
Scope Moss
Cowberry Holes
High Moor
Orleans Lodge
MELTHAM MOOR
Adam Pasture
Sike Clough
West Nab Moss
West Nab Brow
Millstone Hill
Hey Green
Hey Brinks
Hey Sike Head Marsh
Rocking Stone
Wessenden Lodge
Wessenden Brook
Ford
Holly Bank Moss
Raven Rocks
WEST NAB
Great Green
Waterfalls
Little Hey Cote Hill
WESSENDEN RESERVOIR
Round Hills
Cradles
Great Dike Springs
Great Hey Cote Hill
Leyzing Clough
Flake Moss
WESSENDEN MOOR
Lower Hills
Birken Bank
Winter Clough
PEAK DISTRICT NATIONAL PARK
Birk Moss
Pudding Real Moss
Little Moss
Turton's Edge
Jopes Moss
WESSENDEN HEAD RESERVOIR
A635
Greystones
Shiny Brook Clough
WESSENDEN HEAD
Loadley Clough
Wicken Grain
Shiny Brook
West Grain
Hoe Grain
Reap Hill Clough
Great Rushbed
Nearmost Grain
Wessenden Head Moss
Holmfirth
Dean Clough
Black Dyke Head
Black Dike
Dean Head Moss
DEAN HEAD HILL
HD9
WESSENDEN HEAD MOOR
Issue Edge
Issue Clough
Little Home Clough
Black Dyke Head
Great Hill
Far Grain
Home Clough Croft
GREEN HILL
BLACK HILL
WESSENDEN HEAD ROAD
WESSENDEN ROAD
151
168

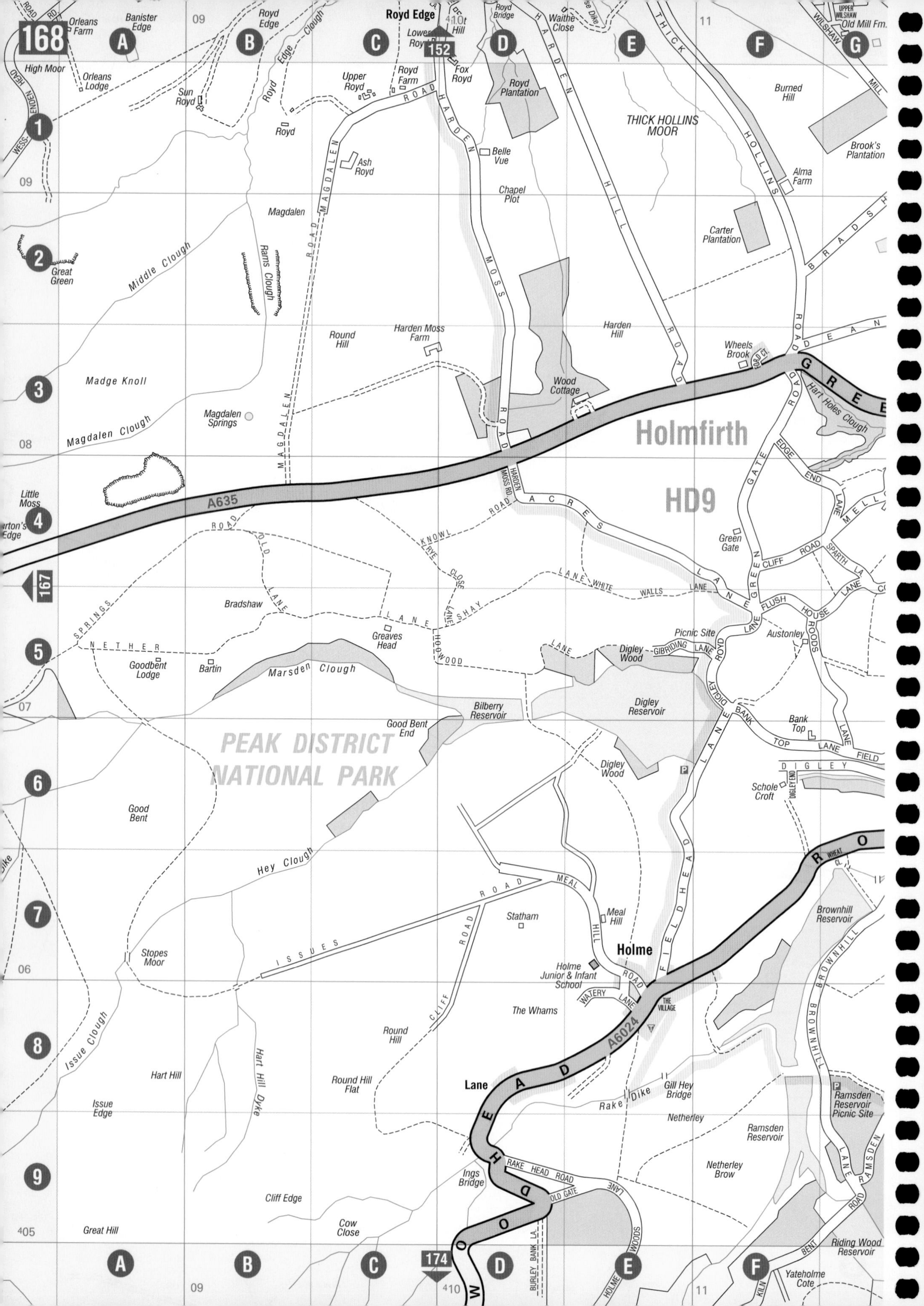
Royd Edge
Orleans Farm
Banister Edge
Royd Edge
Royd Bridge
Waithe Close
Upper Wilshaw
Old Mill Fm.
High Moor
Orleans Lodge
Sun Royd
Royd
Upper Royd
Royd Farm
Lower Royd
Fox Royd
Royd Plantation
Burned Hill
Thick Hollins Moor
Brook's Plantation
Ash Royd
Belle Vue
Chapel Plot
Alma Farm
Carter Plantation
Magdalen
Middle Clough
Rams Clough
Great Green
Round Hill
Harden Moss Farm
Harden Hill
Wheels Brook
Madge Knoll
Wood Cottage
Hart Holes Clough
Magdalen Springs
Holmfirth
Magdalen Clough
HD9
Little Moss
A635
Green Gate
Bradshaw
Greaves Head
Picnic Site
Austonley
Nether
Goodbent Lodge
Bartin
Marsden Clough
Digley Wood
Bilberry Reservoir
Digley Reservoir
Good Bent End
Bank Top
PEAK DISTRICT NATIONAL PARK
Digley Wood
Schole Croft
Good Bent
Hey Clough
Statham
Meal Hill
Brownhill Reservoir
Stopes Moor
Holme
Holme Junior & Infant School
The Whams
Issue Clough
Round Hill
Hart Hill Dyke
Hart Hill
Round Hill Flat
Lane
Gill Hey Bridge
Rake Dike
Ramsden Reservoir Picnic Site
Issue Edge
Netherley
Ramsden Reservoir
Ings Bridge
Netherley Brow
Cliff Edge
Cow Close
Riding Wood Reservoir
Great Hill
Yateholme Cote
A6024
Issues Road
Meal Hill Road
Fieldhead Lane
Woodhead Road
Rake Head Road
Acres Lane
Harden Moss Road
Thick Hollins Road
Harden Hill Road
Magdalen Road
Royd Road
Green Gate Road
Flush House Lane
Digley Royd Lane
Bank Top Lane
Brownhill Lane
Ramsden Road
Holme Woods Lane
Burley Bank La.
Kiln Bent Road
Cliff Road
Watery Lane
Knowl Road
White Walls Lane
Springs Road
Old Lane
Greaves Lane
Rye Close
Shay Lane
Hoowood
Gibriding Lane
Old Gate
152
167
174
A B C D E F G
1 2 3 4 5 6 7 8 9
09 10 11
405 410

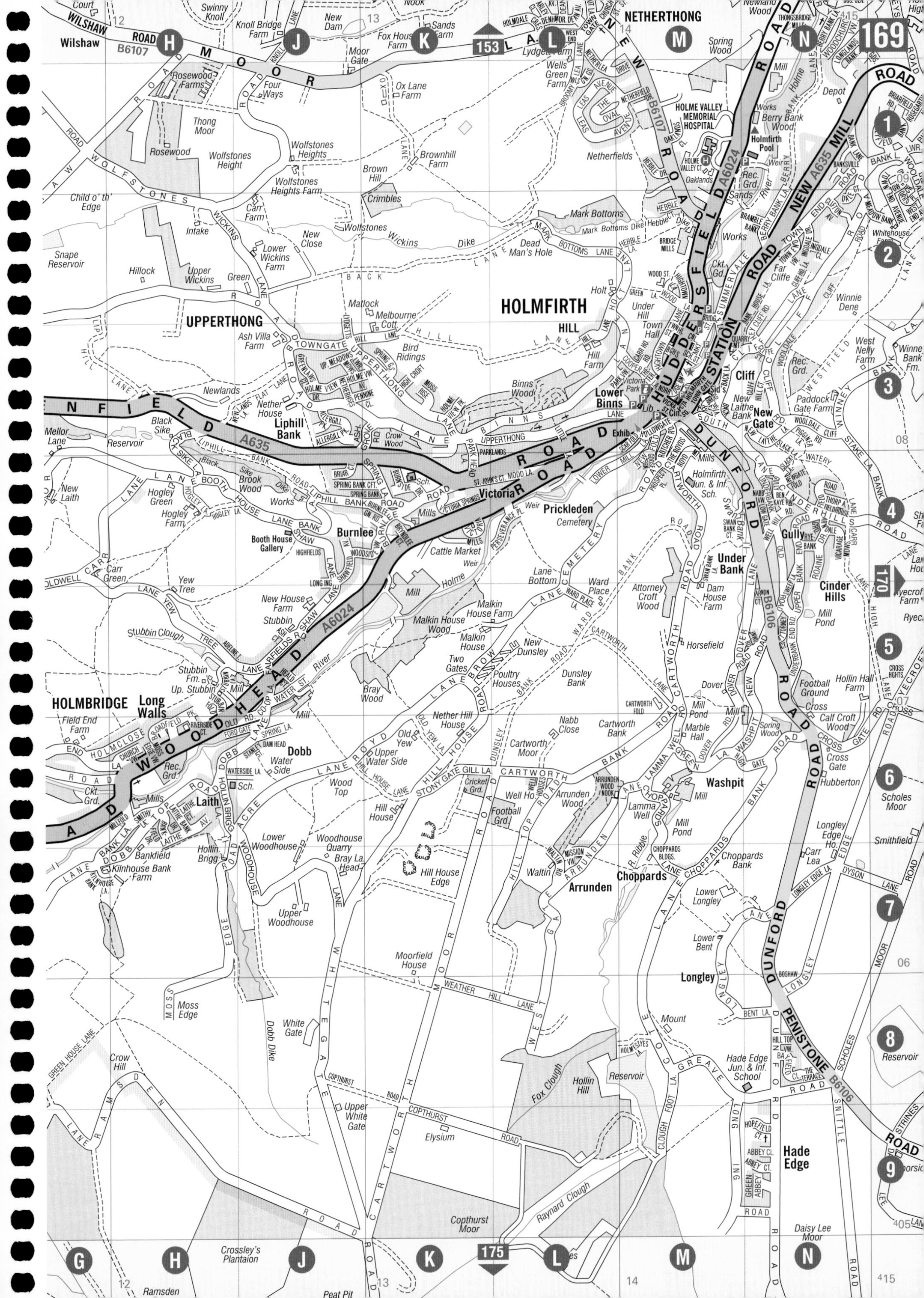

153
175
170
HOLMFIRTH
UPPERTHONG
NETHERTHONG
HOLMBRIDGE
Wilshaw
Netherfields
Cliff
New Gate
Gully
Cinder Hills
Under Bank
Victoria
Burnlee
Liphill Bank
Lower Binns
Prickleden
Washpit
Choppards
Arrunden
Longley
Hade Edge
Dobb
Laith
Long Walls
HOLME VALLEY MEMORIAL HOSPITAL
Holmfirth Pool
Scholes Moor
Smithfield
Copthurst Moor
Crossley's Plantaion
Ramsden
Peat Pit
Daisy Lee Moor
Hollin Hill
Fox Clough
Raynard Clough
Reservoir
Hade Edge Jun. & Inf. School
Snape Reservoir
Thong Moor
Wolfstones Height
Child o' th' Edge
WOODHEAD ROAD
DUNFORD ROAD
PENISTONE ROAD
HUDDERSFIELD ROAD
NEW MILL ROAD
STATION ROAD
A635
A6024
B6106
B6107

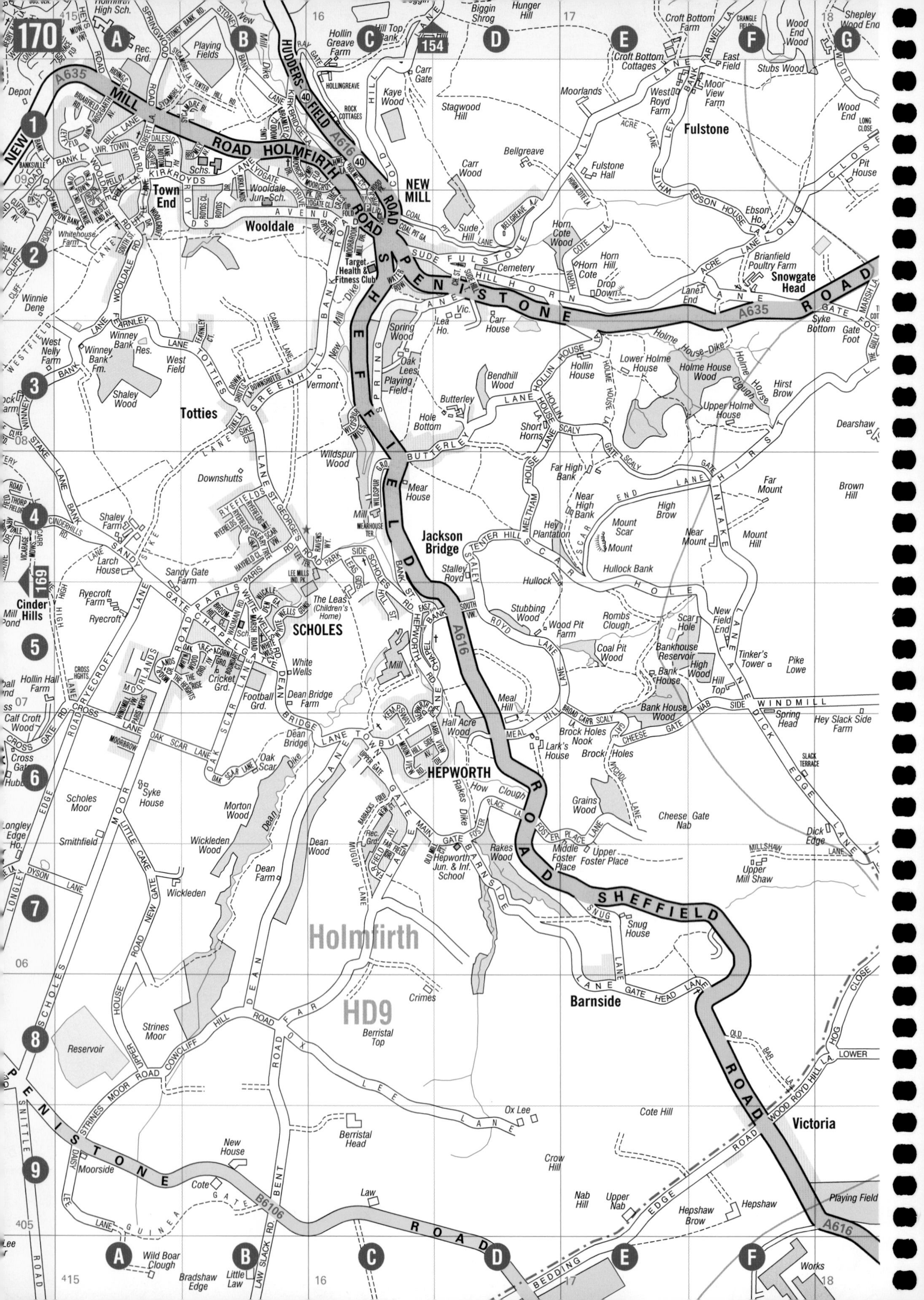

170
A
B
C
D
E
F
G
1
2
3
4
5
6
7
8
9
415
16
17
18
09
08
07
06
405
154
169
40
A635
A616
B6106
HD9
Holmfirth
Holmfirth High Sch.
Rec. Grd.
Playing Fields
Hollin Greave Farm
Hill Top Bank
Biggin Shrog
Hunger Hill
Croft Bottom Farm
Croft Bottom Cottages
Wood End Wood
Shepley Wood End
East Field
Stubs Wood
Carr Gate
Kaye Wood
Hollingreave
Rock Cottages
Stagwood Hill
Moorlands
West Royd Farm
Moor View Farm
Fulstone
Wood End
Long Close
Depot
Mill Road
Holmfirth Road
New Mill Road
Bank L.
Lwr. Town
Bill Lane
Dalesides
Kirkroyds
Lydgate
Town End
Wooldale
Wooldale Jun. Sch.
Schs.
Avenue
New Mill
Bellgreave
Carr Wood
Fulstone Hall
Pit House
Ebson House
Ebson Ho.
Long Close
Whitehouse Farm
Sude Hill
Coal Pit La.
Horn Cote Wood
Horn Hill
Horn Cote
Drop Down
Brianfield Poultry Farm
Snowgate Head
Lane End
Cemetery
Sude Fulstone
Hill Horn
Penistone Road
Target Health & Fitness Club
Winnie Dene
West Nelly Farm
Winney Bank Fm.
Winney Bank Res.
Fearnley Lane
West Field
Totties Lane
Shaley Wood
Totties
Downshutts La.
Greenhill Bank
Vermont
Spring Wood
Oak Lees Playing Field
Lea Ho.
Carr House
Vic.
Syke Bottom
Gate Foot
Marsh La.
Holme House Dike
Lower Holme House
Hollin House
Holme House Wood
Holme House Clough
Hirst Brow
Bendhill Wood
Butterley
Hole Bottom
Short Horns
Upper Holme House
Dearshaw
Sheffield Road
Wildspur Mills
Wildspur Wood
Butterley
Scaly Gate
Far High Bank
Hirst
Far Mount
Brown Hill
Downshutts
Mear House
Mill
Mearhouse Ter.
Near High Bank
High Brow
End Lane
Mount Scar
Mount
Hey Plantation
Jackson Bridge
Tenter Hill
Scar
Near Mount
Mount Hill
Intake
Shaley Farm
Cinderhills Rd.
Sandy Lane
Ryefields
St. George's Road
Larch House
Sandy Gate Farm
Lee Mills Ind. Pk.
Park Side
Stalley Royd
Hullock
Hullock Bank
Hole Lane
Cinder Hills
Mill Pond
Ryecroft Farm
Ryecroft
Paris Road
Paris Gate
Chapelgate
White Wells Rd.
Sch.
Scholes
The Leas (Children's Home)
Scholes Hill
Hepworth Rd.
South Vw.
Stubbing Wood
Wood Pit Farm
Royd Lane
Rombs Clough
Scar Hole
New Field End
Bankhouse Reservoir
Coal Pit Wood
High Wood
Tinker's Tower
Pike Lowe
Bank House
Hill Top
Hollin Hall Farm
Cross Hights
Ryecroft Lane
Moorlands
Cricket Grd.
Football Grd.
White Wells
Dean Bridge Farm
Mill
Chapel
Meal Hill
Windmill Side
Spring Head
Hey Slack Side Farm
Calf Croft Wood
Cross Gate Rd.
Moorbrow
Oak Scar Lane
Dean Bridge
Town Butt
Hall Acre Wood
Broad Carr La.
Brock Holes Nook
Bank House Wood
Nab Gate
Cheese Gate
Lark's House
Brock Holes
Slack Terrace
Cross Gate
Scholes Moor
Syke House
Oak Scar
Hepworth
How Clough
Rakes Dike
Nichol Lane
Dick Edge Lane
Longley Edge Ho.
Smithfield
Morton Wood
Wickleden Wood
Dean Wood
Dean
Grains Wood
Cheese Gate Nab
Foster Place La.
Dick Edge
Millshaw
Dyson Lane
Little Cake
New Gate
Wickleden
Dean Farm
Main Gate
Hepworth Jun. & Inf. School
Rakes Wood
Middle Foster Place
Upper Foster Place
Upper Mill Shaw
Barnside
Longley
Snug
Snug House
Upper House Road
Holmfirth
Gate Head Lane
Crimes
Reservoir
Strines Moor
Cowcliff Hill Road
Far Ox Lee
Berristal Top
Old Bar La.
Hog Close
Lower
Scholes
Strines Moor Road
Ox Lee
Ox Lee Lane
Cote Hill
Wood Royd Hill La.
Victoria
Snittle Road
Penistone
Berristal Head
New House
Moorside
Daisy Lee
Cote
Gate
Crow Hill
Law
Nab Hill
Upper Nab
Edge
Hepshaw Brow
Hepshaw
Playing Field
Guinea Lane
Bent
Law Slack Rd.
Road
Wild Boar Clough
Little Law
Bradshaw Edge
Bedding Edge
Works

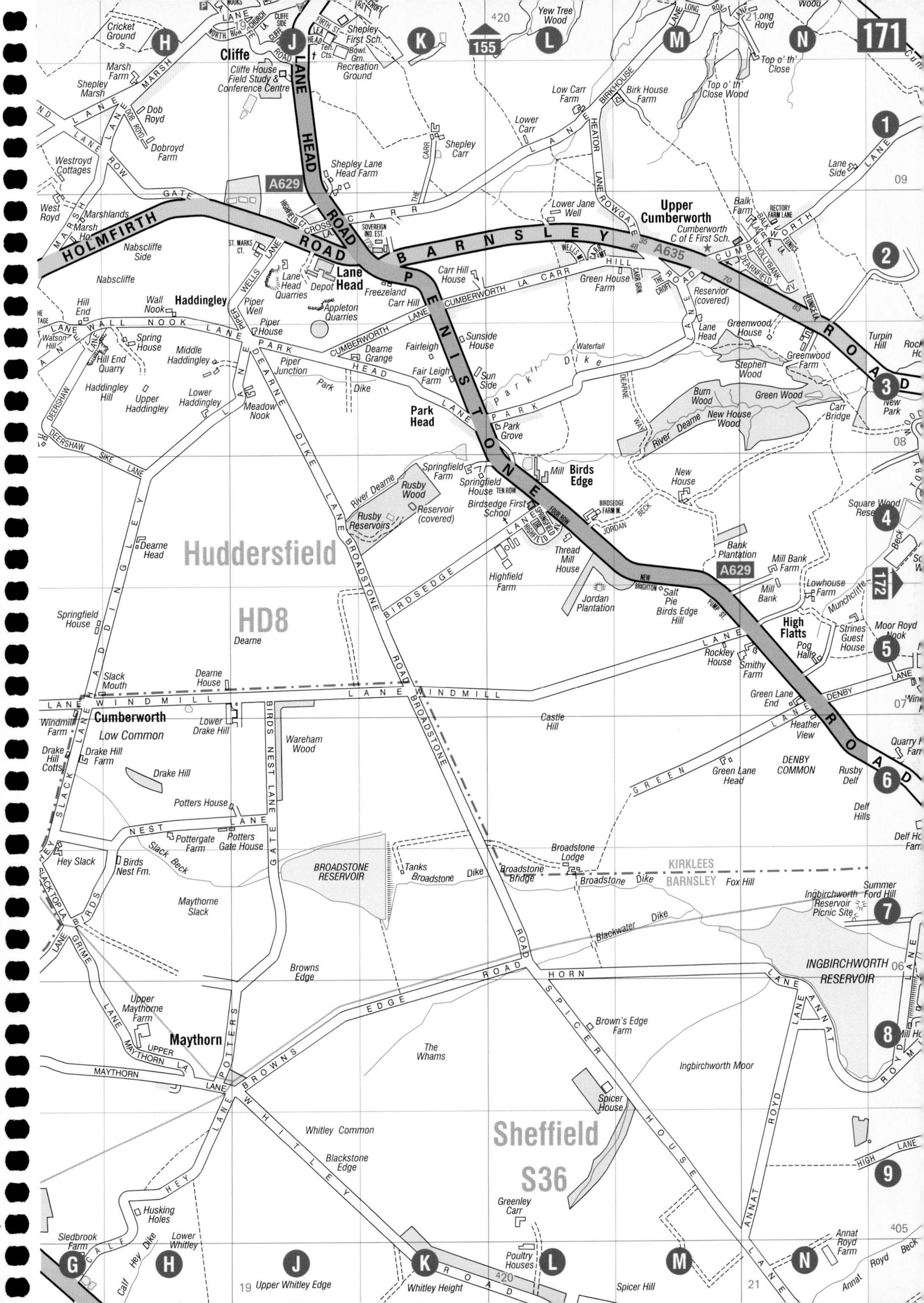

Cliffe
Cliffe House Field Study & Conference Centre
Shepley First Sch.
Recreation Ground
Cricket Ground
Shepley Marsh
Marsh Farm
Dob Royd
Dobroyd Farm
Westroyd Cottages
West Royd
Marshlands
Marsh Ho.
HOLMFIRTH ROAD
LANE HEAD ROAD
A629
A635
BARNSLEY ROAD
PENISTONE ROAD
Shepley Lane Head Farm
Shepley Carr
Lower Carr
Low Carr Farm
Birk House Farm
Top o' th' Close
Top o' th' Close Wood
Yew Tree Wood
Long Royd
Lane Side
Upper Cumberworth
Cumberworth C of E First Sch.
Balk Farm
Lower Jane Well
Nabscliffe Side
Nabscliffe
Lane Head
Lane Head Quarries
Depot
Freezeland
Carr Hill
Carr Hill House
Appleton Quarries
Green House Farm
Reservoir (covered)
Greenwood House
Lane Head
Turpin Hill
Haddingley
Hill End
Wall Nook
Piper Well
Piper House
Spring House
Watson Hill
Hill End Quarry
Middle Haddingley
Haddingley Hill
Upper Haddingley
Lower Haddingley
Meadow Nook
Piper Junction
Dearne Grange
Fairleigh
Sunside House
Fair Leigh Farm
Sun Side
Park Dike
Waterfall
Stephen Wood
Greenwood Farm
Burn Wood
Green Wood
New House Wood
River Dearne
Carr Bridge
New Park
Park Head
Park Grove
Birds Edge
Mill
New House
Springfield Farm
Springfield House
Birdsedge First School
Rusby Wood
River Dearne
Rusby Reservoirs
Reservoir (covered)
Square Wood
Bank Plantation
Thread Mill House
Highfield Farm
Jordan Plantation
Salt Pie
Birds Edge Hill
Mill Bank Farm
Mill Bank
Lowhouse Farm
Huddersfield
HD8
Dearne Head
Springfield House
Dearne
High Flatts
Rockley House
Smithy Farm
Pog Hall
Strines Guest House
Moor Royd Nook
Slack Mouth
Dearne House
WINDMILL LANE
Cumberworth
Low Common
Windmill Farm
Lower Drake Hill
Drake Hill Farm
Drake Hill Cotts
Drake Hill
Wareham Wood
Castle Hill
Green Lane End
Heather View
Green Lane Head
DENBY COMMON
Rusby Delf
Delf Hills
Potters House
Pottergate Farm
Potters Gate House
Hey Slack
Birds Nest Fm.
Slack Beck
BROADSTONE RESERVOIR
Tanks
Broadstone Dike
Broadstone Bridge
Broadstone Lodge
KIRKLEES
BARNSLEY
Fox Hill
Summer Ford Hill
Ingbirchworth Reservoir Picnic Site
Maythorne Slack
Blackwater Dike
Browns Edge
INGBIRCHWORTH RESERVOIR
Upper Maythorne Farm
Maythorn
Brown's Edge Farm
The Whams
Ingbirchworth Moor
Spicer House
Whitley Common
Sheffield
S36
Blackstone Edge
Husking Holes
Sledbrook Farm
Lower Whitley
Greenley Carr
Poultry Houses
Annat Royd Farm
Upper Whitley Edge
Whitley Height
Spicer Hill
Annat Royd Beck
155
172

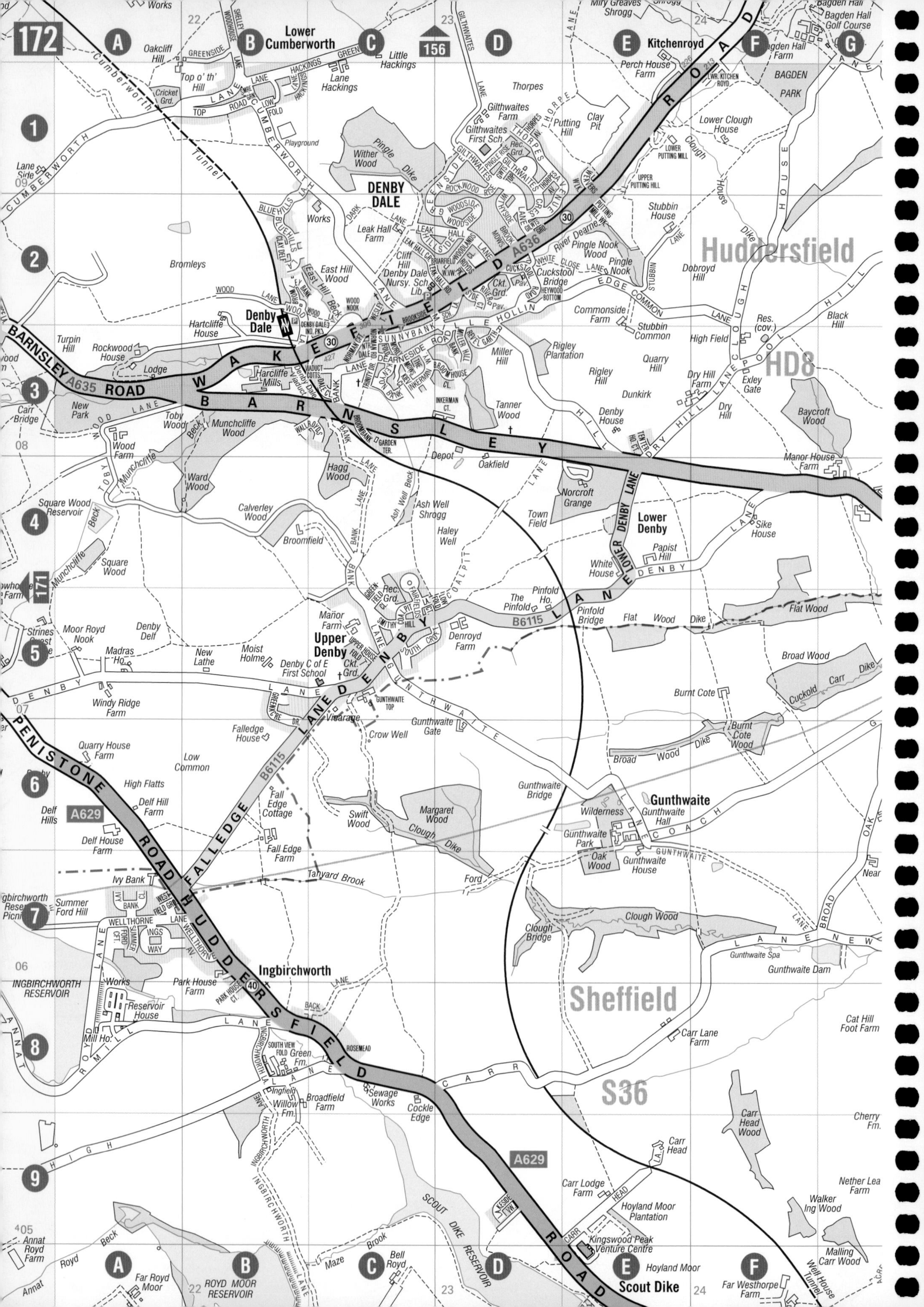
156
171
Lower Cumberworth
Oakcliff Hill
Top o' th' Hill
Cricket Grd.
Little Hackings
Lane Hackings
Kitchenroyd
Perch House Farm
Bagden Hall
Bagden Hall Golf Course
BAGDEN PARK
Thorpes
Gilthwaites Farm
Gilthwaites First Sch.
Putting Hill
Clay Pit
Lower Clough House
Playground
Wither Wood
DENBY DALE
Works
Leak Hall Farm
Cliff Hill
Denby Dale Nursy. Sch.
Lib.
Pingle Nook Wood
Pingle Nook
Stubbin House
Huddersfield
Dobroyd Hill
Bromleys
East Hill Wood
Denby Dale
Hartcliffe House
Turpin Hill
Rockwood House
Lodge
Harcliffe Mills
Cuckstool Bridge
Commonside Farm
Stubbin Common
High Field
Res. (cov.)
Black Hill
Rigley Plantation
Miller Hill
Rigley Hill
Quarry Hill
Dry Hill Farm
Exley Gate
HD8
Dunkirk
Denby House
Tanner Wood
Baycroft Wood
BARNSLEY ROAD
WAKEFIELD ROAD
A635
A636
Carr Bridge
New Park
Toby Wood
Munchcliffe Wood
Wood Farm
Hagg Wood
Depot
Oakfield
Norcroft Grange
Manor House Farm
Ward Wood
Calverley Wood
Ash Well Shrogg
Haley Well
Town Field
Lower Denby
Sike House
Square Wood Reservoir
Broomfield
Papist Hill
White House
Square Wood
The Pinfold
Pinfold Ho.
Pinfold Bridge
Flat Wood
Flat Wood Dike
B6115
Manor Farm
Upper Denby
Denroyd Farm
Moor Royd Nook
Denby Delf
Madras Ho.
New Lathe
Moist Holme
Denby C of E First School
Broad Wood
Cuckold Carr Dike
Burnt Cote
Windy Ridge Farm
Vicarage
Crow Well
Gunthwaite Gate
Burnt Cote Wood
Broad Wood Dike
Falledge House
Quarry House Farm
Low Common
High Flatts
Delf Hill Farm
Delf Hills
A629
Delf House Farm
Fall Edge Cottage
Swift Wood
Margaret Wood
Clough Dike
Gunthwaite Bridge
Gunthwaite
Wilderness
Gunthwaite Hall
Gunthwaite Park
Oak Wood
Gunthwaite House
Fall Edge Farm
Ivy Bank
Tanyard Brook
Ford
Near
Summer Ford Hill
Clough Wood
Clough Bridge
Gunthwaite Spa
Gunthwaite Dam
Ingbirchworth
INGBIRCHWORTH RESERVOIR
Works
Park House Farm
Reservoir House
Sheffield
Cat Hill Foot Farm
Mill Ho.
Carr Lane Farm
Green Fm.
S36
Sewage Works
Broadfield Farm
Willow Fm.
Cockle Edge
Carr Head Wood
Cherry Fm.
PENISTONE ROAD
HUDDERSFIELD ROAD
Carr Head
Carr Lodge Farm
Hoyland Moor Plantation
Nether Lea Farm
Walker Ing Wood
Annat Royd Farm
Maze
Bell Royd
SCOUT DIKE RESERVOIR
Kingswood Peak Venture Centre
Hoyland Moor
Malling Carr Wood
Far Royd Moor
ROYD MOOR RESERVOIR
Scout Dike
Far Westhorpe Farm
Well House Tunnel
A B C D E F G
1 2 3 4 5 6 7 8 9
22 23 24
09 08 07 06 405

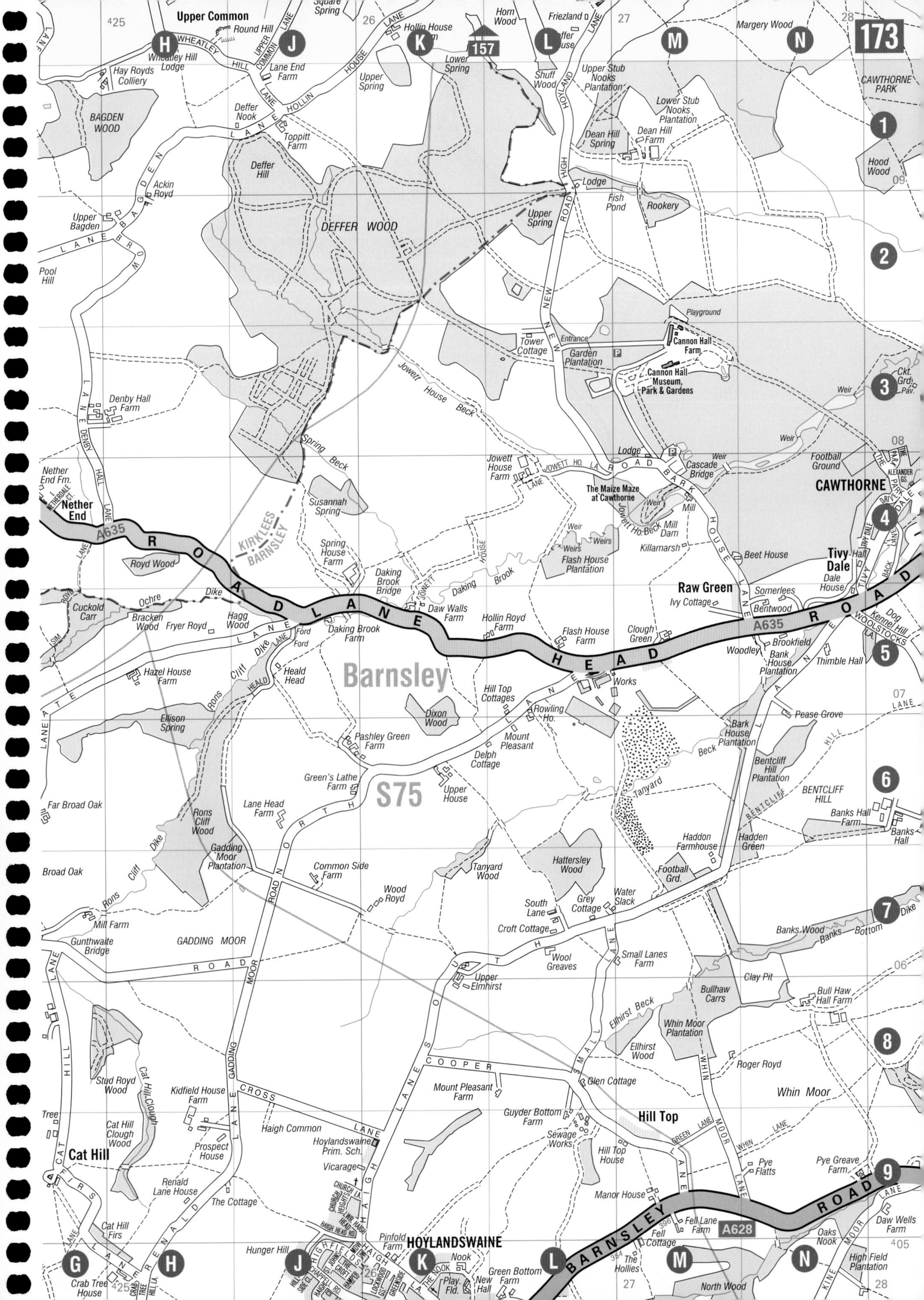

Upper Common
Square Spring
Round Hill
Horn Wood
Friezland
Margery Wood
Hollin House Farm
157
Wheatley Hill Lodge
Lane End Farm
Lower Spring
Shuff Wood
Upper Stub Nooks Plantation
CAWTHORNE PARK
Hay Royds Colliery
Upper Spring
Lower Stub Nooks Plantation
BAGDEN WOOD
Deffer Nook
Toppitt Farm
Dean Hill Farm
Dean Hill Spring
Hood Wood
Deffer Hill
Lodge
Fish Pond
Rookery
Ackin Royd
Upper Bagden
DEFFER WOOD
Upper Spring
Pool Hill
Playground
Tower Cottage
Entrance
Garden Plantation
Cannon Hall Farm
Cannon Hall Museum, Park & Gardens
Weir
Ckt. Grd. Pav.
Denby Hall Farm
Jowett House Beck
Football Ground
Spring Beck
Jowett House Farm
Lodge
Cascade Bridge
CAWTHORNE
Nether End Fm.
Nether End
Susannah Spring
The Maize Maze at Cawthorne
Mill
Jowett Ho. Beck
Mill Dam
Killamarsh
Weirs
Flash House Plantation
KIRKLEES
BARNSLEY
Royd Wood
Spring House Farm
Daking Brook Bridge
Daking Brook
Beet House
Tivy Dale
Dale House
Raw Green
Ivy Cottage
Somerlees
Bentwood
Cuckold Carr
Ochre Dike
Bracken Wood
Fryer Royd
Hagg Wood
Daw Walls Farm
Hollin Royd Farm
Flash House Farm
Clough Green
A635
Brookfield
Dog Kennel Hill
Woodley
Bank House Plantation
Thimble Hall
Daking Brook Farm
Ford
Hazel House Farm
Heald Head
Barnsley
Works
Hill Top Cottages
Rowling Ho.
Pease Grove
Dixon Wood
Ellison Spring
Rons Cliff
Pashley Green Farm
Mount Pleasant
Delph Cottage
Beck
Bark House Plantation
Bentcliff Hill Plantation
Green's Lathe Farm
S75
Upper House
Tanyard
BENTCLIFF HILL
Far Broad Oak
Lane Head Farm
Banks Hall Farm
Banks Hall
Rons Cliff Wood
Gadding Moor Plantation
Haddon Farmhouse
Hadden Green
Hattersley Wood
Broad Oak
Common Side Farm
Tanyard Wood
Football Grd.
Wood Royd
South Lane
Grey Cottage
Water Slack
Dike
Mill Farm
Croft Cottage
Banks Wood
Banks Bottom
Gunthwaite Bridge
GADDING MOOR
Wool Greaves
Small Lanes Farm
Clay Pit
Upper Elmhirst
Bullhaw Carrs
Bull Haw Hall Farm
Ellhirst Beck
Whin Moor Plantation
Ellhirst Wood
Stud Royd Wood
Cat Hill Clough
Roger Royd
Glen Cottage
Kidfield House Farm
Mount Pleasant Farm
Whin Moor
Tree
Guyder Bottom Farm
Hill Top
Cat Hill Clough Wood
Haigh Common
Sewage Works
Hoylandswaine Prim. Sch.
Hill Top House
Prospect House
Pye Flatts
Pye Greave Farm
Cat Hill
Vicarage
Renald Lane House
Manor House
The Cottage
A628
Fell Lane Farm
Fell Cottage
Daw Wells Farm
Cat Hill Firs
Pinfold Farm
HOYLANDSWAINE
Oaks Nook
Hunger Hill
Nook
The Hollies
High Field Plantation
Crab Tree House
Green Bottom Farm
New Hall
Play. Fld.
North Wood
BARNSLEY ROAD
HEAD LANE
ROAD LANE
COOPER LANE
CROSS LANE
GADDING MOOR ROAD
NORTH ROAD
SOUTH ROAD
HIGH HOYLAND NEW ROAD
BARK HOUSE LANE
JOWETT HO. LANE
DENBY HALL LANE
BAGDEN LANE
HOLLIN HOUSE LANE
WHEATLEY HILL LANE
WHIN MOOR LANE
GREEN LANE
SMALL LANE
CAT HILL
KINE MOOR LANE

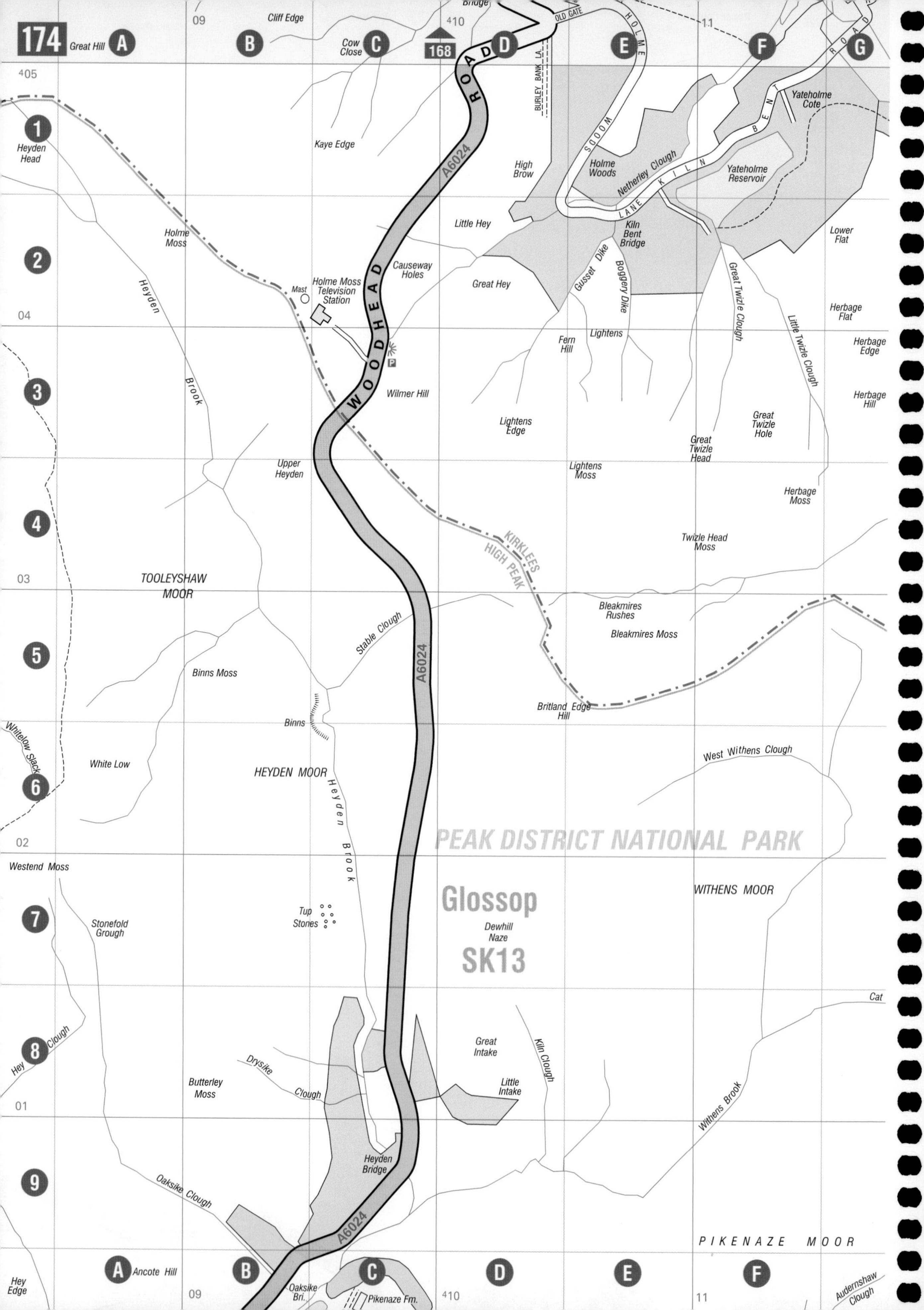

A   B   C   168   D   E   F   G

405

09   Cliff Edge   Cow Close   410   OLD GATE   HOLME   11   ROAD

1 Heyden Head

BURLEY BANK LA.

Kaye Edge

Yateholme Cote

High Brow   Holme Woods   Netherley Clough   Yateholme Reservoir

2 Holme Moss   Mast   Holme Moss Television Station   Causeway Holes   Little Hey   Great Hey   Lower Flat

04   Herbage Flat

Herbage Edge

Wilmer Hill   Fern Hill   Lightens   Gusset Dike   Boggery Dike   Great Twizle Clough   Little Twizle Clough   Herbage Hill

3

WOODHEAD

Lightens Edge   Great Twizle Head   Great Twizle Hole   Herbage Moss

4 Upper Heyden   Lightens Moss

KIRKLEES

03   TOOLEYSHAW MOOR   HIGH PEAK   Twizle Head Moss

A6024

Stable Clough   Bleakmires Rushes

5 Binns Moss   Bleakmires Moss

Binns   Britland Edge Hill

Whitelow Stack

6 White Low   HEYDEN MOOR   West Withens Clough

02

Westend Moss   WITHENS MOOR

Heyden Brook   **PEAK DISTRICT NATIONAL PARK**

7 Stonefold Grough   Tup Stones   **Glossop**   Dewhill Naze   **SK13**   Cat

Hey Edge Clough

8 Drysike Clough   Great Intake   Kiln Clough

Butterley Moss   Little Intake   Withens Brook

01

9 Oaksike Clough   Heyden Bridge

Hey Edge   A6024   PIKENAZE MOOR

A   Ancote Hill   B   C   D   410   E   11   F   Audernshaw Clough

09   Oaksike Bri.   Pikenaze Fm.

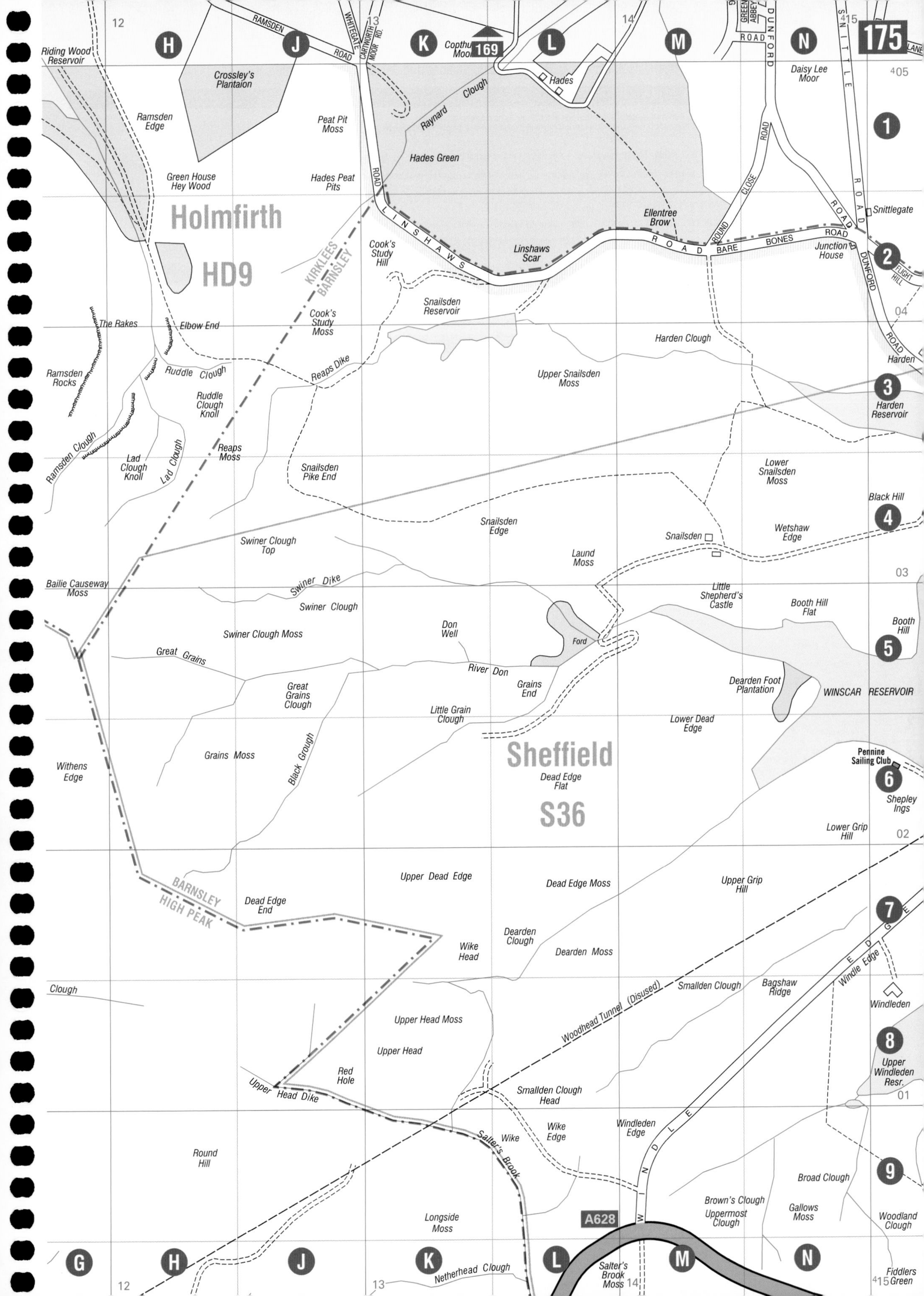

H
J
K
L
M
N
G
Riding Wood Reservoir
Crossley's Plantaion
Ramsden Edge
Peat Pit Moss
Hades
Raynard Clough
Daisy Lee Moor
Hades Green
Green House Hey Wood
Hades Peat Pits
Holmfirth
HD9
Cook's Study Hill
Linshaws Scar
Ellentree Brow
Junction House
Snittlegate
Snailsden Reservoir
Cook's Study Moss
The Rakes
Elbow End
Ramsden Rocks
Ruddle Clough
Ruddle Clough Knoll
Reaps Dike
Reaps Moss
Harden Clough
Upper Snailsden Moss
Harden
Harden Reservoir
Ramsden Clough
Lad Clough Knoll
Lad Clough
Snailsden Pike End
Lower Snailsden Moss
Black Hill
Snailsden Edge
Snailsden
Wetshaw Edge
Laund Moss
Swiner Clough Top
Bailie Causeway Moss
Swiner Dike
Swiner Clough
Little Shepherd's Castle
Booth Hill Flat
Booth Hill
Swiner Clough Moss
Don Well
Ford
Great Grains
River Don
Grains End
Dearden Foot Plantation
WINSCAR RESERVOIR
Great Grains Clough
Little Grain Clough
Lower Dead Edge
Sheffield
S36
Pennine Sailing Club
Withens Edge
Grains Moss
Black Grough
Dead Edge Flat
Shepley Ings
Lower Grip Hill
Upper Dead Edge
Dead Edge Moss
Upper Grip Hill
BARNSLEY
HIGH PEAK
KIRKLEES
BARNSLEY
Dead Edge End
Dearden Clough
Wike Head
Dearden Moss
Clough
Smallden Clough
Bagshaw Ridge
Windle Edge
Windleden
Woodhead Tunnel (Disused)
Upper Head Moss
Upper Windleden Resr.
Upper Head
Red Hole
Upper Head Dike
Smallden Clough Head
Wike Edge
Wike
Windleden Edge
Salter's Brook
Round Hill
Broad Clough
Brown's Clough
Uppermost Clough
Gallows Moss
Woodland Clough
Longside Moss
A628
Netherhead Clough
Salter's Brook Moss
Fiddlers Green
RAMSDEN ROAD
WHITEGATE
CARTWORTH MOOR RD.
LINSHAWS ROAD
ROUND CLOSE ROAD
BARE BONES ROAD
DUNFORD ROAD
GREEN ABBEY ROAD
SNITTLE ROAD
FLIGHT HILL
WINDLE EDGE
Copthu Moor
169
LANE
12
13
14
415
405
04
03
02
01
1
2
3
4
5
6
7
8
9

INDEX

Including Streets, Places & Areas, Industrial Estates,
Selected Flats & Walkways, Service Areas, Stations and Selected Places of Interest.

HOW TO USE THIS INDEX

1. Each street name is followed by its Postcode District, then by its Locality abbreviation(s) and then by its map reference;
   e.g. **Aachen Way** HX1: Hal . . . .7M **97** is in the HX1 Postcode District and the Halifax Locality and is to be found in square 7M on page **97**.
   The page number is shown in bold type.

2. A strict alphabetical order is followed in which Av., Rd., St., etc. (though abbreviated) are read in full and as part of the street name; e.g. **Aireview Cres.** appears after **Aire Vw. Av.** but before **Aire Vw. Dr.**

3. Streets and a selection of flats and walkways that cannot be shown on the mapping, appear in the index with the thoroughfare to which they are connected shown in brackets;
   e.g. **Abbey Ct.** BD8: B'frd . . . . 6A **64** (off Stallabrass St.)

4. Addresses that are in more than one part are referred to as not continuous.

5. Places and areas are shown in the index in BLUE TYPE and the map reference is to the actual map square in which the town centre or area is located and not to the place name shown on the map.
   e.g. **ACKTON** 3A **128**

6. An example of a selected place of interest is Abbey House Mus. 1K 67

7. An example of a station is Baildon Station (Rail) . . . . 4C 46, also included is Park & Ride.
   e.g. King Lane (Park & Ride) 4D 50

8. Service Areas are shown in the index in **BOLD CAPITAL TYPE**; e.g. **BARNSDALE BAR SERVICES** 8G 148

9. Map references for entries that appear on large scale pages **4-9** are shown first, with small scale map references shown in brackets; e.g. **Accent Bus. Cen.** BD1: B'frd 3E **6** (7E **64**)

GENERAL ABBREVIATIONS

All. : Alley	**Cotts.** : Cottages	**Junc.** : Junction	**Ri.** : Rise
App. : Approach	**Ct.** : Court	**La.** : Lane	**Rd.** : Road
Arc. : Arcade	**Cres.** : Crescent	**Lit.** : Little	**Shop.** : Shopping
Av. : Avenue	**Cft.** : Croft	**Lwr.** : Lower	**Sth.** : South
Bk. : Back	**Dr.** : Drive	**Mnr.** : Manor	**Sq.** : Square
Blvd. : Boulevard	**E.** : East	**Mans.** : Mansions	**Sta.** : Station
Bri. : Bridge	**Ent.** : Enterprise	**Mkt.** : Market	**St.** : Street
B'way. : Broadway	**Est.** : Estate	**Mdw.** : Meadow	**Ter.** : Terrace
Bldg. : Building	**Fld.** : Field	**Mdws.** : Meadows	**Twr.** : Tower
Bldgs. : Buildings	**Flds.** : Fields	**M.** : Mews	**Trad.** : Trading
Bungs. : Bungalows	**Gdn.** : Garden	**Mt.** : Mount	**Up.** : Upper
Bus. : Business	**Gdns.** : Gardens	**Mus.** : Museum	**Va.** : Vale
C'way. : Causeway	**Gth.** : Garth	**Nth.** : North	**Vw.** : View
Cen. : Centre	**Ga.** : Gate	**No.** : Number	**Vs.** : Villas
Chu. : Church	**Gt.** : Great	**Pal.** : Palace	**Vis.** : Visitors
Circ. : Circle	**Grn.** : Green	**Pde.** : Parade	**Wlk.** : Walk
Cir. : Circus	**Gro.** : Grove	**Pk.** : Park	**W.** : West
Cl. : Close	**Hgts.** : Heights	**Pas.** : Passage	**Yd.** : Yard
Coll. : College	**Ho.** : House	**Pl.** : Place	
Comn. : Common	**Ho's.** : Houses	**Pct.** : Precinct	
Cnr. : Corner	**Ind.** : Industrial	**Prom.** : Promenade	
Cott. : Cottage	**Info.** : Information	**Res.** : Residential	

LOCALITY ABBREVIATIONS

Aber : **Aberford**	Coll : **Collingham**	Hawk : **Hawksworth**	M'fld : **Micklefield**
A'ton : **Ackton**	Comp : **Compton**	Haw : **Haworth**	M'twn : **Middlestown**
Ackw : **Ackworth**	Cot : **Cottingley**	Haz : **Hazlewood**	Midd : **Middleton**
Add : **Addingham**	Crag V : **Cragg Vale**	Hea : **Heath**	Midg : **Midgley**
Ad St : **Adwick le Street**	Cri S : **Cridling Stubbs**	Heb B : **Hebden Bridge**	Mill B : **Mill Bank**
All : **Allerton**	Crig : **Crigglestone**	Heck : **Heckmondwike**	M Grn : **Millhouse Green**
All B : **Allerton Bywater**	Croft : **Crofton**	Hems : **Hemsworth**	Mir : **Mirfield**
Alt : **Altofts**	Cros R : **Cross Roads**	Hept : **Heptonstall**	Mix : **Mixenden**
Arm B : **Armitage Bridge**	Cro E : **Crow Edge**	H'wth : **Hepworth**	Mon B : **Monk Bretton**
Arth : **Arthington**	Cud : **Cudworth**	H Flat : **High Flatts**	Moor : **Moorhouse**
Askw : **Askwith**	Cull : **Cullingworth**	H Hoy : **High Hoyland**	Morl : **Morley**
Ath : **Athersley**	Cumb : **Cumberworth**	Hip : **Hipperholme**	Mt T : **Mount Tabor**
Bac : **Bacup**	D'ton : **Darrington**	Hol : **Hollingthorpe**	Myth : **Mytholmroyd**
Bads : **Badsworth**	Dart : **Darton**	Holm : **Holmbridge**	Nes : **Nesfield**
Bail : **Baildon**	Del : **Delph**	H'lm : **Holme**	Nether : **Netherthong**
B Bri : **Bailiff Bridge**	Den D : **Denby Dale**	H'frth : **Holmfirth**	Neth : **Netherton**
Bard : **Bardsey**	Denh : **Denholme**	Holy : **Holywell Green**	N Cro : **New Crofton**
Bark : **Barkisland**	Dens : **Denshaw**	Hon : **Honley**	N Far : **New Farnley**
B Grn : **Barugh Green**	Den : **Denton**	Horb : **Horbury**	New M : **New Mill**
Bar E : **Barwick in Elmet**	Dew : **Dewsbury**	Hors : **Horsforth**	New : **Newmillerdam**
Bat : **Batley**	Drau : **Draughton**	Hoy : **Hoylandswaine**	N Sha : **New Sharlston**
Beal : **Beal**	Drig : **Drighlington**	Huby : **Huby**	N Kym : **Newton Kyme**
Beam : **Beamsley**	Dun B : **Dunford Bridge**	Hud : **Huddersfield**	Norl : **Norland**
Bick : **Bickerton**	Dur : **Durkar**	Hun : **Hunsworth**	Norm : **Normanton**
B Ain : **Bilton in Ainsty**	E Ard : **East Ardsley**	I'ly : **Ilkley**	North : **Northowram**
Bgly : **Bingley**	E Bier : **East Bierley**	Illing : **Illingworth**	N Rig : **North Rigton**
Bird E : **Birds Edge**	E Car : **East Carlton**	Ing : **Ingbirchworth**	Nort : **Norton**
B'haw : **Birkenshaw**	E Hard : **East Hardwick**	Jack B : **Jackson Bridge**	Nor G : **Norwood Green**
Birk : **Birkin**	E Kes : **East Keswick**	Kear : **Kearby**	Not : **Notton**
Birs : **Birstall**	E Mor : **East Morton**	Keigh : **Keighley**	O'haw : **Oakenshaw**
Blac H : **Blackshaw Head**	East : **Eastburn**	Kell : **Kellingley**	Oak : **Oakworth**
Bolt A : **Bolton Abbey**	E'by : **Eastby**	Kex : **Kexborough**	Ogd : **Ogden**
B Spa : **Boston Spa**	Ecc : **Eccup**	Kild : **Kildwick**	Old : **Oldfield**
B'frd : **Bradford**	Ell : **Elland**	Kins : **Kinsley**	Old S : **Old Snydale**
Brad : **Bradshaw**	Emb : **Embsay**	Kip : **Kippax**	Oss : **Ossett**
B'ham : **Bramham**	Eml : **Emley**	Kbtn : **Kirkburton**	Otley : **Otley**
B'hpe : **Bramhope**	Esh : **Esholt**	Kirkby : **Kirkby Overblow**	Oul : **Oulton**
B'clif : **Briercliffe**	Fair : **Fairburn**	K Dei : **Kirk Deighton**	Outl : **Outlane**
B'ley : **Brierley**	F'ley : **Farnley**	Kirk : **Kirkhamgate**	Out : **Outwood**
Bries : **Briestfield**	Farn T : **Farnley Tyas**	K'htn : **Kirkheaton**	Over : **Overton**
Brigh : **Brighouse**	Fars : **Farsley**	K S'ton : **Kirk Smeaton**	Ows : **Owston**
Brock : **Brockholes**	F'stne : **Featherstone**	K'thpe : **Kirkthorpe**	Oxen : **Oxenhope**
B'ton : **Brotherton**	Fen B : **Fenay Bridge**	Knot : **Knottingley**	Pan : **Pannal**
Burg : **Burghwallis**	Ferr : **Ferrybridge**	L Bri : **Laneshaw Bridge**	P Wel : **Pecket Well**
Burl W : **Burley in Wharfedale**	Fitz : **Fitzwilliam**	Lay : **Laycock**	Pen : **Penistone**
Bur S : **Burton Salmon**	Fix : **Fixby**	Leat : **Leathley**	Pon : **Pontefract**
Byram : **Byram cum Sutton**	Flock : **Flockton**	Led : **Ledsham**	Pool : **Pool**
Cal G : **Calder Grove**	Foul : **Foulby**	Leds : **Ledston**	Pott : **Potterton**
Cal : **Calverley**	Fric : **Frickley**	Leeds : **Leeds**	Pud : **Pudsey**
Cam : **Campsall**	Gar : **Garforth**	Lept : **Lepton**	Que : **Queensbury**
Carc : **Carcroft**	Gil : **Gildersome**	Lind : **Lindley**	Ras : **Rastrick**
Carl : **Carlton**	Golc : **Golcar**	Linth : **Linthwaite**	Raven : **Ravensthorpe**
Carr G : **Carr Gate**	Gom : **Gomersal**	Lin : **Linton**	Raw : **Rawdon**
C'frd : **Castleford**	G Moor : **Grange Moor**	Lit : **Littleborough**	Rid : **Riddlesden**
Cast : **Castley**	Gt P : **Great Preston**	Lit S : **Little Smeaton**	Ripp : **Ripponden**
Caw : **Cawthorne**	Green : **Greenfield**	Liv : **Liversedge**	Rish : **Rishworth**
Chap : **Chapelthorpe**	Gree : **Greetland**	Loft : **Lofthouse**	Rob H : **Robin Hood**
Chis : **Chiserley**	Grim : **Grimethorpe**	L Bra : **Low Bradley**	Rothw : **Rothwell**
Chur : **Churwell**	Guis : **Guiseley**	Lwr C : **Lower Cumberworth**	Roys : **Royston**
Clay : **Clayton**	Had E : **Hade Edge**	Low M : **Low Moor**	Ryh : **Ryhill**
Clay W : **Clayton West**	Hai : **Haigh**	Lud : **Luddenden**	Saxt : **Saxton**
Cleck : **Cleckheaton**	Hal : **Halifax**	Lud F : **Luddenden Foot**	Scam : **Scammonden**
Cliff : **Clifford**	Hal E : **Halton East**	Map : **Mapplewell**	S'cft : **Scarcroft**
Clift : **Clifton**	Hamp : **Hampole**	Mars : **Marsden**	Scho : **Scholes**
Cliv : **Cliviger**	Har : **Harden**	Mel : **Meltham**	Shad : **Shadwell**
Cold : **Colden**	Hare : **Harewood**	Men : **Menston**	Shaf : **Shafton**
Col H : **Cold Heindley**	H'cft : **Havercroft**	Meth : **Methley**	S Comn : **Sharlston Common**

1st Bowl—Airedale Quay

She : Shelf
Shel : Shelley
Shep : Shepley
Ship : Shipley
Sick : Sicklinghall
Silk : Silkstone
Sils : Silsden
S'brk : Skelbrooke
Skel : Skellow
Skelm : Skelmanthorpe
Slait : Slaithwaite
Smit : Smithies
S Cros : South Crosland
S Elm : South Elmsall
South : Southfield
S Hien : South Hiendley
S Kirk : South Kirkby
S Mil : South Milford
Sou : Southowram
Sow B : Sowerby Bridge
Sow : Sowood
Spof : Spofforth
Stainb : Stainburn
S'ross : Staincross
Stainl : Stainland
S'bury : Stanbury
S'ley : Stanley
Stan : Stanningley
Stap : Stapleton
Stee : Steeton
Stock : Stocksmoor
Stor : Storiths
Street : Streethouse
Stut : Stutton
Sut : Sutton
Swil : Swillington
Swil C : Swillington Common
Tad : Tadcaster
T'bdge : Thongsbridge
T'ner : Thorner
T'hill : Thornhill
Thorn : Thornton
T Arch : Thorpe Arch
Thpe A : Thorpe Audlin
Thpe H : Thorpe on the Hill
Thurs : Thurstonland
Ting : Tingley
Tod : Todmorden
Traw : Trawden
Tri : Triangle
Up C : Upper Cumberworth
Up D : Upper Denby
Up H : Upper Hopton
U'thng : Upperthong
Upt : Upton
Wads : Wadsworth
Wain : Wainstalls
Wake : Wakefield
Wal S : Walden Stubbs
W'den : Walsden
W'ton : Walton
Ward : Wardle
Warm : Warmfield
Wee : Weeton
Went : Wentbridge
W Ard : West Ardsley
W Bret : West Bretton
W Har : West Hardwick
W Mor : West Morton
Weston : Weston
Weth : Wetherby
W'ley : Whitley
Whit : Whitworth
Wid : Widdop
Wig : Wighill
Wike : Wike
Wils : Wilsden
Wint : Wintersett
Wome : Womersley
Wood : Woodlands
W'frd : Woodlesford
Wool : Woolley
W Gran : Woolley Grange
W'orne : Worsthorne
Wrag : Wragby
Wren : Wrenthorpe
Wyke : Wyke
Yead : Yeadon

1st Bowl
Leeds 4F 4 (5E 68)
5 Rise Shop. Cen. BD16: Bgly 4E 44
1853 Art Gallery, The 6M 45

A

A1 Bus. Pk. WF11: Knot 9B 110
Aachen Way HX1: Hal 7M 97
Aaron Wilkinson Ct. WF9: S Kirk 7G 162
Abaseen Cl. BD3: B'frd 7F 64
Abbe's Close, The DN6: Burg 4N 165
Abbe's Walk, The
DN6: Burg, Ows 4N 165
Abbey Av. LS5: Leeds 3J 67
Abbey Cl. HD9: Had E 9N 169
LS29: Add 1N 13
WF3: E Ard 3F 104
WF14: Mir 5J 121
Abbey Ct. BD8: B'frd 6A 64
(off Stallabrass St.)
HD9: Had E 9N 169
LS18: Hors 9E 48
Abbeydale Dr. BD8: B'frd 6J 63
Abbeydale Gdns. LS5: Leeds 9H 49
Abbeydale Gth. LS5: Leeds 9H 49
Abbeydale Gro. LS5: Leeds 9H 49
Abbeydale Mt. LS5: Leeds 9H 49
Abbeydale Oval LS5: Leeds 9H 49
Abbeydale Va. LS5: Leeds 9H 49
Abbeydale Way LS5: Leeds 9H 49
Abbey Dr. HD8: Shep 8K 155
Abbey Farm Dr. HD8: Shep 9K 155
Abbeyfield Gro. Ho. LS29: I'ly 6G 14
(off Riddings Rd.)
Abbey Gdns. WF8: Pon 9K 109
Abbey Gth. LS19: Yead 1M 47
(off Well Hill)
Abbey Gorse LS5: Leeds 1K 67
Abbey House Mus. 1K 67
Abbey La. HX2: Hal 5F 96
Abbey Lea BD15: All 6H 63
Abbey Light Railway 2K 67
Abbey M. WF8: Pon 9K 109
Abbey Mt. LS5: Leeds 3J 67
Abbey Retail Pk. LS5: Leeds 2K 67
Abbey Rd. HD2: Hud 1N 137
HD8: Shep 8K 155
LS5: Leeds 9G 48
WF17: Bat 8C 102
Abbey Rd. Nth. HD8: Shep 8K 155
Abbey Rd. Sth. HD8: Shep 9J 155
Abbey St. LS3: Leeds 6B 68
Abbey Ter. LS5: Leeds 3J 67
Abbey Vw. LS5: Leeds 1K 67
Abbey Wlk. HX3: Hal 8B 98
LS5: Leeds 1J 67
WF8: Pon 9K 109
Abbey Wlk. Sth. HX3: Hal 8C 98
Abbot La. WF4: Wool 3K 159
Abbotside Cl. BD10: B'frd 9G 46
Abbots M. LS4: Leeds 4N 67
Abbots Pl. HD2: Hud 6D 120
Abbot St. HD1: Hud 3K 137
Abbotsway LS25: Gar 8L 71
Abbots Wood BD9: B'frd 3M 63
(off Firth Rd.)
Abbott Ct. LS12: Leeds 6N 67
Abbott Rd. LS12: Leeds 7N 67
Abbotts Cl. LS25: Aber 7E 54
Abbott's Ladies Home HX3: Hal 9B 98
Abbott's Ter. HX1: Hal 5N 97
(off Leafland St.)
Abbott Ter. WF1: Wake 8M 125
Abbott Vw. LS12: Leeds 6N 67
Abb Scott La. BD6: B'frd 7N 81
BD12: Low M 7N 81
Abb St. HD1: Hud 3J 137
Abelia Mt. BD7: B'frd 8K 63
Abel St. BD12: Wyke 9A 82
Aberdeen BD22: Oxen 5B 60
Aberdeen Dr. LS12: Leeds 7K 67
Aberdeen Gro. LS12: Leeds 7K 67
Aberdeen Pl. BD7: B'frd 9M 63
Aberdeen Rd. LS12: Leeds 7K 67
Aberdeen Ter. BD7: B'frd 8M 63
BD14: Clay 1J 81
Aberdeen Wlk. LS12: Leeds 7K 67
Aberfield Bank LS10: Leeds 7G 86
Aberfield Cl. LS10: Leeds 6G 86
Aberfield Crest LS10: Leeds 7G 86
Aberfield Dr. LS10: Leeds 7G 86
WF4: Crig 6G 142
Aberfield Gdns. LS10: Leeds 6G 86
Aberfield Ga. LS10: Leeds 6G 86
Aberfield Mt. LS10: Leeds 7G 86
Aberfield Ri. LS10: Leeds 7G 86
Aberfield Rd. LS10: Leeds 6G 86
Aberfield Wlk. LS10: Leeds 7F 86
ABERFORD 8E 54
Aberford Rd. BD8: B'frd 5N 63
LS15: Bar E 8M 53
LS23: B'ham 7D 38
LS25: Aber, Gar 6N 71
LS26: Oul, W'frd 8D 88
WF1: Wake 1M 9 (3N 125)
WF3: S'ley 3N 125
Abingdon St. BD8: B'frd 5N 63
HD2: Hud 1M 137
Abinger Cl. BD10: B'frd 9G 47
Abraham Hill LS26: Rothw 8A 88
Abram St. BD5: B'frd 8B 6 (1C 82)
Acacia Av. WF9: S Elm 5N 163
Acacia Cl. WF10: C'frd 6K 109
Acacia Dr. BD15: All 2E 62
HX3: Hip 5M 99
WF10: C'frd 6J 109
Acacia Grn. WF8: Pon 2M 129
Acacia Gro. HX7: Myth 3N 95
S72: Shaf 7K 161
Acacia Ho. WF10: C'frd 5E 108
(off Parklands)
Acacia Pk. Cres. BD10: B'frd 5K 47
Acacia Pk. Dr. BD10: B'frd 5K 47
Acacia Pk. Ter. BD10: B'frd 5L 47
Acacia Rd. DN6: Skel 7M 165
Acacia Wlk. WF11: Knot 9C 110
Acaster Dr. BD12: Low M 7A 82
LS25: Gar 8A 72
Accent Bus. Cen. BD1: B'frd 3E 6 (7E 64)
Accommodation Rd. LS9: Leeds 4L 5 (5G 69)
Acer Way BD19: Scho 4D 100
Ackroyd Ct. BD13: Thorn 8C 62
Ackroyd Pl. BD13: Que 4C 80
Ackroyd Sq. BD13: Que 4G 80
(off Highgate Rd.)
Ackroyd St. LS27: Morl 9L 85
OL14: Tod 3D 92
ACKTON 3A 128
Ackton Cl. WF7: A'ton 2A 128
Ackton Hall Cres. WF7: A'ton 3A 128
Ackton La. WF7: A'ton, F'stne 3A 128
Ackton Pasture La. WF10: C'frd 8A 108
Ackton Wood Vs. WF7: A'ton 9B 108
Ackworth Av. LS19: Yead 1N 47
Ackworth Bridle Rd. WF8: E Hard 3L 147
Ackworth Cres. LS19: Yead 1N 47
Ackworth Dr. LS19: Yead 1N 47
Ackworth Ho. Cl. WF7: Ackw 2G 146
Ackworth Lodge WF7: Ackw 2G 147
ACKWORTH MOOR TOP 5E 146
Ackworth Rd. WF7: F'stne 7D 128
WF8: Pon 7H 129
Ackworth St. BD5: B'frd 1C 82
Acme Ter. WF1: Wake 8M 125
Acomb Ter. BD12: Wyke 1A 100
Acorn Bus. Pk. LS14: Leeds 5N 69
Acorn Cl. BD6: B'frd 7K 81
Acorn Dr. LS14: Leeds 7D 52
Acorn Gro. HD9: Scho 5B 170
Acorn Pk. BD17: Bail 5C 46
Acorn Pk. Ind. Est. BD17: Bail 5C 46
Acorn St. BD3: B'frd 5F 6 (8E 64)
BD21: Keigh 2H 43
HX1: Hal 5N 97
Acorn Way LS21: Pool 2G 33
Acre, The BD12: Wyke 8N 81
Acre Av. BD2: B'frd 1F 64
Acre Cir. LS10: Leeds 9E 86
Acre Cl. BD2: B'frd 1F 64
LS10: Leeds 1D 104
Acre Ct. BD6: B'frd 4A 82
LS10: Leeds 9E 86
Acre Cres. BD2: B'frd 1F 64
LS10: Leeds 9E 86
Acre Dr. BD2: B'frd 1F 64
Acre Fold LS29: Add 1L 13
Acre Gro. BD2: B'frd 1F 64
LS10: Leeds 9E 86
Acre Ho. Av. HD3: Hud 2H 137
Acrehowe Ri. BD17: Bail 3C 46
Acre La. BD2: B'frd 2F 64
(not continuous)
BD6: B'frd 4A 82
BD16: Bgly 8D 28
BD22: Haw 8C 42
HD9: Holm 6J 169
HD9: Mel 8E 152
HD9: New M 2F 170
(Ebson Ho. La.)
HD9: New M 1E 170
(White Ley Bank)
HX2: Midg 1C 96
HX7: Hept 7D 76
S36: Hoy 9G 172
Acre Mt. LS10: Leeds 9E 86
Acre Pl. BD6: B'frd 4A 82
(off Acre La.)
LS10: Leeds 9E 86
Acre Ri. BD17: Bail 3A 46
Acre Rd. LS10: Leeds 9D 86
Acres, The LS17: Leeds 2B 50
(off The Avenue)
LS29: Add 9N 11
Acres Hall Av. LS28: Pud 8D 66
Acres Hall Cres. LS28: Pud 8D 66
Acres Hall Dr. LS28: Pud 8D 66
Acres La. HD9: Holm 4D 168
HX7: Hept 9G 76
Acre Sq. LS10: Leeds 9E 86
Acres Rd. WF3: Loft 4L 105
Acres St. BD21: Keigh 1H 43
Acre St. HD3: Hud 2G 137
LS10: Leeds 9F 86
OL12: Whit 9A 112
Acre Ter. LS10: Leeds 9F 86
Acre Vs. HX7: Myth 3M 95
Acrewood Cl. LS17: Leeds 4J 51
Acton Flat La. HD3: Hud 8F 118
Acton Hall Ent. Pk. WF7: F'stne 5C 128
Acton Ho. BD1: B'frd 4D 6
Acton St. BD3: B'frd 7G 65
Acute Ter. WF2: Wake 5G 125
Ada Glassby Ct. LS15: Leeds 5E 70
Adam Ct. HD3: Hud 1G 136
Adam Cft. BD13: Cull 9K 43
Adams Ct. HD6: Brigh 7K 99
Adams Cft. LS21: Otley 1K 31
Adams Gro. LS15: Leeds 2F 70
Adam Slack BD23: Stor 1N 11
Adam St. BD6: B'frd 4N 81
OL14: Tod 6K 93
Adam's Wlk. LS6: Leeds 1A 4 (4B 68)
Ada's Pl. LS28: Stan 4B 66
Ada St. BD13: Que 4C 80
BD17: Bail 5C 46
BD18: Ship 7L 45
BD21: Keigh 9G 27
HX3: Hal 1L 7 (3B 98)
Addenbrook Cl. BD10: B'frd 9G 47
Addersgate La. HX3: North 9D 80
ADDINGFORD 2D 142
Addingford Cl. WF4: Horb 2C 142
Addingford Dr. WF4: Horb 2C 142
Addingford La. WF4: Horb 2B 142
ADDINGHAM 1M 13
Addingham Gdns. LS12: Leeds 7K 67
ADDINGHAM MOORSIDE 5M 13
Addingham Wharfedale Rd.
LS29: Add 7J 11
Addison Av. BD3: B'frd 5H 65
WF6: Norm 2K 127
Addison Ct. LS15: Leeds 8E 70
WF4: Horb 9E 124
Addison Dr. BD22: Haw 9C 42
Addi St. BD4: B'frd 2G 82
Addle Cft. La. HD8: Lept 5J 139
Addlethorpe La. LS22: Sick 3A 22
Addy Cres. WF9: S Elm 6M 163
ADEL 4N 49
Adelaide Ho. BD16: Bgly 5G 44
Adelaide Ri. BD17: Bail 6A 46
Adelaide St. BD5: B'frd 7B 6 (9C 64)
HX1: Hal 5M 97
HX7: Heb B 1G 94
OL14: Tod 6K 93
Adelaide Ter. HX4: Stainl 8M 117
ADEL EAST MOOR 4A 50
Adel Gth. LS16: Leeds 2N 49
Adel Grange Cl. LS16: Leeds 5M 49
Adel Grange Cft. LS16: Leeds 5M 49
Adel Grange M. LS16: Leeds 5M 49
(not continuous)
Adel Grn. LS16: Leeds 3N 49
Adeline Ter. HD9: Holm 5H 169
Adel La. LS16: Leeds 3M 49
Adel Mead LS16: Leeds 3N 49
ADEL MILL 1N 49
Adel Mill LS16: Leeds 1M 49
Adel Pk. Cl. LS16: Leeds 4M 49
Adel Pk. Ct. LS16: Leeds 4M 49
Adel Pk. Cft. LS16: Leeds 4M 49
Adel Pk. Dr. LS16: Leeds 4M 49
Adel Pk. Gdns. LS16: Leeds 4M 49
Adel Pasture LS16: Leeds 4M 49
Adelphi Rd. HD3: Hud 3H 137
Adel Towers Cl. LS16: Leeds 4N 49
Adel Towers Ct. LS16: Leeds 4N 49
Adel Vale LS16: Leeds 3N 49
Adel Wood Cl. LS16: Leeds 4N 49
Adel Wood Dr. LS16: Leeds 4N 49
Adel Wood Gdns. LS16: Leeds 4N 49
Adel Wood Gro. LS16: Leeds 4N 49
Adel Wood Pl. LS16: Leeds 4N 49
Adel Wood Rd. LS16: Leeds 4N 49
Adgil Cres. HX3: Sou 8F 98
Adgil Gro. HX3: Sou 8G 98
Admiral St. LS11: Leeds 1E 86
Admirals Yd. LS10: Leeds 1H 87
Admiral Way BD21: Keigh 8J 27
Adowsley Cl. WF7: Ackw 4E 146
ADWALTON 7D 84
Adwalton Bus. Pk.
BD11: Drig 8D 84
Adwalton Cl. BD11: Drig 8A 84
Adwalton Grn. BD11: Drig 8A 84
Adwalton Gro. BD13: Que 4E 80
Adwalton Moor Bus. Pk.
BD11: B'haw 6M 83
Adwick Gro. WF2: Wake 5K 143
Adwick Pl. LS4: Leeds 4M 67
Adwick Ter. WF8: Pon 1L 129
(off Sandrock Rd.)
Aerial Vw. LS25: M'fld 9F 72
Agar St. BD8: B'frd 6L 63
Agar Ter. BD8: B'frd 6L 63
AGBRIGG 9N 125
Agbrigg Gro. WF2: Wake 9N 125
Agbrigg Rd. WF1: Wake 9N 125
WF2: Wake 9N 125
Agincourt Dr. BD16: Bgly 4G 44
WF6: Alt 8F 106
Agnes Rd. S75: Dart 9G 158
Agnes St. BD20: Keigh 7J 27
Agricultural Ho's. WF8: Lit S 4K 149
Ahlux Ct. LS2: Leeds 4J 5 (5F 68)
Ahlux Ho. LS2: Leeds 4J 5 (5F 68)
Ailsa Dell WF17: Bat 5G 103
Ailsa Ho. BD10: B'frd 8G 47
(off Fairhaven Grn.)
Ails La. HX2: Lud 3D 96
Aimbry Cl. HD5: Hud 8D 138
Ainley Bottom HX5: Ell 6E 118
Ainley Cl. HD3: Hud 9F 118
Ainley Ind. Est. HX5: Ell 6F 118
Ainley Pk. HD7: Golc 6D 136
Ainley Pl. HD7: Slait 8J 135
Ainley Rd. HD3: Hud 8F 118
AINLEYS 7F 118
Ainley St. HX5: Ell 5E 118
Ainsbury Av. BD10: B'frd 5F 46
Ainsdale Cl. S71: Roys 4C 160
Ainsdale Gro. BD13: Cull 9L 43
Ainsdale Rd. S71: Roys 4C 160
Ainsley HD7: Mars 5D 150
Ainsley Ct. LS14: Leeds 1F 70
Ainsley La. HD7: Mars 5D 150
Ainsley M. LS14: Leeds 1F 70
Ainsley Vw. LS14: Leeds 1F 70
Ainsty Cres. LS22: Weth 2M 23
Ainsty Dr. LS22: Weth 2M 23
Ainsty Gth. LS22: Weth 2M 23
Ainsty Rd. LS22: Weth 2L 23
Ainsty Vw. LS22: Weth 2M 23
Aintree Cl. LS25: Kip 3N 89
Aintree Ct. LS10: Leeds 1G 87
Airdale Ter. LS13: Leeds 1C 66
(off Airedale Cft.)
Aire & Calder Cotts. WF1: Wake 1C 126
Aire & Calder Ind. Pk. WF10: C'frd 3D 108
Airebank BD16: Bgly 4E 44
Aireborough Leisure Cen. 8J 31
Aireburn Av. BD20: Stee 3D 26
Aire Cl. BD17: Bail 6N 45
Aire Ct. BD20: Sils 9E 12
(off Calder Way)
LS10: Leeds 9E 86
AIREDALE 5H 109
Airedale Av. BD16: Cot 8F 44
Airedale Cliff LS13: Leeds 1F 66
Airedale Coll. Mt. BD3: B'frd 5E 64
(off Airedale Coll. Rd.)
Airedale Coll. Rd. BD3: B'frd 5E 64
Airedale Coll. Ter. BD3: B'frd 1E 6 (5E 64)
Airedale Community Bus. Cen.
WF10: C'frd 5H 109
Airedale Ct. LS14: Leeds 1A 70
Airedale Cres. BD3: B'frd 5E 64
Airedale Cft. LS13: Leeds 1C 66
Airedale Dr. HX3: She 8G 80
LS18: Hors 7C 48
LS25: Gar 8B 72
WF10: C'frd 2J 109
Airedale Gdns. LS13: Leeds 2C 66
Airedale Gro. LS18: Hors 7C 48
LS26: W'frd 7E 88
Airedale Hgts. WF2: Wake 7E 124
Airedale Ho. LS13: Leeds 2E 66
WF17: Bat 1F 122
(off Dale Cl.)
Airedale M. BD20: Sils 8E 12
Airedale Mills BD16: Bgly 1D 44
Airedale Mt. BD20: Rid 8B 28
LS13: Leeds 1B 66
Airedale Pl. BD17: Bail 5C 46
Airedale Quay LS13: Leeds 2D 66

Airedale Rd.—Almondbury Bank

Airedale Rd. BD3: B'frd 5D 64
BD21: Keigh 8M 27
LS26: W'frd 7E 88
S75: Kex 9E 158
WF10: C'frd 5H 109
Airedale Shop. Cen. BD21: Keigh 9J 27
Airedale St. BD2: B'frd 3F 64
BD16: Bgly 4E 44
BD21: Keigh 8L 27
Airedale Ter. BD17: Bail 5B 46
LS26: W'frd 7E 88
LS27: Morl 9L 85
(off Gillroyd Pde.)
Airedale Vw. *LS13: Leeds 1C 66*
(off Town St.)
LS19: Raw 4A 48
LS26: W'frd 7E 88
Airedale Wharf LS13: Leeds 1C 66
Aire Gro. LS19: Yead 1N 47
Aire Mt. LS22: Weth 2L 23
Aire Pl. LS3: Leeds 5A 68
Aire Quay LS10: Leeds 9H 69
Aire Rd. LS22: Weth 1L 23
Aireside Rd. BD17: Ship 6B 46
Aire St. BD10: B'frd 6E 46
BD16: Bgly 1D 44
BD21: Keigh 8K 27
BD22: Haw 8D 42
HD6: Ras 2N 119
LS1: Leeds 7D 4 (7D 68)
WF10: C'frd 4D 108
WF11: Knot 7F 110
(Chapel St.)
WF11: Knot 7F 110
(The Island)
WF13: Raven 6C 122
Aire Ter. WF10: C'frd 4D 108
Aire Valley Bus. Cen.
BD21: Keigh 8J 27
Aire Valley Ct. BD16: Bgly 5E 44
Aire Valley Marina LS4: Leeds 5L 67
Aire Valley Mt. WF10: C'frd 5G 108
Aire Valley Pk. BD16: Bgly 6G 44
Aire Valley Rd. BD16: Bgly 1C 44
BD21: Keigh 8L 27
LS9: Leeds 9H 69
Aire Vw. BD20: Rid 6M 27
BD20: Sils 8D 12
LS19: Yead 1N 47
WF11: B'ton 5B 110
WF11: Knot 7C 110
Aire Vw. Av. BD16: Cot 7G 44
Aireview Cres. BD17: Bail 6M 45
Aire Vw. Dr. BD20: Rid 9B 28
Aire Vw. Gdns. LS5: Leeds 9J 49
Aire Vw. Nth. BD18: Ship 7M 45
Aire Vw. Ter. LS13: Leeds 2D 66
Aireview Ter. BD21: Keigh 1L 43
Aireville Av. BD9: B'frd 1M 63
BD18: Ship 1N 63
Aireville Cl. BD18: Ship 1N 63
BD20: Keigh 6G 26
Aireville Cres. BD9: B'frd 2N 63
BD20: Sils 8F 12
Aireville Dr. BD18: Ship 1N 63
BD20: Sils 8F 12
Aireville Grange BD18: Ship 1N 63
Aireville Gro. BD18: Ship 1N 63
Aireville Mt. BD20: Rid 8B 28
BD20: Sils 8F 12
Aireville Ri. BD9: B'frd 1N 63
Aireville Rd. BD9: B'frd 1N 63
Aireville St. BD20: Keigh 6G 27
Aireville Ter. LS29: Burl W 8C 16
Aire Wlk. WF11: Knot 7F 110
Aire Way BD17: Bail 6M 45
AIREWORTH 8L 27
Aireworth Cl. BD21: Keigh 7L 27
Aireworth Gro. BD21: Keigh 8L 27
Aireworth Rd. BD21: Keigh 7L 27
Aireworth St. BD21: Keigh 1H 43
Airey St. BD21: Keigh 9G 27
Airlie Av. LS8: Leeds 2H 69
Airlie Pl. LS8: Leeds 2H 69
Airport West LS19: Yead 7B 32
Aislaby Hgts. HX2: Hal 3K 97
Akam Rd. BD1: B'frd 7B 64
Aked's Rd. HX1: Hal 5H 7 (6A 98)
Aked St. BD1: B'frd 4D 6 (7D 64)
Aketon Cft. WF10: C'frd 7B 108
Aketon Dr. WF10: C'frd 6C 108
Aketon Rd. WF10: C'frd 7B 108
Akroyd Cotts. HX7: P Wel 6J 77
Akroyd Ct. HX3: Hal 1K 7
Akroyd La. HX7: Wads 6J 77
AKROYDON 3B 98
Akroyd Pl. HX1: Hal 2K 7 (4B 98)
(not continuous)
Akroyd Ter. HX2: Hal 7M 97
Alabama St. HX1: Hal 5M 97
Alanby Dr. BD10: B'frd 8G 46
Alan Ct. BD13: Thorn 8C 62
Alan Cres. LS15: Leeds 7B 70
Alandale Cres. LS25: Gar 8L 71
Alandale Dr. LS25: Gar 8L 71
Alandale Gro. LS25: Gar 8L 71
Alandale Rd. HD2: Hud 5C 120
LS25: Gar 7L 71
Alan Rd. S75: Dart 9F 158
Alaska Pl. LS7: Leeds 9G 50
Albans Cl. LS17: Bard 3F 36
Alban St. BD4: B'frd 1F 82
Albany Ct. BD20: Keigh 8G 27
WF8: Pon 4K 129
Albany Cres. WF9: S Elm 7M 163
Albany Dr. HD5: Hud 4E 138
Albany Pl. WF9: S Elm 7M 163
Albany Rd. HD5: Hud, K'htn 4E 138
LS26: Rothw 7M 87
Albany St. BD5: B'frd 8B 6 (1C 82)
BD6: B'frd 4A 82
HD1: Hud 8A 8 (6L 137)
HX3: Hal 7C 98
LS12: Leeds 7K 67
WF9: S Elm 7M 163
Albany Ter. HX3: Hal 7C 98
LS12: Leeds 7K 67
Albany Vw. *HX4: Holy 7A 118*
(off Stainland Rd.)
Albany Wlk. LS29: I'ly 6G 14
Alberta Av. LS7: Leeds 9G 50
Albert Av. BD10: B'frd 7G 46
BD18: Ship 6K 45
HX2: Hal 4L 97
Albert Bldgs. BD10: B'frd 9F 46
HX6: Sow B 8J 97
(off Albert Rd.)
Albert Cl. WF17: Bat 1F 122
Albert Ct. HX2: Hal 4L 97
Albert Cres. BD11: B'haw 9M 83
BD13: Que 4D 80
Albert Dr. HX2: Hal 4K 97
LS27: Morl 8N 85
WF5: Oss 5D 124
Albert Edward St. BD13: Que 4D 80
Albert Gdns. HX2: Hal 4L 97
Albert Gro. LS6: Leeds 9N 49
Albert La. OL14: Tod 6K 93
Albert Mt. *LS18: Hors 7G 49*
(off Broadgate La.)
Albert Pl. BD3: B'frd 6J 65
LS18: Hors 6F 48
LS26: Meth 1J 107
Albert Prom. HX3: Hal 8N 97
Albert Rd. BD13: Que 3C 80
BD18: Ship 7L 45
HD8: Clay W 7H 157
HX2: Hal 4K 97
HX6: Sow B 7J 97
LS26: Oul 7D 88
LS27: Morl 8L 85
Albert Simmons Way LS29: Burl W 8C 16
Albert Sq. BD20: Sils 8E 12
LS19: Yead 9N 31
Albert St. BD6: B'frd 5N 81
BD10: B'frd 9F 46
BD12: Wyke 2A 100
BD13: Que 4E 80
BD13: Thorn 8C 62
BD15: Wils 2B 62
BD17: Bail 6A 46
BD19: Cleck 4H 101
BD21: Keigh 9H 27
BD22: Cros R 7F 42
(off Bingley Rd.)
HD1: Hud 8A 8 (7L 137)
HD6: Clift 1A 120
HX1: Hal 3H 7 (5A 98)
HX5: Ell 5E 118
HX7: Heb B 1H 95
HX7: Myth 3M 95
LS28: Pud 8A 66
OL14: Tod 6K 93
S72: Cud 8K 161
WF6: Norm 8K 107
WF7: F'stne 6D 128
(not continuous)
WF10: C'frd 4D 108
WF15: Liv 9N 101
Albert Ter. BD12: O'haw 8D 82
BD12: Wyke 2B 100
BD18: Ship 6L 45
LS19: Yead 9N 31
(off Rockfield Ter.)
Albert Vw. HX2: Hal 4L 97
Albert Wlk. BD18: Ship 7K 45
Albert Way BD11: B'haw 9M 83
Albert Yd. *BD21: Keigh 1J 43*
(off Church St.)
HD1: Hud 6B 8 (4M 137)
Albion Av. LS12: Leeds 7N 67
Albion Cl. LS23: Cliff 3D 38
S75: Map 8K 159
Albion Ct. BD1: B'frd 4B 6 (7C 64)
HD9: Mel 7B 152
HX1: Hal 3K 7
WF1: Wake 5J 9 (5L 125)
WF16: Heck 8A 102
Albion Cft. WF5: Oss 5A 124
Albion Fold BD15: Wils 1B 62
Albion M. HD9: Mel 7B 152
WF4: M'twn 3L 141
Albion Mills Bus. Cen.
HD9: T'bdge 9N 153
Albion Mills Retail Pk.
WF2: Wake 5G 9 (5K 125)
Albion Pk. LS12: Leeds 6A 68
Albion Pl. BD13: Thorn 8B 62
HD6: Brigh 9M 99
(off Waterloo Rd.)
LS1: Leeds 6F 4 (6E 68)
LS20: Guis 7J 31
WF9: S Elm 6N 163
Albion Rd. BD10: B'frd 7F 46
LS28: Stan 4B 66
S71: Carl 9D 160
WF12: T'hill 1H 141
Albion Sq. WF2: Wake 4G 124
Albion St. BD1: B'frd 4A 6 (7C 64)
BD6: B'frd 6K 81
BD13: Denh 6K 61
BD13: Que 4C 80
BD19: Cleck 5J 101
BD22: Cros R 7E 42
HD1: Hud 6B 8 (5M 137)
HD6: Brigh 9M 99
HX1: Hal 4L 7 (5B 98)
HX5: Ell 5F 118
LS1: Leeds 6F 4 (6E 68)
LS2: Leeds 6F 4 (6E 68)
LS21: Otley 1M 31
LS23: Cliff 3D 38
LS27: Morl 9K 85
(Corporation St.)
LS27: Morl 9K 85
(Windsor Ct.)
WF1: Wake 2J 9 (4L 125)
WF3: Carl 1M 105
WF9: Fitz 7A 146
WF10: C'frd 5C 108
Albion St. WF13: Dew 2F 122
WF13: Raven 6C 122
WF15: Liv 8L 101
WF16: Heck 8N 101
WF17: Bat 8G 102
(not continuous)
Albion Ter. *HX7: Heb B 1G 95*
(off Heptonstall Rd.)
LS23: Cliff 3D 38
Albion Way LS12: Leeds 6A 68
Albion Yd. BD1: B'frd 4B 6 (7C 64)
Alcester Gth. BD3: B'frd 6F 64
Alcester Pl. LS8: Leeds 2H 69
Alcester Rd. LS8: Leeds 2H 69
Alcester Ter. LS8: Leeds 2H 69
Aldams Rd. WF12: Dew 4F 122
Aldbeck Cft. S75: Dart 9G 158
Alden Av. LS27: Morl 2K 103
Alden Cl. LS27: Morl 2K 103
Alden Ct. LS27: Morl 2K 103
Alden Cres. WF8: Pon 4H 129
Alden Fold LS27: Morl 2K 103
Alder Av. BD21: Keigh 2L 43
HD9: T'bdge 9A 154
WF2: Wake 3J 125
Alder Carr BD17: Bail 4N 45
Alder Cl. S75: Map 8J 159
Alder Dr. LS28: Pud 6L 65
Alder Gth. LS28: Pud 6M 65
Alder Gro. HX2: Illing 7L 79
WF6: Norm 4J 127
Alder Hill Av. LS6: Leeds 8C 50
Alder Hill Cotts. LS6: Leeds 8B 50
Alder Hill Gro. LS7: Leeds 8C 50
Alderholt Dr. BD6: B'frd 7M 81
Aldermanbury BD1: B'frd 5A 6 (8C 64)
Alder M. WF17: Bat 7D 102
Alderney Rd. WF12: Dew 1J 123
Alders, The LS7: Leeds 8F 50
Alderscholes Cl. *BD13: Thorn 8C 62*
(off Alderscholes La.)
Alderscholes La. BD13: Thorn 9A 62
Aldersgate *LS12: Leeds 7M 67*
(off Wesley Rd.)
Alderson St. BD6: B'frd 6K 81
Alderstone Ri. HD3: Hud 9F 118
Alder St. HD1: Hud 1C 8 (2N 137)
HD2: Hud 2N 137
Aldersyde WF17: Birs 3B 102
Aldersyde Rd. LS20: Guis 8H 31
Aldersyde Way LS20: Guis 8H 31
Alderton Bank LS17: Leeds 5B 50
Alderton Cres. LS17: Leeds 5B 50
Alderton Hgts. LS17: Leeds 5B 50
Alderton Mt. LS17: Leeds 5B 50
Alderton Pl. LS17: Leeds 5B 50
Alderton Ri. LS17: Leeds 5C 50
Alder Vs. LS17: N Rig 4N 19
Aldonley HD5: Hud 5E 138
Alegar St. HD6: Brigh 1A 120
Alexander Av. LS15: Leeds 7A 70
Alexander Ct. BD20: Rid 9C 28
LS1: Leeds 5E 4 (6D 68)
Alexander Cres. WF7: F'stne 4D 128
Alexander Gdns. S75: Caw 4N 173
Alexander Rd. WF7: F'stne 5D 128
Alexander Sq. BD14: Clay 1G 81
Alexander St. BD6: B'frd 5N 81
LS1: Leeds 5E 4 (6D 68)
Alexander Ter. HX1: Hal 5M 97
Alexandra Av. WF17: Birs 3C 102
Alexandra Cl. HX6: Sow B 8J 97
Alexandra Cres. HX5: Ell 4G 119
LS29: I'ly 5F 14
WF13: Dew 2D 122
Alexandra Dr. WF6: Norm 3J 127
Alexandra Gro. LS6: Leeds 4A 68
LS28: Pud 8A 66
Alexandra Mill LS27: Morl 1K 103
Alexandra Pl. *LS29: I'ly 5F 14*
(off Alexandra Cres.)
Alexandra Rd. BD2: B'frd 1G 64
BD18: Ship 8M 45
HD3: Hud 2H 137
HX7: Heb B 1H 95
LS6: Leeds 4A 68
LS18: Hors 6F 48
LS28: Pud 8N 65
WF17: Bat 8G 103
Alexandra Rd. W. HD3: Hud 5H 137
Alexandra Sq. BD18: Ship 7L 45
Alexandra St. BD7: B'frd 9A 64
BD13: Que 4C 80
HX1: Hal 5L 7 (5B 98)
WF15: Liv 8L 101
Alexandra Ter. BD2: B'frd 4G 64
LS19: Yead 9N 31
(not continuous)
Alford Ter. BD7: B'frd 7M 63
Alfred St. HD1: Hud 6B 8 (5M 137)
HD6: Brigh 9N 99
HX1: Hal 5M 97
HX4: Gree 4C 118
LS27: Chur 5M 85
OL12: Whit 9A 112
S71: Roys 5F 160
WF13: Dew 2G 123
WF15: Liv 8M 101
WF16: Heck 9A 102
WF17: Bat 8E 102
Alfred St. E. HX1: Hal 4M 7 (5C 98)
Alfreds Way WF17: Bat 7F 102
Alhambra Theatre & Studio 5A 6 (8C 64)
Alice Smart Cl. LS15: Leeds 5E 70
Alice St. BD8: B'frd 6B 64
BD19: Cleck 4H 101
BD21: Keigh 9J 27
BD22: Haw 9C 42
Alkincote St. BD21: Keigh 1J 43
All Alone BD10: B'frd 8E 46
All Alone Rd. BD10: B'frd 8D 46
Allanbridge Cl. BD10: B'frd 8G 46
Allandale Av. BD6: B'frd 6M 81
Allandale Rd. BD6: B'frd 6M 81
Allanfield Gro. LS22: Weth 2M 23
Allanfield Ter. LS22: Weth 1M 23
Allan Haigh Cl. WF2: Wake 3F 124
Allan Ter. HX6: Sow B 9J 97
Allenby Cres. LS11: Leeds 5C 86
Allenby Dr. LS11: Leeds 5C 86
Allenby Gdns. LS11: Leeds 5C 86
Allenby Gro. LS11: Leeds 5C 86
Allenby Pl. LS11: Leeds 5C 86
Allenby Rd. LS11: Leeds 5C 86
Allenby Vw. LS11: Leeds 4D 86
Allen Cft. BD11: B'haw 8L 83
Allendale Gro. BB10: B'clif 5A 56
Allendale Rd. S75: Kex 9F 158
Allen Row HD1: Hud 5K 137
Allerby Grn. BD6: B'frd 6L 81
Allergill Pk. HD9: U'thng 3J 169
ALLERTON 5G 63
Allerton Av. LS17: Leeds 5F 50
ALLERTON BYWATER 7N 89
Allerton Bywater Bus. Pk. WF10: All B 9D 90
Allerton Cl. BD15: All 5G 63
Allerton Ct. *LS17: Leeds 5F 50*
(off Allerton Gro.)
Allerton Cft. *LS7: Leeds 1G 68*
(off Harehills La.)
Allerton Dr. LS17: E Kes 1D 36
Allerton Grange Av. LS17: Leeds 6G 50
Allerton Grange Cl. BD15: All 5G 62
LS17: Leeds 7E 50
Allerton Grange Cres.
LS17: Leeds 7F 50
Allerton Grange Cft. LS8: Leeds 7G 50
Allerton Grange Dr. BD15: All 5G 62
LS17: Leeds 7F 50
Allerton Grange Gdns.
LS17: Leeds 7F 50
Allerton Grange Ri. LS17: Leeds 7E 50
Allerton Grange Va. LS17: Leeds 7F 50
Allerton Grange Wlk. LS17: Leeds 7F 50
Allerton Grange Way LS8: Leeds 7G 50
LS17: Leeds 7F 50
Allerton Gro. LS17: Leeds 5F 50
Allerton Hall LS7: Leeds 8E 50
Allerton Hill LS7: Leeds 8E 50
Allerton La. BD13: Thorn 7F 62
BD15: All 7F 62
Allerton M. LS17: Leeds 6F 50
Allerton Pk. LS7: Leeds 8F 50
Allerton Pl. HX1: Hal 5N 97
LS17: Leeds 5F 50
Allerton Rd. BD8: B'frd 5H 63
BD15: All 5C 62
(not continuous)
Allerton St. LS4: Leeds 4N 67
Allerton Ter. LS4: Leeds 5N 67
Allerton Up. Grn. BD15: All 6D 62
Allescholes Rd. OL14: W'den 4J 113
Alliance St. LS12: Leeds 7K 67
Allinson St. LS12: Leeds 8A 68
Allison Dr. HD2: Hud 9N 119
Allison La. BD2: B'frd 2B 64
Allison St. WF7: F'stne 6C 128
Allison Ter. WF2: Kirk 1D 124
Alloe Fld. Pl. HX2: Illing 7L 79
Alloe Fld. Vw. HX2: Illing 7L 79
Allotments Rd. BD13: Denh 5L 61
Allott Cl. WF9: S Elm 6M 163
All Saints Av. LS9: Leeds 6M 5
All Saint's Circ. LS26: W'frd 7E 88
All Saints Cl. HD8: Clay W 6J 157
LS23: B'ham 6D 38
All Saints Ct. BD21: Keigh 9H 27
LS21: Otley 9L 17
LS29: I'ly 4G 15
All Saint's Dr. LS26: W'frd 7D 88
All Saints Hall BD5: B'frd 9A 64
All Saints Ind. Est. WF8: Pon 2L 129
All Saints Rd. BD7: B'frd 9N 63
LS9: Leeds 6M 5 (6H 69)
LS26: W'frd 6E 88
All Saints Ter. BD21: Keigh 9H 27
LS9: Leeds 6M 5
All Saint's Vw. LS26: W'frd 6D 88
WF8: Pon 3L 129
(off Baghill La.)
All Saints Wlk. *WF1: Wake 5K 9*
(within Ridings Shop. Cen.)
All Souls' Rd. HX3: Hal 1K 7 (3B 98)
All Souls' St. HX3: Hal 1K 7 (3B 98)
All Souls' Ter. HX3: Hal 1K 7 (3B 98)
Allums La. LS21: Arth 4A 34
Alma Cl. LS28: Fars 3N 65
Alma Cotts. *BD13: Que 5B 80*
(off Moor Cl. La.)
LS6: Leeds 1N 67
Alma Dr. HD5: Hud 4B 138
Alma Gro. BD18: Ship 7B 46
Alma La. HX6: Ripp 4B 116
WF16: Heck 6A 102
Alma Pl. BD3: B'frd 6H 65
BD21: Keigh 2J 43
Alma Rd. LS6: Leeds 1N 67
OL14: W'den 2J 113
Alma St. BD4: B'frd 9G 65
(Buller St.)
BD4: B'frd 1H 83
(Inkerman St.)
BD13: Que 4C 80
BD18: Ship 7B 46
BD21: Keigh 3J 43
(not continuous)
BD22: Haw 7C 42
HX5: Ell 5F 118
(off South La.)
LS9: Leeds 3L 5 (5H 69)
LS19: Yead 9N 31
LS26: W'frd 6D 88
OL14: W'den 2J 113
Alma Ter. BD20: E Mor 7D 28
BD21: Keigh 2J 43
LS26: Rothw 7M 87
Alma Vs. LS26: W'frd 6E 88
Almond Av. S72: Cud 9J 161
ALMONDBURY 7D 138
Almondbury Bank HD5: Hud 5B 138

Almondbury Cl.—Arthur St.

Almondbury Cl. HD5: Hud 7E 138
ALMONDBURY COMMON 8D 138
Almondbury Comn. HD4: Hud 9D 138
Almondbury Sports Cen. 6D 138
Almond Cl. WF9: S Elm 4N 163
Almond Ct. HX3: North 9F 80
Almondroyd WF16: Heck 7N 101
Almond St. BD3: B'frd 8G 64
Almond Way WF17: Bat 3C 102
Almscliffe Av. WF12: Dew 3H 123
Almscliffe Dr. LS17: Huby 5M 19
Almscliffe Gth. LS17: N Rig 2N 19
Almscliffe Pl. BD2: B'frd 2H 65
Almscliffe Ter. LS21: Otley 1M 31
Almsgate WF1: Wake 5K 9
Almshouse Hill LS23: B'ham 6D 38
Almshouse La. WF1: Wake 5K 9 (5L 125)
WF2: New 6K 143
Alnwick Vw. LS16: Leeds 8M 49
Alpha St. BD21: Keigh 9K 27
Alpine Cl. HX2: Illing 6M 79
WF17: Bat 8E 102
Alpine Ct. WF9: Hems 1D 162
WF10: C'frd 7E 108
Alpine Ri. BD13: Thorn 7C 62
Alpine Ter. LS26: Rothw 7N 87
Alpine Vw. WF9: Hems 1D 162
Alred Ct. BD4: B'frd 4F 82
Alston Cl. BD9: B'frd 5J 63
Alston La. LS14: Leeds 3B 70
Alston Retail Pk. BD21: Keigh 7K 27
Alston Rd. BD21: Keigh 7K 27
Altar Dr. BD9: B'frd 3M 63
BD20: Rid 7N 27
Altar La. BD16: Bgly 3M 43
Altar Vw. BD20: Rid 6M 27
Altar Vs. BD21: Rid 7M 27
Althorpe Gro. BD10: B'frd 9E 46
Altinkool St. WF1: Wake 9A 126
ALTOFTS 8G 106
Altofts Hall Rd. WF6: Alt 8G 107
Altofts La. WF10: C'frd 6L 107
Altofts Lodge Dr. WF6: Alt 9F 106
Altofts Rd. WF6: Norm 1H 127
Alton Av. HD5: Hud 3D 138
Alton Cft. BD14: Clay 2F 80
Alton Gro. BD9: B'frd 3L 63
BD18: Ship 1N 63
Alton Way S75: Map 8J 159
Alum Ct. BD9: B'frd 3M 63
Alum Dr. BD9: B'frd 3M 63
Alva Cl. LS20: Guis 6H 31
Alva Ct. LS20: Guis 6H 31
Alvanley Ct. BD8: B'frd 6J 63
Alva Ter. BD18: Ship 9N 45
ALVERTHORPE 4G 124
Alverthorpe Rd. WF2: Wake 4H 125
Alwen Av. HD2: Hud 9L 119
ALWOODLEY 3E 50
Alwoodley Chase LS17: Leeds 2G 50
Alwoodley Ct. LS17: Leeds 2B 50
Alwoodley Ct. Gdns. LS17: Leeds 1C 50
Alwoodley Gdns. LS17: Leeds 2C 50
ALWOODLEY GATES 1G 51
Alwoodley Gates LS17: Leeds 1G 50
Alwoodley Golf Course 1G 51
Alwoodley La. LS17: Leeds 1B 50
ALWOODLEY PARK 1C 50
Amberley Ct. BD3: B'frd 8G 64
(off Amberley St.)
Amberley Gdns. LS12: Leeds 8N 67
Amberley Ri. DN6: Skel 7L 165
Amberley Rd. LS12: Leeds 8M 67
Amberley St. BD3: B'frd 7G 64
(not continuous)
LS12: Leeds 8M 67
Amber St. WF17: Bat 5D 102
Amberton App. LS8: Leeds 2L 69
Amberton Cl. LS8: Leeds 1L 69
Amberton Cres. LS8: Leeds 2L 69
Amberton Gdns. LS8: Leeds 2L 69
Amberton Gth. LS8: Leeds 2L 69
Amberton Gro. LS8: Leeds 2L 69
Amberton La. LS8: Leeds 2L 69
Amberton M. LS8: Leeds 3M 69
Amberton Mt. LS8: Leeds 2L 69
Amberton Pl. LS8: Leeds 2K 69
Amberton Rd. LS8: Leeds 2K 69
LS9: Leeds 2K 69
Amberton St. LS8: Leeds 2L 69
Amberton Ter. LS8: Leeds 2L 69
Ambler Gro. HX2: Illing 7M 79
Amblers Bldgs. LS28: Pud 8B 66
(off Amblers Ct.)
Amblers Bungs. WF3: E Ard 4D 104
Amblers Ct. LS28: Pud 8B 66
Amblers Cft. BD10: B'frd 5F 46
Amblers M. BD17: Bail 3A 46
BD20: E Mor 8C 28
Amblers Row BD17: Bail 3A 46
Amblers Ter. HX3: Hal 1L 7 (3B 98)
Ambler St. BD8: B'frd 5A 64
BD21: Keigh 9K 27
WF10: C'frd 5D 108
AMBLER THORN 6B 80
Amblerthorne BD11: B'haw 8M 83
Ambler Way BD13: Que 6B 80
Ambleside Av. BD9: B'frd 4L 63
Ambleside Dr. WF2: W'ton 4B 144
Ambleside Gdns. LS28: Pud 7N 65
Ambleside Gro. LS26: W'frd 7D 88
Ambleside Rd. WF10: C'frd 3L 109
Ambleside Wlk. LS22: Weth 3J 23
Amble Tonia BD13: Denh 5L 61
Ambleton Way BD13: Que 5B 80
Amelia Stewart La. LS15: Leeds 4E 70
Amelia St. BD18: Ship 6L 45
America La. HD6: Clift 1A 120
America Moor La. LS27: Morl 2K 103
Amisfield Rd. HX3: Hip 4J 99
Amos St. HX1: Hal 5M 97
OL14: Tod 3E 92
Amport Cl. HD6: Ras 2N 119
Amspool Ct. WF3: Carl 1L 105
Amundsen Av. BD2: B'frd 1E 64
Amy Busfield Grn.
LS29: Burl W 8C 16
Amyroyce Dr. BD18: Ship 8C 46
Amy St. BD16: Bgly 4F 44
HX3: Hal 2N 97
Anaheim Dr. WF1: Out 7M 105
Ancaster Cres. LS16: Leeds 8L 49
Ancaster Rd. LS16: Leeds 8L 49
Ancaster Vw. LS16: Leeds 8L 49
Anchorage, The BD16: Bgly 3E 44
Anchor Bri. Way WF12: Dew 4F 122
Anchor Ct. BD8: B'frd 6B 64
(off Jervaulx Cres.)
HD8: Kbtn 3F 154
Anchor Pl. HD6: Brigh 3B 120
Anchor St. OL14: Tod 7L 93
Andersen Ct. WF10: C'frd 7J 109
Anderson Av. LS8: Leeds 1L 5 (4G 69)
Anderson Ho. BD17: Bail 6N 45
(off Fairview Ct.)
Anderson Mt. LS8: Leeds 1L 5 (4G 69)
Anderson St. BD8: B'frd 5A 64
WF2: Wake 5J 125
WF8: Pon 2J 129
Anderton Fold HX3: North 2F 98
Anderton St. WF1: Wake 8N 125
Andover Grn. BD4: B'frd 1J 83
Andrew Cl. HX3: Sou 8F 98
Andrew Cres. HD4: Hud 9F 136
WF1: Out 7K 105
Andrew Ho. LS28: Fars 3A 66
(off Water La.)
Andrews Gro. WF7: Ackw 4F 146
Andrews Mnr. LS19: Yead 9M 31
(off Haworth La.)
Andrew Sq. LS28: Fars 3A 66
Andrew St. LS28: Fars 4A 66
WF1: Wake 1H 9 (3K 125)
WF7: F'stne 7C 128
Anerley St. BD4: B'frd 3F 82
Angel Ct. LS3: Leeds 5B 68
Angel Inn Yd. LS1: Leeds 6F 4
Angel Pl. BD16: Bgly 2F 44
Angel Rd. HX1: Hal 2G 7 (4A 98)
(Crossley Retail Pk.)
HX1: Hal 2J 7 (4A 98)
(Stannary Pl.)
Angel Row LS26: Rothw 8J 87
Angel St. BD17: Bail 3B 46
Angerton Way BD6: B'frd 7M 81
Anglers Country Pk. 5G 145
Angram Rd. BD20: Keigh 5G 26
Angus Av. BD12: Wyke 3A 100
Anlaby St. BD4: B'frd 9H 65
Annandale Ct. LS29: I'ly 6G 15
Annandale Vw. BD13: Que 3G 81
Annat Royd La. S36: Ing 9N 171
Anne Cres. S72: S Hien 4M 161
Anne Ga. BD1: B'frd 3D 6 (7D 64)
Anne's Ct. HX3: Sou 8F 98
Anne St. BD7: B'frd 2L 81
WF17: Bat 5D 102
Annie Smith Way HD2: Hud 2L 137
Annie St. BD18: Ship 9A 46
BD21: Keigh 7J 27
BD22: Cros R 7F 42
HX6: Sow B 8H 97
LS27: Morl 9L 85
WF1: Out 8K 105
WF9: Fitz 6A 146
Anning Fold LS25: Gar 6B 72
Annison St. BD3: B'frd 4E 6 (7E 64)
Annottes Cft. HD5: Hud 3D 138
Ann Pl. BD5: B'frd 7A 6 (9C 64)
Ann St. BD21: Keigh 1H 43
BD22: Haw 8D 42
Another World (Mountainboarding Cen.)
2K 79
Anroyd St. WF13: Dew 2D 122
Anson Gro. BD7: B'frd 3L 81
Anstey Ho. LS3: Leeds 5B 4
Anston Dr. WF9: S Elm 4N 163
Anstone Dr. BD5: B'frd 3A 82
Anthony La. BD16: Har 5A 44
Anthony's La. LS25: Bur S 1F 110
Antler Complex LS27: Morl 9G 85
Anton Rd. LS29: Guis, Men 6G 30
Antony Cl. HD3: Hud 1C 136
Anvil Ct. BD8: B'frd 5N 63
(off Carlisle St.)
BD13: Cull 1K 61
HX2: Illing 8L 79
Anvil St. BD8: B'frd 5N 63
(not continuous)
HD6: Brigh 9M 99
Apex Bus. Cen. LS11: Leeds 9E 68
Apex Vw. LS11: Leeds 9D 68
Apex Way LS11: Leeds 9E 68
APPERLEY BRIDGE 7J 47
Apperley Gdns. BD10: B'frd 7J 47
Apperley La. BD10: B'frd, Yead 7J 47
LS19: Raw, Yead 6K 47
Apperley Rd. BD10: B'frd 7G 46
(not continuous)
Appleby Cl. BD13: Que 4B 80
S75: Dart 8H 159
Appleby La. LS25: Gar 7B 72
Appleby Pl. DN6: Skel 7L 165
LS15: Leeds 6N 69
Appleby Wlk. LS15: Leeds 6N 69
Appleby Way LS22: Weth 2M 23
LS27: Morl 8L 85
Apple Cl. WF17: Birs 2D 102
Applegarth BD14: Clay 2H 81
LS26: W'frd 6D 88
WF2: Wake 3N 143
Applehaigh Cl. BD10: B'frd 8G 46
Applehaigh Ct. WF4: Not 4B 160
Applehaigh Gro. S71: Roys 5B 160
Applehaigh La. WF4: Not 2B 160
Applehaigh Vw. S71: Roys 6B 160
Apple Ho. Ter. HX2: Lud 3E 96
Appleshaw Cres. WF2: Wren 9H 105
Apple St. BD21: Keigh 4G 43
BD22: Oxen 4C 60
Appleton Cl. BD12: O'haw 8D 82
BD16: Bgly 2G 45
LS9: Leeds 6H 69
Appleton Ct. BD13: Thorn 8C 62
(off John St.)
LS9: Leeds 6H 69
WF2: Wake 2H 143
Appleton Gro. LS9: Leeds 6K 69
Appleton Sq. LS9: Leeds 6H 69
Appleton Way LS9: Leeds 6H 69
Apple Tree Cl. WF3: E Ard 4E 104
WF8: Pon 5H 129
Appletree Cl. LS23: B Spa 1D 38
Apple Tree Ct. WF3: E Ard 5E 104
Apple Tree Gdns. LS29: I'ly 5E 14
Apple Tree La. LS25: Kip 5B 90
Apple Tree M. LS25: Kip 4B 90
Apple Tree Rd. WF7: F'stne 7E 128
Apple Tree Wlk. LS25: Kip 4B 90
Applewood Gdns. WF8: D'ton 6B 130
Appleyard Rd. HX7: Myth 3N 95
Appleyard Wing HX1: Hal 8J 7
Approach, The LS15: Scho 8G 52
April Ct. WF15: Liv 1L 121
April Gdns. BD13: Que 4D 80
Aprilia Ct. BD14: Clay 9J 63
Apsley Cres. BD8: B'frd 5A 64
Apsley St. BD21: Keigh 2H 43
BD22: Haw 8D 42
BD22: Oak 4D 42
Apsley Ter. BD22: Oak 4D 42
(off Apsley St.)
Apsley Vs. BD8: B'frd 5B 64
Aquamarine Dr. HD2: Hud 9A 120
Aquila Way WF15: Liv 7H 101
Aragon Ct. LS7: Leeds 8C 50
Arborary La. HD9: Mel 3E 152
Arbour, The LS29: I'ly 3F 14
Arbour Ct. WF16: Heck 7A 102
Arcade, The LS29: I'ly 5G 14
(off Church St.)
WF11: Knot 8D 110
WF13: Dew 3G 122
(off Corporation St.)
Arcade Royale HX1: Hal 4L 7
Arcadia St. BD21: Keigh 2H 43
Archbell Av. HD6: Ras 3N 119
Archer Rd. HD6: Brigh 2B 120
Archer St. WF10: C'frd 6C 108
Archery Pl. LS2: Leeds 1D 4 (4D 68)
Archery Rd. LS2: Leeds 1D 4 (4D 68)
Archery St. LS2: Leeds 2E 4 (4D 68)
Archery Ter. LS2: Leeds 2D 4 (4D 68)
Arches, The HX3: Hal 1M 7 (3B 98)
Arches St. HX1: Hal 5J 7 (6A 98)
Archibald Dr. WF9: Kins 8B 146
Archibald St. BD7: B'frd 7A 64
Arctic Pde. BD7: B'frd 1M 81
Arctic St. BD20: Keigh 6H 27
BD22: Cros R 7E 42
Arden Ct. HD5: K'htn 3G 138
LS16: Leeds 5M 49
WF4: Horb 2C 142
Arden Grange LS16: Leeds 5M 49
Arden Ho. HX1: Hal 7H 7
Arden M. HX1: Hal 6H 7 (7A 98)
Ardennes Cl. BD2: B'frd 2D 64
Arden Rd. BD8: B'frd 7H 63
HX1: Hal 6H 7 (6A 98)
Ardsley Cl. BD4: B'frd 3K 83
Ardsley Ct. WF3: E Ard 4G 105
Arena Pk. LS17: Leeds 9A 36
Argent Way BD4: B'frd 3K 83
Argie Av. LS4: Leeds 3L 67
Argie Gdns. LS4: Leeds 4M 67
Argie Rd. LS4: Leeds 4M 67
Argie Ter. LS4: Leeds 4M 67
Argyle M. LS17: E Kes 3D 36
Argyle Rd. LS9: Leeds 5J 5 (6F 68)
WF11: Ferr 7B 110
Argyle St. BD4: B'frd 2F 82
BD21: Keigh 9H 27
HD7: Mars 5F 150
WF1: Wake 7N 125
Argyll Av. WF8: Pon 3H 129
Argyll Cl. BD17: Bail 5C 46
LS18: Hors 3E 48
Ariba Av. BD3: B'frd 2D 6 (6D 64)
Arkendale M. BD7: B'frd 2K 81
Arkenley La. HD4: Hud 8D 138
HD8: Fen B 8D 138
Arkenmore HD5: Hud 3D 138
Arksey Pl. LS12: Leeds 6M 67
Arksey Ter. LS12: Leeds 6M 67
Arkwright Ct. WF15: Liv 7L 101
Arkwright Hall BD7: B'frd 7B 64
Arkwright St. BD4: B'frd 8J 65
BD14: Clay 1G 81
Arkwright Wlk. LS27: Morl 7K 85
Arlesford Rd. BD4: B'frd 3J 83
Arley Cl. HD9: Nether 9L 153
Arley Gro. LS12: Leeds 6M 67
Arley Pl. LS12: Leeds 6M 67
Arley St. LS12: Leeds 6M 67
Arley Ter. LS12: Leeds 6M 67
Arlington Bus. Cen.
LS11: Leeds 5N 85
Arlington Cres. HX2: Hal 7K 97
Arlington Gro. LS8: Leeds 1K 69
WF10: C'frd 5F 108
Arlington M. WF16: Heck 9A 102
Arlington Rd. LS8: Leeds 2K 69
Arlington St. WF1: Wake 1H 9 (3K 125)
Arlington Way HD5: Hud 3E 138
Armadale Av. BD4: B'frd 5F 82
Armgill La. BD2: B'frd 2B 64
Armidale Way BD2: B'frd 3D 64
Armitage, The BD20: E Mor 8A 28
Armitage Av. HD6: Ras 3N 119
ARMITAGE BRIDGE 1K 153
Armitage Bldgs. WF12: Dew 6L 103
Armitage Cl. HD8: Skelm 7C 156
Armitage Ct. LS28: Pud 8A 66
(off Armitage Sq.)
Armitage Fold HD4: Arm B 1K 153
Armitage Rd. BD12: O'haw 9D 82
HD2: Hud 1L 137
HD3: Hud 5G 136
HD4: Arm B 1K 153
HX1: Hal 7M 97
WF2: Wake 3F 124
Armitage Sq. LS28: Pud 8A 66
Armitage St. HD4: Hud 8B 8 (6M 137)
LS26: Rothw 9N 87
WF10: C'frd 4C 108
WF13: Raven 6A 122
ARMLEY 6N 67
Armley Ct. LS12: Leeds 6N 67
Armley Grange Av. LS12: Leeds 5J 67
Armley Grange Cres. LS12: Leeds 5J 67
Armley Grange Dr. LS12: Leeds 6J 67
Armley Grange Mt. LS12: Leeds 6J 67
Armley Grange Oval LS12: Leeds 5J 67
Armley Grange Ri. LS12: Leeds 6J 67
Armley Grange Vw. LS12: Leeds 6K 67
Armley Grange Wlk. LS12: Leeds 6K 67
Armley Gro. Pl. LS12: Leeds 7N 67
Armley Ho. LS14: Leeds 9N 51
(off Kingsdale Ct.)
Armley Leisure Cen. 7L 67
Armley Lodge Rd. LS12: Leeds 5M 67
Armley Mills Leeds Industrial Mus. 5N 67
Armley Pk. Ct. LS12: Leeds 6M 67
(off Cecil Rd.)
Armley Pk. Rd. LS12: Leeds 5M 67
Armley Ridge Cl. LS12: Leeds 6K 67
Armley Ridge Rd. LS12: Leeds 3J 67
(not continuous)
Armley Ridge Ter.
LS12: Leeds 5K 67
Armley Rd. LS12: Leeds 7A 4 (6M 67)
(not continuous)
Armley Tennis Club 5K 67
Armouries Dr. LS10: Leeds 8J 5 (8F 68)
Armouries Way LS10: Leeds 8J 5 (7F 68)
Armoury Av. WF14: Mir 6L 121
Armstrong Cl. WF6: Alt 8H 107
Armstrong St. BD4: B'frd 8H 65
LS28: Fars 4A 66
Armstrong Ter. WF8: Pon 4H 129
Army Row S71: Roys 5E 160
Armytage Cres. HD1: Hud 7L 137
Armytage Rd. HD6: Brigh 1A 120
Armytage Wlk. WF9: S Kirk 6J 163
Armytage Way HD6: Brigh 2B 120
Arncliffe Av. BD22: Keigh 1G 42
Arncliffe Ct. HD1: Hud 3K 137
Arncliffe Cres. HD6: Ras 3K 119
LS27: Morl 2M 103
Arncliffe Dr. WF11: Ferr 8A 110
Arncliffe Gdns. WF17: Bat 7E 102
Arncliffe Gth. LS28: Stan 4A 66
Arncliffe Grange LS17: Leeds 5F 50
Arncliffe Gro. BD22: Keigh 2G 42
Arncliffe Path BD22: Keigh 1G 42
(off Arncliffe Av.)
Arncliffe Pl. BD22: Keigh 1G 42
(off Arncliffe Av.)
Arncliffe Rd. BD22: Keigh 2G 42
LS16: Leeds 7K 49
WF1: Wake 4N 125
WF17: Bat 7D 102
Arncliffe St. LS28: Stan 4A 66
Arncliffe Ter. BD7: B'frd 8N 63
Arndale Cen. LS6: Leeds 1N 67
Arndale Gro. HD9: H'frth 4N 169
Arndale Ho. BD1: B'frd 4B 6
Arndale Shop. Cen. BD18: Ship 8N 45
(off Market Sq.)
Arnford Cl. BD3: B'frd 1D 6 (6D 64)
Arnhem Cl. BD16: Bgly 4G 45
Arnold Av. HD2: Hud 1L 137
S71: Ath 9A 160
Arnold Pl. BD8: B'frd 6A 64
Arnold Royd HD6: Ras 4K 119
Arnold St. BD8: B'frd 5A 64
HD2: Hud 1L 137
HX1: Hal 5N 97
HX6: Sow B 8H 97
WF15: Liv 8L 101
Arnside Av. BD20: Rid 7L 27
Arnside Cl. WF10: C'frd 4K 109
Arnside Cres. WF10: C'frd 4K 109
Arnside Rd. BD5: B'frd 3C 82
Arran Cl. HD7: Golc 5C 136
Arran Ct. LS25: Gar 9N 71
Arran Dr. LS18: Hors 3E 48
LS25: Gar 9N 71
Arran Way LS26: Rothw 8A 88
Arrow La. WF10: All B, Leds 9E 90
ARRUNDEN 7L 169
Arrunden Ct. HD9: H'frth 5N 169
Arrunden La. HD9: H'frth 7L 169
Arrunden Wood Nook HD9: H'frth 6L 169
ARTHINGTON 2M 33
Arthington Av. LS10: Leeds 3F 86
Arthington Cl. WF3: W Ard 5N 103
Arthington Ct. LS10: Leeds 3F 86
Arthington Gth. LS21: Arth 2J 33
Arthington Gro. LS10: Leeds 3F 86
Arthington La. LS21: Arth, Pool 1G 32
Arthington Lawns LS21: Pool 2H 33
Arthington Pl. LS10: Leeds 3F 86
Arthington Rd. LS16: Leeds 6M 33
Arthington St. BD8: B'frd 6A 64
LS10: Leeds 3F 86
Arthington Ter. LS10: Leeds 3F 86
Arthington Vw. LS10: Leeds 3F 86
Arthur Av. BD8: B'frd 7H 63
Arthur Gro. WF17: Bat 4C 102
ARTHURSDALE 7G 53
Arthursdale Cl. LS15: Scho 8G 53
Arthursdale Dr. LS15: Scho 8G 53
Arthursdale Grange LS15: Scho 8G 52
Arthur St. BD10: B'frd 9F 46
BD16: Bgly 3E 44
BD22: Oak 5C 42
HD6: Brigh 1A 120
HD7: Golc 6D 136
LS28: Fars 4A 66

Arthur St. LS28: Stan 4B **66**
WF1: Wake 8N **125**
Arthur Ter. *LS28: Fars* *4A 66*
(off Arthur St.)
Artillery St. WF16: Heck 9A **102**
Artist St. LS12: Leeds 7B **68**
Aruba LS12: Leeds 7A **4**
Arum St. BD5: B'frd 2A **82**
Arundel Cl. WF1: Wake 2J **9** (4L **125**)
WF17: Bat 2E **102**
Arundel Gdns. S71: Roys 5D **160**
Arundel St. HX1: Hal 5M **97**
LS25: Gar 6B **72**
LS28: Pud 7B **66**
WF1: Wake 2J **9** (4L **125**)
Arundel Ter. *LS15: Leeds* *4D 70*
(off Tranquility Av.)
Arundel Wlk. WF17: Bat 3E **102**
Asco Pl. WF12: Dew 4H **123**
Ascot Av. BD7: B'frd 3K **81**
Ascot Dr. BD7: B'frd 3K **81**
Ascot Gdns. BD7: B'frd 3K **81**
HX6: Sow B 9D **96**
LS10: Leeds 1F **104**
Ascot Gro. HD6: Ras 3K **119**
Ascot Pde. BD7: B'frd 3K **81**
Ascot Rd. LS25: Kip 3N **89**
Ascot Ter. LS9: Leeds 8M **5** (7H **69**)
Asda Ho. LS11: Leeds 8F **4** (8E **68**)
Asdale Rd. WF2: Crig, Wake 2J **143**
Ash Apartments WF1: Wake 1M **9** (3M **125**)
Ash Av. LS6: Leeds 1N **67**
Ashbourne Av. BD2: B'frd 3D **64**
BD19: Cleck 6H **101**
Ashbourne Bank BD2: B'frd 3D **64**
Ashbourne Cl. BD2: B'frd 2D **64**
Ashbourne Cres. BD2: B'frd 3D **64**
BD13: Que 4C **80**
LS25: Gar 9N **71**
Ashbourne Cft. BD19: Cleck 6H **101**
Ashbourne Dr. BD2: B'frd 3D **64**
BD19: Cleck 6H **101**
WF8: Pon 6K **129**
Ashbourne Gdns. BD2: B'frd 3D **64**
BD19: Cleck 6H **101**
Ashbourne Gth. BD2: B'frd 2E **64**
Ashbourne Gro. BD2: B'frd 3D **64**
HX1: Hal 5M **97**
Ashbourne Haven BD2: B'frd 3D **64**
Ashbourne Mt. BD2: B'frd 3D **64**
Ashbourne Oval BD2: B'frd 3D **64**
Ashbourne Ri. BD2: B'frd 3D **64**
Ashbourne Rd. BD2: B'frd 3D **64**
BD21: Keigh 3G **43**
Ashbourne Vw. BD19: Cleck 6H **101**
Ashbourne Way BD2: B'frd 2D **64**
BD19: Cleck 6H **101**
Ashbrook Cl. WF5: Oss 4N **123**
Ashbrooke Pk. LS11: Leeds 3E **86**
Ash Brow WF4: Flock 7F **140**
Ashbrow Rd. HD2: Hud 8N **119**
Ashburn Cl. LS22: Weth 2L **23**
Ashburn Cft. LS22: Weth 2L **23**
Ashburn Dr. LS22: Weth 2L **23**
Ashburn Gro. BD17: Bail 3A **46**
LS22: Weth 2L **23**
Ashburnham Gro. BD9: B'frd 3N **63**
Ashburn Pl. LS29: I'ly 6F **14**
Ashburn Way LS22: Weth 2L **23**
Ashbury Chase WF1: Out 7J **105**
Ashby Av. LS13: Leeds 4G **66**
Ashby Cl. WF15: Liv 2K **121**
Ashby Cres. LS13: Leeds 5G **66**
Ashby Mt. LS13: Leeds 4G **66**
Ashby Sq. LS13: Leeds 4G **67**
Ashby St. BD4: B'frd 1E **82**
Ashby Ter. LS13: Leeds 4G **66**
Ashby Vw. LS13: Leeds 4G **66**
Ash Cl. HX3: Hip 4J **99**
LS27: Gil 7G **84**
LS29: I'ly 5D **14**
WF5: Oss 6N **123**
Ashcombe Dr. WF11: Knot 9E **110**
Ash Ct. BD19: Scho 4D **100**
HD9: Holm 5J **169**
LS14: Leeds 4N **69**
Ash Cres. LS6: Leeds 1N **67**
WF3: S'ley 8A **106**
Ash Cft. BD6: B'frd 5M **81**
Ashcroft Cl. WF17: Bat 9E **102**
Ashdale WF2: Wake 2N **143**
Ashdale La. LS22: K Dei 1L **23**
Ashdale Vw. LS22: K Dei 1M **23**
Ashday La. HX3: Sou 9F **98**
Ashdene LS12: N Far 2G **85**
OL14: W'den 2K **113**
Ashdene App. WF4: Croft 1G **144**
Ashdene Av. WF4: Croft 1G **144**
Ashdene Cl. LS28: Pud 9B **66**
Ashdene Ct. BD13: Cull 9K **43**
Ashdene Cres. LS28: Pud 9B **66**
WF4: Croft 1G **144**
Ashdene Dr. WF4: Croft 1G **144**
Ashdene Gth. WF4: Croft 1G **144**
Ashdene Gro. WF8: Pon 8M **109**
Ashdown Cl. BD6: B'frd 4N **81**
HX2: Hal 6K **97**
Ashdown Ct. BD18: Ship 8M **45**
WF11: Ferr 7B **110**
Ashdowne Pl. *BD8: B'frd* *5A 64*
(off E. Squire La.)
Ashdown Rd. WF1: Wake 8N **125**
Ashdown St. LS13: Leeds 5F **66**
Ash Dyke Cl. S75: Kex 9F **158**
ASHENHURST 7A **138**
Ashenhurst Av. HD4: Hud 7A **138**
Ashenhurst Cl. HD4: Hud 7N **137**
OL14: Tod 5J **93**
Ashenhurst Ri. HD4: Hud 7N **137**
Ashenhurst Rd. HD4: Hud 7N **137**
OL14: Tod 5H **93**
Asherton Gro. LS23: B Spa 1E **38**
Ashes La. HD4: Hud 1N **153**
OL14: Tod 4M **93**
ASHFIELD 9J **107**

Ashfield BD4: B'frd 4H **83**
LS12: N Far 1K **85**
LS22: Weth 3N **23**
WF12: Dew 7G **122**
Ashfield Av. BD9: B'frd 1N **63**
BD18: Ship 1N **63**
HD8: Skelm 8D **156**
LS27: Morl 1J **103**
Ashfield Cl. HX3: Hal 2M **97**
LS12: N Far 1J **85**
LS15: Leeds 2E **70**
WF17: Birs 3D **102**
Ashfield Cotts. *BD16: Bgly* *5F 44*
(off Healey Av.)
Ashfield Ct. BD16: Bgly 5F **44**
Ashfield Cres. BD16: Bgly 5F **44**
LS28: Stan 5A **66**
Ashfield Dr. BD9: B'frd 1N **63**
BD17: Bail 3B **46**
HX3: Hal 2M **97**
Ashfield Gro. BD9: B'frd 1M **63**
LS28: Stan 5B **66**
Ashfield Ho. WF9: Hems 3D **162**
Ashfield Paddock LS23: B Spa 1F **38**
Ashfield Pk. LS6: Leeds 1A **68**
LS21: Otley 9J **17**
Ashfield Pl. BD2: B'frd 4H **65**
LS17: Huby 5M **19**
LS21: Otley 1K **31**
Ashfield Retail Pk.
BD16: Bgly 1C **44**
Ashfield Rd. BD10: B'frd 6F **46**
BD13: Thorn 8C **62**
BD18: Ship 8K **45**
HD2: Hud 1K **137**
HX4: Gree 4A **118**
LS27: Morl 1J **103**
LS28: Stan 5A **66**
WF9: Hems 4D **162**
WF17: Birs 2C **102**
Ashfield St. *BD21: Keigh* *1H 43*
(off Minnie St.)
HD2: Hud 9N **119**
WF6: Norm 9K **107**
Ashfield Ter. BD12: Wyke 9B **82**
BD16: Bgly 5F **44**
BD19: Cleck *5J 101*
(off Neville St.)
BD22: Haw 9C **42**
HD7: Slait 1L **151**
HX4: Gree 3A **118**
LS15: Leeds 2E **70**
WF3: Thpe H 2H **105**
Ashfield Way LS12: N Far 1H **85**
Ash Fold BD7: B'frd 9K **63**
Ashford Ct. HD8: Kbtn 2K **155**
S71: Roys 4D **160**
Ashford Dr. LS28: Pud 8C **66**
Ashford Grn. BD6: B'frd 4L **81**
Ashford Mnr. HD8: Fen B 9H **139**
Ashford Pk. WF7: Golc 5C **136**
Ashgap La. WF6: Norm 1J **127**
Ash Gdns. LS6: Leeds 1N **67**
Ash Ghyll Gdns. BD16: Bgly 3E **44**
Ash Grn. WF8: Pon 2M **129**
Ash Gro. BD11: B'haw 7L **83**
BD16: Bgly 6F **44**
BD19: Cleck 6F **100**
BD19: Gom 3L **101**
BD21: Keigh 3G **43**
HD6: Clift 9A **100**
(not continuous)
LS6: Leeds 3B **68**
LS18: Hors 5F **48**
LS21: Otley 1K **31**
LS28: Pud 8B **66**
LS29: I'ly 4H **15**
WF3: S'ley 1A **126**
WF8: D'ton 6B **130**
WF9: S Elm 5N **163**
WF12: Dew *3K 123*
(off Westfield Av.)
Ashgrove BD2: B'frd 3G **64**
BD7: B'frd 8B **64**
BD10: B'frd 8J **47**
BD20: Stee 3D **26**
Ashgrove Av. HX3: Hal 9C **98**
Ashgrove Cres. LS25: Kip 2B **90**
Ashgrove Cft. LS25: Kip 3B **90**
Ash Gro. Ho. WF9: S Elm 5N **163**
Ashgrove M. LS13: Leeds 2C **66**
Ashgrove Mt. LS25: Kip 2A **90**
Ashgrove Pl. HX3: Hal 9D **98**
Ashgrove Rd. BD20: Keigh 6G **26**
HD2: Hud 9D **120**
HD9: U'thng 3K **169**
Ash Gro. Ter. *HD6: Ras* *2M 119*
(off Thomas St.)
Ash Hall La. HX6: Ripp 3A **116**
Ash Hill Dr. LS17: Shad 3A **52**
Ash Hill Gdns. LS17: Shad 3A **52**
Ash Hill Gth. LS17: Shad 3A **52**
Ash Hill La. LS17: Shad 3A **52**
Ash Hill Wlk. BD4: B'frd 1F **82**
Ash Ho. LS15: Leeds 8N **69**
Ashington Cl. BD2: B'frd 2H **65**
Ashlands Rd. LS29: I'ly 4H **15**
Ash La. HD8: Eml 3H **157**
LS25: Gar 6A **72**
Ashlar Cl. BD22: Haw 8D **42**
Ashlar Gro. BD13: Que 6C **80**
WF10: C'frd 6F **108**
Ash Lea WF3: S'ley 1A **126**
WF11: Fair 9N **91**
Ashlea Av. HD6: Ras 3N **119**
Ashlea Cl. HD6: Ras 3N **119**
LS25: Gar 9N **71**
Ashlea Ct. *LS13: Leeds* *2F 66*
(off Ashlea Ga.)
WF2: New *6L 143*
(off Lake Vw.)
Ashlea Dr. HD6: Ras 3N **119**
Ashlea Ga. LS13: Leeds 3F **66**
Ashlea Grn. LS13: Leeds 3F **66**
Ashleigh S72: B'ley 6A **162**

Ashleigh Av. WF2: Wake 6G **124**
WF8: Pon 4K **129**
Ashleigh Cl. HD8: Shel 7K **155**
Ashleigh Dale HD2: Hud 1J **137**
Ashleigh Gdns. LS26: Oul 7D **88**
WF5: Oss 3M **123**
Ashleigh Rd. LS16: Leeds 7K **49**
Ashleigh St. BD21: Keigh 8J **27**
HX3: Hal 1N **97**
Ashley Av. LS9: Leeds 4J **69**
Ashley Cl. BD19: Gom 2L **101**
WF2: Wren 1H **125**
Ashley Ct. *LS16: Leeds* *6L 49*
(off Otley Rd.)
WF9: S Kirk 8F **162**
Ashley Cft. S71: Roys 5C **160**
Ashley Est. WF10: C'frd 8G **108**
Ashley Gro. HX7: Myth 3M **95**
Ashley Ind. Est. LS7: Leeds 1G **5** (3E **68**)
WF5: Oss 4A **124**
Ashley La. BD17: Ship 7N **45**
Ashley Pk. M. LS25: Gar 5C **72**
Ashley Rd. BD12: Wyke 2A **100**
BD16: Bgly 5F **44**
LS9: Leeds 4H **69**
LS12: Leeds 8L **67**
Ashley St. BD18: Ship 7N **45**
HX1: Hal 5M **97**
Ashley Ter. LS9: Leeds 4J **69**
Ashley Vs. *HX7: Heb B* *9H 77*
(off Moss La.)
Ashmead LS23: Cliff 3D **38**
WF17: Bat 9D **102**
Ash Mdw. Cl. HD8: Hud 8A **120**
Ashmere Gro. HD2: Hud 9A **120**
Ash Mews BD10: B'frd 8J **47**
Ashmore Dr. WF5: Oss 2M **123**
Ashmore Gdns. BD4: B'frd 5F **82**
Ash Mt. BD7: B'frd 9N **63**
BD21: Keigh 2G **42**
S72: Shaf 6K **161**
Ashmount BD14: Clay 1J **81**
Ashmount Ind. Pk. WF9: Kins 8B **146**
Ashmount M. BD22: Haw 7C **42**
Ashmount Pl. BD22: Haw 7C **42**
Ash Rd. DN6: Skel 7N **165**
LS6: Leeds 2M **67**
LS16: Leeds 2M **49**
S72: Shaf 7L **161**
Ashroyd LS26: Rothw 9A **88**
Ash St. BD19: Cleck 5G **101**
BD22: Oxen 3C **60**
HD1: Hud 1A **8** (2M **137**)
(not continuous)
LS29: I'ly 4H **15**
WF3: S'ley 1A **126**
WF4: N Cro 3H **145**
Ash Ter. BD16: Bgly 5E **44**
BD19: Cleck *4H 101*
(off Whitcliffe Rd.)
HX6: Ripp 8C **116**
LS6: Leeds 1N **67**
LS25: Gar 6A **72**
Ashtofts Mt. LS20: Guis 7J **31**
Ashton Av. BD7: B'frd 9K **63**
LS8: Leeds 4H **69**
Ashton Binn HD7: Mars 4G **150**
Ashton Clough Rd. WF15: Liv 8L **101**
Ashton Ct. LS8: Leeds 3J **69**
WF2: New *6L 143*
(off Lake Vw.)
Ashton Cres. WF3: Carl 1M **105**
Ashton Gro. LS8: Leeds 4H **69**
Ashton Ho. BD5: B'frd 7A **6**
Ashton Mt. LS8: Leeds 4H **69**
Ashton Pl. LS8: Leeds 4H **69**
Ashton Rd. *HX7: Myth* *3L 95*
(off Thrush Hill Rd.)
LS8: Leeds 3J **69**
WF10: C'frd 6D **108**
Ashton Rd. Ind. Est. LS8: Leeds 3J **69**
Ashton St. BD1: B'frd 7B **64**
LS8: Leeds 3H **69**
WF10: C'frd 5D **108**
Ashton Ter. LS8: Leeds 4H **69**
WF3: Rob H 9K **87**
Ashton Vw. LS8: Leeds 4H **69**
Ashton Wlk. BD10: B'frd 8E **46**
Ash Tree App. LS14: Leeds 2E **70**
Ash Tree Av. BD13: Thorn 8A **62**
Ash Tree Cl. LS14: Leeds 1E **70**
Ash Tree Fold WF8: D'ton 7C **130**
Ash Tree Gdns. HX2: Mix 8J **79**
LS14: Leeds 1E **70**
WF6: Alt 9G **107**
Ash Tree Gro. LS14: Leeds 1E **70**
Ashtree Gro. BD7: B'frd 3L **81**
LS25: Kip 4B **90**
Ash Tree Pk. LS25: Kip 4B **90**
Ash Tree Rd. HX2: Mix 8J **79**
Ash Tree Vw. *LS14: Leeds* *1E 70*
(off Stanks Gdns.)
Ash Tree Wlk. *LS14: Leeds* *1E 70*
(off Ash Tree Gdns.)
LS24: Tad 7N **39**
LS29: Burl W 8C **16**
Ashtree Way WF11: Ferr 6M **109**
Ash Vw. LS6: Leeds 1N **67**
WF3: E Ard 5E **104**
Ash Vs. LS15: Leeds 2E **70**
Ashville Av. LS6: Leeds 3N **67**
Ashville Cft. HX2: Hal 4K **97**
Ashville Gdns. HX2: Hal 4K **97**
Ashville Gro. HX2: Hal 3K **97**
LS6: Leeds 3N **67**
Ashville Rd. LS4: Leeds 3N **67**
LS6: Leeds 3N **67**
Ashville St. HX3: Hal 3N **97**
Ashville Ter. BD22: Oak 5D **42**
LS6: Leeds 3N **67**
LS28: Fars *4A 66*
(off New St.)
Ashville Vw. LS6: Leeds 4A **68**
Ash Wlk. HD7: Golc 5D **136**
Ash Way LS23: T Arch 8J **25**

Ashwell Cl. S72: Shaf 6K **161**
Ashwell La. BD9: B'frd 2M **63**
Ashwell Rd. BD8: B'frd 5N **63**
BD9: B'frd 2M **63**
Ashwood LS14: Leeds 6C **52**
Ashwood Cl. HD2: Hud 8A **120**
Ashwood Ct. WF5: Oss 2M **123**
WF6: Norm 1J **127**
WF9: Fitz 7A **146**
Ashwood Dr. BD20: Rid 7N **27**
LS27: Gil 6E **84**
Ashwood Gdns. LS27: Gil 6E **84**
Ashwood Grange WF4: Dur 4G **143**
Ashwood Grn. WF4: H'cft 1J **161**
Ashwood Gro. LS27: Gil 6F **84**
WF4: Horb 9E **124**
Ashwood Hgts. WF4: M'twn 3L **141**
Ashwood Mt. WF9: Fitz 7A **146**
Ashwood Pde. *LS27: Gil* *6E 84*
(off Ashwood Gdns.)
WF4: Hol 7H **143**
Ashwood St. BD4: B'frd 4H **83**
Ashwood Ter. LS6: Leeds 2B **68**
Ashwood Vs. LS6: Leeds 2B **68**
WF8: Pon *3J 129*
(off Banks Av.)
Ashworth Cl. WF13: Dew 3F **122**
Ashworth Gdns. WF13: Dew 3F **122**
Ashworth Grn. WF13: Dew 3F **122**
Ashworth Pl. BD6: B'frd 4B **82**
Ashworth Rd. WF8: Pon 9L **109**
WF13: Dew 3F **122**
Ashworth Sq. WF1: Wake 1L **9** (3M **125**)
Askam Av. WF8: Pon 8M **109**
Asket Av. LS14: Leeds 1N **69**
Asket Cl. LS14: Leeds 9N **51**
Asket Cres. LS14: Leeds 1N **69**
Asket Dr. LS14: Leeds 9N **51**
Asket Gdns. LS8: Leeds 9M **51**
Asket Gth. LS14: Leeds 1N **69**
Asket Grn. LS14: Leeds 9N **51**
Asket Hill LS8: Leeds 8M **51**
Asket Pl. LS14: Leeds 1N **69**
Asket Wlk. LS14: Leeds 1N **69**
Askey Av. LS27: Morl 2L **103**
Askey Cres. LS27: Morl 2L **103**
Askham Gro. WF9: Upt 2D **164**
Askham Rd. WF10: C'frd 3K **109**
Askrigg Ct. LS29: Men 6F **30**
Askrigg Dr. BD2: B'frd 3F **64**
ASKWITH 4D **16**
Askwith La. LS21: Askw 4D **16**
Aspden St. OL14: Tod 6K **93**
Aspect 14 LS7: Leeds 3G **5** (5E **68**)
Aspect Gdns. LS28: Pud 6N **65**
Aspect Ter. LS28: Pud 6N **65**
Aspen Cl. BD19: Gom 3M **101**
BD21: Keigh 2L **43**
WF2: Wake 3J **125**
Aspen Ct. HD8: Eml 2F **156**
WF3: Ting 3M **103**
Aspen Grn. LS14: S'cft 8D **36**
Aspen Gro. HX3: North 9F **80**
WF13: Dew 3E **122**
Aspen Mt. LS16: Leeds 5H **49**
Aspen Ri. BD15: All 2E **62**
Aspen Way WF10: C'frd 8F **108**
Aspinalls Fold HX5: Ell 5H **119**
Aspinall St. HX7: Myth 3M **95**
Aspire Citygate BD5: B'frd 7A **6** (9C **64**)
ASPLEY 6E **8** (5A **138**)
Aspley Hgts. HD5: Hud 5B **138**
Aspley Pl. HD1: Hud 5D **8** (4N **137**)
Asprey Dr. BD15: All 6G **62**
Asquith Av. LS27: Morl 7H **85**
Asquith Av. Bus. Pk. LS27: Gil 7H **85**
Asquith Bottom HX6: Sow B 9H **97**
Asquith Bldgs. *BD12: O'haw* *8D 82*
(off Cleckheaton Rd.)
Asquith Cl. LS27: Morl 8J **85**
Asquith Ct. HX2: Hal 5K **97**
Asquith Dr. LS27: Morl 8J **85**
Asquith Flds. WF17: Bat 6B **102**
Asquith St. WF17: Birs 2E **102**
Asquith Ter. *HX6: Sow B* *9H 97*
(off Scar Head Rd.)
Assembly St. LS2: Leeds 7G **5** (7E **68**)
WF6: Norm 1H **127**
Assisi Pl. LS10: Leeds 1G **87**
Asthall Cl. BD21: Keigh 9H **27**
Astley Av. LS26: Swil 4H **89**
Astley La. LS26: Swil 4J **89**
Astley La. Ind. Est. LS26: Swil 5J **89**
Astley Way LS26: Swil 5J **89**
Aston Av. LS13: Leeds 4G **67**
Aston Chase WF9: Hems 3D **162**
Aston Cl. WF15: Liv 1K **121**
Aston Ct. WF5: Oss 7C **124**
Aston Cres. LS13: Leeds 4H **67**
Aston Dr. LS13: Leeds 4H **67**
Aston Gro. LS13: Leeds 4H **67**
Aston Mt. LS13: Leeds 4H **67**
Aston Pl. LS13: Leeds 4H **67**
Aston Rd. BD5: B'frd 2C **82**
LS13: Leeds 4G **67**
Aston St. LS13: Leeds 4G **67**
Aston Ter. LS13: Leeds 4H **67**
Aston Vw. LS13: Leeds 4G **67**
Astor Gro. LS13: Leeds 4D **66**
Astoria Ct. LS8: Leeds 1J **69**
WF6: Norm 2M **127**
Astor St. LS13: Leeds 4D **66**
Astra Bus. Pk. LS11: Leeds 3E **86**
Astral Av. HX3: Hip 4J **99**
Astral Cl. HX3: Hip 4J **99**
Astral Vw. BD6: B'frd 3M **81**
Astronomy Centre, The 8B **92**
Astura Ct. LS7: Leeds 1D **68**
Astwick Cl. BD20: E Mor 7N **27**
Atalanta Ter. HX2: Hal 8L **97**
Atha Cl. LS11: Leeds 4C **86**
Atha Cres. LS11: Leeds 4C **86**
Atha Ho. LS2: Leeds 2E **4**
Atha St. LS11: Leeds 4C **86**
Athelstan La. LS21: Otley 7L **17**

Athene Dr.—Bk. Cross Flatts Cres.

Athene Dr. HD4: Hud 7A 138
Athens LS20: Guis 7H 31
ATHERSLEY NORTH 9A 160
Atherstone Rd. BD15: All 6G 63
Atherton La. HD6: Ras 3N 119
Athlone Dr. WF12: Dew 1H 123
Athlone Gro. LS12: Leeds 7M 67
Athlone Ri. LS25: Gar 7B 72
Athlone St. LS12: Leeds 7M 67
Athlone Ter. LS12: Leeds 7M 67
Athol Cl. HX3: Hal 1N 97
Athol Cres. HX3: Hal 1N 97
Athold Dr. WF5: Oss 6B 124
Athold St. WF5: Oss 6B 124
Athol Gdns. HX3: Hal 1N 97
Athol Grn. HX3: Hal 1N 97
Athol Mt. HX3: Hal 1N 97
Athol Rd. BD9: B'frd 4N 63
HX3: Hal 1N 97
Athol St. BD21: Keigh 7L 27
HX3: Hal 1N 97
Atkinson Ct. WF6: Norm 2H 127
ATKINSON HILL 1H 87
Atkinson La. WF8: Pon 1M 129
Atkinson Quay LS10: Leeds 9G 69
Atkinson's Ct. HX1: Hal 3K 7 (4B 98)
Atkinson St. BD18: Ship 7N 45
LS10: Leeds 9G 69
Atlanta St. LS13: Leeds 4D 66
Atlantic Apartments LS1: Leeds 7D 4
Atlas Mill Caravan Pk.
HD6: Brigh 1M 119
Atlas Mill Rd. HD6: Brigh 1M 119
Atlas St. BD8: B'frd 5N 63
Attlee Av. WF4: H'cft 9K 145
Attlee Cres. WF2: Wake 3N 143
Attlee Gro. WF1: Out 8L 105
Attlee St. WF6: Norm 3J 127
Attorney Ct. HD9: H'frth 5N 169
Auckland Rd. BD6: B'frd 4M 81
Audby Cl. LS22: Weth 2N 23
Audby Ct. LS22: Weth 3N 23
Audby La. LS22: Weth 2N 23
Audrey St. WF5: Oss 7A 124
Audsley's Yd. WF4: Horb 1A 142
Augusta Ct. WF2: Wake 6G 125
Augusta Dr. WF6: Norm 3L 127
Aurelia Ho. BD8: B'frd 4A 64
AUSTHORPE 6F 70
Austhorpe Av. LS15: Leeds 7F 70
Austhorpe Ct. LS15: Leeds 7G 70
Austhorpe Dr. LS15: Leeds 7F 70
Austhorpe Gdns. LS15: Leeds 6G 70
Austhorpe Gro. LS15: Leeds 7F 70
Austhorpe La. LS15: Leeds 5E 70
Austhorpe Rd. LS15: Leeds 4D 70
Austhorpe Vw. LS15: Leeds 6E 70
Austin Av. HD6: Brigh 8L 99
Austin Rd. WF10: C'frd 4K 109
Austin St. BD21: Keigh 8K 27
Austwick Cl. S75: Map 7J 159
Authorpe Rd. LS6: Leeds 9B 50
Autumn Av. LS6: Leeds 4A 68
LS22: Weth 1M 23
Autumn Cl. S71: Roys 6C 160
Autumn Cres. LS18: Hors 8G 48
Autumn Gro. LS6: Leeds 4A 68
Autumn Pl. LS6: Leeds 4A 68
Autumn St. HX1: Hal 7M 97
LS6: Leeds 4A 68
Autumn Ter. LS6: Leeds 4A 68
Auty Cres. WF3: S'ley 7A 106
Auty M. WF3: S'ley 7A 106
Auty Sq. LS27: Morl 1L 103
Avalon Ri. WF9: S Elm 7N 163
Avenel Rd. BD15: All 5G 62
Avenel Ter. BD15: All 6G 63
Avenham Way BD3: B'frd 2E 6 (6E 64)
Avens Cl. WF8: Pon 4K 129
Avenue, The BD10: B'frd 4J 47
BD14: Clay 1F 80
BD15: Wils 2C 62
BD16: Cot 7G 44
BD17: Esh 4J 47
HD5: Hud 5B 138
HX3: Hip 4J 99
LS8: Leeds 7J 51
LS9: Leeds 7K 5 (7G 68)
LS15: Leeds 3E 70
(Sandbed La.)
LS15: Leeds, Swil 3E 88
(Newsam Grn. Rd.)
LS15: Scho 7G 53
LS17: Hare 2J 35
LS17: Leeds 2B 50
LS18: Hors 6C 48
LS22: Coll 8H 23
LS24: Wig 4N 25
S71: Roys 5F 160
WF1: Out 8J 105
WF3: Ting 4C 104
WF4: Croft 1F 144
WF4: W Bret 3A 158
WF13: Dew 9C 102
WF17: Bat 5D 102
WF17: Birs 3B 102
(not continuous)
Avenue A LS23: T Arch 6H 25
Avenue B LS23: T Arch 8G 25
(Street 1)
LS23: T Arch 7H 25
(Street 5)
Avenue C LS23: T Arch 8H 25
Avenue Ct. LS17: Leeds 2B 50
Avenue Cres. LS8: Leeds 2G 69
Avenue D LS23: T Arch 9H 25
Avenue Des Hirondelles LS21: Pool 2F 32
Avenue E East LS23: T Arch 8J 25
Avenue E West LS23: T Arch 9H 25
Avenue F LS23: T Arch 8J 25
Avenue Gdns. LS17: Leeds 2C 50
Avenue Hill LS8: Leeds 2G 69
Avenue Lawns LS17: Leeds 2B 50
Avenue No. 1 HD6: Ras 2M 119
Avenue No. 2 HD6: Ras 2M 119
Avenue Rd. BD5: B'frd 2D 82
WF2: Wake 1N 143
Avenue St. BD4: B'frd 4H 83
Avenue Ter. LS19: Yead 9A 32
LS21: Otley 1K 31
WF8: Pon 3G 129
Avenue Victoria LS8: Leeds 7J 51
Avenue Wlk. LS2: Leeds 1B 4 (3C 68)
LS6: Leeds 3C 68
Averingcliffe Rd. BD10: B'frd 9H 47
Avery Tulip Ct. BD12: Low M 7A 82
(off Edward Turner Cl.)
Aviary Gro. LS12: Leeds 6M 67
Aviary Mt. LS12: Leeds 6M 67
Aviary Pl. LS12: Leeds 6M 67
Aviary Rd. LS12: Leeds 6M 67
Aviary Row LS12: Leeds 6M 67
Aviary St. LS12: Leeds 6M 67
Aviary Ter. LS12: Leeds 6M 67
Aviary Vw. LS12: Leeds 6M 67
Avison Rd. HD4: Hud 7F 136
Avison Yd. WF1: Wake 5L 9 (5M 125)
Avocet Cl. BD8: B'frd 7H 63
Avocet Gth. LS10: Leeds 8F 86
Avon Cl. LS17: Shad 3A 52
Avon Ct. LS17: Shad 2N 51
Avon Cft. WF5: Oss 6M 123
(not continuous)
Avondale BD20: Keigh 8G 26
Avondale Ct. LS17: Leeds 4F 50
Avondale Cres. BD18: Ship 8M 45
Avondale Dr. S71: Carl 8D 160
WF3: S'ley 7N 105
Avondale Gro. BD18: Ship 8M 45
Avondale Mt. BD18: Ship 8M 45
Avondale Pl. HX3: Hal 8A 98
Avondale Rd. BD18: Ship 8K 45
Avondale St. LS13: Leeds 5F 66
WF2: Wake 8J 9 (7L 125)
Avondale Vs. LS14: T'ner 4F 52
Avondale Way WF2: Wake 8K 9 (7L 125)
Avon Dr. LS25: Gar 8N 71
Avon Gth. LS22: Weth 4K 23
Avon Wlk. WF7: F'stne 4D 128
Axeminster Dr. HD6: B Bri 5N 99
Axis Ct. LS27: Gil 8H 85
Aydonway HX3: She 6K 81
Aygill Av. BD9: B'frd 3J 63
Aylesbury St. BD21: Keigh 3G 43
Aylesford Mt. LS15: Leeds 3G 71
Aylesham Ind. Est.
BD12: Low M 7B 82
Aynholme Cl. LS29: Add 1M 13
Aynholme Dr. LS29: Add 1M 13
Aynsley Gro. BD15: All 4G 62
Ayres Dr. HD4: Hud 7F 136
Ayresome Av. LS8: Leeds 5J 51
Ayresome Oval BD15: All 7F 62
Ayresome Ter. LS8: Leeds 5H 51
Ayre Vw. HX7: Wads 7J 77
(off Akroyd La.)
Ayreville Dr. HX3: She 7H 81
Ayrton Cres. BD16: Bgly 4F 44
Aysgarth Av. HX3: Hip 6M 99
Aysgarth Cl. BD12: Wyke 2A 100
LS9: Leeds 7H 69
WF2: Wake 8F 124
Aysgarth Ct. LS29: Men 6F 30
Aysgarth Cres. HX2: Mt T 1G 97
Aysgarth Dr. LS9: Leeds 7H 69
WF2: Wake 8F 124
Aysgarth Fold LS10: Leeds 9E 86
Aysgarth Pl. LS9: Leeds 7M 5 (7H 69)
Aysgarth Rd. HD4: Hud 8N 137
WF17: Bat 7D 102
Aysgarth Wlk. LS9: Leeds 7M 5 (7H 69)
Ayton Cl. BD3: B'frd 2F 6 (6E 64)
Ayton Ho. BD4: B'frd 4K 83
Ayton Rd. HD3: Hud 4D 136
Azealea Ct. BD3: B'frd 6F 64
(not continuous)

B

Baby Ho. Hill La. HX7: P Wel 1G 77
Bachelor La. LS18: Hors 6F 48
Bk. Ada St. BD21: Keigh 9G 27
(off Devonshire St. W.)
Bk. Aire St. HD6: Ras 2N 119
(off Victoria St.)
Bk. Aireview Ter. BD21: Keigh 1L 43
Bk. Aireville St. BD20: Keigh 6G 27
Bk. Airlie Av. LS8: Leeds 2H 69
(off Airlie Av.)
Bk. Airlie Pl. LS8: Leeds 2H 69
(off Airlie Pl.)
Bk. Albert Gro. LS6: Leeds 9N 49
Bk. Albert Ter. LS6: Leeds 4A 68
(off Springrove Ter.)
Bk. Alcester Pl. LS8: Leeds 2H 69
(off Alcester Pl.)
Bk. Alcester Rd. LS8: Leeds 2H 69
(off Alcester Rd.)
Bk. Alcester Ter. LS8: Leeds 2H 69
(off Hill Top Av.)
Bk. Allerton Ter. LS7: Leeds 8F 50
Bk. Alma St. LS19: Yead 9N 31
(off Alma St.)
Bk. Anderton St. WF1: Wake 8N 125
Bk. Ann St. BD13: Denh 5K 61
Bk. Archery Pl. LS2: Leeds 1D 4
Bk. Archery Rd. LS2: Leeds 2E 4
Bk. Archery St. LS2: Leeds 2E 4
Bk. Archery Ter. LS2: Leeds 2D 4
Bk. Armitage Rd.
HD4: Arm B 1K 153
Bk. Ash Gro. LS6: Leeds 3B 68
Bk. Ashgrove W. BD7: B'frd 8B 64
Bk. Ashley Av. LS9: Leeds 4J 69
(off Ashley Rd.)
Bk. Ashley St. LS9: Leeds 4J 69
(off Ashley Rd.)
Bk. Ashville Av. LS6: Leeds 3A 68
(off Cardigan Rd.)
Bk. Ashville Gro. LS6: Leeds 3N 67
(off Cardigan Rd.)
Bk. Ashville Rd. LS6: Leeds 3N 67
(off Cardigan Rd.)
Bk. Ashville Ter. LS6: Leeds 3N 67
(off Cardigan Rd.)
Bk. Ashwood Ter. LS6: Leeds 2B 68
Bk. Aston Pl. LS13: Leeds 4H 67
(off Aston Rd.)
Bk. Aston Rd. LS13: Leeds 4G 67
Bk. Aston St. LS13: Leeds 4G 67
(off Ashton Mt.)
Bk. Aston Ter. LS13: Leeds 4H 67
(off Aston Av.)
Bk. Aston Vw. LS13: Leeds 4H 67
(off Aston Av.)
Bk. Athlone Av. LS12: Leeds 7M 67
Bk. Athlone Gro. LS12: Leeds 7M 67
(off Athlone St.)
Bk. Athlone Ter. LS12: Leeds 7M 67
(off Athlone St.)
Bk. Atlanta St. LS13: Leeds 4D 66
(off Fairfield Av.)
Bk. Austhorpe Rd. LS15: Leeds 4D 70
(off Austhorpe Rd.)
Bk. Autumn Rd. LS6: Leeds 4A 68
(off Autumn Gro.)
Bk. Autumn Ter. LS6: Leeds 4A 68
(off Alexandra Rd.)
Bk. Aviary Rd. LS12: Leeds 6M 67
(off Aviary Gro.)
Bk. Aylesbury St. BD21: Keigh 3G 43
(off Oakfield Rd.)
Bk. Bailey's Pl. LS16: Leeds 9N 49
Bk. Baker St. BD18: Ship 7M 45
Bk. Baldovan Ter. LS8: Leeds 2H 69
(off Baldovan Ter.)
Bk. Balfour St. BD16: Bgly 5E 44
BD21: Keigh 1H 43
Bk. Bank St. WF10: C'frd 4D 108
Bk. Bank Ter. LS28: Stan 4B 66
Bk. Banstead St. LS8: Leeds 3H 69
(off Harehills Rd.)
Bk. Barden Pl. LS12: Leeds 7K 67
(off Conference Rd.)
Bk. Barkly Gro. LS11: Leeds 3C 86
(off Theodore St.)
Bk. Barkly Pde. LS11: Leeds 4C 86
(off Barkly Dr.)
Bk. Barkly Ter. LS11: Leeds 3C 86
(off Barkly Dr.)
Bk. Barrowby Vw. LS15: Leeds 7F 70
Bk. Bath Rd. LS13: Leeds 4F 66
(off Cross Bath Rd.)
Bk. Beacon St. HD2: Hud 1M 137
Bk. Beamsley Gro. LS6: Leeds 4A 68
(off Harold Gro.)
Bk. Beamsley Mt. LS6: Leeds 4A 68
(off Royal Pk. Rd.)
Bk. Beamsley Ter. LS6: Leeds 4A 68
(off Royal Pk. Rd.)
Bk. Beaumont St. WF17: Bat 9F 102
Bk. Beck La. LS29: Add 9M 11
Bk. Beech St. BD16: Bgly 5E 44
Bk. Beech Ter. HD1: Hud 1N 137
Bk. Beechwood Gro. LS4: Leeds 3N 67
Bk. Beechwood Rd. LS4: Leeds 3N 67
(off Beechwood Pl.)
Bk. Bellbrooke Gro. LS9: Leeds 4K 69
(off Bellbrooke St.)
Bk. Bellbrooke Pl. LS9: Leeds 4K 69
(off Bellbrooke St.)
Bk. Bellbrooke Ter. LS9: Leeds 4K 69
(off Coldcotes Av.)
Bk. Belvedere Av. LS11: Leeds 3D 86
(off Harlech Rd.)
Bk. Bentley Av. LS6: Leeds 9B 50
(off Bentley Mt.)
Bk. Bentley Gro. LS6: Leeds 9B 50
(off Bentley Mt.)
Bk. Berkeley Av. LS8: Leeds 3J 69
(off Berkeley Rd.)
Bk. Berkeley Ter. LS8: Leeds 3J 69
(off Berkeley Rd.)
Bk. Blackwood Gro. HX1: Hal 4M 97
Bk. Blenheim Av. LS2: Leeds 1E 4 (4D 68)
Bk. Blenheim Mt. BD8: B'frd 4A 64
Bk. Blenheim Ter. LS2: Leeds 2D 4 (4D 68)
Bk. Blythe Av. BD8: B'frd 6M 63
Bk. Boundary Ter. LS3: Leeds 5A 68
(off Woodsley Rd.)
Bk. Bower Rd. HX5: Ell 4F 118
Bk. Bowling Grn. Rd. HX4: Stainl 8M 117
Bk. Bowman St. WF1: Wake 8A 126
Bk. Bradshaw Rd. HD9: Hon 6L 153
Bk. Branch Pl. LS12: Leeds 1K 85
(off Branch Rd.)
Bk. Breary Av. LS18: Hors 6G 49
Bk. Breary Ter. LS18: Hors 6G 49
(off Breary Av.)
Back Briggate BD20: Sils 7E 12
Bk. Broad La. LS13: Leeds 2G 66
Bk. Broomfield Cres. LS6: Leeds 2N 67
Bk. Broomfield Pl. LS6: Leeds 3N 67
(off Newport Rd.)
Bk. Broomfield Rd. BD21: Keigh 9H 27
LS6: Leeds 3N 67
(off Newport Rd.)
Bk. Broomfield St. BD21: Keigh 9H 27
Bk. Broughton Av. LS9: Leeds 4J 69
(off Foundry App.)
Bk. Broughton Ter. LS9: Leeds 4J 69
(off Foundry App.)
Bk. Brudenell Gro. LS6: Leeds 4B 68
(off Royal Pk. Rd.)
Bk. Brudenell Mt. LS6: Leeds 3A 68
(off Royal Pk. Rd.)
Bk. Brudenell Rd. LS6: Leeds 3A 68
(off Thornville Rd.)
Bk. Brunswick St. LS2: Leeds 4G 5 (5E 68)
WF13: Dew 2D 122
Bk. Burchett Gro. LS6: Leeds 2C 68
(off Hartley Av.)
Bk. Burchett Pl. LS6: Leeds 2C 68
(off Hartley Av.)
Bk. Burley Hill LS4: Leeds 4M 67
Bk. Burley Lodge Rd. LS6: Leeds 4A 68
(off Chiswick St.)
Bk. Burley Lodge Ter. LS6: Leeds 5A 68
(off Burley Lodge Ter.)
Bk. Burley St. LS3: Leeds 5B 4
Bk. Burlington Pl. LS11: Leeds 3D 86
(off Tempest Rd.)
Bk. Burlington Rd. LS11: Leeds 3D 86
(off Harlech Av.)
Bk. Burton Cres. LS6: Leeds 9N 49
Bk. Burton Ter. LS11: Leeds 2E 86
Bk. Buxton St. BD21: Keigh 9K 27
(off Chatsworth St.)
Bk. Byrl St. BD21: Keigh 7J 27
(off Hard Ings Rd.)
Bk. Byrom St. OL14: Tod 6K 93
Bk. Caister St. BD21: Keigh 3H 43
(off Oakfield Rd.)
Bk. Caledonia Rd. BD21: Keigh 8K 27
(off Hard Ings Rd.)
Bk. Camberley St. LS11: Leeds 2D 86
(off Camberley St.)
Bk. Carberry Pl. LS6: Leeds 4A 68
(off Carberry Rd.)
Bk. Carberry Rd. LS6: Leeds 4A 68
(off Chiswick St.)
Bk. Carberry Ter. LS6: Leeds 4A 68
(off Carberry Rd.)
Bk. Carlinghow La. WF17: Bat 5B 102
Bk. Carter Mt. LS15: Leeds 6D 70
(off Carter La.)
Bk. Carter Ter. LS15: Leeds 5D 70
(off Carter La.)
Bk. Cartmel Rd. BD21: Keigh 9G 27
(off Devonshire St. W.)
Bk. Castle Rd. BD21: Keigh 8H 27
Bk. Cavendish Rd. BD10: B'frd 8F 46
Bk. Cavendish St. BD21: Keigh 9J 27
Bk. Cavendish Ter. HX1: Hal 3G 7 (5N 97)
Bk. Cecil St. HD1: Hud 5A 8 (4M 137)
Bk. Chapel La. LS6: Leeds 2N 67
(off Broomfield Rd.)
Bk. Chapel St. BD1: B'frd 4D 6 (7D 64)
Bk. Charles St. HD6: Brigh 9M 99
(off Waterloo Rd.)
Bk. Charlton Rd. LS9: Leeds 7J 69
Bk. Chatsworth Rd. LS8: Leeds 3J 69
(off Harehills La.)
Bk. Chestnut Av. LS15: Leeds 4E 70
(off Railway Rd.)
Bk. Chiswick Ter. LS6: Leeds 4A 68
(off Carberry Rd.)
Bk. Christ Chu. Vw.
LS12: Leeds 6L 67
(off Stanningley Rd.)
Bk. Church La. LS5: Leeds 2K 67
(off Hesketh Rd.)
LS16: Leeds 2N 49
Bk. Church Vw. WF1: Wake 9A 126
Bk. Claremont Av. LS3: Leeds 4B 4
Bk. Claremont Gro. LS3: Leeds 4B 4
Bk. Claremont St. LS26: Oul 7D 88
Bk. Claremont Ter. LS3: Leeds 4B 4
Bk. Claremount Ter. HX3: Hal 2B 98
Bk. Clarence Rd. LS18: Hors 8E 48
Bk. Clarence St. HX1: Hal 4H 7 (5A 98)
LS13: Leeds 5F 66
Bk. Clarendon Pl. HX1: Hal 5N 97
Bk. Clarkson Vw. LS6: Leeds 2C 68
(off Quarry St.)
Bk. Cliffe Ter. BD21: Keigh 3J 43
Bk. Cliff Mt. LS6: Leeds 2C 68
(off Cliff Mt. Ter.)
Bk. Clifton Rd. HD1: Hud 3J 137
Bk. Clifton Ter. LS9: Leeds 4K 69
(off Clifton Av.)
Bk. Clipston Av. LS6: Leeds 9B 50
(off Clipston Av.)
Bk. Clock Vw. St. BD20: Keigh 6H 27
(off Royd St.)
Back Cl. Lea HD6: Ras 2M 119
(off Close Lea)
Back Clough HX3: North 2F 98
Bk. Clovelly Pl. LS11: Leeds 2D 86
(off Rowland Rd.)
Bk. Colenso Mt. LS11: Leeds 1B 86
(off Cleveleys Av.)
Bk. Colenso Rd. BD21: Keigh 7L 27
(off Cornwall Rd.)
LS11: Leeds 1B 86
(off Cleveleys Av.)
Bk. Colton Rd. LS12: Leeds 7M 67
Bk. Colwyn Vw. LS11: Leeds 3D 86
(off Colwyn Av.)
Bk. Commercial St. HX1: Hal 4K 7
OL14: Tod 7L 93
Bk. Compton St. BD21: Keigh 8K 27
(off Compton St.)
Bk. Conway St. LS8: Leeds 3H 69
(off Harehills Rd.)
Bk. Cowper Gro. LS9: Leeds 3J 69
(off Ashley Rd.)
Bk. Cowper St. LS7: Leeds 3G 68
(off Cross Cowper St.)
Bk. Craggwood Rd. LS18: Hors 8F 48
Bk. Crag Rd. BD18: Ship 8A 46
Bk. Cranbrook Av. LS11: Leeds 2C 86
(off Wickham St.)
Bk. Cranbrook Ter. LS11: Leeds 2C 86
(off Hird St.)
Bk. Crescent, The LS2: Leeds 3C 68
(off Woodhouse La.)
Back Cft. HX6: Rish 1C 134
Back Cft. Ho. La. BD20: Keigh 6G 27
Bk. Cromer Av. BD21: Keigh 2H 43
(off Foster Rd.)
Bk. Cromer Gro. BD21: Keigh 3H 43
(off Foster Rd.)
Bk. Cromer Ter. LS2: Leeds 2C 4 (4C 68)
Bk. Cromwell Ter. HX1: Hal 3H 7 (5A 98)
Bk. Cross Flatts Av. LS11: Leeds 3C 86
(off Theodore St.)
Bk. Cross Flatts Cres. LS11: Leeds 3B 86
(off Wooler St.)

A-Z West Yorkshire Atlas 181

Bk. Cross Flatts Gro.—Bk. Nice Vw.

Bk. Cross Flatts Gro. LS11: Leeds 3C 86 (off Wooler Dr.)
Bk. Cross Flatts Mt. LS11: Leeds 3C 86 (off Wooler Gro.)
Bk. Cross Flatts Pl. LS11: Leeds 3B 86 (off Wooler St.)
Bk. Cross Flatts Row LS11: Leeds 3B 86 (off Wooler St.)
Bk. Cross Grn. La. LS9: Leeds 8H 69 (off Cross Grn. La.)
LS9: Leeds 8H 69 (off Cross Grn. Rd.)
Bk. Cross La. HX5: Ell 5D 118 (off Cross La.)
Bk. Cunliffe Rd. LS29: I'ly 5G 14
Bk. Dale St. BD18: Ship 8N 45 (off Dale St.)
Bk. Dalton Gro. LS11: Leeds 3C 86 (off Cross Flatts Av.)
Bk. Dalton Rd. LS11: Leeds 3C 86
Bk. Dawlish Av. LS9: Leeds 6K 69 (off Ivy Av.)
Bk. Dawlish Mt. LS9: Leeds 6K 69 (off Ivy Av.)
Bk. Dawlish Rd. LS9: Leeds 6K 69 (off Dawlish Cres.)
Bk. De Lacy Mt. LS5: Leeds 1K 67 (off Morris La.)
Bk. Delph Mt. LS6: Leeds 2C 68 (off Delph La.)
Bk. Dent St. LS9: Leeds 8M 5
Back Der St. OL14: Tod 7L 93
Bk. Devonshire La. LS8: Leeds 5J 51
Bk. Dewsbury Dr. LS11: Leeds 3E 86 (off Dewsbury Rd.)
Bk. Dorset Mt. LS8: Leeds 2J 69 (off Dorset St.)
Bk. Dorset Rd. LS8: Leeds 2J 69 (off Dorset Av.)
Bk. Dorset Ter. LS8: Leeds 3J 69 (off Harehills La.)
Bk. Dudley Hill Rd. BD2: B'frd 4F 64
Bk. Duke of York St. WF1: Wake 2L 9 (4M 125)
Bk. Duke St. WF7: F'stne 5C 128
Bk. East Pk. Rd. LS9: Leeds 7J 69 (off Garton Rd.)
Bk. Eaton St. BD21: Keigh 3G 43 (off Oakfield Rd.)
Bk. Ecclesburn Gro. LS9: Leeds 7K 69 (off Ivy St.)
Bk. Ecclesburn St. LS9: Leeds 7J 69 (off Park Pde.)
Bk. Edensor Rd. BD21: Keigh 9G 27 (off Devonshire St.)
Bk. Edinburgh Rd. LS12: Leeds 6K 67 (off Moorfield Rd.)
Bk. Eldon Rd. HD1: Hud 3J 137
Bk. Elford Pl. LS8: Leeds 3H 69 (off Roundhay Rd., not continuous)
Bk. Elizabeth St. BD5: B'frd 7A 6 (9C 64)
Bk. Ellers Gro. LS8: Leeds 2H 69 (off Ellers Gro.)
Bk. Ellers Rd. LS8: Leeds 2H 69 (off Ellers Rd.)
Bk. Elmfield Ter. HX1: Hal 8H 7 (7A 98)
Bk. Elsworth St. LS12: Leeds 7N 67
Bk. Emily St. BD21: Keigh 8J 27 (off Lawkholme La.)
Bk. Eric St. BD21: Keigh 8J 27 (off Lawkholme La.)
LS13: Leeds 1F 66
Bk. Eshald Pl. LS26: W'frd 7E 88
Bk. Esmond Ter. LS12: Leeds 7M 67
Bk. Estcourt Av. LS6: Leeds 1M 67 (off Canterbury Dr.)
Bk. Estcourt Ter. LS6: Leeds 2M 67 (off Canterbury Dr.)
Bk. Eversley Mt. HX2: Hal 6L 97
Bk. Fairford Pl. LS11: Leeds 2E 86
Bk. Featherbank Ter. LS18: Hors 8E 48
Bk. Ferguson St. HX1: Hal 4K 7 (6B 98)
Back Fld. BD13: Thorn 8D 62 (off Market St.)
Bk. Fitzwilliam St. HD1: Hud 4A 8 (4L 137)
Bk. Florist St. BD21: Keigh 7L 27 (off Athol St.)
Back Fold BD14: Clay 9G 63
HX6: Ripp 7D 116 (off Back La.)
Bk. Foster Rd. BD21: Keigh 3H 43 (off Oakfield Rd.)
Bk. Garden St. WF10: C'frd 6D 108
Bk. Garton Rd. LS9: Leeds 7J 69 (off East Pk. Rd.)
Bk. Garton Ter. LS9: Leeds 7J 69 (off East Pk. Pde.)
Bk. Gathorne St. LS7: Leeds 1L 5
Bk. Gerrard St. HX1: Hal 4H 7 (5A 98)
Bk. Giles St. Nth. BD5: B'frd 7A 6 (9B 64)
Bk. Giles St. Sth. BD5: B'frd 8A 6 (9B 64)
Bk. Gillett La. LS26: Rothw 8A 88
Bk. Girlington Rd. BD8: B'frd 5L 63 (not continuous)
Bk. Gladstone Rd. HX1: Hal 3G 7 (5A 98)
Bk. Gladstone St. BD16: Bgly 5E 44
Bk. Glebe Ter. LS16: Leeds 9N 49 (off Weetwood La.)
Bk. Glen Ter. HX1: Hal 8J 7 (7A 98)
Bk. Glenthorpe Ter. LS9: Leeds 6J 69 (off Walford Rd.)
Bk. Glossop St. LS6: Leeds 2D 68 (off Elm St.)
Bk. Gooder La. HD6: Ras 2N 119
Bk. Gordon St. WF1: Wake 9A 126
Bk. Gordon Ter. LS6: Leeds 9B 50 (off Gordon Vw.)
Bk. Graham Gro. LS4: Leeds 3N 67
Bk. Granby Gro. LS6: Leeds 2N 67 (off Granby Rd.)
Bk. Grange Av. LS7: Leeds 2F 68 (off Grange Av.)
Bk. Grange Cres. LS7: Leeds 2G 68 (off Hamilton Ter.)
Bk. Grange Ter. LS7: Leeds 2F 68 (off Nassau Pl.)
Bk. Grange Vw. LS7: Leeds 2G 68 (off Nassau Pl.)
Bk. Grantley St. WF1: Wake 4L 9 (5M 125)
Bk. Grant St. BD21: Keigh 9G 26
Bk. Grassington Ter. BD21: Keigh 8J 27 (off Plover St.)
Bk. Gt. Russell St. BD7: B'frd 7A 64
Bk. Greaves St. BD5: B'frd 2B 82 (off Greaves St.)
Back Grn. HD3: Outl 2N 135
LS27: Chur 6M 85
Bk. Greenhead Rd. HD1: Hud 5A 8 (4L 137)
Bk. Greenhow Wlk. LS4: Leeds 4N 67 (off Greenhow Wlk.)
Bk. Greenmount Ter. LS11: Leeds 2D 86 (off Greenmount La.)
Bk. Grosvenor Ter. HX1: Hal 3G 7 (5N 97)
LS6: Leeds 2B 68 (off Cliff La.)
Bk. Grouse St. BD21: Keigh 8K 27 (off Parson St.)
Bk. Grove Gdns. LS6: Leeds 9A 50 (off Grove Av.)
Bk. Grovehall Av. LS11: Leeds 4C 86
Bk. Grovehall Dr. LS11: Leeds 4C 86
Bk. Grove Rd. LS29: I'ly 5G 14
Bk. Haigh Av. LS26: Rothw 6M 87
Bk. Haigh St. LS26: Rothw 6L 87
Bk. Haigh Vw. LS26: Rothw 6L 87
Bk. Halliday Gro. LS12: Leeds 6K 67
Bk. Halliday Pl. LS12: Leeds 6K 67
Bk. Hambleton St. WF1: Wake 2K 9
Bk. Hamilton Av. LS7: Leeds 2G 68 (off Nassau Pl.)
Bk. Hamilton Vw. LS7: Leeds 2G 68 (off Hamilton Ter.)
Bk. Hanson La. HX1: Hal 4L 97 (off Hanson La., not continuous)
Bk. Harehills Av. LS7: Leeds 2G 68 (off Nassau Pl.)
Bk. Harehills Pk. Vw. LS9: Leeds 4K 69 (off Foundry App.)
Bk. Harehills Pl. LS8: Leeds 3H 69 (off Harehills Pl.)
Bk. Harehills Rd. LS8: Leeds 3H 69 (off Harehills Pl.)
Bk. Hares Av. LS8: Leeds 2H 69 (off Hares Av.)
Bk. Hares Mt. LS8: Leeds 2G 69 (off Hares Rd.)
Bk. Hares Ter. LS8: Leeds 2H 69 (off Hares Ter.)
Bk. Hares Vw. LS8: Leeds 2H 69 (off Hares Rd.)
Bk. Harold Gro. LS6: Leeds 4A 68 (off Cardigan Rd.)
Bk. Hartley Av. LS6: Leeds 2D 68 (off Burchett Ter.)
Bk. Hartley Gro. LS6: Leeds 2C 68 (off Glossop Vw.)
Bk. Hartley St. LS27: Morl 1M 103
Bk. Hatfeild St. WF1: Wake 2J 9 (4L 125)
Bk. Hawksworth Gro. LS5: Leeds 9G 49
Bk. Headingley Av. LS6: Leeds 1M 67 (off Canterbury Dr.)
Bk. Headingley Mt. LS6: Leeds 1M 67 (off Canterbury Dr.)
Bk. Heathfield Ter. LS6: Leeds 9N 49 (off Heathfield Ter.)
Bk. Heddon St. LS6: Leeds 9A 50 (off Brookfield Rd.)
Bk. Heights Rd. BD13: Thorn 6A 62
Bk. Henrietta St. WF17: Bat 7F 102
Bk. Hessle Av. LS6: Leeds 3A 68 (off Walmsley Rd.)
Bk. Hessle Mt. LS6: Leeds 3A 68 (off Brundenell Rd.)
Bk. Hessle Ter. LS6: Leeds 3A 68 (off Walmsley Rd.)
Bk. Hessle Vw. LS6: Leeds 3A 68 (off Welton Rd.)
Bk. Highbury Ter. LS6: Leeds 9A 50 (off Highbury Mt.)
Bk. Highfield Rd. LS13: Leeds 4G 67 (off Aston Mt.)
Bk. High St. BD13: Thorn 8C 62
LS19: Yead 9M 31
Bk. Highthorne Gro. LS12: Leeds 6K 67 (off Highthorne St.)
Bk. Highthorne St. LS12: Leeds 6K 67 (off Armley Ridge Rd.)
Bk. Hillcrest Av. LS7: Leeds 2G 69 (off Grange Av.)
Bk. Hillcrest Vw. LS7: Leeds 2G 69 (off Hillcrest Pl.)
Bk. Hilltop Av. LS8: Leeds 2H 69 (off Shepherd's La.)
Bk. Hill Top Mt. LS8: Leeds 2H 69 (off Hill Top Mt.)
Bk. Hilton Pl. LS8: Leeds 1H 69 (off Hilton Pl.)
Bk. Hilton Rd. LS8: Leeds 2H 69 (off Avenue Cres.)
Bk. Hird St. BD21: Keigh 1H 43
Backhold HX3: Hal 9D 98
Backhold Av. HX3: Hal 1D 118
Backhold Dr. HX3: Hal 1C 118
Backhold Hall HX3: Hal 9D 98
Backhold La. HX3: Hal 1C 118
Backhold Rd. HX3: Hal 1D 118
Bk. Hollyshaw Ter. LS15: Leeds 6D 70
Bk. Holywell La. LS17: Shad 2M 51
Bk. Honoria St. HD1: Hud 1M 137
Bk. Hope Hall Ter. HX1: Hal 6L 7 (6B 98)
Backhouse La. WF4: Wool 2H 159
Bk. Hovingham Gro. LS8: Leeds 2J 69 (off Sandhurst Mt.)
Bk. Hovingham Mt. LS8: Leeds 2J 69 (off Dorset Av.)
Bk. Hovingham Ter. LS8: Leeds 2J 69 (off Dorset Av.)
Bk. Hyde Gro. BD21: Keigh 8K 27 (off Kirby St.)
Bk. Hyde Ter. LS2: Leeds 3B 4 (5C 68)
Bk. Ibbetson Pl. LS1: Leeds 3D 4
Bk. Ingledew Cres. LS8: Leeds 5K 51
Bk. Irwell St. BD4: B'frd 8F 6 (9E 64)
Bk. Ivy Av. LS9: Leeds 6J 69 (off Ivy Av.)
Bk. Ivy Gro. LS9: Leeds 7K 69 (off Victoria Av.)
Bk. Ivy Mt. LS9: Leeds 6J 69 (off Ivy Vw.)
Bk. Ivy St. LS9: Leeds 6J 69 (off Ivy Av.)
Bk. John St. BD13: Thorn 8C 62
Bk. Karnac Rd. LS8: Leeds 2H 69 (off Nice St.)
Bk. Kelso Rd. LS2: Leeds 2A 4 (4B 68)
Bk. Kendal La. LS3: Leeds 4B 4
Bk. Kennerleigh Wlk. LS15: Leeds 5D 70 (off Kingswear Pde.)
Bk. Kensington St. BD8: B'frd 5M 63 (off Thorn St.)
Bk. Kensington Ter. LS6: Leeds 3B 68
Bk. Kings Av. LS6: Leeds 4A 68 (off Alexandra Rd.)
Bk. Kirby St. BD21: Keigh 8K 27 (off Caledonia Rd.)
Back Kirkgate BD18: Ship 8M 45
Bk. Kitson St. LS9: Leeds 8M 5
Bk. Knowle Mt. LS4: Leeds 3N 67 (off Stanmore Hill)
Bk. Knowl Rd. WF14: Mir 5K 121
Bk. Laisteridge La. BD7: B'frd 8A 64
Bk. Lake St. LS10: Leeds 3F 86
Bk. Lambton Gro. LS8: Leeds 2H 69 (off Lambton Gro.)
Bk. Landseer Av. LS13: Leeds 3H 67 (off Victoria Pk. Av.)
Bk. Landseer Gro. LS13: Leeds 3H 67 (off Victoria Pk. Av.)
Bk. Landseer Ter. LS13: Leeds 3H 67 (off Victoria Pk. Av.)
Back La. BB10: South 1C 56
BD9: B'frd 2M 63
BD10: B'frd 7F 46
BD11: Drig 6C 84
BD13: Que 3G 80
BD13: Thorn 7C 62
BD14: Clay 1H 81
BD15: All 4C 62
BD20: E Mor 7C 28
BD20: Sils 7E 12
BD22: Lay 9B 26
BD22: S'bury 1J 59
DN6: Nort 7N 149
HD7: Slait 3L 151
HD8: Clay W 6J 157
HD8: Eml 4D 156
HD8: Shel 6M 155
HD9: H'frth 3M 169
HD9: U'thng 2J 169
HX2: Illing 8K 79
HX2: Ogd 2J 79
HX6: Ripp 6C 116 (Hob La.)
HX6: Ripp 3B 116 (Salt Drake)
HX6: Ripp 7D 116 (Spring St.)
HX7: Heb B 3G 95
HX7: Hept 6C 76 (Broad La.)
HX7: Hept 8G 76 (Church St.)
HX7: P Wel 8H 59
LS11: Leeds 4B 86
LS12: N Far 3F 84
LS13: Leeds 5G 66
LS17: Wee 6B 20
LS18: Hors 7E 48
LS19: Yead 1L 47
LS20: Guis 7G 31
LS21: Askw 5E 16
LS22: Sick 4C 22
LS23: B'ham 5D 38
LS25: Kip 4B 90
LS28: Fars 3A 66
LS29: Burl W 8D 16
OL14: Tod 5A 94
S36: Ing 8C 172
S75: Caw 4N 173
WF1: Wake 4H 9 (5K 125)
WF2: Wake 5G 9 (5K 125)
WF3: Loft 3L 105
WF4: Col H 9E 144
WF4: G Moor 5A 140
WF4: M'twn 2L 141
WF4: S Comn 9K 127
WF4: Wint 6J 145
WF4: Wool 3H 159
WF5: Oss 6N 123
WF8: D'ton 6C 130
WF9: Bads 8L 147
WF9: S Elm 3N 163
WF10: All B 1B 108
WF12: Bries, W'ley 3B 140
WF12: W'ley 1B 140
WF14: Mir 6J 121
WF14: Up H 3M 139
WF16: Heck 8A 102
Back La. W. S71: Roys 5B 160
Bk. Langdale Gdns. LS6: Leeds 2M 67 (off Canterbury Dr.)
Bk. Langdale Ter. LS6: Leeds 2M 67 (off Canterbury Dr.)
Bk. Laurel Mt. LS7: Leeds 1F 68
Bk. Leatham St. WF13: Dew 2D 122
Back Leeming BD22: Oxen 5D 60
Bk. Lime St. BD21: Keigh 4H 43 (off Hainworth Wood Rd.)
Bk. Linden Gro. LS11: Leeds 2E 86 (off Linden Gro.)
Bk. Lindum Ter. BD9: B'frd 4A 64 (off Oak La.)
Bk. Lodge La. LS11: Leeds 3D 86 (off Stratford Ter.)
Bk. Lombard St. LS19: Raw 3L 47
Bk. Longfield Rd. OL14: Tod 7K 93 (off Longfield Rd.)
Bk. Longroyd Ter. LS11: Leeds 2E 86 (off Burton Av.)
Bk. Lord St. HX1: Hal 4J 7 (5A 98)
Bk. Low La. LS18: Hors 6G 49 (off Bk. Breary Av.)
Bk. Lucas St. LS6: Leeds 2C 68 (off Delph La.)
Bk. Lumbutts Rd. OL14: Tod 9J 93
Bk. Lunan Pl. LS8: Leeds 2H 69 (off Lunan Pl.)
Bk. Lunan Ter. LS8: Leeds 2H 69 (off Lunan Ter.)
Bk. Lyons St. BD13: Que 4E 80
Bk. Lytton St. HX3: Hal 1L 7 (3B 98)
Bk. Mafeking Av. LS11: Leeds 4C 86 (off Dewsbury Rd.)
Bk. Mafeking Mt. LS11: Leeds 4C 86
Bk. Malt St. BD22: Keigh 3G 42 (off Bracken Rd.)
Bk. Mannville Rd. BD21: Keigh 1G 43 (off Malsis Rd.)
Bk. Manor Dr. LS6: Leeds 2A 68 (off Manor Av.)
Bk. Manor Gro. LS7: Leeds 9F 50 (off St Martin's Dr.)
Bk. Manor St. BD2: B'frd 3F 64
Bk. Market St. BD6: B'frd 4A 82
Bk. Markham Av. LS8: Leeds 2H 69 (off Markham Av.)
Bk. Marriot St. WF13: Dew 2G 123
Bk. Marshall Av. LS15: Leeds 4E 70 (off Railway Rd.)
Bk. Marshall St. LS15: Leeds 4D 70 (off Austhorpe Rd.)
Bk. Marshall Ter. LS15: Leeds 4D 70 (off Railway Rd.)
Bk. Mary St. WF3: E Ard 4G 104
Bk. Masham St. LS12: Leeds 7N 67 (off Bk. Middle Cross St.)
Bk. Maud Av. LS11: Leeds 3D 86 (off Maud Pl.)
Bk. Mayville Av. LS6: Leeds 3A 68 (off Mayville Rd.)
Bk. Mayville Pl. LS6: Leeds 3A 68 (off Cardigan La.)
Bk. Mayville St. LS6: Leeds 3A 68 (off Mayville St.)
Bk. Mayville Ter. LS6: Leeds 3A 68 (off Mayville Rd.)
Bk. Meadow Vw. LS6: Leeds 3A 68 (off Brundenell Rd.)
Bk. Methley Dr. LS7: Leeds 9F 50
Bk. Mexborough Av. LS7: Leeds 2F 68 (off Savile Av.)
Bk. Mexborough Dr. LS7: Leeds 2F 68 (off Savile Av.)
Bk. Mexborough Gro. LS7: Leeds 2F 68 (off Savile Av.)
Bk. Mexborough St. LS7: Leeds 2F 68 (off Savile Av.)
Bk. Meynell Av. LS26: Rothw 8N 87
Bk. Middle Cross St. LS12: Leeds 7N 67
Bk. Middleton Rd. LS29: I'ly 5F 14
Bk. Middleton Vw. LS11: Leeds 2C 86
Bk. Midland Rd. LS6: Leeds 3B 68 (off Hyde Pk. Ter.)
Bk. Milan Av. LS8: Leeds 3H 69 (off Milan Rd.)
Bk. Milan Rd. LS8: Leeds 3H 69 (off Harehills Rd.)
Bk. Milan St. LS8: Leeds 3J 69 (off Harehills La.)
Bk. Mill Hey BD22: Haw 8D 42 (off Mill Hey)
Bk. Milton Ter. HX1: Hal 3H 7 (5A 98)
Bk. Minnie St. BD22: Haw 9C 42 (off Minnie St.)
Bk. Mitchell Ter. BD16: Bgly 5E 44
Bk. Mitford Rd. LS12: Leeds 7N 67
Bk. Model Rd. LS12: Leeds 7N 67
Bk. Model Ter. LS12: Leeds 7N 67
Bk. Model Vw. LS12: Leeds 7N 67
Bk. Monk Bri. Dr. LS6: Leeds 9B 50 (off Bentley Mt.)
Bk. Monk Bri. St. LS6: Leeds 9B 50 (off Monk Bri. St.)
Bk. Montpelier Ter. LS6: Leeds 2C 68 (off Cliff Rd.)
Bk. Moorfield St. HX1: Hal 7N 97
Bk. Moorfield Ter. LS12: Leeds 6K 67
Bk. Moorland Ter. LS2: Leeds 2B 4 (4C 68)
Bk. Moor La. HD4: Neth 2J 153
Bk. Morning St. BD21: Keigh 3H 43 (off Hainworth Wood Rd.)
Bk. Morritt Dr. LS15: Leeds 6A 70
Bk. Mount Av. WF17: Bat 9G 102 (off Mount St.)
Bk. Mount Pleasant LS10: Leeds 8E 86
WF1: Wake 4M 9 (5M 125)
Bk. Mount Royd BD8: B'frd 4A 64
Bk. Mount Vw. LS6: Leeds 2B 68 (off Regent Pk. Ter.)
Bk. Muff St. BD4: B'frd 9F 64
Bk. Myrtle Av. BD16: Bgly 5E 44
Bk. Myrtle Ter. BD22: Cros R 6F 42
Bk. Nansen St. LS13: Leeds 4D 66 (off Fairfield Av.)
Bk. Napier Rd. BD3: B'frd 7H 65
Bk. Nelson Rd. LS29: I'ly 5G 15
Bk. Nelson St. WF13: Dew 3F 122
Bk. Newport Gdns. LS6: Leeds 3N 67 (off Newport Rd.)
Bk. Newport Mt. LS6: Leeds 3N 67 (off Newport Rd.)
Bk. Newport Pl. LS6: Leeds 3N 67 (off Newport Rd.)
Bk. New St. BD12: O'haw 8F 82 (off Mill Carr Hill Rd.)
Bk. Newton Gro. LS7: Leeds 2F 68
Bk. Newton La. WF10: Led, Leds 5D 90
Bk. New York St. LS2: Leeds 7H 5 (7F 68)
Bk. Nice Vw. LS8: Leeds 2H 69 (off Nice Vw.)

Bk. Norman Mt.—Balderstone Hall La.

Bk. Norman Mt. *LS5: Leeds* 2K **67**
(off Morris La.)
Bk. Norman Pl. *LS8: Leeds* 5J **51**
(off Norton Rd.)
Bk. Norman Ter. *LS8: Leeds* 5J **51**
(off Norton Rd.)
Bk. Northbrook St. *LS7: Leeds* 8F **50**
(off Northbrook St.)
Bk. Northfield Pl. *BD8: B'frd* 5A **64**
(off Carlisle Rd.)
Back Northgate WF8: Pon 2K **129**
Bk. North Pk. Av. LS8: Leeds 7H **51**
Bk. North St. BD12: O'haw 9E **82**
OL14: Tod 7K **93**
(off Ridge Rd.)
Bk. Norwood Gro. *LS6: Leeds* 3A **68**
(off Norwood Mt.)
Bk. Norwood Pl. *LS6: Leeds* 3A **68**
(off Norwood Mt.)
Bk. Norwood Rd. *LS6: Leeds* 3A **68**
(off Norwood Vw.)
Bk. Norwood Ter. LS6: Leeds 3A **68**
Bk. Nowell Cres. *LS9: Leeds* 5K **69**
(off Harehills La.)
Bk. Nowell Mt. *LS9: Leeds* 5K **69**
(off Harehills La.)
Bk. Nowell Pl. *LS9: Leeds* 5K **69**
(off Harehills La.)
Bk. Nowell Ter. *LS9: Leeds* 5K **69**
(off Harehills La.)
Bk. Nunington St. *LS12: Leeds* 6N **67**
(off Armley Pk. Rd.)
Bk. Nunington Vw. *LS12: Leeds* 5M **67**
(off Nunnington Vw.)
Bk. Nunroyd Rd. *LS17: Leeds* 6F **50**
(off Nunroyd Ter.)
Bk. Oak Av. BD16: Bgly 6E **44**
Bk. Oakfield Ter. *LS6: Leeds* 9A **50**
(off Brookfield Rd.)
Bk. Oakley St. WF3: Thpe H 3G **104**
Bk. Oakley Ter. *LS11: Leeds* 3E **86**
(off Garnet Rd.)
Bk. Oak Rd. *LS7: Leeds* 1F **68**
(off St Mary's Rd.)
Bk. Oakwood Av. *LS8: Leeds* 9K **51**
(off Oakwood Av.)
Bk. Oakwood Dr. *LS8: Leeds* 9K **51**
(off Oakwood Boundary Rd.)
Back O'dam HD7: Slait 1N **151**
Back of the Mill BD16: Har 6N **43**
Bk. Osmondthorpe La. *LS9: Leeds* 6L **69**
(off Cross Osmondthorpe La.)
Bk. o' th' Height HX6: Rish 9K **115**
Bk. Otterburn St. *BD21: Keigh* 8J **27**
(off Ashleigh St.)
Bk. Outwood La. LS18: Hors 8F **48**
Bk. Overdale Ter. *LS15: Leeds* 6B **70**
(off Cross St.)
Back o'Wall HD7: Slait 7H **135**
Bk. Oxford Pl. LS1: Leeds 5D **4**
Bk. Oxford St. WF3: E Ard 4G **104**
Bk. Paget St. *BD21: Keigh* 9G **27**
(off Devonshire St.)
Bk. Parish Ghyll Rd. LS29: I'ly 6G **14**
Bk. Park Cres. LS8: Leeds 5K **51**
Bk. Parkfield Pl. *LS11: Leeds* 2C **86**
(off Parkfield Row)
Bk. Parkfield Rd. *LS11: Leeds* 2C **86**
(off Parkfield Row)
Bk. Park Ter. HX1: Hal 6N **97**
Bk. Park Vw. *LS11: Leeds* 2C **86**
(off Dawson Rd.)
Bk. Park Vw. Av. LS4: Leeds 3N **67**
Bk. Parkville Rd. LS13: Leeds 3F **66**
Bk. Parnaby Av. *LS10: Leeds* 4H **87**
(off Parnaby Rd.)
Bk. Parnaby St. LS10: Leeds 4H **87**
Bk. Parnaby Ter. *LS10: Leeds* 4H **87**
(off Parnaby Rd.)
Bk. Pasture Gro. *LS7: Leeds* 8F **50**
(off Hillside Rd.)
Bk. Pasture Rd. *LS8: Leeds* 2H **69**
(off Ellers Rd.)
Bk. Pawson St. WF3: E Ard 4G **104**
Bk. Pelham Rd. *BD2: B'frd* 3F **64**
(off Pelham Rd.)
Bk. Pleasant St. HX6: Sow B 8J **97**
Bk. Pollard La. LS13: Leeds 1F **66**
Bk. Pollard St. HD2: Hud 9N **119**
Bk. Poplar Av. *LS15: Leeds* 4E **70**
(off Railway Rd.)
Bk. Poplar Ter. S71: Roys 5F **160**
Bk. Potternewton La. LS7: Leeds 9E **50**
Bk. Potters St. *LS7: Leeds* 9F **50**
(off St Martin's Dr.)
Bk. Prospect Pl. BD21: Keigh 1H **43**
Bk. Prospect Ter. LS9: Leeds 7M **5** (7H **69**)
Bk. Providence Av. *LS6: Leeds* 2C **68**
(off Delph La.)
Bk. Providence St. WF17: Bat 7F **102**
Bk. Purlwell Hall Rd. WF17: Bat 9F **102**
Bk. Purlwell La. WF17: Bat 8F **102**
Bk. Quarry Mt. Ter. *LS6: Leeds* 2C **68**
(off Providence Rd.)
Bk. Queen St. HD1: Hud 6C **8** (4N **137**)
HX4: Gree 5B **118**
Bk. Raglan Rd. LS2: Leeds 1C **4**
Bk. Ravenscar Av. *LS8: Leeds* 9J **51**
(off Ravenscar Wlk.)
Bk. Ravens St. WF13: Dew 5D **122**
Bk. Raynville Mt. *LS13: Leeds* 3H **67**
(off Victoria Pk. Av.)
Bk. Regent Pk. Ter. *LS6: Leeds* 2B **68**
(off Regent Pk. Av.)
Bk. Regent St. WF1: Wake 8N **125**
Bk. Regent Ter. LS6: Leeds 4B **68**
Bk. Reginald Mt. *LS7: Leeds* 2F **68**
(off Hall La.)
Bk. Reginald Pl. *LS7: Leeds* 2F **68**
(off Reginald Row)
Bk. Reginald St. *LS7: Leeds* 2F **68**
(off Reginald St.)
Bk. Rhodes St. HX1: Hal 4H **7** (5A **98**)
Bk. Ribble St. *BD21: Keigh* 8M **27**
(off Airedale Rd.)
Bk. Richardson St. *BD12: O'haw* 9E **82**
(off Bradford Rd.)
Bk. Richmond Mt. *LS6: Leeds* 2A **68**
(off Manor Av.)
Bk. Ridge Mt. Ter. *LS6: Leeds* 2C **68**
(off Cliff Rd.)
Bk. Ridge St. OL14: Tod 7K **93**
Bk. Ridge Vw. LS7: Leeds 1C **68**
Bk. Rigging La. HX6: Sow B 9C **96**
Bk. Ripley St. *BD20: Rid* 7M **27**
(off Canal Rd.)
Bk. Ripon St. HX1: Hal 6L **97**
Bk. Ripon Ter. HX3: Hal 3A **98**
Bk. River St. BD22: Haw 8D **42**
Back Rd. BD3: B'frd 5E **64**
BD12: Wyke 9A **82**
Bk. Roberts St. LS26: W'frd 7D **88**
Bk. Rochester Ter. *LS6: Leeds* 2N **67**
(off Broomfield Rd.)
Bk. Rokeby Gdns. *LS6: Leeds* 1M **67**
(off Ash Rd.)
Bk. Roman Gro. LS8: Leeds 5J **51**
Bk. Roman Pl. LS8: Leeds 5K **51**
Bk. Roman St. LS8: Leeds 5K **51**
Bk. Rose Av. *LS18: Hors* 8E **48**
(off Rose St.)
Bk. Rosebank Cres. LS3: Leeds 2A **4** (4B **68**)
Bk. Rosemont Wlk. *LS13: Leeds* 4F **66**
(off Rosemont St.)
Bk. Rossall Rd. *LS8: Leeds* 2J **69**
(off Nice St.)
Bk. Rossington Rd. *LS8: Leeds* 2G **69**
(off Rossington Gro.)
Bk. Roundhay Cres. *LS8: Leeds* 1H **69**
(off Cross Roundhay Av.)
Bk. Roundhay Gro. *LS8: Leeds* 1H **69**
(off Cross Roundhay Av., not continuous)
Bk. Roundhay Pl. *LS8: Leeds* 1H **69**
(off Harehills La.)
Bk. Roundhay Vw. *LS8: Leeds* 1H **69**
(off Cross Roundhay Av.)
Back Row LS11: Leeds 8D **68**
Bk. Rowland Ter. *LS11: Leeds* 2E **86**
(off Rowland Pl.)
Bk. Rowsley St. *BD21: Keigh* 9K **27**
(off Chatsworth St.)
Bk. Roydwood Ter. BD13: Cull 9K **43**
Bk. Rupert St. *BD21: Keigh* 8J **27**
(off Lawkholme La.)
Bk. Russell St. BD5: B'frd 7A **6** (9B **64**)
Bk. Ruthven Vw. *LS8: Leeds* 3J **69**
(off Ruthven Vw.)
Bk. Rydal St. BD21: Keigh 1G **43**
Bk. Rylstone St. BD21: Keigh 8L **27**
Back St Alban Cres. *LS9: Leeds* 5L **69**
(off Harehills La.)
Back St Elmo Gro. *LS9: Leeds* 6J **69**
(off Vinery Av.)
Back St Ives Mt. LS12: Leeds 6K **67**
Back St Luke's Cres. *LS11: Leeds* 1C **86**
(off St Luke's Cres.)
Back St Mary's Rd. LS7: Leeds 1F **68**
Back St Mary's Rd. W. BD9: B'frd 4A **64**
Back St Paul's Rd. BD18: Ship 8M **45**
Bk. Salisbury Gro. *LS12: Leeds* 6M **67**
(off Armley Lodge Rd.)
Bk. Salisbury Ter. HX3: Hal 3A **98**
LS12: Leeds 6M **67**
(off Armley Lodge Rd.)
Bk. Salisbury Vw. *LS12: Leeds* 6M **67**
(off Armley Lodge Rd.)
Bk. Saltaire Rd. BD18: Ship 7M **45**
Bk. Saltaire Rd. Nth. BD18: Ship 7M **45**
Bk. Sandhurst Gro. *LS8: Leeds* 3J **69**
(off Harehills La.)
Bk. Sandhurst Pl. *LS8: Leeds* 3J **69**
(off Harehills La.)
Bk. Sandhurst Rd. *LS8: Leeds* 3J **69**
(off Harehills La.)
Bk. Savile Pde. HX1: Hal 8H **7** (7A **98**)
Bk. Savile Pl. *LS7: Leeds* 3F **68**
(off Savile Av.)
Bk. Savile Rd. *LS7: Leeds* 3F **68**
(off Savile Av.)
Bk. School St. *LS27: Morl* 9L **85**
(off South St.)
Bk. School Vw. *LS6: Leeds* 3A **68**
(off Welton Rd.)
Bk. Seaforth Av. *LS9: Leeds* 4K **69**
(off Foundry App.)
Bk. Seaforth Pl. *LS9: Leeds* 3J **69**
(off Strathmore Ter.)
Bk. Seaforth Ter. *LS9: Leeds* 3J **69**
(off Strathmore Ter.)
Bk. Sefton Av. *LS11: Leeds* 2C **86**
(off Wickham St.)
Bk. Sefton Ter. *LS11: Leeds* 2C **86**
(off Wickham St.)
Bk. Shaftesbury Av. LS8: Leeds 6J **51**
Bk. Shaw La. BD21: Keigh 3K **43**
Bk. Shepherd's Pl. *LS8: Leeds* 2H **69**
(off Shepherd's Pl.)
Bk. Sholebroke Av. LS7: Leeds 1F **68**
Bk. Sholebroke Pl. *LS7: Leeds* 2F **68**
(off Hall La.)
Bk. Sholebroke Vw. *LS7: Leeds* 2F **68**
(off Hall La.)
Bk. Sidlaw Ter. *LS8: Leeds* 2H **69**
(off Markham Av.)
Bk. Simpson St. *BD21: Keigh* 9G **27**
(off Edensor Rd.)
Bk. Sladen St. BD21: Keigh 9G **27**
Bk. Slaithwaite Rd. WF12: Dew 7F **122**
Bk. Smith Row BD5: B'frd 2A **82**
Bk. South End Gro. *LS13: Leeds* 4H **67**
(off South End Av.)
Bk. Southfield Sq. *BD8: B'frd* 5A **64**
(off Laburnum Pl.)
Bk. South Pde. HX5: Ell 6D **118**
(not continuous)
Bk. South St. HD1: Hud 5J **137**
Bk. Sowerby Cft. HX6: Sow B 1H **117**
Bk. Spencer Mt. *LS8: Leeds* 2G **69**
(off Gathorne St.)
Bk. Springfield Mt. LS12: Leeds 6K **67**
Bk. Springfield Pl. *BD8: B'frd* 5B **64**
(off Cornwall Rd.)
Bk. Springfield Rd. HX5: Ell 4F **118**
Bk. Spring Gro. Wlk. *LS6: Leeds* 4A **68**
(off Harold Ter.)
Bk. Spring St. HD1: Hud 5A **8** (4L **137**)
Bk. Stanley St. HD1: Hud 7K **137**
LS9: Leeds 4H **69**
(off Ashley Rd.)
Bk. Stanmore Pl. *LS4: Leeds* 3M **67**
(off St Michael's La.)
Bk. Stanmore St. *LS4: Leeds* 3M **67**
(off St Michael's La.)
Bk. Station Rd. WF14: Mir 7L **121**
WF17: Bat 8G **103**
Bk. Stonegate Rd. LS6: Leeds 8B **50**
Backstone Gill La. LS17: Wike 7M **35**
Bk. Stone Hall Rd. BD2: B'frd 2F **64**
Backstone La. LS29: I'ly 6H **15**
Backstone Way LS29: I'ly 5J **15**
Bk. Stoney La. HD4: Hud 8L **137**
Bk. Storey Pl. LS14: Leeds 5N **69**
Bk. Stratford Av. *LS11: Leeds* 2C **86**
(off Wickham St.)
Bk. Stratford St. *LS11: Leeds* 2D **86**
(off Rowland Pl.)
Bk. Stratford Ter. *LS11: Leeds* 2D **86**
(off Bude Rd.)
Bk. Strathmore Dr. *LS9: Leeds* 3J **69**
(off Strathmore Dr.)
Back St. LS23: B'ham 6C **38**
WF8: Pon 3J **129**
Back Sunnydene LS14: Leeds 5A **70**
Bk. Sutton App. LS14: Leeds 5N **69**
Bk. Swinton St. HX1: Hal 6M **97**
Bk. Sycamore Av. BD16: Bgly 5E **44**
Bk. Tamworth St. BD4: B'frd 8J **65**
Bk. Tempest Rd. *LS11: Leeds* 2C **86**
(off Sefton Ter.)
Bk. Temple Vw. LS11: Leeds 2C **86**
Bk. Thornhill Rd. HD3: Hud 4F **136**
Bk. Thornhill St. LS28: Cal 9M **47**
Bk. Thornville Row *LS6: Leeds* 3A **68**
(off Thornville St.)
Bk. Tower Gro. LS12: Leeds 6K **67**
Bk. Trafford Av. *LS9: Leeds* 4K **69**
(off Foundry App.)
Bk. Trentham Pl. *LS11: Leeds* 3D **86**
(off Trentham St.)
Bk. Trinity Ter. BD5: B'frd 7A **6** (9B **64**)
Bk. Union St. HD1: Hud 3C **8** (3N **137**)
Bk. Unity St. Nth. BD16: Bgly 5E **44**
Bk. Unity St. Sth. BD16: Bgly 5E **44**
Back Up. Castle HX7: Crag V 9K **95**
Bk. Vicars Rd. *LS8: Leeds* 2H **69**
(off Shepherd's La.)
Bk. Victoria Av. *LS9: Leeds* 6J **69**
(off Dawlish Cres.)
Bk. Victoria Gro. *LS9: Leeds* 6K **69**
(off Dawlish Cres.)
Bk. Victoria St. HX1: Hal 3K **7** (5B **98**)
Bk. Victor Ter. HX1: Hal 4M **97**
Bk. Violet Ter. *HX6: Sow B* 8J **97**
(off Park Rd.)
Bk. Wakefield Rd. HX6: Sow B 8K **97**
Bk. Walmsley Rd. *LS6: Leeds* 3A **68**
(off Mayville Rd.)
Bk. Walnut St. *BD21: Keigh* 3H **43**
(off Hainworth Wood Rd.)
Bk. Warwick Ter. WF17: Bat 9G **102**
Bk. Waverley Rd. HX5: Ell 6E **118**
Bk. Webster St. WF13: Dew 3F **122**
Bk. Welburn Av. LS16: Leeds 8L **49**
Bk. Wellfield Ter. OL14: Tod 8K **93**
Bk. Welton Av. *LS6: Leeds* 3A **68**
(off Welton Rd.)
Bk. Welton Gro. *LS6: Leeds* 3A **68**
(off Welton Rd.)
Bk. Welton Mt. *LS6: Leeds* 3A **68**
(off Welton Rd.)
Bk. Welton Pl. *LS6: Leeds* 3A **68**
(off Welton Rd.)
Bk. Wentworth St. HD1: Hud 3L **137**
Bk. Wesley Rd. LS12: Leeds 7M **67**
Bk. Wesley St. WF10: C'frd 4D **108**
Bk. Westbury St. LS10: Leeds 4H **87**
Bk. Westfield Rd. *LS3: Leeds* 5B **68**
(off Westfield Cres.)
Bk. Westlock Av. *LS9: Leeds* 5J **69**
(off Burton Way)
Bk. Westmorland Mt. LS13: Leeds 2G **67**
Bk. Weston Rd. LS29: I'ly 5G **15**
Bk. West St. HX6: Sow B 9H **97**
Bk. Wetherby Gro. *LS4: Leeds* 4M **67**
(off Argie Av.)
Bk. Wetherby Rd. *LS8: Leeds* 9K **51**
(off Wetherby Rd.)
Bk. Wheat St. *BD22: Keigh* 3G **42**
(off Bracken Rd.)
Bk. Wickham St. *LS11: Leeds* 2C **86**
(off Hardy St.)
Bk. William Av. *LS15: Leeds* 6N **69**
(off Selby Rd.)
Bk. William St. *HD6: Ras* 2M **119**
(off William St.)
Bk. Wilton Gro. *LS6: Leeds* 9A **50**
(off Monk Bri. Rd.)
Bk. Winfield Gro. LS2: Leeds 1E **4**
Bk. Winston Gdns. *LS6: Leeds* 1M **67**
(off Ash Rd.)
Bk. Winterburn St. *BD21: Keigh* 8J **27**
(off Ashleigh St.)
Bk. Wolseley Ter. HX1: Hal 5M **97**
Bk. Woodbine Ter. LS6: Leeds 9A **50**
Bk. Woodland Pk. Rd. *LS6: Leeds* 1A **68**
(off Coniston Av.)
Bk. Woodstock St. LS2: Leeds 1D **4**
Bk. Wright Av. BD22: Oak 4D **42**
Bk. York Pl. LS1: Leeds 7C **4** (7C **68**)
(not continuous)
Bk. York St. LS2: Leeds 7H **5** (7F **68**)
Bacon Av. WF6: Norm 9K **107**
Bacon St. LS20: Guis 8K **31**
Bacup Rd. OL14: Tod 7A **92**
Baddeley Gdns. BD10: B'frd 5E **46**
Baden Powell Cres. WF8: Pon 4K **129**
Baden St. BD22: Haw 7C **42**
Baden Ter. *BD19: Cleck* 5H **101**
(off Tofts Rd.)
LS13: Leeds 6F **66**
(off Pudsey Rd.)
Badger Brow HD9: Mel 7C **152**
Badger Cl. LS29: I'ly 5D **14**
WF4: Dur 3H **143**
Badger Cft. HX7: Blac H 9A **76**
Badger Ga. BD15: Wils 2B **62**
HD9: Mel 7C **152**
Badgergate Av. BD15: Wils 2B **62**
Badger Hill HD6: Ras 5K **119**
Badger La. HX3: Hip 5G **99**
HX7: Blac H 9B **76**
Badgers Drift BD20: Keigh 6H **27**
Badgers Mt. LS15: Leeds 4G **71**
Badgerstone Cl. BD20: E Mor 7C **28**
Badgers Wlk. WF16: Heck 9B **102**
Badgers Way BD2: B'frd 2C **64**
Badger Wood OL14: Tod 7L **93**
Badger Wood Glade LS22: Weth 1M **23**
Badminton Dr. LS10: Leeds 1F **104**
Badminton Vw. LS10: Leeds 1F **104**
BADSWORTH 8L **147**
BADSWORTH COMMON 7H **147**
Badsworth Ct. BD14: Clay 9J **63**
WF9: Bads 7L **147**
Badsworth M. WF9: Bads 8L **147**
Badsworth Vw. WF9: Upt 1N **163**
BAGBY FIELDS 1E **4** (3D **68**)
Bagden Hall Golf Course 9G **156**
Bagden La. HD8: Clay W 2H **173**
(Brow La.)
HD8: Clay W 9G **156**
(Clough Ho. La.)
BAGHILL 6N **103**
Baghill Grn. WF3: W Ard 6N **103**
Baghill La. WF8: Pon 2L **129**
Baghill Rd. WF3: W Ard 5N **103**
BAGLEY 2B **66**
Bagley La. LS13: Fars, Leeds 2B **66**
LS28: Fars 2A **66**
Bagnall Ter. BD6: B'frd 4N **81**
Bagshaw Mus. 4D **102**
BAILDON 4A **46**
Baildon Av. LS25: Kip 2B **90**
Baildon Bri. BD17: Ship 7N **45**
Baildon Chase LS14: Leeds 8D **52**
Baildon Cl. LS14: Leeds 9D **52**
Baildon Dr. LS14: Leeds 9D **52**
Baildon Golf Course 2A **46**
BAILDON GREEN 5N **45**
Baildon Grn. LS14: Leeds 9D **52**
BAILDON HOLMES 6A **46**
Baildon Holmes BD17: Bail 6A **46**
Baildon Mills *BD17: Bail* 3A **46**
(off Providence Row)
Baildon Path LS14: Leeds 9D **52**
Baildon Pl. LS14: Leeds 9D **52**
Baildon Recreation Cen. 6N **45**
Baildon Rd. BD17: Bail 4A **46**
LS14: Leeds 8D **52**
Baildon Station (Rail) 4C **46**
Baildon Wlk. LS14: Leeds 8D **52**
Baildon Way HD8: Skelm 6D **156**
BAILDON WOOD BOTTOM 6A **46**
Baildon Wood Ct. BD17: Bail 6A **46**
Bailes Rd. LS7: Leeds 1C **68**
Bailey Cl. WF8: Pon 1L **129**
Bailey Cres. WF9: S Elm 4N **163**
Bailey Fold BD15: All 5E **62**
Baileygate Ct. *WF8: Pon* 2K **129**
(off Back Northgate)
Baileygate Ind. Est. WF8: Pon 2L **129**
Baileygate M. WF8: Pon 1L **129**
Bailey Hall Bank HX3: Hal 5C **98**
Bailey Hall Bus. Pk. HX3: Hal 4M **7** (5C **98**)
Bailey Hall Rd. HX3: Hal 4M **7** (6C **98**)
Bailey Hall Vw. HX3: Hal 5C **98**
Bailey Hills Rd. BD16: Bgly 3D **44**
Bailey's Cl. LS14: Leeds 9B **52**
Baileys Cft. BD20: Keigh 6H **27**
Bailey's Hill LS14: Leeds 1B **70**
Bailey's La. LS14: Leeds 1B **70**
Bailey's Lawn LS14: Leeds 1B **70**
Bailey St. BD4: B'frd 8D **6** (9D **64**)
Bailey Towers LS14: Leeds 1B **70**
Bailey Wlk. WF4: Hol 7H **143**
Bailey Wells Av. BD5: B'frd 2A **82**
BAILIFF BRIDGE 5N **99**
Bainbrigge Rd. LS6: Leeds 2N **67**
Baines St. HX1: Hal 4N **97**
LS26: Rothw 8N **87**
WF17: Bat 8E **102**
Baird St. BD5: B'frd 1C **82**
Bairstow Ct. HX6: Sow B 6J **97**
Bairstow La. HX2: Hal 6J **97**
HX6: Sow B 6J **97**
Bairstow Mt. HX6: Sow B 7K **97**
Bairstow's Bldgs. HX2: Hal 9M **79**
Bairstow St. BD15: All 3F **62**
Baitings Ga. Rd. HX6: Rish 9K **115**
Baker Cres. LS27: Morl 1K **103**
Baker Fold HX1: Hal 3G **7**
Baker La. WF3: S'ley 6M **105**
Baker Rd. LS27: Morl 1K **103**
Bakers Cotts. *LS28: Pud* 7B **66**
(off Park Vw.)
Baker's St. HX7: Heb B 9H **77**
Baker St. BD2: B'frd 4F **64**
BD18: Ship 7M **45**
HD3: Hud 2G **137**
LS27: Morl 1K **103**
Baker St. Nth. HX2: Hal 8N **79**
Bakes St. BD7: B'frd 1M **81**
Bakston Cl. HD5: Hud 7C **138**
Balbec Av. LS6: Leeds 1A **68**
Balbec St. LS6: Leeds 1A **68**
Balcony BD22: Haw 9B **42**
Balcony Cotts. BD13: Que 5D **80**
Balcony Ter. *BD22: Cros R* 7F **42**
(off Halifax Rd.)
Balderstone Hall La. WF14: Mir 5N **121**

Baldovan Mt.—Barncroft Hgts.

Baldovan Mt. LS8: Leeds 2H 69
Baldovan Pl. LS8: Leeds 2H 69
Baldovan Ter. LS8: Leeds 2H 69
Baldwin La. BD13: Que 3F 80
BD14: Clay 3F 80
Baldwin Ter. HX3: Hal 5C 98
Baldwin Wing HX1: Hal 8K 7
Bale Dr. BD10: B'frd 7D 46
Balfour St. BD4: B'frd 8F 6 (1E 82)
BD16: Bgly 5E 44
BD21: Keigh 1H 43
Balk, The S75: S'ross 7L 159
WF2: W'ton 4B 144
WF4: Croft 1E 144
WF17: Bat 5F 102
Balk Av. WF3: S'ley 1B 126
Balkcliffe La. LS10: Leeds 7C 86
Balk Cres. WF3: S'ley 1B 126
Balk La. BD7: B'frd 1N 81
HD5: K'htn 3F 138
HD8: Shel 7N 155
HD8: Up C 2N 171
WF3: S'ley 1B 126
WF4: Neth 4A 142
WF9: S Elm 5C 164
Balkram Dr. HX2: Mix 8H 79
Balkram Edge HX2: Mt T 8F 78
Balkram Rd. HX2: Mix 8H 79
Balks WF15: Liv 8K 101
Balk St. WF17: Bat 7E 102
Ballantyne Rd. BD10: B'frd 5E 46
Ballater Av. HD4: Hud 8H 137
Ballfield Av. S75: Kex 9E 158
Ballfield Fold S75: Kex 9D 158
Ballfield La. S75: Kex 9E 158
Ballroyd Clough HD3: Hud 3F 136
(not continuous)
Ballroyd La. HD3: Hud 4F 136
Ballroyd Rd. HD2: Hud 9N 119
Ball St. BD13: Thorn 8D 62
Balme La. BD12: Wyke 1B 100
Balme Rd. BD19: Cleck 4H 101
Balme St. BD1: B'frd 3C 6 (7D 64)
BD12: Wyke 1A 100
Balmfield WF15: Liv 1L 121
Balmfield Cres. WF15: Liv 1L 121
Balmfords Yd. W. HD3: Hud 6G 136
(off Market St.)
Balmoral Av. HD4: Hud 8H 137
Balmoral Chase LS10: Leeds 2H 87
Balmoral Cl. WF8: Pon 6H 129
Balmoral Ct. WF3: W Ard 5B 104
Balmoral Dr. LS26: Meth 1K 107
WF11: Ferr 8B 110
Balmoral Ho. LS17: Leeds 2F 50
Balmoral Pl. BD13: Que 5B 80
HX1: Hal 5J 7 (6B 98)
Balmoral St. HX7: Heb B 1H 95
(off Marlborough Rd.)
Balmoral Ter. LS6: Leeds 9A 50
Balmoral Way LS19: Yead 1A 48
Balm Pl. LS11: Leeds 9C 68
Balm Rd. LS10: Leeds 3G 86
Balm Rd. Ind. Est. LS10: Leeds 2F 86
Balm Wlk. LS11: Leeds 9B 68
Balne Av. WF2: Wake 4J 125
Balne La. WF1: Wake 3G 9 (4H 125)
WF2: Wake 3G 9 (4H 125)
Bamborough St. WF1: Wake 8A 126
Bamburgh Cl. LS15: Leeds 3F 70
Bamburgh Rd. LS15: Leeds 3F 70
Bamford Ho. BD4: B'frd 4J 83
(off Tong St.)
Bamlett Brow BD22: Haw 7D 42
Banbury Rd. WF8: Pon 9L 109
Bancroft Av. HD5: Hud 5C 138
Bancroft St. BD22: Cros R 7F 42
(off Halifax Rd.)
Bangor Gro. LS12: Leeds 1K 85
Bangor Pl. LS12: Leeds 1K 85
Bangor St. LS12: Leeds 1K 85
Bangor Ter. LS12: Leeds 1K 85
Bangor Vw. LS12: Leeds 1K 85
BANK 7K 5 (7G 68)
Bank BD22: Oxen 5E 60
Bank, The BD10: B'frd 1G 65
Bank Av. LS18: Hors 7E 48
LS27: Morl 8K 85
Bank Bottom HD7: Mars 3J 151
HX3: Hal 4M 7 (5C 98)
HX6: Rish 2D 134
HX7: Crag V 9K 95
HX7: Myth 2A 96
Bank Bottom Cotts. HD7: Mars 6F 150
Bank Bottom La. HX2: Lud 3F 96
Bank Bottom Ter. HD7: Mars 3J 151
(off Manchester Rd.)
Bank Bldgs. HD9: Mel 8D 152
HX6: Mill B 4C 116
(off Nathan La.)
HX7: Heb B 2K 95
Bank Cl. BD10: B'frd 1G 65
Bank Crest BD17: Bail 4A 46
Bank Crest Ri. BD18: Ship 8H 45
Bank Dr. BD6: B'frd 4B 82
Bank Edge Gdns. HX2: Illing 1L 97
Bank Edge Rd. HX2: Illing 9L 79
BANK END 8B 154
Bank End HD7: Golc 6B 136
HD8: Clay W 8K 157
HX4: Gree 4K 117
Bank End Knoll HD9: Brock 8B 154
Bank End La. HD5: Hud 6C 138
HD8: Clay W 8K 157
S75: H Hoy 8K 157
Bank End Rd. HD7: Golc 7A 136
Banker St. LS4: Leeds 5N 67
Bankfield HD7: Mars 5G 151
(off Manchester Rd.)
HD8: Shel 7K 155
LS17: Bard 4E 36
Bankfield Av. BD18: Ship 8J 45
HD5: K'htn 2F 138
Bankfield Bldgs. OL14: Tod 8J 93
Bankfield Cl. WF5: Oss 7B 124
Bankfield Ct. HD5: Hud 5B 138
WF2: Wren 9H 105
WF14: Mir 6K 121
Bankfield Dr. BD18: Ship 8J 45
BD22: Keigh 9E 26
HD9: Holm 6H 169
WF2: Wren 9H 105
Bankfield Gdns. HX3: Sou 6E 98
LS4: Leeds 4M 67
Bankfield Grange HX4: Gree 4B 118
Bankfield Gro. BD18: Ship 9J 45
LS4: Leeds 3M 67
Bankfield La. HD5: K'htn 2F 138
Bankfield Mills WF14: Mir 6K 121
Bankfield Mt. BD22: Keigh 8E 26
Bankfield Mus. 3B 98
Bankfield Pk. Av. HD4: Hud 9K 137
Bank Fld. Rd. WF17: Bat 7F 102
Bankfield Rd. BD18: Ship 8J 45
BD22: Keigh 8E 26
HD1: Hud 7A 8 (5L 137)
LS4: Leeds 4M 67
Bankfield St. BD22: Keigh 8E 26
Bankfield Ter. BD17: Bail 5B 46
HD1: Hud 7A 8
HD4: Arm B 1K 153
HX6: Sow B 7G 97
LS4: Leeds 4M 67
LS28: Stan 5B 66
(off Richardshaw Rd.)
Bankfield Vw. HX3: Hal 3A 98
Bankfield Wlk. BD22: Keigh 8E 26
Bankfield Yd. HX3: Hal 3A 98
(off Boothtown Rd.)
BANK FOOT
BD6 4A 82
WF17 7F 102
Bankfoot HX7: Heb B 1G 94
Bank Foot La. HD4: Arm B 2K 153
Bankfoot Pl. WF17: Bat 7F 102
Bankfoot Rd. HD4: Hud 1D 154
Bankfoot St. WF17: Bat 7F 102
Bankfoot Ter. HX7: Heb B 1G 94
Bank Gdns. LS18: Hors 7E 48
Bank Gdns. Cl. HX2: Illing 1L 97
Bank Gate HD7: Slait 9M 135
Bank Gro. WF12: Dew 4K 123
Bank Hall Gro. HD8: Shep 9K 155
Bank Hey Bottom HX6: Ripp 8E 116
Bankholme Ct. BD4: B'frd 3K 83
BANKHOUSE 9A 66
Bank Ho. HX4: Holy 7K 117
LS27: Morl 9K 85
(off Queen St.)
Bankhouse LS28: Pud 9A 66
BANKHOUSE BOTTOM 1A 84
Bank Ho. Cl. LS27: Morl 8K 85
Bankhouse Ct. LS28: Pud 9A 66
Bank Ho. La. HD9: H'frth 2N 169
HX2: Lud, Wain 9D 78
Bankhouse La. HD3: Hud 5H 137
HX3: Hal 1C 118
LS28: Pud 9A 66
Bankhouse Rd. HD3: Hud 5G 136
Bank Ho. Ter. HX3: Hal 1C 118
Banklands BD20: Sils 7E 12
Banklands Av. BD20: Sils 7F 12
Banklands La. BD20: Sils 7F 12
Bank La. BD20: Sils 9E 10
BD22: Keigh 9D 26
BD22: Oak 5B 42
BD22: Oxen 4M 59
HD8: Den D, Up D 3C 172
(not continuous)
HD9: H'frth 1N 169
(Banksville)
HD9: H'frth 4J 169
(Shaw La.)
HD9: Holm 7G 169
Bank Pde. LS21: Otley 1K 31
Bank Rd. HX6: Sow B 9H 97
Bank Royd La. HX4: Bark 1H 135
Banks HD9: Hon 5M 153
Banks, The HX6: Sow B 7G 97
Banks App. HD7: Golc 5C 136
Banks Av. HD7: Golc 5B 136
WF7: Ackw 5E 146
WF8: Pon 3J 129
Banks Bldgs. WF7: F'stne 7D 128
(off Ackworth Rd.)
Banks Cres. HD7: Golc 5C 136
Banks Dr. HD7: Golc 5C 136
Banks End HX5: Ell 5H 119
Banks End Rd. HX5: Ell 5H 119
Banksfield Av. HX7: Myth 3M 95
LS19: Yead 8M 31
Banksfield Cl. LS19: Yead 8M 31
Banksfield Cres. HX7: Myth 3M 95
LS19: Yead 8M 31
Banksfield Gro. LS19: Yead 8M 31
Banksfield Mt. LS19: Yead 8M 31
Banksfield Ri. LS19: Yead 8M 31
Banksfield Rd. HX7: Myth 3M 95
Banksfield Ter. HX7: Myth 3M 95
LS19: Yead 9M 31
Banks Gth. WF11: Knot 8E 110
Banks Gth. Cotts.
WF11: Knot 8E 110
(off Banks Gth.)
Banks Gro. HD7: Golc 5C 136
Bankside BD17: Bail 4A 46
HD7: Golc 5C 136
HD8: Shel 7K 155
HX7: Heb B 1H 95
(off Birchcliffe Rd.)
OL14: Tod 8K 93
Bank Side St. LS8: Leeds 3H 69
Bankside Ter. BD17: Bail 5N 45
Banks La. BD20: Rid 4L 27
WF11: Knot 8E 110
Banks M. WF14: Mir 7K 121
Banks Mt. WF8: Pon 3J 129
Bank Sq. LS27: Morl 8K 85
Banks Rd. HD7: Golc 5C 136
HD7: Linth 1A 152
Banks Row LS25: Aber 8E 54
Banks St. WF17: Bat 8F 102
Bank St. BD1: B'frd 4B 6 (7C 64)
BD6: B'frd 4A 82
BD18: Ship 8N 45
BD19: Cleck 5G 100
BD21: Keigh 9J 27
(within Airedale Shop. Cen.)
BD22: Haw 8C 42
(off Main St.)
HD6: Brigh 1M 119
HD9: Jack B 4C 170
LS1: Leeds 7F 4 (7E 68)
(Boar La.)
LS1: Leeds 6F 4
(Commercial St.)
LS22: Weth 4M 23
LS27: Morl 8K 85
OL14: Tod 8K 93
WF1: Wake 5J 9 (5L 125)
WF4: Horb 1C 142
WF5: Oss 6N 123
WF9: Hems 2D 162
WF10: C'frd 4D 108
WF12: Dew 3G 123
WF14: Mir 6J 121
WF15: Liv 8M 101
Banksville HD9: H'frth 1N 169
Bank Ter. HX2: Lud 4E 96
(off High St.)
HX6: Mill B 4C 116
HX7: Crag V 9K 95
HX7: Heb B 1F 94
LS27: Morl 8L 85
LS28: Stan 4B 66
BANK TOP
BD10 1G 64
HX3 7E 98
Bank Top HD7: Slait 9M 135
(off Hill Top Rd.)
HX3: Sou 6D 98
HX4: Gree 3B 118
OL14: Tod 8K 93
(off Honey Hole Rd.)
Bank Top Dr. BD20: Rid 6M 27
Bank Top La. HD9: Holm 5F 168
HX7: Crag V 7G 94
LS21: Arth 4N 33
Bank Top Way
BD21: Keigh 1M 43
Bank Vw. BD11: B'haw 7L 83
BD17: Bail 5N 45
BD22: Oak 5B 42
(off Low Bank La.)
HD9: Brock 7A 154
HX2: Lud F 6D 96
HX4: Bark 6F 116
HX6: Mill B 4D 116
(off Lumb La.)
HX7: Heb B 1F 94
HX7: Myth 3M 95
LS7: Leeds 8D 50
WF12: Dew 4K 123
Bank Vw. Ho. BD17: Bail 5A 46
(off Bank Vw.)
Bank Wlk. BD17: Bail 4A 46
Bankwell Fold BD6: B'frd 4B 82
Bankwell Rd. HD3: Hud 6G 137
Bank Wood Rd. DN6: Wome 7E 130
WF8: Stap 7E 130
Bankwood Way WF17: Birs 9E 84
Bank Yd. WF5: Oss 6N 123
Bannatyne's Health Club
Wakefield 1K 125
Bannerman St. BD12: O'haw 8E 82
Banner St. BD3: B'frd 5F 6 (8E 64)
Bannister La. DN6: S'brk 4G 165
Bannockburn Ct. BD5: B'frd 4F 82
Bannockburn Way WF6: Alt 8F 106
Banstead St. E. LS8: Leeds 3H 69
Banstead St. W. LS8: Leeds 3H 69
Banstead Ter. E. LS8: Leeds 3H 69
Banstead Ter. W. LS8: Leeds 3H 69
Bantam Cl. LS27: Morl 9N 85
BANTAM GROVE 9N 85
Bantam Gro. La. LS27: Morl 9N 85
Bantam Gro. Vw. LS27: Morl 9N 85
Bantree Ct. BD10: B'frd 5E 46
Baptist Fold BD13: Que 4D 80
Baptist La. WF5: Oss 7D 124
Baptist Pl. BD1: B'frd 3A 6 (7B 64)
Baptist St. WF17: Bat 9D 102
Baptist Way LS28: Stan 4D 66
Bar Av. S75: Map 9M 159
Barber Row HD7: Linth 9C 136
Barberry Av. BD3: B'frd 6J 65
Barber Sq. WF16: Heck 8N 101
Barber St. HD6: Brigh 9N 99
Barber Wlk. WF13: Dew 3F 122
(off Willan's Rd.)
Barclay Cl. BD13: Cull 9L 43
Barclay St. LS7: Leeds 3H 5
BARCROFT 7F 42
Bar Cft. HD5: K'htn 1F 138
Barcroft BD22: Cros R 7F 42
Barcroft Gro. LS19: Yead 1L 47
Barcroft Rd. HD4: Hud 8L 137
Barden Av. BD6: B'frd 4J 81
Barden Cl. LS12: Leeds 7K 67
WF17: Bat 7E 102
Barden Dr. BD16: Bgly 3H 45
Barden Grn. LS12: Leeds 7K 67
Barden Gro. LS12: Leeds 7K 67
Barden Mt. LS12: Leeds 7K 67
Barden Pl. LS12: Leeds 7K 67
Barden Rd. BD23: E'by 1A 10
WF1: Wake 5A 126
Barden St. BD8: B'frd 5N 63
Barden Ter. LS12: Leeds 7K 67
Bardon Hall Gdns. LS16: Leeds 7M 49
Bardon Hall M. LS16: Leeds 7M 49
BARDSEY 5E 36
Bardsey Cres. BD3: B'frd 4F 6 (7E 64)
Bardsey Ho. BD4: B'frd 9H 65
(off Parsonage Rd.)
Bardwell Ct. WF3: S'ley 7N 105
Bare Bones Rd. HD9: Had E 2M 175
Bare Head La. HX3: North 8C 80
Barewell Hill S72: B'ley, Hems 5A 162
(not continuous)
Barfield Av. LS19: Yead 1L 47
Barfield Cres. LS17: Leeds 2H 51
Barfield Dr. LS19: Yead 1L 47
Barfield Gro. LS17: Leeds 2J 51
Barfield Mt. LS17: Leeds 2J 51
Barfield Rd. HX3: Hip 5H 99
Barfield Ter. LS27: Morl 2K 103
Bargate HD7: Linth 8C 136
Bargess Ter. LS25: Kip 4B 90
Barge St. HD1: Hud 8A 8 (6L 137)
Bargrange Av. BD18: Ship 9N 45
Bargreen HD5: K'htn 1F 138
Barham Ter. BD10: B'frd 2H 65
Bar Ho. La. BD20: Keigh 5F 26
Bar Ho. Row LS21: Pool 3E 32
Baring Av. BD3: B'frd 6H 65
Baring Gould Way WF4: Horb 1A 142
Bark Cl. HD8: Shel 6L 155
Barker Cl. HX3: Hal 9D 98
Barker Ct. HD2: Hud 1K 137
BARKEREND 3F 6 (7F 64)
Barkerend Rd. BD1: B'frd 3D 6 (7D 64)
BD3: B'frd 3D 6 (7E 64)
Barker Hill LS12: Gil 4E 84
Barker Ho. HX3: Hal 9C 98
Barker Pl. LS13: Leeds 5G 66
Barker Rd. WF4: Horb 9B 124
Barker's Rd. WF4: Dur 4G 143
Barkers Ter. HX7: Heb B 1G 95
(off Hangingroyd Rd.)
Barker St. OL14: Tod 6K 93
WF3: S'ley 6C 106
WF15: Liv 8M 101
Barkers Well Fold LS12: N Far 2G 85
Barkers Well Gth. LS12: N Far 2H 85
Barkers Well Ga. LS12: N Far 2H 85
Barkers Well Lawn LS12: N Far 2H 85
Bark Ho. La. HD8: Shel 6N 155
S75: Caw 4M 173
Barkhouse Wood La. WF11: Birk 1N 111
BARKISLAND 7G 117
Barkisland Mill Colne HX4: Bark 7K 117
Bark La. BD23: E'by 1A 10
LS29: Add 9N 11
Barkly Av. LS11: Leeds 4C 86
Barkly Dr. LS11: Leeds 4C 86
Barkly Gro. LS11: Leeds 3C 86
Barkly Pde. LS11: Leeds 4C 86
Barkly Pl. LS11: Leeds 4C 86
Barkly Rd. LS11: Leeds 3B 86
Barkly St. LS11: Leeds 4C 86
Barkly Ter. LS11: Leeds 4C 86
Barkston Wlk. BD15: All 7F 62
Bar La. BD20: Rid 7M 27
HX6: Ripp 9B 116
LS18: Hors 7B 48
LS23: Cliff 2F 38
LS25: Gar 7A 72
S75: Map, S'ross 9M 159
WF1: Wake 2M 125
WF4: Midg 8K 141
Barlbrough Pl. HD3: Hud 5F 136
Barlby Way LS8: Leeds 9L 51
Barleycorn Cl. WF1: Wake 2N 125
Barleycorn Yd. LS12: Leeds 7L 67
Barley Cote BD20: Rid 6N 27
Barley Cote Av. BD20: Rid 6M 27
Barley Cote Gro. BD20: Rid 6N 27
Barley Cote Rd. BD20: Rid 6N 27
Barley Cft. WF13: Dew 3C 122
Barleyfield Cl. WF1: Wake 3N 125
Barley Fld. Ct. LS15: Leeds 6B 70
Barley Flds. Cl. LS25: Gar 8M 71
Barleyfields Cl. LS22: Weth 2M 23
WF7: Ackw 5E 146
Barleyfields Ct. LS22: Weth 3M 23
Barleyfields La. LS22: Weth 3M 23
Barleyfields M. LS22: Weth 3M 23
Barley Fld. Sq. HX2: Hal 2K 97
Barleyfields Rd. LS22: Weth 2M 23
(not continuous)
Barleyfields Ter. LS22: Weth 3M 23
Barleyfields Wlk. LS22: Weth 4M 23
Barleyhill Cres. LS25: Gar 8M 71
Barleyhill La. LS25: Gar 7M 71
Barleyhill Rd. LS25: Gar 7L 71
Barley M. WF3: Rob H 1K 105
Barley St. BD22: Keigh 3G 43
Barlow Rd. BD21: Keigh 8H 27
Barlow St. BD3: B'frd 7F 64
Barmby Cl. WF5: Oss 7B 124
Barmby Cres. WF5: Oss 7C 124
Barmby Fold WF5: Oss 7B 124
Barmby Pl. BD2: B'frd 5F 64
Barmby Rd. BD2: B'frd 5F 64
Barmby St. BD12: Wyke 9B 82
Bar Mt. LS25: Gar 7A 72
Barmouth Ter. BD3: B'frd 5D 64
Barnaby Rd. BD16: Bgly 3H 45
Barnard Cl. LS15: Leeds 3F 70
Barnard Rd. BD4: B'frd 8E 6 (9E 64)
Barnard Ter. BD4: B'frd 8E 6 (9E 64)
Barnard Way LS15: Leeds 3F 70
BARNBOW CARR 1K 71
Barnbow La. LS15: Leeds 2J 71
Barnbrough St. LS4: Leeds 4M 67
Barnby Av. BD8: B'frd 7H 63
Barnby Royd HD5: Hud 3C 138
Barncliffe Hill HD8: Shel 8N 155
Barn Climbing & Activity Centre, The 1C 44
Barn Cl. LS29: Men 4D 30
Barn Ct. WF4: Wool 2H 159
Barncroft BD18: Ship 8A 46
Barncroft Cl. LS14: Leeds 8A 52
WF7: Ackw 5E 146
Barncroft Ct. LS14: Leeds 9N 51
Barncroft Dr. LS14: Leeds 9N 51
Barncroft Gdns. LS14: Leeds 9A 52
Barncroft Grange LS14: Leeds 9N 51
Barncroft Hgts. LS14: Leeds 8N 51

Barncroft Mt.—Bedlam La.

Barncroft Mt. LS14: Leeds 9N 51
Barncroft Ri. LS14: Leeds 9A 52
Barncroft Rd. LS14: Leeds 9A 52
Barncroft Towers LS14: Leeds 9N 51
Barnes Av. WF1: Wake 9J 105
Barnes Rd. BD8: B'frd 6L 63
WF10: C'frd 6D 108
Barnes St. OL14: W'den 2J 113
Barnet Gro. LS27: Morl 2K 103
Barnet Rd. LS12: Leeds 7N 67
Barnfield WF13: Dew 1E 122
(off Beckett Rd.)
Barnfold Pl. S72: Shaf 7K 161
Barns, The LS29: I'ly 7M 15
BARNSDALE BAR 1F 164
BARNSDALE BAR SERVICES 8G 148
Barnsdale Est. WF10: C'frd 6B 108
Barnsdale M. DN6: Cam 1N 165
Barnsdale Rd. LS26: Meth 3L 107
WF10: All B 9D 90
Barnsdale Vw. DN6: Nort 7N 149
Barnsdale Way WF7: Ackw 5E 146
WF9: Upt 2D 164
BARNSIDE 8E 170
Barnside La. HD9: H'wth 7D 170
Barnsley Beck Gro. BD17: Bail 4B 46
Barnsley Golf Course 7L 159
Barnsley Rd. HD8: Clay W 8H 157
HD8: Den D, Up C 2K 171
S36: Hoy, Pen 9L 173
S72: B'ley, Shaf 7L 161
S72: Cud 9J 161
S75: B Grn, Dart 9G 158
S75: Den D 3B 172
S75: Silk 9L 173
WF1: Wake 8M 9 (7M 125)
WF2: New, Wake 6L 143
WF4: Flock 7B 140
WF4: New, Not, Wool 7K 143
WF7: Ackw 6G 146
WF9: Hems 5A 162
WF9: S Kirk, S Elm 6K 163
Barnstaple Way BD4: B'frd 3H 83
Barnstone Va. WF1: Wake 3N 125
Barn St. BD22: Oxen 4C 60
Barnswick Cl. WF8: Pon 5K 129
Barnswick Vw. LS16: Leeds 3H 49
Baron Cl. LS11: Leeds 1C 86
Baronscourt LS15: Leeds 6E 70
Baronsmead LS15: Leeds 6D 70
Baronsway LS15: Leeds 6D 70
Barplas Ind. Pk. BD5: B'frd 3C 82
Barrack Rd. LS7: Leeds 1J 5 (3F 68)
Barracks Fold HD9: H'wth 6C 170
Barracks St. WF16: Heck 8N 101
Barrack St. LS7: Leeds 1H 5 (4F 68)
Barraclough Bldgs. BD10: B'frd 8J 47
Barraclough Sq. BD12: Wyke 9A 82
Barraclough St. BD12: Low M 7N 81
Barran Ct. LS8: Leeds 1M 5 (3H 69)
Barran St. BD16: Bgly 4F 44
Barras Gth. Ind. Est. LS12: Leeds 8L 67
Barras Gth. Pl. LS12: Leeds 8L 67
Barras Gth. Rd. LS12: Leeds 8L 67
Barras Pl. LS12: Leeds 8L 67
Barras St. LS12: Leeds 8L 67
Barrass Yd. WF2: Wake 6J 125
(off Park Gro. Rd.)
Barras Ter. LS12: Leeds 8L 67
Barratt's Rd. WF1: Wake 1K 9 (3L 125)
Barrett St. BD20: Sils 8D 12
Barrington Cl. HX3: Sou 8F 98
Barrington Pde. BD19: Gom 4L 101
BARROWBY
HG3 5L 21
LS25 6J 71
Barrowby Av. LS15: Leeds 7F 70
Barrowby Carr Dr. LS15: Gar 6H 71
Barrowby Cl. LS29: Men 4F 30
Barrowby Cres. LS15: Leeds 6F 70
Barrowby Dr. LS15: Leeds 7G 70
Barrowby La. HG3: Kirkby 2K 21
LS15: Leeds 6F 70
LS25: Gar, Leeds 6H 71
Barrowby Rd. LS15: Leeds 7G 70
Barrowby Vw. LS25: Gar 6M 71
Barrowclough La. HX3: Sou 5E 98
Barrows La. BD20: Stee 4B 26
Barrowstead HD8: Skelm 8E 156
Barr St. HD1: Hud 2A 138
Barr Ter. BD8: B'frd 6L 63
(off Washington St.)
Barry St. BD1: B'frd 4A 6 (7C 64)
Barsey Grn. La. HX4: Bark 5J 117
Barstow Fall WF8: Pon 9L 109
Barstow Sq. WF1: Wake 4J 9 (5L 125)
Bar St. OL14: Tod 8J 93
WF17: Bat 8G 102
Barthorpe Av. LS17: Leeds 7D 50
Barthorpe Cl. BD4: B'frd 3K 83
Barthorpe Cres. LS17: Leeds 7E 50
Bartle Cl. BD7: B'frd 2L 81
Bartle Ct. BD15: Wils 9A 44
Bartle Fold BD7: B'frd 1M 81
Bartle Gill Dr. BD17: Bail 3C 46
Bartle Gill Ri. BD17: Bail 3C 46
Bartle Gill Vw. BD17: Bail 3C 46
Bartle Gro. BD7: B'frd 2L 81
Bartle La. BD7: B'frd 2L 81
Bartle Pl. BD7: B'frd 2L 81
Bartle Sq. BD7: B'frd 1M 81
BARTON 6J 137
Barton Ct. LS15: Leeds 7D 70
Barton Gro. LS11: Leeds 1C 86
Barton Hill LS11: Leeds 1C 86
Barton Mnr. Cl. HD4: Hud 8G 137
Barton Mt. LS11: Leeds 1C 86
Barton Pl. LS11: Leeds 1C 86
WF17: Bat 8F 102
Barton Rd. LS11: Leeds 1C 86
Barton St. BD5: B'frd 2N 81
HD6: Brigh 9M 99
(off Manley St.)
Barton Ter. LS11: Leeds 1C 86
Barton Vw. LS11: Leeds 1C 86
Barton Way WF9: S Elm 4N 163
Barum Top HX1: Hal 4K 7 (5B 98)
Barwick Ct. LS27: Morl 8L 85
Barwick Grn. BD6: B'frd 4K 81
BARWICK IN ELMET 8L 53
Barwick Rd. LS15: Leeds 3C 70
LS25: Bar E, Gar 6M 71
Barwick Sq. BD22: Cros R 7F 42
Basford Ct. WF2: Wake 6J 125
Basford St. WF2: Wake 6J 125
Basilica LS1: Leeds 6F 4
Basil St. BD5: B'frd 2N 81
HD4: Hud 6J 137
Baslow Gro. BD9: B'frd 4L 63
Bassenthwaite Wlk.
WF11: Knot 1D 130
Bassett Way WF8: Pon 4N 129
Batcliffe Dr. LS6: Leeds 9M 49
Batcliffe Mt. LS6: Leeds 1M 67
Bateman Cl. S72: Cud 7J 161
Bateman Fold BD12: O'haw 8F 82
(off Mill Carr Hill Rd.)
Bateman St. BD8: B'frd 5B 64
Bates Av. HX6: Sow B 9F 96
Bates Hill WF8: Pon 6M 129
Bateson St. BD10: B'frd 8J 47
Bath Cl. LS13: Leeds 4F 66
Bath Gro. LS13: Leeds 4F 66
Bath La. LS13: Leeds 5F 66
Bath Pl. BD19: Cleck 5H 101
HD6: Ras 2M 119
HX3: Hal 1J 7 (3A 98)
Bath Rd. BD19: Cleck 5H 101
HX3: Hal 8B 98
LS11: Leeds 8C 4 (8C 68)
LS13: Leeds 5F 66
WF16: Heck 8A 102
Bath St. BD21: Keigh 9H 27
HD1: Hud 3A 8 (3M 137)
(John William St.)
HD1: Hud 7L 137
(Lockwood Rd.)
HD8: Kbtn 4K 155
HX1: Hal 5M 7 (6C 98)
HX5: Ell 5E 118
LS29: I'ly 4H 15
OL14: Tod 7K 93
(off Dalton St.)
WF13: Dew 2F 122
WF17: Bat 7G 102
BATLEY 8G 103
Batley Art Gallery 7F 102
Batley Av. HD1: Hud 4J 137
Batley Baths & Recreation Cen. 7F 102
Batley Bulldogs RLFC 8F 102
Batley Bus. & Technology Cen. WF17: Bat 8H 103
BATLEY CARR 1F 122
Batley Ct. BD17: Bail 3B 46
Batley Ent. Cen. WF17: Bat 6E 102
Batley Fld. Hill WF17: Bat 6F 102
Batley Rd. WF2: Kirk 6N 103
WF3: W Ard 6N 103
WF16: Heck 8B 102
Batleys Bldgs. HD1: Hud 3K 137
Batley Sports & Tennis Cen. 3E 102
Batley Station (Rail) 8G 103
Batley St. HD5: Hud 4B 138
HX3: Hal 3N 97
Baton Dr. HD3: Hud 1G 137
Batter La. LS19: Raw 3N 47
Battinson Rd. HX1: Hal 4M 97
Battinson St. HX3: Sou 7D 98
Battlefield Vw. BD11: B'haw 6M 83
Battye Av. HD4: Hud 7G 137
BATTYEFORD 6H 121
Battye St. BD4: B'frd 8G 65
WF13: Dew 2G 122
WF16: Heck 8A 102
Battye's Yd. HD1: Hud 5C 8
Baulk Head La. OL14: Tod 5A 94
Bavaria Pl. BD8: B'frd 5N 63
BAWN 9J 67
Bawn App. LS12: Leeds 9H 67
Bawn Av. LS12: Leeds 8H 67
Bawn Chase LS12: Leeds 8H 67
Bawn Dr. LS12: Leeds 8H 67
Bawn Gdns. LS12: Leeds 8H 67
Bawn La. LS12: Leeds 8H 67
Bawn Path LS12: Leeds 8J 67
(off Bawn Av.)
Bawn Va. LS12: Leeds 8H 67
(off Bawn Gdns.)
Bawn Wlk. LS12: Leeds 8J 67
(off Bawn Gdns.)
Bawson Ct. BD19: Gom 3L 101
Baxandall St. BD5: B'frd 2B 82
Baxendale Dr. LS13: Leeds 9E 48
Baxtergate WF8: Pon 3K 129
Baxter La. HX3: North 1F 98
Bay Cl. HD3: Hud 3H 137
Bayfield Cl. HD9: Had E 8N 169
Bay Hall HD1: Hud 1A 8 (2M 137)
Bay Hall Comn. Rd. HD1: Hud 2M 137
Bay Horse Ct. LS21: Otley 9L 17
(off Clapgate)
Bay Horse La. LS14: S'cft 9B 36
LS17: Leeds, S'cft 9B 36
Bay Horse Yd. LS1: Leeds 6G 5
LS28: Fars 3A 66
Bayldons Pl. WF17: Bat 7F 102
Baylee St. WF9: Hems 3E 162
Bayne Dr. BD4: B'frd 5F 82
Bay of Biscay BD15: All 2F 62
Bayonne LS20: Guis 7H 31
(off Silver Cross Way)
Bayswater Cres. LS8: Leeds 1M 5 (3H 69)
Bayswater Gro. BD2: B'frd 4H 65
LS8: Leeds 1M 5 (3H 69)
Bayswater Mt. LS8: Leeds 1M 5 (3H 69)
Bayswater Pl. LS8: Leeds 1M 5 (3H 69)
Bayswater Rd. LS8: Leeds 1L 5 (3G 69)
Bayswater Row LS8: Leeds 1M 5 (3H 69)
Bayswater Ter. HX3: Hal 9B 98
LS8: Leeds 1M 5 (3H 69)
Bayswater Vw. LS8: Leeds 1M 5 (4H 69)
Bayton La. LS18: Hors 1A 48
LS19: Hors, Yead 1A 48
Beachill Cres. WF4: Ryh 9K 145
Beachill Dr. WF4: H'cft 9K 145
Beachill Rd. WF4: Ryh 9K 145
Beacon Av. LS27: Morl 2L 103
Beacon Brow BD6: B'frd 3J 81
Beacon Bus. Cen. HX3: Hal 6D 98
Beacon Cl. BD16: Bgly 4G 45
Beacon Dr. WF9: Upt 1N 163
Beaconfield Rd. WF9: Bads 8M 147
Beacon Gro. BD6: B'frd 4L 81
LS27: Morl 2L 103
Beacon Hill WF9: Upt 1N 163
Beacon Hill Rd. HX3: Hal 2M 7 (4C 98)
Beacon Ho. WF9: Upt 1N 163
Beacon Pl. BD6: B'frd 4K 81
Beacon Ri. LS29: I'ly 5D 14
Beacon Rd. BD6: B'frd 3J 81
Beaconsfield Ct. LS25: Gar 6N 71
Beaconsfield Rd. BD14: Clay 1H 81
Beaconsfield St. HX3: Hal 6D 98
OL14: Tod 7L 93
Beacon St. BD6: B'frd 4M 81
BD7: B'frd 3K 81
HD2: Hud 1M 137
LS29: Add 1N 13
WF13: Raven 5B 122
Beacon Vw. LS27: Morl 2L 103
(off Tingley Comn.)
WF9: S Kirk 6J 163
WF9: Upt 1N 163
Beaden Dr. HD8: Lept 8J 139
Beadon Av. HD5: Hud 5F 138
Beagle Av. HD4: Hud 9H 137
BEAL 5M 111
Beal La. DN14: Beal 5N 111
WF11: Cri S 1L 131
Beamshaw WF9: S Kirk 8H 163
BEAMSLEY 5M 11
Beamsley Cl. LS29: Men 5E 30
Beamsley Ct. LS29: Men 6E 30
Beamsley Cft. LS29: Men 6E 30
Beamsley Gro. BD16: Bgly 4G 45
LS6: Leeds 4A 68
Beamsley Ho. BD18: Ship 1N 63
(off Bradford Rd.)
Beamsley La. BD23: Beam 4M 11
Beamsley Mt. LS6: Leeds 4A 68
Beamsley Pl. LS6: Leeds 4A 68
Beamsley Rd. BD9: B'frd 4N 63
BD18: Ship 1N 63
Beamsley Ter. LS6: Leeds 4A 68
Beamsley Vw. LS29: I'ly 5D 14
Beamsley Wlk. BD9: B'frd 4M 63
LS29: Men 5E 30
Beancroft Rd. WF10: C'frd 5D 108
Beancroft St. WF10: C'frd 6C 108
Beanland Ct. BD18: Ship 1N 63
(off Aireville Av.)
Beanland Gdns. BD6: B'frd 5L 81
Beanlands Pde. LS29: I'ly 4H 15
Bean St. HX5: Ell 5H 119
Bearing Av. LS11: Leeds 3E 86
Bear Pit Gdns. LS6: Leeds 3N 67
(off Chapel La.)
Beastfair WF8: Pon 3J 129
Beast Mkt. HD1: Hud 4C 8 (4N 137)
Beatrice St. BD19: Cleck 4H 101
BD20: Keigh 7J 27
BD22: Oxen 4C 60
Beatrice Taylor Ho. WF8: Pon 2K 129
(off Horsefair)
Beaufort Av. HD8: Shel 6K 155
Beaufort Gro. BD2: B'frd 3E 64
Beaufort M. WF7: Ackw 3H 147
Beaulah Ct. WF11: Knot 8F 110
Beaulieu Cl. S75: Map 9L 159
Beaulieu Vw. S75: Map 9L 159
Beaumont Av. HD5: Hud 5B 138
LS8: Leeds 5J 51
WF9: S Elm 6M 163
Beaumont Cl. WF3: S'ley 7A 106
Beaumont Clough Rd. HX7: Heb B 3F 94
Beaumont Ct. WF17: Bat 8F 102
(off Beaumont St.)
Beaumont Dr. S75: Hai 3B 158
WF4: W Bret 2A 158
(not continuous)
Beaumont Pk. Rd. HD4: Hud 9J 137
Beaumont Pl. WF17: Bat 8C 102
Beaumont Rd. BD8: B'frd 5N 63
S75: Kex 9E 158
Beaumont Sq. LS28: Pud 8A 66
Beaumont St. HD1: Hud 2C 8 (3N 137)
HD3: Hud 5E 136
HD4: Neth 2H 153
HD5: Hud 5B 138
HD8: Eml 2F 156
OL14: Tod 6J 93
WF3: S'ley 7A 106
WF17: Bat 9F 102
Beaumont Vw. HX7: Heb B 2E 94
Beauvais Dr. BD20: Rid 8A 28
Beaver Cl. BD22: Cros R 7E 42
Beaver Dr. WF13: Dew 4C 122
Becca La. LS25: Aber 8E 54
BECK BOTTOM 9E 104
Beck Bottom LS28: Cal 9J 47
LS28: Fars 2B 66
WF2: Kirk 9E 104
Beckbridge Ct. WF6: Norm 9K 107
Beckbridge Grn. WF6: Norm 9K 107
Beckbridge Grn. Ind. Est. WF6: Norm 9L 107
Beckbridge La. WF6: Norm 1K 127
(Hopetown Wlk.)
WF6: Norm 2M 127
(Loscoe La.)
Beckbridge Rd. WF6: Norm 9K 107
Beckbridge Way WF6: Norm 1K 127
Beckbury Cl. LS28: Fars 4A 66
Beckbury St. LS28: Fars 4A 66
Beckenham Pl. HX1: Hal 4L 97
Beckers Av. WF17: Birs 2E 102
Becket La. WF3: Loft 2K 105
Beckett Cl. WF4: Horb 9E 124
Beckett Ct. LS15: Leeds 8E 70
Beckett Cres. WF13: Dew 3C 122
Beckett Gro. WF13: Dew 4C 122
Beckett La. WF13: Dew 4C 122
Beckett Nook WF13: Dew 3C 122
BECKETT PARK 9N 49
Beckett Rd. WF13: Dew 1E 122
(not continuous)
Becketts, The LS6: Leeds 9B 50
(off Monk Bri. Rd.)
Becketts Cl. HX7: Hept 9G 76
Beckett's Pk. Cres.
LS6: Leeds 1M 67
Beckett's Pk. Dr. LS6: Leeds 1M 67
Beckett's Pk. Rd. LS6: Leeds 1N 67
Beckett Sq. HD8: Kbtn 3K 155
(off Riley La.)
Beckett St. LS9: Leeds 4L 5 (5G 69)
WF17: Bat 9F 102
Beckett Wlk. WF13: Dew 4C 122
Beckfield Cl. HD6: B Bri 6N 99
Beckfield La. LS25: Led 8L 91
WF11: Fair 8L 91
Beckfield Rd. BD16: Cot 8E 44
Beckfoot La. BD16: Bgly, Cot 5D 44
BECK HILL 7K 81
Beck Hill BD6: B'frd 6K 81
Beckhill App. LS7: Leeds 9C 50
Beckhill Av. LS7: Leeds 9C 50
Beckhill Chase LS7: Leeds 9C 50
Beckhill Cl. LS7: Leeds 9C 50
Beckhill Dr. LS7: Leeds 8C 50
Beckhill Fold LS7: Leeds 8C 50
Beckhill Gdns. LS7: Leeds 9C 50
Beckhill Gth. LS7: Leeds 9C 50
Beckhill Ga. LS7: Leeds 9C 50
Beckhill Grn. LS7: Leeds 9C 50
Beckhill Gro. LS7: Leeds 9C 50
Beckhill Lawn LS7: Leeds 9C 50
Beckhill Pl. LS7: Leeds 8C 50
Beckhill Row LS7: Leeds 8C 50
Beckhill Va. LS7: Leeds 8C 50
Beckhill Vw. LS7: Leeds 9C 50
Beckhill Wlk. LS7: Leeds 8C 50
Beck Ho's. BD16: Bgly 3F 44
(off Gawthorpe La.)
Beck La. BD16: Bgly 2E 44
LS22: Coll 8J 23
WF16: Heck 9N 101
Beckley Rd. WF2: Wake 5J 125
Beck Mdw. LS15: Bar E 9M 53
Beck Ri. WF9: Hems 2D 162
Beck Rd. BD16: Bgly 8D 28
HD1: Hud 1A 8 (2M 137)
LS8: Leeds 2H 69
Becks Ct. WF12: Dew 5J 123
Beck Side BD21: Keigh 1J 43
Beckside BD1: B'frd 4C 64
HX3: She 6J 81
LS25: Aber 9E 54
WF4: Flock 8F 140
Beckside Cl. LS29: Add 1M 13
LS29: Burl W 8C 16
Beckside Ct. BD20: Sils 8E 12
Beckside Gdns. HD5: Hud 6G 138
LS16: Leeds 8N 49
Beckside La. BD7: B'frd 1M 81
Beckside Rd. BD7: B'frd 9M 63
Beckside Vw. LS27: Morl 9M 85
Becks Rd. BD21: Keigh 1G 42
Beck St. BD21: Keigh 1H 43
Beck Vw. WF4: Not 3B 160
WF17: Birs 2A 102
Beck Way WF3: E Ard 4H 105
Beckwith Dr. BD10: B'frd 1H 65
Bective Rd. WF2: Wake 4G 124
Bedale WF3: W Ard 4N 103
Bedale Av. HD6: Ras 3K 119
HD8: Skelm 8C 156
Bedale Cl. HD8: Skelm 8C 156
Bedale Ct. LS27: Morl 9A 86
Bedale Dr. BD6: B'frd 4K 81
HD8: Skelm 8C 156
WF11: Knot 1D 130
Bedale Rd. WF10: C'frd 6B 108
Bedale Wlk. S72: Shaf 6K 161
Bedding Edge Rd. HD9: H'wth 9D 170
Bede Ct. WF1: Wake 1J 9 (3L 125)
Bede Ho. WF1: Wake 1J 9
Bede's Cl. BD13: Thorn 8C 62
Bedford Av. WF4: G Moor 5B 140
Bedford Chambers LS1: Leeds 6E 4
Bedford Cl. HD8: Lept 7J 139
LS16: Leeds 4H 49
WF4: Croft 2H 145
WF7: F'stne 7D 128
Bedford Ct. LS8: Leeds 9L 51
WF7: F'stne 7D 128
Bedford Dr. LS16: Leeds 4H 49
Bedford Farm Ct. WF4: Croft 2H 145
Bedford Fld. LS6: Leeds 2C 68
Bedford Gdns. LS16: Leeds 4H 49
Bedford Gth. LS16: Leeds 4H 49
Bedford Grn. LS16: Leeds 4H 49
Bedford Gro. LS16: Leeds 5H 49
Bedford Mt. LS16: Leeds 5H 49
(not continuous)
Bedford Pl. LS16: Leeds 4H 49
LS20: Guis 8J 31
(off Otley Rd.)
LS21: Otley 9N 17
Bedford Row LS10: Leeds 1F 86
Bedford St. BD4: B'frd 6C 6 (8D 64)
BD19: Cleck 5G 100
(off Westgate)
BD21: Keigh 9H 27
HX1: Hal 4J 7 (5A 98)
HX5: Ell 5E 118
LS1: Leeds 6E 4 (6D 68)
OL14: Tod 4G 92
Bedford St. Nth. HX1: Hal 3J 7 (5A 98)
Bedford Vw. LS16: Leeds 4H 49
Bedivere Rd. BD8: B'frd 7J 63
Bedlam La. LS21: Arth 3B 34

Bedlam Rd.—Bent Rd.

Bedlam Rd. HD9: Mel .8B 152
Beech Av. BD13: Denh .3J 61
HD5: Hud .5C 138
HD7: Golc .5D 136
HD9: T'bdge .8A 154
HX6: Sow B .7H 97
LS12: Leeds .6M 67
LS18: Hors .8F 48
OL14: Tod .6K 93
S72: Cud .9J 161
WF2: Wake .4H 125
WF3: S'ley .8A 106
WF4: N Cro .3J 145
BEECHCLIFFE .7H 27
Beech Cl. BD10: B'frd .5F 46
HX3: She .7J 81
LS16: Leeds .2M 49
LS29: Men .2E 30
S72: B'ley .6A 162
WF9: S Kirk .7H 163
Beech Cotts. HX7: Crag V .8L 95
Beech Ct. BD17: Bail .6N 45
(off Southcliffe Dr.)
LS14: Leeds .4N 69
WF5: Oss .5M 123
WF10: C'frd .6E 108
WF11: Knot .7F 110
Beech Cres. BD3: B'frd .5F 64
BD17: Bail .6L 45
LS9: Leeds .3M 69
WF8: D'ton .6B 130
WF10: C'frd .6K 109
Beech Cft. WF2: W'ton .3B 144
WF3: Loft .3N 105
WF8: Pon .9L 109
Beechcroft Cl. LS11: Leeds .4N 85
Beechcroft Mead LS17: Leeds .3J 51
Beechcroft Vw. LS11: Leeds .4N 85
Beechdale Av. WF17: Bat .5D 102
Beech Dr. BD13: Denh .3J 61
LS12: Leeds .6M 67
LS14: Leeds .4N 69
LS18: Hors .8E 48
WF7: Ackw .1G 147
Beecher St. BD21: Keigh .8L 27
HX3: Hal .2A 98
Beeches, The BD11: B'haw .8L 83
BD17: Bail .3B 46
LS20: Guis .6J 31
LS21: Pool .1G 32
LS22: Weth .3N 23
LS28: Pud .6M 65
WF4: S Comn .7J 127
Beeches End LS23: B Spa .1E 38
Beeches Rd. BD21: Keigh .8L 27
Beechfield LS12: N Far .2G 84
WF2: Wake .1N 143
Beechfield Av. HD8: Skelm .8D 156
Beechfield Dr. WF4: S Comn .7J 127
Beechfield Rd. HD2: Hud .1K 137
Beechfield Ter. BD19: Cleck .5J 101
(off Neville St.)
Beech Gdns. WF10: C'frd .6K 109
Beech Gro. BD3: B'frd .5F 64
BD14: Clay .9H 63
BD16: Bgly .2H 45
BD19: Gom .3L 101
BD20: Sils .8D 12
HX3: Hip .5M 99
LS6: Leeds .9N 49
LS25: Bur S .1D 110
LS26: Rothw .7A 88
LS27: Morl .1J 103
LS29: Men .5E 30
WF6: Norm .3H 127
WF7: F'stne .7E 128
WF9: Kins .8A 146
WF10: C'frd .7M 107
WF14: Mir .6L 121
WF16: Heck .7N 101
Beech Gro. Av. LS25: Gar .8M 71
Beech Gro. Gdns. LS26: Oul .8D 88
Beech Gro. Ter.
LS2: Leeds .2C 4 (4C 68)
LS25: Gar .8M 71
Beech Hill LS21: Otley .9L 17
WF8: Pon .2L 129
Beech Ho. LS16: Leeds .7M 49
Beechlands WF8: Pon .6M 129
Beech La. LS9: Leeds .3L 69
Beech Lees LS28: Fars .2N 65
Beech Mt. LS9: Leeds .3M 69
Beechmount Cl. BD17: Bail .3B 46
Beechnut La. WF8: Pon .2J 129
Beech Rd. BD6: B'frd .6A 82
DN6: Skel .8M 165
HX6: Sow B .8J 97
LS23: B Spa .9C 24
S72: Shaf .7L 161
WF9: Upt .2A 164
Beechroyd LS28: Pud .8B 66
Beechroyd Ter. BD16: Bgly .5E 44
Beech Spinney LS22: Weth .1N 23
Beech Sq. BD14: Clay .1H 81
Beech St. BD16: Bgly .5E 44
BD20: Stee .3C 26
BD21: Keigh .8L 27
HD1: Hud .5H 137
HD9: H'frth .3M 169
HX1: Hal .3H 7 (4A 98)
HX4: Holy .7N 117
HX5: Ell .5E 118
WF3: Ting .3A 104
WF8: Pon .4K 129
WF9: S Elm .8L 163
WF14: Mir .6L 121
Beech Ter. BD3: B'frd .6F 64
Beech Tree Av. LS5: Leeds .3J 67
Beechtree Ct. BD17: Bail .5M 45
HD2: Hud .8A 120
Beech Tree M. WF17: Bat .6D 102
Beech Tree Rd. WF7: F'stne .7E 128
Beechtree Rd. LS24: Tad .6N 39
Beech Vw. HX6: Sow B .7H 97
LS25: Aber .8D 54
Beech Vw. WF4: Hol .7H 143
WF11: Ferr .5M 109
Beech Vs. HX6: Sow B .8J 97
Beech Wlk. BD11: B'haw .9M 83
LS9: Leeds .3M 69
LS16: Leeds .5N 49
WF13: Dew .3F 122
(off Willan's Rd.)
Beech Way WF17: Birs .2D 102
BEECHWOOD
HX6 .9F 96
LS14 .9A 52
LS18 .4E 48
Beechwood LS26: W'frd .6D 88
LS29: I'ly .6J 15
WF8: Pon .4H 129
Beechwood Av. BD6: B'frd .3M 81
BD11: Drig .6A 84
BD18: Ship .8K 45
BD20: Rid .7M 27
HX2: Hal .8N 79
HX3: She .8G 81
HX6: Sow B .9F 96
LS4: Leeds .3N 67
WF2: Wake .5F 124
WF8: Pon .3H 129
WF14: Mir .6L 121
(not continuous)
Beechwood Cen. LS26: W'frd .6D 88
(off Beechwood)
Beechwood Cl. HX2: Hal .9M 79
LS17: Shad .3N 51
LS18: Hors .4D 48
Beechwood Ct. LS4: Leeds .3N 67
(off Beechwood Gro.)
LS14: Leeds .9N 51
LS16: Leeds .2L 49
Beechwood Cres. HX6: Sow B .9F 96
LS4: Leeds .3N 67
WF8: Pon .4H 129
WF9: Hems .3C 162
Beechwood Dale WF7: Ackw .3H 147
Beechwood Dr. BD6: B'frd .3N 81
HX2: Hal .8M 79
HX6: Sow B .9F 96
Beechwood Gro. BD6: B'frd .3N 81
BD11: Drig .6A 84
BD18: Ship .8K 45
HD2: Fix .7M 119
HX2: Hal .9M 79
LS4: Leeds .3N 67
LS29: I'ly .5E 14
WF4: Horb .1E 142
Beechwood Mt. LS4: Leeds .3N 67
WF9: Hems .3D 162
Beechwood Pk. HD6: B Bri .6N 99
Beechwood Pk. Nature Reserve .8M 79
Beechwood Pl. LS4: Leeds .3N 67
Beechwood Ri. LS22: Weth .2M 23
Beechwood Rd. BD6: B'frd .3M 81
HX2: Hal .9M 79
LS4: Leeds .3N 67
WF14: Mir .5L 121
Beechwood Row LS4: Leeds .3N 67
Beechwood St. LS4: Leeds .3N 67
LS28: Stan .5N 65
Beechwood Ter. LS4: Leeds .3N 67
Beechwood Vw. HX7: Heb B .2E 94
LS4: Leeds .3N 67
Beechwood Vs. HX2: Hal .9M 79
Beechwood Wlk. LS4: Leeds .3N 67
Beecroft Cl. LS13: Leeds .3D 66
Beecroft Cres. LS13: Leeds .3E 66
Beecroft Gdns. LS13: Leeds .3D 66
Beecroft Mt. LS13: Leeds .3D 66
Beecroft St. BD21: Keigh .9K 27
LS5: Leeds .3K 67
Beecroft Wlk. BD15: All .7F 62
Beehive Ct. WF15: Liv .1N 121
Beehive St. BD6: B'frd .6L 81
Beehive Yd. BD6: B'frd .6L 81
BEESTON .4B 86
BEESTON HILL .1C 86
Beeston Hurst HX6: Ripp .8M 115
Beestonley La. HX4: Bark, Holy, Stainl .7K 117
Beeston Pk. Cft. LS11: Leeds .3A 86
Beeston Pk. Gth. LS11: Leeds .3A 86
Beeston Pk. Gro. LS11: Leeds .3A 86
Beeston Pk. Pl. LS11: Leeds .3A 86
BEESTON PARK SIDE .5C 86
Beeston Pk. Ter. LS11: Leeds .3A 86
Beeston Rd. LS11: Leeds .3B 86
BEESTON ROYDS .3L 85
Beeston Royds Ind. Est. LS12: Leeds .2M 85
Beeston's La. LS17: N Rig .2N 19
Beeston Sq. S71: Ath .9A 160
Beeston Way WF10: All B .9B 90
Beevers Cotts. LS25: Gar .6M 71
Beevers Ct. LS16: Leeds .5K 49
BEGGARINGTON HILL .6N 103
Beggartons Row HX6: Mill B .4C 116
(off Lumb La.)
Behrens Warehouse BD1: B'frd .4D 6
Bela Av. BD4: B'frd .3G 82
Belcross Dr. HX3: Hal .1M 7 (3C 98)
Beldon Brook Grn. HD8: Fen B .9H 139
BELDON HILL .3K 81
Beldon La. BD7: B'frd .4L 81
Beldon Pk. Av. BD7: B'frd .3L 81
Beldon Pk. Cl. BD7: B'frd .3L 81
Beldon Pl. BD2: B'frd .4F 64
Beldon Rd. BD7: B'frd .2M 81
Belfast St. HX1: Hal .6M 97
Belford Cl. BD4: B'frd .2H 83
Belford Ct. LS6: Leeds .6A 50
Belfry, The LS19: Yead .1N 47
Belfry Ct. WF1: Out .7L 105
Belfry Rd. LS9: Leeds .9J 69
Belfry Way WF6: Norm .2L 127
Belgrave Av. HX3: Hal .1M 7 (4C 98)
WF5: Oss .7A 124
Belgrave Cl. HX3: Hal .4C 98
Belgrave Ct. HD6: Ras .4K 119
Belgrave Cres. HX3: Hal .4C 98
Belgrave Dr. HX3: Hal .4D 98
Belgrave Gdns. HX3: Hal .1M 7 (3C 98)
Belgrave Gro. HX3: Hal .3C 98
Belgrave M. LS19: Raw .3L 47
Belgrave Mt. HX3: Hal .3C 98
WF1: Wake .1K 9 (3M 125)
Belgrave Pk. HX3: Hal .3C 98
Belgrave Rd. BD16: Bgly .3F 44
BD21: Keigh .8H 27
Belgrave St. HX6: Sow B .7F 96
LS2: Leeds .5F 4 (6E 68)
WF5: Oss .6A 124
Belgrave Ter. HD1: Hud .3A 8 (3L 137)
WF1: Wake .1L 9 (3M 125)
Belgravia Gdns. LS8: Leeds .8L 51
Belgravia Rd. WF1: Wake .1G 9 (3K 125)
Belinda St. LS10: Leeds .1G 87
Belk's Ct. WF8: Pon .3J 129
(off Liquorice Way)
Bell Bank Vw. BD16: Bgly .3D 44
Bellbank Way S71: Ath .9A 160
Bellbrooke Av. LS9: Leeds .4K 69
Bellbrooke Gro. LS9: Leeds .4K 69
Bellbrooke Pl. LS9: Leeds .4K 69
Bellbrooke St. LS9: Leeds .4J 69
Bellcote Dr. HD5: Hud .5B 138
Bell Dean Rd. BD8: B'frd .6G 62
BD15: All .6G 62
BELLE GREEN .9K 161
BELLE ISLE
LS10 .5G 86
WF1 .8M 125
Belle Isle BD22: Haw .9C 42
Belle Isle Av. WF1: Wake .8M 9 (7M 125)
Belle Isle Cir. LS10: Leeds .5G 86
Belle Isle Cl. LS10: Leeds .5G 86
Belle Isle Cres. WF1: Wake .7M 125
Belle Isle Dr. WF1: Wake .8M 9 (7M 125)
Belle Isle Pde. LS10: Leeds .4G 86
Belle Isle Rd. BD22: Haw .8C 42
LS10: Leeds .3G 86
Bellerby Brow BD6: B'frd .4J 81
Bellerby Pl. DN6: Skel .7L 165
Bellerby Rd. DN6: Skel .7L 165
Belle Vw. Ter. LS23: Cliff .3D 38
(off Albion Ter.)
BELLE VUE .7A 126
Belle Vue BD2: B'frd .1G 65
BD8: B'frd .5B 64
BD13: Que .6D 80
HX4: Ripp .7F 116
LS29: I'ly .6H 15
Belle Vue Av. LS8: Leeds .9M 51
LS15: Scho .8G 53
Belle Vue Cl. BD10: B'frd .6F 46
Belle Vue Ct. LS3: Leeds .4A 4
Belle Vue Cres. HD2: Hud .8A 120
HX3: She .8G 81
Belle Vue Dr. LS28: Fars .3N 65
Belle Vue Est. LS15: Scho .9G 53
Belle Vue Ri. HX3: She .8G 81
Belle Vue Rd. HX3: She .8G 81
LS3: Leeds .3A 4 (5B 68)
LS15: Scho .9G 53
WF1: Wake .8N 125
Belle Vue St. WF17: Bat .7C 102
Belle Vue Ter. BD21: Keigh .1K 43
(off Feather St.)
HX2: Lud F .5C 96
HX3: Sou .7D 98
LS20: Guis .8J 31
LS27: Gil .7G 85
Bellflower Cl. WF10: C'frd .7A 108
Bellgreave Av. HD9: New M .2D 170
Bell Gro. LS13: Leeds .3F 66
Bell Hall Mt. HX1: Hal .8G 7 (7N 97)
Bell Hall Ter. HX1: Hal .8G 7 (7N 97)
Bell Hall Vw. HX1: Hal .8H 7 (7A 98)
Bell Ho. Av. BD4: B'frd .4F 82
Bell Ho. Cres. BD4: B'frd .5F 82
Bell La. LS13: Leeds .3F 66
WF7: Ackw .5E 146
Bellmont Cres. WF9: Hems .3E 162
Bellmount Cl. LS13: Leeds .3G 66
Bellmount Gdns. LS13: Leeds .2F 66
Bellmount Grn. LS13: Leeds .3G 66
Bellmount Pl. LS13: Leeds .2F 66
Bellmount Vw. LS13: Leeds .3G 66
Belloe St. BD5: B'frd .1B 82
Bell Rd. LS13: Leeds .3F 66
Bell Row HD6: Ras .2M 119
Bellshaw St. BD8: B'frd .7K 63
Bellspring La.
HD5: K'htn .1J 139
Bell St. BD12: Wyke .9A 82
HD4: Hud .8C 8 (6N 137)
HX3: Hal .1M 7 (3C 98)
LS9: Leeds .5J 5 (6F 68)
WF1: Wake .3H 9 (4K 125)
WF9: Upt .1D 164
WF13: Raven .6B 122
Bellway Ct. WF5: Oss .5E 124
Bellwood Av. LS23: Cliff .2D 38
Belmont WF11: B'ton .3B 110
Belmont Av. BD12: Low M .6C 82
BD17: Bail .4N 45
LS21: Otley .8K 17
Belmont Cl. BD17: Bail .4N 45
HD1: Hud .3A 8 (3M 137)
Belmont Cres. BD12: Low M .6C 82
BD18: Ship .7M 45
Belmont Gdns. BD12: Low M .6B 82
Belmont Grange WF15: Liv .1L 121
(off Cross St.)
Belmont Gro. BD6: B'frd .6B 82
LS2: Leeds .4C 4 (5C 68)
LS19: Raw .2N 47
Belmont Pl. HX1: Hal .6N 97
Belmont Ri. BD12: Low M .6C 82
BD17: Bail .4N 45
Belmont Rd. LS29: I'ly .5K 15
Belmont St. BD2: B'frd .1G 64
HD1: Hud .3A 8 (3M 137)
HD7: Slait .1N 151
HX3: Hal .4D 98
HX6: Sow B .8J 97
Belmont St. WF1: Wake .1H 9 (3K 125)
WF7: Street .6K 127
Belmont Ter. BD18: Ship .7M 45
HD7: Linth .9C 136
HX2: Lud F .7E 96
WF3: Thpe H .2H 105
Belmont Way WF9: S Elm .6A 164
Beltoft Cotts. LS17: Wee .7B 20
Belton Cl. BD7: B'frd .2M 81
Belton Gro. HD3: Hud .9G 118
Belton Rd. BD20: Sils .9E 12
Belton St. HD5: Hud .5C 138
Belvedere Av. LS11: Leeds .3D 86
LS17: Leeds .3F 50
Belvedere Cl. S72: Shaf .7K 161
Belvedere Ct. LS7: Leeds .1G 68
(off Harehills La.)
LS17: Leeds .3G 50
WF1: Out .7L 105
Belvedere Gdns. LS17: Leeds .3G 50
Belvedere Gro. LS17: Leeds .3F 50
Belvedere Mt. LS11: Leeds .3D 86
Belvedere Rd. LS17: Leeds .3F 50
WF17: Bat .8E 102
Belvedere St. BD8: B'frd .5N 63
Belvedere Ter. BD8: B'frd .6N 63
LS11: Leeds .3D 86
Belvedere Vw. LS17: Leeds .3G 50
Belvoir Dr. WF11: Knot .8D 110
Belvoir Gdns. HX3: Hal .9B 98
Bembridge Ct. WF2: Wake .6G 125
Bembridge Ho. WF2: Wake .6G 125
Bempton Ct. BD7: B'frd .1N 81
Bempton Gro. WF17: Birs .2C 102
Bempton Pl. BD7: B'frd .1N 81
Ben Booth La. WF4: G Moor .5B 140
Benbow Av. BD10: B'frd .1J 65
Bence Cl. S75: Dart .9G 158
Bence Farm Ct. S75: Dart .9G 159
Bence La. S75: Dart, Kex .9E 158
Bendigo Rd. WF12: Dew .2J 123
Benjamin St. WF2: Wake .4J 125
WF15: Liv .9M 101
Benjamin Sykes Way WF2: Wake .7E 124
Ben Kaye Row HD9: H'frth .4N 169
Ben La. LS17: N Rig .2B 20
Benn Av. BD7: B'frd .1L 81
Benn Cres. BD7: B'frd .1L 81
Bennet Ct. LS15: Leeds .6E 70
Bennett Av. WF4: Horb .9E 124
Bennett Ct. LS21: Otley .8K 17
Bennett La. WF12: Dew .9H 103
WF17: Bat .9H 103
Bennett Rd. LS6: Leeds .1N 67
Bennett St. HX3: Hal .6D 98
WF15: Liv .8M 101
Bennetts Yd. LS26: Rothw .9N 87
Benn Gdns. BD14: Clay .2G 80
Benn La. HD3: Hud .4E 136
Benn's Av. HD1: Hud .1A 8
Benns La. HX2: Lud .2E 96
Benny La. HD7: Golc .7A 136
Benny Parr Cl. WF17: Bat .7H 103
BENOMLEY .6C 138
Benomley Cres. HD5: Hud .7C 138
Benomley Dr. HD5: Hud .7C 138
Benomley Rd. HD5: Hud .7C 138
BEN RHYDDING .5K 15
Ben Rhydding Dr. LS29: I'ly .5K 15
Ben Rhydding Golf Course .6L 15
Ben Rhydding Rd. LS29: I'ly .6H 15
Ben Rhydding Station (Rail) .5K 15
Ben Royd Ter. HX4: Holy .8B 118
Benson Ct. BD2: B'frd .1B 64
Benson Gdns. LS12: Leeds .8L 67
WF6: Norm .9K 107
Benson La. WF6: Norm .8K 107
Benson's Mobile Home Pk. BD20: Rid .5A 28
Benson St. LS7: Leeds .2H 5 (4F 68)
Bentcliffe Av. LS17: Leeds .5F 50
Bentcliffe Cl. LS17: Leeds .6G 50
Bentcliffe Ct. LS17: Leeds .6G 50
Bentcliffe Dr. LS17: Leeds .5G 50
Bentcliffe Gdns. LS17: Leeds .6G 50
Bentcliffe Gro. LS17: Leeds .6G 50
Bentcliffe La. LS17: Leeds .6F 50
Bentcliffe Mt. LS17: Leeds .6G 50
Bentcliff Hill La. S75: Caw .6N 173
Bentcliff Wlk. BD15: All .7G 62
Bent Cl. La. HX7: Crag V .9L 95
Bentfield Cotts. BD14: Clay .9H 63
Bentfield Ter. BD14: Clay .9H 63
(off Bentfield Cotts.)
Bentham Way S75: Map .7J 159
Bent Head HX7: P Wel .5H 77
Bent Ho. HD9: Mel .8D 152
Bent La. HD9: H'frth .8N 169
Bent Lea HD2: Hud .5D 120
Bentley Av. HX3: Hip .5M 99
Bentley Cl. BD17: Bail .3N 45
Bentley Ct. LS7: Leeds .9B 50
LS26: W'frd .6D 88
Bentley Gdns. LS7: Leeds .9B 50
Bentley Gro. LS6: Leeds .9B 50
Bent Ley Ind. Est. HD9: Mel .6F 152
Bentley La. LS6: Leeds .9B 50
LS7: Leeds .9B 50
Bentley M. LS6: Leeds .9B 50
Bentley Mt. HX6: Sow B .7K 97
LS6: Leeds .9B 50
Bentley Pde. LS6: Leeds .9B 50
Bent Ley Rd. HD9: Mel .6F 152
Bentley Rd. WF2: Wake .7G 125
Bentley Royd Cl. HX6: Sow B .9G 97
Bentley Sq. LS26: Oul .8D 88
Bentley St. BD12: Wyke .1B 100
HD1: Hud .7K 137
Benton Cres. WF4: Horb .9E 124
Benton M. WF4: Horb .9E 124
Benton Office Pk. WF4: Horb .9E 124
Benton Pk. Av. LS19: Raw .2N 47
Benton Pk. Cres. LS19: Raw .2N 47
Benton Pk. Dr. LS19: Raw .2N 47
Benton Pk. Rd. LS19: Raw .2N 47
Bent Rd. HD9: H'wth .9B 170

Bents—Blackmoor La.

Bents BD22: Oxen 2C 60
Bents Foot BD16: Har 7A 44
Bents La. BD15: Wils 2N 61
HD7: Slait 1G 151
Bent St. HD4: Hud 8C 8 (6N 137)
Benwood Vw. WF4: Croft 2G 145
Benyon Pk. Way LS12: Leeds 1N 85
Beresford Rd. BD6: B'frd 6N 81
Beresford St. BD12: O'haw 8E 82
Beringa LS12: Leeds 7B 4 (7C 68)
Berkeley Av. LS8: Leeds 3J 69
Berkeley Cl. BD2: B'frd 3F 64
Berkeley Ct. LS2: Leeds 3A 4 (5B 68)
LS8: Leeds 3J 69
(off Chatsworth Rd.)
Berkeley Cres. LS8: Leeds 3J 69
Berkeley Cft. S71: Roys 5C 160
Berkeley Gro. LS8: Leeds 3J 69
Berkeley Ho. BD4: B'frd 2J 83
(off Stirling Cres.)
Berkeley Mt. LS8: Leeds 3J 69
Berkeley Rd. LS8: Leeds 3J 69
Berkeley St. LS8: Leeds 3J 69
Berkeley Ter. LS8: Leeds 3J 69
Berkeley Vw. LS8: Leeds 3J 69
Berking Av. LS9: Leeds 6M 5 (6H 69)
Berking Row LS9: Leeds 6H 69
Bermondsey M. LS21: Otley 1M 31
Bermondsey St. LS21: Otley 1M 31
Bernard St. HD2: Hud 8C 120
LS26: W'frd 7E 88
Berne Gro. WF1: Wake 2K 9 (4L 125)
Berners St. WF1: Wake 5M 9 (5M 125)
Berrington Way BD22: Oak 4B 42
Berry Bank La. HD9: H'frth, T'bdge 2N 169
BERRY BROW 1L 153
Berry Brow Station (Rail) 1L 153
Berry Cft. HD9: Hon 4L 153
Berrydale Cl. BD15: All 7F 62
Berry Dr. BD17: Bail 6B 46
Berryfield Gth. WF5: Oss 3N 123
Berry Greave HD7: Mars 4D 150
Berry Hill Cl. WF15: Liv 9M 101
Berry La. BD21: Keigh 2H 43
HX1: Hal 4M 7 (5C 98)
LS26: Gt P 5M 89
WF4: Horb 1D 142
Berry Mill La. HD3: Holy 2J 135
HX4: Holy 2J 135
Berry Moor Rd. HX6: Norl 1K 117
Berry Rd. HD9: Mel 6C 152
Berry's Bldgs. HX2: Hal 9M 79
(off Bairstow's Bldgs.)
Berry St. BD21: Keigh 9K 27
Berry's Yd. WF4: Horb 9D 124
Berry Vw. HD4: Hud 9L 137
Bertha St. LS28: Fars 4A 66
Bertie St. BD4: B'frd 2G 83
Bertram Dr. BD17: Bail 6N 45
Bertram Rd. BD8: B'frd 4A 64
Bertrand St. LS11: Leeds 9C 68
Berwick Av. WF16: Heck 6A 102
Berwick St. HX1: Hal 4M 7 (5C 98)
Besancon Bri. HD1: Hud 3A 8 (3M 137)
Bescaby Gro. BD17: Bail 3C 46
Bescot Way BD18: Ship 1C 64
Besha Av. BD12: Low M 7B 82
Besha Gro. BD12: Low M 7B 82
Bessbrook St. LS10: Leeds 2F 86
Bessingham Gdns. BD6: B'frd 5L 81
Best La. BD22: Oxen 4C 60
HD4: Farn T 3B 154
Beswick Cl. BD3: B'frd 7H 65
Beswick St. OL14: W'den 4J 113
Bethan Ct. WF4: H'cft 9L 145
Bethel Gdns. S75: Map 9K 159
Bethel Pl. WF2: Wake 8J 9
Bethel Rd. BD18: Ship 7B 46
Bethel St. BD20: E Mor 8C 28
HD6: Brigh 1N 119
HX3: Hal 2N 97
Bethel Ter. HX2: Lud 3D 96
HX6: Sow B 9K 97
HX7: Heb B 9J 77
Bethesda Row HX7: Heb B 3L 95
Betula Way HD8: Lept 7J 139
Beulah Gro. LS6: Leeds 3D 68
Beulah Mt. LS6: Leeds 3D 68
Beulah Pl. HX2: Lud F 7E 96
Beulah St. LS6: Leeds 3D 68
Beulah Ter. LS6: Leeds 2D 68
(off Beulah Gro.)
LS15: Leeds 4D 70
(off Austhorpe Rd.)
Beulah Vw. LS6: Leeds 3D 68
Bevan Av. WF6: Norm 3J 127
Bevan Ct. BD7: B'frd 2L 81
Bevan Pl. WF2: Wake 7E 124
Beven Gro. WF1: Wake 1M 9 (3M 125)
Beverley Av. BD12: Wyke 2B 100
LS11: Leeds 2D 86
Beverley Cl. HX5: Ell 4G 119
S71: Smit 9N 159
WF6: Norm 3J 127
Beverley Ct. HD2: Hud 9M 119
LS17: Leeds 5F 50
LS28: Fars 4A 66
Beverley Dr. BD12: Wyke 2B 100
WF12: Dew 3J 123
Beverley Gdns. WF17: Bat 2E 102
Beverley Gth. WF7: Ackw 5G 147
Beverley Pl. HX3: Hal 3A 98
Beverley Ri. LS29: I'ly 5D 14
Beverley Sq. LS11: Leeds 2D 86
Beverley St. BD4: B'frd 9H 65
Beverley Ter. HX3: Hal 3A 98
(not continuous)
LS11: Leeds 2D 86
Beverley Wlk. LS25: Gar 8N 71
Bevin Cl. WF1: Out 7L 105
Bevin Cres. WF1: Out 7L 105
Bevitt St. WF1: Wake 8N 125
Bevor Cres. WF16: Heck 6A 102
Bewdley Ct. S71: Roys 5E 160
Bewerley Cres. BD6: B'frd 7M 81
Bewerley Cft. LS11: Leeds 1D 86
Bewick Ct. BD6: B'frd 3G 81
Bewick Dr. BD16: Bgly 3H 45
Bewick Gro. LS10: Leeds 6H 87
Bexhill Cl. WF8: Pon 1M 129
Bexley Av. LS8: Leeds 1M 5 (4H 69)
Bexley Gro. LS8: Leeds 1M 5 (4H 69)
Bexley Mt. LS8: Leeds 1M 5 (4H 69)
Bexley Pl. LS8: Leeds 1M 5 (4H 69)
Bexley Rd. LS8: Leeds 1M 5 (4H 69)
Bexley Ter. LS8: Leeds 1M 5 (4H 69)
Bexley Vw. LS8: Leeds 1M 5 (4H 69)
Beza Ct. LS10: Leeds 3F 86
Beza Rd. LS10: Leeds 2F 86
Beza St. LS10: Leeds 2F 86
Bickerdike Pl. WF10: All B 9B 90
(off Victoria St.)
Bickerdike Ter. LS25: Kip 4A 90
Bickerdyke Bldgs. LS26: Meth 1L 107
(off Main St.)
Bickerton Way LS21: Otley 8J 17
Biddenden Rd. LS15: Leeds 4G 70
Bidder Dr. WF3: E Ard 3E 104
Bideford Av. LS8: Leeds 4H 51
Bideford Mt. BD4: B'frd 2J 83
BIERLEY 4F 82
Bierley Hall Gro. BD4: B'frd 6F 82
Bierley Ho. Av. BD4: B'frd 4F 82
Bierley La. BD4: B'frd 6F 82
Bierley Vw. BD4: B'frd 4G 83
Big Fellas Stadium, The 6D 128
Big Mdw. Dr. LS29: Add 1K 13
Bilberry Cl. BD14: Clay 2H 81
Bilberry Ri. BD22: Haw 9D 42
Bilham Rd. HD8: Clay W 7K 157
Billam's Hill LS21: Otley 8K 17
Billey La. LS12: Leeds 9H 67
Billingbauk Ct. LS13: Leeds 5G 66
Billingbauk Dr. LS13: Leeds 5G 66
Billing Ct. LS19: Raw 4A 48
Billing Dr. LS19: Raw 4B 48
Billingham Cl. WF2: Wake 3F 124
Billingsley Ter. BD4: B'frd 1F 82
Billington Ct. LS13: Leeds 5E 48
Billing Vw. BD10: B'frd 8G 47
LS19: Raw 4A 48
Billingwood Dr. LS19: Raw 4A 48
Bill La. HD9: H'frth 1A 170
Billy La. HX7: Wads 8K 77
Bilsdale Grange BD6: B'frd 5L 81
Bilsdale Way BD17: Bail 5M 45
BILTON IN AINSTY 1N 25
Bilton Pl. BD8: B'frd 6A 64
Bingham Pl. WF3: Loft 7J 105
BINGLEY 4E 44
Bingley Arts Centre & Little Theatre 4E 44
Bingley Bank LS17: Bard 6D 36
Bingley Five-Rise Locks 3E 44
Bingley Pool 4E 44
Bingley Relief Rd.
BD16: Bgly, Cot 1C 44
Bingley Rd. BD9: B'frd 1J 63
BD13: Cull 9K 43
BD17: Bail 1L 45
BD18: Ship 7J 45
BD21: Haw, Keigh 7F 42
BD22: Cros R 7F 42
LS20: Hawk 6M 29
LS29: Men 5C 30
Bingley St Ives Golf Course 5B 44
Bingley Station (Rail) 4E 44
Bingley St. BD8: B'frd 7M 63
BD21: Keigh 9J 27
LS3: Leeds 6A 4 (6B 68)
Binham Rd. HD2: Hud 2J 137
Binks Fold BD12: Wyke 2B 100
Binks St. WF1: Out 8L 105
Binn HD7: Slait 2N 151
Binnie St. BD3: B'frd 7F 64
Binn La. HD7: Mars 7G 150
Binn Rd. HD7: Mars 6F 150
Binns Fold BD15: Wils 1B 62
(off Main St.)
Binns Hill HX2: Hal 6H 97
Binns Hill La. HX2: Hal 6H 97
Binns La. BD7: B'frd 9L 63
HD9: H'frth 3L 169
Binns St. BD16: Bgly 4F 44
Binns Top La. HX3: Sou 9F 98
HX5: Ell 9F 98
Binswell Fold BD17: Bail 3A 46
Bircham Cl. BD16: Bgly 2H 45
Birch Apartments WF1: Wake 1L 9 (3M 125)
Birch Av. BD5: B'frd 3D 82
DN6: Skel 8M 165
HD8: Lept 8J 139
HX6: Rish 1C 134
LS15: Leeds 6B 70
OL14: Tod 5J 93
Birch Cliff BD17: Bail 5N 45
Birchcliffe HX7: Heb B 9J 77
Birchcliffe Centre, The HX7: Heb B 1J 95
(off Birchcliffe Rd.)
Birchcliffe Rd. HX7: Heb B 1H 95
Birch Cl. BD5: B'frd 3D 82
HD6: Clift 9A 100
WF4: H'cft 1J 161
Birch Cl. La. BD16: Bgly 8L 29
Birch Ct. BD11: B'haw 7M 83
LS27: Morl 2L 103
Birch Cres. LS15: Leeds 6B 70
Birchdale BD16: Bgly 1E 44
Birch Dr. LS25: Kip 2A 90
Birchen Av. WF5: Oss 6M 123
BIRCHENCLIFFE 9G 118
Birchencliffe Hill Rd. HD3: Hud 9G 118
Birchen Cl. WF10: C'frd 7A 108
Birchen Hills WF5: Oss 6M 123
Birchenlee Cl. HX7: Myth 3N 95
Birches, The LS16: B'hpe 6J 33
LS20: Guis 6J 31
Birchfield HX6: Norl 1K 117
Birchfield Av. LS27: Gil 7F 84
Birchfield Gro. HD8: Skelm 8D 156
Birchfields Av. LS14: Leeds 7D 52
Birchfields Cl. LS14: Leeds 8D 52
Birchfields Ct. LS14: Leeds 7D 52
Birchfields Cres. LS14: Leeds 7D 52
Birchfields Gth. LS14: Leeds 8D 52
Birchfields Ri. LS14: Leeds 8D 52
Birchfield Vs. HX7: Heb B 1J 95
(off Alexandra Rd.)
Birch Grn. WF8: Pon 2M 129
Birch Gro. BD5: B'frd 4C 82
BD21: Keigh 3H 43
HD7: Golc 5D 136
LS25: Kip 3A 90
WF10: C'frd 6J 109
WF17: Bat 4D 102
Birch Hill Ri. LS18: Hors 7H 49
Birch Ho. LS7: Leeds 8F 50
WF10: C'frd 5E 108
(off Parklands)
Birchington Av. HD3: Hud 9F 118
Birchington Cl. HD3: Hud 9G 118
Birchington Dr. HD3: Hud 9F 118
Birchlands Av. BD15: Wils 9A 44
Birchlands Gro. BD15: Wils 9A 44
Birch La. BD5: B'frd 2C 82
(not continuous)
HX2: Lud 4E 96
Birch M. LS16: Leeds 5N 49
Birch Pk. HD9: Brock 7B 154
LS23: T Arch 8J 25
Birch Rd. HD4: Hud 9K 137
LS25: Kip 2A 90
WF6: Norm 4J 127
Birchroyd LS26: Rothw 9A 88
Birchroyd Cl. HD2: Hud 9J 119
Birch St. BD8: B'frd 6L 63
(not continuous)
LS27: Morl 2L 103
WF1: Wake 7N 125
Birchtree Cl. WF1: Wake 3A 126
Birch Tree Gdns. BD21: Keigh 1L 43
Birchtree Wlk. WF11: Knot 9C 110
Birchtree Way LS16: Leeds 5H 49
Birch Vs. HX7: Heb B 1H 95
(off Birchcliffe Rd.)
Birch Wlk. OL14: Tod 6K 93
Birch Way BD5: B'frd 3D 82
Birchwood HD6: Brigh 9L 99
(off Elmwood Dr.)
Birchwood Av. BD20: Keigh 6H 27
LS17: Leeds 4J 51
WF17: Birs 2C 102
Birchwood Cl. HD3: Hud 1F 136
Birchwood Ct. LS29: I'ly 5F 14
WF15: Liv 9M 101
Birchwood Dr. BD20: Keigh 6G 27
Birchwood Gdns. BD10: B'frd 8G 46
Birchwood Hill LS17: Leeds 3J 51
Birchwood Mt. LS17: Leeds 3J 51
Birchwood Pk. HD9: New M 2C 170
Birchwood Rd. BD20: Keigh 6G 27
BIRDACRE 3M 101
Birdale Fld. La. LS22: Coll 9L 23
Birdcage HX3: Hal 4C 98
Birdcage Ct. LS21: Otley 2L 31
Birdcage Hill HX3: Hal 9N 97
Birdcage La. HX3: Hal 9N 97
Birdcage Wlk. LS21: Otley 2K 31
Bird Holme La. HX3: Hip 3G 99
Bird La. DN5: Clay 9H 163
HX6: Ripp 8C 116
BIRDS EDGE 4L 171
Birdsedge Farm M. HD8: Bird E 4L 171
Birdsedge La. HD8: Bird E 5K 171
Birds Nest La. HD8: Cumb 7G 171
BIRDS ROYD 2N 119
Birds Royd La. HD6: Brigh 2N 119
Birdswell Av. HD6: Clift 9B 100
Birdwalk, The BD6: B'frd 3H 81
BIRDWELL HILL 2J 21
Birfed Cres. LS4: Leeds 3L 67
BIRKBY 1L 137
Birkby Brow Cres. WF17: Birs 2E 102
Birkby Cft. HD2: Hud 1L 137
(off Nursery St.)
Birkby Fold HD2: Hud 2K 137
Birkby Hall Rd. HD2: Hud 1K 137
Birkby Haven BD6: B'frd 5K 81
Birkby La. BD19: Scho 5N 99
HD6: B Bri 5N 99
Birkby Lodge Rd. HD2: Hud 1K 137
Birkby Rd. HD2: Hud 9H 119
Birkby St. BD12: Wyke 9B 82
Birkdale Av. HD3: Hud 2F 136
Birkdale Cl. BD13: Cull 9L 43
LS17: Leeds 3D 50
S72: Cud 9K 161
Birkdale Ct. BD20: Keigh 5G 27
Birkdale Dr. LS17: Leeds 3C 50
Birkdale Grn. LS17: Leeds 3C 50
Birkdale Gro. HX2: Illing 6M 79
LS17: Leeds 3C 50
WF13: Dew 1D 122
Birkdale Mt. LS17: Leeds 3D 50
Birkdale Pl. LS17: Leeds 3C 50
Birkdale Ri. LS17: Leeds 3C 50
Birkdale Rd. S71: Roys 4C 160
WF13: Dew 2E 122
Birkdale Wlk. LS17: Leeds 3C 50
Birkdale Way LS17: Leeds 3C 50
BIRKENSHAW 8L 83
BIRKENSHAW BOTTOMS 9N 83
Birkenshaw La. BD11: B'haw 8M 83
Birkett St. BD19: Cleck 4H 101
Birkhead Cl. HD8: Kbtn 2J 155
Birkhead St. WF16: Heck 9B 102
Birk Hey Cl. HD6: B Bri 6N 99
Birkhill WF10: C'frd 4J 109
Birkhill Cres. BD11: B'haw 8M 83
BIRKHOUSE 6A 100
Birkhouse La. HD1: Hud 5K 137
HD4: Hud 5K 137
HD5: Hud 5B 138
HD6: B Bri 6A 100
HD8: Up C 1L 171
Birkhouse Rd. HD6: B Bri 5A 100
BIRKIN 2M 111
Birkin La. WF11: Birk 5H 111
Birklands Rd. BD18: Ship 8N 45
HD2: Hud 9L 119
Birklands Ter. BD18: Ship 8N 45
Birk La. LS27: Morl 9H 85
Birk Lea St. BD5: B'frd 1D 82
BIRKS
BD7 8L 63
LS27 2L 103
Birks HD7: Slait 8H 135
Birks Av. BD7: B'frd 9L 63
Birks Fold BD7: B'frd 8L 63
Birks Hall La. HX1: Hal 1G 7 (4N 97)
Birkshall La. BD4: B'frd 8F 64
Birks Hall St. HX1: Hal 2G 7 (4N 97)
Birks Hall Ter. HX1: Hal 2G 7 (4N 97)
BIRKSHEAD 2C 62
Birkshead Dr. BD15: Wils 1C 62
Birkshead M. BD15: Wils 1C 62
Birksland Ind. Est. BD4: B'frd 9F 64
Birksland Moor BD11: B'haw 1M 101
Birksland St. BD3: B'frd 9F 64
BD4: B'frd 9F 64
Birks La. HD8: Fen B 7E 138
HD8: Kbtn 6H 155
HX6: Mill B 4D 116
HX6: Ripp 6D 116
OL14: W'den 3K 113
Birks Rd. HD3: Hud 5F 136
Birkwith Cl. LS14: Leeds 7C 52
Birkwood Av. WF4: S Comn 9J 127
Birkwood Rd. WF6: Alt 9C 106
Birmingham La. HD9: Mel 6B 152
Birnam Gro. BD4: B'frd 8E 6 (1E 82)
Birr Rd. BD9: B'frd 3N 63
BIRSTALL 3B 102
Birstall La. BD11: Drig 8B 84
Birstall Retail Pk. WF17: Birs 9D 84
BIRSTALL SMITHIES 4B 102
Birthwaite Rd. S75: Kex 8D 158
Bishopdale Ct. HX1: Hal 8J 7 (7A 98)
Bishopdale Dr. LS22: Coll 9H 23
Bishopdale Holme BD6: B'frd 5K 81
Bishopgate St.
LS1: Leeds 7E 4 (7D 68)
Bishopgate Wlk. WF1: Wake 5K 9
(within Ridings Shop. Cen.)
Bishops Ct. HD4: Hud 2L 153
Bishop's Cft. WF2: Wake 3N 143
Bishop St. BD9: B'frd 3N 63
Bishops Way HD9: Mel 7D 152
LS14: Leeds 1N 69
WF10: C'frd 6B 108
WF14: Mir 4H 121
Bishop Way WF3: Ting 4B 104
Bisley Cl. S71: Roys 6F 160
Bismarck Ct. LS11: Leeds 1D 86
Bismarck Dr. LS11: Leeds 1D 86
Bismarck St. LS11: Leeds 1D 86
Bittern Ct. BD6: B'frd 3H 81
Bittern Cft. WF4: Neth 2A 142
Bittern Ri. LS27: Morl 1M 103
Blackberry Way BD14: Clay 2G 81
HX3: Hal 8D 98
Blackbird Gdns. BD8: B'frd 7G 63
Black Brook Ct. HD6: Brigh 8L 99
Black Brook Way HX4: Gree 5B 118
Black Bull St. LS10: Leeds 8H 5 (8F 68)
Blackburn Bldgs. HD6: Brigh 1A 120
Blackburn Cl. BD8: B'frd 7J 63
HX3: Hal 1M 97
Blackburn Ct. LS26: Rothw 8A 88
WF8: Pon 3J 129
Blackburn Ho. HX3: Hal 1N 97
Blackburn La. WF11: Knot 9H 111
Blackburn Pl. WF17: Bat 7G 102
Blackburn Rd. HD6: Brigh 8L 99
WF17: Birs 3B 102
Black Dyke La. BD13: Thorn 4A 62
Black Edge La. BD13: Denh 8K 61
Blacker Cres. WF4: Neth 4A 142
Blacker La. S72: Shaf 6K 161
WF4: Neth, Crig 3A 142
Blacker Rd. HD1: Hud 1A 8 (2L 137)
HD2: Hud 2L 137
S75: Map, S'ross 8L 159
Blacker Rd. Nth. HD1: Hud 1A 8 (2L 137)
Blackers Ct. WF12: Dew 7D 122
Blackett St. LS28: Cal 8M 47
Black Ga. HX7: P Wel 3L 77
Blackgate M. WF3: Ting 3A 104
BLACK GATES 3B 104
Blackgates Ct. WF3: Ting 4B 104
Blackgates Cres. WF3: Ting 4B 104
Blackgates Dr. WF3: Ting 4B 104
Blackgates Fold WF3: Ting 4B 104
Blackgates Ri. WF3: Ting 4B 104
Blackheath Cl. S71: Ath 9C 160
Blackheath Rd. S71: Ath 9C 160
Blackheath Wlk. S71: Ath 9C 160
BLACK HILL 8F 26
Black Hill HX7: P Wel 5J 77
Black Hill La. BD20: Keigh 7D 26
LS16: Ecc 7M 33
Black Hill Rd. LS21: Arth 4L 33
Black Horse Dr. HX4: Stainl 8L 117
Blackhouse Fold HX2: Illing 8K 79
Blackhouse Rd. HD2: Hud 9N 119
Black La. HD7: Linth 2D 152
Blackledge HX1: Hal 4M 7 (5C 98)
BLACKLEY 7D 118
Blackley Rd. HX5: Ell 6C 118
Blackman La. LS2: Leeds 2E 4 (4D 68)
LS7: Leeds 2E 4 (4D 68)
Blackmires BD13: Que 5C 80
HX2: Hal 8N 79
BLACK MOOR 3C 50
BLACKMOOR 9A 36
Blackmoor Ct. LS17: Leeds 2B 50
BLACKMOORFOOT 2C 152
Blackmoorfoot Rd. HD4: Hud 7H 137
HD7: Linth 2C 152
HD9: Mel 4B 152
Blackmoor La. LS17: Bard, S'cft 8B 36

Black Moor Rd.—Bowling Grn. Ct.

Black Moor Rd. BD22: Oxen ... 4E 60
LS17: Leeds ... 4B 50
Black Moor Top BD22: Haw, Oxen ... 9D 42
Blackpool Gro. LS12: Leeds ... 1K 85
Blackpool Pl. LS12: Leeds ... 1K 85
Blackpool St. LS12: Leeds ... 1K 85
Blackpool Ter. LS12: Leeds ... 1K 85
Blackpool Vw. LS12: Leeds ... 1K 85
Black Rd. WF1: Hea ... 8B 126
Blackshaw Beck La. BD13: Que ... 6F 80
Blackshaw Clough Rd. HX6: Ripp ... 5A 116
Blackshaw Dr. BD6: B'frd ... 5J 81
BLACKSHAW HEAD ... 9A 76
Blackshaw St. OL14: Tod ... 7M 93
Black Shepherd's La. *LS7: Leeds* ... *2G 69*
(off Shepherd's Gro.)
Black Sike La. HD9: H'frth ... 3H 169
Blacksmith Fold BD7: B'frd ... 1M 81
HD5: Hud ... 7D 138
Blacksmith La. LS16: Ecc ... 7B 34
Blacksmith M. WF3: Rob H ... 1K 105
Blacksmiths Fold HD5: Hud ... 8D 138
Blackstone Av. BD12: Wyke ... 2A 100
Blackstone Edge Old Rd. OL15: Lit ... 5A 132
Blackstone Edge Rd.
HX6: Heb B, Ripp ... 7F 114
HX7: Crag V ... 7F 114
Black Swan Ginnell HX1: Hal ... 4K 7
Black Swan Pas. HX1: Hal ... 4K 7
Blackthorn Cl. HX3: North ... 9F 80
Blackthorn Ct. LS10: Leeds ... 5F 86
Blackthorn Dr. HD3: Hud ... 1F 136
Blackthorn Rd. LS29: I'ly ... 4J 15
Blackthorn Way HD8: Clay W ... 7H 157
WF2: Wake ... 3H 125
Black Wlk. WF8: Pon ... 2K 129
Blackwall HX1: Hal ... 5K 7 (6B 98)
Blackwall La. HX6: Sow B ... 7G 97
Blackwall Ri. HX6: Sow B ... 7G 97
Blackwood Av. LS16: Leeds ... 4G 48
Blackwood Edge Rd. HX6: Rish ... 4J 133
Blackwood Gdns. LS16: Leeds ... 4G 48
Blackwood Gro. HX1: Hal ... 4M 97
LS16: Leeds ... 4G 49
Blackwood Hall La. HX2: Lud F ... 6C 96
Blackwood Mt. LS16: Leeds ... 4G 49
Blackwood Ri. LS16: Leeds ... 4G 49
Blacup Moor Vw. BD19: Cleck ... 5H 101
Blagden La. HD4: Hud ... 9L 137
Blairsville Gdns. LS13: Leeds ... 2E 66
Blairsville Gro. LS13: Leeds ... 2F 66
Blaithroyd Ct. HX3: Hal ... 6D 98
Blaith Royd La. HX7: Crag V ... 8G 95
Blaithroyd La. HX3: Hal ... 6D 98
Blake Cres. LS20: Guis ... 8K 31
Blake Gro. LS7: Leeds ... 9F 50
Blake Hall Dr. WF14: Mir ... 7M 121
Blake Hall Rd. WF14: Mir ... 7N 121
Blake Hill HX3: North ... 1D 98
Blakehill Av. BD2: B'frd ... 4G 64
Blake Hill End HX3: North ... 8E 80
Blakehill Ter. BD2: B'frd ... 4G 64
Blakeholme Cl. HD7: Slait ... 9L 135
Blakelaw Dr. HD6: Clift ... 9B 100
Blake Law La. HD6: Clift ... 1D 120
Blake Lee La. HD7: Mars ... 4B 150
Blakeley Cl. S71: Ath ... 9C 160
Blakeley Gro. WF2: Wake ... 5H 125
Blakeney Gro. LS10: Leeds ... 4F 86
Blakeney Rd. LS10: Leeds ... 4F 86
Blakeridge La. WF17: Bat ... 7E 102
BLAKESTONES ... 1L 151
Blakestones Rd. HD7: Slait ... 1L 151
Blakey Rd. WF2: Wake ... 3H 125
Blamires Pl. BD7: B'frd ... 2L 81
Blamires St. BD7: B'frd ... 2L 81
Blanche St. BD4: B'frd ... 8H 65
Blandford Gdns. LS2: Leeds ... 2D 4 (4D 68)
Blandford Gro. LS2: Leeds ... 2D 4
Blands Av. WF10: All B ... 8A 90
Bland's Cl. WF10: C'frd ... 5D 108
Blands Cotts. *LS25: Kip* ... *4B 90*
(off Ashtree Gro.)
Blands Cres. WF10: All B ... 8A 90
Blands Gro. WF10: All B ... 8A 90
Blands Ter. WF10: All B ... 8A 90
Bland St. HD1: Hud ... 8A 8 (6L 137)
HX1: Hal ... 4J 7 (5A 98)
Blanket Hall St. WF16: Heck ... 9N 101
Blantyre Ct. BD13: Cull ... 9K 43
Blayds Gth. LS26: W'frd ... 6B 88
Blayd's M. LS1: Leeds ... 8F 4 (7E 68)
Blayds St. LS9: Leeds ... 7M 5 (7H 69)
Blayd's Yd. LS1: Leeds ... 8F 4 (7E 68)
Bleach Mill La. LS29: Men ... 3B 30
Bleak Av. S72: Shaf ... 7K 161
Bleakley Av. WF4: Not ... 3C 160
Bleakley Cl. S72: Shaf ... 7K 161
Bleakley La. WF4: Not ... 4C 160
Bleakley Ter. WF4: Not ... 3C 160
Bleak St. BD19: Gom ... 4N 101
Bleak St. Lwr. BD19: Gom ... 4N 101
Bleasdale Av. HD2: Hud ... 1L 137
WF11: Knot ... 7E 110
Blencarn Cl. LS14: Leeds ... 2A 70
Blencarn Gth. LS14: Leeds ... 2A 70
Blencarn Lawn LS14: Leeds ... 2A 70
Blencarn Path LS14: Leeds ... 2A 70
Blencarn Rd. LS14: Leeds ... 2A 70
Blencarn Vw. LS14: Leeds ... 2A 70
Blencarn Wlk. LS14: Leeds ... 2A 70
Blenheim Av. LS2: Leeds ... 1E 4 (4D 68)
Blenheim Chase HD8: Clay W ... 8H 157
Blenheim Cl. WF11: Ferr ... 8B 110
Blenheim Ct. HX1: Hal ... 2J 7
LS2: Leeds ... 2E 4
Blenheim Cres. LS2: Leeds ... 1E 4
Blenheim Dr. WF13: Dew ... 2D 122
WF17: Bat ... 6F 102
Blenheim Gro. LS2: Leeds ... 2E 4 (4D 68)
Blenheim Hill WF17: Bat ... 5G 102
Blenheim Mt. BD8: B'frd ... 4A 64
Blenheim Pl. BD10: B'frd ... 6F 46
Blenheim Rd. BD8: B'frd ... 5A 64
WF1: Wake ... 1H 9 (3K 125)
Blenheim Sq. LS2: Leeds ... 1E 4 (4D 68)
WF17: Bat ... 6F 102
Blenheim St. BD21: Keigh ... 2H 43
HX7: Heb B ... 1J 95
Blenheim Ter. LS2: Leeds ... 2D 4
LS27: Morl ... 7K 85
WF17: Bat ... 6F 102
Blenheim Vw. LS2: Leeds ... 1D 4 (4D 68)
Blenheim Wlk. LS2: Leeds ... 1D 4 (4D 68)
Blenkinsop Ct. *LS27: Morl* ... *2L 103*
(off Britannia Rd.)
Blenkinsop Dr. LS10: Leeds ... 9G 87
Blenkinsop Way LS10: Leeds ... 9G 87
Blind La. BD11: Drig ... 6C 84
BD13: Que ... 2B 80
BD16: Har ... 5B 44
HX2: Lud F ... 4B 96
HX2: Ogd ... 5L 79
LS17: Shad ... 3N 51
OL14: Tod ... 6J 93
WF3: E Ard ... 7C 104
WF4: Col H ... 9F 144
YO26: B Ain ... 1M 25
Bloomer Ga. HX7: Myth ... 3A 96
Bloomfield Ri. S75: Dart ... 8J 159
Bloomfield Rd. S75: Dart ... 8H 159
Bloomfield Sq. *LS21: Otley* ... *1L 31*
(off Gay La.)
BLOOMHOUSE ... 7J 159
Bloomhouse La. S75: Dart ... 7G 159
Bloomingdale Ct. S75: W Gran ... 6G 158
Blossom Ct. HD5: Hud ... 4C 138
LS19: Yead ... 1M 47
Blossoms, The LS26: Meth ... 1L 107
Blossom Way WF10: C'frd ... 7N 107
Blucher St. BD4: B'frd ... 9H 65
Blue Ball La. HX6: Ripp ... 8M 115
Blue Ball Rd. HX6: Ripp ... 9K 115
Blue Bell HD7: Slait ... 2K 151
Bluebell Av. LS25: Gar ... 9A 72
Bluebell Cl. BD15: All ... 6G 63
BD18: Ship ... 1B 64
WF8: Pon ... 4K 129
Bluebell Ct. LS14: Leeds ... 7B 52
WF17: Birs ... 2B 102
BLUE BELL HILL ... 8L 137
Blue Bell Hill HD4: Hud ... 8L 137
Blue Bell La. OL14: Tod ... 2E 92
Bluebell M. WF10: C'frd ... 7N 107
Bluebell Rd. S75: Dart ... 6G 159
WF3: E Ard ... 4G 105
Bluebell Wlk. HX2: Lud ... 4E 96
WF12: Dew ... 5J 123
Bluebell Way WF9: Upt ... 2M 163
Bluebird Wlk. BD16: Bgly ... 3H 45
Blue Butts WF5: Oss ... 6M 123
Bluecoat Ct. LS22: Coll ... 9G 22
Blue Hill BD13: Denh ... 5K 61
Blue Hill Cres. LS12: Leeds ... 8K 67
Blue Hill Grange LS12: Leeds ... 9K 67
Blue Hill Gro. LS12: Leeds ... 8K 67
Blue Hill La. LS12: Leeds ... 8K 67
Bluehills La. HD8: Den D ... 2B 172
Blundell Rd. WF9: S Elm ... 6L 163
Blundell St. LS1: Leeds ... 4D 4 (5D 68)
Blythe Av. BD8: B'frd ... 6M 63
Blythe St. BD7: B'frd ... 7B 64
BMK Ind. Est. WF15: Liv ... 8M 101
Boardman St. OL14: Tod ... 6K 93
Boar La. LS1: Leeds ... 7F 4 (7E 68)
Boathouse La. WF14: Mir ... 8N 121
Boat La. LS26: Meth ... 2A 108
WF10: All B ... 1B 108
Bobbin Cl. HD6: B Bri ... 5A 100
HD7: Golc ... 6C 136
Bobbin Mill Cl. *BD20: Stee* ... *3C 26*
(off Bobbin Mill Ct.)
OL14: Tod ... 3D 92
Bobbin Mill Ct. BD20: Stee ... 3C 26
Bobbin St. OL14: Tod ... 3E 92
Bobby's La. HX7: Hept ... 7E 76
Bob La. BD15: All, Wils ... 2C 62
HX2: Hal ... 5K 97
BOCKING ... 7F 42
Bodiham Hill LS25: Gar ... 6B 72
Bodkin BD22: Oxen ... 4M 59
Bodkin La. BD22: Oxen ... 4L 59
Bodley Ter. LS4: Leeds ... 5N 67
Bodmin App. LS10: Leeds ... 8C 86
Bodmin Av. BD18: Ship ... 8D 46
Bodmin Cres. LS10: Leeds ... 8C 86
Bodmin Cft. LS10: Leeds ... 8D 86
Bodmin Dr. WF6: Norm ... 9J 107
Bodmin Gdns. LS10: Leeds ... 9C 86
Bodmin Gth. LS10: Leeds ... 9C 86
Bodmin Pl. LS10: Leeds ... 9D 86
(not continuous)
Bodmin Rd. LS10: Leeds ... 7B 86
Bodmin Sq. LS10: Leeds ... 9C 86
Bodmin St. LS10: Leeds ... 9C 86
Bodmin Ter. LS10: Leeds ... 9C 86
Bodylines Gym
Leeds ... 5K 5
Body Mania Fitness ... *8N 87*
(off Marsh St.)
Bodytech ... *8F 86*
(within Middleton District Cen.)
Boggart Hill LS14: Leeds ... 9N 51
Boggart Hill Cres. LS14: Leeds ... 9N 51
Boggart Hill Dr. LS14: Leeds ... 9N 51
Boggart Hill Gdns. LS14: Leeds ... 9N 51
Boggart Hill Rd. LS14: Leeds ... 9N 51
Boggart La. HD8: Skelm ... 6D 156
HX3: Hip ... 3J 99
HX6: Sow B ... 9H 97
Boggart Wood Vw. BD15: All ... 7G 63
BOG GREEN ... 7G 120
Bog Grn. La. HD5: Hud ... 6F 120
Bog La. LS15: Leeds, Scho ... 1H 71
BOGTHORN ... 3F 42
Boiling M. WF10: C'frd ... 6B 108
Boland Ct. BD22: Oak ... 4E 42
Boldgrove St. WF12: Dew ... 5K 123
Boldmere Rd. LS15: Leeds ... 7N 69
Boldron Holt BD6: B'frd ... 5L 81
Boldshay St. BD3: B'frd ... 6F 64
Bold St. BD8: B'frd ... 5A 64
Bolehill Pk. HD6: Brigh ... 6K 99
Bolingbroke Ct. BD5: B'frd ... 8A 6
Bolingbroke St. BD5: B'frd ... 3B 82
Bolland Bldgs.
BD12: Low M ... 8D 82
Bolland St. BD12: Low M ... 8C 82
Bolling Hall (Museum) ... 2E 82
Bolling Rd. BD4: B'frd ... 6C 6 (8D 64)
LS29: I'ly ... 6J 15
Bolsover Cl. LS25: Gar ... 7B 72
Bolster Gro. HD7: Golc ... 7A 136
BOLSTER MOOR ... 7A 136
Bolstermoor Rd. HD7: Golc ... 6N 135
Boltby La. BD6: B'frd ... 5K 81
BOLTON ... 3D 64
BOLTON ABBEY ... 2L 11
Bolton Abbey Station
Embsay and Bolton Abbey Steam Railway
... 3J 11
BOLTON BRIDGE ... 3K 11
Bolton Bri. Ct. *LS29: I'ly* ... *5F 14*
(off Bolton Bri. Rd.)
Bolton Bri. Rd. LS29: I'ly ... 5F 14
Bolton Brow HX6: Sow B ... 9K 97
Bolton Ct. BD2: B'frd ... 4E 64
Bolton Cres. BD2: B'frd ... 2F 64
Bolton Dr. BD2: B'frd ... 1F 64
Bolton Grange LS19: Yead ... 1N 47
Bolton Gro. BD2: B'frd ... 2F 64
Bolton Hall Rd. BD2: B'frd ... 1B 64
(not continuous)
Bolton La. BD2: B'frd ... 4B 64
BOLTON OUTLANES ... 2E 64
Bolton Priory (remains of) ... 1L 11
Bolton Rd. BD1: B'frd ... 3C 6 (7D 64)
(not continuous)
BD2: B'frd ... 3D 64
BD3: B'frd ... 1C 6 (4D 64)
BD20: Sils ... 7E 12
LS19: Yead ... 1N 47
LS29: Add ... 4L 11
Bolton St. BD3: B'frd ... 3E 6 (7E 64)
BD12: Low M ... 7A 82
(not continuous)
Bolton Ter. BD20: Sils ... 7E 12
Bolton Way LS23: B Spa ... 1C 38
Bolton Wife Hill WF4: Wool ... 9H 143
BOLTON WOODS ... 2C 64
Bolus Cl. WF1: Out ... 8L 105
Bolus La. WF1: Out ... 8K 105
Bonaccord Sq. *WF17: Bat* ... *8F 102*
(off Purlwell La.)
Bonaccord Ter. *WF17: Bat* ... *8F 102*
(off Gt. Wood St.)
Bonaire LS12: Leeds ... 7A 4 (7B 68)
Bond Ct. LS1: Leeds ... 6E 4
Bondgate LS17: Hare ... 1J 35
LS21: Otley ... 1L 31
WF8: Pon ... 1M 129
Bond St. HD6: Brigh ... 9M 99
HX1: Hal ... 5J 7
HX7: Heb B ... 1H 95
LS1: Leeds ... 6E 4 (6D 68)
OL14: Tod ... 7K 93
WF1: Wake ... 3H 9 (4K 125)
WF8: Pon ... 1L 129
WF13: Dew ... 3F 122
WF17: Bat ... 6F 102
WF17: Birs ... 3B 102
Bond Ter. WF1: Wake ... 3J 9
Bonegate Av. HD6: Brigh ... 9N 99
Bonegate Ct. *HD6: Brigh* ... *9N 99*
(off Old La.)
Bonegate Rd. HD6: Brigh ... 9M 99
Bone La. DN6: Cam ... 1N 165
Bonham Ct. *LS27: Morl* ... *9K 85*
(off Queen St.)
Bonn Rd. BD9: B'frd ... 4M 63
Bonny Clough Vw. HD7: Golc ... 6C 136
(Brook La.)
HD7: Golc ... 4B 136
(New La.)
Bonwick Mall BD6: B'frd ... 6K 81
Boocock St. *LS28: Stan* ... *5B 66*
(off Varley St.)
Bookbinders, The *LS2: Leeds* ... *7H 5*
(off Bk. York St.)
Bookers Fld. BD19: Gom ... 6N 101
BOOTH ... 9E 78
Bootham Pk. BD9: B'frd ... 4J 63
Booth Hill HX2: Lud ... 9E 78
Booth House Gallery ... 4J 169
Booth Ho. La. HD9: H'frth ... 4H 169
Booth Ho. Rd. HX2: Lud F ... 5C 96
Booth Ho. Ter. HX2: Lud F ... 5C 96
Booth La. HD8: Skelm ... 5D 156
Boothman Wlk. BD21: Keigh ... 2G 43
BOOTHROYD ... 3D 122
Boothroyd BD10: B'frd ... 6F 46
Boothroyd Ct. HD8: Kbtn ... 3G 154
Booth Royd Dr. BD10: B'frd ... 6F 46
Boothroyd Dr. HD4: Hud ... 7G 137
LS6: Leeds ... 1B 68
Boothroyd Grn. WF13: Dew ... 3E 122
Boothroyd La. HD6: Ras ... 3J 119
WF13: Dew ... 3D 122
Boothroyds Way WF7: F'stne ... 5A 128
Booths, The WF8: Pon ... 2L 129
Booth's Bldgs. *HD6: B Bri* ... *5N 99*
(off Field Top)
Booth St. BD10: B'frd ... 8F 46
BD13: Que ... 4C 80
BD18: Ship ... 8B 46
BD19: Cleck ... 4H 101
LS29: Burl W ... 7C 16
WF10: C'frd ... 4D 108
Booth's Yd. LS28: Pud ... 6B 66
Booth Ter. HX2: Lud ... 1E 96
BOOTHTOWN ... 3N 97
Boothtown Rd. HX3: Hal ... 1K 7 (1A 98)
Border Cl. HD3: Hud ... 1E 136
BOROUGH CORNER ... 6H 125
Boroughgate LS21: Otley ... 9L 17
Borough Mkt. HX1: Hal ... 4L 7
Borough Rd.
WF1: Wake ... 3J 9 (4L 125)
(not continuous)
Borrin's Way BD17: Bail ... 4B 46
Borrough Av. LS8: Leeds ... 7G 51
Borrough Vw. LS8: Leeds ... 7G 51
Borrowdale Cl. LS12: Leeds ... 4J 67
Borrowdale Ct. LS29: Men ... 6F 30
Borrowdale Cres.
LS12: Leeds ... 4J 67
Borrowdale Cft. LS19: Yead ... 9M 31
Borrowdale Dr. WF10: C'frd ... 3K 109
Borrowdale Rd. WF2: Wake ... 4G 125
WF12: Dew ... 1H 123
Borrowdale Ter. LS14: Leeds ... 3A 70
Boshaw HD9: H'frth ... 8N 169
Boston Av. LS5: Leeds ... 3J 67
Boston Hill HX7: Wads ... 7J 77
Boston M. LS23: B Spa ... 1E 38
Boston Rd. LS22: Coll, Weth ... 5M 23
LS23: Cliff ... 2D 38
BOSTON SPA ... 9E 24
Boston St. HX1: Hal ... 5M 97
HX6: Sow B ... 9G 97
WF10: C'frd ... 4E 108
Boston Towers LS9: Leeds ... 4K 5
Boston Wlk. BD6: B'frd ... 5L 81
Boswell Cl. S71: Roys ... 5C 160
Bosworth Av. WF6: Alt ... 8F 106
Bosworth Cl. BD15: All ... 4G 63
BOTANY ... 6D 28
Botany Av. BD2: B'frd ... 2D 64
Botany Dr. BD20: E Mor ... 6D 28
Botany La. HD8: Lept ... 5J 139
Botham Flds. HD3: Hud ... 5F 136
Botham Hall Rd. HD3: Hud ... 4E 136
BOTTOM BOAT ... 6C 106
Bottom Boat Rd. WF3: S'ley ... 6C 106
BOTTOMLEY ... 9K 117
BOTTOMLEY HOLES ... 9N 61
Bottomley La. HX4: Bark ... 9H 117
Bottomley Rd. OL14: W'den ... 5L 113
Bottomley St. BD5: B'frd ... 1B 82
BD6: B'frd ... 6L 81
HD6: Brigh ... 8N 99
Bottoms HX3: Hal ... 9C 98
HX7: Crag V ... 8L 95
Bottoms La. BD11: B'haw ... 9M 83
Boulder Bri. La. S71: Carl ... 7G 160
BOULDER CLOUGH ... 8D 96
Bouldergate HD7: Mars ... 5H 151
Boulevard, The
LS10: Leeds ... 8J 5 (8F 68)
LS12: Leeds ... 2N 85
LS28: Fars ... 4A 66
Boulevard Ct. *HD8: Kbtn* ... *3G 154*
(off Storthes Hall La.)
Boulevard Ri. LS10: Leeds ... 9G 86
Boundary, The BD8: B'frd ... 5K 63
Boundary Cl. BD17: Bail ... 2B 46
LS15: Leeds ... 7F 70
Boundary Ct. HD9: Scho ... 5B 170
Boundary Dr. S72: B'ley ... 6A 162
WF1: Wake ... 2L 125
Boundary Farm Rd.
LS17: Leeds ... 4C 50
Boundary La. WF6: Warm ... 4F 126
Boundary Pl. *BD2: B'frd* ... *4F 64*
(off Baker St.)
LS7: Leeds ... 1K 5 (4G 68)
Boundary Rd. WF13: Dew ... 1C 122
Boundary St. LS7: Leeds ... 1K 5 (4G 68)
WF16: Heck ... 8N 101
Boundary Ter. *WF13: Dew* ... *9C 102*
(off Kilpin Hill La.)
Bourbon Cl. BD6: B'frd ... 5N 81
Bourne Ct. S75: S'ross ... 7L 159
WF16: Heck ... 7A 102
Bourne St. BD10: B'frd ... 6F 46
Bourne Wlk. S75: S'ross ... 7L 159
Bourn Vw. Cl. HD4: Neth ... 2J 153
Bourn Vw. Rd. HD4: Neth ... 2J 153
Bourse, The LS1: Leeds ... 7F 4
Bouverie Ct. LS9: Leeds ... 8L 5 (8G 69)
Bowater Ct. BD4: B'frd ... 3K 83
Bow Beck BD4: B'frd ... 7F 6 (9E 64)
Bowbridge Rd. BD5: B'frd ... 1C 82
Bowcliffe Grange LS23: B'ham ... 7D 38
Bowcliffe Rd. LS10: Leeds ... 1H 87
LS23: B'ham ... 6C 38
Bower, The WF17: Bat ... 5C 102
Bower Grn. BD3: B'frd ... 7G 64
Bower Hill La. WF4: W Bret ... 9N 141
Bower La. WF13: Dew ... 9C 102
Bower Rd. LS15: Leeds ... 3F 70
Bower Slack Rd. HX6: Tri ... 2N 115
Bowers La. HX4: Bark ... 5K 117
Bowers Mill Ind. Est.
HX4: Bark ... 6K 117
Bowers Row LS26: W'frd ... 7M 89
Bower St. BD5: B'frd ... 7A 6
Bowes Nook BD6: B'frd ... 6K 81
Bowfell Cl. LS14: Leeds ... 2B 70
Bow Grn. BD14: Clay ... 1K 81
Bowland Av. BD17: Bail ... 6K 45
Bowland Cl. LS15: Leeds ... 7N 69
Bowland St. BD1: B'frd ... 6B 64
Bow La. HX7: Blac H ... 9B 76
Bowler Cl. BD12: Low M ... 7A 82
Bowlers Ct. WF1: Wake ... 2L 125
BOWLING ... 1F 82
Bowling All. HD6: Ras ... 3M 119
Bowling All. Ter. HD6: Ras ... 3M 119
Bowling Av. WF1: Wake ... 1H 125
Bowling Bk. La. BD4: B'frd ... 7F 6 (9E 64)
Bowling Ct. HD6: Brigh ... 9L 99
WF2: Wake ... *8K 125*
(off Major St.)
Bowling Ct. Ind. Est. BD4: B'frd ... 9G 64
Bowling Dyke HX1: Hal ... 1L 7 (4B 98)
HX3: Hal ... 1L 7 (4B 98)
Bowling Grn. Ct. HD3: Hud ... 3D 136
HX4: Stainl ... *8M 117*
(off Bk. Bowling Grn. Rd.)

Bowling Grn. Fold—Brearcliffe Cl.

Bowling Grn. Fold BD12: Wyke 1A 100
Bowling Grn. Rd. HX4: Stainl 8M 117
Bowling Grn. Ter. LS11: Leeds 9D 68
Bowling Grn. Vw. BD11: Drig 7B 84
Bowling Hall Rd. BD4: B'frd 1E 82
Bowling La. WF1: Wake 1H 125
WF2: Wren 1H 125
Bowling Mill HX3: Hal 2K 7 (4B 98)
Bowling Old La. BD5: B'frd 1C 82
(Albany St.)
BD5: B'frd 8A 6 (3B 82)
(Manchester Rd.)
Bowling Pk. Cl. BD4: B'frd 1D 82
Bowling Pk. Dr. BD4: B'frd 2D 82
Bowling St. HD4: Hud 6F 136
Bowling Swimming Pool 2E 82
Bowlplex
Glass Houghton 8F 108
(within Xscape)
Bowl Shaw La. HX3: North 7E 80
Bowman Av. BD6: B'frd 6N 81
Bowman Gro. HX1: Hal 5N 97
Bowman La. LS10: Leeds 8H 5 (7F 68)
Bowman Pl. HX1: Hal 5N 97
Bowman Rd. BD6: B'frd 6N 81
Bowman St. HX1: Hal 5N 97
WF1: Wake 9A 126
Bowman Ter. HX1: Hal 5N 97
Bowmere Dr. BD15: All 6G 63
Bownas Rd. LS23: B Spa 9C 24
Bowness Av. BD10: B'frd 2H 65
WF10: C'frd 3L 109
Bowness Dr. HD5: Hud 3B 138
Bowood Av. LS7: Leeds 8C 50
Bowood Cres. LS7: Leeds 8C 50
Bowood Gro. LS7: Leeds 8C 50
Bowood La. HX6: Tri 2D 116
Bowood Rd. HX5: Ell 6E 118
Bow St. BD21: Keigh 9J 27
HD1: Hud 6A 8 (5L 137)
LS9: Leeds 8K 5 (7G 68)
Bowwood Dr. BD20: Rid 8A 28
Boxhall Rd. HX5: Ell 4E 118
Box Ings La.
HD8: Kbtn, Shel 6J 155
Box La. WF8: Pon 1L 129
Box's Bldgs. WF17: Bat 6C 102
Box Tree Cl. BD8: B'frd 5K 63
Box Tree Gro. BD21: Keigh 1L 43
Box Trees HX2: Mix 1K 97
Box Trees La. HX2: Mix 1K 97
Boycott Dr. WF7: Ackw 5G 146
Boycott Way WF9: S Elm 5N 163
Boyd Av. BD3: B'frd 5J 65
Boyfe Hall HD5: Hud 7J 121
Boy Home La.
HX2: Lud F 6D 96
Boy La. BD4: B'frd 6F 82
HX3: Hal 2K 97
Boyle, The LS15: Bar E 7L 53
Boyne Dr. WF2: Wake 5J 143
Boyne Hill WF4: Chap 6J 143
Boyne St. HX1: Hal 4J 7 (5A 98)
Boynton St. BD5: B'frd 2B 82
Boynton Ter. BD5: B'frd 2C 82
Boys La. HX3: Hal 7M 7 (7C 98)
Boys Scarr HX2: Lud F 6D 96
Bracewell Av. BD15: All 6F 62
Bracewell Bank HX3: Hal 2N 97
Bracewell Dr. HX3: Hal 2M 97
Bracewell Gro. HX3: Hal 3N 97
Bracewell Mt. *HX3: Hal 2M 97*
(off Bracewell Dr.)
Bracewell Rd. HD9: Mel 8B 152
Bracewell St. BD21: Keigh 9L 27
Bracken Av. HD6: Brigh 7M 99
BRACKEN BANK 4F 42
Bracken Bank Av. BD22: Keigh 5F 42
Bracken Bank Cres. BD22: Keigh 4F 42
Bracken Bank Gro. BD22: Keigh 4F 42
Bracken Bank Wlk.
BD22: Keigh 5F 42
Bracken Bank Way BD22: Keigh 4F 42
Brackenbeck Rd. BD7: B'frd 1L 81
Brackenbed Grange HX2: Hal 3L 97
Brackenbed La. HX2: Hal 3M 97
Brackenbed Ter. *HX2: Hal 3M 97*
(off Brackenbed La.)
Bracken Cl. HD6: Brigh 7M 99
WF14: Mir 4H 121
Bracken Ct. LS12: Leeds 9A 68
LS17: Leeds 6E 50
Brackendale BD10: B'frd 5D 46
Brackendale Av. BD10: B'frd 5E 46
Brackendale Dr. BD10: B'frd 5D 46
Brackendale Gro. BD10: B'frd 5D 46
Brackendale Lodge BD10: B'frd 5D 46
Brackendale Pde. BD10: B'frd 5D 46
Brackendale Rd. WF2: Wake 8J 125
Bracken Edge BD10: B'frd 8G 47
LS8: Leeds 1H 69
Bracken Ghyll Dr. BD20: Sils 7D 12
Bracken Ghyll Golf Course 9K 11
Bracken Grange Ct. BD18: Ship 8J 45
Bracken Grn. WF3: E Ard 4G 105
Bracken Gro. HD2: Hud 7N 119
WF14: Mir 4H 121
BRACKENHALL 7A 120
Bracken Hall (Countryside Cen.) 4K 45
Brackenhall Ct. BD7: B'frd 1L 81
Bracken Hall Rd. HD2: Hud 8A 120
BRACKEN HILL 4H 121
BRACKENHILL 5D 146
Bracken Hill HX2: Hal 3L 97
LS17: Leeds 6E 50
WF7: Ackw 4D 146
WF9: S Kirk 5K 163
WF14: Mir 4H 121
Brackenhill Dr. BD7: B'frd 2L 81
Brackenhill M. BD7: B'frd 1L 81
Bracken Hill Vw. WF4: Horb 9B 124
Brackenholme Royd BD6: B'frd 5K 81
Brackenhurst Dr. LS17: Leeds 5E 50
Brackenhurst Pl. LS17: Leeds 5E 50
Bracken Mt. BD20: Sils 7D 12
Bracken Pk. BD16: Bgly 4H 45
(Gilstead La.)
BD16: Bgly 2G 45
(Moor Cft.)
LS14: S'cft 8B 36
Bracken Rd. BD20: East 3A 26
BD22: Keigh 3G 42
HD6: Brigh 7M 99
Brackens La. HX3: She 6G 81
Bracken Sq. HD2: Hud 7A 120
Bracken St. BD21: Keigh 3H 43
Bracken Way HX5: Ell 4G 119
Brackenwell La. LS17: N Rig 2N 19
Brackenwood Cl. LS8: Leeds 8G 51
LS29: I'ly 5K 15
Brackenwood Ct. WF1: Out 7M 105
Brackenwood Dr. LS8: Leeds 7G 50
Brackenwood Grn. LS8: Leeds 7G 51
Brackenwood Rd. WF1: Out 7M 105
Bradbeck Rd. BD7: B'frd 7L 63
Bradburn Rd. WF3: Rob H 1J 105
Bradbury St. WF13: Raven 6A 122
Bradcroft *HD1: Hud 1N 137*
(off Cobcroft Rd.)
Bradd Cl. WF15: Liv 7M 101
Bradfield Cl. HD2: Hud 6C 120
BRADFORD 3A 6 (7C 64)
Bradford 1 Gallery 5A 6 (8C 64)
Bradford & Heckmondwike Rd. BD4: E Bier 5K 83
Bradford & Wakefield Rd. BD4: B'frd 6N 83
Bradford Bulls RLFC 5C 82
Bradford Bus. Pk. BD1: B'frd 5C 64
Bradford Cathedral Church of St Peter
3C 6 (7D 64)
Bradford Chamber Bus. Pk. BD4: B'frd 8H 65
Bradford City AFC 5C 64
Bradford City Farm 6N 63
Bradford City Hall 5B 6 (8C 64)
Bradford Design Exchange 4D 6
Bradford Forster Square Station (Rail)
3B 6 (7C 64)
Bradford Golf Course 9E 30
Bradford Ice Arena 6A 6 (8C 64)
Bradford Industrial Mus. 3H 65
Bradford Interchange Station (Rail) 5C 6 (8D 64)
Bradford Kart Racing 8C 6 (9D 64)
Bradford La. BD3: B'frd 7H 65
BRADFORD MOOR 6G 64
Bradford Moor Golf Course 5G 64
Bradford Old Rd. BD16: Cot 8G 45
(not continuous)
HX3: Hal 1B 98
Bradford Park Avenue FC 6N 81
Bradford Playhouse and Film Theatre 4D 6
Bradford Rd. BD3: B'frd 5K 65
BD4: E Bier 5K 83
BD10: B'frd 1E 64
BD11: B'haw 9L 83
BD11: Drig 8E 84
(Buttercup Way)
BD11: Drig 6A 84
(Woodview)
BD12: O'haw 9E 82
BD14: Clay 9H 63
BD16: Bgly, Cot 5F 44
BD18: Ship 8M 45
BD19: Cleck 9E 82
BD19: Gom 9L 83
BD20: Rid 7L 27
BD21: Keigh, Rid 9K 27
HD1: Hud 3B 8 (3M 137)
HD2: Fix, Hud 5N 119
HD6: B Bri, Brigh 4N 99
HX3: North 1F 98
(Oaklands Av.)
HX3: North 3F 98
(Park Vw. Av.)
LS20: Guis 4F 30
LS21: Otley 2F 30
LS27: Gil 8E 84
LS28: Pud, Stan 5N 65
LS29: Burl W 9D 16
LS29: Men 4F 30
WF1: Wake 1G 9 (9H 105)
((Ruskin Av.))
WF1: Wake 1G 9 (3K 125)
(Wentworth St.)
WF2: Carr G, Wren 7G 104
(not continuous)
WF3: E Ard, Ting 3N 103
WF13: Dew 2F 122
WF15: Liv 6J 101
WF17: Bat, Birs 2N 101
Bradfords Cl. LS23: B'ham 5C 38
Bradford St. BD21: Keigh 8J 27
WF13: Dew 2G 122
Bradlaugh Rd. BD6: B'frd 4N 81
Bradlaugh Ter. BD6: B'frd 4A 82
Bradleigh Cl. BD21: Keigh 2L 43
BRADLEY 6D 120
Bradley Av. BD20: Sils 7D 12
WF10: C'frd 4C 108
Bradley Blvd. HD2: Hud 8A 120
Bradley Bus. Pk. HD2: Hud 6B 120
Bradley Carr Ter. WF9: S Elm 9M 163
Bradley Colliery La. HD2: Hud 7D 120
Bradley Ct. HX4: Gree 5A 118
Bradley Dr. BD20: Sils 7D 12
Bradley Grange Gdns. HD2: Hud 5D 120
Bradley Gro. BD20: Sils 7D 12
BRADLEY HILL 3D 66
Bradley Hill Vw. *LS28: Stan 4D 66*
(off Swinnow La.)
Bradley Junc. Ind. Est. HD2: Hud 7E 120
Bradley La. DN6: Wome 7M 131
HX4: Gree 5A 118
LS28: Pud 7M 65
BRADLEY MILLS 2B 138
Bradley Mills HD5: Hud 2B 138
Bradley Mills La. HD1: Hud 1F 8 (2A 138)
Bradley Mills Rd. HD1: Hud 1F 8 (2A 138)
HD5: Hud 2B 138
Bradley Pk. Golf Course 5B 120
Bradley Quarry Cl. HD2: Hud 5E 120
Bradley Quarry Nature Reserve 5E 120
Bradley Ri. BD20: Sils 7D 12
Bradley Rd. BD20: Sils 6D 12
HD2: Hud 6A 120
Bradley Sq. BD16: Har 6A 44
Bradley St. BD9: B'frd 2A 64
BD16: Bgly 3E 44
WF10: C'frd 4D 108
Bradley Ter. LS17: Leeds 3J 51
Bradley Vw. HX4: Holy 7N 117
BRADSHAW 4M 79
Bradshaw Av. HD9: Hon 6K 153
Bradshaw Cl. HD9: Hon 6K 153
Bradshaw Cres. HD9: Hon 6K 153
Bradshaw Dr. HD9: Hon 6K 153
Bradshaw La. HD7: Slait 9F 134
HX2: Brad 5M 79
Bradshaw Rd. HD9: H'frth 2G 168
HD9: Hon 8K 153
Bradshaw Row HX2: Brad 3M 79
Bradshaw Vw. BD13: Que 4B 80
HX2: Illing 6L 79
(off W. Scausby Pk.)
Bradstock Gdns. LS27: Morl 7K 85
Bradup BD20: Rid 3B 28
Bradwell La. WF5: Oss 6A 124
Brae Av. BD2: B'frd 3D 64
Braemar Cft. S72: S Hien 2L 161
Braemar Dr. LS25: Gar 6B 72
Braemar Ri. S72: S Hien 2L 161
Braeside HX2: Hal 5K 97
Brafferton Arbor BD6: B'frd 5K 81
Braine Cft. BD6: B'frd 6L 81
Braine Rd. LS22: Weth 3N 23
BRAITHWAITE 8E 26
Braithwaite Av. BD22: Keigh 8E 26
Braithwaite Ct. WF9: Hems 1E 162
Braithwaite Cres. BD22: Keigh 9F 26
Braithwaite Dr. BD22: Keigh 9F 26
Braithwaite Edge Rd.
BD22: Keigh 8D 26
Braithwaite Gro. BD22: Keigh 9F 26
Braithwaite M. *S75: Map 8L 159*
(off Braithwaite St.)
Braithwaite Rd. BD22: Keigh 9D 26
Braithwaite Row LS10: Leeds 3G 86
Braithwaite St. LS11: Leeds 8B 68
S75: S'ross 8L 159
BRAITHWAITE VILLAGE 9D 26
Braithwaite Wlk. BD22: Keigh 9F 26
Braithwaite Way BD22: Keigh 9F 26
Bramah St. S71: Carl 8D 160
Bramall Bus. Pk. BD5: B'frd 8A 6 (1C 82)
Bramall Ho. *BD3: B'frd 6K 65*
(off Chapman Rd.)
Bramble Av. LS23: B Spa 1B 38
Bramble Bank HD9: H'frth 2N 169
Bramble Cl. BD14: Clay 2H 81
BD22: Haw 9D 42
HX3: Hal 8D 98
WF8: Pon 5H 129
Bramble Ct. LS21: Pool 2G 33
WF1: Out 7J 105
Bramble Gro. HX5: Ell 4G 119
LS21: Pool 2G 33
Bramble M. LS17: Leeds 2L 51
Bramble Rd. S72: S Hien 3M 161
Brambles, The LS29: I'ly 5E 14
S71: Roys 5B 160
Brambleside BD13: Denh 5L 61
Bramble Sq. WF3: E Ard 4H 105
Bramble Wlk. WF17: Bat 3C 102
Brambling Dr. BD6: B'frd 3H 81
Brambling M. LS27: Morl 9M 85
Bramblings, The WF10: C'frd 7A 108
Bramcote Av. S71: Ath 9N 159
BRAMHAM 6C 38
Bramham Dr. BD17: Bail 3B 46
Bramham La. LS23: B'ham 4G 36
Bramham Pk. 8N 37
Bramham Pk. Ct. LS10: Leeds 1F 104
Bramham Rd. BD16: Bgly 3F 44
LS14: T'ner 1H 53
LS23: Cliff 4D 38
WF10: C'frd 6A 108
Bramham's Yd. LS25: Kip 4B 90
BRAMHOPE 5H 33
Bramhope Rd. BD19: Cleck 4G 101
Bramleigh Dr. LS27: Morl 7K 85
Bramleigh Gro. LS27: Morl 7K 85
BRAMLEY 3G 66
Bramley Baths (Swimming Pool) 3E 66
Bramley Cen. LS13: Leeds 3G 66
Bramley Cl. BD22: Oak 4B 42
HD9: New M 1B 170
Bramley Cres. WF1: Out 8K 105
Bramley Fold HX3: Hip 4J 99
Bramley Gdns. LS14: Leeds 6D 52
Bramley La. HX3: Hip 4H 99
WF4: W Bret, Wool 1C 158
Bramley Station (Rail) 5E 66
Bramley St. BD5: B'frd 8A 6 (9C 64)
(not continuous)
Bramley's Yd. LS1: Leeds 6G 5
Bramley Vw. HX3: Hip 4K 99
Brampton HX2: Lud F 3B 96
Brampton Ct. WF9: S Elm 4N 163
Bramsche Sq. *OL14: Tod 7K 93*
(off Brook St.)
Bramstan Av. LS13: Leeds 3D 66
Bramstan Cl. LS13: Leeds 3D 66
Bramstan Gdns. LS13: Leeds 3D 66
Bramston Gdns. HD6: Ras 3M 119
Bramston St. HD6: Ras 2M 119
Bramwell Rd. WF10: All B 8C 90
Bramwell Way
HX1: Hal 8J 7 (7A 98)
Branby Av. BD20: E Mor 7N 27
Brancepeth Pl. LS12: Leeds 7A 68
Branch Cl. LS12: Leeds 1K 85
Branch End LS27: Gil 6G 85
Branch La. HD2: Hud 8G 118
Branch Pl. LS12: Leeds 1K 85
Branch Rd. BD19: Scho 3D 100
HD2: Hud 7F 118
HX4: Bark, Gree 7K 117
Branch Rd. LS12: Leeds 6M 67
(Beech Dr.)
LS12: Leeds 1K 85
(Branch Pl.)
WF4: Cal G 6E 142
WF13: Dew 3F 122
WF17: Bat 7F 102
Branch St. HD1: Hud 5J 137
LS12: Leeds 1K 85
Brander App. LS9: Leeds 5M 69
Brander Cl. BD10: B'frd 9F 46
LS9: Leeds 5M 69
Brander Dr. LS9: Leeds 5L 69
Brander Gro. LS9: Leeds 5L 69
Brander Rd. LS9: Leeds 4M 69
Brander St. LS9: Leeds 4M 69
Brandfort St. BD7: B'frd 9M 63
Brand Hill App. WF4: Croft 1F 144
Brand Hill Dr. WF4: Croft 1F 144
Brandling Ct. LS10: Leeds 8E 86
BRANDON 2N 51
Brandon Cl. LS17: Leeds 6A 52
Brandon Ct. LS17: Leeds 2L 51
WF1: Out 8K 105
Brandon Cres. LS17: Leeds 9N 35
Brandon Golf Course 2M 51
Brandon Ho. *BD4: B'frd 3J 83*
(off Fontmell Cl.)
Brandon La. LS17: Leeds 9A 36
LS17: Wike 8M 35
Brandon Rd. LS3: Leeds 5B 4 (6C 68)
Brandon St. LS12: Leeds 7B 68
Brandon Ter. LS17: Leeds 2K 51
Brandon Vw. LS17: Shad 2M 51
Brandon Way LS7: Leeds 1F 68
Brandon Way Cres. LS7: Leeds 1G 68
BRANDY CARR 8F 104
Brandy Carr Rd. WF2: Kirk, Wren 1D 124
Branksome Ct. BD9: B'frd 4L 63
Branksome Cres. BD9: B'frd 3L 63
Branksome Dr. BD18: Ship 7H 45
Branksome Gro. BD18: Ship 7H 45
Branksome Pl. LS6: Leeds 4A 68
Branksome St. *LS6: Leeds 4A 68*
(off Queen's Rd.)
Branksome Ter. *LS6: Leeds 4A 68*
(off Queen's Rd.)
Bransby Cl. LS28: Fars 4B 66
Bransby Ct. LS28: Fars 4B 66
Bransby Ri. LS28: Fars 3B 66
Bransdale Av. LS20: Guis 8J 31
WF6: Alt 8H 107
Bransdale Cl. BD17: Bail 5M 45
LS20: Guis 8J 31
WF6: Alt 8H 107
Bransdale Clough BD6: B'frd 4K 81
Bransdale Gdns. LS20: Guis 8J 31
Bransdale Gth. LS20: Guis 8J 31
Bransdale M. WF6: Alt 8H 107
Bransdale Wlk. WF6: Alt 8H 107
Branshaw Dr. BD22: Keigh 2E 42
Branshaw Golf Course 4D 42
Branshaw Gro. BD22: Keigh 2E 42
Branshaw Mt. BD22: Keigh 2E 42
Branstone Gro. WF5: Oss 2N 123
Bran St. BD21: Keigh 3H 43
Brant Av. HX2: Illing 9M 79
Brant Bank La. LS29: Nes 3C 14
Brantcliffe Dr. BD17: Bail 3N 45
Brantcliffe Way BD17: Bail 2A 46
Brantdale Cl. BD9: B'frd 2H 63
Brantdale Rd. BD9: B'frd 2H 63
Brantford St. LS7: Leeds 9F 50
Brant La. LS24: Stut 9N 39
Brantom HX2: Lud F 7C 96
Brantwood Av. BD9: B'frd 2H 63
Brantwood Cl. BD9: B'frd 2H 63
Brantwood Cres. BD9: B'frd 2G 63
Brantwood Dr. BD9: B'frd 2H 63
Brantwood Gro. BD9: B'frd 2H 63
Brantwood Oval BD9: B'frd 2H 63
Brantwood Rd. BD9: B'frd 2G 63
Brantwood Vs. BD9: B'frd 2H 63
Branwell Av. LS20: Guis 7H 31
WF17: Birs 1B 102
Branwell Cl. LS20: Guis 7H 31
Branwell Ct. BD9: B'frd 4K 63
Branwell Dr. BD22: Haw 7C 42
Branwell Lodge BD7: B'frd 2M 81
Branwell Rd. LS20: Guis 7H 31
Branwell Wlk. WF17: Birs 1C 102
Branxholme Ind. Est. HD6: B Bri 5N 99
Brassey Rd. BD4: B'frd 1E 82
Brassey St. HX1: Hal 6J 7 (6A 98)
Brassey Ter. BD4: B'frd 8F 6 (1E 82)
Brathay Gdns. LS14: Leeds 3B 70
Braunstone Ct. LS29: Men 4D 30
Braybrook Ct. BD8: B'frd 3A 64
Bray Cl. BD7: B'frd 3J 81
Brayshaw Dr. BD7: B'frd 3J 81
Brayshaw Fold BD12: Low M 7C 82
Brayshaw Rd. WF3: E Ard 6E 104
Brayside Av. HD2: Hud 9L 119
BRAYTHORNE 2G 18
Braythorne La.
LS21: Stainb 2G 18
Brayton App. LS14: Leeds 1D 70
Brayton Cl. LS14: Leeds 1D 70
Brayton Gdns. DN6: Cam 9N 149
Brayton Gth. LS14: Leeds 1E 70
Brayton Grange LS14: Leeds 1E 70
Brayton Grn. LS14: Leeds 1E 70
Brayton Gro. LS14: Leeds 1D 70
Brayton Pl. LS14: Leeds 1E 70
Brayton Sq. LS14: Leeds 1E 70
Brayton Ter. LS14: Leeds 1D 70
Brayton Wlk. LS14: Leeds 1D 70
Brazil St. WF10: C'frd 4E 108
Bread St. WF1: Wake 4J 9 (5L 125)
Breakmoor Av. BD20: Sils 7E 12
Break Neck HX3: Hip 4F 98
Breaks Fold BD12: Wyke 2B 100
Breaks Rd. BD12: Low M 7C 82
Bream Av. BD19: Cleck 5G 100
Brearcliffe Cl. BD6: B'frd 5N 81

Brearcliffe Dr.—Broadmeadows

Brearcliffe Dr. BD6: B'frd 6M 81
Brearcliffe Gro. BD6: B'frd 6M 81
Brearcliffe Rd. BD6: B'frd 6N 81
Brearcliffe St. BD6: B'frd 6M 81
Brearley Gdns. WF15: Liv 9L 101
Brearley La. HX2: Lud F 3A 96
Brearley La. Top HX2: Lud F 3B 96
Brearley St. WF17: Bat 8E 102
Brearton St. BD1: B'frd 1A 6 (6C 64)
Breary Av. LS18: Hors 6G 49
(not continuous)
Breary Ct. LS16: B'hpe 5H 33
Breary La. LS16: B'hpe 5H 33
Breary La. E. LS16: B'hpe 5J 33
Breary Ri. LS16: B'hpe 5H 33
Breary Ter. LS18: Hors 6G 49
Breary Wlk. LS18: Hors 6G 49
Breck Lea HX6: Sow B 1G 116
Brecks BD14: Clay 9J 63
Brecks Gdns. LS25: Kip 2N 89
Brecks La. LS25: Kip 2M 89
LS26: Swil 1K 89
Brecks Rd. BD14: Clay 9J 63
Breck Willows HX6: Sow B 1F 116
Brecon App. LS9: Leeds 5M 69
Brecon Av. HD3: Hud 1F 136
Brecon Cl. BD10: B'frd 8F 46
Brecon Ct. LS9: Leeds 5M 69
Brecon Ri. LS9: Leeds 5M 69
Bredon Av. BD18: Ship 8D 46
Bredon Cl. WF9: Hems 2F 162
Breighton Adown
BD6: B'frd 5J 81
Bremit Wlk. BD6: B'frd 5N 81
Bremner St. LS21: Otley 9M 17
Brendon Ct. BD4: B'frd 2H 83
WF14: Up H 9K 121
Brendon Dr. HD2: Hud 1J 137
Brendon Wlk. BD4: B'frd 3H 83
Brentford Rd. BD12: Low M 6A 82
Brentlea Av. WF2: Wake 8K 125
Brentwood Cl. WF8: Thpe A 5N 147
WF17: Bat 7H 103
Brentwood Ct. LS16: Leeds 7K 49
Brentwood Gdns. BD6: B'frd 5B 82
Brentwood Gro. LS12: Leeds 7M 67
Brentwood Ho. WF7: F'stne 8C 128
Brentwood St. LS12: Leeds 7M 67
Brentwood Ter. LS12: Leeds 7M 67
Bretfield Ct. WF12: Dew 6G 122
Brettegate WF9: Hems 2C 162
Brett Gdns. LS11: Leeds 1D 86
Bretton Cl. S72: B'ley 7A 162
S75: Kex 9E 158
Bretton Country Pk. 4A 158
Bretton Ct. BD6: B'frd 5L 81
Bretton Lakes Nature Reserve 4N 157
Bretton La. WF4: W Bret, Crig 1B 158
Bretton Pk. Way WF12: Dew 6H 123
Bretton Rd. S75: Kex 9E 158
Bretton St. WF12: Dew 6G 123
Bretton St. Ent. Cen. WF12: Dew 6G 122
Brewerton La. WF13: Dew 1C 122
Brewery Ct. HD3: Hud 1F 136
Brewery Dr. HD4: Hud 8K 137
Brewery La. BD13: Que 6B 80
(Ambler Way)
BD13: Que 2C 80
(Carter La.)
WF11: Knot 8E 110
WF12: Dew 7F 122
Brewery Pl. LS10: Leeds 8H 5
Brewery Rd. BD21: Keigh 4G 43
LS29: I'ly 5H 15
Brewery St. BD21: Keigh 9K 27
HX3: Hal 2B 98
OL14: Tod 4G 92
WF16: Heck 9A 102
Brewery Wharf LS10: Leeds 8H 5 (7F 68)
(Bowman La.)
LS10: Leeds 8G 5
(Waterloo St.)
WF14: Mir 7L 121
Brewery Yd. HD8: Fen B 7G 138
Brexdale Av. LS25: Kip 2N 89
Brian Av. HD5: Hud 5C 138
Brian Cres. LS15: Leeds 4C 70
Brian Jackson Centre, The HD1: Hud 4A 8
Brian Pl. LS15: Leeds 3C 70
Brian Royd La. HX4: Gree 4M 117
Brian Royd Mills HX4: Gree 4M 117
BRIANSIDE 3B 70
Brian St. HD3: Hud 1G 136
Brian Vw. LS15: Leeds 3D 70
Briar Av. HD9: Mel 6B 152
Briar Bank WF9: Kins 8A 146
Briar Cl. HX5: Ell 6D 118
LS28: Fars 4A 66
WF16: Heck 7A 102
Briar Ct. HD9: H'frth 4J 169
WF16: Heck 8B 102
Briardale Rd. BD9: B'frd 2G 63
Briardene LS26: Oul 9D 88
Briar Dr. WF13: Dew 1C 122
Briarfield HD8: Den D 2D 172
Briarfield Av. BD10: B'frd 8E 46
Briarfield Cl. BD10: B'frd 8E 46
LS29: I'ly 6J 15
Briarfield Gdns. BD18: Ship 9N 45
HD5: Hud 4C 138
LS27: Gil 7F 84
Briarfield Gro. BD10: B'frd 8E 46
Briarfield Rd. BD18: Ship 1A 64
HD9: H'frth 1A 170
Briar Ga. LS22: Weth 2M 23
Briar Gro. S72: B'ley 6A 162
WF1: Wake 8N 125
Briar La. HD3: Hud 9N 119
Briarlea Cl. LS19: Yead 2K 47
Briarlyn Av. HD3: Hud 9F 118
Briarlyn Rd. HD3: Hud 9F 118
Briarmains Rd. WF17: Birs 2C 102
Briar Rhydding BD17: Bail 5C 46
Briar Rd. DN6: Skel 8M 165
Briarsdale Ct. LS8: Leeds 3L 69
Briarsdale Cft. LS8: Leeds 3L 69
Briarsdale Gth. LS8: Leeds 3K 69
Briarsdale Hgts. LS9: Leeds 3L 69
Briarsdale M. LS8: Leeds 3K 69
Briar Wood BD18: Ship 8C 46
Briarwood Av. BD6: B'frd 4N 81
BD20: Rid 7M 27
Briarwood Cl. WF1: Out 7M 105
Briarwood Cres. BD6: B'frd 4N 81
Briarwood Dr. BD6: B'frd 4N 81
Briarwood Gro. BD6: B'frd 3N 81
Briary Cl. WF1: Wake 9A 126
Brick & Tile Ter. HD6: Ras 2M 119
Brick Bank HD5: Hud 7D 138
Brickfield Gro. HX2: Hal 8N 79
Brickfield La. HX2: Hal 8N 79
Brickfield Ter. HX2: Hal 8N 79
Brick Mill Rd. LS28: Pud 8C 66
Brick Row BD12: Wyke 1A 100
HX3: Hal *8C 98*
(off Siddal La.)
WF13: Dew 3C 122
Brick St. BD19: Cleck 5G 100
BD21: Keigh 1J 43
LS9: Leeds 7J 5 (7F 68)
WF2: Wake 4F 124
Brick Ter. HD6: Ras 2N 119
Brickyard WF14: Mir 6K 121
Brickyard, The S72: Shaf 8K 161
Bride St. OL14: Tod 6K 93
Bridge, The LS10: Leeds 8G 5
Bridge Av. LS21: Otley 9L 17
Bridge Cl. HD8: Clay W 7H 157
LS23: B Spa 9E 24
WF4: Horb 1A 142
Bridge Cotts. LS25: Aber 8E 54
Bridge Ct. HD6: B Bri 5N 99
LS11: Leeds 9C 68
LS17: Hare 8G 21
LS22: Weth 5M 23
LS27: Morl 1L 103
WF9: Fitz 8A 146
Bridge Cft. HD3: Hud 6G 136
Bridge End HD6: Ras 2M 119
HX7: Myth 3M 95
LS1: Leeds 7F 4 (7E 68)
LS11: Leeds 8G 5
LS22: Weth 5N 23
Bridge End St. OL14: Tod 3E 92
Bridge End Wharfe WF1: Wake 7L 9
Bridge Fold LS5: Leeds 2J 67
Bridge Foot LS23: T Arch 9E 24
Bridge Gth. LS23: Cliff 2D 38
Bridge Ga. HX7: Heb B 1H 95
Bridgegate Fold BD10: B'frd 1H 65
Bridgegate Way BD10: B'frd 9H 47
Bridgehouse La. BD22: Haw 9C 42
Bridge La. HD9: H'frth 2M 169
HX3: She 7F 80
LS29: I'ly 4F 14
WF8: Thpe A 6N 147
WF11: Knot 7E 110
Bridge Lanes HX7: Heb B 1G 94
Bridge Mills HD9: H'frth 2M 169
Bridge Paddock LS22: Coll 8J 23
Bridge Pl. LS18: Hors 5F 48
Bridge Rd. BD20: Sils 7E 12
HD5: Hud 6E 120
HD6: Brigh 1M 119
LS5: Leeds 2J 67
LS11: Leeds 9C 68
LS13: Leeds 1B 66
LS23: B Spa 9E 24
WF4: Horb 2A 142
Bridge Row HD4: Neth 4H 153
Bridge Royd Bank OL14: Tod 6A 94
Bridge St. BD1: B'frd 5B 6 (8C 64)
BD13: Thorn 8D 62
BD20: Sils 7E 12
BD21: Keigh 1H 43
BD22: Oak 5B 42
HD4: Hud 7L 137
(Lockwood Rd.)
HD4: Hud 1L 153
(School La.)
HD7: Slait 1N 151
HX6: Sow B 9H 97
LS2: Leeds 6H 5 (6F 68)
LS21: Otley 9L 17
LS27: Morl 1L 103
OL14: Tod 7K 93
S75: Dart 8G 159
WF1: Wake 8M 9 (7M 125)
WF6: Norm 9K 107
WF8: Pon 2K 129
WF10: C'frd 4E 108
WF13: Raven 5C 122
WF16: Heck 8N 101
WF17: Bat 7G 102
WF17: Birs 4B 102
Bridge Ter. HX2: Wain 7E 78
LS17: Shad 3B 52
LS27: Morl 1L 103
Bridge Vw. LS13: Leeds 1B 66
Bridgewater Ct. LS6: Leeds 9B 50
Bridgewater Pk. Dr. DN6: Skel 7L 165
Bridgewater Pl. LS11: Leeds 8E 4 (8D 68)
Bridgewater Rd. LS9: Leeds 9H 69
Bridgeway BD4: B'frd 3H 83
Bridge Wood Cl. LS18: Hors 6G 48
Bridge Wood Vw. LS18: Hors 5G 48
Bridgland Av. LS29: Men 3E 30
Bridgwater Rd. BD9: B'frd 4M 63
Bridle Av. WF5: Oss 3M 123
Bridle Cl. WF4: Neth 3A 142
Bridle Dene HX3: She 8H 81
Bridle La. WF4: Neth 3A 142
WF5: Oss 3M 123
Bridle Path Rd. LS17: Leeds 2M 51
Bridle Path Wlk. LS15: Leeds 4B 70
Bridle Pl. WF5: Oss 3N 123
Bridle Stile HX3: She 8H 81
Bridle Stile La. BD13: Que 3D 80
Bridle St. WF17: Bat 7H 103
Bridleway LS27: Chur 6L 85
Bridley Dr. HD7: Slait 1N 151
Bridon Way BD19: Cleck 6J 101
Brierdene BD20: Sils 7E 12
Brierey Cl. S75: Dart 9J 159
Brier Hey HX7: Myth 3N 95
Brier Hey Cl. HX7: Myth 3N 95
Brier Hey Ind. Units HX7: Myth 4N 95
Brier Hey La. HX7: Myth 3N 95
Brier Hill Cl. BD19: Cleck 6E 100
Brier Hill Vw. HD2: Hud 6B 120
Brierlands Cl. LS25: Gar 6B 72
Brierlands Fold LS25: Gar 6B 72
Brier La. HD6: Brigh 1J 119
S72: S Hien 1J 161
WF4: H'cft 1J 161
BRIERLEY 6N 161
Brierley Cl. BD18: Ship 9A 46
Brierley Cres. WF9: S Kirk 6J 163
BRIERLEY GAP 8D 162
Brierley Rd. S72: B'ley, Grim 8N 161
S72: S Hien 4L 161
S72: Shaf 7L 161
Brier St. BD21: Keigh 3H 43
HX3: Hal 2B 98
Briery Cl. LS29: I'ly 5D 14
Briery Ct. WF2: Wake 7B 144
Briery Fld. BD18: Ship 1N 63
Briery Gro. WF14: Mir 9L 121
Briery Hall Farm WF2: Wake 7B 144
BRIESTFIELD 3D 140
Briestfield Rd. WF4: G Moor 5B 140
WF12: Bries, T'hill 3D 140
Brigantian Way
WF9: Hems, S Kirk 5G 162
Briggate BD17: Ship 7N 45
BD18: Ship 8A 46
BD20: Sils 7E 12
HD5: Hud 3E 138
HD6: Brigh 1M 119
(not continuous)
HX5: Ell 4E 118
LS1: Leeds 7F 4 (7E 68)
LS29: Nes 1B 14
Brigg Gdns. BD22: Keigh 9F 26
Briggland Ct. BD15: Wils 1B 62
Briggs Av. BD6: B'frd 4M 81
WF10: C'frd 6D 108
Briggs Bldgs. *LS27: Morl* *9L 85*
(off Melbourne St.)
Briggs Gro. BD6: B'frd 4M 81
Briggs La. WF4: Over 2H 141
Briggs Pl. BD6: B'frd 4M 81
Brigg's Row WF7: F'stne 7D 128
Briggs St. BD13: Que 4C 80
S71: Carl 8D 160
Briggs Ter. HD5: Hud 4A 138
Briggs Vs. *BD13: Que* *4D 80*
(off Briggs St.)
Briggs Yd. WF5: Oss 6M 123
Brigg Well Head Ga. HX7: Wads 7L 77
BRIGHOUSE 9M 99
Brighouse & Denholme Gate Rd.
HX3: North, She 9G 81
HX3: She 7F 80
Brighouse & Denholme Rd.
BD13: Denh, Que, Thorn 8L 61
Brighouse Rd. BD12: Low M 8B 82
BD13: Que 4E 80
HD2: Hud 8G 118
HX3: Hip 5H 99
HX3: She 4E 80
Brighouse Station (Rail) 2N 119
Brighouse Swimming Pool & Fitness Cen. 9N 99
Brighouse Wood La. HD6: Brigh 9L 99
Brighouse Wood Row HD6: Brigh 9L 99
Brighton Av. LS27: Morl 8J 85
Brighton Cliff LS13: Leeds 4F 66
Brighton Cl. WF17: Bat 6B 102
Brighton Gro. *HX1: Hal* *4N 97*
(off Pellon La.)
LS13: Leeds 5G 66
Brighton Rd. LS29: I'ly 6K 15
Brighton St. BD10: B'frd 6E 46
BD17: Ship 7N 45
HX3: Hal 3N 97
OL14: Tod 3E 92
WF2: Wake 6J 125
WF16: Heck 7A 102
Brighton Ter. BD19: Scho 4D 100
OL14: Tod *3E 92*
(off Brighton St.)
Bright St. BD4: B'frd 3G 83
BD13: Que 4E 80
BD14: Clay 1G 81
BD15: All 5G 63
BD22: Haw 8D 42
HX6: Sow B 7H 97
LS27: Morl 9J 85
LS28: Stan 4C 66
OL14: Tod 9J 93
WF3: E Ard 4F 104
WF13: Dew 2F 122
WF14: Mir 3K 121
Brignall Cft. LS9: Leeds 4M 5 (5H 69)
Brignall Gth. LS9: Leeds 4M 5 (5H 69)
Brignall Way LS9: Leeds 4M 5 (5H 69)
BRIG ROYD 6D 116
Brig Royd HX6: Ripp 6E 116
Brigshaw Dr. WF10: All B 6N 89
Brigshaw La. LS25: Kip 6N 89
WF10: All B 6N 89
Brindle Cl. BD15: All 7F 62
Brindle Pk. Dr. WF10: C'frd 6G 108
Brindley Gro. BD8: B'frd 7H 63
Brindley Rd. BD20: Sils 9F 12
Brindley Way WF2: Carr G 8H 105
Brink Bottom OL14: Tod 8A 94
Brink Top OL14: Tod 8A 94
Brinsmead Ct. LS26: Rothw 6A 88
Brisbane Av. BD2: B'frd 3C 64
Briscoe La. HX4: Gree 4A 118
Bristol Av. *BD20: Rid* *8A 28*
(off Ford Rd.)
Bristol St. HX3: Hal 9C 98
LS7: Leeds 3J 5 (5F 68)
Britannia Bldgs. *LS27: Morl* *2J 103*
(off Britannia Rd.)
Britannia Bus. Ent. Cen. WF5: Oss 5L 123
Britannia Cl. LS28: Stan 4C 66
Britannia Ct. LS13: Leeds 6D 66
Britannia Cres. HD2: Hud 2L 137
Britannia Ho. LS1: Leeds 6D 4
Britannia M. LS28: Pud 6D 66
Britannia Mills HD1: Hud 8B 8 (6M 137)
HD7: Slait *1N 151*
(off Britannia Rd.)
Britannia Rd. HD3: Hud 7D 136
HD7: Golc 7D 136
HD7: Slait 1M 151
LS27: Morl 2J 103
Britannia Sq. LS27: Morl 2J 103
Britannia St. BD5: B'frd 6C 6 (8D 64)
BD16: Bgly 4F 44
LS1: Leeds 7D 4 (7D 68)
LS28: Stan 4C 66
Britannia Ter. BD19: Cleck 4H 101
Britannia Trad. Est. HD3: Hud 6E 136
Britannia Wharf BD16: Bgly 4F 44
British Library
Boston Spa 6H 25
Britton St. BD19: Cleck 6K 101
Broadacre Rd. WF5: Oss 6A 124
Broadacres HD6: B Bri 5N 99
HD9: Hon 6L 153
WF4: Dur 3J 143
Broadacres Dr. LS22: Weth 4K 23
Broadacre Way BD17: Bail 2D 46
Broadbent Cft. HD9: Hon 5L 153
Broad Bottom HX7: Heb B 2L 95
BROAD CARR 7B 118
Broad Carr La. HD9: Jack B 5E 170
HX4: Holy 7B 118
Broad Carr Ter. HX4: Holy 6C 118
Broadcasting Pl. LS2: Leeds 2E 4
Broadcroft Chase WF3: Ting 5A 104
Broadcroft Dr. WF3: Ting 5A 104
Broadcroft Gro. WF3: Ting 4A 104
Broadcroft Way WF3: Ting 4A 104
Broad Cut WF4: Cal G 3F 142
Broad Cut Rd. WF4: Cal G 4E 142
Broad Dale Cl. BD20: E Mor 7A 28
Broadfield HD7: Slait 2M 151
Broadfield Cl. BD4: B'frd 4J 83
Broadfield Ind. Est. HD4: Hud 7L 137
Broadfield Pk. HD9: Holm 6H 169
Broadfields LS18: Hors 6G 48
Broadfield Way LS29: Add 1K 13
BROAD FOLDS 1H 81
Broadfolds BD14: Clay 1H 81
Broad Ga. OL14: Tod 7B 94
(Lee Bottom Rd.)
OL14: Tod 5L 93
(Scrapers La., not continuous)
Broadgate HD5: Hud 6B 138
HX4: Sow 9M 117
LS2: Leeds 5F 4 (6E 68)
WF5: Oss 6A 124
Broadgate Av. LS18: Hors 6G 49
Broadgate Ct. LS18: Hors 7G 49
Broadgate Cres. HD5: Hud 6B 138
LS18: Hors 7F 48
Broadgate Dr. LS18: Hors 6G 48
Broadgate Ho. BD1: B'frd 3B 6
Broadgate La. LS18: Hors 6F 48
Broadgate M. LS18: Hors 7G 49
Broadgate Ri. LS18: Hors 7G 49
Broadgates HD5: Hud 6B 138
Broadgate Wlk. LS18: Hors 7F 48
Broad Head La. BD22: Oak 4K 41
Broadheads Yd. *WF5: Oss* *6N 123*
(off Bank St.)
Broad Ings Way HX3: She 8H 81
Broadlands BD20: Keigh 8F 26
Broadlands Av. LS28: Pud 7C 66
Broadlands Ct. LS28: Pud 7C 66
Broadlands Gdns. LS28: Pud 7D 66
Broadlands Pl. LS28: Pud 7C 66
Broadlands Rd. HD9: Mel 6C 152
Broadlands St. BD4: B'frd 1H 83
Broadlands Vw. LS28: Pud 7D 66
Broadland Way WF3: Loft 4L 105
Broad La. BD4: B'frd 9H 65
DN14: Beal 5M 111
HD4: Thurs 6D 154
HD5: Hud 4B 138
HD9: U'thng 3J 169
HX2: Lud F 7C 96
(not continuous)
HX7: Heb B 3G 94
HX7: Hept 7C 76
LS5: Leeds 2F 66
LS13: Leeds 2F 66
LS28: Leeds 4D 66
OL14: Tod 2M 93
WF8: Pon 2K 129
WF9: S Kirk, S Elm 8G 163
Broad La. Bus. Cen. WF9: S Elm 8M 163
Broad La. Cl. LS13: Leeds 2H 67
Broadlea Av. LS13: Leeds 2H 67
Broadlea Cl. LS13: Leeds 2H 67
Broadlea Cres. BD5: B'frd 2D 82
LS13: Leeds 2H 67
Broadlea Gdns. LS13: Leeds 2H 67
Broadlea Gro. LS13: Leeds 2H 67
Broadlea Hill LS13: Leeds 2H 67
Broadlea Mt. LS13: Leeds 3J 67
Broadlea Oval LS13: Leeds 2H 67
Broadlea Pl. LS13: Leeds 3H 67
Broadlea Rd. LS13: Leeds 2H 67
Broadlea St. LS13: Leeds 2H 67
Broadlea Ter. LS13: Leeds 2H 67
Broadlea Vw. LS13: Leeds 2G 67
Broadley Av. HX2: Hal 2H 97
Broadley Cl. HX2: Hal 3J 97
Broadley Cres. HX2: Hal 3H 97
Broadley Gro. HX2: Hal 3J 97
Broadley Lathe HX2: Hal 3J 97
Broadley Rd. HX2: Hal 3H 97
Broadmead WF10: C'frd 4F 108
Broadmeadows WF1: Out 7L 105

Broad Oak—Brow Wood Ter.

Broad Oak HD7: Linth 8D 136
HX3: Hip 6J 99
Broad Oak La. HX3: Hip 6J 99
S36: Pen 7G 172
Broad Oak Pl. HX3: Hip 6J 99
Broadoaks Cl. WF12: Dew 4K 123
Broad Oak St. HX3: Hip 6J 99
Broad Oak Ter. HX3: Hip 6J 99
Broadowler La. WF5: Oss 6A 124
Broad Royd HX4: Stainl 8L 117
Broadstone Rd. HD8: Cumb 4J 171
Broadstones Pk. BD16: Bgly 5J 45
Broadstone St. OL14: Tod 6M 93
Broadstone Way BD4: B'frd 4J 83
Broad St. BD1: B'frd 3B 6 (7C 64)
HX1: Hal 4K 7 (5B 98)
HX6: Ripp 8C 116
LS28: Fars 3N 65
OL14: Tod 6K 93
WF13: Dew 5D 122
Broad St. Plaza HX1: Hal 3L 7
Broad Tree Rd. HX3: Hal 2N 97
Broad Vw. WF5: Oss 6B 124
Broad Wlk. LS2: Leeds 1B 4 (3C 68)
Broadwalk, The LS21: Otley 8J 17
Broadway BD1: B'frd 4B 6 (7C 64)
BD16: Bgly 4F 44
HD1: Hud 3C 8 (3N 137)
HX3: Sou 7D 98
HX6: Sow B 9E 96
LS5: Leeds 8H 49
LS15: Leeds 8A 70
LS18: Hors 9B 48
LS20: Guis 8G 30
S75: Map 8K 159
WF2: Wake 6E 124
WF8: Pon 3L 129
(not continuous)
WF9: S Elm 8L 163
Broadway Av. BD5: B'frd 3B 82
LS6: Leeds 4A 68
Broadway Cl. BD5: B'frd 3B 82
Broad Way Ct. WF12: T'hill 1H 141
Broadway Ct. HX6: Sow B 9E 96
Broadway Dr. LS18: Hors 7E 48
Broadway Shop. Cen. BD1: B'frd 4C 6 (7D 64)
Broadway Ter. WF9: S Elm 8L 163
Broadwell Dr. BD18: Ship 9C 46
Broadwell Rd. WF5: Oss 6B 124
Broadwood Av. HX2: Hal 3J 97
Brockadale Av. WF8: Pon 6K 129
Brockadale Nature Reserve 3G 148
Brock Bank HD5: Hud 3D 138
BROCKHOLES 7A 154
Brockholes Ind. Pk. HD9: Brock 7A 154
Brockholes La. HD4: Farn T 5B 154
HD9: Brock 7A 154
Brockholes Station (Rail) 6A 154
Brocklebank Cl. BD20: E Mor 7A 28
Brocklesby Dr. BD15: All 6G 62
Brocklyn Yd. HX1: Hal 5M 7
Brocks HX2: Lud F 7C 96
Brockswood Ct. WF2: W'ton 4D 144
Brockwell Gdns. HX6: Sow B 9G 96
Brockwell Ga. HX6: Sow B 9G 96
Brockwell La. HX6: Sow B 9F 96
(not continuous)
HX6: Tri 1F 116
Broc-O-Bank DN6: Nort 7N 149
Brodley Cl. HX3: Hip 4H 99
Brodrick Ct. LS6: Leeds 1N 67
Brodrick Dr. LS29: I'ly 6F 14
Brodwell Grange LS18: Hors 7H 49
Brogans Yd. *LS21: Otley 1M 31*
(off Cambridge St.)
Brogdens Fold LS17: N Rig 2N 19
Broken Cross HD5: Hud 8C 138
Broken Way *BD5: B'frd 3B 82*
(off Delamere St.)
Bromet Pl. BD2: B'frd 2F 64
Bromfield Ct. S71: Roys 5E 160
Bromford Rd. BD4: B'frd 1F 82
Bromley Av. HD9: New M 1B 170
Bromley Bank HD8: Den D 2B 172
Bromley Gro. BD22: Keigh 2E 42
Bromley Mt. WF1: Wake 7M 125
Bromley Rd. BD16: Bgly 3E 44
BD18: Ship 7K 45
HD2: Hud 1L 137
WF17: Bat 9H 103
Bromley St. WF17: Bat 9G 103
Brompton Av. BD4: B'frd 2E 82
Brompton Gro. LS11: Leeds 3D 86
Brompton Mt. LS11: Leeds 3D 86
Brompton Rd. BD4: B'frd 1E 82
Brompton Row LS11: Leeds 3D 86
Brompton Ter. BD4: B'frd 1E 82
LS11: Leeds 3D 86
Brompton Vw. LS11: Leeds 3D 86
Bronshill Gro. BD15: All 5H 63
Bronte Av. WF11: Ferr 8A 110
Bronte Caravan Pk. BD22: Cros R 6F 42
Bronte Cl. BD9: B'frd 4K 63
BD19: Gom 3M 101
HD4: Hud 7J 137
WF3: E Ard 3F 104
WF13: Dew 1C 122
Bronte Ct. WF8: Pon 1K 129
Bronte Dr. BD22: Oak 4E 42
Bronte Gro. WF9: Hems 3C 162
WF14: Mir 7N 121
Bronte Ho. LS7: Leeds 3E 68
Bronte Old Rd. BD13: Thorn 8D 62
Bronte Pl. BD13: Thorn 8D 62
Bronte Ri. WF10: C'frd 7K 109
Bronte Rd. WF17: Birs 3B 102
Bronte St. BD21: Keigh 8K 27
BD22: Haw 8B 42
Bronte Vs. BD22: Cros R 7F 42
Bronte Way WF14: Mir 7N 121
Brontë Parsonage Mus. 8B 42
Brook, The HX7: Myth 4L 95
Brook Cl. WF5: Oss 8B 124
Brook Cotts. HX6: Ripp 4B 116
Brook Cres. WF1: Wake 8N 125
Brookdale OL14: W'den 1J 113
Brookdale Av. WF5: Oss 2M 123
Brookdale Bank HD3: Hud 5F 136
Brookdale Ct. HX2: Hal 3M 97
Brook Dr. HX4: Holy 7B 118
Brooke Ct. WF8: Pon 6J 129
Brooke Fold HD9: Hon 4L 153
Brooke Grn. HX3: Hip 4H 99
Brookelea HX3: Hip 5K 99
Brooke St. BD19: Cleck 5J 101
HD6: Ras 2M 119
WF16: Heck 9A 102
Brookeville *HX3: Hip 5J 99*
(off Brighouse Rd.)
Brookeville Av. HX3: Hip 5H 99
Brook Farm Ct. *HX3: She 6J 81*
(off Cooper La.)
Brook Fld. WF14: Up H 9K 121
Brookfield HD8: Kbtn 3H 155
Brookfield Av. BD18: Ship 7B 46
BD19: Cleck 3H 101
LS8: Leeds 2H 69
LS13: Leeds 9A 48
WF10: C'frd 5F 108
Brookfield Ct. LS13: Leeds 9A 48
WF6: Norm 1K 127
Brookfield Dr. WF7: Ackw 2J 147
Brookfield Gdns. LS13: Leeds 1A 66
Brookfield Pl. LS6: Leeds 9A 50
(not continuous)
Brookfield Rd. BD3: B'frd 2F 6 (6E 64)
BD18: Ship 7B 46
LS6: Leeds 9A 50
Brookfields WF4: Neth 5N 141
Brookfields Av. BD12: Wyke 3C 100
Brookfields Cres. WF4: H'cft 8L 145
Brookfields Rd. BD12: Wyke 3C 100
Brookfield St. LS10: Leeds 9F 68
OL14: Tod 3E 92
Brookfield Ter. BD19: Cleck 3H 101
LS6: Leeds 9A 50
(off Brookfield Rd.)
LS10: Leeds 9F 68
OL14: Tod 3E 92
(off Brighton St.)
S71: Carl 9D 160
Brookfield Vw. BD19: Cleck 3J 101
BROOKFOOT 9L 99
Brookfoot Av. BD11: B'haw 8L 83
Brookfoot Bus. Pk. HD6: Brigh 9L 99
Brookfoot Ind. Est. HD6: Brigh 1L 119
Brookfoot La. HD6: Brigh 9L 99
HX3: Sou 9J 99
Brookfoot Old La. HD6: Brigh 9L 99
Brook Gdns. HD9: Mel 7C 152
WF13: Dew 3E 122
(off Travis Lacey Ter.)
Brook Grain Hill HD6: Ras 3M 119
Brook Grains La. HX6: Ripp 9D 116
BROOK HILL 4B 46
Brook Hill BD17: Bail 4B 46
Brookhill Av. LS17: Leeds 3G 51
Brookhill Cl. LS17: Leeds 3G 51
Brookhill Cres. LS17: Leeds 3G 51
Brookhill Dr. LS17: Leeds 3G 51
Brookhill Gro. LS17: Leeds 3G 51
Brookhill Rd. S75: Kex 9D 158
BROOKHOUSE 5J 79
Brookhouse Gdns. BD10: B'frd 7K 47
Brook Ho. La. HD8: Shel 7M 155
BROOKLANDS 2A 70
Brooklands HD2: Hud 6D 120
HX3: Hip 5J 99
LS17: E Kes 3D 36
WF2: W'ton 3C 144
Brooklands Av. BD13: Thorn 8E 62
HX4: Holy 7A 118
LS14: Leeds 2N 69
Brooklands Cl. HX4: Holy 7A 118
LS14: Leeds 2N 69
LS29: Men 3F 30
Brooklands Ct. LS14: Leeds 2A 70
WF5: Oss 7C 124
Brooklands Cres. LS14: Leeds 2N 69
LS19: Yead 1M 47
WF4: H'cft 9L 145
Brooklands Dr. LS14: Leeds 2N 69
LS19: Yead 1M 47
Brooklands Gth. LS14: Leeds 2A 70
Brooklands Gro. LS29: Men 3F 30
Brooklands La. LS14: Leeds 2A 70
LS29: Men 3E 30
Brooklands Pk. LS29: Men 3F 30
Brooklands Rd. WF2: W'ton 3C 144
Brooklands Towers LS14: Leeds 1B 70
Brooklands Vw. LS14: Leeds 2A 70
(not continuous)
WF2: W'ton 3D 144
Brooklands Wlk. LS29: Men 3F 30
Brooklands Way LS29: Men 3F 30
Brook La. BD14: Clay 2F 80
HD7: Golc 6C 136
LS17: Wee 6B 20
WF15: Liv 8G 101
Brookleigh LS28: Cal 9M 47
Brooklyn WF9: S Elm 6N 163
Brooklyn Av. HD5: Hud 4D 138
LS12: Leeds 7M 67
Brooklyn Cl. WF13: Dew 8C 102
Brooklyn Ct. BD19: Cleck 4H 101
Brooklyn Dr. BD19: Cleck 4H 101
Brooklyn Grange BD19: Cleck 3J 101
Brooklyn Pl. LS12: Leeds 7M 67
Brooklyn Rd. BD19: Cleck 4H 101
Brooklyn St. BD20: Keigh 5G 26
LS12: Leeds 7M 67
Brooklyn Ter. HD6: Brigh 7K 99
LS12: Leeds 7M 67
WF12: Dew 7G 122
Brook Mdws. HD8: Den D 2D 172
Brook Rd. WF13: Dew 4E 122
Brook Row BD22: Oak 6D 42
HX4: Holy 7B 118
BROOKROYD 4D 102
Brookroyd Av. HD6: B Bri 6N 99
Brookroyd Gdns. WF17: Bat 4C 102
Brookroyd La. WF17: Bat 3C 102
BROOKS BANK 5G 9 (5K 125)
Brooksbank WF2: Wake 5G 9 (5K 125)
Brooksbank Av. BD7: B'frd 9K 63
Brooksbank Dr. LS15: Leeds 6B 70
Brooksbank Gdns. HX5: Ell 5E 118
Brooks Bldgs. HD1: Hud 4J 137
Brooksfield WF9: S Kirk 5K 163
Brook Side HD7: Slait 8M 135
Brookside BD13: Cull 9K 43
HD8: Den D 2C 172
HX7: Heb B 9F 76
LS17: Leeds 2G 50
LS22: Coll 9J 23
WF9: Hems 2E 162
Brookside Fold BD22: Oxen 4C 60
Brookside St. WF9: S Elm 6M 163
Brookside Ter. WF9: S Elm 6M 163
Brooks Ter. BD13: Que 3G 81
Brook St. BD12: O'haw 8F 82
BD21: Keigh 2H 43
HD1: Hud 6K 137
(Crosland Rd.)
HD1: Hud 3B 8 (3M 137)
(Viaduct St., not continuous)
HD5: Hud 4B 138
HX2: Lud 3E 96
(off High St.)
HX5: Ell 5F 118
HX7: Heb B 9H 77
LS29: I'ly 5G 14
OL14: Tod 7K 93
WF1: Wake 4K 9 (5L 125)
WF5: Oss 6N 123
WF6: Alt 9G 106
WF10: C'frd 1J 109
WF13: Dew 2C 122
Brooks Yd. HD1: Hud 5B 8 (4M 137)
HD2: Hud 5E 120
WF13: Dew 4E 122
Brook Ter. HD7: Slait 8N 135
HX2: Lud 2E 96
Brookwater Cl. HX3: Hal 9C 98
Brookwater Dr. BD18: Ship 9C 46
Brookway WF7: F'stne 6D 128
Brookwood Ho. *HX7: Heb B 1G 94*
(off Bankfoot)
Brookwoods Ind. Est. HX4: Holy 6A 118
Broombank HD2: Hud 9J 119
HD8: Den D 3C 172
Broomcliffe Gdns. S72: Shaf 7K 161
Broom Cl. LS10: Leeds 6H 87
S75: Dart 8J 159
Broom Ct. LS10: Leeds 7H 87
Broom Cres. LS10: Leeds 6G 87
Broomcroft BD14: Clay 1G 81
Broomcroft Rd. WF5: Oss 7N 123
Broom Cross LS10: Leeds 6G 87
Broome Av. BD2: B'frd 3C 64
Broome Cl. WF6: Alt 8H 107
Broomer St. WF13: Raven 5B 122
Broomfield BD14: Clay 2F 80
BD15: Wils 1C 62
BD19: Cleck 6G 100
(off West End Dr.)
HX5: Ell 5C 118
LS16: Leeds 3L 49
Broomfield Av. HX3: Hal 9A 98
Broomfield Bus. Pk. HD1: Hud 8A 8 (6M 137)
Broomfield Cl. HD8: Eml 2F 156
Broomfield Cres. LS6: Leeds 2N 67
Broom Fld. La. HD8: Eml 1E 156
Broomfield M. S71: Roys 6E 160
Broomfield Pl. BD14: Clay 2F 80
BD21: Keigh 9H 27
LS6: Leeds 3N 67
Broomfield Rd. BD21: Keigh 9H 27
HD1: Hud 4J 137
HD2: Fix 7M 119
LS6: Leeds 2N 67
BROOMFIELDS 8B 6 (9C 64)
Broomfield St. BD13: Que 4D 80
BD21: Keigh 9H 27
LS6: Leeds 3N 67
Broomfield Ter. BD19: Cleck 6F 100
HD1: Hud 3J 137
LS6: Leeds 3N 67
Broomfield Vw. LS6: Leeds 3N 67
Broom Gdns. LS10: Leeds 6G 87
Broom Gth. LS10: Leeds 6H 87
Broom Gro. LS10: Leeds 6G 87
Broomhall Av. WF1: Wake 1J 125
Broomhall Cres. WF1: Wake 1J 125
Broomhead Cl. HX2: Illing 8K 79
Broomhead Ct. S75: Map 9K 159
Broomhey Av. HD8: Eml 3G 156
BROOMHILL 9G 111
Broomhill BD21: Keigh 9M 27
WF10: C'frd 6G 109
Broomhill Av. BD21: Keigh 2G 42
LS17: Leeds 5F 50
WF11: Knot 9G 110
Broomhill Bottom HX4: Stainl 1L 135
Broomhill Cl. HD9: Scho 5B 170
WF11: Knot 9G 111
Broomhill Cres. LS17: Leeds 5F 50
WF11: Knot 9G 110
Broomhill Dr. BD21: Keigh 2G 43
LS17: Leeds 6E 50
(not continuous)
WF11: Knot 9G 111
Broomhill Gro. BD21: Keigh 2G 43
WF11: Knot 9G 110
Broomhill Mt. BD21: Keigh 2G 43
Broomhill Pl. WF11: Knot 9G 111
Broom Hill Rd. HX4: Stainl 3K 135
LS9: Leeds 5K 69
Broomhill Sq. WF11: Knot 9G 111
Broomhill St. BD21: Keigh 3G 43
Broomhill Ter. WF17: Bat 9G 102
Broomhill Wlk. BD21: Keigh 2G 43
WF11: Knot 9G 110
Broomhill Way BD21: Keigh 2G 43
Broomhouse Cl. HD8: Den D 3D 172
Broom Lawn LS10: Leeds 6G 87
Broom Mills Rd. LS28: Fars 3B 66
Broom Mt. LS10: Leeds 7H 87
Broom Nook LS10: Leeds 6H 87
Broom Pl. LS10: Leeds 6H 87
Broom Rd. LS10: Leeds 7G 87
LS24: Tad 6N 39
Broomroyd HD3: Hud 4E 136
Broomsdale Rd. WF17: Bat 6H 103
Broom St. BD4: B'frd 6C 6 (8D 64)
BD19: Cleck 6F 100
BD21: Keigh 1J 43
Broom Ter. BD22: Oak 4D 42
LS17: Leeds 6H 87
Broom Vw. LS10: Leeds 6H 87
Broom Wlk. LS10: Leeds 7H 87
WF17: Bat 7H 103
Broomy Lea La. HD9: Nether 1L 169
Broster Av. BD22: Keigh 9F 26
BROTHERTON 4B 110
Brotherton Av. WF1: Wake 4N 125
Brotherton By-Pass WF11: B'ton 3B 110
Brotherton Ct. WF11: Knot 7D 110
Brougham Rd. HD7: Mars 5F 150
HX3: Hal 3B 98
Brougham St. HX3: Hal 3B 98
Brougham Ter. HX3: Hal 2B 98
Broughton Av. BD4: B'frd 4F 82
LS9: Leeds 4J 69
Broughton Ho. BD4: B'frd 4K 83
Broughton Rd. HD4: Hud 7G 137
Broughton St. HX7: Heb B 9H 77
Broughtons Yd. WF11: Ferr 7B 110
Broughton Ter. LS9: Leeds 4J 69
LS28: Stan 6B 66
Brow, The *BD17: Bail 4A 46*
(off Bank Wlk.)
BROW BOTTOM 8G 79
Brow Bottom La. HX2: Mix 7G 79
Browcliff BD20: Sils 7E 12
Brow Cotts. HD6: Brigh 7J 99
Browfield Ter. BD20: Sils 7E 12
Browfield Vw. BD22: Keigh 2E 42
Browfoot BD18: Ship 7B 46
Browfoot Dr. HX2: Hal 6K 97
Brow Foot Ga. *HX2: Hal 6K 97*
(off Brow Foot Ga. La.)
Brow Foot Ga. La. HX2: Hal 6K 97
Browgate BD17: Bail 4A 46
Brow Grains Rd. HD9: Mel 8N 151
Brow La. BD14: Clay 2D 80
HD8: Den D 2H 173
HD9: H'frth 5K 169
HX3: Hal 7N 79
HX3: North 9D 80
HX3: She 7J 81
Brow Mills Ind. Est. HX3: Hip 6J 99
Brown Av. LS11: Leeds 1A 86
Brown Bank Caravan Pk. BD20: Sils 5H 13
Brown Bank La. BD20: Sils 7F 12
Brownberrie Av. LS18: Hors 4F 48
Brownberrie Cres. LS18: Hors 4E 48
Brownberrie Dr. LS18: Hors 4F 48
(not continuous)
Brownberrie Gdns. LS18: Hors 4E 48
Brownberrie La. LS18: Hors 4C 48
Brownberrie Wlk. LS18: Hors 4F 48
Brownberry Gro. HX3: She 6J 81
Brown Birks St. OL14: Tod 3D 92
BROWN HILL 4C 102
Brown Hill Av. LS9: Leeds 4J 69
Brownhill Cl. BD11: B'haw 6L 83
WF17: Bat 3C 102
Brown Hill Cres. LS9: Leeds 4J 69
Brownhill Cres. WF9: Kins 8A 146
Brown Hill Dr. BD11: B'haw 7L 83
BROWNHILL END 3C 102
Brownhill Gth. WF17: Bat 3C 102
Brown Hill La. HX7: Blac H 9N 75
Brownhill La. HD9: Holm 8F 168
Brownhill Rd. WF17: Bat 3C 102
Brown Hill Ter. LS9: Leeds 4J 69
Brown Ho's. HX2: Mt T 2H 97
Browning Av. HX3: Hal 9C 98
Browning Rd. HD2: Hud 8B 120
Browning St. BD3: B'frd 7F 64
Brown La. E. LS11: Leeds 9B 68
Brown La. W. LS11: Leeds 9A 68
LS12: Leeds 9A 68
Brownlea Cl. LS19: Yead 2K 47
Brown Lee La. BD15: Wils 2N 61
Brown Pl. LS11: Leeds 1A 86
Brown Rd. LS11: Leeds 1A 86
BROWN ROYD 6N 63
Brown Royd Av. HD5: Hud 3B 138
Brownroyd Av. S71: Roys 7D 160
Brownroyd Fold BD5: B'frd 3N 81
BROWNROYD HILL 3A 82
Brownroyd Hill Rd. BD6: B'frd 4N 81
Brownroyd Rd. HD9: Hon 5K 153
Brownroyd St. BD7: B'frd 8N 63
BD8: B'frd 6N 63
Brownroyd Wlk. BD6: B'frd 3N 81
Browns Edge Rd. S36: M Grn 8J 171
Browns Grn. WF6: Norm 3H 127
Brown's Knoll Rd. HD4: Thurs 6E 154
Brown's Pl. WF17: Bat 8E 102
Brown Springs BD22: Oak 3E 42
Brown Springs La. BD22: Oak 3E 42
Brown's St. WF17: Bat 8F 102
Brown St. BD21: Keigh 8K 27
WF14: Mir 6K 121
Brown Wood BD10: B'frd 5D 46
Brow Rd. BD22: Haw 9D 42
HD1: Hud 5K 137
Browsfield Rd. LS29: Add 1K 13
Browsholme St. BD21: Keigh 1J 43
Brow St. BD21: Keigh 1K 43
Brow Top BD14: Clay 3F 80
Brow Top Rd. BD22: Cros R 9D 42
Brow Wood Cres. BD2: B'frd 3C 64
Brow Wood Ri. HX3: She 7J 81
Brow Wood Rd. HX3: She 7J 81
WF17: Bat 3E 102
Brow Wood Ter. BD6: B'frd 6L 81

Bruce Gdns.—Butts Yd.

Bruce Gdns. LS12: Leeds 7A 68
Bruce Lawn LS12: Leeds 7A 68
Bruce St. HX1: Hal 7M 97
Brudenell Av. LS6: Leeds 3B 68
Brudenell Gro. LS6: Leeds 3B 68
Brudenell Mt. LS6: Leeds 3A 68
Brudenell Rd. LS6: Leeds 3A 68
Brudenell St. LS6: Leeds 1A 4 (3B 68)
Brudenell Vw. LS6: Leeds 1A 4 (3B 68)
Brumfitt Hill LS29: Add 1M 13
Brunel Cl. BD9: B'frd 4M 63
WF2: Carr G 8H 105
Brunel Ct. BD3: B'frd 4E 64
HX3: Hal 2A 98
(off Mill La.)
Brunel Gdns. *BD5: B'frd 2A 82*
(off Ida St.)
Brunel Rd. WF2: Carr G 7H 105
Brunswick WF4: Ryh 8J 145
Brunswick Arc. *BD21: Keigh 9J 27*
(within Airedale Shop. Cen.)
Brunswick Cl. WF1: Wake 5M 9 (5M 125)
Brunswick Ct. LS2: Leeds 4H 5 (5F 68)
Brunswick Dr. WF13: Dew 2D 122
Brunswick Gdns. HX1: Hal 4J 7 (5A 98)
LS25: Gar 7N 71
Brunswick Gro. WF1: Wake 5M 9 (5M 125)
Brunswick Ho. BD16: Bgly 5G 44
Brunswick Ind. Est. HX1: Hal 6H 7 (6A 98)
Brunswick Pl. BD10: B'frd 8H 47
LS27: Morl 9L 85
WF16: Heck 9A 102
Brunswick Rd. BD10: B'frd 8H 47
LS28: Pud 6B 66
Brunswick Row LS2: Leeds 4H 5 (5F 68)
Brunswick St. BD13: Cull 9L 43
BD13: Que 4E 80
BD16: Bgly 4G 44
HD1: Hud 4A 8 (4M 137)
HX7: Heb B 1G 95
LS27: Morl 8K 85
OL14: W'den 4J 113
(off Beswick St.)
WF1: Wake 6L 9 (6M 125)
WF13: Dew 2D 122
WF16: Heck 9A 102
WF17: Bat 7F 102
Brunswick Ter. BD12: Low M 6A 82
LS2: Leeds 4F 4 (5E 68)
LS27: Morl 9M 85
BRUNTCLIFFE 9G 85
Bruntcliffe Av. LS27: Morl 9H 85
Bruntcliffe Cl. LS27: Morl 9J 85
Bruntcliffe Dr. LS27: Morl 9J 85
Bruntcliffe La. LS27: Morl 9H 85
Bruntcliffe Rd. LS27: Morl 9G 85
Bruntcliffe Way LS27: Morl 9H 85
BRUNTHWAITE 8G 12
Brunthwaite Bri. La. BD20: Sils 1F 26
Brunthwaite Cotts. BD20: Sils 8G 12
Brunthwaite La. BD20: Sils 8G 12
Brunthwaite Ter. BD20: Sils 8G 12
Brussels Ct. HX1: Hal 5L 7
Brussels St. LS9: Leeds 7J 5 (7F 68)
Bryan Cl. WF10: C'frd 4A 108
Bryan La. HD2: Hud 8H 119
Bryan Rd. HD2: Hud 2J 137
HX5: Ell 5C 118
Bryanstone Rd. BD4: B'frd 9H 65
Bryan St. HD6: Ras 2M 119
LS28: Fars 2A 66
Bryan St. Nth. LS28: Fars 2A 66
Bryan Ter. HD7: Golc 4D 136
Bryden Cl. HD6: Brigh 7L 99
Bryer St. WF13: Dew 3F 122
Bryndlee Ct. HD9: H'frth 4K 169
Bryngate LS26: Oul 7D 88
Bryony Ct. LS10: Leeds 8H 87
Bubwith Gro. *HX2: Hal 6L 97*
(off Bk. Eversley Mt.)
Buchan Towers BD5: B'frd 7A 6
Buckden Ct. BD20: Sils 7E 12
HD3: Hud 3G 136
(off Chesil Bank)
LS29: Men 5F 30
(off Jackson Wlk.)
Buckden Rd. HD3: Hud 2J 137
Buckfast Ct. BD10: B'frd 8F 46
Buckingham Av. LS6: Leeds 2A 68
Buckingham Ct. S71: Roys 5C 160
WF1: Wake 7A 126
Buckingham Cres. BD14: Clay 9J 63
Buckingham Dr. LS6: Leeds 2A 68
WF1: Wake 8A 126
Buckingham Gro. LS6: Leeds 2A 68
Buckingham Ho. LS6: Leeds 2A 68
Buckingham Mt. LS6: Leeds 3A 68
Buckingham Rd. LS6: Leeds 3A 68
Buckingham Way S71: Roys 5C 160
WF10: C'frd 5C 108
WF11: Byram 5D 110
Buckland Pl. HX1: Hal 6L 97
Buckland Rd. BD8: B'frd 6L 63
Buck La. BD17: Bail 4D 46
Buckle La. LS29: Men 5F 30
WF6: Norm 1H 127
Buckley Av. LS11: Leeds 2D 86
Buckley La. HX2: Hal 2J 97
Buckley Vw. OL14: Tod 6J 93
Buckley Wood Bottom *OL14: Tod 7K 93*
(off Doghouse La.)
Buck Mill La. BD10: B'frd 5E 46
Buckrose St. HD1: Hud 1M 137
Buckrose Ter. *HD1: Hud 1M 137*
(off Buckrose St.)
Buckstone Av. LS17: Leeds 3B 50
Buckstone Cl. LS17: Leeds 3C 50
Buckstone Cres. LS17: Leeds 3B 50
Buckstone Dr. LS17: Leeds 3B 50
LS19: Raw 4L 47
(not continuous)
Buckstone Gdns. LS17: Leeds 3C 50
Buckstone Gth. BD20: E Mor 7C 28
Buckstone Grn. LS17: Leeds 3B 50
Buckstone Gro. LS17: Leeds 3B 50
Buckstone Mt. LS17: Leeds 3B 50
Buckstone Oval LS17: Leeds 3B 50
Buckstone Ri. LS17: Leeds 3B 50
Buckstone Rd. LS17: Leeds 3B 50
Buckstones Cl. HX4: Holy 7A 118
Buckstone Vw. LS17: Leeds 3B 50
Buckstone Way LS17: Leeds 3B 50
Buck St. BD3: B'frd 6E 6 (8E 64)
BD13: Denh 6L 61
Buckthorne Cl. WF3: E Ard 4F 104
Buckthorne Ct. WF3: E Ard 4F 104
Buckthorne Dr. WF3: E Ard 4F 104
Buckthorne Fold WF3: E Ard 4F 104
Buckton Cl. LS11: Leeds 1C 86
Buckton Mt. LS11: Leeds 1C 86
Buckton Vw. LS11: Leeds 1C 86
Bude Rd. BD5: B'frd 4D 82
LS11: Leeds 2D 86
Bugler Ter. WF4: Horb 1A 142
Bula Cl. LS25: Kip 3B 90
Bulay Rd. HD1: Hud 6L 137
Bullace Trees La. WF15: Liv 9J 101
Bullcliff Old La. WF4: W Bret 7B 142
Bull Cl. La. HX1: Hal 5J 7 (6A 98)
Bullcroft Cl. DN6: Carc 8N 165
Bullenshaw Rd. WF9: Hems 3D 162
Bullenshaw Vs. WF9: Hems 3G 163
Buller Cl. LS9: Leeds 5L 69
Buller Ct. LS9: Leeds 5L 69
Buller Gro. LS9: Leeds 5K 69
Buller St. BD4: B'frd 9G 65
LS26: W'frd 7E 88
Bullerthorpe La. LS15: Leeds 8G 70
LS26: Swil 5F 88
Bullfield, The BD16: Har 7A 44
Bullfields Cl. WF12: T'hill 9H 123
Bull Grn. HX1: Hal 4K 7 (5B 98)
Bull Grn. Rd. HD3: Hud 4E 136
Bull Hill BD22: Oxen 5C 60
Bull La. WF4: Crig 5H 143
WF9: S Kirk 7J 163
Bullough La. LS26: Rothw 6A 88
Bull Ring WF1: Wake 4J 9 (5L 125)
Bullroyd Av. BD8: B'frd 6K 63
Bullroyd Cres. BD8: B'frd 6K 63
Bullroyd Dr. BD8: B'frd 6K 63
Bull Royd Ind. Est. BD8: B'frd 6K 63
Bullroyd La. BD8: B'frd 6K 63
Bullstyle Rd. WF8: Pon 5J 129
Bulrush Bus. Pk. WF17: Bat 5E 102
Bungalow, The BD5: B'frd 8A 6 (1C 82)
Bungalows, The HX2: Hal 3K 97
HX3: Hal 1D 118
(Backhold Av.)
HX3: Hal 2M 97
(High Cft.)
HX6: Sow B 8G 97
LS15: Leeds 3E 70
(off Church La.)
LS25: Kip 3D 90
LS25: M'fld 8G 73
WF6: Alt 7H 107
WF7: F'stne 7D 128
(off Bedford Cl.)
Bunkers *BD22: Haw 9C 42*
(off Bridgehouse La.)
Bunkers Hill BD17: Esh 2F 46
HD9: H'frth 3M 169
LS25: Aber 9E 54
WF2: Wren 1H 125
Bunker's Hill La. BD22: Keigh 2D 42
Bunkers La. WF17: Bat 8C 102
Bunkers M. *WF11: B'ton 4B 110*
(off Cross Hill)
Bunney Grn. HX3: North 9E 80
Bunny Pk. HD4: Hud 7J 137
(not continuous)
Bunting Dr. BD6: B'frd 3G 81
Burbeary Rd. HD1: Hud 7K 137
Burberry Cl. BD4: B'frd 5G 83
Burchett Gro. LS6: Leeds 2C 68
Burchett Pl. LS6: Leeds 2C 68
Burchett Ter. LS6: Leeds 2D 68
Burcote Dr. HD3: Outl 1A 136
Burdale Pl. BD7: B'frd 8N 63
Burdett Ter. LS4: Leeds 4M 67
Burdock Way HX1: Hal 5J 7 (6A 98)
HX3: Hal 1L 7 (6A 98)
Burfitts Rd. HD3: Hud 3G 136
Burgage Sq. WF1: Wake 4H 9 (5K 125)
Burghley M. LS10: Leeds 1F 104
Burghley Wlk. BD18: Ship 9C 46
Burgh Mill Gdns. WF13: Dew 4D 122
Burgh Mill La. WF13: Dew 4C 122
BURGHWALLIS 5M 165
Burghwallis La. DN6: Sut 4N 165
Burghwallis Rd. DN6: Burg, Cam 4N 165
Burhouse Ct. *HD9: Hon 5L 153*
(off Cuckoo La.)
Burhouse St. *HD9: Hon 5L 153*
(off High St.)
Burkill St. WF1: Wake 9M 125
Burking Rd. WF13: Dew 3E 122
Burland Ter. LS26: Swil 3H 89
Burlees Cotts. HX7: Heb B 1K 95
Burlees La. HX7: Heb B 1K 95
Burleigh St. HX1: Hal 7M 97
BURLEY 4N 67
Burley Bank La. HD9: H'lm 1D 174
Burley Carr HX7: Heb B 1K 95
Burley Ct. BD20: Stee 3C 26
Burley Grange Rd. LS4: Leeds 4M 67
Burley Hill Cres. LS4: Leeds 3L 67
Burley Hill Dr. LS4: Leeds 3L 67
Burley Hill Trad. Est. LS4: Leeds 3M 67
BURLEY IN WHARFEDALE 8D 16
Burley in Wharfedale Station (Rail) 9C 16
Burley La. LS18: Hors 7E 48
LS29: Men 3D 30
Burley Lodge Pl. *LS6: Leeds 5A 68*
(off Burley Lodge Rd.)
Burley Lodge Rd. LS6: Leeds 4A 68
Burley Lodge St. LS6: Leeds 5A 68
Burley Lodge Ter. LS6: Leeds 5A 68
Burley M. BD20: Stee 3C 26
Burley Park Station (Rail) 3N 67
Burley Pl. LS4: Leeds 5N 67
Burley Rd. LS3: Leeds 4A 4 (3M 67)
LS4: Leeds 3M 67
LS29: Men 2E 30
Burley St. BD2: B'frd 2B 64
HX5: Ell 5E 118
LS3: Leeds 5A 4 (6B 68)
Burley Wlk. WF17: Bat 7E 102
Burley Wood Ct. LS4: Leeds 3L 67
Burley Wood Cres. LS4: Leeds 3L 67
BURLEY WOODHEAD 2A 30
Burley Wood La. LS4: Leeds 3M 67
Burley Wood Mt. LS4: Leeds 3L 67
Burley Wood Vw. LS4: Leeds 3M 67
Burlington Av. BD3: B'frd 5J 65
Burlington Pl. LS11: Leeds 3D 86
Burlington Rd. LS11: Leeds 3D 86
Burlington St. BD8: B'frd 5B 64
HX1: Hal 5M 97
Burmah St. HX1: Hal 5M 97
BURMANTOFTS 5H 69
Burmantofts St. LS9: Leeds 5K 5 (6G 68)
Burn Cl. LS26: W'frd 7M 89
Burned Gro. HX3: She 6H 81
Burned Rd. HX3: She 6H 81
Burneston Gdns. BD6: B'frd 5K 81
Burnett Av. BD5: B'frd 2B 82
Burnett Pl. BD5: B'frd 2B 82
Burnett Ri. BD13: Que 5B 80
Burnett St. BD1: B'frd 4D 6 (7D 64)
Burnham Av. BD4: B'frd 3F 82
S75: Map 8K 159
Burnham Ct. LS22: Weth 3K 23
Burnham Rd. LS25: Gar 9N 71
Burnham Wlk. BD4: B'frd 4G 82
Burnhill La. WF9: Bads 4M 147
Burnholme BD13: Denh 6K 61
Burniston Cl. BD15: Wils 2B 62
Burniston Dr. HD3: Hud 2F 136
BURNLEE 4J 169
Burnlee Grn. Rd. HD9: H'frth 4K 169
Burnlee Rd. HD9: H'frth 4K 169
Burnley Hill HX3: North 9F 80
Burnley Hill Ter. HX3: She 9G 80
Burnley Rd. HX2: Hal 6K 97
HX2: Lud F 6D 96
HX6: Sow B 6D 96
HX7: Heb B, Myth 2J 95
OL14: Tod 1A 92
Burnleys Bldgs. WF4: Flock 8E 140
Burnleys Ct. LS26: Meth 4L 107
Burnleys Dr. LS26: Meth 4L 107
Burnleys M. LS26: Meth 4L 107
Burnley's Mill Rd. BD19: Gom 4L 101
Burnleys Vw. LS26: Meth 3L 107
Burnleyville BD19: Gom 3M 101
Burn Rd. HD2: Hud 9H 119
HD3: Hud 9H 119
Burnsall Av. WF17: Bat 7D 102
Burnsall Ct. *HD3: Hud 4G 137*
(off Reinwood Rd.)
LS12: Leeds 6L 67
Burnsall Cft. LS12: Leeds 6L 67
Burnsall Gdns. LS12: Leeds 6L 67
Burnsall Grange *LS12: Leeds 6L 67*
(off Theaker La.)
Burnsall M. BD20: Sils 7D 12
Burnsall Rd. BD3: B'frd 7F 64
(not continuous)
HD6: Ras 3K 119
WF15: Liv 8K 101
WF17: Bat 7D 102
Burns Av. WF9: S Kirk 8F 162
Burns Ct. WF17: Birs 2A 102
Burnsdale BD15: All 3F 62
Burnshaw M. LS10: Leeds 1E 104
Burns Hill LS29: Add 1L 13
Burnside LS29: Add 1M 13
Burnside Av. HX3: She 6J 81
Burnside Cl. WF17: Bat 3D 102
Burnside Dr. HD9: H'frth 4K 169
Burns St. HX3: Hal 9M 79
Burnstall Cl. LS29: Men 5F 30
Burnstall Cres. LS29: Men 6E 30
Burns Way LS23: Cliff 2D 38
Burnt Acres OL14: Tod 4C 94
Burnt Acres La. OL14: Tod 4C 94
Burnt Edge La. HX7: Blac H 9M 75
Burnt Ho. Cl. OL14: Tod 6L 93
Burnt Plats La. HD7: Slait 8F 134
Burnt Side Rd. LS12: N Far 3F 84
Burntwood Av. WF9: S Kirk 7J 163
Burntwood Bank WF9: Hems 4D 162
Burntwood Court Health & Fitness Cen. 7C 162
Burntwood Cres. WF9: S Kirk 7J 163
Burntwood Dr. WF9: S Kirk 7H 163
Burntwood Gro. WF9: S Kirk 8J 163
Burnt Wood La. S72: B'ley 9E 162
Burnup Gro. BD19: Cleck 5G 101
BURNWELLS 5E 46
Burnwells BD10: B'frd 5E 46
Burnwells Av. BD10: B'frd 5E 46
Burrage St. BD16: Bgly 4E 44
Burras Av. LS21: Otley 1K 31
Burras Dr. LS21: Otley 1K 31
Burras La. LS21: Otley 1K 31
Burras Rd. BD4: B'frd 3F 82
Burrell Cl. LS22: Weth 4A 24
Burrell St. WF1: Wake 5M 9 (5M 125)
Burrows, The WF17: Bat 5C 102
Burrow St. BD5: B'frd 6A 6 (8C 64)
Burr Tree Dr. LS15: Leeds 7E 70
Burr Tree Gth. LS15: Leeds 7E 70
Burr Tree Va. LS15: Leeds 7E 70
Burrwood Ter. HX4: Holy 6A 118
Burrwood Way HX4: Holy 6A 118
Burton Acres Dr. HD8: Kbtn 2J 155
Burton Acres La. HD8: Kbtn 1J 155
(not continuous)
Burton Acres M. HD8: Kbtn 1J 155
Burton Acres Way HD8: Kbtn 2J 155
Burton Av. LS11: Leeds 2E 86
Burton Comn. La. LS25: Bur S 1D 110
Burton Cres. LS6: Leeds 9N 49
Burton Ho. LS17: Leeds 3H 51
Burton M. LS17: Leeds 2F 50
Burton Rd. LS11: Leeds 2E 86
Burton Row LS11: Leeds 1E 86
Burton Royd La. HD8: Kbtn 2L 155
BURTON SALMON 1D 110
Burton St. BD4: B'frd 1E 82
BD20: Keigh 6H 27
HX2: Hal 8N 79
LS11: Leeds 1E 86
LS28: Fars 3A 66
WF1: Wake 3H 9 (4K 125)
WF9: S Elm 7M 163
Burton Ter. LS11: Leeds 2E 86
Burton Way LS9: Leeds 5J 69
Burwood Rd. HD3: Hud 2G 137
Bury La. BD20: E Mor 7B 28
Busely Ct. LS27: Morl 8J 85
Busfeild St. BD16: Bgly 4E 44
Busfield St. BD4: B'frd 2F 82
Bush Hill Fold BD13: Que 3B 80
Bush St. WF9: Hems 3E 162
Busker La. HD8: Clay W 8F 156
BUSLINGTHORPE 2E 68
Buslingthorpe Grn. LS7: Leeds 3E 68
Buslingthorpe La. LS7: Leeds 2E 68
Buslingthorpe Va. LS7: Leeds 2E 68
Bussey Ct. LS6: Leeds 3C 68
Busy La. BD18: Ship 6C 46
Butcher Hill LS5: Leeds 7H 49
LS16: Leeds 7H 49
LS18: Hors 7H 49
WF9: Hems 1E 162
Butcher La. LS26: Rothw 8N 87
Butcher's Gap La. WF1: Warm 5H 127
Butchers Row LS2: Leeds 6G 5
Butcher St. LS11: Leeds 8D 4 (8D 68)
Bute Av. HD6: Brigh 7M 99
Bute St. BD2: B'frd 2B 64
Butler La. BD17: Bail 3B 46
(not continuous)
Butler's Fold BD16: Bgly 9E 28
Butler St. E. BD3: B'frd 2F 6 (6E 64)
Butler St. W. BD3: B'frd 2E 6 (6E 64)
Butlers Vw. *HX3: Hal 2A 98*
(off Crown Rd.)
Butler Way LS28: Stan 4B 66
Butterbowl Dr. LS12: Leeds 9H 67
Butterbowl Gdns. LS12: Leeds 9J 67
Butterbowl Gth. LS12: Leeds 9H 67
Butterbowl Gro. LS12: Leeds 9H 67
Butterbowl Lawn LS12: Leeds 9H 67
Butterbowl Mt. LS12: Leeds 9J 67
Butterbowl Rd. LS12: Leeds 9J 67
Buttercross DN6: Skel 8M 165
Buttercross Ct. DN6: Skel 7M 165
Buttercup Cl. WF9: Upt 2M 163
Buttercup La. WF3: E Ard 3G 105
Buttercup Way BD11: Drig 8E 84
WF10: C'frd 7A 108
Butterfield Homes *BD16: Cot 9G 45*
(off Cottingley Moor Rd.)
Butterfield Ind. Est. BD17: Bail 5C 46
Butterfield's Bldgs. LS27: Morl 8J 85
Butterfield St. LS9: Leeds 7M 5 (7H 69)
Butterley La. HD9: New M 4C 170
Butterley St. LS10: Leeds 9E 68
Buttermead Cl. BD6: B'frd 6M 81
Buttermere Av. LS22: Weth 3K 23
Buttermere Cl. DN6: Carc 8N 165
Buttermere Cft. WF2: W'ton 4B 144
Buttermere Dr. HD5: Hud 4B 138
Buttermere Rd. BD2: B'frd 3E 64
Buttermere Wlk. WF11: Knot 1D 130
Butternab Ridge HD4: Hud 1J 153
Butternab Rd. HD4: Hud 9H 137
BUTTERSHAW 5K 81
Buttershaw Dr. BD6: B'frd 5K 81
Buttershaw La. BD6: B'frd 6N 81
WF15: Liv 7F 100
Butterton Cl. S75: Map 8L 159
Butterwick Gdns. LS22: Weth 4K 23
Butterwood Cl. HD4: Hud 1J 153
Butterworth End La. HX6: Norl 3G 117
Butterworth Hill HD3: Outl 3N 135
Butterworth La. HX6: Tri 1E 116
Butterworth St. *OL14: Tod 7K 93*
(off Calder St.)
Butt Hill LS25: Kip 4A 90
Buttholme Ga. BD6: B'frd 5L 81
Butt La. BD10: B'frd 7F 46
BD22: Haw 8C 42
DN6: Hamp 9F 164
HD9: H'wth 6C 170
LS12: Leeds 8G 67
LS13: Leeds 7H 67
Button Hill LS7: Leeds 2F 68
Button Pk. WF8: Pon 4J 129
Buttress HX2: Lud 3E 96
HX7: Heb B 9H 77
Buttress La. HX2: Lud 3E 96
Butt Row LS12: Leeds 8H 67
Butts HX7: Myth 2M 95
Butts, The BD20: E Mor 8C 28
WF8: Pon 2K 129
Butts Bottom HX7: Heb B 3H 95
Butts Cl. HD4: Farn T 3C 154
Butts Ct. LS1: Leeds 6F 4 (6E 68)
Butts Gth. LS14: T'ner 2G 53
Butts Gth. Ct. LS14: T'ner 2G 53
Butts Gth. Farm LS14: T'ner 2G 53
Butts Gth. Vw. LS14: T'ner 2G 53
Butts Gth. Wlk. LS14: T'ner 2G 52
Butts Grn. La. HX2: Hal 5F 96
Butts Grn. Rd. HX2: Lud F 5E 96
Butts Hill BD19: Gom 4M 101
Butts La. LS20: Guis 7J 31
OL14: Tod 3M 93
WF4: M'twn 3L 141
Butts Mt. LS12: Leeds 7N 67
Butts Rd. HD4: Farn T 3C 154
Butts Ter. HD4: Farn T 3C 154
LS20: Guis 7J 31
Butts Way HD4: Farn T 3C 154
Butts Yd. BD19: Cleck 5H 101

Buxton Av.—Carlton Gro.

Buxton Av. BD9: B'frd 1A 64
Buxton Ho. HD1: Hud 6B 8
Buxton La. BD9: B'frd 2A 64
HX4: Stainl 7M 117
Buxton Pl. WF1: Wake 1H 9 (3K 125)
Buxton St. BD9: B'frd 4N 63
BD21: Keigh 9K 27
HX3: Hal 3N 97
Buxton Way HD1: Hud 6B 8
HX3: Hal 1M 97
Byeway LS20: Guis 7G 30
Byland HX2: Illing 6L 79
Byland Cl. LS23: B Spa 1C 38
Byland Gro. BD15: All 4E 62
Bylands Av. BD20: Rid 6L 27
BYRAM 4C 110
Byram Arc. HD1: Hud 4B 8
Byram Ct. HD1: Hud 4B 8
Byram Ind. Pk. WF11: B'ton 5B 110
Byram Pk. Av. WF11: Byram 4D 110
Byram Pk. Rd. WF11: Byram 4C 110
Byram St. HD1: Hud 4B 8 (4N 137)
Byre Way BD22: Keigh 2E 42
Byrl St. BD21: Keigh 7K 27
Byrom St. OL14: Tod 6K 93
Byron Av. HX6: Sow B 7H 97
Byron Cl. WF11: Ferr 8A 110
Byron Gro. WF3: S'ley 6N 105
WF13: Dew 1B 122
Byron Halls BD3: B'frd 6F 64
Byron Ho. LS29: I'ly 5J 15
Byron M. BD16: Bgly 2F 44
Byron St. BD3: B'frd 6F 64
HX1: Hal 5M 97
HX6: Sow B 7H 97
LS2: Leeds 4H 5 (5F 68)
Byron Studios BD3: B'frd 6F 64
(off Barkerend Rd.)
Byron Ter. HX6: Sow B 7H 97
(off Byron St.)
Bywater Ct. WF10: All B 9C 90
Bywater Row BD11: B'haw 8M 83
Bywater Vs. WF11: Knot 7E 110
Bywater Wlk. WF10: All B 9C 90
(off Letchmire Rd.)
Byways, The WF8: Pon 5K 129
Bywell Cl. WF12: Dew 3J 123
Bywell Rd. WF12: Dew 2J 123

C

CABBAGE HILL 8K 67
Cabbage Hill LS12: Leeds 8L 67
Cabin La. HD9: New M 2B 170
Cabin Rd. LS21: Pool 3E 32
Cable Pl. LS10: Leeds 1G 87
Cable St. HD1: Hud 8A 8 (6M 137)
CACKLESHAW 5E 42
Cad Beeston LS11: Leeds 2C 86
Cad Beeston M. LS11: Leeds 2C 86
Caddon Av. WF9: S Elm 8A 164
CADDY FIELD 6D 98
Caddy Fld. St. HX3: Hal 6C 98
(off Jubilee St.)
Cadman Ct. LS27: Morl 1K 103
Cadney Cft. HX1: Hal 5K 7
Cadogan Av. HD3: Hud 2G 137
Cadwell Cl. S72: Cud 9K 161
Caernarvon Av. LS25: Gar 7B 72
Caernarvon Cl. WF17: Bat 3D 102
Cain Cl. LS9: Leeds 8M 5 (7H 69)
(not continuous)
Cain La. HX3: Sou 8F 98
Cairn Av. LS20: Guis 6G 30
Cairn Cl. BD20: Keigh 6G 26
Cairn Ct. WF16: Heck 7B 102
Cairn Gth. LS20: Guis 6G 31
Cairns Cl. BD2: B'frd 3D 64
Cairns Wlk. HX6: Ripp 8C 116
Cairn Vw. LS29: I'ly 4J 15
(off Hauxley Ct.)
Caister Cl. WF17: Birs 2D 102
Caister Gro. BD21: Keigh 3H 43
(off Oakfield Rd.)
Caister St. BD21: Keigh 3H 43
Caister Way BD21: Keigh 3H 43
Caistor Gth. BD10: B'frd 9G 47
(off Rowantree Dr.)
Calde Ct. BD12: Low M 7C 82
Caldene Av. BD12: Low M 7C 82
HX7: Myth 3L 95
Caldene Bus. Pk. HX7: Myth 4N 95
Caldene Cft. HX7: Myth 3K 95
Calder HX4: Bark 7K 117
Calder Av. HX2: Hal 7M 97
S71: Roys 6F 160
Calder Bank Rd. WF12: Dew 5E 122
CALDER BANKS 4F 80
Calder Banks BD13: Que 4F 80
CALDERBROOK 9L 113
Calder Brook HX7: Heb B 3K 95
Calder Brook Ind. Est. HX7: Heb B 3K 95
Calderbrook Rd. OL15: Lit 9L 113
Caldercliffe Rd. HD4: Hud 9K 137
Calder Cl. HX4: Gree 4C 118
(off Calder St.)
LS22: Weth 1L 23
S71: Roys 6F 160
WF4: Wake 2H 143
WF5: Oss 6M 123
WF10: C'frd 4H 109
WF14: Mir 7K 121
Calder Ct. HX1: Hal 3L 7
WF14: Mir 7K 121
Caldercroft HX5: Ell 5F 118
Calderdale Bus. Pk. HX2: Hal 1M 97
Calderdale Way HX5: Ell 4D 118
Calder Dr. HD4: Hud 1L 153
CALDER GROVE 4F 142
Calder Gro. HX7: Myth 3M 95
Calder Ho. HX5: Ell 4E 118
(off St Mary's Ga.)
WF1: Wake 6M 9 (6M 125)
Calder Island Way WF2: Wake 9K 125
Caldermill Way WF12: Dew 6E 122
Calder Mt. WF4: Crig 5G 143
CALDER PARK 2H 143
Calder Pk. WF2: Wake 2J 143
Calder Pl. HX7: Heb B 1G 94
(off Bridge Lanes)
Calder Rd. WF12: Dew 7C 122
WF13: Raven 6B 122
WF14: Mir 8L 121
Calder Row WF1: Wake 1C 126
CALDERSIDE 1E 94
Calderstone Av. BD6: B'frd 5J 81
Calderstone Ct. WF4: M'twn 3K 141
Calder St. HD6: Brigh 2A 120
HX4: Gree 4C 118
OL14: Tod 7K 93
WF1: Wake 8L 9 (7M 125)
WF10: C'frd 4C 108
Calder Ter. HX3: Hal 2N 117
HX7: Heb B 1G 95
HX7: Myth 3L 95
WF4: Horb 2E 142
Calder Trad. Est. HD5: Hud 5E 120
HD6: B Bri 6N 99
CALDER VALE 6N 125
Caldervale S71: Roys 5F 160
Calder Vale Rd. WF1: Wake 6M 9 (6M 125)
WF4: Horb 2E 142
Calder Vw. HD6: Ras 2L 119
OL14: Tod 6N 93
(off Halifax Rd.)
WF4: Crig 5G 143
WF5: Oss 6L 123
WF14: Mir 7K 121
Calder Vw. Ct. HX3: She 7F 80
Calder Way BD20: Sils 9E 12
Calderwood Cl. BD18: B'frd, Ship 1C 64
Caldicott Cl. OL14: Tod 9H 93
Caledonia Ct. WF2: Kirk 1D 124
Caledonian Rd. WF12: Dew 5F 122
Caledonia Rd. BD21: Keigh 8K 27
WF17: Bat 7G 102
Caledonia St. BD4: B'frd 7B 6 (9C 64)
BD5: B'frd 7B 6 (9C 64)
Calf Hey La. S36: Cro E 9G 171
Calf Hey Ter. OL14: W'den 2H 113
Calf Hill Rd. HD9: T'bdge 8N 153
Calgary Cres. WF3: W Ard 5B 104
Calgary Pl. LS7: Leeds 9F 50
California Dr. OL14: Tod 9J 93
WF4: Horb 1E 142
WF10: C'frd 7L 107
California La. BD19: Gom 5M 101
California M. LS27: Morl 7L 85
California St. LS27: Morl 9L 85
Callis Wood Bottom HX7: Heb B 3D 94
Call La. LS1: Leeds 8G 5 (7E 68)
Calls, The LS2: Leeds 7G 5 (7E 68)
Cally Cotts. HX7: Blac H 9C 76
CALMLANDS 8D 152
Calmlands Rd. HD9: Mel 8C 152
Calpin Cl. BD10: B'frd 7F 46
Calton Gro. BD21: Keigh 1M 43
Calton Rd. BD21: Keigh 1M 43
Calton St. BD21: Keigh 2H 43
(not continuous)
HD1: Hud 1C 8 (2N 137)
Calver Av. BD21: Keigh 8F 26
Calver Gro. BD21: Keigh 8G 26
CALVERLEY 8M 47
Calverley Av. BD3: B'frd 6H 65
LS13: Leeds 3E 66
CALVERLEY BRIDGE 9B 48
Calverley Ct. LS13: Leeds 3E 66
LS26: Oul 8C 88
Calverley Cutting BD10: B'frd 7K 47
LS28: Cal 7K 47
Calverley Dr. LS13: Leeds 3E 66
Calverley Gdns. LS13: Leeds 2D 66
Calverley Gth. LS13: Leeds 3E 66
Calverley Golf Course 3L 65
Calverley Grn. Rd. WF6: Alt 9G 106
Calverley Gro. LS13: Leeds 3E 66
Calverley La. LS13: Leeds 2C 66
LS18: Hors 8B 48
LS28: Cal, Fars 9N 47
(not continuous)
Calverley Moor Av. LS28: Pud 5L 65
Calverley Rd. LS26: Oul 8D 88
Calverley St. LS1: Leeds 4D 4 (5D 68)
Calverley Ter. LS13: Leeds 3E 66
Calver Rd. BD21: Keigh 9G 26
Calversyke St. BD21: Keigh 9G 26
Calvert Cl. LS25: Kip 2A 90
Calverts Wlk. WF5: Oss 7B 124
Camargue Fold BD2: B'frd 2D 64
Camberley Cl. LS28: Pud 8B 66
Camberley Mt. BD4: B'frd 1J 83
Camberley St. LS11: Leeds 2E 86
Camberley Way LS28: Pud 8B 66
Camborne Dr. HD2: Fix 8L 119
Camborne Way BD22: Keigh 2E 42
Cambrian Bar BD12: Low M 7N 81
Cambrian St. LS11: Leeds 1C 86
Cambrian Ter. LS11: Leeds 1C 86
CAMBRIDGE 1M 31
Cambridge Chase BD19: Gom 2M 101
Cambridge Cl. LS27: Morl 8L 85
Cambridge Ct. LS27: Morl 9L 85
Cambridge Cres. WF4: Croft 8D 126
Cambridge Dr. LS13: Leeds 3E 66
LS21: Otley 1M 31
Cambridge Gdns. LS13: Leeds 3E 66
Cambridge Gro. LS21: Otley 1M 31
LS25: Kip 4A 90
Cambridge Pl. BD3: B'frd 1D 6 (6D 64)
BD13: Que 4D 80
OL14: Tod 7K 93
Cambridge Rd. HD1: Hud 2A 8 (3M 137)
LS6: Leeds 1F 4 (3D 68)
WF17: Birs 3A 102
Cambridge St. BD7: B'frd 1N 81
BD13: Que 4E 80
BD14: Clay 1G 81
HX7: Heb B 1G 94
Cambridge St. LS20: Guis 7J 31
LS21: Otley 1L 31
OL14: Tod 7K 93
WF2: Wake 6J 125
WF6: Norm 2H 127
WF9: S Elm 6L 163
WF10: C'frd 5D 108
WF16: Heck 9B 102
WF17: Bat 7F 102
Cambridge Ter. LS21: Otley 1L 31
Cambridge Way LS21: Otley 1M 31
Camden Rd. WF10: C'frd 4K 109
Camden St. HX6: Sow B 9H 97
Camden Ter. BD8: B'frd 5B 64
Camellia Cl. WF2: Wake 8F 124
Camellia Ct. BD18: Ship 1B 64
Camellia Mt. BD7: B'frd 8K 63
Camelot Ct. WF8: Pon 3L 129
Camelot Way WF9: S Elm 7N 163
Cameron Av. BD12: Wyke 3N 99
Cameron Gro. BD2: B'frd 3F 64
Cameronian Ct. BD21: Keigh 9J 27
Camerton Grn. BD5: B'frd 3D 82
Camilla Ct. WF12: Dew 4J 123
Cam La. HD6: Clift 8B 100
Camm La. WF14: Mir 5M 121
Camm St. HD6: Brigh 9N 99
Camomile Ct. BD13: Thorn 8A 62
Campbell St. BD13: Que 4E 80
BD21: Keigh 9J 27
LS28: Stan 4A 66
Campden Rd. HX7: Heb B 9F 76
CAMP FIELD 8D 4 (8D 68)
Campinot Va. HD7: Slait 9M 135
Campion Cl. WF8: Pon 4K 129
Camp Mt. WF8: Pon 3H 129
Camp Ri. WF8: Pon 3H 129
Camp Rd. LS16: B'hpe 7G 33
WF9: S Kirk 8F 162
CAMPSALL 1N 165
Campsmount Dr. DN6: Cam 1N 165
Camp Sq. LS14: T'ner 2G 52
CAMP TOWN 3D 50
Campus Rd. BD7: B'frd 8A 64
Camroyd St. WF13: Dew 2G 123
Camwood Ct. BD20: E Mor 7A 28
Canada Cres. LS19: Raw 3N 47
Canada Dr. LS19: Raw 2N 47
Canada Rd. LS19: Raw 2N 47
Canada Ter. LS19: Raw 3N 47
Canalbank Vw. LS13: Leeds 1C 66
Canal Ct. WF3: Loft 6M 105
Canal Gdns. 6K 51
Canal La. BD20: Sils 1G 27
WF3: Loft, S'ley 6L 105
Canal Pl. LS12: Leeds 7A 4 (7B 68)
Canal Rd. BD1: B'frd 4C 64
BD2: B'frd 1B 6 (1A 64)
BD16: Bgly 1D 44
BD20: Rid 7L 27
HX6: Sow B 8L 97
LS12: Leeds 6M 67
LS13: Leeds 9B 48
Canal Side BD20: Sils 9E 12
Canalside Sports Complex 1B 138
Canal St. HD1: Hud 1E 8 (2A 138)
HD6: Brigh 1N 119
HX3: Hal 6M 7 (6C 98)
LS12: Leeds 8A 4 (7A 68)
OL14: Tod 7K 93
Canal Vw. HX6: Sow B 8G 96
Canal Wlk. WF3: S'ley 6A 106
Canal Wharf LS5: Leeds 3J 67
LS11: Leeds 8D 4 (7D 68)
Canal Works HX7: Heb B 1H 95
(off Fielding St.)
Canary Dr. BD16: Bgly 3H 45
Canary St. BD19: Cleck 4H 101
Canberra Cl. BD22: Cros R 7F 42
Canberra Dr. BD22: Cros R 7F 42
Canby Gro. HD5: Hud 5F 138
Candle Ho. LS1: Leeds 8D 4
Candleworks Yd. LS21: Otley 1L 31
Canford Dr. BD15: All 5G 63
Canford Gro. BD15: All 5H 63
Canford Rd. BD15: All 5G 63
Canker La. HD2: Hud 1A 138
HX3: Hal 1N 97
Canning Av. WF2: Wake 3F 124
Cannon Gro. WF16: Heck 7B 102
Cannon Hall Ct. HD6: Clift 9B 100
Cannon Hall Dr. HD6: Clift 1B 120
Cannon Hall Farm 3M 173
Cannon Hall Museum, Park & Gardens 3M 173
Cannon Mill La. BD7: B'frd 1M 81
Cannon St. BD16: Bgly 5F 44
HX1: Hal 7M 97
OL14: Tod 9J 93
WF10: C'frd 7E 108
Cannon Wlk. LS2: Leeds 1B 4 (4C 68)
Cannon Way WF12: Dew 4F 122
Canonbury Ter. LS11: Leeds 2A 86
Canon Pinnington M. BD16: Cot 8F 44
(off Littlelands)
Canteen Mill Ind. Est. OL14: Tod 4G 92
Canter, The LS10: Leeds 1F 104
Canterbury Av. BD5: B'frd 2A 82
Canterbury Ct. WF8: Pon 9L 109
Canterbury Cres. HX3: Hal 3A 98
Canterbury Dr. LS6: Leeds 2M 67
Canterbury Ho. HX6: Sow B 8J 97
Canterbury Rd. LS6: Leeds 2M 67
WF12: Dew 2J 123
Canwick Cl. BD20: E Mor 7A 28
Capas Hgts. Way WF16: Heck 9B 102
Cape Ind. Est. LS28: Fars 3B 66
Capel Ct. LS28: Cal 9M 47
Capel St. HD6: Ras 2M 119
LS28: Cal 9M 47
Cape of Good Hope BD13: Que 5B 80
Cape St. BD1: B'frd 1B 6 (6C 64)
Capitol Blvd. LS27: Morl 3M 103
Capitol Cl. LS27: Morl 2M 103
Capitol Pde. LS6: Leeds 8B 50
Caprington Ct. WF6: Norm 2L 127
Captain St. BD1: B'frd 2C 6 (7D 64)
Caraway Ct. LS6: Leeds 6B 50
Caraway Dr. LS6: Leeds 6B 50
Caraway M. LS6: Leeds 6B 50
Carberry Pl. LS6: Leeds 4A 68
Carberry Rd. LS6: Leeds 4A 68
Carberry Ter. LS6: Leeds 4A 68
(off Carberry Rd.)
CARCROFT 9N 165
Carcroft Ent. Pk. DN6: Carc 9N 165
Cardan Dr. LS29: I'ly 5K 15
Carden Av. LS15: Leeds 7N 69
Carden Gro. LS15: Leeds 7N 69
Carden Rd. BD4: B'frd 9J 65
Cardigan Av. LS27: Morl 2K 103
Cardigan Cl. WF17: Bat 7H 103
Cardigan Ct. LS6: Leeds 2A 68
Cardigan Flds. Rd. LS4: Leeds 5M 67
Cardigan La. LS4: Leeds 4N 67
(not continuous)
LS6: Leeds 3A 68
WF5: Oss 8C 124
Cardigan Rd. LS6: Leeds 2N 67
Cardigan St. BD13: Que 4E 80
Cardigan Ter. WF1: Wake 3H 9 (4L 125)
WF3: E Ard 4G 104
Cardigan Trad. Est. LS4: Leeds 5N 67
Cardinal Av. LS11: Leeds 5B 86
Cardinal Cl. HD9: Mel 7D 152
Cardinal Ct. LS11: Leeds 4A 86
Cardinal Cres. LS11: Leeds 5B 86
Cardinal Gdns. DN6: Burg 5M 165
LS11: Leeds 5A 86
Cardinal Gro. LS11: Leeds 5A 86
Cardinal Rd. LS11: Leeds 5A 86
Cardinal Sq. LS11: Leeds 4B 86
Cardinal Wlk. LS11: Leeds 4A 86
Cardwell Ter. WF11: Knot 8G 110
(off Fernley Grn. Rd.)
WF12: Dew 5F 122
Carisbrooke Cres. BD6: B'frd 5N 81
Carisbrooke La. LS25: Gar 6B 72
Carisbrooke Rd. LS16: Leeds 8L 49
Cark Rd. BD21: Keigh 8J 27
Carlby Gro. BD22: Keigh 1G 43
(off Carlby St.)
Carlby St. BD22: Keigh 1G 43
CARLETON 6M 129
Carleton Cl. LS23: B Spa 9B 24
WF8: Pon 4K 129
Carleton Crest WF8: Pon 5L 129
Carleton Dr. LS23: B Spa 1B 38
Carleton Ga. WF8: Pon 5K 129
Carleton Glen WF8: Pon 3K 129
Carleton Grange Stables WF8: Pon 6M 129
Carleton Grn. WF8: Pon 6L 129
Carleton Grn. Cl. WF8: Pon 5L 129
Carleton Pk. Av. WF8: Pon 5K 129
Carleton Pk. Rd. WF8: Pon 5K 129
Carleton Rd. WF8: D'ton, Pon 4K 129
Carleton St. BD20: Keigh 7H 27
Carleton Vw. WF8: Pon 5K 129
Carlile St. HD9: Mel 7D 152
Carling Cl. BD7: B'frd 2L 81
CARLINGHOW 6D 102
Carlinghow Ct. WF13: Dew 9C 102
(off Occupation La.)
Carlinghow Hill WF17: Bat 6E 102
Carlinghow La. WF17: Bat 5B 102
Carlisle Av. LS19: Yead 1N 47
Carlisle Bus. Cen. BD8: B'frd 5A 64
(off Carlisle Rd.)
Carlisle Cl. WF13: Dew 1F 122
Carlisle Dr. LS28: Pud 8A 66
Carlisle Gro. LS28: Pud 8A 66
Carlisle Pl. BD8: B'frd 5A 64
Carlisle Rd. BD8: B'frd 5N 63
LS10: Leeds 8F 68
LS28: Pud 8A 66
Carlisle St. BD8: B'frd 5A 64
BD21: Keigh 9K 27
HX2: Hal 4L 97
LS28: Stan 5N 65
Carlisle Ter. BD8: B'frd 5A 64
Carlrayne La. LS29: Men 3E 30
CARLTON
S71 8E 160
WF3 1M 105
Carlton App. LS22: Weth 3K 23
Carlton Av. BD18: Ship 7K 45
LS28: Pud 7B 66
WF10: C'frd 5F 108
WF17: Bat 9E 102
Carlton Carr LS7: Leeds 2F 4 (4E 68)
Carlton Cl. BD19: Cleck 5H 101
LS7: Leeds 2F 4
WF6: Norm 1J 127
WF9: Hems 4C 162
Carlton Ct. BD19: Cleck 4H 101
LS12: Leeds 1A 86
S71: Ath 9D 160
WF5: Oss 5N 123
WF9: S Elm 6M 163
(off Carlton Gdns.)
Carlton Cft. LS7: Leeds 1G 5
WF2: Wake 4M 143
Carlton Dr. BD9: B'frd 2N 63
BD17: Bail 3A 46
BD18: Ship 1M 63
LS20: Guis 6K 31
LS25: Gar 9N 71
Carlton Gdns. LS7: Leeds 2G 5 (4E 68)
WF6: Norm 1K 127
WF9: S Elm 6M 163
Carlton Gth. LS7: Leeds 2F 4 (4E 68)
LS17: Leeds 2J 51
Carlton Ga. LS7: Leeds 2F 4 (4E 68)
Carlton Grange LS19: Yead 9N 31
CARLTON GREEN 9E 160
Carlton Grn. S71: Carl 9D 160
WF6: Norm 1K 127
Carlton Gro. BD5: B'frd 2B 82
BD18: Ship 1N 63
HX5: Ell 4G 119
LS7: Leeds 1F 4 (4E 68)

Carlton Hill—Cavendish Rd.

Carlton Hill LS2: Leeds 2F 4 (4E 68)
LS7: Leeds 2F 4 (4E 68)
Carlton Ho. Ter. HX1: Hal 7G 7 (7N 97)
Carlton Ind. Est. S71: Carl 9D 160
Carlton La. LS19: E Car 5A 32
LS20: Guis 6K 31
LS26: Rothw 9M 87
WF3: Loft 3L 105
Carlton Lanes Shop. Cen.
WF10: C'frd 4D 108
Carlton Marsh Nature Reserve 9G 161
Carlton M. LS20: Guis 7K 31
S71: Carl 8D 160
Carlton Mill *HX6: Sow B* 8J 97
(off Old Cawsey)
Carlton Moor M. LS10: Leeds 8H 87
Carlton Mt. LS19: Yead 8N 31
Carlton Pde. LS7: Leeds 2G 5 (4E 68)
Carlton Pl.
HX1: Hal 5K 7 (6B 98)
LS7: Leeds 1F 4 (4E 68)
Carlton Ri. LS7: Leeds 2F 4 (4E 68)
LS28: Pud 7B 66
Carlton Rd. BD18: Ship 7K 45
S71: Ath, Carl, Smit 9C 160
WF9: S Elm 6M 163
WF13: Dew 2F 122
WF15: Liv 9L 101
WF16: Heck 6N 101
Carlton Row LS12: Leeds 7K 67
Carlton St. BD7: B'frd 8B 64
BD22: Haw 8D 42
HX1: Hal 5K 7 (6B 98)
HX7: Heb B 1H 95
LS21: Otley 1M 31
WF2: Wake 6J 125
WF4: Horb 1C 142
WF6: Norm 1J 127
WF7: F'stne 4D 128
WF10: C'frd 4D 108
Carlton Ter. HX1: Hal 5K 7 (6B 98)
LS19: Yead 9N 31
LS28: Pud 6B 66
WF12: Dew 5G 122
WF17: Bat 9D 102
Carlton Towers LS7: Leeds 2G 5 (4E 68)
Carlton Trad. Est. LS12: Leeds 6N 67
Carlton Vw. LS7: Leeds 1F 4 (4E 68)
WF10: All B 7N 89
Carlton Wlk. BD18: Ship 7L 45
LS7: Leeds 2F 4 (4E 68)
Carlton Way BD19: Cleck 5H 101
Carlyle Cres. WF10: C'frd 5G 109
Carlyle Rd. WF10: C'frd 5G 109
Carmel Rd. HX3: Hal 2B 98
Carmine Cl. HD5: Hud 4C 138
Carmona Av. BD18: Ship 1N 63
Carmona Gdns. BD18: Ship 1N 63
Carnaby Rd. BD7: B'frd 3K 81
Carnation St. BD3: B'frd 8G 64
Carnegie Ct. LS29: I'ly 5H 15
Carnegie Dr. BD18: Ship 8A 46
Carnegie Landing *BD18: Ship* 8A 46
(off Carr La.)
Carnegie Regional Indoor Tennis Cen. 9L 49
Carnlea Gro. WF2: Wake 8L 125
Carnoustie Gdns. WF6: Norm 2L 127
Carnoustie Gro. BD16: Cot 8G 44
Carolan Ct. HD7: Golc 6C 136
Caroline St. BD18: Ship 7L 45
BD19: Cleck 4H 101
(off Carver St.)
Carperley Cres. BD13: Denh 6L 61
Carr, The HD8: Shep 2K 171
Carr Bank BD20: E Mor 7B 28
LS21: Otley 7K 17
Carr Bank Bottom LS21: Otley 7K 17
Carr Beck Cl. LS23: B'ham 6D 38
Carr Beck Dr. WF10: C'frd 7A 108
Carr Beck Rd. WF10: C'frd 7A 108
Carr Beck Vw. WF10: C'frd 7A 108
Carr Bottom Av. BD5: B'frd 3N 81
Carr Bottom Fold BD5: B'frd 4A 82
Carr Bottom Gro. BD5: B'frd 3N 81
Carr Bottom Rd. BD5: B'frd 3N 81
BD10: B'frd 8J 47
Carr Bri. WF7: Ackw 4G 147
Carr Bri. Av. LS16: Leeds 4G 49
Carr Bri. Cl. LS16: Leeds 4G 49
Carr Bri. Dr. LS16: Leeds 4G 48
Carr Bri. Vw. LS16: Leeds 4G 48
Carr Cl. LS19: Raw 4A 48
Carr Ct. *WF17: Bat* 1F 122
(off Trinity St.)
CARR CROFTS 7L 67
Carr Crofts LS12: Leeds 7L 67
Carr Crofts Dr. LS12: Leeds 7L 67
Carrfield Cl. S75: Kex 9F 158
Carr Fld. Dr. HX2: Lud 4E 96
Carrfield Dr. LS15: Bar E 8L 53
Carrfield La. LS15: Bar E 8K 53
Carrfield Rd. LS15: Bar E 8L 53
Carrfield Vs. OL14: Tod 3C 92
Carr Furlong S71: Ath 8A 160
CARR GATE 7G 104
Carrgate WF9: Kins 8B 146
Carr Gate Cres. WF2: Carr G 7F 104
Carr Gate Dr. WF2: Carr G 7F 104
Carr Gate Mt. WF2: Carr G 7F 104
Carr Grn. HD8: Up C 2M 171
S75: Map 9L 159
Carr Grn. Av. HD6: Ras 5L 119
Carr Grn. Cl. HD6: Ras 5L 119
Carr Grn. Dr. HD6: Ras 5L 119
Carr Grn. La. HD5: Hud 3B 138
HD6: Ras 4L 119
S75: Map 9L 159
Carr Gro. BD20: Rid 7N 27
Carr Hall La. HX4: Holy 8N 117
Carr Hall Rd. BD12: Wyke 1A 100
Carr Head La. S36: Pen 9E 172
Carr Hill Av. LS28: Cal 9L 47
Carr Hill Dr. LS28: Cal 9L 47
Carr Hill Gro. LS28: Cal 9L 47
Carr Hill Nook LS28: Cal 9L 47
Carr Hill Ri. LS28: Cal 9L 47
Carr Hill Rd. HD8: Up C 2L 171
LS28: Cal 9L 47
Carrholm Cres. LS7: Leeds 8D 50
Carrholm Dr. LS7: Leeds 8D 50
Carrholme Ct. *HX1: Hal* 7M 97
(off Dundas St.)
Carrholm Grn. BD6: B'frd 7N 81
Carrholm Gro. LS7: Leeds 8D 50
Carrholm Mt. LS7: Leeds 8D 50
Carrholm Rd. LS7: Leeds 8D 50
Carrholm Vw. LS7: Leeds 8D 50
Carr Ho. HX2: Lud 1D 96
WF1: Wake 5J 9 (5L 125)
Carr Ho. Fold OL14: Tod 6M 93
CARR HOUSE GATE 9A 82
Carr Ho. Ga. BD12: Wyke 9A 82
Carr Ho. Gro. BD12: Wyke 9A 82
Carr Ho. La. BD12: Wyke 8N 81
HX3: She 6J 81
OL14: Tod 6M 93
Carr Ho. Mt. BD12: Wyke 9A 82
Carr Ho. Rd. HD9: H'frth 3M 169
HX3: She 7J 81
Carr Ho's. LS26: Meth 4M 107
Carriage Dr. BD19: Gom 2M 101
HD4: Hud 1K 153
Carriage Drive, The
HX4: Gree 3B 118
HX4: Stainl 7N 117
LS8: Leeds 6L 51
Carriage Fold BD13: Cull 1K 61
Carriage Way WF16: Heck 9A 102
Carriageworks Theatre, The 5E 4 (6D 68)
Carrick Dr. BD3: B'frd 6K 65
Carricks Cl. BD12: Low M 7C 82
Carrier St. HX1: Hal 4L 7 (5B 98)
Carrington Grn. WF17: Bat 6C 102
Carrington St. BD3: B'frd 7G 65
(not continuous)
Carrington Ter. LS20: Guis 8H 31
Carr La. BD12: Low M 9B 82
BD13: Denh 4L 61
BD16: Bgly 8D 28
BD18: Ship 7A 46
BD20: E Mor 7B 28
BD20: Rid 7N 27
HD7: Slait 9N 135
HD8: Shep 2K 171
HD9: H'frth 4N 169
(Cinderhills Rd.)
HD9: H'frth 4G 169
(Coldwell La.)
HX7: Heb B 3K 95
HX7: P Wel 6H 77
LS14: T'ner 3B 52
LS19: Raw 4A 48
LS22: Weth 2A 24
S36: Pen 8D 172
WF2: Wake 3M 143
WF3: Carl 1N 105
WF4: M'twn, Neth 4L 141
WF9: Kins 7N 145
WF9: S Kirk 5J 163
WF10: C'frd 6E 108
WF12: Bries 2E 140
WF13: Dew 3B 122
WF16: Heck 2A 122
Carr La. Av. WF10: C'frd 7E 108
Carr Mnr. Av. LS17: Leeds 7D 50
Carr Mnr. Cres. LS17: Leeds 6D 50
Carr Mnr. Cft. LS17: Leeds 8D 50
Carr Mnr. Dr. LS17: Leeds 7D 50
Carr Mnr. Gdns. LS17: Leeds 7D 50
Carr Mnr. Gth. LS17: Leeds 6D 50
Carr Mnr. Gro. LS17: Leeds 7D 50
Carr Mnr. Mt. LS17: Leeds 7D 50
Carr Mnr. Pde. LS17: Leeds 7D 50
Carr Mnr. Pl. LS17: Leeds 7D 50
Carr Mnr. Rd. LS17: Leeds 8D 50
Carr Mnr. Vw. LS17: Leeds 6D 50
Carr Mnr. Wlk. LS17: Leeds 8D 50
Carr Mills LS7: Leeds 2D 68
Carr Moor Side LS11: Leeds 2E 86
Carr Moor St. LS10: Leeds 3F 86
Carr Mt. HD5: K'htn 3J 139
HD8: Up C 2L 171
Carroll Ct. WF9: S Elm 6L 163
Carroll St. BD3: B'frd 5E 6 (8E 64)
Carron Dr. S75: Map 9J 159
Carr Pit Rd. HD5: Hud 6E 8 (5A 138)
Carr Rd. BD12: Wyke 1A 100
LS28: Cal 8K 47
OL14: Tod 3B 92
Carr Row BD12: Wyke 1A 100
Carrs Cl. WF13: Dew 9C 102
Carr Side Cres. WF17: Bat 9F 102
Carrs Rd. HD7: Mars 6F 150
Carrs Side St. No. 1 HD7: Mars 5G 151
Carrs Side St. No. 2 HD7: Mars 5G 151
Carrs St. HD7: Mars 5G 151
Carr St. BD5: B'frd 3B 82
BD19: Cleck 5H 101
BD21: Keigh 9J 27
HD3: Hud 3H 137
HD6: Brigh 8M 99
WF13: Dew 1F 122
WF15: Liv 7L 101
WF17: Birs 3B 102
Carr Ter. HX2: Lud 4D 96
Carr Top Cl. WF17: Bat 1E 122
Carr Top La. HD7: Golc 6C 136
Carr Vw. HX2: Lud 4D 96
WF9: S Kirk 5J 163
Carr Vw. Rd. HD9: H'wth 6D 170
Carr Wood Cl. LS28: Cal 9L 47
Carr Wood Gdns. LS28: Cal 9L 47
Carr Wood Ind. Est. WF10: C'frd 7F 108
Carr Wood Rd. WF10: C'frd 7F 108
Carr Wood Way LS28: Cal 8L 47
Carter Av. LS15: Leeds 6D 70
Carter La. BD13: Que 2C 80
LS15: Leeds 5D 70
Carter Mt. LS15: Leeds 6D 70
Carter's La. LS29: I'ly, Midd 2H 15
Carter St. BD4: B'frd 6D 6 (8D 64)
WF1: Wake 4H 9 (5K 125)
Carter Ter. LS15: Leeds 5D 70
Cart Ga. BD6: B'frd 4B 82
Cartier Ho. LS10: Leeds 8J 5 (8F 68)
Cartmel La. BD20: Stee 3C 26
Cartmell Ct. LS15: Leeds 7M 69
Cartmell Dr. LS15: Leeds 7M 69
Cartmel Rd. BD21: Keigh 8G 27
Carton Ct. *BD5: B'frd* 2C 82
(off New Cross St.)
Cartworth Bank Rd. HD9: H'frth 6L 169
Cartworth Fold HD9: H'frth 5M 169
Cartworth La. HD9: H'frth 5L 169
Cartworth Moor Rd. HD9: H'frth 9K 169
Cartworth Rd. HD9: H'frth 4M 169
Cartwright Fold WF2: Wake 4F 124
Cartwright Gdns. HD4: Hud 7H 137
Cartwright Hall Art Gallery 3A 64
Cartwright Ho. *WF15: Liv* 7L 101
(off Carr St.)
Cartwright St. BD19: Cleck 6J 101
Carver St. BD19: Cleck 4H 101
Caryl Rd. BD4: B'frd 2E 82
Cashmere St. BD21: Keigh 9G 27
Cask Ct. HX2: Hal 2J 97
Caspar Apartments LS2: Leeds 4G 5
Casson Av. WF3: E Ard 3D 104
Casson Dr. WF3: E Ard 3D 104
Casson Fold HX3: North 2F 98
Casson Gro. WF3: E Ard 3D 104
Casson St. HD4: Hud 6F 136
Cass Yd. WF1: Wake 5L 9
Castle, The OL14: Tod 6M 93
Castle Av. HD4: Hud 9M 137
HD6: Ras 3L 119
WF2: Wake 9M 125
Castle Carr Rd. HX2: Midg, Wain 4A 78
Castle Chain WF8: Pon 2L 129
Castle Cl. LS17: Bard 5E 36
WF17: Birs 3D 102
Castle Clough OL14: Tod 6N 93
Castle Cres. WF2: Wake 2M 143
WF12: T'hill 1F 140
Castle Cft. BD16: Har 6N 43
Castle Est. HX6: Ripp 8C 116
Castlefield Ct. WF10: C'frd 4D 108
Castlefields BD16: Bgly 2C 44
LS26: Rothw 8K 87
Castlefields Cres. HD6: Ras 3L 119
Castlefields Dr. HD6: Ras 3L 119
Castlefields Golf Course 3M 119
Castlefields Ind. Est. BD16: Bgly 2C 44
Castlefields La. BD16: Bgly 2C 44
HD6: Ras 3L 119
Castlefields Rd. BD16: Bgly 1C 44
HD6: Ras 3L 119
Castlefields Trad. Est. BD16: Bgly 2C 44
CASTLEFORD 4D 108
CASTLEFORD INGS 3D 108
Castleford La. WF7: A'ton 2A 128
WF11: Ferr 7A 110
Castleford Mkt. Hall *WF10: C'frd* 4D 108
(off Jessop St.)
Castleford Mus. 4D 108
Castleford Rd. WF6: Norm 1J 127
Castleford Station (Rail) 5D 108
Castleford Swimming Pool 6B 108
Castleford Tigers RLFC 3F 108
Castle Gth. WF8: Pon 2L 129
Castle Gate HX7: Crag V 8K 95
LS22: Weth 4M 23
LS26: Oul 4N 105
LS29: I'ly 5G 14
WF3: S'ley 4B 106
Castlegate HD1: Hud 4A 8 (5M 137)
Castlegate Dr. BD10: B'frd 9G 47
WF8: Pon 6H 129
Castlegate Ho. *HX5: Ell* 4E 118
(off Huddersfield Rd.)
Castlegate Loop HD1: Hud 4A 8 (3M 137)
Castlegate Slip HD1: Hud 3A 8 (3M 137)
Castle Grange LS19: Yead 1A 48
Castle Gro. BD16: Har 6N 43
LS17: Bard 5E 36
OL14: Tod 6M 93
WF4: Horb 2E 142
WF8: Pon 2K 129
Castle Gro. Av. LS6: Leeds 8N 49
Castle Gro. Dr. LS6: Leeds 9N 49
Castle Head Cl. WF3: Loft 4L 105
Castle Head La. WF3: Loft 5H 105
WF3: Thpe H 4H 105
Castle Hill BD22: Keigh 1G 42
HD6: Ras 3L 119
LS29: I'ly 5G 14
WF2: Wake 7E 124
Castle Hill & Victoria Tower 1A 154
Castle Hill Rd. BD19: Gom 6M 101
Castle Hill Side HD4: Hud 1A 154
Castle Hills Rd. DN6: Stap 7H 131
Castle Hill Vw. LS17: Bard 5D 36
WF16: Heck 9C 102
Castle Houses HD4: Hud 1N 153
Castle Ings Cl. LS12: N Far 2G 84
Castle Ings Dr. LS12: N Far 2G 84
Castle Ings Gdns. LS12: N Far 2G 84
Castle Keep LS22: Weth 4M 23
Castle La. HD7: Slait 7K 135
HX6: Ripp 8C 116
OL14: Tod 6M 93
Castle Lodge HX7: Crag V 9K 95
Castle Lodge Av. LS26: Rothw 6K 87
Castle Lodge Ct. LS26: Rothw 7L 87
Castle Lodge Gdns. LS26: Rothw 7K 87
Castle Lodge Gth. LS26: Rothw 6L 87
Castle Lodge M. LS26: Rothw 7L 87
Castle Lodge Sq. LS26: Rothw 6L 87
Castle Lodge Way LS26: Rothw 7K 87
Castle Mdws. WF4: Hol 7H 143
Castle M. BD18: Ship 8N 45
WF8: Pon 2K 129
Castlemore Rd. BD17: Bail 5B 46
CASTLE MOUNT 1G 141
Castle Mt. WF12: T'hill 9G 123
Castle Pde. WF10: C'frd 6F 108
Castle Pl. HD6: Ras 3M 119
Castlerigg Grn. BD6: B'frd 7L 81
Castle Rd. BD18: Ship 8N 45
BD21: Keigh 8H 27
LS26: Rothw 8M 87
LS29: I'ly 5G 14
(not continuous)
WF2: Wake 1M 143
Castle Rd. W. WF2: Wake 1M 143
CASTLE STREET 6M 93
Castle St. BD5: B'frd 8B 6 (9C 64)
LS1: Leeds 6C 4 (6C 68)
WF2: Wake 6H 125
Castle Syke Hill WF7: Ackw 8H 129
Castle Syke Vw. WF8: Pon 5J 129
Castle Ter. HD6: Ras 3L 119
WF2: Wake 2M 143
Castleton Cl. LS12: Leeds 7A 4 (7B 68)
Castleton Rd. LS12: Leeds 6A 68
Castle Va. WF8: Pon 1M 129
Castle Vw. HD9: Hon 6L 153
LS17: Leeds 6D 50
OL14: Tod 8K 93
(off Well St.)
WF2: Wake 2M 143
WF4: Horb 2E 142
WF8: Pon 2K 129
WF14: Mir 6M 121
Castlewood Cl. LS17: Hare 1J 35
LS18: Hors 7G 49
CASTLEY 9L 19
Castle Yd. LS29: I'ly 5G 14
Castley La. LS21: Cast, Leat 9G 18
Catalina LS12: Leeds 8B 4 (7C 68)
Cater La. WF16: Heck 9A 102
Cater St. BD1: B'frd 4D 6 (7D 64)
Cathcart St. HX3: Hal 3A 98
LS6: Leeds 3C 68
Cathedral Church of All Saints, The 4K 9 (5L 125)
Cathedral Cl. BD1: B'frd 3C 6 (7D 64)
WF1: Wake 3H 9 (4K 125)
Cathedral Retail Pk.
WF2: Wake 6H 9 (6K 125)
Cathedral Wlk. WF1: Wake 4K 9 (5L 125)
Catherine Cl. HD3: Hud 9F 118
Catherine Cres. HX5: Ell 5E 118
Catherine Gro. LS11: Leeds 2D 86
Catherine Ho. La. HX2: Midg 6A 78
Catherine Rd. HD2: Hud 7N 119
CATHERINE SLACK 7A 80
Catherine Slack HD6: Brigh 6L 99
Catherine St. BD21: Keigh 2H 43
(not continuous)
HD6: Brigh 9M 99
HX5: Ell 5E 118
WF9: Fitz 6A 146
Catherines Wlk. S71: Ath 9B 160
CAT HILL 9G 173
Cat Hill La. S36: Hoy 9G 173
Cat La. HX2: Lud F 7A 96
HX4: Gree 4L 117
Catlow St. WF10: C'frd 5C 108
Catstones Wood BD18: Ship 8C 46
Cattlelaith La. WF11: Knot 9B 110
Cattle La. LS25: Aber 8E 54
Cattle Mkt. St. LS21: Otley 9L 17
Caudle Hill WF11: Fair 9M 91
Cauldwell Gdns. BD5: B'frd 1C 82
Caulms Wood Rd. WF12: Dew 2G 122
WF13: Dew 2G 122
Causeway HD3: Outl 6M 135
HD7: Slait 7M 135
(Highfield Rd.)
HD7: Slait 7J 135
(Worts Hill Side)
HX1: Hal 4M 7 (5C 98)
HX4: Bark 8G 116
Causeway Cres. HD7: Linth 9C 136
CAUSEWAY FOOT
HD8 4J 155
HX2 3L 79
Causeway Foot HX2: Ogd 2K 79
Causeway Gth. La.
WF8: Thpe A 6A 148
Causeway Head HX6: Sow B 7H 97
Causeway Head La. HX6: Ripp 6B 116
Causeway Side HD7: Linth 9C 136
Causeway Wood Rd. OL14: Tod 8N 93
Cautley Rd. LS9: Leeds 8H 69
Cavalier App. LS9: Leeds 8H 69
Cavalier Cl. LS9: Leeds 8H 69
Cavalier Ct. LS9: Leeds 8H 69
Cavalier Dr. BD10: B'frd 7J 47
Cavalier Gdns. LS9: Leeds 8H 69
Cavalier Ga. LS9: Leeds 8H 69
Cavalier Grn. LS9: Leeds 8H 69
CAVALIER HILL 8L 5 (7G 69)
Cavalier M. LS9: Leeds 8H 69
Cavalier Vw. LS9: Leeds 8H 69
Cave Cres. WF2: Wake 7G 125
Cave Hill HX3: North 9E 80
Cave La. WF3: E Ard 4F 104
Cavendish App. BD11: Drig 7B 84
Cavendish Av. WF8: Pon 9L 109
Cavendish Ct. *BD10: B'frd* 1G 65
(off Park Rd.)
BD11: Drig 7B 84
(off Cavendish App.)
BD21: Keigh 9J 27
HD7: Mars 5F 150
Cavendish Dr. BD16: Bgly 3G 44
LS20: Guis 8H 31
Cavendish Gro. LS20: Guis 8H 31
Cavendish M. BD11: Drig 7B 84
LS17: Leeds 3F 50
Cavendish Pl. LS28: Stan 5A 66
Cavendish Ri. LS28: Pud 7D 66
Cavendish Rd. BD2: B'frd 1G 65
BD10: B'frd 8F 46
(Buckfast Ct.)
BD10: B'frd 1G 65
(Park Rd.)
LS2: Leeds 2D 4 (4D 68)
LS20: Guis 8H 31

Cavendish Sq.—Charlesworth Way

Cavendish Sq. LS28: Stan 5B 66
Cavendish St. BD21: Keigh 9J 27
HX1: Hal 3G 7 (5N 97)
LS3: Leeds 5A 4 (6B 68)
LS19: Yead 9N 31
LS28: Pud 7D 66
Cavendish Ter. HX1: Hal 3G 7 (5N 97)
(not continuous)
Cavewell Cl. WF5: Oss 8B 124
Cavewell Gdns. WF5: Oss 8B 124
Cawcliffe Dr. HD6: Brigh 7M 99
Cawcliffe Rd. HD6: Brigh 8M 99
Cawley Gth. WF16: Heck 9B 102
Cawley La. WF16: Heck 8B 102
Cawood Haven BD6: B'frd 5K 81
CAWTHORNE 4N 173
Cawthorne Av. HD2: Hud 9M 119
Cawthorne La. S75: Caw, Kex 9D 158
Cawthorne Rd. WF2: Wake 4K 143
Caxton Gdns. WF8: Pon 9K 109
Caxton Rd. LS21: Otley 2J 31
Caxton St. LS22: Weth 4M 23
Caycroft Nook HX7: Hept 8G 77
Caygill Ter. HX1: Hal 7K 7 (7B 98)
Caythorpe Rd. LS16: Leeds 8L 49
Caythorpe Wlk. BD10: B'frd 1G 65
Cecil Av. BD7: B'frd 1N 81
BD17: Bail 3A 46
HX3: Hip 4K 99
Cecil Gro. LS12: Leeds 6M 67
Cecil Mt. LS12: Leeds 6M 67
Cecil Rd. LS12: Leeds 6M 67
Cecil St. BD22: Cros R 7F 42
HD1: Hud 5A 8 (4M 137)
LS12: Leeds 6M 67
Cecily Cl. WF6: Norm 3J 127
Cedar Apartments WF1: Wake 1M 9 (3M 125)
Cedar Av. HD1: Hud 3L 137
LS12: Leeds 7M 67
WF5: Oss 7A 124
Cedar Cl. BD4: B'frd 5G 82
HD7: Golc 5E 136
LS12: Leeds 7M 67
OL14: Tod 5J 93
S71: Roys 5B 160
WF8: Pon 6J 129
Cedar Ct. HD1: Hud 3K 137
LS17: Leeds 5F 50
(off Harrogate Rd.)
LS26: W'frd 6F 88
WF10: C'frd 5E 108
WF11: Knot 7F 110
Cedar Ct. Office Pk. WF4: Cal G 3F 142
Cedar Covert LS22: Weth 1M 23
Cedar Dr. BD12: Wyke 9C 82
LS14: Leeds 4N 69
WF12: Dew 5L 123
Cedar Gro. BD17: Bail 6K 45
HD6: B Bri 6N 99
HX4: Gree 4A 118
WF7: F'stne 4D 128
WF17: Bat 1F 122
Cedar M. WF2: Wake 9J 125
Cedar Mt. HD1: Hud 3L 137
LS12: Leeds 7L 67
Cedar Pl. LS12: Leeds 7L 67
Cedar Ridge LS25: Gar 5B 72
Cedar Rd. LS12: Leeds 7L 67
WF6: Norm 4J 127
WF12: Dew 5K 123
Cedars, The LS16: B'hpe 6J 33
Cedars Bus. Pk. WF9: Hems 2D 162
Cedar St. BD16: Bgly 2D 44
BD21: Keigh 3H 43
HD1: Hud 3K 137
HX1: Hal 6M 97
LS12: Leeds 7L 67
OL14: W'den 3J 113
Cedar Ter. LS12: Leeds 7L 67
Cedar Wlk. DN6: Cam 1N 165
WF7: F'stne 5D 128
WF11: Knot 1C 130
(not continuous)
Cedar Way BD19: Gom 4L 101
Celandine Av. HD3: Hud 2D 136
Celandine Cl. WF8: Pon 4K 129
Celandine Dr. HD3: Hud 2D 136
Celette Ind. Pk. BD19: Cleck 5G 101
Cemetery La. BD20: Keigh 6H 27
HX6: Sow B 8G 96
WF3: Carl 3L 105
Cemetery Rd. BD6: B'frd 6N 81
BD7: B'frd 6L 63
BD8: B'frd 6L 63
BD12: Low M 6N 81
BD16: Bgly 3D 44
BD22: Haw 9N 41
HD1: Hud 3L 137
HD9: H'frth 4L 169
LS11: Leeds 1C 86
LS19: E Car, Yead 9N 31
LS28: Pud 6N 65
WF4: Ryh 9J 145
WF6: Norm 1K 127
WF9: Hems 2C 162
WF13: Dew 4D 122
WF16: Heck 8A 102
WF17: Bat 7E 102
Cemetery Wlk. HD5: Hud 7D 138
Centaur Ho. LS1: Leeds 5C 4 (6C 68)
Centenary Rd. BD17: Bail 3D 46
Centenary Sq. BD1: B'frd 5B 6 (8C 64)
WF12: Dew 7E 122
Centenary Way WF17: Bat 6E 102
Central Arc. *BD19: Cleck 5J 101*
(off Cheapside)
Central Av. BD5: B'frd 1A 82
BD17: Bail 5N 45
BD18: Ship 8N 45
BD22: Keigh 4F 42
HD2: Hud 8N 119
S72: Grim 9A 162
WF9: Fitz 6A 146
WF9: S Elm 7M 163
WF15: Liv 7F 100
Central Bldgs. *HX4: Stainl 7M 117*
(off Stainland Rd.)
HX6: Sow B 8H 97
(off Town Hall St.)
Central Cl. HD2: Hud 8N 119
Central Ct. WF7: F'stne 7C 128
Central Dr. BD22: Keigh 4F 42
HD2: Hud 8N 119
S71: Roys 6D 160
WF10: C'frd 5N 107
Central M. WF7: F'stne 7C 128
Central Pde. *BD19: Cleck 5J 101*
(off Dewsbury Rd.)
Central Pk. HX1: Hal 7J 7 (7A 98)
LS11: Leeds 8D 68
Central Pl. *BD14: Clay 1G 81*
(off Clayton La.)
Central Rd. LS1: Leeds 7G 5 (7E 68)
Central St. HX1: Hal 4K 7 (5B 98)
HX7: Heb B 1H 95
LS1: Leeds 6D 4 (6D 68)
WF13: Dew 3E 122
Central Village Leeds LS1: Leeds 3D 4
Centre 27 Bus. Pk. WF17: Birs 1E 102
Centre St. BD5: B'frd 2A 82
WF9: Hems 2D 162
WF9: S Elm 6N 163
WF16: Heck 8N 101
Centre Va. *HX6: Tri 2E 116*
(off Rochdale Rd.)
Centuria Wlk. HD3: Hud 2D 136
Centurion Way BD19: Cleck 2G 101
Century Pl. BD8: B'frd 5A 64
Century Rd. HX5: Ell 4E 118
Century St. *BD21: Keigh 3J 43*
(off Percy St.)
Century Way LS15: Leeds 7G 70
Ceres Ct. LS22: Weth 4A 24
Ceres Rd. LS22: Weth 4A 24
Chaddlewood Cl. LS18: Hors 6F 48
Chadwell Springs BD16: Cot 8F 44
Chadwick Cres. WF13: Dew 2E 122
Chadwick Fold La. WF14: Mir 7K 121
Chadwick Hall Gdns. WF14: Mir 7K 121
Chadwick La. WF14: Mir 8K 121
Chadwick St. LS10: Leeds 8H 5 (8F 68)
Chadwick St. Sth. LS10: Leeds 8F 68
Chaffinch Rd. BD8: B'frd 7H 63
Chaffinch Wlk. HD4: Neth 2K 153
Chain Bar Rd. BD19: Cleck 3G 101
Chain Rd. HD7: Slait 4L 151
Chain St. BD1: B'frd 3A 6 (7B 64)
WF10: C'frd 4C 108
Chak Gdns. BD9: B'frd 1J 63
Chalcroft Cl. WF16: Heck 7B 102
Chald La. WF2: Wake 6G 9 (6K 125)
Chalfont Rd. LS16: Leeds 7L 49
Chalice Cl. LS10: Leeds 6G 86
Challenge Way BD4: B'frd 1H 83
WF17: Bat 8J 103
Challis Gro. BD5: B'frd 2C 82
Chalner Av. LS27: Morl 2J 103
Chalner Cl. LS27: Morl 2J 103
Chaloner Grn. WF1: Wake 1M 9 (3M 125)
Chaloner Gro. WF1: Wake 1M 9 (3M 125)
Chalwood HD2: Hud 7C 120
Chaly Flds. LS23: B Spa 1D 38
Champion Av. WF10: C'frd 7E 108
Chancel Ct. HD3: Hud 4F 136
Chancellor Ct. LS2: Leeds 7G 5 (7E 68)
Chancellor St. LS6: Leeds 3D 68
Chancel Rd. WF1: Wake 8M 9 (7M 125)
Chancel Sq. LS6: Leeds 6B 50
Chancery Cl. HD1: Hud 5B 8
Chancery La. HD1: Hud 5B 8 (4M 137)
WF1: Wake 4J 9 (5L 125)
WF5: Oss 3L 123
Chancery Rd. WF5: Oss 3L 123
Chancery Ter. HX3: Hal 1B 118
Chandler Cl. WF17: Birs 3B 102
Chandler La. HD9: Hon 5J 153
Chandlers, The LS2: Leeds 8H 5
Chandlers Cl. WF1: Out 7K 105
Chandlers Wharf LS13: Leeds 9B 48
Chandos Av. LS8: Leeds 7G 51
Chandos Fold LS8: Leeds 8G 51
Chandos Gdns. LS8: Leeds 7G 51
Chandos Gth. LS8: Leeds 7G 51
Chandos Grn. LS8: Leeds 7G 51
Chandos M. LS8: Leeds 8G 51
Chandos Pl. LS8: Leeds 7H 51
Chandos St. BD4: B'frd 6C 6 (8D 64)
BD21: Keigh 2H 43
(not continuous)
Chandos Ter. LS8: Leeds 7H 51
Chandos Wlk. LS8: Leeds 7G 51
Change All. LS1: Leeds 6F 4
Changegate BD22: Haw 8B 42
Changegate Ct. BD22: Haw 8B 42
Change La. HX3: Hal 1D 118
Channing Way BD1: B'frd 5B 6 (8C 64)
Chantrell Ct. LS2: Leeds 7H 5 (7F 68)
Chantry Bri. Ind. Est. WF1: Wake 7L 9 (6M 125)
Chantry Chapel of St Mary 7M 9 (6M 125)
Chantry Cl. LS29: I'ly 6G 15
WF8: Pon 4H 129
Chantry Ct. LS27: Morl 8L 85
Chantry Cft. LS15: Leeds 7E 70
WF9: Kins 8A 146
Chantry Dr. LS29: I'ly 6G 15
Chantry Gth. LS15: Leeds 7E 70
Chantry Gro. S71: Roys 6D 160
Chantry Ho. *HD1: Hud 5C 8*
(off Oldgate)
WF1: Wake 5L 9
Chantry La. LS24: Stut 3J 55
Chantry Rd. WF2: Wake 7G 124
Chantry Waters WF1: Wake 8M 9 (7M 125)
Chapel, The *LS26: Oul 8D 88*
(off Calverley Rd.)
CHAPEL ALLERTON 9D 50
Chapel Allerton Lawn Tennis, Squash & Gym 8E 50
Chapel Av. HX7: Heb B 1J 95
WF16: Heck 7B 102
Chapel Bank HD9: Jack B 5C 170
Chapel Cl. *BD22: Cros R 7E 42*
(off East Ter.)
HD4: Hud 1L 153
HD8: Skelm 7D 156
HX3: She 7J 81
HX4: Holy 7A 118
LS25: Gar 7M 71
OL14: W'den 5K 113
S72: Shaf 6K 161
WF4: Wrag 3N 145
WF12: T'hill 9G 122
Chapel Ct. *BD13: Que 3G 80*
(off Chapel La.)
BD15: Wils 9B 44
HD6: Brigh 9N 119
(off Park St.)
LS15: Leeds 6B 70
LS25: M'fld 7G 73
Chapel Cft. BD22: Lay 9C 26
HD6: Ras 4L 119
Chapelfields WF9: S Kirk 7H 163
CHAPEL FOLD 1D 122
Chapel Fold BD6: B'frd 4N 81
BD12: Wyke 4A 100
HX3: She 7J 81
LS6: Leeds 3N 67
LS11: Leeds 3A 86
LS12: Leeds 7M 67
(off Wesley Rd.)
LS15: Leeds 6B 70
LS28: Pud 8B 66
(off Littlemoor Rd.)
WF17: Bat 9D 102
Chapel Gth. WF7: Ackw 4G 146
Chapelgate HD9: Scho 5B 170
CHAPEL GREEN 2B 82
Chapel Grn. LS28: Pud 8A 66
Chapel Gro. BD16: Bgly 2D 44
CHAPEL HILL 7N 21
Chapel Hill HD1: Hud 8A 8 (6M 137)
HD7: Linth 9C 136
HD8: Clay W 7H 157
LS10: Leeds 8F 86
LS19: Yead 9M 31
LS22: Kear 7L 21
LS27: Morl 8K 85
WF8: D'ton 7D 130
WF14: Up H 9K 121
Chapel Hill La. HD3: Scam 4H 135
LS21: Cast 9L 19
WF4: Over 5K 141
Chapel Hill Rd. LS21: Pool 2G 32
Chapel Ho. *LS29: I'ly 6G 14*
(off Wells Prom.)
Chapel Ho. Apartments
HX2: Hal 1M 97
(off Club La.)
Chapel Ho. Bldgs. *BD12: Low M 7C 82*
(off Chapel Ho. Rd.)
Chapel Ho. Rd. BD12: Low M 6B 82
Chapel Ho's. *OL12: Whit 7A 112*
(off Oak St.)
CHAPEL LANE 6C 42
Chapel La. BD13: Que 4C 80
(Foxhill Gro.)
BD13: Que 3G 80
(Highgate)
BD15: All 6H 63
BD16: Bgly 4E 44
BD17: Esh 2G 46
BD21: Keigh 9H 27
BD22: Lay 9C 26
BD22: Oak 5C 42
BD23: Hal E 1E 10
HD5: Hud 5B 138
HD7: Golc 6C 136
HD8: Eml 2E 156
HX2: Midg 2B 96
HX3: Hal 1C 118
HX3: Sou 8F 98
HX6: Sow B 8K 97
LS6: Leeds 2N 67
LS12: Leeds 7M 67
LS12: N Far 9G 67
LS15: Bar E 8M 53
LS19: Yead 9M 31
LS23: Cliff 2D 38
LS25: Gar 7M 71
LS25: Kip 4B 90
LS29: I'ly 5F 14
S71: Carl 9D 160
WF8: Lit S 4K 149
WF9: Bads 8L 147
WF9: S Elm 6A 164
WF9: S Kirk 6J 163
WF12: T'hill 9G 122
WF16: Heck 7B 102
WF17: Birs 3B 102
Chapel Lofts *LS27: Morl 9L 85*
(off Commercial St.)
Chapel M. BD15: All 6H 63
LS23: Cliff 2D 38
S75: S'ross 8L 159
Chapel Pl. LS6: Leeds 1N 67
Chapel Rd. BD12: Low M 7B 82
(not continuous)
BD16: Bgly 2D 44
BD20: Stee 3C 26
LS7: Leeds 1F 68
Chapel Row BD15: Wils 9B 44
LS21: Pool 1F 32
(off Main St.)
WF4: G Moor 6B 140
Chapel Royd HD8: Eml 2G 156
Chapel Sq. *LS6: Leeds 1N 67*
(off Chapel St.)
Chapel St. BD1: B'frd 4D 6 (7D 64)
BD2: B'frd 2H 65
BD5: B'frd 1B 82
BD6: B'frd 4A 82
BD13: Denh 6K 61
BD13: Que 4D 80
BD13: Thorn 8C 62
BD16: Bgly 2D 44
Chapel St. BD19: Cleck 4J 101
BD20: Sils 7E 12
DN6: Carc 9N 165
HD1: Hud 7B 8 (5M 137)
HD4: Hud 8K 137
HD4: Neth 2H 153
HD5: Hud 5B 138
HD6: Brigh 7K 99
HD7: Golc 5A 136
HX2: Hal 4L 97
HX3: Nor G 1L 99
HX4: Holy 7A 118
LS6: Leeds 1N 67
LS13: Leeds 1B 66
LS15: Leeds 6B 70
LS19: Raw 3M 47
LS28: Cal 8M 47
LS28: Stan 5B 66
LS29: Add 1M 13
OL14: Tod 6M 93
OL15: Lit 9M 113
S72: Shaf 6K 161
WF3: Carl 1M 105
WF3: E Ard 5E 104
WF3: S'ley 7N 105
WF3: Ting 3B 104
WF4: Ryh 9J 145
WF5: Oss 7C 124
WF11: Knot 7F 110
WF12: Dew 5F 122
WF14: Mir 6L 121
WF15: Liv 8N 101
(Flush)
WF15: Liv 7G 101
(The Shearings)
Chapel St. Nth. HX3: Hal 1M 97
Chapel St. Sth. *OL14: W'den 2J 113*
(off Barnes St.)
Chapel Ter. BD13: Thorn 8C 62
BD15: All 5G 62
HD4: Hud 6J 137
HD9: Hon 5L 153
HX4: Bark 4J 117
HX6: Sow B 9D 96
LS6: Leeds 1N 67
(off Chapel St.)
CHAPELTHORPE 6H 143
CHAPELTOWN 2F 68
Chapeltown HX1: Hal 3J 7 (5B 98)
LS28: Pud 8A 66
Chapeltown Bus. Cen. *LS7: Leeds 2F 68*
(off Chapeltown Rd.)
Chapeltown Rd. LS7: Leeds 1H 5 (3F 68)
Chapel Vw. LS26: W'frd 7M 89
LS27: Gil 5F 84
Chapel Wlk. BD2: B'frd 2H 65
Chapel Yd. *LS15: Leeds 8E 70*
(off Meynell Rd.)
LS26: Oul 8D 88
WF11: Fair 9N 91
(off Gauk St.)
Chapman Rd. BD3: B'frd 6K 65
Chapman St. BD4: B'frd 8H 65
Chappell Rd. S36: Hoy 9J 173
Chariot Pl. WF11: Ferr 7A 110
Chariot Way WF8: Thpe A 6N 147
Charles Apartments LS3: Leeds 5B 4
Charles Av. BD3: B'frd 7H 65
HD3: Hud 2F 136
HX3: Sou 8F 98
LS9: Leeds 8H 69
WF1: Out 7K 105
WF1: Wake 8A 126
Charles Cotton Cl. WF2: Wake 3F 124
Charles Ct. *BD22: Oxen 4C 60*
(off Station Rd.)
LS26: W'frd 7M 89
Charles Gdns. LS11: Leeds 9C 68
Charles Gro. LS26: Oul 7D 88
Charles Jones Ct. WF17: Bat 7E 102
Charles Morris Hall BD5: B'frd 9A 64
LS2: Leeds 3B 4 (5C 68)
Charles Pl. OL14: Tod 9J 93
Charles Robert St. WF4: Horb 3E 142
Charles St. BD1: B'frd 4B 6 (7C 64)
BD13: Que 4C 80
BD16: Bgly 4E 44
BD17: Ship 7N 45
BD19: Gom 4M 101
DN6: Carc, Skel 7N 165
HD4: Hud 6J 137
(not continuous)
HD6: Brigh 9M 99
HX1: Hal 4M 7 (5C 98)
HX5: Ell 5E 118
HX6: Sow B 8H 97
LS18: Hors 7E 48
LS21: Otley 1L 31
LS27: Morl 9L 85
LS28: Fars 3A 66
S72: Cud 9K 161
S72: S Hien 4M 161
WF1: Wake 6M 9 (6M 125)
WF4: Ryh 9H 145
WF5: Oss 8B 124
WF10: C'frd 5E 108
WF12: Dew 3H 123
WF13: Dew 3C 122
WF13: Raven 6B 122
WF17: Bat 8F 102
CHARLESTOWN
BD17 ....5C 46
HX7 ....2E 94
Charlestown WF7: Ackw 5G 146
Charlestown Rd. HX3: Hal 2M 7 (4C 98)
Charles Vw. WF4: Hol 7H 143
Charlesworth Ct. WF12: T'hill 9G 123
Charlesworth Gro. HX2: Hal 4L 97
Charlesworth Pl. WF3: S'ley 6D 106
Charlesworth's Bldgs. *WF4: Horb 1C 142*
(off Claytons Cotts.)
Charlesworth Sq. BD19: Gom 4L 101
Charlesworth St. WF12: Dew 7F 122
Charlesworth Ter. HX2: Hal 4L 97
Charlesworth Way WF2: Wake 7H 9 (6K 125)

Charleville—Churchill St.

Charleville WF9: S Elm 5L 163
Charlotte Cl. HX1: Hal 7B 98
WF17: Birs 1C 102
Charlotte Ct. BD7: B'frd 2M 81
BD22: Haw 7D 42
Charlotte Gro. LS15: Leeds 6C 70
WF5: Oss 7B 124
Charlotte St. WF1: Wake 6K 9 (6M 125)
Charlotte Yd. WF1: Wake 6L 9
Charlton Cl. BD2: B'frd 2F 64
Charlton Ct. *HX2: Hal* *4L 97*
(off Reservoir Rd.)
Charlton Gro. BD20: Sils 9F 12
LS9: Leeds 7J 69
Charlton Pl. LS9: Leeds 7J 69
Charlton Rd. LS9: Leeds 7J 69
Charlton St. LS9: Leeds 7J 69
Charnley Dr. LS7: Leeds 9G 50
Charnock Cl. HX1: Hal 8K 7 (7B 98)
Charnwood Bank WF17: Bat 8B 102
Charnwood Cl. BD2: B'frd 4G 64
WF17: Bat *8B 102*
(off Charnwood Bank)
Charnwood Gro. BD2: B'frd 4G 64
Charnwood Rd. BD2: B'frd 4G 64
Chart Cl. LS25: Gar 7M 71
Charterhouse Rd. BD10: B'frd 6F 46
Charteris Rd. BD8: B'frd 7H 63
Chartist's Ct. *LS27: Morl* *1K 103*
(off Gt. Northern St.)
Chartists Way LS27: Morl 1K 103
Chartwell Ct. *LS17: Leeds* *2K 51*
(off Shadwell La.)
Chartwell Dr. BD6: B'frd 4K 81
Charville Gdns. LS17: Shad 4A 52
Chase, The BD20: Keigh 8F 26
LS19: Raw 3L 47
LS22: Weth 3N 23
LS25: Gar 7B 72
LS29: Burl W 1D 30
WF3: S'ley 6B 106
WF3: Ting 3A 104
Chase Av. LS27: Morl 3L 103
Chase Ct. LS27: Morl 3L 103
Chase Way BD5: B'frd 3C 82
Chassum Gro. BD9: B'frd 4M 63
Chaster St. WF17: Bat 6D 102
(not continuous)
Chatham St. BD3: B'frd 5D 64
HX1: Hal 3H 7 (5A 98)
HX6: Sow B 7H 97
Chat Hill Rd. BD13: Thorn 9E 62
Chatswood Av. LS11: Leeds 5B 86
Chatswood Cres. LS11: Leeds 5B 86
Chatswood Dr. LS11: Leeds 4B 86
Chatsworth Av. LS28: Pud 6L 65
WF8: Pon 9L 109
Chatsworth Cl. HD5: Hud 6B 138
LS8: Leeds 3J 69
Chatsworth Ct. *BD8: B'frd* *6M 63*
(off Girlington Rd.)
WF12: Dew 4J 123
Chatsworth Cres. LS28: Pud 6L 65
Chatsworth Dr. LS22: Weth 3K 23
LS28: Pud 6L 65
Chatsworth Fall LS28: Pud 6L 65
Chatsworth Ind. Est. LS12: Leeds 8N 67
Chatsworth M. LS27: Morl 1M 103
Chatsworth Pl. BD8: B'frd 4N 63
Chatsworth Ri. LS28: Pud 6L 65
Chatsworth Rd. LS8: Leeds 3J 69
LS28: Pud 6L 65
S71: Ath 9B 160
Chatsworth St. BD21: Keigh 9K 27
Chatsworth Ter. WF12: Dew 4J 123
Chatts Wood Fold BD12: O'haw 8F 82
Chaucer Av. LS28: Pud 8C 66
WF3: S'ley 6N 105
Chaucer Cl. HD9: Hon 6L 153
Chaucer Gdns. LS28: Pud 8C 66
Chaucer Gro. LS28: Pud 8C 66
Chaucer St. HX1: Hal 6M 97
Cheapside BD1: B'frd 3B 6 (7C 64)
BD19: Cleck 5J 101
HX1: Hal 4L 7 (5B 98)
HX3: She 7H 81
LS27: Morl *8K 85*
(off Chapel Hill)
WF1: Wake 4H 9 (5K 125)
WF6: Norm 1J 127
WF17: Bat 7G 103
Checkstone Av. WF10: C'frd 7A 108
Cheddington Gro. BD15: All 6G 62
Cheese Ga. Nab Side HD8: Cumb 6E 170
HD9: Jack B 6E 170
Cheetham Hill OL12: Whit 8A 112
Cheetham St. HX7: Heb B 1H 95
Chelburn Vw. OL15: Lit 9L 113
Chelker Cl. BD6: B'frd 3J 81
Chellowfield Ct. BD9: B'frd 3H 63
Chellow Gdns. *BD15: All* *4F 62*
(off Deanwood Cres.)
Chellow Grange Rd. BD9: B'frd 3H 63
Chellow La. BD9: B'frd 4H 63
Chellow St. BD5: B'frd 3B 82
Chellow Ter. BD9: B'frd 5J 63
BD11: B'haw 9M 83
Chellow Way WF12: Dew 4F 122
Chelmsford Rd. BD3: B'frd 6G 65
(not continuous)
Chelmsford Ter. BD3: B'frd 7G 65
Chelsea Cl. LS12: Leeds 8M 67
Chelsea Mans. HX3: North 2F 98
Chelsea Rd. BD7: B'frd 1L 81
Chelsea St. BD21: Keigh 1H 43
Chelsea Vw. HX3: North 3F 98
Chelsfield Ct. LS15: Leeds 3G 71
Chelsfield Way LS15: Leeds 3G 70
Chelston Pk. BD16: Har 6A 44
Cheltenham Av. LS29: I'ly 5L 15
Cheltenham Ct. HX3: Hal 8C 98
Cheltenham Gdns. HX3: Hal 8C 98
Cheltenham Pl. HX3: Hal 8C 98
Cheltenham Rd. BD2: B'frd 1D 64
Cheltenham St. LS12: Leeds 8N 67
Chelwood Av. LS8: Leeds 4H 51
Chelwood Cres. LS8: Leeds 5H 51
Chelwood Dr. BD15: All 7F 62
LS8: Leeds 4H 51
Chelwood Gro. LS8: Leeds 4H 51
Chelwood Mt. LS8: Leeds 4H 51
Chelwood Pl. LS8: Leeds 4G 51
Chenies Cl. LS14: Leeds 5N 69
Chepstow Cl. LS25: Gar 7B 72
Chepstow Dr. LS10: Leeds 1F 104
CHEQUERFIELD 4L 129
Chequerfield Av. WF8: Pon 3M 129
Chequerfield Cl. WF10: C'frd 6A 108
Chequerfield Ct. WF8: Pon 3M 129
Chequerfield Dr. WF8: Pon 4M 129
Chequerfield La. WF8: Pon 3M 129
Chequerfield Mt. WF8: Pon 4M 129
Chequerfield Rd. WF8: Pon 4L 129
Chequers, The HD9: Mel 7D 152
Chequers Cl. WF8: Pon 4M 129
Cherington Ct. LS29: Burl W 9D 16
Cheriton Dr. BD13: Que 4E 80
Cherry Cl. S71: Roys 5B 160
S72: Cud 9J 161
Cherry Ct. HX1: Hal 2G 7
LS6: Leeds 9B 50
LS9: Leeds 4K 5
LS19: Yead 1M 47
Cherry Flds. BD2: B'frd 2C 64
Cherry Gth. DN6: Cam 1N 165
WF9: Hems 3C 162
Cherry Gro. LS6: Leeds 1B 68
LS29: I'ly 5E 14
Cherry Hills S75: Dart 8J 159
Cherry La. HD8: Clay W 7J 157
Cherry Lea Ct. LS19: Raw 2M 47
Cherry Nook Rd. HD2: Hud 8C 120
Cherry Pl. LS9: Leeds 4K 5 (5G 68)
Cherry Ri. LS14: Leeds 7D 52
Cherry Row LS9: Leeds 4K 5 (5G 68)
Cherry St. BD21: Keigh 8L 27
BD22: Haw 7E 42
Cherry Tree Av. BD10: B'frd 8H 47
WF11: Knot 9D 110
Cherry Tree Cen. HD1: Hud 5B 8
Cherry Tree Cl. HD7: Golc 5D 136
S75: S'ross 8L 159
WF10: C'frd 7A 108
Cherrytree Cl. WF9: Kins 8B 146
Cherry Tree Ct. HD8: Shep 8J 155
WF3: E Ard 5E 104
Cherry Tree Cres. LS28: Fars 3A 66
WF2: W'ton 3C 144
Cherry Tree Dr. HX4: Gree 4A 118
LS28: Fars 3A 66
WF2: W'ton 3C 144
Cherry Tree Gdns. BD10: B'frd 6D 46
Cherry Tree Ri. BD21: Keigh 2K 43
Cherry Tree Rd. WF2: W'ton 3C 144
Cherry Tree Row BD16: Har 8A 44
Cherry Trees S75: H Hoy 8M 157
Cherry Tree Wlk. HD9: Scho 4B 170
LS2: Leeds 7G 5
WF3: E Ard 5E 104
WF11: Knot 9D 110
Cherrywood Cl. LS14: Leeds 6C 52
Cherrywood Gdns. LS14: Leeds 6C 52
Chervana Ct. BD4: B'frd 1J 83
Cherwell Cft. LS25: Gar 9B 72
Cherwell Dr. BD6: B'frd 6M 81
Chesham St. BD21: Keigh 9K 27
Chesil Bank HD3: Hud 3G 136
Chesilton Av. HD3: Hud 3G 136
Chesney Av. LS10: Leeds 1F 86
Chessington Dr. WF4: Flock 7G 140
Chester Cl. HX3: Hal 3A 98
Chester Ct. HX3: Hal 3A 98
WF9: Hems 3D 162
Chester Gro. HX3: Hal 3A 98
Chester Pl. HX3: Hal 3A 98
Chester Rd. HX3: Hal 3A 98
Chester St. BD5: B'frd 5A 6 (8C 64)
BD7: B'frd 6A 6 (8B 64)
HX3: Hal 3A 98
HX6: Sow B 8H 97
LS12: Leeds 6M 67
Chester Ter. HX3: Hal 3A 98
Chesterton Ct. LS15: Leeds 8E 70
WF4: Horb 9E 124
Chesterton Dr. HD9: Hon 6L 153
Chestnut Av. DN6: Carc 8N 165
LS6: Leeds 3A 68
LS15: Leeds 4E 70
LS22: Weth 3L 23
LS23: B Spa 9C 24
OL14: Tod 5J 93
S72: B'ley 7N 161
WF2: W'ton 4B 144
WF17: Bat 8D 102
Chestnut Cl. BD22: Keigh 1F 42
HD4: Hud 8M 137
HX4: Gree 3A 118
LS29: I'ly 6K 15
WF4: Horb 1D 142
WF7: F'stne 4D 128
Chestnut Ct. BD18: Ship 8L 45
HX6: Ripp *7D 116*
(off Halifax Rd.)
Chestnut Cres. WF6: Norm 4H 127
Chestnut Dr. LS16: Leeds 2L 49
S72: S Hien 4L 161
Chestnut End LS23: B Spa 1E 38
Chestnut Gdns. LS12: Leeds 8M 67
LS27: Chur 6K 85
Chestnut Gth. HD3: Hud 3G 136
Chestnut Grn. WF8: Pon 2M 129
Chestnut Gro. BD2: B'frd 2B 64
LS6: Leeds 3A 68
LS23: B Spa 9C 24
LS26: W'frd 7F 88
LS28: Cal 9M 47
WF4: Croft 1G 144
WF8: Pon 5K 129
WF9: Hems 3F 162
WF10: C'frd 7A 108
Chestnut La. LS14: Leeds 4N 69
Chestnut Mdws. WF14: Mir 4K 121
Chestnut M. S72: S Hien 4L 161
Chestnut Pl. LS6: Leeds 3A 68
Chestnut Ri. LS12: Leeds 8L 67
Chestnuts, The WF8: Pon 8N 109
Chestnut St. HD2: Hud 8A 120
HX1: Hal 6M 97
LS6: Leeds 3A 68
WF9: S Elm 8L 163
Chestnut Ter. WF12: Dew 8F 122
Chestnut Vw. LS27: Chur 6K 85
Chestnut Wlk. WF2: Wake 3J 125
WF11: Knot 9C 110
Chestnut Way LS16: Leeds 2L 49
Chevet Ct. WF2: Wake 2M 143
Chevet Cft. WF2: Wake 3N 143
Chevet Gdns. WF2: Wake 3N 143
Chevet Gro. WF2: Wake 3N 143
Chevet Hill WF2: Wake 7A 144
Chevet La. WF2: Wake 2N 143
WF4: Not 2N 143
Chevet Level WF2: Wake 6A 144
Chevet M. WF2: Wake 2N 143
Chevet Mt. BD15: All 7F 62
Chevet Pk. Ct. WF2: Wake 7N 143
Chevet Ri. S71: Roys 5C 160
Chevet Ter. WF1: W'ton 1B 144
Chevet Vw. S71: Roys 5B 160
Chevin Av. LS21: Otley 2M 31
LS29: Men 3F 30
(Bradford Rd.)
LS29: Men 3E 30
(Bridgland Av.)
Chevin Ct. *LS21: Otley* *9L 17*
(off Courthouse St.)
Chevinedge Cres. HX3: Hal 2C 118
Chevin End LS29: Guis, Men 5F 30
Chevin End Rd. LS20: Guis 5H 31
Chevin Fold LS21: Otley 1M 31
Chevington Ct. LS19: Raw 4L 47
Chevin Ho. *LS29: Men* *5F 30*
(off High Royds Dr.)
Chevins Cl. WF17: Bat 4C 102
Chevin Side LS21: Otley 2L 31
Chevin Ter. LS21: Otley 2L 31
Chevin Vw. *LS21: Pool* *1F 32*
(off Main St.)
Cheviot Av. HD9: Mel 8E 152
Cheviot Cl. WF9: Hems 2F 162
Cheviot Ct. LS25: Gar 9N 71
Cheviot Ga. BD12: Low M 7N 81
Cheviot Pl. WF11: Knot 8E 110
Cheviot Way WF14: Up H 9K 121
Cheyne Wlk. BD22: Keigh 1G 43
Chichester St. LS12: Leeds 6M 67
CHICKENLEY 4K 123
Chickenley La. WF12: Dew 4K 123
CHIDSWELL 9K 103
Chidswell Gdns. WF12: Dew 9L 103
Chidswell La. WF5: Dew, Oss 1L 123
WF12: Dew 9L 103
Child La. WF15: Liv 1K 121
Childs La. BD18: Ship 9C 46
Childs Rd. WF2: Wake 3F 124
Chiltern Av. HD3: Hud 1F 136
WF10: C'frd 7N 107
WF11: Knot 8D 110
Chiltern Cl. LS25: Gar 9N 71
Chiltern Ct. LS13: Leeds 1B 66
LS25: Gar 9N 71
WF7: Ackw 5F 146
WF9: Hems 2F 162
Chiltern Dr. WF7: Ackw 5F 146
WF14: Up H 9K 121
Chiltern Rd. WF12: Dew 2J 123
Chiltern Way WF15: Liv 7H 101
Chilver Dr. BD4: B'frd 3L 83
Chilwell Cl. S71: Ath 8A 160
Chilwell Gdns. S71: Ath 8A 160
Chilwell M. S71: Ath 8A 160
Chimes Ct. HD5: K'htn 3G 138
Chimney La. HD8: Lept 6H 139
Chinewood Av. WF17: Bat 6E 102
Chippendale Ct. LS29: Men 4F 30
Chippendale Ri. BD8: B'frd 6J 63
LS21: Otley 8L 17
Chippindale Swimming Pool 8L 17
Chirton Gro. LS8: Leeds 1J 69
CHISERLEY 8K 77
Chiserley Fld. Side *HX7: Chis* *8K 77*
(off Old Mill Ridge)
Chiserley Gdns. HX7: Chis 8K 77
Chiserley Stile HX7: Chis 8K 77
Chiserley Ter. HX7: Wads 8K 77
Chislehurst Pl. BD5: B'frd 2A 82
Chiswick St. LS6: Leeds 5A 68
Chiswick Ter. *LS6: Leeds* *4A 68*
(off Carberry Rd.)
CHOPPARDS 7M 169
Choppards Bank Rd. HD9: H'frth 7M 169
Choppards Bldgs. HD9: H'frth 7M 169
Choppards La. HD9: H'frth 6M 169
Chorley La. LS2: Leeds 4C 4 (5C 68)
LS3: Leeds 5C 4 (6C 68)
Chrisharben Ct. *BD14: Clay* *1H 81*
(off Henry St.)
Chrisharben Pk. BD14: Clay 1H 81
Chrismoor BD10: B'frd 8E 46
Christ Chu. Av. LS12: Leeds 6L 67
Christ Chu. Mt. LS12: Leeds 6L 67
Christ Chu. Pde. LS12: Leeds 6L 67
Christ Chu. Pl. LS12: Leeds 6L 67
Christ Chu. Rd. LS12: Leeds 6L 67
Christ Chu. Ter. LS12: Leeds 6L 67
Christ Chu. Vw. LS12: Leeds 6L 67
Christiana Ter. LS27: Morl 8L 85
Christopher Cl. BD20: Sils 8E 12
Christopher Rd. LS6: Leeds 3D 68
Christopher St. BD5: B'frd 2A 82
Christopher Ter. BD5: B'frd 2A 82
Church App. LS25: Gar 7N 71
Church Av. HD4: Hud 6K 137
HD7: Linth 7D 136
LS6: Leeds 8B 50
Church Av. LS18: Hors 6E 48
LS26: Swil 3H 89
LS27: Gil 5F 84
WF1: K'thpe 4D 126
WF9: S Kirk 7J 163
Churchbalk Dr. WF8: Pon 5L 129
Churchbalk La. WF8: Pon 4L 129
Church Bank BD1: B'frd 4C 6 (7D 64)
HX2: Hal 6K 97
HX6: Sow B 8J 97
HX7: Crag V 9K 95
Church Bank La. HX7: Crag V 9J 95
Churchbank Way WF12: Dew 7F 122
Church C'way. LS23: T Arch 9E 24
Church Cl. BD20: Stee 3C 26
BD22: Oak *5B 42*
(off Commercial St.)
HD8: Shep 9J 155
HX1: Hal 4H 7
HX2: Illing 8K 79
HX6: Sow B 9E 96
LS14: Leeds 2C 70
(not continuous)
LS21: Pool 1F 32
LS25: M'fld 6G 72
LS26: Swil 3H 89
S75: Dart 9G 158
WF4: S Comn 9J 127
WF9: Hems 2D 162
Church Ct. BD7: B'frd 9L 63
BD20: Rid 6M 27
LS19: Yead 1M 47
LS24: Saxt 9N 55
LS27: Morl 8K 85
S72: B'ley 6A 162
WF5: Oss 4N 123
WF6: Norm 2H 127
Church Cres. LS17: Leeds 4E 50
LS18: Hors 6E 48
LS19: Yead 1L 47
LS26: Swil 4J 89
WF4: Neth 4A 142
Church Cft. LS29: Men 4D 30
WF3: Loft 4L 105
Church Dr. LS17: E Kes 3C 36
S72: B'ley 7N 161
WF9: S Kirk 7J 163
Church Farm HD6: Clift 1C 120
LS14: T'ner 1G 53
Church Farm Cl. WF3: Loft 4L 105
WF6: Alt 8G 106
Church Farm Gth. LS17: Shad 3A 52
Church Farm Vw. LS15: Bar E 8M 53
Churchfield Av. S75: Kex 9E 158
Churchfield Cl. S75: Kex 9D 158
WF15: Liv 8L 101
Churchfield Ct. S75: Kex 9F 158
Churchfield Cft. LS26: Rothw 8A 88
WF6: Alt 8G 107
Churchfield Gdns. S71: Carl 8E 160
Churchfield Gro. LS26: Rothw 7N 87
Churchfield La.
DN6: Lit S, Wome 9N 131
LS26: Rothw 7N 87
S75: Dart, Kex 9D 158
WF8: Lit S 4L 149
WF10: C'frd 6F 108
Churchfield Rd. LS26: Rothw 8N 87
Church Flds. HD2: Hud 8D 120
WF6: Norm 2H 127
Churchfields BD2: B'frd 4H 65
WF4: Croft 1G 145
WF4: Ryh 8J 145
Churchfields Cl. LS23: B Spa 9D 24
Church Flds. M. WF10: C'frd 6F 108
Churchfields Rd. HD6: Brigh 9M 99
Churchfield St. WF17: Bat 7F 102
Churchfield Ter. WF15: Liv 8L 101
WF17: Bat *7F 102*
(off Churchfield St.)
Church Forge WF9: S Kirk 6J 163
Church Gdns. LS17: Leeds 4F 50
LS25: Gar 7N 71
LS27: Gil 6F 84
WF4: M'twn 3L 141
CHURCH GARFORTH 8N 71
Church Gth. LS19: E Car 5B 32
LS21: Pool 1F 32
WF10: C'frd 6F 108
Church Ga. LS18: Hors 6E 48
S72: B'ley 7A 162
Churchgate LS16: B'hpe 5G 32
LS27: Gil 6F 84
Church Grange BD19: Cleck 5J 101
Church Grn. *BD8: B'frd* *5A 64*
(off Church St.)
HD8: Kbtn 4K 155
HX2: Hal 3L 97
Church Gro. LS6: Leeds 8A 50
LS18: Hors 6E 48
WF9: S Kirk 7J 163
Church Hgts. S36: Hoy 9J 173
Church Hill BD17: Bail 3B 46
HX2: Lud 3E 96
LS14: T'ner 1H 53
LS16: B'hpe 5G 33
LS17: N Rig 2N 19
LS23: B'ham 6D 38
OL14: Tod 4G 93
S71: Roys 6E 160
WF13: Dew 2G 123
Church Hill Farm WF4: Croft 1G 144
Church Hill Gdns. LS28: Stan 4C 66
Church Hill Grn. LS28: Stan 4C 66
Church Hill Mt. LS28: Stan 4C 66
Church Ho. *HX5: Ell* *4E 118*
(off St Mary's Ga.)
Churchill Flats LS21: Pool 1F 32
Churchill Gdns. LS2: Leeds 2E 4
Churchill Gro. WF2: Wake 2N 143
WF16: Heck 9B 102
Churchill Ho. *BD4: B'frd* *1J 83*
(off Tyersal La.)
Churchill Rd. BD13: Thorn 8E 62
Churchill St. OL14: Tod 5G 92

Church La.—Cleckheaton Rd.

Church La. BD6: B'frd .5N **81**
BD17: Esh .2G **46**
BD19: Gom .4N **101**
HD4: Hud .8M **137**
HD4: S Cros .3G **152**
HD5: Hud .4B **138**
HD5: K'htn .3F **138**
HD6: Brigh .9M **99**
(not continuous)
HD7: Linth .9D **136**
HD7: Mars .5F **150**
HD8: Clay W .7J **157**
HD8: Shep .9J **155**
HX2: Hal .3L **97**
HX3: Sou .8G **99**
HX4: Bark .5F **134**
HX4: Holy, Stainl .7N **117**
(not continuous)
HX5: Ell .4J **119**
HX6: Ripp .8D **116**
HX7: Heb B .1F **94**
HX7: Hept .9G **76**
LS2: Leeds .7H **5** (7F **68**)
LS6: Leeds .8B **50**
LS7: Leeds .9F **50**
LS15: Leeds .4D **70**
LS16: Leeds .3M **49**
LS17: Bard .6C **36**
LS17: Hare .1G **35**
LS18: Hors .6E **48**
LS21: Otley .1L **31**
LS21: Pool .1F **32**
LS21: Stainb .3G **18**
LS21: Weston .7F **16**
LS22: Coll .8J **23**
LS24: Wig .7N **25**
LS25: Gar .7N **71**
LS25: Kip .4B **90**
LS25: M'fld .7E **72**
LS26: Meth .2J **107**
LS26: Swil .4G **89**
LS28: Pud .7B **66**
S36: Hoy .9J **173**
S72: S Hien .2H **161**
S75: H Hoy .8M **157**
WF1: Out .7K **105**
WF3: E Ard .5E **104**
WF3: W Ard .5N **103**
WF4: Chap .6J **143**
WF4: H'cft .2F **160**
WF4: Horb .1D **142**
WF4: Neth .3A **142**
WF6: Norm .1H **127**
(High St., not continuous)
WF6: Norm .2H **127**
(Wakefield Rd.)
WF7: F'stne .2C **128**
WF7: Old S .3L **127**
WF8: D'ton .6C **130**
WF8: E Hard .9L **129**
WF8: Pon .3K **129**
WF12: T'hill .9H **123**
WF13: Dew .3C **122**
WF14: Mir .6N **121**
WF15: Liv .9F **100**
(Hartshead La.)
WF15: Liv .7L **101**
(Knowler Way)
WF16: Heck .9A **102**
WF17: Birs .4N **101**
Church La. Av. WF1: Out .7K **105**
Church La. Nth. LS25: Kip .4B **90**
Church Mdws. HX6: Ripp .8D **116**
LS23: B'ham .5D **38**
WF17: Birs .3A **102**
Church M. *BD6: B'frd .6K 81*
(off School St.)
LS5: Leeds .9H **49**
LS23: B Spa .9D **24**
Church Mt. LS18: Hors .6E **48**
WF9: S Kirk .7J **163**
Church Paddocks HD6: Clift .1C **120**
Church Pk. WF15: Liv .1J **121**
Church Pl. HX1: Hal .4H **7** (5A **98**)
LS25: Gar .7N **71**
Church Rd. BD6: B'frd .5N **81**
LS9: Leeds .8K **5**
LS12: Leeds .7M **67**
LS18: Hors .7E **48**
LS26: Gt P .5M **89**
OL14: Tod .4G **93**
WF3: S'ley .7A **106**
WF6: Alt .8F **106**
WF15: Liv .1H **121**
WF17: Bat .4C **102**
Church Row LS2: Leeds .7H **5** (7F **68**)
LS29: Den .3M **15**
Church Side LS26: Meth .2J **107**
Church Side Cl. HX3: Hal .1L **7** (3B **98**)
Church Side Dr. HX3: Hal .1L **7** (3B **98**)
Churchside Vs. LS26: Meth .2K **107**
Church Sq. LS25: Gar .7N **71**
Church Stile Farm HX6: Sow B .9E **96**
CHURCH STREET .5B **42**
Church St. BD6: B'frd .6K **81**
BD8: B'frd .5N **63**
BD13: Cull .9K **43**
BD16: Bgly .5F **44**
BD18: Ship .7B **46**
BD19: Cleck .5J **101**
BD21: Keigh .9K **27**
(Bradford Rd.)
BD21: Keigh .1H **43**
(Bridge St.)
BD22: Haw .8B **42**
BD22: Oxen .4C **60**
HD1: Hud .5J **137**
(North St.)
HD1: Hud .4B **8** (4M **137**)
(St Peter's St.)
HD3: Hud .4F **136**
HD4: Hud .6K **137**
HD5: Hud .5B **138**
HD6: Ras .3L **119**
HD7: Golc .6C **136**
Church St. HD7: Slait .1M **151**
HD8: Eml .2F **156**
HD9: Hon .4L **153**
HD9: Nether .9L **153**
HD9: New M .2D **170**
HX1: Hal .4M **7** (5C **98**)
(Alfred St. E.)
HX1: Hal .5M **7** (6C **98**)
(Lily La.)
HX4: Gree .4C **118**
HX5: Ell .4E **118**
HX7: Hept .8G **76**
HX7: Myth .4M **95**
LS5: Leeds .2K **67**
LS10: Leeds .1F **86**
LS19: Yead .1L **47**
LS20: Guis .7J **31**
LS22: Weth .4M **23**
LS23: B Spa, Cliff .1D **38**
LS26: Rothw .8N **87**
LS26: W'frd .6D **88**
LS27: Gil .6F **84**
LS27: Morl .8K **85**
LS29: Add .1N **13**
LS29: I'ly .5F **14**
OL14: Tod .4G **93**
S71: Carl .8E **160**
S71: Roys .6D **160**
S72: B'ley .6N **161**
S75: Dart .9G **158**
S75: S'ross .8L **159**
WF1: Wake .8K **9** (7L **125**)
WF4: Horb .1D **142**
WF4: Wool .2H **159**
WF5: Oss .4N **123**
WF6: Alt .7J **107**
WF9: S Elm .7N **163**
WF10: C'frd .4D **108**
WF11: B'ton .4B **110**
WF13: Dew .3G **122**
WF13: Raven .6B **122**
WF15: Liv .7L **101**
(Rock Edge)
WF15: Liv .7G **101**
(Roundwell Rd.)
WF16: Heck .9A **102**
WF17: Birs .3B **102**
YO26: B Ain .1N **25**
Church Ter. HD4: Hud .1L **153**
HD8: Clay W .8G **156**
HD9: H'frth .3M **169**
HX2: Illing .8K **79**
HX4: Bark .7G **117**
HX6: Sow B .9E **96**
LS25: Aber .8E **54**
WF6: Alt .7H **107**
Church Top WF9: S Kirk .7J **163**
Church Town Vw. HD3: Hud .1G **137**
Church Vw. BD19: Cleck .4F **100**
HD9: Holm .6H **169**
HX3: Nor G .2L **99**
HX6: Sow B .8J **97**
HX7: Hept .9F **76**
LS5: Leeds .2L **67**
LS14: T'ner .1G **53**
LS16: Leeds .2M **49**
LS21: Pool .1G **32**
LS25: Kip .3D **90**
LS29: Men .4D **30**
WF1: Wake .9N **125**
WF4: Crig .5H **143**
WF7: F'stne .6C **128**
WF8: Pon .6M **129**
WF9: S Kirk .7J **163**
WF10: C'frd .5B **108**
WF15: Liv .7G **101**
Church Vw. Cl. WF4: H'cft .9K **145**
Church Vw. Ho. *HD1: Hud .5K 137*
(off Church St.)
Church Vw. M. LS23: Cliff .3D **38**
Church Vs. WF9: S Kirk .7J **163**
Churchville LS25: M'fld .7G **72**
Churchville Av. LS25: M'fld .7F **72**
Churchville Dr. LS25: M'fld .7G **72**
Churchville Ter. LS25: M'fld .7G **72**
Church Wlk. HD8: Kbtn .4K **155**
HX3: North .2F **98**
LS2: Leeds .7H **5** (7F **68**)
OL14: W'den .2J **113**
WF12: T'hill .9H **123**
WF17: Bat .9D **102**
Church Way BD21: Keigh .1J **43**
LS27: Morl .8K **85**
WF4: Croft .1H **145**
Church Wood Av. LS6: Leeds .9L **49**
LS16: Leeds .9M **49**
Churchwood Cl. HD7: Slait .9M **135**
Church Wood Mt. LS16: Leeds .8M **49**
Church Wood Rd. LS16: Leeds .9M **49**
Church Yd. Bottom *HX7: Hept .8G 76*
(off Church La.)
Churn Dr. BD6: B'frd .5K **81**
Churn La. HX2: Hal .5K **97**
Churn Milk La. HX3: Hal .9N **79**
CHURWELL .5M **85**
Churwell Av. WF13: Dew .9C **102**
Churwell Cl. WF10: C'frd .6D **108**
Churwell Va. WF12: Dew .1J **123**
Cinder Hill HD8: Kbtn .2M **155**
Cinder Hill Ct. HD8: Kbtn .3F **154**
Cinder Hill Rd. OL14: Tod .6N **93**
CINDER HILLS .4N **169**
Cinderhills La. HX3: Hal .9D **98**
Cinderhills Rd. HD9: H'frth .4N **169**
Cinder La. LS21: F'ley, Lind .4A **18**
LS23: Cliff .2E **38**
WF10: C'frd .4C **108**
Cineworld Cinema
Bradford .5D **6** (8D **64**)
Glass Houghton .8F 108
(within Xscape)
Wakefield .7H **9** (6K **125**)
Circle, The WF8: Pon .4L **129**
Cirrus Vw. WF7: Ackw .5F **146**
CITY .9L **85**
City Bloc Indoor Climbing Wall .9F **68**
City Gate LS3: Leeds .6A **4** (6B **68**)
City Golf Course .5M **67**
City High Community Sports Cen. .4A **126**
City La. HX3: Hal .3L **97**
City Link Ind. Pk. BD4: B'frd .8J **65**
City Mills *LS27: Morl .9L 85*
(off Peel St.)
City of Wakefield Golf Course .9H **125**
City Pk. Ind. Est. LS12: Leeds .2M **85**
City Rd. BD1: B'frd .6A **64**
BD8: B'frd .6A **64**
City Sports *.7F 64*
(within Greystone Mill)
City Sq. LS1: Leeds .7E **4** (7D **68**)
City Ter. HX3: Hal .2M **97**
City Varieties Music Hall .6F **4** (6E **68**)
City Vw. *LS11: Leeds .3B 86*
(off Kirk Beston Rd.)
City Wlk. LS11: Leeds .8D **68**
Cityway Ind. Est. BD4: B'frd .8F **6** (9F **64**)
City West One Office Pk. LS12: Leeds .2N **85**
Civil Justice Centre
Wakefield .5H **9** (5K **125**)
Claire's Ho. WF1: Wake .4L **9**
Clapgate LS21: Otley .9L **17**
Clapgate La. HX6: Ripp .4D **116**
LS10: Leeds .8H **87**
Clapham Dene Rd. LS15: Leeds .5C **70**
Clapham St. BD13: Denh .6L **61**
Claphouse Fold S75: Hai .4C **158**
Clapton Av. HX1: Hal .6G **7** (6N **97**)
Clapton Gro. HX1: Hal .6G **7** (6N **97**)
Clapton Mt. HX1: Hal .6G **7**
Clara Dr. LS28: Cal .8K **47**
Clara Rd. BD2: B'frd .1D **64**
Clara St. HD1: Hud .2M **137**
HD4: Hud .7F **136**
HD6: Ras .2M **119**
LS28: Fars .4A **66**
Clare Ct. HX1: Hal .6L **7**
Clare Cres. BD12: Wyke .2A **100**
Clare Hall HX1: Hal .6K **7**
Clare Hall La. HX1: Hal .6L **7** (6B **98**)
Clare Hill HD1: Hud .1A **8** (2M **137**)
Claremont BD7: B'frd .8B **64**
BD12: Wyke .2A **100**
LS28: Pud .7C **66**
WF16: Heck .8A **102**
Claremont Av. BD18: Ship .9C **46**
LS3: Leeds .4B **4** (5C **68**)
Claremont Ct. LS6: Leeds .9A **50**
Claremont Cres. BD18: Ship .9C **46**
LS6: Leeds .1B **68**
WF4: Croft .2G **145**
Claremont Dr. LS6: Leeds .9A **50**
Claremont Gdns. BD16: Bgly .3F **44**
LS28: Fars .4A **66**
Claremont Gro. BD18: Ship .9D **46**
LS3: Leeds .4B **4** (5C **68**)
LS28: Pud .7B **66**
Claremont Pl. LS12: Leeds .7K **67**
OL14: Tod .6K 93
(off Stansfield Rd.)
Claremont Rd. BD18: Ship .9C **46**
LS6: Leeds .9A **50**
WF13: Dew .2E **122**
Claremont St. BD19: Cleck .4H **101**
HD1: Hud .2A **8** (3M **137**)
HX5: Ell .5F **118**
HX6: Sow B .7J **97**
LS12: Leeds .7K **67**
LS26: Oul .7D **88**
WF1: Wake .8N **125**
Claremont Ter. BD5: B'frd .8B **64**
LS12: Leeds .7K **67**
OL14: W'den .6M **113**
WF2: Wake .6J **125**
Claremont Vw. LS3: Leeds .4B **4** (5C **68**)
LS26: Oul .7D **88**
Claremont Vs. *BD5: B'frd .8B 64*
(off Claremont Ter.)
HX6: Sow B .8J 97
(off Victoria Av.)
LS2: Leeds .4C 4
(off Clarendon Rd.)
CLAREMOUNT .4C **98**
Claremount LS6: Leeds .9A **50**
Claremount Ho. *HX3: Hal .4C 98*
(off Claremount Rd.)
Claremount Rd. HX3: Hal .1M **7** (2A **98**)
Claremount Ter. HX3: Hal .2B **98**
Clarence Dock LS10: Leeds .8J **5** (8F **68**)
Clarence Dr. LS18: Hors .8E **48**
LS29: Men .2D **30**
Clarence Gdns. LS18: Hors .8E **48**
Clarence Gro. LS18: Hors .8E **48**
Clarence Ho. LS10: Leeds .8F **68**
Clarence M. LS18: Hors .8E **48**
Clarence Pl. LS29: Burl W .8D **16**
Clarence Rd. BD18: Ship .7L **45**
LS10: Leeds .8G **68**
LS18: Hors .8E **48**
WF2: Wake .8K **125**
Clarence St. BD19: Cleck .5H **101**
HX1: Hal .4J **7** (5A **98**)
LS13: Leeds .5F **66**
WF17: Bat .7G **102**
Clarence Ter. LS28: Pud .6B **66**
WF12: Dew .5G **122**
Clarence Wlk. WF2: Wake .6J **125**
Clarendon Cotts. WF5: Oss .8A **124**
Clarendon Ct. BD8: B'frd .5B **64**
WF1: Wake .2K **9** (4L **125**)
Clarendon Pl. BD13: Que .5B **80**
HX1: Hal .5N **97**
LS2: Leeds .2B **4** (4C **68**)
Clarendon Rd. BD16: Bgly .3G **44**
LS2: Leeds .3B **4** (4C **68**)
LS23: B Spa .1C **38**
Clarendon St. BD21: Keigh .2H **43**
BD22: Haw .9C **42**
HX7: Myth .3M **95**
WF1: Wake .2J **9** (4L **125**)
(not continuous)
Clarendon Ter. LS27: Chur .5M **85**
LS28: Pud .8B **66**
Clarendon Way LS2: Leeds .4C **4** (5C **68**)
Clare Rd. BD12: Wyke .2A **100**
BD19: Cleck .5H **101**
HX1: Hal .5L **7** (6B **98**)
HX7: Myth .3L **95**
Clare Rd. Flats HX1: Hal .6L **7** (6B **98**)
Clare Royd HX3: Hip .5M **99**
Clare St. HX1: Hal .5L **7** (6B **98**)
Clarges St. BD5: B'frd .2A **82**
Clarion Camp LS29: Men .3H **31**
Clarion Fld. LS29: Men .3H **31**
Clarion St. WF1: Wake .7N **125**
Clark Av. LS9: Leeds .8M **5** (7H **69**)
Clark Ct. WF7: F'stne .2C **128**
Clark Cres. LS9: Leeds .8M **5** (7H **69**)
Clarke Cres. WF6: Norm .4H **127**
Clarke Gro. WF1: Wake .2N **125**
Clarke Hall Rd. WF3: S'ley .1N **125**
Clarke La. HD9: Mel .7D **152**
Clarke Rd. WF3: W Ard .7A **104**
Clarke St. LS28: Cal .9M **47**
WF13: Dew .2D **122**
Clark Gro. LS9: Leeds .8H **69**
Clark Hall Educational Museum & Visitor Cen.
.2N **125**
Clark La. LS9: Leeds .8M **5** (7H **69**)
(not continuous)
Clark Mt. LS9: Leeds .8M **5** (7H **69**)
Clark Rd. LS9: Leeds .8H **69**
Clark Row LS9: Leeds .8H **69**
Clarkson Av. WF16: Heck .8B **102**
Clarkson Cl. WF16: Heck .8B **102**
Clarkson Ct. WF6: Norm .2K **127**
WF10: C'frd .5A **108**
Clarkson Dr. LS25: Bur S .1D **110**
Clarkson St. WF13: Raven .5A **122**
Clarkson Ter. LS27: Chur .5M **85**
Clarkson Vw. LS6: Leeds .2C **68**
Clark Spring Cl. LS27: Morl .6K **85**
Clark Spring Ct. LS27: Morl .6L **85**
Clark Spring Ri. LS27: Morl .6L **85**
Clark Ter. LS9: Leeds .7H **69**
Clark Vw. LS9: Leeds .8H **69**
Clarydon Pl. *WF16: Heck .8A 102*
(off Darley St.)
Clattering Stones Rd. HX7: Crag V .1L **115**
Clayborn Vw. BD19: Cleck .6J **101**
Clay Brow *BD22: Haw .7C 42*
(off North Vw. Ter.)
Clay Butts HD2: Hud .9K **119**
Clay Delf HD8: Den D .2B **172**
Clayfield Bungs. WF11: Ferr .8B **110**
Clayfield Dr. BD7: B'frd .3M **81**
Clay Ga. HX7: P Wel .2L **77**
Clay Hill Dr. BD12: Wyke .1B **100**
(not continuous)
Clay Ho. La. HX4: Gree .4B **118**
Clay La. HD7: Slait .9N **135**
Claymore Ri. BD20: Sils .9F **12**
Clay Pit La. HX4: Sow .1M **135**
LS2: Leeds .4F **4** (5E **68**)
LS7: Leeds .3G **5** (5E **68**)
Claypit La. LS14: T'ner .2G **53**
LS25: Led .6G **90**
WF10: Leds .6G **90**
Clay Pits La. HX1: Hal .4L **97**
HX6: Ripp .4B **116**
Clay Royd La. HX3: Sou .7H **99**
Clay St. HX1: Hal .5M **97**
HX6: Sow B .8J **97**
(Bk. Pleasant St.)
HX6: Sow B .8H **97**
(John St. W.)
CLAYTON .1G **81**
Clayton Av. LS25: Kip .3B **90**
WF9: Upt .1D **164**
Clayton Bus. Cen. LS10: Leeds .2G **87**
Clayton Cl. LS10: Leeds .3H **87**
Clayton Ct. LS10: Leeds .3H **87**
LS16: Leeds .7J **49**
WF7: F'stne .6C **128**
Clayton Dr. LS10: Leeds .3H **87**
CLAYTON EDGE .3C **80**
Clayton Flds. HD2: Hud .2L **137**
Clayton Golf Course .2H **81**
Clayton Grange LS16: Leeds .7J **49**
Clayton Gro. LS19: Yead .9M **31**
CLAYTON HEIGHTS .4G **80**
Clayton Holt WF9: S Kirk .8H **163**
Clayton La. BD5: B'frd .8A **6** (1C **82**)
BD14: Clay .2G **80**
Clayton M. WF6: Alt .8H **107**
Clayton Pl. WF6: Alt .8H **107**
Clayton Ri. BD20: Keigh .8G **27**
WF1: Out .7K **105**
Clayton Rd. BD7: B'frd .1K **81**
LS10: Leeds .3H **87**
Claytons Bldgs. WF7: F'stne .3D **128**
Claytons Cl. LS26: Meth .1J **107**
Claytons Cotts. WF4: Horb .1C **142**
Clayton St. LS26: Rothw .8A **88**
WF2: Wake .6J **125**
Clayton Ter. BD13: Cull .1K **61**
Clayton Vw. WF9: S Kirk .8H **163**
Clayton Way LS10: Leeds .3H **87**
CLAYTON WEST .7J **157**
Clayton West Station
Kirklees Light Railway .6J **157**
Clayton West Station Vis. Cen. .6J **157**
Clayton Wood Bank LS16: Leeds .6J **49**
Clayton Wood Cl. LS16: Leeds .6J **49**
Clayton Wood Ct. LS16: Leeds .6J **49**
Clayton Wood Ri. LS16: Leeds .6J **49**
Clayton Wood Rd. LS16: Leeds .6H **49**
Clay Well HD7: Golc .6C **136**
Clearings, The LS10: Leeds .5F **86**
Clear Vw. S72: Grim .9A **162**
Cleasby Rd. LS29: Men .5E **30**
Cleavesty La. LS17: E Kes .1C **36**
CLECKHEATON .5H **101**
Cleckheaton & District Golf Course .2F **100**
Cleckheaton Rd. BD6: B'frd .7B **82**
BD12: Low M, O'haw .7B **82**

Cobden St.—Copley Ter.

Cobden St. LS27: Morl 8K 85
OL14: Tod 7K 93
Cobden Ter. HX3: Hip 4H 99
HX5: Ell 6E 118
LS12: Leeds 1J 85
Cobham Pde. WF1: Out 8K 105
Cobham Wlk. LS15: Leeds 4G 71
Cockburn Cl. LS11: Leeds 2E 86
Cockburn Way LS11: Leeds 2E 86
Cock Cft. Fold BD16: Har 6A 44
Cockcroft Ho. LS6: Leeds 3N 67
(off Chapel La.)
Cockcroft La. HX6: Rish 1A 134
Cockermouth La. WF4: Flock 8A 140
COCKERSDALE 5D 84
Cock Hill HX3: She 7G 80
Cock Hill La. HX3: She 7F 80
Cock Hill Rd. HX7: Crag V 1L 115
Cocking La. LS29: Add 4J 13
Cocking Steps La. HD4: Neth 4H 153
Cockin La. BD14: Clay 2C 80
Cock La. WF4: Croft 1F 144
Cockley Cote HD7: Slait 8J 135
Cockley Hill La. HD5: K'htn 1G 139
Cockley Mdws. HD5: K'htn 1G 139
Cockpit OL14: Tod 8K 93
Cock Pit La. HX6: Rish 2D 134
Cockpit La. WF8: Pon 2K 129
Cockroft Gro. BD3: B'frd 3F 6 (7E 64)
Cockshot Pit La. S75: Map 9J 159
Cockshott Cl. LS12: Leeds 5J 67
Cockshott Dr. LS12: Leeds 5J 67
Cockshott Hill LS28: Fars 3A 66
Cockshott La. BD10: B'frd 7E 46
LS12: Leeds 5J 67
(not continuous)
Cockshott Pl. LS29: Add 1L 13
Coiners Fold HX7: Myth 4K 95
Colbeck Av. WF17: Bat 7D 102
(off Nelson St.)
Colbeck Row WF17: Birs 3B 102
Colbeck Ter. WF17: Bat 7D 102
(off Nelson St.)
Colbert Av. LS29: I'ly 4J 15
Colby Ri. LS15: Leeds 7N 69
Coldbeck Dr. BD6: B'frd 5K 81
Coldcotes Av. LS9: Leeds 4K 69
Coldcotes Cir. LS9: Leeds 4L 69
Coldcotes Cl. LS9: Leeds 4L 69
Coldcotes Cres. LS9: Leeds 4M 69
Coldcotes Dr. LS9: Leeds 4L 69
Coldcotes Gth. LS9: Leeds 4M 69
Coldcotes Gro. LS9: Leeds 4M 69
Coldcotes Vw. LS9: Leeds 4M 69
Coldcotes Wlk. LS9: Leeds 4M 69
Cold Edge Bottom HX2: Wain 7F 78
Cold Edge Rd. HX2: Wain 8F 78
(Mt. Tabor Rd.)
HX2: Wain 9C 60
(Nab Water La.)
COLDEN 8B 76
Colden Cl. HX7: Heb B 1G 94
Colden La. HX7: Hept 7A 76
Colden Rd. HX7: Heb B 8E 76
Colders Dr. HD9: Mel 8C 152
Colders Grn. HD9: Mel 7C 152
Colders La. HD9: Mel 8C 152
COLD HIENDLEY 9E 144
Cold Hiendley Comn. La. WF4: Col H 8D 144
Cold Hill La. HD4: Hud 1M 153
HD9: New M 1C 170
Coldhill La. LS24: Saxt 2L 73
LS25: Aber, Saxt 2L 73
Cold Royd La. HD5: K'htn 3E 138
(not continuous)
Coldshaw BD22: Oxen 3A 60
Coldshaw Top BD22: Haw 1C 60
Cold St. BD22: Haw 1C 60
Coldwell Activity Cen. 1C 56
Coldwell La. HD9: Holm 4G 169
Coldwell Rd. LS15: Leeds 5C 70
Coldwells Hill HX4: Stainl 8L 117
Coldwell Sq. LS15: Leeds 5C 70
Coldwell St. HD7: Linth 9C 136
Coleman St. BD3: B'frd 1C 6 (5D 64)
LS12: Leeds 8A 4 (8B 68)
Colenso Gdns. LS11: Leeds 9B 68
Colenso Gro. BD21: Keigh 7L 27
(off Aireworth Cl.)
LS11: Leeds 1B 86
Colenso Mt. LS11: Leeds 1B 86
Colenso Pl. LS11: Leeds 1B 86
Colenso Rd. LS11: Leeds 1B 86
Colenso Ter. LS11: Leeds 1B 86
Colenso Wlk. BD21: Keigh 7L 27
(off Cornwall Rd.)
Colenso Way BD21: Keigh 7L 27
(off Cornwall Rd.)
Coleridge Cl. LS26: Oul 1D 106
Coleridge Cres. WF2: Wren 9H 105
Coleridge Gdns. BD10: B'frd 7G 46
Coleridge La. LS28: Pud 9C 66
Coleridge St. HX1: Hal 5L 7 (6B 98)
Coleridge Way WF8: Pon 1K 129
Coleshill Way BD4: B'frd 5F 82
Coles Way BD20: Rid 6K 27
COLEY 2J 99
Coley Hall La. HX3: Nor G 2J 99
Coley Rd. HX3: North 9H 81
Coley Vw. HX3: Hip 4J 99
HX3: North 1F 98
Colin Barnaby Ct. WF2: Wake 3F 124
Colinsway WF2: Wake 7G 9 (6K 125)
Collbrook Av. BD6: B'frd 5A 82
Colleen Rd. WF4: Dur 5G 143
College Av. HD3: Hud 1H 137
College Ct. LS27: Gil 7G 85
College Dr. LS29: I'ly 6G 14
College Farm La. LS22: Lin 6J 23
College Flds. WF10: C'frd 6B 108
(off Barnsdale Rd.)
College Gdns. BD16: Bgly 2F 44
College Gro. WF1: Wake 1J 9 (3L 125)
WF10: C'frd 6A 108
College Gro. Cl. WF1: Wake 1K 9 (3L 125)
College Gro. Rd. WF1: Wake 2J 9 (4L 125)
College Gro. Vw. WF1: Wake 1J 9 (3L 125)
College La. BD20: L Bra, Sils 2A 12
College Lawns LS12: Leeds 6J 67
College Rd. BD16: Bgly 1F 44
LS27: Gil 7G 85
WF10: C'frd 5H 109
College St. HD4: Hud 6J 137
OL14: Tod 3E 92
WF17: Birs 3B 102
College St. E. HD4: Hud 6J 137
College Ter. HX1: Hal 7N 97
(off Skircoat Moor Rd.)
WF7: Ackw 4E 146
College Vw. LS12: Leeds 7J 67
WF7: Ackw 4E 146
WF13: Dew 2F 122
College Wlk. BD21: Keigh 9J 27
(within Airedale Shop. Cen.)
Colley Gdns. WF3: S'ley 6A 106
Collier Cl. BD18: Ship 8K 45
Collier La. BD17: Bail 3N 45
LS25: Aber 2F 72
Collier Rd. S72: Shaf 8K 161
Colliers La. LS17: Shad 3N 51
Colliers Way HD8: Clay W 5J 157
Colliery App. WF3: Loft 6K 105
Collindale Cl. BD10: B'frd 9J 47
Collinfield Ri. BD6: B'frd 7L 81
COLLINGHAM 9J 23
Collingham Av. BD6: B'frd 5K 81
Collingham Dr. LS25: Gar 8N 71
COLLINGHAM FIELDS 9L 23
Collingwood Ct. BD5: B'frd 2C 82
(off Ladywell Cl.)
Collingwood Rd. WF6: Norm 1J 127
Collin Moor La. HX4: Gree 3B 118
Collin Rd. LS14: Leeds 5A 70
Collins Cl. BD22: Haw 7E 42
Collinson St. BD19: Cleck 4H 101
Collins St. BD4: B'frd 1F 82
BD7: B'frd 2M 81
COLL PLACE 6B 82
Coll Pl. BD6: B'frd 5B 82
Collyer Vw. LS29: I'ly 4K 15
Colmore Gro. LS12: Leeds 9N 67
Colmore Rd. LS12: Leeds 9N 67
Colmore St. LS12: Leeds 8N 67
Colne Hurst HD2: Hud 7C 120
Colne Rd. BD22: Oak 5B 42
HD1: Hud 8B 8 (6M 137)
Colne St. HD1: Hud 6E 8 (5A 138)
(Day St.)
HD1: Hud 5K 137
(Market St.)
Colne Vale Rd. HD3: Hud 6F 136
Colne Valley Bus. Pk. HD7: Linth 9C 136
Colne Valley Leisure Cen. 9N 135
Colne Valley Mus. 6C 136
Colne Valley Specialist Arts College Sports Cen. 9D 136
Colne Vw. HD7: Linth 9C 136
HD7: Slait 9N 135
Colonel's Wlk. WF8: Pon 2J 129
Colonial Bldg. BD1: B'frd 4A 6
Colorado Way WF10: C'frd 7E 108
Colour Experience 4A 6 (7B 64)
Colston Cl. BD8: B'frd 5K 63
Colston Dr. LS29: Burl W 9A 16
COLTON 8E 70
Colton Cl. LS15: Leeds 7E 70
Colton Cft. LS15: Leeds 7E 70
Colton Gth. LS15: Leeds 7E 70
Colton La. LS15: Leeds 7E 70
Colton Lodges LS15: Leeds 7F 70
Colton Mill LS15: Leeds 7G 70
Colton Retail Pk. LS15: Leeds 7F 70
Colton Rd. LS12: Leeds 7M 67
LS15: Leeds 7D 70
Colton Rd. E. LS15: Leeds 8F 70
Colton St. LS12: Leeds 7M 67
Coltsfoot Cl. WF8: Pon 4K 129
Columbus St. HX3: Hal 3N 97
Colville Ter. LS11: Leeds 1D 86
WF3: Thpe H 3G 104
Colwyn Av. LS11: Leeds 3D 86
Colwyn Mt. LS11: Leeds 3D 86
Colwyn Pl. LS11: Leeds 3D 86
Colwyn Rd. LS11: Leeds 3D 86
Colwyn St. HD1: Hud 3J 137
Colwyn Ter. LS11: Leeds 3D 86
WF7: F'stne 5D 128
Colwyn Vw. LS11: Leeds 3D 86
Colyton Mt. BD15: All 5F 62
Combined Court Cen.
Bradford 5C 6 (8D 64)
Leeds 5D 4 (6D 68)
COMBS 8H 123
Combs, The WF12: T'hill 8H 123
Combs Rd. WF12: T'hill 9G 123
Commerce Ct. BD4: B'frd 1H 83
Commerce Pk. WF10: C'frd 7N 107
Commerce St. BD1: B'frd 3B 6 (7C 64)
Commercial Bldgs. BD12: O'haw 9F 82
Commercial Mills HX6: Ripp 8D 116
Commercial Rd. HD8: Skelm 7D 156
LS5: Leeds 2K 67
WF13: Dew 2F 122
Commercial St. BD1: B'frd 3C 6
BD13: Denh 6K 61
BD13: Que 4C 80
BD13: Thorn 8D 62
BD18: Ship 7N 45
BD19: Cleck 5J 101
BD22: Oak 5B 42
HD1: Hud 7C 8 (6N 137)
HD6: Brigh 1M 119
HD7: Slait 1N 151
HX1: Hal 4K 7 (5B 98)
(not continuous)
HX7: Heb B 1H 95
LS1: Leeds 6F 4 (6E 68)
LS26: Rothw 8N 87
LS27: Morl 9K 85
OL14: Tod 7L 93
Commercial St. WF1: Wake 8L 9 (7M 125)
WF10: C'frd 4D 108
WF12: Dew 4J 123
WF13: Raven 5C 122
WF16: Heck 8B 102
WF17: Bat 7F 102
Commercial Vs. LS28: Pud 8A 66
Commercial Way LS28: Pud 6C 66
Common, The S72: S Hien 4M 161
WF12: T'hill 8H 123
Commondale Way BD4: B'frd 7E 82
COMMON END
HD8 7C 156
WF9 3F 162
Common End HD6: B Bri 6A 100
Common End La. HD8: Fen B, Lept 7H 139
Common Holme La. LS29: Nes 3C 14
Common Ing La. WF4: Ryh 8J 145
Common La. DN14: Beal 7M 111
HD8: Den D 2E 172
HD8: Eml 2B 156
HX3: Sou 7E 98
S71: Roys 5D 160
(not continuous)
WF2: W'ton 5A 144
WF3: E Ard 4D 104
WF4: Flock 8D 140
WF4: Wool 1F 158
WF8: Thpe A 6A 148
WF9: Upt 2M 163
WF11: Knot 8G 110
(not continuous)
Common La. Bungs. WF9: Upt 2M 163
Common Piece La. WF8: E Hard 1L 147
Common Rd. BD12: Low M 7N 81
HD1: Hud 1A 8 (2M 137)
HX5: Ell 5H 119
S72: B'ley 7A 162
WF3: S'ley 5A 106
WF9: Kins 8A 146
WF9: S Kirk 8D 162
WF17: Bat 8C 102
Common Rd. Av. WF9: S Kirk 8G 162
Common Rd. Ind. Est. BD12: Low M 7B 82
Common Royd HX4: Bark 6G 117
COMMON SIDE 3M 155
Common Side LS26: Meth 3M 107
Commonside WF15: Liv 1J 121
WF17: Bat 1G 122
Common Side La. WF7: A'ton, F'stne 6A 128
Common Ter. HD6: Ras 2M 119
COMMON TOP 7H 139
Como Av. BD8: B'frd 5L 63
Como Dr. BD8: B'frd 6L 63
Como Gdns. BD8: B'frd 5L 63
Como Gro. BD8: B'frd 5L 63
Compeigne Av. BD21: Rid 7M 27
COMPTON 2K 37
Compton Av. LS9: Leeds 4J 69
Compton Ct. LS22: Coll 8J 23
Compton Cres. LS9: Leeds 4J 69
Compton La. LS22: Comp 2K 37
(not continuous)
LS23: B'ham 3G 36
Compton Pl. LS9: Leeds 4J 69
Compton Rd. LS9: Leeds 4J 69
Compton Row LS9: Leeds 4J 69
Compton St. BD4: B'frd 3G 82
BD21: Keigh 8K 27
Compton Ter. LS9: Leeds 4J 69
Compton Vw. LS9: Leeds 4J 69
Concept LS7: Leeds 8E 50
Concept Pl. LS3: Leeds 4A 4 (5B 68)
Concordia St. LS1: Leeds 8F 4 (7E 68)
Concord St. HD9: Hon 5L 153
LS2: Leeds 4H 5 (5F 68)
Concourse Ho. LS11: Leeds 5B 86
(off Dewsbury Rd.)
Concrete St. HX3: Hal 3N 97
Condor Cl. BD6: B'frd 3H 81
Conduit St. BD8: B'frd 5A 64
Coney La. BD21: Keigh 9J 27
HX2: Hal 7N 79
Coney Moor Gro. LS26: Meth 1N 107
Coney Pk. Ind. Pk. LS19: Yead 7B 32
Coney Wlk. WF13: Dew 3C 122
Coney Warren La. WF3: S'ley 4N 105
Conference Pl. LS12: Leeds 7K 67
Conference Rd. LS12: Leeds 7K 67
Conference Ter. LS12: Leeds 7K 67
Congress Mt. LS12: Leeds 7K 67
Congress St. LS12: Leeds 7K 67
Congreve App. LS17: Bard 3F 36
Congreve Way LS17: Bard 2F 36
Conisborough Cl. LS29: Burl W 9B 16
Conisborough La. LS25: Gar 7B 72
Conisborough Way WF9: Hems 1E 162
Coniston Av. BD13: Que 4C 80
HD5: Hud 3B 138
LS6: Leeds 1A 68
S75: S'ross 7J 159
Coniston Cl. BD13: Que 4C 80
HX5: Ell 4G 118
Coniston Ct. WF3: Loft 6K 105
Coniston Cres. WF1: Wake 3N 125
Coniston Dr. WF10: C'frd 5L 109
Coniston Gdns. LS15: Leeds 8N 69
WF10: C'frd 5L 109
Coniston Gro. BD9: B'frd 4L 63
BD17: Bail 6K 45
Coniston Ho. HX5: Ell 4E 118
(off St Mary's Ga.)
Coniston M. HD5: Hud 4B 138
Coniston Pl. WF11: Knot 2D 130
Coniston Rd. BD7: B'frd 2K 81
HD9: Mel 8D 152
LS26: W'frd 6D 88
WF12: Dew 1J 123
Coniston Way LS22: Weth 3J 23
LS26: W'frd 7D 88
Connaught Fold HD2: Hud 6C 120
Connaught Rd. LS29: I'ly 6J 15
Conservation Greenhouse
Birstall 4E 102
Consort St. LS3: Leeds 4A 4 (5B 68)
Consort Ter. LS3: Leeds 4A 4 (5B 68)
Consort Vw. LS3: Leeds 3A 4 (5B 68)
Consort Wlk. LS3: Leeds 4A 4 (5B 68)
(not continuous)
Constable Dr. WF5: Oss 5N 123
Constable Gro. WF3: S'ley 6N 105
Constable Rd. LS29: I'ly 6J 15
WF3: Ting 4A 104
Constance Gdns. LS7: Leeds 1E 4 (4D 68)
Constance St. BD18: Ship 7L 45
Constance Way LS7: Leeds 1E 4 (4D 68)
Constitutional St. HX1: Hal 7N 97
Convent Av. WF9: S Kirk 7J 163
Conway Av. LS8: Leeds 3H 69
Conway Cres. HD9: Mel 8C 152
WF17: Bat 1F 122
Conway Dr. LS8: Leeds 3H 69
Conway Gro. LS8: Leeds 3H 69
Conway Mt. LS8: Leeds 3H 69
Conway Pl. LS8: Leeds 3H 69
Conway Rd. LS8: Leeds 3H 69
WF2: Wake 4G 125
Conway St. BD4: B'frd 8C 6 (9D 64)
HX1: Hal 6N 97
LS8: Leeds 3H 69
LS28: Stan 5A 66
Conway Ter. LS8: Leeds 3H 69
Conway Vw. LS8: Leeds 3H 69
Conyer's Yd. WF5: Oss 4A 124
Cooke Cres. BD19: Gom 4L 101
Cooke St. BD21: Keigh 9J 27
Cook La. BD21: Keigh 9J 27
WF16: Heck 8N 101
COOKRIDGE 2G 49
Cookridge Av. LS16: Leeds 1H 49
Cookridge Dr. LS16: Leeds 1G 49
Cookridge Gro. LS16: Leeds 1H 49
Cookridge Hall Golf Course 1J 49
Cookridge La. LS16: Leeds 8G 33
Cookridge St. LS1: Leeds 5E 4 (6D 68)
LS2: Leeds 4E 4 (6D 68)
(not continuous)
Cooksland La. WF7: Old S 3M 127
Cookson Cl. WF10: C'frd 7K 109
Cookson St. HD6: Brigh 9L 99
Coombe Hill BD13: Que 3G 81
Coombe Rd. HD3: Hud 5E 136
Co-op Bldgs. HX7: P Wel 5J 77
Co-operation St. LS12: Leeds 1K 85
Cooperative Bldgs. HD6: B Bri 5N 99
Co-operative Bldgs. HX3: Hal 2M 97
Co-operative Cotts. HX7: Blac H 9B 76
S72: B'ley 6N 161
Cooperative Rd. LS27: Morl 2J 103
Co-operative St. BD21: Keigh 4G 43
LS27: Chur 5M 85
LS27: Morl 8K 85
OL14: W'den 4J 113
WF2: Wake 6J 125
WF3: Loft 3L 105
WF4: Horb 1C 142
WF12: Dew 3L 123
WF14: Mir 8L 121
Cooperative Ter. HX7: Hept 8G 77
(off Northgate)
Co-operative Ter. HD9: H'frth 1A 170
HX4: Stainl 8M 117
(off Stainland Rd.)
Co-operative Yd. BD19: Cleck 3H 101
(off Heaton St.)
Cooper Bri. Rd. WF14: Mir 5F 120
Cooper Cl. BD16: Bgly 2F 44
Cooperfields HX2: Lud F 6E 96
Cooper Gro. HX3: She 6J 81
Cooper Hill LS28: Pud 9C 66
Cooper Ho. WF9: Hems 3D 162
(off Lilley St.)
Cooper La. BD6: B'frd 3J 81
HD9: H'frth 3M 169
HX3: She 3J 81
S36: Hoy 8K 173
Cooper Rd. LS22: Weth 4M 23
S75: Kex 9E 158
Coopers Cl. HX2: Hal 2K 97
WF7: Ackw 4E 146
Coopers Fold LS23: B Spa 9D 24
Cooper St. OL14: Tod 6N 93
Co-op La. HD9: Holm 5J 169
Coop Pl. BD5: B'frd 4E 82
Copeland St. BD4: B'frd 9H 65
Copeworth Dr. WF4: Hol 7H 143
Copgrove Cl. BD4: B'frd 2J 83
Copgrove Ct. BD4: B'frd 2J 83
Copgrove Rd. BD4: B'frd 2J 83
LS8: Leeds 2J 69
Cop Hill End HD7: Slait 1J 151
Cop Hill La. HD7: Slait 1H 151
Cop Hill Side HD7: Slait 1H 151
COPLEY 1N 117
Copley Av. HD9: Mel 7B 152
HX2: Hal 7M 97
Copley Bank Rd. HD7: Golc 7B 136
Copley Circ. HX3: Hal 2N 117
Copley Cl. HX3: Hal 2A 118
Copley Dr. HX3: Hal 1N 117
Copley Glen HX3: Hal 1A 118
Copley Gro. HX3: Hal 1A 118
Copley Hall St. HX3: Hal 2A 118
Copley Hall Ter. HX3: Hal 1A 118
COPLEY HILL 2D 102
Copley Hill LS12: Leeds 8A 68
WF17: Birs 3C 102
Copley Hill Trad. Est. LS12: Leeds 9A 68
Copley Hill Way LS12: Leeds 9A 68
Copley La. HD8: Shel 9M 155
HX3: Hal 2N 117
LS25: Aber 1J 73
WF3: Rob H 9K 87
Copley Mill Ho. HX3: Hal 1N 117
(off St Stephen's St.)
Copley Mt. HX3: Hal 1A 118
Copley St. BD5: B'frd 2N 81
LS12: Leeds 8A 68
WF17: Bat 5D 102
Copley Ter. HX3: Hal 1A 118

Copley Vw.—Cranmore La.

Copley Vw. HX3: Hal 1A 118
Copley Wood Ter. HX3: Hal 1A 118
Copley Yd. LS12: Leeds 8A 68
Coplowe La. BD15: Wils 8C 44
Copmanroyd LS21: Clift 6L 17
Copperas HD9: Hon 4N 153
Copperas Ho. Ter. OL14: W'den 1H 113
Copperas Row HX4: Gree 4L 117
Copper Beech Cl. WF8: Pon 5L 129
Copper Beech Ct. WF2: W'ton 4B 144
Copperfield Av. LS9: Leeds 8H 69
Copperfield Cres. LS9: Leeds 8H 69
Copperfield Dr. LS9: Leeds 8H 69
Copperfield Gro. LS9: Leeds 8H 69
Copperfield Mt. LS9: Leeds 8J 69
Copperfield Pl. LS9: Leeds 8H 69
Copperfield Row LS9: Leeds 8H 69
Copperfield Ter. LS9: Leeds 8H 69
Copperfield Vw. LS9: Leeds 8H 69
Copperfield Wlk. LS9: Leeds 8H 69
Coppertop M. WF8: Pon 9L 109
Coppice, The BD19: Gom 3A 102
HD2: Fix 7N 119
HD3: Hud 1F 136
HX1: Hal 7H 7 (7A 98)
LS15: Bar E 9L 53
LS19: Yead 2K 47
LS29: I'ly 3F 14
WF14: Mir 3K 121
Coppice Cl. WF1: Wake 3N 125
Coppice Dr. HD4: Neth 3H 153
Coppice Grange LS19: Yead 8M 31
Coppice Head LS26: Rothw 8A 88
Coppice Vw. BD10: B'frd 7E 46
Coppice Way LS8: Leeds 9J 51
Coppice Wood Av. LS19: Yead 8L 31
LS20: Guis, Yead 8L 31
Coppicewood Av. BD7: B'frd 8M 63
Coppice Wood Cl. LS20: Guis 7L 31
Coppice Wood Cres. LS19: Yead 8L 31
Coppice Wood Gro. LS20: Guis 8L 31
Coppicewood Gro. BD7: B'frd 8M 63
Coppice Wood Ri. LS19: Yead 8M 31
Coppies, The BD12: Wyke 9N 81
Coppin Hall Gro. WF14: Mir 5H 121
Coppin Hall La. WF14: Mir 4H 121
Copplestone Wlk. BD4: B'frd 3J 83
Coppy Cl. BD16: Cot 9F 44
Coppy La. BD22: Oak 1K 41
HX7: P Wel 2G 77
LS13: Leeds 2F 66
Coppy Nook La. HX7: Crag V 1L 115
Coppy Rd. BD20: Stee 3B 26
LS29: Add 1L 13
Coppy Row BD22: Oak 5B 42
Coppy Wood Dr. LS29: I'ly 2G 15
Copres Av. HD3: Hud 1G 136
Cop Royd HD9: Hon 4N 153
Copse, The BD16: Bgly 4J 45
BD19: Scho 5D 100
HD6: Brigh 8L 99
LS23: B Spa 8C 24
LS29: Burl W 9C 16
WF3: E Ard 5D 104
WF7: F'stne 2C 128
Copthorne Gdns. HD2: Hud 6D 120
Copthorne Sq. HD2: Hud 6D 120
Copthurst Rd. HD9: Holm, H'frth 8J 169
Copt Royd Gro. LS19: Yead 9L 31
Copy Nook HX4: Gree 4N 117
Copy St. BD15: All 5G 63
Coral Windows Stadium 5B 64
Corban St. BD4: B'frd 2G 82
Corby St. HD2: Hud 1M 137
Cordingley Cl. BD4: B'frd 4J 83
Cordingley Grn. *HX4: Stainl* 8M 117
(off Bk. Bowling Grn.)
Cordingley St. BD4: B'frd 4J 83
Core Shop. Centre, The LS1: Leeds 6F 4 (6E 68)
Corfe Cl. WF17: Bat 2E 102
Coriander Cl. BD15: All 6F 62
Corn Bank HD4: Neth 3H 153
Corner Ho. Shops LS17: Leeds 5F 50
Cornerstones Cl. LS29: Add 1N 13
Cornet Cl. HD3: Hud 1H 137
Cornfield WF13: Dew 2C 122
Cornfield Av. HD3: Hud 3F 136
Cornfield St. OL14: Tod 6M 93
Cornflower M. WF10: C'frd 7B 108
CORNHOLME 3D 92
Cornholme Ter. *OL14: Tod* 3D 92
(off Ackroyd St.)
Corn Mkt. HX1: Hal 4L 7 (5B 98)
Cornmarket WF8: Pon 3J 129
Corn Mill LS29: Men 4F 30
Cornmill App. LS28: Pud 7N 65
Cornmill Av. WF15: Liv 9N 101
Corn Mill Bottom HD8: Shel 7J 155
Cornmill Cl. LS17: Bard 5E 36
Corn Mill Ct. LS13: Leeds 6G 67
Cornmill Cres. WF15: Liv 9M 101
Cornmill Dr. WF15: Liv 9M 101
Corn Mill Fold BD6: B'frd 7K 81
Corn Mill La. BD14: Clay 9E 62
LS29: Burl W 8E 16
Cornmill La. LS17: Bard 5E 36
WF15: Liv 9M 101
Cornmill Vw. LS18: Hors 7H 49
Cornrace Vw.
HD1: Hud 8D 8 (6N 137)
Cornstone Fold LS12: Leeds 7F 66
Corn St. BD21: Keigh 3G 43
Cornus Gdns. LS10: Leeds 5F 86
Cornwall Av. BD20: Sils 8C 12
Cornwall Cl. LS26: Rothw 7M 87
Cornwall Cres. BD17: Bail 3N 45
HD6: B Bri 6N 99
LS26: Rothw 7M 87
Cornwall Ho. *HX5: Ell* 5E 118
(off Crown St.)
Cornwall Pl. BD8: B'frd 1A 6 (5B 64)
Cornwall Rd. BD8: B'frd 1A 6 (5B 64)
BD16: Bgly 5G 44
BD21: Keigh 7L 27
Cornwall Ter. BD8: B'frd 1A 6 (5B 64)
Coronation Av. BD17: Esh 3H 47
LS25: Kip 4C 90
S71: Roys 5F 160
S72: Shaf 6J 161
WF6: Alt 8G 106
Coronation Bungs. *HD9: Mel* 8D 152
(off Calmlands Rd.)
LS25: Kip 4C 90
WF11: Knot 8C 110
Coronation Bus. Cen. BD21: Keigh 7K 27
Coronation Mt. BD22: Keigh 9F 26
Coronation Pde. LS15: Leeds 8N 69
(not continuous)
Coronation Rd. HX3: Hal 8B 98
WF4: S Comn 8J 127
Coronation St. BD12: O'haw 9E 82
HX4: Gree 3B 118
HX5: Ell 5E 118
WF2: Wren 1H 125
WF3: Carl 1M 105
WF6: Norm 9L 107
WF10: C'frd 3F 108
Coronation Ter. HX6: Ripp 5E 116
HX7: Wads 8K 77
WF10: C'frd 6G 108
WF17: Birs 3C 102
Coronation Wlk. BD22: Keigh 8F 26
Coronation Way BD22: Keigh 9E 26
Corporal La. BD13: North 7D 80
HX3: North 7D 80
Corporation St. BD2: B'frd 3G 64
HD1: Hud 6B 8 (5M 137)
HX1: Hal 2K 7 (4B 98)
HX6: Sow B 8H 97
LS27: Morl 8J 85
WF13: Dew 3G 122
Corrance Rd. BD12: Wyke 3B 100
Corrie Fold *BD13: Thorn* 8D 62
(off Corrie St.)
Corrie St. BD13: Thorn 8D 62
Corsair Av. BD10: B'frd 9G 47
Cotchers La. LS24: Saxt 7N 55
Cotchers Ri. LS24: Saxt 8N 55
Cote, The LS28: Fars 4N 65
Cote Cl. HD8: Shel 6J 155
Cote Farm La. BD10: B'frd 6D 46
Cotefields Av. LS28: Fars 3N 65
Cote Hill HX2: Hal 6J 97
Cote Hill Fold HX2: Hal 6K 97
Cote La. BD15: All 5F 62
HD6: Ras 6K 119
HD9: H'frth 8M 169
LS28: Fars, Stan 4N 65
Cote Rd. HX6: Ripp 7B 116
Coteroyd Av. LS27: Chur 5M 85
Coteroyd Dr. LS27: Chur 6M 85
Cote Wall M. WF14: Mir 8A 122
Cotewall Rd. BD5: B'frd 2B 82
Cotswold Av. BD18: Ship 8C 46
Cotswold Cl. WF9: Hems 2F 162
Cotswold Dr. LS25: Gar 9N 71
LS26: Rothw 7M 87
WF11: Knot 8D 110
WF15: Liv 7H 101
Cotswold M. HD8: Kbtn 2K 155
Cotswold Rd. LS26: Rothw 7N 87
WF2: Wake 6F 124
Cottage, The HD8: Shep 2G 171
Cottage Grn. *BD8: B'frd* 6L 63
(off Lane Ends Cl.)
Cottage Homes HD5: Hud 4E 138
Cottage Rd. BD10: B'frd 8H 47
LS6: Leeds 9N 49
Cottage Road Cinema
Headingley 9N 49
Cottam Av. BD7: B'frd 8N 63
Cottam Cft. WF9: Hems 2E 162
Cottam Ter. BD7: B'frd 8N 63
Cotterdale BD15: All 3F 62
LS29: Men 5F 30
(off Clifford Dr.)
Cotterdale Holt LS22: Coll 8H 23
Cotterdale Vw. LS15: Leeds 8N 69
Cotterill Rd. WF11: Knot 9C 110
COTTINGLEY
BD16 9G 45
LS11 4N 85
Cottingley App. LS11: Leeds 4N 85
Cottingley Bus. Pk. BD16: Cot 8G 44
Cottingley Chase LS11: Leeds 4M 85
Cottingley Cliffe Rd. BD16: Cot 9H 45
Cottingley Ct. LS11: Leeds 4N 85
Cottingley Cres. LS11: Leeds 4N 85
Cottingley Dr. BD16: Cot 7F 44
LS11: Leeds 3M 85
Cottingley Fold LS11: Leeds 3M 85
Cottingley Gdns. LS11: Leeds 4N 85
Cottingley Grn. LS11: Leeds 4N 85
Cottingley Gro. LS11: Leeds 4N 85
Cottingley Hall Crematorium LS11: Leeds 3N 85
Cottingley Hgts. LS11: Leeds 4N 85
Cottingley Mnr. Pk. BD16: Cot 8G 45
Cottingley Moor Rd. BD16: Cot 2F 62
Cottingley New Rd. BD16: Cot 8G 45
Cottingley Rd. BD15: All 3F 62
LS11: Leeds 3M 85
Cottingley Springs Caravan Site
LS27: Gil 4K 85
Cottingley Station (Rail) 4M 85
Cottingley Ter. BD8: B'frd 5B 64
Cottingley Towers LS11: Leeds 4N 85
Cottingley Va. LS11: Leeds 4N 85
Cottingley Wood BD16: Cot 7F 44
COTTON STONES 4C 116
Cotton St. LS9: Leeds 7J 5 (7G 68)
WF2: Wake 8J 9 (7L 125)
Couford Gro. HD2: Hud 7D 120
Cougar Park 7K 27
Coule Royd HD5: Hud 3C 138
Coulsdon Ho. *BD8: B'frd* 5A 64
(off Green La.)
Coultas Cl. LS29: Men 4F 30
Council Ter. HD9: Hon 4M 153
County Arc. LS1: Leeds 6G 5 (6E 68)
County Bri. BD13: Denh 9K 61
County Cl. WF17: Bat 6F 102
County Court
Halifax 5L 7
Huddersfield 7B 8 (5M 137)
Wakefield 2K 129
Coupe Gro. WF6: Alt 7G 107
Coupland Pl. LS11: Leeds 1D 86
Coupland Rd. LS11: Leeds 1D 86
LS25: Gar 7M 71
Coupland St. LS11: Leeds 2D 86
OL14: Tod 7K 93
Court, The BD18: Ship 8K 45
LS17: Leeds 2B 50
WF7: Ackw 2H 147
WF15: Liv 8J 101
Court Barton La. LS23: Cliff 3E 38
Courtenay Cl. BD3: B'frd 7J 65
Courtenays LS14: Leeds 2C 70
Courthouse St. LS21: Otley 9L 17
Court La. HX2: Hal 5K 97
Courtney Ho. *BD8: B'frd* 5B 64
(off Trenton Dr.)
Court No. 6 WF17: Bat 8F 102
Courts Leet BD12: Wyke 9A 82
Court Way, The WF7: Ackw 3H 147
Court Yard, The *BD17: Bail* 3B 46
(off East Pde.)
Courtyard, The BD7: B'frd 3K 81
HD4: Hud 6J 137
HD8: Fen B 6G 139
LS10: Leeds 1F 86
LS12: Leeds 5J 67
WF2: Wake 8F 124
WF4: Wool 2J 159
WF8: Pon 9L 109
WF17: Birs 2C 102
Courtyard M. BD20: Sils 2F 26
Courtyards, The LS14: Leeds 8C 52
Cousen Av. BD7: B'frd 9L 63
Cousen Pl. BD7: B'frd 1N 81
Cousen Rd. BD7: B'frd 1N 81
Cousin La. HX2: Illing 8L 79
Coutances Way LS29: Burl W, I'ly 4L 15
Coventry St. BD4: B'frd 1F 82
HX2: Hal 5L 97
Coverdale Cl. LS12: Leeds 4J 67
Coverdale Gth. LS22: Coll 9H 23
Coverdale Way BD17: Bail 3C 46
Cover Dr. BD6: B'frd 5M 81
Coverley Gth. LS19: Yead 9K 31
Coverley Ri. LS19: Yead 9K 31
Covert, The WF17: Bat 5C 102
Covet, The BD10: B'frd 7H 47
Covey Clough Ct. WF14: Up H 1K 139
Cow & Calf Rocks 7K 15
COWCLIFFE 9M 119
Cowcliffe Hill Rd. HD2: Fix, Hud 7L 119
Cowcliff Hill Rd. HD9: Had E 8A 170
Cow Cl. Cotts. BD12: Wyke 2D 100
Cow Cl. Gro. LS12: Leeds 1K 85
Cow Cl. La. BD12: Wyke 2C 100
Cow Cl. Rd. LS12: Leeds 1J 85
Cowdray Dr. BD19: Scho 4D 100
Cowdry Cl. WF12: T'hill 9H 123
Cowfold St. OL14: Tod 6K 93
Cow Ga. HD3: Hud 4E 136
Cowgill St. BD8: B'frd 5A 64
Cow Grn. HX1: Hal 4K 7 (5B 98)
Cow Hey La. HX7: Heb B 2E 76
Cow Heys HD5: Hud 3C 138
Cow Hill Ga. La. HX2: Ogd 5L 79
Cowhouse Bri. BD13: Cull 8K 43
Cowhurst Av. OL14: Tod 5H 93
Cow La. DN6: Wome 8L 131
HX3: Hal 1B 118
HX3: Sou 8J 99
HX6: Ripp 5D 116
(Soyland Town Rd.)
HX6: Ripp 3A 116
(Wicking La.)
HX7: Heb B 5F 76
LS25: Bur S 1E 110
WF4: H'cft 1J 161
WF4: S Comn 7H 127
WF11: Knot 8F 110
COWLERSLEY 7E 136
Cowlersley La. HD4: Hud 9D 136
HD7: Linth 9D 136
Cowley Cres. BD9: B'frd 2H 63
Cowley Rd. LS13: Leeds 1C 66
Cowling La. HX3: North 7E 80
COWMES 5G 138
Cowm St. OL12: Whit 6A 112
Cowpasture Rd. LS29: I'ly 5G 15
Cowper Av. LS9: Leeds 4J 69
Cowper Cres. LS9: Leeds 4J 69
Cowper Gro. LS8: Leeds 3J 69
Cowper Mt. LS9: Leeds 4J 69
Cowper Rd. LS9: Leeds 4J 69
Cowper St. LS7: Leeds 2F 68
WF12: Dew 5F 122
Cowper Ter. LS9: Leeds 4J 69
Cowrakes Cl. HD3: Hud 1F 136
Cowrakes Ct. HD3: Hud 1F 136
Cowrakes Rd. HD3: Hud 1E 136
Cowroyd Pl. HX3: Hal 1M 7 (3C 98)
Cowslip La. WF10: C'frd 7A 108
Cowslip St. HD1: Hud 5J 137
COXLEY 3N 141
Coxley Cres. WF4: Neth 4N 141
Coxley Dell WF4: Neth 2A 142
Coxley La. WF4: M'twn 3N 141
Coxley Vw. WF4: Neth 5M 141
Coxwold Hill LS22: Weth 2M 23
Coxwold Vw. LS22: Weth 2M 23
Coxwold Wlk. BD15: All 7F 62
Crabby La. HD5: Hud 1E 138
Crabgate Dr. DN6: Skel 7K 165
Crabgate La. DN6: Skel 8K 165
Crab Hill WF8: Pon 3J 129
Crab La. LS12: Leeds 6M 67
WF2: New 6K 143
Crabtree Av. WF16: Heck 7B 102
Crabtree Fold HX7: Wads 8J 77
Crabtree Grn. LS22: Coll 9H 23
Crabtree Hill LS22: Coll 9J 23
Crab Tree Hill La. S36: Hoy 9H 173
Crab Tree La. WF8: K S'ton 8G 148
WF9: S Elm 6B 164
Crabtree La. LS17: E Kes 2D 36
Crabtree Pl. BD7: B'frd 1N 81
OL14: Tod 3D 92
Crabtree St. BD7: B'frd 1M 81
HX1: Hal 5M 97
Crabtree Way WF3: W Ard 4B 104
CRACKENEDGE 2G 122
Crackenedge La. WF13: Dew 1G 122
(not continuous)
Crackenedge Ter. WF13: Dew 2G 122
Crackhills La. LS22: Sick 4C 22
Crack La. BD15: Wils 1B 62
Cracoe Rd. BD3: B'frd 8F 64
Crag, The LS23: B'ham 6D 38
Crag Cl. HX2: Mix 9K 79
Crag Ct. HX2: Mix 9K 79
Crag Gdns. LS23: B'ham 6D 38
Cragg Av. LS18: Hors 7E 48
Cragg Bottom Rd. BD22: Old 7F 40
Cragg Dr. LS29: I'ly 6L 15
Cragg Hill LS18: Hors 7F 48
Cragg La. BD7: B'frd 2M 81
BD13: Denh 9L 61
BD13: Thorn 9M 61
HX7: Crag V 6K 95
Cragg Rd. HX7: Crag V 6G 94
(Dick's La.)
HX7: Crag V, Myth 9K 95
(Blackstone Edge Rd.)
LS18: Hors 7F 48
Cragg Side HX7: Hept 6D 76
Cragg St. BD7: B'frd 2M 81
Cragg Ter. BD7: B'frd 2M 81
LS18: Hors 7E 48
(not continuous)
LS19: Raw 5M 47
Cragg Top BD13: Denh 9L 61
WF11: Fair 9N 91
(off Gauk St.)
CRAGG VALE 9K 95
Cragg Vw. BD20: Sils 7E 12
LS21: Pool 3E 32
LS29: Add 1M 13
(off Bolton Rd.)
Craggwell Ter. *LS18: Hors* 8F 48
(off Wood La.)
Craggwood Cl. LS18: Hors 8F 48
Cragg Wood Dr. LS19: Raw 5L 47
Craggwood Rd. LS18: Hors 8F 48
Craggwood Ter. *LS18: Hors* 8F 48
(off Craggwood Rd.)
Crag Hill Av. LS16: Leeds 9H 33
Crag Hill Rd. BD10: B'frd 5E 46
Crag Hill Vw. LS16: Leeds 1H 49
Crag La. HX2: Mix 9K 79
LS17: Huby 5M 19
(Almscliffe Dr.)
LS17: Huby, N Rig 3L 19
(Merrybank La.)
LS17: Leeds 2A 50
Crag Mt. WF8: Pon 3J 129
Crag Pl. BD21: Keigh 3J 43
Crag Rd. BD18: Ship 8A 46
Cragside BD10: B'frd 6D 46
Cragside Cl. LS5: Leeds 8H 49
Cragside Cres. LS5: Leeds 8H 49
Cragside Gdns. LS5: Leeds 8H 49
Cragside Gro. LS5: Leeds 9G 49
Cragside Mt. LS5: Leeds 8H 49
Cragside Pl. LS5: Leeds 8H 49
Cragside Wlk. LS5: Leeds 9G 49
Crag Vw. BD10: B'frd 9G 47
LS17: Huby 5M 19
Crag Vw. Cotts. LS17: Huby 5M 19
Craig Cl. WF17: Bat 6F 102
Craiglands HX3: Hip 4J 99
Craiglands Pk. LS29: I'ly 6H 15
Craiglands Rd. LS29: I'ly 6H 15
Craiglea Dr. BD12: Wyke 2B 100
Craigmore Ct. BD4: B'frd 3K 83
Craigmore Dr. LS29: I'ly 5K 15
Craig Vw. BD18: Ship 8J 45
Craig-y-Don WF12: Dew 4J 123
Crake Dr. BD6: B'frd 4H 81
Cranberry Av. OL14: W'den 4K 113
Cranborne Dr. S75: Dart 8H 159
Cranbourne Rd. BD9: B'frd 4J 63
Cranbrook Av. BD6: B'frd 5A 82
LS11: Leeds 2C 86
Cranbrook Pl. BD5: B'frd 2C 82
Cranbrook St. BD5: B'frd 2C 82
BD14: Clay 1G 80
Cranbrook Vw. LS28: Pud 9D 66
Cranbrook Way WF8: Pon 9L 109
Cranewells Dr. LS15: Leeds 8E 70
Cranewells Grn. LS15: Leeds 8D 70
Cranewells Ri. LS15: Leeds 8D 70
Cranewells Va. LS15: Leeds 8D 70
Cranewells Vw. LS15: Leeds 7D 70
Cranfield Dr. DN6: Skel 7M 165
Cranford Gdns. LS29: I'ly 6E 14
S71: Roys 5C 160
Cranford Pl. BD15: Wils 1B 62
Crangle Flds. HD4: Stock 7G 154
HD9: New M 9F 154
Cranleigh Mt. BD21: Keigh 2G 42
Cranmer Bank LS17: Leeds 4C 50
Cranmer Cl. LS17: Leeds 4C 50
Cranmer Gdns. HD9: Mel 7D 152
LS17: Leeds 4C 50
Cranmer Ri. LS17: Leeds 3C 50
Cranmer Rd. BD3: B'frd 5D 64
LS17: Leeds 4C 50
(not continuous)
Cranmore Cres. LS10: Leeds 8H 87
Cranmore Dr. LS10: Leeds 8H 87
Cranmore Gdns. LS10: Leeds 8G 87
Cranmore Gth. LS10: Leeds 8G 87
Cranmore Grn. LS10: Leeds 8G 87
Cranmore Gro. LS10: Leeds 8G 87
Cranmore La. LS10: Leeds 8H 87

Cranmore Ri.—Crossflatts Station (Rail)

Cranmore Ri. LS10: Leeds 8H 87
Cranmore Rd. LS10: Leeds 8G 87
Cranwood Dr. HD5: Hud 4E 138
Craven Av. BD13: Thorn 8D 62
BD20: Sils 8E 12
Craven Cl. BD19: Gom 4N 101
S71: Roys 5C 160
Craven Ct. *BD8: B'frd 6L 63*
(off Lane Ends Cl.)
BD20: Sils 8F 12
LS11: Leeds 4A 86
Craven Cres. LS29: Add 1L 13
Cravendale Rd. WF13: Raven 5A 122
Craven Dr. BD19: Gom 4N 101
BD20: Sils 8E 12
Craven Edge HX1: Hal 6N 97
Craven Ent. Cen. *HX1: Hal 6N 97*
(off Hopwood La.)
Craven Gth. DN14: Beal 5M 111
Craven Gro. BD20: Sils 8F 12
Craven La. BD19: Gom 4N 101
Craven Mt. *HX1: Hal 6N 97*
(off Lister La.)
Craven Pk. LS29: Men 3D 30
Craven Pl. HX1: Hal 5G 7
Craven Rd. BD21: Keigh 8L 27
LS6: Leeds 3D 68
WF9: Hems 3D 162
WF13: Dew 5D 122
Craven St. BD3: B'frd 2D 6 (6D 64)
HD4: Hud 6F 136
LS21: Otley 1M 31
WF13: Raven 5A 122
Craven Ter. BD2: B'frd 3G 64
HX1: Hal 6N 97
LS21: Otley 1M 31
(off Fairfax St.)
Crawford Av. BD6: B'frd 5A 82
Crawford Cl. BD6: B'frd 5A 82
Crawford Dr. WF2: Wake 4H 125
Crawford St. BD4: B'frd 1E 82
OL14: W'den 3K 113
Crawley Av. WF9: S Kirk 6K 163
Crawshaw Av. LS28: Pud 7C 66
Crawshaw Cl. LS28: Pud 7B 66
Crawshaw Gdns. LS28: Pud 7C 66
Crawshaw Hill LS28: Pud 7B 66
Crawshaw La. HD8: Dew, Eml 9D 140
WF4: Flock 8C 140
Crawshaw Pk. LS28: Pud 7B 66
Crawshaw Ri. LS28: Pud 8B 66
Crawshaw Rd. LS28: Pud 7B 66
Crawshaw St. WF13: Raven 5C 122
Crawthorne Cres. HD2: Hud 7C 120
Crayford Dr. WF4: Croft 1G 145
Cray La. HX4: Holy 9K 117
Crediton Av. BD15: All 6G 62
Crediton Ct. BD15: All 6G 63
Crescent, The BD6: B'frd 5K 81
BD11: B'haw 6L 83
BD16: Bgly 1D 44
BD17: Bail 5A 46
HD6: Brigh 9N 99
HD8: Kbtn 2L 155
HD9: New M 2C 170
HX3: Hip 4J 99
HX3: Sou 6E 98
HX4: Holy 7N 117
LS6: Leeds 3C 68
(off Woodhouse La.)
LS13: Leeds 3F 66
LS15: Leeds 6C 70
LS16: Leeds 3K 49
LS17: Leeds 1B 50
LS17: N Rig 3N 19
LS18: Hors 6C 48
LS20: Guis 8G 30
LS21: Otley 7L 17
LS22: Sick 4D 22
LS25: Gar 6A 72
LS25: Kip 4A 90
LS25: M'fld 8G 73
LS28: Pud 6C 66
LS29: Burl W 9C 16
LS29: I'ly 4K 15
LS29: Men 4F 30
S72: Cud 9J 161
WF3: Ting 4C 104
WF4: Neth 5M 141
WF6: Alt 8G 106
WF7: Street 6L 127
WF10: C'frd 6F 108
WF13: Raven 6A 122
WF15: Liv 7H 101
Crescent Av. HD4: Neth 2J 153
LS26: Rothw 6A 88
WF13: Raven 6A 122
Crescent Bungs. WF3: Thpe H 2F 104
Crescent Ct. LS17: Leeds 1B 50
Crescent Gdns. LS17: Leeds 3F 50
Crescent Grange LS11: Leeds 1E 86
Crescent Rd. HD2: Hud 1L 137
HD4: Neth 2J 153
WF4: H'cft 9L 145
Crescent Royd HD5: Hud 5E 138
Crescent St. OL14: Tod 7K 93
Crescent Ter. LS29: I'ly 5G 15
Crescent Towers LS11: Leeds 1E 86
Crescent Vw. BD22: Keigh 4G 42
LS17: Leeds 1B 50
Crescent Vs. WF9: Kins 8B 146
Crescent Wlk. BD14: Clay 9J 63
WF13: Raven 6A 122
Creskeld Cres. LS16: B'hpe 5J 33
Creskeld Dr. LS16: B'hpe 4H 33
Creskeld Gdns. LS16: B'hpe 5H 33
Creskeld Gth. LS16: B'hpe 5J 33
Creskeld La. LS16: Arth, B'hpe 4J 33
LS21: Arth 4J 33
Creskeld Pk. LS16: B'hpe 5J 33
Creskeld Vw. LS16: B'hpe 5H 33
Creskeld Way BD15: All 4F 62
Cressfield Rd. HD3: Hud 2H 137
Cressingham Vs. *BD13: Cull 1K 61*
(off Cullingworth Ga.)
Cresswell Mt. BD7: B'frd 3K 81
Cresswell Pl. BD7: B'frd 3K 81
Cresswell Ter. BD7: B'frd 3K 81
HX3: Hip 4K 99
Crest, The HD2: Hud 5C 120
LS25: Kip 4A 90
LS26: Swil 4H 89
Crest Av. BD12: Wyke 3A 100
HD5: Hud 5C 138
Crest Dr. WF8: Pon 5L 129
Crestfield Av. HX5: Ell 5D 118
Crestfield Cres. HX5: Ell 6D 118
Crestfield Dr. HX2: Hal 7L 97
HX5: Ell 6D 118
Crestfield Rd. HX5: Ell 6D 118
Crest Hill Rd. HD2: Hud 8A 120
Crest Mt. WF8: Pon 5L 129
Crest Pl. *HD6: Brigh 7K 99*
(off Halifax Rd.)
Crest Rd. HD3: Hud 8F 118
Crest Vw. HD6: Brigh 7K 99
Crestville Cl. BD14: Clay 9J 63
Crestville Rd. BD14: Clay 9H 63
Crestville Ter. BD14: Clay 9J 63
Crestwood Cl. BD5: B'frd 4F 82
Creswell La. WF13: Dew 9C 102
Crewe Av. WF11: Ferr 8A 110
Crewe Rd. WF10: C'frd 5J 109
Crib La. HX1: Hal 2K 7 (4B 98)
Cricketers, The LS5: Leeds 2L 67
Cricketers App. WF2: Wren 9G 105
Cricketers Cl. LS25: Gar 7A 72
WF7: Ackw 5G 147
Cricketers Fold HX3: Hal 1C 118
LS17: Shad 3N 51
Cricketers Grn. LS19: Yead 1N 47
Cricketers Ter. LS12: Leeds 7M 67
Cricketers Vw. LS17: Shad 3N 51
Cricketers Wlk. BD20: Stee 3D 26
LS15: Leeds 7F 70
Cricklegate LS15: Leeds 6C 70
Cridling Pk. WF11: Cri S 3J 131
Cridling Pk. Cotts. WF11: Knot 1H 131
CRIDLING STUBBS 4J 131
CRIGGLESTONE 5G 142
Crimble Bank HD7: Slait 9M 135
Crimble Cl. HX3: Hip 5K 99
Crimble Clough HD7: Slait 8M 135
CRIMBLES 7C 66
Crimbles, The WF4: Dur 3H 143
Crimbles Ct. LS28: Pud 7C 66
Crimbles Pl. LS28: Pud 7C 66
Crimbles Rd. LS28: Pud 7C 66
Crimbles Ter. LS28: Pud 7C 66
Crimea La. HD7: Slait 7K 135
Crimple Grn. LS25: Gar 9B 72
Crimshaw La. BD18: Ship 9B 46
Crimsworth La. HX7: P Wel 5H 77
Crimsworth Ter. HX7: Heb B 6H 77
Crinan Ct. WF6: Alt 8H 107
CRINGLES 4F 12
Cringles La. BD20: Sils 2E 12
Cringles Pk. Mobile Home Pk. BD20: Sils 4F 12
Cripplegate HX1: Hal 3M 7 (5C 98)
Cripple Syke LS18: Hors 5F 48
Crispin Ho. LS2: Leeds 5H 5
Croasdale Gdns. DN6: Carc 8N 165
(not continuous)
Crodingley HD9: T'bdge 9N 153
Crodingley Farm Ct. HD9: T'bdge 9M 153
Croft HD7: Linth 9D 136
Croft, The BD11: Drig 8B 84
BD12: O'haw 9D 82
BD17: Bail 4A 46
BD21: Keigh 9M 27
BD23: Drau 5D 10
HD8: Shep 9K 155
(off Lydgate Rd.)
HD8: Up C 2M 171
LS14: S'cft 8E 36
LS15: Leeds 5C 70
LS22: Coll 9H 23
LS24: Saxt 9N 55
LS26: Oul 8D 88
S36: Hoy 9J 173
WF3: W Ard 7N 103
WF4: W Bret 1B 158
WF9: Bads 7K 147
WF10: C'frd 6F 108
WF11: Knot 7F 110
Croft Av. BD16: Bgly 1C 44
LS21: Otley 8K 17
LS28: Fars 3A 66
S71: Roys 6C 160
WF3: E Ard 5F 104
WF6: Alt 9G 106
WF6: Norm 9K 107
WF11: Knot 7F 110
Croft Bank BD11: B'haw 8L 83
OL12: Whit 9A 112
Croft Bri. LS26: Oul 8D 88
Croft Carr OL14: Tod 9N 93
Croft Cl. LS29: Men 4D 30
S75: Map 8K 159
Croft Cott. La. HD1: Hud 1C 8 (2N 137)
Croft Cotts. LS12: N Far 2H 85
LS23: B'ham 6D 38
Croft Ct. HD6: Ras 5K 119
HD9: Hon 6L 153
LS18: Hors 6F 48
LS29: Men 4E 30
Croftdale Gro. LS15: Leeds 4E 70
Croft Dr. HD9: Hon 5K 153
LS23: B'ham 5C 38
LS29: Men 4E 30
S75: Map 8J 159
Croft End LS22: Weth 4K 23
Crofters Ct. WF4: H'cft 9K 145
Crofters Grn. BD10: B'frd 7E 46
Crofters Lea LS19: Yead 1K 47
Croft Fld. BD20: Sils 9E 12
Croftflat Dr. HD8: Fen B 6G 139
Croft Fold HX3: Hal 2M 97
Croft Foulds Ct. LS25: Gar 7N 71
Croft Gdns. HD2: Hud 1K 137
Croft Head HD8: Skelm 7D 156
LS20: Guis 7J 31
Croft Head La. WF1: Warm 4F 126
Croft Ho. HD9: Nether 9M 153
HX2: Lud 3D 96
HX5: Ell 4E 118
(off St Mary's Ga.)
Croft Ho. Av. LS27: Morl 8L 85
Croft Ho. Cl. BD6: B'frd 5N 81
LS27: Morl 7L 85
Croft Ho. Ct. LS28: Pud 6B 66
Croft Ho. Dr. LS21: Otley 8K 17
LS27: Morl 8L 85
Croft Ho. Fold LS29: Add 1N 13
Croft Ho. Gdns. LS27: Morl 8L 85
Croft Ho. Gro. LS27: Morl 8L 85
Croft Ho. La. BD20: Keigh 6G 27
HD1: Hud 3K 137
LS27: Morl 8L 85
Croft Ho. M. LS27: Morl 8L 85
Croft Ho. Mt. LS27: Morl 7L 85
Croft Ho. Ri. LS27: Morl 7L 85
Croft Ho. Rd. BD6: B'frd 5N 81
HD3: Scam 5K 135
LS27: Morl 8L 85
Croft Ho. Vw. LS27: Morl 8L 85
Croft Ho. Wlk. LS27: Morl 7L 85
Croft Ho. Way LS27: Morl 7L 85
Croftlands BD10: B'frd 7E 46
HD4: Hud 8M 137
WF5: Oss 6A 124
WF11: Knot 7F 110
WF12: Dew 9J 103
WF17: Bat 9J 103
Croft La. LS23: W'ton 5G 24
LS24: N Kym 2K 39
Croft Lea WF11: Cri S 4J 131
Croft Leigh Ct. BD5: B'frd 4E 82
Croft Mills Apartments *HX7: Heb B 1H 95*
(off Albert St.)
Croft Mill Yd. *HX7: Heb B 1H 95*
(off Albert St.)
CROFTON 2G 145
Crofton Cl. HD7: Linth 1C 152
Crofton Ct. *BD9: B'frd 2L 63*
(off Crofton Rd.)
WF4: Croft 2G 145
Crofton Ri. LS17: Shad 3B 52
Crofton Rd. BD9: B'frd 3M 63
Crofton Ter. LS17: Shad 3B 52
Croft Pk. LS29: Men 4D 30
Croft Pl. BD6: B'frd 4L 81
BD22: Cros R 7F 42
HD6: Brigh 8N 99
Croft Ri. HX3: Hal 2M 97
LS29: Men 4E 30
Croft Rd. BD16: Bgly 1C 44
BD20: E Mor 7C 28
LS23: B'ham 5C 38
Croft Row BD13: Denh 8L 61
Crofts, The HD8: Eml 2F 156
WF16: Heck 8C 102
Croft's Ct. LS1: Leeds 6E 4 (6D 68)
Croftside Cl. LS14: Leeds 3C 70
Croft St. BD5: B'frd 6B 6 (8C 64)
(not continuous)
BD6: B'frd 4A 82
BD10: B'frd 7G 46
BD11: B'haw 8L 83
(not continuous)
BD18: Ship 8N 45
BD20: Stee 3C 26
BD21: Keigh 1H 43
BD22: Haw 8C 42
HD1: Hud 5H 137
HD6: Brigh 1M 119
HX6: Sow B 8J 97
HX7: Heb B 1H 95
(off Hope St.)
LS21: Otley 1M 31
LS28: Fars 3A 66
WF13: Dew 3F 122
WF16: Heck 9A 102
Croft Ter. *BD22: Oak 5D 42*
(off Dockroyd La.)
LS12: N Far 2H 85
Croft Top HD3: Outl 2N 135
Croft Way LS29: Men 4E 30
Croftway LS15: Bar E 8M 53
Croisdale Cl. WF15: Liv 8J 101
Cromack Vw. LS28: Pud 7N 65
Cromarty Av. HD4: Hud 8H 137
Cromarty Dr. HD4: Hud 8H 137
Cromer Av. *BD21: Keigh 2H 43*
(off Foster Rd.)
Cromer Gro. BD21: Keigh 2H 43
Cromer Pl. LS2: Leeds 2B 4 (4C 68)
(not continuous)
Cromer Rd. BD21: Keigh 2H 43
LS2: Leeds 2B 4 (4C 68)
Cromer St. BD21: Keigh 2H 43
HX1: Hal 7M 97
LS2: Leeds 2B 4 (4C 68)
Cromer Ter. LS2: Leeds 3B 4 (5C 68)
Crompton Dr. LS27: Morl 7J 85
Cromwell Bottom Dr. HD6: Brigh 2H 119
Cromwell Bottom Nature Reserve 2J 119
Cromwell Cl. HX3: Sou 8F 98
WF11: B'ton 4C 110
Cromwell Ct. BD9: B'frd 1H 63
BD11: Drig 8A 84
DN6: Skel 8L 165
HD5: Hud 8D 138
Cromwell Cres. WF8: Pon 3L 129
Cromwell Gro. DN6: Skel 7M 165
Cromwell Hgts. LS9: Leeds 5K 5
Cromwell M. LS9: Leeds 4K 5 (5G 68)
Cromwell Mt. LS9: Leeds 4K 5 (5G 68)
LS10: Leeds 5F 86
WF8: Pon 1K 129
Cromwell Pl. WF5: Oss 4A 124
Cromwell Ri. LS25: Kip 5A 90
Cromwell Rd. HX3: Sou 8F 98
WF10: C'frd 5K 109
Cromwells Mt. HX2: Hal 5H 97
Cromwell St. LS9: Leeds 5K 5 (6G 68)
Cromwell Ter. HX1: Hal 3H 7 (5A 98)
(not continuous)
Cromwell Vw. HX3: Sou 8G 98
Cromwell Wood La. HD6: Brigh 1J 119
Cronkhill La. S71: Carl 8E 160
(Royston La.)
S71: Carl, Roys 7F 160
(Low Cronkhill La.)
Crooked La. BD10: B'frd 6D 46
HX3: Hal 7A 80
Crooke La. BD15: Wils 2B 62
Crookes La. S71: Carl 8C 160
Crook Farm Caravan Pk. BD17: Bail 4L 45
Crooklands *LS20: Guis 7J 31*
(off Kelcliffe La.)
Cropper Fold BD16: Bgly 1J 45
Cropper Ga. LS1: Leeds 6B 4 (6C 68)
Cropredy Cl. BD13: Que 4E 80
Cropstones LS23: B'ham 6D 38
Cropton Rd. S71: Roys 6C 160
Crosby Av. LS11: Leeds 1B 86
Crosby Pl. LS11: Leeds 9C 68
Crosby Rd. LS11: Leeds 1B 86
Crosby St. BD21: Keigh 8H 27
LS11: Leeds 9B 68
S72: Cud 9J 161
Crosby Ter. LS11: Leeds 9C 68
Crosby Vw. LS11: Leeds 9C 68
Croscombe Wlk. BD5: B'frd 7A 6 (9C 64)
Croset Av. HD1: Hud 3E 8 (3A 138)
Crosland Bank HD4: Neth 4F 152
Crosland Ct. HD3: Hud 1E 136
Crosland Edge HD9: Mel 4E 152
Crosland Factory La. HD4: Neth 4F 152
Crosland Heath Golf Course 9F 136
CROSLAND HILL 8G 137
Crosland Hill Rd. HD4: Hud 7G 136
CROSLAND MOOR 7G 137
Crosland Rd. HD1: Hud 6K 137
HD3: Hud 9E 118
Crosland Rd. Ind. Est. HD4: Neth 4G 152
Crosland Spring Rd. HD4: S Cros 3F 152
Crosland St. HD4: Hud 6K 137
Crosley Ho. BD16: Bgly 5F 44
Crosley Vw. BD16: Bgly 5G 45
Crosley Wood Rd. BD16: Bgly 5G 44
Cross, The HX4: Bark 6F 116
LS15: Bar E 8L 53
LS16: B'hpe 5G 33
WF12: T'hill 9G 123
Cross Albert Pl. LS12: Leeds 8N 67
Cross Arc. LS1: Leeds 6G 5
Cross Aston Gro. LS13: Leeds 4H 67
Cross Av. LS26: Rothw 6A 88
Cross Aysgarth Mt. LS9: Leeds 6M 5 (6H 69)
CROSS BANK 6E 102
Cross Bank Rd. WF17: Bat 6D 102
Crossbank Rd. LS29: Add 1J 13
Cross Banks BD18: Ship 8N 45
Cross Bank St. WF12: Dew 3G 123
WF14: Mir 8L 121
Cross Banstead St. LS8: Leeds 3H 69
Cross Bath Rd. LS13: Leeds 4F 66
Crossbeck Cl. LS29: I'ly 6G 15
Crossbeck Rd. LS29: I'ly 6G 15
Cross Belgrave St. LS2: Leeds 5G 5 (6E 68)
Cross Bellbrooke Av. *LS9: Leeds 4K 69*
(off Bellbrooke Av.)
Cross Bell St. LS9: Leeds 5J 5
Cross Bentley La. LS6: Leeds 9B 50
Cross Burley Lodge Rd. *LS6: Leeds 4A 68*
(off Broadway Av.)
Cross Cardigan Ter. LS4: Leeds 5M 67
Cross Catherine St. LS9: Leeds 7L 5 (7G 69)
Cross Chancellor St. LS6: Leeds 3D 68
Cross Chapel St. LS6: Leeds 1N 67
Cross Chestnut Gro. *LS6: Leeds 3A 68*
(off Chestnut Gro.)
Cross Chu. St. BD19: Cleck 5J 101
HD1: Hud 5J 137
(Church St.)
HD1: Hud 5C 8 (4N 137)
(Kirkgate)
Cross Cliff Rd. LS6: Leeds 2B 68
Cross Conway Mt. LS8: Leeds 3H 69
Cross Cotts. *HD1: Hud 3K 137*
(off Grasscroft Rd.)
Cross Cowper St. LS7: Leeds 3F 68
Cross Crown St. BD19: Cleck 5H 101
Crossdale Av. BD6: B'frd 5K 81
Cross Dawlish Gro. LS9: Leeds 6K 69
Cross Dikes Rd. HX6: Ripp 4A 116
Cross Easy Rd. LS9: Leeds 8M 5 (8H 69)
Cross Elford St. *LS8: Leeds 3H 69*
(off Elford Gro.)
Cross Emily St. BD21: Keigh 8J 27
Cross End Fold LS29: Add 1N 13
Cross Ends La. HX7: P Wel 1H 77
Cross Farm Ct. BD22: Oxen 3C 60
Cross Fld. HX4: Holy 7N 117
Crossfield Cl. BD22: Oxen 3B 60
Crossfield Ct. WF4: Over 4J 141
Crossfield Dr. DN6: Skel 7M 165
Crossfield Ho. Cl. DN6: Skel 7M 165
Crossfield La. DN6: Skel 8M 165
Crossfield Rd. BD22: Oxen 3B 60
Crossfields HD5: Hud 3C 138
WF4: Over 4K 141
Crossfields Cl. HX4: Gree 4A 118
Crossfield St. LS2: Leeds 1C 4 (3C 68)
Crossfield Ter. *WF4: Horb 1A 142*
(off Storrs Hill Rd.)
Cross Firs St. HD3: Hud 5G 137
CROSSFLATTS 1D 44
Cross Flatts Av. LS11: Leeds 3C 86
Cross Flatts Cres. LS11: Leeds 3B 86
Cross Flatts Dr. LS11: Leeds 2B 86
Cross Flatts Gro. LS11: Leeds 3B 86
Cross Flatts Mt. LS11: Leeds 3C 86
Cross Flatts Pde. LS11: Leeds 3B 86
Cross Flatts Pl. LS11: Leeds 3B 86
Cross Flatts Rd. LS11: Leeds 3B 86
Cross Flatts Row LS11: Leeds 3B 86
Crossflatts Station (Rail) 2D 44

Cross Flatts St.—Daisy Cft.

Cross Flatts St. LS11: Leeds 3B 86
Cross Flatts Ter. LS11: Leeds 3B 86
Cross Foundry St. WF13: Raven 6B 122
Cross Francis St. LS7: Leeds 3F 68
Crossgate LS21: Otley 1L 31
S75: Map 8K 159
Cross Ga. Rd. HD9: H'frth 6N 169
CROSS GATES 4D 70
Cross Gates Av. LS15: Leeds 3D 70
Cross Gates La. BD16: Har 3B 44
LS15: Leeds 3C 70
Cross Gates Rd. LS15: Leeds 4B 70
(not continuous)
Crossgates Shop. Cen. LS15: Leeds 4D 70
Cross Gates Station (Rail) 5D 70
Cross Glen Rd. LS16: Leeds 8M 49
Cross Granby Ter. LS6: Leeds 1N 67
Cross Grange Av. LS7: Leeds 3G 69
Cross Grasmere St. LS12: Leeds 7N 67
CROSS GREEN 9J 69
Cross Grn. BD4: B'frd 1J 83
LS21: Otley 9M 17
Cross Grn. App. LS9: Leeds 9J 69
Cross Grn. Av. LS9: Leeds 8H 69
Cross Grn. Cl. LS9: Leeds 9J 69
Cross Grn. Ct. LS9: Leeds 9K 69
Cross Grn. Cres. LS9: Leeds 8H 69
Cross Grn. Dr. HD5: Hud 4E 138
LS9: Leeds 9J 69
Cross Grn. Gth. LS9: Leeds 9J 69
Cross Grn. Gro. LS9: Leeds 8H 69
Cross Grn. Ind. Est. LS9: Leeds 9K 69
Cross Grn. Ind. Pk. LS9: Leeds 8L 69
Cross Grn. La. LS9: Leeds 8G 69
LS15: Leeds 6B 70
Cross Grn. Ri. LS9: Leeds 9J 69
Cross Grn. Rd. HD5: Hud 4E 138
LS9: Leeds 8H 69
Cross Grn. Row LS6: Leeds 8A 50
Cross Grn. Va. LS9: Leeds 1J 87
Cross Grn. Way LS9: Leeds 9J 69
Cross Greenwood Mt.
LS6: Leeds 8A 50
Cross Gro. St. HD1: Hud 6A 8 (5M 137)
Cross Hands La. WF4: Wrag 4B 146
Cross Hartley Av. *LS6: Leeds* *2C 68*
(off Lucas Pl.)
Cross Heath Gro. LS11: Leeds 2A 86
Cross Hgts. HD9: Scho 5A 170
Cross Henley Rd. LS13: Leeds 4F 66
CROSS HILL
HX4 4B 118
WF9 2D 162
Cross Hill DN6: Skel 8L 165
HX4: Gree 4B 118
LS11: Leeds 4A 86
S72: B'ley 6N 161
WF7: Ackw 1G 146
WF9: Hems 2D 162
WF11: B'ton 4B 110
Cross Hill Ct. DN6: Skel 7L 165
Cross Hill La. S72: S Hien 1M 161
WF15: Liv 2F 120
Cross Hills HX1: Hal 2L 7 (4B 98)
LS25: Kip 4A 90
Cross Hills Ct. LS25: Kip 4A 90
Cross Hills Dr. LS25: Kip 4A 90
Cross Hills Gdns. LS25: Kip 4A 90
Crosshills Mt. HX4: Gree 4B 118
Cross Hilton Gro. LS8: Leeds 1H 69
Cross Ho. Ct. BD12: O'haw 9E 82
Cross Ingledew Cres. LS8: Leeds 5K 51
Cross Ingram Rd. LS11: Leeds 9B 68
Crossings, The WF17: Bat 4C 102
Cross Kelso Rd. LS2: Leeds 3A 4 (5B 68)
Cross Keys WF5: Oss 4C 124
Cross Keys Ct. WF4: Horb 1D 142
Crossland Ct. *BD12: Wyke* *9A 82*
(off Carr Ho. La.)
LS11: Leeds 8C 68
Crossland Rd. LS27: Chur 6L 85
Crossland Ter. LS11: Leeds 2E 86
Cross La. BD7: B'frd 1N 81
(Cousen Pl.)
BD7: B'frd 2M 81
(Low Green)
BD11: B'haw 6M 83
BD13: Que 5B 80
BD15: Wils 9B 44
BD16: Bgly 3E 44
BD22: Oxen 3C 60
HD4: Hud 8M 137
HD4: Stock 7G 154
HD6: Clift 2C 120
HD8: Eml 1G 157
HD8: Kbtn, Shel 5L 155
HD8: Shep 2J 171
HD8: Skelm 8D 156
HD9: Hon 7K 153
HD9: Scho 5A 170
HX3: She 7F 80
(Brighouse & Denholme Gate Rd.)
HX3: She 9G 81
(West St.)
HX5: Ell 5D 118
LS12: Leeds 7L 67
(Privilege St.)
LS12: Leeds 9H 67
(Stonebridge La.)
LS20: Guis 4K 31
OL14: Tod 8A 94
S36: Hoy 8J 173
S71: Roys 6F 160
WF2: Wake 6H 125
Cross Lanes *HX7: Heb B* *9H 77*
(off Lee Wood Rd.)
Cross Lea Farm Rd. LS5: Leeds 8J 49
Cross Lee OL14: Tod 5H 93
Cross Leeds St. BD21: Keigh 9H 27
Cross Lee Ga. OL14: Tod 5H 93
Cross Lee Rd. OL14: Tod 5H 93
CROSSLEY 4M 121
Crossley Bri. BD22: Oxen 5D 60
Crossley Cl. HX1: Hal 2G 7
WF14: Mir 3L 121
Crossley Gdns. HX1: Hal 3G 7 (5N 97)
(Bowman Ter.)
HX1: Hal 2G 7 (4N 97)
(Halifax Ind. Cen.)
Crossley Gro. WF14: Mir 3L 121
CROSSLEY HALL 7K 63
Crossley Hall M. BD8: B'frd 7K 63
Crossley Hall St. BD8: B'frd 7J 63
Crossley Hill HX3: Hal 9C 98
Crossley Hill La. *HX3: Hal* *9C 98*
(off Westbourne Rd.)
Crossley Ho. *HX1: Hal* *3L 7*
(off Town Hall St. E.)
Crossley La. HD5: Hud, K'htn 3E 138
WF14: Mir 3L 121
Crossley New Rd. OL14: Tod 4N 93
Crossley Pl. HD7: Linth 1B 152
Crossley Retail Pk. HX1: Hal 2H 7 (4A 98)
Crossleys Bldgs. HX3: Hal 6D 98
Crossley St. BD7: B'frd 9N 63
BD13: Que 4E 80
HD6: Ras 2N 119
HX1: Hal 3K 7 (5B 98)
LS22: Weth 4M 23
OL14: Tod 7K 93
WF1: Warm 5G 126
WF4: N Sha 5G 126
WF7: F'stne 6D 128
WF15: Liv 1N 121
Crossley Ter. *HX7: Heb B* *1H 95*
(off Commercial St.)
WF17: Bat 9F 102
Crossley Ter. Nth. HX3: Hal 9N 79
Crossley Ter. Sth. HX3: Hal 9N 79
Crossley Vw. WF14: Mir 3M 121
Crossley Wing HX1: Hal 8J 7
Cross Lidgett Pl. LS8: Leeds 7H 51
Cross Lister St. *BD21: Keigh* *1G 43*
(off Lister St.)
Cross Louis St. LS7: Leeds 3F 68
Crossman Dr. WF6: Norm 9K 107
Cross Maude St. LS2: Leeds 7H 5
Cross Mitford Rd. LS12: Leeds 7N 67
Cross Moor Cl. BD20: Sils 8C 12
Cross Mt. St. WF17: Bat 9F 102
Cross Myrtle St. LS11: Leeds 9E 68
Cross Normanton St. WF4: Horb 2E 142
Cross Osmondthorpe La. LS9: Leeds 6L 69
Cross Pk. Av. WF10: C'frd 5F 108
Cross Pk. St. LS15: Leeds 6B 70
WF4: Horb 1C 142
WF12: Dew 3J 123
WF17: Bat 7G 102
Cross Peel St. LS27: Morl 9L 85
Cross Pipes Rd. WF2: Wake 3G 124
Cross Pl. *HD6: Brigh* *8N 99*
(off Cross St.)
Cross Platts HX3: Sou 8H 99
Cross Quarry St. LS6: Leeds 2C 68
Cross Queen St. WF6: Norm 1H 127
Cross Regent Pk. Av. *LS6: Leeds* *2B 68*
(off Regent Pk. Av.)
Cross Reginald Mt. LS7: Leeds 2F 68
Cross Rink St. WF17: Bat 9G 102
Cross River St. *BD21: Keigh* *7L 27*
(off Dale St.)
Cross Rd. BD8: B'frd 5N 63
BD10: B'frd 7G 46
BD12: O'haw 8D 82
LS18: Hors 7D 48
WF4: Hol 7H 143
WF4: M'twn 3L 141
WF12: T'hill 9F 122
CROSS ROADS 7E 42
Cross Roads BD22: Cros R 7F 42
HX3: She 9G 81
Cross Roseville Rd. *LS8: Leeds* *3G 69*
(off Bayswater Rd.)
Cross Rosse St. BD18: Ship 7N 45
Cross Roundhay Av. LS8: Leeds 1H 69
Cross Row LS15: Swil C 8H 71
Cross Rydal St. BD21: Keigh 1G 43
Cross Ryecroft St. WF5: Oss 4M 123
Cross St Michaels La. LS6: Leeds 2N 67
Cross Speedwell St. LS6: Leeds 3D 68
Cross Sq. WF1: Wake 4J 9 (5L 125)
Cross Stamford St. LS7: Leeds 3J 5 (5F 68)
CROSS STONE 6M 93
Cross Stone Fold OL14: Tod 6M 93
Cross Stone Rd. OL14: Tod 6L 93
Cross St. BD6: B'frd 6L 81
BD12: O'haw 9E 82
BD14: Clay 1H 81
HD4: Hud 6K 137
HD6: Brigh 8M 99
HD7: Slait 9N 135
HD9: Hon 5L 153
HX1: Hal 5M 7 (6C 98)
(Blackledge)
HX1: Hal 3L 7 (5B 98)
(Winding Rd.)
HX4: Gree 4C 118
HX4: Holy 7A 118
LS15: Leeds 6B 70
LS22: Weth 4M 23
LS26: Rothw 8N 87
WF1: Wake 4J 9 (5L 125)
WF3: E Ard 4G 104
WF4: Horb 1D 142
WF5: Oss 2M 123
WF8: Pon 3K 129
WF9: Hems 2C 162
WF9: Upt 1C 164
WF10: C'frd 4B 108
(Pottery St.)
WF10: C'frd 4C 108
(Wilson St.)
WF12: Dew 4G 122
(Wharf St.)
WF12: Dew 3G 123
(Woodville Rd.)
WF15: Liv 1L 121
WF17: Bat 7G 102
Cross St. W. HX2: Hal 4L 97
Cross Sun St. BD1: B'frd 2C 6 (6D 64)
Cross Ter. LS26: Rothw 8N 87
Crossthwaite Ct. WF8: Pon 2K 129
Cross Valley Dr. LS15: Leeds 5C 70
Cross Vw. BD22: Oak 4D 42
Cross Vs. HX4: Bark 7F 116
Crossway BD16: Cot 8E 44
Crossways, The LS21: Otley 7L 17
Cross Wellington St. BD1: B'frd 3D 6
Cross Wells Rd. HX6: Ripp 6B 116
Cross Westfield Rd. LS3: Leeds 4A 4
Cross Wingham St. LS7: Leeds 1J 5 (4F 68)
Cross Woodstock St. *LS2: Leeds* *1D 4*
(off Blenheim Wlk.)
Cross Woodview St. *LS11: Leeds* *3D 86*
(off Woodview St.)
Cross York St. LS2: Leeds 7H 5 (7F 68)
Crowcrowns La. WF8: Pon 1A 130
Crowgill Rd. BD18: Ship 7N 45
Crow Hill End Rd. HX6: Tri 1N 115
Crow Hill Rd. HX6: Tri 2N 115
HX7: Crag V 9N 95
Crowhurst Gdns. HD6: Brigh 6L 99
Crow La. HD3: Hud 5F 136
LS21: Otley 1L 31
Crow La. M. *LS21: Otley* *1L 31*
(off Crow La.)
Crowlees Cl. WF14: Mir 6M 121
Crowlees Gdns. WF14: Mir 6M 121
Crowlees Rd. WF14: Mir 6L 121
Crown & Anchor Yd. WF8: Pon 3J 129
Crown Bldgs. *HD8: Clay W* *6J 157*
(off Scott Hill)
Crown Cl. WF12: Dew 4K 123
Crown Ct. LS2: Leeds 7G 5 (7E 68)
WF1: Wake *4J 9*
(off Chancery La.)
Crown Dr. BD12: Wyke 9A 82
CROW NEST 4F 44
Crow Nest Cotts. HX3: Hip 5K 99
Crow Nest Ct. *WF14: Mir* *6K 121*
(off York Rd.)
Crow Nest Dr. LS11: Leeds 3A 86
Crow Nest La. LS11: Leeds 3N 85
Crownest La. BD16: Bgly 3F 44
Crow Nest M. LS11: Leeds 3A 86
Crow Nest Pk. Golf Course 6L 99
Crow Nest Rd. HX7: Heb B 2J 95
Crownest Rd. BD16: Bgly 4F 44
Crow Nest Ter. *WF13: Dew* *4E 122*
(off High St.)
Crow Nest Vw. WF13: Dew 4D 122
Crown Flatt Way WF12: Dew 2H 123
Crown Grn. HD4: Hud 6F 136
Crownlands La. WF5: Oss 5N 123
Crown La. HD9: H'frth 3M 169
CROWN POINT 8H 5 (7F 68)
Crown Point HX7: Hept 8F 76
Crown Point Cl. WF5: Oss 5M 123
Crown Point Dr. WF5: Oss 5M 123
Crown Point Retail Pk. LS10: Leeds 8E 68
Crown Point Rd. LS2: Leeds 8H 5 (7F 68)
LS9: Leeds 8H 5 (7F 68)
LS10: Leeds 8G 5 (8E 68)
WF5: Oss 5M 123
Crown Rd. HX3: Hal 2A 98
Crown Sq. HD3: Hud 5G 137
Crown St. BD1: B'frd 7A 64
BD12: Wyke 9A 82
BD19: Cleck 5H 101
HD6: Brigh 9M 99
HD8: Clay W 8G 157
HD9: Hon 4L 153
HX1: Hal 4K 7 (5B 98)
HX5: Ell 4E 118
HX7: Heb B 1H 95
LS2: Leeds 7G 5 (7E 68)
LS29: Burl W 8D 16
WF5: Oss 8A 124
Crown St. Bldg. *LS2: Leeds* *7G 5*
(off Crown St.)
Crown Ter. HD8: Clay W 6J 157
Crown Vs. *HD8: Clay W* *8G 157*
(off Crown St.)
Crown Yd. WF9: S Kirk 6K 163
Crowther Av. LS28: Cal 9K 47
Crowther Bruce Mill Rd. HD7: Mars 5G 150
Crowther Cl. HD7: Slait 8N 135
Crowther Fold BD16: Har 6A 44
Crowther Pl. LS6: Leeds 3D 68
WF10: C'frd 5D 108
Crowther Rd. WF14: Mir 6K 121
WF16: Heck 7B 102
Crowthers St. BD12: Wyke 9A 82
Crowther St. BD10: B'frd 8H 47
BD19: Cleck 4H 101
HD1: Hud 6D 8 (5N 137)
(Firth St.)
HD1: Hud 7L 137
(Lockwood Rd.)
WF10: C'frd 5C 108
WF17: Bat 7C 102
Crowthers Yd. LS28: Pud 8B 66
Crowther Ter. HX7: Heb B 9F 76
Crow Tree Cl. BD17: Bail 4B 46
Crow Tree La. BD8: B'frd 5K 63
Crowtrees Ct. LS19: Raw 3N 47
Crowtrees Cres. HD6: Ras 3L 119
Crowtrees La. HD6: Ras 4L 119
Crowtrees Pde. *HD6: Ras* *4L 119*
(off Crowtrees La.)
Crow Trees Pk. LS19: Raw 3M 47
Crowtrees Pk. HD6: Ras 4L 119
Crow Trees Rd. HD7: Slait 3H 151
Crow Wood La. HX4: Holy 9J 117
Crow Wood Pk. HX2: Hal 7K 97
Croxall Dr. WF3: S'ley 7N 105
Croydon Rd. BD7: B'frd 1L 81
Croydon St. BD13: Que 4D 80
LS11: Leeds 8B 68
Crozier Ho. LS10: Leeds 8F 68
Crumack La. BD22: Oxen 3E 60
Crummock Pl. WF11: Knot 1D 130
Crunwelle Ct. BD15: All 2F 62
Cryer Mdws. BD22: Haw 7D 42
Crystal Ct. HX1: Hal 3G 7
Crystal Pl. WF1: Wake 5M 9 (5M 125)
Crystal Ter. BD4: B'frd 2G 83
Cubley Av. WF2: Wake 4K 143
Cuckoo La. HD9: Hon 5L 153
Cuckoo Nest BD7: B'frd 7A 64
BD16: Har 5B 44
Cuckoo Nest Ind. Est. BD7: B'frd 7A 64
Cuckoo Pk. La. BD22: Oxen 2E 60
Cuckoo's Nest Halt Station
Kirklees Light Railway 7F 156
Cuckstool Rd. HD8: Den D 2D 172
Cudbear St. LS10: Leeds 8H 5 (8F 68)
CUDWORTH 9J 161
Cudworth Parkway S72: Cud 9H 161
CULLINGWORTH 9K 43
Cullingworth Bldgs. BD21: Keigh 8H 43
Cullingworth Ga. BD13: Cull 1K 61
Cullingworth Rd. BD13: Cull 1K 61
Cullingworth St. WF13: Dew 9D 102
Culpans Rd. HX2: Lud F 8A 96
Culver St. HX1: Hal 3L 7 (5B 98)
Culvert BD12: Wyke 4N 99
Cumberland Av. HD2: Fix 6M 119
Cumberland Cl. HX2: Illing 9L 79
Cumberland Ct. HX2: Illing 1L 97
LS6: Leeds 3N 67
Cumberland Rd. BD7: B'frd 9M 63
LS6: Leeds 2B 68
WF10: C'frd 2L 109
CUMBERWORTH 5G 171
Cumberworth La. HD8: Bird E, Up C 3J 171
HD8: Den D, Lwr C 1B 172
HD8: Lwr C, Up C 2M 171
Cumberworth Rd. HD8: Skelm 8C 156
Cumbrian Way WF2: Wake 8G 124
Cuniver Ct. WF15: Liv 7G 101
Cunliffe La. BD17: Esh 2F 46
Cunliffe Rd. BD8: B'frd 4A 64
LS29: I'ly 5G 14
Cunliffe Ter. BD8: B'frd 4B 64
Cunliffe Vs. BD8: B'frd 3B 64
Cunningham Ct. WF3: Rob H 9J 87
Cupstone Cl. BD20: E Mor 7C 28
Cure Hill BD22: Oak 4B 42
Curlew Cl. LS29: I'ly 5D 14
WF10: C'frd 6D 108
Curlew Ct. BD20: Stee 2B 26
Curlew Ri. LS27: Morl 1N 103
Curlew St. BD5: B'frd 2A 82
Curly Hill LS29: I'ly 3F 14
Currer Av. BD4: B'frd 4F 82
Currerbell M. BD13: Thorn 8E 62
Currer Gro. WF10: C'frd 6M 107
Currer St. BD1: B'frd 4C 6 (7D 64)
BD12: O'haw 9E 82
Currer Wlk. BD20: Stee 2B 26
Curtis Ct. *BD13: Cull* *9K 43*
(off Halifax Rd.)
Curwen Cres. WF16: Heck 7B 102
Curzon Rd. BD3: B'frd 7F 64
(not continuous)
Curzon St. HD2: Hud 5E 120
Cusworth Cl. HX1: Hal 4M 97
Cuthberts Cl. BD13: Que 5C 80
Cut La. HX3: North 8E 80
CUTLER HEIGHTS 2G 83
Cutler Hgts. La. BD4: B'frd 2G 83
Cutler La. LS26: Meth 1M 107
Cutler Pl. BD4: B'frd 1H 83
Cut Rd. WF11: B'ton 3B 110
WF11: Fair 9N 91
CUTSYKE 6C 108
Cutsyke Av. WF10: C'frd 6B 108
Cutsyke Crest WF10: C'frd 6B 108
Cutsyke Hill WF10: C'frd 6B 108
Cutsyke Rd. WF7: F'stne 9B 108
WF10: C'frd 8B 108
Cutsyke Wlk. WF10: C'frd 7C 108
Cutting, The HD9: Brock 7A 154
Cuttlehurst HD8: Clay W 9G 156
Cutts Fld. Vw. S71: Roys 4C 160
Cyndor Ct. WF10: C'frd 6L 109
Cypress Ct. HX3: She 6K 81
WF2: Wake 9J 125
Cypress Fold HD8: Lept 7J 139
Cypress Ho. *WF10: C'frd* *5E 108*
(off Parklands)
Cypress Point LS7: Leeds 3H 5
Cypress Rd. WF6: Norm 3J 127
Cyprus Av. BD10: B'frd 6D 46
WF1: Wake 3J 125
Cyprus Cres. WF14: Mir 4A 122
Cyprus Dr. BD10: B'frd 6E 46
Cyprus Gro. LS25: Gar 7M 71
WF1: Wake 3J 125
Cyprus Mt. WF1: Wake 1G 9 (3J 125)
Cyprus Rd. LS25: Gar 7M 71
Cyprus St. WF1: Wake 1G 9 (3K 125)
WF5: Oss 3M 123
Cyprus Ter. LS25: Gar 7M 71
Czar St. LS11: Leeds 9C 68

D

Dacre Av. WF2: Wake 7E 124
Dacre Cl. WF15: Liv 7K 101
Dacre Ct. LS24: Saxt 9N 55
Dacre St. BD3: B'frd 1E 6 (6D 64)
Daffels Wood Cl. BD4: B'frd 5F 82
Daffil Av. LS27: Chur 6L 85
Daffil Grange M. LS27: Morl 6L 85
Daffil Grange Way LS27: Morl 6L 85
Daffil Gro. LS27: Chur 6L 85
Daffil Rd. LS27: Chur 6L 85
Daffodil Ct. BD15: All 6G 63
Dahl Dr. WF10: C'frd 7J 109
Daily Ct. BD5: B'frd 2N 81
Dairies, The WF6: Norm 9K 107
Daisy Bank HX1: Hal 8J 7 (7A 98)
HX3: Nor G 2M 99
HX7: Heb B 1K 95
Daisy Bank St. OL14: Tod 3D 92
Daisy Cl. WF17: Birs 2B 102
Daisy Cft. BD20: Sils 8F 12

Daisyfield Grange—Dell Av.

Daisyfield Grange *LS13: Leeds* 5G 66
(off Rossefield App.)
Daisyfield Rd. LS13: Leeds 4G 66
Daisy Fold WF9: Upt 2M 163
Daisy Grn. HD7: Linth 2B 152
DAISY HILL
BD9 4K 63
LS27 8M 85
Daisy Hill BD12: Wyke 1A 100
BD20: Sils 8F 12
LS27: Morl 8M 85
WF13: Dew 3F 122
Daisy Hill Av. LS27: Morl 7M 85
Daisy Hill Bk. La. BD9: B'frd 4K 63
Daisy Hill Cl. HX2: Lud F 5D 96
LS27: Morl 7L 85
Daisy Hill Gro. BD9: B'frd 4K 63
Daisy Hill La. BD9: B'frd 4K 63
Daisy La. *HD9: H'frth* 3M 169
(off Holmfirth Town Ga.)
WF3: E Ard 4H 105
Daisy Lea *HD3: Outl* 2N 135
(off New Hey Rd.)
HX6: Sow B 8F 96
Daisy Lea La. HD3: Hud 1G 137
Daisy Lee La. HD9: Had E 9A 170
Daisy Mt. HX6: Sow B 7G 97
Daisy Pl. *BD18: Ship* 7L 45
(off Saltaire Rd.)
Daisy Rd. HD6: Ras 2N 119
Daisy Row LS13: Leeds 5G 66
Daisy Royd HD4: Hud 8M 137
Daisy St. BD7: B'frd 2M 81
BD22: Haw 7E 42
HD6: Brigh 1M 119
HX1: Hal 5H 7 (6A 98)
Daisy Va. M. WF3: Thpe H 3G 104
Daisy Va. Ter. WF3: Thpe H 3G 104
Daisy Way WF10: C'frd 7B 108
Dalby Av. BD3: B'frd 5G 65
Dalby Ct. BD19: Gom 5M 101
Dalby St. BD3: B'frd 6G 65
Dalby Way LS10: Leeds 9G 86
Dalcross Gro. BD5: B'frd 1D 82
Dalcross St. BD5: B'frd 1C 82
Dale, The LS25: Aber 6E 54
Dale Av. OL14: Tod 7M 93
Dale Cl. HD8: Den D 3C 172
LS20: Guis 8F 30
WF5: Oss 5A 124
WF17: Bat 1F 122
Dale Ct. HD9: H'frth 2N 169
WF5: Oss 5N 123
WF8: Pon 6K 129
Dale Cres. BD20: Stee 3C 26
Dale Cft. HD8: Skelm 7D 156
LS25: Gar 6M 71
LS29: I'ly 5D 14
Dale Cft. Ri. BD15: All 4E 62
Dalecroft Rd. DN6: Carc 9N 165
Dalefield Av. WF6: Norm 2J 127
Dalefield Rd. WF6: Norm 2H 127
Dalefield Way WF6: Norm 3J 127
Dale Gth. BD17: Bail 4N 45
Dale Gro. BD10: B'frd 6C 46
Dale La. WF9: S Elm 4A 164
WF16: Heck 7A 102
Dale La. Ent. Zone WF9: S Elm 5A 164
Dale M. WF8: Pon 6K 129
Dale Pk. Av. LS16: Leeds 3G 49
Dale Pk. Cl. LS16: Leeds 3G 48
Dale Pk. Gdns. LS16: Leeds 3G 49
Dale Pk. Ri. LS16: Leeds 3G 48
Dale Pk. Vw. LS16: Leeds 3G 49
Dale Pk. Wlk. LS16: Leeds 3G 48
Dale Rd. BD11: Drig 4D 84
Dales Bank Holiday Pk. BD20: Sils 4D 12
Dales Dr. LS20: Guis 8F 30
Daleside HX4: Gree 4N 117
OL14: Tod 8J 93
WF12: T'hill 1F 140
Daleside Av. HD9: New M 1A 170
LS28: Pud 6L 65
Daleside Cl. LS28: Pud 5K 65
Daleside Gro. BD12: O'haw 9D 82
LS28: Pud 6L 65
Dale Side Ho. BD8: B'frd 4B 64
Daleside Rd. BD18: Ship 6C 46
BD20: Rid 7N 27
LS28: Pud 5K 65
Daleside Wlk. BD5: B'frd 3D 82
Daleson Cl. HX3: North 1F 98
Dale Stone Cl. WF11: B'ton 3B 110
Dale St. BD1: B'frd 3B 6 (7C 64)
BD18: Ship 8N 45
BD21: Keigh 7L 27
HD1: Hud 7B 8 (5M 137)
HD3: Hud 4F 136
HD8: Skelm 7D 156
HX6: Sow B 8H 97
OL14: Tod 7K 93
WF5: Oss 5N 123
WF12: Dew 6E 122
Dale St. Nth. HX3: Hal 3C 98
Dales Way LS20: Guis 8F 30
Dalesway BD16: Bgly 2G 45
Dale Ter. *HX6: Sow B* 8H 97
(off Greenups Ter.)
Dale Vw. BD11: Drig 7C 84
BD20: Sils 7E 12
BD20: Stee 3C 26
HX2: Lud F 5D 96
HX7: Myth 4M 95
LS29: I'ly 5D 14
WF8: Pon 6K 129
WF9: Hems 3F 162
Dale Vw. Cl. BD21: Keigh 2J 43
Daleview Ct. BD17: Bail 5M 45
Dale Vw. Gro. BD21: Keigh 1L 43
Dale Vw. Rd. BD21: Keigh 2L 43
Dale Vw. Way BD21: Keigh 1L 43
Dale Vs. LS18: Hors 8G 49
WF10: C'frd 5J 109
Dale Wlk. WF7: F'stne 7C 128
Dallam Av. BD18: Ship 7K 45
Dallam Gro. BD18: Ship 6K 45
Dallam Rd. BD18: Ship 7K 45
Dallam Wlk. BD18: Ship 6K 45
Dalmeny Av. HD4: Hud 8H 137
Dalmeny Cl. HD4: Hud 7H 137
DALTON 3D 138
Dalton Av. LS11: Leeds 3C 86
Dalton Bank Rd. HD5: Hud 1E 138
Dalton Clowes HD5: Hud 3C 138
DALTON FOLD 2F 8 (3B 138)
Dalton Fold Rd. HD5: Hud 3B 138
DALTON GREEN 4E 138
Dalton Grn. La. HD5: Hud 3E 138
Dalton Gro. HD5: Hud 3C 138
LS11: Leeds 3C 86
Dalton La. BD21: Keigh 9K 27
LS23: B'ham 6M 37
Dalton Mills Bus. Complex BD21: Keigh 9K 27
Dalton Rd. BD21: Keigh 9L 27
LS11: Leeds 3C 86
Dalton St. HX6: Sow B 7H 97
OL14: Tod 7K 93
Dalton Ter. BD8: B'frd 6N 63
BD21: Keigh 8L 27
(off Sussex St.)
WF10: C'frd 5D 108
Dalton Wlk. DN6: Burg 4N 165
Damask St. HX1: Hal 2J 7 (4A 98)
Damems BD22: Keigh 5F 42
Damems La. BD22: Keigh 5F 42
Damems Rd. BD21: Keigh 5G 42
Damems Station
Keighley & Worth Valley Railway 5G 42
Damfield M. HD4: Hud 8L 137
DAM HEAD 1D 98
Dam Head HD9: Holm 6J 169
Dam Head La. HD8: Lept 4K 139
Dam Head Rd. HX6: Sow B 7J 97
Dam Hill HD8: Kbtn, Shel 6H 155
Dam La. LS19: Yead 9N 31
LS24: Saxt 8M 55
Damon Av. BD10: B'frd 2J 65
Dampier St. OL14: W'den 2J 113
Damside BD21: Keigh 1H 43
Damside Rd. HD4: Hud 8C 8 (6M 137)
Damson Cl. HX6: Sow B 9H 97
Damson Ct. BD14: Clay 2H 81
Damson Pl. HX1: Hal 6M 97
Dam Top HX6: Ripp 7D 116
Danby Av. BD4: B'frd 5F 82
Danby Ct. WF3: Rob H 9J 87
Danby La. WF2: New, Wake 6L 143
Danby Wlk. LS9: Leeds 7M 5 (7H 69)
Dancroft BD22: Haw 9C 42
Dandelion Cl. WF10: C'frd 7B 108
Dando Way WF7: Ackw 6D 146
Dandy Mill Av. WF8: Pon 1M 129
Dandy Mill Ct. WF8: Pon 1M 129
Dandy Mill Cft. WF8: Pon 1M 129
Dandy Mill Vw. WF8: Pon 1M 129
Danebury Rd. HD6: Ras 2N 119
Danecourt Rd. BD4: B'frd 2J 83
Danefield Ter. LS21: Otley 9M 17
Dane Hill Dr. BD4: B'frd 1J 83
Danehurst WF8: Pon 3K 129
Danella Cres. WF2: Wren 1H 125
Danella Gro. WF2: Wren 1H 125
Danes La. WF4: M'twn 4L 141
Danesleigh Dr. WF4: M'twn 4L 141
Daniel Cl. BD21: Keigh 4G 43
Daniel Ct. BD4: B'frd 3K 83
Daniel St. BD3: B'frd 7H 65
Dan La. BD6: B'frd 4H 81
(not continuous)
Danny La. HX2: Lud F 5D 96
Dansk Way LS29: I'ly 4J 15
Danum Dr. BD17: Bail 5A 46
Danum Ter. HX3: North 1F 98
Darbyfields HD7: Golc 4D 136
Darby Way WF10: All B 9C 90
Darcey Hey La. HX2: Hal 7L 97
Darcy Ct. LS15: Leeds 6D 70
Darfield Av. LS8: Leeds 3J 69
Darfield Cres. LS8: Leeds 3J 69
Darfield Gro. LS8: Leeds 3H 69
Darfield Pl. LS8: Leeds 3J 69
Darfield Rd. LS8: Leeds 3J 69
Darfield St. BD1: B'frd 2A 6 (6B 64)
LS8: Leeds 3J 69
Darfield Vs. *LS8: Leeds* 4J 69
(off Darfield Cres.)
Darkfield La. WF8: Pon 8M 109
Dark Future Laser Quest
Huddersfield 2A 8 (2M 137)
Dark La. BD22: Oak 7N 41
BD22: Oxen 3C 60
HD4: Hud 8E 138
HD7: Mars 4B 150
HD8: Den D 2C 172
HX2: Hal 6H 97
HX3: Hip 5F 98
HX3: Sou 8G 99
HX6: Ripp 8A 116
HX7: Blac H 1D 94
HX7: Cold 6N 75
HX7: Myth 2N 95
LS15: Bar E 6L 53
LS21: Stainb 4G 18
WF8: Pon 4J 129
WF17: Bat 8E 102
WF17: Birs 1C 102
Dark Neville St. LS1: Leeds 8E 4
Darkwood Cl. LS17: Leeds 3J 51
Darkwood Way LS17: Leeds 3J 51
Darley Av. LS10: Leeds 6F 86
Darley Mall BD1: B'frd 4B 6
Darley Rd. WF15: Liv 7K 101
Darley St. BD1: B'frd 3A 6 (7C 64)
(not continuous)
BD20: Keigh 7H 27
WF16: Heck 8A 102
Darnay La. BD5: B'frd 2C 82
Darnes Av. HX2: Hal 7L 97
Darning La. WF8: Thpe A 5A 148
Darnley Av. WF2: Wake 4J 125
Darnley Cl. HD9: Mel 8D 152
Darnley La. LS15: Leeds 8D 70
Darnley Rd. LS16: Leeds 8L 49
Darren St. BD4: B'frd 8J 65
DARRINGTON 6B 130
Darrington Rd. WF8: E Hard 1L 147
Dartmouth Av. HD5: Hud 7E 138
LS27: Morl 2K 103
Dartmouth M. LS27: Morl 1J 103
Dartmouth St. HD7: Slait 9M 135
Dartmouth Ter. BD8: B'frd 4A 64
HD4: Farn T 2C 154
Dartmouth Way LS11: Leeds 3E 86
DARTON 8G 159
Darton Bus. Pk. S75: Dart 9G 159
Darton Common Sports Cen. 9D 158
Darton Hall Cl. S75: Dart 8H 159
Darton Hall Dr. S75: Dart 8H 159
Darton La. S75: Dart, Map 9H 159
Darton Station (Rail) 8G 158
Darwin St. BD5: B'frd 2A 82
Daughter's Ct. WF5: Oss 5E 124
Davey La. HX7: Blac H 1A 94
David La. WF13: Dew 1F 122
David Lloyd Leisure
Leeds 5D 50
David St. LS11: Leeds 8D 4 (8D 68)
WF1: Wake 7N 125
Davies Av. LS8: Leeds 7H 51
Davis Av. WF10: C'frd 6K 109
Davy Cotts. HX7: Blac H 1A 94
Davy Rd. WF10: All B 9C 90
Dawes Av. WF10: C'frd 6F 108
DAW GREEN 3E 122
Daw Green Av. WF4: Crig 6G 142
Daw Knowle HD5: K'htn 2G 138
Daw La. WF4: Crig 7F 142
WF4: Horb 2D 142
Dawlish Av. LS9: Leeds 6K 69
Dawlish Cres. LS9: Leeds 6K 69
Dawlish Gro. LS9: Leeds 7K 69
Dawlish Mt. LS9: Leeds 6K 69
Dawlish Pl. LS9: Leeds 6K 69
Dawlish Rd. LS9: Leeds 6K 69
Dawlish Row LS9: Leeds 6K 69
Dawlish St. LS9: Leeds 6K 69
Dawlish Ter. LS9: Leeds 6K 69
Dawlish Wlk. LS9: Leeds 6K 69
Dawnay Rd. BD5: B'frd 2N 81
Daw Royds HD5: Hud 5E 138
Dawslack *BD20: Keigh* 5G 27
(off Parker's La.)
Dawson Av. BD6: B'frd 5A 82
Dawson Gdns. *WF13: Dew* 3E 122
(off Vulcan Rd.)
Dawson Hill LS27: Morl 8K 85
Dawson Hill Yd. WF4: Horb 1D 142
Dawson La. BD4: B'frd 4G 83
(Dawson Mt.)
BD4: B'frd 3B 84
(Keeper La.)
LS26: Rothw 7N 87
Dawson Mt. BD4: B'frd 4G 83
Dawson Pl. BD4: B'frd 4H 83
BD21: Keigh 2J 43
Dawson Rd. BD21: Keigh 2J 43
HD4: Hud 7N 137
LS11: Leeds 2C 86
Dawsons Cnr. LS28: Stan 4N 65
Dawsons Ct. LS14: Leeds 2C 70
Dawsons Mdw. LS28: Stan 4N 65
Dawsons Ter. LS28: Stan 4N 65
Dawson St. BD4: B'frd 3G 83
BD10: B'frd 5F 46
LS28: Stan 5A 66
WF3: Ting 3N 103
Dawsons Yd. LS21: Otley 1K 31
Dawson Ter. BD4: B'frd 4H 83
Dawson Way BD21: Keigh 2J 43
Dawtrie Cl. WF10: C'frd 5K 109
(not continuous)
Dawtrie St. WF10: C'frd 4K 109
Daykin Cl. S75: Kex 9F 158
Day St. HD1: Hud 6E 8 (5A 138)
WF13: Raven 6B 122
Deacon Cl. BD2: B'frd 4H 65
HD9: Mel 7D 152
Deaconess Ct. LS29: I'ly 6G 14
Deacons Wlk. WF16: Heck 8B 102
Deadmanstone HD4: Hud 1L 153
Dealburn Rd. BD12: Low M 8C 82
Deal La. HD7: Golc 6C 136
Deal St. BD21: Keigh 8L 27
HX1: Hal 5M 7 (6C 98)
Dean Av. HD9: Nether 9L 153
LS8: Leeds 9J 51
Dean Beck Av. BD6: B'frd 4C 82
Dean Beck Ct. BD6: B'frd 4D 82
Dean Bottom HD8: Kbtn 2H 155
Dean Bri. La. HD9: H'wth 5B 170
Dean Brook Rd. HD4: Arm B 1K 153
HD9: Nether, T'bdge 9L 153
Dean Cl. BD8: B'frd 5J 63
WF2: Wren 1H 125
Dean Clough 1K 7 (4B 98)
Dean Clough HX3: Hal 2K 7 (4B 98)
Dean Clough Galleries 1K 7
(within Dean Clough)
Dean Clough Office Pk. HX3: Hal 1J 7 (4A 98)
Dean Ct. HX3: Hal 1N 117
LS8: Leeds 9J 51
Dean Edge Rd. BD22: Old 7G 41
Dean End HX4: Gree 3B 118
Deanery Gdns. BD10: B'frd 1G 65
Deanfield Av. LS27: Morl 8J 85
Dean Fold HD8: Kbtn 1H 155
Dean Hall Cl. LS27: Morl 9J 85
Dean Head LS18: Hors 8D 32
OL15: Lit 8M 113
Dean Hey Country Bus. Pk.
HX7: Crag V 6L 95
Deanhouse HD9: Nether 9L 153
Dean Ho. La. HX2: Lud 2D 96
HX4: Stainl 2J 135
Deanhurst Gdns. LS27: Gil 7G 85
Deanhurst Ind. Cen. LS27: Gil 7G 85
Dean La. BD13: Thorn 5B 62
BD22: Oak 1M 41
HD9: H'wth 8B 170
HX6: Sow B 1E 116
HX6: Tri 3E 116
LS18: Hors, Yead 8D 32
LS20: Hawk 8D 30
Dean La. Head BD13: Thorn 5B 62
Dean M. LS18: Hors 8E 32
Dean Pk. Av. BD11: Drig 6B 84
Dean Pk. Dr. BD11: Drig 6B 84
Dean Pastures BD11: Drig 7B 84
Dean Rd. BD6: B'frd 5B 82
HD9: H'frth, U'thng 3G 168
Deanroyd Rd. OL14: W'den 4K 113
Deans Ct. WF8: Pon 2K 129
Deans Laithe BD21: Keigh 9K 27
Dean's Ter. HX3: Hal 1A 98
Deanstones Cres. BD13: Que 5D 80
Deanstones La. BD13: Que 5C 80
Dean St. BD22: Haw 8D 42
HD3: Hud 2G 137
HX4: Gree 5B 118
HX5: Ell 5E 118
LS29: I'ly 4H 15
Deansway LS27: Morl 7J 85
Deanswood Cl. LS17: Leeds 4C 50
Deanswood Dr. LS17: Leeds 4B 50
Deanswood Gdns. LS17: Leeds 4B 50
Deanswood Gth. LS17: Leeds 4C 50
Deanswood Grn. LS17: Leeds 4B 50
Deanswood Hill LS17: Leeds 4B 50
Deanswood Pl. LS17: Leeds 4C 50
Deanswood Ri. LS17: Leeds 4C 50
Deanswood Vw. LS17: Leeds 4C 50
Dean Vw. WF17: Birs 2C 102
Dean Vs. OL14: W'den 4K 113
Deanwood Av. BD15: All 4F 62
Deanwood Cres. BD15: All 3F 62
Dean Wood Vw. HX3: Hal 1B 118
Deanwood Wlk. BD15: All 4F 62
Dearden St. HX6: Sow B 7H 97
WF5: Oss 6N 123
Dearne Ct. S75: W Gran 6G 158
Dearne Courthouse *HD8: Clay W* 8G 157
(off Wakefield Rd.)
Dearne Cft. LS22: Weth 1M 23
Dearne Dike La. HD8: Cumb 3J 171
Dearne Fold HD3: Hud 1G 136
Dearne Mills S75: Dart 9G 159
Dearne Pk. HD8: Clay W 7H 157
Dearne Pk. Est. HD8: Clay W 6J 157
Dearne Royd HD8: Clay W 7H 157
Dearneside Rd. HD8: Den D 3C 172
Dearne St. HD8: Clay W 8G 157
S75: Dart 8H 159
WF9: S Elm 6M 163
Dearne Ter. *HD8: Clay W* 8H 157
(off Barnsley Rd.)
Dearne Way HD8: Bird E 3M 171
Dearnfield HD8: Up C 2N 171
Dearnley St. WF13: Raven 5B 122
Dee Ct. BD22: Oak 5C 42
Deep Dale LS23: B Spa 8C 24
Deepdale Cl. BD17: Bail 5M 45
Deepdale Ho. *WF17: Bat* 1F 122
(off Wilson Wood St.)
Deepdale La. LS23: B Spa 8B 24
Deep La. BD13: Thorn 1N 79
BD14: Clay 9H 63
HD4: Hud 7G 136
HD6: Clift 1C 120
HX2: Lud F 5F 96
HX6: Tri 3B 116
Deer Cft. Av. HD3: Hud 2E 136
Deer Cft. Cres. HD3: Hud 2E 136
Deer Cft. Dr. HD3: Hud 2E 136
Deer Cft. Rd. HD3: Hud 1E 136
Deer Hill Cl. HD7: Mars 6F 150
Deer Hill Ct. HD9: Mel 7B 152
Deer Hill Cft. *HD7: Mars* 6F 150
(off Deer Hill Dr.)
Deer Hill Dr. HD7: Mars 6F 150
Deer Hill End Rd. HD9: Mel 6M 151
Deershaw La. HD8: Cumb 3G 171
Deershaw Sike La. HD8: Cumb 3G 171
Deerstone Ridge LS22: Weth 1M 23
DEERSTONES 3N 11
Defarge Ct. BD5: B'frd 2C 82
Deffer Rd. WF2: Wake 4L 143
Deganwy Dr. HD5: K'htn 9G 120
DEIGHTON 7C 120
Deighton Cl. LS22: Weth 3N 23
DEIGHTON GATES 1M 23
Deighton La. WF17: Bat 7D 102
Deighton Rd. HD2: Hud 8B 120
LS22: Weth 1M 23
Deighton Sports Arena 8B 120
Deighton Station (Rail) 8C 120
Deighton Vw. LS6: Leeds 6A 50
De Lacies Ct. LS26: W'frd 6B 88
De Lacies Rd. LS26: W'frd 6B 88
De Lacy Av. BD4: B'frd 5F 82
HD5: Hud 6D 138
WF7: F'stne 2C 128
Delacy Cres. WF10: C'frd 3K 109
De Lacy Mt. LS5: Leeds 2K 67
De Lacy Ter. WF8: Pon 3L 129
Delamere Gdns. WF1: Wake 4L 9 (5M 125)
Delamere St. BD5: B'frd 3B 82
Delauney Cl. BD6: B'frd 5L 81
Delaware Ct. BD4: B'frd 5F 82
Delf Cl. HX3: She 6K 81
Delf Hill HD6: Ras 4K 119
Delf La. HX7: Wads 5K 77
OL14: Tod 1E 92
Delf Pl. HD6: Ras 4K 119
Delfs La. HX6: Tri 3N 115
Delius Av. BD10: B'frd 1J 65
Dell, The BD13: Cull 9K 43
HD2: Fix 7N 119
LS17: Bard 5E 36
WF10: C'frd 6A 108
Dell Av. S72: Grim 9A 162

Dell Cft.—Doubting Rd.

Dell Cft. BD20: Sils .8C 12
Dellside Fold BD13: Cull .9K 43
Dellside Gdns. BD13: Cull .9K 43
Delmont Cl. WF17: Bat .6B 102
Delph, The WF7: F'stne .6F 128
Delph Brow HX3: Hal .8M 97
Delph Cotts. HX4: Bark .4K 117
Delph Ct. LS6: Leeds .2C 68
Delph Cres. BD14: Clay .1G 80
Delph Cft. Vw. BD21: Keigh .1K 43
Delph Dr. BD14: Clay .1G 80
DELPH END .7M 65
Delph End LS28: Pud .7M 65
Delph Gro. BD14: Clay .1G 80
DELPH HILL
BD12 .8A 82
HX3 .8N 97
Delph Hill BD17: Bail .3A 46
HX2: Hal .8N 97
HX4: Sow .9M 117
(off Thornhill Hey)
LS28: Pud .6B 66
(off Clifton Hill)
Delph Hill Fold HX2: Hal .8M 97
Delph Hill La. HX2: Lud .2D 96
Delph Hill Rd. HX2: Hal .8M 97
Delph Hill Ter. HX2: Hal .8M 97
(off Delph Hill Rd.)
Delph Ho. BD21: Keigh .2J 43
Delph La. HD4: Neth .2J 153
LS6: Leeds .2C 68
Delph Mt. LS6: Leeds .2C 68
Delph St. HX1: Hal .5J 7 (6A 98)
Delph Ter. BD14: Clay .1G 80
HX4: Bark .4K 117
(off Barsey Grn. La.)
Delph Vw. LS6: Leeds .2C 68
Delph Wood Cl. BD16: Bgly .4H 45
Delver Fold BD2: B'frd .4F 64
(off Idle Rd.)
Delverne Gro. BD2: B'frd .3G 64
Delves Ga. HD7: Slait .3M 151
Delves Wood Rd. HD4: Hud .9H 137
Denbigh App. LS9: Leeds .4M 69
Denbigh Cft. LS9: Leeds .4M 69
Denbigh Hgts. LS9: Leeds .4M 69
Denbrook Av. BD4: B'frd .4K 83
Denbrook Cl. BD4: B'frd .4K 83
Denbrook Cres. BD4: B'frd .5K 83
Denbrook Wlk. BD4: B'frd .4K 83
Denbrook Way BD4: B'frd .4K 83
Denbury Mt. BD4: B'frd .3J 83
Denby Cl. WF15: Liv .7K 101
WF17: Birs .3A 102
Denby Ct. BD22: Oak .5B 42
Denby Crest WF8: D'ton .6B 130
DENBY DALE .3C 172
Denby Dale Ind. Pk. HD8: Den D .2C 172
Denby Dale Rd. WF1: Wake .7J 9 (6L 125)
WF2: Wake .8H 9 (8K 125)
WF4: Cal G, W Bret .2M 157
WF4: Dur .3H 143
Denby Dale Rd. E. WF4: Dur .3G 143
Denby Dale Rd. W. WF4: Cal G .4F 142
Denby Dale Station (Rail) .2B 172
Denby Dr. BD17: Bail .6N 45
Denby Grange La. WF4: G Moor .6D 140
Denby Hall La. HD8: Den D .3G 173
DENBY HILL .5A 42
Denby Hill Rd. BD22: Oak .5B 42
Denby Ho. BD4: B'frd .4K 83
BD17: Bail .6A 46
(off Denby Dr.)
Denby La. BD15: All .5G 63
HD8: Den D, Up D .5N 171
WF4: G Moor .5B 140
WF12: Bries .4F 140
Denby La. Cres. WF4: G Moor .5B 140
Denby Mt. BD22: Oak .5B 42
BD22: Oxen .4C 60
Denby Pk. Dr. WF4: G Moor .5B 140
Denby Pl. HX6: Sow B .7H 97
Denby Rd. BD21: Keigh .2J 43
WF8: D'ton .6B 130
Denby St. BD8: B'frd .6A 64
Denby Vw. WF12: T'hill .1G 141
Dence Grn. BD4: B'frd .9J 65
Dence Pl. LS15: Leeds .6N 69
Dencombe Ter. WF9: S Kirk .8G 162
Dendrum Cl. BD22: Oak .4C 42
Dene Bank BD16: Bgly .1F 44
Dene Cl. HX5: Ell .6D 118
Dene Cres. BD7: B'frd .1K 81
Dene Gro. BD20: Sils .7E 12
Dene Hill BD17: Bail .4L 45
Denehill BD9: B'frd .4J 63
Dene Ho. Ct. LS2: Leeds .1E 4 (4D 68)
Dene Mt. BD15: All .5H 63
Dene Pk. HD8: Kbtn .2K 155
Dene Pl. HX1: Hal .2J 7 (4A 98)
Dene Rd. BD6: B'frd .4J 81
HD8: Skelm .8C 156
Dene Royd HX4: Stainl .8M 117
(off Stainland Rd.)
Dene Royd Cl. HX4: Stainl .8M 117
Dene Royd Ct. HX4: Stainl .8M 117
Deneside WF5: Oss .4M 123
Deneside Mt. BD5: B'frd .3B 82
Deneside Ter. BD5: B'frd .3B 82
Denesway LS25: Gar .9A 72
Dene Vw. HX2: Lud F .4D 96
Deneway LS28: Stan .4N 65
Denfield Av. HX3: Hal .2L 97
Denfield Cres. HX3: Hal .2M 97
Denfield Edge HX3: Hal .2M 97
Denfield Gdns. HX3: Hal .2M 97
Denfield La. HX3: Hal .2L 97
Denfield Sq. HX3: Hal .2M 97
Denhale Av. WF2: Wake .5G 125
Denham Av. LS27: Morl .2K 103
Denham Ct. WF17: Bat .5D 102
Denham Dr. HD9: Nether .9L 153
Denham St. HD6: Ras .2M 119
WF17: Bat .5D 102
DENHOLME .5L 61
DENHOLME CLOUGH .8L 61
Denholme Dr. WF5: Oss .4N 123
DENHOLME GATE .9K 61
Denholme Ga. BD13: Denh .7L 61
Denholme Ga. Rd. HX3: Hip, North .2H 99
Denholme Ho. Farm Dr. BD13: Denh .7L 61
Denholme Mdw. WF9: S Elm .5M 163
Denholme Rd. BD22: Oxen .4D 60
Denison Hall LS3: Leeds .4B 4 (5C 68)
Denison Rd. LS3: Leeds .5B 4 (6C 68)
Denison St. LS19: Yead .9M 31
WF17: Bat .8F 102
Denmark St. WF1: Wake .7N 125
Dennil Cres. LS15: Leeds .2E 70
Dennil Rd. LS15: Leeds .3E 70
DENNINGTON .7E 142
Dennington La. WF4: Crig .6E 142
Dennis Bellamy Hall BD5: B'frd .9A 64
Dennis La. BD20: Sils .6A 12
Dennison Fold BD4: B'frd .9J 65
Dennison Hill LS21: Otley .9M 17
Dennison Ter. LS17: N Rig .2N 19
Dennistead Cres. LS6: Leeds .1N 67
Denshaw Dr. LS27: Morl .9M 85
Denshaw Gro. LS27: Morl .9M 85
Denshaw La. WF3: Ting .1B 104
Denstone St. WF1: Wake .3L 9 (4M 125)
Dent Dr. WF1: Wake .3A 126
DENTON .3M 15
Denton Av. LS8: Leeds .7H 51
Denton Bri. HX6: Ripp .4E 116
Denton Dr. BD16: Bgly .3H 45
Denton Gdns. WF7: Ackw .5G 146
Denton Gro. LS8: Leeds .7H 51
Denton Ho. LS14: Leeds .9N 51
(off Kingsdale Ct.)
Denton Rd. LS29: Den .1L 15
LS29: I'ly .5K 15
(Margerison Rd.)
LS29: I'ly .4F 14
(Olicana Pk.)
Denton Row BD13: Denh .6K 61
HX4: Holy .7B 118
LS12: Leeds .8K 67
Denton Ter. LS27: Morl .2K 103
WF10: C'frd .4E 108
Dent St. LS9: Leeds .8M 5 (7H 69)
Denwell Ter. WF8: Pon .2K 129
Derald Ho. HX1: Hal .5J 7
(off King Cross St.)
Derby Pl. BD3: B'frd .7H 65
LS19: Raw .3M 47
(off North St.)
Derby Rd. BD3: B'frd .7J 65
LS19: Raw .3M 47
Derbyshire St. LS10: Leeds .2H 87
Derby St. BD7: B'frd .1N 81
BD13: Que .4C 80
BD14: Clay .1G 80
HX6: Sow B .7K 97
OL14: Tod .7M 93
Derby Ter. BD10: B'frd .7J 47
HD7: Mars .5F 150
Derdale St. OL14: Tod .7L 93
Derry Hill LS29: Men .5D 30
Derry Hill Gdns. LS29: Men .4D 30
Derry La. LS29: Men .4D 30
Der St. OL14: Tod .7L 93
Derwent Av. BD15: Wils .2B 62
BD17: Bail .6K 45
(not continuous)
LS25: Gar .8N 71
LS26: W'frd .7D 88
Derwent Cl. HX7: Heb B .9H 77
Derwent Ct. BD20: Sils .9E 12
HX6: Ripp .9C 116
Derwent Dr. HD5: Hud .3B 138
LS16: Leeds .3N 49
WF10: C'frd .3L 109
Derwent Gro. WF2: Wake .5H 125
Derwent Ho. HX3: Hal .3N 97
Derwent Pl. BD13: Que .3B 80
LS11: Leeds .8C 68
WF11: Knot .2D 130
Derwent Ri. LS22: Weth .1L 23
Derwent Rd. BD2: B'frd .3E 64
HD9: Hon .6K 153
HD9: Mel .8D 152
WF2: Wake .5H 125
WF12: Dew .9J 103
Derwent St. BD21: Keigh .8M 27
Derwentwater Gro. LS6: Leeds .1N 67
Derwentwater Ter. LS6: Leeds .1N 67
Derwin Av. HD4: Stock .7G 154
De Trafford St. HD4: Hud .6J 137
Detroit Av. LS15: Leeds .6E 70
Detroit Dr. LS15: Leeds .6F 70
Deveron Gro. HD2: Hud .2K 137
Devilliers Way WF7: A'ton .1N 127
Devon Cl. LS2: Leeds .1D 4 (4D 68)
Devon Gro. WF5: Oss .7M 123
Devon Rd. LS2: Leeds .1D 4 (4D 68)
Devonshire Av. LS8: Leeds .6J 51
Devonshire Cl. LS8: Leeds .5J 51
(not continuous)
Devonshire Ct. WF11: Knot .8E 110
Devonshire Cres. LS8: Leeds .6J 51
Devonshire Gdns. LS2: Leeds .1D 4 (3D 68)
Devonshire La. LS8: Leeds .5J 51
Devonshire Pl. LS19: Yead .9M 31
Devonshire St. BD21: Keigh .9G 26
HD1: Hud .7K 137
Devonshire St. W. BD21: Keigh .9G 27
Devonshire Ter. BD9: B'frd .4A 64
Devon St. HX1: Hal .6M 97
Devon Wlk. WF13: Dew .3E 122
Devon Way HD6: B Bri .6N 99
Devro Ct. LS9: Leeds .1K 87
Dewar Cl. LS22: Coll .8J 23
Dewberry Cl. BD7: B'frd .2K 81
Dewfield Cl. BD4: B'frd .4G 82
Dewhirst Cl. BD17: Bail .5B 46
Dewhirst Pl. BD4: B'frd .9H 65
Dewhirst Rd. BD17: Bail .5B 46
HD6: Brigh .8M 99
Dewhirst St. BD15: Wils .1B 62
Dewhurst Rd. HD2: Hud .9N 119
DEWSBURY .3G 123
Dewsbury Bus Mus. .6B 122
Dewsbury District Golf Course .8A 122
Dewsbury Ga. Rd. WF13: Dew .9C 102
Dewsbury Little Theatre .1F 122
Dewsbury Mills WF12: Dew .5F 122
Dewsbury Minster .4G 122
DEWSBURY MOOR .3C 122
Dewsbury Moor Crematorium WF13: Dew .3D 122
Dewsbury Mus. .4D 122
Dewsbury Rams RLFC .1K 123
Dewsbury Ring Rd. WF13: Dew .3F 122
Dewsbury Rd. BD19: Cleck .5J 101
BD19: Gom .1M 101
HD6: Ras .5F 118
HX5: Ell .5F 118
LS11: Leeds .8E 68
(Meadow La.)
LS11: Leeds .6B 86
(Park Wood Cl.)
LS27: Leeds, Morl .2A 104
WF2: Wake .6E 124
WF3: Ting .4N 103
(not continuous)
WF5: Oss .3M 123
WF12: Dew, E Ard .6L 103
WF17: Birs .1M 101
Dewsbury Sports Cen. .3G 123
Dewsbury Station (Rail) .3F 122
Deyne Rd. HD4: Neth .2H 153
Diadem Dr. LS14: Leeds .5N 69
Dial St. LS9: Leeds .8M 5 (8H 69)
Diamond Av. WF9: S Elm .6L 163
Diamond St. BD22: Keigh .3G 42
HD1: Hud .1D 8 (2N 137)
HD5: Hud .5B 138
HX1: Hal .4N 97
WF17: Bat .6E 102
Diamond Ter. HX1: Hal .4N 97
HX2: Hal .7M 97
Dibb La. LS19: Yead .9K 31
Dib Cl. LS8: Leeds .1M 69
Dib La. LS8: Leeds .1M 69
Dick Dean La. HX7: P Wel .9H 59
Dick Edge La. HD8: Cumb .6F 170
Dickens Dr. WF10: C'frd .7K 109
Dickens St. BD5: B'frd .2C 82
HX2: Hal .5L 97
Dickin Ct. HX6: Ripp .7E 116
Dickinson Ct. WF1: Wake .1K 9 (3L 125)
Dickinson Gdns. WF13: Dew .3E 122
(off Greenwood St.)
Dickinson St. LS18: Hors .5F 48
WF1: Wake .2K 9 (4L 125)
Dickinson Ter. WF7: F'stne .5D 128
Dick La. BD3: B'frd .7J 65
BD4: B'frd .1H 83
HX6: Ripp .9B 116
Dick's Gth. Rd. LS29: Men .4D 30
Dick's La. HX7: Crag V .7F 94
Dickson Fold WF15: Liv .8K 101
Dicky Sykes La. WF7: Ackw .5D 146
Digby Rd. LS29: Men .4E 30
Diggerland
Whitwood .6N 107
Digley Av. BD6: B'frd .3H 81
Digley Rd. HD9: Holm .6F 168
Digley Royd La. HD9: Holm .5F 168
Digpal Rd. LS27: Chur .4M 85
Dike La. HX7: Wads .9L 77
Dimple Gdns. WF5: Oss .7N 123
Dimples La. BD20: E Mor .8C 28
BD22: Haw .8B 42
Dimple Wells Cl. WF5: Oss .7N 123
Dimple Wells La. WF5: Oss .7N 123
Dimple Wells Rd. WF5: Oss .7N 123
Dineley Av. OL14: Tod .5H 93
Dingle Rd. HD1: Hud .4J 137
Dingley Rd. HD3: Hud .2H 137
Dinsdale Bldgs. LS19: Yead .1L 47
Dirker HD7: Mars .4F 150
Dirker Av. HD7: Mars .4G 150
Dirker Bank Rd. HD7: Mars .4F 150
Dirker Dr. HD7: Mars .5F 150
DIRK HILL .9A 64
Dirkhill Rd. BD7: B'frd .9A 64
Dirkhill St. BD7: B'frd .9N 63
Discovery Rd. HX1: Hal .6M 7 (6C 98)
Dish Hill WF11: Byram .5C 110
Dish Hill Fly-Over WF11: B'ton .5B 110
Disney Cl. HD4: Hud .7J 137
Dispensary Wlk. HX1: Hal .4M 7 (5C 98)
Disraeli Gdns. LS11: Leeds .1D 86
Disraeli Ter. LS11: Leeds .1D 86
DITCHES .3F 112
Dixon Av. BD7: B'frd .9L 63
Dixon Cl. BD20: Stee .3C 26
HX4: Gree .3A 118
Dixon Ct. LS12: N Far .2L 85
Dixon La. LS12: Leeds .9M 67
Dixon La. Rd. LS12: Leeds .9M 67
Dixon St. WF7: F'stne .4D 128
Dixon's Yd. WF1: Wake .5L 9 (5M 125)
Dob HX6: Sow B .9D 96
DOBB .6J 169
Dobb Kiln La. BD16: Bgly .6G 45
Dobb La. HD9: Holm .6H 169
Dobb Top Rd. HD9: Holm .7H 169
Dob La. HX6: Sow B .9D 96
Dob Pk. Rd. LS21: Clift .2K 17
Dob Royd HD8: Shep .1H 171
Dobroyd Ct. OL14: Tod .8J 93
Dobroyd Rd. OL14: Tod .8J 93
DOBRUDDEN .2L 45
Dobrudden Caravan Pk. BD17: Bail .2L 45
Dobson Av. LS11: Leeds .2E 86
Dobson Gro. LS11: Leeds .2E 86
Dobson Locks BD10: B'frd .6H 47
Dobson Pl. LS11: Leeds .2E 86
Dobsons Row WF3: Carl .2M 105
Dobsons Wharf BD20: Sils .9E 12
Dobson's Yd. WF11: B'ton .3B 110
Dobson Ter. LS11: Leeds .2E 86
Dobson Vw. LS11: Leeds .2E 86
Dockery HD1: Hud .7L 137
Dockfield Ind. Pk. BD17: Ship .6B 46
Dockfield Pl. BD17: Ship .7A 46
Dockfield Rd. BD17: Ship .7A 46
Dockfield Ter. BD17: Ship .6A 46
Dock Hill HD9: Nether .9L 153
Dock La. BD17: Ship .7A 46
BD18: Ship .7A 46
Dock Mills BD17: Ship .6A 46
Dockroyd BD22: Oak .6D 42
Dockroyd La. BD22: Oak .5C 42
Dock St. LS10: Leeds .8G 5 (7E 68)
Doctor Fold HD9: Hon .4L 153
Doctor Hill BD10: B'frd .8F 46
(Evesham Gro.)
BD10: B'frd .9E 46
(The Stray)
HX2: Hal .3K 97
Doctor La. BD10: B'frd .6F 46
HD8: Shel .6L 155
WF4: Flock .8E 140
WF14: Mir .7L 121
Doctors La. WF10: All B .8A 90
Doctors Row HD5: K'htn .2G 138
DODD NAZE .1J 95
Dodds Royd HD4: Hud .1K 153
Dodge Holme Cl. HX2: Mix .9K 79
Dodge Holme Ct. HX2: Mix .9K 79
(off Dodge Holme Cl.)
Dodge Holme Dr. HX2: Mix .9J 79
Dodge Holme Gdns. HX2: Mix .9K 79
Dodge Holme Rd. HX2: Mix .9K 79
Dodgson Av. LS7: Leeds .3G 68
Dodgson St. HX5: Ell .6E 118
Dodlee La. HD3: Hud .3D 136
Dodsworth Cres. WF6: Norm .3J 127
Dodworth Dr. WF2: Wake .5K 143
Doe Pk. BD13: Denh .5L 61
Doe Pk. Water Activities Cen. .5M 61
Dog Hill S72: Shaf .6J 161
Dog Hill Dr. S72: Shaf .6K 161
Doghouse La. OL14: Tod .7H 93
Dog Kennel Bank HD5: Hud .7F 8 (5A 138)
Dog Kennel La. HX3: Sou .7D 98
Dog La. HX4: Gree .4K 117
HX4: Holy .9K 117
DOGLEY LANE .9H 139
Dogley La. HD8: Fen B .9H 139
Dogley Villa Ct. HD8: Fen B .9H 139
Dol BD22: Oxen .5E 60
Doldram La. HX6: Norl .2G 116
Dole La. HX7: Heb B .3H 95
Doles Av. S71: Roys .6C 160
Doles Cres. S71: Roys .6C 160
Doles La. HD6: Clift .8C 100
Dole St. BD13: Thorn .8D 62
Dolfin Pl. HD2: Hud .6D 120
Doll La. BD13: Cull .2L 61
Dolly La. LS9: Leeds .3K 5 (5G 68)
Dolly La. Bus. Cen.
LS9: Leeds .2L 5 (4G 69)
Dolphin Ct. LS9: Leeds .7L 5 (7G 69)
LS13: Leeds .5E 66
Dolphin La. BD16: Har .7L 43
WF3: Thpe H .3G 105
(not continuous)
Dolphin Rd. LS10: Leeds .8G 87
Dolphin St. LS9: Leeds .7L 5 (7G 68)
Dolphin Ter. BD13: Que .5B 80
Dombey St. HX1: Hal .4G 7 (5N 97)
Domestic Rd. LS12: Leeds .9B 68
Domestic St. LS11: Leeds .8B 68
Dominion Av. LS7: Leeds .9F 50
Dominion Cl. LS7: Leeds .9F 50
Dominion Ind. Pk. HX3: Hip .4H 99
Dom Pedro Cotts. WF6: Norm .1M 127
Donald Aldred Dr. LS29: Burl W .9C 16
Donald Av. BD6: B'frd .5A 82
Donald St. LS28: Fars .4A 66
Don Av. LS22: Weth .1L 23
Doncaster La. DN6: Hamp, S'brk .5G 165
Doncaster Rd.
WF1: Wake .7M 9 (6M 125)
WF4: Croft, Foul, Wrag .9F 126
WF7: Ackw, S Elm, Upt .5G 146
WF8: E Hard, Thpe A, Went .1L 147
WF9: Bads, S Elm, Upt .5G 146
WF9: S Elm .7N 163
WF11: Ferr .8B 110
Doncaster Rd. Est. WF7: Ackw .5G 146
Doncaster Sq. WF11: Ferr .7B 110
Doncaster St. HX3: Hal .9C 98
Don Ct. BD20: Sils .8E 12
Donisthorpe St. BD5: B'frd .2B 82
LS10: Leeds .9G 68
Don Pedro Av. WF6: Norm .1L 127
Don Pedro Cl. WF6: Norm .2L 127
Don St. BD21: Keigh .8H 27
Dorchester Av. WF8: Pon .3H 129
Dorchester Ct. BD4: B'frd .2J 83
Dorchester Cres. BD4: B'frd .2J 83
BD17: Bail .3D 46
Dorchester Dr. HX2: Hal .7L 97
LS19: Yead .1A 48
Dorchester Rd. HD2: Fix .6N 119
Dorian Cl. BD10: B'frd .9H 47
Dorman Av. WF9: Upt .1C 164
Dorothy St. BD21: Keigh .4G 43
Dorset Av. LS8: Leeds .2J 69
Dorset Cl. BD5: B'frd .2A 82
WF9: Hems .1D 162
Dorset Gro. LS28: Stan .6B 66
Dorset Mt. LS8: Leeds .3J 69
Dorset Rd. LS8: Leeds .2J 69
Dorset St. BD5: B'frd .2A 82
HD1: Hud .1A 8 (2L 137)
LS8: Leeds .2J 69
Dorset Ter. LS8: Leeds .3J 69
Dorset Wlk. WF13: Dew .3E 122
(off Lacey St.)
Dortmund Sq. LS2: Leeds .5F 4
Dotterel Glen LS27: Morl .1M 103
Doubting La. WF12: T'hill .1G 141
Doubting Rd. WF12: T'hill .1G 141

Douglas Av.—East M.

Douglas Av. HD3: Hud .5G 137
HD5: Hud .5C 138
WF17: Bat .7J 103
Douglas Cres. BD18: Ship .9B 46
Douglas Dr. BD4: B'frd .1G 83
Douglas Rd. BD4: B'frd .1G 83
Douglas St. BD22: Cros R .7E 42
HX3: Hal .2A 98
WF12: Dew .7F 122
Douglas Towers BD5: B'frd .7A 6
Dove Cl. LS22: Weth .1M 23
Dovecote Cl. WF4: Horb .9D 124
Dovecote Dr. WF10: Leds .7E 90
Dovecote La. WF4: Horb .9C 124
Dovecote Lodge WF4: Horb .9D 124
Dovedale Cl. HX3: She .7G 81
WF4: Croft .1H 145
Dovedale Gdns. LS15: Leeds .4G 70
Dovedale Gth. LS15: Leeds .3G 70
Dove Dr. WF10: C'frd .4H 109
Dove Hill S71: Roys .5E 160
Dover La. HD9: H'frth .5M 169
Dover Rd. HD9: H'frth .6M 169
Dover St. BD3: B'frd .5D 64
LS25: Gar .7B 72
OL14: Tod .6M 93
Dovesdale Gro. BD5: B'frd .3A 82
Dovesdale Rd. BD5: B'frd .3B 82
Dove St. BD18: Ship .7L 45
BD22: Haw .8D 42
Dowkell La. LS23: T Arch .8E 24
Dowker St. HD3: Hud .5G 136
HX1: Hal .7M 97
DOWLEY GAP .6H 45
Dowley Gap La. BD16: Bgly .6G 44
Downham St. BD3: B'frd .5F 6 (8E 64)
Downing Cl. BD3: B'frd .7F 64
Downing St. HD7: Linth .1B 152
Downland Cres. WF11: Knot .1G 130
Downs Ho. Cl. S72: S Hien .3L 161
Downshutts La. HD9: New M .3B 170
Downside Cres. BD15: All .5F 62
Dowry HD7: Slait .3L 151
DPM Ind. Est. BD4: B'frd .1H 83
Dracup Av. BD7: B'frd .9K 63
Dracup Rd. BD7: B'frd .2L 81
Dradishaw Rd. BD20: Sils .8D 12
Dragon Ct. LS12: Leeds .8A 4 (8B 68)
Dragon Cres. LS12: Leeds .9N 67
Dragon Dr. LS12: Leeds .9M 67
Dragon Rd. LS12: Leeds .9N 67
Drake Fold BD12: Wyke .1A 100
Drake Hill La. BD16: Bgly .8F 28
Drake La. BD11: Drig .8B 84
Drakes Ind. Est. HX3: Hal .9N 79
Drake St. BD1: B'frd .5C 6 (8D 64)
BD21: Keigh .8J 27
Draper Cnr. HX7: Hept .7F 76
Draper La. HX7: Hept .7F 76
DRAUGHTON .5D 10
Draughton Gro. BD5: B'frd .3B 82
Draughton St. BD5: B'frd .4B 82
Draycott Wlk. BD4: B'frd .3J 83
DN6: Carc .9N 165
Draymans Ct. HX2: Hal .2K 97
Drayton Mnr. Yd. *LS11: Leeds .1E 86*
(off Moor Cres.)
Dray Vw. WF13: Dew .1C 122
Drewry Rd. BD21: Keigh .9H 27
Drewton Rd. BD1: B'frd .3A 6 (7B 64)
Driftholme Rd. BD11: Drig .6C 84
DRIGHLINGTON .7B 84
Drighlington By-Pass BD11: Drig .6N 83
LS27: Gil .8A 84
Drill Hall, The HX1: Hal .5L 7
Drill Hall Bus. Cen. LS29: I'ly .5H 15
Drill Pde. BD8: B'frd .5B 64
Drill St. BD21: Keigh .9J 27
BD22: Haw .9C 42
Drinker La. HD8: Shel .4A 156
Drive, The BD10: B'frd .9H 47
BD13: Denh .6J 61
BD16: Bgly .1D 44
HX3: Hip .4J 99
HX7: Myth .3L 95
LS8: Leeds .7H 51
LS9: Leeds .8K 5 (7G 68)
LS15: Leeds .4E 70
LS16: Leeds .4K 49
LS17: Bard .4E 36
LS17: Leeds .1B 50
LS25: Kip .4A 90
LS26: Swil .4H 89
LS29: Burl W .9C 16
WF17: Bat .6D 102
Driver Pl. LS12: Leeds .8A 68
Drivers Row WF8: Pon .4H 129
Driver St. LS12: Leeds .8B 68
Driver Ter. BD20: Sils .7E 12
LS12: Leeds .8A 68
Drove Rd. Ho. *BD5: B'frd .2C 82*
(off Bowling Old La.)
Drovers Way BD2: B'frd .2C 64
DRUB .2J 101
Drub La. BD19: Cleck .2J 101
Druggist La. LS29: Add .1M 13
Druids St. BD14: Clay .1G 81
Druids Vw. BD16: Bgly .9C 28
Drumlin Ct. WF16: Heck .7B 102
Drummer La. HD7: Golc .7N 135
Drummond Av. LS16: Leeds .9M 49
Drummond Ct. LS16: Leeds .9M 49
Drummond Rd. BD8: B'frd .5A 64
LS16: Leeds .8M 49
Drummond Trad. Est. BD8: B'frd .6B 64
Drury Av. LS18: Hors .7E 48
Drury Cl. LS18: Hors .7E 48
Drury La. HX4: Stainl .7M 117
LS18: Hors .7E 48
(not continuous)
WF1: Wake .4H 9 (5K 125)
WF6: Alt .9G 106
Dry Carr La. HX2: Midg .8C 78
Dryclough Av. HD4: Hud .8H 137
Dryclough Cl. HX3: Hal .9B 98
Dryclough La. HX3: Hal .9B 98
Dryclough Rd. HD4: Hud .7H 137
Dryden St. BD1: B'frd .6D 6 (8D 64)
BD16: Bgly .4E 44
Dry Hill La. HD8: Den D .3E 172
Drysdale Fold HD2: Hud .7A 120
Dry Soil HX7: Blac H .9B 76
Dubb La. BD16: Bgly .4E 44
Duchy Av. BD9: B'frd .3K 63
Duchy Cres. BD9: B'frd .3K 63
Duchy Dr. BD9: B'frd .4K 63
Duchy Gro. BD9: B'frd .3K 63
Duchy Vs. BD9: B'frd .3K 63
Duchywood BD9: B'frd .3K 63
Ducie St. BD10: B'frd .6F 46
Duckett Gro. LS28: Pud .6K 65
Duckett La. BD1: B'frd .3A 6 (7C 64)
Duck Hill HX7: P Wel .4H 77
Ducking Pond Cl. BD22: Haw .9C 42
Duckworth Gro. BD9: B'frd .4L 63
Duckworth La. BD9: B'frd .5K 63
Duckworth Ter. BD9: B'frd .4L 63
Dudfleet La. WF4: Horb .2D 142
Dudfleet Yd. WF4: Horb .3E 142
Dudley Av. HD1: Hud .4J 137
WF17: Birs .2D 102
Dudley Cres. HX2: Illing .8K 79
Dudley Gro. BD4: B'frd .9J 65
DUDLEY HILL .3G 83
Dudley Hill Bus. Cen. BD4: B'frd .3G 83
Dudley Hill Rd. BD2: B'frd .3F 64
Dudley Rd. HD1: Hud .4J 137
Dudley St. BD4: B'frd .9J 65
(Dennison Fold)
BD4: B'frd .2G 83
(School St.)
BD4: B'frd .2F 82
(Vestry St.)
Dudwell Av. HX3: Hal .1C 118
Dudwell Gro. HX3: Hal .1B 118
Dudwell La. HX3: Hal .1B 118
Dufton App. LS14: Leeds .3B 70
Duich Rd. BD6: B'frd .7K 81
Duinen St. BD5: B'frd .7C 6 (9D 64)
Duke of Wellington Regimental Mus. .3B 98
(within Bankfield Mus.)
Duke of York Av. WF2: Wake .1L 143
Duke of York St. WF1: Wake .2L 9 (4M 125)
WF2: Wren .2H 125
Dukes Chase WF8: Pon .9K 109
Dukes Cut HX7: Blac H .1J 93
Dukes Hill LS29: I'ly .3F 14
Duke St. BD1: B'frd .3B 6 (7C 64)
BD20: Keigh .7J 27
BD22: Haw .8D 42
HX2: Lud .3D 96
HX5: Ell .5E 118
LS9: Leeds .7J 5 (7F 68)
OL14: Tod .5B 94
WF9: Fitz .7A 146
WF10: C'frd .4B 108
WF12: Dew .4L 123
WF13: Raven .6B 122
Dukewood Rd. HD8: Clay W .7H 157
Dulverton Cl. LS11: Leeds .4N 85
WF8: Pon .9M 109
Dulverton Ct. LS11: Leeds .4N 85
Dulverton Gdns. LS11: Leeds .3M 85
Dulverton Gth. LS11: Leeds .4M 85
Dulverton Grn. LS11: Leeds .4N 85
Dulverton Gro. BD4: B'frd .2H 83
LS11: Leeds .4M 85
Dulverton Pl. LS11: Leeds .4M 85
Dulverton Ri. WF8: Pon .9M 109
Dulverton Sq. LS11: Leeds .4N 85
Dulverton Way WF8: Pon .9M 109
Dunbar Ct. LS26: Meth .1K 107
Dunbar Cft. BD13: Que .4E 80
Dunbar St. WF1: Wake .7A 126
Dunbottle Cl. WF14: Mir .6M 121
Dunbottle La. WF14: Mir .5M 121
Dunbottle Way WF14: Mir .5N 121
Duncan Av. LS21: Otley .2H 31
WF2: Wake .9N 125
Duncan St. BD5: B'frd .7B 6 (9C 64)
LS1: Leeds .7G 5 (7E 68)
Dunce Pk. Cl. HX5: Ell .6E 118
Duncombe Rd. BD8: B'frd .7L 63
Duncombe St. BD8: B'frd .7M 63
LS1: Leeds .5B 4 (6C 68)
Duncombe Way BD8: B'frd .7M 63
Dundalk Ct. WF5: Oss .5N 123
Dundas St. BD21: Keigh .1K 43
HD1: Hud .5A 8 (4M 137)
HX1: Hal .7M 97
Dundee Rd. OL14: Tod .4F 92
Dunderdale Cres. WF10: C'frd .3K 109
Dunford Rd. HD9: Had E, H'frth .3M 169
Dungeon La. LS26: Oul .2A 106
Dunham Ct. HD1: Hud .3B 8
Dunhill Cres. LS9: Leeds .6N 69
Dunhill Ri. LS9: Leeds .6N 69
DUNKESWICK .7F 20
Dunkeswick La. LS17: N Rig, Wee .2C 20
Dunkhill Cft. BD10: B'frd .8F 46
DUNKIRK .8D 80
Dunkirk Cres. HX1: Hal .6L 97
Dunkirk Gdns. HX1: Hal .7L 97
Dunkirk Hill LS12: Leeds .5N 67
Dunkirk La. HX1: Hal .7L 97
Dunkirk Ri. BD20: Rid .6L 27
Dunkirk St. HX1: Hal .6L 97
Dunkirk Ter. HX1: Hal .6M 97
Dunlands La. WF4: M'twn .2L 141
Dunlin Cl. LS27: Morl .1N 103
Dunlin Ct. LS10: Leeds .8F 86
Dunlin Cft. LS10: Leeds .8F 86
Dunlin Dr. LS10: Leeds .8F 86
Dunlin Fold LS10: Leeds .8F 86
Dunlin Way BD8: B'frd .7H 63
Dunlop Av. LS12: N Far .1K 85
Dunmore Av. BD13: Que .4B 80
Dunn Cl. WF2: Wren .9H 105
Dunningley La. WF3: Ting .1B 104
Dunnington Wlk. BD6: B'frd .7M 81
Dunniwood Cl. WF10: C'frd .7N 107
Dunniwood Dr. WF10: C'frd .7A 108
Dunnock Av. BD6: B'frd .4G 81
Dunnock Cft. LS27: Morl .1M 103
Dunnock Rd. HD9: Mel .5B 152
Dunrobin Av. LS25: Gar .6B 72
Dunsford Av. BD4: B'frd .5F 82
Dunsil Vs. WF9: S Elm .8M 163
Dunsley Bank Rd. HD9: H'frth .6L 169
Dunsley La. S72: B'ley .7E 162
WF9: Hems .5F 162
Dunsley Ter. WF9: S Kirk .7G 162
Dunsmore Dr. HD3: Hud .2E 136
Dunstan Cl. WF5: Oss .7A 124
Dunstan Gro. BD19: Cleck .4J 101
Dunstarn Ct. LS16: Leeds .4N 49
Dunstarn Dr. LS16: Leeds .4N 49
Dunstarn Gdns. LS16: Leeds .4A 50
Dunstarn La. LS16: Leeds .5N 49
Durban Av. LS11: Leeds .3B 86
Durban Cl. WF7: F'stne .5C 128
Durban Cres. LS11: Leeds .3B 86
Durham Ct. LS28: Fars .3A 66
Durham Rd. BD8: B'frd .5M 63
Durham St. HX2: Hal .4L 97
WF10: C'frd .7E 108
Durham Ter. BD8: B'frd .5M 63
DURKAR .3H 143
Durkar Ct. WF4: Dur .3G 143
Durkar Flds. WF4: Dur .4G 143
Durkar La. WF4: Crig, Dur .3G 143
Durkar Low La. WF4: Dur .3H 143
Durkar Ri. WF4: Crig .4H 143
Durkheim Ct. *BD3: B'frd .7G 64*
(off Amberley St.)
Durley Av. BD9: B'frd .3M 63
Durling Dr. BD18: Ship .8C 46
Durlston Gro. BD12: Wyke .9B 82
Durlston Ter. BD12: Wyke .9B 82
Durn St. OL14: Tod .3B 92
Durrance St. BD22: Keigh .1F 42
Durrant Cl. LS22: Weth .4N 23
Dutton Grn. LS14: Leeds .7B 52
Dutton Way LS14: Leeds .8B 52
Duxbury Ri. LS7: Leeds .1E 4 (4D 68)
DW Fitness
Birstall .2C 102
Halifax .2M 7 (4C 98)
Dyehouse BD15: Wils .1A 62
Dyehouse Dr. BD19: Cleck .2G 101
Dyehouse Fold BD12: O'haw .8E 82
Dye Ho. La. HX6: Norl .2L 117
Dyehouse La. BD15: Wils .1N 61
HD6: Brigh .2N 119
LS28: Pud .1B 84
(not continuous)
Dyehouse Rd. BD12: O'haw .8D 82
Dyer La. HX3: Hal .3M 97
Dyers Ct. LS6: Leeds .2B 68
Dyer St. LS2: Leeds .6H 5 (6F 68)
Dyke BD22: Haw .8N 41
Dyke Bottom HD8: Shep .8K 155
Dyke Cl. WF14: Mir .3L 121
Dyke End HD7: Golc .7A 136
Dyke La. OL14: Tod .5C 94
Dyke Nook BD22: Oxen .5A 60
Dymond Gro. WF15: Liv .9L 101
Dymond Rd. WF15: Liv .9M 101
Dymond Vw. WF15: Liv .9L 101
Dyneley Grange LS16: B'hpe .5H 33
Dyson Ho. LS4: Leeds .3L 67
DYSON LANE .8C 116
Dyson La. HD9: Scho .7N 169
HX6: Ripp .8C 116
Dyson Pl. HX3: Hal .9C 98
Dyson Rd. HX1: Hal .4M 97
Dyson's Hill HD9: Hon .4L 153
Dyson St. BD1: B'frd .7B 64
BD9: B'frd .2M 63
HD5: Hud .4C 138
HD6: Brigh .9M 99
Dyson Wood Way HD2: Hud .6A 120

E

Eagle Gro. WF2: Wake .5F 124
Eaglescliffe *HX6: Sow B .8J 97*
(off Beech Rd.)
Eaglesfield Dr. BD6: B'frd .7L 81
Eagle St. BD21: Keigh .9H 27
BD22: Haw .8D 42
OL14: Tod .7K 93
Eagley Bank OL12: Whit .5A 112
Ealand Av. WF17: Bat .5C 102
Ealand Cres. WF17: Bat .5D 102
Ealand Rd. WF17: Bat .4C 102
(not continuous)
Ealing Ct. WF17: Bat .6D 102
Earles Av. HD5: Hud .5C 138
Earle St. WF7: F'stne .5C 128
Earls Chase WF8: Pon .9K 109
EARLSHEATON .4J 123
Earlsmere Dr. LS27: Morl .8J 85
Earl St. BD21: Keigh .8H 27
BD22: Haw .9C 42
WF1: Wake .3L 9 (4M 125)
WF9: Fitz .7A 146
WF12: Dew .3L 123
Earlswood BD12: Wyke .1B 100
Earlswood Av. LS8: Leeds .5H 51
Earlswood Chase LS28: Pud .8B 66
Earlswood Cres. LS25: Kip .3N 89
Earlswood Mead LS28: Pud .8A 66
Earl Ter. HX3: Hal .2N 97
Early Butts HD9: Hon .4L 153
Earnshaw Pl. WF2: Wake .3G 9 (4K 125)
Easby Av. WF17: Bat .8C 102
Easby Cl. LS29: I'ly .5E 14
Easby Dr. LS29: I'ly .5E 14
Easby Rd. BD7: B'frd .9B 64
Easdale Cl. LS14: Leeds .1A 70
Easdale Cres. LS14: Leeds .1B 70
Easdale Mt. LS14: Leeds .2A 70
Easdale Rd. LS14: Leeds .2A 70
Easedale Gdns. HD3: Hud .1F 136
Easington Av. BD6: B'frd .5K 81
Easingwood Dr. HD5: K'htn .1F 138
East Acres WF11: Byram .5D 110
EAST ARDSLEY .5E 104
East Av. BD21: Keigh .8J 27
(not continuous)
HD3: Hud .1H 137
WF4: Horb .1E 142
WF8: Pon .4H 129
WF9: S Elm .5A 164
WF9: Upt .2N 163
E. Av. Loop WF7: F'stne .8C 128
E. Bath St. WF17: Bat .7G 103
E. Beck Ct. LS21: Askw .4D 16
EAST BIERLEY .6K 83
East Bierley Golf Course .6J 83
EASTBOROUGH .2G 123
Eastborough Cres. WF13: Dew .2G 123
EASTBOURNE .3N 129
Eastbourne Av. WF7: F'stne .5E 128
Eastbourne Cl. WF8: Pon .3N 129
Eastbourne Cres. WF8: Pon .3N 129
Eastbourne Dr. WF8: Pon .3N 129
Eastbourne Rd. BD9: B'frd .1N 63
Eastbourne Ter. WF8: Pon .3M 129
Eastbourne Vw. WF8: Pon .3M 129
EAST BOWLING .3E 82
EASTBROOK .5D 6 (8D 64)
Eastbrook Ct. *LS23: B'ham .6D 38*
(off Low Way)
East Brookhall BD1: B'frd .4D 6
EASTBURN .3A 26
Eastbury Av. BD6: B'frd .4J 81
E. Busk La. LS21: Otley .9N 17
EASTBY .1A 10
Eastby Bank BD23: E'by .1A 10
East Byland HX2: Illing .7L 79
EAST CARLTON .5A 32
East Causeway LS16: Leeds .2N 49
E. Causeway Cl. LS16: Leeds .2N 49
E. Causeway Cres. LS16: Leeds .3N 49
E. Causeway Va. LS16: Leeds .3A 50
E. Chevin Rd. LS21: Otley .2M 31
East Cliffe HX3: Sou .6D 98
East Cl. HD2: Hud .9N 119
WF8: Pon .6L 129
East Ct. *LS28: Fars .3A 66*
(off Water La.)
East Cft. BD12: Wyke .2B 100
East Cft. M. *BD12: Wyke .2B 100*
(off Garden Fld.)
East Dale Cl. WF9: Hems .2F 162
Eastdean Bank LS14: Leeds .9B 52
Eastdean Dr. LS14: Leeds .9B 52
Eastdean Gdns. LS14: Leeds .9C 52
Eastdean Ga. LS14: Leeds .1C 70
Eastdean Grange
LS14: Leeds .1C 70
Eastdean Gro. LS14: Leeds .9C 52
Eastdean Ri. LS14: Leeds .9C 52
Eastdean Rd. LS14: Leeds .9B 52
East Dene BD20: Sils .7E 12
Eastdown WF10: C'frd .4G 108
East Dr. WF8: Pon .4M 129
East End Cres. S71: Roys .6F 160
Easterly Av. LS8: Leeds .2J 69
Easterly Cl. LS8: Leeds .3K 69
Easterly Cres. LS8: Leeds .2J 69
Easterly Cross LS8: Leeds .2K 69
Easterly Gth. LS8: Leeds .2K 69
Easterly Gro. LS8: Leeds .2J 69
Easterly Mt. LS8: Leeds .2K 69
Easterly Rd. LS8: Leeds .2J 69
Easterly Sq. LS8: Leeds .2K 69
Easterly Vw. LS8: Leeds .2K 69
Eastfield BD13: Denh .6K 61
HD8: Shep .9K 155
Eastfield Av. WF11: Knot .9E 110
Eastfield Cl. S75: S'ross .9M 159
Eastfield Cres. LS26: W'frd .7C 88
S75: S'ross .9M 159
Eastfield Dr. HD8: Kbtn .2J 155
LS26: W'frd .7C 88
WF8: Pon .2M 129
Eastfield Gdns. BD4: B'frd .2J 83
Eastfield Gro. WF6: Norm .9K 107
Eastfield La. LS29: Burl W .9E 16
WF10: C'frd .4E 108
Eastfield Rd. WF11: Knot .8E 110
WF14: Mir .5A 122
East Fld. St. LS9: Leeds .7L 5 (7G 69)
East Fold HD8: Clay W .8F 156
East Fountains *HX2: Illing .6K 79*
(off Field Head La.)
EAST GARFORTH .6B 72
East Garforth Station (Rail) .7A 72
Eastgate HD9: Hon .4L 153
HX5: Ell .4E 118
LS2: Leeds .6G 5 (6E 68)
LS16: B'hpe .5G 33
WF9: Hems .3E 162
Eastgate Cl. LS16: B'hpe .5G 33
E. Grange Cl. LS10: Leeds .4G 87
E. Grange Dr. LS10: Leeds .4G 86
E. Grange Gth. LS10: Leeds .4G 87
E. Grange Ri. LS10: Leeds .4G 87
E. Grange Rd. LS10: Leeds .4G 86
E. Grange Sq. LS10: Leeds .4G 86
E. Grange Vw. LS10: Leeds .4G 86
East Gro. HD5: K'htn .2G 138
EAST HARDWICK .9L 129
Easthorpe Ct. BD2: B'frd .2H 65
EAST KESWICK .3D 36
East King St. LS9: Leeds .8K 5 (7G 68)
Eastlands HD5: Hud .6E 138
Eastland Wlk. LS13: Leeds .5H 67
East Lee La. OL14: Tod .4A 94
Eastleigh Ct. WF3: Ting .4C 104
Eastleigh Dr. WF3: Ting .4B 104
Eastleigh Gro. BD5: B'frd .2B 82
Eastleigh M. WF3: Ting .4C 104
East Longley HX6: Norl .2G 117
East Manywells BD13: Cull .2L 61
East M. WF7: F'stne .7C 128

East Moor—Ellen Holme

EAST MOOR
LS16 . . . 3N 49
WF1 . . . 3M 9 (4N 125)
East Moor Av. LS8: Leeds . . . 6H 51
East Moor Cl. LS8: Leeds . . . 6H 51
East Moor Cres. LS8: Leeds . . . 5H 51
East Moor Dr. LS8: Leeds . . . 6J 51
Eastmoor Gro. S71: Carl . . . 7D 160
Eastmoor Ho. BD4: B'frd . . . 3K 83
East Moor La. LS16: Leeds . . . 3N 49
East Moor Rd. LS8: Leeds . . . 5H 51
Eastmoor Rd. WF1: Wake . . . 1K 9 (3L 125)
EAST MORTON . . . 8C 28
East Mt. HD6: Brigh . . . 9M 99
WF4: H'cft . . . 1J 161
East Mt. Pl. HD6: Brigh . . . 9M 99
Easton Pl. HD3: Hud . . . 3G 136
East Pde. BD1: B'frd . . . 4D 6 (7D 64)
(not continuous)
BD17: Bail . . . 3B 46
BD20: Stee . . . 3D 26
BD21: Keigh . . . 9J 27
HX6: Sow B . . . 8K 97
LS1: Leeds . . . 6E 4 (6D 68)
LS29: I'ly . . . 5H 15
LS29: Men . . . 4E 30
East Pk. Dr. LS9: Leeds . . . 7H 69
East Pk. Gro. LS9: Leeds . . . 7J 69
East Pk. Mt. LS9: Leeds . . . 7J 69
East Pk. Pde. LS9: Leeds . . . 7J 69
East Pk. Pl. LS9: Leeds . . . 7J 69
East Pk. Rd. HX3: Hal . . . 3N 97
LS9: Leeds . . . 8M 5 (7H 69)
East Pk. St. LS9: Leeds . . . 7J 69
LS27: Morl . . . 1J 103
East Pk. Ter. LS9: Leeds . . . 7J 69
East Pk. Vw. LS9: Leeds . . . 7J 69
East Pinfold S71: Roys . . . 6D 160
East Riddlesden Hall . . . 7M 27
E. Ridge Vw. LS25: Gar . . . 5C 72
EAST RIGTON . . . 4E 36
East Rd. BD12: Low M . . . 7C 82
East Royd BD22: Oak . . . 5D 42
HX3: Hip . . . 3H 99
(off Northedge La.)
E. Side Ct. LS28: Pud . . . 9E 66
E. Squire La. BD8: B'frd . . . 5A 64
East St. HD3: Hud . . . 1G 136
HD6: Ras . . . 2M 119
HD7: Golc . . . 6D 136
HD9: Jack B . . . 5C 170
HX3: Hip . . . 5M 99
HX6: Tri . . . 1E 116
LS2: Leeds . . . 7J 5 (7F 68)
LS9: Leeds . . . 8J 5 (7F 68)
S72: S Hien . . . 4M 161
WF1: Wake . . . 1L 125
WF3: S'ley . . . 1B 126
WF4: H'cft . . . 9L 145
WF9: S Elm . . . 5A 164
WF17: Bat . . . 7F 102
East Ter. BD22: Cros R . . . 7E 42
EAST THORPE . . . 7K 121
E. Thorpe Pl. WF14: Mir . . . 7M 121
East Vw. BD12: O'haw . . . 8D 82
BD13: Que . . . 3H 81
BD13: Thorn . . . 6B 62
BD19: Cleck . . . 6E 100
BD20: Sils . . . 8E 12
HD1: Hud . . . 3K 137
(off Mitre St.)
HD8: Shel . . . 6M 155
HX3: Hip . . . 5M 99
HX4: Holy . . . 7B 118
HX5: Ell . . . 5H 119
HX6: Sow B . . . 7J 97
HX7: Crag V . . . 1K 115
HX7: Heb B . . . 1F 94
HX7: Myth . . . 5L 95
LS15: Leeds . . . 4D 70
LS19: Yead . . . 1N 47
LS25: Kip . . . 3B 90
LS25: M'fld . . . 9H 73
LS26: Oul . . . 8D 88
LS27: Gil . . . 8F 84
LS28: Pud . . . 9B 66
OL12: Whit . . . 6A 112
WF5: Oss . . . 8A 124
WF6: Alt . . . 9F 106
WF10: C'frd . . . 5A 108
WF11: Knot . . . 8F 110
WF12: T'hill . . . 9G 123
WF14: Mir . . . 5K 121
East Vw. Cotts. *LS28: Pud . . . 6C 66*
(off Priestley Gdns.)
East Vw. Rd. LS19: Yead . . . 1N 47
East Vw. Ter. BD12: Wyke . . . 9C 82
LS21: Otley . . . 1M 31
(off Carlton St.)
Eastville Rd. WF4: S Comn . . . 8J 127
Eastway WF14: Mir . . . 4K 121
Eastway Pk. WF14: Mir . . . 4L 121
EASTWOOD
BD21 . . . 8K 27
OL14 . . . 4C 94
Eastwood Av. HX2: Illing . . . 6L 79
HX6: Sow B . . . 9F 96
WF2: Wake . . . 4H 125
Eastwood Cl. HX2: Illing . . . 6L 79
WF4: Dur . . . 3H 143
Eastwood Ct. HX3: Hal . . . 8N 97
Eastwood Cres. BD16: Cot . . . 7G 44
LS14: Leeds . . . 2E 70
Eastwood Dr. LS14: Leeds . . . 1E 70
Eastwood Gdns.
LS14: Leeds . . . 2D 70
Eastwood Gth. LS14: Leeds . . . 2E 70
Eastwood Gro. HX2: Illing . . . 6L 79
LS25: Gar . . . 9A 72
Eastwood La. LS14: Leeds . . . 2E 70
OL14: Tod . . . 3B 94
Eastwood Nook LS14: Leeds . . . 2E 70
Eastwood Rd. OL14: Tod . . . 1J 93
Eastwood's Farm *HX2: Illing . . . 6L 79*
(off Keighley Rd.)
Eastwood St. BD4: B'frd . . . 8D 6 (9D 64)
HD5: Hud . . . 5B 138
HD6: Brigh . . . 9N 99
HX3: Hal . . . 2N 97
Eastwood Ter. WF5: Oss . . . 5N 123
Easy Rd. LS9: Leeds . . . 8M 5 (8H 69)
Eaton Hill LS16: Leeds . . . 4H 49
Eaton M. LS10: Leeds . . . 8E 86
Eaton Pl. WF9: Hems . . . 2E 162
Eaton Rd. LS29: I'ly . . . 6F 14
Eaton Sq. LS10: Leeds . . . 9E 86
Eaton St. BD21: Keigh . . . 3G 43
Eaton Wlk. WF9: S Elm . . . 4N 163
Eaves Av. HX7: Heb B . . . 9F 76
Eaves La. HX7: Hept . . . 9G 76
Eaves Mt. HX7: Hept . . . 9F 76
Eaves Rd. HX7: Heb B . . . 9F 76
Ebberston Gro. LS6: Leeds . . . 3B 68
Ebberston Pl. LS6: Leeds . . . 3B 68
Ebberston Ter. LS6: Leeds . . . 3B 68
Ebberton Cl. WF9: Hems . . . 2E 162
Ebenezer Ho. *LS27: Morl . . . 9K 85*
(off Fountain St.)
Ebenezer Pl. BD7: B'frd . . . 1M 81
Ebenezer St. BD1: B'frd . . . 5C 6 (8D 64)
LS28: Fars . . . 3A 66
WF3: Rob H . . . 1K 105
Ebony Vw. BD22: Keigh . . . 3G 43
Ebor Ct. *BD21: Keigh . . . 1H 43*
(off Aireworth St.)
Ebor Gdns. WF14: Mir . . . 6K 121
Ebor La. BD22: Haw . . . 7C 42
Ebor Mt. LS6: Leeds . . . 4B 68
LS25: Kip . . . 3A 90
Ebor Pl. LS6: Leeds . . . 4B 68
Ebor St. LS6: Leeds . . . 1A 4 (4B 68)
Ebor Ter. *LS10: Leeds . . . 3G 87*
(off Woodhouse Hill Rd.)
Ebridge Ct. *BD16: Bgly . . . 4F 44*
(off Edward St.)
Ebson Ho. La. HD9: New M . . . 2F 170
Ebury Cl. WF17: Bat . . . 6G 102
Ebury St. WF17: Bat . . . 6G 102
Ecclesburn Av. LS9: Leeds . . . 7J 69
Ecclesburn Rd. LS9: Leeds . . . 7J 69
Ecclesburn St. LS9: Leeds . . . 7J 69
Ecclesburn Ter. LS9: Leeds . . . 7J 69
Eccles Ct. BD2: B'frd . . . 2F 64
ECCLESHILL . . . 1G 65
Eccleshill Swimming Pool . . . 9H 47
Eccles Parlour HX6: Ripp . . . 4A 116
ECCUP . . . 7B 34
Eccup La. LS16: Ecc, Leeds . . . 1N 49
Eccup Moor Rd. LS16: Ecc . . . 8A 34
Echo Central LS9: Leeds . . . 8G 69
Echo Central Two *LS9: Leeds . . . 8G 69*
(off Cross Grn. La.)
Echo St. WF15: Liv . . . 1K 121
Edale Av. HD4: Hud . . . 9L 137
Edale Cl. HD5: K'htn . . . 1F 138
Edale Gro. BD13: Que . . . 5B 80
Edale Way LS16: Leeds . . . 4J 49
Eddercliff Cres. WF15: Liv . . . 6L 101
Edderthorpe St. BD3: B'frd . . . 5F 6 (8E 64)
Eddison Cl. LS16: Leeds . . . 2N 49
Eddison St. LS28: Fars . . . 4A 66
Eddison Wlk. LS16: Leeds . . . 2N 49
Eddystone Ri. WF11: Knot . . . 8C 110
(not continuous)
Edelshain Gro. WF2: Wake . . . 2A 144
Eden Av. WF2: Wake . . . 6F 124
WF5: Oss . . . 5N 123
Eden Cl. BD12: Wyke . . . 1B 100
Eden Cres. LS4: Leeds . . . 2L 67
Edendale WF10: C'frd . . . 4F 108
Eden Dr. LS4: Leeds . . . 3L 67
Eden Gdns. LS4: Leeds . . . 3L 67
Eden Gro. LS4: Leeds . . . 3L 67
Eden Mt. LS4: Leeds . . . 3L 67
Eden Rd. LS4: Leeds . . . 2L 67
Edensor Rd. BD21: Keigh . . . 9G 27
Eden Wlk. LS4: Leeds . . . 3L 67
Eden Way LS4: Leeds . . . 3L 67
Ederoyd Av. LS28: Stan . . . 5M 65
Ederoyd Cres. LS28: Stan . . . 5L 65
Ederoyd Dr. LS28: Stan . . . 5M 65
Ederoyd Gro. LS28: Stan . . . 5M 65
Ederoyd Mt. LS28: Stan . . . 5M 65
Ederoyd Ri. LS28: Stan . . . 5L 65
Edgar St. BD14: Clay . . . 1J 81
Edgbaston Cl. LS17: Leeds . . . 1C 50
Edgbaston Wlk. LS17: Leeds . . . 1C 50
Edge Arpers Ct. WF12: T'hill . . . 1H 141
Edge Av. WF12: T'hill . . . 1G 140
Edgebank Av. BD6: B'frd . . . 7L 81
Edge Bottom BD13: Denh . . . 5K 61
Edge Cl. HD7: Golc . . . 6D 136
WF12: T'hill . . . 1H 141
Edge Ct. WF16: Heck . . . 7B 102
Edgecumbe Ho. HX1: Hal . . . 8J 7
Edge End *BD13: Denh . . . 5L 61*
(off Pleasant Views)
Edge End Gdns. BD6: B'frd . . . 6K 81
Edge End La. HD9: H'frth . . . 3F 168
Edge End Rd. BD6: B'frd . . . 5K 81
Edgefield Gro. HX3: Hal . . . 9N 97
Edgehey Grn. HX7: Hept . . . 7C 76
Edge Hill HD7: Linth . . . 9D 136
Edge Hill Cl. HD5: Hud . . . 3B 138
Edgehill Cl. BD13: Que . . . 4E 80
Edgehill Rd. S75: S'ross . . . 7J 159
Edgeholme La. HX2: Hal . . . 5H 97
Edge Junc. WF12: T'hill . . . 1G 141
Edge La. HX7: Hept . . . 5M 75
WF12: T'hill . . . 9H 123
Edgemoor Cl. BD4: B'frd . . . 5J 83
HX3: Hal . . . 8A 98
OL12: Whit . . . 6A 112
Edgemoor Rd. HD9: Hon . . . 6K 153
WF4: Hol . . . 7H 143
Edge Nook *BD6: B'frd . . . 4M 81*
(off Windmill Hill)
Edge Rd. WF12: T'hill . . . 1H 141
EDGERTON . . . 2H 137
Edgerton Grn. HD1: Hud . . . 3K 137
Edgerton Gro. Rd. HD1: Hud . . . 3K 137
Edgerton Ho. HD2: Hud . . . 1J 137
Edgerton La. HD1: Hud . . . 3K 137
Edgerton Rd. HD1: Hud . . . 2K 137
HD3: Hud . . . 2K 137
LS16: Leeds . . . 7L 49
Edge Ter. HD3: Hud . . . 3E 136
Edge Top Rd. WF12: T'hill . . . 1F 140
Edge Vw. HD7: Golc . . . 6D 136
WF12: T'hill . . . 1H 141
Edgeware Rd. HD5: Hud . . . 4E 138
Edgware Av. LS8: Leeds . . . 1M 5 (4H 69)
Edgware Gro. LS8: Leeds . . . 1M 5 (4H 69)
Edgware Mt. LS8: Leeds . . . 1M 5 (4H 69)
Edgware Pl. LS8: Leeds . . . 1M 5 (4H 69)
Edgware Row LS8: Leeds . . . 1M 5 (4H 69)
Edgware St. LS8: Leeds . . . 1L 5 (4H 69)
Edgware Ter. LS8: Leeds . . . 1M 5 (4H 69)
Edgware Vw. LS8: Leeds . . . 1M 5 (4H 69)
Edinburgh Av. LS12: Leeds . . . 6K 67
Edinburgh Gro. LS12: Leeds . . . 6K 67
Edinburgh Pl. LS12: Leeds . . . 6K 67
LS25: Gar . . . 7B 72
Edinburgh Rd. LS12: Leeds . . . 6K 67
Edinburgh Ter. LS12: Leeds . . . 6K 67
Edison Gdns. *LS20: Guis . . . 6H 31*
(off Netherfield Rd.)
Edison Ho. LS20: Guis . . . 7H 31
Edison Way LS20: Guis . . . 6H 31
Ediths Vw. HX6: Sow B . . . 8H 97
Edith Syke Dr. LS15: Leeds . . . 5F 70
Edlington Cl. BD4: B'frd . . . 2J 83
Edlington Vw. WF11: Knot . . . 7D 110
Edmonton Pl. LS7: Leeds . . . 9F 50
Edmund St. BD5: B'frd . . . 6A 6 (8B 64)
OL14: W'den . . . 3J 113
Edna St. WF9: S Elm . . . 6N 163
Edrich Cl. BD12: Low M . . . 7C 82
Edroyd Pl. LS28: Fars . . . 3A 66
Edroyd St. LS28: Fars . . . 3A 66
Edson Cl. BD6: B'frd . . . 5K 81
Education Rd. LS7: Leeds . . . 3E 68
Edward Cl. HX3: Sou . . . 8F 98
LS28: Pud . . . 7A 66
WF12: Dew . . . 8E 122
Edward Ct. WF2: Carr G . . . 7G 104
Edward Dr. WF1: Out . . . 7K 105
Edward Rd. DN6: Skel, Carc . . . 7N 165
WF14: Mir . . . 6K 121
Edwards Rd. HX2: Hal . . . 7L 97
Edward St. BD4: B'frd . . . 6C 6 (8D 64)
(Bedford St.)
BD4: B'frd . . . 4J 83
(Lister St.)
BD16: Bgly . . . 4F 44
BD18: Ship . . . 6L 45
HD6: Brigh . . . 9M 99
HD6: Clift . . . 1A 120
HX6: Sow B . . . 8H 97
HX7: Heb B . . . 1J 95
LS2: Leeds . . . 5G 5 (6E 68)
OL12: Whit . . . 9A 112
S75: Map . . . 9L 159
WF1: Wake . . . 2L 9 (4M 125)
WF6: Alt . . . 7H 107
WF15: Liv . . . 7L 101
(Garden Wlk.)
WF15: Liv . . . 8L 101
(Knowler Hill)
Edward Turner Cl. BD12: Low M . . . 7A 82
Edwin Av. LS20: Guis . . . 7H 31
Edwin Rd. LS6: Leeds . . . 4A 68
Edwins Cl. S71: Ath . . . 9A 160
Eelholme Vw. St. BD20: Keigh . . . 6H 27
Eel Mires Gth. LS22: Weth . . . 3N 23
Effingham Rd. BD16: Har . . . 6N 43
Egerton Gro. BD15: All . . . 5F 62
Egerton St. HX6: Sow B . . . 8H 97
Egerton Ter. *LS19: Raw . . . 4A 48*
(off Town St.)
Eggleston Dr. BD4: B'frd . . . 3K 83
Egglestone Sq. LS23: B Spa . . . 1C 38
Eggleston St. LS13: Leeds . . . 1C 66
Egham Grn. *BD10: B'frd . . . 8F 46*
(off Booth St.)
Egmanton Rd. S71: Ath . . . 8A 160
Egremont Cres. BD6: B'frd . . . 7L 81
Egremont St. HX6: Sow B . . . 9G 97
Egremont Ter. *HX6: Sow B . . . 9G 97*
(off Sowerby New Rd.)
EGYPT . . . 6B 62
Egypt Rd. BD13: Thorn . . . 6B 62
Eider Cl. BD6: B'frd . . . 4H 81
Eiffel Bldgs. HX7: Heb B . . . 1H 95
Eiffel St. HX7: Heb B . . . 1J 95
Eighth Av. LS12: Leeds . . . 8N 67
LS26: Rothw . . . 6B 88
WF15: Liv . . . 7F 100
EIGHTLANDS . . . 3F 122
Eightlands Av. LS13: Leeds . . . 4G 67
Eightlands La. LS13: Leeds . . . 4G 67
Eightlands Rd. WF13: Dew . . . 3F 122
Ekota Pl. LS8: Leeds . . . 2H 69
Elam Grange BD20: Rid . . . 6J 27
Elam Wood BD20: Rid . . . 5K 27
Elam Wood Rd. BD20: Rid . . . 4J 27
Eland Ho. *HX5: Ell . . . 4E 118*
(off Westgate)
Elba LS12: Leeds . . . 7A 4 (7B 68)
Elba Ter. WF4: Horb . . . 8D 124
Elbow La. BD2: B'frd . . . 4F 64
HX2: Lud . . . 3E 96
Elder Av. WF2: Wake . . . 4J 125
WF9: Upt . . . 1B 164
Elder Bank *BD13: Cull . . . 9K 43*
(off Keighley Rd.)
Elderberry Cl. BD20: E Mor . . . 7A 28
Elderberry Dr. HX3: Hal . . . 8D 98
Elderberry Vw. WF10: C'frd . . . 7A 108
Elder Cl. WF17: Birs . . . 2C 102
Elder Cft. LS13: Leeds . . . 5F 66
Elder Dr. WF9: Upt . . . 1A 164
WF12: Dew . . . 8G 122
Elder Gth. LS25: Gar . . . 8B 72
Elder Grn. WF2: Wake . . . 4J 125
Elder Gro. HD4: Neth . . . 3J 153
WF2: Wake . . . 4J 125
Elder Gro. M. HD4: Neth . . . 3J 153
Elder La. HD2: Hud . . . 6E 120
Elder Lea HX2: Brad . . . 4N 79
WF5: Oss . . . 7A 124
Elder M. HD8: Shel . . . 6K 155
WF5: Oss . . . 7D 124
Elder Mt. LS13: Leeds . . . 5F 66
Elder Pl. LS13: Leeds . . . 5F 66
Elder Ri. LS26: W'frd . . . 7F 88
Elder Rd. HD2: Hud . . . 6D 120
LS13: Leeds . . . 5F 66
Elder St. BD10: B'frd . . . 8J 47
BD20: Keigh . . . 6G 27
LS13: Leeds . . . 5F 66
Elder Way S72: S Hien . . . 3M 161
Elderwood Gdns. BD10: B'frd . . . 1J 65
Eldon Ct. LS2: Leeds . . . 1D 4 (4D 68)
Eldon Mt. LS20: Guis . . . 7J 31
Eldon Pl. BD1: B'frd . . . 2A 6 (6B 64)
BD4: B'frd . . . 1H 83
BD19: Cleck . . . 5J 101
(off Dewsbury Rd.)
Eldon Rd. HD1: Hud . . . 4J 137
Eldon St. HX3: Hal . . . 1L 7 (3B 98)
OL14: Tod . . . 7L 93
WF5: Oss . . . 4B 124
WF16: Heck . . . 8A 102
Eldon Ter. BD1: B'frd . . . 6B 64
LS2: Leeds . . . 1D 4
Eldroth Mt. HX1: Hal . . . 7N 97
Eldroth Rd. HX1: Hal . . . 8G 7 (7N 97)
ELDWICK . . . 3G 45
ELDWICK BECK . . . 2H 45
Eldwick Beck BD16: Bgly . . . 1J 45
Eldwick Cft. BD16: Bgly . . . 2H 45
Eleanor Dr. LS28: Cal . . . 8K 47
Eleanor St. HD1: Hud . . . 2M 137
HD6: Ras . . . 2M 119
Elephants Yd. *WF8: Pon . . . 3K 129*
(off Market Pl.)
Eleventh Av. WF15: Liv . . . 7G 100
Elford Gro. LS8: Leeds . . . 1M 5 (3H 69)
Elford Pl. E. LS8: Leeds . . . 3H 69
Elford Pl. W. LS8: Leeds . . . 3H 69
Elford Rd. LS8: Leeds . . . 3H 69
Elgar Wlk. WF3: S'ley . . . 7N 105
Elgin Cl. HD4: Hud . . . 8H 137
Elia St. BD21: Keigh . . . 8K 27
Elim Wlk. *WF13: Dew . . . 3F 122*
(off Willan's Rd.)
Eliot Gro. LS20: Guis . . . 8K 31
Eliots Cl. WF10: C'frd . . . 7J 109
Eli St. BD5: B'frd . . . 2D 82
Elizabethan Ct. WF8: Pon . . . 1L 129
Elizabethan Manor House Art Gallery & Museum . . . 5G 14
Elizabeth Av. BD12: Wyke . . . 9B 82
S72: S Hien . . . 4M 161
Elizabeth Cl. BD12: Wyke . . . 9B 82
Elizabeth Ct. LS22: Coll . . . 9J 23
LS28: Pud . . . 7A 66
WF9: Hems . . . 3F 162
WF10: C'frd . . . 4J 109
Elizabeth Cres. BD12: Wyke . . . 9B 82
Elizabeth Dr. BD12: Wyke . . . 9B 82
WF10: C'frd . . . 3J 109
WF11: Ferr . . . 8B 110
Elizabeth Gdns. WF1: Wake . . . 1K 9 (3L 125)
Elizabeth Gro. LS27: Morl . . . 7M 85
Elizabeth Ho. *HX2: Illing . . . 9L 79*
(off Furness Pl.)
Elizabeth Ind. Est. HX3: Hal . . . 1G 7 (4N 97)
Elizabeth Pl. LS14: Leeds . . . 1B 70
Elizabeth Rd. LS26: W'frd . . . 7M 89
Elizabeth St. BD5: B'frd . . . 7A 6 (9C 64)
BD12: Wyke . . . 9A 82
BD16: Bgly . . . 4F 44
BD21: Keigh . . . 9L 27
BD22: Oak . . . 5D 42
HD4: Hud . . . 7M 137
HX4: Gree . . . 4C 118
HX5: Ell . . . 5E 118
LS6: Leeds . . . 3A 68
WF1: Wake . . . 9N 125
WF15: Liv . . . 8J 101
ELLAND . . . 5E 118
Elland Bri. HX5: Ell . . . 4E 118
Elland Golf Course . . . 6C 118
Elland Hall Farm Caravan Pk. HX5: Ell . . . 4D 118
Elland Ho. *LS14: Leeds . . . 9N 51*
(off Kingsdale Ct.)
Elland La. HD6: Brigh . . . 1M 119
HX5: Ell . . . 4F 118
(not continuous)
ELLAND LOWER EDGE . . . 4J 119
Elland Riorges Link HX5: Ell . . . 4F 118
Elland Road . . . 2A 86
Elland Rd. HD6: Brigh . . . 2F 118
HX4: Bark . . . 7E 116
HX5: Ell . . . 4F 118
(Elland Riorges Link)
HX5: Ell, Hal . . . 2F 118
(Park Rd.)
HX6: Hal, Ripp . . . 7E 116
LS11: Leeds . . . 3N 85
(Crow Nest La.)
LS11: Leeds . . . 6L 85
(Daffil Rd.)
LS11: Leeds . . . 1B 86
(Tilbury Rd.)
LS27: Chur . . . 6L 85
Elland Rd. Ind. Pk. LS11: Leeds . . . 2N 85
Elland St. WF10: C'frd . . . 3E 108
Elland Ter. LS11: Leeds . . . 9D 68
ELLAND UPPER EDGE . . . 5H 119
Elland Way LS11: Leeds . . . 3N 85
Elland Wood Bottom HX3: Hal . . . 2C 118
Ellar Carr Rd. BD10: B'frd . . . 5G 46
BD13: Cull . . . 8J 43
Ellar Gdns. LS29: Men . . . 2E 30
Ellar Ghyll LS21: Otley . . . 3G 30
Ella St. WF9: Fitz . . . 6A 146
Ellen Holme HX2: Lud F . . . 6D 96

Ellen Holme Rd.—Fagley Ter.

Ellen Holme Rd. HX2: Lud F .6D 96
Ellen Royd La. HX2: Lud F, Midg .4C 96
Ellen Royd St. HX3: Hal .1L 7 (4B 98)
Ellen St. BD16: Bgly .4F 44
Ellenthorpe Rd. BD17: Bail .5K 45
ELLENTREES .8H 107
Ellentrees La. WF6: Alt .7H 107
Ellerburn Dr. BD6: B'frd .5K 81
Ellerby La. LS9: Leeds .8L 5 (8G 69)
Ellerby Rd. LS9: Leeds .8K 5 (7G 68)
Eller Ct. LS8: Leeds .9L 51
Ellercroft Av. BD7: B'frd .9M 63
Ellercroft Rd. BD7: B'frd .8M 63
Ellercroft Ter. BD7: B'frd .8M 63
Ellerker La. LS14: T'ner .2J 53
Ellerker Rd. LS14: T'ner .1H 53
Ellers Gro. LS8: Leeds .2H 69
Ellerslie Cl. HD2: Hud .2K 137
Ellerslie Ct. HD2: Hud .2J 137
Ellerslie Hall LS2: Leeds .2B 4
Ellers Rd. LS8: Leeds .2H 69
Ellerton St. BD3: B'frd .7G 65
Ellicott Ct. LS29: Men .4E 30
Ellies Ct. LS17: Leeds .3J 51
Ellingham Ct. BD13: Thorn .8D 62
(off Havelock Sq.)
Ellin's Ter. WF6: Norm .3H 127
Ellinthorpe St. BD4: B'frd .9F 64
Elliot Ct. BD13: Que .4C 80
LS13: Leeds .2D 66
Elliotsdale St. WF7: F'stne .5C 128
Elliott St. BD18: Ship .7M 45
BD20: Sils .8D 12
Ellis Ct. HX3: Nor G .1L 99
WF5: Oss .8A 124
Ellis Fold LS12: Leeds .7L 67
Ellis Laithe Fold WF4: H'cft .2F 160
Ellis La. LS25: Gar .4L 71
Ellison Fold BD17: Bail .3A 46
Ellison Gro. BD11: B'haw .7L 83
Ellison St. HD4: Hud .6J 137
HX3: Hal .3N 97
Ellis St. BD5: B'frd .2B 82
WF4: Horb .1C 142
Ellis Ter. LS6: Leeds .9N 49
(off Glebe Ter.)
Elliston Av. S75: S'ross .8L 159
Ellistones Gdns. HX4: Gree .4N 117
Ellistones La. HX4: Gree .5N 117
Ellistones Pl. HX4: Gree .5N 117
Ellmont Av. HD8: Eml .3F 156
Ellton Gro. BD6: B'frd .4M 81
Ellwood Cl. LS7: Leeds .8B 50
Elm Apartments WF1: Wake .1M 9
Elm Av. HD9: T'bdge .9A 154
HX6: Sow B .7H 97
LS25: Kip .2N 89
OL14: Tod .5K 93
WF3: S'ley .8A 106
Elmbridge Cl. S71: Roys .6F 160
Elm Cl. WF5: Oss .8A 124
WF8: D'ton .6B 130
WF8: Pon .1L 129
Elm Cotts. WF1: Hea .7D 126
Elm Ct. BD11: B'haw .9M 83
BD15: Wils .2B 62
HD8: Kbtn .2K 155
Elm Cres. BD20: E Mor .8C 28
WF9: Kins .8B 146
Elm Cft. LS14: Leeds .7D 52
Elmet Dr. LS15: Bar E .8M 53
Elmete Av. LS8: Leeds .8L 51
LS15: Scho .9G 52
Elmete Cl. LS8: Leeds .9M 51
Elmete Ct. LS8: Leeds .9L 51
Elmete Cft. LS15: Scho .9G 53
Elmete Dr. LS8: Leeds .8M 51
Elmete Grange LS29: Men .4E 30
Elmete Gro. LS8: Leeds .8L 51
Elmete Hill LS8: Leeds .9M 51
Elmete La. LS8: Leeds .8M 51
LS17: Shad .5N 51
Elmete Mt. LS8: Leeds .9M 51
Elmete Rd. WF10: C'frd .3K 109
Elmete Wlk. LS8: Leeds .9L 51
Elmete Way LS8: Leeds .9M 51
Elmet Rd. LS15: Bar E .9M 53
Elmet Way LS14: Leeds .2D 70
Elmfield BD17: Bail .3B 46
LS26: Oul .8E 88
Elmfield Av. HD3: Hud .5E 136
Elmfield Bus. Pk. LS25: Gar .6A 72
Elmfield Ct. BD11: B'haw .9L 83
LS13: Leeds .5G 67
LS27: Morl .1L 103
Elmfield Dr. BD6: B'frd .5A 82
HD8: Skelm .8D 156
Elmfield Gro. LS12: Leeds .8N 67
Elmfield Pde. LS27: Morl .2L 103
Elmfield Pl. LS12: Leeds .8N 67
Elmfield Rd. HD2: Hud .1K 137
LS12: Leeds .8N 67
LS27: Morl .2L 103
Elmfield Ter. HX1: Hal .8H 7 (7A 98)
Elmfield Way LS13: Leeds .5G 67
Elm Gdns. HD8: Skelm .7D 156
HX3: Hal .8L 7 (7B 98)
WF10: C'frd .7K 109
Elm Gro. BD18: Ship .8C 46
BD19: Gom .4L 101
BD20: E Mor .8C 28
BD20: Sils .8D 12
BD21: Keigh .3G 43
HX3: She .7J 81
LS29: Burl W .9D 16
WF4: Horb .1D 142
WF9: S Elm .6M 163
WF16: Heck .7N 101
Elm Ho. LS7: Leeds .8G 50
(off Allerton Pk.)
LS15: Leeds .8N 69
Elmhurst Cl. LS17: Leeds .3J 51
Elmhurst Gdns. LS17: Leeds .3J 51
Elmhurst Gro. WF11: Knot .9E 110
Elm M. WF4: Horb .1D 142
Elm Pk. WF8: Pon .5J 129
Elm Pl. HX1: Hal .5M 97
HX6: Sow B .7H 97
WF11: Knot .9D 110
Elm Rd. BD18: Ship .8B 46
DN6: Skel .8M 165
WF6: Norm .4J 127
WF9: Hems .2E 162
WF13: Dew .3C 122
Elmroyd LS26: Rothw .9A 88
Elms, The LS7: Leeds .9F 50
LS13: Leeds .5H 67
LS20: Guis .7J 31
WF7: Ackw .5F 146
Elmsall Dr. WF9: S Elm .4B 164
Elmsall La. DN6: Moor .9A 164
Elmsall Way WF9: S Elm .4A 164
Elms Ct. HX2: Illing .8L 79
Elmsdale Cl. WF9: S Elm .7A 164
Elms Hill HD7: Slait .1M 151
Elmsley St. BD20: Stee .3C 26
Elm St. BD22: Oxen .3C 60
HD4: Hud .8C 8 (6N 137)
HD8: Skelm .7D 156
HX4: Holy .7N 117
LS6: Leeds .2D 68
WF4: N Cro .3J 145
Elm Ter. HD6: Brigh .7N 99
LS21: Otley .9N 17
WF8: Pon .3J 129
Elmton Cl. LS10: Leeds .6F 86
Elm Tree Av. BD6: B'frd .5A 82
Elm Tree Cl. BD6: B'frd .5B 82
BD21: Keigh .1K 43
LS15: Leeds .8F 70
LS28: Pud .8B 66
WF15: Liv .1N 121
Elm Tree Gdns. BD6: B'frd .4A 82
Elmtree La. LS10: Leeds .1F 86
Elm Tree St. WF1: Wake .7N 125
Elm Vw. BD20: Stee .2B 26
HX3: Hal .8L 7
Elm Walk, The LS15: Leeds .9C 70
Elm Way WF17: Birs .2D 102
Elmwood Av. HD1: Hud .3A 8 (3M 137)
LS15: Bar E .8L 53
WF2: W'ton .3C 144
Elmwood Chase LS15: Bar E .8L 53
Elmwood Cl. HD1: Hud .3A 8 (3M 137)
WF2: W'ton .3C 144
WF14: Up H .1K 139
Elmwood Ct. LS15: Bar E .8L 53
Elmwood Dr. BD22: Keigh .3F 42
HD6: Brigh .9L 99
WF2: W'ton .3C 144
Elmwood Gth. WF2: W'ton .3C 144
Elmwood Gro. WF4: Horb .1E 142
WF17: Bat .9G 102
Elmwood La. LS2: Leeds .3G 5 (5E 68)
LS15: Bar E .8L 53
Elmwood Pl. BD2: B'frd .5G 64
(off Fagley Rd.)
Elmwood Rd. BD22: Keigh .4F 42
Elmwood St. HD6: Brigh .8N 99
HX1: Hal .7N 97
Elmwood Ter. BD22: Keigh .3F 42
LS22: Coll .9J 23
WF13: Dew .2F 122
Elphaborough Cl. HX7: Myth .4M 95
Elphin Ct. HX7: Myth .4L 95
Elphin Gro. HX7: Myth .4L 95
Elsdon Gro. BD5: B'frd .8A 6 (9C 64)
Elsham Fold WF9: Hems .2E 162
Elsham Mdws. WF12: Dew .5J 123
Elsham Ter. LS4: Leeds .4M 67
Elsicker La. WF1: Warm .5G 126
Elsie Bruce Gro. LS15: Leeds .5F 70
Elsie St. BD20: Keigh .6H 27
BD22: Cros R .7F 42
Elsie Whiteley Innovation Cen. .4J 7
Elsinore Av. HX5: Ell .5D 118
Elsinore Ct. HX5: Ell .5D 118
Elston Dr. BD20: Rid .8A 28
(off Ford Rd.)
Elstone Vw. WF1: Out .8J 105
Elsworth Av. BD3: B'frd .5H 65
Elsworth Ho. LS5: Leeds .2J 67
Elsworth St. LS12: Leeds .7N 67
Eltham Av. LS6: Leeds .3D 68
Eltham Cl. LS6: Leeds .3D 68
Eltham Ct. LS6: Leeds .3D 68
Eltham Dr. LS6: Leeds .3D 68
Eltham Gdns. LS6: Leeds .3D 68
Eltham Gro. BD6: B'frd .5M 81
Eltham Ri. LS6: Leeds .3D 68
Elvaston Rd. LS27: Morl .1K 103
Elvey Cl. BD2: B'frd .2H 65
Elvey St. WF1: Wake .2K 9 (4L 125)
Elwell Cl. HX3: She .6J 81
Elwell St. WF3: Thpe H .3G 104
Elwyn Gro. BD5: B'frd .2C 82
Elwyn Rd. BD5: B'frd .2D 82
Ely St. HX4: Gree .5C 118
LS12: Leeds .6M 67
Embankment, The LS1: Leeds .8F 4 (7E 68)
LS4: Leeds .4N 67
WF14: Mir .6L 121
Emblem Ct. BD13: Que .5C 80
Emblem Ter. WF1: Wake .8M 125
Embleton Rd. LS26: Meth .3K 107
Embsay and Bolton Abbey Steam Railway
Bolton Abbey Station .3J 11
Holywell Halt Station .3B 10
Emerald St. BD22: Keigh .3G 42
HD1: Hud .1C 8 (2N 137)
WF17: Bat .6E 102
Emerson Av. BD9: B'frd .3J 63
Emily Ct. BD7: B'frd .2N 81
(off Oakwell Cl.)
Emily Hall Gdns. BD15: Wils .1B 62
Emily St. BD21: Keigh .8J 27
BD22: Haw .8D 42
(off Victoria Rd.)
WF9: S Kirk .6K 163
Emily Way HX1: Hal .8K 7 (7B 98)
EMLEY .2F 156
Emley Moor Bus. Pk. HD8: Eml .3D 156
Emley Vw. LS25: Kip .2N 89
Emmanuel Ter. HD4: Hud .8L 137
Emmanuel Trad. Est. LS12: Leeds .8C 68
Emmeline Cl. BD10: B'frd .7F 46
Emmet Cl. BD11: B'haw .8M 83
Emmfield Dr. BD9: B'frd .2M 63
Emm La. BD9: B'frd .3M 63
Emmott Dr. LS19: Raw .4A 48
Emmott Farm Fold BD22: Haw .9C 42
Emmott Vw. LS19: Raw .4A 48
Empire Bus. Cen. HX2: Hal .9N 79
Empire Ct. HD6: B Bri .5N 99
Empire Ter. S71: Roys .5E 160
Empsall Row HD6: Brigh .9N 99
(off Bonegate Rd.)
Emscote Av. HX1: Hal .7G 7 (7N 97)
Emscote Gdns. HX1: Hal .7G 7 (7N 97)
Emscote Gro. HX1: Hal .7G 7 (7N 97)
Emscote Pl. HX1: Hal .7G 7 (7N 97)
Emscote St. Sth. HX1: Hal .7G 7 (7N 97)
Emsley Cl. BD4: B'frd .5F 82
Emsley Pl. LS10: Leeds .9G 68
Emsley's Farm Shop Vis. Cen. .2L 47
Emville Av. LS17: Leeds .2L 51
Endecliff M. LS6: Leeds .2B 68
Enderby Cl. HX3: Hal .1M 97
Enderley Rd. BD13: Thorn .8C 62
Endor Cres. LS29: Burl W .1D 30
Endor Gro. LS29: Burl W .1D 30
Endsleigh Pl. BD14: Clay .1G 81
Enfield LS19: Yead .1M 47
Enfield Av. LS7: Leeds .1K 5 (4G 68)
Enfield Cl. WF17: Bat .6C 102
Enfield Dr. BD6: B'frd .4M 81
WF17: Bat .6C 102
Enfield Pde. BD6: B'frd .4M 81
Enfield Rd. BD17: Bail .5A 46
Enfield Side Rd. BD22: S'bury .1L 59
Enfield St. BD21: Keigh .9J 27
LS7: Leeds .1J 5 (4F 68)
Enfield Ter. LS7: Leeds .1K 5 (4G 68)
Enfield Wlk. BD6: B'frd .4M 81
Engine Fields Nature Reserve .1L 47
Engine Fold WF2: Kirk .1E 124
Engine La. S72: Shaf .8L 161
WF4: Horb .1B 142
WF4: W Har, Wrag .1N 145
Engine La. Cl. S72: Shaf .8L 161
ENGLAND LANE .9E 110
England La. WF11: Knot .9E 110
Englefield Cl. BD4: B'frd .3J 83
Englefield Cres. BD4: B'frd .3J 83
Ennerdale Av. WF12: Dew .1H 123
Ennerdale Cl. LS22: Weth .3K 23
Ennerdale Cres. WF12: Dew .1H 123
Ennerdale Dr. BD2: B'frd .3F 64
HX5: Ell .4G 119
WF11: Knot .1D 130
Ennerdale Rd. BD2: B'frd .3E 64
LS12: N Far .3G 84
WF2: Wake .4H 125
WF12: Dew .1H 123
Ennerdale Way LS12: N Far .2G 84
Enoch La. HD4: Hud .7L 137
Enterprise 5 Lane Ends
BD10: B'frd .9F 46
Enterprise Ct. BD4: B'frd .4G 83
LS25: M'fld .8G 72
Enterprise Park Ind. Est.
LS11: Leeds .4B 86
Enterprise Way BD10: B'frd .9F 46
LS10: Leeds .4H 87
WF10: C'frd .5C 108
Envoy St. LS11: Leeds .1E 86
Epsom Gro. HX3: Sou .7D 98
Epsom Rd. LS25: Kip .3N 89
Epsom Way HD5: K'htn .1G 139
Epworth Pl. BD22: Oak .4B 42
LS10: Leeds .1G 86
Equilibrium HD3: Hud .2G 136
Equity Chambers BD1: B'frd .3B 6
Eric St. BD21: Keigh .8J 27
LS13: Leeds .1F 66
WF9: S Elm .6N 163
Erivan Pk. LS22: Weth .3A 24
Ernest St. OL14: Tod .3E 92
WF13: Dew .2G 123
Erringden Rd. HX7: Myth .3L 95
(not continuous)
Erringden St. OL14: Tod .7L 93
Escroft Cl. BD12: Wyke .3B 100
Escroft Ct. LS29: Men .5F 30
(off Clifford Dr.)
Eshald La. LS26: W'frd .8E 88
Eshald Mans. LS26: W'frd .7E 88
Eshald Pl. LS26: W'frd .7E 88
ESHOLT .2G 46
Esholt Av. LS20: Guis .9H 31
Esholt Hall Est. BD17: Esh .3H 47
Esholt La. BD17: Bail, B'frd .3D 46
Eshton Av. BD12: O'haw .8D 82
Eshton Ct. S75: Map .7J 159
Esk Av. WF10: C'frd .4H 109
Eskdale Av. HX3: She .8G 81
WF6: Alt .8H 107
Eskdale Cl. LS20: Guis .8J 31
WF6: Alt .8H 107
WF12: Dew .9H 103
Eskdale Ct. WF6: Alt .8H 107
Eskdale Cft. LS20: Guis .8J 31
WF6: Alt .8H 107
Eskdale Gro. LS25: Gar .8A 72
Eskdale Mt. HX7: Heb B .9H 77
Eskdale Ri. BD15: All .6G 63
Eskdale Rd. WF2: Wake .4G 125
Esk Gdns. LS22: Weth .1M 23
Eskine Pde. BD6: B'frd .7L 81
Esmond St. BD7: B'frd .2L 81
LS12: Leeds .7M 67
Esmond Ter. LS12: Leeds .7M 67
Esporta Health & Fitness
Cookridge .1J 49
Essex Pk. Ind. Est. BD4: B'frd .6E 6 (8E 64)
Essex St. BD4: B'frd .6E 6 (8E 64)
HX1: Hal .6M 97
HX7: Heb B .1H 95
Estcourt Av. LS6: Leeds .1M 67
Estcourt Dr. WF8: D'ton .7C 130
Estcourt Gro. BD7: B'frd .9M 63
Estcourt Rd. BD7: B'frd .9M 63
WF8: D'ton .6B 130
Estcourt Ter. LS6: Leeds .1M 67
Esther Av. WF2: Wake .7H 125
Esther Gro. WF2: Wake .7H 125
Esthwaite Gdns. LS15: Leeds .8N 69
Ethel Jackson Rd. LS15: Leeds .4F 70
Ethel St. BD20: Keigh .7H 27
OL12: Whit .9A 112
Etna St. BD7: B'frd .2L 81
Eton Av. HD5: Hud .4D 138
Eton Ct. LS7: Leeds .8G 50
Eton Fold BD8: B'frd .6J 63
Eton St. HX1: Hal .5M 97
HX7: Heb B .1G 94
Eton Ter. HX7: Myth .4M 95
Euden Edge Rd. HD7: Golc .7N 135
Eunice La. HD8: Up C .2N 171
(not continuous)
Eureka! The National Children's Mus.
.5M 7 (6C 98)
Eurocam Technology Pk. BD5: B'frd .3C 82
Euroway Trad. Est. BD4: B'frd .7E 82
Euston Gro. LS11: Leeds .1B 86
Euston Mt. LS11: Leeds .1B 86
Euston Ter. LS11: Leeds .1B 86
Evanston Av. LS4: Leeds .5M 67
Evans Towers BD5: B'frd .7B 6
Evelyn Av. BD3: B'frd .6J 65
Evelyn Pl. LS12: Leeds .8M 67
Evelyn Ter. BD13: Que .3B 80
Evens Ter. BD5: B'frd .3C 82
Everard St. HD4: Hud .6J 137
Everdale Mt. WF9: Hems .3C 162
WF9: S Elm .6L 163
Everest Av. BD18: Ship .8C 46
Evergreen Wlk. BD16: Bgly .2D 44
(off Canal Rd.)
Everleigh St. LS9: Leeds .6J 69
Eversley Dr. BD4: B'frd .1J 83
Eversley Mt. HX2: Hal .6L 97
(off Bk. Eversley Mt.)
Eversley Pl. HX2: Hal .6L 97
Eversley Rd. HX7: Heb B .9H 77
Eversley Vw. LS14: S'cft .9D 36
Every St. OL14: Tod .7L 93
Evesham Gro. BD10: B'frd .8F 46
Ewart Pl. BD7: B'frd .2M 81
Ewart St. BD7: B'frd .2M 81
BD13: Que .4D 80
EWOOD .3N 95
Ewood Ct. HX7: Myth .3A 96
Ewood Dr. HX7: Myth .3N 95
Ewood Hall Av. HX7: Myth .3N 95
Ewood La. OL14: Tod .6H 93
Excalibur Dr. WF9: S Elm .7N 163
Excelsior Cl. HX6: Ripp .8C 116
Excelsior Mill HX6: Ripp .9D 116
Exchange HD9: Hon .5L 153
Exchange St. BD19: Cleck .3H 101
HX4: Gree .5C 118
WF6: Norm .1H 127
WF9: S Elm .6M 163
Exe St. BD5: B'frd .2A 82
Exeter Dr. LS10: Leeds .6F 86
Exeter St. HX3: Hal .9C 98
HX6: Sow B .7J 97
Exhibition Rd. BD18: Ship .7L 45
EXLEY .2C 118
Exley Av. BD21: Keigh .3G 42
Exley Bank HX3: Hal .1C 118
Exley Bank Top HX3: Hal .2C 118
Exley Cres. BD21: Keigh .2G 42
(not continuous)
Exley Dr. BD21: Keigh .2G 43
Exley Gdns. HX3: Hal .2C 118
Exley Gro. BD21: Keigh .2G 42
EXLEY HEAD .2F 42
Exley Head Vw. BD22: Keigh .8E 26
Exley La. HX3: Hal .2C 118
HX5: Ell, Hal .2C 118
Exley Mt. BD7: B'frd .8L 63
BD21: Keigh .2G 42
Exley Rd. BD21: Keigh .2G 42
Exley St. BD22: Keigh .1G 43
Exley Way BD21: Keigh .3G 43
Exmoor St. HX1: Hal .6M 97
Exmouth Pl. BD3: B'frd .5D 64
Express Way WF6: Alt .6H 107
WF10: C'frd .6H 107
Eyres Av. LS12: Leeds .6M 67
Eyres Gro. LS12: Leeds .6M 67
(off Eyres Ter.)
Eyres Mill Side LS12: Leeds .6L 67
Eyres St. LS12: Leeds .6M 67
(off Eyres Ter.)
Eyres Ter. LS12: Leeds .6M 67
Eyre St. WF12: Dew .7E 122
WF17: Bat .8G 102
Eyrie App. LS27: Morl .1M 103

F

F1 Karting
Wakefield .8K 125
FACIT .9A 112
Factory La. BD4: B'frd .3F 82
HD3: Hud .6G 137
HD8: Eml .1B 156
Factory St. BD4: B'frd .3F 82
FAGLEY .4H 65
Fagley Cres. BD2: B'frd .4G 65
Fagley Cft. BD2: B'frd .4H 65
Fagley Dr. BD2: B'frd .4G 65
Fagley La. BD2: B'frd .2H 65
Fagley Pl. BD2: B'frd .5G 65
Fagley Rd. BD2: B'frd .5G 64
Fagley Ter. BD2: B'frd .5G 65

Fairbairn Fold—Featherstone Swimming Pool

Fairbairn Fold BD4: B'frd . . . 8J 65
Fair Bank BD18: Ship . . . 9A 46
Fairbank Pl. *BD18: Ship* . . . *9A 46*
(off Fair Bank)
Fairbank Rd. BD8: B'frd . . . 5M 63
Fairbanks HX6: Sow B . . . 8J 97
Fairbank Ter. BD8: B'frd . . . 5M 63
Fairbrook Rd. WF2: Wake . . . 6J 143
FAIRBURN . . . 9N 91
Fairburn Ct. HX3: Sou . . . 8F 98
Fairburn Dr. LS25: Gar . . . 7A 72
Fairburn Gdns. BD2: B'frd . . . 2G 64
Fairburn Ho. *LS18: Hors* . . . *8E 48*
(off Regent Cres.)
Fairburn Ings Cen. . . . 9J 91
Fairburn Ings Nature Reserve . . . 1H 109
Fairburn St. WF10: C'frd . . . 4C 108
Fairclough Gro. HX3: Hal . . . 1M 97
Fairfax Av. BD4: B'frd . . . 4G 82
BD11: Drig . . . 7D 84
LS29: Men . . . 3E 30
WF7: F'stne . . . 2C 128
WF11: Knot . . . 9C 110
Fairfax Cl. LS14: Leeds . . . 3C 70
Fairfax Ct. LS11: Leeds . . . 2C 86
Fairfax Cres. BD4: B'frd . . . 4G 82
HX3: Sou . . . 7F 98
Fairfax Dr. WF8: Pon . . . 2K 129
Fairfax Flats *LS21: Otley* . . . *1M 31*
(off Fairfax St.)
Fairfax Gdns. LS29: Men . . . 3E 30
Fairfax Gro. LS19: Yead . . . 9K 31
Fairfax Ho. BD1: B'frd . . . 3D 6
Fairfax Rd. BD13: Cull . . . 8K 43
BD16: Bgly . . . 2E 44
LS11: Leeds . . . 2C 86
LS29: Men . . . 3D 30
WF8: Pon . . . 3L 129
Fairfax St. BD4: B'frd . . . 7D 6 (9D 64)
BD20: Sils . . . 8D 12
BD22: Haw . . . 8D 42
LS21: Otley . . . 1M 31
Fairfax Vw. BD4: E Bier . . . 6K 83
LS18: Hors . . . 3E 48
FAIRFIELD . . . 2H 95
Fairfield BD13: Denh . . . 6K 61
HX7: Heb B . . . 2H 95
(not continuous)
LS18: Hors . . . 6F 48
WF11: Fair . . . 8N 91
Fairfield Av. LS13: Leeds . . . 4D 66
LS28: Pud . . . 6B 66
WF3: W Ard . . . 5N 103
WF5: Oss . . . 7B 124
WF6: Alt . . . 9F 106
WF8: Pon . . . 3H 129
WF12: Dew . . . *3J 123*
(off Fairfield Ter.)
WF16: Heck . . . 7B 102
Fairfield Cl. LS13: Leeds . . . 4E 66
LS26: Rothw . . . 9K 87
WF5: Oss . . . 7B 124
WF10: C'frd . . . 3L 109
Fairfield Ct. BD17: Bail . . . 3C 46
LS17: Leeds . . . 2G 50
WF10: C'frd . . . 5G 108
WF15: Liv . . . 8K 101
Fairfield Cres. LS13: Leeds . . . 4D 66
WF13: Dew . . . 2D 122
Fairfield Dr. BD17: Bail . . . 3C 46
LS26: Rothw . . . 9K 87
WF5: Oss . . . 7B 124
(not continuous)
WF16: Heck . . . 7B 102
Fairfield Gdns. LS26: Rothw . . . 9K 87
WF5: Oss . . . 7B 124
Fairfield Gro. LS13: Leeds . . . 4E 66
LS26: Rothw . . . 9K 87
Fairfield Hill LS13: Leeds . . . 4E 66
Fairfield La. LS13: Leeds . . . 4E 66
LS25: Bur S . . . 1G 110
LS26: Rothw . . . 9K 87
Fairfield M. LS13: Leeds . . . 4E 66
WF13: Dew . . . 2D 122
Fairfield Mills HD1: Hud . . . 7B 8 (5M 137)
Fairfield Mt. LS13: Leeds . . . 4E 66
WF5: Oss . . . 7B 124
Fairfield Pde. WF16: Heck . . . 7B 102
Fairfield Ri. HD8: Kbtn . . . 4L 155
Fairfield Rd. BD8: B'frd . . . 5N 63
BD12: Wyke . . . 1B 100
LS13: Leeds . . . 4D 66
WF5: Oss . . . 7B 124
WF16: Heck . . . 7B 102
Fairfields HD8: Up D . . . 5C 172
WF10: C'frd . . . 5L 109
Fairfield Sq. LS13: Leeds . . . 4E 66
Fairfields Rd. HD9: Holm . . . 5J 169
Fairfield St. BD4: B'frd . . . 4H 83
LS13: Leeds . . . 4D 66
(not continuous)
Fairfield Ter. *BD19: Cleck* . . . *5J 101*
(off Neville St.)
LS13: Leeds . . . 4E 66
WF5: Oss . . . 7A 124
WF12: Dew . . . 3J 123
Fairfield Wlk. WF5: Oss . . . 7B 124
Fairford Av. LS11: Leeds . . . 2E 86
Fairford Ct. BD2: B'frd . . . 3F 64
Fairford Mt. LS6: Leeds . . . 6A 50
Fairford Ter. LS11: Leeds . . . 2E 86
Fairhaven Grn. BD10: B'frd . . . 8G 46
Fair Isle Ct. *BD21: Keigh* . . . *9J 27*
(off Alice St.)
Fairlands Cl. HX2: Illing . . . 7M 79
Fairlea Av. HD4: Hud . . . 9K 137
Fair Lea Rd. HD4: Hud . . . 9K 137
Fairleigh Cres. WF3: Ting . . . 4B 104
Fairleigh Rd. WF3: Ting . . . 4B 104
Fairless Av. HX3: Hip . . . 5M 99
Fairmoor Way WF16: Heck . . . 7B 102
Fair Mt. OL14: W'den . . . 2J 113
Fairmount BD9: B'frd . . . 4A 64
BD21: Keigh . . . *1M 43*
(off Fairmount Ter.)
Fairmount Pk. BD18: Ship . . . 8K 45
(not continuous)
Fairmount Ter. BD21: Keigh . . . 1M 43
WF12: Dew . . . 5H 123
Fair Rd. BD6: B'frd . . . 4N 81
Fair St. HD1: Hud . . . 7L 137
Fair Vw. HX4: Bark . . . 7F 116
HX7: Heb B . . . 3J 95
LS11: Leeds . . . 4N 85
WF7: Ackw . . . 5G 147
WF8: Pon . . . 6L 129
WF10: C'frd . . . 3H 109
WF15: Liv . . . 7K 101
Fairview BD12: O'haw . . . 9E 82
Fairview Av. WF17: Bat . . . 6C 102
Fairview Ct. BD17: Bail . . . 6N 45
Fairview Cres. WF17: Bat . . . 6D 102
Fairview Rd. WF17: Bat . . . 6D 102
Fair Vw. St. OL14: Tod . . . 8K 93
Fairview Ter. HX3: Hal . . . 1H 7 (3N 97)
Fairway BD7: B'frd . . . 4L 81
BD10: B'frd . . . 6L 47
BD18: Ship . . . 8L 45
LS20: Guis . . . 7F 30
WF6: Norm . . . 2K 127
Fairway, The HD2: Fix . . . 7M 119
HX2: Illing . . . 6M 79
LS17: Leeds . . . 1D 50
LS28: Stan . . . 5M 65
WF7: F'stne . . . 2D 128
Fairway App. WF6: Norm . . . 1K 127
Fairway Av. BD7: B'frd . . . 4L 81
S75: S'ross . . . 7L 159
WF6: Norm . . . 1K 127
Fairway Cl. BD7: B'frd . . . 4L 81
LS20: Guis . . . 8G 30
WF6: Norm . . . 1K 127
Fairway Cres. BD22: Haw . . . 9D 42
Fairway Dr. BD7: B'frd . . . 3L 81
WF6: Norm . . . 2K 127
Fairway Gdns. WF6: Norm . . . 1K 127
Fairway Gro. BD7: B'frd . . . 3L 81
Fairway Ind. Pk. WF17: Birs . . . 2C 102
Fairway Mdws. WF6: Norm . . . 1K 127
Fair Ways WF14: Up H . . . 9K 121
Fairways, The BD9: B'frd . . . 1K 63
BD20: Keigh . . . 5G 27
Fairways Ct. WF8: D'ton . . . 7D 130
Fairway Vw. WF2: Wake . . . 8H 125
Fairway Wlk. BD7: B'frd . . . 3L 81
FAIRWEATHER GREEN . . . 7J 63
Fairweather M. BD8: B'frd . . . 7K 63
Fairwood Gro. BD10: B'frd . . . 3J 65
Fairy Cotts. WF4: Wrag . . . 3N 145
Fairy Dell BD16: Cot . . . 8F 44
FAIRY HILL . . . 7K 109
Fairy Hill La. WF8: Pon . . . 7K 109
(not continuous)
Faith St. WF9: S Kirk . . . 5K 163
Falcon Cliffe BD20: Stee . . . 3D 26
Falcon Cl. LS21: Otley . . . 1L 31
Falcon Dr. WF10: C'frd . . . 6C 108
Falconer Cl. S75: Kex . . . 8F 158
Falconers Ride HD4: Neth . . . 3K 153
Falcon Knowle Ing S75: Kex . . . 8E 158
Falcon M. BD8: B'frd . . . 6H 63
LS27: Morl . . . 1M 103
WF15: Liv . . . 8K 101
Falcon Rd. BD16: Bgly . . . 2E 44
WF12: Dew . . . 5G 122
Falcon St. BD7: B'frd . . . 9N 63
HD4: Hud . . . 9L 137
HX3: Hal . . . 9C 98
FALHOUSE GREEN . . . 2A 140
Falhouse La. WF12: W'ley . . . 3A 140
Falkland Ct. BD16: Bgly . . . 4F 44
LS17: Leeds . . . 6E 50
Falkland Cres. LS17: Leeds . . . 6E 50
Falkland Gdns. LS17: Leeds . . . 6E 50
Falkland Gro. LS17: Leeds . . . 6E 50
Falkland Mt. LS17: Leeds . . . 6E 50
Falkland Ri. LS17: Leeds . . . 6E 50
Falkland Rd. BD10: B'frd . . . 2J 65
LS17: Leeds . . . 6E 50
FALL, THE . . . 4F 104
Fall Brow Cl. BD14: Clay . . . 2F 80
Falledge La. HD8: Up D . . . 7B 172
Falling Royd HX7: Heb B . . . 2K 95
FALL INGS . . . 8M 9 (7M 125)
Fall Ings Rd. WF1: Wake . . . 7N 125
Fall La. HD7: Mars . . . 6F 150
HX3: North . . . 8C 80
HX6: Sow B . . . 9K 97
WF3: E Ard . . . 4F 104
WF13: Dew . . . 5E 122
WF15: Liv . . . 1H 121
Fallow Cft. HD2: Hud . . . 6D 120
Fallowfield Cl. BD4: B'frd . . . 5G 83
Fallowfield Dr. BD4: B'frd . . . 4G 83
Fallowfield Gdns. BD4: B'frd . . . 4G 82
Fallow La. BD22: Oak . . . 1A 42
Fall Pk. Ct. LS13: Leeds . . . 1G 67
Fall Rd. WF14: Mir . . . 3J 121
Fall Spring Gdns. HX4: Stainl . . . 8M 117
Fall Spring Grn. HX4: Stainl . . . 8M 117
Fallswood Gro. LS13: Leeds . . . 2G 66
Fallwood Marina LS13: Leeds . . . 1E 66
Fallwood St. BD22: Haw . . . 9D 42
Falmers Cotts. *LS6: Leeds* . . . *2B 68*
(off Cliff La.)
Falmouth Av. BD3: B'frd . . . 1D 6 (5D 64)
WF6: Norm . . . 9J 107
Falmouth Cres. WF6: Norm . . . 9J 107
Falmouth Rd. WF6: Norm . . . 9J 107
Falsgrave Av. BD2: B'frd . . . 4H 65
Faltis Sq. BD10: B'frd . . . 9G 47
Fanny La. LS24: Stut . . . 9N 39
Fanny Moor Cres. HD4: Hud . . . 8A 138
Fanny Moor La. HD4: Hud . . . 8A 138
Fanny St. BD18: Ship . . . 6L 45
BD21: Keigh . . . 1H 43
Faraday *LS20: Guis* . . . *6H 31*
(off Netherfield Rd.)
Faraday Sq. *HD3: Hud* . . . *6F 136*
(off Hoffman St.)
Far Bank HD8: Shel . . . 7L 155
Far Banks HD9: Hon . . . 6M 153
Farcliffe Pl. BD8: B'frd . . . 5N 63
Farcliffe Rd. BD8: B'frd . . . 5N 63
Farcliffe Ter. BD8: B'frd . . . 5N 63
Far Comn. Rd. WF14: Mir . . . 3J 121
Far Cotton Stones HX6: Ripp . . . 3B 116
Far Cft. HD8: Lept . . . 8L 139
Far Cft. Ter. LS12: Leeds . . . 8N 67
Far Crook BD10: B'frd . . . 6D 46
Far Dene HD8: Kbtn . . . 1H 155
Fardene St. BD20: Sils . . . 7D 12
Fardew Ct. BD16: Bgly . . . 3E 44
Fardew Golf Course . . . 8B 28
Fare Hill Flats *HD4: Hud* . . . *1L 153*
(off Wain Brow)
Farehill Rd. HD4: Hud . . . 1L 153
Far End La. HD9: Hon . . . 5M 153
Farfield Av. BD6: B'frd . . . 6K 81
HD9: H'wth . . . 7C 170
LS28: Fars . . . 3N 65
WF17: Bat . . . 6C 102
Farfield Ct. LS25: Gar . . . 7L 71
WF9: S Elm . . . 5N 163
Farfield Cres. BD6: B'frd . . . 6L 81
Far Field Dr. HD9: H'wth . . . 7C 170
Farfield Dr. LS28: Fars . . . 4N 65
Farfield Gro. BD6: B'frd . . . 6L 81
LS28: Fars . . . 3N 65
Farfield La. S72: S Hien . . . 2L 161
Farfield Ri. HD6: B Bri . . . 6N 99
LS28: Fars . . . 3N 65
Farfield Rd. BD6: B'frd . . . 6M 81
BD17: Bail . . . 5B 46
BD18: Ship . . . 8L 45
HD5: Hud . . . 7D 138
Far Flds. La. HD4: S Cros . . . 4E 152
Farfield St. BD9: B'frd . . . 4M 63
BD19: Cleck . . . 3H 101
Farfield Ter. BD9: B'frd . . . 4M 63
FAR FOLD . . . 6L 67
Fargate Cl. WF9: S Kirk . . . 7H 163
FAR HEADINGLEY . . . 9B 50
Far Highfield BD22: Oak . . . 4C 42
Far Highfield Cl. BD10: B'frd . . . 8E 46
Farhills BD6: B'frd . . . 4L 81
Far Laithe BD22: Lay . . . 8C 26
Far La. HD9: H'wth . . . 8B 170
HX2: Midg . . . 2A 96
LS9: Leeds . . . 9L 69
Far Lawns S71: Carl . . . 8E 160
Farlea Dr. BD2: B'frd . . . 3G 65
Farleton Dr. BD2: B'frd . . . 3H 65
Farley Cres. BD22: Oak . . . 4B 42
Far Low Bank *BD22: Oak* . . . *4B 42*
(off Kelburn Gro.)
Farm Cl. LS23: W'ton . . . 5G 25
WF6: Alt . . . 8G 106
Farm Ct. LS15: Leeds . . . 4C 70
Farm Cft. WF7: Street . . . 6M 127
Far Mead Cft. LS29: Burl W . . . 7C 16
Farmfield Dr. WF9: Fitz . . . 7A 146
Farm Gdns. WF7: Street . . . 6M 127
Farm Hill Ct. BD10: B'frd . . . 1F 64
Farm Hill Cres. LS7: Leeds . . . 1C 68
Farm Hill M. LS27: Morl . . . 8H 85
Farm Hill Nth. LS7: Leeds . . . 9C 50
Farm Hill Ri. LS7: Leeds . . . 1C 68
Farm Hill Rd. BD10: B'frd . . . 9F 46
LS27: Morl . . . 7J 85
Farm Hill Sth. LS7: Leeds . . . 1C 68
Farm Hill Way LS7: Leeds . . . 1C 68
Farmhouse Ct. HD4: Hud . . . 8G 136
Farm La. WF9: Fitz . . . 8A 146
Farm Mt. LS15: Leeds . . . 4D 70
WF4: Neth . . . 4A 142
Far Moss LS17: Leeds . . . 2C 50
Farm Rd. LS15: Leeds . . . 4C 70
WF7: F'stne . . . 6D 128
Farmstead Rd. BD10: B'frd . . . 9G 47
Farnboro St. OL14: W'den . . . 1J 113
Farndale App. LS14: Leeds . . . 1D 70
Farndale Cl. LS14: Leeds . . . 1D 70
LS22: Weth . . . 3J 23
Farndale Ct. LS25: Gar . . . 9N 71
Farndale Gdns. LS14: Leeds . . . 9D 52
Farndale Gth. LS14: Leeds . . . 9D 52
Farndale Pl. LS14: Leeds . . . 9D 52
Farndale Rd. BD15: Wils . . . 2B 62
BD17: Bail . . . 5M 45
Farndale Sq. LS14: Leeds . . . 1D 70
Farndale Ter. LS14: Leeds . . . 1D 70
Farndale Vw. *LS14: Leeds* . . . *9D 52*
(off Stanks Dr.)
Farne Av. WF2: Wake . . . 5H 125
Farnham Cl. BD17: Bail . . . 3B 46
LS14: Leeds . . . 6C 52
LS16: Leeds . . . 8M 49
Farnham Cft. LS14: Leeds . . . 6C 52
Farnham Rd. BD7: B'frd . . . 9N 63
Farnham Way WF4: Croft . . . 1G 145
Farnlee HD3: Hud . . . 1G 136
FARNLEY
LS12 . . . 9H 67
LS21 . . . 5A 18
Farnley Cl. LS29: Men . . . 4F 30
Farnley Cres. LS12: Leeds . . . 8H 67
Farnley Hey HD4: Farn T . . . 2A 154
Farnley Ho. *LS14: Leeds* . . . *9N 51*
(off Kingsdale Ct.)
Farnley La. LS21: F'ley . . . 4N 17
LS21: Otley . . . 8L 17
Farnley Moor HD4: Farn T . . . 4C 154
Farnley Pk. LS21: F'ley, Leat . . . 6A 18
Farnley Rd. HD4: Farn T . . . 3D 154
LS29: Men . . . 4E 30
FARNLEY TYAS . . . 3D 154
Farnley Vw. BD11: Drig . . . 8D 84
Faroe LS12: Leeds . . . 8B 4 (7C 68)
Far Peat La. BD22: Oxen . . . 7B 60
Farrar Av. WF14: Mir . . . 5K 121
Farrar Bldgs. *BD12: Wyke* . . . *1A 100*
(off Brick Row)
Farrar Cl. HX5: Ell . . . 4G 119
Farrar Ct. LS13: Leeds . . . 3F 66
Farrar Cft. LS16: Leeds . . . 3K 49
Farrar Dr. WF14: Mir . . . 5J 121
Farrar Gro. LS16: Leeds . . . 3K 49
Farrar Height La. HX6: Ripp . . . 7B 116
Farrar La. LS16: Leeds . . . 3J 49
(not continuous)
Farrar Mill La. HX3: Hal . . . 8C 98
Farra St. BD22: Oxen . . . 4C 60
Far Reef Cl. LS18: Hors . . . 5F 48
Farrer La. LS26: Oul . . . 8D 88
Far Richard Cl. WF5: Oss . . . 4N 123
Farriers Ct. BD11: Drig . . . 7B 84
LS22: Weth . . . 4N 23
Farriers Cft. BD2: B'frd . . . 2D 64
Farriers Pl. WF10: C'frd . . . 6H 109
Farrier Way WF3: Rob H . . . 1K 105
Farringdon Cl. BD4: B'frd . . . 1H 83
WF9: Hems . . . 3D 162
Farringdon Dr. BD4: B'frd . . . 2J 83
Farringdon Gro. BD6: B'frd . . . 6M 81
Farringdon Sq. BD4: B'frd . . . 1J 83
Far Row LS21: Pool . . . 3F 32
Farrow Bank LS12: Leeds . . . 7H 67
Farrow Grn. LS12: Leeds . . . 7J 67
Farrow Hill LS12: Leeds . . . 7J 67
Farrow Rd. LS12: Leeds . . . 7H 67
Farrow Va. LS12: Leeds . . . 7H 67
Far Royd HX3: Hal . . . 9N 79
FAR ROYDS . . . 1M 85
Farr Royd LS29: Burl W . . . 7C 16
Farside Grn. BD5: B'frd . . . 2A 82
FARSLEY . . . 3A 66
FARSLEY BECK BOTTOM . . . 3B 66
Farsley Beck M. LS13: Leeds . . . 3B 66
Far Sowood HX4: Sow . . . 1N 135
Farthing Av. WF8: Pon . . . 4G 129
FARTOWN . . . 9N 119
Fartown LS28: Pud . . . 8A 66
Fartown Cl. LS28: Pud . . . 9B 66
Fartown Grn. Rd. HD2: Hud . . . 1N 137
Far Vw. HX2: Illing . . . 7L 79
Far Vw. Bank HD5: Hud . . . 5C 138
Far Vw. Cres. HD5: Hud . . . 5C 138
Farway BD4: B'frd . . . 1J 83
Far Well Fold LS19: Raw . . . 4A 48
Far Well La. HD9: New M . . . 9F 154
Far Well Rd. LS19: Raw . . . 4A 48
Fascination Pl. *BD13: Que* . . . *3B 80*
(off Mill La.)
Faugh La. HX7: Hept . . . 7D 76
Faulkland Ho. *BD8: B'frd* . . . *5A 64*
(off Green La.)
Favell Av. WF6: Norm . . . 2J 127
Faversham Wlk. BD4: B'frd . . . 1J 83
Fawcett Av. LS12: Leeds . . . 9L 67
Fawcett Bank LS12: Leeds . . . 9K 67
Fawcett Cl. LS12: Leeds . . . 9K 67
Fawcett Dr. LS12: Leeds . . . 9K 67
Fawcett Gdns. LS12: Leeds . . . 9K 67
Fawcett La. LS12: Leeds . . . 9K 67
Fawcett Pl. BD4: B'frd . . . 5G 82
LS12: Leeds . . . 9K 67
Fawcett Rd. LS12: Leeds . . . 9K 67
Fawcett St. WF2: Wake . . . 7L 125
Fawcett Va. LS12: Leeds . . . 9K 67
Fawcett Vw. *LS12: Leeds* . . . *9K 67*
(off Fawcett Va.)
Fawcett Way LS12: Leeds . . . 9K 67
Fawdon Dr. LS14: Leeds . . . 1E 70
Fawdon Pl. LS14: Leeds . . . 1F 70
Fawkes Dr. LS21: Otley . . . 2H 31
Faxfleet St. BD5: B'frd . . . 4B 82
Faye Gdns. BD4: B'frd . . . 4H 83
FC Halifax Town . . . 7L 7 (6B 98)
Fearnley Av. WF5: Oss . . . 4M 123
Fearnley Cl. LS12: Leeds . . . 7N 67
Fearnley Cotts. HX7: Heb B . . . 1D 94
Fearnley Ct. HD9: H'rth . . . 3B 170
Fearnley Cft. BD19: Gom . . . 4M 101
Fearnley Dr. WF5: Oss . . . 4M 123
Fearnley La. HD9: H'rth . . . 3A 170
Fearnley Mill Dr. HD5: Hud . . . 5E 120
Fearnley Pl. LS12: Leeds . . . 7N 67
Fearnley St. WF7: F'stne . . . 6C 128
WF13: Dew . . . 4E 122
Fearnside Fold *WF4: Horb* . . . *9C 124*
(off Northgate)
Fearnside's Ct. WF4: Horb . . . 1C 142
Fearnsides St. BD8: B'frd . . . 6N 63
Fearnsides Ter. BD8: B'frd . . . 6N 63
FEARN'S ISLAND . . . 8K 5 (8G 68)
FEARNVILLE . . . 2M 69
Fearnville Av. LS8: Leeds . . . 2M 69
Fearnville Cl. LS8: Leeds . . . 1M 69
Fearnville Dr. BD4: B'frd . . . 9H 65
LS8: Leeds . . . 2M 69
Fearnville Gro. LS8: Leeds . . . 1M 69
S71: Roys . . . 6D 160
Fearnville Leisure Cen. . . . 3M 69
Fearnville Mt. LS8: Leeds . . . 1M 69
Fearnville Pl. LS8: Leeds . . . 1N 69
Fearnville Rd. LS8: Leeds . . . 2M 69
Fearnville Ter. LS8: Leeds . . . 1N 69
Fearnville Vw. LS8: Leeds . . . 2M 69
Feast Fld. LS18: Hors . . . 6E 48
Feather Bank BD22: Keigh . . . 3G 42
Featherbank Av. LS18: Hors . . . 8E 48
Featherbank Ct. *LS18: Hors* . . . *8E 48*
(off Featherbank La.)
Featherbank Gro. LS18: Hors . . . 7E 48
Featherbank La. LS18: Hors . . . 7E 48
Featherbank Mt. LS18: Hors . . . 7E 48
Featherbank Ter. LS18: Hors . . . 8E 48
Featherbank Wlk. LS18: Hors . . . 8E 48
Featherbed Cl. HX4: Gree . . . 5C 118
Featherbed La. HX4: Gree . . . 5C 118
LS24: Wig . . . 3K 25
Feather Rd. BD3: B'frd . . . 7F 64
FEATHERSTONE . . . 6C 128
Featherstone Dr. WF7: F'stne . . . 4D 128
Featherstone Gro. WF7: F'stne . . . 4D 128
Featherstone La. WF7: F'stne . . . 3C 128
Featherstone Rovers RLFC . . . 5D 128
Featherstone Station (Rail) . . . 6C 128
Featherstone Swimming Pool . . . *6F 128*
(off Pontefract Rd.)

Featherstone Technology College Sports Complex—Fitness Studio, The

Featherstone Technology College Sports Complex ... 6F 128
Feather St. BD21: Keigh ... 1K 43
Federation St. BD5: B'frd ... 3D 82
Felbrigg Av. BD22: Keigh ... 1F 42
Felcote Av. HD5: Hud ... 5C 138
Felcourt Dr. BD4: B'frd ... 3J 83
Felcourt Fold BD4: B'frd ... 3J 83
FELKIRK ... 3J 161
Felkirk Cotts. S72: S Hien ... 4J 161
Felkirk Dr. WF4: Ryh ... 1H 161
Felkirk Vw. S72: Shaf ... 6J 161
Felks Stile Rd. HD4: Hud ... 8E 136
Fell Cres. BD22: Keigh ... 2E 42
Fell Greave Rd. HD2: Hud ... 6N 119
Fell Gro. BD22: Keigh ... 1F 42
HD2: Hud ... 7A 120
Fell La. BD22: Keigh ... 2E 42
Fellows, The HD4: Neth ... 2H 153
Fellowsides La. WF5: Oss ... 6A 124
Fellowsides M. WF5: Oss ... 6A 124
Fellside OL14: Tod ... 7C 94
Fellside Cl. BD5: B'frd ... 3D 82
Fellwood Av. BD22: Haw ... 7E 42
Fellwood Cl. BD22: Haw ... 7E 42
Felnex Cl. LS9: Leeds ... 9L 69
Felnex Cres. LS9: Leeds ... 9L 69
Felnex Rd. LS9: Leeds ... 9K 69
Felnex Sq. LS9: Leeds ... 9K 69
Felnex Way LS9: Leeds ... 9L 69
Fenay Bankside HD8: Fen B ... 7H 139
FENAY BRIDGE ... 6G 139
Fenay Bri. Rd. HD8: Fen B ... 5G 138
Fenay Cres. HD5: Hud ... 7E 138
Fenay Dr. HD8: Fen B ... 7G 139
Fenay La. HD5: Hud ... 7D 138
HD8: Fen B ... 7D 138
Fenay Lea Dr. HD5: Hud ... 6F 138
Fenby Av. BD4: B'frd ... 1F 82
(not continuous)
Fenby Cl. BD4: B'frd ... 2G 82
(not continuous)
Fenby Gdns. BD4: B'frd ... 2G 82
Fenby Gro. BD4: B'frd ... 2G 82
Fencote Cres. BD2: B'frd ... 3H 65
Fender Rd. BD6: B'frd ... 4L 81
Fennec Rd. BD17: Bail ... 3C 46
Fennel Ct. LS26: Meth ... 1K 107
Fennell Ct. WF2: Wake ... 3N 143
Fenny Royd HX3: Hip ... 4G 99
Fenton Av. LS26: W'frd ... 6C 88
Fenton Cl. LS26: W'frd ... 6C 88
WF9: S Kirk ... 8H 163
Fenton Ct. BD13: Cull ... 9K 43
Fenton Fold BD12: O'haw ... 9D 82
Fenton Ga. LS10: Leeds ... 9G 86
Fenton Pl. LS10: Leeds ... 9G 87
Fenton Rd. HD1: Hud ... 7L 137
HX1: Hal ... 7M 97
WF3: S'ley ... 5A 106
Fentonsgate WF3: Loft ... 3L 105
Fenton Sq. HD1: Hud ... 5L 137
Fenton St. LS1: Leeds ... 3E 4 (5D 68)
LS29: Burl W ... 8D 16
WF3: Ting ... 3B 104
WF14: Mir ... 7L 121
Fenwick Dr. BD6: B'frd ... 6L 81
Ferguson St. HX1: Hal ... 5K 7 (6B 98)
Fern Av. HD9: Mel ... 6B 152
Fern Bank HX6: Sow B ... 9H 97
HX7: Myth ... 4L 95
LS21: Otley ... 9M 17
Fernbank Av. BD16: Bgly ... 4F 44
BD22: Oak ... 3F 42
LS13: Leeds ... 3C 66
Fernbank Cl. LS13: Leeds ... 3C 66
Fernbank Dr. BD16: Bgly ... 4F 44
BD17: Bail ... 6M 45
LS13: Leeds ... 3C 66
Fernbank Gdns. LS13: Leeds ... 3C 66
Fernbank Pl. LS13: Leeds ... 3C 66
Fernbank Rd. BD3: B'frd ... 5F 64
LS13: Leeds ... 3C 66
Fernbank St. BD16: Bgly ... 4F 44
Fernbank Ter. BD16: Bgly ... 4F 44
LS19: Yead ... 9L 31
(off Park Av.)
Fernbank Wlk. LS13: Leeds ... 3C 66
Fern Chase LS14: S'cft ... 9B 36
FERNCLIFFE ... 4H 45
Ferncliffe Ct. BD18: Ship ... 7L 45
Ferncliffe Dr. BD17: Bail ... 4N 45
BD20: Keigh ... 6F 26
Ferncliffe Rd. BD16: Bgly ... 4E 44
BD18: Ship ... 7L 45
LS13: Leeds ... 4F 66
Ferncliffe Ter. LS13: Leeds ... 4E 66
Fern Cl. WF17: Bat ... 7J 103
Fern Ct. BD20: Keigh ... 6G 26
Fern Cft. LS14: S'cft ... 9B 36
WF2: Wren ... 9G 105
Ferncroft WF15: Liv ... 8G 100
Ferndale BD14: Clay ... 2F 80
WF7: F'stne ... 7D 128
Ferndale Av. BD14: Clay ... 2F 80
Ferndale Ct. HD2: Hud ... 7N 119
LS29: I'ly ... 6F 14
Ferndale Gro. BD9: B'frd ... 2A 64
HD2: Hud ... 7N 119
Ferndale Pl. WF9: Hems ... 3D 162
Ferndene BD16: Bgly ... 4G 44
Ferndene Av. WF17: Birs ... 1C 102
Ferndene Wlk. WF17: Birs ... 1C 102
Ferndown Grn. BD5: B'frd ... 2B 82
Ferney Lee Rd. OL14: Tod ... 6J 93
Ferney St. OL14: Tod ... 6J 93
(off Ferney Lee Rd.)
Fernfield Ter. HX3: Hal ... 2B 98
Fern Gdns. LS29: I'ly ... 6F 14
Fern Gro. LS5: Leeds ... 2K 67
(off Tordoff Pl.)
Fernhill BD16: Bgly ... 2F 44
Fern Hill Av. BD18: Ship ... 8L 45
Fern Hill Gro. BD18: Ship ... 8L 45
Fern Hill Mt. BD18: Ship ... 8L 45
Fern Hill Rd. BD18: Ship ... 8L 45
Fernhurst Cl. WF14: Mir ... 5L 121
Fernhurst Cres. WF14: Mir ... 5L 121
Fernhurst Lea WF14: Mir ... 5M 121
Fernhurst Rd. WF14: Mir ... 5L 121
Fernhurst Way WF14: Mir ... 5L 121
Ferniehurst BD17: Bail ... 6A 46
Fern Lea BD13: Que ... 4E 80
(off Sandbeds)
Fernlea LS26: Rothw ... 7A 88
Fernlea Cl. WF4: Croft ... 1H 145
WF16: Heck ... 9B 102
Fern Lea Flats HD3: Hud ... 1F 136
Fernlea Gro. HD7: Golc ... 7C 136
Fern Lea Rd. HD3: Hud ... 1F 136
Fern Lea St. HX6: Sow B ... 7H 97
Fern Lea Vw. LS28: Stan ... 4B 66
Fern Leigh HD3: Hud ... 5F 136
Fernleigh Ct. WF2: Wake ... 6H 125
Fernleigh Dr. HD3: Hud ... 5F 136
Fernley Gdns. BD12: Wyke ... 9A 82
FERNLEY GREEN ... 8G 111
Fernley Grn. Cl. WF11: Knot ... 8G 110
Fernley Grn. Ct. WF11: Knot ... 8G 111
(off Fernley Grn. Rd.)
Fernley Green Ind. Est. WF11: Knot ... 8G 110
Fernley Grn. Rd. WF11: Knot ... 8G 110
Fernley Hill Dr. WF6: Alt ... 7G 106
Fern Pl. BD18: Ship ... 7L 45
(off Saltaire Rd.)
Fern Ri. HX5: Ell ... 4G 119
Fernside WF4: S Comn ... 8K 127
Fernside Av. HD5: Hud ... 6C 138
Fernside Cl. HD5: Hud ... 5E 138
Fernside Ct. HD5: Hud ... 5E 138
Fernside Cres. HD5: Hud ... 5D 138
Fern St. BD4: B'frd ... 2H 83
BD21: Keigh ... 8J 27
BD22: Haw ... 9C 42
(off Sun St.)
HD1: Hud ... 2M 137
HX3: Hal ... 2A 98
Fern St. E. HD1: Hud ... 5E 8 (4A 138)
Fern Ter. BD8: B'frd ... 4A 64
BD20: Rid ... 7M 27
(off Carr La.)
LS28: Stan ... 4B 66
Fern Valley Chase OL14: Tod ... 6H 93
Fern Vw. BD19: Gom ... 3L 101
Fern Vs. HX7: Heb B ... 2E 94
Fern Way LS14: S'cft ... 9B 36
Fernwood LS8: Leeds ... 6J 51
Fernwood Ct. LS8: Leeds ... 6J 51
Ferrand Av. BD4: B'frd ... 5G 82
Ferrand La. BD16: Bgly ... 4E 44
BD19: Gom ... 3L 101
Ferrand Rd. BD18: Ship ... 7L 45
Ferrands Cl. BD16: Har ... 6A 44
Ferrands Pk. Way BD16: Har ... 6A 44
Ferrand St. BD16: Bgly ... 4F 44
Ferriby Cl. BD2: B'frd ... 3H 65
Ferriby Towers LS9: Leeds ... 3L 5
FERRYBRIDGE ... 7B 110
Ferrybridge Bus. Pk. WF11: Ferr ... 7C 110
Ferrybridge By-Pass WF11: Knot ... 9B 110
FERRYBRIDGE HILL ... 8C 110
Ferrybridge Rd. WF8: Pon ... 1L 129
WF10: C'frd ... 4E 108
WF11: Knot ... 7C 110
FERRYBRIDGE SERVICE AREA ... 1C 130
Ferrybridge Workspace WF11: Ferr ... 7B 110
Ferry Ct. WF3: S'ley ... 1A 126
Ferry La. WF3: S'ley ... 9A 106
Ferry Top La. WF4: Wint ... 9H 145
Festival Av. BD18: Ship ... 1B 64
Feversham Grange HX3: Hal ... 9A 98
Feversham St. BD3: B'frd ... 5E 6 (8E 64)
Fewston Av. BD6: B'frd ... 3H 81
LS9: Leeds ... 8H 69
(not continuous)
WF1: Wake ... 3A 126
Fewston Ct. LS9: Leeds ... 8M 5 (8H 69)
Fiddle La. HX4: Bark ... 7F 116
Fiddler Hill WF12: Dew ... 7E 122
Fiddlers Mill BD16: Bgly ... 1D 44
(off Wood St.)
Fidler Cl. LS25: Gar ... 7M 71
Fidler La. LS25: Gar ... 7M 71
Fidler Ter. LS25: Gar ... 7M 71
Field Cl. HX3: Hal ... 3M 97
WF16: Heck ... 6A 102
Field Ct. BD13: Thorn ... 8D 62
Field Cres. WF9: S Elm ... 7M 163
Field Cft. Ct. WF14: Mir ... 6K 121
Fieldedge La. BD20: Rid ... 6N 27
Field End LS15: Leeds ... 7B 70
Field End Cl. LS15: Leeds ... 7B 70
Field End Ct. LS15: Leeds ... 7B 70
Field End Cres. LS15: Leeds ... 7B 70
Field End Gdns. LS15: Leeds ... 7B 70
Field End Gth. LS15: Leeds ... 7B 70
Field End Grn. LS15: Leeds ... 7B 70
Field End Gro. LS15: Leeds ... 6C 70
Field End La. HD9: Holm ... 6G 168
HD9: Hon ... 5M 153
Field End Mt. LS15: Leeds ... 7B 70
Field End Rd. LS15: Leeds ... 7B 70
Fieldens Pl. WF17: Bat ... 6D 102
Fielden Sq. OL14: Tod ... 8K 93
Fielden St. OL14: Tod ... 6N 93
OL15: Lit ... 9M 113
(off Todmorden Rd.)
Fielden Ter. OL14: Tod ... 6K 93
Fieldfare Dr. BD6: B'frd ... 4G 81
WF10: All B ... 9C 90
Fieldfares, The BD20: Sils ... 8E 12
(off The Mallards)
Field Gdns. WF2: Wake ... 8L 125
Fieldgate Rd. BD10: B'frd ... 8H 47
Field Head BD22: Oxen ... 1B 60
HD5: K'htn ... 2F 138
HD7: Golc ... 5C 136
HD8: Shep ... 8J 155
HX2: Ogd ... 6K 79
WF7: Ackw ... 4D 146
Fieldhead WF17: Birs ... 1B 102
Fieldhead Bus. Cen. BD7: B'frd ... 7A 64
(off Gt. Russell Ct.)
Fieldhead Cl. WF8: Pon ... 2M 129
Fieldhead Ct. LS23: B Spa ... 1C 38
Fieldhead Cres. WF17: Birs ... 1B 102
Fieldhead Dr. LS15: Bar E ... 8N 53
LS20: Guis ... 8G 31
Field Head Farm Ct. HD8: Shep ... 8J 155
Fieldhead Gdns. WF12: Dew ... 9L 103
Fieldhead Gro. LS20: Guis ... 8G 31
Field Head La. BD11: Drig ... 8B 84
BD22: Oxen ... 1A 60
HX2: Illing ... 6K 79
HX7: Crag V ... 8J 95
WF17: Birs ... 2B 102
Fieldhead La. HD9: Holm, H'lm ... 7E 168
Fieldhead Paddock LS23: B Spa ... 9C 24
Field Head Pde. WF17: Birs ... 2C 102
Fieldhead Rd. LS20: Guis ... 8G 31
Fieldhead St. BD7: B'frd ... 8N 63
Field Head Way HX2: Illing ... 6K 79
Fieldhead Way WF16: Heck ... 7N 101
Fieldhouse HD9: H'frth ... 4N 169
Field Ho. Cl. LS22: Weth ... 4K 23
Fieldhouse Cl. LS17: Leeds ... 5E 50
Field Ho. Cotts. HX1: Hal ... 7G 7
Fieldhouse Ct. BD14: Clay ... 2H 81
Fieldhouse Dr. HD7: Slait ... 8N 135
LS17: Leeds ... 5E 50
Fieldhouse Gro. LS28: Fars ... 4N 65
Fieldhouse Lawn LS17: Leeds ... 5E 50
Fieldhouse Rd. HD1: Hud ... 1E 8 (2A 138)
Fieldhouse St. BD3: B'frd ... 7H 65
WF1: Wake ... 8A 126
Fieldhouse Wlk. LS17: Leeds ... 5E 50
(not continuous)
Field Hurst BD19: Scho ... 5D 100
HX4: Bark ... 6H 117
Fieldhurst Ct. BD4: B'frd ... 5G 82
Fielding Ct. LS27: Morl ... 8J 85
Fielding Ga. LS12: Leeds ... 6N 67
Fielding Ga. M. LS12: Leeds ... 6N 67
Fielding St. HX7: Heb B ... 1H 95
Fielding Way LS27: Morl ... 8J 85
FIELD LANE ... 3K 119
Field La. HD4: Farn T ... 3D 154
HD6: Ras ... 3L 119
LS25: Aber ... 8E 54
(not continuous)
WF2: Wake ... 8L 125
WF5: Oss ... 5N 123
WF9: S Elm ... 5A 164
WF9: Upt ... 2N 163
WF13: Raven ... 5A 122
WF17: Bat ... 8F 102
Fieldmoor Lodge LS28: Pud ... 8B 66
Field Pk. Grange LS27: Gil ... 7G 84
Field Pl. WF2: Wake ... 6J 125
Field Rd. HD9: H'frth ... 4N 169
Fields, The WF3: Loft ... 3M 105
Fieldsend Ct. WF9: Upt ... 1N 163
Flds. Head HD7: Linth ... 2C 152
Fieldshead Bungs. HD7: Linth ... 2C 152
Field Side HX1: Hal ... 4M 97
Fieldside BD13: Cull ... 9K 43
Fieldside Cl. BD4: B'frd ... 3K 83
Fieldside Rd. WF9: Kins ... 8B 146
Fields Ri. HD5: K'htn ... 1F 138
Fields Rd. BD12: Low M ... 8C 82
HD8: Lept ... 7H 139
Field St. BD1: B'frd ... 4C 6 (7D 64)
WF13: Raven ... 5B 122
Fields Way HD5: K'htn ... 1F 138
Field Ter. LS15: Leeds ... 6B 70
(Cross St.)
LS15: Leeds ... 5C 70
(Hermon Rd.)
Field Top HD6: B Bri ... 5N 99
Field Top Rd. HD6: Ras ... 3L 119
Field Tops HD3: Hud ... 1G 136
Field Vw. HX2: Illing ... 8L 79
HX3: Hal ... 2M 97
LS25: M'fld ... 8G 73
S71: Roys ... 6D 160
WF10: C'frd ... 6A 108
WF11: Byram ... 5C 110
Field Vw. Cotts. WF7: F'stne ... 7D 128
(off Katrina Gro.)
Field Way HD8: Shep ... 9J 155
Fieldway BD14: Clay ... 9G 63
LS29: I'ly ... 4K 15
Fieldway Av. LS13: Leeds ... 2D 66
Fieldway Chase LS26: Oul ... 8E 88
Fieldway Cl. LS13: Leeds ... 2D 66
Fieldway Ri. LS13: Leeds ... 2D 66
Fife St. BD22: Haw ... 8D 42
Fifth Av. BD3: B'frd ... 5G 65
LS26: Rothw ... 6B 88
Fifth Av. E. WF15: Liv ... 7F 100
Fifth Av. W. WF15: Liv ... 8F 100
Fifth St. BD12: Low M ... 7B 82
Filbert St. HD1: Hud ... 1M 137
Filey Av. S71: Roys ... 5E 160
Filey St. BD1: B'frd ... 5D 6 (8D 64)
Filley Royd BD19: Cleck ... 6H 101
Fillingfir Dr. LS16: Leeds ... 7J 49
Fillingfir Rd. LS16: Leeds ... 7J 49
Fillingfir Wlk. LS16: Leeds ... 7J 49
Finch Av. WF2: Wake ... 5M 143
Finch Cl. BD16: Bgly ... 3H 45
Finch Dr. LS15: Leeds ... 8G 70
Finching Gro. WF14: Mir ... 3L 121
Finchley St. BD5: B'frd ... 2B 82
Finchley Way LS27: Morl ... 1K 103
Finch St. BD5: B'frd ... 1B 82
Findon Ter. BD10: B'frd ... 2J 65
Fine Gth. Cl. LS23: B'ham ... 5D 38
Finghall Rd. DN6: Skel ... 7L 165
Fink Hill LS18: Hors ... 7D 48
Finkil St. HD6: Brigh ... 7K 99
Finkin Av. WF3: S'ley ... 1N 125
Finkin Cft. WF3: S'ley ... 1N 125
Finkin La. WF3: S'ley ... 1N 125
Finkle Cl. WF4: Wool ... 2H 159
Finkle Ct. LS27: Gil ... 7F 84
Finkle La. LS27: Gil ... 7F 84
Finkle St. HX6: Sow B ... 8D 96
WF4: Wool ... 2H 159
WF8: Pon ... 2K 129
Finsbury Dr. BD2: B'frd ... 9D 46
Finsbury Rd. LS1: Leeds ... 3D 4 (5D 68)
Finthorpe La. HD5: Hud ... 7E 138
Fir Av. LS16: Leeds ... 2M 49
WF13: Raven ... 6A 122
Fir Bank WF13: Dew ... 2D 122
Firbank Grn. BD2: B'frd ... 3H 65
Firbank Gro. LS15: Leeds ... 8N 69
Firbeck BD16: Har ... 7A 44
Firbeck Rd. LS23: B'ham ... 5D 38
Fireclay Bus. Pk. BD13: Thorn ... 8A 62
Firethorn Cl. BD8: B'frd ... 6M 63
Fir Gro. WF13: Raven ... 6A 122
Firham Cl. S71: Roys ... 5B 160
Fir Pde. WF13: Raven ... 6A 122
Fir Rd. HD1: Hud ... 4H 137
Firs, The LS14: S'cft ... 9D 36
S71: Roys ... 5B 160
Firs La. S36: Hoy ... 9G 173
First Av. BD3: B'frd ... 5G 65
BD21: Keigh ... 1H 43
HD5: Hud ... 3D 138
HD7: Golc ... 6C 136
HX3: Hal ... 8J 7 (8A 98)
LS12: Leeds ... 7N 67
LS17: Bard ... 3F 36
LS19: Raw ... 2N 47
LS22: Weth ... 4N 23
LS26: Rothw ... 6A 88
LS28: Stan ... 5B 66
S71: Roys ... 5E 160
WF1: Wake ... 1K 125
WF4: Horb ... 1B 142
WF9: Fitz ... 6A 146
WF9: S Kirk ... 8F 162
WF9: Upt ... 2N 163
WF15: Liv ... 7G 100
First Av. Ind. Est. LS28: Stan ... 5B 66
Fir St. BD21: Keigh ... 3H 43
BD22: Haw ... 9C 42
OL14: W'den ... 3J 113
First St. BD12: Low M ... 7C 82
Firth Av. HD6: Brigh ... 9M 99
LS11: Leeds ... 3C 86
Firth Carr BD18: Ship ... 1N 63
Firthcliffe Dr. WF15: Liv ... 7M 101
Firthcliffe Gro. WF15: Liv ... 7M 101
Firthcliffe La. WF15: Liv ... 7M 101
Firthcliffe Mt. WF15: Liv ... 6M 101
Firthcliffe Pde. WF15: Liv ... 6M 101
Firthcliffe Pl. WF15: Liv ... 7N 101
Firthcliffe Rd. WF15: Liv ... 7M 101
Firthcliffe Ter. WF15: Liv ... 7M 101
Firthcliffe Vw. WF15: Liv ... 7M 101
Firthcliffe Wlk. WF15: Liv ... 7M 101
Firth Cl. WF3: S'ley ... 7N 105
Firthfield La. WF9: Bads ... 6L 147
Firthfields LS25: Gar ... 7A 72
Firth Gro. LS11: Leeds ... 3C 86
Firth Ho. WF1: Wake ... 5J 9 (5L 125)
Firth Ho. La. HD6: Ras ... 4N 119
HX4: Holy ... 1J 135
Firth Ho. Mdws. HX4: Holy ... 1J 135
Firth La. BD15: Wils ... 1B 62
Firth Mt. LS11: Leeds ... 3C 86
Firth Rd. BD9: B'frd ... 3M 63
LS11: Leeds ... 3C 86
Firth Row BD4: B'frd ... 5F 82
Firths Ter. HX3: Hal ... 2M 97
(off Wheatley Rd.)
Firth St. BD13: Thorn ... 8C 62
HD1: Hud ... 8C 8 (6N 137)
HD6: Ras ... 2M 119
HD8: Shep ... 9J 155
LS9: Leeds ... 3J 5 (5G 68)
Firth Ter. LS9: Leeds ... 3K 5 (5G 68)
Firth Vw. LS11: Leeds ... 3C 86
Fir Tree App. LS17: Leeds ... 3D 50
Firtree Av. LS25: Gar ... 8B 72
Fir Tree Cl. LS17: Leeds ... 3E 50
Fir Tree Gdns. BD10: B'frd ... 9H 47
LS17: Leeds ... 3D 50
Fir Tree Grn. LS17: Leeds ... 3E 50
Fir Tree Gro. LS17: Leeds ... 4E 50
Fir Tree La. LS17: Leeds ... 4F 50
Fir Tree Ri. LS17: Leeds ... 4E 50
Fir Tree Va. LS17: Leeds ... 4E 50
Fir Tree Vw. LS26: Meth ... 1M 107
Firville Av. WF6: Norm ... 2J 127
Firville Cres. WF6: Norm ... 3J 127
Fir Wlk. WF13: Raven ... 6A 122
Fir Wood Cl. OL14: W'den ... 2J 113
Fishbeck La. BD20: Sils ... 5G 12
Fish Dam La.
S71: Carl, Mon B ... 9E 160
Fishergate WF11: Ferr ... 7B 110
Fisher Grn. HD9: Hon ... 5K 153
Fisher Gro. WF5: Oss ... 7B 124
Fisher St. WF11: Knot ... 8D 110
Fisher Way WF16: Heck ... 9B 102
Fishpond La. WF4: Wake ... 5H 143
Fishponds Dr. WF4: Crig ... 5G 143
FISHPOOL ... 6D 18
Fish St. LS1: Leeds ... 6G 5 (6E 68)
Fitness Connection ... 6B 122
(off Foundry St.)
Fitness Fast ... 5E 118
(off Burley St.)
Fitness First
Halifax ... 1H 7 (4A 98)
Huddlesfield ... 8K 137
Keighley ... 1J 43
Leeds ... 5M 67
Pontefract ... 2J 129
Wakefield ... 6J 125
Fitness First for Women
Bradford ... 4A 6
Fitness Studio, The
Brighouse ... 1N 119
(off Park Row)

Francis St.—Gatesgarth Cres.

Francis St. WF7: Ackw . . . 5D 146
WF10: C'frd . . . 4E 108
WF14: Mir . . . 6J 121
WF16: Heck . . . 9B 102
Francis Ter. WF7: Ackw . . . 5D 146
Francis Vw. WF14: Mir . . . 6K 121
Francus Royd S71: Carl . . . 8D 160
Frank Cl. WF12: T'hill . . . 9H 123
Frankland Gro. LS7: Leeds . . . 3G 68
Frankland Pl. LS7: Leeds . . . 1L 5 (3G 68)
(not continuous)
Frank La. HD8: Eml . . . 3E 156
HX2: Midg . . . 2B 96
WF12: T'hill . . . 9H 123
Franklin St. HX1: Hal . . . 5M 97
Frank Parkinson Ct. *LS20: Guis* . . . *7J 31*
(off W. Villa Rd.)
Frank Parkinson Homes *LS20: Guis* . . . *7J 31*
(off Lands La.)
Frank Peel Cl. WF16: Heck . . . 8A 102
Frank Pl. BD7: B'frd . . . 1N 81
Frank St. BD7: B'frd . . . 1N 81
HX1: Hal . . . 6N 97
Fraser Av. LS18: Hors . . . 7C 48
Fraser Rd. LS28: Cal . . . 9K 47
Fraser St. BD8: B'frd . . . 6A 64
LS9: Leeds . . . 4M 5 (5H 69)
Freakfield La. WF15: Liv . . . 1F 120
Fred Atkinson Way BD17: Bail . . . 6B 46
Frederick Av. LS9: Leeds . . . 8J 69
WF1: Wake . . . 8A 126
Frederick Cl. BD10: B'frd . . . 6D 46
Frederick St. BD21: Keigh . . . 9K 27
HD4: Hud . . . 6H 137
LS28: Fars . . . 3N 65
WF1: Wake . . . 4K 9 (5L 125)
WF15: Liv . . . 9M 101
Frederick Walker Gdns. WF17: Bat . . . 8G 102
Fred's Pl. BD4: B'frd . . . 2G 83
Fred St. BD21: Keigh . . . 1H 43
Freeholds Rd. OL12: Whit . . . 5A 112
Freeholds Ter. OL12: Whit . . . 5A 112
Freely Flds. LS23: B'ham . . . 6D 38
Freely La. LS23: B'ham . . . 6D 38
Freeman Ct. *HD6: B Bri* . . . *5N 99*
(off Axminster Dr.)
Freeman Rd. HX3: Sou . . . 7F 98
Freemans Way LS22: Weth . . . 3N 23
Freeman's Yd. *WF8: Pon* . . . *3J 129*
(off Ropergate Service Rd.)
Freemantle Pl. LS15: Leeds . . . 7N 69
Freemont St. LS13: Leeds . . . 4D 66
Free School La. HX1: Hal . . . 8G 7 (7N 97)
HX3: Hal . . . 8G 7 (7N 97)
Freeston Av. WF1: K'thpe . . . 4E 126
Freeston Ct. WF6: Norm . . . 9J 107
Freeston Dr. WF1: K'thpe . . . 5D 126
WF6: Norm . . . 9J 107
Freestone M. LS12: Leeds . . . 7F 66
Freestone Way WF6: Alt . . . 8F 106
Freeway Dr. WF10: C'frd . . . 7L 107
Fremantle Gro. BD4: B'frd . . . 9J 65
French St. DN6: Skel . . . 8M 165
Frensham Av. LS27: Morl . . . 1J 103
Frensham Dr. BD7: B'frd . . . 2J 81
WF10: C'frd . . . 5K 109
Frensham Gro. BD7: B'frd . . . 2J 81
Frensham Way BD7: B'frd . . . 2J 81
Freshfield Gdns. BD15: All . . . 5G 63
Fresh Mdws. WF6: Norm . . . 2K 127
Friar Ct. BD10: B'frd . . . 9G 46
Friar Pl. HD2: Hud . . . 6D 120
Friar's Cl. WF7: F'stne . . . 7D 128
Friars Ind. Est. BD10: B'frd . . . 8F 46
Friars Nook WF8: Pon . . . 4L 129
Friarwood La. WF8: Pon . . . 3K 129
Friar Wood Steps WF8: Pon . . . 3K 129
Friarwood Ter. WF8: Pon . . . 3K 129
Friary Ct. WF17: Birs . . . 3A 102
Frickley Athletic FC . . . 8M 163
Frickley Bri. La. S72: B'ley . . . 5M 161
Frickley Country Pk. . . . 9M 163
Frickley La. DN5: Fric . . . 9N 163
WF9: S Elm . . . 9N 163
Frieldhurst Rd. OL14: Tod . . . 3E 92
FRIENDLY . . . 7H 97
Friendly Av. HX6: Sow B . . . 7G 97
Friendly Fold HX3: Hal . . . 2N 97
Friendly Fold Ho. *HX3: Hal* . . . *2N 97*
(off Lentilfield St.)
Friendly Fold Rd. HX3: Hal . . . 2N 97
Friendly St. BD13: Thorn . . . 8C 62
HD1: Hud . . . 4C 8 (4N 137)
HX3: Hal . . . 2N 97
Frimley Dr. BD5: B'frd . . . 3A 82
Frisian Cl. WF10: C'frd . . . 3J 109
Frith St. BD22: Cros R . . . 7E 42
FRIZINGHALL . . . 2N 63
Frizinghall Rd. BD9: B'frd . . . 2A 64
Frizinghall Station (Rail) . . . 2A 64
Frizley Gdns. BD9: B'frd . . . 2A 64
Frobisher Gro. WF2: Wake . . . 6G 125
Frodingham Vs. BD2: B'frd . . . 4H 65
Frogmoor Av. BD12: O'haw . . . 8D 82
Frogmore Ter. BD12: O'haw . . . 8D 82
Frontline Cl. LS8: Leeds . . . 9J 51
Front Row LS11: Leeds . . . 8D 4 (8D 68)
(not continuous)
Front St. LS11: Leeds . . . 8D 68
LS23: B'ham . . . 6C 38
WF8: Pon . . . 3J 129
WF10: C'frd . . . 6F 108
Front Vw. HX3: She . . . 8H 81
Frost Hill WF15: Liv . . . 8M 101
Frost Hole La. HX7: Crag V . . . 6K 95
Frostholme OL14: Tod . . . 3D 92
Fruit St. BD21: Keigh . . . 8L 27
Fryergate WF2: Wake . . . 4H 125
Fryersway WF5: Oss . . . 5D 124
Fryston La. WF11: Ferr . . . 6M 109
(not continuous)
Fryston Rd. WF10: C'frd . . . 2J 109
Fuchsia Cft. LS26: W'frd . . . 7F 88
Fulbeck Cl. BD15: All . . . 7F 62
Fulford Av. HD2: Hud . . . 9M 119
Fulford Cl. S75: Dart . . . 8J 159
WF6: Norm . . . 2L 127
Fulford St. WF10: C'frd . . . 5C 108
Fulford Wlk. BD2: B'frd . . . 4H 65
Fulham La. DN6: Wome . . . 8N 131
Fulham Pl. LS11: Leeds . . . 2D 86
Fulham Sq. *LS11: Leeds* . . . *2D 86*
(off Fulham St.)
Fulham St. LS11: Leeds . . . 2D 86
Fullers Ho. *LS9: Leeds* . . . *8K 5*
(off East St.)
Fullerton Cl. DN6: Skel . . . 7L 165
Fullerton St. BD3: B'frd . . . 5E 6 (8E 64)
Fullerton Ter. LS22: Coll . . . 9J 23
Fullwood Dr. HD7: Golc . . . 6C 136
Fulmar Ct. LS10: Leeds . . . 8F 86
Fulmar M. BD8: B'frd . . . 7H 63
Fulmar Rd. WF10: C'frd . . . 6C 108
FULNECK . . . 9B 66
Fulneck LS28: Pud . . . 1A 84
Fulneck Cl. HD2: Fix . . . 8L 119
LS11: Leeds . . . 6C 86
Fulneck Ct. LS28: Pud . . . 9C 66
Fulneck Golf Course . . . 1A 84
Fulneck M. LS28: Pud . . . 9C 66
FULSTONE . . . 1E 170
Fulstone Hall La. HD9: New M . . . 2D 170
Fulstone Rd. HD4: Stock . . . 9F 154
Fulton Pl. LS16: Leeds . . . 8M 49
Fulton St. BD1: B'frd . . . 4A 6 (7B 64)
Fulwood Gro. WF2: Wake . . . 5K 143
Furlong La. WF8: Pon . . . 7L 129
Furnace Gro. BD12: O'haw . . . 8D 82
Furnace Inn St. BD4: B'frd . . . 9H 65
Furnace La. BD11: B'haw . . . 7L 83
Furnace Rd. BD12: O'haw . . . 8D 82
(not continuous)
Furnbrook Gdns. HD5: K'htn . . . 3F 138
Furness Av. HX2: Illing . . . 8K 79
WF2: Wren . . . 1G 124
Furness Cres. HX2: Illing . . . 8K 79
Furness Dr. HX2: Illing . . . 8K 79
WF2: Wren . . . 1G 125
Furness Gdns. HX2: Illing . . . 9L 79
Furness Gro. HX2: Illing . . . 9K 79
Furness Pl. HX2: Illing . . . 1L 97
Fusden La. BD19: Gom . . . 3L 101
Fusion Point LS25: Gar . . . 6A 72
Future Bodies Gym
Morley . . . *8K 85*
(off Bank Av.)
Future Flds. BD6: B'frd . . . 4K 81
Futures Way BD4: B'frd . . . 8C 6 (9D 64)
Fyfe Cres. BD17: Bail . . . 5C 46
Fyfe Gro. BD17: Bail . . . 5C 46
Fyfe La. BD17: Bail . . . 5C 46

G

Gable End Ter. LS28: Pud . . . 7C 66
Gables, The BD17: Bail . . . 4C 46
BD21: Keigh . . . *9G 27*
(off W. Leeds St.)
DN14: Beal . . . 5N 111
LS17: Leeds . . . 3J 51
LS18: Hors . . . 4F 48
WF8: Pon . . . 1M 129
Gables Cl. DN14: Beal . . . 5N 111
Gabriel Ct. *LS10: Leeds* . . . *1F 86*
(off Hunslet Grn. Way)
Gabriel's Cnr. WF7: Ackw . . . 5F 146
Gadding Moor La. S75: Hoy . . . 8H 173
Gadding Moor Rd. S36: Hoy . . . 8H 173
Gadwall Dr. WF10: All B . . . 9B 90
Gagewell Dr. WF4: Horb . . . 9D 124
Gagewell La. WF4: Horb . . . 9D 124
Gagewell Vw. WF4: Horb . . . 9D 124
Gainest HX2: Hal . . . 7M 97
Gainford Dr. LS25: Gar . . . 8N 71
Gain La. BD2: B'frd . . . 5H 65
BD3: B'frd . . . 5H 65
Gainsborough Av. LS16: Leeds . . . 2L 49
Gainsborough Cl. BD3: B'frd . . . 4E 64
Gainsborough Ct. LS16: Leeds . . . 2L 49
Gainsborough Flds. *LS12: N Far* . . . *2H 85*
(off Coach Rd.)
Gainsborough Pl. *LS12: N Far* . . . *2H 85*
(off Coach Rd.)
Gainsborough Way WF3: S'ley . . . 7N 105
GAISBY . . . 1B 64
Gaisby La. BD2: B'frd, Ship . . . 2B 64
BD18: Ship . . . 9B 46
Gaisby Mt. BD18: Ship . . . 1B 64
Gaisby Pl. BD18: Ship . . . 9B 46
Gaisby Ri. BD18: Ship . . . 9B 46
Gaitskell Ct. LS11: Leeds . . . 9C 68
Gaitskell Grange LS11: Leeds . . . 9C 68
Gaitskell Wlk. LS11: Leeds . . . 9C 68
Gala Bingo
Bradford . . . 4J 83
Castleford . . . 7F 108
Leeds . . . 8J 67
Wakefield . . . 6J 9 (6L 125)
Gala Casino
Leeds . . . 6A 4 (6B 68)
Galahad Way WF9: S Elm . . . 7N 163
Galecommon La. DN6: Wome . . . 7M 131
Galefield Grn. BD6: B'frd . . . 7L 81
Gale La. LS21: Stainb . . . 2E 18
Gale St. BD21: Keigh . . . 8J 27
BD22: Cros R . . . 7F 42
Gallagher Leisure Pk. BD3: B'frd . . . 6K 65
Gallagher Retail Pk. HD5: Hud . . . 4F 138
Gallery 339
Halifax . . . 9B 98
Gallery Health & Fitness Club
Wakefield . . . 5J 9
Gall La. OL14: Tod . . . 2E 92
Gallogate La. LS17: Wee . . . 7A 20
Gallon Cft. WF9: S Elm . . . 6L 163
Gallops, The LS27: Morl . . . 3L 103
Galloway Ct. LS28: Pud . . . 6L 65
Galloway La. LS28: Pud . . . 5L 65
Galloway Rd. BD10: B'frd . . . 8H 47
Galloway St. HD1: Hud . . . 1D 8 (2N 137)
Gallows Hill WF10: C'frd . . . 5J 109
Gallows La. WF4: Wool . . . 9H 143
Galsworthy Av. BD9: B'frd . . . 3H 63
Galway Cl. S71: Roys . . . 5D 160
GAMBLE HILL . . . 6G 67
Gamble Hill LS13: Leeds . . . 6G 67
Gamble Hill Chase LS13: Leeds . . . 6G 67
Gamble Hill Cl. LS13: Leeds . . . 6G 67
Gamble Hill Cft. *LS13: Leeds* . . . *6G 67*
(off Gamble Hill Vw.)
Gamble Hill Cross *LS13: Leeds* . . . *6G 67*
(off Gamble Hill Lawn)
Gamble Hill Dr. LS13: Leeds . . . 6G 67
Gamble Hill Fold *LS13: Leeds* . . . *6G 67*
(off Gamble Hill Lawn)
Gamble Hill Grange *LS13: Leeds* . . . *6G 67*
(off Gamble Hill Dr.)
Gamble Hill Grn. LS13: Leeds . . . 6G 66
Gamble Hill Lawn LS13: Leeds . . . 6G 67
Gamble Hill Path *LS13: Leeds* . . . *6G 66*
(off Gamble Hill Grn.)
Gamble Hill Pl. LS13: Leeds . . . 6G 67
Gamble Hill Ri. LS13: Leeds . . . 6G 66
Gamble Hill Va. LS13: Leeds . . . 6G 66
Gamble Hill Vw. LS13: Leeds . . . 6G 67
Gamble Hill Wlk. *LS13: Leeds* . . . *6G 66*
(off Gamble Hill Ri.)
Gamble La. LS12: Leeds . . . 8F 66
Gambles Hill LS28: Fars . . . 3A 66
Gamel Vw. BD20: Stee . . . 2B 26
Game Scar La.
BD22: Lay, Oak . . . 1B 42
Gang, The *LS12: Leeds* . . . *7M 67*
(off Town St.)
Ganners Cl. LS13: Leeds . . . 2F 66
Ganners Gth. LS13: Leeds . . . 2G 66
Ganners Grn. LS13: Leeds . . . 2F 66
Ganners Gro. LS13: Leeds . . . 2G 66
Ganners Hill LS13: Leeds . . . 2G 66
Ganners La. LS13: Leeds . . . 2F 66
Ganners Mt. LS13: Leeds . . . 2F 66
Ganners Ri. LS13: Leeds . . . 2G 66
Ganners Rd. LS13: Leeds . . . 2F 66
Ganners Wlk. LS13: Leeds . . . 2F 66
Ganners Way LS13: Leeds . . . 2F 66
Gannerthorpe Cl. BD12: Wyke . . . 1A 100
Gannet Cl. WF10: C'frd . . . 6C 108
Ganny Rd. HD6: Brigh . . . 1N 119
Ganton Cl. LS6: Leeds . . . 2D 68
Ganton Ct. WF6: Norm . . . 2L 127
Ganton Way HD2: Fix . . . 8L 119
Gant Pl. BD2: B'frd . . . 3D 64
Gaol La. HX1: Hal . . . 3L 7 (5B 98)
Garden, The *WF1: Wake* . . . *5K 9*
(within Ridings Shop. Cen.)
Garden Av. WF15: Liv . . . 6L 101
Garden Cl. BD12: Wyke . . . 9A 82
WF5: Oss . . . 8A 124
WF15: Liv . . . 7L 101
Garden Ct. HD1: Hud . . . 8A 8
WF15: Liv . . . 7H 101
Garden Cft. WF17: Bat . . . 9D 102
Gardeners Ct. LS10: Leeds . . . 1F 86
Gardeners' Wlk. HD8: Skelm . . . 8C 156
Garden Fld. BD12: Wyke . . . 1A 100
Garden Fold HX3: Hip . . . 4H 99
Garden Ho. Cl. LS26: Meth . . . 1L 107
Garden Ho. La. WF3: Ting . . . 4C 104
Gardenhurst LS6: Leeds . . . 2A 68
Garden La. BD9: B'frd . . . 3L 63
HX4: Bark . . . 4H 117
WF8: Went . . . 2C 148
WF11: Knot . . . 7F 110
Garden Pde. WF15: Liv . . . 6L 101
Garden Pl. WF13: Dew . . . 2C 122
Garden Rd. HD6: Brigh . . . 8L 99
Garden Row WF4: Croft . . . 1G 145
Gardens, The BD16: Bgly . . . 4J 45
HX1: Hal . . . 8K 7 (7B 98)
LS10: Leeds . . . 9E 86
LS27: Morl . . . 2J 103
LS28: Fars . . . 3N 65
WF8: Pon . . . 4H 129
Gardens Cres. WF13: Raven . . . 5B 122
Gardens Dr. WF13: Raven . . . 5B 122
Gardens Rd. WF13: Raven . . . 5B 122
Gardens Ter. WF13: Raven . . . 5B 122
Garden St. BD9: B'frd . . . 2L 63
BD22: Cros R . . . 7F 42
HD1: Hud . . . 8A 8 (6L 137)
HX7: Heb B . . . *1H 95*
(off Albert St.)
OL14: Tod . . . 6K 93
WF1: Wake . . . 5H 9 (5K 125)
WF6: Alt . . . 9F 106
WF6: Norm . . . 1J 127
WF7: Ackw . . . 5D 146
WF10: C'frd . . . 6G 108
(Holywell Dene)
WF10: C'frd . . . 6D 108
(Longacre)
WF13: Raven . . . 5A 122
WF16: Heck . . . 9A 102
Garden St. Mill HX3: Hal . . . 2M 7
Garden St. Nth. HX3: Hal . . . 2M 7 (4C 98)
Garden Ter. BD9: B'frd . . . 3M 63
HD8: Den D . . . 3C 172
HX7: Heb B . . . 1H 95
WF4: Crig . . . 6G 142
WF4: Ryh . . . 9J 145
Garden Vw. BD15: Wils . . . 9B 44
BD16: Bgly . . . 4H 45
WF15: Liv . . . 6L 101
Garden Vw. Ct. LS8: Leeds . . . 6K 51
Garden Village LS25: M'fld . . . 8G 73
Garden Vs. *HX7: Hept* . . . *8G 76*
(off Church La.)
Garden Wlk. WF15: Liv . . . 7L 101
Gardiner Row BD4: B'frd . . . 3F 82
Gardiners Sq. HX3: Hip . . . 4H 99
Garfield Av. BD8: B'frd . . . 4N 63
Garfield Pl. *BD15: All* . . . *5F 62*
(off North Vw.)
HD7: Mars . . . 5F 150
Garfield St. BD15: All . . . 5F 62
HX3: Hal . . . 3N 97
OL14: Tod . . . 3E 92
Garfit Hill BD19: Gom . . . 4A 102
WF17: Gom . . . 4A 102
GARFORTH . . . 7M 71
Garforth Av. BD20: Stee . . . 2C 26
GARFORTH BRIDGE . . . 9K 71
Garforth Cl. WF6: Alt . . . 9F 106
Garforth Ct. WF14: Mir . . . 4L 121
Garforth Dr. WF6: Alt . . . 9F 106
Garforth Golf Course . . . 3M 71
Garforth Rd. BD21: Keigh . . . 8L 27
Garforth Squash & Leisure Cen. . . . 8A 72
Garforth Station (Rail) . . . 7N 71
Garforth St. BD15: All . . . 5G 63
HD1: Hud . . . 7E 8 (5A 138)
HD4: Neth . . . 2H 153
Gargrave App. LS9: Leeds . . . 5M 5 (5H 69)
Gargrave Cl. HD6: Ras . . . 3J 119
Gargrave Ct. LS9: Leeds . . . 4M 5 (5H 69)
Gargrave Cres. WF9: Hems . . . 3C 162
Gargrave Pl. LS9: Leeds . . . 4M 5 (5H 69)
WF2: Wake . . . 6E 124
WF9: Hems . . . 3C 162
Garibaldi St. BD3: B'frd . . . 7J 65
(not continuous)
Garland Dr. LS15: Leeds . . . 7E 70
Garlick St. HD6: Ras . . . 5K 119
Garmil Head La. WF9: Fitz . . . 5N 145
Garmil La. WF4: Wrag . . . 5N 145
Garmont M. LS7: Leeds . . . 9F 50
Garmont Rd. LS7: Leeds . . . 9F 50
Garner La. HD8: Kbtn . . . 1H 155
HD9: Hon . . . 5J 153
Garnet Av. LS11: Leeds . . . 2E 86
Garnet Cres. LS11: Leeds . . . 2E 86
Garnet Gro. LS11: Leeds . . . 2E 86
Garnet La. LS24: Tad . . . 8M 39
Garnet Pde. LS11: Leeds . . . 2E 86
Garnet Pl. LS11: Leeds . . . 2E 86
Garnet Rd. LS11: Leeds . . . 3E 86
Garnet Ter. LS11: Leeds . . . 2E 86
LS24: Tad . . . 7N 39
Garnett St. BD3: B'frd . . . 4E 6 (7E 64)
HX7: Heb B . . . 1H 95
LS21: Otley . . . 9L 17
WF13: Dew . . . 9C 102
Garnet Vw. LS11: Leeds . . . 2E 86
Garrett Cl. HD8: Skelm . . . 7C 156
Garrison Ct. WF8: Pon . . . 4G 129
Garros La. BD23: E'by . . . 1A 10
Garrowby Ho. *BD10: B'frd* . . . *7F 46*
(off Thorp Gth.)
Garsdale Av. BD10: B'frd . . . 8G 46
Garsdale Cres. BD17: Bail . . . 3C 46
Garsdale Fold LS22: Coll . . . 8H 23
Garsdale Gro. WF1: Wake . . . 3A 126
Garsdale Rd. HD4: Hud . . . 8N 137
Garsdale Wlk. WF11: Knot . . . 1D 130
Garside Dr. HX2: Hal . . . 9M 79
Garth, The LS9: Leeds . . . 7K 5 (7G 68)
LS22: Coll . . . 9J 23
LS25: Gar . . . 7A 72
Garth Av. LS17: Leeds . . . 6D 50
LS22: Coll . . . 9J 23
WF6: Norm . . . 3H 127
Garth Barn Cl. BD9: B'frd . . . 3M 63
Garth Cotts. WF11: Knot . . . 8G 110
Garth Dr. LS17: Leeds . . . 6D 50
Garth Edge OL12: Whit . . . 6A 112
Garth End LS22: Coll . . . 9J 23
LS22: K Dei . . . 1L 23
Garth Fold BD10: B'frd . . . 7F 46
Garth Gro. LS29: Men . . . 4E 30
Garth Ho. M. WF6: Norm . . . 3H 127
Garthland Way BD4: B'frd . . . 2G 83
Garth Rd. LS17: Leeds . . . 6D 50
Garth St. BD21: Keigh . . . 9H 27
WF10: C'frd . . . 6C 108
Garthwaite Mt. BD15: All . . . 4G 62
Garth Wlk. LS17: Leeds . . . 6D 50
Garthwood Cl. BD4: B'frd . . . 5F 82
Garton Av. LS9: Leeds . . . 7J 69
Garton Dr. BD10: B'frd . . . 1H 65
Garton Gro. LS9: Leeds . . . 7J 69
Garton Rd. LS9: Leeds . . . 7J 69
Garton Ter. LS9: Leeds . . . 7J 69
Garton Vw. LS9: Leeds . . . 7J 69
Garvey Vw. BD5: B'frd . . . 1C 82
Garwick Ter. HX4: Gree . . . 4C 118
Gascoigne Av. LS15: Bar E . . . 9L 53
Gascoigne Ct. LS15: Bar E . . . 9M 53
Gascoigne Ho. *WF8: Pon* . . . *1K 129*
(off Cromwell Mt.)
Gascoigne Rd. LS15: Bar E . . . 9L 53
WF3: Thpe H . . . 3G 105
Gascoigne Vw. LS15: Bar E . . . 9L 53
Gashouse La. LS22: Weth . . . 4N 23
Gas Ho. Yd. BD12: O'haw . . . 8C 82
Gaskell Dr. WF4: Horb . . . 9C 124
Gaskell St. WF2: Wake . . . 6J 125
Gas St. BD22: Haw . . . 8D 42
Gas Works La. HX5: Ell . . . 4E 118
Gas Works Rd. BD21: Keigh . . . 8M 27
(not continuous)
HX6: Sow B . . . 8K 97
Gasworks St. HD1: Hud . . . 3D 8 (3N 137)
WF15: Liv . . . 8M 101
Gatefield Mt. BD6: B'frd . . . 7N 81
Gate Foot La. HD8: Shep . . . 2G 170
Gatehaus, The BD1: B'frd . . . 4D 6 (7D 64)
Gate Head HD7: Mars . . . 5H 151
Gatehead HX4: Gree . . . 5M 117
Gatehead Bank HD7: Mars . . . 4H 151
Gate Head La. HD9: H'wth . . . 8E 170
HX4: Gree . . . 6M 117
Gatehouse Cen. *HD1: Hud* . . . *7L 137*
(off Albert St.)
Gate Ho. Ct. LS26: W'frd . . . 6F 88
Gateland Dr. LS17: Shad . . . 3N 51
Gateland La. LS17: Shad . . . 4N 51
Gatenby Cl. BD6: B'frd . . . 4K 81
Gateon Ho. La. LS17: E Kes . . . 4B 36
Gatesgarth Cres. HD3: Hud . . . 1F 136

Gatesway—Glen Mt.

Gatesway BD16: Har 6N 43
Gateway, The LS26: Rothw 9N 87
Gate Way Dr. LS19: Yead 9L 31
Gateway E. LS9: Leeds 7J 5
Gateway Nth. LS9: Leeds 7J 5
Gateways WF1: Out 7L 105
Gateways, The BD12: Low M 8A 82
Gateway Sth. LS9: Leeds 8J 5
Gateway W. LS9: Leeds 8J 5
Gathorne Cl. LS8: Leeds 3G 69
Gathorne St. BD7: B'frd 1N 81
HD6: Brigh 9N 99
LS8: Leeds 1L 5 (3G 69)
(not continuous)
Gathorne Ter. LS8: Leeds 1L 5 (3G 69)
(not continuous)
Gaukroger La. HX1: Hal 7M 7 (7C 98)
Gauk St. WF11: B'ton 4B 110
WF11: Fair 9N 91
Gaunts Pl. LS28: Fars 3B 66
GAUXHOLME 9J 93
Gauxholme Fold OL14: Tod 9H 93
Gauxholme Ind. Est. OL14: Tod 9H 93
Gavin Cl. BD3: B'frd 7J 65
Gawcliffe Rd. BD18: Ship 9A 46
Gaw La. BD23: Hal E 1F 10
GAWTHORPE
HD5 5H 139
WF5 2M 123
Gawthorpe BD16: Bgly 2F 44
Gawthorpe Av. BD16: Bgly 2F 44
Gawthorpe Dr. BD16: Bgly 2F 44
GAWTHORPE GREEN 4J 139
Gawthorpe Grn. La. HD5: K'htn 4J 139
Gawthorpe La. BD16: Bgly 3F 44
HD5: K'htn 5H 139
WF2: Kirk 1C 124
WF5: Oss 2N 123
Gay La. LS21: Otley 1L 31
Gayle Cl. BD12: Wyke 2A 100
Gaynor St. BD1: B'frd 7B 64
Gaythorne Rd. BD2: B'frd 3G 65
BD5: B'frd 2C 82
Gaythorne Ter. BD14: Clay 1H 81
HX3: Hip 3H 99
Geary Cl. WF2: Wake 3F 124
Geary Dr. WF2: Wake 3F 124
Gedham WF5: Oss 5N 123
Geecroft La. LS22: Sick 4C 22
Geelong Cl. BD2: B'frd 3D 64
Gelder Ct. WF2: Wake 3F 124
Gelder Cft. WF2: Wake 3F 124
Gelderd Bus. Pk. LS12: Leeds 1N 85
Gelderd Cl. LS12: Leeds 1N 85
Gelderd La. LS12: Leeds 1N 85
Gelderd Pl. LS12: Leeds 8A 68
Gelderd Rd. LS12: Gil, Leeds 5J 85
LS27: Gil 8F 84
WF17: Birs 3C 102
Gelderd Trad. Est. LS12: Leeds 9A 68
Gelder Rd. LS12: Leeds 7L 67
Gelder Ter. HD5: Hud 7F 8 (5A 138)
Gelderwood HD8: Shep 7K 155
Gemini Bus. Pk. LS7: Leeds 1H 5 (3F 68)
Gemini Ct. WF8: Pon 9K 109
General Wood OL14: W'den 2J 113
Geneva Gro. WF1: Wake 2K 9 (4M 125)
Genista Dr. LS10: Leeds 5F 86
Gentian Ct. WF2: Wake 4G 125
George, The HX6: Mill B 4D 116
George-A-Green Ct. WF2: Wake 7G 125
George-a-Green Rd. WF2: Wake 6G 124
George and Crown Yd. WF1: Wake 4J 9 (5L 125)
George Av. HD2: Hud 2K 137
George Buckley Ct. WF9: S Kirk 7G 162
George La. HX6: Ripp 9B 116
(not continuous)
WF4: Not 3M 159
George Mann Rd. LS10: Leeds 2J 87
George Mann Way LS10: Leeds 2H 87
George Sq. HX1: Hal 4K 7 (5B 98)
George's Sq. BD13: Cull 9K 43
BD21: Keigh 1H 43
George's St. HX3: Hal 1M 97
George St. BD1: B'frd 5D 6 (8D 64)
BD13: Denh 5L 61
BD13: Thorn 8C 62
BD17: Bail 6A 46
BD18: Ship 7L 45
BD19: Cleck 4H 101
DN6: Carc, Skel 7N 165
HD1: Hud 5B 8 (4M 137)
HD3: Hud 1G 137
(East St.)
HD3: Hud 5G 136
(Market St.)
HD4: Hud 6K 137
HD6: Brigh 1A 120
HD6: Ras 2M 119
HD7: Slait 9M 135
HD8: Kbtn 3K 155
HX1: Hal 4K 7 (5B 98)
HX3: Hip 5J 99
HX4: Gree 4C 118
HX5: Ell 5E 118
HX6: Sow B 9H 97
HX7: Myth 4M 95
LS2: Leeds 6G 5 (6E 68)
LS19: Raw 3M 47
LS26: W'frd 7M 89
LS29: Add 1M 13
OL14: Tod 7K 93
(off Union St. Sth.)
S72: Cud 9K 161
S72: S Hien 3L 161
S75: Map 8K 159
WF1: Out 7K 105
WF1: Wake 5J 9 (5L 125)
WF4: Horb 1D 142
WF4: Ryh 8J 145
WF5: Oss 4M 123
WF6: Alt 9G 106
WF7: F'stne 6C 128
WF7: Street 6L 127
WF9: Hems 3E 162
George St. WF13: Dew 3C 122
(Barley Cft.)
WF13: Dew 3F 122
(Central St.)
WF13: Raven 6B 122
WF15: Liv 8L 101
WF16: Heck 8N 101
WF17: Bat 8F 102
George Wright Ho. *WF8: Pon 3K 129*
(off Horsefair)
Georgia M. WF5: Oss 7B 124
Georgian Sq. LS13: Leeds 1B 66
Geraldton Av. BD2: B'frd 3C 64
Gerard Av. LS27: Morl 9J 85
Gerard Ho. *BD10: B'frd 8G 47*
(off Fairhaven Grn.)
Germaine Ter. LS14: T'ner 4F 52
Gernhill Av. HD2: Fix 6L 119
Gerrard St. HX1: Hal 4H 7 (5A 98)
Gertrude St. OL12: Whit 5A 112
Gervase Rd. WF4: Horb 9C 124
Ghyll, The BD16: Cot 7F 44
HD2: Fix 7M 119
Ghyllbank BD20: Sils 7E 12
Ghyll Beck Dr. LS19: Raw 4B 48
LS21: Otley 2H 31
Ghyll Cl. BD20: Stee 3C 26
Ghyll Dr. BD22: Haw 9C 42
Ghyll Grange La. BD20: Sils 8J 13
Ghyll Lodge BD16: Cot 7F 44
Ghyll M. LS29: I'ly 6F 14
Ghyll Mt. LS19: Yead 1K 47
Ghyll Rd. LS6: Leeds 9K 49
Ghyll Royd LS20: Guis 9J 31
(not continuous)
LS29: I'ly 5E 14
Ghyllroyd LS19: Yead 2L 47
Ghyllroyd Av. BD11: B'haw 8M 83
Ghyllroyd Dr. BD11: B'haw 8M 83
Ghyll Wood LS29: I'ly 6D 14
Ghyll Wood Dr. BD16: Cot 7F 44
Gibbet, The 3J 7
Gibbet St. HX1: Hal 4G 7 (5N 97)
HX2: Hal 5K 97
Gibb La. HX2: Mt T 1H 97
Gib La. HD8: Skelm 7D 156
HD9: Hon 7M 153
HX7: P Wel 2J 77
Gibraltar HX1: Hal 6L 97
Gibraltar Av. HX1: Hal 6L 97
Gibraltar Island Rd. LS10: Leeds 1H 87
Gibraltar Rd. HX1: Hal 5L 97
LS28: Pud 7M 65
Gibriding La. HD9: Holm 5E 168
Gibson Av. WF2: Wake 4H 125
Gibson Cl. WF2: Wake 4J 125
Gibson Dr. LS15: Leeds 7D 70
Gibson La. LS25: Kip 3B 90
Gibson Mill 5D 76
Gibson St. BD3: B'frd 8F 64
HD3: Hud 3H 137
OL14: Tod 7L 93
Gilbert Chase LS5: Leeds 3K 67
Gilbert Cl. LS5: Leeds 3L 67
Gilbert Cotts. HX4: Bark 4K 117
Gilbert Gdns. HX4: Bark 5K 117
Gilbert Gro. HD4: Hud 8J 137
Gilbert Mt. LS5: Leeds 3L 67
Gilbert St. LS28: Fars 4A 66
Gilbert Wilkinson Ho. *WF8: Pon 2K 129*
(off Horsefair)
GILCAR 7K 107
Gilcar St. WF6: Norm 8L 107
Gilcar Vs. WF6: Norm 8L 107
Gilcar Way WF10: C'frd 7J 107
GILDERSOME 6F 84
Gildersome Cross LS27: Gil 7F 84
Gildersome La. LS12: Gil, N Far 5E 84
LS27: Gil 5E 84
Gildersome Spur LS27: Gil 8G 84
GILDERSOME STREET 8E 84
Gilder Way S72: Shaf 7K 161
Gilead Rd. HD3: Hud 3D 136
Giles Hill La. HX3: She 6F 80
Giles St. BD5: B'frd 8A 6 (9B 64)
BD6: B'frd 4M 81
HD9: Nether 9L 153
Giles' Wlk. BD16: Bgly 5H 45
Gillann St. WF11: Knot 8F 110
Gill Bank Rd. LS29: I'ly 3F 14
Gill Beck Cl. BD17: Bail 3C 46
Gill Cl. LS29: Add 1K 13
Gillett Dr. LS26: Rothw 8A 88
Gillett La. LS26: Rothw 8A 88
Gilling Av. LS25: Gar 6B 72
Gillingham Grn. BD4: B'frd 2J 83
Gillion Cres. WF4: Dur 4G 142
Gill La. BD13: Thorn 9B 62
BD22: Oak 3A 42
HD9: H'frth 6K 169
LS19: Yead 3J 47
LS22: Kear 6A 22
LS29: Nes 2B 14
Gillrene Av. BD15: Wils 2C 62
GILLROYD 9M 85
Gillroyd La. HD7: Linth 2C 152
Gillroyd Mt. LS27: Morl 9M 85
Gillroyd Pde. LS27: Morl 1L 103
Gillroyd Pl. LS27: Morl 9L 85
Gillroyd Ri. BD7: B'frd 7N 63
Gillroyd Ter. LS27: Morl 9M 85
Gills, The LS21: Otley 7L 17
LS27: Morl 9M 85
Gill's Bldgs. *WF2: Wake 5J 125*
(off Alverthorpe Rd.)
Gill's Ct. HX1: Hal 4L 7 (5B 98)
Gill Sike Av. WF2: Wake 7H 125
Gill Sike Bungs. WF2: Wake 7H 125
Gill Sike Gro. WF2: Wake 7H 125
Gill Sike Ho. WF2: Wake 7H 125
Gill Sike Rd. WF2: Wake 7H 125
Gillstead Ho. *LS14: Leeds 9A 52*
(off Kingsdale Ct.)
Gillstone Dr. BD22: Cros R 8D 42
Gill St. WF1: Wake 4J 9 (5L 125)
Gill's Yd. WF1: Wake 3J 9 (4L 125)
Gillygate WF8: Pon 3K 129
Gilmour St. HX3: Hal 1H 7 (3A 98)
Gilpin Pl. LS12: Leeds 8N 67
Gilpin St. BD3: B'frd 6F 64
LS12: Leeds 8N 67
Gilpin Ter. LS12: Leeds 8N 67
Gilpin Vw. LS12: Leeds 8N 67
GILSTEAD 3H 45
Gilstead Ct. BD16: Bgly 4H 45
Gilstead Dr. BD16: Bgly 4H 45
Gilstead La. BD16: Bgly 4G 45
Gilstead Way LS29: I'ly 4F 14
Gilthwaites Cres. HD8: Den D 1D 172
Gilthwaites Gro. HD8: Den D 2D 172
Gilthwaites La.
HD8: Den D, Skelm 9D 156
Gilthwaites Top HD8: Den D 1D 172
Gilwell Ct. WF3: Thpe H 2H 105
Gilynda Cl. BD8: B'frd 7K 63
Gindhill La. LS21: Stainb 2K 19
Gin La. WF7: Street 6K 127
Ginnel, The LS17: Bard 6D 36
LS22: Weth 4M 23
Gipsy Hill LS26: W'frd 7C 88
Gipsy La. LS11: Leeds 5C 86
LS26: W'frd 7C 88
WF2: Wake 3N 143
Gipsy Mead LS26: W'frd 7C 88
Gipsy St. BD3: B'frd 6J 65
GIPTON 3K 69
Gipton App. LS9: Leeds 5L 69
Gipton Av. LS7: Leeds 3G 69
Gipton Ga. E. LS9: Leeds 3L 69
Gipton Ga. W. LS9: Leeds 3K 69
Gipton Lodge *LS8: Leeds 2J 69*
(off Copgrove Rd.)
Gipton Sq. LS9: Leeds 5M 69
Gipton St. LS8: Leeds 3G 69
GIPTON WOOD 1K 69
Gipton Wood Av. LS8: Leeds 1K 69
Gipton Wood Cres. LS8: Leeds 1K 69
Gipton Wood Gro. LS8: Leeds 1K 69
Gipton Wood Pl. LS8: Leeds 1K 69
Gipton Wood Rd. LS8: Leeds 1K 69
GIRLINGTON 5M 63
Girlington Ind. Cen. *BD8: B'frd 6M 63*
(off Girlington Rd.)
Girlington Rd. BD8: B'frd 5L 63
Girnhill La. WF7: F'stne 7C 128
Gisbourne Rd. HD2: Hud 6C 120
Gisburn Rd. WF1: Wake 3A 126
Gisburn St. BD21: Keigh 8H 27
Gissing Cen. 4J 9
(off Thompson's Yd.)
Gissing Rd. WF2: Wake 7F 124
Glade, The BD17: Bail 5L 45
LS14: S'cft 9C 36
LS28: Stan 4L 65
Gladedale Av. LS8: Leeds 4L 69
Glade Wlk. LS10: Leeds 9H 87
Gladstone Ct. *LS28: Stan 4C 66*
(off Gladstone Ter.)
WF13: Dew 2D 122
(off Bk. Leatham St.)
Gladstone Cres. LS19: Raw 2M 47
Gladstone Ho. *BD4: B'frd 1J 83*
(off Tyersal La.)
Gladstone Pl. BD13: Denh 6K 61
BD22: Oak 5D 42
(off Keighley Rd.)
Gladstone Rd. HX1: Hal 3G 7 (5N 97)
LS19: Raw 3M 47
Gladstone St. BD3: B'frd 8G 64
BD13: Que 4E 80
BD15: All 5G 63
BD16: Bgly 5E 44
BD19: Cleck 5H 101
BD21: Keigh 1H 43
HX4: Holy 7N 117
LS28: Fars 3A 66
OL14: Tod 3D 92
WF6: Norm 9K 107
WF7: F'stne 4D 128
Gladstone Ter. LS27: Morl 9K 85
LS28: Stan 4C 66
WF10: C'frd 4E 108
Gladstone Vw. HX3: Hal 9D 98
Gladstone Vs. LS17: Shad 4N 51
Gladwin St. WF17: Bat 8E 102
Glaisdale Cl. BD20: Sils 8E 12
Glaisdale Ct. BD15: All 3F 62
Glaisdale Gro. HX3: Hip 5J 99
Glamis Cl. LS25: Gar 6B 72
Glanville Ter. LS26: Rothw 8N 87
GLASS HOUGHTON 6F 108
Glasshoughton Cultural Industries Cen. 6F 108
Glasshoughton Station (Rail) 8E 108
Glasshouse St. LS10: Leeds 9F 68
Glasshouse Vw. LS10: Leeds 9D 86
Glastonbury Av. WF1: Wake 2A 126
Glastonbury Ct. BD4: B'frd 1H 83
Glastonbury Dr. HD3: Hud 5E 136
Glazier Rd. BD13: Que 3B 80
Gleanings Av. HX2: Hal 5J 97
Gleanings Dr. HX2: Hal 5H 97
Glebe Av. LS5: Leeds 2L 67
Glebe Cl. HD8: Eml 2G 157
Glebe Ct. LS26: Rothw 8J 87
Glebe Field Chase LS22: Weth 3L 23
Glebe Field Cl. LS22: Weth 3L 23
Glebe Field Cft. LS22: Weth 3L 23
Glebe Field Dr. LS22: Weth 3L 23
Glebe Field Gth. LS22: Weth 3K 23
Glebe Field Holt LS22: Weth 3L 23
Glebe Fold BD20: Rid 6M 27
Glebe Gdns. HX1: Hal 8G 7 (7N 97)
Glebe Ga. WF12: T'hill 1H 141
Glebelands WF11: Kell 8L 111
Glebelands Cl. LS25: Gar 8N 71
Glebelands Dr. LS6: Leeds 9N 49
Glebe La. WF11: Knot 8E 110
Glebe Mt. LS28: Pud 8B 66
Glebe Pl. LS5: Leeds 2L 67
Glebe Side HD5: K'htn 9G 120
Glebe St. HD1: Hud 3K 137
LS28: Pud 8B 66
WF6: Norm 3K 127
WF10: C'frd 5D 108
Glebe Ter. LS16: Leeds 8N 49
Gledcliffe HX3: Hal 2M 7
Gleddings Cl. HX3: Hal 9N 97
Gledhill Rd. BD3: B'frd 8F 64
Gledhill St. OL14: Tod 6K 93
Gledhills Yd. *HX1: Hal 7M 97*
(off Haugh Shaw Rd. W.)
Gledhill Ter. WF13: Dew 3C 122
GLEDHOLT 4K 137
Gledholt Bank HD1: Hud 4K 137
Gledholt Ind. Pk. HD1: Hud 5K 137
Gledholt Rd. HD1: Hud 3K 137
GLEDHOW 8H 51
Gledhow Av. LS8: Leeds 7H 51
Gledhow Ct. LS7: Leeds 8G 50
Gledhow Dr. BD22: Oxen 2C 60
Gledhow Grange Vw. LS8: Leeds 8H 51
Gledhow Grange Wlk.
LS8: Leeds 8H 51
Gledhow La. LS7: Leeds 8F 50
LS8: Leeds 8G 51
Gledhow La. End LS7: Leeds 8F 50
Gledhow Mt. LS8: Leeds 1L 5 (4G 69)
Gledhow Pk. Av. LS7: Leeds 9G 50
Gledhow Pk. Cres. LS7: Leeds 9G 50
Gledhow Pk. Dr. LS7: Leeds 9F 50
Gledhow Pk. Gro. LS7: Leeds 9G 51
Gledhow Pk. Rd. LS7: Leeds 9G 50
Gledhow Pk. Vw. LS7: Leeds 9G 50
Gledhow Pl. LS8: Leeds 1L 5 (4G 69)
Gledhow Ri. LS8: Leeds 9K 51
Gledhow Rd. LS8: Leeds 1L 5 (4G 69)
Gledhow Ter. LS8: Leeds 1L 5 (4G 69)
Gledhow Towers LS8: Leeds 8G 51
Gledhow Valley Rd. LS7: Leeds 7F 50
LS8: Leeds 7F 50
LS17: Leeds 7E 50
Gledhow Wood Av. LS8: Leeds 8H 51
Gledhow Wood Cl. LS8: Leeds 8H 51
Gledhow Wood Ct. LS8: Leeds 1J 69
Gledhow Wood Gro. LS8: Leeds 8H 51
Gledhow Wood Rd. LS8: Leeds 8H 51
Glen, The OL14: Tod 5H 93
Glenaire BD18: Ship 6C 46
Glenaire Dr. BD17: Bail 6M 45
Glen Av. OL14: Tod 5H 93
WF17: Bat 6F 102
Glenbrook Dr. BD7: B'frd 7K 63
Glencoe HX3: She 7H 81
Glencoe Cl. LS25: Kip 5N 89
Glencoe Cft. LS25: Kip 5N 89
Glencoe Gdns. LS25: Kip 5N 89
Glencoe Ter. LS25: Kip 5N 89
WF15: Liv 9M 101
Glencoe Vw. LS9: Leeds 8H 69
Glen Ct. LS27: Morl 1L 103
WF10: C'frd 6A 108
WF16: Heck 7B 102
(off Fairmoor Way)
Glendale BD16: Bgly 4H 45
BD16: Cot 8E 44
WF4: Horb 1B 142
Glendale Av. LS25: Gar 8N 71
Glendale Cl. BD6: B'frd 6M 81
Glendale Dr. BD6: B'frd 6M 81
Glendale Gdns. LS27: Morl 1L 103
Glendare Av. BD7: B'frd 8L 63
Glendare Rd. BD7: B'frd 8L 63
Glendare Ter. BD7: B'frd 8L 63
Glen Dene BD16: Cot 8E 44
LS29: Men 4F 30
Glen Dene Cl. BD13: Que 6C 80
Glendene Ct. HD3: Outl 2N 135
Glendene M. HD3: Hud 6G 136
Glendorne Dr. HD5: K'htn 1G 139
Glendower Pk. LS16: Leeds 5N 49
Gleneagles Cl. BD4: B'frd 5F 82
Gleneagles Ct. WF6: Norm 2L 127
Gleneagles Dr. WF6: Norm 2L 127
Gleneagles Rd. LS17: Leeds 3D 50
WF7: F'stne 2D 128
Gleneagles Way HD2: Fix 8L 119
Glenfield BD18: Ship 6C 46
HX4: Gree 4A 118
Glenfield Av. BD6: B'frd 5B 82
HD2: Hud 8D 120
LS22: Weth 5N 23
Glenfield Caravan Pk. LS17: Bard 7B 36
Glenfield Mt. BD6: B'frd 5B 82
Glenfield Pl. HX6: Sow B 6J 97
Glenfields WF4: Neth 5N 141
Glenfields Cl. WF4: Neth 5N 141
Glen Garth BD21: Keigh 2K 43
Glen Gro. LS27: Morl 1L 103
Glen Hey HD3: Scam 3J 135
Glenholm BD18: Ship 6C 46
Glenholme Heath HX1: Hal 2L 97
Glenholme Pk. BD14: Clay 2H 81
Glenholme Rd. BD8: B'frd 5N 63
LS28: Fars 4N 65
Glenholme Ter. WF5: Oss 2M 123
Glenholm Rd. BD17: Bail 5A 46
Glenhurst BD4: B'frd 4H 83
Glenhurst Av. BD21: Keigh 2J 43
Glenhurst Dr. BD21: Keigh 2K 43
Glenhurst Gro. BD21: Keigh 2K 43
Glenhurst Rd. BD18: Ship 7K 45
Glen Lea HX6: Sow B 7H 97
Glenlea Cl. LS28: Stan 3D 66
Glenlea Gdns. LS28: Stan 3D 66
Glen Lee La. BD21: Keigh 3K 43
Glenlee Rd. BD7: B'frd 7L 63
Glenlow Rd. WF12: Dew 9J 103
Glenlyon Av. BD20: Keigh 7G 27
Glenlyon Dr. BD20: Keigh 7G 27
Glenmere Mt. LS19: Yead 9A 32
Glenmore Cl. BD2: B'frd 5G 64
Glenmore Ct. LS16: B'hpe 5H 33
Glen Mt. HX3: Hal 2L 97
LS27: Morl 1L 103
LS29: Men 5F 30

Glenmount—Granville St.

Glenmount BD16: Cot .8E **44**
Glen Mt. Cl. HX3: Hal .2L **97**
Glenmount Ter. LS27: Morl .2M **103**
Glenn Way WF4: Croft .2H **145**
Glen Ri. BD17: Bail .5L **45**
Glen Rd. BD16: Bgly .2H **45**
BD17: Bail .3J **45**
LS16: Leeds .8M **49**
LS27: Morl .1L **103**
Glenrose Dr. BD7: B'frd .8K **63**
Glen Royd HX4: Holy .7N **117**
Glenroyd BD18: Ship .6C **46**
HD7: Mars .5E **150**
HX6: Ripp .7D **116**
Glenroyd Av. BD6: B'frd .5B **82**
Glenroyd Cl. LS28: Pud .1M **65**
Glensdale Gro. LS9: Leeds .7H **69**
Glensdale Mt. LS9: Leeds .7H **69**
Glensdale Rd. LS9: Leeds .7H **69**
Glensdale St. LS9: Leeds .7H **69**
Glensdale Ter. LS9: Leeds .7H **69**
Glenside HD3: Outl .2N **135**
Glenside Av. BD18: Ship .6C **46**
Glenside Cl. HD3: Hud .2J **137**
Glen Side Rd. HD7: Slait .1N **151**
Glenside Rd. BD18: Ship .6C **46**
Glenstone Gro. BD7: B'frd .7L **63**
Glen Ter. HX1: Hal .8J **7** (7A **98**)
HX3: Hip .*5H* ***99***
(off Waverley Cres.)
OL14: Tod .4G **93**
Glenthorpe Av. LS9: Leeds .6J **69**
Glenthorpe Cres. LS9: Leeds .6J **69**
Glenthorpe Ter. LS9: Leeds .6J **69**
Glenton Sq. BD9: B'frd .4N **63**
Glen Vw. BD16: Har .6A **44**
HX1: Hal .7J **7** (7A **98**)
HX6: Sow B .8C **96**
HX7: Heb B .1F **94**
LS27: Morl .1L **103**
Glenview Av. BD9: B'frd .3K **63**
Glenview Cl. BD18: Ship .8H **45**
Glenview Dr. BD18: Ship .9H **45**
Glenview Gro. BD18: Ship .8J **45**
Glen Vw. Rd. BD16: Bgly .2H **45**
HD8: Shel .7L **155**
HX7: Heb B .1F **94**
Glenview Rd. BD18: Ship .9H **45**
Glen Vw. St. OL14: Tod .3E **92**
Glenview Ter. BD18: Ship .7L **45**
Glen Way BD16: Bgly .2J **45**
(Heather Vw.)
BD16: Bgly .1H **45**
(The Green)
Glenwood Av. BD17: Bail .6K **45**
Global Av. LS11: Leeds .4A **86**
Global Ct. LS11: Leeds .5A **86**
Globe Ct. WF15: Liv .8M **101**
Globe Fold BD8: B'frd .6A **64**
Globe Rd. LS11: Leeds .8B **4** (7C **68**)
Glossop Gro. *LS6: Leeds* .*2D* ***68***
(off Glossop Vw.)
Glossop Mt. LS6: Leeds .2D **68**
Glossop St. LS6: Leeds .2D **68**
Glossop Vw. LS6: Leeds .2D **68**
Gloucester Av. BD3: B'frd .5H **65**
BD20: Sils .8C **12**
Gloucester Ct. LS12: Leeds .7A **68**
WF2: Wren .9H **105**
Gloucester Gro. WF2: Wake .6F **124**
Gloucester Pl. WF2: Wake .6F **124**
Gloucester Rd. BD16: Bgly .5G **44**
WF2: Wake .6F **124**
Gloucester Ter. LS12: Leeds .6A **68**
Glover Ct. BD5: B'frd .1C **82**
Glovershaw La. BD16: Bgly .1K **45**
Glover Way LS11: Leeds .3E **86**
Glydegate BD5: B'frd .5A **6** (8C **64**)
Glyndon Ct. HD6: Ras .3N **119**
Glynn Ter. BD8: B'frd .6N **63**
G Mill Yd. HX3: Hal .2K **7**
Goals Soccer Cen.
Leeds .5M 67
Gobind Marg BD3: B'frd .4E **6** (7E **64**)
Godfrey Rd. HX3: Hal .1B **118**
Godfrey St. BD8: B'frd .7J **63**
Godley Branch Rd. HX3: Hal .4D **98**
Godley Cl. S71: Roys .5E **160**
Godley Gdns. HX3: Hal .3E **98**
Godley La. HX3: Hal .4D **98**
Godley Rd. HX3: Hal .2M **7** (4C **98**)
Godley Row HX6: Ripp .7E **116**
Godley St. S71: Roys .5E **160**
Godly Cl. HX6: Rish .1C **134**
Godly La. HX6: Rish .1C **134**
Godwin Pl. HD2: Hud .6D **120**
Godwin St. BD1: B'frd .4A **6** (7C **64**)
Goffee Way LS27: Chur .5M **85**
Goff Well La. BD21: Keigh .4J **43**
Gog Hill HX5: Ell .4E **118**
Goit Side BD1: B'frd .4A **6** (7B **64**)
(not continuous)
HX2: Lud .9E **78**
Goit Stock La. BD16: Har .7A **44**
Goit Stock Ter. BD16: Har .7A **44**
GOLCAR .6C 136
GOLCAR BROW .7B 152
Golcar Brow Rd. HD9: Mel .7B **152**
Goldcrest Av. BD8: B'frd .7G **63**
Goldcrest Ct. HD4: Neth .2K **153**
Goldcrest Rd. WF10: All B .9B **90**
Golden Bank LS18: Hors .6F **48**
Golden Butts Rd. LS29: I'ly .5H **15**
Golden Elders WF2: Kirk .9C **104**
Golden Sq. WF4: Horb .1D **142**
Golden Ter. LS12: Leeds .1K **85**
Golden Vw. Dr. BD21: Keigh .1M **43**
Goldfields Av. HX4: Gree .3A **118**
Goldfields Cl. HX4: Gree .3A **118**
Goldfields Vw. HX4: Gree .3A **118**
Goldfields Way HX4: Gree .3A **118**
Golding Hop Cl. HX2: Hal .2K **97**
Goldington Av. HD3: Hud .1E **136**
Goldington Dr. HD3: Hud .2F **136**
Goldsmith Av. WF5: Oss .5E **124**
Goldsmith Dr. WF3: Rob H .1K **105**
Goldsworthy Way S75: W Gran .6F **158**
Golf Av. HX2: Hal .5J **97**
Golf Cres. HX2: Hal .5J **97**
Golf La. LS27: Morl .3H **103**
GOMERSAL .3M 101
GOMERSAL HILL TOP .4M 101
Gomersal La. BD19: Cleck .5K **101**
Gomersall Ho. BD11: Drig .7A **84**
Gomersal Rd. WF16: Heck .6N **101**
Gondal Ct. BD5: B'frd .2A **82**
Goodcomb Pl. LS25: M'fld .2C **90**
Gooder Av. S71: Roys .6D **160**
Gooder La. HD6: Ras .2M **119**
Gooder St. HD6: Brigh .1M **119**
Goodfellow Cl. BD16: Cot .9G **44**
Good Hope Cl. WF6: Norm .9L **107**
GOODLEY .4C 42
Goodman St. LS10: Leeds .9G **68**
Goodrick La. LS17: Leeds .9D **34**
Goods La. WF12: Dew .4G **123**
Goodwin Ho. *BD13: Que* .*4D* ***80***
(off Minstrel Dr.)
Goodwin Rd. LS12: Leeds .8M **67**
Goodwood LS10: Leeds .1F **104**
LS29: Nes .3E **14**
Goodwood Av. LS25: Kip .3N **89**
GOODY CROSS .3K 89
Goody Cross La. LS26: Swil .3J **89**
Goody Cross Va. LS26: Swil .3J **89**
Goose Cote La. BD22: Oak .4E **42**
Goose Cote Way BD22: Oak .4E **42**
Goosedale Ct. BD4: B'frd .4L **83**
GOOSE EYE .1B 42
Goose Eye BD22: Oak .1B **42**
Goose Eye Brow BD22: Oak .1B **42**
Goosefield Ri. LS25: Gar .9L **71**
Goose Grn. BD22: Oxen .4C **60**
HD9: H'frth .4M **169**
GOOSE HILL .3F 82
GOOSEHILL .4F 126
Goose Hill WF16: Heck .8A **102**
Goosehill La. WF6: Norm .3F **126**
Goosehill Rd. WF6: Norm .3H **127**
Goosehole La. WF9: S Elm .8A **164**
Goose La. LS20: Hawk .6N **29**
Goose Nest La. HX6: Sow B .1H **117**
Goose Pond La. HX4: Gree .2L **117**
HX6: Norl .2L **117**
Gordale Cl. WF17: Bat .7E **102**
Gordon Av. WF5: Oss .5N **123**
Gordon Ct. WF14: Mir .5N **121**
Gordon Dr. LS6: Leeds .9A **50**
Gordon Larking Ct. LS21: Otley .1J **31**
Gordon Pl. LS6: Leeds .9B **50**
WF9: S Elm .7M **163**
(not continuous)
Gordonsfield WF7: Ackw .5F **146**
Gordon St. BD5: B'frd .7C **6** (9D **64**)
BD14: Clay .1G **81**
BD21: Keigh .9H **27**
BD22: Cros R .7E **42**
HD7: Slait .1N **151**
HX3: Hal .2A **98**
HX5: Ell .5E **118**
HX6: Sow B .9G **97**
LS29: I'ly .5H **15**
OL14: Tod .7L **93**
WF1: Wake .9A **126**
WF3: E Ard .4G **104**
WF7: F'stne .4D **128**
Gordon Ter. BD10: B'frd .6F **46**
HD7: Linth .8C **136**
LS6: Leeds .9B **50**
WF11: Knot .9G **110**
Gordon Vw. LS6: Leeds .9B **50**
Goring Pk. Av. WF5: Oss .7C **124**
Gorple Cotts. HX7: Hept .2M **75**
Gorple Ga. HX7: Wid .9F **56**
Gorple Rd. BB10: W'orne .9A **56**
Gorpley Clough Nature Reserve .9F 92
Gorpley La. OL14: Tod .8D **92**
Gorse Av. BD17: Bail .6K **45**
Gorse La. LS25: S Mil .9N **73**
Gorse Lea LS10: Leeds .5F **86**
Gorse Rd. HD3: Hud .4H **137**
Gorton St. WF9: Kins .9B **146**
Goshen Vw. *OL14: Tod* .*8K* ***93***
(off Bank St.)
Gosling La. HX4: Bark .9F **116**
Gosport Bri. Cotts. HD3: Outl .2N **135**
Gosport Cl. HD3: Outl .2N **135**
Gosport La. HD3: Outl .2N **135**
HX4: Sow .2N **135**
Gosside Gro. WF6: Norm .2L **127**
Gothic Mt. WF7: A'ton .3A **128**
Gothic St. BD13: Que .4D **80**
Gotts Pk. Av. LS12: Leeds .5J **67**
Gotts Pk. Cres. LS12: Leeds .5J **67**
Gotts Pk. Golf Course .5K 67
Gotts Pk. Vw. LS12: Leeds .4J **67**
Gotts Rd. LS12: Leeds .7A **4** (7B **68**)
Gotts Ter. BD20: Keigh .6G **27**
Gott St. BD22: Cros R .7F **42**
Gough La. HX6: Ripp .5B **116**
Goulbourne St. BD21: Keigh .1H **43**
Governor's Yd. WF1: Wake .2M **9** (4M **125**)
Gower St. BD5: B'frd .8B **6** (1C **82**)
LS2: Leeds .5H **5** (6F **68**)
Gracechurch St. BD8: B'frd .6B **64**
Grace Leather La. WF17: Bat .7H **103**
Grace St. BD21: Keigh .9K **27**
LS1: Leeds .6C **4** (6C **68**)
Gracey La. BD6: B'frd .4L **81**
Grady Cl. BD10: B'frd .9F **46**
Grafton Cl. BD17: Bail .3B **46**
WF11: Knot .7E **110**
Grafton Pl. HX3: Hal .1N **97**
Grafton Rd. BD21: Keigh .2G **42**
Grafton St. BD5: B'frd .7A **6** (9C **64**)
BD21: Keigh .2H **43**
LS7: Leeds .4G **5** (5E **68**)
WF10: C'frd .7E **108**
WF17: Bat .9G **102**
Grafton Vs. LS15: Leeds .2E **70**
Graham Av. LS4: Leeds .3N **67**
WF9: Upt .1C **164**
Graham Dr. WF10: C'frd .5H **109**
Graham Gro. LS4: Leeds .3N **67**
Graham Ho. *LS5: Leeds* .*3J* ***67***
(off Broad La.)
Graham La. HD4: Hud .7G **136**
Graham Mt. LS4: Leeds .3N **67**
Graham St. BD9: B'frd .4M **63**
LS4: Leeds .3N **67**
Graham Ter. LS4: Leeds .3N **67**
Graham Vw. LS4: Leeds .3N **67**
Graham Wlk. LS27: Gil .6G **84**
Graingers Way LS12: Leeds .8A **4** (7B **68**)
Grain St. BD5: B'frd .3N **81**
Gramfield Rd. HD4: Hud .7G **137**
Grammar School Pl. *HD6: Ras* .*3L* ***119***
(off Thornhill Rd.)
Grammar School St. BD1: B'frd .2A **6** (6C **64**)
Grammar Sq. WF1: Wake .3K **9** (4L **125**)
Grampian Av. WF2: Wake .8G **124**
Grampian Cl. HD8: Shel .6K **155**
Granary Ct. BD2: B'frd .1G **65**
Granary Wharf LS1: Leeds .8E **4** (7D **68**)
Granby Av. LS6: Leeds .1N **67**
Granby Cl. LS6: Leeds .2N **67**
Granby Ct. WF9: S Elm .4N **163**
Granby Dr. BD20: Rid .7M **27**
Granby Flats HD1: Hud .5K **137**
Granby Gro. LS6: Leeds .2N **67**
Granby La. BD20: Rid .7M **27**
Granby Mt. LS6: Leeds .1N **67**
Granby Pl. LS6: Leeds .1N **67**
Granby Rd. LS6: Leeds .2N **67**
Granby St. BD4: B'frd .7C **6** (9D **64**)
(not continuous)
BD13: Que .4D **80**
LS6: Leeds .1N **67**
Granby Ter. LS6: Leeds .1N **67**
Granby Vw. LS6: Leeds .1N **67**
Grandage Ter. BD8: B'frd .6N **63**
Grand Arc. LS1: Leeds .5G **5**
Grand Cross Rd. HD5: Hud .4C **138**
Grandsmere Pl. HX3: Hal .8J **7** (8A **98**)
Grand Stand HD7: Golc .5A **136**
Grandstand Rd. WF2: Carr G .7G **105**
WF3: Loft .7G **105**
Grand Theatre & Opera House .5G 5 (6E 68)
Grand Vw. BD13: Que .2B **80**
HX3: Hal .*3N* ***97***
(off Ovenden Av.)
HX6: Mill B .*4D* ***116***
(off Lumb La.)
HX6: Sow B .*9H* ***97***
(off Lwr. Clyde St.)
Grange, The DN6: Skel .7M **165**
HD5: Hud .3D **138**
HX3: Hal .9A **98**
LS6: Leeds .1A **68**
LS11: Leeds .3C **86**
LS12: Leeds .5J **67**
LS13: Leeds .5F **66**
LS25: Gar .7B **72**
S75: W Gran .6F **158**
WF3: Carl .1M **105**
Grange Av. BD3: B'frd .6K **65**
BD4: E Bier .5L **83**
BD15: All .6H **63**
BD18: Ship .7K **45**
HD2: Hud .1L **137**
HD7: Mars .5G **150**
HX2: Hal .8M **79**
LS7: Leeds .2G **68**
LS19: Yead .1N **47**
LS23: T Arch .6G **24**
LS25: Gar .7N **71**
LS29: I'ly .5J **15**
LS29: Men .3D **30**
WF9: S Elm .6N **163**
WF17: Bat .9E **102**
Grange Bank HX3: She .7H **81**
Grange Bank Cl. HD5: Hud .3B **138**
Grange Bldgs. *LS27: Morl* .*2M* ***103***
(off Hodgson St.)
Grange Cl. HD3: Outl .2N **135**
LS10: Leeds .1F **86**
LS17: Bard .4E **36**
LS18: Hors .7C **48**
LS29: I'ly .5J **15**
S72: B'ley .6N **161**
WF9: Bads .8L **147**
WF11: Knot .8C **110**
Grange Cotts. BD13: Cull .9L **43**
BD19: Cleck .*4G* ***101***
(off Whitcliffe Rd.)
HD7: Mars .4G **150**
Grange Ct. BD16: Cot .8F **44**
HX3: Sou .9F **98**
LS6: Leeds .1B **68**
LS15: Scho .9G **53**
LS17: Leeds .2E **50**
LS26: W'frd .6D **88**
S72: B'ley .*6N* ***161***
(off Grange Cl.)
WF9: Bads .8L **147**
Grange Cres. BD20: Rid .7L **27**
LS7: Leeds .2G **68**
LS19: Yead .1N **47**
Grange Cft. LS17: Leeds .2E **50**
Grange Dr. BD15: All .6H **63**
HD8: Eml .1G **156**
LS18: Hors .7C **48**
WF5: Oss .8B **124**
Grange Est. LS29: I'ly .5J **15**
Grange Farm Cl. LS29: Men .3D **30**
Grangefield Av. LS29: Burl W .8D **16**
WF17: Bat .9E **102**
Grangefield Ct. LS25: Gar .7N **71**
Grangefield Ind. Est. LS28: Stan .5B **66**
Grangefield Rd. LS28: Stan .4B **66**
(not continuous)
Grange Flds. Mt. LS10: Leeds .6H **87**
Grange Flds. Rd. LS10: Leeds .7H **87**
Grange Flds. Way LS10: Leeds .7H **87**
Grange Fold BD15: All .6G **63**
Grange Gro. BD3: B'frd .6K **65**
BD20: Rid .7L **27**
Grange Hgts. HX3: Sou .9F **98**
Grange Holt LS17: Leeds .2E **50**
Grange La. BD20: Kild .8A **12**
BD22: Oak .4M **41**
DN6: Burg .6L **165**
HD6: Clift .1C **120**
HD8: Kbtn .6H **155**
LS25: Kip .3B **90**
WF4: Flock .6G **140**
GRANGE MOOR .5B 140
Grange Mt. LS19: Yead .1N **47**
Grange Pk. BD17: Bail .4C **46**
HX3: Hal .9A **98**
Grange Pk. Av. LS8: Leeds .1M **69**
Grange Pk. Cl. LS8: Leeds .1N **69**
LS27: Morl .6L **85**
WF10: All B .8A **90**
Grange Pk. Ct. *LS27: Morl* .*6L* ***85***
(off Grange Pk. Dr.)
Grange Pk. Cres. LS8: Leeds .1M **69**
Grange Pk. Dr. BD16: Cot .7F **44**
LS27: Morl .6L **85**
Grange Pk. Gro. LS8: Leeds .1M **69**
Grange Pk. M. LS8: Leeds .1M **69**
LS27: Morl .6L **85**
Grange Pk. Pl. LS8: Leeds .1M **69**
Grange Pk. Ri. LS8: Leeds .1M **69**
Grange Pk. Rd. BD16: Cot .7F **44**
LS8: Leeds .1M **69**
Grange Pk. Ter. LS8: Leeds .1N **69**
Grange Pk. Wlk. LS8: Leeds .1M **69**
Grange Pk. Way LS27: Morl .6L **85**
Grange Ri. WF9: Hems .2D **162**
Grange Rd. BD15: All .6H **63**
BD16: Bgly .3G **44**
BD19: Cleck .4G **101**
BD20: East .3A **26**
BD20: Rid .7L **27**
HD7: Golc .4D **136**
LS10: Leeds .1F **86**
LS19: Yead .1N **47**
LS29: Burl W .8D **16**
OL12: Whit .8A **112**
S71: Roys .6B **160**
S72: B'ley .6N **161**
WF10: C'frd .3L **109**
WF12: Dew .9K **103**
WF17: Bat .9D **102**
(Chapel Fold)
WF17: Bat .8H **103**
(Technology Dr., not continuous)
Grange Road, The LS16: Leeds .6L **49**
Grange Rd. Bus. Pk. WF17: Bat .8H **103**
Grange Rd. Ind. Est. WF17: Bat .8H **103**
Grange St. BD21: Keigh .8J **27**
HX3: Hal .3N **97**
LS27: Chur .5M **85**
WF2: Wake .6J **125**
Grange Ter. BD15: All .6H **63**
BD18: Ship .9N **45**
BD20: East .3A **26**
HD7: Mars .4G **150**
LS7: Leeds .2F **68**
LS19: Yead .*1N* ***47***
(off Grange Rd.)
LS27: Morl .6L **85**
LS28: Pud .6B **66**
Grange Valley Rd. WF17: Bat .8J **103**
Grange Vw. BD3: B'frd .6K **65**
BD20: East .3A **26**
LS7: Leeds .2G **68**
LS15: Leeds .8E **70**
LS21: Otley .8K **17**
LS22: Weth .5M **23**
LS28: Pud .6B **66**
WF9: Hems .3D **162**
WF12: T'hill .1G **140**
Grange Vw. Gdns. LS17: Leeds .6A **52**
Grangeway BD15: All .6H **63**
WF9: Hems .2D **162**
Grangewood Ct. LS16: Leeds .6L **49**
WF1: Out .7M **105**
Grangewood Gdns. LS16: Leeds .6L **49**
Granham Acre S72: Shaf .7K **161**
Granhamthorpe LS13: Leeds .4F **66**
Granny Av. LS27: Chur .5M **85**
Granny Hall Gro. HD6: Brigh .8L **99**
Granny Hall La. HD6: Brigh .8L **99**
Granny Hall Pk. HD6: Brigh .8L **99**
Granny Hill Ter. HX1: Hal .7M **97**
Granny La. LS12: Leeds .9K **67**
WF14: Mir .8L **121**
Granny Pl. LS27: Chur .5M **85**
Grant Av. LS7: Leeds .1K **5** (4G **68**)
Grantham Pl. BD7: B'frd .9A **64**
HX3: Hal .2A **98**
Grantham Rd. BD7: B'frd .9A **64**
HX3: Hal .2A **98**
Grantham Ter. BD7: B'frd .9A **64**
Grantham Towers LS9: Leeds .3L **5**
Grantley Pl. HD2: Hud .6B **120**
Grantley St. WF1: Wake .3L **9** (4M **125**)
Grantley Way WF1: Wake .3M **9** (4M **125**)
Granton Rd. LS7: Leeds .1F **68**
Granton St. BD3: B'frd .7G **65**
Grant St. BD3: B'frd .3F **6** (7E **64**)
BD21: Keigh .9G **26**
BD22: Oxen .4C **60**
Granville Av. WF8: Pon .3J **129**
Granville Ct. *LS21: Otley* .*1K* ***31***
(off Granville Mt.)
Granville Mt. LS21: Otley .1K **31**
Granville Pl. BD15: All .5G **63**
LS21: Otley .1K **31**
Granville Rd. BD9: B'frd .1N **63**
BD18: Ship .1N **63**
LS9: Leeds .3L **5** (5G **69**)
Granville St. BD14: Clay .9H **63**
BD21: Keigh .*9H* ***27***
(off Enfield St.)
HX5: Ell .5E **118**
LS28: Pud .6N **65**
LS28: Stan .4C **66**

Granville St.—Greenlea Av.

Granville St. OL14: W'den . . . 2J **113**
WF6: Norm . . . 1J **127**
WF7: F'stne . . . 7C **128**
WF10: C'frd . . . 7C **108**
WF13: Dew . . . 3F **122**
WF15: Liv . . . 9M **101**
Granville Ter. BD16: Bgly . . . 4F **44**
BD18: Ship . . . 1N **63**
HD1: Hud . . . 5K **137**
LS19: Yead . . . 9N **31**
LS20: Guis . . . 6K **31**
LS21: Otley . . . 1K **31**
Grape St. BD15: All . . . 5H **63**
BD21: Keigh . . . 8L **27**
HX1: Hal . . . 3H **7** (5A **98**)
LS10: Leeds . . . 9F **68**
Grasleigh Av. BD15: All . . . 4F **62**
Grasleigh Way BD15: All . . . 4E **62**
Grasmere Av. LS22: Weth . . . 4K **23**
Grasmere Cl. LS12: Leeds . . . 8N **67**
WF10: C'frd . . . 3L **109**
Grasmere Ct. LS12: Leeds . . . 7N **67**
Grasmere Cres. S75: S'ross . . . 7J **159**
Grasmere Dr. HX5: Ell . . . 4G **119**
LS22: Weth . . . 4K **23**
Grasmere Pl. HX3: Hal . . . 9N **79**
Grasmere Rd. BD2: B'frd . . . 3E **64**
BD12: Wyke . . . 3C **100**
DN6: Carc . . . 8N **165**
HD1: Hud . . . 3K **137**
HD9: Mel . . . 8D **152**
LS12: Leeds . . . 8N **67**
WF2: Wake . . . 4G **124**
WF11: Knot . . . 1D **130**
WF12: Dew . . . 1H **123**
Grasscroft HD5: Hud . . . 8D **138**
Grasscroft Av. HD9: Hon . . . 5K **153**
Grasscroft Rd. HD1: Hud . . . 3K **137**
HD9: Hon . . . 5K **153**
Grassmoor Fold HD9: Hon . . . 6M **153**
Grass Rd. BD20: E Mor, W Mor . . . 5B **28**
Grassy Bottoms HX6: Tri . . . 2E **116**
Gratrix La. HX6: Sow B . . . 7J **97**
Grattan Rd. BD1: B'frd . . . 4A **6** (7B **64**)
GRAVELEYTHORPE . . . 6B **70**
Graveleythorpe Ri. LS15: Leeds . . . 5C **70**
Graveleythorpe Rd. LS15: Leeds . . . 5C **70**
Gravelly Hill La. LS17: Wee . . . 6K **19**
Gray Av. BD18: Ship . . . 1B **64**
Gray Ct. LS15: Leeds . . . 6E **70**
Gray Hall Cl. HX4: Stainl . . . 8M **117**
Grayrigg Cl. LS15: Leeds . . . 7N **69**
Grayshon Dr. BD6: B'frd . . . 4A **82**
Grayshon St. BD11: Drig . . . 8C **84**
Grayson Crest LS4: Leeds . . . 3L **67**
Grayson Hgts. LS4: Leeds . . . 3L **67**
Gray's Rd. S71: Carl . . . 8D **160**
Gray St. WF15: Liv . . . 8J **101**
Grayswood Cres. BD4: B'frd . . . 2H **83**
Grayswood Dr. BD4: B'frd . . . 1H **83**
Gt. Albion St. HX1: Hal . . . 3K **7** (5B **98**)
Great Ben La. HD7: Slait . . . 6L **135**
GREAT CLIFF . . . 6F **142**
Gt. Cross St. BD1: B'frd . . . 5C **6** (8D **64**)
Gt. Edge Rd. HX2: Hal . . . 5F **96**
Greater Elland Historical Society . . . 4E 118
(off Northgate)
Greatfield Cl. WF5: Oss . . . 5A **124**
Greatfield Ct. WF5: Oss . . . 6A **124**
Greatfield Dr. WF5: Oss . . . 5A **124**
Greatfield Gdns. WF5: Oss . . . 6A **124**
Greatfield Rd. WF5: Oss . . . 6A **124**
Gt. George St. LS1: Leeds . . . 5D **4** (6D **68**)
LS2: Leeds . . . 5D **4** (6D **68**)
GREAT HORTON . . . 1M **81**
Gt. Horton Rd. BD7: B'frd . . . 5A **6** (3J **81**)
Great Ho. La. HX6: Ripp . . . 8A **116**
Great Ho. Rd. OL14: Tod . . . 4N **93**
Gt. Northern Retail Pk. HD1: Hud . . . 2C **8** (3N **137**)
Gt. Northern Rd. BD21: Keigh . . . 1J **43**
Gt. Northern St. HD1: Hud . . . 2C **8** (3N **137**)
LS27: Morl . . . 1K **103**
Great Nth. Rd.
DN6: Hamp, S'brk, Skel, Wood, Ad St . . . 3J **165**
LS25: Aber . . . 2E **72**
LS25: S Mil . . . 1J **91**
WF8: D'ton, Pon, Went . . . 1C **148**
WF11: B'ton, Fair . . . 9N **91**
WF11: D'ton, Knot . . . 9B **110**
Great Nth. Rd. Nth. LS25: Aber . . . 5E **54**
Great Pasture LS29: Burl W . . . 7D **16**
Gt. Pasture La. LS29: Burl W . . . 7D **16**
Gt. Pond St. WF13: Raven . . . 6C **122**
GREAT PRESTON . . . 5M **89**
Gt. Russell Ct. BD7: B'frd . . . 7A **64**
Gt. Russell St. BD7: B'frd . . . 7A **64**
Great Scout HX2: Lud F . . . 4A **96**
Gt. Wilson St. LS11: Leeds . . . 8E **4** (8D **68**)
Gt. Wood Gdns. HD8: Lept . . . 8J **139**
Gt. Wood St. WF17: Bat . . . 8F **102**
Greave Cl. HD2: Hud . . . 7N **119**
Greavefield La. WF8: Pon . . . 3N **129**
Greave Ho. Dr. HX2: Lud F . . . 5D **96**
Greave Ho. Flds. HX2: Lud F . . . 4E **96**
Greave Ho. La. HD8: Lept . . . 7H **139**
Greave Ho. Pk. HX2: Lud F . . . 5D **96**
Greave Ho. Ter. HD8: Lept . . . 7H **139**
Greave Rd.
HD9: Had E, H'frth . . . 8M **169**
HX6: Ripp . . . 5M **115**
Greaves Av. WF2: Wake . . . 6E **124**
Greaves Cft. HD8: Lept . . . 7H **139**
Greaves Fold HX4: Holy . . . 7B **118**
Greaves Pl. HX4: Holy . . . 7B **118**
Greaves Rd. WF13: Dew . . . 2F **122**
Greaves St. BD5: B'frd . . . 2B **82**
WF10: C'frd . . . 4D **108**
Greave St. OL14: Tod . . . 7M **93**
Greaves Yd. LS28: Pud . . . 9B **66**
Grebe Cl. BD6: B'frd . . . 4H **81**
Greek St. LS1: Leeds . . . 6E **4** (6D **68**)
WF10: C'frd . . . 4E **108**
GREEN, THE
LS14 . . . 2C **70**
LS28 . . . 2A **66**
Green, The BD4: E Bier . . . 6K **83**
BD7: B'frd . . . 8B **64**
BD10: B'frd . . . 7F **46**
BD16: Bgly . . . 1F **44**
(College Rd.)
BD16: Bgly . . . 1H **45**
(Stead La.)
BD16: Bgly . . . 4J **45**
(The Gardens)
BD16: Bgly . . . 9D **28**
(Victoria St.)
HD2: Hud . . . 6B **120**
HD4: Thurs . . . 7D **154**
HD7: Mars . . . 5F **150**
LS14: Leeds . . . 1B **70**
(not continuous)
LS17: Leeds . . . 5G **50**
LS18: Hors . . . 7E **48**
LS19: Yead . . . 9M 31
(off Town St.)
LS20: Guis . . . 8J **31**
LS21: Leat . . . 6D **18**
LS21: Otley . . . 8K **17**
LS23: T Arch . . . 9E **24**
LS25: Gar . . . 8A **72**
LS25: Kip . . . 4A **90**
LS27: Gil . . . 6G **84**
LS28: Fars . . . 2A **66**
LS29: Add . . . 9L **11**
S71: Roys . . . 6D **160**
(not continuous)
S72: Shaf . . . 6J **161**
WF2: Wren . . . 9H **105**
WF4: S Comn . . . 9K **127**
WF4: Wool . . . 2J **159**
WF5: Oss . . . 7N **123**
WF6: Norm . . . 2H **127**
WF7: F'stne . . . 7E **128**
WF9: S Kirk . . . 6J **163**
WF10: C'frd . . . 4K **109**
(not continuous)
WF14: Mir . . . 5J **121**
WF17: Birs . . . 2C **102**
Green Abbey HD9: Had E . . . 9N **169**
Greenacre Av. BD12: Wyke . . . 2B **100**
Green Acre Cl. BD17: Bail . . . 4B **46**
Greenacre Cl. BD12: Wyke . . . 2B **100**
Greenacre Ct. LS25: Gar . . . 7A **72**
Greenacre Dr. BD12: Wyke . . . 2B **100**
HD8: Up D . . . 5B **172**
Greenacre Ga. HD8: Lept . . . 7L **139**
Greenacre Pk. LS19: Raw . . . 2M **47**
Greenacre Pk. Av. LS19: Raw . . . 2M **47**
Greenacre Pk. M. LS19: Raw . . . 2N **47**
Greenacre Pk. Ri. LS19: Raw . . . 2M **47**
Greenacre Rd. WF9: Upt . . . 1B **164**
Green Acres BD21: Keigh . . . 2L **43**
LS29: Burl W . . . 9B **16**
S72: Grim . . . 9A **162**
WF4: Dur . . . 3J **143**
WF7: F'stne . . . 8E **128**
Greenacres HX3: She . . . 7J **81**
HX6: Ripp . . . 7E **116**
WF5: Oss . . . 2N **123**
Greenacres Av. HX3: She . . . 7J **81**
Green Acres Cl. HD8: Eml . . . 3F **156**
Greenacres Cl. WF5: Oss . . . 2N **123**
Greenacres Ct. WF10: C'frd . . . 4G **109**
Greenacres Dr. BD20: Keigh . . . 7G **26**
HX3: She . . . 7J **81**
WF10: C'frd . . . 4G **108**
WF17: Birs . . . 2C **102**
Greenacres Gro. HX3: She . . . 7J **81**
Greenacre Wlk. WF4: H'cft . . . 8L **145**
Greenacre Way BD12: Wyke . . . 2B **100**
Greenaire Pl. BD1: B'frd . . . 7B **64**
Green Av. BD20: Sils . . . 7D **12**
LS25: Kip . . . 2N **89**
WF16: Heck . . . 8B **102**
Green Balk La. HD8: Lept . . . 7K **139**
Green Bank BD19: Cleck . . . 6K **101**
HX7: Crag V . . . 2K **115**
WF3: Loft . . . 3M **105**
Greenbank BD17: Bail . . . 6N **45**
S71: Ath . . . 8A **160**
Greenbank Cl. WF10: C'frd . . . 7A **108**
Greenbank Gro. WF6: Alt . . . 9G **106**
Greenbank Rd. BD15: All . . . 6H **63**
WF6: Alt . . . 9G **106**
Greenbanks Av. LS18: Hors . . . 5F **48**
Greenbanks Cl. LS18: Hors . . . 5F **48**
Greenbanks Dr. LS18: Hors . . . 5E **48**
GREENBOTTOM . . . 8J **31**
Green Bottom HD9: Mel . . . 9D **152**
Green Bower HD7: Mars . . . 5G **150**
Green Chase LS6: Leeds . . . 8A **50**
Green Cliff HD9: Hon . . . 4L **153**
Greencliffe Av. BD17: Bail . . . 4A **46**
Green Cl. BD8: B'frd . . . 6K **63**
BD20: East . . . 2A **26**
LS6: Leeds . . . 8B **50**
WF13: Dew . . . 1D **122**
WF17: Bat . . . 7H **103**
Green Ct. BD7: B'frd . . . 9L **63**
BD19: Scho . . . 4D **100**
LS15: Scho . . . 8G **52**
LS17: Leeds . . . 5F **50**
Green Cres. HD7: Golc . . . 5D **136**
LS6: Leeds . . . 8A **50**
Greencroft WF9: Kins . . . 8B **146**
Greencroft Av. HX3: North . . . 1G **98**
Greencroft Cl. BD10: B'frd . . . 8E **46**
Greencroft M. LS20: Guis . . . 7J **31**
Greendale Ct. HD9: Hon . . . 4L **153**
Greendown Cl. LS29: I'ly . . . 5J **15**
Green Dragon Yd. LS1: Leeds . . . 6E **4**
Green Edge HD7: Golc . . . 4B **136**
GREEN END . . . 7D **28**
Green End BD14: Clay . . . 1G **81**
HD6: Ras . . . 2M **119**
HX7: Chis . . . 8K **77**
Green End La. WF2: Wake . . . 8K **125**
Green End Rd. BD6: B'frd . . . 5N **81**
BD20: E Mor . . . 7D **28**
Greenfell Cl. BD22: Keigh . . . 1F **42**
Greenfield BD22: Haw . . . 8C **42**
Greenfield Av. BD18: Ship . . . 9A **46**
HD3: Hud . . . 2F **136**
HX3: Hip . . . 5M **99**
LS20: Guis . . . 9F **30**
LS25: Kip . . . 3A **90**
LS27: Gil . . . 6E **84**
WF5: Oss . . . 7C **124**
Greenfield Cl. HD8: Up D . . . 5C **172**
HX3: North . . . 1F **98**
HX4: Sow . . . 9M **117**
LS25: Kip . . . 3A **90**
LS29: Burl W . . . 1D **30**
WF2: Wren . . . 1H **125**
WF5: Oss . . . 7C **124**
Greenfield Cotts. S71: Carl . . . 9D **160**
Greenfield Ct. BD7: B'frd . . . 1L **81**
BD22: Keigh . . . 9G **27**
LS16: Leeds . . . 3L **49**
Greenfield Cres. BD13: Cull . . . 9L **43**
WF4: G Moor . . . 6B **140**
Greenfield Dr. BD19: Scho . . . 4D **100**
LS27: Gil . . . 6E **84**
Greenfield Gdns. S71: Ath . . . 8N **159**
Greenfield Gth. LS25: Kip . . . 3A **90**
Greenfield La. BD4: B'frd . . . 7F **82**
BD7: B'frd . . . 1L **81**
BD10: B'frd . . . 6E **46**
LS20: Guis . . . 9E **30**
Greenfield Mt. WF2: Wren . . . 1H **125**
Greenfield Pl. BD8: B'frd . . . 5A **64**
HX3: Hip . . . 5M **99**
Greenfield Ri. LS25: Kip . . . 3A **90**
Greenfield Rd. HD9: H'frth . . . 3G **168**
LS9: Leeds . . . 7L **5** (7G **69**)
WF5: Oss . . . 7C **124**
WF6: Alt . . . 1G **127**
WF9: Hems . . . 4D **162**
Greenfields HX6: Sow B . . . 9E **96**
WF16: Heck . . . 7N **101**
Greenfields Way LS29: Burl W . . . 1D **30**
Greenfield Ter. BD22: Haw . . . 8C **42**
LS26: Meth . . . 1M **107**
OL14: Tod . . . 3C **92**
Greenfield Va. LS25: Kip . . . 3A **90**
Greenfield Vw. LS25: Kip . . . 3A **90**
WF17: Bat . . . 6C **102**
Greenfield Way WF2: Wren . . . 1H **125**
Greenfinch Gro. HD4: Neth . . . 3K **153**
Greenfinch Way BD15: All . . . 7G **62**
Green Fold *BD2: B'frd . . . 4F 64*
(off Idle Rd.)
BD17: Bail . . . 5N **45**
Greenfold La. LS22: Weth . . . 4N **23**
Green Gdns. HD7: Golc . . . 5D **136**
Greengate BD20: Sils . . . 7D **12**
LS26: Oul . . . 7D **88**
Greengate Head HX4: Sow . . . 2M **135**
Green Gate La. HD7: Slait . . . 4N **151**
Green Gate Rd. HD9: H'frth . . . 4F **168**
Greengate Rd. BD21: Keigh . . . 1J **43**
WF8: K S'ton . . . 8L **149**
GREENGATES . . . 8J **47**
Greengates Av. BD12: Wyke . . . 3A **100**
Green Gro. HD8: Kbtn . . . 1J **155**
Green Hall Pk. HX3: She . . . 8J **81**
Green Head HD7: Linth . . . 2A **152**
Green Head Av. BD20: Keigh . . . 6G **26**
Greenhead Av. HD5: Hud . . . 5D **138**
Greenhead Ct. HD1: Hud . . . 3K **137**
Green Head Dr. BD20: Keigh . . . 6G **26**
Green Head La. BD20: Keigh . . . 6G **26**
Greenhead La. HD5: Hud . . . 5D **138**
HD6: Ras . . . 5K **119**
Green Head Rd. BD20: Keigh . . . 6G **27**
Greenhead Rd. HD1: Hud . . . 5A **8** (4K **137**)
LS16: Leeds . . . 7L **49**
GREEN HILL
LS25 . . . 7E **54**
WF9 . . . 2D **162**
Green Hill HD2: Hud . . . 7N **119**
HX2: Hal . . . 6H **97**
Greenhill Av. WF8: Pon . . . 5L **129**
Greenhill Bank Rd. HD9: New M . . . 3B **170**
Green Hill Chase LS12: Leeds . . . 8L **67**
Green Hill Cl. LS12: Leeds . . . 5J **67**
Greenhill Ct. WF17: Bat . . . 9H **103**
Green Hill Cres. LS12: Leeds . . . 8L **67**
Green Hill Cft. LS12: Leeds . . . 8L **67**
Green Hill Dr. LS13: Leeds . . . 5H **67**
Greenhill Dr. BD16: Bgly . . . 9D **28**
Green Hill Gdns. LS12: Leeds . . . 8L **67**
Green Hill Holt LS12: Leeds . . . 8L **67**
Greenhill Ind. Est. HX7: Myth . . . 4N **95**
Green Hill La. LS12: Leeds . . . 9K **67**
Greenhill La. BD3: B'frd . . . 7G **65**
BD16: Bgly . . . 1E **44**
HD9: New M . . . 2C **170**
Green Hill Mt. LS13: Leeds . . . 5H **67**
Greenhill Mt. WF8: Pon . . . 5L **129**
Green Hill Pk. HX3: She . . . 5J **81**
Green Hill Pl. LS13: Leeds . . . 5H **67**
Green Hill Rd. LS12: Leeds . . . 5J **67**
LS13: Leeds . . . 5H **67**
Greenhill Rd. HD3: Hud . . . 3D **136**
WF1: Wake . . . 3M **9** (4M **125**)
Greenhills LS19: Raw . . . 4N **47**
Greenhill St. BD3: B'frd . . . 7G **65**
Green Hill Way LS13: Leeds . . . 5H **67**
Greenholme Cl. LS29: Burl W . . . 7D **16**
Green Holme Cotts. LS29: Burl W . . . 6D **16**
Greenholme Ct. BD4: B'frd . . . 3K **83**
HX4: Gree . . . 4B **118**
Greenholme Mills LS29: Burl W . . . 7D **16**
Greenholme Trad. Est. LS29: Burl W . . . 7D **16**
Greenhouse *LS11: Leeds . . . 1D 86*
(off Beeston Rd.)
Greenhouse, The LS11: Leeds . . . 1D **86**
Green Ho. Hill HD8: Shel . . . 5N **155**
Green Ho. La. HD8: Shel . . . 5N **155**
HD9: Holm . . . 8G **169**
Greenhouse Rd. HD2: Hud . . . 1M **137**
Green Houses HX2: Midg . . . 1D **96**
Greenhow Cl. LS4: Leeds . . . 4N **67**
Greenhow Gdns. LS4: Leeds . . . 4N **67**
Greenhow Pk. LS29: Burl W . . . 8B **16**
Greenhow Rd. LS4: Leeds . . . 4N **67**
Greenhow Wlk. LS4: Leeds . . . 4N **67**
Greenland S75: H Hoy . . . 9L **157**
Greenland Av. BD13: Que . . . 5D **80**
Greenland Ct. LS26: Oul . . . 8D **88**
Greenland Rd. HX7: Cold . . . 7K **75**
Greenland Vs. BD13: Que . . . 5D **80**
Green La. BD2: B'frd . . . 3H **65**
BD7: B'frd . . . 9M **63**
BD8: B'frd . . . 5A **64**
BD10: B'frd . . . 7G **47**
(Apperley Rd.)
BD10: B'frd . . . 8E **46**
(Sandhill Fold)
BD12: O'haw . . . 9D **82**
BD12: Wyke . . . 2N **99**
BD13: Que . . . 7D **80**
(Corporal La.)
BD13: Que . . . 3A **80**
(White Castle Ct.)
BD13: Thorn . . . 8D **62**
BD17: Bail . . . 6M **45**
(Milner Rd., not continuous)
BD17: Bail . . . 3M **45**
(Somerset Av.)
BD19: Hun . . . 2H **101**
BD20: East . . . 2A **26**
BD20: Sils . . . 3A **12**
BD22: Oak . . . 3N **41**
(Gill La.)
BD22: Oak . . . 5D **42**
(Keighley Rd.)
BD22: Oxen . . . 4M **59**
(Bodkin La.)
BD22: Oxen . . . 6D **60**
(Isle La.)
BD23: Hal E . . . 1E **10**
DN6: Skel . . . 6K **165**
HD6: Brigh . . . 7K **99**
HD6: Clift . . . 9D **100**
HD7: Slait . . . 1K **151**
(Haw Cote)
HD7: Slait . . . 1H **151**
(Marsden La.)
HD8: H Flat . . . 6M **171**
HD9: H'frth . . . 6M **169**
(Lamma Well Rd.)
HD9: H'frth . . . 2M **169**
(Wood La.)
HD9: Mel . . . 8D **152**
HX2: Hal . . . 7L **97**
HX2: Illing . . . 5L **79**
HX2: Lud . . . 3D **96**
HX3: North . . . 8D **80**
HX3: She . . . 6J **81**
(Cloverdale)
HX3: She . . . 7J **81**
(Willow Pk. Dr.)
HX3: Sou . . . 6D **98**
HX4: Bark . . . 2F **134**
HX4: Gree . . . 5B **118**
HX4: Sow . . . 1M **135**
HX6: Ripp . . . 8B **116**
HX6: Sow B . . . 2C **116**
HX7: Hept . . . 8F **76**
LS11: Leeds . . . 4B **86**
LS12: Leeds . . . 8A **68**
LS12: N Far . . . 9F **66**
LS14: Leeds . . . 7B **52**
LS15: Leeds . . . 5C **70**
LS16: Leeds . . . 3G **48**
LS17: Wee . . . 5D **20**
LS18: Hors . . . 8E **48**
LS19: Yead . . . 2M **47**
LS21: Otley . . . 8K **17**
LS22: Coll . . . 9H **23**
LS23: B Spa . . . 1E **38**
LS25: Gar . . . 7A **72**
(Greenacre Ct.)
LS25: Gar . . . 8B **72**
(Ribblesdale Av.)
LS25: Kip . . . 2N **89**
LS26: Meth . . . 3N **107**
LS28: Pud . . . 8A **66**
LS29: Add . . . 9L **11**
LS29: Burl W . . . 6C **16**
(Leather Bank)
LS29: Burl W . . . 2N **29**
(Moor Rd.)
S75: Silk . . . 9M **173**
WF1: K'thpe . . . 5D **126**
WF2: Wake . . . 4G **124**
WF3: Loft . . . 3L **105**
WF4: Horb . . . 2E **142**
WF4: Neth . . . 5N **141**
WF4: Not . . . 3B **160**
WF4: Over . . . 4J **141**
WF7: Ackw . . . 4D **146**
WF7: F'stne . . . 5A **128**
(not continuous)
WF8: Pon . . . 6L **129**
(Furlong La.)
WF8: Pon . . . 4K **129**
(Mayor's Wlk.)
WF8: Thpe A . . . 5B **148**
WF9: S Kirk . . . 7H **163**
WF9: Upt . . . 9B **148**
WF10: C'frd . . . 3F **108**
(Smith St.)
WF10: C'frd . . . 7C **108**
(Westfields)
WF10: Leds . . . 7D **90**
WF11: Birk . . . 4L **111**
WF13: Dew . . . 2D **122**
WF15: Liv . . . 9H **101**
Green La. Cl. WF4: Over . . . 3K **141**
Green La. Ind. Pk. WF7: F'stne . . . 6A **128**
(not continuous)
Green La. Ter. HD7: Golc . . . 4B **136**
Green La. Vs. LS25: Gar . . . 7A **72**
Greenlaws Cl. HD9: U'thng . . . 3J **169**
Greenlay Dr. WF2: Kirk . . . 1D **124**
Green Lea LS26: Oul . . . 7C **88**
Greenlea Av. LS19: Yead . . . 1K **47**

Green Lea Cl.—Groveville

Green Lea Cl. LS23: B Spa 1E 38
Greenlea Cl. LS19: Yead 2K 47
Greenlea Ct. HD5: Hud 5E 138
HD9: Hon 4L 153
Greenlea Fold LS19: Yead 2K 47
Greenlea Mt. LS19: Yead 1K 47
Green Lea Rd. HD5: Hud 4D 138
Greenlea Rd. LS19: Yead 1K 47
Greenley Hill BD15: Wils 2A 62
Green Mdw. BD15: Wils 2C 62
Greenmires La. LS21: Stainb 1G 19
Greenmoor Av. LS12: Leeds 7G 66
WF3: Loft 3L 105
Greenmoor Cl. WF3: Loft 3L 105
Greenmoor Ct.
WF3: Carl, Loft 3L 105
Greenmoor Cres. WF3: Loft 3M 105
Green Mt. BD4: B'frd 1H 83
BD17: Bail 5M 45
HD5: Hud 4B 138
HX3: Nor G 1L 99
WF5: Oss 7A 124
Greenmount Ct. *LS11: Leeds* *2D 86*
(off Fulham St.)
Greenmount La. LS11: Leeds 2D 86
Greenmount Pl.
LS11: Leeds 2D 86
Green Mt. Retail Pk.
HX1: Hal 3H 7 (5A 98)
Green Mt. Rd. BD13: Thorn 8D 62
Greenmount St. LS11: Leeds 2D 86
Greenmount Ter. LS11: Leeds 2D 86
Greenock Pl. LS12: Leeds 6K 67
Greenock Rd. LS12: Leeds 6K 67
Greenock St. LS12: Leeds 6K 67
Greenock Ter. LS12: Leeds 6K 67
Green Pk. LS17: Leeds 5G 50
WF1: Wake 5N 125
Green Pk. Av. HX3: Hal 1B 118
WF4: Horb 9B 124
WF5: Oss 8A 124
Green Pk. Dr. HX3: Hal 1B 118
Green Pk. Ga. HX3: Hal 1B 118
Green Pk. Rd. HX3: Hal 1B 118
Green Pk. St. HX3: Hal 9C 98
Green Pasture Cl.
LS9: Leeds 6L 69
Green Pl. BD2: B'frd 4F 64
Green Rd. BD17: Bail 5M 45
LS6: Leeds 7A 50
WF15: Liv 7L 101
Green Row BD10: B'frd 9F 46
LS6: Leeds 8A 50
LS26: Meth 3L 107
Green Row Fold LS26: Meth 3L 107
Green Royd HX2: Mt T 9H 79
HX3: Nor G 2M 99
HX4: Gree 5B 118
(not continuous)
Greenroyd Av. BD19: Hun 2H 101
HX3: Hal 9A 98
Greenroyd Cl. HX3: Hal 1A 118
Greenroyd Ct. WF8: D'ton 7B 130
Greenroyd Cres. HX2: Hal 3M 97
Greenroyd Cft. HD2: Hud 1K 137
Greenroyd Gdns. WF8: D'ton 6B 130
Greenroyd La. HX2: Hal 3L 97
Greenroyd Ter. HX3: Hal 1B 118
Greens End Rd. HD9: Mel 7C 152
Greenset Vw. S71: Ath 8N 159
Greenshank M. LS27: Morl 9N 85
Greenshaw Ct. *LS20: Guis* *7H 31*
(off Branwell Av.)
Greenshaw Ter. LS20: Guis 7H 31
GREEN SIDE
BD8 7L 63
HD4 5E 154
GREENSIDE
HD5 5E 138
S75 8L 159
Green Side WF7: F'stne 5D 128
Greenside BD12: O'haw 9E 82
BD14: Clay 1G 81
BD19: Cleck 5J 101
HD8: Den D 2C 172
HD8: Lwr C 9B 156
LS19: Yead *2L 47*
(off Warm La.)
LS28: Pud 8A 66
S36: Hoy 9K 173
S72: Shaf 5J 161
S75: Map, S'ross 8L 159
WF2: W'ton 3B 144
WF4: H'cft 1J 161
WF16: Heck 8N 101
Greenside Av. HD5: Hud 5E 138
LS12: Leeds 9L 67
S75: S'ross 8L 159
Greenside Cl. LS12: Leeds 9M 67
Greenside Ct. LS27: Gil 6G 84
WF4: N Cro 3J 145
WF14: Mir 5M 121
Greenside Cres. HD5: Hud 5E 138
Greenside Dr. HD5: Hud 5E 138
LS12: Leeds 9M 67
Greenside Est. WF14: Mir 4L 121
Greenside Gro. LS28: Pud 8A 66
Greenside Ho. S75: S'ross 8L 159
Greenside La. BD8: B'frd 7L 63
BD13: Cull 9K 43
Greenside Mt. WF14: Mir 4M 121
Greenside Pk. BD8: B'frd 7L 63
WF4: N Cro 3J 145
Greenside Pl. S75: Map 8L 159
Greenside Rd. HD4: Thurs 6D 154
LS12: Leeds 9M 67
WF14: Mir 4L 121
Greenside Ter. LS12: Leeds 9L 67
WF13: Dew 1B 122
Greenside Wlk. LS12: Leeds 9L 67
Green Slacks La. HD3: Scam 5H 135
Green Springs HX7: Heb B 1F 94
Green Sq. LS25: Kip 4A 90
Green's Sq. HX2: Hal 4L 97
Green's Ter. BD12: O'haw 9D 82
Green St. BD1: B'frd 4D 6 (7D 64)
BD12: O'haw 8F 82
BD22: Haw 9C 42
BD22: Oxen 4C 60
HD1: Hud 3B 8 (3M 137)
(not continuous)
HD9: Mel 7C 152
HX4: Holy 7B 118
WF10: C'frd 3D 108
Greensway LS25: Gar 7M 71
Green Sykes Rd. BD22: Oak 8A 26
Green Ter. *BD2: B'frd* *4F 64*
(off Idle Rd.)
LS11: Leeds 2E 86
LS20: Guis 8J 31
WF13: Dew 1D 122
WF14: Mir *5K 121*
(off Nab La.)
Green Ter. Sq. HX1: Hal 8G 7 (7N 97)
Greenthorpe Ct. LS13: Leeds 7H 67
Greenthorpe Hill LS13: Leeds 7H 67
Greenthorpe Mt. LS13: Leeds 6H 67
Greenthorpe Rd. LS13: Leeds 6H 67
Greenthorpe St. LS13: Leeds 7H 67
Greenthorpe Wlk. LS13: Leeds 6H 67
Greenthwaite Cl. BD20: Keigh 7G 27
Greenton Av. BD19: Scho 3C 100
Greenton Cres. BD13: Que 5C 80
Green Top HD7: Mars 7E 150
LS12: Leeds 9L 67
Greentop LS28: Pud 8A 66
WF4: N Cro 3J 145
Green Top Gdns. LS12: Leeds 9L 67
Green Top St. BD8: B'frd 7K 63
Greentrees BD6: B'frd 7N 81
Greenups Mill *HX6: Sow B* *8J 97*
(off Old Cawsey)
Greenups Ter. HX6: Sow B 8H 97
Green Vw. LS6: Leeds 8A 50
LS14: S'cft 8D 36
Green View, The S72: Shaf 5J 161
Greenview WF4: N Cro 3J 145
Greenview Cl. LS9: Leeds 4L 69
Greenview Ct. LS8: Leeds 7J 51
Greenville Av. LS12: Leeds 9L 67
Greenville Dr. BD12: Low M 6C 82
Greenville Gdns. LS12: Leeds 9L 67
Green Way HX2: Illing 5L 79
LS14: S'cft 8D 36
Greenway HD3: Hud 5E 136
HD9: Hon 4L 153
LS15: Leeds 5D 70
LS20: Guis 9G 30
Greenway, The BD3: B'frd 1E 6 (6E 64)
Greenway Cl. LS15: Leeds 5D 70
Greenway Dr. BD15: All 7G 62
Greenway Rd. BD5: B'frd 3C 82
Greenwell Ct. LS9: Leeds 6L 69
Greenwell Row BD14: Clay 1G 81
Greenwood Av. BD2: B'frd 1E 64
WF9: Upt 1B 164
WF12: Dew 4J 123
Greenwood Bldgs. HD5: K'htn 2G 138
Greenwood Cl. WF6: Norm 4J 127
WF9: Upt 1B 164
Greenwood Ct. BD1: B'frd 5B 6 (8C 64)
LS6: Leeds 7A 50
Greenwood Cres. S71: Roys 5C 160
Greenwood Dr. BD2: B'frd 2E 64
Greenwood Fold BD4: B'frd 6F 82
Greenwood Ho. WF1: Wake 5K 9
Greenwood Mt. BD2: B'frd 2E 64
LS6: Leeds 8A 50
Greenwood Pk. LS6: Leeds 8A 50
Greenwood Rd. BD17: Bail 6N 45
WF1: Wake 3M 9 (4M 125)
WF3: Ting 4B 104
Greenwood Row LS28: Pud 7C 66
Greenwood's Ter. HX3: Hal 3M 97
Greenwood St. HD4: Hud 8B 8 (6M 137)
HX7: Heb B *1H 95*
(off Hangingroyd La.)
WF12: Dew 5F 122
WF13: Dew 3E 122
GREETLAND 4A 118
Greetland Moor Vw. HX3: Hal 1M 7
Greetland Rd. HX4: Bark 6G 116
Gregory Ct. BD14: Clay 1H 81
Gregory Cres. BD7: B'frd 3K 81
Gregory Dr. HD8: Kbtn 2K 155
Gregory La. WF14: Up H 3L 139
Gregory Rd. WF10: C'frd 6E 108
Gregory Springs La. WF14: Mir 9L 121
Gregory Springs Mt. WF14: Mir 9M 121
Gregory Springs Rd. WF14: Mir 9M 121
Gregory St. WF17: Bat 7H 103
Greigs Yd. *WF4: Horb* *1A 142*
(off St John's St.)
Grenfell Dr. BD3: B'frd 6H 65
Grenfell Rd. BD3: B'frd 6H 65
Grenfell Ter. BD3: B'frd 6H 65
Grenley St. WF11: Knot 8F 110
Grennshaw M. *LS20: Guis* *7H 31*
(off Branwell Av.)
Grenoside Vw. HD8: Kbtn 2J 155
Grenville Wlk. WF4: Hol 7H 143
Gresford Cl. S75: W Gran 6F 158
Gresham Av. BD2: B'frd 2D 64
Gresley Ho. *LS18: Hors* *4F 48*
(off Sussex Av.)
Gresley Rd. BD21: Keigh 9J 27
Grey Cl. WF1: Out 9K 105
Grey Ct. WF1: Out 9K 105
Greycourt Cl. BD10: B'frd 9E 46
HX1: Hal 6N 97
Greycourt Ho. *HX1: Hal* *6N 97*
(off Greycourt Cl.)
Greyfriars Av. HD2: Hud 7C 120
Greyfriar Wlk. BD7: B'frd 2K 81
Grey Gables WF4: Neth 4A 142
Grey Horse Yd. HD1: Hud 7A 8 (5M 137)
Greyhound Dr. BD7: B'frd 8N 63
Grey Scar Ct. *BD22: Oak* *5B 42*
(off Grey Scar Rd.)
Grey Scar Rd. BD22: Oak 5A 42
Greyshaw Syke HX2: Ogd 3K 79
Greyshiels Av. LS6: Leeds 2M 67
Greyshiels Cl. LS6: Leeds 2M 67
Greystone HD4: Hud 8G 136
Greystone Av. HX5: Ell 6D 118
Greystone Cl. LS23: B Spa 1E 38
LS29: Burl W 7C 16
Greystone Ct. HD6: Ras 4M 119
Greystone Cres. BD10: B'frd 9G 46
Grey Stone La. OL14: Tod 4A 94
Greystone M. WF7: Ackw 2G 146
Greystone Mill BD3: B'frd 7F 64
Greystone Mt. LS15: Leeds 7N 69
Greystone Pk. LS25: Aber 6E 54
Greystones HX2: Mix 1K 97
Greystones Cl. LS25: Aber 6E 54
Greystones Ct. LS8: Leeds 8L 51
LS17: Leeds 3E 50
Greystones Dr. BD22: Keigh 5F 42
WF5: Oss 8A 124
Grey Stones La. HX7: P Wel 9H 59
Greystones La. BD22: Lay 1K 41
Greystones Mt. BD22: Keigh 5F 42
Greystones Ri. BD22: Keigh 4F 42
Greystones Rd. HX2: Lud F 5E 96
Grey St. WF1: Out 9K 105
Griffe Dr. BD12: Wyke 3A 100
Griffe Gdns. BD22: Oak 4B 42
Griffe Head Cres. BD12: Wyke 2A 100
Griffe Head Rd. BD12: Wyke 2A 100
Griffe Rd. BD12: Wyke 2A 100
BD22: Old, S'bury 7L 41
Griffe Ter. BD12: Wyke 3A 100
Griffe Vw. BD22: Oak 4B 42
Griff Ho. La. WF3: E Ard 4D 104
Grime La. HD9: H'wth 7G 171
WF4: S Comn 8J 127
Grimescar Mdws. HD2: Hud 9J 119
Grimescar Rd. HD2: Hud 7G 118
GRIMETHORPE 9A 162
Grimethorpe St. WF9: S Elm 6M 163
Grimpit Hill WF4: Not 3B 160
Grimscar Av. HD2: Hud 9L 119
Grimthorpe Av. LS6: Leeds 1M 67
Grimthorpe Pl. LS6: Leeds 1N 67
Grimthorpe St. LS6: Leeds 1M 67
Grimthorpe Ter. LS6: Leeds 1N 67
Grindlestone Bank HX2: Mt T 9J 79
Grisedale Av. HD2: Hud 1L 137
Grisedale Cl. BD7: B'frd 2L 81
HX2: Hal 3K 97
Gritstone Cl. LS29: Burl W 7C 16
Grizedale Cl. LS22: Weth 3J 23
Grosmont Pl. LS13: Leeds 3F 66
Grosmont Rd. LS13: Leeds 4F 66
Grosmont Ter. LS13: Leeds 3F 66
Grosvenor Av. BD18: Ship 7L 45
HD8: Lept 7J 139
WF8: Pon 2G 129
WF9: Upt 2N 163
Grosvenor Ct. LS16: Leeds 3G 49
Grosvenor Gdns. LS17: Huby 6M 19
Grosvenor Hill LS7: Leeds 1F 4 (4E 68)
Grosvenor M. LS19: Raw 3L 47
Grosvenor Mt. LS6: Leeds 2B 68
Grosvenor Pk. LS7: Leeds 8E 50
Grosvenor Pk. Gdns. LS6: Leeds 2B 68
Grosvenor Pl. HX2: Lud F 5D 96
Grosvenor Rd. BD8: B'frd 5B 64
BD18: Ship 8L 45
HD5: Hud 4C 138
LS6: Leeds 2B 68
WF17: Bat 6G 102
Grosvenor St. BD8: B'frd 5B 64
HX5: Ell 5E 118
WF1: Wake 8A 126
WF12: Dew 4F 122
WF16: Heck 7A 102
Grosvenor Ter. BD8: B'frd 5B 64
HD8: Clay W 7J 157
HX1: Hal *5N 97*
(off West Hill St.)
HX1: Hal 3G 7 (5N 97)
(Stansfield Cl.)
LS6: Leeds 2B 68
LS21: Otley *9M 17*
(off Cross Grn.)
LS22: Weth 3M 23
WF16: Heck 8A 102
Grosvenor Way HD8: Lept 7J 139
Grotto Ter. HX2: Wain 8E 78
Groudle Glen HX7: Heb B 2E 94
Grouse Moor La. BD13: Que 3B 80
Grouse St. BD21: Keigh 8K 27
Grove, The BD10: B'frd 8H 47
(Galloway Rd.)
BD10: B'frd 8F 46
(Woodbine Ter.)
BD13: Que *4C 80*
(off New Pk. Rd.)
BD16: Bgly 1D 44
BD17: Bail 3A 46
BD18: Ship 8K 45
HD2: Hud 9N 119
HD9: Mel 8E 152
HX3: Hip 4J 99
HX3: She 7H 81
LS8: Leeds 9M 51
LS17: E Kes 2C 36
LS17: Leeds 2B 50
LS18: Hors 7E 48
LS19: Yead 1M 47
LS23: B Spa 1F 38
LS25: Kip 4A 90
LS26: Swil 3J 89
LS27: Gil 6G 84
LS28: Pud 7A 66
LS29: I'ly 5F 14
S72: Cud 8J 161
WF2: W'ton 3C 144
WF3: E Ard 4D 104
WF4: Ryh 9H 145
WF6: Norm 1J 127
WF9: S Elm 5M 163
WF9: S Kirk 7J 163
Grove, The WF16: Heck 6N 101
WF17: Bat 5D 102
Grove Av. BD18: Ship 1N 63
HX3: Hal 2M 97
LS6: Leeds 9A 50
LS28: Pud 7A 66
LS29: I'ly 6E 14
WF8: Pon 3L 129
WF9: Hems 3E 162
WF9: S Kirk 7J 163
Grove Cl. BD2: B'frd 2E 64
BD19: Gom 3M 101
WF9: Hems 3F 162
Grove Cotts. HD6: Brigh 1K 119
Grove Ct. HX3: Hal 1N 97
LS6: Leeds 9A 50
LS28: Pud 7A 66
Grove Cres. HX2: Lud F 5D 96
LS23: B Spa 1F 38
WF2: W'ton 3C 144
Grove Cres. Sth. LS23: B Spa 1F 38
Grove Cft. HX3: Hal 2M 97
Grove Dr. HX3: Hal 2M 97
WF9: S Kirk 7H 163
Grove Edge HX3: Hal 2M 97
Grove Farm Cl. LS16: Leeds 3J 49
Grove Farm Cres. LS16: Leeds 4H 49
Grove Farm Cft. LS16: Leeds 3H 49
Grove Farm Dr. LS16: Leeds 3H 49
Grove Gdns. HX3: Hal 2N 97
LS6: Leeds 9A 50
LS23: B Spa 1F 38
WF12: Dew 5K 123
Grovehall Av. LS11: Leeds 4B 86
Grove Hall Caravan Site WF11: Knot 2C 130
Grovehall Dr. LS11: Leeds 4B 86
Grovehall La. WF8: Pon 3A 130
Grovehall Pde. LS11: Leeds 4B 86
Grovehall Rd. LS11: Leeds 4B 86
Grove Head WF9: S Kirk 7H 163
Grove Ho. *LS7: Leeds* *2G 68*
(off Woodland Gro.)
WF9: Hems 3E 162
Grove Ho. Ct. *LS8: Leeds* *9M 51*
(off Nth. Grove Cl.)
Grove Ho. Cres. BD2: B'frd 2E 64
Grove Ho. Dr. BD2: B'frd 3E 64
HD8: Clay W 7H 157
Grove Ho. Rd. BD2: B'frd 2E 64
Grove Ho's. HD9: Hon 4M 153
Grovelands BD2: B'frd 2E 64
Grove La. BD19: Gom 3M 101
LS6: Leeds 9N 49
WF9: Bads 7L 147
WF9: Hems 3E 162
WF9: S Kirk 7H 163
WF11: Knot 8D 110
Grove Lawn Tennis Club 4K 137
Grove Lea Cl. WF9: Hems 3E 162
Grove Lea Cres. WF8: Pon 4L 129
Grove Lea Wlk. WF8: Pon 4L 129
Grove Mill Ct. LS21: Otley 1J 31
Grove Mill Dr. BD21: Keigh 4G 43
Grove Mill La. HX3: Hal 2N 97
Grove Mt. WF8: Pon 3L 129
WF9: S Kirk 7H 163
Grove Nook HD3: Hud 4E 136
Grove Pk. HX3: Hal 1M 97
LS6: Leeds 1B 68
WF4: Cal G 4F 142
Grove Pl. LS23: B Spa 1E 38
WF9: Hems 3E 162
Grove Promenade, The *LS29: I'ly* *5G 14*
(off West St.)
Grove Ri. LS17: Leeds 2B 50
WF8: Pon 3L 129
Grove Rd. BD16: Bgly 5E 44
BD18: Ship 1N 63
HD1: Hud 2D 8 (3N 137)
HX5: Ell 4F 118
HX7: Heb B 9H 77
LS6: Leeds 1A 68
LS10: Leeds 2G 86
LS15: Leeds 7B 70
LS18: Hors 7E 48
LS23: B Spa 1E 38
LS28: Pud 7A 66
LS29: I'ly 5D 14
LS29: Men 4E 30
S75: Map 8J 159
WF1: Wake 6K 9 (6L 125)
WF4: Horb 1C 142
WF8: Pon 3K 129
WF16: Heck 8B 102
Grove Row HX2: Mt T 1G 97
Grove Royd HX3: Hal 2N 97
Groves Hall Rd. WF13: Dew 3C 122
Grove Sq. BD19: Gom 3M 101
HX3: Hal 2M 97
Grove St. HD3: Hud 4D 136
HD6: Brigh 1N 119
HD7: Slait 9M 135
HX2: Hal 1M 97
HX6: Sow B 8K 97
LS1: Leeds 6B 4
LS28: Stan 4B 66
WF1: Wake 6L 9 (6M 125)
WF5: Oss 7N 123
WF9: S Kirk 7H 163
WF13: Dew 3F 122
WF14: Mir 5M 121
WF15: Liv 1M 121
WF16: Heck 8B 102
Grove St. Sth. HX1: Hal 5M 97
Grove Ter. BD7: B'frd 5A 6 (8B 64)
BD11: B'haw 9L 83
HD6: Brigh 1K 119
HX7: Myth 4M 95
LS21: Pool 3E 32
LS23: B Spa 1E 38
LS28: Pud 7A 66
WF9: Hems 3E 162
GROVE TOWN 4L 129
Grove Vs. WF10: All B 7A 90
Groveville HX3: Hip 3H 99

Grove Way—Hampton Pl.

Grove Way WF9: S Kirk 7H 163
Groveway BD2: B'frd 2E 64
Grovewood LS6: Leeds 9N 49
Grunberg Pl. LS6: Leeds 1N 67
Grunberg St. LS6: Leeds 1N 67
Gryce Hall HD8: Shel 3N 155
GUARD HOUSE 9E 26
Guard Ho. Av. BD22: Keigh 9G 26
Guard Ho. Dr. BD22: Keigh 9G 26
Guard Ho. Gro. BD22: Keigh 9F 26
Guard Ho. Rd. BD22: Keigh 9G 26
Guardian Ct. *LS29: I'ly* 5G 14
(off Wells Prom.)
Guardian M. *LS12: Leeds* 9M 67
(off Lynwood Gth.)
Guernsey Rd. WF12: Dew 1J 123
Guide Post Farm *HX2: Illing* 6L 79
(off Keighley Rd.)
Guildford Rd. S71: Roys 4C 160
Guildford St. HX7: Heb B 2H 95
WF5: Oss 7N 123
Guild Way HX2: Hal 5H 97
Guillemot App. LS27: Morl 1N 103
Guinea Ga. HD9: Had E 9A 170
Guinevere Dr. WF9: S Elm 7N 163
GUISELEY 7J 31
Guiseley Dr. LS29: Men 6F 30
Guiseley Retail Pk. LS20: Guis 8J 31
Guiseley Station (Rail) 7H 31
Guiseley Theatre 8J 31
GULLY 4N 169
Gully, The HD8: Shep 3G 170
Gully Ter. HD9: H'frth 4N 169
Gunson Cres. WF5: Oss 5N 123
Gunter Rd. LS22: Weth 4A 24
GUNTHWAITE 6E 172
Gunthwaite La. HD8: Up D 5C 172
S36: Pen 6E 172
Gunthwaite Top HD8: Up D 5C 172
Gurbax Ct. BD3: B'frd 7J 65
Gurney Cl. BD5: B'frd 2B 82
GUYCROFT 1K 31
Guycroft LS21: Otley 1K 31
Guys Cft. BD16: Bgly 2J 45
WF2: Wake 7E 124
Guy St. BD4: B'frd 6C 6 (8D 64)
Gwynne Av. BD3: B'frd 5J 65
Gym Health & Fitness Club, The
Leeds 4J 69
Gynn La. HD9: Hon 5M 153
Gypsy Ct. WF10: C'frd 6J 109
Gypsy La. WF4: Wool 4G 159
WF10: C'frd 6J 109
Gypsy Wood Cl. LS15: Leeds 7E 70
Gypsy Wood Crest LS15: Leeds 7E 70

H

HACKING HILL 6A 164
Hacking La. OL14: Tod 9J 93
WF9: S Elm 6A 164
Hadassah St. HX3: Hal 8C 98
HADDINGLEY 2H 171
Haddingley La. HD8: Cumb 5G 171
Haddlesey Rd. WF11: Birk 2M 111
Haddon Av. HX3: Hal 9B 98
LS4: Leeds 4M 67
Haddon Cl. BD19: Gom 4M 101
WF9: S Elm 4N 163
Haddon Pl. LS4: Leeds 4M 67
Haddon Rd. LS4: Leeds 4N 67
HADE EDGE 9N 169
Hadfield Rd. WF16: Heck 7A 102
Hadleigh Ct. LS17: Leeds 5F 50
Hadleigh Ri. WF8: Pon 6H 129
Hadley's Ct. *LS27: Gil* 7G 85
(off Gelderd Rd.)
Hadrian Cl. WF10: C'frd 3J 109
Hadrians Cl. HD3: Hud 2D 136
WF8: Thpe A 5N 147
Hag Farm Rd. LS29: Burl W 2B 30
Hagg La. WF11: Birk 1N 111
WF14: Mir 8M 121
Haggroyd La. HD9: Brock 7N 153
HAGGS HILL 6C 124
Haggs Hill Rd. WF5: Oss 6C 124
(not continuous)
Haggs La. WF5: Oss 6E 124
Hagg Wood Rd. HD9: T'bdge 7N 153
Hag Hill HD8: Eml 3G 157
Hag Hill La. HD8: Eml 3H 157
Hag La. HX3: Hal 1B 98
Hague Cres. WF9: Hems 4E 162
Hague La. WF9: S Kirk 7G 162
Hague Pk. Cl. WF9: S Kirk 6H 163
Hague Pk. Coppice WF9: S Kirk 6H 163
Hague Pk. Dr. WF9: S Kirk 6H 163
Hague Pk. Gdns. WF9: S Kirk 6H 163
Hague Pk. La. WF9: S Kirk 6H 163
Hague Pk. Wlk. WF9: S Kirk 6H 163
Hague Ter. WF9: Hems 3E 162
Haigh Av. LS26: Rothw 6L 87
Haigh Beck Vw. BD10: B'frd 8G 47
Haigh Cl. S36: Hoy 9J 173
Haigh Cnr. BD10: B'frd 8H 47
Haigh Cft. S71: Roys 5C 160
Haighfield Caravan Site LS17: Bard 6C 36
HAIGH FOLD 3G 65
Haigh Fold BD2: B'frd 3G 65
Haigh Gdns. LS26: Rothw 6L 87
Haigh Hall BD10: B'frd 8H 47
Haigh Hall Rd. BD10: B'frd 8H 47
Haigh Head Rd. S36: Hoy 9J 173
Haigh Hill S75: Hai 3E 158
HAIGH HOUSE HILL 8D 118
Haigh Ho. Rd. HD3: Hud 8D 118
Haigh La. HD9: Nether 9L 153
HX3: Hal 8M 7 (8C 98)
S36: Hoy 9K 173
S75: Hai 4E 158
WF4: Flock 8D 140
Haigh M. S75: Hai 4E 158
HAIGH MOOR 6A 104
Haigh Moor Av. WF3: W Ard 6A 104
Haigh Moor Cres. WF3: W Ard 6A 104
Haigh Moor Rd. WF3: W Ard 7A 104
Haigh Moor St. WF1: Wake 1L 9 (3M 125)
Haigh Moor Vw. WF3: W Ard 6A 104
Haigh Moor Way S71: Roys 4D 160
WF10: All B 9C 90
Haigh Pk. Rd. LS10: Leeds 3K 87
Haigh Rd. LS26: Rothw 7N 87
Haigh Row HD8: Skelm 6D 156
Haigh's Bldgs. HD1: Hud 8C 8
Haighside LS26: Rothw 7L 87
Haighside Cl. LS26: Rothw 7L 87
Haighside Dr. LS26: Rothw 7L 87
Haighside Way LS26: Rothw 7L 87
Haighs Sq. HD5: Hud 3B 138
Haigh St. BD4: B'frd 2F 82
HD1: Hud 7L 137
HD6: Brigh 9M 99
HX1: Hal 4M 97
HX4: Gree 4A 118
Haigh Ter. LS26: Rothw 6L 87
Haigh Vw. LS26: Rothw 6L 87
Haigh Wood Cres. LS16: Leeds 4G 48
Haigh Wood Grn. LS16: Leeds 5G 48
Haigh Wood Rd. LS16: Leeds 4F 48
Hailey St. WF13: Dew 3F 122
Hailhead Dr. WF8: Pon 2M 129
Haincliffe Pl. BD21: Keigh 3H 43
Haincliffe Rd. BD21: Keigh 3H 43
Haines Pk. LS7: Leeds 1L 5 (4G 68)
Hainsworth Ct. *LS28: Fars* 3A 66
(off Ebenezer St.)
Hainsworth Moor Cres. BD13: Que 5C 80
Hainsworth Moor Dr. BD13: Que 5C 80
Hainsworth Moor Gth. BD13: Que 5C 80
Hainsworth Moor Gro. BD13: Que 5C 80
Hainsworth Moor Vw. BD13: Que 5C 80
Hainsworth Rd. BD20: Sils 8E 12
(not continuous)
Hainsworth Sq. LS28: Fars 3A 66
Hainsworth St. *BD20: Sils* 8E 12
(off Howden Rd.)
LS12: Leeds 8A 68
LS26: Rothw 9N 87
HAINWORTH 4H 43
Hainworth Crag Rd. BD21: Keigh 5G 43
Hainworth La. BD21: Keigh 3H 43
Hainworth Rd. BD21: Keigh 4H 43
HAINWORTH SHAW 4K 43
Hainworth Wood Rd. BD21: Keigh 4H 43
Hainworth Wood Rd. Nth. BD21: Keigh 2J 43
Haise Mt. S75: Dart 8J 159
Halberg Ho. WF8: Pon 3L 129
Halcyon Hill LS7: Leeds 7E 50
Halcyon Way BD5: B'frd 2A 82
Haldane Ct. S72: B'ley 6N 161
Haldane Cres. WF1: Wake 3N 125
Hales Ct. WF8: Pon 8K 109
Hales Rd. LS12: Leeds 9L 67
Halesworth Cres. BD4: B'frd 2J 83
Haley Ct. HX3: Hal 1K 7
Haley Hill HX3: Hal 1K 7 (3B 98)
Haley's Yd. LS13: Leeds 3F 66
Half Acre Rd. BD13: Thorn 7A 62
HALF ACRES 6C 108
Half Ho. La. HD6: Brigh 7J 99
HALF MILE 3C 66
Half Mile LS13: Leeds 4C 66
Half Mile Cl. LS28: Stan 4C 66
Half Mile Ct. LS28: Stan 4C 66
Half Mile Gdns. LS13: Leeds 4C 66
Half Mile Grn. LS28: Stan 4C 66
Half Mile La. LS13: Leeds 3C 66
LS28: Fars 3C 66
Half Moon La. WF1: K'thpe 5C 126
Half Moon St. HD1: Hud 5B 8 (4M 137)
Halfpenny La. WF7: F'stne 5D 128
WF8: Pon 4G 129
Half St. BD21: Keigh 8H 27
HALIFAX 4L 7 (5B 98)
Halifax Antiques Cen. *HX1: Hal* 5M 97
(off Queen's Rd.)
Halifax Body Station, The 2L 7
Halifax Bradley Hall Golf Course 6N 117
Halifax Golf Course 4J 79
Halifax Ho. WF13: Dew 9D 102
Halifax Ind. Cen. HX1: Hal 2G 7 (4N 97)
Halifax La. HX2: Lud 4E 96
HX7: Blac H 9N 75
Halifax Old Rd. HD1: Hud 1B 8 (9K 119)
HD2: Hud 9K 119
HX3: Hip 4G 98
Halifax Playhouse 5J 7 (6A 98)
Halifax Retail Pk. HX1: Hal 3J 7 (5A 98)
Halifax RLFC 7L 7 (7B 98)
Halifax Rd. BB10: B'clif 3A 56
BD6: B'frd 6K 81
BD13: Cull 1K 61
BD13: Denh 1K 79
(Foreside Bottom La.)
BD13: Denh 7K 61
(Old Rd.)
BD13: Que 7B 80
BD19: Cleck, Scho 5C 100
BD21: Cros R, Keigh 8F 42
BD21: Keigh 4H 43
BD22: Cros R 6F 42
HD3: Hud 8G 118
HD6: Brigh 6J 99
HD7: Golc 4A 136
HX3: Hip 6J 99
(Broad Oak La.)
HX3: Hip 4G 98
(Halifax Old Rd.)
HX3: North, She 1G 98
HX5: Ell, Hal 3D 118
HX6: Ripp 7D 116
HX7: Heb B 7K 93
OL14: Tod 7K 93
OL15: Lit 3A 132
WF13: Dew 3F 122
WF15: Liv 5C 100
WF16: Heck 8C 102
WF17: Bat 8C 102
Halifax Sailing Club 1C 78
Halifax Ski & Snowboarding Centre, The 1B 98
Halifax Station (Rail) 5M 7 (6C 98)
Halifax Swimming Pool 6L 7 (6B 98)
Halifax Vw. HX3: Hal 1M 7
Halifax Vis. Cen. *5C 98*
(within The Piece Hall)
Hall, The LS7: Leeds 8E 50
Hallamfield LS20: Guis 8J 31
Hallam La. LS21: Askw 4E 16
Hallamshire M. WF2: Wake 7E 124
Hallam St. LS20: Guis 8H 31
HALLAS BRIDGE 9M 43
Hallas Bri. Mill BD13: Cull 1M 61
Hallas Gro. HD5: Hud 5C 138
Hallas La. BD13: Cull 1L 61
(not continuous)
HD8: Kbtn 3M 155
Hallas Rd. HD8: Kbtn 3K 155
Hall Av. BD2: B'frd 1H 65
HD1: Hud 5L 137
Hallbank Cl. BD5: B'frd 4B 82
Hall Bank Dr. BD16: Bgly 3F 44
Hallbank Dr. BD5: B'frd 4B 82
Hall Bank La. HX7: Myth 4M 95
HALL BOWER 9N 137
Hall Bower La. HD4: Hud 1N 153
HALL CLIFFE 9C 124
Hallcliffe BD17: Bail 3B 46
Hall Cliffe Ct. WF4: Horb 9C 124
Hall Cliffe Cres. WF4: Horb 9C 124
Hall Cliffe Gro. WF4: Horb 9C 124
Hall Cliffe Ri. WF4: Horb 9D 124
Hall Cliffe Rd. WF4: Horb 9C 124
Hall Cl. HD9: Mel 7E 152
HX3: North 1F 98
LS16: B'hpe 4H 33
LS23: B Spa 1E 38
LS29: Burl W 8B 16
WF5: Oss 2L 123
WF9: Hems 2D 162
WF15: Liv 9L 101
Hall Ct. LS7: Leeds 2F 68
WF11: B'ton 4B 110
Hall Cft. BD20: Sils 7E 12
WF4: Neth 3A 142
WF6: Norm 1J 127
Hallcroft BD16: Bgly 2E 44
Hallcroft Cl. WF4: Horb 1D 142
Hallcroft Dr. LS29: Add 2A 14
WF4: Horb 1D 142
Hallcroft Ri. S71: Roys 6C 160
Hall Cross Gro. HD5: Hud 7A 138
Hall Cross Rd. HD5: Hud 7A 138
Hall Dr. LS16: B'hpe 4G 33
LS29: Burl W 8B 16
WF15: Liv 1M 121
Hall Farm M. LS25: M'fld 6G 72
Hall Farm Pk. LS25: M'fld 6F 72
HALLFIELD 4N 23
Hallfield Av. LS25: M'fld 7F 72
Hallfield Ct. LS22: Weth 3N 23
Hallfield Cres. LS22: Weth 4N 23
Hallfield Dr. BD17: Bail 4A 46
Hall Fld. La. WF4: H'cft 2H 161
Hallfield La. LS22: Weth 3N 23
Hallfield Pl. BD1: B'frd 1A 6 (6C 64)
Hallfield Rd. BD1: B'frd 2A 6 (6B 64)
Hallfield St. BD1: B'frd 2A 6 (6C 64)
Hallfield Ter. LS25: M'fld 7F 72
Hall Gth. HD5: K'htn 4G 138
Hall Gth. Rd. WF8: Thpe A 5N 147
Hall Gate HX7: Myth 4M 95
Hallgate BD1: B'frd 2A 6 (6C 64)
HALL GREEN 7H 143
Hall Grn. La. HX6: Rish 2D 134
LS17: N Rig 2A 20
Hall Gro. LS6: Leeds 4B 68
S75: S'ross 8L 159
Halliday Av. LS12: Leeds 6K 67
Halliday Ct. BD3: B'frd 6K 65
LS25: Gar 7M 71
Halliday Dr. LS12: Leeds 6K 67
Halliday Gro. LS12: Leeds 6K 67
Halliday Mt. LS12: Leeds 6K 67
Halliday Pl. LS12: Leeds 6K 67
Halliday Rd. LS12: Leeds 6K 67
LS25: Gar 7M 71
Halliday St. LS28: Pud 6B 66
Halliley Gdns.
WF13: Dew 3F 122
(off Vulcan Rd.)
Halliley St. WF13: Dew 3E 122
Hall Ing La. HD4: Farn T 5B 154
HD9: Hon 4N 153
Halling Pl. OL14: Tod 8J 93
HALL INGS 5C 136
Hall Ings BD1: B'frd 5B 6 (8C 64)
HX3: Sou 9F 98
Hall La. BD4: B'frd 7D 6 (9D 64)
BD18: Ship 7A 46
HD7: Golc 4A 136
HD8: Kbtn 2J 155
HX3: North 9E 80
HX6: Ripp 4A 116
LS7: Leeds 1F 68
LS12: Leeds 7M 67
LS12: N Far 8F 66
LS16: Leeds 1H 49
LS18: Hors 7C 48
LS21: Askw 2C 16
LS21: Leat 7D 18
LS25: S Mil 9M 73
WF4: Chap 6H 143
WF9: S Elm 3A 164
WF10: Leds 7E 90
WF12: T'hill 9H 123
Hall Lee Fold HD3: Hud 1H 137
Hall Mews LS23: B Spa 1E 38
Hall Orchards Av. LS22: Weth 3N 23
Hallowes Gro. BD13: Cull 1K 61
Hallowes Pk. Rd. BD13: Cull 1K 61
Hallows, The BD20: Keigh 8G 26
Hallows Ct. *HD5: Hud* 7D 138
(off Old School La.)
Hallows Rd. BD21: Keigh 7L 27
Hall Park Av. LS18: Hors 6D 48
WF4: Croft 9G 126
WF15: Liv 1L 121
Hall Park Cl. LS18: Hors 6D 48
Hall Park Ct. LS25: Kip 4B 90
Hall Park Cft. LS25: Kip 5B 90
Hall Park Gth. LS18: Hors 6D 48
Hall Park Mdws. LS25: Kip 5B 90
Hall Park Mt. LS18: Hors 6D 48
Hall Park Orchards LS25: Kip 5B 90
Hall Park Ri. LS18: Hors 6D 48
LS25: Kip 4B 90
Hall Park Rd. LS23: W'ton 5G 25
Hall Pl. LS9: Leeds 7M 5 (7H 69)
Hall Ri. LS16: B'hpe 5H 33
LS29: Burl W 8B 16
Hall Rise Cl. LS16: B'hpe 5H 33
Hall Rise Cft. LS16: B'hpe 5H 33
Hall Rd. BD2: B'frd 1G 65
LS12: Leeds 7M 67
LS26: Swil 4J 89
WF2: Wake 7F 124
Hall Royd BD18: Ship 8N 45
Hallroyd Cres. OL14: Tod 7L 93
Hallroyd Pl. OL14: Tod 7L 93
Hallroyd Rd. OL14: Tod 6L 93
Hall's Ct. WF7: Ackw 2G 146
Hallside Cl. BD17: Bail 3D 46
Hall Sq. LS28: Cal 8M 47
Hall Stone Ct. HX3: She 8H 81
Hall St. BD6: B'frd 4A 82
BD22: Haw 9C 42
BD22: Oak 5D 42
(off Clough La.)
HD3: Hud 3E 136
HD6: Brigh 1N 119
HX1: Hal 4J 7 (5A 98)
OL14: Tod 7K 93
WF7: F'stne 7D 128
Hall St. Nth. HX3: Hal 2A 98
Hall Syke HD8: Shep 9H 155
Hall Ter. BD2: B'frd 1G 65
BD21: Rid 7M 27
Hallwood Grn. BD10: B'frd 1J 65
Halstead Cl. HX6: Ripp 9C 116
Halstead Dr. LS29: Men 3E 30
Halstead Grn. HX7: Hept 7B 76
Halstead Gro. S75: Map 7J 159
Halstead La. HD4: Thurs 9D 154
Halstead Pl. BD7: B'frd 2N 81
Halsteads Way BD20: Stee 2B 26
HALTON 6A 70
Halton Cl. HD5: Hud 6D 138
Halton Dr. LS15: Leeds 6B 70
HALTON EAST 1E 10
HALTON GREEN 1E 10
Halton Hill LS15: Leeds 6A 70
HALTON MOOR 7N 69
Halton Moor Av. LS9: Leeds 8M 69
Halton Moor Rd. LS9: Leeds 8J 69
(not continuous)
LS15: Leeds 8N 69
Halton Pl. BD5: B'frd 2N 81
Halton Rd. WF1: Wake 3A 126
Halton St. WF7: F'stne 4D 128
Hamble Ct. S75: Map 9L 159
Hambledon Av. BD4: B'frd 4F 82
HD9: Mel 8E 152
Hambleton Bank HX2: Mix 7H 79
Hambleton Cotts. BD23: Bolt A 2H 11
Hambleton Cres. HX2: Mix 8H 79
Hambleton Dr. HX2: Mix 8G 79
Hambleton La. BD22: Oxen 7F 60
Hambleton St. WF1: Wake 2K 9 (4L 125)
Hame, The HX4: Stainl 8M 117
Hamel Ri. WF9: Hems 3D 162
Hamilton Av. LS7: Leeds 2G 68
Hamilton Ct. WF6: Norm 9J 107
Hamilton Gdns. LS7: Leeds 3F 68
Hamilton Pl. LS7: Leeds 3G 68
Hamilton St. BD1: B'frd 6B 64
Hamilton Ter. LS7: Leeds 3G 68
LS21: Otley 9M 17
(off North Av.)
Hamilton Vw. LS7: Leeds 2G 68
Hammer La. WF4: N Sha, S Comn 6J 127
Hammerstone Leach La. HX5: Ell 6C 118
Hammerstones Rd. HX5: Ell 5C 118
Hammerton Cl. HX5: Ell 4E 118
Hammerton Dr. LS25: Gar 9A 72
Hammerton Farm Av. WF4: Ryh 9J 145
Hammerton Gro. LS28: Pud 7C 66
WF4: Ryh 9J 145
Hammerton Rd. HD2: Hud 9M 119
Hammerton St. BD3: B'frd 5E 6 (8E 64)
LS28: Pud 7B 66
Hammerton Ter. OL14: Tod 6K 93
Hammond Cres. BD11: Drig 6A 84
Hammond Pl. BD9: B'frd 3M 63
Hammond Rd. WF11: Knot 9C 110
Hammonds Landing HX6: Sow B 8J 97
Hammond Sq. BD9: B'frd 3M 63
Hammond St. HD2: Hud 1N 137
HX1: Hal 6M 97
Hammond's Yd. HD1: Hud 5C 8
Hamm Strasse BD1: B'frd 2B 6 (6C 64)
Hampden Cl. WF11: Ferr 7A 110
Hampden Pl. BD5: B'frd 1B 82
HX1: Hal 4H 7 (5A 98)
Hampden St. BD5: B'frd 1B 82
Hamper La. S36: Hoy, Pen 9J 173
HAMPOLE 8G 164
Hampole Balk La. DN6: Skel 8K 165
Hampole Fld. La. DN6: Hamp 8E 164
Hampole Rd. LS23: B Spa 9D 24
Hampole Way LS23: B Spa 9D 24
Hampshire Cl. LS29: I'ly 5J 15
WF8: Pon 9L 109
Hampshire St. HD5: Hud 4B 138
Hampson St. WF17: Bat 5D 102
Hampton Ct. *LS29: I'ly* 5F 14
(off Grove Rd.)
Hampton Cres. LS9: Leeds 8M 5
Hampton Pl. BD10: B'frd 7F 46
LS9: Leeds 8M 5 (7H 69)

Hampton St.—Hatfield Rd.

Hampton St. HX1: Hal 7M 97
Hampton Ter. LS9: Leeds 8M 5 (7H 69)
Hamworth Dr. BD22: Oak 5D 42
Hamza St. WF17: Bat 8E 102
Hanbury Gdns. LS25: Gar 6N 71
Hanby Av. WF6: Alt 9G 107
Hanby Cl. HD8: Fen B 6G 139
Hand Bank La. WF14: Mir 9L 121
Hand Carr La. HX2: Lud F 5B 96
Handel St. BD7: B'frd 7A 64
HD7: Golc 6C 136
Handel Ter. HD5: Hud 5B 138
(off The Avenue)
Handsworth Rd. WF2: Wake 6J 143
Hanging Ga. La. BD22: Oxen 1A 60
HANGING HEATON 1H 123
Hanging Heaton Golf Course 2H 123
Hanging Lee HX6: Ripp 8N 115
Hanging Royd HD7: Golc 6C 136
Hangingroyd Cl. HX7: Heb B 1H 95
Hangingroyd La. HX7: Heb B 1H 95
Hangingroyd Rd. HX7: Heb B 1H 95
Hanging Stone Rd. HD4: Hud 2L 153
Hangingstone Rd. LS29: I'ly 6J 15
Hanging Stones La. HX6: Ripp 7E 116
Hanging Wood Way BD19: Cleck 2G 101
Hangram St. HD6: Brigh 1N 119
Hanley Rd. LS27: Morl 1K 103
Hannah Ct. BD12: Wyke 1A 100
Hanover Av. LS3: Leeds 4B 4 (6C 68)
Hanover Cl. BD8: B'frd 5M 63
Hanover Ct. LS27: Morl 8L 85
WF13: Dew 2D 122
(off Russell St.)
Hanover Cres. WF8: Pon 6J 129
Hanover Gdns. BD5: B'frd 9B 64
LS29: Burl W 9C 16
WF13: Dew 3E 122
Hanover Grn. WF11: Cri S 4K 131
Hanover Ho. BD1: B'frd 4D 6
(off Chapel St.)
HX2: Hal 7L 97
LS19: Yead 9N 31
(off Harper La.)
Hanover La. LS3: Leeds 5C 4 (6C 68)
Hanover Mt. LS3: Leeds 4A 4 (5C 68)
Hanover Pl. LS25: Kip 4B 90
WF11: B'ton 3B 110
WF17: Bat 7G 102
Hanover Sq. BD1: B'frd 1A 6 (6B 64)
BD12: Wyke 1A 100
LS3: Leeds 4B 4 (5C 68)
Hanover St. BD21: Keigh 9J 27
HX1: Hal 5J 7 (6A 98)
HX6: Sow B 8K 97
WF2: Wake 6J 125
WF13: Dew 3E 122
WF17: Bat 7F 102
Hanover Wlk. LS3: Leeds 5C 4 (6C 68)
Hanover Way LS3: Leeds 5B 4 (6C 68)
LS29: Burl W 9C 16
Hansby Av. LS14: Leeds 1C 70
Hansby Bank LS14: Leeds 1C 70
Hansby Cl. LS14: Leeds 2C 70
Hansby Dr. LS14: Leeds 1C 70
Hansby Gdns. LS14: Leeds 2C 70
Hansby Ga. LS14: Leeds 1C 70
Hansby Grange LS14: Leeds 1C 70
Hansby Pl. LS14: Leeds 1C 70
Hansel Fold HX4: Bark 8F 116
Hanson Av. WF6: Norm 2J 127
Hanson Ct. BD12: Wyke 2A 100
WF6: Norm 2J 127
Hanson Fold BD12: Wyke 1A 100
Hanson La. HD1: Hud 8K 137
HD4: Hud 8K 137
HX1: Hal 3G 7 (5L 97)
Hanson Mt. BD12: Wyke 2A 100
Hanson Pl. BD12: Wyke 1A 100
Hanson Rd. HD6: Ras 3K 119
HD9: Mel 8B 152
Hanworth Rd. BD12: Low M 7B 82
Hapsburg Ct. BD5: B'frd 8A 6
Harbeck Dr. BD16: Har 6A 44
Harborough Grn. BD10: B'frd 7J 47
Harbour Cres. BD6: B'frd 5M 81
Harbour Pk. BD6: B'frd 5L 81
Harbour Rd. BD6: B'frd 5L 81
Harclo Rd. BD21: Keigh 8L 27
Harcourt Av. BD13: Thorn 7C 62
Harcourt Dr. LS27: Morl 8J 85
LS29: Add 9M 11
Harcourt Pl. LS1: Leeds 6A 4 (6B 68)
Harcourt St. BD4: B'frd 7C 82
WF2: Wake 6H 125
Hardaker Cft. BD17: Bail 5M 45
Hardaker La. BD17: Bail 5M 45
Hardaker's App. WF7: Ackw 5F 146
Hardaker's La. WF7: Ackw 4E 146
Hardaker St. BD8: B'frd 6B 64
Hardcastle Av. WF8: Pon 2J 129
Hardcastle Craggs 4D 76
Hardcastle La. WF4: Flock 7G 141
HARDEN 6A 44
Harden & Bingley Caravan Pk. BD16: Har 8N 43
Harden Brow La. BD16: Har 5N 43
Harden Gro. BD10: B'frd 3J 65
BD21: Keigh 2L 43
Harden Hill Rd. HD9: H'frth, Mel 9D 152
Harden La. BD15: Wils 8A 44
BD16: Har 8A 44
Harden Moss Rd. HD9: H'frth, Mel 1D 168
Harden Rd. BD16: Bgly, Har 6A 44
BD21: Keigh 2L 43
Hardgate La. BD21: Cros R 8F 42
Hardhill Ho's. BD16: Har 6A 44
(off Wilsden Rd.)
Hardie Rd. WF4: H'cft 9K 145
Hardingley HD8: Shel 9M 155
Hardings La. LS29: I'ly 3E 14
LS29: Midd 1E 14
Hard Ings Rd. BD21: Keigh 7J 27
Hardistry Dr. WF8: Pon 3H 129
Hardistry-le-Court WF8: Pon 9N 109
Hardknot Cl. BD7: B'frd 2K 81
Hardnaze BD22: Oxen 5N 59
Hard Nese La. BD22: Oxen 5N 59
Hard Platts La. HX4: Stainl 8M 117
Hardrow Grn. LS12: Leeds 9N 67
Hardrow Gro. LS12: Leeds 9N 67
Hardrow Rd. LS12: Leeds 9M 67
Hardrow Ter. LS12: Leeds 9N 67
Hardwick Cl. HX1: Hal 5L 97
S71: Roys 5E 160
WF4: Ryh 1H 161
Hardwick Ct. WF8: Pon 4J 129
Hardwick Cres. WF8: Pon 6K 129
Hardwick Cft. LS7: Leeds 9F 50
Hardwick La. WF4: W Har 1B 146
Hardwick Rd. WF7: F'stne 7C 128
WF8: Pon 8M 129
(Darrington Rd.)
WF8: Pon, E Hard 5K 129
(Ackworth Rd.)
Hardwick St. BD21: Keigh 1G 43
Hardy Av. BD6: B'frd 5A 82
LS27: Chur 5M 85
Hardy Ct. LS27: Morl 9L 85
Hardy Cft. WF1: Wake 5L 9 (5M 125)
Hardy Gro. LS11: Leeds 2C 86
Hardy Pl. HD6: Brigh 7K 99
Hardy St. BD4: B'frd 6C 6 (8D 64)
BD6: B'frd 4A 82
HD6: Brigh 9N 99
LS11: Leeds 2C 86
LS27: Morl 9L 85
Hardy Ter. BD6: B'frd 4A 82
(off Hardy St.)
LS11: Leeds 2D 86
Hardy Vw. LS11: Leeds 2C 86
Harebell Av. WF2: Wake 4G 125
Hare Ct. OL14: Tod 6J 93
HARE CROFT 2N 61
Harecroft Rd. LS21: Otley 8L 17
Haredon Cl. S75: Map 7J 159
Hare Farm Av. LS12: Leeds 7G 67
Hare Farm Cl. LS12: Leeds 6G 67
Harefield Cl. BD20: East 3A 26
Harefield Dr. WF17: Bat 3D 102
Harefield E. LS15: Leeds 7N 69
Harefield Pk. HD2: Hud 9H 119
Harefield Rd. WF8: Pon 3M 129
Harefield W. LS15: Leeds 7N 69
Harehill OL14: Tod 6J 93
Harehill Av. OL14: Tod 6J 93
Harehill Cl. BD10: B'frd 6F 46
Hare Hill Edge BD22: Old 6J 41
Harehill Rd. BD10: B'frd 6F 46
HAREHILLS 4K 69
Harehills Av. LS7: Leeds 2G 68
LS8: Leeds 2G 68
HAREHILLS CORNER 2H 69
Harehills La. BD22: Old 6M 41
LS7: Leeds 1G 68
LS8: Leeds 2J 69
LS9: Leeds 2J 69
Harehills Pk. Av. LS9: Leeds 4K 69
Harehills Pk. Cotts. LS9: Leeds 4L 69
Harehills Pk. Rd. LS9: Leeds 4K 69
Harehills Pk. Ter. LS9: Leeds 4K 69
Harehills Pk. Vw. LS9: Leeds 4K 69
Harehills Pl. LS8: Leeds 3H 69
Harehills Rd. LS8: Leeds 2H 69
Harehill St. OL14: Tod 6J 93
Hare La. LS28: Pud 9B 66
Hare Pk. Av. WF15: Liv 8G 100
Hare Pk. Cl. WF15: Liv 8G 100
Hare Pk. Dr. WF15: Liv 8G 101
Hare Pk. Grange WF15: Liv 8G 101
(off Hare Pk. La.)
Hare Pk. La. WF4: Croft 3G 144
WF15: Liv 9G 100
Hare Pk. Mt. LS12: Leeds 7F 66
Hare Pk. Vw. WF4: Croft 2G 145
Hares Av. LS8: Leeds 2H 69
Hares Mt. LS8: Leeds 2G 69
Hares Rd. LS8: Leeds 2G 69
Hares Ter. LS8: Leeds 2H 69
Hare St. HX1: Hal 5M 97
Hares Vw. LS8: Leeds 2H 69
HAREWOOD 2J 35
Harewood Av. BD20: East 3A 26
HX2: Hal 4K 97
LS17: Bard, Hare 2K 35
WF6: Norm 9K 107
WF8: Pon 4L 129
WF16: Heck 9B 102
Harewood Cl. WF11: Ferr 8B 110
Harewood Ct. LS14: Leeds 2B 70
LS17: Leeds 6F 50
Harewood Cres. BD22: Oak 4E 42
Harewood Dr. BD20: East 3A 26
WF2: Wren 2F 124
Harewood Ga. LS17: Hare 1J 35
Harewood Gro. WF16: Heck 9B 102
Harewood House 2G 34
Harewood House Bird Garden 2F 34
Harewood La. WF8: Thpe A 9D 148
WF9: Upt 9D 148
(Sheepwalk La.)
WF9: Upt 1B 164
(Wrangbrook Rd.)
Harewood M. LS17: Hare 1J 35
Harewood Mt. HD9: Mel 7E 152
WF8: Pon 3L 129
HAREWOOD PARK 3L 129
Harewood Pl. HX2: Hal 6L 97
Harewood Ri. BD22: Oak 4F 42
WF8: Pon 3L 129
Harewood Rd. BD22: Oak 5E 42
LS17: E Kes 1B 36
LS21: Arth 2M 33
LS22: Coll 1B 36
WF1: Wake 3A 126
Harewood St. BD3: B'frd 3F 6 (7F 64)
(not continuous)
LS2: Leeds 6G 5 (6E 68)
Harewood Vw. WF8: Pon 3L 129
Harewood Way LS13: Leeds 6E 66
Hargrave Cres. LS29: Men 4D 30
Hargreaves Av. WF3: S'ley 7N 105
Hargreaves Cl. LS27: Morl 6J 85
Hargreaves St. LS26: Rothw 8A 88
Hargreaves Yd. WF4: Horb 1C 142
Harker Rd. BD12: Low M 6A 82
Harker St. WF11: Knot 8G 110
Harker Ter. LS28: Stan 5A 66
Harland Cl. BD2: B'frd 4C 64
Harland Sq. LS2: Leeds 3C 68
(off Moorfield St.)
Harlech Av. LS11: Leeds 3D 86
Harlech Cres. LS11: Leeds 3D 86
Harlech Gro. LS11: Leeds 3D 86
Harlech Mt. LS11: Leeds 3D 86
Harlech Pk. Ct. LS11: Leeds 3D 86
Harlech Rd. LS11: Leeds 3D 86
Harlech St. LS11: Leeds 3D 86
Harlech Ter. LS11: Leeds 3D 86
Harlech Way LS25: Gar 7B 72
Harley Cl. LS13: Leeds 6D 66
Harley Ct. LS13: Leeds 6D 66
Harley Dr. LS13: Leeds 6D 66
Harley Gdns. LS13: Leeds 6D 66
Harley Grn. LS13: Leeds 6D 66
Harley Pl. HD6: Ras 2M 119
(off Harley St.)
Harley Ri. LS13: Leeds 6D 66
Harley Rd. LS13: Leeds 6D 66
Harley St. HD6: Ras 2M 119
OL14: Tod 6K 93
Harley Ter. LS13: Leeds 6D 66
Harley Vw. LS13: Leeds 6D 66
Harley Vs. OL14: Tod 6K 93
(off Wood St.)
Harley Wlk. LS13: Leeds 6D 66
HARLEY WOOD 5J 93
Harley Wood OL14: Tod 4G 93
Harley Wood Vw. OL14: Tod 4G 93
(off Church St.)
Harlington Ct. LS27: Morl 2K 103
Harlington Rd. LS27: Morl 2K 103
Harlock St. WF1: Wake 9N 125
Harlow Ct. LS8: Leeds 8L 51
Harlow Rd. BD7: B'frd 9M 63
Harmby Cl. DN6: Skel 7L 165
Harmon Cl. BD4: B'frd 5G 82
Harmony Pl. BD13: Que 2B 80
Harold Av. LS6: Leeds 4A 68
Harold Ct. BD12: Low M 8A 82
Harold Gdns. LS27: Morl 9M 85
Harold Gro. LS6: Leeds 4A 68
Harold Mt. LS6: Leeds 4A 68
Harold Pl. BD18: Ship 7L 45
LS6: Leeds 4A 68
Harold Rd. LS6: Leeds 4A 68
Harold Sq. LS6: Leeds 4A 68
Harold St. BD16: Bgly 3D 44
LS6: Leeds 4A 68
Harold Ter. LS6: Leeds 4A 68
Harold Vw. LS6: Leeds 4A 68
Harold Wlk. LS6: Leeds 4A 68
Harold Wilson Ho. WF6: Norm 2H 127
Harpe Inge HD5: Hud 3C 138
Harper Av. BD10: B'frd 6F 46
Harper Cres. BD10: B'frd 6G 46
Harper Ga. BD4: B'frd 1K 83
Harper Gro. BD10: B'frd 6F 46
Harper La. LS19: Yead 1M 47
Harper Rock LS19: Yead 1M 47
(off Harper La.)
Harper Royd HX6: Sow B 1J 117
Harper Royd La. HX6: Sow B 1H 117
Harper St. LS2: Leeds 7H 5 (7F 68)
Harper Ter. LS19: Yead 1M 47
(off Harper La.)
Harp La. BD13: Que 3C 80
Harp Rd. HD3: Hud 5G 137
Harrap St. WF2: Wake 4F 124
Harrier Cl. BD8: B'frd 7G 63
Harriers Ct. WF9: S Elm 8M 163
Harrier Way LS27: Morl 9N 85
Harriet St. BD8: B'frd 6N 63
HD6: Brigh 8M 99
LS7: Leeds 3F 68
Harrington Ct. HD9: Mel 8E 152
Harris Ct. BD7: B'frd 2M 81
Harrison and Potter Trust Homes, The
LS2: Leeds 4G 5
Harrison Cres. LS9: Leeds 5M 69
Harrison La. HD9: Mel 5D 152
Harrison Potter Trust Almshouses
LS2: Leeds 3C 68
(off Raglan Rd.)
Harrison Rd. HX1: Hal 5K 7 (6B 98)
WF4: Croft 1F 144
Harrison's Av. LS28: Stan 4C 66
Harrison St. BD16: Bgly 5F 44
LS1: Leeds 5G 5 (6E 68)
OL14: Tod 3D 92
WF1: Wake 6K 9 (6L 125)
Harris St. BD1: B'frd 4E 6 (7E 64)
BD16: Bgly 5F 44
Harrogate Av. BD3: B'frd 4E 64
Harrogate Pde. LS17: Leeds 5F 50
Harrogate Pl. BD3: B'frd 4E 64
Harrogate Rd. BD2: B'frd 4F 64
BD10: B'frd 2H 65
LS7: Leeds 7E 50
LS16: B'hpe 8B 32
LS17: Hare 4F 20
LS17: Huby, N Rig, Wee 8G 19
LS17: Leeds 6E 50
LS19: B'hpe, Yead 8B 32
LS19: Raw, Yead 3M 47
(not continuous)
LS21: Cast, Leat 8G 19
LS22: Weth 1G 22
Harrogate St. BD3: B'frd 4E 64
Harrogate Ter. BD3: B'frd 4E 64
Harrogate Vw. LS17: Leeds 2L 51
Harrop Av. LS27: Morl 2L 103
HARROP EDGE 4B 62
Harrop Gro. LS27: Morl 2L 103
Harrop La. BD15: Wils 3N 61
Harrop Ter. LS27: Morl 2L 103
Harrop Well La. WF8: Pon 2K 129
Harrowby Cres. LS16: Leeds 8L 49
Harrowby Rd. LS16: Leeds 8L 49
Harrows, The BD20: E Mor 8A 28
Harrow St. HX1: Hal 5M 97
WF9: S Elm 6L 163
Harry La. BD14: Clay 1G 80
BD22: Oxen 3C 60
Harry St. BD4: B'frd 2G 82
Harthill LS27: Gil 6G 85
Harthill Av. LS27: Gil 6G 84
Harthill Cl. LS27: Gil 6G 84
Harthill La. LS27: Gil 6G 84
Harthill Paddock LS27: Gil 6G 85
Harthill Pde. LS27: Gil 6G 85
(off Town St.)
Harthill Ri. LS27: Gil 6G 84
Hartington St. BD21: Keigh 8J 27
WF17: Bat 9F 102
Hartington Ter. BD7: B'frd 9M 63
Hartland Rd. BD4: B'frd 1J 83
Hartley Av. LS6: Leeds 2C 68
Hartley Bank La. HX3: North 2H 99
Hartley Bus. Pk. BD4: B'frd 8H 65
Hartley Cl. WF9: S Elm 5N 163
Hartley Ct. WF15: Liv 9L 101
Hartley Cres. LS6: Leeds 2C 68
Hartley Gdns. LS6: Leeds 2D 68
Hartley Gro. LS6: Leeds 2C 68
WF13: Dew 1F 122
Hartley Hill LS2: Leeds 4G 5 (5E 68)
Hartley Pk. Av. WF8: Pon 3H 129
Hartley Pk. Vw. WF8: Pon 3H 129
Hartley Pl. LS27: Morl 1L 103
Hartley's Bldgs. LS27: Morl 1L 103
Hartley Sq. BD13: Que 2N 79
Hartley's Sq. BD20: E Mor 7C 28
Hartley St. BD4: B'frd 9E 64
HX1: Hal 4N 97
LS27: Chur 6L 85
LS27: Morl 9L 85
WF7: F'stne 7C 128
(off Priory Rd.)
WF10: C'frd 5C 108
WF13: Dew 2F 122
Hartley's Yd. LS12: Leeds 7L 67
Hartley Ter. WF7: F'stne 7C 128
Hartley Wood Cotts. LS25: M'fld 6J 73
Hartlington Ct. BD17: Bail 4C 46
Hartman Pl. BD9: B'frd 4L 63
Hart Rhydding La. LS29: Add 2M 13
HARTSHEAD 1G 121
Hartshead Ct. WF15: Liv 8F 100
Hartshead Hall La. WF15: Liv 3G 120
Hartshead La. WF15: Liv 1F 120
HARTSHEAD MOOR SERVICE AREA 7E 100
HARTSHEAD MOOR SIDE 6E 100
HARTSHEAD MOOR TOP 6D 100
Harts Hole HD7: Golc 5N 135
Hart St. BD7: B'frd 1M 81
HD4: Hud 8M 137
Hartwell Rd. LS6: Leeds 4A 68
Harvelin Pk. OL14: Tod 7B 94
Harvest Cl. LS25: Gar 9A 72
WF8: Pon 9L 109
Harvest Ct. HX1: Hal 4H 7 (5A 98)
Harvest Cft. LS29: Burl W 8B 16
Harvest M. WF5: Oss 8A 124
Harvest Mt. BD10: B'frd 7D 46
Harvey Royd HD5: Hud 6E 138
Harvey St. WF1: Wake 8N 125
Harwill App. LS27: Chur 6M 85
Harwill Av. LS27: Chur 6M 85
Harwill Cft. LS27: Chur 6M 85
Harwill Gro. LS27: Chur 6M 85
Harwill Ri. LS27: Chur 6M 85
Harwill Rd. LS27: Chur 6M 85
Harwin Cl. HX3: North 1F 98
Harwood Cl. HD5: Hud 6C 138
(Almondbury Bank)
HD5: Hud 5D 138
(Greenhead La.)
WF2: Wake 1N 143
Haselden Cres. WF2: Wake 6G 124
Haselden Rd. WF2: Wake 6F 124
Haslam Cl. BD3: B'frd 2F 6 (6E 64)
Haslam Gro. BD18: Ship 9C 46
Haslegrave Pk. WF4: Crig 6G 143
Haslemere Cl. BD4: B'frd 2H 83
Haslewood Cl. LS9: Leeds 6L 5 (6G 69)
Haslewood Ct. LS9: Leeds 6M 5 (6H 69)
Haslewood Dene LS9: Leeds 6M 5 (6H 69)
Haslewood Dr. LS9: Leeds 5L 5 (6G 69)
Haslewood Gdns. LS9: Leeds 6M 5 (6H 69)
Haslewood Grn. LS9: Leeds 6M 5 (6H 69)
Haslewood M. LS9: Leeds 6M 5 (6H 69)
Haslewood Pl. LS9: Leeds 6M 5 (6H 69)
Haslewood Sq. LS9: Leeds 6M 5 (6H 69)
Haslewood Vw. LS9: Leeds 5M 5 (6H 69)
Hasley Rd. LS29: Burl W 9D 16
Haslingden Dr. BD9: B'frd 4L 63
Hassocks La. HD9: Hon 5H 153
Hassocks Rd. HD9: Mel 6A 152
Haste St. WF10: C'frd 4B 108
Hastings Av. BD5: B'frd 3B 82
WF2: Wake 9L 125
Hastings Ct. LS17: Shad 3N 51
LS22: Coll 9J 23
WF6: Alt 8F 106
Hastings Cres. WF10: C'frd 5H 109
Hastings Gro. WF2: Wake 9M 125
Hastings Pl. BD5: B'frd 2B 82
Hastings St. BD5: B'frd 3B 82
Hastings Ter. BD5: B'frd 3B 82
Hastings Wlk. WF10: C'frd 5H 109
Hastings Way HX1: Hal 8J 7 (7A 98)
LS22: Coll 9G 23
Hatcham Cl. BD15: All 7F 62
Hatchet La. BD12: O'haw 9E 82
Hatfeild Ct. WF1: Wake 2J 9 (4L 125)
Hatfeild St. WF1: Wake 2J 9 (4L 125)
Hatfield Cl. S71: Smit 9N 159
Hatfield Gdns. S71: Roys 5C 160
Hatfield Pl. WF4: H'cft 8L 145
Hatfield Rd. BD2: B'frd 4F 64

Hatfield Vw.—Heather Va.

Hatfield Vw. WF1: Wake 1L 125
Hathaway Av. BD9: B'frd 3J 63
Hathaway Cotts. WF5: Oss 7N 123
Hathaway Dr. LS14: Leeds 6C 52
Hathaway La. LS14: Leeds 7C 52
Hathaway M. LS14: Leeds 6C 52
Hathaway Wlk. LS14: Leeds 7C 52
Hathenshaw La. LS29: Den 1K 15
Hathershelf La. HX2: Lud F 6A 96
Hatters Fold HX1: Hal 4M 7 (5C 98)
(not continuous)
Hatton Cl. BD6: B'frd 5B 82
Haugh End La. HX6: Sow B 9G 96
Haugh Rd. OL14: Tod 6N 93
HAUGHS GREEN 5A 136
Haugh Shaw Cft. HX1: Hal 7G 7 (7N 97)
Haugh Shaw Rd. HX1: Hal 7G 7 (7N 97)
Haugh Shaw Rd. W. HX1: Hal 7M 97
Haughs La. HD3: Hud 3E 136
Haughs Rd. HD3: Hud 3F 136
Hauxley Ct. LS29: I'ly 4J 15
Hauxwell Cl. DN6: Skel 7L 165
Hauxwell Dr. LS19: Yead 1M 47
Havelock Sq. BD13: Thorn 8D 62
Havelock St. BD7: B'frd 1L 81
BD13: Thorn 8D 62
WF13: Raven 6B 122
Haven, The BD10: B'frd 9G 47
LS15: Leeds 6E 70
Haven Chase LS16: Leeds 4H 49
Haven Cl. HX3: North 1F 98
LS16: Leeds 3J 49
Haven Ct. LS16: Leeds 4J 49
WF8: Pon 6H 129
Haven Cft. LS16: Leeds 4J 49
Haven Gdns. LS16: Leeds 4H 49
Haven Gth. LS16: Leeds 4H 49
Haven Grn. LS16: Leeds 4H 49
Haven La. HX7: Heb B 4J 95
Haven Mt. LS16: Leeds 4H 49
Haven Ri. LS16: Leeds 4H 49
Haven St. OL14: Tod 7L 93
Haven Vw. LS16: Leeds 4H 49
HAVERCROFT 9K 145
Havercroft LS12: Leeds 9H 67
WF5: Oss 6A 124
WF17: Bat 7F 102
(off Hanover St.)
Havercroft & Ryhill Sports & Youth Cen. 9J 145
Havercroft Gdns. LS12: Leeds 9H 67
Havercroft Grn. WF4: H'cft 1J 161
Havercroft La. WF8: D'ton 5C 130
Havercroft Ri. S72: S Hien 3M 161
Havercroft Way WF17: Bat 7C 102
Haverdale Rd. WF4: H'cft 9K 145
Haverlands, The WF9: Hems 3E 162
Haveroid La. WF4: Crig 6G 143
Haveroid Way WF4: Crig 5H 143
Haverthwaites Dr. LS25: Aber 6E 54
Haverthwaites La. LS25: Aber 6E 54
Havertop La. WF7: A'ton 1N 127
Haw Av. LS19: Yead 8N 31
Hawber Cote Dr. BD20: Sils 7F 12
Hawber Cote La. BD20: Sils 7F 12
Hawber La. BD20: Sils 8F 12
Haw Cliff La. HD4: Thurs 8D 154
Haw Cote HD7: Slait 1K 151
Hawes Av. BD5: B'frd 3A 82
HD3: Hud 4G 136
Hawes Cl. WF10: C'frd 4H 109
(not continuous)
Hawes Cres. BD5: B'frd 3A 82
(not continuous)
Hawes Dr. BD5: B'frd 3A 82
Hawes Gro. BD5: B'frd 3A 82
Hawes Mt. BD5: B'frd 3A 82
Hawes Rd. BD5: B'frd 3A 82
Hawes Ter. BD5: B'frd 3A 82
Haweswater Cl. LS22: Weth 4J 23
Haweswater Pl. WF11: Knot 2D 130
Haw Hill Vw. WF6: Norm 9K 107
Hawkcliffe Vw. BD20: Sils 8C 12
Hawke Av. WF16: Heck 8B 102
Hawke Way BD12: Low M 7C 82
Hawkhill Av. LS15: Leeds 4C 70
LS20: Guis 8H 31
Hawkhill Dr. LS15: Leeds 3C 70
Hawkhill Gdns. LS15: Leeds 3C 70
Hawkhills LS7: Leeds 8G 50
Hawkhurst Rd. LS12: Leeds 8M 67
Hawkingcroft Rd. WF4: Horb 1B 142
Hawkins Dr. LS7: Leeds 1F 4 (4E 68)
Hawkroyd Bank Rd. HD4: Neth 2K 153
Hawksbridge La. BD22: Oxen 3A 60
HAWKS CLOUGH 3L 95
Hawkshead Cl. BD5: B'frd 8A 6 (9C 64)
Hawkshead Cres. LS14: Leeds 3A 70
Hawkshead Dr. BD5: B'frd 8A 6 (9C 64)
Hawkshead Wlk. BD5: B'frd 8A 6 (9C 64)
Hawkshead Way BD5: B'frd 8A 6
Hawksley Ct. LS27: Morl 6J 85
Hawk's Nest Gdns. E. LS17: Leeds 3F 50
Hawk's Nest Gdns. Sth. LS17: Leeds 3F 50
Hawk's Nest Gdns. W. LS17: Leeds 3F 50
Hawk's Nest Ri. LS17: Leeds 3F 50
Hawkstone Av. LS20: Guis 9G 31
Hawkstone Dr. BD20: Keigh 7G 26
Hawkstone Vw. LS20: Guis 9G 31
Hawk St. BD21: Keigh 8K 27
(off Parson St.)
Hawkswood Av. BD9: B'frd 3L 63
LS5: Leeds 8H 49
Hawkswood Cres. LS5: Leeds 8H 49
Hawkswood Gro. LS5: Leeds 8H 49
Hawkswood Mt. LS5: Leeds 8H 49
Hawkswood Pl. LS5: Leeds 9H 49
Hawkswood St. LS5: Leeds 9J 49
Hawkswood Ter. LS5: Leeds 9J 49
Hawkswood Vw. LS5: Leeds 8H 49
HAWKSWORTH
LS5 .... 9H 49
LS20 .... 8D 30
Hawksworth Av. LS20: Guis 9H 31
Hawksworth Cl. LS29: Men 5E 30
Hawksworth Commercial Pk. LS13: Leeds 5F 66
Hawksworth Dr. LS20: Guis 9H 31
LS29: Men 4D 30
Hawksworth Gro. LS5: Leeds 9G 49
Hawksworth La. LS20: Guis 8D 30
Hawksworth Rd. BD17: Bail 1A 46
LS18: Hors 8G 48
Hawksworth St. LS29: I'ly 5G 14
Haw La. LS19: Yead 9M 31
Hawley Cl. LS27: Morl 2J 103
Hawley Ter. BD10: B'frd 2J 65
Hawley Way LS27: Morl 2J 103
HAWORTH 8C 42
Haworth Cl. HX1: Hal 8J 7 (7A 98)
WF14: Mir 5K 121
Haworth Ct. LS19: Yead 9M 31
(off Chapel La.)
Haworth Gro. BD9: B'frd 3K 63
Haworth La. LS19: Yead 9M 31
Haworth M. BD22: Haw 8C 42
Haworth Rd. BD9: B'frd 3K 63
BD13: Cull 9G 42
BD15: All 3F 62
BD15: Wils 2C 62
(Bob La.)
BD15: Wils 2M 61
(Cullingworth Rd.)
BD21: Keigh 9F 42
BD22: Cros R 7E 42
WF17: Birs 2C 102
Haworth Station
Keighley & Worth Valley Railway 8C 42
Haw Pk. La. WF2: Col H 8C 144
WF4: Wint 7F 144
Hawthorn Av. LS19: Yead 9M 31
LS21: Pool 2G 33
WF4: Croft 1F 144
WF11: Knot 9C 110
WF17: Bat 9D 102
Hawthorn Cl. HD6: Clift 9A 100
LS29: Add 1K 13
Hawthorn Ct. WF4: Croft 1F 144
Hawthorn Cres. BD17: Bail 4B 46
LS7: Leeds 8F 50
LS19: Yead 9M 31
Hawthorn Cft. WF3: Loft 3L 105
Hawthorn Dr. BD10: B'frd 8G 47
LS13: Leeds 9A 48
LS19: Yead 8N 31
Hawthorne Av. BD3: B'frd 6J 65
BD18: Ship 1B 64
LS22: Weth 2L 23
WF9: Hems 3D 162
WF10: C'frd 6H 109
Hawthorne Cl. HD8: Fen B 7H 139
LS27: Gil 6G 85
WF2: Kirk 9D 104
WF4: Flock 7G 140
Hawthorne Cotts. WF5: Oss 7A 124
Hawthorne Ct. S75: Kex 9D 158
WF11: Knot 7G 110
Hawthorne Cres. DN6: Skel 8M 165
WF9: Hems 3C 162
Hawthorne Dr. LS27: Gil 6H 85
Hawthorne Gdns. LS16: Leeds 2L 49
Hawthorne Gro. LS29: Burl W 9D 16
WF2: Wake 4G 125
Hawthorne Mills LS12: Leeds 1K 85
(off Cobden Rd.)
Hawthorne Mt. WF6: Norm 4J 127
Hawthorne Ri. LS14: Leeds 7D 52
WF7: Ackw 5D 146
Hawthorne St. BD20: Sils 8D 12
S72: Shaf 6K 161
Hawthorne Ter. HD4: Hud 6H 137
WF2: Wake 4G 125
WF5: Oss 8A 124
Hawthorne Vw. LS27: Gil 6H 85
Hawthorne Way BD20: E Mor 8D 28
HD8: Shel 6K 155
S72: Shaf 6K 161
Hawthorn Gro. LS13: Leeds 1A 66
LS26: Rothw 9A 88
WF7: Ackw 5F 146
Hawthorn La. BD19: Cleck 3G 101
LS7: Leeds 8F 50
Hawthorn M. LS14: Leeds 7C 52
Hawthorn Mt. LS7: Leeds 8F 50
Hawthorn Pk. LS14: Leeds 7B 52
Hawthorn Pl. OL14: Tod 6K 93
Hawthorn Rd. HD7: Slait 8M 135
LS7: Leeds 8F 50
LS19: Yead 9M 31
Hawthorns, The WF1: Out 7M 105
WF5: Oss 8A 124
WF8: Pon 8N 109
Hawthorn Sq. WF3: E Ard 4G 105
Hawthorn St. BD3: B'frd 6J 65
HX1: Hal 7N 97
HX3: Hip 4J 99
Hawthorn Ter. HD1: Hud 1C 8
HX1: Hal 7N 97
(off Hawthorn St.)
LS25: Gar 9K 71
Hawthorn Va. LS7: Leeds 8F 50
Hawthorn Vw. BD17: Bail 4B 46
LS7: Leeds 8F 50
Hawthorn Way HX2: Illing 6K 79
Hawtop La. WF4: Wool 3H 159
Haw Vw. LS19: Yead 8N 31
Hayburn Gdns. WF17: Bat 7E 102
Hayburn Rd. WF17: Bat 7D 102
Haycliffe Av. BD7: B'frd 3M 81
Haycliffe Dr. BD7: B'frd 3L 81
Haycliffe Gro. BD7: B'frd 3M 81
HAYCLIFFE HILL 3N 81
Haycliffe Hill Rd. BD5: B'frd 3N 81
Haycliffe La. BD5: B'frd 3M 81
BD6: B'frd 3M 81
Haycliffe Mill Fold BD7: B'frd 3M 81
Haycliffe Rd. BD5: B'frd 2N 81
Haycliffe Ter. BD5: B'frd 2N 81
Hayclose Mead BD6: B'frd 7M 81
Hay Cft. BD10: B'frd 7D 46
Hayden St. BD3: B'frd 8F 64
Haydn Av. WF3: S'ley 6N 105
Haydn Cl. LS27: Morl 9K 85
Haydn Ct. LS27: Morl 9K 85
Haydn Pl. BD13: Que 4B 80
Haydn's Ter. LS28: Stan 4B 66
Hayfield Av. HD3: Hud 3F 136
LS23: B Spa 9C 24
Hayfield Cl. BD17: Bail 2C 46
HD9: Scho 4B 170
WF6: Norm 3J 127
Hayfields, The BD22: Haw 7C 42
Hayfields Cl. BD22: Keigh 2E 42
Hayfield Ter. LS12: Leeds 8M 67
Hayfield Way WF7: Ackw 5D 146
Haygill Nook BD20: Sils 8D 10
Hayhills La. BD20: Sils 5D 12
Hayhills Rd. BD20: Sils 7E 12
Hayleigh Av. LS13: Leeds 3F 66
Hayleigh Mt. LS13: Leeds 3F 66
Hayleigh St. LS13: Leeds 3F 66
Hayleigh Ter. LS13: Leeds 4F 66
Hayne La. WF4: Over 5H 141
Haynes St. BD21: Keigh 1K 43
Hays La. HX2: Mix 6H 79
Hayson Cl. WF12: Dew 2J 123
Haythorns Av. BD20: Sils 8D 12
Haythorns Mt. BD20: Sils 8D 12
Hayton Dr. LS22: Weth 5N 23
Hayton Wood Vw. LS25: Aber 7E 54
Haywain, The LS29: I'ly 6J 15
Haywood Av. HD3: Hud 4H 137
Hazebrouck Dr. BD17: Bail 3N 45
Hazel Av. LS14: Leeds 7D 52
WF12: Dew 4L 123
Hazel Bank WF2: Wake 3G 125
Hazel Beck BD16: Cot 7E 44
Hazel Cl. BD11: B'haw 7L 83
WF12: Dew 4L 123
Hazel Ct. HD4: Hud 7E 136
HX2: Illing 1L 97
(off Cumberland Cl.)
LS26: Rothw 9A 88
WF2: Wake 3J 125
Hazel Cres. WF12: Dew 4L 123
Hazel Cft. BD18: Ship 9A 46
Hazelcroft BD2: B'frd 2H 65
Hazeldene BD13: Que 5C 80
Hazeldene Cotts. LS22: Sick 4D 22
Hazel Dr. HX2: Illing 6K 79
HX4: Bark 8F 116
WF12: Dew 4L 123
Hazel Gdns. WF10: C'frd 6K 109
HAZEL GROVE 8D 136
Hazel Gro. HD2: Fix 6N 119
HD7: Linth 8D 136
HX3: Hip 5M 99
WF4: Flock 7G 140
WF8: Pon 1L 129
WF17: Bat 8D 102
Hazelheads BD17: Bail 3A 46
Hazelhurst Av. BD16: Cot 7E 44
Hazelhurst Brow BD9: B'frd 4J 63
Hazelhurst Ct. BD3: B'frd 7G 65
BD9: B'frd 4J 63
LS28: Pud 7C 66
Hazelhurst Gro. BD13: Que 6C 80
Hazelhurst Rd. BD9: B'frd 4J 63
BD13: Que 6C 80
Hazelhurst Ter. BD9: B'frd 4J 63
Hazel La. DN6: Hamp 7F 164
WF3: E Ard 4H 105
WF11: Knot 3E 130
Hazelmere Av. BD16: Cot 7F 44
Hazel M. LS25: Gar 7A 72
Hazel Mt. BD18: Ship 8A 46
Hazel Ri. LS26: Meth 3K 107
Hazel Rd. WF11: Knot 9D 110
Hazeltine Ct. WF6: Norm 2K 127
Hazelton Cl. BD18: Ship 9C 46
Hazel Wlk. BD9: B'frd 4J 63
Hazelwood Av. BD20: Rid 7M 27
LS25: Gar 9A 72
Hazelwood Castle 3H 55
Hazelwood Ct. HX1: Hal 8L 7 (7B 98)
WF1: Out 7M 105
Hazelwood Gdns. WF9: Hems 3E 162
Hazelwood Rd. BD9: B'frd 3H 63
WF1: Out 7M 105
WF9: Kins 9B 146
Hazelwood St. OL14: Tod 7K 93
Hazledene Cres. S72: Shaf 8L 161
Hazledene Rd. S72: Shaf 8K 161
Headfield La. WF12: Dew 6F 122
Headfield Rd. HD4: Hud 7M 137
WF12: Dew 5F 122
(not continuous)
Headfield Vw. WF12: Dew 7G 122
HEADINGLEY 1N 67
Headingley 2N 67
Headingley Av. LS6: Leeds 1M 67
Headingley Ct. LS6: Leeds 2B 68
Headingley Cres. LS6: Leeds 2N 67
Headingley Golf Course 2N 49
HEADINGLEY HILL 2A 68
Headingley Ho. BD3: B'frd 6K 65
(off Chapman Rd.)
Headingley La. LS6: Leeds 2A 68
Headingley M. WF1: Wake 2K 125
Headingley Mt. LS6: Leeds 1M 67
Headingley Office Pk. LS6: Leeds 2B 68
Headingley Ri. LS6: Leeds 3B 68
(off Welton Rd.)
Headingley Station (Rail) 2L 67
Headingley Ter. LS6: Leeds 2B 68
Headingley Vw. LS6: Leeds 2N 67
Headland Ct. LS25: Gar 6M 71
(off Aberford Rd.)
Headland Gro. BD6: B'frd 4L 81
Headland La. WF12: Dew 5J 123
Headlands WF15: Liv 9L 101
Headlands Av. WF5: Oss 6M 123
Headlands Cl. WF15: Liv 9M 101
Headlands Gro. WF5: Oss 6M 123
Headlands La. WF8: Pon 2J 129
WF11: Knot 8D 110
Headlands Pk. WF5: Oss 6M 123
Headlands Rd. HD1: Hud 2B 8 (3M 137)
WF5: Oss 6M 123
WF8: Pon 3K 129
WF15: Liv 8L 101
Headlands Rd. Bus. Pk. WF15: Liv 8L 101
Headlands St. WF15: Liv 9L 101
Headlands Wlk. WF5: Oss 6M 123
Headley Cotts. LS24: Tad 8G 39
Headley Golf Course 9B 62
Headley La. BD13: Thorn 1B 80
LS23: B'ham 6D 38
Headrow, The LS1: Leeds 5E 4 (6D 68)
Headrow Ct. BD13: Thorn 8C 62
(off Thornton Rd.)
HEADWALL GREEN 7A 136
Headway Bus. Cen. BD4: B'frd 3G 83
Headway Bus. Pk. WF2: Wake 8K 125
Headwell La. LS24: Saxt 9N 55
Heald Ct. HD9: Holm 5J 169
Healdfield Rd. WF10: C'frd 4E 108
Heald La. S75: Caw 5J 173
Healds Av. WF15: Liv 8M 101
Healds Rd. WF13: Dew 1D 122
Heald St. WF10: C'frd 4F 108
Heald Ter. HX4: Bark 6G 117
Healdwood Cl. WF10: C'frd 4G 109
Healdwood Rd. WF10: C'frd 4G 109
HEALEY
WF5 .... 8M 123
WF17 .... 7C 102
Healey HD8: Shel 5J 155
Healey Av. BD16: Bgly 5F 44
Healey Cl. WF17: Bat 7C 102
Healey Cres. WF5: Oss 8N 123
Healey Cft. WF3: W Ard 5D 104
Healey Cft. La. WF3: E Ard 5D 104
Healey Dr. WF5: Oss 8N 123
Healey Grn. La. HD5: K'htn 4K 139
Healey Ho's. HD4: Neth 5F 152
Healey La. BD16: Bgly 5F 44
WF12: Bries 4C 140
WF17: Bat 8C 102
(not continuous)
Healey La. Bus. Cen. WF17: Bat 7C 102
Healey New Mills WF5: Oss 9L 123
Healey Old Mills WF5: Oss 8L 123
Healey Rd. WF5: Oss 8M 123
Healey St. WF17: Bat 7C 102
Healey Vw. WF5: Oss 7N 123
Healey Wood Bottom HD6: Ras 2N 119
(off Gooder La.)
Healey Wood Cres. HD6: Ras 3M 119
Healey Wood Gdns. HD6: Ras 3M 119
Healey Wood Gro. HD6: Ras 3N 119
Healey Wood Rd. HD6: Ras 3M 119
Heap La. BD3: B'frd 3E 6 (7E 64)
(not continuous)
Heap St. BD3: B'frd 3E 6 (7E 64)
HX3: Hal 2B 98
HEATH 6B 126
Heath Av. HX3: Hal 8A 98
Heathcliff BD22: Haw 8B 42
Heathcliffe Cl. WF17: Birs 1C 102
Heathcliffe Ct. LS27: Morl 9G 85
(off Bruntcliffe Rd.)
Heathcliffe M. BD22: Haw 8C 42
Heathcliff M. BD13: Thorn 8D 62
Heath Cl. HD7: Linth 2D 152
WF12: Dew 3L 123
Heath Common Caravan Pk.
WF1: Wake 7B 126
Heathcote Av. LS14: T'ner 2G 53
Heathcote Cl. S75: W Gran 6G 158
Heathcote Ri. BD22: Haw 7D 42
Heath Cres. HX1: Hal 8K 7 (7B 98)
LS11: Leeds 2A 86
Heathcroft Bank LS11: Leeds 3A 86
Heathcroft Cres. LS11: Leeds 3A 86
Heathcroft Dr. LS11: Leeds 3A 86
Heathcroft Lawn LS11: Leeds 3A 86
Heathcroft Ri. LS11: Leeds 3A 86
Heathcroft Va. LS11: Leeds 3A 86
Heathdale Av. HD2: Hud 1L 137
Heath Dr. LS23: B Spa 1B 38
Heather Av. HD9: Mel 8D 152
Heather Bank HX2: Hal 7M 97
(off Darcey Hey La.)
OL14: W'den 2K 113
Heather Bank Av. BD22: Oak 3F 42
Heather Bank Cl. BD13: Cull 1J 61
Heather Cl. WF1: Out 7M 105
WF5: Oss 8B 124
WF9: S Kirk 6K 163
Heather Ct. BD16: Bgly 2F 44
HD3: Hud 2E 136
LS29: I'ly 6G 14
WF1: Out 7N 105
WF10: C'frd 7B 108
WF17: Birs 2B 102
Heather Cft. WF4: S Comn 8K 127
Heathercroft LS7: Leeds 9G 51
Heatherdale Cl. HX3: Hal 3M 97
Heatherdale Ct. WF3: Ting 4A 104
Heatherdale Dr. WF3: Ting 4A 104
Heatherdale Fold WF3: Ting 4A 104
Heatherdale Rd. WF3: Ting 4N 103
Heather Dr. HX2: Mt T 1G 97
Heatherfield Cres. HD1: Hud 4J 137
Heatherfield Rd. HD1: Hud 4J 137
Heather Fold HD8: Skelm 7C 156
Heather Gdns. LS13: Leeds 6H 67
LS14: S'cft 9D 36
Heather Gro. BD9: B'frd 3G 63
BD21: Keigh 8F 26
LS13: Leeds 5H 67
Heathergrove Fold HD5: Hud 3B 138
Heatherlands Av. BD13: Denh 4K 61
Heather Pl. BD13: Que 3A 80
Heather Ri. LS29: Burl W 9C 16
Heather Rd. BD17: Bail 3B 46
HD9: Mel 8C 152
Heathers, The WF4: S Comn 8K 127
Heatherside BD17: Bail 2N 45
Heatherstones HX3: Hal 8H 7 (8A 98)
Heather Va. LS14: S'cft 9C 36

Heather Vw.—Heys Ho.

Heather Vw. BD16: Bgly 2J 45
HX5: Ell 4G 119
WF4: S Comn 8K 127
WF5: Oss 6N 123
Heatherville Cl. BD16: Bgly 2H 45
HEATHFIELD 4F 118
Heathfield LS16: Leeds 3K 49
WF14: Mir 5K 121
Heathfield Av. HX5: Ell 4G 118
Heathfield Cl. BD16: Bgly 3F 44
WF3: W Ard 5B 104
Heathfield Gro. BD7: B'frd 1K 81
HX3: Hal 8L 7
Heathfield Ind. Est. HX5: Ell 4F 118
Heathfield La. BD11: B'haw 9L 83
LS23: B Spa 9B 24
Heathfield M. HD7: Golc 6D 136
Heathfield Pl. HX3: Hal 8L 7 (8B 98)
Heathfield Ri. HX6: Rish 1C 134
Heathfield Rd. HD7: Golc 6D 136
Heathfield St. HX5: Ell 5F 118
Heathfield Ter. HX3: Hal 8L 7 (8B 98)
LS6: Leeds 9N 49
Heathfield Wlk. LS16: Leeds 2K 49
Heath Gdns. HX3: Hal 8B 98
Heath Gro. BD20: E Mor 8C 28
HD4: Hud 8K 137
LS11: Leeds 2A 86
LS28: Pud 8N 65
WF17: Bat 7J 103
Heath Hall HX1: Hal 8K 7 (7B 98)
Heath Hall Av. BD4: B'frd 4F 82
Heath Hall Cotts. WF1: Hea 6B 126
Heath Hill HD7: Golc 4B 136
Heath Hill Rd. HX2: Hal, Mt T 4G 97
Heath Ho. La. HD7: Golc 6A 136
Heath Ho. Mill HD7: Golc 6A 136
Heath Ho's. HD7: Golc 6A 136
Heath La. HX3: Hal 8L 7 (8B 98)
Heath Lea HX1: Hal 7K 7 (7B 98)
Heath Mnr. WF1: Hea 7C 126
Heathmoor Cl. BD10: B'frd 7E 46
HX2: Illing 7K 79
Heathmoor Mt. HX2: Illing 7K 79
Heathmoor Pk. Rd. HX2: Illing 6K 79
Heathmoor Way HX2: Illing 7K 79
Heath Mt. HX1: Hal 8J 7 (8A 98)
LS11: Leeds 2A 86
Heath Mt. Rd. HD6: Ras 3M 119
Heathness Rd. LS29: Add 9K 11
Heath Pk. LS29: I'ly 6E 14
Heath Pk. Av. HX1: Hal 8L 7 (7B 98)
Heath Pl. LS11: Leeds 2A 86
Heath Ri. LS11: Leeds 3A 86
Heath Rd. BD3: B'frd 5F 64
HD7: Linth 2D 152
HX1: Hal 8K 7 (8B 98)
HX3: Hal 8K 7 (8B 98)
LS11: Leeds 2A 86
WF12: Dew 3L 123
(not continuous)
Heath Royd HX3: Hal 8B 98
Heath St. BD3: B'frd 7G 64
BD16: Bgly 4F 44
HX3: Hal 8J 7 (8A 98)
WF15: Liv 1M 121
Heath Ter. BD3: B'frd 7F 64
Heath Vw. HX1: Hal 6L 7
Heath Vw. St. HX1: Hal 6L 7 (6C 98)
(not continuous)
Heath Vs. HX3: Hal 8K 7 (8B 98)
Heath Wlk. WF12: Dew 3L 123
Heathwood Dr. HD7: Golc 5B 136
Heathy Av. HX2: Hal 8N 79
Heathy La. HX2: Hal 7M 79
HEATON 3M 63
Heaton Av. BD19: Cleck 5G 101
BD20: Rid 9B 28
HD5: K'htn 1G 139
LS12: Leeds 9M 67
WF12: Dew 3H 123
Heaton Cl. BD16: Bgly 3G 44
BD17: Bail 2N 45
Heaton Ct. *BD16: Bgly 5E 44*
(off Bk. Unity St. Nth.)
LS14: Leeds 9A 52
(off Kingsdale Ct.)
Heaton Cres. BD16: Bgly 3G 45
BD17: Bail 2N 45
Heaton Dr. BD16: Bgly 3G 44
BD17: Bail 2N 45
HD5: K'htn 9G 120
Heaton Fold La. HD1: Hud 5J 137
Heaton Gdns. HD1: Hud 4J 137
Heaton Grange WF17: Bat 9H 103
HEATON GROVE 2N 63
Heaton Gro. BD9: B'frd 2N 63
BD18: Ship 8A 46
BD19: Cleck 5G 101
Heaton Hill BD6: B'frd 6K 81
Heaton Lodge WF17: Birs 2B 102
Heaton Moor Rd. HD5: K'htn 1G 139
Heaton Pk. Dr. BD9: B'frd 3L 63
Heaton Pk. Rd. BD9: B'frd 3L 63
Heaton Pk. Vs. HD1: Hud 4K 137
Heaton Rd. BD8: B'frd 3M 63
BD9: B'frd 3M 63
HD1: Hud 5J 137
WF17: Bat 5F 102
Heaton Royd *BD16: Bgly 4G 44*
(off Fernbank Dr.)
HEATON ROYDS 1L 63
Heaton Royds La. BD9: B'frd, Ship 1L 63
BD18: Ship 1L 63
Heaton's Ct. LS1: Leeds 8F 4 (7E 68)
HEATON SHAY 1K 63
Heaton St. BD4: B'frd 7E 6 (9E 64)
BD19: Cleck 4H 101
HD6: Brigh 1M 119
WF7: Ackw 5E 146
Heatons Yd. HD6: Ras 2N 119
Heator La. HD8: Up C 1L 171
Hebble Brook Bus. Pk. HX2: Mix 6J 79
Hebble Brook Cl. HX2: Mix 9J 79
Hebble Cotts. HX2: Hal 3L 97
Hebble Ct. HD9: H'frth 2M 169
HX2: Mix 9K 79
WF12: Dew 7G 122
Hebble Dean HX2: Hal 3M 97
Hebble Dr. HD9: H'frth 1M 169
HEBBLE END 1G 95
Hebble End HX7: Heb B 1G 95
Hebble Gdns. HX2: Hal 3L 97
Hebble La. HD9: H'frth 2M 169
HD9: Mel 9C 152
HX3: Hal 3M 97
Hebble Mt. HD9: Mel 8D 152
Hebble Oval WF9: S Elm 7A 164
Hebble Row BD22: Haw 6C 42
Hebble St. HD1: Hud 1C 8 (2N 137)
WF13: Raven 6C 122
Hebble Va. Dr. HX2: Hal 2L 97
Hebble Vw. HX3: Hal 9D 98
(Cinderhills La.)
HX3: Hal 2L 97
(Meadow Dr.)
WF12: Dew 5G 123
Hebble Way WF9: S Elm 7A 164
Hebble Wharf WF1: Wake 8L 9 (7M 125)
Hebb Vw. BD6: B'frd 3K 81
Hebden App. LS14: Leeds 9C 52
HEBDEN BRIDGE 1H 95
Hebden Bridge Alternative Technology Cen. *1G 95*
(off Hebble End)
Hebden Bridge Golf Course 1L 95
Hebden Bridge Little Theatre 1H 95
Hebden Bridge Picture House 1H 95
Hebden Bri. Rd. BD22: Oxen 9L 59
Hebden Bridge Station (Rail) 2H 95
Hebden Bridge Vis. & Canal Cen. 1H 95
Hebden Chase LS14: Leeds 9C 52
Hebden Cl. LS14: Leeds 9C 52
Hebden Ct. *HD3: Hud 3G 136*
(off Chesil Bank)
Hebden Grn. LS14: Leeds 9C 52
Hebden Gro. HX7: Heb B 8H 77
Hebden Path LS14: Leeds 9C 52
Hebden Pl. LS14: Leeds 9C 52
Hebden Rd. BD22: Haw, Oxen 1D 60
WF1: Wake 3N 125
Hebden Ter. HX7: Heb B 6H 77
Hebden Vw. *HX7: Wads 7J 77*
(off Akroyd La.)
Hebden Wlk. LS14: Leeds 9C 52
Heber Cl. BD20: Sils 9F 12
Heber's Ghyll Dr. LS29: I'ly 6C 14
Heber's Gro. LS29: I'ly 5D 14
Heber St. BD21: Keigh 1H 43
HECKMONDWIKE 9A 102
Heckmondwike Rd. WF13: Dew 1B 122
Heckmondwyke Sports Cen. 8A 102
Hector Cl. BD6: B'frd 4A 82
Heddle Ri. WF2: Wake 4G 124
Heddon Cl. BD5: B'frd 8A 6 (9C 64)
Heddon Gro. BD5: B'frd 8B 6 (9C 64)
Heddon Pl. LS6: Leeds 9A 50
Heddon St. LS6: Leeds 9A 50
Heddon Wlk. BD5: B'frd 8A 6
Hedge Cl. BD8: B'frd 5J 63
Hedge La. S75: Dart 9F 158
(not continuous)
Hedge Nook BD12: Wyke 9A 82
Hedge Side BD8: B'frd 6K 63
Hedge Top La. HX3: North 2G 98
Hedge Way BD8: B'frd 5K 63
Hedley Chase LS12: Leeds 7A 68
Hedley Cres. WF1: Wake 9K 105
Hedley Gdns. LS12: Leeds 7A 68
Hedley Grn. LS12: Leeds 7A 68
Heeley Rd. WF2: Wake 6J 143
Heidelberg Rd. BD9: B'frd 4M 63
HEIGHT 1C 152
Height Grn. HX6: Sow B 8H 97
Height La. BD22: Oxen 4D 60
BD23: Drau 8D 10
HX6: Ripp 7B 116
Heights HX6: Ripp 8D 116
Heights, The HD9: Scho 5A 170
Heights Bank LS12: Leeds 7J 67
Heights Cl. LS12: Leeds 7H 67
Heights Ct. WF15: Liv 7F 100
Heights Dr. HD7: Linth 2C 152
LS12: Leeds 6H 67
Heights East, The LS12: Leeds 7J 67
Heights Gth. LS12: Leeds 7H 67
Heights Grn. LS12: Leeds 7J 67
Heights La. BD9: B'frd 3J 63
BD16: Bgly 7E 28
BD20: Sils 5A 12
LS12: Leeds 7J 67
WF16: Heck 9B 102
Heights Pde. LS12: Leeds 7H 67
Heights Rd. HX2: Midg 1L 95
HX7: Heb B, Myth, Wads 1L 95
Heights Wlk. LS12: Leeds 7J 67
Heights Way LS12: Leeds 7H 67
Heights West, The LS12: Leeds 7H 67
Height Wlk. HX6: Ripp 8E 116
Helena Ct. LS25: Kip 4N 89
Helena Pl. LS25: Kip 5N 89
Helena St. LS25: Kip 5N 89
Helena Way BD4: B'frd 5G 82
Helene Ct. HD3: Hud 2D 136
Helen Rose Ct. BD18: Ship 6C 46
Helens Ct. WF8: Pon 1K 129
Helen St. BD18: Ship 7L 45
HD1: Hud 7K 137
Helen Ter. HD6: Brigh 9L 99
Helios 47 LS25: Gar 6B 72
Hellen Edge HX6: Sow B 1H 117
Hellewell St. BD6: B'frd 6L 81
Helliwells Row WF4: Horb 1N 141
Hell La. WF1: Hea 7D 126
WF4: N Sha 7D 126
Hellwood La. LS14: S'cft 9D 36
HELME 5C 152
Helme La. HD5: Hud 6G 121
HD9: Mel 6C 152
Helme Pk. HD9: Mel 6C 152
Helmet La. HD9: Mel 8C 152
Helm La. HX6: Tri 2C 116
Helmsley Ct. LS10: Leeds 9E 86
Helmsley Dr. LS16: Leeds 8L 49
Helmsley Rd. LS16: Leeds 8L 49
LS23: B Spa 1C 38
WF2: Wake 1A 144
Helmsley St. BD4: B'frd 8F 6 (1E 82)
Helston Cft. LS10: Leeds 8C 86
Helston Gth. LS10: Leeds 8C 86
Helston Grn. LS10: Leeds 8C 86
Helston Gro. HD9: Hon 5K 153
Helston Pl. LS10: Leeds 8C 86
Helston Rd. LS10: Leeds 7C 86
WF6: Norm 9J 107
Helston Sq. LS10: Leeds 7B 86
Helston St. LS10: Leeds 7B 86
Helston Wlk. LS10: Leeds 8C 86
(not continuous)
Helston Way LS10: Leeds 7C 86
Helted Way HD5: Hud 7C 138
Hembrigg Gdns. LS27: Morl 2K 103
Hembrigg Ter. LS27: Morl 2K 103
Heming's Way WF9: S Elm 6A 164
Hemingway Cl. LS10: Leeds 1G 87
WF10: C'frd 7K 109
Hemingway Gth. LS10: Leeds 2G 87
Hemingway Grn. LS10: Leeds 2G 87
Hemingway Rd. BD10: B'frd 7H 47
Hemishor Dr. LS26: Gt P 5M 89
Hemmingway Cl. WF4: Ryh 9K 145
Hemsby Gro. *BD21: Keigh 3H 43*
(off Hemsby St.)
Hemsby Rd. WF10: C'frd 5C 108
Hemsby St. BD21: Keigh 3H 43
HEMSWORTH 2D 162
Hemsworth By-Pass S72: B'ley 5B 162
WF9: Hems 8F 146
Hemsworth La. WF9: Fitz 6A 146
HEMSWORTH MARSH 9F 146
Hemsworth Rd. WF9: Hems, S Kirk 4E 162
Hemsworth Sports Cen. 1E 162
Hemsworth Water Pk. 9C 146
Henacre Wood Ct. BD13: Que 6D 80
Henage St. BD13: Que 4C 80
Henbury St. LS7: Leeds 3J 5 (5F 68)
Henconner Av. LS7: Leeds 9E 50
Henconner Cres. LS7: Leeds 9E 50
Henconner Dr. LS7: Leeds 9E 50
Henconner Gdns. LS7: Leeds 9E 50
Henconner Gth. LS7: Leeds 9E 50
Henconner Gro. LS7: Leeds 9E 50
Henconner La. LS7: Leeds 9E 50
LS13: Leeds 5H 67
Henconner Rd. LS7: Leeds 9E 50
Hendal La. WF2: Wake 6J 143
Henderson Av. WF6: Norm 3J 127
Henderson Glen S71: Roys 6B 160
Henderson Pl. BD6: B'frd 4A 82
Hendford Dr. BD3: B'frd 3F 6 (6E 64)
Hen Holme La. BD20: Sils 1E 26
Henley Av. BD5: B'frd 3C 82
LS13: Leeds 4F 66
LS19: Raw 4A 48
WF12: T'hill 9G 123
Henley Cl. LS19: Raw 4A 48
Henley Ct. BD5: B'frd 3D 82
Henley Cres. LS13: Leeds 4F 66
LS19: Raw 4A 48
Henley Cft. HD5: Hud 4C 138
Henley Dr. LS19: Raw 4N 47
WF7: F'stne 8D 128
Henley Gro. BD5: B'frd 3C 82
LS13: Leeds 4F 66
Henley Hill LS19: Raw 4N 47
Henley Mt. LS19: Raw 4A 48
Henley Pl. LS13: Leeds 4F 66
Henley Rd. BD5: B'frd 3D 82
LS13: Leeds 4F 66
WF12: T'hill 9H 123
Henley St. LS13: Leeds 4F 66
Henley Ter. LS13: Leeds 4F 66
Henley Vw. LS13: Leeds 4F 66
LS19: Raw 4N 47
Henley Vs. *LS19: Raw 4N 47*
(off Well La.)
Henna Cl. BD7: B'frd 3K 81
Henrietta St. WF17: Bat 7F 102
Henry Av. LS12: Leeds 9M 67
WF4: H'cft 1K 161
Henry Cl. S72: Shaf 6K 161
Henry Frederick Av. HD4: Neth 3H 153
Henry Gro. LS28: Pud 7A 66
Henry Moore Ct. S75: W Gran 6F 158
WF10: C'frd 5H 109
Henry Moore Foundation Studio, The *1K 7*
(within Dean Clough)
Henry Moore Institute 5E 4
Henry Moore Pl. WF10: C'frd 6E 108
Henry Pl. LS27: Morl 9K 85
Henry Price Bldgs. LS2: Leeds 1B 4 (4C 68)
Henry Ralph Av. HD4: Hud 9H 137
Henry St. BD13: Thorn 8C 62
BD14: Clay 1H 81
BD21: Keigh 9J 27
HD1: Hud 5A 8 (4M 137)
HD6: Brigh 8M 99
HX1: Hal 5J 7 (6A 98)
WF2: Wake 5J 125
WF17: Bat 1F 122
Henry Ter. LS19: Yead 9K 31
HENSHAW 1L 47
Henshaw Av. LS19: Yead 1M 47
Henshaw Cres. LS19: Yead 1M 47
Henshaw La. LS19: Yead 2L 47
Henshaw M. LS19: Yead 2M 47
Henshaw Oval LS19: Yead 1M 47
Henshaw Rd. OL14: W'den 2J 113
Henshaw Woods OL14: W'den 1J 113
Henson Gro. WF10: C'frd 5H 109
Hepley Vw. WF4: Flock 8F 140
Heppenstall St. HD4: Hud 8C 8 (6N 137)
Hepton Ct. LS9: Leeds 6K 69
Hepton Dr. HX7: Hept 9G 76
Hepton Edge HX7: Hept 9F 76
HEPTONSTALL 8G 76
Heptonstall Mus. 8G 76
Heptonstall Rd. HX7: Heb B, Hept 9G 77
Heptonstall Social & Bowling Club *9G 77*
(off Acres La.)
HEPWORTH 6C 170
Hepworth Av. LS27: Chur 5L 85
Hepworth Cl. S75: W Gran 6G 158
WF14: Mir 5M 121
Hepworth Cres. HD9: H'wth 5C 170
LS27: Chur 5L 85
Hepworth Dr. WF14: Mir 5N 121
Hepworth La. WF14: Mir 5M 121
Hepworth Rd. HD9: Jack B 5C 170
Hepworth St. WF10: C'frd 3F 108
Herbalist St. LS12: Leeds 8A 68
Herbert Pl. BD3: B'frd 6J 65
Herbert St. BD5: B'frd 1B 82
BD14: Clay 2H 81
BD16: Bgly 4F 44
BD16: Cot 9G 45
BD18: Ship 6L 45
HX1: Hal 6M 97
WF10: C'frd 5D 108
Herdwick Vw. BD20: Rid 7A 28
Hereford Cl. WF9: Hems 1D 162
Hereford St. LS12: Leeds 6M 67
Hereford Way BD4: B'frd 1E 82
Heritage Ct. HD9: Mel 6C 152
Heritage M. HX1: Hal 5M 7
Heritage Pk. BD16: Bgly 1F 44
Heritage Rd. WF17: Bat 8F 102
Heritage Way BD22: Oak 5B 42
Hermitage Pk. HD8: Fen B 8J 139
HERMIT HOLE 5G 43
Hermit St. BD22: Keigh 5G 42
Hermon Av. HX1: Hal 6N 97
Hermon Gro. HX1: Hal 6N 97
Hermon Rd. LS15: Leeds 5C 70
Hermon St. LS15: Leeds 5C 70
Heron Cl. BD13: Que 3B 80
BD16: Har 6N 43
BD20: Stee 2B 26
LS17: Leeds 3H 51
WF13: Raven 5B 122
Heron Ct. LS27: Morl 9N 85
Heron Dr. WF2: Wake 5L 143
Heron Gro. LS17: Leeds 3H 51
Herons, The HX6: Tri 2E 116
Herries Ct. *LS29: Men 4F 30*
(off Leathley Rd.)
Herriot M. WF10: C'frd 7K 109
Herriot Way WF1: Wake 1K 125
Herschel Rd. BD8: B'frd 7J 63
Hertford Chase LS15: Leeds 8D 70
Hertford Cl. LS15: Leeds 8E 70
Hertford Cft. LS15: Leeds 8E 70
Hertford Fold LS15: Leeds 8D 70
Hertford Lawn LS15: Leeds 8D 70
Heseltine Cl. WF6: Norm 2H 127
Heseltine La. HX7: Crag V 8H 95
Heshbon St. BD4: B'frd 2G 82
Hesketh Av. LS5: Leeds 1K 67
WF3: Ting 4N 103
Hesketh Farm Pk. 2H 11
Hesketh La. WF3: Ting, W Ard 4N 103
Hesketh Mt. LS5: Leeds 1K 67
Hesketh Pl. HX3: Hip 5M 99
LS5: Leeds 1K 67
Hesketh Rd. LS5: Leeds 1K 67
Hesketh Ter. LS5: Leeds 2K 67
Hesley Rd. WF2: Wake 5K 143
Hessel Ct. WF8: Pon 3H 129
HESSLE 3E 146
Hessle WF4: W Har 3E 146
Hessle Av. LS6: Leeds 3A 68
Hessle Comn. La. WF4: W Har 4D 146
Hessle La. WF4: W Har 1D 146
Hessle Mt. LS6: Leeds 3A 68
Hessle Pl. LS6: Leeds 3A 68
Hessle Rd. LS6: Leeds 3A 68
Hessle St. LS6: Leeds 3A 68
Hessle Ter. LS6: Leeds 3A 68
Hessle Vw. LS6: Leeds 3A 68
Hessle Wlk. LS6: Leeds 3A 68
Hetchell Ct. LS17: Bard 5E 36
Hetchell Vw. LS17: Bard 6E 36
Hetchell Wood Nature Reserve 6G 36
Hetton Ct. LS10: Leeds 2F 86
Hetton Dr. BD3: B'frd 8H 65
Hetton Rd. LS8: Leeds 1K 69
Heuthwaite Av. LS22: Weth 5N 23
Heuthwaite La. LS22: Weth 5A 24
Hever Gro. HD5: Hud 3E 138
Hew Clews BD7: B'frd 2K 81
HEWENDEN 2M 61
Hewenden Vw. BD13: Denh 4K 61
Hew Royd BD10: B'frd 7D 46
Hexham Grn. HD3: Hud 5E 136
HEY BECK 7M 103
Heybeck La. WF12: Dew 7M 103
Heybeck Wlk. BD4: B'frd 3K 83
Hey Cliff Rd. HD9: H'frth 3N 169
Hey Cres. HD9: Mel 7C 152
(not continuous)
Heydon Cl. LS6: Leeds 6B 50
Heyford Ct. BD2: B'frd 3B 64
Heygate Cl. BD17: Bail 3B 46
Heygate La. BD17: Bail 3B 46
LS23: B'ham 5E 38
Hey Head La. OL14: Tod 3L 93
Hey La. BD22: S'bury 7N 41
HD3: Scam 3J 135
HD4: Farn T, Hud 2N 153
HD5: Hud 7B 138
Hey Moor La. HD8: Shel 7L 155
Heyroyd La. HD7: Slait 2L 151
Heys Av. BD13: Thorn 8E 62
Hey's Bldgs. WF6: Alt 8H 107
Heys Cl. WF11: Knot 8E 110
Heys Cres. BD13: Thorn 8F 62
Heys Gdns. HD9: T'bdge 9N 153
Heysham Dr. BD4: B'frd 2J 83
Heys Ho. *HX2: Hal 4L 97*
(off Cross St. W.)

Hey Slack La.—High Wicken Cl.

Hey Slack La. HD8: Cumb 6G 171
Heys La. HD7: Slait 8K 135
HX2: Wain 7B 78
HX6: Rish 9D 116
Heys Rd. HD9: H'frth, T'bdge 9A 154
Hey St. BD7: B'frd 7B 64
HD6: Brigh 8N 99
OL14: Tod 7L 93
Hey Top BD22: Old 7K 41
Heywood Bottom HD8: Den D 2D 172
Heywood Cl. HX3: North 2F 98
Heywood Ct. HX3: North 2F 98
Heywood M. HX1: Hal 4L 97
Heywoods HD7: Linth 1A 152
Hick La. WF17: Bat 7G 102
Hicks La. LS26: Meth 1L 107
Hick St. BD1: B'frd 4D 6 (7D 64)
Hi Energy Dance, Health & Fitness Cen.
Keighley 9H 27
(off Russell St.)
Higgin Chamber HX2: Lud F 7C 96
Higgin La. HX3: Sou 7D 98
HIGH ACKWORTH 2G 146
Higham HX6: Sow B 8C 96
Higham and Dob La. HX6: Sow B 8C 96
Higham Vw. S75: Kex 9F 158
Higham Way LS25: Gar 6N 71
High Ash BD18: Ship 8C 46
High Ash Av. HD8: Clay W 7K 157
LS17: Leeds 2G 51
High Ash Cl. WF4: Not 2A 160
High Ash Cres. LS17: Leeds 2G 51
High Ash Dr. LS17: Leeds 2G 51
High Ash Mt. LS17: Leeds 2G 51
High Ash Pk. BD15: All 5E 62
High Bank App. LS15: Leeds 7E 70
High Bank Cl. HX5: Ell 4H 119
LS15: Leeds 7E 70
LS29: Add 1M 13
High Bank Gdns. LS15: Leeds 7F 70
High Bank Ga. LS15: Leeds 7E 70
High Bank La. BD18: Ship 9J 45
High Bank Pl. LS15: Leeds 7E 70
High Banks Cl. BD20: Rid 6M 27
High Bank St. *LS28: Fars* *3A 66*
(off Low Bank St.)
High Bank Vw. LS15: Leeds 7E 70
High Bank Way LS15: Leeds 7E 70
High Bentley HX3: She 8K 81
High Binns La. BD22: Oxen 4D 60
Highbridge La. HD8: Clay W 8F 156
Highbridge Ter. BD5: B'frd 4D 82
High Brook Fall WF3: Loft 6L 105
High Brooms HD2: Hud 1K 137
High Brunthwaite BD20: Sils 8G 13
HIGHBURTON 2K 155
Highbury Cl. BD13: Que 5B 80
LS6: Leeds 9A 50
Highbury La. LS6: Leeds 9A 50
Highbury Mt. LS6: Leeds 9A 50
Highbury Pl. LS6: Leeds 9A 50
LS13: Leeds 6D 66
Highbury Rd. LS6: Leeds 9A 50
Highbury St. LS6: Leeds 9A 50
Highbury Ter. LS6: Leeds 9A 50
WF12: Dew *3G 123*
(off Highgate Rd.)
High Busy La. BD10: B'frd 7D 46
BD18: Ship 7C 46
Highclere Ct. WF9: S Elm 6A 164
High Cliffe *LS4: Leeds* *3M 67*
(off St Michael's La.)
Highcliffe Av. HD2: Hud 9L 119
High Cliffe Cl. BD13: Thorn 8D 62
Highcliffe Ct. HX3: She 8G 81
LS22: Weth 4N 23
Highcliffe Dr. HX2: Hal 5K 97
Highcliffe Ind. Est. LS27: Morl 8H 85
Highcliffe Rd. LS27: Morl 9J 85
WF17: Bat 9F 102
High Cliffe Ter. LS22: Weth 4M 23
High Cl. HD5: Hud 7C 138
HD7: Linth 1D 152
LS19: Raw 4M 47
LS20: Guis 8F 30
S75: Kex 8F 158
WF5: Oss 2N 123
WF12: Dew 4J 123
High Cote BD20: Rid 6K 27
High Ct. HX7: Hept 7E 76
LS2: Leeds 7H 5 (7F 68)
High Ct. La. LS2: Leeds 7H 5 (7F 68)
High Crest HD7: Linth 8D 136
High Cft. BD13: Que 4D 80
HD9: U'thng 3K 169
HX3: Hal 2M 97
LS29: Add 1M 13
Highcroft LS22: Coll 9H 23
WF17: Bat *9F 102*
(off Highcliffe Rd.)
Highcroft Cl. LS28: Pud 6N 65
Highcroft Cres. HD5: Hud 7D 138
High Cft. Dr. S71: Ath 9A 160
Highcroft Gdns. BD21: Keigh 1M 43
High Cft. Rd. OL14: Tod 6L 93
High Cross La. BD13: Que 6E 80
HX3: She 6E 80
Highdale WF12: Dew 1H 123
Highdale Cft. BD10: B'frd 7F 46
High End BD17: Esh 2G 46
Higher Ashenhurst OL14: Tod 5J 93
Higher Back La. HX7: Blac H 9N 75
Higher Brockwell HX6: Sow B 9F 96
Higher Calderbrook OL15: Lit 9L 113
Higher Calderbrook Rd. OL15: Lit 9L 113
Higher Coach Rd. BD16: Bail, Bgly 5H 45
BD17: Bail 5K 45
Higher Crimsworth HX7: P Wel 5H 77
Higher Downs BD8: B'frd 6J 63
Higher Grange Rd. LS28: Pud 6B 66
Higher Intake Rd. BD2: B'frd 4G 64
Higher Needless HX7: Heb B 1K 95
Higher Pk. Royd Dr. HX6: Ripp 4E 116
Higher Row BD21: Keigh 4K 43
Higher Scholes BD22: Oak 6N 41
Higher School St. BD18: Ship 7L 45
Higher Springhead BD22: Oak 4E 42
Higherwood Cl. BD21: Keigh 9L 27
High Farm Fold WF9: Bads 8L 147
High Farm Mdw. WF9: Bads 8L 147
Highfell Ri. BD22: Keigh 2E 42
High Fernley Ct. BD12: Wyke 9A 82
High Fernley Rd. BD12: Wyke 1M 99
(not continuous)
HIGHFIELD
BD21 9G 26
WF9 3D 162
Highfield BD4: B'frd 4H 83
HD7: Slait 7M 135
HX3: She 8G 81
LS23: B Spa *9E 24*
(off Bridge Rd.)
WF3: Ting 3N 103
Highfield Av. BD10: B'frd 8E 46
HD6: B Bri 4N 99
HD8: Bird E 4L 171
HD9: Mel 6C 152
HX3: She 6J 81
HX4: Gree 4A 118
LS12: Leeds 8M 67
WF8: Pon 4J 129
(Mill Hill La.)
WF8: Pon 8N 109
(Pontefract Rd.)
Highfield Cen. WF9: Hems 3D 162
Highfield Chase WF13: Dew 9C 102
Highfield Cl. BD20: E Mor 7C 28
LS12: Leeds 9N 67
LS27: Gil 6H 85
WF7: F'stne 3D 128
Highfield Ct. BD13: Cull 9K 43
BD22: Oak 5C 42
HD8: Shep 2J 171
LS12: Leeds *9M 67*
(off Highfield Av.)
LS25: Aber 7E 54
WF5: Oss 4N 123
WF10: C'frd 6D 108
WF15: Liv 1K 121
WF17: Bat 7J 103
Highfield Cres. BD9: B'frd 2J 63
BD17: Bail 3A 46
HD9: Mel 6C 152
HX7: Heb B 9H 77
LS12: Leeds 8N 67
LS26: W'frd 6D 88
LS28: Pud 6A 66
WF4: Over 4J 141
WF10: All B *8N 89*
(off Highfield Dr.)
Highfield Dr. BD9: B'frd 2J 63
HX2: Lud 4E 96
LS19: Raw 4N 47
LS25: Gar 9N 71
LS27: Gil 6G 85
WF2: Wake 4G 124
WF10: All B 8N 89
WF15: Liv 8J 101
WF17: Birs 2B 102
Highfield Gdns. BD9: B'frd 3J 63
LS12: Leeds 8M 67
LS27: Gil 6G 85
WF12: T'hill 8G 123
Highfield Gth. LS12: Leeds 9N 67
Highfield Grange WF4: Horb 1C 142
Highfield Grn. LS28: Pud 6A 66
WF10: All B 7N 89
Highfield Gro. BD10: B'frd 9E 46
HX5: Ell 3D 118
WF10: All B 7N 89
High Fld. La. BD22: Oak 4C 42
HX6: Ripp 5D 116
Highfield La. BD20: Sils 7E 12
BD21: Keigh 8G 26
BD22: Oak 5C 42
DN6: Wome 9N 131
HD5: K'htn 5G 139
HD8: Lept 5G 139
HD9: Mel 6B 152
LS15: Bar E 1L 71
LS25: S Mil 1J 91
LS26: W'frd 6D 88
WF13: Dew 9C 102
Highfield M. BD17: Bail 3A 46
BD20: E Mor 7C 28
LS25: Gar 9N 71
Highfield Mt. LS26: Oul 7D 88
WF12: T'hill 1H 141
Highfield Pl. *BD8: B'frd* *5A 64*
(off Church St.)
HX1: Hal 6M 97
(not continuous)
HX6: Sow B *9E 96*
(off Towngate)
LS25: Gar 7M 71
LS27: Morl 1L 103
WF4: Horb 1C 142
WF7: F'stne 3D 128
WF9: Hems 3C 162
WF10: All B 7A 90
Highfield Ri. WF2: Wake 3G 124
WF4: H'cft 8L 145
Highfield Rd. BD2: B'frd 9E 46
BD9: B'frd 1A 64
BD10: B'frd 9E 46
BD19: Cleck 5G 100
BD21: Keigh 9G 26
HD6: Ras 3K 119
HD7: Slait 7M 135
HD8: Kbtn 2J 155
HD9: Mel 6C 152
HX2: Lud 4E 96
HX5: Ell 5E 118
LS13: Leeds 4G 67
LS25: Aber 7E 54
LS28: Pud 6N 65
WF4: Horb 1C 142
WF4: Neth 5N 141
WF8: Pon 5J 129
WF9: Hems 4C 162
High Flds. HX6: Sow B 8L 97
Highfields HD1: Hud 2A 8 (3L 137)
HD9: H'frth 4J 169
S36: Hoy 9J 173
WF4: H'cft 8L 145
WF4: Neth 5N 141
Highfields Ct. HD1: Hud 3A 8
Highfields Rd. HD1: Hud 3A 8 (3L 137)
S75: Kex 9D 158
Highfield St. BD21: Keigh 9H 27
LS13: Leeds 4G 67
LS28: Pud 6N 65
Highfield Ter. BD13: Cull 9K 43
BD13: Que 5C 80
BD16: Bgly 4F 44
BD18: Ship 7K 45
BD19: Cleck 5G 100
HX1: Hal *6M 97*
(off Highfield Pl.)
HX6: Ripp 5E 116
LS19: Raw 4N 47
LS28: Pud 6N 65
WF12: Dew 8G 122
Highfield Vw. *LS12: Leeds* *9N 67*
(off Hardrow Grn.)
LS27: Gil 6H 85
HIGH FLATTS 5N 171
High Fold BD16: Bgly 8D 28
BD17: Bail 3A 46
BD20: E Mor *7C 28*
(off Stocks Hill Cl.)
BD22: Keigh 2F 42
Highfold LS19: Yead 2L 47
High Fold La. BD20: Keigh 6G 27
High Gate HD9: H'frth 6M 169
Highgate BD9: B'frd 2L 63
BD13: Denh 8L 61
Highgate Av. HD8: Lept 7K 139
Highgate Cl. BD13: Que 3H 81
Highgate Cres. HD8: Lept 7J 139
Highgate Dr. HD8: Lept 7K 139
Highgate Gdns. *HX2: Hal* *4K 97*
(off Reservoir Rd.)
Highgate Gro. BD13: Que 3H 81
Highgate La. HD5: K'htn 9H 121
HD8: Lept 7J 139
Highgate Mill Fold BD13: Que 3H 81
Highgate Mills BD13: Que 3H 81
Highgate Rd. BD13: Que 4F 80
WF12: Dew 3G 123
High Gate St. LS10: Leeds 1G 86
Highgate St. WF17: Bat 9J 103
Highgate Ter. *HD8: Lept* *7K 139*
(off Highgate Av.)
WF12: Dew *3G 123*
(off Highgate Rd.)
Highgate Wlk. HD8: Lept 7K 139
High Gate Way S72: Shaf 7K 161
HIGH GREEN 7J 139
High Grn. Ct. *HD8: Kbtn* *3G 154*
(off Storthes Hall La.)
High Grn. Dr. BD20: Sils 7D 12
High Grn. Rd. WF6: Alt 8F 106
Highgrove Ct. WF6: Alt 7G 107
WF6: Norm 3L 127
High Gro. La. HX3: Hal 7D 98
High Gro. Pl. HX3: Hal 7D 98
High Holly Gth. BD21: Keigh 1K 43
High Ho. Av. BD2: B'frd 2E 64
High Ho. Edge HD7: Linth 2A 152
High Ho. La. HD7: Linth 2A 152
HX2: Midg 9C 78
High Ho. M. LS29: Add 1M 13
High Ho. Rd. BD2: B'frd 2E 64
HIGH HOYLAND 8M 157
High Hoyland La. S75: H Hoy 1L 173
High Keep Fold WF4: Hol 7H 143
Highland HX3: North 9E 80
Highland Cl. WF8: Pon 9M 109
Highlands LS17: Leeds 2G 50
LS29: Burl W 9C 16
Highlands, The WF5: Oss 6M 123
WF15: Liv 7H 101
Highlands Av. HD5: Hud 7D 138
Highlands Cl. BD7: B'frd 2K 81
LS10: Leeds 5H 87
Highlands Dr. LS10: Leeds 5H 87
Highlands Gro. BD7: B'frd 2K 81
LS10: Leeds 5H 87
Highlands La. HX2: Illing 7M 79
Highlands Pk. HX2: Illing 7M 79
Highlands Wlk. LS10: Leeds 5H 87
Highland Ville HX3: Hip 4J 99
High La. HD4: Hud 8N 137
HD9: Scho 5A 170
HG3: Spof 1N 21
HX2: Hal 4H 97
HX7: Crag V 9K 95
S36: Ing 9A 172
High Lea HD7: Mars 5F 150
Highlea Cl. LS19: Yead 2K 47
High Lee HX2: Lud F 6C 96
High Lee Grn. HX2: Lud F 6B 96
Highlee La. HX4: Bark 4F 116
HX6: Ripp 4E 116
High Lees Rd. HX2: Mix 8H 79
High Level Way HX1: Hal 4M 97
Highley Hall Cft. HD6: Clift 9B 100
Highley Pk. HD6: Clift 1C 120
High Mdw. BD20: Keigh 7F 26
High Mdws. BD15: Wils 1B 62
HX4: Gree 4B 118
WF2: W'ton 4C 144
WF12: T'hill 1F 140
High Mill LS29: Add 9N 11
High Mill Bus. Pk. LS27: Morl 1K 103
High Mill La. LS29: Add 9N 11
High Moor Av. LS17: Leeds 5G 51
High Moor Cl. LS17: Leeds 4G 50
High Moor Ct. LS17: Leeds 5G 51
High Moor Cres. LS17: Leeds 4G 50
Highmoor Cres. HD6: Clift 9B 100
High Moor Dr. LS17: Leeds 4G 51
High Moor End Rd. HD9: Mel 8N 151
High Moor Grange LS16: B'hpe 5G 32
High Moor Gro. LS17: Leeds 4G 51
High Moor La. HD8: Shep 9L 155
Highmoor La. BD19: Cleck 7E 100
HD6: Clift 9B 100
(not continuous)
High Moor Rd. LS17: N Rig 1M 19
Highmoor Wlk. BD17: Bail 5M 45
Highoak Gth. BD22: Oak 5C 42
High Oxford St. WF10: C'frd 5C 108
High Pk. Cres. BD9: B'frd 3K 63
High Pk. Dr. BD9: B'frd 3K 63
High Pk. Gro. BD9: B'frd 3K 63
High Pk. Vw. WF2: Wren 2H 125
High Pastures BD22: Keigh 2E 42
High Peak OL15: Lit 5A 132
High Peal Ct. BD13: Que 4C 80
High Poplars BD2: B'frd 2D 64
High Ridge WF4: Neth 4A 142
High Ridge Av. LS26: Rothw 6M 87
High Ridge Ct. LS26: Rothw 7N 87
High Ridge Pk. LS26: Rothw 6M 87
High Ridge Way LS16: B'hpe 6J 33
High Rd. WF12: Dew 4H 123
HIGHROAD WELL 5K 97
Highroad Well HX2: Hal 5K 97
Highroad Well Ct. HX2: Hal 5K 97
Highroad Well La. HX2: Hal 5J 97
High Royd HX6: Sow B 7F 96
Highroyd HD8: Lept 7J 139
Highroyd Cres. HD5: Hud 4B 138
Highroyd La. HD5: Hud 4B 138
High Royds Dr. LS29: Men 5E 30
High Shann Farm BD20: Keigh 8G 26
High Spring Gdns. La. BD20: Keigh 7G 27
High Spring Rd. BD21: Keigh 1M 43
High Stones Rd. HX7: Crag V 9M 95
High St. BD6: B'frd 4N 81
BD10: B'frd 7F 46
BD13: Que 4D 80
BD13: Thorn 8C 62
BD19: Cleck 4H 101
BD20: Stee 3C 26
BD21: Keigh 9H 27
DN6: Carc 9N 165
HD1: Hud 6B 8 (5M 137)
(Huddersfield)
HD1: Hud 5K 137
(Paddock)
HD6: Brigh 9M 99
HD7: Golc 5A 136
HD8: Clay W 7J 157
HD9: Hon 5L 153
HX1: Hal 5J 7 (6A 98)
(not continuous)
HX2: Lud 3E 96
HX4: Gree 5C 118
HX4: Stainl 8L 117
HX7: Blac H 8B 76
LS19: Yead 9M 31
LS22: Weth 4M 23
LS23: B Spa 9B 24
LS23: B'ham 6D 38
LS23: Cliff 3D 38
LS25: Kip 4B 90
LS27: Morl 2K 103
LS28: Fars 3A 66
OL14: Tod *9J 93*
(off Littleholme St.)
S71: Roys 6B 160
S72: S Hien 4M 161
S72: Shaf 6K 161
S75: S'ross 7J 159
WF4: Crig 5G 142
WF4: Croft 2G 145
WF4: Horb 1C 142
WF4: N Sha 7H 127
WF4: Wool 2H 159
WF5: Oss 2M 123
WF6: Alt 9G 106
WF6: Norm 1H 127
WF9: S Elm 6N 163
WF9: Upt 2N 163
WF10: C'frd 5C 108
WF11: B'ton 3B 110
WF11: Ferr 7B 110
WF12: Dew 4J 123
WF12: T'hill 1F 140
WF13: Dew 4E 122
WF16: Heck 8A 102
WF17: Bat 9H 103
WF17: Birs 3B 102
High St. Ct. HX2: Lud 3E 96
High St. Fold HX2: Lud 3E 96
High St. Pl. BD10: B'frd 7F 46
BD13: Que *4D 80*
(off High St.)
High Sunderland La. HX3: Hal 3C 98
Highthorne Av. BD3: B'frd 5G 65
Highthorne Ct. LS17: Leeds 3H 51
Highthorne Dr. LS17: Leeds 3H 51
Highthorne Gro. LS12: Leeds 6K 67
LS17: Leeds 3J 51
Highthorne Mt. LS17: Leeds 3H 51
Highthorne St. LS12: Leeds 6K 67
Highthorne Vw. LS12: Leeds 6K 67
HIGHTOWN
WF10 5A 108
WF15 7G 100
HIGHTOWN HEIGHTS 7F 100
Hightown La. HD9: H'frth 2M 169
Hightown Rd. BD19: Cleck 5H 101
WF15: Liv 7H 101
Hightown Vw. WF15: Liv 7H 101
High Trees Gdns. LS23: Cliff 2E 38
High Trees La. HX4: Gree 5K 117
HIGH UTLEY 7G 27
High Vw. S71: Roys 6C 160
WF4: Crig 5G 142
Highway LS20: Guis 7F 30
Highways LS14: Leeds 5N 69
HIGH WEARDLEY 2D 34
High Weardley La. LS17: Hare 2C 34
High Well Hill La. S72: S Hien 3J 161
High Wheatley LS29: I'ly 6K 15
High Wicken Cl. BD13: Thorn 8B 62

High Wood—Hollings, The

High Wood LS29: I'ly . 6L 15
Highwood Av. LS17: Leeds . 4E 50
Highwood Cl. S75: Kex . 9E 158
High Wood Ct. LS6: Leeds . 1A 68
Highwood Cres. LS17: Leeds . 4E 50
Highwood Gro. LS17: Leeds . 5E 50
High Wood Head BD20: Rid . 4K 27
High Woodlands WF3: E Ard . 5E 104
High Wood La. HD8: Kbtn . 4M 155
High Wood Path HD7: Slait . 8N 135
High Wood Rd. WF17: Birs . 9D 84
Higson Ct. HD5: Hud . 3E 138
Higson Row HD8: Clay W . 6J 157
Hilberoyd Rd. WF17: Bat . 7G 102
Hilda St. BD9: B'frd . 2M 63
WF5: Oss . 7A 124
HILL . 3L 169
Hillam Ct. Ind. Est. BD2: B'frd . 3B 64
Hillam Rd. BD2: B'frd . 3B 64
Hillam St. BD5: B'frd . 2N 81
Hillary Pl. LS2: Leeds . 2D 4 (4D 68)
Hillary Rd. BD18: Ship . 8C 46
Hillary St. WF13: Dew . 9C 102
Hillas Ct. HX3: Hal . 9C 98
Hillas Ind. Est. HX6: Sow B . 8K 97
Hillbeck HX3: Hal . 2M 97
Hillbrook Ri. LS29: I'ly . 6E 14
Hill Brow Cl. BD15: All . 5F 62
Hill Cl. BD17: Bail . 5N 45
HD3: Hud . 1E 136
WF8: Pon . 4K 129
Hill Clough BD22: Lay . 9D 26
Hill Clough Gro. BD22: Lay . 9C 26
Hillcote Dr. BD5: B'frd . 1C 82
Hill Ct. WF10: C'frd . 6F 108
Hill Ct. Av. LS13: Leeds . 2F 66
Hillcourt Cft. LS13: Leeds . 2F 66
Hill Ct. Dr. LS13: Leeds . 2F 66
Hill Ct. Fold LS13: Leeds . 2F 66
Hill Ct. Gro. LS13: Leeds . 2F 66
Hill Ct. Vw. LS13: Leeds . 2E 66
Hill Cres. HX3: Sou . 7E 98
LS19: Raw . 2N 47
LS29: Burl W . 1D 30
WF17: Birs . 2D 102
Hill Crest DN6: Skel . 8K 165
HX6: Rish . 1C 134
HX6: Sow B . 7H 97
HX7: Heb B . 1G 95
(off Lime Av.)
LS26: Swil . 4H 89
Hillcrest LS16: B'hpe . 4D 32
LS22: Coll . 9F 22
LS27: Gil . 5E 84
WF4: H'cft . 9K 145
WF6: Alt . 8F 106
WF9: Hems . 3D 162
(off Highfield Rd.)
Hill Crest Av. BD13: Denh . 5K 61
HX6: Sow B . 7H 97
(off Dearden St.)
Hillcrest Av. BD13: Que . 5E 80
BD20: Sils . 7E 12
LS7: Leeds . 3G 69
WF5: Oss . 3M 123
WF7: F'stne . 6B 128
WF10: C'frd . 6K 109
WF17: Bat . 7D 102
Hill Crest Cl. HX6: Sow B . 7H 97
LS26: Swil . 4G 89
Hillcrest Cl. WF10: C'frd . 6K 109
Hillcrest Ct. LS16: Leeds . 3H 49
Hill Crest Dr. BD13: Denh . 5K 61
Hillcrest Dr. BD13: Que . 5E 80
WF10: C'frd . 6K 109
Hillcrest Mdws. WF10: C'frd . 6L 109
Hill Crest Mt. BD13: Denh . 5K 61
Hillcrest Mt. BD19: Scho . 5D 100
LS16: Leeds . 3H 49
WF10: C'frd . 6L 109
Hillcrest Pl. LS7: Leeds . 2G 69
Hillcrest Ri. LS16: Leeds . 3G 49
Hill Crest Rd. BD13: Denh . 5K 61
BD13: Thorn . 7C 62
Hillcrest Rd. BD13: Que . 5E 80
WF10: C'frd . 5L 109
WF12: Dew . 6F 122
Hill Crest Vw. BD13: Denh . 5K 61
Hillcrest Vw. LS7: Leeds . 2G 69
Hill Cft. BD13: Thorn . 7D 62
HX6: Rish . 1C 134
Hillcroft WF8: Pon . 6M 129
Hillcroft Cl. WF8: D'ton . 6C 130
Hill Dr. WF7: Ackw . 2G 146
HILL END . 6H 67
Hill End BD7: B'frd . 2K 81
WF12: Dew . 3H 123
Hill End Cl. HX3: Hip . 5H 99
HX3: Nor G . 2M 99
LS12: Leeds . 6J 67
Hill End Cres. LS12: Leeds . 6J 67
Hill End Gro. BD7: B'frd . 2K 81
Hill End La. BD13: Que . 5C 80
BD16: Har . 7L 43
Hill End Rd. LS12: Leeds . 6J 67
S75: Map . 9L 159
Hillesley Rd.
WF12: Dew . 9K 103
Hill Est. WF9: Upt . 1A 164
Hillfold WF9: S Elm . 6A 164
HILLFOOT . 6M 65
Hillfoot BD18: Ship . 8K 45
Hillfoot Av. LS28: Pud . 6M 65
Hillfoot Cotts. LS28: Pud . 6L 65
Hillfoot Cres. LS28: Pud . 6M 65
Hillfoot Dr. LS28: Pud . 6M 65
Hillfoot Ri. LS28: Pud . 6M 65
Hillgarth WF11: Knot . 9D 110
WF12: T'hill . 8G 123
HILL GREEN . 3B 84
Hill Grn. Ct. BD4: B'frd . 3B 84
Hill Gro. HD3: Hud . 1E 136
Hill Gro. Lea HD3: Hud . 1E 136
Hillhead Dr. WF17: Bat . 3C 102
Hill Head Gdns. WF13: Dew . 1E 122
Hill Ho. Edge La. BD22: Oxen . 5B 60
Hill Ho. La. BD22: Oxen . 5C 60
HD9: H'frth . 6K 169
Hillhouse La. HD1: Hud . 1B 8 (2M 137)
(not continuous)
Hill Ho. Rd. HD9: H'frth . 6K 169
Hillidge Rd. LS10: Leeds . 1F 86
Hillidge Sq. LS10: Leeds . 1F 86
Hillingdon Way LS17: Leeds . 1C 50
Hillings La. LS20: Hawk, Men . 7B 30
LS29: Men . 4B 30
Hill Lands BD12: Wyke . 8A 82
Hill La. HD9: H'frth, U'thng . 3J 169
Hill Pk. WF14: Up H . 9K 121
Hill Pk. Av. HX3: Hal . 3M 97
Hill Pk. Mt. HX6: Ripp . 5E 116
Hill Pl. OL14: Tod . 9J 93
Hill Ri. WF17: Bat . 8J 103
Hill Ri. Av. LS13: Leeds . 2F 66
Hill Ri. Gro. LS13: Leeds . 2F 66
Hill Rd. WF2: New . 6L 143
WF10: C'frd . 5F 108
Hill Royd Cl. HX2: Illing . 6L 79
Hillsborough Vs. WF9: S Elm . 8M 163
(off Broad La.)
HILL SIDE . 3F 138
HILLSIDE . 7A 162
Hill Side HD4: Hud . 1A 154
Hillside HD8: Den D . 2C 172
LS25: Gar . 8A 72
WF11: Byram . 5C 110
Hill Side Av. HD9: H'wth . 6C 170
Hillside Av. BD22: Oak . 5B 42
HD2: Hud . 9N 119
HX2: Lud F . 5D 96
HX6: Ripp . 5E 116
LS20: Guis . 5H 31
Hillside Bldgs. LS11: Leeds . 2C 86
(off Beeston Rd.)
Hillside Cl. LS29: Add . 1L 13
S36: Hoy . 9J 173
WF2: Wake . 8F 124
Hillside Ct. LS7: Leeds . 8G 50
LS29: Men . 4D 30
WF9: S Elm . 5N 163
Hillside Cres. HD4: Hud . 8N 137
S72: B'ley . 7A 162
Hillside Gro. BD22: Oak . 5B 42
LS28: Pud . 7C 66
S72: B'ley . 7N 161
Hill Side Mt. LS28: Stan . 4B 66
Hillside Mt. LS28: Pud . 7D 66
S72: B'ley . 7A 162
WF8: Pon . 3L 129
Hill Side Ri. WF15: Liv . 9L 101
Hillside Ri. LS20: Guis . 5H 31
Hill Side Rd. BD3: B'frd . 3E 6 (7E 64)
Hillside Rd. BD16: Bgly . 3E 44
BD18: Ship . 9A 46
LS7: Leeds . 8F 50
WF7: Ackw . 4F 146
WF8: Pon . 3L 129
Hill Side Ter. BD3: B'frd . 2E 6 (6E 64)
Hillside Ter. BD17: Bail . 4A 46
Hillside Vw. HD7: Linth . 9C 136
HX6: Sow B . 8G 97
LS28: Pud . 7D 66
Hillside Works Ind. Est. BD19: Hun . 2H 101
Hill St. BD4: B'frd . 9F 64
BD6: B'frd . 4M 81
BD19: Cleck . 5G 101
BD22: Haw . 9C 42
HD9: Jack B . 5C 170
HX1: Hal . 6J 7 (6A 98)
LS9: Leeds . 3K 5 (5G 68)
LS11: Leeds . 2D 86
OL14: Tod . 6N 93
Hillthorpe LS28: Pud . 9B 66
Hillthorpe Ct. LS10: Leeds . 1E 104
Hillthorpe Dr. WF8: Thpe A . 5N 147
Hillthorpe Ri. LS28: Pud . 9B 66
Hillthorpe Rd. LS28: Pud . 9B 66
Hillthorpe Sq. LS28: Pud . 9B 66
Hillthorpe St. LS28: Pud . 9B 66
Hillthorpe Ter. LS28: Pud . 9B 66
HILL TOP
BD13 . 7B 62
HD7 . 9M 135
HD8 . 7J 157
LS6 . 7A 50
LS12 . 6J 67
S36 . 9M 173
WF2 . 6L 143
Hill Top BD13: Que . 3D 80
BD16: Cot . 9H 45
BD20: Stee . 3C 26
HD4: Neth . 3J 153
HX2: Hal . 7L 97
HX6: Sow B . 7G 96
LS29: Burl W . 6C 16
LS29: I'ly . 7F 14
WF9: Fitz . 7A 146
WF10: C'frd . 5N 107
WF11: Knot . 8D 110
Hilltop S72: B'ley . 6N 161
Hill Top Av. HD2: Hud . 7G 118
LS8: Leeds . 2H 69
S71: Ath . 8N 159
Hill Top Bank HD4: Neth . 3H 153
Hill Top Cl. LS12: Leeds . 6J 67
WF3: W Ard . 6A 104
WF4: Not . 3C 160
WF9: Fitz . 7A 146
Hilltop Cl. WF10: C'frd . 3G 108
Hill Top Cotts. BD9: B'frd . 4K 63
Hilltop Cotts. LS17: N Rig . 2N 19
Hill Top Ct. WF2: New . 6L 143
WF3: W Ard . 6A 104
Hill Top Cres. WF14: Up H . 1K 139
Hill Top Cft. HD4: Neth . 3H 153
Hill Top Dr. HD3: Hud . 2F 136
Hill Top Est. WF9: S Kirk . 8F 162
WF16: Heck . 9B 102
Hill Top Fold BD12: Low M . 7B 82
(off Low Moor St.)
Hill Top Fold HD7: Slait . 9M 135
(off Olney St.)
Hill Top Gdns. WF3: W Ard . 6A 104
Hill Top Grn. WF3: W Ard . 6N 103
Hill Top Gro. BD15: All . 5F 62
WF3: W Ard . 6A 104
Hill Top La. BD15: All . 5F 62
BD16: Bgly . 8E 28
HX7: Crag V . 9J 95
WF3: W Ard . 7N 103
WF4: W Har . 1C 146
Hill Top M. WF11: Knot . 8E 110
Hill Top Mt. LS8: Leeds . 2H 69
Hill Top Pl. LS6: Leeds . 4B 68
LS8: Leeds . 2H 69
Hill Top Rd. BD13: Thorn . 7A 62
BD21: Keigh . 6G 42
BD22: Oak . 5B 42
HD1: Hud . 5K 137
HD3: Hud . 2E 136
HD5: Hud . 4B 138
HD7: Slait . 9M 135
HD9: H'frth . 7L 169
LS6: Leeds . 4B 68
LS12: Leeds . 6J 67
WF2: New . 6L 143
WF4: Flock . 7G 140
Hill Top St. LS6: Leeds . 4B 68
Hill Top Ter. HD8: Clay W . 7K 157
Hill Top Vw. HD9: Had E . 8N 169
WF3: W Ard . 6N 103
WF6: Norm . 4H 127
Hilltop Vs. WF3: W Ard . 6N 103
Hill Top Wlk. BD22: Keigh . 9F 26
Hill Top Way BD22: Keigh . 9F 26
HILL TREE PARK . 9F 136
Hill Vw. HX2: Illing . 6M 79
HX7: Myth . 4N 95
OL15: Lit . 9M 113
Hill Vw. Av. LS7: Leeds . 8F 50
Hill Vw. Gdns. HX3: North . 3F 98
Hill Vw. Mt. LS7: Leeds . 8F 50
Hill Vw. Pl. LS7: Leeds . 8F 50
Hillview Ri. BD4: B'frd . 1J 83
Hill Vw. Ter. LS7: Leeds . 8F 50
Hillway LS20: Guis . 9G 30
Hillworth Ho. BD21: Keigh . 1H 43
(off Oakworth Rd.)
Hillworth Village
BD21: Keigh . 1H 43
Hilmian Way WF9: Hems . 4F 162
Hilton Av. BD18: Ship . 1N 63
Hilton Ct. LS16: B'hpe . 4D 32
Hilton Cres. BD17: Bail . 5A 46
Hilton Dr. BD18: Ship . 1N 63
Hilton Grange LS16: B'hpe . 4D 32
Hilton Gro. BD7: B'frd . 8M 63
BD18: Ship . 1N 63
LS8: Leeds . 1H 69
Hilton M. LS16: B'hpe . 5D 32
Hilton Pl. LS8: Leeds . 2H 69
Hilton Rd. BD7: B'frd . 8M 63
BD18: Ship . 1N 63
LS8: Leeds . 2H 69
Hilton St. HX7: Heb B . 1H 95
(off Market St.)
LS8: Leeds . 2H 69
Hilton Ter. LS8: Leeds . 2H 69
Hinchcliffe Av. WF5: Oss . 6B 124
Hinchcliffe St. BD3: B'frd . 6F 64
Hinchliffe Av. BD17: Bail . 5B 46
Hind Ct. HD9: Mel . 6B 152
Hindle Pl. LS27: Chur . 6L 85
Hindley Rd. WF15: Liv . 9L 101
Hindley Wlk. BD7: B'frd . 3J 81
Hinds Cres. WF9: S Elm . 6M 163
Hind St. BD8: B'frd . 6A 64
BD12: Wyke . 2A 100
Hinsley Ct. LS6: Leeds . 1A 68
Hinton Cl. WF8: Pon . 9L 109
Hinton La. WF11: Ferr . 6N 109
Hions Cl. HD6: Ras . 3M 119
HIPPERHOLME . 4J 99
Hipswell St. BD3: B'frd . 6G 65
Hird Av. BD6: B'frd . 5A 82
Hird Rd. BD12: Low M . 7B 82
Hird St. BD17: Ship . 7N 45
BD21: Keigh . 2H 43
LS11: Leeds . 2C 86
Hirst Av. WF16: Heck . 6A 102
Hirst Fold BD12: Wyke . 1A 100
(off Town Ga.)
Hirst Gro. HX7: Heb B . 1J 95
Hirstlands Av. WF5: Oss . 3M 123
Hirstlands Dr. WF5: Oss . 3M 123
Hirst La. BD18: Ship . 6K 45
HD8: Cumb . 4F 170
Hirst Lodge Ct. BD2: B'frd . 1D 64
Hirst Mill Cres. BD18: Ship . 6K 45
Hirst Rd. WF2: Wake . 6F 124
WF13: Dew . 2F 122
Hirst St. OL14: Tod . 3D 92
WF10: All B . 6M 89
WF14: Mir . 8L 121
Hirst's Yd. LS1: Leeds . 7G 5
Hirstwood HX6: Ripp . 7E 116
Hirst Wood Cres. BD18: Ship . 7K 45
Hirst Wood Rd. BD18: Ship . 7J 45
Hive St. BD22: Keigh . 1G 43
HMP & YOI New Hall WF4: Flock . 6J 141
HMP Leeds LS12: Leeds . 7N 67
HMP Wakefield
WF2: Wake . 4G 9 (5K 125)
HMP Wealstun LS23: T Arch . 7G 24
HMYOI Wetherby LS22: Weth . 2A 24
Hobart Bldgs. HX7: Myth . 3L 95
Hobart Rd. WF10: C'frd . 3K 109
WF12: Dew . 2J 123
Hobb End BD13: Thorn . 6B 62
Hobberley La. LS17: Leeds, Shad . 3A 52
Hobb Nook La. LS21: Askw . 2E 16
Hob Cote HX7: Heb B . 6H 77
Hob Cote La. BD22: Oak . 6N 41
Hobcroft Ter. DN6: Carc . 8N 165
Hob Hill BD22: S'bury . 9K 41
Hob La. BD22: S'bury . 8K 41
HD4: Hud . 8G 137
HX2: Lud F . 4A 96
HX6: Norl . 2H 117
HX6: Ripp . 6C 116
Hobson Fold BD12: Wyke . 2B 100
(off Wyke La.)
Hockney Rd. BD8: B'frd . 6N 63
Hockney Rd. Ind. Est. BD8: B'frd . 6N 63
Hoctun Cl. WF10: C'frd . 7E 108
Hodge La. WF8: K S'ton, Lit S . 4K 149
Hodgewood La. WF8: D'ton . 5C 130
Hodgson Av. BD3: B'frd . 6H 65
LS17: Leeds . 4J 51
Hodgson Cres. LS17: Leeds . 4J 51
Hodgson Fold BD2: B'frd . 2D 64
LS29: Add . 9K 11
Hodgson La. BD11: B'haw . 6M 83
BD11: Drig . 7A 84
Hodgson Pl. LS27: Chur . 6L 85
Hodgson St. LS27: Morl . 3M 103
WF1: Wake . 2G 9 (4K 125)
Hodgson Ter. WF12: Dew . 5G 122
Hodgson Yd. BD2: B'frd . 1G 65
(off Sovereign Ct.)
Hodroyd Cl. S72: Shaf . 8L 161
Hodroyd Cotts. S72: B'ley . 7A 162
Hodroyd La. S72: Shaf . 8L 161
Hoffman St. HD3: Hud . 6F 136
Hog Cl. La. HD9: H'wth . 8G 170
Hogley La. HD9: H'frth . 4H 169
Holays HD5: Hud . 3C 138
HOLBECK . 9C 68
Holbeck La. LS11: Leeds . 8B 68
Holbeck Moor Rd. LS11: Leeds . 9C 68
Holbeck Towers LS11: Leeds . 9C 68
Holborn App. LS6: Leeds . 3C 68
Holborn Central LS6: Leeds . 3C 68
(off Rampart Rd.)
Holborn Ct. BD12: Low M . 7A 82
LS6: Leeds . 3D 68
Holborn Gdns. LS6: Leeds . 3C 68
Holborn Grn. LS6: Leeds . 3C 68
Holborn Gro. LS6: Leeds . 3C 68
Holborn St. LS6: Leeds . 3D 68
Holborn Ter. LS6: Leeds . 3C 68
Holborn Towers LS6: Leeds . 1D 4 (3D 68)
Holborn Vw. LS6: Leeds . 3C 68
Holborn Wlk. LS6: Leeds . 3C 68
Holby Bus. Pk. HX6: Sow B . 9H 97
Holby Sq. WF2: Wake . 7E 124
Holden Ing Way WF17: Birs . 9D 84
Holden La. BD17: Bail . 3B 46
(not continuous)
BD20: Sils . 9G 12
BD22: Oxen . 5N 59
Holden Rd. BD6: B'frd . 4N 81
Holderness Rd. WF11: Knot . 7D 110
Holderness St. OL14: Tod . 7L 93
Holdforth Cl. LS12: Leeds . 7A 68
Holdforth Gdns. LS12: Leeds . 7A 68
Holdforth Grn. LS12: Leeds . 7A 68
Holdforth Pl. LS12: Leeds . 7A 68
Holdgatehill La. WF8: D'ton . 5E 130
HOLDSWORTH . 7N 79
Holdsworth Bldgs. BD2: B'frd . 2H 65
(off Elvey Cl.)
BD12: Wyke . 9A 82
(off Huddersfield Rd.)
Holdsworth Ct. BD19: Cleck . 5H 101
Holdsworth Pl. LS12: Leeds . 7L 67
Holdsworth Rd. HX2: Hal . 6N 79
HX3: Hal . 6N 79
Holdsworth Sq. BD2: B'frd . 2H 65
Holdsworth St. BD1: B'frd . 2C 6 (6D 64)
BD18: Ship . 9A 46
BD19: Cleck . 4H 101
Holdsworth Ter. HX1: Hal . 8M 7 (7C 98)
Holdsworth Yd. BD1: B'frd . 7B 64
(off Thornton Rd.)
Hole BD22: Haw . 9B 42
HOLE BOTTOM . 5K 93
Hole Bottom Rd. OL14: Tod . 6K 93
Hole La. BD20: Sils . 5A 12
WF4: Crig . 7E 142
Holes, The WF11: Knot . 7D 110
Holes La. WF11: Knot . 8D 110
Holgate Av. WF9: Fitz . 7B 146
Holgate Cres. WF9: Hems . 2C 162
Holgate Gdns. WF9: Hems . 2C 162
Holgate Hospital WF9: Hems . 3A 162
Holgate La. LS23: B Spa . 9D 24
Holgate Rd. WF8: Pon . 6J 129
Holgate Ter. WF9: Fitz . 7B 146
Holgate Vw. S72: B'ley . 6A 162
WF9: Fitz . 7B 146
(off Wakefield Rd.)
Holker St. BD8: B'frd . 6N 63
BD21: Keigh . 8J 27
Holland Mt. LS16: B'hpe . 5G 33
Holland Pk. BD9: B'frd . 4K 63
Holland Rd. LS25: Kip . 3C 90
Holland St. BD4: B'frd . 8J 65
WF17: Bat . 7G 102
Hollas La. HX6: Norl . 1L 117
(not continuous)
Hollerton La. WF3: W Ard . 4B 104
Hollies, The LS12: Leeds . 7M 67
LS21: Pool . 2G 32
Hollin Av. HD3: Hud . 3J 137
Hollinbank La. WF16: Heck . 7B 102
Hollin Brigg La. HD9: Holm . 6H 169
Hollin Cl. La. BD2: B'frd . 3C 64
Hollin Ct. BD18: Ship . 9A 46
LS16: Leeds . 8N 49
Hollin Cres. LS16: Leeds . 8N 49
Hollin Dr. LS16: Leeds . 8A 50
WF4: Dur . 4G 142
Hollin Edge HD8: Den D . 2D 172
Hollin Gdns. LS16: Leeds . 8M 49
Hollin Ga. LS21: Otley . 7H 17
Hollingbourne Rd. LS15: Leeds . 4G 70
Hollingreave HD9: New M . 1C 170
Hollin Greaves La. HX3: Hal . 1M 7 (3C 98)
Hollings, The LS26: Meth . 1J 107

Hollings Gro.—Hopefield Dr.

Hollings Gro. HX6: Sow B . . . 7G 97
Hollings Rd. BD8: B'frd . . . 5N 63
Hollings Sq. BD8: B'frd . . . 6N 63
Hollings St. BD8: B'frd . . . 6N 63
BD16: Cot . . . 8G 45
Hollings Ter. BD8: B'frd . . . 6N 63
HOLLINGTHORPE . . . 7G 143
Hollingthorpe Av. WF4: Hol . . . 7G 143
Hollingthorpe Ct. WF4: Hol . . . 8H 143
Hollingthorpe Gro. WF4: Hol . . . 7G 143
Hollingthorpe La. WF4: Hol . . . 6G 142
Hollingthorpe Rd. WF4: Hol . . . 7G 143
Hollingwell Hill BD14: Clay . . . 2D 80
Hollingwood Av. BD7: B'frd . . . 1L 81
Hollingwood Dr. BD7: B'frd . . . 1K 81
Hollingwood Ga. LS29: I'ly . . . 6E 14
Hollingwood La. BD7: B'frd . . . 2J 81
Hollingwood Mt. BD7: B'frd . . . 1K 81
Hollingwood Pk. LS29: I'ly . . . 6E 14
Hollingwood Ri. LS29: I'ly . . . 6E 14
Hollingworth La. OL14: W'den . . . 3K 113
WF11: Knot . . . 8F 110
Hollin Hall Dr. LS29: I'ly . . . 6D 14
Hollin Hall La. HD7: Golc . . . 5B 136
(not continuous)
WF14: K'htn . . . 9H 121
Hollin Hall Rd. BD18: Ship . . . 9K 45
Hollin Head BD17: Bail . . . 3D 46
Hollin Hill Av. LS8: Leeds . . . 1L 69
Hollin Hill Cotts. LS8: Leeds . . . 1L 69
Hollin Hill Dr. LS8: Leeds . . . 1L 69
Hollinhirst La. WF4: Neth . . . 5B 142
Hollin Ho. La. HD8: Clay W . . . 1J 173
HD9: New M . . . 3D 170
Hollinhurst WF10: All B . . . 7M 89
Hollin La. BD18: Ship . . . 9B 46
HX2: Midg . . . 8A 78
HX6: Norl . . . 2H 117
HX6: Ripp . . . 8N 115
LS16: Leeds . . . 8N 49
WF4: Cal G . . . 4F 142
Hollin M. LS16: Leeds . . . 8N 49
Hollin Mt. LS16: Leeds . . . 8M 49
Hollin Nook HD3: Hud . . . 3H 137
HOLLIN PARK . . . 1M 69
Hollin Pk. Av. LS8: Leeds . . . 1M 69
Hollin Pk. Ct. LS28: Cal . . . 9L 47
Hollin Pk. Cres. LS8: Leeds . . . 1M 69
Hollin Pk. Dr. LS28: Cal . . . 9L 47
Hollin Pk. Mt. LS8: Leeds . . . 9M 51
Hollin Pk. Pde. LS8: Leeds . . . 1L 69
Hollin Pk. Pl. LS8: Leeds . . . 1L 69
Hollin Pk. Rd. LS8: Leeds . . . 1L 69
LS28: Cal . . . 9L 47
Hollin Pk. Ter. LS8: Leeds . . . 1L 69
Hollin Pk. Vw. LS8: Leeds . . . 1L 69
Hollin Ri. BD18: Ship . . . 9A 46
Hollin Rd. BD18: Ship . . . 9A 46
LS16: Leeds . . . 8N 49
Hollinroyd Rd. WF12: Dew . . . 3H 123
Hollins HX2: Lud F . . . 7C 96
HX6: Tri . . . 2E 116
HX7: Heb B . . . 8H 77
Hollins, The HX6: Ripp . . . 8C 116
HX6: Sow B . . . 8H 97
OL14: Tod . . . 6K 93
WF13: Dew . . . 1B 122
Hollins Av. WF13: Dew . . . 9C 102
Hollins Bank HX6: Sow B . . . 8H 97
Hollins Bank La. BD20: Stee . . . 3D 26
Hollins Beck Cl. LS25: Kip . . . 5A 90
Hollins Cl. BD20: Keigh . . . 6F 26
Hollins Cres. *HX7: Heb B* . . . *1H 95*
(off Osborne St.)
Hollins Ga. HX2: Lud F . . . 7B 96
Hollins Glen HD7: Slait . . . 1N 151
Hollins Grn. OL14: Tod . . . 8E 92
Hollins Gro. WF10: All B . . . 7N 89
Hollins Hall Golf Course . . . 1E 46
Hollins Hey Rd. HX4: Holy . . . 7C 118
Hollins Hill BD17: Bail . . . 2E 46
LS20: Guis . . . 2E 46
Hollins La. BD20: Keigh . . . 5F 26
DN6: S'brk . . . 4E 164
HD7: Slait . . . 3K 151
HX2: Lud F . . . 7B 96
HX2: Mix . . . 8J 79
HX6: Sow B . . . 7G 96
Hollins Mdw. OL14: W'den . . . 2J 113
Hollins Mill Bus. Cen. *OL14: W'den* . . . *2J 113*
(off Rochdale Rd.)
Hollins Mill La. HX6: Sow B . . . 8G 97
Hollins Mt. WF9: Hems . . . 2C 162
Hollins Pk. LS25: Kip . . . 4A 90
Hollins Pl. HX7: Heb B . . . 1H 95
OL14: W'den . . . 2J 113
Hollins Rd. OL14: W'den . . . 1J 113
WF13: Dew . . . 1C 122
Hollins Row HD7: Slait . . . 1N 151
Hollins St. OL14: W'den . . . 3K 113
Hollins Ter. HX6: Tri . . . 2E 116
Hollin St. HX6: Tri . . . 2E 116
Hollin Ter. BD18: Ship . . . 9A 46
HD3: Hud . . . 3H 137
HOLLINTHORPE . . . 1H 89
Hollin Vw. LS16: Leeds . . . 8N 49
Hollin Wood Cl. BD18: Ship . . . 8K 45
Hollinwood Vw. BD16: Bgly . . . 9C 28
Hollis Pl. LS3: Leeds . . . 4A 4 (5B 68)
Hollow, The HD9: Mel . . . 7B 152
Hollowfield Cft. BD12: O'haw . . . 8F 82
Hollowgate HD4: Thurs . . . 8C 154
HD9: H'frth . . . 3M 169
Holly App. WF5: Oss . . . 3N 123
Holly Av. LS16: Leeds . . . 4G 48
Holly Bank HD5: K'htn . . . 2F 138
HX5: Ell . . . 6D 118
LS6: Leeds . . . 9N 49
LS20: Guis . . . 7H 31
LS25: Gar . . . 8B 72
WF7: Ackw . . . 4E 146
WF9: Hems . . . *1D 162*
(off Wakefield Rd.)
Hollybank Av. HD8: Up C . . . 2N 171
WF17: Bat . . . 5F 102
Holly Bank Ct. HD3: Hud . . . 3F 136
HX3: Hip . . . 4J 99
Holly Bank Dr. HX3: Hip . . . 4J 99
Hollybank Gdns. BD7: B'frd . . . 2K 81
Hollybank Gro. BD7: B'frd . . . 2K 81
Holly Bank Ho. *HD6: Ras* . . . *3L 119*
(off Holly Bank Pk.)
Holly Bank Pk. HD6: Ras . . . 3L 119
Holly Bank Rd. HD3: Hud . . . 1G 137
HD6: Ras . . . 3K 119
Hollybank Rd. BD7: B'frd . . . 2K 81
Holly Bush Ct. LS23: B Spa . . . 1E 38
Hollybush Grn. LS22: Coll . . . 9K 23
Holly Cl. LS10: Leeds . . . 9D 86
WF4: Croft . . . 1F 144
WF8: Pon . . . 4N 129
WF9: S Elm . . . 7M 163
Holly Ct. LS20: Guis . . . 8H 31
WF1: Out . . . 7L 105
WF3: W Ard . . . 6A 104
Holly Cres. HX6: Ripp . . . 8C 116
WF3: E Ard . . . 4H 105
WF4: Croft . . . 1F 144
Hollycroft Av. S71: Roys . . . 6C 160
Hollycroft Ct. LS16: Leeds . . . 4K 49
Holly Dene WF5: Oss . . . 3N 123
Holly Dr. LS16: Leeds . . . 4G 48
Holly Farm S72: Shaf . . . 6K 161
Holly Farm Ct. DN6: Burg . . . 5M 165
Hollyfield Av. HD3: Hud . . . 3F 136
Hollygarth Ct. WF9: Hems . . . 2D 162
Hollygarth Gdns. DN14: Beal . . . 5M 111
Hollygarth La. DN14: Beal . . . 5M 111
Holly Gro. HD3: Hud . . . 1H 137
HX1: Hal . . . 6N 97
HX2: Lud . . . 9E 78
S72: B'ley . . . 6A 162
WF17: Bat . . . 8E 102
Holly Hall La. BD12: Low M . . . 8A 82
Holly Hill LS17: Huby . . . 4M 19
Holly Hill Cotts. LS17: Huby . . . 4M 19
Hollyhock Cl. HX6: Sow B . . . 9H 97
Holly Ho. *WF10: C'frd* . . . *5E 108*
(off Parklands)
Holly Mede WF5: Oss . . . 3N 123
Holly Mt. *HX3: Hal* . . . *7D 98*
(off High Gro. La.)
Hollynsmill HX4: Gree . . . 4C 118
Hollyns Ter. HX4: Gree . . . 4C 118
Holly Pk. LS17: Huby . . . 4N 19
LS18: Hors . . . 6C 48
Holly Pk. Dr. BD7: B'frd . . . 1K 81
Holly Pk. Gro. BD7: B'frd . . . 1K 81
Holly Pk. Mills LS28: Cal . . . 9L 47
Holly Pk. Way HX2: Hal . . . 9M 79
Holly Rd. HD1: Hud . . . 6K 137
HD8: Clay W . . . 7H 157
LS23: B Spa . . . 9B 24
Holly Royd HX3: Sou . . . 8H 99
HX6: Ripp . . . 5D 116
Hollyshaw Cres. LS15: Leeds . . . 6D 70
Hollyshaw Gro. LS15: Leeds . . . 6D 70
Hollyshaw La. LS15: Leeds . . . 5D 70
Hollyshaw St. LS15: Leeds . . . 6D 70
Hollyshaw Ter. LS15: Leeds . . . 6D 70
Hollyshaw Wlk. LS15: Leeds . . . 5D 70
Holly St. BD6: B'frd . . . 3J 81
WF2: Wake . . . 4H 125
WF9: Hems . . . 2D 162
Holly Ter. HD1: Hud . . . 1C 8
Holly Tree La. LS15: Leeds . . . 8F 70
Holly Tree Wlk. LS24: Tad . . . 7N 39
Holly Vw. HX6: Tri . . . 2E 116
Holly Way LS14: Leeds . . . 4N 69
Hollywell Gro. LS12: Leeds . . . 6L 67
Hollywell La. LS12: Leeds . . . 7L 67
Hollywood Bowl
Bradford . . . 5C 6 (8D 64)
Leeds . . . 5N 67
Holman Av. LS25: Gar . . . 9N 71
HOLMBRIDGE . . . 6H 169
Holmcliffe Av. HD4: Hud . . . 9L 137
Holmclose HD9: Holm . . . 6G 169
Holmdale Cres. HD9: Nether . . . 9L 153
Holmdene Dr. WF14: Mir . . . 5L 121
HOLME . . . 7E 168
Holme Av. HD5: Hud . . . 5C 138
Holme Bank BD4: B'frd . . . 1K 83
Holme Bank Cl. BD4: B'frd . . . 3K 83
Holmebank M. HD9: Brock . . . 6A 154
Holme Bottom *HD9: New M* . . . *1C 170*
(off Holme La.)
Holmecarr Ct. BD16: Bgly . . . 3F 44
Holme Cl. WF4: G Moor . . . 5B 140
Holme Ct. HD9: New M . . . 1C 170
Holme Cft. WF4: Dur . . . 3H 143
Holme Dr. HX2: Hal . . . 6H 97
Holme End Rd. HX7: Heb B . . . 3K 95
Holme Farm Ct. LS12: N Far . . . 2G 84
Holme Farm La.
LS17: Bard, Coll . . . 4F 36
LS23: B'ham . . . 4F 36
Holme Fld. WF5: Oss . . . 4M 123
Holmefield Vw. BD4: B'frd . . . 1K 83
Holme Gro. LS29: Burl W . . . 1D 30
Holme Ho. OL15: Lit . . . 9M 113
Holme Ho. La. BD22: Oak . . . 1B 42
HD9: New M . . . 3E 170
HX2: Lud . . . 9E 78
HX6: Rish . . . 9D 116
Holme Ho. Rd. OL14: Tod . . . 3E 92
Holme Ho. St. OL15: Lit . . . 9M 113
Holme Ings LS29: Add . . . 2B 14
Holme La. BD4: B'frd . . . 2K 83
BD23: Hal E . . . 2C 10
HD7: Slait . . . 1J 151
HD9: New M . . . 1C 170
WF2: Wake . . . 8K 125
Holmelea Cft. *LS6: Leeds* . . . *8A 50*
(off Church Gro.)
Holme Leas Dr. WF5: Oss . . . 4M 123
Holme Mill La. BD22: Keigh . . . 1F 42
Holme Mills Ind. Pk. HD7: Slait . . . 3J 151
Holme Pk. LS29: Burl W . . . 1D 30
Holme Pk. Ct. HD4: Hud . . . 1L 153
Holme Pl. HD1: Hud . . . 3J 137
HX7: Heb B . . . 9H 77
Holme Ri. WF9: S Elm . . . 7N 163
Holme Rd. HX2: Hal . . . 6H 97
Holmeside Cl. HD4: Hud . . . 1K 153
Holmeside M. HD4: Hud . . . 1K 153
Holmes Rd. HX6: Sow B . . . 8J 97
Holmes St. BD1: B'frd . . . 6B 64
LS11: Leeds . . . 8E 68
Holme's Ter. HX2: Hal . . . 4L 97
Holme St. BD5: B'frd . . . 1B 82
BD22: Oxen . . . 4C 60
HX3: Hip . . . 5M 99
HX7: Heb B . . . 1H 95
OL14: Tod . . . 5G 93
WF15: Liv . . . 8M 101
Holmestyes La. HD9: H'frth . . . 8M 169
Holme Ter. HX7: Myth . . . 5L 95
OL15: Lit . . . 9M 113
HOLME TOP . . . 1B 82
Holme Top La. BD5: B'frd . . . 1B 82
Holme Top St. BD5: B'frd . . . 1B 82
Holme Valley Camping & Caravan Pk.
HD9: T'bdge . . . 8A 154
Holme Valley Ct. HD9: H'frth . . . 1M 169
Holme Vw. LS21: Arth . . . 2M 33
LS29: I'ly . . . 5F 14
Holme Vw. Av. HD9: U'thng . . . 3J 169
Holme Vw. Dr. HD9: U'thng . . . 3J 169
Holme Vw. Pk. HD9: U'thng . . . 3K 169
Holme Vw. Rd. S75: Kex . . . 9D 158
HOLME VILLAGE . . . 2K 83
Holme Vs. HD7: Mars . . . 3J 151
Holme Way WF5: Oss . . . 4M 123
HOLME WOOD . . . 2H 83
Holme Wood BD22: Keigh . . . 1G 42
Holme Wood Rd. BD4: B'frd . . . 2H 83
BD22: Keigh . . . 1F 42
Holme Woods La. HD9: H'lm . . . 1E 174
HOLMFIELD . . . 8N 79
Holmfield BD22: Oxen . . . 5C 60
HD8: Clay W . . . 7J 157
Holmfield Av. HD8: Clay W . . . 7J 157
WF2: Wake . . . 8K 125
Holmfield Chase WF3: S'ley . . . 6C 106
Holmfield Cl. HD8: Clay W . . . 7J 157
WF8: Pon . . . 8M 109
Holmfield Cotts. LS26: Meth . . . 1M 107
Holmfield Ct. BD1: B'frd . . . 4A 6
WF8: Pon . . . 9M 109
Holmfield Dr. HD7: Golc . . . 6E 136
LS8: Leeds . . . 6J 51
Holmfield Gdns. HX2: Hal . . . 8N 79
Holmfield Gro. WF2: Wake . . . 8K 125
Holmfield Ho. HX3: Hal . . . 8N 79
Holmfield Ind. Est. HX2: Hal . . . 6N 79
Holmfield Ind. Est. Rd. HX2: Hal . . . 6N 79
Holmfield La. WF2: Wake . . . 8K 125
WF8: Pon . . . 9M 109
WF11: Ferr . . . 7M 109
Holmfield Rd. HD3: Hud . . . 4C 136
HD8: Clay W . . . 7J 157
Holmfield St. BD1: B'frd . . . 7B 64
Holmfield Ter. *HD8: Clay W* . . . *7J 157*
(off Holmfield Av.)
HOLMFIRTH . . . 3M 169
Holmfirth Picturedrome . . . 3M 169
Holmfirth Pool . . . 1N 169
Holmfirth Rd. HD8: Shep . . . 2G 171
HD9: Mel . . . 8D 152
HD9: New M . . . 1B 170
OL3: Green . . . 9A 166
Holmfirth Town Ga. HD9: H'frth . . . 3M 169
Holmsley Av. WF9: S Kirk . . . 7G 162
Holmsley Crest LS26: W'frd . . . 6B 88
Holmsley Fld. Ct. LS26: Oul . . . 7D 88
Holmsley Fld. La. LS26: Oul . . . 7C 88
Holmsley Gth. LS26: W'frd . . . 6C 88
Holmsley Grn. LS26: W'frd . . . 6C 88
Holmsley Gro. WF9: S Kirk . . . 7G 163
Holmsley La. LS26: W'frd . . . 7B 88
S72: B'ley . . . 8E 162
WF9: S Kirk . . . 8E 162
Holmsley Mt. WF9: S Kirk . . . 7G 163
Holmsley Wlk. LS26: Oul . . . 7C 88
Holmwood LS8: Leeds . . . 5J 51
Holmwood Av. LS6: Leeds . . . 7A 50
Holmwood Cl. LS6: Leeds . . . 7B 50
Holmwood Cres. LS6: Leeds . . . 7B 50
Holmwood Dr. LS6: Leeds . . . 7A 50
Holmwood Gro. LS6: Leeds . . . 7B 50
Holmwood Mt. LS6: Leeds . . . 7B 50
Holmwood Vw. LS6: Leeds . . . 7A 50
Holroyd Hill BD6: B'frd . . . 4A 82
Holroyd Mill La. BD16: Bgly . . . 8D 28
Holroyd Sq. HX4: Stainl . . . 7M 117
Holroyd St. LS7: Leeds . . . 2J 5 (4F 68)
Holsworthy Rd. BD4: B'frd . . . 3J 83
Holt, The BD18: Ship . . . 7A 46
Holt Av. LS16: Leeds . . . 2M 49
Holtby Gro. HX3: Hip . . . 5M 99
Holt Cl. LS16: Leeds . . . 3M 49
Holt Cres. LS16: Leeds . . . 2J 49
Holtdale App. LS16: Leeds . . . 2H 49
Holtdale Av. LS16: Leeds . . . 2J 49
Holtdale Cl. LS16: Leeds . . . 2J 49
Holtdale Cft. LS16: Leeds . . . 2J 49
Holtdale Dr. LS16: Leeds . . . 2J 49
Holtdale Fold LS16: Leeds . . . 2J 49
Holtdale Gdns. LS16: Leeds . . . 2J 49
Holtdale Gth. LS16: Leeds . . . 2J 49
Holtdale Grn. LS16: Leeds . . . 2J 49
Holtdale Gro. LS16: Leeds . . . 2H 49
Holtdale Lawn LS16: Leeds . . . 2J 49
Holtdale Pl. LS16: Leeds . . . 2J 49
Holtdale Rd. LS16: Leeds . . . 2J 49
Holtdale Vw. LS16: Leeds . . . 2J 49
Holtdale Way LS16: Leeds . . . 2J 49
Holt Dr. LS16: Leeds . . . 2K 49
Holt Farm Cl. LS16: Leeds . . . 2J 49
Holt Farm Ri. LS16: Leeds . . . 2J 49
Holt Gdns. BD10: B'frd . . . 7E 46
LS16: Leeds . . . 2M 49
Holt Gth. LS16: Leeds . . . 2K 49
Holt Ga. LS16: Leeds . . . 2K 49
Holt Grn. LS16: Leeds . . . 2K 49
HOLT HEAD . . . 4M 151
Holt Head Rd. HD7: Linth, Slait . . . 4N 151
Holt La. HD9: H'frth . . . 2M 169
LS16: Leeds . . . 2H 49
Holt La. Ct. LS16: Leeds . . . 3L 49
HOLT PARK . . . 2J 49
Holt Pk. App. LS16: Leeds . . . 2K 49
Holt Pk. Av. LS16: Leeds . . . 2K 49
Holt Pk. Cl. LS16: Leeds . . . 2K 49
Holt Pk. Cres. LS16: Leeds . . . 2J 49
Holt Pk. District Cen. LS16: Leeds . . . 2J 49
Holt Pk. Dr. LS16: Leeds . . . 2K 49
Holt Pk. Gdns. LS16: Leeds . . . 2K 49
Holt Pk. Ga. LS16: Leeds . . . 2K 49
Holt Pk. Grange LS16: Leeds . . . 2K 49
Holt Pk. Grn. LS16: Leeds . . . 2K 49
Holt Pk. Gro. LS16: Leeds . . . 2J 49
Holt Pk. La. LS16: Leeds . . . 2K 49
Holt Pk. Leisure Cen. . . . 3J 49
Holt Pk. Ri. LS16: Leeds . . . 2K 49
Holt Pk. Rd. LS16: Leeds . . . 2K 49
Holt Pk. Va. LS16: Leeds . . . 2K 49
Holt Pk. Vw. LS16: Leeds . . . 2J 49
Holt Pk. Way LS16: Leeds . . . 2K 49
Holt Ri. LS16: Leeds . . . 2K 49
Holt Rd. LS16: Leeds . . . 2K 49
Holts La. BD14: Clay . . . 9G 62
Holts Ter. HX3: Hal . . . 8C 98
Holt St. OL15: Lit . . . 9M 113
Holt's Yd. WF1: Wake . . . 5H 9 (5K 125)
Holt Va. LS16: Leeds . . . 2K 49
Holt Wlk. LS16: Leeds . . . 2K 49
Holt Way LS16: Leeds . . . 2K 49
Holybrook Av. BD10: B'frd . . . 9H 47
Holybrook Ct. HX4: Holy . . . 7B 118
HOLY CROFT . . . 1H 43
Holycroft St. BD21: Keigh . . . 1H 43
Holyoake Av. BD16: Bgly . . . 6E 44
HD7: Linth . . . 1B 152
WF17: Bat . . . 7D 102
Holyoake St. OL14: Tod . . . 3C 92
Holyoake Ter. HD7: Linth . . . 9B 136
WF4: Horb . . . 1A 142
Holyrood Chase WF10: C'frd . . . 5C 108
Holyrood Cres. WF6: Alt . . . 8G 107
Holyrood La. LS25: Led . . . 5K 91
Holywell HD7: Linth . . . 9B 136
Holywell Ash La. BD8: B'frd . . . 1A 6 (5B 64)
Holywell Av. WF10: C'frd . . . 6H 109
Holywell Dene WF10: C'frd . . . 6G 108
Holywell Gdns. WF10: C'frd . . . 6G 108
HOLYWELL GREEN . . . 7A 118
Holywell Gro. *WF10: C'frd* . . . *6G 108*
(off Rock Hill)
Holywell Hall HX4: Holy . . . 7A 118
Holywell Halt Nature Trail . . . 3B 10
Holywell Halt Station
Embsay and Bolton Abbey Steam Railway . . . 3B 10
Holywell Ho. *HX4: Holy* . . . *7A 118*
(off Station Rd.)
Holywell La. LS17: Shad . . . 2M 51
WF10: C'frd . . . 6G 108
Holywell Mt. WF10: C'frd . . . 6H 109
Holywell Vw. LS17: Shad . . . 2M 51
Home Farm Cl. BD6: B'frd . . . 4J 81
Home Farm Ct. WF4: W Bret . . . 2B 158
Home Farm Dr. LS29: Men . . . 5D 30
Home Farm M. LS29: Men . . . 5E 30
Homefield Av. LS27: Morl . . . 2K 103
Home Lea LS26: Rothw . . . 6M 87
Home Lea Dr. LS26: Rothw . . . 6M 87
Homepaddock Ho. LS22: Weth . . . 3N 23
Homes, The HD2: Hud . . . 7D 120
Homestead, The WF16: Heck . . . 8B 102
Homestead Dr. WF2: Wake . . . 5H 125
Homestead Est. LS29: Men . . . 3E 30
Home Vw. Ter. BD8: B'frd . . . 5N 63
Honey Halling HD2: Hud . . . 7A 120
Honey Head La. HD9: Hon . . . 6L 153
Honey Hole Cl. OL14: Tod . . . 8K 93
Honey Hole Ct. *OL14: Tod* . . . *8K 93*
(off Honey Hole Rd.)
Honey Hole Rd. OL14: Tod . . . 8K 93
Honey Pot BD15: Wils . . . 3B 62
Honey Pot Dr. BD17: Bail . . . 4M 45
Honey Pot Fold BD17: Bail . . . 4M 45
Honey Pot La. BD17: Bail . . . 4M 45
Honey Pot Vw. *BD22: Oxen* . . . *4C 60*
(off Station Rd.)
Honeysuckle Cl. LS25: M'fld . . . 9H 73
WF2: Wake . . . 4G 125
Honeysuckle Dr. WF12: Dew . . . 8G 122
Honeysuckle Way WF10: C'frd . . . 7B 108
HONLEY . . . 4L 153
Honley Bus. Cen. HD9: Hon . . . 5M 153
Honley Ho. *WF4: Horb* . . . *1C 142*
(off Honley Sq.)
Honley La. HD4: Farn T . . . 3A 154
HONLEY MOOR . . . 6K 153
Honley Sq. WF4: Horb . . . 1C 142
Honley Station (Rail) . . . 4N 153
Honoria St. HD1: Hud . . . 1M 137
Hoods, The HD6: Ras . . . 4L 119
Hood St. HD4: Hud . . . 1L 153
WF9: S Elm . . . 8L 163
Hoo Hole La. HX7: Crag V . . . 5K 95
Hoopoe M. BD15: All . . . 7G 63
Hooton Cres. WF4: Ryh . . . 9H 145
Hoowood La. HD9: H'lm . . . 5D 168
Hopbine Av. BD5: B'frd . . . 3C 82
Hopbine Rd. BD5: B'frd . . . 3C 82
Hope Av. BD5: B'frd . . . 3A 82
BD18: Ship . . . 7B 46
Hope Bank HD9: Hon . . . 6N 153
Hope Bldgs. *OL14: Tod* . . . *7L 93*
(off Every St.)
Hopefield Chase LS26: Rothw . . . 9K 87
Hopefield Cl. LS26: Rothw . . . 9K 87
Hopefield Ct. HD9: Had E . . . 9N 169
LS26: Rothw . . . 9K 87
WF3: E Ard . . . 5E 104
Hopefield Cres. LS26: Rothw . . . 9K 87
Hopefield Dr. LS26: Rothw . . . 9K 87

Hopefield Gdns.—Hyde Pl.

Hopefield Gdns. LS26: Rothw 9K 87
Hopefield Grn. LS26: Rothw 9K 87
Hopefield Gro. LS26: Rothw 9K 87
Hopefield M. LS26: Rothw 9K 87
Hopefield Pl. LS26: Rothw 9K 87
Hopefield Vw. LS26: Rothw 9K 87
Hopefield Wlk. LS26: Rothw 9K 87
Hopefield Way BD5: B'frd 4F 82
LS26: Rothw 9K 87
Hope Hall St. HX1: Hal 6L 7 (6B 98)
Hope Hall Ter. HX1: Hal 6L 7
Hope Hill Vw. BD16: Cot 8F 44
Hope La. BD17: Bail 3N 45
Hope Pk. BD5: B'frd 4D 82
Hope Pastures 5M 49
Hope Pl. BD21: Keigh 2J 43
Hope Rd. LS9: Leeds 5J 5 (6F 68)
Hopes Farm Mt. LS10: Leeds 6H 87
Hopes Farm Rd. LS10: Leeds 6H 87
Hopes Farm Vw. LS10: Leeds 6H 87
Hope St. HD3: Hud 5G 136
HX1: Hal 3H 7 (5A 98)
HX3: She 9G 80
HX6: Sow B 9H 97
HX7: Heb B 1H 95
LS27: Morl 9K 85
OL14: Tod 7L 93
S75: S'ross 9L 159
WF1: Wake 2K 9 (4L 125)
WF4: H'cft 2K 161
WF5: Oss 8B 124
WF6: Norm 3H 127
WF10: C'frd 2J 109
WF13: Dew 2E 122
WF16: Heck 8A 102
Hope St. E. WF10: C'frd 4D 108
Hope St. W. WF10: C'frd 5C 108
Hope Ter. HD7: Golc 7C 136
WF4: Croft 2G 145
HOPETOWN 9L 107
Hopetown Wlk. WF6: Norm 9L 107
Hope Vw. BD18: Ship 8B 46
Hopewell Pl. LS6: Leeds 4A 68
Hopewell St. WF17: Bat 6E 102
Hopewell Ter. LS18: Hors 8E 48
LS25: Kip 4B 90
Hopewell Vw. LS10: Leeds 8F 86
Hopewell Way WF4: Crig 5G 142
Hopkinson Bldgs. *HX3: Hal* *1M 97*
(off Foundry St. Nth.)
Hopkinson Dr. BD4: B'frd 5G 82
Hopkinson Rd. HD2: Hud 7N 119
Hopkinson St. HX3: Hal 1M 97
Hopkin St. BD4: B'frd 4J 83
Hops Dr. HD2: Hud 2L 137
Hops La. HX3: Hal 2K 97
Hopton Av. BD4: B'frd 4F 82
WF14: Up H 9J 121
Hopton Ct. *LS12: Leeds* *7L 67*
(off Hopton M.)
Hopton Dr. WF14: Up H 9J 121
Hopton Hall La. WF14: Up H 2K 139
Hopton La. WF14: Mir, Up H 9J 121
Hopton M. LS12: Leeds 7L 67
Hopton New Rd. WF14: Mir 8L 121
Hopwood Bank LS18: Hors 5F 48
Hopwood Cl. LS18: Hors 5F 48
Hopwood Gro. WF10: C'frd 5H 109
Hopwood La. HX1: Hal 5G 7 (6L 97)
(not continuous)
Hopwood Rd. LS18: Hors 5F 48
Horace Waller VC Pde.
WF12: Dew 1K 123
HORBURY 1D 142
HORBURY BRIDGE 1A 142
HORBURY JUNCTION 2E 142
Horbury M. WF4: Horb 9B 124
Horbury Rd. S72: Cud 9J 161
WF2: Wake 8F 124
WF5: Oss 8A 124
Horley Grn. La. HX3: Hal 3D 98
Horley Grn. Rd. HX3: Hal 3D 98
Hornbeam Av. WF2: Wake 3J 125
Hornbeam Cl. BD15: All 2E 62
Hornbeam Ct. LS20: Guis 7H 31
Hornbeam Grn. WF8: Pon 2M 129
Hornbeam Gro. HX3: North 9E 80
Hornbeam Way LS14: Leeds 7D 52
Hornby St. HX1: Hal 6M 97
Hornby Ter. HX1: Hal 6M 97
Horncastle St. BD19: Cleck 5J 101
Horncastle Vw. WF4: H'cft 8L 145
Horn Cote La. HD9: New M 1E 170
(not continuous)
Horner Av. WF17: Bat 6C 102
Horner Cres. WF17: Bat 6C 102
Horner Pl. WF6: Norm 1H 127
Horner's Bldgs. *HX2: Hal* *8N 79*
(off Shay La.)
Horners Fold BD20: E Mor 7C 28
Hornes La. S75: S'ross 8L 159
Horne St. HX1: Hal 3H 7 (5A 98)
WF2: Wake 8J 9 (7L 125)
Horn La. BD20: Sils 4B 12
HD9: New M 2D 170
S36: Ing 7L 171
Hornsea Dr. BD15: Wils 2B 62
Horse Bank Dr. HD4: Hud 8J 137
Horse Cl. BD12: Wyke 9M 81
Horse Cft. La. HD8: Shel 6M 155
Horsefair LS22: Weth 4N 23
WF8: Pon 2K 129
Horsefair Centre, The LS22: Weth 4N 23
Horsehold La. HX7: Heb B 2F 94
Horsehold Rd. HX7: Heb B 2F 94
Horse Pond La. HD3: Outl 3N 135
HORSE RACE END 7D 126
Horseshoe Ct. BD15: Wils 2A 62
Horse Shoe Yd. HD1: Hud 1A 8
HORSEWOOD 9N 93
Horsfall Stadium 6N 81
Horsfall St. HX1: Hal 7N 97
LS27: Morl 7J 85
OL14: Tod 6N 93
Horsforde Vw. LS13: Leeds 9E 48
HORSFORTH 7E 48
Horsforth Golf Course 4C 48
Horsforth New Rd. LS13: Leeds 9B 48
Horsforth Station (Rail) 4F 48
Horsforth Village Mus. 7E 48
Horsham Ct. BD22: Keigh 2E 42
Horsham Rd. BD4: B'frd 3J 83
Horsley Fold HD6: Clift 1C 120
Horsley St. BD6: B'frd 4A 82
Horsman St. BD4: B'frd 4J 83
HORTON BANK 2J 81
HORTON BANK BOTTOM 3M 81
Horton Bank Country Pk. 2J 81
HORTON BANK TOP 3J 81
Horton Cl. LS13: Leeds 2C 66
Horton Gth. LS13: Leeds 2C 66
Horton Grange Rd. BD7: B'frd 8N 63
Horton Hall Cl. BD5: B'frd 9B 64
Horton Ho. *BD3: B'frd* *6K 65*
(off Chapman Rd.)
Horton Ind. Est. BD7: B'frd 2M 81
Horton Pk. Av. BD5: B'frd 9N 63
BD7: B'frd 9N 63
Horton Pl. HX2: Brad 5M 79
Horton Ri. LS13: Leeds 2C 66
Horton St. HX1: Hal 5L 7 (6B 98)
WF5: Oss 5M 123
WF16: Heck 9A 102
Horton Ter. HX3: Hip 4G 99
Hospital La. LS16: Leeds 4J 49
Hospital Rd. BD20: Rid 7M 27
Hostingley La. WF4: M'twn 9J 123
WF12: T'hill 9J 123
Hothfield St. BD20: Sils 8D 12
Hot La. HX7: Hept 6A 76
Hough HX3: North 3E 98
Hough Cl. LS13: Leeds 6E 66
HOUGH END 6F 66
Hough End Av. LS13: Leeds 5G 66
Hough End Cl. LS13: Leeds 5G 66
Hough End Ct. LS13: Leeds 5G 66
Hough End Cres. LS13: Leeds 5F 66
Hough End Gdns. LS13: Leeds 5G 66
Hough End Gth. LS13: Leeds 5F 66
Hough End La. LS13: Leeds 5F 66
Hough Gro. LS13: Leeds 4F 66
Hough La. LS13: Leeds 4F 66
Houghley Av. LS12: Leeds 4J 67
Houghley Cl. LS13: Leeds 4H 67
Houghley Cres. LS12: Leeds 4J 67
Houghley La. LS12: Leeds 4H 67
LS13: Leeds 4H 67
Houghley Rd. LS12: Leeds 4J 67
Houghley Sq. LS12: Leeds 4J 67
HOUGH SIDE 7E 66
Hough Side Cl. LS28: Pud 7E 66
Hough Side La. LS28: Pud 7D 66
Hough Side Rd. LS28: Pud 7C 66
Hough Ter. LS13: Leeds 4F 66
Houghton Av. WF11: Ferr 7A 110
Houghton Pl. BD1: B'frd 2A 6 (6B 64)
Houghton's Almshouses HD5: Hud 7D 138
Houghton St. HD6: Brigh 9N 99
Houghton Towers HX6: Sow B 8H 97
Hough Top LS13: Leeds 7D 66
Hough Tree Rd. LS13: Leeds 6F 66
Hough Tree Ter. LS13: Leeds 6F 66
Hougomont BD13: Que 2B 80
Houldsworth Av. WF16: Heck 5B 102
Hoults La. HX4: Gree 3A 118
Houndhill La. WF7: F'stne 6F 128
HOUSES HILL 4K 139
Hove Ct. WF16: Heck 8A 102
HOVE EDGE 7L 99
Hovingham Av. LS8: Leeds 2J 69
Hovingham Gro. LS8: Leeds 2J 69
Hovingham Mt. LS8: Leeds 2J 69
Hovingham Ter. LS8: Leeds 2J 69
Howard Av. HD3: Hud 2H 137
LS15: Leeds 7A 70
Howard Ct. LS15: Leeds 7A 70
Howard Cres. WF4: Dur 4G 142
Howard Dr. WF7: Ackw 6F 146
Howard Pk. BD19: Cleck 5J 101
Howard Pl. WF17: Bat 9F 102
Howard Rd. HD3: Hud 2H 137
Howards Dean BD22: Haw 7D 42
Howard St. BD5: B'frd 6A 6 (8B 64)
HX1: Hal 4N 97
WF1: Wake 2J 9 (4L 125)
WF5: Oss 4N 123
WF17: Bat 9F 102
Howard Way HD9: Mel 8D 152
Howarth Av. BD2: B'frd 1E 64
Howarth Cres. BD2: B'frd 1E 64
Howarth La. HD1: Hud 7K 137
Howbeck Av. BD20: Rid 8N 27
Howbeck Dr. BD20: Rid 8N 27
Howcans La. HX3: Hal 8N 79
Howcroft Ct. WF2: Wake 3N 143
Howcroft Gdns. WF2: Wake 3N 143
Howden Av. BD20: Keigh 6G 26
DN6: Skel 8K 165
Howdenbrook HX3: She 6K 81
Howden Cl. BD4: B'frd 4K 83
HD4: Hud 8E 136
S75: Dart 8H 159
HOWDEN CLOUGH 2E 102
Howden Clough Ind. Est. WF17: Birs 1E 102
Howden Clough Rd. LS27: Morl 1F 102
Howden Gdns. LS6: Leeds 4A 68
Howden Pl. LS6: Leeds 4A 68
Howden Rd. BD20: Sils 8E 12
HOWDEN ROUGH 4H 27
Howden Way LS27: Morl 9G 85
WF1: Wake 5N 125
Howell M. WF9: S Kirk 7F 162
Howell Wood Country Pk. 9E 162
Howes La. HX3: North 1E 98
Howgate BD10: B'frd 7G 46
Howgate Hill HX3: Sou 7E 98
Howgate Ho. *WF13: Dew* *3F 122*
(off Wellington Rd.)
Howgate Rd. HD7: Slait 1M 151
Howgill Grn. BD6: B'frd 7M 81
Howley Cl. BD19: Gom 3L 101
Howley Hall Golf Course 5H 103
Howley Mill La. WF17: Bat 5G 103
Howley Pk. Bus. Village LS27: Morl 3J 103
Howley Pk. Cl. LS27: Morl 2J 103
Howley Pk. Rd. LS27: Morl 2J 103
Howley Pk. Rd. E. LS27: Morl 3J 103
Howley Pk. Ter. LS27: Morl 2J 103
Howley Pk. Trad. Est. LS27: Morl 2J 103
Howley Pk. Vw. LS27: Morl 2M 103
Howley St. WF17: Bat 6G 103
Howley Wlk. WF17: Bat 7H 103
Howorth St. OL14: Tod 4G 92
Howroyd La. HX4: Bark 7H 117
WF12: W'ley 2B 140
Howroyd's Yd. WF5: Oss 2M 123
Howson Cl. LS20: Guis 7K 31
Hoxton Mt. LS11: Leeds 2B 86
Hoxton St. BD8: B'frd 6M 63
Hoylake Av. HD2: Fix 8L 119
Hoyland Rd. WF2: Wake 5K 143
HOYLANDSWAINE 9K 173
Hoyland Ter. WF9: S Kirk 7G 163
Hoyle Beck Cl. HD7: Linth 9C 136
Hoyle Ct. Av. BD17: Bail 4C 46
Hoyle Ct. Dr. BD17: Bail 4C 46
Hoyle Ct. Rd. BD17: Bail 4C 46
Hoyle Fold BD22: Keigh 2F 42
Hoyle Ho. Fold HD7: Linth 9C 136
Hoyle Ing HD7: Linth 9C 136
Hoyle Ing Rd. BD13: Thorn 8E 62
Hoyle Mill Rd. WF9: Hems, Kins 9C 146
Hoyle Syke BD22: Oxen 2B 60
HUBBERTON GREEN 1C 116
Hubberton Grn. Rd. HX6: Sow B 1C 116
Hubert St. BD3: B'frd 8F 64
HD3: Hud 1D 136
HX2: Hal 5K 97
HUBY 5M 19
Huby Banks LS17: Huby 6M 19
Huby Pk. LS17: Huby 6M 19
Huck Hill La. HD7: Mars 5F 150
HUDDERSFIELD 4C 8 (5M 137)
Huddersfield Crematorium HD2: Fix 5M 119
Huddersfield Giants RLFC 1F 8 (2A 138)
Huddersfield Golf Course 8K 119
Huddersfield Lawn Tennis & Squash Club 3L 137
Huddersfield Library & Art Gallery 6C 8 (5N 137)
Huddersfield Rd. BD5: B'frd 7A 82
BD6: B'frd 7A 82
BD12: Low M, Wyke 4N 99
(not continuous)
HD3: Hud 7F 118
HD4: Neth 5F 152
HD6: Brigh, Ras 4N 119
HD8: Kbtn, Shel, Skelm 4K 155
(not continuous)
HD9: H'frth, T'bdge 3M 169
HD9: Hon 4M 153
HD9: Mel 7D 152
HD9: New M 9B 154
HX3: Hal 8L 7 (7B 98)
(not continuous)
HX5: Ell 7F 118
OL3: Del 9A 150
S36: Ing, Pen 7B 172
S75: Dart, Hai, Kex 5D 158
S75: Hai 1B 158
WF4: W Bret 9A 142
(Bower Hill La.)
WF4: W Bret 1B 158
(Bretton La.)
WF13: Dew, Raven 7L 121
WF14: Mir 4G 121
WF15: Liv 2L 121
WF16: Heck 5B 102
WF17: Birs 5B 102
Huddersfield RUFC 8K 137
Huddersfield Sports Cen. 4D 8 (4N 137)
Huddersfield Station (Rail) 4B 8 (4M 137)
Huddersfield Town FC 1F 8 (2A 138)
HUDDLESTON 6N 73
Huddleston Ct. WF12: Dew 3J 123
WF14: Mir 7L 121
Hud Hill HX3: She 9G 80
Hudroyd HD5: Hud 7D 138
Hudson, The BD12: Wyke 1A 100
Hudson Av. BD7: B'frd 1N 81
WF4: Not 3C 160
Hudson Cl. BD7: B'frd 2N 81
LS22: Weth 4M 23
Hudson Cres. BD7: B'frd 2N 81
Hudson Cft. HX4: Bark 4F 134
Hudson Gdns. BD7: B'frd 1N 81
Hudson Ga. BD12: Wyke 1A 100
Hudson Gro. LS9: Leeds 5J 69
Hudson M. LS23: B Spa 1E 38
Hudson Mill Rd. HX7: Blac H 8B 76
Hudson Pl. LS9: Leeds 5J 69
Hudson Rd. LS9: Leeds 4J 69
Hudson's Ter. LS19: Yead 9N 31
Hudson St. BD3: B'frd 7H 65
LS9: Leeds 5J 69
LS28: Fars 5A 66
OL14: Tod 3E 92
Hudson Vw. BD12: Wyke 1N 99
Hudson Way LS22: Weth 1M 23
Hudswell Rd. LS10: Leeds 1F 86
Hudswell St. WF1: Wake 8N 125
Huffa La. BD23: Bolt A 3K 11
Huggan Row *LS28: Pud* *7C 66*
(off Hammerton Gro.)
Hughenden Vw. LS27: Morl 7K 85
Hughendon Dr. BD13: Thorn 8F 62
Hughendon Wlk. BD13: Thorn 8F 62
Hugh St. WF10: C'frd 5D 108
(not continuous)
Hugill St. BD13: Thorn 8C 62
Hulbert Cft. HD5: Hud 6D 138
Hulbert St. BD16: Bgly 5F 44
Hullenedge Gdns. HX5: Ell 5C 118
Hullenedge La. HX4: Gree 5B 118
HX5: Ell 5B 118
Hullenedge Rd. HX5: Ell 5C 118
Hullen Rd. HX5: Ell 5C 118
Hullett Cl. HX7: Myth 3N 95
Hullett Dr. HX7: Myth 3N 95
Hull St. LS27: Morl 9L 85
Hulme Sq. WF10: C'frd 3K 109
Hulme St. *HX6: Sow B* *9H 97*
(off Syke La.)
Humber Cl. DN6: Skel 8M 165
HD7: Linth 9C 136
WF10: C'frd 4H 109
Humber Ct. DN6: Skel 8M 165
Humber Pl. WF4: Horb 9C 124
Humboldt St. BD1: B'frd 3E 6 (7E 64)
Hume Crest WF17: Bat 7F 102
Humley Rd. WF2: Wake 5K 143
Hundhill WF8: E Hard 9K 129
Hundhill La. WF8: E Hard 9K 129
HUNGATE 4F 106
Hungate Cl. LS24: Saxt 9N 55
Hungate La. LS26: Meth 4F 106
Hungerford Rd. HD3: Hud 2J 137
HUNGER HILL 5E 80
Hunger Hill HX1: Hal 6L 7 (6B 98)
LS27: Morl 1K 103
LS29: Midd 1G 15
Hunger Hill Rd. LS29: Midd 1H 15
Hunger Hills Av. LS18: Hors 6D 48
Hunger Hills Dr. LS18: Hors 6D 48
HUNSLET 1F 86
Hunslet Bus. Pk. LS10: Leeds 9G 68
HUNSLET CARR 4F 86
Hunslet Distributor LS10: Leeds 1F 86
Hunslet Grn. Retail Cen. LS10: Leeds 2F 86
Hunslet Grn. Way LS10: Leeds 1F 86
Hunslet Hall Rd. LS11: Leeds 1D 86
Hunslet Hawks 5E 86
Hunslet Ho. LS10: Leeds 8G 5
Hunslet La. LS10: Leeds 8E 68
(Crown Point Rd.)
LS10: Leeds 8G 5 (8E 68)
(Salem Pl.)
Hunslet Rd. LS10: Leeds 8F 68
(Sheaf St., not continuous)
LS10: Leeds 8G 5 (7E 68)
(Waterloo St.)
Hunslet Trad. Est. LS10: Leeds 1H 87
Hunston Av. HD3: Hud 3G 136
HUNSWORTH 2H 101
Hunsworth La. BD4: E Bier 1H 101
BD19: Cleck, Hun 3H 101
(not continuous)
Hunt Ct. WF2: Wake 5G 124
Hunter Hill Rd. HX2: Mix 8G 79
Hunterscombe Ct. BD16: Bgly 2J 45
Hunters Ct. BD9: B'frd 2H 63
LS15: Leeds 7B 70
Hunters Farm Glade WF9: Kins 9B 146
Hunters Glen BD20: Sils 7E 12
Hunters Grn. BD13: Cull 8K 43
Hunters La. OL14: Tod 6H 93
Hunters Mdw. BD20: Sils 7E 12
Hunters Nab HD4: Farn T 1D 154
Hunters Pk. Av. BD14: Clay 9J 63
Hunters Wlk. LS22: Weth 1M 23
Hunters Way LS15: Leeds 7B 70
Huntingdon Av. HD2: Hud 6D 120
Huntingdon Rd. HD6: Brigh 2A 120
Huntington Cres. LS16: Leeds 8M 49
Huntock Pl. HD6: Brigh 7L 99
Huntsman Fold WF2: Wake 5F 124
Huntsman Ho.
LS10: Leeds 8G 5 (8E 68)
Huntsmans Cl. BD16: Bgly 2H 45
BD20: Keigh 8G 27
HD4: Hud 1J 153
Huntsmans Way WF9: Bads 8L 147
Hunt St. WF10: C'frd 3D 108
(Lock La.)
WF10: C'frd 4B 108
(Methley Rd.)
Huntwick Av. WF7: F'stne 7C 128
Huntwick Cres. WF7: F'stne 7B 128
Huntwick Dr. WF7: F'stne 7B 128
Huntwick La. WF7: Street 9N 127
Huntwick Rd. WF7: F'stne 7C 128
Hunt Yd. BD7: B'frd 1M 81
Hurst Knowle HD5: Hud 6E 138
Hurst La. WF14: Mir 8M 121
Hurst Rd. HX7: Heb B 9J 77
Hurst Royd HX7: Heb B 9J 77
Hurstville Av. BD4: E Bier 7K 83
Hurstwood HD2: Hud 7C 120
Husler Gro. LS7: Leeds 3F 68
Husler Pl. LS7: Leeds 3F 68
Hustings, The WF15: Liv 8K 101
Hustlergate BD1: B'frd 4B 6 (7C 64)
Hustler's Row LS6: Leeds 7N 49
Hustler St. BD3: B'frd 1F 6 (5E 64)
(not continuous)
Hutchinson La. HD6: Brigh 1N 119
Hutchinson Pl. LS5: Leeds 3K 67
Hutson St. BD5: B'frd 1B 82
Hutton Cl. BD3: B'frd 6K 65
Hutton Dr. WF9: S Elm 5N 163
WF16: Heck 8B 102
Hutton Rd. BD5: B'frd 3A 82
Hutton Ter. BD2: B'frd 1H 65
LS28: Pud 7B 66
Huxley Mt. BD2: B'frd 1G 64
Hydale Cl. BD21: Keigh 2L 43
Hydale Ct. BD12: Low M 7A 82
Hyde Gro. *BD21: Keigh* *8K 27*
(off Kirby St.)
HYDE PARK 3A 68
Hyde Pk. HX1: Hal 6G 7 (6N 97)
WF1: Wake 5N 125
Hyde Pk. Cl. LS6: Leeds 2A 4 (4B 68)
Hyde Pk. Cnr. LS6: Leeds 3B 68
Hyde Pk. Pl. LS6: Leeds 3B 68
Hyde Pk. Rd. HX1: Hal 7G 7 (7N 97)
LS6: Leeds 1A 4 (4B 68)
Hyde Pk. St. HX1: Hal 6G 7 (7N 97)
Hyde Pk. Ter. LS6: Leeds 3B 68
Hyde Pk. Vs. *LS6: Leeds* *3B 68*
(off Bk. Kensington Ter.)
Hyde Pl. LS2: Leeds 4B 4 (5C 68)

Hyde St.—Jaggar La.

Hyde St. BD10: B'frd 6F 46
LS2: Leeds 4B 4 (5C 68)
Hyde Ter. LS2: Leeds 3B 4 (5C 68)
Hyde Way WF3: Thpe H 2H 105
Hydro Cl. LS29: I'ly 6L 15
Hyman Wlk. WF9: S Elm 5N 163
Hyne Av. BD4: B'frd 4F 82
Hyrst Gth. WF17: Bat 9E 102
Hyrstlands Rd. WF17: Bat 9E 102
Hyrst Wlk. WF17: Bat 9F 102

I

Ibberson Av. S75: Map 9K 159
Ibbetson Cl. LS27: Chur 6K 85
Ibbetson Ct. LS27: Chur 6K 85
Ibbetson Cft. LS27: Chur 6K 85
Ibbetson Dr. LS27: Chur 6K 85
Ibbetson M. LS27: Chur 6K 85
Ibbetson Oval LS27: Chur 6K 85
Ibbetson Ri. LS27: Chur 6K 85
Ibbetson Rd. LS27: Chur 6K 85
Ibbotroyd Av. OL14: Tod 5J 93
Ibbotson Flats HD1: Hud 3C 8
Ibbottson St. WF1: Wake 8A 126
Ida's, The LS10: Leeds 3J 87
Ida St. BD5: B'frd 2A 82
LS10: Leeds 3J 87
Iddesleigh St. BD4: B'frd 8G 65
IDLE 7F 46
Idlecroft Rd. BD10: B'frd 7F 46
IDLE MOOR 8D 46
Idle Rd. BD2: B'frd 1E 64
Idlethorp Way BD10: B'frd 8G 46
Ilbert Av. BD4: B'frd 4G 82
Ilford St. LS27: Morl 9L 85
ILKLEY 5G 14
Ilkley Golf Course 3E 14
Ilkley Hall M. LS29: I'ly 6G 15
Ilkley Hall Pk. LS29: I'ly 6G 15
Ilkley Lawn Tennis & Squash Club 4E 14
Ilkley Playhouse *5G 15*
(off Weston Rd.)
Ilkley Pool & Lido 3G 15
Ilkley Rd. BD20: Rid 6M 27
LS21: Otley 1J 31
LS29: Add 2N 13
LS29: Burl W 6B 16
Ilkley Station (Rail) 5G 15
Ilkley Toy Mus. *5G 15*
(off Whitton Cft. Rd.)
ILLINGWORTH 7L 79
Illingworth Av. HX2: Illing 5L 79
WF6: Alt 8F 106
Illingworth Bldgs. *BD12: O'haw* *9D 82*
(off Illingworth Rd.)
Illingworth Cl. BD21: Keigh 4G 43
HX2: Illing 6L 79
LS19: Yead 2N 47
Illingworth Cres. HX2: Illing 6L 79
Illingworth Dr. HX2: Illing 6L 79
Illingworth Gdns. HX2: Illing 7L 79
Illingworth Gro. HX2: Illing 6L 79
Illingworth Rd. BD12: O'haw 9D 82
HX2: Illing 7L 79
Illingworth St. WF5: Oss 6N 123
Illingworth Vs. *HX7: Heb B* *9H 77*
(off Lee Mill Rd.)
Illingworth Way HX2: Illing 6L 79
IMAX Cinema
Bradford 6A 6
Imex Bus. Cen. *BD19: Cleck* *4H 101*
(off Balme Rd.)
Imperial Arc. HD1: Hud 5B 8
Imperial Av. WF2: Wren 1H 125
Imperial Cl. HD6: B Bri 5N 99
Imperial Rd. HD1: Hud 3J 137
HD3: Hud 3J 137
Imperial Ter. *LS12: Leeds* *6L 67*
(off Theaker La.)
Inchfield Rd. OL14: W'den 3H 113
Inch La. WF9: S Elm 3M 163
Incline, The HX3: Hal 4D 98
Independent Ho. WF16: Heck 8B 102
Independent St. BD5: B'frd 2A 82
Indigoblu *LS10: Leeds* *8E 68*
(off Crown Point Rd.)
Indoor Bowls & Athletic Cen.
Beeston 4E 86
Indus Cl. WF16: Heck 8B 102
Industrial Av. WF17: Birs 3A 102
Industrial Pl. HX1: Hal 5L 7
Industrial Rd. HX6: Sow B 8G 97
Industrial St. BD16: Bgly 4E 44
BD19: Scho 4D 100
BD22: Keigh 1G 42
HD4: Hud 7M 137
HD6: Brigh 9N 99
LS9: Leeds 3M 5 (5H 69)
OL14: Tod 7K 93
WF1: Wake 3K 9 (4L 125)
WF4: Horb 2E 142
WF15: Liv 8J 101
Industrial Ter. HD5: Hud 5E 138
HX1: Hal 8H 7 (7A 98)
Industry Rd. S71: Carl 9D 160
Industry St. OL14: W'den 2J 113
Infirmary Rd. WF13: Dew 2E 122
Infirmary St. BD1: B'frd 3A 6 (6B 64)
(not continuous)
LS1: Leeds 6E 4 (6D 68)
INGBIRCHWORTH 7B 172
Ingbirchworth La. S36: Ing 8B 172
Ingdale Dr. HD9: H'frth 2N 169
Ingester St. *BD22: Haw* *8B 42*
(off West La.)
Ing Fld. BD12: O'haw 9E 82
Ingfield Av. HD5: Hud 4B 138
WF5: Oss 5A 124
Ingfield Ter. *HD7: Slait* *9N 135*
(off Knowle Rd.)
OL14: Tod 3E 92
Ingham Cl. HX2: Brad 5M 79
WF14: Mir 6N 121
Ingham Cft. WF14: Mir 7N 121
Ingham Gth. WF14: Mir 6N 121
Ingham La. HX2: Brad 4L 79
Ingham Rd. WF12: Dew 8F 122
Inghams Av. LS28: Pud 7M 65
Inghams Ct. HX3: Hal 3N 97
Inghams Ter. LS28: Pud 6M 65
Inghams Vw. LS28: Pud 6M 65
Ing Head HD7: Slait 9L 135
Ing Head Cotts. HX3: She 9H 81
Ing Head Gdns. HX3: She 9G 81
Ing Head La. HD4: Thurs 7E 154
Ing Head Rd. HD7: Slait 9K 135
Ing Head Ter. HX3: She 9G 81
(not continuous)
Ing La. HD4: Hud 8M 137
HD7: Slait 1J 151
Ingle Av. LS27: Morl 7J 85
Ingleborough Cl. BD4: B'frd 2J 83
Ingleborough Dr. LS27: Morl 1M 103
(not continuous)
Ingleby Pl. BD7: B'frd 8M 63
Ingleby Rd. BD7: B'frd 6M 63
BD8: B'frd 6M 63
Ingleby St. BD8: B'frd 7M 63
Ingleby Way LS10: Leeds 6G 86
Ingle Ct. LS27: Morl 8J 85
(Earlsmere Dr.)
LS27: Morl 7J 85
(Springfield Av.)
Ingle Cres. LS27: Morl 7K 85
Ingle Dene HX7: Heb B 2E 94
Ingledew Cl. LS17: Leeds 3F 50
Ingledew Cres. LS8: Leeds 5K 51
Ingledew Dr. LS8: Leeds 6K 51
Ingle Gro. LS27: Morl 8J 85
Ingle La. LS29: Men 5F 30
Ingle Row LS7: Leeds 9F 50
Ingleton Cl. LS11: Leeds 2D 86
Ingleton Dr. LS15: Leeds 7N 69
Ingleton Gro. LS11: Leeds 2D 86
Ingleton Pl. LS11: Leeds 2D 86
Ingleton Rd. HD4: Hud 8N 137
Ingleton St. LS11: Leeds 2D 86
Inglewood S75: Dart 8J 159
WF1: Wake 1L 9 (3M 125)
Inglewood App.
LS14: Leeds 3C 70
Inglewood Av. HD2: Hud 1H 137
Inglewood Ct. HX3: Hip 4J 99
Inglewood Dr. LS14: Leeds 3C 70
LS21: Otley 1K 31
Inglewood Est. LS21: Otley 1K 31
Inglewood Pl. LS14: Leeds 3C 70
Inglewood Ter. *LS6: Leeds* *2C 68*
(off Delph La.)
Ingram Cl. LS11: Leeds 9B 68
Ingram Ct. LS11: Leeds 9B 68
Ingram Cres. LS11: Leeds 1B 86
WF11: Knot 9C 110
Ingram Gdns. LS11: Leeds 9B 68
Ingram Pde. LS26: Rothw 8N 87
Ingram Rd. LS11: Leeds 1B 86
Ingram Row LS11: Leeds 8D 68
Ingram Sq. HX1: Hal 7N 97
Ingram St. BD21: Keigh 4H 43
HX1: Hal 7N 97
LS11: Leeds 8D 68
Ingram Vw. LS11: Leeds 9B 68
INGROW 4G 42
Ingrow Bri. BD21: Keigh 3H 43
Ingrow La. BD21: Keigh 3G 43
BD22: Keigh 3F 42
Ingrow Railway Cen. 3H 43
Ingrow West Station
Keighley & Worth Valley Railway 3H 43
Ings, The HD8: Clay W 7J 157
HX3: Hip 6M 99
Ings Av. LS20: Guis 6H 31
Ingsback M. WF1: Wake 6K 9 (6L 125)
Ings Cl. WF4: H'cft 9K 145
WF9: S Kirk 6K 163
Ings Ct. LS20: Guis 6G 31
Ings Cres. LS9: Leeds 7K 69
LS20: Guis 7G 31
WF12: T'hill 9F 122
WF15: Liv 8M 101
Ings Cft. HX3: She 7H 81
Ings Dr. LS26: Meth 1M 107
Ings Grange *WF15: Liv* *7M 101*
(off Ings Rd.)
Ings Holt WF9: S Kirk 5K 163
Ings Ho. WF9: Kins 9B 146
Ings La. DN6: Skel 9M 165
DN14: Beal 5M 111
LS20: Guis 7G 31
LS21: Otley 9M 17
LS23: T Arch 9G 25
LS24: Tad 9N 25
WF10: All B 9D 90
WF10: C'frd 2F 108
WF12: T'hill 9F 122
Ings Mere Ct. WF11: Fair 9N 91
Ings Mill WF5: Oss 5A 124
Ings Mill Av. HD8: Clay W 6J 157
Ings Mill Dr. HD8: Clay W 6J 157
Ings Mill Yd. WF16: Heck 8N 101
Ings Ri. WF17: Bat 6E 102
Ings Rd. BD20: Stee 1B 26
HD5: Hud 6E 138
LS9: Leeds 7K 69
WF1: Wake 6J 9 (6L 125)
WF2: Wake 6G 9 (6K 125)
WF9: Kins 9B 146
WF13: Dew 2H 123
WF15: Liv 7M 101
WF16: Heck 8A 102
WF17: Bat 6D 102
Ing St. BD3: B'frd 7H 65
Ings Vw. LS26: Meth 1M 107
WF10: C'frd 4H 109
Ings Villa WF15: Liv 1N 121
Ings Wlk. WF9: S Kirk 6K 163
Ings Way BD8: B'frd 6K 63
BD20: Sils 8E 12
Ings Way HD8: Lept 7J 139
S36: Ing 7A 172
Ings Way E. HD8: Lept 7J 139
Ings Way W. HD8: Lept 7J 139
Ingswell Av. WF4: Not 2A 160
Ingswell Dr. WF4: Not 2A 160
Ingwell Ct. WF1: Wake 5M 9 (5M 125)
Ingwell St. WF1: Wake 5L 9 (5M 125)
Ingwell Ter. BD19: Cleck 5J 101
Ingwood Pde. HX4: Gree 5B 118
Inholmes La. LS23: W'ton 5H 25
Inkerman Ct. HD8: Den D 3D 172
Inkerman St. BD2: B'frd 2H 65
BD4: B'frd 1H 83
Inkerman Way HD8: Den D 3C 172
Inkersley Rd. BD1: B'frd 1A 6 (5C 64)
Inmoor Rd. BD11: B'haw 6M 83
Inner Hey HD7: Mars 5G 150
Inner Ring Rd. LS1: Leeds 4C 4 (5C 68)
LS2: Leeds 3E 4 (5C 68)
Innfold Farm WF4: W Bret 1B 158
Innings, The BD10: B'frd 7E 46
Innovation Sq. WF7: F'stne 5B 128
Institute Rd. BD2: B'frd 1G 64
INTAKE 2D 66
Intake BD22: Keigh 1E 42
HD7: Golc 5D 136
Intake, The *LS25: Kip* *4B 90*
(off Roger Fold)
Intake Cl. WF3: S'ley 7A 106
Intake Gro. BD2: B'frd 4G 65
Intake Head HD7: Mars 5D 150
Intake Laithe BD22: Old 7K 41
Intake La. BD20: Stee 4A 26
BD22: Oxen 6A 60
HD4: S Cros 2E 152
HD7: Slait 5M 151
HD8: Cumb 4F 170
LS10: Leeds 1E 104
LS13: Leeds 3C 66
LS14: T'ner 4E 52
LS19: Raw 4A 48
LS28: Stan 3C 66
S72: Cud 9K 161
WF3: S'ley 7A 106
(not continuous)
WF4: Wool 2F 158
WF5: Oss 6A 124
WF11: Birk 3M 111
WF17: Bat 4C 102
Intake Mt. LS10: Leeds 9E 86
Intake Rd. BD2: B'frd 4G 64
HD7: Slait 8J 135
LS28: Pud 6C 66
Intake Sq. LS10: Leeds 9E 86
Intake Ter. BD2: B'frd 5G 65
Intake Vw. LS10: Leeds 9E 86
LS13: Leeds 3D 66
Intercity Way LS13: Leeds 5C 66
Intermezzo Dr. LS10: Leeds 4K 87
International Ho. BD5: B'frd 9A 64
Invargarry Cl. LS25: Gar 6B 72
Inverness Rd. LS25: Gar 7B 72
Invertrees Av. LS19: Raw 3N 47
Iona Pl. HX3: Hal 2B 98
Iona St. HX3: Hal 2B 98
Iqbal Ct. BD3: B'frd 8H 65
Ireland Cres. LS16: Leeds 4J 49
Ireland St. BD16: Bgly 4D 44
Ireland Ter. BD16: Bgly 4D 44
IRELAND WOOD 5J 49
Ireton St. BD7: B'frd 2N 81
Irish La. BD22: Oak 5A 42
Iron Row LS29: Burl W 8D 16
(Back La.)
LS29: Burl W 7D 16
(Gt. Pasture La.)
Ironstone Dr. LS12: N Far 1K 85
Ironstone Gdns. LS12: N Far 2K 85
Iron St. BD19: Cleck 5G 101
Ironwood App. LS14: Leeds 3B 70
Ironwood Cres. LS14: Leeds 3B 70
Ironwood Vw. LS14: Leeds 2B 70
Irving St. HX1: Hal 7M 97
Irving Ter. BD14: Clay 2H 81
Irvin Ter. *WF10: C'frd* *5C 108*
(off High Oxford St.)
Irwell St. BD4: B'frd 8F 6 (9E 64)
Irwin App. LS15: Leeds 7A 70
Irwin Av. WF1: Wake 4A 126
Irwin Cres. WF1: Wake 4N 125
Irwin St. LS28: Fars 4A 66
(not continuous)
Isaac St. BD8: B'frd 6N 63
Isabella Rd. LS25: Gar 6A 72
Island, The WF11: Knot 7F 110
Island Dr. HD9: Brock 7A 154
Island Vw. WF12: Dew 5E 122
Islay Cl. LS26: Rothw 8A 88
Isle La. BD22: Oxen 7C 60
Isles St. BD8: B'frd 6L 63
ISLINGTON 1N 85
Issues Rd. HD9: H'lm 7B 168
Ivanhoe Rd. BD7: B'frd 9N 63
Ivegate BD1: B'frd 4B 6 (7C 64)
LS19: Yead 9M 31
Ive Ho. La. HX2: Lud 4E 96
Iveson App. LS16: Leeds 5J 49
Iveson Cl. LS16: Leeds 5J 49
Iveson Ct. LS16: Leeds 5J 49
Iveson Cres. LS16: Leeds 5J 49
Iveson Dr. LS16: Leeds 5J 49
Iveson Gdns. LS16: Leeds 5J 49
Iveson Gth. LS16: Leeds 5K 49
Iveson Grn. LS16: Leeds 5J 49
Iveson Gro. LS16: Leeds 5J 49
Iveson Lawn LS16: Leeds 5K 49
Iveson Ri. LS16: Leeds 5K 49
Iveson Rd. LS16: Leeds 5J 49
Iveson Wood Ri. LS16: Leeds 5K 49
Ives St. BD17: Ship 7N 45
(not continuous)
Ivey Way BD18: Ship 8M 45
Ivies, The *LS28: Pud* *7B 66*
(off Lidget Hill)
Ivory St. LS10: Leeds 9E 68
Ivy Av. LS9: Leeds 6J 69
Ivy Bank BD12: Wyke 9A 82
HX7: Heb B 2E 94
LS19: Yead 9L 31
OL12: Whit 8A 112
Ivy Bank Cl. S36: Ing 7A 172
Ivy Bank Ct. *BD17: Bail* *5B 46*
(off Dewhirst Cl.)
Ivy Bank La. BD22: Haw 9C 42
Ivy Chase LS28: Pud 6E 66
Ivy Cl. WF1: Wake 1M 9 (3N 125)
WF9: S Elm 7L 163
Ivy Cotts. HX1: Hal 8G 7
HX4: Bark 7F 116
S71: Roys 5E 160
Ivy Ct. LS7: Leeds 9F 50
LS29: I'ly 6G 14
Ivy Cres. HX3: Hip 5K 99
LS9: Leeds 6J 69
Ivy Farm Cl. S71: Carl 8E 160
Ivy Gdns. LS13: Leeds 2G 66
WF10: C'frd 7K 109
Ivy Gth. LS7: Leeds 9F 50
Ivy Gro. BD18: Ship 8K 45
LS9: Leeds 7K 69
WF1: Wake 1M 9 (3N 125)
Ivy Ho. Rd. BD5: B'frd 4C 82
Ivy Houses HX4: Bark 7F 116
Ivy La. BD15: All 4F 62
HX2: Mix 7K 79
LS23: B Spa 1C 38
WF1: Wake 1M 9 (3N 125)
Ivy Mt. HD7: Slait 9M 135
HX3: Hal 1C 118
LS9: Leeds 6J 69
Ivy Pl. BD2: B'frd 2F 64
LS13: Leeds 2G 66
OL14: Tod 3B 92
Ivy Rd. BD18: Ship 8K 45
BD21: Keigh 1L 43
LS9: Leeds 7J 69
Ivy St. BD21: Keigh 8H 27
HD4: Hud 6H 137
HD5: Hud 6E 8 (5A 138)
HD6: Brigh 9L 99
HX1: Hal 8G 7 (7N 97)
LS9: Leeds 6J 69
WF7: F'stne 5D 128
Ivy St. Sth. BD21: Keigh 3H 43
HX1: Hal 8G 7 (7N 97)
Ivy Ter. BD6: B'frd 6N 81
BD21: Keigh 1M 43
HD6: Brigh *9L 99*
(off Ivy St.)
HX1: Hal 8G 7
HX3: Hip 5K 99
OL15: Lit 9M 113
WF4: Horb 9C 124
WF9: S Elm 6N 163
Ivy Vw. LS9: Leeds 6J 69
Ivy Vs. *OL14: Tod* *8K 93*
(off Longfield Rd.)
Ivywood Ct. BD7: B'frd 2K 81

J

Jacana Way BD6: B'frd 4H 81
Jacinth Ct. HD2: Hud 9A 120
Jack Bri. Cotts. HX7: Cold 8B 76
Jack Cl. Orchard S71: Roys 5D 160
Jackdaw Cl. BD15: All 7G 62
Jackdaw La. LS23: B Spa 9C 24
Jack Hill HD2: Hud 1M 137
Jackie Smart Ct. LS7: Leeds 3G 68
Jackie Smart Rd. BD5: B'frd 1C 82
Jack La. LS10: Leeds 9E 68
(Parkfield St.)
LS10: Leeds 1G 86
(Whitfield Sq.)
LS11: Leeds 9D 68
(Nineveh Rd.)
LS11: Leeds 9E 68
(Parkfield St.)
WF17: Bat 1G 122
Jack Lee Ga. OL14: Tod 9N 93
Jackman Dr. LS18: Hors 7G 48
Jackman St. OL14: Tod 7K 93
Jackroyd HX3: Hal 2M 97
Jackroyd La. HD4: Hud 8M 137
WF14: Up H 9J 121
Jackson Av. LS8: Leeds 8H 51
JACKSON BRIDGE 5D 170
Jackson Hill BD13: Que 6E 80
(not continuous)
Jackson Ho. *WF9: Hems* *3D 162*
(off Lilley St.)
Jackson La. HX4: Bark 6G 116
Jackson Mdws. HX4: Bark 6G 116
Jackson Rd. LS7: Leeds 3E 68
Jacksons Ct. *WF8: Pon* *3J 129*
(off Liquorice Way)
Jacksons La. WF8: Went 3C 148
WF12: T'hill 1D 140
Jackson St. BD3: B'frd 6F 6 (8E 64)
Jackson Wlk. LS29: Men 5F 30
Jacks Way WF9: Upt 1B 164
Jacky La. BD22: Haw 9C 42
Jacobs Ct. LS5: Leeds 3L 67
WF4: Horb 2E 142
Jacobs Cft. BD14: Clay 1G 81
Jacobs Hall Ct. S75: Kex 9E 158
Jacobs La. BD22: Haw 7D 42
Jacob's Row HD4: Hud 7L 137
Jacob St. BD5: B'frd 1B 82
LS2: Leeds 4G 5 (5E 68)
Jacobs Well BD1: B'frd 5B 6 (8C 64)
Jacob's Well La. WF1: Wake 3K 9 (4M 125)
Jacquard Ct. HD6: B Bri 5A 100
Jacquard Sq. LS10: Leeds 1G 87
Jacques Fold BD20: Sils 8F 12
Jacques Gro. BD20: Sils 8F 12
Jade Pl. HD2: Hud 9A 120
Jaggar La. HD9: Hon 5L 153

Jagger Green—Kelso Pl.

JAGGER GREEN 8B 118
Jagger Grn. Dean HX4: Holy 8A 118
Jagger Grn. La. HX4: Holy 9A 118
(not continuous)
Jagger La. HD5: Hud 2E 138
HD8: Eml 3A 156
Jaglin Ct. WF7: F'stne 7E 128
Jail Rd. WF17: Bat 7C 102
Jail Yd. LS26: Rothw 8A 88
Jail Yd. Pde. *LS26: Rothw* *8A 88*
(off Jail Yd.)
Jakeman Cl. WF3: Ting 4A 104
Jakeman Ct. WF3: Ting 4A 104
Jakeman Cft. WF3: Ting 4A 104
Jakeman Dr. WF3: Ting 4A 104
Jakeman Fold WF3: Ting 4A 104
James Av. BD20: East 3A 26
LS8: Leeds 7H 51
James Baillie Pk. LS6: Leeds 1B 68
James Cl. LS25: Gar 7B 72
James Ct. HD4: Hud 8E 138
LS22: Coll *9J 23*
(off Station La.)
LS27: Morl 8M 85
WF9: Hems 2C 162
James Duggan Av. WF7: F'stne 5D 128
James Ga. BD1: B'frd 3A 6 (7C 64)
James Gibbs Cl. WF7: F'stne 5D 128
James La. HD4: S Cros 3F 152
James Mason Ct. HD1: Hud 3J 137
James St. BD1: B'frd 3A 6 (7C 64)
BD11: B'haw 7L 83
BD13: Thorn 8C 62
BD15: All 5H 63
BD22: Oak 5B 42
HD6: Brigh 8M 99
HD7: Golc 6C 136
HD7: Slait 9N 135
HX4: Holy 7A 118
HX5: Ell 5E 118
LS19: Raw 3M 47
OL14: Tod *6K 93*
(off Meadow Bottom Rd.)
S72: S Hien 4N 161
WF10: C'frd 3D 108
WF13: Dew 2E 122
WF14: Mir 4L 121
WF15: Liv 9M 101
WF17: Bat 8E 102
James St. E. BD21: Keigh 1J 43
James St. Mkt. BD1: B'frd 3A 6
Jamie Ct. BD10: B'frd 9H 47
Jane Few Ho. LS15: Leeds 4F 70
Jane Grn. HX2: Ogd 3K 79
Jane Hills *BD17: Ship* *7M 45*
(off Riverside Est.)
Jane's Hill WF5: Oss 4E 124
Jane St. BD13: Denh 5K 61
BD18: Ship 7L 45
BD22: Haw *8D 42*
(off Park St.)
OL12: Whit 5A 112
Janesway LS25: Kip 3N 89
Janet St. BD22: Haw 7E 42
Jans Cl. WF9: Upt 1A 164
Japonica Way BD3: B'frd 5G 65
Jaques Cl. LS6: Leeds 2L 67
Jardine Av. WF7: F'stne 5D 128
Jardine Rd. BD16: Bgly 4F 44
Jardine St. BD16: Bgly 4F 44
Jarratt St. BD8: B'frd 5N 63
Jarratt St. E. BD8: B'frd 5N 63
Jarrom Cl. BD4: B'frd 1H 83
Jarvis Sq. WF3: Rob H 1J 105
Jarvis Wlk. WF3: Rob H 1J 105
Jasmine Gdns. HX1: Hal 6M 97
WF10: C'frd 7A 108
Jasmin Ter. BD8: B'frd 6A 64
Jason Ter. WF17: Birs 2D 102
Jasper La. HG3: Kirkby 3K 21
Jasper St. BD10: B'frd 7F 46
HX1: Hal 5M 97
Javelin Cl. BD10: B'frd 9F 46
JAW HILL 9C 104
Jay Ho. La. HD6: Clift 7A 100
Jay St. BD22: Haw 8D 42
Jean Av. LS15: Leeds 7B 70
Jeanwood Rd. HD9: H'frth 5N 169
Jebb La. S75: Hai 6N 157
Jemmy La. BD23: E'by 1A 10
HX3: Hal 2L 7
Jenkin Dr. WF4: Horb 1B 142
Jenkin La. WF4: Horb 9B 124
Jenkin Rd. WF4: Horb 1B 142
Jenkinson Cl. LS11: Leeds 9C 68
Jenkinson Ct. HD8: Kbtn 3G 154
Jenkinson Lawn LS11: Leeds 9C 68
Jenkinsons Pl. LS10: Leeds 5F 86
Jenkinson St. WF17: Bat 1F 122
Jenkyn Gdns. HD8: Shep 9H 155
Jenkyn La. HD8: Shep 9H 155
Jennetts Cres. LS21: Otley 1K 31
Jennie Blackamore Way LS15: Leeds 4E 70
Jennings Cl. BD20: Sils 9F 12
Jennings Pl. BD7: B'frd 1M 81
Jennings St. BD7: B'frd 1M 81
Jenny La. BD17: Bail 3B 46
WF14: Mir 4M 121
Jenson Av. WF13: Dew 9C 102
Jepson La. HX5: Ell 5E 118
Jeremy La. WF16: Heck 8N 101
Jer Gro. BD7: B'frd 3K 81
Jer La. BD7: B'frd 3K 81
Jermyn St. BD1: B'frd 3D 6 (7D 64)
Jerry Clay Dr. WF2: Wren 1G 124
Jerry Clay La. WF2: Kirk, Wren 9E 104
Jerry La. BD20: Sils 8M 13
HX6: Sow B 9G 97
Jerry Spring Rd. HX2: Lud F 6D 96
Jersey Cl. WF12: Dew 1J 123
Jerusalem Farm Camp Site HX2: Midg 9D 78
Jerusalem Farm Nature Reserve 8D 78
Jerusalem Farm Workshops 9D 78
Jerusalem La. HX2: Lud, Midg 9C 78
Jerusalem Rd. HD7: Linth 3A 152
Jervaulx Cl. LS23: B Spa 1C 38
Jervaulx Cres. BD8: B'frd 6A 64
Jerwood Hill Cl. HX3: Hal 3C 98
Jerwood Hill Rd. HX3: Hal 3C 98
Jesmond Av. BD9: B'frd 4L 63
S71: Roys 6C 160
Jesmond Gro. BD9: B'frd 4L 63
WF13: Dew 2E 122
Jesmond Sq. LS28: Fars 3B 66
Jessamine Av. LS11: Leeds 4B 86
Jessamine St. WF13: Raven 6A 122
Jesse St. BD5: B'frd 8B 6 (9C 64)
BD8: B'frd 7J 63
Jessop Av. HD5: Hud 7E 138
Jessop Fold HD9: Hon 4L 153
Jessop Row LS12: Leeds 7K 67
Jessop St. WF2: Wake 7L 125
WF10: C'frd 4D 108
Jester Pl. BD13: Que 3B 80
Jewitt La. LS22: Coll 2J 37
Jew La. BD22: Oxen 4C 60
Jilley Royd La. HD2: Fix 7M 119
(not continuous)
Jilling Gdns. WF12: Dew 4K 123
(not continuous)
Jilling Ing Pk. WF12: Dew 4J 123
Jill Kilner Dr. LS29: Burl W 9B 16
Jill La. WF14: Mir 4N 121
Jim Allen La. HX2: Midg 3C 96
Jim Laker Pl. BD18: Ship 8L 45
Jim La. HD1: Hud 4J 137
Jimmy Gees 7L 45
Jinnah Ct. BD8: B'frd 6B 64
Jinny Moor La. LS26: Swil 5F 88
Jin Whin Ct. WF10: C'frd 4A 108
Jin-Whin Hill WF10: C'frd 4A 108
Jin Whin Ter. WF10: C'frd 4A 108
Joan Royd WF16: Heck 6A 102
Joba Av. BD3: B'frd 7F 64
Joffre Av. WF10: C'frd 6E 108
Joffre Mt. *LS19: Yead* *1N 47*
(off Springwell Cl.)
John Barker St. OL14: Tod 4G 93
John Booth Cl. WF15: Liv 1K 121
John Carr Av. WF4: Horb 9C 124
John Charles App. LS11: Leeds 5E 86
John Charles Centre for Sport 5E 86
John Charles Way LS12: Leeds 1N 85
John Escritt Rd. BD16: Bgly 5F 44
John Gilmour Way LS29: Burl W 9B 16
John Haigh Rd. HD7: Slait 1N 151
John Hanson Ct. BD13: Denh 8L 61
John Henry St. OL12: Whit 7A 112
John Naylor La. HX2: Lud F 7E 96
John Nelson Cl. WF17: Bat 3C 102
Johnny La. LS21: Otley 2L 31
JOHN O'GAUNTS 6A 88
John O'Gaunts Trad. Est. LS26: Rothw 6N 87
John O'Gaunts Wlk. LS26: Rothw 7A 88
John Ormsby VC Way WF12: Dew 9K 103
John Ramsden Ct. HD1: Hud 6D 8
Johns Av. WF3: Loft 6L 105
John's Cres. WF2: Wren 1G 125
Johns La. HX5: Ell 7E 118
John Smeaton Leisure Cen. 3F 70
John Smith's Stadium, The 1F 8 (3A 138)
Johnson St. BD3: B'frd 7H 65
BD16: Bgly 3E 44
WF14: Mir 8L 121
Johnsons Yd. LS29: Burl W 8D 16
Johnson Ter. LS27: Morl 9L 85
Johnston St. LS6: Leeds 3D 68
WF1: Wake 4M 9 (5M 125)
John St. BD1: B'frd 3A 6 (7C 64)
BD4: B'frd 4J 83
BD13: Cull 9K 43
BD13: Denh 5K 61
BD13: Thorn 8C 62
BD14: Clay 1H 81
BD17: Bail 6A 46
BD18: Ship 7M 45
BD22: Oak 5D 42
HD3: Hud 6G 136
HD6: Brigh 9M 99
HX1: Hal 4K 7 (5B 98)
HX4: Gree 4B 118
HX5: Ell 5E 118
LS6: Leeds 3A 68
LS19: Raw 3M 47
OL14: Tod *7K 93*
(off Dalton St.)
WF1: Wake 5M 9 (5M 125)
WF9: S Elm 7M 163
WF10: C'frd 6C 108
WF12: Dew 2H 123
WF13: Dew 1F 122
WF13: Raven 6B 122
WF16: Heck 9A 102
WF17: Birs 3B 102
John St. W. HX6: Sow B 8H 97
John William St. BD19: Cleck 4H 101
HD1: Hud 3B 8 (3M 137)
HX5: Ell 5E 118
WF15: Liv 8N 101
(Flush)
WF15: Liv 9M 101
(Union Rd.)
Jolly Sailor Yd. WF11: B'ton 4B 110
Jonathan Gth. LS29: Add 1L 13
Jons Av. WF9: S Kirk 7G 163
Jonscroft BD13: Que 6C 80
Jordan Beck HD8: Bird E 4L 171
Jordan Rd. LS28: Stan 4D 66
Jordan Way BD2: B'frd 4G 65
Joseph Av. HX3: North 2F 98
Joseph Crossley's Almshouses
HX1: Hal 6H 7 (6A 98)
Joseph Dobson's Sweet Factory 4E 118
Josephine Rd. HD4: Hud 7F 136
Joseph Stones Ho. *LS2: Leeds* *6J 5*
(off St Cecilia St.)
Joseph St. BD3: B'frd 4E 6 (7E 64)
BD4: B'frd 4J 83
LS10: Leeds 1G 86
Joseph's Well LS3: Leeds 5C 4
Joseph Wright Ct. *BD10: B'frd* *6E 46*
(off Brighton St.)
Joshua St. OL14: Tod 6K 93
Jos La. HD8: Shep 8J 155
Jos Way HD8: Shep 9J 155
Jowett Ho. La. S75: Caw 5K 173
Jowett Pk. Cres. BD10: B'frd 5E 46
Jowett's La. BD20: Sils 1D 12
Jowett St. BD1: B'frd 7A 64
Jowett Ter. LS27: Morl 2K 103
Jowler HX2: Lud 9D 78
Jubilee Av. HD8: Shel 7L 155
WF1: Out 8L 105
WF6: Norm 3H 127
Jubilee Bungs. WF11: Knot 8D 110
Jubilee Cl. WF9: Hems 4F 162
Jubilee Cotts. WF4: H'cft 1K 161
WF7: Street 6L 127
Jubilee Ct. BD18: Ship 7A 46
LS27: Morl *9L 85*
(off Marshall St.)
WF9: Fitz 6A 146
Jubilee Cres. BD11: Drig 6D 84
WF1: Out 8L 105
WF4: S Comn 8J 127
Jubilee Cft. BD11: Drig 6C 84
Jubilee Dr. BD21: Keigh 2G 42
Jubilee Gdns. LS26: W'frd 7M 89
S71: Roys 5E 160
WF8: Pon 2K 129
Jubilee Ho. *HX6: Sow B* *9H 97*
(off West St.)
Jubilee La. HD4: Hud 7E 136
Jubilee Mt. HD6: Ras 1L 119
Jubilee Pl. LS27: Morl 9L 85
Jubilee Rd. HX3: Hal 1C 118
WF4: S Comn 8J 127
Jubilee St. BD1: B'frd 5B 64
HX3: Hal 6C 98
HX7: Myth 3M 95
LS27: Morl 9L 85
WF4: Hol 7H 143
Jubilee St. Nth. HX3: Hal 1N 97
Jubilee Ter. *HX3: Hal* *6C 98*
(off Jubilee St.)
HX6: Ripp 5E 116
LS27: Morl 9L 85
WF7: Ackw 2G 146
Jubilee Trees LS29: Burl W 1A 30
Jubilee Way BD18: Ship 7B 46
OL14: Tod 3C 92
WF4: G Moor 6B 140
WF8: Pon 3J 129
Jude Ct. LS13: Leeds 3H 67
Judy Haigh La. WF12: T'hill 2G 141
Judy La. HD2: Fix 8N 119
Julian Dr. BD13: Que 3H 81
Julian St. HD5: Hud 5C 138
Julie Av. WF4: Dur 5G 142
Jumb Beck Cl. LS29: Burl W 9D 16
Jumble Dyke HD6: Ras 3L 119
Jumble Hole Rd. OL14: Tod 3C 94
Jumbles Ct. WF3: Loft 3L 105
Jumbles La. WF3: Loft 3L 105
Jumble Wood HD8: Fen B 7H 139
Jumples HX2: Mix 9K 79
Jumples Cl. HX2: Mix 9K 79
Jumples Ct. HX2: Mix 9J 79
Jumples Crag HX2: Mix 9K 79
Jumps La. HX7: Heb B 3G 95
OL14: Tod 4G 93
Jumps Rd. OL14: Tod 4G 92
Junction 1 Retail Pk. LS11: Leeds 3M 85
Junction 25 Bus. Pk. WF14: Mir 6K 121
Junction 32 Outlet Village WF10: C'frd 7F 108
Junction Cl. WF7: F'stne 5B 128
Junction Ho's. WF10: All B 3D 108
Junction La. WF5: Oss 7C 124
(not continuous)
Junction Rd. BD17: Ship 7A 46
WF13: Dew 4E 122
Junction Row BD2: B'frd 2F 64
Junction St. LS10: Leeds 8E 68
Junction Ter. *BD2: B'frd* *2F 64*
(off Bolton Rd.)
June St. BD21: Keigh 8J 27
Juniper Av. LS26: W'frd 6E 88
Juniper Cl. BD8: B'frd 6N 63
WF2: Wake 3G 124
Juniper Ct. HX3: North 9F 80
Juniper Gro. HD4: Neth 3J 153
Juniper Gro. M. HD4: Neth 3J 153
Juniper Pl. LS9: Leeds 5K 69
Junxion, The *LS5: Leeds* *2L 67*
(off Station App.)
Jupiter Cres. BD2: B'frd 9E 46
Justin Way HD4: Hud 9F 136

K

Kaffir Rd. HD2: Hud 2J 137
Karam Cl. BD3: B'frd 7G 65
Karnac Rd. LS8: Leeds 2H 69
Karon Dr. WF4: Horb 1D 142
Kashmir Ct. WF13: Raven 6B 122
Kashmir Pk. HX1: Hal 5M 97
Katherine St. BD18: Ship 7L 45
Katrina Gro. WF7: F'stne 8D 128
Kaycell St. BD4: B'frd 3F 82
Kay Cl. LS27: Morl 6J 85
Kaye Hill *BD13: Cull* *9K 43*
(off Old La.)
Kaye La. HD5: Hud 8B 138
HD7: Linth 7D 136
Kaye St. WF12: Dew 5G 122
WF16: Heck 9A 102
Kay St. BD18: Ship 1A 64
WF1: Wake 5M 9 (5M 125)
Kearby Cliff LS22: Kear 6L 21
KEARBY TOWN END 6N 21
KEARBY WITH NETHERBY 6M 21
Kearsley Ter. LS10: Leeds 3G 86
Keasden Cl. BD10: B'frd 5E 46
Keats Av. OL14: Tod 6M 93
Keats Cl. WF8: Pon 1K 129
Keats Dr. WF16: Heck 1B 122
Keats Gro. WF3: S'ley 6N 105
Keats Ho. LS29: I'ly 5K 15
Keat St. HD4: Hud 6K 137
Kebble Ct. BD19: Gom 5M 101
KEBCOTE 2H 93
Keble Gth. LS25: Kip 3C 90
KEBROYD 5E 116
Kebroyd Av. HX6: Ripp 4E 116
Kebroyd La. HX6: Ripp 4E 116
Kebroyd Mt. HX6: Ripp 4E 116
Kebs Rd. HX7: Blac H 1J 93
OL14: Tod 9F 74
Kedleston Rd. LS8: Leeds 5H 51
Keeble Ho. *BD2: B'frd* *4H 65*
(off St Clare's Av.)
Keelam Ga. HX7: Wads 8M 77
Keelam La. HX7: Wads 8L 77
Keeldar Cl. BD7: B'frd 2N 81
KEELHAM 9L 61
Keelham Dr. LS19: Raw 3N 47
Keelham La. BD20: Keigh 6G 27
OL14: Tod 3M 93
Keelham Pl. BD13: Denh 9M 61
Keel Moorings LS13: Leeds 1C 66
Keenan Av. WF9: S Elm 8L 163
Keeper La. BD4: B'frd 2A 84
WF4: Not 4M 159
Keepers Fold BD10: B'frd 5F 46
Keeton St. LS9: Leeds 6L 5 (6H 69)
KEIGHLEY 9J 27
Keighley & Worth Valley Railway
Damems Station 5G 42
Haworth Station 8C 42
Ingrow West Station 3H 43
Oakworth Station 6D 42
Oxenhope Station 3C 60
Keighley & Worth Valley Railway Exhibition Shed
3C 60
Keighley Cl. HX2: Illing 7K 79
Keighley Cougars RLFC 7K 27
Keighley Dr. HX2: Illing 8L 79
Keighley Golf Course 4H 27
Keighley Ind. Pk. BD21: Keigh 7J 27
Keighley Leisure Cen. 8K 27
Keighley Pl. LS28: Stan 4B 66
Keighley Playhouse 9H 27
Keighley Retail Pk. BD21: Keigh 7J 27
Keighley Rd. BD8: B'frd 2N 63
BD9: B'frd 2N 63
BD13: Cull 8J 43
BD13: Denh 3J 61
BD16: Bgly 1C 44
BD16: Har 3M 43
BD20: Sils 1D 26
BD20: Stee 3D 26
BD21: Har 3M 43
BD22: Oak 5D 42
BD22: Oxen 3C 60
HX2: Hal, Illing 8L 79
HX2: Illing, Ogd 4K 79
(not continuous)
HX3: Hal 8L 79
HX7: Heb B, Wads 1H 95
HX7: P Wel 3H 77
LS29: I'ly 1D 28
Keighley Station (Rail) 9K 27
Keilder Cres. BD6: B'frd 3H 81
Keir Hardie Cl. WF15: Liv 8M 101
Kelburn Gro. BD22: Oak 4B 42
Kelcbar Hill LS24: Tad 4N 39
KELCLIFFE 6H 31
Kelcliffe Av. LS20: Guis 7J 31
Kelcliffe Gro. LS20: Guis 7J 31
Kelcliffe La. LS20: Guis 6H 31
(not continuous)
Keldholme Cl. LS13: Leeds 1B 66
Keldholme Rd. LS13: Leeds 1B 66
Keldregate HD2: Hud 8C 120
Kell Beck LS21: Otley 7K 17
Kell Butts HX2: Wain 7F 78
Kellett Av. LS12: Leeds 1M 85
Kellett Bldgs. BD12: Low M 8B 82
Kellett Cres. LS12: Leeds 1M 85
Kellett Dr. BD13: Thorn 8A 62
LS12: Leeds 1M 85
Kellett Gro. LS12: Leeds 1M 85
Kellett La. LS12: Leeds 9L 67
Kellett Mt. LS12: Leeds 1M 85
Kellett Pl. LS12: Leeds 1M 85
Kellett Rd. LS12: Leeds 9L 67
Kellett Ter. LS12: Leeds 1M 85
Kellett Wlk. LS12: Leeds 1M 85
KELLINGLEY 8L 111
Kellingley Rd. WF11: Kell 8L 111
Kell La. HX2: Wain 8E 78
HX3: North 1E 98
Kelloe St. BD19: Cleck 3H 101
Kell St. BD16: Bgly 4F 44
Kellymoor Wlk. BD10: B'frd 8D 46
Kelmore Gro. BD6: B'frd 7K 81
Kelmscott Av. LS15: Leeds 3E 70
Kelmscott Cres. LS15: Leeds 3E 70
Kelmscott Gdns. LS15: Leeds 3E 70
Kelmscott Gth. LS15: Leeds 2F 70
Kelmscott Grn. LS15: Leeds 3E 70
Kelmscott Gro. LS15: Leeds 3E 70
Kelmscott La. LS15: Leeds 3E 70
Kelsall Av. LS6: Leeds 4A 68
Kelsall Gro. LS6: Leeds 5A 68
Kelsall Ho. BD3: B'frd 2D 6
Kelsall Pl. LS6: Leeds 4A 68
Kelsall Rd. LS6: Leeds 4A 68
Kelsall Ter. LS6: Leeds 4A 68
Kelseys Ct. *HX2: Hal* *4L 97*
(off Stretchgate La.)
Kelsey St. HX1: Hal 4M 97
Kelso Ct. LS3: Leeds 3A 4 (5B 68)
Kelso Gdns. LS2: Leeds 2A 4 (5B 68)
Kelso Gro. HD5: Hud 4E 138
Kelso Hgts. LS3: Leeds 2A 4 (4B 68)
Kelso Ho. *BD4: B'frd* *2J 83*
(off Stirling Cres.)
Kelso Pl. LS2: Leeds 2A 4 (4B 68)

Kingsway BD2: B'frd 8D 46
BD11: Drig 7B 84
BD16: Bgly 4F 44
BD20: Rid 7N 27
LS15: Leeds 6D 70
LS17: Huby 5N 19
LS25: Gar 8L 71
S75: Map 8J 159
WF3: S'ley 1A 126
WF5: Oss 3M 123
WF6: Norm 3H 127
WF8: Pon 9K 109
WF13: Dew 3G 122
(off Foundry St.)
WF17: Birs 2B 102
Kingsway Arc. *WF13: Dew 3G 122*
(off Northgate)
Kingsway Cl. WF5: Oss 4M 123
Kingsway Ct. LS17: Leeds 6F 50
WF5: Oss 3M 123
(Kingsmead)
WF5: Oss 4M 123
(Kingsway Cl.)
Kingsway Dr. LS29: I'ly 5F 14
Kingsway Gdns. WF5: Oss 3M 123
Kingsway Gth. LS25: Gar 8L 71
Kingsway M. WF5: Oss 3M 123
Kingswear Cl. LS15: Leeds 5E 70
Kingswear Cres. LS15: Leeds 5E 70
Kingswear Gth. LS15: Leeds 5E 70
Kingswear Glen LS15: Leeds 5E 70
Kingswear Gro. LS15: Leeds 5E 70
Kingswear Pde. LS15: Leeds 5E 70
Kingswear Ri. LS15: Leeds 5E 70
Kingswear Vw. LS15: Leeds 5E 70
Kingswell Av. WF1: Out 8L 105
Kingswood Av. LS8: Leeds 4J 51
Kingswood Cres. LS8: Leeds 4H 51
Kingswood Dr. LS8: Leeds 4H 51
Kingswood Gdns. LS8: Leeds 4H 51
Kingswood Grn. HX3: North 3E 98
Kingswood Gro. LS8: Leeds 4J 51
Kingswood Pl. BD7: B'frd 1M 81
Kingswood Rd. LS12: Leeds 8M 67
Kingswood St. BD7: B'frd 1M 81
Kingswood Ter. BD7: B'frd 1M 81
Kinnaird Cl. HX5: Ell 5E 118
WF17: Bat 7J 103
Kinroyd La. HD5: Hud 6B 138
KINSLEY 9B 146
Kinsley Church Apartments
WF9: Hems 9C 146
Kinsley Ent. Zone WF9: Kins 9C 146
Kinsley Ho. Cres. WF9: Fitz 8A 146
Kinsley Ind. Est. WF9: Kins 8C 146
Kinsley Stadium (Greyhound) 8B 146
Kinsley St. WF9: Kins 9B 146
Kipling Cl. HD4: Hud 7J 137
Kipling Ct. BD10: B'frd 8H 47
Kipling Gro. WF8: Pon 9K 109
KIPPAX 3A 90
KIPPAX COMMON 2N 89
Kippax La. End LS25: Gar 9M 71
Kippax Leisure Cen. 5N 89
Kippax Mt. LS9: Leeds 8M 5 (7H 69)
Kippax Pk. Fishery 6B 90
Kippax Pl. LS9: Leeds 8M 5 (7H 69)
Kipping La. BD13: Thorn 8C 62
Kipping Pl. BD13: Thorn 8C 62
Kirby Cote La.
HX7: Crag V 9L 95
Kirby Leas HX1: Hal 6K 7 (6B 98)
Kirby Row HD5: K'htn 1G 138
Kirby St. BD21: Keigh 8K 27
Kirk Beston Cl. LS11: Leeds 3A 86
Kirkbourne Gro. BD17: Bail 5C 46
Kirkbridge La. HD9: New M 1B 170
Kirkbridge Way WF9: S Elm 6M 163
Kirkburn Pl. BD7: B'frd 8N 63
KIRKBURTON 3K 155
Kirkby Av. LS25: Gar 9A 72
S71: Ath 9B 160
Kirkby Cl. WF9: S Kirk 6J 163
Kirkby Gth. LS14: T'ner 1G 53
Kirkbygate WF9: Hems 4E 162
Kirkby La. HD8: Eml 1E 156
HG3: Kirkby 5L 21
LS22: Kear, Sick 6N 21
WF4: Flock 1E 156
KIRKBY OVERBLOW 2K 21
Kirkby Rd. WF9: Hems 3E 162
Kirkcaldy Fold
WF6: Norm 2L 127
Kirk Cliff HX6: Ripp 6D 116
Kirk Cl. WF12: Dew 3L 123
Kirkcroft BD13: Denh 6K 61
Kirk Cross Cres. S71: Roys 7D 160
Kirkdale WF10: C'frd 4J 109
Kirkdale Av. LS12: Leeds 1L 85
Kirkdale Cres. LS12: Leeds 2L 85
Kirkdale Dr. LS12: Leeds 1L 85
WF4: Cal G 4F 142
Kirkdale Gdns. LS12: Leeds 1L 85
Kirkdale Gro. LS12: N Far 1K 85
Kirkdale Mt. LS12: Leeds 2L 85
Kirkdale Ter. LS12: Leeds 2L 85
Kirkdale Vw. LS12: Leeds 2L 85
Kirkdale Way BD4: B'frd 4K 83
KIRK DEIGHTON 1L 23
Kirk Dr. BD17: Bail 3B 46
Kirkfield Av. LS14: T'ner 1H 53
Kirkfield Cres. LS14: T'ner 1H 53
Kirkfield Dr. LS15: Leeds 7E 70
Kirkfield Gdns. LS15: Leeds 7E 70
Kirkfield La. LS14: T'ner 2H 53
Kirkfields BD17: Bail 3C 46
Kirkfields Ind. Cen.
LS19: Yead 9L 31
Kirkfield Vw. LS15: Leeds 7E 70
Kirkfield Way S71: Roys 7D 160
Kirk Ga. BD11: B'haw 6K 83
Kirkgate BD1: B'frd 4A 6 (7C 64)
(not continuous)
BD18: Ship 7M 45
BD20: Sils 8E 12
Kirkgate HD1: Hud 5C 8 (4N 137)
LS1: Leeds 6G 5 (6E 68)
(not continuous)
LS2: Leeds 7H 5 (7E 68)
LS21: Otley 9L 17
(not continuous)
WF1: Wake 4K 9 (5L 125)
(not continuous)
WF17: Bat 9H 103
WF17: Birs 3A 102
Kirkgate Arc. LS21: Otley 1L 31
Kirkgate Bus. Cen.
WF1: Wake 7M 9 (6M 125)
Kirkgate Cen. BD1: B'frd 4A 6 (7C 64)
Kirkgate Commercial Cen.
WF1: Wake 7M 9 (6M 125)
Kirkgate La. S72: S Hien 3J 161
Kirkgate Mall BD1: B'frd 4B 6
Kirkgate Mkt. LS2: Leeds 6G 5 (6E 68)
Kirkgate Sq. BD1: B'frd 4B 6
Kirkham Av. WF2: Kirk 9D 104
KIRKHAMGATE 1D 124
Kirkham Rd. BD7: B'frd 8N 63
Kirkham St. LS13: Leeds 1C 66
Kirkhaw La. WF11: Ferr 5A 110
KIRKHEATON 2G 138
Kirkhills LS14: T'ner 2H 53
Kirklands BD19: Cleck 5J 101
HD9: New M 1B 170
LS14: T'ner 2G 52
WF15: Liv 8L 101
Kirklands Av. BD13: Thorn 8D 62
BD17: Bail 4C 46
Kirklands Cl. BD17: Bail 5C 46
LS19: Yead 9L 31
LS29: Men 4E 30
Kirklands Gdns. BD17: Bail 5C 46
Kirklands La. BD17: Bail 4C 46
Kirklands Rd. BD17: Bail 4B 46
Kirkland Vs. LS28: Pud 8B 66
Kirk La. HX3: Hip 4H 99
LS19: Yead 9K 31
Kirklea HD8: Shel 6N 155
Kirk Lea Cres. HD3: Hud 1H 137
Kirklees Cl. LS28: Fars 2A 66
Kirklees Cft. LS28: Fars 2A 66
Kirklees Dr. LS28: Fars 2A 66
Kirklees Gth. LS28: Fars 2A 66
Kirklees Light Railway
Clayton West Station 6J 157
Cuckoo's Nest Halt Station 7F 156
Shelley Station 8M 155
Skelmanthorpe Station 6D 156
Kirklees Ri. LS28: Fars 2A 66
Kirklees Rd. BD15: All 7G 63
Kirkley Av. BD12: Wyke 3A 100
Kirkness Cl. LS27: Morl 9K 85
Kirkroyds La. HD9: New M 1A 170
KIRK SMEATON 4J 149
KIRKSTALL 2K 67
Kirkstall Abbey (remains) 1J 67
Kirkstall Av. LS5: Leeds 3J 67
Kirkstall Brewery *LS5: Leeds 2J 67*
(off Broad La.)
Kirkstall Gdns. BD21: Keigh 2J 43
Kirkstall Gro. BD8: B'frd 7J 63
Kirkstall Hill LS4: Leeds 2L 67
LS5: Leeds 2L 67
Kirkstall Ind. Pk. LS4: Leeds 5N 67
Kirkstall La. LS5: Leeds 2K 67
LS6: Leeds 2K 67
Kirkstall Leisure Cen. 2K 67
Kirkstall Mt. LS5: Leeds 3J 67
Kirkstall Rd. LS3: Leeds 5A 4 (6B 68)
LS4: Leeds 3L 67
S71: Smit 9N 159
Kirkstall Valley Nature Reserve 4K 67
Kirkstall Valley Retail Pk. LS5: Leeds 3K 67
Kirkstone Av. HD5: Hud 4A 138
Kirkstone Dr. BD19: Gom 4M 101
HX2: Hal 4H 97
Kirkstone Hall BD7: B'frd 8A 64
Kirkstone Ter. LS27: Morl 7K 85
KIRKTHORPE 4E 126
Kirkthorpe La. WF1: Hea, K'thpe 8B 126
Kirkwall Av. LS9: Leeds 7K 69
Kirkwall Dr. BD4: B'frd 2J 83
Kirkwood Av. LS16: Leeds 3G 49
Kirkwood Cl. LS16: Leeds 2G 49
Kirkwood Cres. LS16: Leeds 2H 49
Kirkwood Dr. HD3: Hud 2F 136
LS16: Leeds 2G 49
Kirkwood Gdns. LS16: Leeds 2H 49
Kirkwood Grn. HD3: Hud 2G 136
Kirkwood Gro. LS16: Leeds 3G 49
WF3: Ting 4B 104
Kirkwood La. LS16: Leeds 2G 49
Kirkwood Ri. LS16: Leeds 2H 49
Kirkwood Vw. LS16: Leeds 2H 49
Kirkwood Way LS16: Leeds 2H 49
Kismet Cl. HX1: Hal 3G 7 (5N 97)
Kismet Gdns. BD3: B'frd 6G 65
Kistvaen Gdns. HD9: Mel 6B 152
Kitchener Av. LS9: Leeds 5K 69
Kitchener Gro. LS9: Leeds 4K 69
Kitchener Mt. LS9: Leeds 5K 69
Kitchener Pl. LS9: Leeds 5K 69
Kitchener St. BD12: O'haw 8E 82
LS9: Leeds 5K 69
LS26: W'frd 7D 88
Kitchen Fold HD7: Slait 1N 151
Kitchenman Ter. HX1: Hal 8K 7
KITCHENROYD 1E 172
Kite M. BD8: B'frd 7H 63
Kit La. BD20: Sils 4B 12
Kitson Cl. LS12: Leeds 8M 67
Kitson Gdns. LS12: Leeds 8M 67
KITSON HILL 5K 121
Kitson Hill Cres. WF14: Mir 4K 121
Kitson Hill Rd. WF14: Mir 5J 121
Kitson La. HX6: Norl 2K 117
Kitson Rd. LS10: Leeds 9F 68
Kitson St. BD18: Ship 9A 46
LS9: Leeds 8M 5 (7H 69)
WF3: Ting 3N 103
Kitson Wood Rd. OL14: Tod 4G 92
Kitten Clough HX2: Hal 3L 97
Kitty Fold LS29: Add 1M 13
Kit Wood Cl. BD4: B'frd 3K 83
Klick Fitness
Bradford 1A 82
Kliffen Pl. HX3: Hal 8C 98
Knap Yd. LS17: Hare 2E 34
Knaresborough Dr. HD2: Hud 9M 119
Knave Cl. WF4: Horb 9F 124
Knavesmire LS26: Rothw 8K 87
(not continuous)
Knightsbridge Ct. HD6: Brigh 9M 99
Knightsbridge Wlk. BD4: B'frd 6F 82
Knights Cl. LS15: Leeds 6D 70
Knights Cft. LS22: Weth 2N 23
Knightscroft Av. LS26: Rothw 7N 87
Knightscroft Dr. LS26: Rothw 7N 87
Knightscroft Pde.
WF9: S Elm 7N 163
Knight's Fold BD7: B'frd 1M 81
Knightshill LS15: Leeds 6E 70
Knight St. HD1: Hud 3C 8 (3N 137)
HX1: Hal 7M 97
Knights Way BD16: Bgly 3H 45
Knightsway LS15: Leeds 5D 70
LS25: Gar 9L 71
WF2: Wake 4L 143
WF3: Loft 2K 105
Knightsway Ct. BD3: B'frd 5K 65
Knoll, The LS23: B'ham 5C 38
LS28: Cal 4L 65
Knoll Cl. WF5: Oss 4N 123
Knoll Gdns. BD17: Bail 6N 45
Knoll La. HD9: Nether 9J 153
Knoll M. S75: W Gran 6G 158
Knoll Pk. WF3: E Ard 5F 104
Knoll Pk. Dr. BD17: Bail 6N 45
Knoll Ter. BD17: Bail 6N 45
Knoll Vw. BD17: Bail 5N 45
HX6: Mill B 4C 116
LS28: Cal 2B 66
Knoll Wood Pk. LS18: Hors 7G 49
Knostrop La. LS9: Leeds 1K 87
Knostrop Quay LS10: Leeds 1G 87
KNOTFORD 8B 18
Knott Hill OL12: Whit 5A 112
Knott Hill St. OL12: Whit 5A 112
KNOTTINGLEY 8D 110
Knottingley Rd. WF8: Pon 1N 129
WF11: Knot 1N 129
Knottingley Sports Cen. 8E 110
Knottingley Station (Rail) 8D 110
Knott La. LS19: Raw 7A 48
Knotts Rd. OL14: Tod 4F 92
Knotty La. HD8: Lept 7K 139
Knowl, The WF14: Mir 6K 121
Knowl Bank HD7: Golc 6D 136
Knowle, The HD8: Shep 9K 155
Knowle Av. HD5: Hud 5C 138
LS4: Leeds 3N 67
Knowle Cl. BD21: Keigh 4G 43
Knowle Gro. LS4: Leeds 3N 67
Knowle La. BD12: Wyke 2B 100
HD9: Mel 7E 152
Knowle Mt. LS4: Leeds 3N 67
KNOWLE PARK 2G 43
Knowle Pk. Av. HD8: Shep 9K 155
Knowle Pl. LS4: Leeds 3N 67
Knowler Cl. WF15: Liv 7L 101
KNOWLER HILL 7L 101
Knowler Hill WF15: Liv 8L 101
Knowle Rd. HD5: K'htn 2G 138
HD7: Slait 9N 135
LS4: Leeds 3N 67
Knowler Way WF15: Liv 7L 101
Knowles Av. BD4: B'frd 3H 83
Knowles Cft. *WF13: Dew 1C 122*
(off Staincliffe Rd.)
KNOWLES HILL 1C 122
Knowles Hill WF13: Dew 1C 122
Knowles Hill Rd. WF13: Dew 2C 122
Knowles La. BD4: B'frd 3G 83
BD19: Gom 1M 101
WF17: Bat 8E 102
Knowle Spring Rd. BD21: Keigh 3H 43
(Foster Rd.)
BD21: Keigh 2H 43
(Up. Calton St.)
Knowles Rd. HD6: Ras 3M 119
WF17: Bat 8E 102
Knowles St. BD4: B'frd 3G 82
BD13: Denh 6K 61
Knowles Vw. BD4: B'frd 3H 83
Knowles Wlk. *WF9: S Elm 4N 163*
(off Hutton Dr.)
Knowle Ter. LS4: Leeds 4M 67
Knowle Top HX4: Sow 9N 117
Knowle Top Dr. HX3: Hip 4K 99
Knowle Top Rd. HX3: Hip 4K 99
Knowl Grange WF14: Mir 6L 121
Knowl Gro. WF14: Mir 6L 121
Knowl Rd. HD7: Golc 6C 136
HD9: H'lm 4C 168
WF14: Mir 5K 121
Knowl Top HX7: Hept 7D 76
KNOWL WOOD 1J 113
Knowlwood Bottom OL14: Tod 1H 113
Knowlwood Rd. OL14: Tod 1J 113
Knowsley Av. OL14: W'den 2J 113
Knowsley Cres. OL12: Whit 5A 112
Knowsley St. BD3: B'frd 4F 6 (7E 64)
KNOWSTHORPE 9G 69
Knowsthorpe Cres. LS9: Leeds 9H 69
Knowsthorpe Ga. LS9: Leeds 1K 87
Knowsthorpe La. LS9: Leeds 9H 69
Knowsthorpe Rd. LS9: Leeds 9L 69
Knowsthorpe Way LS9: Leeds 1K 87
Knox St. LS13: Leeds 1A 66
Knutsford Gro. BD4: B'frd 3J 83
Komla Cl. BD1: B'frd 3D 6
Krives La. HD7: Slait 4L 151
KRUMLIN 9H 117
Krumlin Hall Cotts. HX4: Bark 9H 117
Krumlin Rd. HX4: Bark 9H 117
Kyffin Av. LS15: Leeds 7N 69
Kyffin Pl. BD4: B'frd 9J 65

L

Laburnum Cl. WF3: E Ard 5E 104
Laburnum Ct. WF4: Horb 1B 142
WF10: C'frd 6E 108
Laburnum Dr. BD17: Bail 3B 46
Laburnum Gro. BD19: Gom 3L 101
BD22: Cros R 7E 42
HD7: Golc 5E 136
HD8: Skelm 8D 156
HX3: Hip 6M 99
WF4: Horb 1B 142
Laburnum Pl. BD8: B'frd 5A 64
BD10: B'frd 7J 47
Laburnum Rd. BD18: Ship 1B 64
WF1: Wake 3H 9 (4K 125)
WF13: Dew 1B 122
Laburnum St. BD8: B'frd 5A 64
LS28: Fars 5A 66
LS28: Pud 6N 65
Laburnum Ter. *HD1: Hud 1C 8*
(off Calton St.)
HX3: Nor G 2M 99
(off Rookes La.)
Laceby Cl. BD10: B'frd 7G 46
Lacey Gro. LS22: Weth 5N 23
Lacey M. BD4: B'frd 3G 83
Lacey St. WF4: Horb 9E 124
WF13: Dew 3E 122
Lacy Av. OL14: W'den 2J 113
Lacy St. WF9: Hems 2C 162
Lacy Way HX5: Ell 2G 118
Ladbroke Gro. BD4: B'frd 4J 83
Ladderbanks La.
BD17: Bail 3B 46
Ladstone Pk. HX6: Norl 4G 117
Ladstone Towers HX6: Sow B 8H 97
Lady Ann Bus. Pk. WF17: Bat 6G 103
Lady Ann Rd. WF17: Bat 7H 103
LADY BALK 9K 109
Lady Balk La. WF8: Pon 1K 129
Ladybeck Cl. LS2: Leeds 5H 5 (6F 68)
Ladybower Av. HD4: Hud 8E 136
Lady Cl. WF5: Oss 3M 123
Ladyfield BD13: Thorn 8C 62
Lady Heton Av. WF14: Mir 5K 121
Lady Heton Cl. WF14: Mir 5J 121
Lady Heton Dr. WF14: Mir 5J 121
Lady Heton Gro. WF14: Mir 5J 121
Lady Ho. La. HD4: Hud 1L 153
Lady La. BD16: Bgly 1F 44
HD5: Hud 3E 138
LS2: Leeds 5G 5 (6E 68)
WF1: Wake 6H 9 (6K 125)
Lady Mill La. WF12: T'hill 1L 141
Lady Pk. Av. BD16: Bgly 1F 44
Lady Pk. Ct. LS17: Leeds 3H 51
Lady Pit Ct. *LS11: Leeds 1D 86*
(off Lady Pit La.)
Lady Pit La. LS11: Leeds 1D 86
(not continuous)
Ladyroyd Dr. BD4: E Bier 7J 83
Ladysmith Cl. WF7: F'stne 5C 128
Ladysmith Rd. BD13: Que 5B 80
Lady's Wlk. LS29: Den 2N 15
Ladywell Cl. BD5: B'frd 2C 82
Ladywell La. WF15: Liv 9F 100
LADY WOOD 8L 51
Ladywood Grange LS8: Leeds 9M 51
Ladywood Mead LS8: Leeds 9M 51
Ladywood Rd. LS8: Leeds 9K 51
WF13: Dew 5D 122
Ladywood Ter. HX1: Hal 4N 97
Ladywood Way WF13: Raven 7B 122
Lafflands La. WF4: Ryh 9H 145
LA Fitness
Yeadon 9M 31
Lagentium Plaza WF10: C'frd 6E 108
Lairum Ri. LS23: Cliff 3D 38
LAISTERDYKE 8H 65
Laisterdyke BD4: B'frd 8H 65
Laisteridge La. BD5: B'frd 8A 64
BD7: B'frd 8A 64
LAITH 6H 169
Laith Cl. LS16: Leeds 4J 49
Laithe Av. HD9: Holm 6H 169
Laithe Bank Dr. HD9: Holm 6H 169
Laithe Cl. BD20: Sils 7D 12
Laithe Ct. HD9: Holm 6H 169
Laithe Cft. WF17: Bat 7H 103
Laithe Cft. Rd. WF17: Bat 7H 103
Laithe Fld. HX4: Bark 6K 117
Laithe Gro. BD6: B'frd 3M 81
Laithe Hall Av. BD19: Cleck 3G 100
Laithe Rd. BD6: B'frd 4N 81
Laithes Chase WF2: Wake 4F 124
Laithes Cl. S71: Ath 9C 160
WF2: Wake 4F 124
Laithes Ct. WF2: Wake 4F 124
Laithes Cres. S71: Ath 9A 160
WF2: Wake 4F 124
Laithes Cft. WF12: Dew 5H 123
Laithes Dr. WF2: Wake 4F 124
Laithes Fold WF2: Wake 4F 124
Laithes La. S71: Ath 9A 160
Laithes Shop. Cen. S71: Ath 9A 160
Laithes Vw. WF2: Wake 4F 124
Laith Gdns. LS16: Leeds 4K 49
Laith Gth. LS16: Leeds 4J 49
Laith Grn. LS16: Leeds 4J 49
Laith Rd. LS16: Leeds 4J 49
Laith Staid La. LS25: S Mil 5M 73
Laith Wlk. LS16: Leeds 4J 49
Lake Ct. *WF2: New 6L 143*
(off Lake Vw.)
Lakeland Ct. LS15: Leeds 8M 69
Lakeland Cres. LS17: Leeds 1C 50
Lakeland Dr. LS17: Leeds 1D 50
Lakeland Way WF2: W'ton 4B 144
LAKE LOCK 7B 106
Lake Lock Dr. WF3: S'ley 6A 106

Laverock Pl.—Lesmere Gro.

Laverock Pl. HD6: Brigh . . . 7L 99
(off Laverock La.)
Laverton Rd. BD4: B'frd . . . 1F 82
Lavery Cl. WF5: Oss . . . 5M 123
Lavinia Ter. BD14: Clay . . . 1J 81
Lawcliffe Cres. BD22: Haw . . . 7D 42
Law Cl. LS22: Weth . . . 2N 23
Lawefield Gro. WF2: Wake . . . 6J 125
Lawefield La. WF2: Wake . . . 7G 9 (6J 125)
Lawfield Av. LS26: Rothw . . . 7L 87
Lawkholme Cres. BD21: Keigh . . . 9J 27
Lawkholme La. BD21: Keigh . . . 9J 27
Law La. HX3: Sou . . . 7E 98
HX7: Heb B . . . 9J 77
Lawler Cl. HX3: Hal . . . 1M 97
(off Rugby Gdns.)
Lawn, The LS29: Burl W . . . 8D 16
Lawn Av. LS29: Burl W . . . 8D 16
Lawndale DN6: Skel . . . 7L 165
Lawndale Fold S75: Dart . . . 8H 159
Lawnhurst M. WF13: Dew . . . 9C 102
Lawn Rd. LS29: Burl W . . . 8D 16
LAWNS . . . 6G 105
Lawns WF2: Carr G . . . 6G 105
Lawns, The HX3: Hal . . . 9A 98
LS29: I'ly . . . 5F 14
(off Church St.)
WF4: Over . . . 4K 141
Lawns Av. LS12: N Far . . . 2G 84
Lawns Cl. LS12: N Far . . . 2G 84
WF6: Alt . . . 8F 106
Lawns Ct. WF2: Carr G . . . 7G 105
Lawns Cres. LS12: N Far . . . 2G 84
Lawns Cft. LS12: N Far . . . 2G 84
Lawns Dene LS12: N Far . . . 2G 84
Lawns Dr. LS12: N Far . . . 2G 84
Lawns Grn. LS12: N Far . . . 2G 85
Lawns Hall Cl. LS16: Leeds . . . 4L 49
Lawns La. LS10: Leeds . . . 2G 86
LS12: N Far . . . 1G 85
WF2: Carr G . . . 7G 104
Lawns Mt. LS12: N Far . . . 2G 85
Lawns Sq. LS12: N Far . . . 2G 85
Lawns Ter. LS12: N Far . . . 2G 84
WF3: E Ard . . . 5F 104
Lawns Vw. WF6: Alt . . . 8F 106
(off Agincourt Dr.)
LAWNSWOOD . . . 5K 49
Lawnswood Bus. Pk. LS16: Leeds . . . 6K 49
Lawnswood Crematorium LS16: Leeds . . . 4L 49
Lawnswood Gdns. LS16: Leeds . . . 5L 49
Lawnswood Rd. BD21: Keigh . . . 2G 42
Lawn Wlk. LS29: Burl W . . . 8D 16
Lawrence Av. LS8: Leeds . . . 2L 69
WF8: Pon . . . 3H 129
Lawrence Batley Theatre . . . 5C 8 (4N 137)
Lawrence Ct. LS28: Pud . . . 8A 66
Lawrence Cres. LS8: Leeds . . . 2L 69
WF16: Heck . . . 6A 102
Lawrence Dr. BD7: B'frd . . . 3K 81
Lawrence Gdns. LS8: Leeds . . . 1L 69
Lawrence M. HD1: Hud . . . 4K 137
Lawrence Rd. HD1: Hud . . . 3K 137
HX3: Hal . . . 9A 98
LS8: Leeds . . . 2L 69
Lawrence St. HX3: Hal . . . 3N 97
Lawrence Wlk. LS8: Leeds . . . 2L 69
Law Slack Rd. HD9: Had E . . . 9B 170
Lawson Ct. LS28: Fars . . . 3B 66
Lawson Rd. HD6: Brigh . . . 1N 119
Lawson St. BD3: B'frd . . . 1C 6 (6D 64)
LS12: Leeds . . . 7L 67
Lawson Wood Ct. LS6: Leeds . . . 6B 50
Lawson Wood Dr. LS6: Leeds . . . 6B 50
Law St. BD4: B'frd . . . 3G 82
BD19: Cleck . . . 3H 101
OL14: Tod . . . 3D 92
OL14: W'den . . . 4K 113
WF17: Bat . . . 4C 102
Lawton St. HD4: Hud . . . 7M 137
Laxton Rd. S71: Ath . . . 9A 160
LAYCOCK . . . 9C 26
Laycock Ct. HD8: Kbtn . . . 3G 154
Laycock La. BD22: Lay . . . 1B 42
Laycock Pl. LS7: Leeds . . . 3F 68
Lay Garth LS26: Rothw . . . 9N 87
Lay Gth. Cl. LS26: Rothw . . . 8N 87
Lay Gth. Ct. LS26: Rothw . . . 9N 87
Laygarth Dr. HD5: K'htn . . . 4G 138
Lay Gth. Fold LS26: Rothw . . . 9N 87
Lay Gth. Gdns. LS26: Rothw . . . 9N 87
Lay Gth. Grn. LS26: Rothw . . . 9N 87
Lay Gth. Mead LS26: Rothw . . . 9N 87
Lay Gth. Pl. LS26: Rothw . . . 9N 87
Lay Gth. Sq. LS26: Rothw . . . 8N 87
Laythorp Ter. BD20: E Mor . . . 7C 28
Layton Av. LS19: Raw . . . 4A 48
Layton Cl. LS19: Raw . . . 5B 48
Layton Cres. LS19: Raw . . . 4A 48
Layton Dr. LS19: Raw . . . 4B 48
Layton La. LS19: Raw . . . 5B 48
Layton Mt. LS19: Raw . . . 4A 48
Layton Pk. Av. LS19: Raw . . . 5B 48
Layton Pk. Cl. LS19: Raw . . . 4A 48
Layton Pk. Cft. LS19: Raw . . . 5B 48
Layton Pk. Dr. LS19: Raw . . . 4A 48
Layton Ri. LS18: Hors . . . 4C 48
Layton Rd. LS18: Hors . . . 4B 48
LS19: Raw . . . 4B 48
Lazenby Dr. LS22: Weth . . . 3L 23
Lazenby Fold LS22: Weth . . . 3L 23
Lea, The LS25: Gar . . . 9N 71
Lea Av. HX3: Hal . . . 9B 98
Leabank Av. LS25: Gar . . . 9A 72
Leach Cres. BD20: Rid . . . 6L 27
Leach Ri. BD20: Rid . . . 6L 27
Leach Rd. BD20: Rid . . . 6K 27
Leach Way BD20: Rid . . . 6L 27
Lea Cl. HD6: Brigh . . . 8M 99
Lea Ct. BD7: B'frd . . . 3K 81
Lea Cft. LS21: Otley . . . 1L 31
LS23: Cliff . . . 3D 38
WF14: Mir . . . 5L 121
Leadenhall St. HX1: Hal . . . 7M 97
Lea Dr. HD8: Shep . . . 9K 155
Leadwell La. LS26: Rothw . . . 1K 105
WF3: Rob H . . . 1K 105
Lea Farm Cres. LS5: Leeds . . . 9J 49
Lea Farm Dr. LS5: Leeds . . . 9J 49
Lea Farm Gro. LS5: Leeds . . . 9J 49
Lea Farm Mt. LS5: Leeds . . . 8J 49
Lea Farm Pl. LS5: Leeds . . . 9J 49
Lea Farm Rd. LS5: Leeds . . . 8H 49
Lea Farm Row LS5: Leeds . . . 9J 49
Lea Farm Wlk. LS5: Leeds . . . 8J 49
Leafield Av. BD2: B'frd . . . 2G 64
HD3: Hud . . . 4D 136
Leafield Bank HD3: Hud . . . 4D 136
Leafield Cl. HD2: Hud . . . 7B 120
LS17: Leeds . . . 5D 50
Leafield Cres. BD2: B'frd . . . 2F 64
Leafield Dr. BD2: B'frd . . . 2G 64
LS17: Leeds . . . 5D 50
LS28: Pud . . . 9C 66
Leafield Grange LS17: Leeds . . . 5D 50
Leafield Gro. BD2: B'frd . . . 3G 64
Leafield La. LS21: Leat . . . 7F 18
Leafield Pl. LS19: Yead . . . 9K 31
Leafield Ter. BD2: B'frd . . . 3G 64
Leafield Towers LS17: Leeds . . . 5D 50
Leafield Vs. LS19: Yead . . . 9K 31
(off Leafield Pl.)
Leafield Way BD2: B'frd . . . 3G 64
Leafland St. HX1: Hal . . . 5N 97
Leaf St. BD22: Haw . . . 7E 42
WF10: C'frd . . . 5C 108
Leafsway BD6: B'frd . . . 7L 81
Lea Head HD8: Shep . . . 9J 155
Leah Pl. LS12: Leeds . . . 8B 68
Leah Row LS12: Leeds . . . 8B 68
Leake St. WF10: C'frd . . . 5E 108
Leak Hall Cres. HD8: Den D . . . 2C 172
Leak Hall La. HD8: Den D . . . 2C 172
Leak Hall Rd. HD8: Den D . . . 2C 172
Lea La. HD4: Neth . . . 3H 153
WF7: F'stne . . . 7E 128
Lea Mill Pk. Cl. LS19: Yead . . . 9L 31
Lea Mill Pk. Dr. LS19: Yead . . . 9L 31
Leamington Dr. BD10: B'frd . . . 7G 47
Leamington Rd. LS29: I'ly . . . 4H 15
Leamington St. BD9: B'frd . . . 4N 63
Leamington Ter. LS29: I'ly . . . 4H 15
WF12: Dew . . . 5G 123
Leamside Wlk. BD4: B'frd . . . 3J 83
Lea Pk. Cl. LS10: Leeds . . . 6H 87
Lea Pk. Cft. LS10: Leeds . . . 6J 87
Lea Pk. Dr. LS10: Leeds . . . 6H 87
Lea Pk. Gdns. LS10: Leeds . . . 6H 87
Lea Pk. Gth. LS10: Leeds . . . 6H 87
Lea Pk. Gro. LS10: Leeds . . . 6H 87
Lea Pk. Va. LS10: Leeds . . . 6J 87
Lea Ri. HD9: Hon . . . 6L 153
Lea Rd. WF17: Bat . . . 5C 102
Learoyd St. HD1: Hud . . . 2D 8 (3N 137)
Leas Av. HD9: H'frth . . . 1L 169
Leas Gdns. HD9: Jack B . . . 4C 170
Leaside Dr. BD13: Thorn . . . 7C 62
Lea Side Gdns. HD3: Hud . . . 4D 136
Leasowe Av. LS10: Leeds . . . 3G 86
Leasowe Cl. LS10: Leeds . . . 3G 87
Leasowe Ct. LS10: Leeds . . . 3G 87
(off Springfield Pl.)
Leasowe Gdns. LS10: Leeds . . . 3H 87
Leasowe Gth. LS10: Leeds . . . 3G 87
Leasowe Rd. LS10: Leeds . . . 3G 87
Lea St. HD1: Hud . . . 2M 137
(not continuous)
HD3: Hud . . . 1H 137
Lea Ter. HD8: Skelm . . . 7D 156
LS17: Leeds . . . 6E 50
Leatham Av. WF7: F'stne . . . 7E 128
Leatham Cres. WF7: F'stne . . . 7E 128
Leatham Dr. WF7: F'stne . . . 7F 128
Leatham Pk. Rd. WF7: F'stne . . . 7E 128
Leatham Royd HD7: Mars . . . 5F 150
(off Manchester Rd.)
Leather Bank LS29: Burl W . . . 6C 16
LEATHLEY . . . 6D 18
Leathley Av. LS29: Men . . . 5F 30
Leathley Cl. LS29: Men . . . 4F 30
Leathley Cres. LS29: Men . . . 5F 30
Leathley La. LS21: Leat, Otley . . . 5D 18
LS29: Men . . . 4F 30
Leathley Rd. LS10: Leeds . . . 9E 68
LS29: Men . . . 4F 30
Leavens, The BD10: B'frd . . . 7H 47
LEAVENTHORPE . . . 8H 63
Leaventhorpe Av. BD8: B'frd . . . 7H 63
Leaventhorpe Cl. BD8: B'frd . . . 7J 63
Leaventhorpe Gro. BD13: Thorn . . . 8H 63
Leaventhorpe La. BD8: B'frd . . . 8G 63
BD13: Thorn . . . 8G 63
Leaventhorpe Way BD8: B'frd . . . 7J 63
Lea Vw. LS18: Hors . . . 6E 48
WF17: Bat . . . 4D 102
Leavington Cl. BD6: B'frd . . . 7N 81
Leconfield Ct. LS22: Weth . . . 3K 23
Leconfield Ho. BD10: B'frd . . . 8G 46
LS29: I'ly . . . 5G 15
(off Springs La.)
Ledbury Av. LS10: Leeds . . . 9H 87
Ledbury Cl. LS10: Leeds . . . 9H 87
Ledbury Cft. LS10: Leeds . . . 9H 87
Ledbury Dr. LS10: Leeds . . . 9H 87
Ledbury Grn. LS10: Leeds . . . 9H 87
Ledbury Gro. LS10: Leeds . . . 9G 87
Ledbury Pl. BD4: B'frd . . . 1F 82
Ledgard Dr. WF4: Dur . . . 3H 143
Ledgard Way LS12: Leeds . . . 6M 67
Ledgard Wharf WF14: Mir . . . 8L 121
Ledgate La. LS25: Bur S . . . 1D 110
Ledger La. WF1: Out . . . 7K 105
WF3: Loft . . . 3L 105
Ledger Pl. WF1: Out . . . 8K 105
LEDSHAM . . . 5K 91
LEDSTON . . . 7E 90
Ledston Av. LS25: Gar . . . 9A 72
LEDSTON LUCK . . . 3D 90
Ledston Luck Cotts. LS25: Kip . . . 3E 90
Ledston Luck Ent. Pk. LS25: Kip . . . 3D 90
Ledston Luck Vs. LS25: Kip . . . 3D 90
Ledston Mill La. WF10: Leds . . . 6E 90
Lee Bank HX3: Hal . . . 1H 7 (3A 98)
Lee Beck Gro. WF3: S'ley . . . 4N 105
Lee Bottom Rd. OL14: Tod . . . 7B 94
Lee Bri. HX3: Hal . . . 1H 7 (4A 98)
Lee Bri. Ind. Est. HX3: Hal . . . 1H 7 (4A 98)
Lee Brig WF6: Alt . . . 9F 106
Leech La. BD16: Har . . . 7M 43
Lee Cl. BD15: Wils . . . 9B 44
Lee Clough Dr. HX7: Myth . . . 3N 95
Lee Ct. BD21: Keigh . . . 1M 43
WF5: Oss . . . 7B 124
WF15: Liv . . . 7L 101
Lee Cres. WF4: Dur . . . 3H 143
LEEDS . . . 6F 4 (6E 68)
Leeds 27 Ind. Est. LS27: Morl . . . 8H 85
Leeds and Bradford Rd. LS5: Leeds . . . 1F 66
LS13: Leeds . . . 1F 66
LS28: Stan . . . 4C 66
Leeds Aquatic Cen. . . . 5E 86
Leeds Arena . . . 4F 4 (5E 68)
Leeds Barnsdale Rd. WF10: C'frd . . . 6A 108
LEEDS BRADFORD INTERNATIONAL AIRPORT . . . 9B 32
Leeds Bus. Centre, The LS27: Morl . . . 8H 85
Leeds Carnegie RUFC
Headingley Carnegie Stadium . . . 2N 67
Leeds City Art Gallery . . . 5E 4 (6D 68)
Leeds City Mus. . . . 4E 4 (5D 68)
Leeds City Office Pk. LS11: Leeds . . . 8E 68
Leeds Corn Exchange LS2: Leeds . . . 7G 5
Leeds Golf Cen. . . . 8L 35
Leeds Golf Course . . . 7M 51
Leeds La. LS26: Swil . . . 9H 71
Leeds Metropolitan University
City Campus . . . 3E 4 (5D 68)
Headingley Campus . . . 9L 49
Leslie Silver Building . . . 3E 4 (5D 68)
Leeds Metropolitan University Sports Cen. . . . 9L 49
Leeds Museum Discovery Cen. . . . 8G 68
Leeds Old Rd. BD3: B'frd . . . 6H 65
WF16: Heck . . . 7N 101
WF17: Bat . . . 7N 101
Leeds Rhinos RLFC . . . 2N 67
Leeds Rd. BD1: B'frd . . . 4C 6 (7D 64)
(not continuous)
BD2: B'frd . . . 2F 64
BD3: B'frd . . . 4C 6 (7D 64)
BD10: B'frd . . . 5F 46
BD18: B'frd, Ship . . . 7A 46
HD1: Hud . . . 3C 8 (3N 137)
HD2: Hud . . . 3N 137
HD5: Hud . . . 3N 137
HX3: Hal . . . 3E 98
HX3: Hip . . . 4J 99
LS15: Bar E, Scho . . . 2F 70
LS16: B'hpe . . . 4F 32
LS19: Raw . . . 3M 47
LS20: Guis . . . 8J 31
LS21: Otley, Pool . . . 1M 31
(not continuous)
LS22: Coll . . . 1G 37
(Wetherby Rd.)
LS22: Coll, Weth . . . 8L 23
(Wattlesyke)
LS24: Tad . . . 3A 54
LS25: Gar, Kip . . . 1N 89
LS26: Meth . . . 1H 107
LS26: Oul, Rothw . . . 6A 88
LS29: I'ly . . . 5G 15
WF1: Out, Wake . . . 1G 9 (8K 105)
WF3: Loft, Rob H . . . 1K 105
WF5: Oss . . . 2L 123
(not continuous)
WF10: All B . . . 7M 89
WF10: C'frd . . . 7C 108
(Aketon Rd.)
WF10: C'frd . . . 4A 108
(Methley Rd.)
WF12: Dew . . . 3G 123
WF14: Liv, Mir . . . 4F 120
WF15: Liv . . . 8M 101
WF16: Heck . . . 8M 101
WF17: Bat, Birs . . . 3C 102
Leeds Road Athletic Arena . . . 9C 120
Leeds Rd. Retail Pk. HD1: Hud . . . 1F 8 (2B 138)
Leeds Road Sports Complex . . . 9C 120
Leeds Rugby Academy . . . 3K 67
Leeds Sailing & Activity Cen. . . . 1H 43
Leeds Station (Rail) . . . 8E 4 (7D 68)
Leeds St. BD21: Keigh . . . 9H 27
Leeds United FC . . . 2A 86
Leeds University Business School . . . 2A 4 (4B 68)
Leeds University Medical Cen. . . . 2E 4
(off Blenheim Wlk.)
Leeds Valley Pk. LS10: Leeds . . . 5K 87
Leeds Wall, The . . . 9N 67
Lee Edge LS10: Leeds . . . 9F 86
Lee Fair Ct. WF3: W Ard . . . 6N 103
Leefield Rd. WF17: Bat . . . 6B 102
Leef St. HD5: Hud . . . 4B 138
Lee Grn. HX4: Holy . . . 9A 118
WF14: Mir . . . 4L 121
Lee Head HD2: Hud . . . 2L 137
Lee Head Ct. HD5: Hud . . . 3E 138
Leeke Av. WF4: Horb . . . 9C 124
Lee La. BD15: Wils . . . 9A 44
BD16: Cot . . . 8B 44
BD22: Oxen . . . 3N 59
HD8: Kbtn . . . 3J 155
HX3: Hal . . . 1B 98
OL14: Tod . . . 9N 93
S71: Roys, S'ross . . . 7M 159
WF7: Ackw . . . 1H 147
Lee La. E. LS18: Hors . . . 5E 48
Lee La. W. LS18: Hors . . . 5C 48
Lee Mill Rd. HX7: Heb B . . . 8H 77
Lee Mills Ind. Pk. HD9: Scho . . . 4B 170
LEEMING . . . 5D 60
Leemingbeck Cl. BD22: Oxen . . . 3C 60
(off West Dr.)
Leeming St. BD1: B'frd . . . 2C 6 (6D 64)
LEE MOOR . . . 5N 105
Lee Moor La. WF3: S'ley . . . 4N 105
Lee Moor Rd. WF3: S'ley . . . 5N 105
LEE MOUNT
HX3 . . . 3N 97
WF3 . . . 6A 106
Lee Mt. Gdns. HX3: Hal . . . 3N 97
Lee Mt. Rd. HX3: Hal . . . 3N 97
Lee Orchards LS23: B Spa . . . 9E 24
Lee Rd. WF13: Raven . . . 6A 122
Lee Royd HX7: Heb B . . . 1G 95
LEES . . . 7E 42
Lees HD7: Linth . . . 9B 136
Lees Av. WF12: Dew . . . 7F 122
Lees Bank Av. BD22: Cros R . . . 7E 42
Lees Bank Dr. BD22: Cros R . . . 7E 42
Lees Bank Hill BD22: Cros R . . . 7E 42
Lees Bank Rd. BD22: Cros R . . . 7E 42
Lees Bldgs. HX3: Hip . . . 4H 99
Lees Cl. BD13: Cull . . . 9J 43
HD5: Hud . . . 3D 138
Lees Dr. WF12: Dew . . . 7F 122
Lees Hall Rd. WF12: Dew . . . 7D 122
Lees Holm WF12: Dew . . . 7F 122
Lees Ho. Rd. WF12: Dew . . . 6F 122
Leeside Av. HD2: Hud . . . 7A 120
Leeside Rd. WF16: Heck . . . 6B 102
WF17: Bat . . . 6B 102
Lees La. BD22: Haw . . . 8D 42
HX3: Hip . . . 3K 99
LS28: Fars . . . 2A 66
Lees Mill La. HD7: Linth . . . 9A 136
Lees Moor . . . 7H 43
Lees Moor Mdw. BD13: Cull . . . 9J 43
Lees Moor Rd. BD13: Cull . . . 9J 43
Lees Rd. HX7: Heb B . . . 9H 77
Lee St. BD13: Que . . . 5C 80
HD6: Brigh . . . 8M 99
WF1: Wake . . . 4J 9 (5L 125)
WF13: Raven . . . 5B 122
WF15: Liv . . . 7L 101
Leesworth Ct. BD22: Cros R . . . 7E 42
(off Haworth Rd.)
Lees Yd. HX7: Heb B . . . 1H 95
(off Bridge Ga.)
Lee Ter. BD12: O'haw . . . 8D 82
HD9: Scho . . . 4B 170
Lee Vw. HX7: Heb B . . . 9H 77
Lee Vw. Rd. HX7: Heb B . . . 9H 77
Lee Way HD8: Kbtn . . . 2J 155
WF10: C'frd . . . 7E 108
Lee Wood Rd. HX7: Hept . . . 7G 77
Legrams Av. BD7: B'frd . . . 9L 63
Legrams La. BD7: B'frd . . . 9M 63
Legrams Mill La. BD7: B'frd . . . 8M 63
Legrams St. BD7: B'frd . . . 7N 63
Legrams Ter. BD7: B'frd . . . 7A 64
Leicester Cl. LS7: Leeds . . . 1E 4 (4D 68)
Leicester Cres. LS29: I'ly . . . 5G 15
Leicester Gro. LS7: Leeds . . . 1E 4 (4D 68)
Leicester Pl. LS2: Leeds . . . 1E 4 (4D 68)
LS7: Leeds . . . 1E 4 (4D 68)
Leicester St. BD4: B'frd . . . 1E 82
Leicester Ter. HX3: Hal . . . 8A 98
Leigh Av. WF3: Ting . . . 4C 104
Leigh Rd. WF3: Ting . . . 4C 104
Leigh St. HX6: Sow B . . . 7J 97
WF7: Ackw . . . 5D 146
Leighton La. LS1: Leeds . . . 5C 4
Leighton Pl. LS1: Leeds . . . 5D 4
Leighton St. LS1: Leeds . . . 5C 4 (6D 68)
Leigh Vw. WF3: Ting . . . 4B 104
Leisure Exchange, The
Bradford . . . 5D 6
Leisure La. HD8: Eml . . . 1H 157
Leith Ct. WF12: T'hill . . . 1H 141
Leith Ho. BD4: B'frd . . . 2J 83
(off Stirling Cres.)
Leith St. BD21: Keigh . . . 8H 27
Lemans Dr. WF13: Dew . . . 9C 102
Le Marchant Av. HD3: Hud . . . 2H 137
Le Mar Vw. HX3: Sou . . . 6D 98
Lemington Av. HX1: Hal . . . 6G 7 (6N 97)
Lemonroyd Marina LS26: Oul . . . 8H 89
Lemon St. BD5: B'frd . . . 2A 82
HX1: Hal . . . 5M 97
Lemon Tree Cl. WF8: Pon . . . 5H 129
Lenacre La. HD8: Eml . . . 9A 140
Leng Dr. BD3: B'frd . . . 7K 65
Lenham Cl. LS27: Morl . . . 2K 103
Lenhurst Av. LS12: Leeds . . . 3J 67
Lennie St. BD21: Keigh . . . 1H 43
Lennon Dr. BD8: B'frd . . . 6N 63
Lennox Dr. WF2: Wake . . . 9F 124
Lennox Gdns. LS15: Leeds . . . 7D 70
Lennox Rd. LS4: Leeds . . . 5N 67
OL14: Tod . . . 3B 92
(not continuous)
Lenny Balk DN6: Hamp . . . 9C 164
Lens Dr. BD17: Bail . . . 3A 46
Lentilfield St. HX3: Hal . . . 2N 97
Lentilfield Ter. HX3: Hal . . . 2N 97
Lenton Dr. LS11: Leeds . . . 3E 86
Lenton Vs. BD10: B'frd . . . 6F 46
Leodis Ct. LS11: Leeds . . . 8D 68
Leodis Ho. LS10: Leeds . . . 4L 87
Leodis Residences LS6: Leeds . . . 1E 4 (3D 68)
Leodis Way LS10: Leeds . . . 5K 87
Leonard's Pl. BD16: Bgly . . . 5F 44
Leonard St. BD12: Wyke . . . 1B 100
BD16: Bgly . . . 5F 44
HD2: Hud . . . 1N 137
Leonore Cft. HX3: North . . . 2F 98
Leopold Gdns. LS7: Leeds . . . 3G 68
Leopold Gro. LS7: Leeds . . . 1J 5 (3F 68)
Leopold St. LS7: Leeds . . . 1L 5 (3F 68)
WF5: Oss . . . 7C 124
LEPTON . . . 7L 139
LEPTON EDGE . . . 7N 139
Lepton Hare Chase LS10: Leeds . . . 2E 104
Lepton La. HD8: Kbtn, Lept . . . 9K 139
Lepton Pl. LS27: Gil . . . 6G 84
Lesley Way HD4: Hud . . . 9F 136
Leslie Av. LS19: Yead . . . 8N 31
Leslie St. HD2: Hud . . . 1M 137
Leslie Ter. LS6: Leeds . . . 3C 68
Lesmere Gro. BD7: B'frd . . . 3L 81

Lip Hill La.—Longside Gallery

Lip Hill La. HD9: H'frth 3G 169
Lippersley La. BD20: Sils 3G 12
(not continuous)
Lipscomb St. HD3: Hud 5F 136
Liquorice Way WF8: Pon 3J 129
Lisbon Sq. LS1: Leeds 6B 4
Lisbon St. LS1: Leeds 6C 4 (6C 68)
Lisheen Av. WF10: C'frd 5E 108
Lisheen Gro. WF10: C'frd 5E 108
Lisker Av. LS21: Otley 1M 31
Lisker Ct. LS21: Otley 1M 31
Lisker Dr. LS21: Otley 1M 31
Lismore Cl. LS26: Rothw 8A 88
Lismore Rd. BD20: Keigh 8H 27
Lisset M. BD20: Rid 7N 27
Lister Av. BD4: B'frd 2F 82
Lister Cl. WF7: F'stne 6C 128
Lister Ct. HX1: Hal 4K 7
LS29: I'ly 5F 14
(off Church St.)
Listerdale WF15: Liv 7L 101
Lister Dr. WF7: F'stne 6C 128
Lister Gdns. BD8: B'frd 4B 64
Lister Hill LS18: Hors 5F 48
LISTER HILLS 7A 64
Listerhills Ind. Est. BD1: B'frd 7B 64
Listerhills Rd. BD7: B'frd 8A 64
Listerhills Science Pk. BD7: B'frd 7A 64
Lister Ho. LS23: B Spa 9E 24
Lister La. BD2: B'frd 4D 64
HX1: Hal 4G 7 (5N 97)
(not continuous)
Lister Pk. WF7: F'stne 5B 128
Lister Rd. WF7: F'stne 6C 128
Lister's Ct. HX1: Hal 3G 7 (5N 97)
Listers Rd. HX3: Hal 4D 98
Lister St. BD4: B'frd 3G 83
(Bela Av.)
BD4: B'frd 4J 83
(Edward St.)
BD21: Keigh 1G 43
HD5: Hud 4C 138
HD6: Brigh 9M 99
LS29: I'ly 5F 14
WF10: C'frd 4C 108
Lister Vw. BD8: B'frd 5A 64
Lister Ville BD15: Wils 1B 62
Lister Wlk. LS27: Morl 7J 85
Listing Av. WF15: Liv 7M 101
Listing Ct. WF15: Liv 7M 101
Listing Dr. WF15: Liv 7M 101
Listing La. BD19: Gom 7M 101
WF15: Liv 7M 101
Litell Royd WF7: Street 6L 127
Litherop La. HD8: Clay W 3M 157
Litherop Rd. S75: H Hoy 5N 157
Lit. Baines St. HX1: Hal 5N 97
Littlebeck Dr. BD16: Bgly 4H 45
Little Bradley HX4: Gree 5B 118
Lit. Brunswick St. HD1: Hud 3A 8 (3M 137)
Little Cake HD9: Scho 6A 170
Lit. Church La. LS26: Meth 2K 107
Little Cote BD10: B'frd 6E 46
Lit. Cote Farm Cl. BD10: B'frd 6E 46
Lit. Cross St. BD5: B'frd 3C 82
LS1: Leeds 6F 4
Littlefield Gro. WF5: Oss 5A 124
Littlefield Rd. WF5: Oss 6A 124
Littlefield Wlk. BD6: B'frd 5N 81
Lit. Fountain St. LS27: Morl 1K 103
Lit. Green La. WF16: Heck 7N 101
Little Haley BD22: Oxen 3D 60
Little Hallas HD8: Kbtn 3K 155
LITTLE HEMSWORTH 3E 162
Little Hemsworth WF9: Hems 3E 162
Lit. Hew Royd BD10: B'frd 6D 46
Lit. Hollin Hey HX7: Myth 5M 95
Littleholme St. OL14: Tod 9J 93
LITTLE HORTON 1A 82
LITTLE HORTON GREEN 9B 64
Lit. Horton Grn. BD5: B'frd 9B 64
Lit. Horton La. BD5: B'frd 2A 82
(Canterbury Av.)
BD5: B'frd 8A 6 (9B 64)
(Melbourne Pl., not continuous)
Lit. John Cres. WF2: Wake 7G 124
Lit. King St. LS1: Leeds 7D 4 (7D 68)
Littlelands BD16: Cot 8F 44
Little La. BD9: B'frd 4L 63
BD20: E Mor 7D 28
HD9: H'frth 3L 169
(Upperthong La.)
HD9: H'frth 2A 170
(Woolcroft Dr.)
HX3: Hal 5F 98
HX7: P Wel 8H 59
LS27: Chur 5M 85
LS27: Morl 9K 85
LS29: I'ly 5G 15
S75: H Hoy 8M 157
WF3: Carl 1N 105
WF7: F'stne 7E 128
WF8: Lit S 3M 149
WF9: S Elm 6M 163
(Beaumont Av.)
WF9: S Elm 6A 164
(Heming's Way)
WF9: Upt 2A 164
Lit. Lane Ct. LS27: Chur 5M 85
LITTLE LEPTON 8L 139
LITTLE LONDON
LS7 2G 5 (4E 68)
LS19 3L 47
Little London HX3: North 9E 80
LITTLE MOOR 4F 80
Little Moor BD13: Que 4F 80
LITTLEMOOR BOTTOM 9B 66
Littlemoor Ct. LS28: Pud 8B 66
Littlemoor Cres. LS28: Pud 9B 66
Littlemoor Cres. Sth.
LS28: Pud 9B 66
Littlemoor Gdns. HX2: Illing 7L 79
LS28: Pud 9B 66
Littlemoor Gro. WF14: Mir 6K 121
Littlemoor La. LS14: T'ner 2G 53
Lit. Moor Pl. LS12: Leeds 7L 67
Littlemoor Rd. HX2: Illing 6L 79
LS28: Pud 8B 66
WF14: Mir 6K 121
Littlemoor Vw. LS28: Pud 8C 66
Lit. Neville St. LS1: Leeds 8E 4 (7D 68)
Little Park BD10: B'frd 6J 47
Lit. Pilling La. HD8: Skelm 7E 156
LITTLE PRESTON 4J 89
Lit. Preston Hall LS26: Swil 4J 89
Lit. Queen St. LS1: Leeds 7C 4 (7C 68)
LITTLE SMEATON 4K 149
Little St. BD22: Haw 8C 42
Lit. Taylor Hall La. WF14: Liv, Mir 2J 121
LITTLE THORPE 2H 121
Littlethorpe Hill WF15: Liv 2H 121
Littlethorpe Rd. WF15: Liv 2H 121
LITTLETOWN 7M 101
Littleway LS17: Leeds 6E 50
Little Westfields S71: Roys 5B 160
Littlewood HX7: Crag V 2K 115
Littlewood Cl. BD6: B'frd 6A 82
Littlewood Cft. HD4: Hud 8M 137
Littlewood Dr. BD19: Cleck 2H 101
LITTLE WOODHOUSE 3B 4 (5C 68)
Little Woodhouse HD6: Ras 1M 119
Lit. Woodhouse St. LS2: Leeds 4C 4 (5C 68)
Litton Cl. S72: Shaf 6K 161
Litton Ct. LS29: Men 5F 30
Litton Cft. WF1: Wake 4A 126
Littondale Cl. BD17: Bail 3C 46
Litton Rd. BD22: Keigh 1G 42
Litton Wlk. S72: Shaf 6K 161
Litton Way LS14: Leeds 7C 52
Liverpool Row *HX2: Hal 6H 97*
(off Stock La.)
LIVERSEDGE 8L 101
Liversedge Hall La. WF15: Liv 9L 101
Liversedge Row *BD7: B'frd 2M 81*
(off Perseverance La.)
Livingstone Cl. BD2: B'frd 9D 46
Livingstone Rd. BD2: B'frd 1D 64
(Cheltenham Rd.)
BD2: B'frd 2B 64
(Gaisby La.)
Livingstone St. HX3: Hal 3N 97
Livingstone St. Nth. HX2: Hal 8N 79
Livingston Ho. BD10: B'frd 9G 46
Livinia Gro. LS7: Leeds 1F 4 (4E 68)
Lloyds Dr. BD12: Low M 7C 82
Lloyd St. OL14: Tod 6K 93
Lobley St. WF16: Heck 8B 102
Lob Quarry OL14: Tod 9H 93
Locarno Av. BD9: B'frd 4K 63
Locherbie Grn. BD15: All 5G 62
Lochy Rd. BD6: B'frd 7L 81
Lockbridge Way HD3: Hud 6G 137
Lock Hill WF11: Ferr 7B 110
Lock La. WF6: Alt 6G 107
WF10: C'frd 3D 108
Lock Lane RL & Sports Club 3E 108
Locks, The BD16: Bgly 3E 44
LS26: W'frd 6E 88
Lockside Rd. LS10: Leeds 2J 87
Locksley Rd. HD6: Brigh 2B 120
Lock St. HX3: Hal 6M 7 (6C 98)
OL14: Tod 9J 93
WF12: Dew 7G 123
Lock Vw. BD16: Bgly 3D 44
HX5: Ell 3F 118
Lock Way WF13: Raven 7B 122
LOCKWOOD 7K 137
Lockwood Av. WF14: Mir 4M 121
Lockwood Cl. HD3: Hud 3H 137
LS11: Leeds 4E 86
Lockwood Ct. LS11: Leeds 4E 86
Lockwood Gdns. S36: Hoy 9K 173
Lockwood Pk. HD1: Hud 8K 137
LS11: Leeds 4E 86
Lockwood Rd. HD1: Hud 8A 8 (7L 137)
Lockwood Scar HD4: Hud 7L 137
Lockwood Station (Rail) 7K 137
Lockwood St. BD6: B'frd 4A 82
BD12: Low M 8C 82
BD18: Ship 7L 45
Lockwoods Yd. HD1: Hud 5B 8 (4M 137)
HD7: Golc 5B 136
Lockwood Way LS11: Leeds 4E 86
Lode Pit La. BD16: Bgly 3J 45
Lodge, The HD7: Linth 8D 136
Lodge Av. HX5: Ell 4H 119
WF10: C'frd 5J 109
Lodge Cl. HD4: Hud 9K 137
HX2: Lud F 6D 96
(off Boy Home La.)
Lodge Ct. BD13: Cull 9K 43
Lodge Dr. HX5: Ell 4H 119
LS23: B'ham 6D 38
WF14: Mir 7N 121
Lodge Farm Cl. WF12: Dew 7G 123
Lodge Farm Gdns. WF6: Alt 9F 106
Lodge Gdns. LS23: B'ham 6D 38
Lodge Ga. BD13: Denh 5L 61
Lodge Ga. Cl. BD13: Denh 5L 61
LODGE HILL 3A 124
Lodge Hill BD17: Bail 4L 45
LS29: Add 1M 13
(off Main St.)
Lodge Hill Cl. LS12: N Far 2H 85
Lodge Hill Rd. WF5: Oss 3N 123
Lodge Hill Wlk. LS12: N Far 2H 85
Lodge La. LS11: Leeds 2D 86
LS22: Weth 5M 23
WF2: New 6M 143
WF4: Croft 9F 126
WF15: Liv 1N 121
Lodge Pl. HX5: Ell 4H 119
Lodge Rd. BD10: B'frd 5F 46
DN6: Carc, Skel 7N 165
LS28: Pud 6A 66
Lodge Row *LS15: Leeds 4D 70*
(off Tranquility Av.)
Lodges Cl. WF4: H'cft 8K 145
Lodge St. BD13: Cull 9K 43
BD22: Haw 8B 42
Lodge St. HD8: Skelm 7D 156
LS2: Leeds 2D 4 (4D 68)
(not continuous)
WF9: Hems 1D 162
Lodge Ter. LS11: Leeds 3D 86
Lodore Av. BD2: B'frd 3E 64
Lodore Pl. BD2: B'frd 3F 64
Lodore Rd. BD2: B'frd 3E 64
LOFTHOUSE 3L 105
Lofthouse Farm Fold WF3: Loft 5L 105
LOFTHOUSE GATE 6K 105
Lofthouse Hill Golf Course 5L 105
Lofthouse Pl. LS2: Leeds 2E 4 (4D 68)
Loft St. BD8: B'frd 6L 63
Lo Grove WF1: Out 8K 105
Logwood St. HD1: Hud 8A 8 (6M 137)
Loiner Ct. LS9: Leeds 9L 69
Lombardi Ct. WF5: Oss 7B 124
Lombard St. HX1: Hal 7M 97
LS15: Leeds 7A 70
LS19: Raw 3L 47
Lombardy Cl. HD9: Hon 6L 153
Lombardy Gth. WF2: Wake 3J 125
Lomond Av. LS18: Hors 3E 48
Londesboro Gro. LS9: Leeds 7J 69
Londesboro Ter. LS9: Leeds 7J 69
London La. LS19: Raw 3L 47
London Pk. Est. WF14: Mir 4K 121
London Rd. HD7: Slait 9N 135
HX6: Norl 9K 97
OL14: Tod 7C 94
(not continuous)
London Spring Rd. HX6: Ripp 7A 116
London Sq. LS19: Raw 3L 47
London St. LS19: Raw 3L 47
Long Acre S71: Carl 8C 160
Longacre WF10: C'frd 6D 108
Longacre La. BD22: Haw 7D 42
Longacres BD22: Haw 7E 42
Longacres Dr. OL12: Whit 9A 112
Longacres La. OL12: Whit 9A 112
Longbottom Av. BD20: Sils 8F 12
HX6: Sow B 9E 96
Longbottom Ter. HX3: Hal 8C 98
Longbow Av. LS26: Meth 1K 107
Longbow Cl. HD2: Hud 6B 120
Long Causeway BB10: Cliv 6A 74
BD13: Denh 5F 60
BD22: Denh 5F 60
BD23: Hal E 3D 10
HX2: Ogd 2K 79
HX6: Rish 1M 133
LS9: Leeds 9H 69
LS16: Leeds 5N 49
OL14: Tod 9A 94
WF1: Wake 1L 9 (3M 125)
WF3: S'ley 7A 106
WF14: Mir 9B 122
Long Causeway, The HX2: Lud F 6A 96
HX7: Blac H 9L 75
Longcauseway WF12: Dew 8G 122
(Ingham Rd.)
WF12: Dew 3G 122
(Vicarage Rd., not continuous)
Long Cliffe Cl. S72: Shaf 7K 161
Long Cl. BD12: Wyke 9N 81
HD8: Shep 1G 170
Long Cl. La. HD8: Shep 2F 170
HD9: New M 2F 170
LS9: Leeds 8M 5 (7H 69)
WF9: S Elm 2B 164
Long Crest WF8: Pon 5L 129
Long Cft. S75: Map 8K 159
Longcroft BD21: Keigh 1J 43
HD5: Hud 7C 138
Longcroft Link BD1: B'frd 7B 64
Longcroft Pl. BD1: B'frd 3A 6 (7B 64)
Longcroft Rd. LS29: I'ly 6K 15
Long Cft. St. HD7: Golc 6D 136
Long Cft. Vw. WF17: Bat 4F 102
Long Cft. Yd. *HD7: Golc 6D 136*
(off Long Cft. St.)
Longdale Dr. WF9: S Elm 5L 163
Long Dales WF8: Pon 1A 130
Long Dam La. WF4: Wint 6H 145
Longden Av. HD4: Hud 8H 137
HD8: Lept 7J 139
Longden Wlk. HD8: Lept 7J 139
Longdike Ct. LS25: Kip 4B 90
Longdike La. LS25: Kip 5C 90
Long Edge Low Rd. HX6: Sow B 1B 116
Long Edge Middle Rd. HX6: Sow B 9A 96
Long Edge Rd. HX6: Sow B 9A 96
Long Fallas Cres. HD6: Ras 4N 119
Longfellow Ct. HX7: Myth 3M 95
Longfellow Gro. WF3: S'ley 6N 105
Longfield HX4: Holy 7A 118
HX7: Hept 9G 76
Longfield Av. HD5: Hud 3B 138
HD7: Golc 5D 136
HX3: North 3F 98
LS28: Pud 7C 66
Longfield Cl. HD5: Hud 3B 138
OL14: Tod 8K 93
Longfield Ct. LS28: Pud 7C 66
WF16: Heck 8B 102
Longfield Dr. BD4: B'frd 2G 82
LS13: Leeds 1C 66
LS15: Leeds 6B 70
S75: Map 8K 159
WF7: Ackw 3J 147
Longfield Gth. LS13: Leeds 1C 66
Longfield Gro. LS28: Pud 7C 66
OL14: Tod 8K 93
Longfield La. OL14: Tod 9K 93
Longfield Mt. LS28: Pud 7C 66
Longfield Ri. OL14: Tod 8K 93
Longfield Rd. LS28: Pud 7B 66
OL14: Tod 8K 93
WF16: Heck 8A 102
Longfields Ct. S71: Ath 9C 160
Longfields Rd. S71: Carl 9C 160
Longfield Ter. *HX3: North 3F 98*
(off Bradford Rd.)
LS28: Pud 7B 66
Longfield Ter. OL14: Tod 8K 93
WF2: Wake 4H 125
Longfield Vw. *LS28: Fars 3A 66*
(off Croft St.)
Longfield Way OL14: Tod 8K 93
Longford Ter. BD7: B'frd 9L 63
Long Gate BD22: Oak 1K 41
HX6: Rish 2A 134
Long Gro. Av. HD5: Hud 4C 138
Long Hall Pk. LS29: I'ly 3E 14
Long Hey La. OL14: Tod 9L 93
Long Heys HX4: Gree 5B 118
Long Hey Top HX7: Blac H 2C 94
Long Hill Rd. HD2: Hud 7N 119
Longhouse Dr. BD13: Denh 6K 61
Longhouse La. BD13: Denh 6K 61
Long Ho. Rd. HX2: Mix 7J 79
Long Ing HD9: H'frth 4J 169
Long Ing Rd. HD9: Had E 9M 169
Longland La. DN6: Burg, Cam, Nort 3M 165
Longlands BD10: B'frd 7F 46
Longlands Av. BD13: Denh 5K 61
HD7: Slait 9L 135
Longlands Bank HD9: T'bdge 9N 153
Longlands Cl. WF5: Oss 5A 124
Longlands Dr. BD22: Haw 7D 42
S75: Map 9K 159
Longlands Ind. Est. WF5: Oss 5A 124
(not continuous)
Longlands La. LS22: Sick 4D 22
Longlands Rd. HD7: Slait 9L 135
WF5: Oss 5A 124
WF13: Dew 1D 122
Longlands St. BD1: B'frd 7B 64
(Baptist Pl.)
BD1: B'frd 3A 6 (7B 64)
(Providence St.)
Longlands Trad. Est. WF5: Oss 5A 124
Longlands Vw. WF17: Bat 9D 102
Long La. BD9: B'frd 1J 63
BD13: Que 6C 80
BD15: All 5C 62
BD16: Har 6N 43
HD5: Hud 4B 138
HD8: Clay W 6J 157
HD8: Shel, Shep 8J 155
HD9: Hon 6L 153
HX2: Hal 2L 97
HX3: Hal 2L 97
HX3: Sou 5E 98
HX6: Sow B 1G 117
HX7: Crag V 9E 94
HX7: Heb B 3F 94
HX7: Myth 5M 95
LS15: Bar E 8M 53
LS25: Gar 8M 53
OL14: Tod 6N 93
WF4: Flock 9A 140
WF7: Ackw 1G 147
WF8: K S'ton 1H 165
WF8: Pon 5M 129
WF12: Dew 5H 123
LONG LEE 1L 43
Long Lee La. BD21: Keigh 2K 43
Long Lee Ter. BD21: Keigh 2L 43
LONGLEY
HD4 8A 138
HD9 8N 169
Longley Edge La. HD9: H'frth 7N 169
Longley Edge Rd. HD9: H'frth 8N 169
Longley La. HD4: Hud 8A 138
HD9: H'frth 8M 169
HX6: Norl, Sow B 2F 116
(not continuous)
Longley Old Hall 7A 138
Longley Pk. Golf Course 7E 8 (5A 138)
Longley Rd. HD5: Hud 7B 138
Longley's Yd. LS10: Leeds 3G 86
Long Lover La. HX1: Hal 4L 97
HX2: Hal 4L 97
Long Meadow WF7: Ackw 1G 147
Longmeadow HX4: Bark 6G 116
(not continuous)
Long Meadow Ct. LS25: Gar 9A 72
Long Meadow Ga. LS25: Gar 9N 71
Long Meadows BD2: B'frd 2C 64
LS16: B'hpe 6H 33
LS25: Gar 9N 71
LS29: Burl W 7C 16
Long Moor La. HD8: Shel 8M 155
Long Preston Chase BD10: B'frd 8H 47
Long Pye Cl. S75: W Gran 6G 158
Long Reach HX2: Mt T 1G 97
Long Riddings LS29: Add 9L 11
Long Ridge HD6: Ras 4M 119
Long Row BD12: Low M 8B 82
BD13: Thorn 7B 62
HX7: Blac H 1M 93
LS18: Hors 6F 48
(not continuous)
WF4: N Sha 6H 127
Long Row Ct. BD5: B'frd 2C 82
Longroyd BD10: B'frd 7D 46
Longroyd Av. LS11: Leeds 2E 86
Long Royd Cl. BD17: Bail 3B 46
Longroyd Cres. HD7: Slait 9L 135
LS11: Leeds 2E 86
Longroyd Cres. Nth. LS11: Leeds 2E 86
Long Royd Dr. BD17: Bail 3C 46
Longroyde Cl. HD6: Ras 3L 119
Longroyde Gro. HD6: Ras 3L 119
Longroyde Rd. HD6: Ras 2L 119
Longroyd Farm WF4: M'twn 3L 141
Longroyd Gro. LS11: Leeds 2E 86
Long Royd La. HD8: Up C 9M 155
Longroyd La. HD1: Hud 5K 137
Longroyd Pl. HD1: Hud 5K 137
LS11: Leeds 2E 86
Long Royd Rd. HX6: Sow B 1C 116
Longroyd St. LS11: Leeds 2E 86
Longroyd St. Nth. LS11: Leeds 2E 86
Longroyd Ter. LS11: Leeds 2E 86
Longroyd Vw. LS11: Leeds 2E 86
Long Shaw La. OL14: Tod 8A 94
Longside Gallery 6A 158

Longside Hall BD7: B'frd . . . 8A 64
Longside La. BD7: B'frd . . . 8A 64
Longsight Rd. S75: Map . . . 8J 159
Longsight Ter. WF9: Kins . . . 9B 146
Longstaff Ct. HX7: Heb B . . . 1F 94
Long St. BD4: B'frd . . . 9F 64
Long Tail La. HX7: Hept . . . 6A 76
Long Thorpe La. WF3: Loft, Thpe H . . . 3H 105
Long Tongue Scrog La. HD5: K'htn . . . 3J 139
Longviews WF9: Upt . . . 1N 163
Long Wall HX5: Ell . . . 4C 118
LONG WALLS . . . 5H 169
LONGWOOD . . . 4E 136
Longwood Av. BD16: Bgly . . . 2C 44
Longwood Cl. HX3: Hal . . . 9A 98
LS17: Leeds . . . 2K 51
WF3: Ting . . . 4N 103
Longwood Ct. WF3: Ting . . . 4A 104
Longwood Cres. LS17: Leeds . . . 2K 51
LONGWOOD EDGE . . . 3D 136
Longwood Edge Rd. HD3: Hud . . . 2C 136
Longwood Fold WF3: Ting . . . 4A 104
Longwood Gth. WF3: Ting . . . 4A 104
Longwood Ga. HD3: Hud . . . 3D 136
Longwood Ho. Rd. HD2: Fix . . . 8M 119
Longwood Rd. HD3: Hud . . . 5G 137
WF3: Ting . . . 4N 103
Longwoods Wlk. WF11: Knot . . . 7F 110
Longwood Va. WF3: Ting . . . 4A 104
Longwood Vw. BD16: Bgly . . . 2D 44
Longwood Way LS17: Leeds . . . 2K 51
Longworth Rd. WF9: Hems . . . 3D 162
Lonk Ho. La. BD17: Bail . . . 2D 46
Lonsborough Way WF9: S Elm . . . 5N 163
Lonsbrough Av. WF16: Heck . . . 7A 102
Lonsbrough Flats HD1: Hud . . . 4C 8
Lonsdale Av. WF17: Bat . . . 5C 102
Lonsdale Cl. LS10: Leeds . . . 4F 86
Lonsdale Mdws. LS23: B Spa . . . 1D 38
Lonsdale Ri. WF3: W Ard . . . 4A 104
Lonsdale Rd. WF1: Wake . . . 1G 9 (3K 125)
Lonsdale St. BD3: B'frd . . . 6F 64
Lonsdale Ter. WF15: Liv . . . 8L 101
Loom Ho. LS9: Leeds . . . 8K 5
Lord La. BD22: Haw . . . 7B 42
Lord's Bldgs. LS27: Morl . . . 2K 103
Lords Chase WF8: Pon . . . 9K 109
Lordsfield Pl. BD4: B'frd . . . 4H 83
Lord's La. HD6: Ras . . . 2N 119
Lord St. BD21: Keigh . . . 9J 27
BD22: Haw . . . 8D 42
HD1: Hud . . . 3C 8 (4N 137)
HD7: Slait . . . 9M 135
HX1: Hal . . . 4K 7 (5B 98)
HX6: Sow B . . . 7J 97
LS12: Leeds . . . 8A 4 (8B 68)
OL14: W'den . . . 2J 113
WF1: Wake . . . 8A 126
WF12: Dew . . . 4L 123
WF13: Dew . . . 8C 102
Lordswood Grange LS28: Pud . . . 7M 65
Lord Ter. LS12: Leeds . . . 8A 4 (8B 68)
Loris St. BD4: B'frd . . . 4H 83
Lorna Cotts. *WF8: Pon* . . . *9K 109*
(off Skinner La.)
Lorne St. BD4: B'frd . . . 2F 82
BD21: Keigh . . . 8L 27
BD22: Cros R . . . *7F 42*
(off Bingley Rd.)
Lorry Bank LS7: Leeds . . . 2E 68
LOSCOE . . . 1N 127
Loscoe Cl. WF6: Norm . . . 9M 107
Loscoe La. WF6: Norm . . . 1M 127
WF7: A'ton . . . 2N 127
Lotherton Bus. Pk. LS25: Gar . . . 6N 71
(not continuous)
Lotherton Hall . . . 1H 73
Lotherton La. LS25: Aber . . . 9E 54
(not continuous)
Lotherton Rd. WF9: Hems . . . 2E 162
Lotherton Way LS25: Gar . . . 6N 71
Lot St. BD22: Haw . . . 8D 42
Loughrigg St. BD5: B'frd . . . 2C 82
Loughrigg Wlk. WF7: Ackw . . . 4E 146
Louisa St. BD10: B'frd . . . 7F 46
WF10: C'frd . . . 4C 108
Louis Av. BD5: B'frd . . . 1A 82
Louis Ct. LS7: Leeds . . . 3F 68
Louis Gro. LS7: Leeds . . . 3G 68
Louis Ho. *LS27: Morl* . . . *8L 85*
(off Pullman Ct.)
Louis Le Prince Ct. LS8: Leeds . . . 1M 5
Louis St. LS7: Leeds . . . 3F 68
Lounge Apartments *LS6: Leeds* . . . *1N 67*
(off North La.)
Lovaine Gro. WF2: Wake . . . 1M 143
Lovatt Fold BD17: Bail . . . 6B 46
Love La. HX1: Hal . . . 6J 7 (7A 98)
LS26: Rothw . . . 8N 87
WF2: Wake . . . 4G 9 (5K 125)
WF5: Oss . . . 5M 123
WF8: Pon . . . 4H 129
WF10: C'frd . . . 6C 108
Love La. Ter. WF8: Pon . . . 3J 129
Lovell Ho. LS7: Leeds . . . 3H 5
Lovell Pk. Cl. LS7: Leeds . . . 3H 5 (5F 68)
Lovell Pk. Ct. LS7: Leeds . . . 3G 5 (5F 68)
Lovell Pk. Ga. LS7: Leeds . . . 3G 5 (5E 68)
Lovell Pk. Grange LS7: Leeds . . . 3H 5
Lovell Pk. Hgts. LS7: Leeds . . . 3H 5
Lovell Pk. Hill LS7: Leeds . . . 3G 5 (5E 68)
Lovell Pk. M. LS7: Leeds . . . 3H 5 (5F 68)
Lovell Pk. Rd. LS2: Leeds . . . 4G 5 (5E 68)
LS7: Leeds . . . 4G 5 (5E 68)
Lovell Pk. Towers LS7: Leeds . . . 3G 5
Lovell Pk. Vw. LS7: Leeds . . . 3H 5 (5F 68)
Lovell Vw. WF4: Croft . . . 2H 145
Lovers Wlk. OL14: Tod . . . 7J 93
LOW ACKWORTH . . . 3H 147
Low Ash Av. BD18: Ship . . . 8B 46
Low Ash Cres. BD18: Ship . . . 8B 46
Low Ash Dr. BD18: Ship . . . 8B 46
Low Ash Gro. BD18: Ship . . . 8B 46
Low Ash Rd. BD18: Ship . . . 8C 46
LOW BAILDON . . . 3A 46
LOW BANK . . . 4B 42
Low Bank Dr. BD22: Oak . . . 4B 42
Low Bank La. BD22: Oak . . . 4B 42
LOW BANKS . . . 6M 27
Low Banks BD20: Rid . . . 7M 27
Low Bank St. LS28: Fars . . . 3A 66
Low Beck LS29: I'ly . . . 4J 15
Low Bentley HX3: She . . . 8K 81
Low Cliff Wlk. WF16: Heck . . . 1B 122
Low Cl. BD16: Bgly . . . 5G 45
LS29: I'ly . . . 3C 14
Low Cl. St. LS2: Leeds . . . 1C 4 (3C 68)
LOW COMMON
LS26 . . . 3M 107
WF5 . . . 6B 124
Low Cft. S71: Roys . . . 6E 160
Lowcroft LS22: Coll . . . 9H 23
Low Cft. Ct. LS16: B'hpe . . . 5H 33
Low Cronkhill La. S71: Carl . . . 7F 160
Low Cross Ct. WF11: Knot . . . 7F 110
Lowdale WF12: Dew . . . 1H 123
Lowell Av. BD7: B'frd . . . 9L 63
Lowell Gro. LS13: Leeds . . . 6D 66
Lowell Pl. LS13: Leeds . . . 6D 66
Lower Ainley *HX2: Illing* . . . *7M 79*
(off Whitehill Rd.)
LOWER ALTOFTS . . . 7H 107
Lower Ashgrove BD5: B'frd . . . 8B 64
Lower Bk. La. HX7: Blac H . . . 9A 76
Lower Bankhouse LS28: Pud . . . 1A 84
Lwr. Bank Ho's. HX4: Holy . . . 7K 117
Lwr. Basinghall St. LS1: Leeds . . . 6E 4 (6D 68)
Lwr. Bentley Royd HX6: Sow B . . . 8G 97
LOWER BINNS . . . 3M 169
Lwr. Bower La. WF13: Dew . . . 9C 102
Lwr. Bracken Bank *BD22: Keigh* . . . *3G 42*
(off Diamond St.)
Lower Brea HX3: Hal . . . 4F 98
Lwr. Brig Royd HX6: Ripp . . . 7E 116
Lower Brockholes HX2: Ogd . . . 6K 79
Lwr. Brockwell La. HX6: Tri . . . 1F 116
Lwr. Brown Hurst HX2: Mt T . . . 1J 97
Lwr. Brunswick St.
LS2: Leeds . . . 4H 5 (5F 68)
Lwr. Cambridge St. WF10: C'frd . . . 4E 108
Lower Chiserley HX7: Chis . . . 8K 77
Lwr. Clay Pits HX1: Hal . . . 4L 97
Lwr. Clifton St. HX6: Sow B . . . 8J 97
LOWER CLOUGH . . . 1C 152
Lwr. Clough Foot Caravan Club Site
HX7: Crag V . . . 6L 95
Lwr. Clyde St. HX6: Sow B . . . 9H 97
Lwr. Common La. HD8: Clay W . . . 9G 157
Lwr. Constable Fold *LS29: I'ly* . . . *6J 15*
(off Lwr. Constable Rd.)
Lwr. Constable Rd. LS29: I'ly . . . 6J 15
Lower Copy BD15: All . . . 5G 63
Lwr. Cross St. HX1: Hal . . . 3M 7 (5C 98)
WF13: Dew . . . 2F 122
Lwr. Crow Nest Dr. HX3: Hip . . . 5N 99
LOWER CUMBERWORTH . . . 1B 172
LOWER DENBY
HD8 . . . 4E 172
WF4 . . . 4F 140
Lwr. Denby La. HD8: Den D . . . 4E 172
LOWER EDGE BOTTOM . . . 4G 118
Lwr. Edge Rd. HD6: Ras . . . 4G 119
HX5: Brigh, Ell . . . 4G 119
Lower Ellistones *HX4: Gree* . . . *4N 117*
(off Saddleworth Rd.)
Lower Exley HX3: Hal . . . 2C 118
LOWER FAGLEY . . . 3J 65
Lwr. Ferney Lee OL14: Tod . . . 6J 93
Lwr. Finkil St. HD6: Brigh . . . 7K 99
Lwr. Fitzwilliam St. HD1: Hud . . . 3C 8 (3N 137)
Lower Fleet BD13: Que . . . 4B 80
Lower Fold HD6: Ras . . . 5L 119
HD9: Hon . . . 4L 153
HX1: Hal . . . 4K 7
HX4: Bark . . . 5K 117
Lowergate HD3: Hud . . . 5G 136
Lower Gaukrodger HX6: Sow B . . . 9F 96
Lwr. George St. BD6: B'frd . . . 4N 81
OL14: Tod . . . 7K 93
Lwr. Gilbert Flds. HX4: Bark . . . 5J 117
Lwr. Globe St. BD8: B'frd . . . 6A 64
LOWER GRANGE . . . 7G 62
Lower Grange HD2: Hud . . . 5C 120
Lwr. Grange Cl. BD8: B'frd . . . 7H 63
Lwr. Grattan Rd. BD1: B'frd . . . 7B 64
Lwr. Greave Rd. HD9: Mel . . . 9G 152
Lower Grn. BD17: Bail . . . 5N 45
Lower Grn. Av. BD19: Scho . . . 4D 100
Lower Greenside HD4: Thurs . . . 5E 154
Lwr. Haigh Head S36: Hoy . . . 9J 173
Lwr. Hall Cl. WF15: Liv . . . 8K 101
Lwr. Hall Cres. HD5: K'htn . . . 4G 138
Lwr. Hall Dr. WF15: Liv . . . 8K 101
Lwr. Hall La. WF15: Liv . . . 8K 101
Lwr. Hall Mt. WF15: Liv . . . 8K 101
Lwr. Hall Rd. HD5: K'htn . . . 4G 138
Lwr. Hartley Ct. HD8: Kbtn . . . 3G 154
Lower Hathershelf HX2: Lud F . . . 5B 96
Lower Hazelhurst BD13: Que . . . 6D 80
Lower Hgts. Rd. BD13: Thorn . . . 6B 62
Lower Hey HD9: Mel . . . 7C 152
(not continuous)
Lwr. Hey Grn. HD7: Mars . . . 4C 150
Lwr. High Royds S75: Dart . . . 9J 159
Lower Hollins HX6: Sow B . . . 8H 97
LOWER HOLME . . . 9K 135
Lower Holme BD17: Bail . . . 6A 46
LOWER HOPTON . . . 8L 121
Lwr. Horley Grn. HX3: Hal . . . 3D 98
Lower Ho. Cl. BD10: B'frd . . . 6D 46
Lower Ho. La. HD8: Lept . . . 8M 139
LOWER HOUSES . . . 7B 138
Lowerhouses La. HD5: Hud . . . 7A 138
Lowerhouses Rd. HD3: Hud . . . 4G 136
Lower Ings HX2: Ogd . . . 4J 79
Lwr. Kipping La. BD13: Thorn . . . 8C 62
Lower Kirkgate BD1: B'frd . . . 4B 6 (7C 64)
HX1: Hal . . . 4M 7 (5C 98)
Lwr. Kitchen Royd HD8: Den D . . . 1F 172
Lwr. Laith Av. OL14: Tod . . . 7L 93
Lower La. BD4: B'frd . . . 1F 82
BD4: E Bier . . . 8H 83
BD19: Gom . . . 5M 101
HD9: Hon . . . 5J 153
HX7: Blac H . . . 1M 93
Lower Langwith LS22: Coll . . . 9H 23
Lwr. Lark Hill BD19: Cleck . . . 5F 100
Lower Laund HD7: Slait . . . 7J 135
Lwr. Lumb La. HX7: Crag V . . . 8K 95
Lwr. Maythorn La. HD9: H'wth . . . 8G 170
Lower Mdws. HD9: U'thng . . . 3J 169
LOWER MICKLETOWN . . . 1N 107
Lower Mickletown LS26: Meth . . . 1M 107
Lwr. Mill Bank Rd. HX6: Mill B . . . 4D 116
Lwr. Mill La. HD9: H'frth . . . 4L 169
Lwr. Mill M. HD9: Mel . . . 7B 152
Lower Moor HX6: Ripp . . . 6C 116
Lower Newlands HD6: Ras . . . 2N 119
Lower Northcroft WF9: S Elm . . . 6N 163
Lwr. Northfield La. WF9: S Kirk . . . 5J 163
Lwr. North St. WF17: Bat . . . 8E 102
Lower Oak HX6: Tri . . . 3E 116
Lwr. Oxford St. WF10: C'frd . . . 5D 108
Lwr. Ox Heys HX3: Nor G . . . 1L 99
Lwr. Ozzings HD8: Shel . . . 8N 155
Lwr. Park Grn. BD20: Sils . . . 8C 12
Lwr. Park Royd Dr. HX6: Ripp . . . 4E 116
Lwr. Peel St. WF13: Dew . . . 2F 122
Lwr. Pierce Cl. BD22: Cros R . . . 6F 42
LOWER POPELEY . . . 7N 101
Lwr. Putting Mill HD8: Den D . . . 1E 172
Lwr. Quarry Rd. HD2: Hud . . . 4D 120
HD5: Hud . . . 4D 120
Lwr. Railway Rd. LS29: I'ly . . . 5H 15
Lower Range HX3: Hal . . . 1L 7 (3B 98)
Lwr. Range Ter. HX3: Hal . . . 1L 7
Lwr. Rayleigh St. BD4: B'frd . . . 8F 6 (1E 82)
Lower Reins HD9: Hon . . . 3M 153
Lower Rd. HX4: Bark . . . 5F 134
(not continuous)
Lower Rotcher HD7: Slait . . . 1L 151
Lwr. Royd HD9: Hon . . . 4N 153
Lwr. Rushton Rd. BD3: B'frd . . . 7J 65
Lower Saltonstall HX2: Wain . . . 8D 78
Lower Sandhills LS14: T'ner . . . 4F 52
Lower Scholes BD22: Oak . . . 7N 41
Lwr. School St. BD12: Low M . . . 7A 82
BD18: Ship . . . 7L 45
Lwr. Skircoat Grn. *HX3: Hal* . . . *1B 118*
(off Cow La.)
Lower Slack HX2: Wain . . . 7F 78
Lower Slaids HD7: Linth . . . 9E 136
Lower Smithy HX7: Hept . . . 8B 76
LOWER SOOTHILL . . . 7H 103
Lower Springhead BD22: Oak . . . 4E 42
Lwr. Station Rd. WF6: Norm . . . 1H 127
Lower Stubbins HX6: Tri . . . 3E 116
Lwr. Sunny Bank Ct. HD9: Mel . . . 7B 152
Lwr. Swift Pl. HX6: Rish . . . 9B 116
Lwr. Taythes La. WF8: Pon . . . 2N 129
LOWER THIRSTIN . . . 4K 153
Lwr. Tofts Rd. LS28: Pud . . . 7B 66
LOWER TOWN . . . 4D 60
Lowertown BD22: Oxen . . . 4C 60
Lwr. Town End Rd. HD9: H'frth . . . 1A 170
Lwr. Town Mills *BD22: Oxen* . . . *4C 60*
(off Lower Town)
Lwr. Town St. LS13: Leeds . . . 3G 66
Lwr. Viaduct St. HD1: Hud . . . 3B 8 (3N 137)
(not continuous)
Lower Warrengate WF1: Wake . . . 4L 9 (5M 125)
Lower Wellgate HX4: Gree . . . 4B 118
Lower Wellhouse HD7: Golc . . . 7B 136
Lwr. Wellington Rd. LS29: I'ly . . . 5H 15
Lwr. Westfield Rd. BD9: B'frd . . . 5M 63
Lwr. West Ho's. *HD9: Hon* . . . *5L 153*
(off Moor Bottom)
Lwr. Wheat Royd HD4: Hud . . . 8D 138
Lwr. Whitegate Rd. HD4: Hud . . . 7N 137
Lwr. White Lee HX7: Myth . . . 3N 95
Lwr. Whiteshaw M. BD13: Denh . . . 3K 61
Lower Woodhead HX4: Bark . . . 2H 135
LOWER WOODLANDS . . . 8F 82
Lower Wormald HX6: Rish . . . 1N 133
LOWER WORTLEY . . . 9M 67
Lwr. Wortley Rd. LS12: Leeds . . . 9K 67
LOWER WYKE . . . 4A 100
Lwr. Wyke Grn. BD12: Wyke . . . 4N 99
Lwr. Wyke La. BD12: Wyke . . . 4N 99
Lwr. York Ct. WF1: Wake . . . 2K 9
Lwr. York St. WF1: Wake . . . 2J 9 (4L 125)
LOWESTWOOD . . . 8C 136
Loweswater Av. BD6: B'frd . . . 7L 81
Loweswater Rd. WF11: Knot . . . 1D 130
LOW FARM . . . 3J 49
Low Farm LS26: Gt P . . . 5M 89
Low Farm Gdns. WF9: Upt . . . 2A 164
Low Farm La. WF7: Ackw . . . 4G 147
Low Fell Cl. BD22: Keigh . . . 1E 42
Lowfield Cl. BD12: Low M . . . 8C 82
Lowfield Cres. BD20: Sils . . . 9F 12
WF9: Hems . . . 2E 162
Lowfield La. BD23: Beam . . . 5M 11
Lowfield Rd. WF9: Hems . . . 2E 162
WF13: Dew . . . 3C 122
Lowfields Av. LS12: Leeds . . . 1A 86
Lowfields Bus. Pk. HX5: Ell . . . 3G 118
(not continuous)
Lowfields Cl. HX5: Ell . . . 3F 118
Lowfields Rd. LS11: Leeds . . . 2A 86
LS12: Leeds . . . 1A 86
(not continuous)
Low Flds. Way LS12: Leeds . . . 1A 86
Lowfields Way HX5: Ell . . . 3F 118
LOW FOLD
LS12 . . . 8H 67
LS18 . . . 7D 48
Low Fold BD2: B'frd . . . 3D 64
BD13: Que . . . 3D 80
BD17: Bail . . . *3A 46*
(off Moorgate)
BD19: Scho . . . 4D 100
BD20: Stee . . . 3C 26
HD5: K'htn . . . 2F 138
HD8: Lwr C . . . 1B 172
Low Fold LS9: Leeds . . . 8G 68
LS18: Hors . . . 8D 48
LS19: Raw . . . 3M 47
WF5: Oss . . . 5A 124
WF14: Mir . . . 6J 121
Low Fold Ct. HD8: Up D . . . 5D 172
Low Gate HD8: Kbtn . . . 3K 155
HD9: H'frth . . . 4N 169
WF9: S Elm . . . 6N 163
Low Grange Cres. LS10: Leeds . . . 4G 86
Low Grange Vw. LS10: Leeds . . . 5G 87
LOW GREEN . . . 4N 47
Low Green BD7: B'frd . . . 2M 81
LS19: Raw . . . 4N 47
WF7: Ackw . . . 3H 147
WF11: Knot . . . 8G 110
Low Grn. Ter. BD7: B'frd . . . 2N 81
Low Hall Cl. LS29: Men . . . 4E 30
Low Hall Pl. LS11: Leeds . . . 8C 68
Low Hall Rd. LS18: Hors . . . 7B 48
LS29: Men . . . 4F 30
Low Hill BD17: Bail . . . 1A 46
Low Hills La. HD3: Hud . . . 1F 136
Low Holland WF11: Fair . . . 9N 91
Low Ho. Cl. BD19: Cleck . . . 5H 101
Low Ho. Dr. BD20: Sils . . . 9E 12
Low Ho. Farm Ct. BD20: Sils . . . 9E 12
Low Ho. Fold WF15: Liv . . . 8K 101
Low Ings Grn. HD8: Clay W . . . 6H 157
Low Laithe Fold BD22: Lay . . . 9C 26
LOW LAITHES . . . 3D 124
Low Laithes HX6: Sow B . . . 9G 96
Low Laithes Golf Course . . . 3D 124
Lowlands Rd. WF14: Mir . . . 7L 121
Low La. BD13: Que . . . 2B 80
BD14: Clay . . . 9E 62
BD20: Sils . . . 3C 12
BD23: Drau . . . 5D 10
BD23: Emb, Hal E . . . 2A 10
HD6: B Bri . . . 6A 100
HG3: Spof . . . 1A 22
HX2: Wain . . . 6A 78
LS17: Stainb . . . 4G 19
LS18: Hors . . . 5F 48
LS21: Stainb . . . 4G 19
WF4: M'twn . . . 2K 141
WF17: Birs . . . 3B 102
Low Ling La. HX7: Cold . . . 7L 75
Low Lit. Moor WF14: Mir . . . 7K 121
Low Mill LS29: Add . . . 2B 14
Low Mill La. BD21: Keigh . . . 9K 27
LS29: Add . . . 1A 14
WF13: Raven . . . 7A 122
Low Mill Rd. WF5: Oss . . . 8M 123
Low Mills Ind. Est. WF13: Raven . . . 7A 122
Low Mills Rd. LS12: Leeds . . . 1L 85
LOW MILL VILLAGE . . . 2A 14
LOW MOOR . . . 7A 82
Low Moor Bus. Pk. BD12: Low M . . . 7A 82
Low Moor Cres. WF4: Hol . . . 7H 143
Low Moor La. WF4: Wool . . . 9F 142
LOW MOOR SIDE . . . 3F 84
Low Moor Side LS12: N Far . . . 2G 84
Low Moorside Cl. LS12: N Far . . . 2H 85
Low Moorside Ct. LS12: N Far . . . 2H 85
Low Moor Side La. LS12: N Far . . . 3F 84
Low Moor St. BD12: Low M . . . 7B 82
Low Moor Ter. HX2: Hal . . . 6K 97
LS11: Leeds . . . 3D 86
Low Newall Fold BD5: B'frd . . . 4C 82
Lowood La. WF17: Birs . . . 1B 102
Low Pk. Rd. LS29: Den . . . 4M 15
Low Platt La. HD3: Scam . . . 5H 135
Low Rd. HD4: Hud . . . 1L 153
LS10: Leeds . . . 1G 86
WF12: Dew . . . 4H 123
WF12: T'hill . . . 1E 140
WF13: Dew . . . 3C 122
Low Row S75: Dart . . . 6G 159
Low Royds Grn. LS26: Oul . . . 4B 106
Lowry Rd. WF3: Ting . . . 4N 103
Lowry Vw. BD21: Keigh . . . 1J 43
Low Shops La. LS26: Rothw . . . 7L 87
Low Spring Rd. BD21: Keigh . . . 1L 43
LOW SPRINGS . . . 9A 30
Low St. BD21: Keigh . . . 9J 27
(not continuous)
WF3: Ting . . . 3B 104
WF11: B'ton . . . 4B 110
WF13: Dew . . . 2F 122
Lowther Av. LS25: Gar . . . 8M 71
Lowther Cres. LS26: Swil . . . 3H 89
Lowther Dr. LS25: Gar . . . 8M 71
LS26: Swil . . . 3G 89
Lowther Gro. LS25: Gar . . . 8M 71
Lowther Rd. LS25: Gar . . . 8M 71
Lowther St. BD2: B'frd . . . 4F 64
LS8: Leeds . . . 3H 69
Lowther Ter. LS15: Swil C . . . 8H 71
Low Town HD8: Kbtn . . . 4K 155
Lowtown LS28: Pud . . . 6C 66
LOW TOWN END . . . 1L 103
LOW UTLEY . . . 6G 27
Low Way LS23: B'ham . . . 6D 38
LS23: Cliff . . . 2D 38
Low Well St. BD5: B'frd . . . 2B 82
Low Westwood La. HD7: Golc . . . 7C 136
HD7: Linth . . . 8C 136
Low Whitehouse Row LS10: Leeds . . . 9F 68
Low Wood BD15: Wils . . . 2C 62
Low Wood Ct. BD20: Keigh . . . 5H 27
Low Wood Head BD20: Rid . . . 5K 27
Low Wood Ri. LS29: I'ly . . . 6L 15
Loxley Cl. BD2: B'frd . . . 4H 65
Loxley Gro. LS22: Weth . . . 1L 23
Loxley St. WF17: Bat . . . 5D 102
Lucas Ct. LS6: Leeds . . . 3E 68
Lucas Pl. LS6: Leeds . . . 2C 68
Lucas St. LS6: Leeds . . . 2C 68
Luck La. HD1: Hud . . . 4H 137
HD3: Hud . . . 3J 137
Lucy Av. LS15: Leeds . . . 6N 69
Lucy Hall Dr. BD17: Bail . . . 5K 45
Lucy Hall Farm Cl. BD17: Bail . . . 4L 45
Lucy La. HD8: Lept . . . 5H 139

Lucy St.—Manley St.

Lucy St. HX3: Hal 1M 7 (4C 98)
LUDDENDEN 3E 96
LUDDENDEN FOOT 5D 96
Luddenden La. HX2: Lud F 5D 96
Luddendon Pl. BD13: Que 3B 80
(off Mill La.)
Luddite Ho. WF15: Liv 7L 101
(off Carr St.)
Ludgate Hill LS2: Leeds 6G 5 (6E 68)
Ludhill La. HD4: Farn T 4A 154
Ludlam St. BD5: B'frd 8B 6 (9C 64)
(not continuous)
Ludlow Av. LS25: Gar 7B 72
Ludolf Dr. LS17: Shad 3N 51
Ludwell Cl. WF12: T'hill 1J 141
Ludwood Cl. HD9: Hon 4N 153
Luis Ct. BD17: Bail 3N 45
Luke La. HD9: T'bdge 9A 154
Luke Rd. BD5: B'frd 1A 82
Luke Williams Ho.
WF8: Pon 2K 129
Lulworth Av. LS15: Leeds 5E 70
Lulworth Cl. LS15: Leeds 5E 70
Lulworth Cres. LS15: Leeds 5E 70
Lulworth Dr. LS15: Leeds 6E 70
Lulworth Gth. LS15: Leeds 6E 70
Lulworth Gro. BD4: B'frd 3H 83
(not continuous)
Lulworth Vw. LS15: Leeds 5E 70
Lulworth Wlk. LS15: Leeds 5E 70
LUMB 1A 154
Lumb Bottom BD11: Drig 6C 84
Lumbfoot BD22: S'bury 8M 41
Lumbfoot Rd. BD22: S'bury 8M 41
Lumb Gill La. LS29: Add 3A 14
Lumb Hall Way BD11: Drig 6C 84
Lumb La. BD8: B'frd 5A 64
HD4: Hud 1A 154
HX2: Wain 7F 78
HX3: Hal 2A 98
HX6: Mill B 4C 116
HX7: P Wel 2H 77
WF15: Liv 1K 121
Lumb La. Mills BD8: B'frd 6B 64
Lumb Rd. HX7: Hept 8E 76
Lumbrook HX3: North 1H 99
Lumbrook Cl. HX3: North 1H 99
Lumb Ter. HX2: Wain 7F 78
LUMBUTTS 8A 94
Lumbutts La. OL14: Tod 8A 94
Lumbutts Rd. OL14: Tod 1J 113
(not continuous)
Lumby Cl. LS28: Pud 9C 66
Lumby Gth. LS17: E Kes 2C 36
Lumby La. LS17: E Kes 1B 36
LS28: Pud 9C 66
Lumby Leys La. LS25: S Mil 5M 91
Lumby St. BD10: B'frd 7F 46
Lumley Av. LS4: Leeds 3N 67
WF10: C'frd 5A 108
Lumley Gro. LS4: Leeds 3N 67
Lumley Hill WF10: C'frd 5A 108
Lumley Mt. LS4: Leeds 3N 67
WF10: C'frd 6A 108
Lumley Mt. Bungs.
WF10: C'frd 5A 108
Lumley Pl. LS4: Leeds 3N 67
Lumley Rd. LS4: Leeds 3N 67
WF12: Dew 1H 123
Lumley St. LS4: Leeds 3N 67
WF10: C'frd 6A 108
Lumley Ter. LS4: Leeds 3N 67
Lumley Vw. LS4: Leeds 3N 67
Lumley Wlk. LS4: Leeds 3N 67
Lunan Pl. LS8: Leeds 2H 69
Lunan Ter. LS8: Leeds 2H 69
Lund Dr. WF16: Heck 9B 102
Lund Head La. HG3: Kirkby 4M 21
Lund Hill La. S71: Roys 5G 160
Lund La. BD22: Oak 1B 42
Lund St. BD8: B'frd 7K 63
BD16: Bgly 4F 44
BD21: Keigh 8J 27
Lundy Ct. BD5: B'frd 2C 82
Lune St. BD22: Cros R 7F 42
Lunnfields La. WF11: Fair 8N 91
Lunn La. DN14: Beal 7N 111
LUPSET 7G 124
Lupset Cres. WF2: Wake 8G 125
Lupton Av. LS9: Leeds 6J 69
Lupton Flats LS6: Leeds 1N 67
Lupton's Bldgs. LS12: Leeds 7L 67
Lupton Sq. HD9: Hon 5L 153
(off Westgate)
Lupton Square Gallery 5L 153
Lupton St. BD8: B'frd 1A 6 (5C 64)
LS10: Leeds 2G 86
Lustre St. BD21: Keigh 9G 27
Luther Pl. HD3: Hud 2K 137
Luther St. LS13: Leeds 1B 66
Luther Way BD2: B'frd 3D 64
Luton St. BD21: Keigh 9H 27
HD4: Hud 7E 136
HX1: Hal 5M 97
Luttrell Cl. LS16: Leeds 5K 49
Luttrell Cres. LS16: Leeds 5K 49
Luttrell Gdns. LS16: Leeds 5K 49
Luttrell Pl. LS16: Leeds 5K 49
Luttrell Rd. LS16: Leeds 5K 49
Lutyens, The LS29: I'ly 5E 14
Luxor Av. LS8: Leeds 2H 69
Luxor Rd. LS8: Leeds 2H 69
Luxor St. LS8: Leeds 2H 69
Luxor Vw. LS8: Leeds 2H 69
Lydbrook Pk. HX3: Hal 1N 117
Lyddon Hall LS2: Leeds 2C 4 (4C 68)
Lyddon Ter. LS2: Leeds 2B 4 (4C 68)
LYDGATE
HX3 5K 99
OL14 4G 93
OL15 5A 132
Lydgate HD8: Lept 7L 139
HX3: North 1F 98
LS9: Leeds 5H 69
Lydgate Cl. HD9: New M 2C 170
Lydgate Dr. BD7: B'frd 8L 63
HD8: Lept 7L 139
HD9: New M 1B 170
Lydgate Pk. HX3: Hip 5K 99
Lydgate Pl. LS28: Cal 8L 47
Lydgate Ri. WF9: S Kirk 6K 163
Lydgate Rd. HD8: Shep 9J 155
WF17: Bat 7J 103
Lydgate St. LS28: Cal 8L 47
Lydgate Vs. WF4: Horb 1C 142
Lydget Ct. BD20: Keigh 7G 26
Lydgetts HD9: U'thng 2J 169
Lydia Hill HD6: Ras 2M 119
(off East St.)
Lydia St. LS2: Leeds 6H 5
Lyme Chase LS14: Leeds 4A 70
Lyme Ter. DN6: Skel 8K 165
Lymington Dr. BD4: B'frd 1J 83
Lynch Av. BD7: B'frd 2L 81
Lyncroft BD2: B'frd 2D 64
Lynda Gro. WF5: Oss 7C 124
Lyndale LS25: Kip 5A 90
Lyndale Cres. WF16: Heck 8B 102
Lyndale Dr. BD18: Ship 8D 46
WF2: Wren 1G 125
(not continuous)
Lyndale Gro. WF6: Norm 2K 127
Lyndale M. WF13: Dew 9C 102
Lyndale Rd. BD16: Bgly 2H 45
Lyndean Gdns. BD10: B'frd 8E 46
Lynden Av. BD18: Ship 7C 46
Lynden Ct. BD6: B'frd 6M 81
Lyndhurst BD16: Bgly 3E 44
(off Hall Bank Dr.)
Lyndhurst Av. HD6: Ras 4M 119
Lyndhurst Cl. LS15: Scho 8G 53
Lyndhurst Cres. LS15: Scho 8G 52
Lyndhurst Gro. BD15: All 5H 63
Lyndhurst Gro. Rd.
HD6: Ras 4M 119
Lyndhurst Rd. HD3: Hud 2G 137
HD6: Ras 3M 119
LS15: Scho 9G 52
Lyndhurst Vw. LS15: Scho 9G 53
Lyndon Av. LS23: B'ham 5C 38
LS25: Gar 7M 71
Lyndon Cl. LS23: B'ham 5C 38
Lyndon Cres. LS23: B'ham 5C 38
Lyndon Rd. LS23: B'ham 5C 38
Lyndon Sq. LS23: B'ham 5C 38
Lyndon Ter. BD16: Bgly 4F 44
Lyndon Way LS23: B'ham 5C 38
Lyndsey Ct. BD22: Oak 5B 42
Lyndum Gro. LS25: Kip 3A 90
Lynfield Dr. BD9: B'frd 3H 63
WF15: Liv 7F 100
Lynfield Mt. BD18: Ship 7C 46
Lyng Ct. WF11: Knot 8D 110
Lynmoor Ct. BD10: B'frd 8D 46
Lynndale Av. HD2: Hud 1L 137
Lynnfield Gdns. LS15: Scho 9G 52
Lynnwood Gdns. LS28: Pud 7N 65
Lyn Royd Flats HD7: Linth 8C 136
Lynsey Gdns. BD4: B'frd 6F 82
Lynthorne Rd. BD9: B'frd 2A 64
Lynton Av. BD9: B'frd 4L 63
HD1: Hud 4L 137
LS23: B Spa 9D 24
WF3: Thpe H 2G 105
Lynton Dr. BD9: B'frd 4K 63
BD18: Ship 8M 45
BD20: Rid 7M 27
Lynton Gro. BD9: B'frd 4L 63
HX2: Brad 4M 79
Lynton Pl. S75: Kex 9F 158
Lynton Ter. BD19: Cleck 4H 101
(off Mount St.)
Lynton Vs. BD9: B'frd 4L 63
Lynwood Av. BD18: Ship 7C 46
LS12: Leeds 9M 67
LS26: W'frd 7E 88
Lynwood Cl. BD11: B'haw 9M 83
WF7: Street 7L 127
WF11: Knot 7F 110
Lynwood Ct. BD22: Keigh 2E 42
Lynwood Cres. HX1: Hal 7M 97
LS12: Leeds 9M 67
LS26: W'frd 7E 88
WF8: Pon 5K 129
WF9: Fitz 6A 146
Lynwood Dr. S71: Carl 8D 160
WF2: Wake 4L 143
Lynwood Gth. LS12: Leeds 9M 67
Lynwood Gro. LS12: Leeds 1M 85
Lynwood M. BD4: B'frd 3K 83
Lynwood Mt. LS12: Leeds 9M 67
Lynwood Ri. LS12: Leeds 9M 67
Lynwood Vw. LS12: Leeds 9M 67
Lyon Rd. BD20: East 2A 26
WF8: Pon 5K 129
Lyons St. BD13: Que 4E 80
Lyon St. BD13: Thorn 7C 62
Lysander Way BD16: Cot 9G 44
Lytham Cl. WF6: Norm 2L 127
Lytham Dr. BD13: Que 3G 81
Lytham Gro. LS12: Leeds 1K 85
Lytham Pl. LS12: Leeds 1K 85
Lytham St. HX1: Hal 5M 97
Lytham Way HD3: Hud 2G 136
Lytton Rd. BD8: B'frd 6L 63
Lytton St. HX3: Hal 1L 7
LS10: Leeds 2F 86

M

M1 Ind. Est. LS10: Leeds 2F 86
Mabel Royd BD7: B'frd 9L 63
Mabel St. HX7: Myth 3M 95
MABGATE 4H 5 (5F 68)
Mabgate LS9: Leeds 5J 5 (6F 68)
Mabgate Grn. LS9: Leeds 5J 5 (6F 68)
Mabgate Mills Industrial & Commercial Cen.
LS9: Leeds 4K 5 (5G 68)
Macaulay Rd. HD2: Hud 1L 137
Macaulay St. HD1: Hud 5A 8
LS9: Leeds 5K 5 (5G 68)
Macauley Pl. WF7: F'stne 7C 128
McBride Way LS22: Weth 4N 23
McBurney Cl. HX3: Hal 2A 98
McClintock Ho. LS10: Leeds 8F 68
(off The Boulevard)
McClure Ho. LS10: Leeds 8F 68
(off The Boulevard)
McCrea Wing HX1: Hal 8K 7
Macham St. HD1: Hud 6L 137
MACHPELAH 2J 95
Machpelah Works HX7: Heb B 2H 95
(off Burnley Rd.)
McKenzie Ct. WF17: Bat 1F 122
(off Trinity St.)
Mackenzie Ho. LS10: Leeds 8J 5
Mackey Cres. S72: B'ley 6M 161
Mackey La. S72: B'ley 6M 161
Mackie Hill Cl. WF4: Crig 6F 142
Mackingstone Dr. BD22: Oak 4B 42
Mackingstone La. BD22: Oak 3B 42
Mackinnon Av. WF6: Norm 9K 107
Mackintosh Memorial Homes, The HX3: Hal 8N 97
(off Albert Prom.)
McLaren Av. WF9: Upt 1C 164
McLaren Flds. LS13: Leeds 4G 67
McMahon Dr. BD13: Que 3H 81
McMillan Gdns. BD6: B'frd 6B 82
Macturk Gro. BD8: B'frd 5M 63
Maddocks St. BD18: Ship 7M 45
Madeley Rd. WF4: H'cft 9K 145
Madeley Sq. WF10: C'frd 3J 109
Madeline Joy Apartments LS6: Leeds 2N 67
(off Broomfield Cres.)
Madewel Ho. HX5: Ell 6F 118
Madgin La. HD4: S Cros 3F 152
Madison Av. BD4: B'frd 4J 83
Madison Cl. WF7: Ackw 5D 146
Madison Wlk. WF7: Ackw 4D 146
Madni Cl. HX1: Hal 4H 7 (5A 98)
Mafeking Av. LS11: Leeds 4C 86
Mafeking Gro. LS11: Leeds 4C 86
Mafeking Mt. LS11: Leeds 4C 86
Mafeking Ter. BD18: Ship 1B 64
MAG DALE 3K 153
Magdale HD9: Hon 3L 153
Magdalene Cl. LS16: Leeds 4K 49
Magdalene Flds. WF6: Norm 3L 127
Magdalene Rd. WF2: Wake 6E 124
Magdalen Rd. HD9: H'frth, Mel 3B 168
Magdalin Dr. LS28: Stan 4D 66
Magellan Ho. LS10: Leeds 8J 5 (8F 68)
Magistrate Barker Av. LS15: Leeds 4E 70
Magistrates' Court
Bradford & Keighley 5A 6 (8C 64)
Halifax 5K 7 (6B 98)
Huddersfield 6B 8 (5M 137)
Leeds 5D 4 (6D 68)
Wakefield 4H 9 (5L 125)
Magna Gro. WF2: Wake 1N 143
Magnolia Cl. S72: Shaf 7L 161
Magnolia Dr. BD15: All 2E 62
Magnolia Ho. WF10: C'frd 5E 108
(off Parklands)
Magnolias WF17: Bat 5B 102
Magpie Cl. BD6: B'frd 4H 81
Magpie La. LS27: Morl 1L 103
Mahim Cres. BD17: Bail 5C 46
Maidstone St. BD3: B'frd 7G 65
Maidwell Way BD6: B'frd 7M 81
Mail Cl. LS15: Leeds 3F 70
Main Av. HD4: Hud 7E 136
Main Ga. HD9: H'wth 6C 170
Main Rd. BD13: Denh 6K 61
BD20: E Mor 8C 28
BD20: East 2A 26
Mainspring Rd. BD15: Wils 1B 62
Main St. BD12: Low M 7C 82
BD12: Wyke 9A 82
BD15: Wils 1B 62
BD16: Bgly 4E 44
BD16: Cot 9G 44
BD17: Esh 2G 47
BD22: Haw 8C 42
BD22: S'bury 9L 41
DN6: Hamp 8G 164
DN6: Wome 8L 131
DN14: Beal 5M 111
HG3: Kirkby 2K 21
LS14: T'ner 3G 52
LS15: Bar E 8L 53
LS15: Scho 9G 53
LS17: E Kes 3D 36
LS17: Shad 2M 51
LS17: Wee 7A 20
LS20: Hawk 8C 30
LS21: Pool 1F 32
LS22: Coll 9J 23
LS22: Lin 7J 23
LS22: Sick 4C 22
LS23: W'ton 5G 24
LS24: N Kym 1L 39
LS24: Saxt 9N 55
LS25: Bur S 1D 110
LS25: Gar 7M 71
LS26: Meth 1L 107
LS29: Add 1L 13
LS29: Burl W 7C 16
LS29: Men 3D 30
S72: S Hien 3L 161
WF3: Carl 1M 105
WF3: E Ard 5F 104
WF8: K S'ton 4J 149
WF9: Bads 7L 147
WF9: Upt 1C 164
WF10: All B 9B 90
WF10: Leds 8E 90
WF11: Birk 2M 111
Main St. Nth. LS25: Aber 8E 54
Main St. Sth. LS25: Aber 9E 54
Mairs Ct. WF9: Kins 9B 146
Maister Pl. BD22: Oak 4B 42
Maitland Cl. BD15: All 7G 62
OL14: W'den 3J 113
Maitland Pl. LS11: Leeds 1C 86
Maitland St. OL14: W'den 3J 113
Maizebrook WF13: Dew 2C 122
Maize Maze at Cawthorne, The 4L 173
Maize St. BD21: Keigh 3G 43
Majestic Ct. S75: Dart 8G 159
Majestic Way BD22: Keigh 3G 43
(off Wirefield Rd.)
Major St. OL14: Tod 7L 93
WF2: Wake 8K 125
Makin St. WF2: Wake 6J 125
Malden Rd. LS6: Leeds 6B 50
Malham Av. BD9: B'frd 3H 63
HD6: Ras 3K 119
Malham Cl. LS14: Leeds 2B 70
S72: Shaf 6K 161
Malham Ct. BD20: Sils 9E 12
(off Ings Way)
HD3: Hud 3G 137
(off Willwood Av.)
Malham Dr. WF15: Liv 2K 121
WF17: Bat 7D 102
Malham Ho. LS29: Men 5E 30
Malham Rd. HD6: Ras 4K 119
WF1: Wake 4A 126
Malham Sq. WF1: Wake 4A 126
Malincroft S75: Map 9K 159
Malin Rd. WF12: Dew 9J 103
Mallard Av. WF2: Wake 5L 143
Mallard Cl. BD10: B'frd 1G 65
LS10: Leeds 6H 87
WF16: Heck 9A 102
Mallard Ct. BD8: B'frd 7H 63
Mallard M. BD10: B'frd 1G 65
WF9: S Elm 6N 163
Mallard Rd. WF10: C'frd 6C 108
Mallards, The BD20: Sils 8E 12
Mallard Vw. BD22: Oxen 4C 60
Mallard Way HD7: Slait 1M 151
LS27: Morl 9N 85
Mallinson St. WF13: Dew 2D 122
Mall La. LS20: Guis 5M 31
LS21: Otley 5M 31
Mallory Cl. BD7: B'frd 8L 63
Mallory Way S72: Cud 9K 161
Malmesbury Cl. BD4: B'frd 4J 83
LS12: Leeds 8M 67
Malmesbury Gro. LS12: Leeds 8M 67
Malmesbury Pl. LS12: Leeds 8M 67
Malmesbury Ter. LS12: Leeds 8M 67
Malsis Cres. BD21: Keigh 1G 43
Malsis Rd. BD21: Keigh 1G 43
Maltby Av. S75: W Gran 7G 158
Maltby Ct. LS15: Leeds 7E 70
Malthouse Cl. LS14: S'cft 8D 36
WF10: C'frd 5C 108
Malthouse Ct. WF15: Liv 8M 101
Malting Cl. WF3: Rob H 1K 105
Malting Ri. WF3: Rob H 1K 105
Maltings, The BD14: Clay 9G 63
BD19: Cleck 4G 101
BD20: Sils 7E 12
HD8: Shep 8K 155
LS6: Leeds 4A 68
(off Spring Gro. Wlk.)
WF3: Rob H 1K 105
WF8: Pon 2K 129
WF14: Mir 6K 121
Maltings Ct. LS11: Leeds 1E 86
(off Maltings Rd.)
Maltings Rd. HX2: Hal 2K 97
LS11: Leeds 2E 86
Maltins, The WF10: C'frd 4E 108
Malt Kiln BD14: Clay 1G 81
(off Gordon St.)
Maltkiln Cotts. HG3: Kirkby 1J 21
Malt Kiln Cft. WF2: Wake 1N 143
Maltkiln Dr. WF4: W Bret 1B 158
Malt Kiln La. BD13: Thorn 9A 62
Maltkiln La. LS25: Kip 4B 90
WF10: C'frd 4E 108
Malton Rd. WF9: Upt 1C 164
Malton St. HX3: Hal 2B 98
HX6: Sow B 7H 97
Malt Shovel Yd. BD10: B'frd 7F 46
(off Town La.)
Malt St. BD22: Keigh 3G 42
Malvern Brow BD9: B'frd 4J 63
Malvern Cl. WF10: C'frd 7N 107
Malvern Cres. BD20: Rid 5L 27
Malvern Gro. BD9: B'frd 5J 63
LS11: Leeds 1C 86
Malvern Ri. HD4: Hud 7M 137
LS11: Leeds 1C 86
Malvern Rd. BD9: B'frd 5J 63
HD4: Hud 8C 8 (6N 137)
LS11: Leeds 1C 86
WF11: Knot 8D 110
WF12: Dew 2J 123
Malvern St. LS11: Leeds 1C 86
Malvern Vw. LS11: Leeds 1C 86
Manchester Rd. BD5: B'frd 6B 6 (3B 82)
HD1: Hud 7A 8 (5M 137)
HD4: Hud 7E 136
HD7: Linth, Mars, Slait, Hud 9A 150
Manchester Sq. LS21: Otley 9L 17
Mandale Gro. BD6: B'frd 5J 81
Mandale Rd. BD6: B'frd 5J 81
Mandarin Way LS10: Leeds 6H 87
Mandela Ct. LS7: Leeds 1F 68
Mandela Ho. LS7: Leeds 1H 5 (3F 68)
Manderlay Gdns. HD8: Eml 3F 156
Manderston Chase LS12: Leeds 4J 67
Mandeville Cres. BD6: B'frd 5L 81
Mangrill La. LS14: Pott 9L 37
LS23: B'ham 9L 37
Manitoba Pl. LS7: Leeds 9G 50
MANKINHOLES 9A 94
Mankinholes Bank OL14: Tod 9A 94
Manley Ct. LS25: Gar 9N 71
Manley Dr. LS22: Weth 3J 23
Manley Gro. LS29: I'ly 5J 15
Manley Ri. LS29: I'ly 6J 15
Manley Rd. LS29: I'ly 6J 15
Manley St. HD6: Brigh 9M 99

Manley St. Pl.—Marley Pl.

Manley St. Pl. HD6: Brigh 9N 99
(off Bonegate Rd.)
Mannerley Gro. BD19: Gom 6M 101
Mannheim Rd. BD9: B'frd 4M 63
MANNINGHAM 4N 63
Manningham La. BD1: B'frd 1A 6 (4A 64)
BD8: B'frd 4A 64
Manningham La. Pk. BD1: B'frd 2A 6 (6B 64)
Manningham Sports Cen. 5N 63
Mann's Bldgs. WF17: Bat 2E 102
Mann's Ct. BD1: B'frd 4B 6
Mannville Gro. BD22: Keigh 1G 42
Mannville Pl. BD22: Keigh 1G 42
Mannville Rd. BD22: Keigh 2G 43
Mannville St. BD22: Keigh 1G 42
Mannville Ter. BD7: B'frd 8B 64
Mannville Wlk. BD22: Keigh 1G 42
(off Mannville Pl.)
Mannville Way BD22: Keigh 1G 42
Manor, The LS8: Leeds 9L 51
(off Ladywood Rd.)
Manor Av. LS6: Leeds 2A 68
WF5: Oss 8B 124
Mnr. Barn Stables LS21: Otley 9L 17
(off Kirkgate)
Manor Cl. BD8: B'frd 6J 63
BD11: Drig 6B 84
HX3: Hal 8A 98
LS16: B'hpe 5G 33
LS19: Yead 9M 31
LS26: Rothw 7N 87
OL14: Tod 8B 94
WF4: Not 2A 160
WF5: Oss 8B 124
WF8: K S'ton 5J 149
WF9: Bads 8L 147
Manor Cott. M. LS14: S'cft 1D 52
Manor Ct. BD16: Cot 8F 44
BD19: Scho 5D 100
LS11: Leeds 4A 86
LS17: Shad 3A 52
LS21: Otley 9L 17
LS25: Aber 8E 54
S71: Roys 6B 160
WF5: Oss 8B 124
WF6: Norm 1J 127
WF11: Fair 9N 91
Manor Cres. LS21: Pool 1F 32
LS26: Rothw 7M 87
S72: Grim 9A 162
WF2: Wake 7G 124
WF2: W'ton 2B 144
Manor Crest WF4: Crig 5F 142
Manor Cft. HD8: Skelm 7D 156
HX7: Heb B 1J 95
LS15: Leeds 7D 70
S72: S Hien 3L 161
Manorcroft WF6: Norm 1J 127
Manordale Cl. WF4: Flock 7G 141
Manor Dr. BD16: Cot 7F 44
HD8: Skelm 8D 156
(not continuous)
HX3: Hal 8J 7 (8A 98)
HX7: Heb B 1J 95
LS6: Leeds 3A 68
(not continuous)
S71: Roys 6C 160
S72: S Hien 3L 161
WF4: Flock 7G 141
WF4: N Cro 3H 145
WF5: Oss 8B 124
WF7: F'stne 2C 128
WF14: Mir 4H 121
Manor Farm WF9: Bads 8L 147
Mnr. Farm Cl. BD16: Cot 9G 44
LS10: Leeds 7F 86
S71: Carl 9E 160
Mnr. Farm Ct. BD4: E Bier 6J 83
LS20: Guis 7J 31
WF4: Crig 6G 142
Mnr. Farm Cres. LS27: Chur 5M 85
Mnr. Farm Dr. LS10: Leeds 7E 86
LS27: Chur 5M 85
WF17: Bat 6J 103
Mnr. Farm Est. WF9: S Elm 6N 163
Mnr. Farm Gdns. LS10: Leeds 7E 86
Mnr. Farm Grn. LS10: Leeds 7E 86
Mnr. Farm Gro. LS10: Leeds 7E 86
Mnr. Farm La. WF4: Wrag 4A 146
Mnr. Farm Ri. LS10: Leeds 7F 86
Mnr. Farm Rd. LS10: Leeds 7E 86
WF4: Crig 6G 142
Mnr. Farm Wlk. LS10: Leeds 7F 86
Mnr. Farm Way LS10: Leeds 7E 86
Manorfield LS11: Leeds 2B 86
Manorfield Dr. WF4: Horb 9C 124
Manorfields LS20: Hawk 8D 30
Manorfields Av. WF4: Croft 2H 145
Manorfields Ct. WF4: Croft 2H 145
Manor Fold BD16: Cot 9G 44
LS18: Hors 7D 48
Manor Gdns. BD13: Cull 1K 61
LS14: T'ner 1H 53
LS21: Pool 1F 32
S72: Shaf 7K 161
WF10: C'frd 7E 108
WF12: Dew 1K 123
Manor Gth. LS15: Leeds 7D 70
LS25: Led 5K 91
WF2: W'ton 2B 144
Manor Gth. Rd. LS25: Kip 3B 90
WF12: Dew 4J 123
Manor Gates LS16: B'hpe 5G 33
Manor Golf Course, The 6B 84
Manor Grange HD8: Shep 9H 155
Manor Gro. BD20: Rid 8N 27
LS7: Leeds 9F 50
S71: Roys 6C 160
S72: Grim 9N 161
WF5: Oss 8B 124
WF9: S Kirk 8G 162
WF10: C'frd 6E 108
Mnr. Haigh Rd. WF2: Wake 7G 124
Manor Heath Park & Jungle Experience 8A 98
Mnr. Heath Rd. HX3: Hal 8A 98
Manor Ho. LS21: Otley 9L 17
(off Kirkgate)
WF1: Wake 5L 9
WF4: Flock 7G 140
Manor Ho. Bungalows WF11: Knot 7E 110
Manor Ho. Caravan Site WF4: Flock 7G 141
Manor Ho. Cft. LS16: Leeds 4N 49
Manor Ho. La. LS17: Leeds 9H 35
Manor Ho. Rd. BD15: Wils 9B 44
Manor Ho's. BD22: Oak 5C 42
(off Colne La.)
HD9: Mel 7E 152
Manor Ho. St. LS28: Pud 7B 66
Manor La. BD18: Ship 8N 45
(not continuous)
LS26: Oul 8D 88
(off Aberford Rd.)
WF5: Oss 8B 124
Manorley La. BD6: B'frd 7K 81
Mnr. Mill La. LS11: Leeds 4A 86
Manor Mills LS11: Leeds 4A 86
(Manor Ct.)
LS11: Leeds 8D 68
(Manor Rd.)
Manor Mills Cotts. HD9: Mel 7E 152
Mnr. Occupation Rd. S71: Roys 5C 160
MANOR PARK 6A 16
Manor Pk. BD8: B'frd 6J 63
BD22: Oak 5C 42
LS14: S'cft 9D 36
WF8: D'ton 6C 130
WF10: Leds 7E 90
WF12: Dew 9L 103
(Chidswell La.)
WF12: Dew 1L 123
(Windsor Rd.)
WF14: Mir 4G 121
Manor Pk. Av. WF8: Pon 9M 109
WF10: All B 8A 90
Manor Pk. Gdns. BD19: Gom 1M 101
Manor Pk. Ri. WF8: D'ton 6C 130
Manor Pk. Rd. BD19: Cleck 6J 101
Manor Pk. Way HD8: Lept 7H 139
Manor Pl. WF4: Horb 1C 142
Manor Ri. HD4: Hud 8D 8 (6N 137)
HD8: Skelm 8D 156
LS29: I'ly 5J 15
WF2: W'ton 3B 144
WF4: Crig 5G 142
Manor Rd. BD16: Cot 8F 44
BD20: Keigh 6G 27
DN14: Beal 5L 111
HD4: Farn T 3D 154
HD7: Golc 6C 136
HD8: Clay W 5K 157
LS11: Leeds 8D 68
LS12: Leeds 9M 67
LS18: Hors 7D 48
LS26: Rothw 7M 87
LS27: Chur 5M 85
WF2: Wake 6H 125
WF2: W'ton 3B 144
WF4: Horb 1C 142
WF5: Oss 7A 124
WF13: Dew 4E 122
WF17: Bat 7J 103
Manor Row BD1: B'frd 2A 6 (6C 64)
BD12: Low M 6A 82
Manor Royd HX3: Hal 8B 98
Manor Sq. LS19: Yead 9M 31
LS21: Otley 9L 17
Manorstead HD8: Skelm 8D 156
Manor St. BD2: B'frd 3F 64
BD19: Scho 6D 100
HD4: Hud 8D 8 (6N 137)
LS7: Leeds 2J 5 (4F 68)
LS21: Otley 9L 17
S71: Carl 9E 160
WF12: Dew 3G 122
Manor St. Ind. Est. LS7: Leeds 1J 5 (4G 68)
(not continuous)
Manor Ter. BD2: B'frd 3F 64
LS6: Leeds 2A 68
LS19: Yead 9M 31
LS25: Kip 4B 90
(off Roger Fold)
Manor Vw. BD20: East 3A 26
(off Moor La.)
LS6: Leeds 2A 68
LS28: Pud 7B 66
S72: Shaf 7K 161
WF9: Upt 1N 163
WF10: C'frd 7E 108
Manor Way WF17: Bat 8D 102
Manscombe Rd. BD15: All 5H 63
Manse Cres. LS29: Burl W 8C 16
Manse Dr. HD4: Hud 7F 136
Manse Farm M. S72: Cud 9J 161
Mansel M. BD4: B'frd 4J 83
Manse Rd. LS29: Burl W 8C 16
Manse St. BD3: B'frd 7G 65
Mansfield Av. BD16: Bgly 2H 45
Mansfield Cres. DN6: Skel 7N 165
Mansfield Pl. LS6: Leeds 9N 49
Mansfield Rd. BD8: B'frd 4A 64
LS29: Burl W 8B 16
S71: Ath 9A 160
Mansion Gdns. HD4: Hud 9L 137
Mansion Ga. LS7: Leeds 9G 50
Mansion Ga. Dr. LS7: Leeds 9G 50
Mansion Ga. M. LS7: Leeds 9G 50
Mansion Ga. Sq. LS7: Leeds 9G 50
Mansion La. HX3: Hal 8M 7 (8B 98)
LS8: Leeds 6K 51
MANSTON 3E 70
Manston App. LS15: Leeds 3D 70
Manston Av. LS15: Leeds 3D 70
Manston Cres. LS15: Leeds 3D 70
Manston Dr. LS15: Leeds 3D 70
Manston Gdns. LS15: Leeds 3E 70
Manston Gro. LS15: Leeds 4D 70
Manston La. LS15: Leeds 4E 70
Manston Ri. LS15: Leeds 3D 70
Manston Ter. LS15: Leeds 3E 70
Manston Way LS15: Leeds 3D 70
Mantra Ho. Bus. Cen. BD21: Keigh 1H 43
(off South St.)
Manygates Av. WF1: Wake 8M 125
Manygates Ct. WF1: Wake 8M 125
Manygates Cres. WF1: Wake 8M 125
Manygates La. WF1: Wake 9M 125
WF2: Wake 9M 125
Manygates Pk. WF1: Wake 8M 125
Manywells Brow BD13: Cull 2J 61
(not continuous)
Manywells Brow Ind. Est. BD13: Cull 1K 61
Manywells Cres. BD13: Cull 1K 61
Manywells La. BD13: Cull 1H 61
Maple Apartments WF1: Wake 1M 9
Maple Av. BD3: B'frd 6J 65
BD22: Oak 5D 42
HD7: Golc 5E 136
WF8: Pon 6J 129
Maple Cl. HD5: K'htn 1G 138
WF10: C'frd 7B 108
Maple Ct. BD16: Bgly 5E 44
(off Ash Ter.)
HX2: Illing 6L 79
LS11: Leeds 3B 86
LS14: Leeds 4A 70
LS26: W'frd 6C 88
WF5: Oss 8A 124
Maple Cft. HD4: Neth 3J 153
LS12: N Far 9G 67
LS17: Leeds 4G 50
Maple Dr. LS12: N Far 9G 67
LS22: Weth 2M 23
WF8: Pon 5J 129
Maple Fold HX5: Ell 6D 118
LS12: N Far 9G 67
Maple Gdns. LS17: Bard 3F 36
Maple Gro. BD17: Bail 6K 45
BD19: Gom 3L 101
BD20: Keigh 7G 26
HD2: Fix 6M 119
LS12: N Far 9H 67
WF6: Norm 4H 127
WF8: Pon 6J 129
Maple Ri. LS26: Rothw 9N 87
Maple Rd. S75: Map 8J 159
WF12: Dew 4L 123
Maple St. HD5: Hud 7E 8 (5A 138)
HX1: Hal 7M 97
OL14: W'den 4J 113
WF2: Wake 3H 125
Maple Ter. LS19: Yead 9K 31
Maple Wlk. WF11: Knot 9D 110
WF12: Dew 4L 123
Maple Way LS14: Leeds 7D 52
Maplin Av. HD3: Hud 1E 136
Maplin Dr. HD3: Hud 1E 136
MAPPLEWELL 9J 159
Mapplewell Cres. WF5: Oss 6A 124
Mapplewell Dr. S75: Map 9L 159
WF5: Oss 6A 124
Mapplewell Rd. WF10: C'frd 2J 109
Marbridge Ct. BD6: B'frd 3N 81
Marchant St. WF10: C'frd 4C 108
Marchant Way LS27: Chur 4M 85
Marchbank Rd. BD3: B'frd 6G 65
March Cote La. BD16: Cot 9E 44
Marchmont Cres. LS25: Kip 5N 89
March St. WF6: Norm 2H 127
Marchwood Gro. BD14: Clay 9J 63
Marcia Cl. BD10: B'frd 9G 46
Marcus Way HD3: Hud 1C 136
Mardale Cres. LS14: Leeds 3B 70
Mardale Rd. WF12: Dew 1H 123
Margaret Av. LS17: Bard 4E 36
Margaret Cl. LS27: Morl 8M 85
Margaret St. BD21: Keigh 8G 27
HX1: Hal 4H 7 (5A 98)
WF1: Out 8J 105
WF1: Wake 2G 9 (4K 125)
Margate LS26: Oul 7D 88
Margate Rd. BD4: B'frd 1E 82
Margate St. HX6: Sow B 9G 97
Margerison Cres. LS29: I'ly 6K 15
Margerison Rd. LS29: I'ly 6K 15
Margetson Rd. BD11: Drig 8D 84
Margram Bus. Cen. HX1: Hal 2H 7
Marguerite Gdns. WF9: Upt 1D 164
Marian Gro. LS11: Leeds 2D 86
Marian Rd. LS6: Leeds 3D 68
Marian Ter. LS6: Leeds 3D 68
Maria St. LS29: Burl W 7C 16
Marie Cl. HD5: K'htn 4G 138
Marina Cres. LS27: Morl 1J 103
Marina Gdns. HX6: Sow B 8K 97
(off Park Rd.)
Marina Ter. HD7: Golc 5D 136
Mariner Ct. WF4: Wake 2H 143
Marine Villa Rd. WF11: Knot 8E 110
Marion Av. WF2: Wake 3F 124
Marion Cl. WF9: S Kirk 7G 163
Marion Dr. BD18: Ship 8A 46
Marion Gro. WF2: Wake 3F 124
Marion St. BD7: B'frd 7A 64
BD16: Bgly 4F 44
HD6: Brigh 8M 99
Marizon Gro. WF1: Wake 2L 9 (4M 125)
Mark Bottoms La. HD9: H'frth 2L 169
Mark Brooks Yd. HD1: Hud 1D 8 (2N 137)
Mark Cl. BD10: B'frd 7G 46
Market, The WF6: Norm 1H 127
Market Arc. BD19: Cleck 5J 101
(off Albion St.)
HX1: Hal 4L 7
Market Av. HD1: Hud 5B 8
Market Balcony HX1: Hal 4L 7
Market Bldgs. LS2: Leeds 6H 5 (6F 68)
Market Bus. Centre, The HX1: Hal 5M 97
Market Ct. BD13: Thorn 8D 62
Market Hall LS27: Morl 9K 85
(off Hope St.)
Market Hall Kiosks WF10: C'frd 4D 108
(off Carlton St.)
Market Pl. BD21: Keigh 9J 27
HD1: Hud 5B 8 (4M 137)
HD7: Mars 5F 150
Market Pl. HD7: Slait 1M 151
HD9: Hon 5L 153
HD9: Mel 7C 152
LS21: Otley 9L 17
LS22: Weth 4M 23
LS28: Pud 7B 66
WF5: Oss 6N 123
WF6: Norm 1H 127
WF8: Pon 3K 129
WF9: Hems 3E 162
WF13: Dew 3G 122
WF16: Heck 9A 102
WF17: Bat 7F 102
Market Place, The WF10: C'frd 4D 108
(off Carlton St.)
Market Sq. BD18: Ship 8N 45
LS27: Morl 9L 85
(off Hope St.)
WF17: Bat 7F 102
(off Market Pl.)
Market Stall HX1: Hal 4L 7
(off Market St.)
Market St. BD1: B'frd 4B 6 (7C 64)
BD6: B'frd 4A 82
BD13: Thorn 8D 62
BD16: Bgly 4E 44
BD18: Ship 8N 45
BD19: Cleck 5J 101
BD20: Stee 3D 26
BD21: Keigh 1J 43
HD1: Hud 6A 8 (5M 137)
(Castlegate)
HD1: Hud 5K 137
(Hill Top Rd.)
HD3: Hud 5G 136
HD6: Brigh 1N 119
(not continuous)
HD9: H'frth 3M 169
HX1: Hal 4L 7 (5B 98)
HX7: Heb B 1H 95
LS21: Otley 9L 17
OL12: Bac, Whit 4A 112
OL14: Tod 9J 93
(off Rochdale Rd.)
WF1: Wake 5J 9 (5L 125)
WF6: Norm 1H 127
WF7: F'stne 5C 128
WF9: Hems 2D 162
WF13: Dew 3G 122
WF16: Heck 9A 102
(not continuous)
WF17: Birs 3B 102
Market St. Arc. LS1: Leeds 7G 5 (7E 68)
Market Wlk. HD1: Hud 5C 8
HD7: Mars 5F 150
(off Market Pl.)
HD9: H'frth 3M 169
(off Victoria St.)
WF1: Wake 3K 9
Market Way WF1: Wake 4K 9 (5L 125)
Markfield Av. BD12: Low M 8A 82
Markfield Cl. BD12: Low M 8A 82
Markfield Cres. BD12: Low M 8A 82
Markfield Dr. BD12: Low M 8A 82
Markham Av. LS8: Leeds 2H 69
LS19: Raw 2N 47
Markham Cotts. LS25: Aber 7E 54
Markham Cres. LS19: Raw 2N 47
Markham Cft. LS19: Raw 2N 47
Markham Mkt. HX2: Hal 7L 97
Markham St. WF2: Wake 5J 125
WF17: Bat 8E 102
Markington M. LS10: Leeds 1E 104
Markington Pl. LS10: Leeds 1E 104
Mark La. LS2: Leeds 5F 4 (6E 68)
OL14: Tod 5H 93
Mark St. BD5: B'frd 2C 82
HD1: Hud 5K 137
WF1: Wake 8K 9 (7L 125)
WF15: Liv 8M 101
Marland Rd. BD21: Keigh 8L 27
Marlbeck Cl. HD9: Hon 6L 153
Marlborough Av. HX3: Hal 8J 7 (8A 98)
LS24: Tad 6N 39
WF11: Byram 5C 110
Marlborough Cotts. LS29: Men 4F 30
(off Leathley La.)
Marlborough Ct. LS14: S'cft 8D 36
LS29: Men 4F 30
Marlborough Cft. WF9: S Elm 5M 163
Marlborough Dr. LS24: Tad 6N 39
Marlborough Gdns. LS2: Leeds 2D 4
WF13: Dew 1E 122
Marlborough Grange LS1: Leeds 5B 4
Marlborough Gro. HX7: Heb B 1H 95
(off Marlborough Ter.)
LS2: Leeds 2D 4
LS29: I'ly 6J 15
Marlborough Ho. HX5: Ell 4E 118
(off St Mary's Ga.)
Marlborough M. WF15: Liv 9M 101
Marlborough Rd. BD8: B'frd 5A 64
BD10: B'frd 7G 47
BD18: Ship 8M 45
HD2: Fix 6N 119
HX7: Heb B 1H 95
Marlborough Sq. LS29: I'ly 6J 15
Marlborough St. BD21: Keigh 8K 27
LS1: Leeds 6B 4 (6C 68)
WF2: Wake 5J 125
WF5: Oss 6M 123
Marlborough Ter. HX7: Heb B 1H 95
WF13: Dew 1E 122
(off Beckett Rd.)
Marlborough Towers LS1: Leeds 5B 4 (6C 68)
Marlborough Vs. LS29: Men 4F 30
Marldon Rd. HX3: North 3F 98
Marled Cl. WF16: Heck 7A 102
MARLEY 1A 44
Marley Activities & Coaching Cen. 8M 27
Marley Cl. BD8: B'frd 6K 63
Marley Ct. BD16: Bgly 9C 28
Marley Gro. LS11: Leeds 2B 86
Marley La. BD14: Clay 2D 80
Marley Pl. LS11: Leeds 2B 86

Marley Rd.—Meanwood Valley Dr.

Marley Rd. BD21: Keigh ... 8M 27
Marley St. BD3: B'frd ... 4F 6 (7E 64)
BD21: Keigh ... 1H 43
LS11: Leeds ... 2B 86
Marley Ter. LS11: Leeds ... 2B 86
Marley Vw. BD16: Bgly ... 9C 28
LS11: Leeds ... 2B 86
Marling Rd. HD2: Hud ... 8G 118
Marlington Dr. HD2: Hud ... 8A 120
Marlo Rd. WF12: Dew ... 1K 123
Marlott Rd. BD18: Ship ... 7B 46
Marlow Cl. HD5: Hud ... 4D 138
Marlowe Cl. LS28: Pud ... 9C 66
Marlowe Ct. *LS20: Guis* ... *7H 31*
(off Holly Bank)
LS25: Gar ... 7N 71
Marlpit La. WF8: D'ton ... 5A 130
Marmaville Ct. WF14: Mir ... 6N 121
Marmion Av. BD8: B'frd ... 7H 63
Marne Av. BD14: Clay ... 2H 81
Marne Ct. BD14: Clay ... 2H 81
Marne Cres. BD10: B'frd ... 8F 46
Marquis Av. BD12: O'haw ... 8F 82
Marriner Cl. LS21: Otley ... 7K 17
Marriner Rd. BD21: Keigh ... 1J 43
Marriner's Dr. BD9: B'frd ... 2N 63
Marriner's Wlk. BD21: Keigh ... 2J 43
Marriott Gro. WF2: Wake ... 2A 144
Marrtree Bus. Pk. BD20: Sils ... 9E 12
MARSDEN ... 5F 150
Marsden Av. LS11: Leeds ... 3C 86
Marsden Ct. *LS28: Fars* ... *3A 66*
(off Water La.)
Marsden Ga. HX4: Stainl ... 4L 135
Marsden Golf Course ... 8E 150
Marsden Gro. LS11: Leeds ... 3C 86
Marsden La. HD7: Mars ... 5G 150
HD7: Slait ... 3H 151
Marsden Memorial Homes
LS28: Fars ... *4A 66*
(off Newlands)
Marsden M. WF9: Hems ... 3D 162
Marsden Mt. LS11: Leeds ... 3C 86
Marsden Pl. LS11: Leeds ... 3C 86
Marsden Station (Rail) ... 5F 150
Marsden St. HD8: Skelm ... 7D 156
LS12: Leeds ... 8J 67
Marsden Vw. LS11: Leeds ... 3C 86
Marsett Way LS14: Leeds ... 7C 52
MARSH
BD19 ... 6J 101
BD22 ... 2B 60
HD1 ... 3J 137
Marsh HD9: Hon ... 5L 153
LS28: Pud ... 7N 65
Marsh, The BD4: E Bier ... 6K 83
Marshall Av. LS15: Leeds ... 4E 70
WF4: Hol ... 7H 143
Marshall Cl. *LS27: Morl* ... *9K 85*
(off Marshall St.)
Marshall Ct. LS11: Leeds ... 8C 4 (8C 68)
LS19: Yead ... 9M 31
Marshall Cres. LS27: Morl ... 2L 103
Marshall Dr. WF9: S Elm ... 6M 163
Marshall Hill WF6: Norm ... 4E 126
Marshall M. WF10: C'frd ... 4D 108
Marshall Mill Ct. HD8: Clay W ... 8H 157
Marshall Mills LS11: Leeds ... 8C 68
Marshall St. BD20: Keigh ... 7H 27
LS11: Leeds ... 8D 4 (8D 68)
LS15: Leeds ... 4D 70
LS19: Yead ... 9M 31
LS27: Morl ... 9K 85
WF3: S'ley ... 7A 106
WF14: Mir ... 8K 121
Marshall Ter. LS15: Leeds ... 4D 70
Marsham Gro. HD3: Hud ... 3H 137
Marshaw Bri. HX7: Crag V ... 9K 95
Marsh Ct. LS28: Pud ... 7N 65
Marsh Cft. WF11: B'ton ... 5B 110
Marsh Delves HX3: Sou ... 6E 98
Marsh Delves La. HX3: Sou ... 6E 98
Marsh End WF11: Knot ... 7G 110
Marshfield Pl. BD5: B'frd ... 2B 82
MARSHFIELDS ... 3B 82
Marshfield St. BD5: B'frd ... 2B 82
Marsh Gdns. HD9: Hon ... 5L 153
Marsh Gro. BD5: B'frd ... 2A 82
(not continuous)
HX7: Crag V ... 9J 95
Marsh Gro. Rd. HD3: Hud ... 2J 137
Marsh Hall La. HD4: Thurs ... 6D 154
Marsh La. BD11: B'haw ... 8L 83
BD22: Oxen ... 2A 60
DN14: Beal ... 5M 111
HD8: Shep ... 2G 170
(not continuous)
HG3: Kirkby ... 3L 21
HX3: Sou ... 6D 98
HX7: Blac H ... 1B 94
LS9: Leeds ... 7J 5 (7F 68)
(not continuous)
WF11: Byram ... 5D 110
WF11: Knot ... 7G 110
Marsh Lea Gro. WF9: Hems ... 2F 162
Marsh Mills HD3: Hud ... 3J 137
Marsh Platt HD9: Hon ... 5M 153
Marsh Ri. LS28: Pud ... 7N 65
Marsh Rd. HD9: Scho ... 5B 170
WF10: C'frd ... 7A 108
Marsh St. BD5: B'frd ... 2B 82
BD19: Cleck ... 6J 101
LS6: Leeds ... 3C 68
LS26: Rothw ... 9N 87
Marsh Ter. LS28: Pud ... 7N 65
MARSH TOP ... 2C 60
Marsh Va. LS6: Leeds ... 3C 68
Marsh Vw. LS28: Pud ... 7N 65
Marsh Way WF1: Wake ... 4L 9 (5M 125)
(Kirkgate)
WF1: Wake ... 3J 9 (4L 125)
(Northgate)
Marshway HX1: Hal ... 2G 7 (4N 97)
Marsland Av. WF1: Wake ... 5M 9 (5M 125)
Marsland Ct. BD19: Hun ... 2H 101
Marsland Pl. BD3: B'frd ... 7H 65
WF1: Wake ... 4M 9 (5M 125)
Marsland St. WF1: Wake ... 5M 9 (5M 125)
Marsland Ter. WF1: Wake ... 4M 9 (5M 125)
Marston Av. LS27: Morl ... 1K 103
Marston Cl. BD13: Que ... 4E 80
Marston Ct. WF10: C'frd ... 6A 108
Marston Mt. LS9: Leeds ... 3K 5
Marston Wlk. WF6: Alt ... 8F 106
Marston Way LS22: Weth ... 3K 23
Marten Dr. HD4: Neth ... 2J 153
Marten Gro. HD4: Neth ... 2J 153
Marten Rd. BD5: B'frd ... 2A 82
Martin Bank Wood HD5: Hud ... 5B 138
Martin Cl. LS27: Morl ... 9M 85
Martin Ct. BD6: B'frd ... 4H 81
LS15: Leeds ... 6E 70
Martindale Cl. BD2: B'frd ... 3H 65
Martindale Dr. LS13: Leeds ... 5H 67
Martindale Wlk. DN6: Carc ... 9N 165
Martin Frobisher Dr. WF6: Alt ... 9G 107
Martingale Dr. LS10: Leeds ... 1E 104
Martingale Fold LS15: Bar E ... 8L 53
Martin Grn. La. HX4: Gree ... 4N 117
(not continuous)
Martin Gro. WF2: Wake ... 4N 143
Martin St. HD6: Brigh ... 9N 99
WF6: Norm ... 3H 127
WF17: Birs ... 3B 102
Martin Ter. LS4: Leeds ... 4M 67
Martlett Dr. BD5: B'frd ... 3D 82
Marton Av. WF9: Hems ... 3C 162
Marton Ct. BD3: B'frd ... 7H 65
Marton Hgts. HX6: Sow B ... 8G 97
Marwood Rd. LS13: Leeds ... 7H 67
Maryfield Av. LS15: Leeds ... 4B 70
Maryfield Cl. LS15: Leeds ... 4B 70
Maryfield Ct. LS15: Leeds ... 4C 70
Maryfield Cres. LS15: Leeds ... 4C 70
Maryfield Gdns. LS15: Leeds ... 4B 70
WF5: Oss ... 7B 124
Maryfield Grn. LS15: Leeds ... 4B 70
Maryfield M. LS15: Leeds ... 4B 70
Maryfield Va. LS15: Leeds ... 4B 70
Marygate WF1: Wake ... 4J 9 (5L 125)
Mary Rose Ct. *WF7: F'stne* ... *7C 128*
(off Granville St.)
Mary Seacole Cl. BD5: B'frd ... 8A 6 (9B 64)
Mary Seacole Ct. BD5: B'frd ... 8A 6
Mary St. BD4: B'frd ... 9G 64
BD12: Wyke ... 9A 82
BD13: Denh ... 5K 61
BD13: Thorn ... 8C 62
BD18: Ship ... 7L 45
BD22: Oxen ... 4C 60
HD6: Brigh ... 8M 99
LS28: Fars ... 2B 66
WF3: E Ard ... 4G 104
Mary St. Caravan Site BD4: B'frd ... 9G 64
Mary Sunley Ho. *LS8: Leeds* ... *3H 69*
(off Banstead St. W.)
Mary's Way HX6: Sow B ... 9G 96
Maryville Av. HD6: Brigh ... 7K 99
Masefield Av. BD9: B'frd ... 3H 63
Masefield St. LS20: Guis ... 8K 31
Masham Ct. LS6: Leeds ... 9N 49
Masham Gro. LS12: Leeds ... 7N 67
Masham Pl. BD9: B'frd ... 4L 63
Masham St. LS12: Leeds ... 7N 67
Masino Ter. *BD7: B'frd* ... *1M 81*
(off Paternoster La.)
Mason Ct. HD4: Hud ... 8G 136
Masonic St. HX1: Hal ... 6L 97
Mason's Grn. HX2: Illing ... 8L 79
Masons Mill BD17: Ship ... 6N 45
Mason Sq. *HX2: Hal* ... *1M 97*
(off Keighley Rd.)
Mason St. HX7: Heb B ... 1H 95
Massey Flds. BD22: Haw ... 7D 42
Master La. HX2: Hal ... 8M 97
Matherville HD8: Skelm ... 8D 156
Matlock St. HD4: Hud ... 6H 137
HX3: Hal ... 3N 97
Matrix Ct. LS11: Leeds ... 3D 86
Matterdale Cl. WF12: Dew ... 1H 123
Matterdale Rd. WF12: Dew ... 1H 123
Matthew Cl. BD20: Rid ... 7L 27
Matthew Gro. HD9: Mel ... 7B 152
Matthew La. HD9: Mel ... 7B 152
OL14: Tod ... 5N 93
Matty La. LS26: Rothw ... 9K 87
Matty Marsden La. WF4: Horb ... 9A 124
Maud Av. LS11: Leeds ... 3D 86
Maude Av. BD17: Bail ... 5A 46
Maude Cres. HX6: Sow B ... 9E 96
Maude La. HX6: Ripp ... 7D 116
Maude St. HX3: Hal ... 9N 79
HX4: Gree ... 4C 118
LS2: Leeds ... 7H 5 (7F 68)
Maud Pl. LS11: Leeds ... 3D 86
Maudsley St. BD3: B'frd ... 4F 6 (7E 64)
Maud St. BD3: B'frd ... 8F 64
Mauds Yd. WF8: Pon ... 3K 129
Maufe Way LS29: I'ly ... 6G 15
Maurice Av. HD6: Brigh ... 8L 99
Maustin Caravan Pk. LS22: Kear ... 7L 21
Mavis Av. LS16: Leeds ... 1H 49
WF13: Dew ... 5D 122
Mavis Gro. LS16: Leeds ... 2H 49
Mavis La. LS16: Leeds ... 1H 49
Mavis Rd. WF13: Dew ... 9C 102
Mavis St. BD3: B'frd ... 7F 64
WF13: Dew ... 5D 122
Mawcroft Cl. LS19: Yead ... 2L 47
Mawcroft Grange Dr. LS19: Yead ... 2L 47
Mawcroft M. LS19: Yead ... 2M 47
Mawson Ct. BD1: B'frd ... 4A 6
Mawson St. BD18: Ship ... 7L 45
Maw St. BD4: B'frd ... 8D 6 (9D 64)
Maxwell Av. WF17: Bat ... 1F 122
Maxwell Rd. BD6: B'frd ... 5L 81
LS29: I'ly ... 6J 15
Maxwell St. WF7: F'stne ... 6C 128
May Av. BD13: Thorn ... 8D 62
LS27: Chur ... 5M 85
Maybrook Ind. Pk.
LS12: Leeds ... 6A 68
Maybury Av. WF4: Dur ... 2J 143
Maybush Ct. WF1: Wake ... 8N 125
Maybush Rd. WF1: Wake ... 8N 125
May Ct. LS27: Chur ... 4M 85
Maydal Dr. S75: W Gran ... 6F 158
Mayfair BD5: B'frd ... 1B 82
Mayfair Av. HX4: Sow ... 9M 117
Mayfair Ct. *WF2: Wake* ... *6J 125*
(off Park Gro. Rd.)
Mayfair Pl. WF9: Hems ... 2D 162
Mayfair Way BD4: B'frd ... 9H 65
Mayfield HX3: Hip ... 3H 99
HX3: Nor G ... 2L 99
Mayfield Av. BD12: Wyke ... 1A 100
HD5: Hud ... 4D 138
HD6: B Bri ... 4N 99
HX1: Hal ... 6G 7 (6N 97)
LS29: I'ly ... 5J 15
Mayfield Cl. LS29: I'ly ... 5J 15
Mayfield Ct. LS18: Hors ... 6F 48
WF5: Oss ... 8A 124
Mayfield Dr. BD20: Rid ... 8B 28
HX1: Hal ... 6N 97
Mayfield Gdns. HX1: Hal ... 6N 97
HX6: Sow B ... *8K 97*
(off Park Rd.)
LS29: I'ly ... 4J 15
WF5: Oss ... 3M 123
Mayfield Gro. BD15: Wils ... 9A 44
BD17: Bail ... 4B 46
HD5: Hud ... 4D 138
HD6: B Bri ... 4N 99
HX1: Hal ... 6N 97
Mayfield Mt. HX1: Hal ... 6N 97
Mayfield Pl. BD12: Wyke ... 1A 100
WF13: Dew ... 2D 122
Mayfield Ri. BD12: Wyke ... 1B 100
WF4: Ryh ... 9H 145
Mayfield Rd. BD20: Keigh ... 8H 27
HX7: Heb B ... 9H 77
LS15: Leeds ... 6C 70
LS29: I'ly ... 5H 15
Mayfield St.
HX1: Hal ... 7G 7 (7N 97)
Mayfields Way WF9: S Kirk ... 8H 163
Mayfield Ter. BD12: Wyke ... 1B 100
BD14: Clay ... 2H 81
BD19: Cleck ... *5J 101*
(off Neville St.)
HX1: Hal ... 5M 97
Mayfield Ter. Sth. HX1: Hal ... 6G 7
Mayfield Vw. BD12: Wyke ... 1B 100
Mayflower Ho. LS10: Leeds ... 3J 87
Mayhall Av. BD20: Rid ... 7N 27
Maylea Dr. LS21: Otley ... 2H 31
Mayman Cl. WF17: Bat ... 7F 102
Mayman La. WF17: Bat ... 7E 102
Maynes Cl. WF12: T'hill ... 9G 123
Mayo Av. BD5: B'frd ... 3B 82
Mayo Cl. LS8: Leeds ... 9M 51
Mayo Cres. BD5: B'frd ... 4C 82
Mayo Dr. BD5: B'frd ... 4C 82
Mayo Gro. BD5: B'frd ... 4C 82
Mayo Rd. BD5: B'frd ... 4C 82
Mayor's Wlk. WF8: Pon ... 4K 129
WF10: C'frd ... 5L 109
Mayor's Wlk. Av. WF8: Pon ... 4K 129
Mayors Wlk. Cl. WF8: Pon ... 4K 129
Maypole M. LS15: Bar E ... 7L 53
Mayroyde HX3: Hip ... 5J 99
Mayroyd La. HX7: Heb B ... 2J 95
Mayster Gro. HD6: Ras ... 4K 119
Mayster Rd. HD6: Ras ... 4L 119
May St. BD19: Cleck ... 4H 101
BD21: Keigh ... 8J 27
BD22: Haw ... 9D 42
HD4: Hud ... 6J 137
May Ter. LS9: Leeds ... 8H 69
MAYTHORN ... 8H 171
Maythorne Av. WF17: Bat ... 9D 102
Maythorne Cl. BD4: B'frd ... 3K 83
S75: S'ross ... 9L 159
Maythorne Cres. BD14: Clay ... 1J 81
Maythorne Dr. BD14: Clay ... 1K 81
May Tree Cl. BD14: Clay ... 9J 63
Mayville Av. BD20: Rid ... 8A 28
LS6: Leeds ... 3A 68
Mayville Pl. LS6: Leeds ... 3A 68
Mayville Rd. LS6: Leeds ... 3A 68
Mayville St. LS6: Leeds ... 3A 68
Mayville Ter. LS6: Leeds ... 3A 68
Mazebrook Av. BD19: Cleck ... 2J 101
Mazebrook Cres. BD19: Cleck ... 2J 101
Mead Cl. LS15: Leeds ... 8F 70
Meade, The LS25: Gar ... 7N 71
Mead Gro. LS15: Leeds ... 8F 70
Meadow, The LS14: S'cft ... 8E 36
WF6: Norm ... 4H 127
Meadow Bank HD9: H'frth ... 2A 170
WF4: H'cft ... 9K 145
WF7: Ackw ... 1G 146
WF13: Dew ... 3C 122
Meadowbank Av. BD15: All ... 5G 62
Meadow Bank Cres. WF14: Mir ... 6J 121
Meadow Bottom Rd. OL14: Tod ... 6K 93
Meadow Brook Chase WF6: Norm ... 2K 127
Meadow Brook Cl. WF6: Norm ... 2K 127
Meadow Brook Ct. WF6: Norm ... 3K 127
Meadowbrook Ct. LS27: Morl ... 1H 103
Meadow Brook Grn. WF6: Norm ... 2K 127
Meadow Cl. BD16: Har ... 6A 44
HX3: She ... 7J 81
LS17: Bard ... 2F 36
LS23: B Spa ... 9C 24
WF1: Out ... 7M 105
WF9: Hems ... 3C 162
WF15: Liv ... 2K 121
WF17: Bat ... 3D 102
Meadow Ct. BD15: All ... 2F 62
HD6: Clift ... 1C 120
S71: Roys ... 6E 160
WF2: Wake ... 5H 125
WF4: Neth ... 3A 142
Meadow Ct. WF5: Oss ... 4M 123
WF9: S Elm ... 6A 164
WF10: C'frd ... 6K 109
Meadow Cres. HX3: Hal ... 2L 97
S71: Roys ... 5E 160
S72: Grim ... 9N 161
Meadow Cft. BD11: Drig ... 7A 84
BD22: Keigh ... 1E 42
BD23: Drau ... 4D 10
HD2: Hud ... 6D 120
HX4: Bark ... 7H 117
LS11: Leeds ... 9D 68
LS17: E Kes ... 3D 36
LS29: Men ... 5E 30
S72: Shaf ... 6K 161
WF1: Out ... 7L 105
WF2: Wake ... 4H 125
WF9: Hems ... 4E 162
Meadowcroft BD5: B'frd ... 4D 82
HD9: Hon ... 5K 153
Meadowcroft Cl. BD10: B'frd ... 7D 46
WF1: Out ... 7M 105
Meadowcroft Ct. WF1: Out ... 7M 105
WF7: Ackw ... 5E 146
Meadowcroft Cres. WF10: C'frd ... 4G 108
Meadowcroft La. HX6: Ripp ... 6E 116
Meadowcroft M. LS9: Leeds ... 8L 5 (7G 69)
WF10: C'frd ... 4G 108
Meadowcroft Ri. BD4: B'frd ... 5G 82
Meadowcroft Rd. WF1: Out ... 7M 105
Meadow Dr. HX3: Hal ... 2L 97
WF15: Liv ... 2K 121
Meadow End LS16: B'hpe ... 6H 33
Meadowfield Cl. WF9: Fitz ... 8A 146
Meadowfield Ri. WF3: S'ley ... 6C 106
Meadowfields Cl. WF4: Croft ... 2H 145
Meadowfields Dr. WF4: Croft ... 2H 145
Meadowfields Rd. WF4: Croft ... 2H 145
Meadow Fold BD15: Wils ... 2C 62
Meadow Gth. LS16: B'hpe ... 7J 33
WF1: Out ... 7L 105
Meadowgate WF5: Oss ... 4M 123
Meadowgate Cft. WF3: Loft ... 2K 105
Meadowgate Dr. WF3: Loft ... 2K 105
Meadowgate Va. WF3: Loft ... 3K 105
Meadow Grn. HD7: Linth ... 1C 152
Meadowhurst Gdns. LS28: Pud ... 7A 66
Meadowlands BD19: Scho ... 3C 100
Meadow La. BD20: Sils ... 1H 27
HD7: Slait ... 9M 135
HX3: Hal ... 2L 97
LS11: Leeds ... 8F 4 (8E 68)
LS23: Cliff ... 6C 38
S75: Dart ... 9G 158
WF2: Wake ... 4H 125
WF13: Dew ... 2F 122
WF15: Liv ... 2K 121
Meadow Pk. HD5: K'htn ... 9F 120
Meadow Pk. Cres. LS28: Stan ... 4M 65
Meadow Pk. Dr. LS28: Stan ... 4M 65
Meadow Ri. WF9: Hems ... 2C 162
Meadow Rd. BD10: B'frd ... 7J 47
LS11: Leeds ... 9D 68
LS25: Gar ... 7A 72
S71: Roys ... 6E 160
WF10: C'frd ... 7B 108
Meadows, The BD6: B'frd ... 4A 82
HD8: Den D ... 3C 172
HD8: Lept ... 8J 139
HX6: Lud F ... 7G 96
LS16: Leeds ... 4M 49
LS21: Askw ... 4E 16
WF10: All B ... 7N 89
Meadow Side Rd. WF3: E Ard ... 3G 104
Meadowside Rd. BD17: Bail ... 3C 46
Meadow St. HD1: Hud ... 3J 137
OL14: Tod ... *6K 93*
(off Meadow Bottom Rd.)
Meadow Va. WF1: Out ... 7L 105
WF4: Neth ... 5N 141
Meadow Valley LS17: Leeds ... 2D 50
Meadow Vw. BD12: Wyke ... 3A 100
BD22: Oak ... 5D 42
HD8: Skelm ... 8E 156
HD9: T'bdge ... 9A 154
LS6: Leeds ... 3A 68
LS15: Bar E ... 7M 53
LS28: Pud ... 7N 65
OL14: Tod ... 6K 93
S36: Hoy ... 9J 173
WF5: Oss ... 4M 123
WF11: Fair ... 9N 91
Meadow Wlk. *HX3: Hal* ... *2L 97*
(off Meadow Dr.)
LS7: Leeds ... 9G 51
WF9: Bads ... 7L 147
Meadow Way LS17: Leeds ... 2C 50
WF3: W Ard ... 5N 103
WF7: Ackw ... 1G 147
WF10: C'frd ... 4G 108
Mead Rd. LS15: Leeds ... 8F 70
Meadstead Dr. S71: Roys ... 6C 160
Meadstead Fold S71: Roys ... 6C 160
Mead St. HD1: Hud ... 1M 137
Mead Vw. BD4: B'frd ... 2J 83
Mead Way HD8: Kbtn ... 2J 155
LS15: Leeds ... 8F 70
Meadway BD6: B'frd ... 7K 81
WF7: Street ... 6K 127
Meagill Ri. LS21: Otley ... 7H 17
Meal Hill HD7: Slait ... 8M 135
Meal Hill La. HD7: Slait ... 7L 135
HD9: Jack B ... 6D 170
Meal Hill Rd. HD9: H'lm ... 7E 168
Mean La. BD22: Old ... 6K 41
HD9: Mel ... 7C 152
MEANWOOD ... 8B 50
Meanwood Cl. LS7: Leeds ... 2D 68
MEANWOOD GROVE ... 6A 50
Meanwood Gro. LS6: Leeds ... 6A 50
Meanwood Rd. LS6: Leeds ... 1F 4 (9B 50)
LS7: Leeds ... 2D 68
Meanwood Towers LS6: Leeds ... 7C 50
Meanwood Valley Cl. LS7: Leeds ... 9B 50
Meanwood Valley Dr. LS7: Leeds ... 9B 50

Meanwood Valley Grn.—Mill Grn.

Meanwood Valley Grn. LS7: Leeds . . . 9B 50
Meanwood Valley Gro. LS7: Leeds . . . 9B 50
Meanwood Valley Mt. LS7: Leeds . . . 9B 50
Meanwood Valley Urban Farm . . . 1D 68
Meanwood Valley Wlk. LS7: Leeds . . . 9B 50
Mearclough Rd. HX6: Sow B . . . 8K 97
Mearhouse Ter. HD9: New M . . . 4C 170
Mecca Bingo
Bradford . . . 6A 6
Dewsbury . . . 3G 123
(within Library)
Halifax . . . 3K 7
Huddersfield . . . 8A 8 (5M 137)
Leeds, Balm Rd. . . . 2F 86
Leeds, Cross Gates Rd. . . . 4D 70
Leeds, New York St. . . . 7H 5
Wakefield . . . 7G 9 (6K 125)
Medeway LS28: Stan . . . 4N 65
Medhurst Av. LS25: Kip . . . 3B 90
Medley La. HX3: North . . . 9E 80
Medley St. WF10: C'frd . . . 5E 108
Medlock Rd. WF4: Horb . . . 1C 142
Medway BD13: Que . . . 5E 80
HD5: K'htn . . . 9F 120
Medway Av. LS25: Gar . . . 9A 72
Meeting Ho. La. HD7: Golc . . . 6N 135
Meggison Gro. BD5: B'frd . . . 1A 82
Meg La. HD3: Hud . . . 5G 136
Megna Way BD5: B'frd . . . 1C 82
Melba Rd. BD5: B'frd . . . 2N 81
Melbourne Av. WF2: Wren . . . 9H 105
Melbourne Gro. BD3: B'frd . . . 6J 65
LS13: Leeds . . . 4F 66
Melbourne Ho. BD5: B'frd . . . 6A 6
Melbourne M. WF2: Wren . . . 8G 104
Melbourne Mills LS27: Morl . . . 9L 85
(off Melbourne St.)
Melbourne Mill Yd. LS27: Morl . . . 9L 85
(off Middleton Rd.)
Melbourne Pl. BD5: B'frd . . . 7A 6 (9B 64)
Melbourne Rd. OL14: W'den . . . 2J 113
WF1: Wake . . . 3J 125
Melbourne St. BD18: Ship . . . 7M 45
HX3: Hal . . . 3N 97
HX7: Heb B . . . 1G 95
LS2: Leeds . . . 4H 5 (5F 68)
LS13: Leeds . . . 4F 66
LS27: Morl . . . 9L 85
LS28: Fars . . . 4A 66
WF15: Liv . . . 9M 101
Melbourne Ter. BD5: B'frd . . . 7A 6 (9C 64)
Melbourne Vs. WF9: Hems . . . 3B 162
Melcombe Wlk. BD4: B'frd . . . 1J 83
Meldon Way BD6: B'frd . . . 4H 81
Melford Cl. S75: Map . . . 8K 159
Melford St. BD4: B'frd . . . 3G 82
Melilot Cl. BD16: Bgly . . . 5G 45
Mellor Brook HD7: Golc . . . 6M 135
Mellor La. HD9: H'frth . . . 4G 168
Mellor Mill La. HX4: Holy . . . 7A 118
Mellor St. HX1: Hal . . . 8G 7 (7N 97)
OL14: Tod . . . 4G 93
Mellor Ter. HX1: Hal . . . 8G 7 (7N 97)
Mellwood Ho. WF9: S Elm . . . 6L 163
(off Little La.)
Mellwood La. WF9: S Elm . . . 6L 163
Melrose BD22: Haw . . . 9C 42
Melrose Cl. HD5: Hud . . . 4D 138
Melrose Ct. HX5: Ell . . . 5D 118
Melrose Dr. LS29: Burl W . . . 7C 16
Melrose Gro. LS18: Hors . . . 7H 49
Melrose Pl. LS18: Hors . . . 7G 49
LS28: Pud . . . 8A 66
Melrose St. BD7: B'frd . . . 1M 81
HX3: Hal . . . 3N 97
Melrose Ter. HX5: Ell . . . 5E 118
LS18: Hors . . . 7G 49
Melrose Vs. LS18: Hors . . . 7G 49
(off Melrose Ter.)
Melrose Wlk. LS18: Hors . . . 7G 49
MELTHAM . . . 7C 152
Meltham Golf Course . . . 8E 152
Meltham Hall HD9: Mel . . . 7E 152
Meltham Ho. La. HD9: New M . . . 4D 170
Meltham Mills Ind. Est. HD9: Mel . . . 7E 152
Meltham Mills Rd. HD9: Mel . . . 7E 152
Meltham Rd. HD1: Hud . . . 3H 153
HD4: Hud, Neth . . . 3H 153
HD7: Hud, Mars . . . 5G 151
HD9: Hon . . . 6H 153
Melton Av. LS10: Leeds . . . 9H 87
Melton Cl. LS10: Leeds . . . 9H 87
WF9: S Elm . . . 4N 163
Meltonfield M. WF2: Wake . . . 7H 125
Melton Gth. LS10: Leeds . . . 9H 87
Melton M. BD22: Haw . . . 7D 42
Melton Rd. WF2: Wake . . . 6J 143
Melton St. WF17: Bat . . . 6E 102
Melton Ter. BD10: B'frd . . . 2J 65
Melton Way S71: Roys . . . 4D 160
WF15: Liv . . . 2K 121
Melville Cl. LS6: Leeds . . . 3D 68
Melville Gdns. LS6: Leeds . . . 2D 68
Melville Gro. LS29: I'ly . . . 5K 15
Melville Ho. BD7: B'frd . . . 7A 64
(off Preston St.)
Melville Pl. LS6: Leeds . . . 2D 68
Melville Rd. LS6: Leeds . . . 3D 68
Melville St. BD7: B'frd . . . 7A 64
Memorial Cotts. LS12: N Far . . . 2G 85
(off Lawn La.)
Memorial Dr. LS6: Leeds . . . 8B 50
Mendip Av. HD3: Hud . . . 1F 136
Mendip Cl. LS25: Gar . . . 9N 71
Mendip Ho. Gdns. LS29: I'ly . . . 2H 15
Mendip Rd. WF12: Dew . . . 2J 123
Mendip Way BD12: Low M . . . 7N 81
Menin Dr. BD17: Bail . . . 2A 46
MENSTON . . . 4D 30
Menston Dr. LS29: Men . . . 5E 30
Menstone St. BD8: B'frd . . . 6A 64
Menston Hall LS29: Men . . . 4F 30
Menston Ho. LS29: Men . . . 5E 30
(off High Royds Dr.)
Menston Old La. LS29: Burl W . . . 2D 30
Menston Station (Rail) . . . 3E 30
Mercer Cl. HD4: Neth . . . 2H 153
Merchant Ga. WF1: Wake . . . 4H 9 (5K 125)
Merchants Ct. BD4: B'frd . . . 8F 6 (9E 64)
BD16: Bgly . . . 5F 44
Merchants Ho. LS2: Leeds . . . 4H 5
(off North St.)
Merchants Quay LS9: Leeds . . . 8J 5 (7F 68)
Mercia Way LS15: Leeds . . . 3F 70
Mercury Row LS21: Otley . . . 1L 31
Merefield Way WF10: C'frd . . . 7E 108
Mereside HD5: Fen B, Hud . . . 5F 138
Merewood Rd. WF10: C'frd . . . 5N 107
Meriden Av. LS25: Gar . . . 9N 71
Merlin Cl. LS27: Morl . . . 1M 103
WF9: S Elm . . . 7N 163
Merlin Ct. BD21: Keigh . . . 2H 43
HD4: Neth . . . 2K 153
WF17: Bat . . . 4D 102
Merlin Gro. BD8: B'frd . . . 7H 63
Merlinwood Dr. BD17: Bail . . . 3B 46
Merlyn-Rees Av. LS27: Morl . . . 9K 85
Merrall Cl. BD22: Haw . . . 7D 42
Merrion Cen. LS2: Leeds . . . 4F 4 (5E 68)
Merrion Cres. HX3: Sou . . . 7D 98
Merrion Pl. LS1: Leeds . . . 5G 5 (6E 68)
(not continuous)
LS2: Leeds . . . 6E 68
Merrion St. HX3: Sou . . . 7D 98
LS1: Leeds . . . 5G 5 (6E 68)
LS2: Leeds . . . 5F 4 (6E 68)
(not continuous)
Merrion Way LS2: Leeds . . . 4F 4 (5E 68)
Merrivale Rd. BD15: All . . . 6F 62
Merriville LS18: Hors . . . 8G 49
Merry Bank Cotts. LS17: Huby . . . 4L 19
Merrybank La. LS17: Huby . . . 3L 19
Merry Bent La. HX6: Ripp . . . 6A 116
Merrybents St. OL14: Tod . . . 7M 93
Merrydale Rd. BD4: B'frd . . . 7E 82
Merton Av. LS28: Fars . . . 4A 66
Merton Cl. LS25: Kip . . . 3C 90
Merton Dr. LS28: Fars . . . 4N 65
Merton Fold BD5: B'frd . . . 1C 82
Merton Gdns. LS28: Fars . . . 4N 65
Merton Rd. BD7: B'frd . . . 9B 64
Merton St. HD1: Hud . . . 6A 8 (5M 137)
Merville Av. BD17: Bail . . . 2A 46
Metcalfe St. BD4: B'frd . . . 1F 82
METHLEY . . . 2K 107
Methley Dr. LS7: Leeds . . . 9E 50
Methley Gro. LS7: Leeds . . . 9E 50
METHLEY JUNCTION . . . 4L 107
Methley La. LS7: Leeds . . . 9F 50
LS26: Oul . . . 9D 88
METHLEY LANES . . . 5F 106
Methley Mt. LS7: Leeds . . . 9F 50
Methley Pl. LS7: Leeds . . . 9E 50
Methley Rd. WF10: C'frd . . . 4A 108
Methley Rd. Ind. Pk. WF10: C'frd . . . 4B 108
Methley Ter. LS7: Leeds . . . 9F 50
Methley Vw. LS7: Leeds . . . 9F 50
Methuen Oval BD12: Wyke . . . 3A 100
Mews, The WF6: Norm . . . 9J 107
Mews Ct. WF7: F'stne . . . 7C 128
(East Av. Loop)
WF7: F'stne . . . 6D 128
(Victoria St.)
Mexborough Av. LS7: Leeds . . . 2F 68
Mexborough Ct. LS14: T'ner . . . 2G 53
Mexborough Dr. LS7: Leeds . . . 2F 68
Mexborough Gro. LS7: Leeds . . . 2F 68
Mexborough Ho. HX5: Ell . . . 4E 118
(off Westgate)
Mexborough Pl. LS7: Leeds . . . 3F 68
Mexborough Rd. BD2: B'frd . . . 1B 64
LS7: Leeds . . . 3F 68
Mexborough St. LS7: Leeds . . . 2F 68
Meynell App. LS11: Leeds . . . 9C 68
Meynell Av. LS26: Rothw . . . 8N 87
Meynell Ct. LS15: Leeds . . . 7E 70
Meynell Fold LS15: Leeds . . . 8E 70
Meynell Hgts. LS11: Leeds . . . 9C 68
Meynell La. LS15: Leeds . . . 8E 70
Meynell Mt. LS26: Rothw . . . 8A 88
Meynell Rd. LS15: Leeds . . . 7E 70
Meynell Sq. LS11: Leeds . . . 9C 68
Meynell Wlk. LS11: Leeds . . . 9C 68
Meyrick Av. LS22: Weth . . . 3A 24
Meyrick Dr. S75: Dart . . . 9F 158
Miall St. HX1: Hal . . . 4N 97
Michael Av. WF3: S'ley . . . 7N 105
Michael's Est. S72: Grim . . . 9A 162
Mickle Ct. WF10: C'frd . . . 5C 108
Mickledore Ridge BD7: B'frd . . . 2K 81
MICKLEFIELD . . . 7G 72
Micklefield Ct. LS19: Raw . . . 3M 47
Micklefield La. LS19: Raw . . . 3L 47
Micklefield Rd. LS19: Raw . . . 3M 47
Micklefield Station (Rail) . . . 8G 73
Micklegate WF8: Pon . . . 2K 129
Micklegate Sq. WF8: Pon . . . 2K 129
Micklemoss Dr. BD13: Que . . . 3B 80
MICKLETHWAITE . . . 9D 28
Micklethwaite Dr. BD13: Que . . . 5C 80
Micklethwaite Gro. LS22: Weth . . . 5M 23
Micklethwaite La. BD16: Bgly . . . 1D 44
Micklethwaite M. LS22: Weth . . . 5M 23
Micklethwaite Rd. WF4: Hol . . . 7H 143
Micklethwaite Stables LS22: Weth . . . 5M 23
Micklethwaite Steps LS22: Weth . . . 5M 23
Micklethwaite Vw. LS22: Weth . . . 5M 23
MICKLETOWN . . . 1L 107
Mickletown Rd. LS26: Meth . . . 1L 107
Mickley St. LS12: Leeds . . . 7N 67
Mid Birk HX7: Crag V . . . 7L 95
Middlebrook Cl. BD8: B'frd . . . 7J 63
Middlebrook Cres. BD8: B'frd . . . 8J 63
Middlebrook Dr. BD8: B'frd . . . 7J 63
Middlebrook Hill BD8: B'frd . . . 7J 63
Middlebrook Ri. BD8: B'frd . . . 7J 63
Middlebrook Vw. BD8: B'frd . . . 7K 63
Middlebrook Wlk. BD8: B'frd . . . 7K 63
Middlebrook Way BD8: B'frd . . . 8J 63
Middle Calderbrook OL15: Lit . . . 9L 113
Middle Cl. S75: Kex . . . 8E 158
Middlecroft Cl. LS10: Leeds . . . 5H 87
Middlecroft Rd. LS10: Leeds . . . 5H 87
Middle Cross St. LS12: Leeds . . . 7N 67
(not continuous)
Middle Dean St. HX4: Gree . . . 5B 118
Middle Ellistones HX4: Gree . . . 4N 117
(off Saddleworth Rd.)
Middlefield Ct. BD20: E Mor . . . 7A 28
Middle Fld. La. WF4: Wool . . . 3G 158
Middlefield La. WF8: K S'ton . . . 6F 148
Middle Fold LS9: Leeds . . . 5J 5 (6F 68)
Middlegate WF17: Birs . . . 3B 102
Middlegate Ct. BD4: B'frd . . . 5F 82
Middle Hall Cl. WF15: Liv . . . 8K 101
Middleham Ct. BD4: B'frd . . . 2J 83
Middleham Moor LS10: Leeds . . . 1F 104
Middle Harper Royd HX6: Norl . . . 1H 117
Middle La. BD14: Clay . . . 9H 63
LS22: Lin . . . 7J 23
WF4: N Cro . . . 3J 145
WF11: Knot . . . 8F 110
(not continuous)
Middlemoor LS14: Leeds . . . 7C 52
Middlemost Cl. HD2: Hud . . . 1L 137
Middle Nook HX7: Wads . . . 9L 77
Middle Oxford St. WF10: C'frd . . . 5C 108
Middle Rd. LS9: Leeds . . . 3M 87
WF12: Dew . . . 4H 123
WF13: Dew . . . 4E 122
MIDDLESTOWN . . . 3L 141
Middle St. BD1: B'frd . . . 3B 6 (7C 64)
HX6: Tri . . . 2E 116
Middlethorne Cl. LS17: Leeds . . . 2K 51
Middlethorne Ct. LS17: Leeds . . . 2J 51
Middlethorne M. LS17: Leeds . . . 2K 51
Middlethorne Ri. LS17: Leeds . . . 2J 51
MIDDLETON
LS10 . . . 8D 86
LS29 . . . 2H 15
Middleton Av. LS9: Leeds . . . 4M 5 (5H 69)
LS26: Rothw . . . 8J 87
LS29: I'ly . . . 3G 14
Middleton Cl. LS27: Morl . . . 9M 85
Middleton Ct. WF15: Liv . . . 8J 101
Middleton Cres. LS11: Leeds . . . 3D 86
Middleton District Cen. LS10: Leeds . . . 8F 86
Middleton Gro. LS11: Leeds . . . 4D 86
LS27: Morl . . . 9M 85
Middleton La. LS26: Rothw . . . 8J 87
(not continuous)
WF3: Thpe H . . . 1F 104
Middleton Leisure Cen. . . . 8F 86
Middleton Lit. Rd. WF10: All B . . . 9C 90
Middleton Pk. Av. LS10: Leeds . . . 9D 86
Middleton Pk. Cir. LS10: Leeds . . . 8D 86
Middleton Pk. Ct. LS10: Leeds . . . 9D 86
Middleton Pk. Cres. LS10: Leeds . . . 9E 86
Middleton Pk. Equestrian Cen. . . . 5E 86
Middleton Pk. Golf Course . . . 8C 86
Middleton Pk. Grn. LS10: Leeds . . . 9D 86
Middleton Pk. Gro. LS10: Leeds . . . 8D 86
Middleton Pk. Mt. LS10: Leeds . . . 9D 86
Middleton Pk. Rd. LS10: Leeds . . . 8D 86
Middleton Pk. Ter. LS10: Leeds . . . 9E 86
Middleton Railway
Moor Road Station . . . 2F 86
Park Halt Station . . . 5F 86
Middleton Rd. LS10: Leeds . . . 6G 87
LS27: Morl . . . 9L 85
LS29: I'ly . . . 5F 14
Middleton St. BD8: B'frd . . . 5N 63
Middleton Ter. LS27: Morl . . . 9M 85
Middleton Way LS10: Leeds . . . 7H 87
WF11: Knot . . . 7E 110
Middle Wlk. LS8: Leeds . . . 6L 51
Middle Way BD21: Keigh . . . 9L 27
Middleway BD20: Sils . . . 8F 12
Middlewoods Way S71: Ath . . . 9C 160
Midge Hall Cl. LS29: Burl W . . . 8C 16
Midgeham Gro. BD16: Har . . . 6N 43
Midgehole La. HX7: Heb B . . . 6H 77
Midgehole Rd. HX7: Heb B . . . 6G 77
Midgeley Rd. BD17: Bail . . . 6M 45
MIDGLEY
HX2 . . . 3C 96
WF4 . . . 8M 141
Midgley Dr. BD22: Haw . . . 7D 42
Midgley Gdns. LS6: Leeds . . . 3C 68
Midgley Pl. LS6: Leeds . . . 3D 68
Midgley Ri. WF8: Pon . . . 9K 109
Midgley Rd. HX7: Myth . . . 3M 95
LS29: Burl W . . . 8C 16
Midgley Row BD4: B'frd . . . 4F 82
Midgley Ter. LS6: Leeds . . . 3D 68
Midland Cl. LS10: Leeds . . . 2H 87
Midland Cotts. S71: Roys . . . 2E 160
Midland Gth. LS10: Leeds . . . 2G 87
Midland Hill BD16: Bgly . . . 4E 44
Midland Ho. LS26: W'frd . . . 7E 88
(off Midland St.)
Midland Pas. LS6: Leeds . . . 3B 68
Midland Pl. LS11: Leeds . . . 8C 68
Midland Rd. BD1: B'frd . . . 4B 64
BD8: B'frd . . . 1A 6 (4B 64)
BD9: B'frd . . . 1A 64
BD17: Bail . . . 5B 46
LS6: Leeds . . . 3B 68
LS10: Leeds . . . 2G 86
S71: Roys . . . 5D 160
WF8: Pon . . . 3L 129
Midland St. HD1: Hud . . . 1C 8 (2N 137)
LS26: Oul . . . 7D 88
Midland Ter. BD2: B'frd . . . 3B 64
BD21: Keigh . . . 8J 27
Mid Point BD3: B'frd . . . 6K 65
Mid Point Bus. Pk. BD3: B'frd . . . 6K 65
Midway HD4: S Cros . . . 3F 152
Midway Av. BD16: Cot . . . 8F 44
Mid Yorkshire Golf Course . . . 6D 130
Milan Rd. LS8: Leeds . . . 3H 69
Milan St. LS8: Leeds . . . 3J 69
Milbrook Gdns. WF13: Dew . . . 1D 122
Mildred St. BD3: B'frd . . . 1E 6 (5E 64)
Mildred Sylvester Way WF6: Norm . . . 1L 127
Mile Cross Gdns. HX1: Hal . . . 6L 97
Mile Cross Pl. HX1: Hal . . . 6L 97
Mile Cross Rd. HX1: Hal . . . 6L 97
Mile Cross Ter. HX1: Hal . . . 6L 97
Mile End HD9: Mel . . . 8C 152
Miles Gth. LS17: Bard . . . 2G 36
MILES HILL . . . 9D 50
Miles Hill Av. LS7: Leeds . . . 9D 50
Miles Hill Cres. BD4: B'frd . . . 4G 83
LS7: Leeds . . . 9D 50
Miles Hill Dr. BD4: B'frd . . . 4G 82
Miles Hill Gro. LS7: Leeds . . . 9D 50
Miles Hill Mt. LS7: Leeds . . . 8C 50
Miles Hill Pl. LS7: Leeds . . . 8D 50
Miles Hill Rd. LS7: Leeds . . . 8D 50
Miles Hill Sq. LS7: Leeds . . . 9D 50
Miles Hill St. LS7: Leeds . . . 9D 50
Miles Hill Ter. LS7: Leeds . . . 9D 50
Miles Hill Vw. LS7: Leeds . . . 9D 50
Milestone Ct. LS28: Stan . . . 4C 66
Mile Thorn St. HX1: Hal . . . 5M 97
Milford Ct. HD1: Hud . . . 7B 8
Milford Gro. BD19: Gom . . . 1L 101
Milford Pl. BD9: B'frd . . . 3M 63
LS4: Leeds . . . 5N 67
Milford St. HD1: Hud . . . 7B 8 (5M 137)
Milgate St. S71: Roys . . . 5E 160
Millars Wlk. WF9: S Kirk . . . 8G 163
Mill Av. HD5: Hud . . . 3E 138
MILL BANK . . . 4C 116
Mill Bank WF12: Dew . . . 9L 123
Millbank LS19: Yead . . . 8M 31
Mill Bank Cl. HX6: Mill B . . . 4C 116
Millbank Ct. LS28: Pud . . . 8C 66
Millbank Fold LS28: Pud . . . 8C 66
Mill Bank Rd. HD9: Mel . . . 8D 152
HX6: Mill B . . . 4D 116
Mill Banks BD20: Sils . . . 8E 12
Millbank Vw. LS28: Pud . . . 8C 66
Millbeck App. LS27: Morl . . . 9M 85
Mill Beck Cl. LS28: Fars . . . 2B 66
Millbeck Cl. BD8: B'frd . . . 8H 63
Millbeck Dr. BD16: Har . . . 5N 43
Millbeck Grn. LS22: Coll . . . 9H 23
Millbeck Vw. WF8: Pon . . . 9J 109
MILL BRIDGE . . . 8M 101
Millbrook Gdns. WF13: Dew . . . 1D 122
Mill Carr Hill Rd. BD4: B'frd . . . 9F 82
BD12: O'haw . . . 9F 82
Mill Chase Cl. WF2: Wake . . . 5J 125
Mill Chase Cft. WF2: Wake . . . 5J 125
(off Mill Chase Rd.)
Mill Chase Gdns. WF2: Wake . . . 5J 125
Mill Chase Rd. WF2: Wake . . . 5J 125
Mill Cl. HD9: Mel . . . 7C 152
WF7: Ackw . . . 4G 147
WF9: S Kirk . . . 7G 162
WF16: Heck . . . 8A 102
Mill Cotts. LS21: Pool . . . 1G 32
WF7: F'stne . . . 6B 128
Mill Ct. BD22: Oxen . . . 4C 60
WF10: C'frd . . . 5B 108
(off Mill St.)
Mill Cft. LS27: Gil . . . 6G 84
Millcroft WF3: Loft . . . 6N 105
Millcroft Cl. WF3: Loft . . . 6M 105
Millcroft Est. LS21: Pool . . . 1G 32
Millcroft Ri. WF3: Loft . . . 6N 105
Mill Dale Ct. BD11: Drig . . . 7C 84
(off Moorside Va.)
Mill Dam LS23: Cliff . . . 3E 38
Mill Dam La. WF8: Pon . . . 1L 129
Millennia Pk. WF2: Wake . . . 8K 125
Millennium Bus. Pk. BD20: Stee . . . 2C 26
Millennium Ct. LS28: Pud . . . 6C 66
(off Lowtown)
Millennium Dr. LS11: Leeds . . . 4D 86
Millennium Sq. LS2: Leeds . . . 4E 4 (5D 68)
Millennium Way LS11: Leeds . . . 4D 86
Miller Av. WF2: Wake . . . 9M 125
Miller Cl. BD2: B'frd . . . 1B 64
Miller Ct. HD6: B Bri . . . 5N 99
(off Axminster Dr.)
WF2: New . . . 6K 143
Miller Gth. WF7: Ackw . . . 5G 146
Millergate BD1: B'frd . . . 4A 6 (7C 64)
Miller Hill HD8: Den D . . . 3D 172
Miller Hill Bank HD8: Den D . . . 3D 172
Millers Ct. WF15: Liv . . . 1M 121
Millers Cft. S71: Roys . . . 5D 160
WF7: Ackw . . . 4G 147
WF10: C'frd . . . 5B 108
WF17: Bat . . . 3E 102
Millers Dale LS27: Morl . . . 7J 85
Millersdale Cl. BD4: B'frd . . . 6E 82
Mill Farm Dr. WF2: New . . . 6L 143
Millfield Cl. HD3: Hud . . . 3H 137
Millfield Cotts. WF4: Horb . . . 2F 142
Mill Fld. Ct. BD20: Sils . . . 8E 12
Millfield Cres. WF8: Pon . . . 5J 129
Mill Fld. End HX2: Midg . . . 4C 96
Mill Fld. Rd. BD16: Cot . . . 8G 44
Millfield Rd. WF4: Horb . . . 2E 142
Millfields BD20: Sils . . . 8D 12
WF5: Oss . . . 6M 123
Mill Fold HX6: Ripp . . . 7E 116
LS27: Gil . . . 6G 84
LS29: Add . . . 2B 14
Millfold HD9: Holm . . . 6H 169
Mill Fold Way HX6: Ripp . . . 7D 116
Mill Forest Way WF17: Bat . . . 7J 103
Mill Garth DN14: Beal . . . 4M 111
Mill Gth. LS27: Gil . . . 6G 84
WF8: Pon . . . 4J 129
Millgarth Ct. LS22: Coll . . . 9J 23
Millgarth St. LS2: Leeds . . . 6H 5 (6F 68)
MILLGATE . . . 6A 112
Millgate BD16: Bgly . . . 4E 44
HD1: Hud . . . 5K 137
HD8: Fen B . . . 8F 138
HX5: Ell . . . 4E 118
WF7: Ackw . . . 4G 147
Millgate Ter. OL12: Whit . . . 6A 112
MILL GREEN . . . 1C 70
Mill Grn. LS12: Leeds . . . 8B 68

Mill Grn. Cl.—Moor End Gdns.

Mill Grn. Cl. LS14: Leeds . . . 1D **70**
Mill Grn. Gdns. LS14: Leeds . . . 1D **70**
Mill Grn. Gth. LS14: Leeds . . . 1D **70**
Mill Grn. Pl. LS14: Leeds . . . 1D **70**
Mill Grn. Rd. LS14: Leeds . . . 1D **70**
Mill Grn. Vw. LS14: Leeds . . . 1D **70**
Mill Gro. HD6: Brigh . . . 8L **99**
Millhaven M. BD8: B'frd . . . 1A **6**
Mill Hey BD22: Haw . . . 8D **42**
MILL HILL . . . 4K **127**
Mill Hill BD22: Haw . . . 8C **42**
HX2: Lud F . . . 4B **96**
LS1: Leeds . . . 7F **4** (7E **68**)
LS26: Rothw . . . 8N **87**
LS28: Pud . . . 9B **66**
WF6: Norm . . . 2H **127**
WF7: Ackw . . . 2G **146**
Mill Hill Av. WF8: Pon . . . 4H **129**
Mill Hill Cl. WF8: D'ton . . . 6C **130**
Mill Hill Grn. LS26: Rothw . . . 8N **87**
Mill Hill La. HD6: Brigh . . . 8K **99**
(Springvale Works)
HD6: Brigh . . . 2D **120**
(Wakefield Rd.)
WF8: Pon . . . 4H **129**
Mill Hill Rd. WF8: Pon . . . 4J **129**
Mill Hill Sq. LS26: Rothw . . . 8N **87**
Mill Hill Top BD16: Har . . . 7A **44**
Mill Ho. La. HX6: Tri . . . 1F **116**
Mill Ho. Ri. BD5: B'frd . . . 4F **82**
Milligan Av. BD2: B'frd . . . 1D **64**
Milligan Ct. BD16: Har . . . 6N **43**
Mill La. BD4: B'frd . . . 8B **6** (9C **64**)
(Manchester Rd.)
BD4: B'frd . . . 2C **84**
(Tong La.)
BD5: B'frd . . . 8B **6** (9C **64**)
BD6: B'frd . . . 7K **81**
BD11: B'haw . . . 7L **83**
BD13: Que . . . 3B **80**
BD16: Bgly . . . 1H **45**
BD19: Cleck, Hun . . . 2H **101**
BD20: Stee . . . 3C **26**
BD22: Oak . . . 5B **42**
(Commercial St.)
BD22: Oak . . . 5C **42**
(Providence La.)
BD22: Oxen . . . 3C **60**
DN6: Skel . . . 6L **165**
HD4: Farn T . . . 2E **154**
HD5: Hud . . . 6F **120**
HD6: Brigh . . . 1N **119**
HX2: Lud . . . 2E **96**
HX2: Mix . . . 6J **79**
HX3: Hal . . . 2A **98**
HX4: Holy . . . 7B **118**
LS13: Leeds . . . 3D **66**
LS17: Bard . . . 4F **36**
LS20: Hawk . . . 9A **30**
LS21: Otley . . . 9L **17**
LS21: Pool . . . 1F **32**
LS22: Coll . . . 9J **23**
LS22: Kear . . . 6N **21**
LS23: T Arch . . . 9E **24**
LS26: Meth . . . 1K **107**
LS27: Gil . . . 6G **84**
S36: Ing . . . 8A **172**
S75: Dart . . . 8G **158**
WF3: E Ard . . . 4F **104**
WF4: Flock . . . 7G **140**
WF4: Ryh . . . 9J **145**
WF6: Norm . . . 8L **107**
WF7: Ackw . . . 5G **146**
WF7: Old S, Street . . . 6K **127**
WF8: Pon . . . 9M **109**
WF9: S Elm . . . 4N **163**
WF9: S Kirk . . . 8G **163**
WF10: C'frd . . . 3D **108**
WF12: Dew . . . 4K **123**
WF14: Mir . . . 4H **121**
WF17: Bat . . . 8G **103**
(not continuous)
WF17: Birs . . . 2E **102**
Millmoor Cl. BD9: B'frd . . . 4J **63**
Mill Moor Rd. HD9: Mel . . . 7A **152**
Mill Pit La. LS26: Rothw . . . 6M **87**
Mill Pl. WF10: C'frd . . . 5B **108**
Mill Pond Cl. LS6: Leeds . . . 9A **50**
Millpond Gdns. *LS12: Leeds* . . . *6L 67*
(off Eyres Mill Side)
Mill Pond Gro. LS6: Leeds . . . 9A **50**
Mill Pond La. LS6: Leeds . . . 8A **50**
Mill Pond Sq. LS6: Leeds . . . 8A **50**
Mill Race Fold HD9: T'bdge . . . 9A **154**
Mill Race La. BD4: B'frd . . . 8H **65**
Mill Rd. WF13: Dew . . . 1F **122**
Mill Row BD20: East . . . 2A **26**
Mill Royd St. HD6: Brigh . . . 1N **119**
MILL SHAW . . . 4A **86**
Millshaw LS11: Leeds . . . 4N **85**
Millshaw La. HD9: H'wth . . . 7F **170**
Millshaw Mt. LS11: Leeds . . . 5A **86**
Millshaw Pk. Av. LS11: Leeds . . . 5N **85**
Millshaw Pk. Cl. LS11: Leeds . . . 5N **85**
Millshaw Pk. Dr. LS11: Leeds . . . 4N **85**
Millshaw Pk. La. LS11: Leeds . . . 5N **85**
Millshaw Pk. Trad. Est. LS11: Leeds . . . 5A **86**
Millshaw Pk. Way LS11: Leeds . . . 4N **85**
Millshaw Rd. LS11: Leeds . . . 6A **86**
Millside S72: Shaf . . . 6K **161**
Millside Wlk. LS27: Morl . . . 9M **85**
S72: Shaf . . . 6K **161**
Millside Way HX3: Hal . . . 9C **98**
Millstone Cl. WF7: Ackw . . . 5G **147**
Millstone Ri. WF15: Liv . . . 1M **121**
Millstream Cl. BD20: E Mor . . . 7A **28**
Mill Stream Dr. HX2: Lud F . . . 5D **96**
Mill St. BD1: B'frd . . . 2C **6** (6D **64**)
BD6: B'frd . . . 4M **81**
BD13: Cull . . . 9K **43**
HD4: Hud . . . 6K **137**
HX3: Hal . . . 2N **117**
LS9: Leeds . . . 7J **5** (7G **68**)
LS27: Morl . . . 1K **103**
WF9: S Kirk . . . 7G **163**
Mill St. WF10: C'frd . . . 5B **108**
WF17: Birs . . . 4B **102**
Mill St. E. WF12: Dew . . . 4G **122**
Mill St. W. WF12: Dew . . . 4F **122**
Mill Vw. BD18: Ship . . . 7M **45**
HX6: Ripp . . . 7D **116**
LS29: Burl W . . . 7C **16**
WF2: Wake . . . 4F **124**
WF9: Hems . . . 3C **162**
WF11: Ferr . . . 8A **110**
Millward St. WF4: Ryh . . . 9H **145**
Millwater Av. WF12: Dew . . . 6E **122**
Mill West *HX6: Sow B* . . . *9H 97*
(off West St.)
MILLWOOD . . . 7L **93**
Millwood La. OL14: Tod . . . 7M **93**
Millwright Cl. HD7: Mars . . . 5E **150**
Millwright St. LS2: Leeds . . . 4J **5** (5F **68**)
Milne Ct. LS15: Leeds . . . 8E **70**
Milner Bank LS21: Otley . . . 2H **31**
Milner Cl. HX4: Gree . . . 4B **118**
Milner Ct. BD18: Ship . . . 7K **45**
Milner Fold LS28: Pud . . . 9A **66**
Milner Gdns. LS9: Leeds . . . 8M **5** (8H **69**)
Milner Ga. HX2: Lud F . . . 6C **96**
Milner Ing BD12: Wyke . . . 9A **82**
Milner La. HX4: Gree . . . 4B **118**
LS14: S'cft, T'ner . . . 8G **36**
LS24: Saxt . . . 8N **55**
WF3: Rob H . . . 1J **105**
Milner Pl. HX2: Lud F . . . 6D **96**
Milner Rd. BD17: Bail . . . 6M **45**
Milner Royd La. HX6: Norl . . . 9L **97**
Milner Royd Nature Reserve . . . 8L **97**
Milner's La. WF8: D'ton . . . 7C **130**
Milner's Rd. LS19: Yead . . . 9K **31**
Milner St. HD1: Hud . . . 7K **137**
HX1: Hal . . . 3H **7** (5A **98**)
WF5: Oss . . . 2M **123**
Milner Way WF5: Oss . . . 5A **124**
Milne's Av. WF2: Wake . . . 8H **125**
Milnes Ct. BD6: B'frd . . . 5M **81**
Milnes Gro. WF10: C'frd . . . 5H **109**
Milnes St. LS12: Leeds . . . 8A **68**
Miln Rd. HD1: Hud . . . 1A **8** (2M **137**)
MILNSBRIDGE . . . 6F **136**
MILNTHORPE . . . 3M **143**
Milnthorpe Cl. LS23: B'ham . . . 5C **38**
Milnthorpe Cres. WF2: Wake . . . 3M **143**
Milnthorpe Dr. WF2: Wake . . . 2M **143**
Milnthorpe Gdns.
LS23: B'ham . . . 5C **38**
Milnthorpe Gth. LS23: B'ham . . . 5C **38**
Milnthorpe Grn. WF2: Wake . . . 3M **143**
Milnthorpe La. LS23: B'ham . . . 5C **38**
WF2: Wake . . . 1L **143**
(Milnthorpe Dr.)
WF2: Wake . . . 9M **125**
(Newlyn Dr.)
Milnthorpe Way LS23: B'ham . . . 5C **38**
Milroyd Cres. WF17: Birs . . . 2D **102**
Milton Av. HX6: Sow B . . . 7H **97**
WF15: Liv . . . 9N **101**
Milton Cl. WF4: Cal G . . . 4F **142**
WF15: Liv . . . 1N **121**
Milton Ct. WF3: S'ley . . . 6A **106**
Milton Cres. WF2: Wake . . . 7E **124**
Milton Dr. LS15: Scho . . . 8G **52**
WF9: Kins . . . 8B **146**
WF15: Liv . . . 1N **121**
Milton Gdns. WF7: F'stne . . . 6D **128**
WF15: Liv . . . 9N **101**
Milton Gro. WF13: Dew . . . 1F **122**
Milton Pl. HX1: Hal . . . 4H **7** (5A **98**)
HX6: Sow B . . . *7H 97*
(off Milton St.)
WF5: Oss . . . 4N **123**
Milton Rd. DN6: Carc . . . 8N **165**
WF2: Wake . . . 7E **124**
WF15: Liv . . . 9N **101**
Milton Sq. WF16: Heck . . . 8A **102**
Milton St. BD7: B'frd . . . 7A **64**
BD13: Denh . . . 6L **61**
HX6: Sow B . . . 7H **97**
WF2: Wake . . . 6J **125**
WF10: C'frd . . . 4C **108**
WF16: Heck . . . 8A **102**
Milton Ter. BD19: Cleck . . . 4G **101**
HX1: Hal . . . 3H **7** (5A **98**)
LS5: Leeds . . . 2K **67**
LS19: Yead . . . 9K **31**
WF9: Fitz . . . 6A **146**
Milton Wlk. *WF13: Dew* . . . *3F 122*
(off Wellington Wlk.)
Minden Cl. WF8: Pon . . . 4G **129**
Minden Way WF8: Pon . . . 3G **129**
Miners M. *LS25: M'fld* . . . *8G 73*
(off Pit La.)
Miners Way HX3: Sou . . . 8F **98**
Minerva Ind. Est. LS26: W'frd . . . 6F **88**
Minerva St. HD4: Hud . . . 7E **136**
Minnie St. BD21: Keigh . . . 1H **43**
BD22: Haw . . . 9C **42**
Minor and Scurr's Yd. LS1: Leeds . . . 6F **4**
Minorca Mt. BD13: Denh . . . 5K **61**
Minstead Av. HX5: Ell . . . 4J **119**
Minster Cl. HX4: Gree . . . 4A **118**
Minster Dr. BD4: B'frd . . . 9H **65**
MINSTHORPE . . . 4N **163**
Minsthorpe La. WF9: S Elm, S Kirk . . . 3N **163**
Minsthorpe Swimming Pool . . . 5N **163**
Minsthorpe Va. WF9: S Elm . . . 5M **163**
Minstrel Dr. BD13: Que . . . 4D **80**
Mint St. BD2: B'frd . . . 4F **64**
HD1: Hud . . . 3J **137**
Miramar HD2: Hud . . . 6B **120**
Mires Beck Cl. BD18: Ship . . . 7C **46**
Mirey Butt La. WF11: Knot . . . 9B **110**
(not continuous)
Mirey La. HX6: Sow B . . . 8B **96**
MIRFIELD . . . 7L **121**
Mirfield Av. BD2: B'frd . . . 1E **64**
MIRFIELD MOOR . . . 4K **121**
Mirfield Station (Rail) . . . 8L **121**
Mirycarr La. LS14: Leeds, T'ner . . . 5F **52**
Miry Grn. Ter. HD9: Nether . . . 9L **153**
Miry La. HD9: Nether . . . 8K **153**
HD9: T'bdge . . . 9N **153**
HX7: Crag V . . . 6N **95**
LS15: Pott . . . 5M **53**
LS19: Yead . . . 9M **31**
WF15: Liv . . . 8F **100**
(not continuous)
Mission Ct. *S75: W Gran* . . . *6G 158*
(off Wooley Edge La.)
Mission St. HD6: Brigh . . . 2A **120**
Mission Vw. HD9: H'frth . . . 7L **169**
Mistal, The BD10: B'frd . . . 7D **46**
LS21: F'ley . . . 6A **18**
Mistral Cl. BD12: Wyke . . . 2A **100**
Mistral Gro. WF15: Liv . . . 7F **100**
Mistress La. LS12: Leeds . . . 6M **67**
Mitcham Dr. BD9: B'frd . . . 4M **63**
Mitchell Av. HD5: Hud . . . 5F **138**
WF13: Dew . . . 1E **122**
Mitchell Cl. BD10: B'frd . . . 6G **46**
Mitchell La. BD10: B'frd . . . 6G **46**
BD20: Sils . . . 8E **12**
Mitchell Sq. BD5: B'frd . . . 1C **82**
BD20: Sils . . . *8E 12*
(off Elliot St.)
Mitchell St. BD21: Keigh . . . 8K **27**
HD6: Brigh . . . 9M **99**
HX6: Sow B . . . 8J **97**
HX7: Heb B . . . 2H **95**
OL14: Tod . . . 5G **92**
Mitchell's Yd. WF5: Oss . . . 4A **124**
Mitchell Ter. BD16: Bgly . . . 5E **44**
Mitford Pl. LS12: Leeds . . . 7N **67**
Mitford Rd. LS12: Leeds . . . 7N **67**
Mitford Ter. LS12: Leeds . . . 7N **67**
Mitford Vw. LS12: Leeds . . . 7N **67**
Mitre Ct. BD4: B'frd . . . 2H **83**
Mitre St. HD1: Hud . . . 3K **137**
WF13: Dew . . . 3D **122**
Mitton St. BD5: B'frd . . . 2A **82**
BD16: Cot . . . 9G **44**
MIXENDEN . . . 8J **79**
Mixenden Activity Cen. . . . 7H **79**
Mixenden Cl. HX2: Mix . . . 8J **79**
Mixenden Ct. *HX2: Mix* . . . *9K 79*
(off Jumples Cl.)
Mixenden Grn. HX2: Mix . . . 6H **79**
Mixenden La. HX2: Mix . . . 7K **79**
Mixenden La. Ends HX2: Mt T . . . 9H **79**
Mixenden Rd. HX2: Mix . . . 7J **79**
Mixenden Stones HX2: Mix . . . 7J **79**
Moat Cres. BD10: B'frd . . . 7G **46**
Moat End LS14: T'ner . . . 2G **53**
Moat Hill WF17: Birs . . . 2C **102**
Moat Hill Farm Dr. WF17: Birs . . . 2D **102**
Moat Ho. Sq. LS23: T Arch . . . 8K **25**
Mobray Dr. S75: W Gran . . . 6G **158**
Modder Av. LS12: Leeds . . . 7L **67**
Modder Pl. LS12: Leeds . . . 7L **67**
Modd La. HD9: H'frth . . . 4L **169**
Model Av. LS12: Leeds . . . 7N **67**
Model Rd. LS12: Leeds . . . 7N **67**
Model Ter. LS12: Leeds . . . 7N **67**
Moderna Bus. Pk. HX7: Myth . . . 4N **95**
Moderna Way HX7: Myth . . . 4N **95**
Moffat Cl. BD6: B'frd . . . 6L **81**
Moffatt Cl. HX3: Hal . . . 1L **97**
Moins Cl. HX2: Mix . . . 8H **79**
MOLDGREEN . . . 6F **8** (4B **138**)
Moles Head HD7: Golc . . . 4B **136**
MOLL SPRINGS . . . 4J **153**
Molly Hurst La. WF4: Wool . . . 2H **159**
Monarch Ga. BD13: Denh . . . 8L **61**
Mona's Ter. OL14: W'den . . . 1H **113**
Mona St. HD7: Slait . . . 9M **135**
WF2: Wake . . . 5G **124**
Monckton Dr. WF10: C'frd . . . 6J **109**
Monckton Rd. WF2: Wake . . . 9J **125**
Monckton Rd. Ind. Est. WF2: Wake . . . 9J **125**
Mond Av. BD3: B'frd . . . 5H **65**
Monk Barn Cl. BD16: Bgly . . . 3F **44**
Monk Bri. Av. LS6: Leeds . . . 9B **50**
Monk Bri. Dr. LS6: Leeds . . . 9B **50**
Monk Bri. Gro. LS6: Leeds . . . 9A **50**
Monk Bri. Mt. LS6: Leeds . . . 9B **50**
Monk Bri. Pl. LS6: Leeds . . . 9A **50**
Monk Bri. Rd. LS6: Leeds . . . 9A **50**
Monk Bri. St. LS6: Leeds . . . 9B **50**
Monk Bri. Ter. LS6: Leeds . . . 9A **50**
Monkfield WF14: Mir . . . 5J **121**
MONKHILL . . . 1K **129**
Monkhill Av. WF8: Pon . . . 1K **129**
Monkhill Dr. WF8: Pon . . . 1K **129**
Monkhill La. WF8: Pon . . . 8K **109**
Monkhill Mt. WF8: Pon . . . 1K **129**
Monk Ings WF17: Birs . . . 3A **102**
Monk Ings Av. WF17: Birs . . . 3N **101**
Monkmans Wharf BD20: Sils . . . 8E **12**
Monk St. BD7: B'frd . . . 7A **64**
WF1: Wake . . . 6L **9** (6M **125**)
Monkswood LS5: Leeds . . . 9J **49**
Monkswood Av. LS14: Leeds . . . 7A **52**
Monkswood Bank LS14: Leeds . . . 7A **52**
Monkswood Cl. LS14: Leeds . . . 7A **52**
Monkswood Dr. LS14: Leeds . . . 7A **52**
Monkswood Ga. LS14: Leeds . . . 7B **52**
Monkswood Grn. LS14: Leeds . . . 7A **52**
Monkswood Hill LS14: Leeds . . . 7A **52**
Monkswood Ho. LS5: Leeds . . . 2J **67**
Monkswood Ri. LS14: Leeds . . . 7A **52**
Monkswood Wlk.
LS14: Leeds . . . 7B **52**
Monkton Way S71: Roys . . . 4D **160**
Monkwood Rd. WF1: Out . . . 7K **105**
Monson Av. LS28: Cal . . . 9M **47**
Mons Rd. OL14: Tod . . . 5H **93**
Montagu Av. LS8: Leeds . . . 1K **69**
Montagu Ct. LS8: Leeds . . . 9K **51**
Montagu Cres. LS8: Leeds . . . 1L **69**
Montagu Dr. LS8: Leeds . . . 1K **69**
Montague LS12: Leeds . . . 7A **4**
Montague Ct. LS12: Leeds . . . 7K **67**
Montague Cres. LS25: Gar . . . 6A **72**
Montague Pl. LS25: Gar . . . 7A **72**
Montague St. BD5: B'frd . . . 2A **82**
HX6: Sow B . . . 9G **97**
S72: Cud . . . 9K **161**
WF1: Wake . . . 8A **126**
Montagu Gdns. LS8: Leeds . . . 1K **69**
Montagu Gro. LS8: Leeds . . . 1L **69**
Montagu La. LS22: Weth . . . 1C **24**
Montagu M. LS22: Weth . . . 1C **24**
Montagu Pl. LS8: Leeds . . . 1K **69**
Montagu Ri. LS8: Leeds . . . 1L **69**
Montagu Rd. LS22: Weth . . . 4A **24**
Montagu Vw. LS8: Leeds . . . 1K **69**
Montagu Way LS22: Weth . . . 1C **24**
Montcalm Cres. LS10: Leeds . . . 3G **87**
WF3: S'ley . . . 9A **106**
Monterey Dr. BD15: All . . . 3E **62**
Montfort Cl. LS18: Hors . . . 4E **48**
Montgomery Av. LS16: Leeds . . . 8M **49**
Montgomery Ho. *BD8: B'frd* . . . *5A 64*
(off Trenton Dr.)
Mont Gro. *BD5: B'frd* . . . *2A 82*
(off Montague St.)
Montpelier Ter. LS6: Leeds . . . 2C **68**
Montreal Av. LS7: Leeds . . . 9F **50**
Montreal St. OL14: W'den . . . 2J **113**
Montreal Ter. LS13: Leeds . . . 6D **66**
Montrose Av. S75: Dart . . . 8H **159**
Montrose Bldgs. HX7: Heb B . . . 9H **77**
Montrose Gdns. WF10: C'frd . . . 5B **108**
Montrose Pl. BD13: Que . . . 3B **80**
Montrose St. BD2: B'frd . . . 2B **64**
Montrose Ter. *HX7: Heb B* . . . *9H 77*
(off Lee Mill Rd.)
Montserrat Rd. BD4: B'frd . . . 4K **83**
Monument Dr. S72: B'ley . . . 7N **161**
Monument La. WF8: Pon . . . 4L **129**
Monument M. WF8: Pon . . . 4L **129**
Moody St. BD4: B'frd . . . 7C **6** (9D **64**)
Moon Cl. WF17: Birs . . . 3C **102**
Moon Hill Ct. LS25: Aber . . . 8E **54**
MOOR ALLERTON . . . 4E **50**
Moor Allerton Av. LS17: Leeds . . . 5G **51**
Moor Allerton Cen. LS17: Leeds . . . 5D **50**
Moor Allerton Cres. LS17: Leeds . . . 5G **51**
Moor Allerton Dr. LS17: Leeds . . . 5G **51**
Moor Allerton Gdns. LS17: Leeds . . . 5F **50**
Moor Allerton Golf Course . . . 8N **35**
Moor Allerton Hall LS8: Leeds . . . 6H **51**
Moor Allerton Way LS17: Leeds . . . 5G **51**
Moor Av. LS15: Leeds . . . 7A **70**
LS23: Cliff . . . 2D **38**
WF3: S'ley . . . 6N **105**
Moor Bank BD4: B'frd . . . 6L **83**
Moorbank Ct. LS6: Leeds . . . 1A **68**
MOOR BOTTOM . . . 4C **122**
MOORBOTTOM . . . 5F **100**
Moor Bottom HD9: Hon . . . 5L **153**
HX2: Mt T . . . 2G **96**
Moorbottom BD19: Cleck . . . 5F **100**
HD9: Hon . . . 5L **153**
Moor Bottom La. BD21: Keigh . . . 5H **43**
HX2: Lud F . . . 8B **96**
HX4: Gree . . . 2N **117**
HX6: Norl . . . 3G **117**
HX7: Crag V . . . 7N **95**
Moorbottom La. BD16: Bgly . . . 4F **44**
Moor Bottom Rd. HX2: Illing . . . 7M **79**
HX4: Bark . . . 6F **116**
Moorbottom Rd. HD1: Hud . . . 6K **137**
Moorbrook Mill Dr. HD9: New M . . . 2C **170**
Moorbrow HD9: Scho . . . 6A **170**
Moor Cl. HD4: Hud . . . 9H **137**
LS10: Leeds . . . 3F **86**
Moor Cl. Av. BD13: Que . . . 5B **80**
Moor Cl. Farm M. BD13: Que . . . 5B **80**
Moor Cl. La. BD13: Que . . . 5B **80**
Moor Cl. Pde. BD13: Que . . . 4B **80**
Moor Cl. Rd. BD13: Que . . . 5B **80**
Moorcock La. HX7: Blac H . . . 7K **75**
Moorcock Rd. HX7: Blac H . . . 8L **75**
Moor Cott. Cl. HD4: Neth . . . 2J **153**
Moor Cres. LS11: Leeds . . . 1E **86**
Moor Cres. Chase LS11: Leeds . . . 1E **86**
Moorcrest Ri. S75: S'ross . . . 7K **159**
Moor Crest Rd. HD4: Hud . . . 7H **137**
Moor Cft. BD16: Bgly . . . 2G **45**
LS16: Leeds . . . 3N **49**
Moorcroft HD7: Golc . . . 5C **136**
WF5: Oss . . . 5N **123**
WF13: Dew . . . 2D **122**
Moorcroft Av. BD3: B'frd . . . 5H **65**
BD22: Oak . . . 4E **42**
HD7: Golc . . . 5C **136**
Moorcroft Ct. *WF5: Oss* . . . *5N 123*
(off Moorcroft)
Moorcroft Dr. BD4: B'frd . . . 4K **83**
HD9: New M . . . 1B **170**
WF13: Dew . . . 2C **122**
Moorcroft Pk. Dr. HD9: New M . . . 1C **170**
Moorcroft Rd. BD4: B'frd . . . 4K **83**
WF13: Dew . . . 2C **122**
Moorcroft Ter. BD4: B'frd . . . 4K **83**
Moor Dr. BD22: Oak . . . 4C **42**
LS6: Leeds . . . 9A **50**
LS21: Otley . . . 9A **18**
LS28: Pud . . . 9C **66**
Moore Av. BD6: B'frd . . . 2L **81**
BD7: B'frd . . . 2L **81**
MOOR EDGE . . . 5N **43**
Moor Edge High Side BD16: Har . . . 5N **43**
Moor Edge Low Side BD16: Har . . . 5N **43**
Moorehouse Gro.
LS9: Leeds . . . 3K **5** (5G **68**)
MOOR END
BD2 . . . 9E **46**
HX2 . . . 9H **79**
LS12 . . . 7K **67**
LS17 . . . 6F **20**
MOOREND . . . 3H **101**
Moor End BD22: Oxen . . . 9D **42**
HX6: Norl . . . 1K **117**
LS23: B Spa . . . 9A **24**
Moor End Av. HX2: Hal . . . 3J **97**
Moor End Gdns. HX2: Hal . . . 3K **97**
LS23: B Spa . . . 9B **24**

Moor End La.—Moseley Wood La.

Moor End La. HX6: Norl 1K 117
(not continuous)
WF13: Dew 1B 122
Moor End Rd. HD4: Hud 7K 137
HX2: Hal, Mt T 8H 79
Moor End Vw. HX2: Hal 4L 97
Moore St. BD21: Keigh 1J 43
Moore Vw. BD7: B'frd 2L 81
Moor Farm Gdns. LS7: Leeds 8E 50
Moorfield HX7: Wads 8K 77
LS27: Gil 6F 84
Moorfield Av. BD3: B'frd 5H 65
BD19: Scho 5C 100
LS12: Leeds 6K 67
LS29: Men 4D 30
Moorfield Bus. Pk. LS19: Yead 1A 48
Moorfield Cl. LS19: Yead 1A 48
Moorfield Ct. LS19: Yead 1A 48
WF4: G Moor 5B 140
Moorfield Cres. LS12: Leeds 6K 67
LS19: Yead 1N 47
LS28: Pud 8A 66
WF9: Hems 3C 162
Moorfield Cft. LS19: Yead 1A 48
Moorfield Dr. BD17: Bail 2A 46
BD22: Oak 4D 42
LS19: Yead 1A 48
Moorfield Gdns. LS28: Pud 8N 65
Moorfield Gro. LS12: Leeds 6K 67
LS28: Pud 8N 65
Moorfield Ind. Est. LS19: Yead 9A 32
Moorfield Pl. BD10: B'frd 7F 46
(not continuous)
WF9: Hems 3C 162
Moor Fld. Rd. HX4: Bark 1G 135
Moorfield Rd. BD16: Cot 8F 44
HD1: Hud 1N 137
LS12: Leeds 6K 67
LS19: Yead 1A 48
LS29: I'ly 5L 15
Moorfields LS13: Leeds 3F 66
LS17: Leeds 5F 50
Moorfield Shop. Cen. HD4: Hud 6J 137
Moorfield St. HX1: Hal 8G 7 (7N 97)
LS2: Leeds 1C 4 (3C 68)
LS12: Leeds 6K 67
Moorfield Ter. LS19: Yead 9N 31
Moorfield Vw. WF15: Liv 2K 121
Moorfield Way BD19: Scho 5C 100
LS29: I'ly 5L 15
Moor Flatts Av. LS10: Leeds 8E 86
Moor Flatts Rd. LS10: Leeds 8E 86
Moor Fold HD9: New M 1C 170
MOOR GARFORTH 6N 71
Moorgarth Av. BD3: B'frd 5H 65
MOOR GATE 3A 90
Moor Ga. OL14: Tod 9L 93
Moorgate BD17: Bail 3A 46
Moorgate Av. BD3: B'frd 5H 65
LS25: Kip 2A 90
Moorgate Cl. LS25: Kip 3A 90
Moorgate Dr. LS25: Kip 3B 90
Moorgate Flats HD9: Mel 7C 152
Moorgate Ri. LS25: Kip 3A 90
Moorgate Rd. LS25: Kip 2A 90
Moorgate St. HX1: Hal 7M 97
Moor Grange LS19: Yead 1A 48
Moor Grange Ct. LS16: Leeds 7J 49
Moor Grange Dr. LS16: Leeds 7K 49
Moor Grange Ri. LS16: Leeds 7K 49
Moor Grange Vw. LS16: Leeds 7K 49
Moorgreen Fold BD10: B'frd 8E 46
Moor Gro. HX3: She 6H 81
LS28: Pud 9C 66
WF3: S'ley 6N 105
Moor Haven LS17: Leeds 4C 50
Moorhaven Ct. LS17: Leeds 4C 50
MOOR HEAD 5F 84
MOORHEAD 8K 45
Moorhead Cl. HD9: Mel 7C 152
Moorhead Cres. BD18: Ship 8K 45
Moorhead La. BD18: Ship 8K 45
Moorhead Ter. BD18: Ship 8K 45
Moorhead Vs. LS27: Gil 4E 84
Moor Hey HX4: Sow 9M 117
Moor Hey La. HD2: Fix 6H 119
HX4: Stainl 1L 135
Moor Hill Ct. HD3: Hud 2E 136
Moor Hill Rd. HD3: Hud 2E 136
MOORHOUSE 8C 164
Moorhouse BD22: Oxen 2B 60
Moorhouse Av. BD2: B'frd 1E 64
LS11: Leeds 4B 86
WF2: Wake 5J 125
WF3: S'ley 5C 106
Moorhouse Bri. BD22: Oxen 3C 60
Moorhouse Cl. BD22: Oxen 3C 60
WF3: S'ley 5C 106
WF6: Norm 9K 107
MOORHOUSE COMMON 9A 164
Moor Ho. Ct. LS17: Leeds 3K 51
Moorhouse Ct. BD22: Oxen 3C 60
WF9: S Elm 8N 163
Moorhouse Ct. M. WF9: S Elm 8N 163
Moorhouse Cres. WF2: Wake 5J 125
Moorhouse Dr. BD11: B'haw 6K 83
Moorhouse Gap DN6: Moor 8D 164
Moorhouse Gro. WF3: S'ley 5C 106
Moorhouse La. BD11: B'haw 6L 83
BD22: Oxen 2B 60
DN6: Moor 9B 164
S75: Hai 4E 158
WF4: Wint 6K 145
Moorhouse Ter. HX3: Hal 3A 98
WF3: S'ley 6C 106
Moor Ho. Vw. HX7: Blac H 9A 76
Moorhouse Vw. WF3: S'ley 5C 106
WF9: S Elm 7A 164
Moorings, The BD10: B'frd 7H 47
LS10: Leeds 2K 87
LS17: Leeds 2G 50
WF3: S'ley 6C 106
Moor Knoll Cl. WF3: E Ard 4F 104
Moor Knoll Dr. WF3: E Ard 4E 104
Moor Knoll Gdns. WF3: E Ard 3E 104
Moor Knoll La. WF3: E Ard 3E 104
Moorland Av. BD16: Bgly 2H 45
BD17: Bail 3B 46
LS6: Leeds 1A 4 (4B 68)
LS20: Guis 7J 31
LS27: Gil 5E 84
S75: S'ross 7K 159
Moorland Cl. HD7: Linth 2D 152
HX2: Illing 1L 97
LS17: Leeds 6F 50
LS27: Gil 5F 84
Moorland Cres. BD17: Bail 3B 46
LS17: Leeds 6E 50
LS20: Guis 6J 31
LS27: Gil 5E 84
LS28: Pud 6L 65
LS29: Men 6G 30
(Bradford Rd.)
LS29: Men 3E 30
(Chevin Av.)
S75: S'ross 7K 159
Moorland Dr. BD11: B'haw 6M 83
LS17: Leeds 6E 50
LS20: Guis 6J 31
LS28: Pud 5L 65
WF4: Hol 8H 143
Moorland Gdns. LS17: Leeds 6F 50
Moorland Gth. LS17: Leeds 6E 50
Moorland Gro. LS17: Leeds 5E 50
LS28: Pud 5L 65
Moorland Ho. HD4: S Cros 3G 152
Moorland Ings LS17: Leeds 6E 50
Moorland Leys LS17: Leeds 6E 50
Moorland Mills BD19: Cleck 3H 101
Moorland Mt. BD19: Cleck 6F 100
Moorland Pl. BD12: Low M 8C 82
WF3: S'ley 4N 105
Moorland Ri. HD9: Mel 8B 152
LS17: Leeds 6E 50
Moorland Rd. BD11: Drig 7B 84
LS6: Leeds 1A 4 (4B 68)
LS16: B'hpe 6E 32
LS28: Pud 5L 65
Moorlands HD9: Scho 5A 170
LS29: I'ly 7F 14
Moorlands, The LS17: Leeds 3G 51
LS22: Weth 4N 23
LS23: B Spa 9C 24
Moorlands Av. BD3: B'frd 5H 65
BD11: B'haw 6L 83
BD22: Oak 3F 42
HX2: Illing 1L 97
LS19: Yead 1A 48
WF5: Oss 3M 123
WF13: Dew 2F 122
WF14: Mir 5K 121
Moorlands Av. Nth. WF13: Dew 2E 122
Moorlands Av. W. WF13: Dew 2E 122
Moorlands Bus. Cen. *BD19: Cleck* 4H 101
(off Balme Rd.)
Moorlands Cl. WF13: Dew 9C 102
Moorlands Ct. HX4: Gree 3A 118
LS22: Weth 4N 23
Moorlands Cres. HD3: Hud 1C 136
HD9: Scho 5A 170
HX2: Illing 1L 97
Moorlands Dr. HX3: Illing 2L 97
LS19: Yead 1A 48
Moorlands Edge HD3: Hud 1C 136
Moorlands Pl. HX1: Hal 8J 7 (7A 98)
Moorlands Rd. BD11: B'haw 6L 83
HD3: Hud 1C 136
HX4: Gree 3A 118
WF13: Dew 3E 122
Moorlands Ter. WF13: Dew 2E 122
Moorlands Vw. HD8: Clay W 7K 157
HX1: Hal 8H 7 (7A 98)
LS22: Weth 4N 23
Moorland Ter. BD21: Keigh 1M 43
LS25: Gar 8M 71
Moorland Vw. BD12: Low M 8C 82
BD15: Wils 2C 62
HD8: Eml 2D 156
HX6: Sow B 9F 96
LS13: Leeds 2E 66
LS17: Leeds 5E 50
Moorland Villa HX6: Sow B 2F 116
Moorland Wlk. LS17: Leeds 5E 50
Moor La. BD11: B'haw 9N 83
BD19: Gom 2M 101
BD20: East 3A 26
HD4: Farn T 4C 154
HD4: Neth 2H 153
HD7: Slait 3L 151
HD8: Kbtn 1J 155
HD9: Nether 9H 153
HG3: Kirkby 6L 21
HX2: Illing 9L 79
HX7: Cold 6L 75
LS17: E Kes 2A 36
LS20: Guis 5J 31
LS21: Askw 3E 16
LS21: Weston 6F 16
LS22: Coll 2N 37
LS23: W'ton 4D 24
LS24: Stut, Tad 8M 39
LS29: Add 8G 10
(not continuous)
LS29: Burl W 1A 30
LS29: Men 3B 30
OL14: Tod 9K 93
S72: B'ley 8D 162
WF8: E Hard, Pon 7N 129
WF8: Pon 7K 129
WF9: Upt 2M 163
Moorlea Dr. BD17: Bail 4B 46
Moorleigh Cl. LS25: Kip 3B 90
Moorleigh Dr. LS25: Kip 3B 90
Moor Lodge Caravan Pk. LS17: Bard 7B 36
Moor Pk. Av. HD4: Hud 9H 137
LS6: Leeds 9N 49
Moor Park Bus. Cen. WF2: Wake 8J 125
Moor Pk. Cl. BD3: B'frd 6G 65
LS29: Add 1K 13
Moor Pk. Ct. WF12: Dew 2H 123
Moor Pk. Cres. LS29: Add 1K 13
Moor Pk. Dr. BD3: B'frd 6H 65
LS6: Leeds 9N 49
LS29: Add 1K 13
Moor Pk. Gdns. WF12: Dew 3H 123
Moor Pk. Gro. LS29: Add 1L 13
Moor Pk. La. WF12: Dew 3H 123
Moor Pk. Mt. LS6: Leeds 9N 49
Moor Pk. Rd. BD3: B'frd 6G 65
Moor Pk. Vs. LS6: Leeds 9A 50
Moor Pk. Way LS29: Add 1L 13
Moor Rd. LS6: Leeds 9N 49
LS10: Leeds 1F 86
LS11: Leeds 1E 86
LS16: B'hpe 5G 33
LS29: Burl W, I'ly 8K 15
OL15: Lit 9L 113
WF3: S'ley 6N 105
WF7: F'stne 6D 128
Moor Road Station
Middleton Railway 2F 86
Moor Royd HD9: Hon 6K 153
HX3: Hal 8N 97
Moors Centre, The *LS29: I'ly* 5G 14
(off Cunliffe Rd.)
Moorshutt Rd. WF9: Hems 3C 162
MOOR SIDE
BD2 4F 64
BD12 8A 82
MOORSIDE
BD11 8C 84
LS13 2F 66
Moor Side LS23: B Spa 9B 24
Moorside BD9: B'frd 4K 63
BD17: Bail 2A 46
BD19: Cleck 6E 100
(not continuous)
BD22: Oxen 2A 60
Moorside App. BD11: Drig 8C 84
Moorside Av. BD2: B'frd 4G 65
BD11: B'haw 6L 83
BD11: Drig 8C 84
BD20: East 3A 26
HD4: Hud 6J 137
WF13: Dew 1C 122
Moorside Cl. BD2: B'frd 3G 65
BD11: Drig 8C 84
S75: Map 9K 159
Moorside Ct. LS29: I'ly 6H 15
Moorside Cres. BD11: Drig 8B 84
WF4: Hol 8H 143
WF13: Dew 1C 122
Moorside Cft. BD2: B'frd 4G 65
Moorside Dr. BD11: Drig 8C 84
LS13: Leeds 2F 66
MOORSIDE EDGE 7L 135
Moorside End WF13: Dew 1C 122
Moorside Fold BD13: Que 3A 80
Moorside Gdns. BD2: B'frd 3G 65
BD11: Drig 8C 84
HX3: Hal 9M 79
Moorside Grn. BD11: Drig 7C 84
Moor Side La. HD7: Slait 7K 135
Moorside La. BD3: B'frd 7H 65
BD22: Haw, Oxen 1N 59
LS21: Askw 2D 16
LS29: Add 5L 13
Moorside Maltings LS11: Leeds 1E 86
Moorside Mdws. BD2: B'frd 4H 65
Moorside M. BD2: B'frd 3G 65
Moorside Mt. BD11: Drig 8B 84
Moorside Paddock BD19: Cleck 6F 100
Moorside Pde. BD11: Drig 8C 84
Moorside Pl. BD3: B'frd 7H 65
WF13: Dew 1C 122
Moorside Ri. BD19: Cleck 5F 100
Moorside Rd. BD2: B'frd 2G 64
BD3: B'frd 7H 65
(off Moorside La.)
BD11: Drig 8B 84
BD15: Wils 2B 62
HD5: K'htn 9G 120
HD9: Hon 6K 153
WF13: Dew 1C 122
Moorside St. BD12: Low M 7N 81
LS13: Leeds 2F 66
Moorside Ter. BD2: B'frd 4H 65
BD11: Drig 8C 84
HD5: K'htn 1G 138
LS13: Leeds 2F 66
Moorside Va. BD11: Drig 7C 84
Moorside Vw. BD11: Drig 8C 84
Moorside Wlk. BD11: Drig 7C 84
Moor Smith Copse HX2: Illing 6L 79
Moor Stone Pl. HX3: She 8H 81
Moor St. BD13: Que 4D 80
BD22: Oak 4D 42
Moor Ter. *BD2: B'frd* 5G 64
(off Higher Intake Rd.)
MOORTHORPE 6M 163
Moorthorpe Av. BD3: B'frd 5H 65
Moorthorpe Station (Rail) 6L 163
MOOR TOP
BD6 7N 81
LS12 7L 67
WF14 3J 121
Moor Top BD11: Drig 7A 84
(not continuous)
LS12: N Far 3F 84
LS20: Guis 3H 31
LS29: Men 3H 31
WF14: Mir 5J 121
Moor Top Av. HD4: Thurs 7D 154
WF7: Ackw 5E 146
Moor Top Dr. WF9: Hems 4D 162
Moor Top Gdns. HX2: Illing 5L 79
Moor Top La. WF4: Flock 9A 140
Moor Top Rd. BD12: Low M 7N 81
HD5: K'htn 9G 120
HX2: Hal 4H 97
MOORTOWN 4F 50
Moortown Cnr. LS17: Leeds 5F 50
Moortown Golf Course 2F 50
Moorvale HD7: Mars 4G 151
Moor Valley Pk. LS20: Hawk 9A 30
Moor Vw. BD4: B'frd 6L 83
HD9: Mel 6B 152
LS6: Leeds 3B 68
(off Hyde Pk. Rd.)
LS11: Leeds 9C 68
LS12: Leeds 7L 67
LS19: Yead 9A 32
WF4: Crig 5H 143
WF4: Flock 7F 140
WF14: Mir 2L 121
WF16: Heck 1B 122
Moorview LS26: Meth 1N 107
Moor Vw. Av. BD18: Ship 7M 45
Moor Vw. Cl. WF10: C'frd 5F 108
Moor Vw. Ct. BD20: Rid 9B 28
Moorview Ct. *BD10: B'frd* 6E 46
(off Northlea Av.)
Moor Vw. Cres. BD16: Cot 9D 44
Moorview Cft. LS29: Men 3D 30
Moorview Dr. BD16: Cot 9D 44
BD18: Ship 8D 46
Moorview Gro. BD21: Keigh 2K 43
Moor Vw. Ter. BD22: S'bury 8L 41
Moorville Av. BD3: B'frd 5H 65
Moorville Cl. LS11: Leeds 1D 86
Moorville Ct. LS11: Leeds 1D 86
Moorville Dr. BD11: B'haw 6L 83
Moorville Gro. LS11: Leeds 1C 86
Moorville Rd. LS11: Leeds 1D 86
Moor Way BD22: Oak 4C 42
Moorway LS20: Guis 7F 30
Moorwell Pl. BD2: B'frd 2G 64
Moravia Bank *LS28: Pud* 9B 66
(off Fartown)
Moravian Museum & Settlement 9B 66
Moravian Pl. BD5: B'frd 1B 82
Moravian Ter. *HX3: Hip* 5J 99
(off Victoria Rd.)
Morefield Bank HD9: T'bdge 9A 154
More Fitness
Heckmondwike 7K 101
More Pleasant HD3: Outl 3M 135
Moresby Rd. BD6: B'frd 7K 81
Moresdale La. LS14: Leeds 3A 70
MORLEY 9K 85
Morley Av. BD3: B'frd 5H 65
WF11: Knot 8F 110
Morley Bottoms LS27: Morl 8K 85
MORLEY CARR 8B 82
Morley Carr Rd. BD12: Low M 8B 82
Morley Fold HD8: Den D 3C 172
Morley Hall La. HX2: Lud F 6C 96
Morley Hall Ter. HX2: Lud F 6C 96
MORLEY HOLE 8J 85
Morley La. HD3: Hud 6F 136
Morley Leisure Cen. 9K 85
Morley Mkt. *LS27: Morl* 9K 85
(off Hope St.)
Morley Station (Rail) 8M 85
Morley St. BD7: B'frd 6A 6 (8B 64)
Morley Vw. HX3: Hal 9D 98
Morningside BD8: B'frd 5N 63
BD13: Denh 4K 61
Morning St. BD21: Keigh 3H 43
Mornington Rd. BD16: Bgly 4F 44
LS29: I'ly 5H 15
Mornington St. BD21: Keigh 8H 27
Mornington Vs. BD8: B'frd 5B 64
Morpeth Pl. LS9: Leeds 8K 5 (7G 68)
Morpeth St. BD7: B'frd 7A 64
BD13: Que 4D 80
Morrell Ct. BD4: B'frd 2H 83
Morrell Cres. WF2: Wren 9H 105
Morris Av. LS5: Leeds 1K 67
Morris Cl. WF9: Kins 8B 146
Morris Flds. WF6: Norm 2K 127
Morris Gro. LS5: Leeds 2K 67
Morris La. LS5: Leeds 1K 67
Morris Mt. LS5: Leeds 2K 67
Morrison St. WF10: C'frd 5E 108
Morris Pl. LS27: Morl 8J 85
Morris Vw. LS5: Leeds 2K 67
Morritt Av. LS15: Leeds 5C 70
Morritt Dr. LS15: Leeds 6A 70
Morritt Gro. LS15: Leeds 6A 70
Mortec Pk. LS15: Leeds 8F 52
Mortimer Av. BD3: B'frd 5H 65
WF17: Bat 7C 102
Mortimer Cl. LS25: Gar 7M 71
Mortimer Ri. WF5: Oss 5B 124
Mortimer Row BD3: B'frd 7H 65
WF4: Horb 1B 142
Mortimer St. BD8: B'frd 6L 63
BD19: Cleck 5H 101
WF17: Bat 7C 102
Mortimer Ter. WF17: Bat 7C 102
Morton Cres. WF10: C'frd 5F 108
Morton Grn. HD5: Hud 6E 138
Morton Gro. BD20: E Mor 8C 28
WF12: Dew 8E 122
Morton La. BD16: Bgly 1C 44
BD20: E Mor 8C 28
Morton Pde. WF2: Wake 5J 125
Morton Rd. BD4: B'frd 9H 65
Mortons, The HD3: Hud 2E 136
Mortons Cl. HX3: Hal 9D 98
Morton Ter. LS20: Guis 7H 31
Morton Way HD3: Hud 1D 136
Morton Wood Gro. HD9: Scho 5B 170
Morvern Mdws. WF9: Hems 2F 162
Morwick Gro. LS15: Scho 9G 52
Morwick Ter. LS14: Leeds 7F 52
Moselden La. HX6: Rish 4C 134
Moseley Pl. LS6: Leeds 3D 68
Moseley Wood App. LS16: Leeds 3G 48
Moseley Wood Av. LS16: Leeds 1G 49
Moseley Wood Bank LS16: Leeds 2G 48
Moseley Wood Cl. LS16: Leeds 3G 48
Moseley Wood Cres. LS16: Leeds 2G 48
Moseley Wood Cft. LS16: Leeds 3F 48
Moseley Wood Dr. LS16: Leeds 2G 48
Moseley Wood Gdns. LS16: Leeds 2G 48
Moseley Wood Grn. LS16: Leeds 2G 48
Moseley Wood Gro. LS16: Leeds 2G 48
Moseley Wood La. LS16: Leeds 2H 49

Moseley Wood Ri.—Navigation Yd.

Moseley Wood Ri. LS16: Leeds 2G 48
Moseley Wood Vw. LS16: Leeds 1H 49
Moseley Wood Wlk. LS16: Leeds 2G 48
Moseley Wood Way LS16: Leeds 1G 49
Moser Av. BD2: B'frd 1E 64
Moser Cres. BD2: B'frd 1E 64
Mosley Ho. *BD4: B'frd 9H 65*
(off Parsonage Rd.)
Mosley La. HD8: Shel 6N 155
Moss Bri. Rd. LS13: Leeds 1C 66
Moss Brook Ct. LS29: Burl W 1E 30
Moss Carr Av. BD21: Keigh 2M 43
Moss Carr Gro. BD21: Keigh 2M 43
Moss Carr Rd. BD21: Keigh 2M 43
Moss Carr Ter. BD21: Keigh 1M 43
Mossdale Av. BD9: B'frd 3H 63
Moss Dr. HX2: Illing 7L 79
Moss Edge Rd. HD9: Holm 8H 169
Moss Edge Vw. HD9: Holm 6H 169
Moss Gdns. LS17: Leeds 2C 50
Moss Hall La. HX7: Blac H 9N 75
Moss La. HX2: Illing 7L 79
HX7: Heb B 9H 77
Moss Lea LS27: Chur 6L 85
Moss Ri. HD9: U'thng 3K 169
LS17: Leeds 2C 50
Moss Row BD15: Wils 9B 44
Moss Side BD9: B'frd 4K 63
Moss Side St. OL12: Whit 6A 112
Moss St. BD13: Thorn 7B 62
BD22: Cros R 7E 42
HD4: Hud 8D 8 (6N 137)
WF10: C'frd 4B 108
Moss Syke LS14: S'cft 8D 36
Mosstree Cl. BD13: Que 3B 80
Moss Valley LS17: Leeds 2C 50
Mossy Bank Cl. BD13: Que 3D 80
Mostyn Gro. BD6: B'frd 5M 81
Mostyn Mt. HX3: Hal 1N 97
Mostyn Wlk. WF4: Hol 7H 143
Mothers Way WF5: Oss 5E 124
Moth Hole La. HX7: Hept 5M 75
Motley La. LS20: Guis 6J 31
Motley Row *LS20: Guis 6J 31*
(off Motley La.)
Mould Greave BD22: Oxen 2B 60
Mouldson Pl. HX4: Bark 4J 117
Moule Ri. LS25: Gar 5B 72
Moulson Cl. BD6: B'frd 4N 81
Moulson Ct. BD5: B'frd 2C 82
Moulson Ter. BD13: Denh 6K 61
Moulton Chase WF9: Hems 2E 162
MOUNT 2C 136
Mount, The BD17: Bail 5B 46
LS15: Bar E 9L 53
LS15: Leeds 5C 70
LS17: Leeds 1D 50
LS19: Raw 4A 48
LS25: Kip 6A 90
LS26: Rothw 6A 88
LS27: Chur 6L 85
(off Elland Rd.)
OL14: Tod 6L 93
WF2: Wake 8H 125
WF2: Wren 2F 124
WF6: Norm 1J 127
WF8: Pon 3J 129
WF10: C'frd 5J 109
WF17: Birs 2B 102
MOUNTAIN 3B 80
Mountain Cres. WF12: T'hill 9G 122
Mountain Rd. WF12: T'hill 9G 122
Mountain Vw. BD18: Ship 9B 46
HX2: Illing 7N 79
WF12: T'hill 9G 122
(off Edge Top Rd.)
Mountain Way HD5: K'htn 3G 139
Mount Av. BD2: B'frd 1F 64
HD3: Hud 1C 136
HX2: Hal 5J 97
S72: Grim 9A 162
WF2: Wren 9H 105
WF9: Hems 1D 162
WF16: Heck 6B 102
WF17: Bat 9G 102
(off Mount St.)
Mountbatten Av. WF1: Out 7L 105
WF2: Wake 3N 143
Mountbatten Ct. BD5: B'frd 3C 82
Mountbatten Cres. WF1: Out 7L 105
Mountbatten Gdns. HD3: Hud 3G 137
Mountbatten Gro. WF1: Out 8M 105
Mountcliffe Vw. LS27: Chur 6L 85
Mount Cres. BD19: Cleck 4H 101
HX2: Hal 5J 97
WF2: Wake 8H 125
Mount Dr. LS17: Leeds 1D 50
Mountfield Av. HD5: Hud 5F 138
Mountfield Rd. HD5: Hud 5F 138
Mountfields HX3: Hip 4K 99
LS2: Leeds 3A 4
Mountfields Wlk. WF9: S Kirk 8H 163
Mount Gdns. BD19: Cleck 4H 101
LS17: Leeds 1D 50
Mount Gro. BD2: B'frd 1F 64
Mountjoy Rd. HD1: Hud 3K 137
Mount La. HD6: Ras 4K 119
OL14: Tod 1E 92
Mountleigh Cl. BD4: B'frd 7E 82
Mt. Pellon HX2: Hal 4L 97
Mt. Pellon Rd. HX2: Hal 4L 97
Mt. Pisgah LS21: Otley 1L 31
Mt. Pisgah Ter. *LS21: Otley 1L 31*
(off Well Hill)
Mount Pl. BD18: Ship 7M 45
OL14: W'den 2J 113
MOUNT PLEASANT
LS25 4B 90
WF17 9F 102
Mount Pleasant 9F 102
Mt. Pleasant BD6: B'frd 6K 81
BD9: B'frd 4A 64
BD13: Denh 6K 61
BD17: Bail 4A 46
BD19: Cleck 5K 101
Mt. Pleasant BD20: Rid 9B 28
HD1: Hud 7L 137
HD6: Ras 4K 119
HD7: Golc 6C 136
(off Knowl Rd.)
HD8: Eml 2G 156
HX2: Midg 3C 96
HX3: Sou 8F 98
(off Cain La.)
HX6: Ripp 7E 116
HX6: Sow B 9D 96
LS10: Leeds 8E 86
LS13: Leeds 2E 66
LS18: Hors 7G 49
(off Broadgate La.)
LS20: Guis 6J 31
LS25: Kip 5B 90
LS28: Stan 5A 66
(off Westbourne Pl.)
LS29: Add 1M 13
LS29: I'ly 6H 15
OL14: Tod 7K 93
S72: Grim 9A 162
WF4: Croft 8B 126
WF7: Ackw 4F 146
WF8: Lit S 4M 149
WF10: C'frd 5F 108
WF12: Dew 4H 123
Mt. Pleasant Av. HX1: Hal 2H 7 (4A 98)
LS8: Leeds 1H 69
Mt. Pleasant Ct. LS28: Pud 6B 66
Mt. Pleasant Dr. HX7: Myth 3M 95
Mt. Pleasant Gdns. *LS8: Leeds 1H 69*
(off Sycamore Av.)
LS25: Kip 5B 90
Mt. Pleasant Hgts. *LS28: Pud 6B 66*
(off Mt. Pleasant Rd.)
Mt. Pleasant La. HD8: Fen B 6G 138
Mt. Pleasant Mills *HX7: Myth 3M 95*
(off Midgley Rd.)
Mt. Pleasant Rd. LS28: Pud 6B 66
Mt. Pleasant St. BD13: Que 4D 80
HD5: Hud 4B 138
LS28: Pud 6C 66
OL14: Tod 3C 92
WF7: F'stne 5D 128
Mt. Preston LS2: Leeds 3B 4
Mt. Preston St. LS2: Leeds 3B 4 (5C 68)
Mount Ri. LS17: Leeds 1D 50
Mount Rd. BD2: B'frd 1G 64
BD6: B'frd 4M 81
HD1: Hud 4J 137
HD7: Mars 8B 150
S72: Grim 9A 162
WF3: S'ley 6A 106
Mount Royal HX4: Sow 1M 135
LS18: Hors 7E 48
Mount Royd BD8: B'frd 4B 64
Mt. Royd Cotts. *DN6: Nort 7N 149*
(off Ryecroft Rd.)
Mt. Scar Vw. HD9: Scho 4B 170
Mount St. BD2: B'frd 1F 64
BD3: B'frd 5F 6 (8E 64)
BD4: B'frd 8F 64
BD19: Cleck 4H 101
BD21: Keigh 9H 27
HD1: Hud 7L 137
HD4: Hud 6F 136
HX1: Hal 4K 7 (5B 98)
HX6: Sow B 8H 97
OL14: Tod 6K 93
(off Meadow Bottom Rd.)
WF17: Bat 9G 102
Mount St. W. HX2: Hal 4L 97
MOUNT TABOR 1G 97
Mt. Tabor Rd. HX2: Mt T 8F 78
Mt. Tabor St. LS28: Pud 7N 65
Mount Ter. BD2: B'frd 1F 64
HX2: Hal 4L 97
HX2: Midg 3C 96
HX6: Sow B 8H 97
WF17: Bat 9F 102
Mt. Vernon Rd. LS19: Raw 3N 47
Mount Vw. BD13: Que 4C 80
BD16: Bgly 4G 44
BD22: Oak 5B 42
HX2: Mt T 1G 97
LS27: Chur 6L 85
OL14: Tod 6K 93
WF10: C'frd 5D 108
Mount Vw. Ct. BD19: Cleck 4G 100
Mount Vw. Rd. HD9: H'wth 6C 170
Mount Wlk. WF10: C'frd 7D 108
Mt. Zion Ct. OL14: Tod 3C 92
Mt. Zion Rd. HD5: Hud 5F 8 (4A 138)
Mourning Fld. La.
WF8: Thpe A 7C 148
Mouse Hole La. WF14: Mir 1A 140
Moverley Flats WF8: Pon 4L 129
Moverley St. OL14: W'den 4K 113
Moverley Way WF10: C'frd 6G 109
Mowat Ct. WF15: Liv 7F 100
Mowbray Chase LS26: W'frd 6C 88
Mowbray Cl. BD13: Cull 1J 61
Mowbray Ct. LS14: Leeds 3B 70
WF11: Knot 7G 110
Mowbray Cres. LS14: Leeds 3B 70
Mowell Cft. WF8: D'ton 7D 130
Moxon Cl. WF8: Pon 5K 129
Moxon Gro. WF1: Wake 9K 105
Moxon Pl. WF2: Wake 6E 124
Moxon Sq. WF1: Wake 2M 9 (4M 125)
(not continuous)
Moxon St. WF1: Out 8L 105
Moxon Way WF1: Out 8L 105
Moynihan Cl. LS8: Leeds 2K 69
Mozart Way LS27: Chur 5M 85
Mozeley Dr. HX2: Illing 7M 79
Mucky La. HX4: Holy 7C 118
Muddy La. LS22: Lin 6J 23
Muffit La. BD19: Gom 4N 101
Muff St. BD4: B'frd 9F 64
Muff Ter. BD6: B'frd 4M 81
Mug Mill La. WF12: T'hill 2H 141
Mugup La. HD9: H'wth 7C 170
Muir Ct. *LS6: Leeds 2N 67*
(off Sagar Pl.)
Muirfield Av. WF7: F'stne 2C 128
Muirfield Cl. S72: Cud 8K 161
Muirfield Dr. WF2: Wake 9J 125
Muirfields, The S75: Dart 8J 159
Muirhead Ct. BD4: B'frd 3J 83
Muirhead Dr. BD4: B'frd 3J 83
Muirhead Fold BD4: B'frd 3J 83
Muirlands, The HD2: Hud 6C 120
Mulberry Av. LS16: Leeds 3N 49
WF4: Ryh 9J 145
Mulberry Chase LS21: Pool 2G 33
Mulberry Ct. HD7: Golc 5D 136
Mulberry Gdns. LS26: Meth 2J 107
Mulberry Gth. LS16: Leeds 4A 50
LS23: T Arch 8E 24
Mulberry Ho. WF1: Wake 4H 9
WF10: C'frd 5E 108
(off Parklands)
Mulberry La. BD20: Stee 3C 26
Mulberry Pl. WF4: Ryh 9J 145
Mulberry Ri. LS16: Leeds 3N 49
Mulberry St. BD21: Keigh 8K 27
HD5: Hud 6F 8 (5A 138)
LS28: Pud 7B 66
Mulberry Ter. *HD1: Hud 1C 8*
(off Calton St.)
Mulberry Vw. LS16: Leeds 4N 49
Mulberry Way HX3: North 9F 80
WF1: Wake 4H 9 (5K 125)
Mulcture Hall Rd. HX1: Hal 3M 7 (5C 98)
Mulehouse La. HD3: Outl 1A 136
Mulgrave St. BD3: B'frd 8F 64
Mulhalls Mill HX6: Sow B 8J 97
Mullins Ct. LS9: Leeds 8M 5 (7H 69)
Mullion Av. HD9: Hon 5K 153
Mullions, The OL14: W'den 4H 113
Mumford St. BD5: B'frd 2C 82
Munby St. BD8: B'frd 7K 63
Muncaster Rd. LS25: Gar 6B 72
Munster St. BD4: B'frd 2F 82
Munton Cl. BD6: B'frd 7K 81
Murdoch St. BD21: Keigh 8M 27
Murdstone Cl. BD5: B'frd 2C 82
Murgatroyd St. BD5: B'frd 3C 82
(not continuous)
BD18: Ship 7N 45
Murking La. HX7: Hept 7E 76
Murray Av. LS10: Leeds 9G 87
Murray Ct. LS18: Hors 7H 49
Murray Dr. LS10: Leeds 9G 87
Murray Rd. HD2: Hud 2L 137
Murray St. BD5: B'frd 2A 82
Murray Vw. LS10: Leeds 9G 86
Murray Way LS10: Leeds 9G 87
Murton Cl. LS14: Leeds 2B 70
Murton Gro. *BD20: Stee 3D 26*
(off East Pde.)
Museum Ct. BD2: B'frd 4G 65
Museum St. LS9: Leeds 3M 5 (5H 69)
Musgrave Bank LS13: Leeds 4H 67
Musgrave Bldgs. LS28: Pud 6C 66
Musgrave Ct. LS28: Pud 7B 66
WF2: Wake 6F 124
Musgrave Dr. BD2: B'frd 4G 65
Musgrave Gro. BD2: B'frd 4G 65
Musgrave Mt. BD2: B'frd 4G 65
LS13: Leeds 4H 67
Musgrave Ri. LS13: Leeds 4H 67
Musgrave Rd. BD2: B'frd 4G 64
Musgrave St. WF17: Birs 3B 102
Musgrave Vw. LS13: Leeds 4H 67
Musgrove Ho. *LS5: Leeds 2J 67*
(off Broad La.)
Mushroom St. LS9: Leeds 3J 5 (5F 68)
Musselburgh St. BD7: B'frd 7A 64
Mutton Fold *HX3: North 2F 98*
(off Towngate)
Mutton La. BD15: All 4C 62
Myers Av. BD2: B'frd 2E 64
Myers Cl. BD10: B'frd 7F 46
Myers Ct. HD8: Kbtn 3G 154
Myers Cft. HD5: Hud 4D 138
LS21: Otley 1L 31
WF4: Horb 2C 142
Myers Dr. LS13: Leeds 9E 48
Myers La. BD2: B'frd 2E 64
Myrtle Av. BD16: Bgly 5E 44
HX2: Illing 9L 79
WF13: Raven 6B 122
Myrtle Bank HX3: Hal 8C 98
Myrtle Ct. BD16: Bgly 5E 44
Myrtle Dr. BD22: Cros R 6F 42
HX2: Illing 9L 79
Myrtle Gdns. HX2: Illing 9L 79
Myrtle Gro. BD13: Que 6B 80
BD16: Bgly 5E 44
HD3: Hud 4G 136
HX2: Illing 9L 79
HX6: Ripp 5E 116
HX7: Heb B 9J 77
HX7: Myth 4M 95
(off Scout Rd.)
Myrtle La. LS29: Burl W 3B 30
Myrtle Pl. BD16: Bgly 4E 44
BD18: Ship 7L 45
HX2: Illing 9L 79
Myrtle Rd. HD7: Golc 6C 136
HX5: Ell 6E 118
WF13: Raven 6B 122
Myrtle St. BD3: B'frd 8G 64
BD16: Bgly 4F 44
HD1: Hud 2C 8 (3N 137)
OL14: Tod 7K 93
Myrtle Ter. BD22: Cros R 6F 42
HX6: Sow B 8H 97
Myrtle Vw. BD22: Oak 4D 42
Myrtle Wlk. *BD16: Bgly 4E 44*
(off Main St.)
Myson Av. WF8: Pon 8M 109
MYTHOLM 1F 94
Mytholm Bank HX7: Heb B 1F 94
MYTHOLM BRIDGE 8A 154
Mytholm Cl. HX7: Heb B 1G 94
Mytholm Ct. HX7: Heb B 1F 94
MYTHOLMES 7C 42
Mytholmes BD22: Haw 7C 42
Mytholmes La. BD22: Haw, Oak 8C 42
Mytholmes Ter. BD22: Haw 7C 42
Mytholm Mdws. HX7: Heb B 1F 94
MYTHOLMROYD 3M 95
Mytholmroyd Community and Leisure Cen. 4M 95
Mytholmroyd Station (Rail) 4M 95

N

NAB 5J 121
Nab, The HD1: Hud 5H 137
WF14: Mir 5J 121
Nabbs La. HD7: Slait 1M 151
Nabb Vw. HD9: H'frth 4N 169
Nab Cres. HD9: Mel 7B 152
Nab Cft. WF14: Mir 5J 121
Nabcroft La. HD4: Hud 6J 137
Nabcroft Ri. HD4: Hud 6J 137
NAB END 3H 81
Nab End BD12: Wyke 2B 100
Nab End Rd. HX4: Gree 4C 118
Nab La. BD18: Ship 8J 45
WF14: Mir 5J 121
WF17: Birs 2D 102
(not continuous)
Naburn App. LS14: Leeds 6C 52
Naburn Chase LS14: Leeds 8D 52
Naburn Cl. LS14: Leeds 8D 52
Naburn Ct. LS14: Leeds 7C 52
Naburn Dr. LS14: Leeds 8C 52
Naburn Fold LS14: Leeds 8D 52
Naburn Gdns. LS14: Leeds 8C 52
Naburn Grn. LS14: Leeds 8C 52
Naburn Pl. LS14: Leeds 7C 52
Naburn Rd. LS14: Leeds 8C 52
Naburn Vw. LS14: Leeds 8D 52
Naburn Wlk. LS14: Leeds 8C 52
Nab Vw. BD20: Sils 6F 12
Nab Water La. BD22: Oxen 8B 60
NAB WOOD 8J 45
Nab Wood Bank BD18: Ship 8J 45
Nab Wood Cl. BD18: Ship 8K 45
Nab Wood Crematorium BD18: Ship 7J 45
Nab Wood Cres. BD18: Ship 8J 45
Nab Wood Dr. BD18: Ship 9J 45
Nab Wood Gdns. BD18: Ship 8K 45
Nab Wood Gro. BD18: Ship 8J 45
Nab Wood Mt. BD18: Ship 8J 45
Nab Wood Pl. BD18: Ship 8J 45
Nab Wood Ri. BD18: Ship 8J 45
Nab Wood Rd. BD18: Ship 9J 45
Nab Wood School Sports Cen. 8H 45
Nab Wood Ter. BD18: Ship 8J 45
Naden Cl. BD6: B'frd 3H 81
Nags La. LS22: Weth 4N 23
Nairn Cl. HD4: Hud 8H 137
Nancroft Cres. LS12: Leeds 7M 67
Nancroft Mt. LS12: Leeds 7M 67
Nancroft Ter. LS12: Leeds 7M 67
Nann Hall Glade BD19: Cleck 3J 101
Nanny Goat La. LS25: Gar 6L 71
Nansen Av. LS13: Leeds 4E 66
Nansen Gro. LS13: Leeds 4E 66
Nansen Mt. LS13: Leeds 4E 66
Nansen Pl. LS13: Leeds 4E 66
Nansen St. LS13: Leeds 4D 66
Nansen Ter. LS13: Leeds 4E 66
Nansen Vw. LS13: Leeds 4E 66
Naomi Rd. HD4: Hud 8M 137
Napier Rd. BD3: B'frd 7H 65
HX5: Ell 5D 118
Napier St. BD3: B'frd 7H 65
BD13: Que 4E 80
BD21: Keigh 1K 43
Napier Ter. BD3: B'frd 7H 65
Naples St. BD8: B'frd 5N 63
Napoleon Bus. Pk. BD4: B'frd 9F 64
Nares St. BD21: Keigh 9H 27
BD22: Cros R 7E 42
Narrowboat Wharf LS13: Leeds 1C 66
Narrow La. BD16: Har 6A 44
Narrows, The BD16: Har 6A 44
Naseby Gdns. LS9: Leeds 5K 5 (6G 68)
Naseby Gth. LS9: Leeds 4K 5 (5G 68)
Naseby Grange LS9: Leeds 5K 5
Naseby Ho. BD4: B'frd 4K 83
Naseby Pl. LS9: Leeds 5K 5 (6G 68)
Naseby Ri. BD13: Que 4E 80
Naseby Ter. LS9: Leeds 5L 5 (6G 69)
Naseby Vw. LS9: Leeds 5K 5 (6G 68)
Naseby Wlk. LS9: Leeds 5L 5 (6G 69)
Nashville Rd. BD22: Keigh 1G 43
Nashville St. BD22: Keigh 1G 43
Nashville Ter. *BD22: Keigh 1G 43*
(off Salisbury Rd.)
Nassau Pl. LS7: Leeds 3G 68
Nateby Ri. WF3: Carl 1M 105
Nathaniel Waterhouse Homes HX1: Hal 5K 7
Nathan La. HX6: Mill B 4C 116
Nathans Folly HX6: Mill B 4D 116
National Coalmining Museum for England 5H 141
National Media Mus. 5A 6 (8C 64)
National Pk. LS10: Leeds 1G 87
National Rd. LS10: Leeds 9G 69
Nat La. LS17: Huby 4K 19
Natty Flds. Cl. HX2: Illing 6L 79
Natty La. HX2: Illing 6L 79
Nature Way BD6: B'frd 6K 81
Nautilus Weight Management 2J 129
Navigation Cl. HX5: Ell 3F 118
Navigation Ct. LS13: Leeds 9B 48
WF2: Wake 1J 143
Navigation Dr. BD10: B'frd 7J 47
Navigation Gdns. WF12: Dew 7E 122
Navigation Ri. HD3: Hud 6H 137
Navigation Rd. HX3: Hal 5M 7 (6C 98)
WF10: C'frd 3D 108
WF12: Dew 7E 122
Navigation Wlk. LS10: Leeds 8G 5 (7E 68)
WF1: Wake 8L 9 (7M 125)
Navigation Yd. WF1: Wake 7M 9 (6M 125)

Navvy La.—New Mill

Navvy La. S71: Roys .2E 160
Naylor Ct. WF13: Dew .2G 122
Naylor Gth. LS6: Leeds .1B 68
Naylor La. HX2: Midg .4C 96
Naylor Pl. LS11: Leeds .1D 86
Naylor's Bldgs. BD19: Scho .4D 100 (off Tabbs La.)
Naylor St. HX1: Hal .5M 97
WF5: Oss .3M 123
WF13: Dew .1E 122
Naze Rd. OL14: Tod .1H 113
Naze Vw. OL14: Tod .9H 93
Neale Rd. HD1: Hud .7L 137
Neale St. HX7: Heb B .2H 95
Neal St. BD5: B'frd .6A 6 (8C 64)
Near Bank HD8: Shel .6M 155
Nearcliffe Rd. BD9: B'frd .4M 63
Near Crook BD10: B'frd .6D 46
Near Highfield BD22: Oak .4C 42
Near Hob Cote BD22: Oak .6A 42
Near La. HD9: Mel .7D 152
Near Peat La. BD22: Oxen .7A 60
Near Royd HX3: Hal .1N 97
Neath Gdns. LS9: Leeds .3M 69
Necropolis Rd. BD7: B'frd .9L 63
Ned Hill Rd. HX2: Ogd .3L 79
Ned La. BD4: B'frd .1J 83
HD7: Slait .1M 151
Needless Inn La. LS26: W'frd .6D 88
NEILEY .5N 153
Nell Gap Av. WF4: M'twn .3K 141
Nell Gap Cres. WF4: Over .4K 141
Nell Gap La. WF4: M'twn .3K 141 (not continuous)
Nelson Ct. LS26: Meth .1L 107
LS27: Morl .2J 103
LS29: I'ly .5G 15 (off Nelson Rd.)
Nelson Cft. LS25: Gar .8L 71
Nelson Pl. BD13: Que .4D 80
HX6: Sow B .8K 97
LS27: Morl .8K 85 (off Croft Ho. Rd.)
Nelson Rd. LS29: I'ly .5G 15
Nelson St. BD1: B'frd .6B 6 (8C 64)
BD5: B'frd .6B 6 (8C 64)
BD13: Que .4D 80
BD15: All .5H 63
BD22: Cros R .7E 42 (Albion St.)
BD22: Cros R .7E 42 (East Ter.)
HD1: Hud .6L 137
HX6: Sow B .8J 97
LS21: Otley .1L 31
OL14: W'den .3J 113
S72: S Hien .4M 161
WF6: Norm .9K 107
WF13: Dew .3F 122
WF15: Liv .9M 101
WF17: Bat .7D 102
WF17: Birs .3C 102
Nene St. BD5: B'frd .1A 82
Nepshaw La. LS27: Gil .9G 85
LS27: Morl .8J 85
Nepshaw La. Nth. LS27: Morl .8H 85
Nepshaw La. Sth. LS27: Gil .8H 85
Neptune St. LS9: Leeds .8J 5 (7F 68)
Neptune Way HD2: Hud .8D 120
NESFIELD .2B 14
Nesfield Cl. LS10: Leeds .7H 87
Nesfield Cres. LS10: Leeds .7H 87
Nesfield Gdns. LS10: Leeds .7G 87
Nesfield Gth. LS10: Leeds .7G 87
Nesfield Grn. LS10: Leeds .7G 87
Nesfield La. LS29: Nes .1B 14
Nesfield Rd. LS10: Leeds .7G 87
LS29: I'ly, Nes .3E 14
Nesfield St. BD1: B'frd .1A 6 (6C 64)
Nesfield Vw. LS10: Leeds .7G 87
LS29: I'ly .5D 14
Nesfield Wlk. LS10: Leeds .7G 87
Nessfield Dr. BD22: Keigh .2F 42
Nessfield Gro. BD22: Keigh .2F 42
Nessfield Rd. BD22: Keigh .2F 42
Nest Est. HX7: Myth .3L 95
Nest Est. E. HX7: Myth .3L 95
Nestfield Cl. WF8: Pon .9K 109
Nest La. HX7: Myth .4L 95
Neston Way WF5: Oss .2N 123
Netherby St. BD3: B'frd .7F 64
Nethercliffe Cres. LS20: Guis .6H 31
Nethercliffe Rd. LS20: Guis .6H 31
Nether Cl. HD5: Hud .2C 138
Nether Cres. HD5: Hud .2C 138
Nethercroft WF17: Bat .7H 103
Nether Dale HD8: Den D .3C 172
Netherdale Ct. HD8: Den D .4G 173
LS22: Weth .3A 24
NETHER END .4G 173
Netherend Rd. HD7: Slait .9M 135
Netherfield Av. WF4: Neth .4N 141
Netherfield Cl. HD8: Kbtn .3K 155
LS19: Yead .9M 31
WF10: C'frd .7N 107
Netherfield Ct. LS20: Guis .7H 31 (off Netherfield Rd.)
Netherfield Cres. WF4: Neth .5N 141
Netherfield Cft. S72: Shaf .7K 161
Netherfield Dr. HD9: H'frth .1M 169
LS20: Guis .6H 31
Netherfield Ind. Est. WF13: Raven .6B 122
Netherfield Pl. BD19: Cleck .5J 101
WF4: Neth .4N 141
Netherfield Ri. LS20: Guis .7H 31
Netherfield Rd. LS20: Guis .6H 31
WF13: Raven .6B 122
Netherfield Ter. LS19: Yead .9M 31
LS20: Guis .7H 31 (off Netherfield Rd.)
Nether Hall Av. HD5: Hud .2C 138
Netherhall Pk. BD17: Bail .4B 46 (off Netherhall Rd.)
Netherhall Rd. BD17: Bail .4B 46
Netherhouses HD9: U'thng .3J 169
Netherlands Av. BD6: B'frd .6A 82
BD12: Low M .6A 82
Netherlands Sq. BD12: Low M .6B 82
Nether La. HD9: H'lm .5A 168
Netherlea Dr. HD9: Nether .9L 153
NETHERLEY .7E 150
Netherley Brow WF5: Oss .8A 124
Netherley Dr. HD7: Mars .7E 150
Nether Moor Rd. HD4: Hud .1G 153
Nethermoor Vw. BD16: Bgly .4F 44
Netheroyd WF7: Street .6K 127
Netheroyd Ct. WF4: S Comn .7K 127
NETHEROYD HILL .8M 119
Netheroyd Hill Rd. HD2: Fix .8M 119
Netheroyd Pl. WF4: S Comn .7J 127
Nether St. LS28: Fars .3A 66
NETHERTHONG .9L 153
Netherthong Rd. HD9: Mel .9E 152
NETHERTON
HD4, Armitage Bridge .2H 153
HD4, Farnley Tyas .3E 154
WF4 .5N 141
Netherton Fold HD4: Neth .3H 153
Netherton Hall Dr. WF4: Neth .4N 141
Netherton Hall Gdns. WF4: Neth .3N 141
Netherton La. WF4: Neth .2A 142
NETHERTON MOOR .3J 153
Netherton Moor Rd. HD4: Neth .2J 153
NETHERTOWN .6D 84
Netherwood BD13: Denh .6K 61
Netherwood Cl. HD2: Fix .8M 119
NETHERWOOD HEYS .3G 150
Netherwood La. HD7: Mars .3G 150
NETHER YEADON .3M 47
Nettle Gro. HX3: North .3F 98
Nettle La. WF1: Wake .4L 9
Nettleton Av. WF14: Mir .6K 121
Nettleton Chase WF5: Oss .2M 123
Nettleton Cl. BD4: B'frd .3B 84
Nettleton Ct. LS15: Leeds .6E 70
NETTLETON HILL .4B 136
Nettleton Hill Rd. HD7: Golc .4A 136
Nettleton Ho. WF9: Hems .3D 162 (off Lilley St.)
Nettleton Rd. HD5: Hud .2E 138
WF14: Mir .6K 121
Nettleton St. WF3: S'ley .6C 106
WF5: Oss .5M 123
Nettleton Ter. HD5: Hud .2E 138
Network Way WF6: Norm .9N 107
Neville App. LS9: Leeds .8L 69
Neville Av. BD4: B'frd .4F 82
LS9: Leeds .8L 69
Neville Cl. LS9: Leeds .8L 69
WF9: S Kirk .6J 163
Neville Ct. BD18: Ship .7L 45
Neville Cres. LS9: Leeds .6M 69
Neville Gth. LS9: Leeds .8L 69
Neville Gro. HD5: Hud .6D 138
LS9: Leeds .8L 69
LS26: Swil .3H 89
Neville Mt. LS9: Leeds .8L 69
Neville Pde. LS9: Leeds .8L 69
Neville Pl. LS9: Leeds .7M 69
Neville Rd. BD4: B'frd .1F 82
LS9: Leeds .6M 69
LS15: Leeds .7N 69
LS21: Otley .1M 31
WF2: Wake .6E 124
Neville Row LS9: Leeds .8L 69
Neville Sq. LS9: Leeds .7M 69
Neville St. BD19: Cleck .6J 101
BD21: Keigh .8K 27
LS1: Leeds .8E 4 (8D 68)
LS11: Leeds .8E 4 (8D 68)
WF1: Wake .7A 126
WF6: Norm .2J 127
Neville Ter. LS9: Leeds .8L 69
Neville Vw. LS9: Leeds .8L 69
Neville Wlk. LS9: Leeds .7L 69
Nevill Gro. BD9: B'frd .3J 63
Nevins Rd. WF13: Raven .5A 122
Nevison Av. WF8: Pon .9L 109
New Adel Av. LS16: Leeds .4K 49
New Adel Gdns. LS16: Leeds .4K 49
New Adel La. LS16: Leeds .5K 49
NEWALL .8K 17
Newall Av. LS21: Otley .8K 17
Newall Carr Rd. LS21: Clift, Otley .3J 17
Newall Cl. LS21: Otley .8K 17 (not continuous)
LS29: Men .3F 30
Newall Cres. WF9: Fitz .7N 145
Newall Hall M. LS21: Otley .8L 17
Newall Hall Pk. LS21: Otley .8L 17
Newall Mt. LS21: Otley .9K 17
Newall St. BD5: B'frd .1B 82
OL14: W'den .3J 113
New Arc. WF9: S Kirk .7H 163
Newark Cl. S75: S'ross .7K 159
Newark Rd. BD16: Bgly .2E 44
Newark St. BD4: B'frd .9F 64
Newark Va. WF3: Rob H .1J 105
New Augustus St. BD1: B'frd .6D 6 (8D 64)
New Av. HD5: K'htn .1F 138
New Bank HX3: Hal .1L 7 (4C 98)
New Bank Ri. BD4: B'frd .2H 83
New Bank St. LS27: Morl .8L 85
New Barton HX6: Sow B .1C 116
Newberry Cl. BD5: B'frd .1B 82
NEW BIGGIN HILL .5L 143
NEW BLACKPOOL .1K 85
New Bond St. HX1: Hal .4J 7 (6A 98)
NEW BRIDGE .6H 77
Newbridge Ind. Est. BD21: Keigh .9K 27
Newbridge La. BD23: Hal E .2D 10
New Bridge Rd. HD9: Mel .7A 152
New Briggate LS1: Leeds .5G 5 (6E 68)
LS2: Leeds .5G 5 (6E 68)
NEW BRIGHTON
BD16 .9H 45
LS27 .9K 85
WF2 .7G 9 (6J 125)
New Brighton BD12: O'haw .8E 82 (off Dyehouse Rd.)
New Brighton BD16: Cot .9H 45
HD8: Bird E .4M 171
New Brook St. LS29: I'ly .5G 14
New Brunswick St. HX1: Hal .4J 7 (5A 98)
WF1: Wake .8K 9 (7L 125)
Newburn Rd. BD7: B'frd .9N 63
Newbury Cl. BD17: Bail .3B 46
Newbury Dr. WF9: S Elm .4N 163
Newbury Rd. HD6: Ras .4L 119
Newbury Wlk. HD5: K'htn .1G 139
Newby Cl. LS29: Men .5F 30
Newby Ct. LS29: Men .5F 30
WF9: Hems .2E 162
Newby Gth. LS17: Leeds .2K 51
Newby Ho. BD2: B'frd .4F 64 (off Mint St.)
Newby St. BD5: B'frd .8A 6 (1C 82)
Newcastle Cl. BD11: Drig .8A 84
Newcastle Farm Ct. WF11: Fair .9N 91
Newcastle Ho. BD3: B'frd .3D 6
New Centaur Ho. LS11: Leeds .8E 4 (7D 68)
New Clayton Ter. BD13: Cull .1K 61
New Cl. BD13: Thorn .9M 61
New Cl. Av. BD20: Sils .8E 12
New Cl. La. DN6: S'brk .3J 165
HD7: Slait .9H 135
New Cl. Mill Fold BD20: Sils .8E 12
New Cl. Rd. BD18: Ship .8H 45
New Clough Rd. HX6: Norl .1K 117
Newcombe St. HX5: Ell .6F 118
New Cote Cotts. LS28: Fars .3B 66
New Craven Ga. LS11: Leeds .9E 68
New Cres. LS18: Hors .7E 48
New Cft. LS18: Hors .7E 48
NEW CROFTON .3J 145
New Cross St. BD5: B'frd .3C 82 (not continuous)
BD12: O'haw .8F 82
New Delight HX2: Mix .6J 79
HX7: Myth .4M 95
HX7: P Wel .4H 77
Newell Sq. LS28: Pud .8A 66 (off Smalewell Rd.)
New England Rd. BD21: Keigh .2J 43
New Fairfield St. LS13: Leeds .4E 66
New Farmers Hill LS26: W'frd .6E 88
NEW FARNLEY .2G 85
Newfield Av. WF6: Norm .2K 127
WF10: C'frd .5E 108
Newfield Chase LS25: Gar .9B 72
Newfield Cl. WF6: Norm .2K 127
Newfield Ct. WF6: Norm .1K 127
Newfield Cres. LS25: Gar .1B 90
WF6: Norm .2K 127
Newfield Dr. LS25: Gar .1B 90
LS29: Men .4E 30
Newfield Ho. WF6: Norm .1K 127
Newfield La. LS25: Led .5K 91
WF10: Leds .8J 91
New Fields Dr. BD3: B'frd .2E 6 (6E 64)
New Fields Wlk. BD3: B'frd .2E 6 (6E 64)
New Fold BD6: B'frd .6K 81
HD9: H'frth .4M 169
New Forest Way LS10: Leeds .9G 86
Newforth Gro. BD5: B'frd .2A 82
NEW FRYSTON .1J 109
NEW GATE .3N 169
New Gate HD9: Scho .7A 170
HX6: Rish .1N 133
Newgate WF8: Pon .3J 129
WF14: Mir .7L 121
Newgate Fold HD9: H'frth .4N 169
Newgate La. HD9: Mel .7D 152
Newgate St. WF17: Bat .9J 103
New Grange Vw. HX2: Brad .5M 79
New Gro. Dr. HD5: Hud .3C 138
NEWHALL .4E 82
New Hall App. WF4: Flock .6H 141
Newhall Bank LS10: Leeds .8F 86
Newhall Chase LS10: Leeds .7F 86
New Hall Cl. WF4: Crig .6G 142
Newhall Cl. LS10: Leeds .7F 86
Newhall Cres. LS10: Leeds .7F 86
Newhall Cft. LS10: Leeds .6G 86
Newhall Dr. BD6: B'frd .5D 82
Newhall Gdns. LS10: Leeds .8F 86
Newhall Gth. LS10: Leeds .8F 86
Newhall Ga. LS10: Leeds .6F 86
Newhall Grn. LS10: Leeds .7G 86
New Hall La. WF4: Flock .7J 141
WF4: Over .6J 141
Newhall La. WF14: Mir .9M 121
Newhall Mt. BD6: B'frd .5D 82
LS10: Leeds .8F 86
Newhall Pk. Dr. BD5: B'frd .4E 82
New Hall Rd. WF8: Pon .9L 109
Newhall Rd. BD4: B'frd .4F 82
LS10: Leeds .7F 86
Newhall Wlk. LS10: Leeds .7G 86
New Hall Way WF4: Flock .7J 141
Newhall Way BD5: B'frd .4E 82
Newhaven WF4: Chap .6H 143
Newhaven Bus. Pk. HD3: Hud .5F 136
New Hey HD7: Mars .6E 150
New Hey Moor Ho's. HD8: Shep .7K 155
New Hey Rd. BD4: B'frd .1E 82
HD2: Fix .7H 119
HD3: Hud .7G 118
HD3: Hud .1B 136
HD3: Outl, Scam .1A 150
HD6: Ras .7H 119
Newhill WF9: S Kirk .8H 163
New Hold LS25: Gar .6A 72
Newhold Ind. Est. LS25: Gar .6A 72
New Holme HX3: Hip .5H 99
New Holme Cotts. HX2: Wain .8F 78
New Holme Rd. BD22: Haw .9D 42
New House HX7: Myth .4M 95
New Ho. La. BD13: Que .5G 80
Newhouse Pl. HD1: Hud .3A 8 (3M 137)
New Ho. Rd. HD2: Hud .7B 120
Newill Cl. BD5: B'frd .3E 82
New Image Health & Fitness Studio
Royston .6D 160 (off High St.)
Newington Av. S72: Cud .9J 161
New Inn Ct. LS21: Otley .1L 31
New Inn St. LS12: Leeds .7K 67
New John St. BD1: B'frd .4A 6 (7B 64)
New Kirkgate BD18: Ship .7N 45
New Laithe HX2: Illing .8L 79
HX4: Bark .1H 135
HX4: Sow .2M 135
New Laithe Cl. HD4: Hud .8A 138
New Laithe Hill HD4: Hud .8N 137
New Laithe La. HD9: H'frth .3N 169
New Laithe Rd. BD6: B'frd .4M 81
BD22: Old .7F 40
HD4: Hud .8A 138
Newlaithes Cres. WF6: Norm .1K 127
Newlaithes Gdns. LS18: Hors .8E 48
Newlaithes Gth. LS18: Hors .9D 48
Newlaithes Rd. LS18: Hors .9D 48
Newland Av. HD2: Hud .1L 137
Newland Ct. HD2: Hud .1L 137
WF1: Wake .9N 125
Newland Cres. WF4: Dur .3G 143
Newland Fold HD7: Linth .2C 152
Newland La. WF6: Norm .2F 126
Newland Rd. HD5: K'htn .2E 138
Newlands LS28: Fars .4A 66
Newlands, The HX6: Sow B .1E 116
Newlands Av. BD3: B'frd .5H 65
DN6: Skel .7K 165
HD8: Clay W .7J 157
HX3: North .9F 80
HX6: Sow B .9E 96
LS19: Yead .8L 31
Newlands Cl. HD6: Ras .2N 119
Newlands Cres. HX3: North .1F 98
LS27: Morl .9N 85
Newlands Dr. BD16: Bgly .1D 44
HX3: North .1F 98
LS27: Morl .8N 85
WF3: S'ley .7N 105
Newlands Ga. HX2: Hal .5G 97
Newlands Gro. HX3: North .1F 98
Newlands La. HD9: U'thng .3J 169
Newlands Pl. BD3: B'frd .5F 64
Newlands Ri. LS19: Yead .9L 31
Newlands Rd. HX2: Hal .5G 97
Newland St. WF1: Wake .9N 125
Newlands Vw. HX3: North .1G 98
Newlands Wlk. WF3: S'ley .7N 105
Newlands Way BD10: B'frd .1H 65
Newland Vw. WF6: Alt .1G 126
New La. BD3: B'frd .8H 65
BD4: B'frd .8H 65 (Armstrong St.)
BD4: B'frd .3M 83 (Raikes La.)
BD11: Drig .5D 84
BD19: Cleck .6E 100
BD20: Kild, Sils .6A 12
DN14: Beal .7N 111
HD3: Scam .6E 134
HD7: Golc .3A 136 (Shaw La.)
HD7: Golc .7N 135 (Westwood Edge Rd.)
HD8: Skelm .8E 156
HX2: Lud F .7B 96
HX3: Hal .9N 97 (Birdcage La.)
HX3: Hal .8C 98 (Whitegate)
HX7: Blac H .9E 76
HX7: Crag V .9L 95
LS10: Leeds .8D 86
LS11: Leeds .8D 68
LS21: Stainb .1G 18
LS25: Bur S .1C 110
LS27: Gil .5D 84
WF2: Wake .2G 143
WF3: E Ard .4D 104 (not continuous)
WF8: Pon .2K 129
WF9: Upt .3N 163
New La. Cres. WF9: Upt .2N 163
New La. Ter. HD4: Farn T .3D 154
NEWLAY .9E 48
Newlay Bridle Path LS18: Hors .8E 48
Newlay Cl. BD10: B'frd .8J 47
Newlay Gro. LS18: Hors .9E 48
Newlay La. LS13: Leeds .2F 66
LS18: Hors .8E 48
Newlay La. Pl. LS13: Leeds .2F 66
Newlay Mt. LS18: Hors .9E 48
Newlay Wood Av. LS18: Hors .8F 48
Newlay Wood Cl. LS18: Hors .8F 48
Newlay Wood Cres. LS18: Hors .8F 48
Newlay Wood Dr. LS18: Hors .8F 48
Newlay Wood Fold LS18: Hors .8E 48
Newlay Wood Gdns. LS18: Hors .8F 48
Newlay Wood Ri. LS18: Hors .8F 48
Newlay Wood Rd. LS18: Hors .8E 48
New Leeds LS13: Leeds .1E 66
Newley Av. WF17: Bat .4C 102
New Line BD10: B'frd .8H 47
NEW LODGE .9A 160
New Lodge Cres. S71: Smit .9N 159
New Longley HX6: Norl .2G 117
New Longley La. HX6: Norl .2G 117
Newlyn Dr. WF2: Wake .9M 125
Newlyn Rd. BD20: Rid .7N 27
Newman Av. S71: Carl .8D 160
Newman St. BD4: B'frd .3F 82
New Market LS21: Otley .1L 31
Newmarket App. LS9: Leeds .9K 69
Newmarket Grn. LS9: Leeds .9K 69
Newmarket La. LS9: Leeds .9K 69
LS26: Meth .5C 106
WF3: S'ley .5C 106
New Mkt. Pl. BD1: B'frd .4B 6
New Market St. LS1: Leeds .7G 5 (7E 68)
New Marsh HX6: Sow B .7H 97
NEW MICKLEFIELD .9G 73
NEW MILL .2C 170
New Mill BD17: Ship .7N 45
HX2: Wain .7E 78

Newmillerdam—Northcote Cres.

NEWMILLERDAM 6L 143
Newmillerdam Country Pk. 8L 143
New Mill La. LS23: Cliff 3E 38
New Mill Rd. HD9: H'frth, Hon 5M 153
(Gynn La.)
HD9: H'frth, New M 2N 169
(Town End Rd.)
New Moon Apartments LS6: Leeds 1A 68
New Moor HX6: Ripp 6C 116
New North Pde. HD1: Hud 4A 8 (4M 137)
New North Rd. HD1: Hud 3A 8 (3L 137)
HD7: Slait 8N 135
WF16: Heck 7N 101
New Occupation La. LS28: Pud 8N 65
New Otley Rd. BD3: B'frd 2E 6 (6E 64)
New Pk. Av. LS28: Fars 3B 66
New Pk. Cl. LS28: Fars 3B 66
New Pk. Cft. LS28: Fars 3B 66
New Pk. Gro. LS28: Fars 3A 66
New Pk. La. WF5: Oss 3D 124
New Pk. Pl. LS28: Fars 3B 66
New Pk. Rd. BD13: Que 3C 80
New Pk. St. LS27: Morl 1J 103
New Pk. Va. LS28: Fars 3B 66
New Pk. Vw. LS28: Fars 4B 66
New Pk. Wlk. LS28: Fars 4A 66
New Pk. Way LS28: Fars 3B 66
New Pepper Rd. LS10: Leeds 2H 87
New Popplewell La. BD19: Scho 4D 100
Newport Av. LS13: Leeds 4D 66
Newport Cres. LS6: Leeds 3N 67
Newport Gdns. LS6: Leeds 3N 67
Newport Mt. LS6: Leeds 3N 67
Newport Pl. BD8: B'frd 5A 64
Newport Rd. BD8: B'frd 5A 64
LS6: Leeds 3N 67
Newport St. WF8: Pon 2J 129
Newport Vw. LS6: Leeds 2N 67
New Princess St. LS11: Leeds 9D 68
New Priory WF7: F'stne 7B 128
New Pudsey Sq. LS28: Stan 5N 65
New Pudsey Station (Rail) 5N 65
New Rd. BD13: Denh 6K 61
BD20: Sils 8D 12
DN6: Cam 1M 165
HD5: K'htn 9F 120
HD9: H'frth, Nether 9M 153
HX1: Hal 5L 7 (6B 98)
HX2: Lud 3D 96
HX4: Gree 4N 117
HX4: Holy 8B 118
HX4: Sow 1N 135
HX7: Cold 7N 75
HX7: Crag V 3K 115
HX7: Heb B 1G 94
HX7: Myth 4M 95
LS19: Yead 9K 31
LS23: B'ham 5D 38
LS25: Led 4K 91
OL14: Tod 8A 94
(Cross La.)
OL14: Tod 4N 93
(Gt. House Rd.)
OL14: Tod 8E 74
(Kebs Rd.)
S36: Hoy 7G 172
S75: Caw 2L 173
S75: Map, S'ross 7J 159
WF3: Carl 1M 105
WF4: Horb 1D 142
WF4: M'twn, Over 5H 141
WF4: W Har 1B 146
WF4: Wool 2J 159
WF7: Old S 3L 127
WF8: Lit S 2J 149
WF9: Bads 8J 147
WF11: Ferr 7N 109
New Rd. E. BD19: Scho 4D 100
NEW ROAD SIDE 9B 82
New Rd. Side LS18: Hors 7D 48
LS19: Raw 2M 47
New Rd. Sq. HD6: Ras 5K 119
New Row BD9: B'frd 4K 63
BD12: Wyke 2B 100
BD16: Cot 7G 44
HD9: H'frth 3M 169
(off Rotcher Rd.)
HX4: Holy 7B 118
LS15: Leeds 8F 70
LS25: M'fld 7G 73
LS28: Cal 3K 65
WF2: Kirk 1D 124
WF8: D'ton 6B 130
WF9: Bads 8L 147
Newroyd Rd. BD5: B'frd 3C 82
Newsam Ct. LS15: Leeds 7B 70
Newsam Dr. LS15: Leeds 7N 69
NEWSAM GREEN 3E 88
Newsam Grn. Rd. LS26: W'frd 3E 88
NEW SCARBOROUGH
LS13 . . . . . 5G 66
LS19 . . . . . 9K 31
WF4 . . . . . 3A 142
NEW SCARBRO' 6M 121
New Scarbro' Rd. LS13: Leeds 4G 66
New School La. BD13: Cull 1K 61
NEW SHARLSTON 7H 127
New Shaw La. HX7: Blac H 8A 76
NEWSHOLME 3A 42
Newsholme La. WF4: Dur 3H 143
Newsholme New Rd. BD22: Oak 3A 42
NEWSOME 8M 137
Newsome Av. HD4: Hud 9M 137
Newsome Mills HD4: Hud 8M 137
Newsome Rd. HD4: Hud 8C 8 (6N 137)
Newsome Rd. Sth. HD4: Hud 1M 153
Newsomes Row WF17: Bat 8E 102
(off Brown's Pl.)
Newsome St. WF13: Dew 2E 122
New Station St. LS1: Leeds 7E 4 (7D 68)
NEWSTEAD 8L 145
Newstead Av. HX1: Hal 5L 97
WF1: Out 7J 105
WF9: Fitz 7A 146
Newstead Cres. WF9: Fitz 6A 146
Newstead Dr. WF9: Fitz 7A 146
Newstead Gdns. HX1: Hal 5L 97
Newstead Gro. HX1: Hal 5L 97
WF9: Fitz 7A 146
Newstead Heath HX1: Hal 5L 97
Newstead La. WF4: Fitz 7M 145
WF9: Fitz 7M 145
Newstead Mt. WF9: Fitz 7A 146
(off Wakefield Rd.)
Newstead Pl. HX1: Hal 5L 97
New Stead Ri. BD20: E Mor 7A 28
Newstead Rd. LS21: Otley 1L 31
S71: Ath 9N 159
WF1: Wake 3H 9 (4K 125)
Newstead Ter. HX1: Hal 5L 97
WF9: Fitz 7A 146
Newstead Vw. WF9: Fitz 7A 146
New St. BD4: B'frd 5F 82
BD10: B'frd 7F 46
BD12: O'haw 8F 82
BD13: Denh 6K 61
BD16: Bgly 9D 28
BD19: Cleck 6K 101
BD22: Haw 9C 42
BD22: Oak 5D 42
HD1: Hud 6B 8 (5M 137)
(Princess St.)
HD1: Hud 5K 137
(Quaker La.)
HD3: Hud 6F 136
HD4: Neth 2H 153
HD5: K'htn 2G 138
HD6: B Bri 5N 99
HD6: Clift 9B 100
HD7: Golc 6D 136
HD7: Slait 9N 135
HD8: Clay W 8G 157
HD8: Skelm 7D 156
HD9: Hon 5L 153
HD9: H'wth 6C 170
HD9: Mel 7C 152
HX2: Hal 4L 97
HX3: Sou 8F 98
HX4: Stainl 8M 117
LS18: Hors 7E 48
LS25: Kip 4B 90
LS28: Fars 5A 66
LS28: Pud 8A 66
S71: Roys 6D 160
S72: S Hien 3L 161
S75: Map 8K 159
WF4: Horb 1D 142
WF5: Oss 6N 123
WF7: Ackw 5F 146
WF9: Kins 9C 146
WF9: S Elm 6L 163
WF10: C'frd 3E 108
WF12: Dew 4J 123
WF17: Bat 9H 103
(Bromley Rd.)
WF17: Bat 7F 102
(East St.)
New St. Cl. LS28: Pud 8B 66
New St. Gdns. LS28: Pud 8B 66
New St. Gro. LS28: Pud 8B 66
New Sturton La. LS25: Gar 6B 72
New Tanhouse WF14: Mir 6K 121
New Temple Ga. LS15: Leeds 8B 70
NEWTHORPE 9N 73
Newthorpe La. LS25: S Mil 1M 91
Newthorpe Rd. DN6: Nort 7N 149
NEW TOFTSHAW 5H 83
New Toftshaw BD4: B'frd 5H 83
NEWTON 9H 91
Newton Av. WF1: Wake 1K 125
Newton Bar WF1: Wake 3K 125
Newton Cl. BD20: Sils 8D 12
LS26: Rothw 9K 87
WF1: Wake 2K 125
Newton Ct. LS8: Leeds 9L 51
LS26: Rothw 9K 87
WF1: Out 8K 105
Newton Dr. WF1: Out 9L 105
WF10: C'frd 5H 109
Newton Gdns. WF1: Wake 2K 125
Newton Gth. LS7: Leeds 1G 68
Newton Grange WF9: Hems 3D 162
Newton Grn. OL14: Tod 5H 93
(off Pine Rd.)
WF1: Wake 2K 125
Newton Gro. LS7: Leeds 2G 68
OL14: Tod 5H 93
NEWTON HILL 1K 125
Newton Hill Rd. LS7: Leeds 1F 68
NEWTON KYME 2M 39
Newton La. WF1: Out 8K 105
WF10: All B, Leds 9D 90
WF11: Fair 9J 91
Newton Lodge Cl. LS7: Leeds 1E 68
Newton Lodge Dr. LS7: Leeds 1E 68
Newton Pde. LS7: Leeds 1F 68
Newton Pk. HD6: Brigh 6L 99
Newton Pk. Ct. LS7: Leeds 1G 68
Newton Pk. Dr. LS7: Leeds 1G 68
Newton Pk. Vw. LS7: Leeds 2G 68
Newton Pl. BD5: B'frd 1B 82
Newton Rd. LS7: Leeds 2F 68
Newton Sq. LS12: N Far 2G 84
Newton St. BD5: B'frd 1C 82
(Ripley St.)
BD5: B'frd 2C 82
(St Stephen's Ter.)
HX6: Sow B 8H 97
Newton Ter. HX6: Sow B 9H 97
LS7: Leeds 9E 50
Newton Vw. LS7: Leeds 1F 68
Newton Vs. LS7: Leeds 9E 50
Newton Wlk. LS7: Leeds 2G 68
Newton Way BD17: Bail 3A 46
NEW TOWN
BD22 . . . . . 1G 42
LS9 . . . . . 3L 5 (4G 69)
LS29 . . . . . 1M 13
WF8 . . . . . 9K 109
NEWTOWN 1A 8 (2M 137)
New Town HX3: Hal 3B 98
(off Boothtown Rd.)
Newtown HD9: Hon 4M 153
Newtown Av. S71: Roys 5C 160
New Town Cl. BD21: Keigh 9H 27
New Town Ct. BD21: Keigh 9H 27
New Village M. LS27: Chur 5M 85
(off New Village Way)
New Village Way LS27: Chur 4M 85
New Wlk. LS8: Leeds 6K 51
New Way LS20: Guis 7F 30
WF17: Bat 7F 102
New Wellgate WF10: C'frd 6F 108
New Wells WF1: Wake 6K 9 (6L 125)
New Wells Ter. WF1: Wake 6K 9
New Windsor Dr. LS26: Rothw 7A 88
New Works Rd. BD12: Low M 8A 82
NEW WORTLEY 7A 68
New York Cotts. LS19: Raw 5A 48
New York La. LS19: Raw 5A 48
New York Rd. LS2: Leeds 5H 5 (6F 68)
(not continuous)
LS9: Leeds 5J 5 (6F 68)
New York St. LS2: Leeds 7G 5 (7F 68)
Nialls Ct. BD10: B'frd 5F 46
Nibshaw La. BD19: Gom 4L 101
Nibshaw Rd. BD19: Gom 4L 101
Nice Av. LS8: Leeds 2H 69
Nice St. LS8: Leeds 2J 69
Nice Vw. LS8: Leeds 2H 69
Nicholas Cl. BD7: B'frd 7L 63
Nichol La. HD9: H'wth 6E 170
Nichols Cl. LS22: Weth 4K 23
Nicholson Cl. BD16: Bgly 1F 44
Nicholson Ct. LS8: Leeds 9J 51
Nicholson St. WF10: C'frd 5C 108
Nichols Way LS22: Weth 4J 23
Nichols Yd. HX6: Sow B 8J 97
Nickleby Rd. LS9: Leeds 6J 69
Nicola Ct. BD5: B'frd 1B 82
Nicolsons Pl. BD20: Sils 8E 12
Nidd App. LS22: Weth 1L 23
Nidd Ct. BD20: Sils 8E 12
Nidd Dr. WF10: C'frd 4H 109
Nidderdale Cl. LS25: Gar 9B 72
Nidderdale Wlk. BD17: Bail 3C 46
Nidd St. BD3: B'frd 8F 64
Nields Rd. HD7: Slait 1M 151
Nightingale Crest WF2: Wake 6E 124
Nightingale St. BD21: Keigh 8J 27
(off Parson St.)
Nightingale Wlk. BD16: Bgly 3H 45
Nijinsky Way LS10: Leeds 4K 87
Nile Cres. BD22: Keigh 1F 42
Nile Rd. LS29: I'ly 5G 15
Nile St. BD22: Cros R 7E 42
BD22: Keigh 1F 42
HD1: Hud 7A 8 (5L 137)
LS2: Leeds 4H 5 (5F 68)
Nina Rd. BD7: B'frd 2L 81
Ninelands La. LS25: Gar 9A 72
Ninelands Spur LS25: Gar 8A 72
Ninelands Vw. LS25: Gar 7A 72
NINEVAH 7K 147
Ninevah Cotts. WF9: Bads 7K 147
Ninevah La. WF9: Bads 7K 147
WF10: All B 8N 89
Nineveh Gdns. LS11: Leeds 9C 68
Nineveh Pde. LS11: Leeds 9C 68
Nineveh Rd. LS11: Leeds 9C 68
Ninth Av. WF15: Liv 7F 100
Nippet La. LS9: Leeds 5L 5 (6G 69)
Nixon Av. LS9: Leeds 7K 69
Nixon Cl. WF12: T'hill 1J 141
Noble Ct. HD4: Neth 3J 153
Noble Hop Way HX2: Hal 2J 97
Noble Rd. WF1: Out 9K 105
Noble St. BD7: B'frd 9N 63
Nog La. BD9: B'frd 2M 63
NOOK 3D 102
Nook, The BD19: Cleck 4J 101
HX6: Sow B 9H 97
LS17: Leeds 2F 50
S36: Hoy 9K 173
WF3: W Ard 6A 104
Nook Gdns. LS15: Scho 7G 53
Nook Grn. WF3: W Ard 5B 104
WF12: T'hill 9G 122
Nooking WF2: Kirk 9D 104
Nooking, The WF2: Kirk 9D 104
Nook La. HX6: Tri 3N 115
HX7: Wads 9L 77
Nook Rd. LS15: Scho 7G 53
Nooks, The HD8: Shep 9J 155
LS27: Gil 6G 84
Nook Vw. WF3: W Ard 6A 104
Nook Wlk. WF13: Dew 3C 122
Noon Cl. WF3: S'ley 7N 105
NOON NICK 2H 63
Nopper Rd. HD7: Linth 2E 152
Nora Pl. LS13: Leeds 3D 66
Nora Rd. LS13: Leeds 3D 66
Nora Ter. LS13: Leeds 3D 66
Norbreck Dr. BD22: Cros R 7E 42
Norbury Rd. BD10: B'frd 1J 65
Norcliffe La. HX3: Hip, Sou 6F 98
Norcroft Brow BD7: B'frd 8B 64
Norcroft Ind. Est. BD7: B'frd 7A 64
Norcroft St. BD7: B'frd 7A 64
Norcross Av. HD3: Hud 3F 136
Nordale Cl. LS29: I'ly 4H 15
Nordene Cl. HX7: Myth 3L 95
Norfield HD2: Fix 7M 119
Norfolk Av. HD2: Hud 8A 120
WF17: Bat 9E 102
Norfolk Cl. HD1: Hud 3L 137
LS7: Leeds 8F 50
LS26: Oul 8E 88
WF11: B'ton 4B 110
Norfolk Dr. LS26: Oul 8E 88
Norfolk Gdns. BD1: B'frd 5B 6 (8C 64)
LS7: Leeds 8F 50
Norfolk Grn. LS7: Leeds 8F 50
Norfolk Ho. WF1: Wake 8A 126
Norfolk Mt. LS7: Leeds 8F 50
Norfolk Pl. HX1: Hal 6G 7 (6N 97)
LS7: Leeds 8F 50
Norfolk St. BD16: Bgly 4F 44
HX7: Heb B 2H 95
WF17: Bat 8E 102
Norfolk Ter. LS7: Leeds 8F 50
Norfolk Vw. LS7: Leeds 8F 50
Norfolk Wlk. LS7: Leeds 8F 50
WF13: Dew 3E 122
(off Lacey St.)
Norgarth Cl. WF17: Bat 7J 103
Norham Gro. BD12: Wyke 2B 100
Norland Rd. HX4: Gree 4K 117
HX6: Sow B 9H 97
Norland St. BD7: B'frd 2L 81
NORLAND TOWN 1K 117
Norland Town Rd. HX6: Norl 1K 117
Norland Vw. HX2: Hal 8N 97
(off Delph Hill Rd.)
HX6: Sow B 8K 97
Norman Av. BD2: B'frd 1F 64
HX5: Ell 5F 118
Norman Cres. BD2: B'frd 1F 64
Norman Cft. HD8: Den D 3C 172
Norman Dr. WF14: Mir 5K 121
Normandy Ct. WF10: Alt 7K 107
Norman Gro. BD2: B'frd 1F 64
HX5: Ell 5F 118
LS5: Leeds 2K 67
Norman La. BD2: B'frd 1F 64
Norman Mt. BD2: B'frd 1F 64
LS5: Leeds 2K 67
Norman Pl. LS8: Leeds 5J 51
WF4: Horb 1D 142
Norman Rd. HD2: Hud 1M 137
(not continuous)
HD8: Den D 3C 172
WF14: Mir 5K 121
Norman Row LS5: Leeds 2K 67
Norman St. BD16: Bgly 4F 44
BD22: Haw 8D 42
HX1: Hal 7M 97
HX5: Ell 5F 118
LS5: Leeds 2K 67
Normans Way WF2: Wake 1A 144
Norman Ter. BD2: B'frd 1F 64
HX5: Ell 5F 118
LS8: Leeds 5J 51
NORMANTON 1H 127
Normanton By-Pass WF6: Norm 4H 127
NORMANTON COMMON 9K 107
Normanton Golf Course 9N 105
Normanton Gro. LS11: Leeds 1C 86
Normanton Ind. Est. WF6: Norm 9A 108
(Premier Way Nth.)
WF6: Norm 8L 107
(Pontefract Rd.)
WF6: Norm 9L 107
(Ripley Dr., not continuous)
WF7: A'ton 1N 127
Normanton Jubilee Swimming Pool 1H 127
Normanton North Ind. Est. WF6: Norm 9M 107
Normanton Pl. LS11: Leeds 1C 86
Normanton Station (Rail) 1H 127
Normanton St. WF4: Horb 2E 142
Normanton Vw. WF6: Norm 3J 127
Norman Towers LS16: Leeds 9K 49
Norman Vw. LS5: Leeds 2K 67
Normington Ho. LS13: Leeds 1B 66
No Rd. DN6: Cam 1N 165
Norquest Ind. Pk. WF17: Birs 1D 102
NORR 9C 44
Norr Grn. Ter. BD15: Wils 9C 44
Norridge Bottom HD9: H'frth 3M 169
Norris Cl. HD5: Hud 6E 138
NORRISTHORPE 1M 121
Norristhorpe Av. WF15: Liv 1L 121
Norristhorpe La. WF15: Liv 1L 121
Norset Ho. HX3: Hal 2A 98
(off West Vw.)
Nortech Cl. LS7: Leeds 2J 5 (4F 68)
Northallerton Rd. BD3: B'frd 5D 64
Northampton St. BD3: B'frd 1D 6 (5D 64)
North App. LS24: Stut 2G 54
North Av. BD8: B'frd 3B 64
LS21: Otley 9L 17
WF1: Wake 1K 9 (3L 125)
WF4: Horb 1E 142
WF8: Pon 4H 129
WF9: S Elm 7L 163
WF10: C'frd 5N 107
North Baileygate WF8: Pon 2K 129
Nth. Bank Rd. BD16: Cot 1F 62
HD2: Hud 1L 137
WF17: Bat 7D 102
Nth. Beck Ho. BD21: Keigh 1H 43
(off Aireworth St.)
North Bri. HX1: Hal 2L 7 (4B 98)
North Bridge Leisure Cen.
Halifax 2L 7 (4B 98)
North Bri. St. HX1: Hal 2L 7 (4B 98)
Nth. Broadgate La. LS18: Hors 6F 48
Northbrook Cft. LS7: Leeds 8F 50
(off Hill Vw. Mt.)
Northbrook Pl. LS7: Leeds 8F 50
Northbrook St. BD1: B'frd 2C 6 (6D 64)
BD3: B'frd 2C 6 (6D 64)
LS7: Leeds 8F 50
North Byland HX2: Illing 6L 79
North Carr HD5: Hud 3C 138
Nth. Carr Cft. HD5: Hud 3C 138
North Cliffe HX6: Sow B 9H 97
Nth. Cliffe Av. BD13: Thorn 8E 62
Nth. Cliffe Cl. BD13: Thorn 7D 62
Nth. Cliffe Dr. BD13: Thorn 8D 62
Northcliffe Golf Course 9K 45
Nth. Cliffe Gro. BD13: Thorn 7D 62
Nth. Cliffe La. BD13: Thorn 7E 62
Northcliffe Rd. BD18: Ship 9M 45
North Cl. LS8: Leeds 9M 51
S71: Roys 6D 160
WF7: F'stne 2C 128
Nth. Clough Head HX2: Hal 4H 97
Northcote WF5: Oss 2M 123
Northcote Cres. LS11: Leeds 1D 86

Oak Av.—Old Cross Stone Rd.

Oak Av. WF3: S'ley 8A 106
WF6: Norm 3H 127
Oak Bank BD16: Bgly 5F 44
BD18: Ship 1B 64
Oakbank Av. BD22: Keigh 2F 42
Oak Bank B'way. BD22: Oak 3F 42
Oak Bank Ct. BD22: Oak 3F 42
Oak Bank Cres. BD22: Oak 3F 42
Oakbank Dr. BD22: Keigh 2F 42
Oakbank Gro. BD22: Keigh 2F 42
Oak Bank La. BD22: Oak 3F 42
Oak Bank Mt. BD22: Oak 3F 42
Oakburn Rd. LS29: I'ly 6F 14
Oak Cl. LS29: Burl W 9D 16
OL12: Whit 7A 112
Oak Cotts. LS23: Cliff 3D 38
OL14: Tod 1J 113
Oak Cres. LS15: Leeds 7A 70
LS25: Gar 7N 71
WF4: H'cft 1J 161
Oakdale BD16: Bgly 2F 44
Oakdale Av. BD6: B'frd 4N 81
BD18: Ship 9B 46
Oakdale Cl. BD10: B'frd 3J 65
HX3: Hal 2N 97
WF3: Loft 6K 105
Oakdale Cres. BD6: B'frd 4N 81
HD3: Hud 2F 136
Oakdale Dr. BD10: B'frd 3J 65
BD18: Ship 9C 46
LS21: Pool 2G 33
Oakdale Gth. LS14: Leeds 6C 52
Oakdale Gro. BD18: Ship 9C 46
Oakdale Mdw. LS14: Leeds 6C 52
Oakdale Pk. LS21: Pool 2G 33
Oakdale Rd. BD18: Ship 9C 46
WF9: Kins 8B 146
Oakdale Ter. BD6: B'frd 4N 81
Oakdean HD2: Fix 7M 119
Oakdene LS26: W'frd 6E 88
Oakdene Cl. LS28: Pud 9C 66
Oakdene Ct. LS17: Leeds 3J 51
Oakdene Dr. LS17: Leeds 3J 51
WF4: Croft 2J 145
Oakdene Gdns. LS17: Leeds 3J 51
Oakdene Mt. BD14: Clay 2F 80
Oakdene Va. LS17: Leeds 3J 51
Oakdene Way LS17: Leeds 3J 51
Oak Dr. HD7: Golc 7C 136
LS10: Leeds 9F 86
LS16: Leeds 5L 49
LS25: Gar 7N 71
Oaken Bank Cres. HD5: Hud 7A 138
OAKENSHAW 8D 82
Oakenshaw Ct. BD12: Wyke 2A 100
Oakenshaw La. BD12: O'haw 2E 100
BD19: Cleck 2E 100
WF1: W'ton 3B 144
WF2: W'ton 3B 144
WF4: Croft 8B 126
Oakenshaw St. WF1: Wake 8A 126
OAKES 3G 136
Oakes, The WF1: Wake 1N 125
Oakes Av. HD9: Brock 7A 154
Oakes Fold HD8: Lept 7L 139
Oakes Gdns. HX4: Holy 7A 118
Oakes La. HD9: Brock 7A 154
Oakes Rd. HD3: Hud 2G 136
Oakes Rd. Sth. HD3: Hud 3G 136
Oakes St. WF2: Wake 5F 124
Oakfield LS6: Leeds 2A 68
Oakfield Av. BD16: Bgly 5H 45
LS26: Rothw 7N 87
Oakfield Cl. HX5: Ell 5D 118
LS25: Gar 8N 71
LS29: Men 2E 30
Oakfield Ct. S75: Map 8J 159
Oakfield Cres. WF11: Knot 9E 110
Oakfield Dr. BD17: Bail 5B 46
WF14: Mir 8K 121
Oakfield Gro. BD9: B'frd 4A 64
HD8: Skelm 8D 156
Oakfield Pk. WF8: Thpe A 6A 148
Oakfield Rd. BD21: Keigh 3G 43
HD2: Hud 1K 137
Oakfield Ter. BD18: Ship 8B 46
LS18: Hors 7H 49
(off Woodville St.)
Oakford Ter. LS18: Hors 6H 49
Oak Gro. BD20: Rid 6M 27
BD21: Keigh 4G 43
LS14: Leeds 2D 70
LS25: Gar 7A 72
LS27: Morl 1L 103
Oak Hall Pk. WF4: Crig 6E 142
Oakhall Pk. BD13: Thorn 7C 62
Oakham Gth. LS9: Leeds 7L 69
Oakham M. LS9: Leeds 7K 69
Oakhampton Ct. LS8: Leeds 7L 51
Oakham Wlk. BD4: B'frd 1E 82
Oakham Way LS9: Leeds 7K 69
Oak Hill HX6: Tri 3E 116
Oak Hill Clough OL14: Tod 5K 93
Oak Hill Rd. HD6: Brigh 9N 99
Oakhill Rd. WF17: Bat 5D 102
Oak Ho. LS5: Leeds 2J 67
LS7: Leeds 8F 50
(off Allerton Pk.)
LS15: Leeds 8N 69
WF10: C'frd 5E 108
(off Parklands)
Oakhurst LS6: Leeds 2A 68
Oakhurst Av. LS11: Leeds 4C 86
Oakhurst Ct. BD8: B'frd 4B 64
Oakhurst Gro. LS11: Leeds 4B 86
Oakhurst Mt. LS11: Leeds 4B 86
Oakhurst Rd. LS11: Leeds 4B 86
Oakhurst St. LS11: Leeds 4C 86
Oakland Ct. HD8: Kbtn 2K 155
WF17: Bat 6F 102
(off Princess St.)
Oakland Crest WF4: M'twn 3K 141
Oakland Dr. WF4: Neth 5M 141
Oakland Hill Pk. Home Est. WF11: Ferr 5M 109
Oakland Hills WF6: Norm 2K 127
Oakland Rd. WF1: Wake 8N 125
WF4: Neth 5N 141
Oaklands BD10: B'frd 7E 46
BD18: Ship 8J 45
HD6: Ras 2L 119
LS29: I'ly 6F 14
WF3: Rob H 1J 105
Oaklands Av. HX3: North 1G 98
LS13: Leeds 1B 66
LS16: Leeds 4N 49
Oaklands Cl. HD9: H'frth 1M 169
LS8: Leeds 2L 69
LS16: Leeds 4N 49
Oaklands Ct. LS8: Leeds 3L 69
Oaklands Cres. LS8: Leeds 3L 69
Oaklands Cft. WF2: W'ton 4C 144
Oaklands Dr. HD5: Hud 5D 138
LS8: Leeds 3L 69
LS16: Leeds 5N 49
WF17: Bat 7J 103
Oaklands Fold LS8: Leeds 2L 69
LS16: Leeds 4N 49
Oaklands Gro. LS8: Leeds 3L 69
LS13: Leeds 1B 66
LS16: Leeds 4N 49
Oaklands Pl. LS8: Leeds 3L 69
Oaklands Rd. LS13: Leeds 1B 66
Oaklands St. LS8: Leeds 3L 69
Oakland St. BD20: Sils 8D 12
Oak La. BD9: B'frd 4N 63
HX1: Hal 5N 97
HX6: Tri 3E 116
Oaklea Cl. S75: S'ross 7K 159
Oaklea Gdns. LS16: Leeds 5N 49
Oaklea Hall Cl. LS16: Leeds 5N 49
Oaklea Rd. LS15: Scho 9G 52
Oakleigh *HX7: Myth 4M 95*
(off Scout Rd.)
Oakleigh Av. BD14: Clay 2G 80
(not continuous)
HX3: Hal 9B 98
WF2: Wake 6G 124
Oakleigh Cl. BD14: Clay 1G 81
WF4: S Comn 7J 127
Oakleigh Gdns. BD14: Clay 2G 80
WF14: Mir 8K 121
Oakleigh Gro. BD14: Clay 2G 80
(not continuous)
Oakleigh M. BD22: Oak 5C 42
Oakleigh Rd. BD14: Clay 2G 80
Oakleigh Ter. BD14: Clay 1G 80
OL14: Tod 3D 92
Oakleigh Vw. BD17: Bail 4N 45
Oakley Gro. LS11: Leeds 2E 86
Oakley St. WF3: Thpe H 3G 104
Oakley Ter. LS11: Leeds 3E 86
Oakley Vw. LS11: Leeds 3E 86
Oakmont Cl. WF6: Norm 2K 127
Oak Mt. BD8: B'frd 4B 64
HX3: Hip 4K 99
OL14: Tod 6K 93
Oak Pk. Cl. LS16: Leeds 5H 49
Oak Pk. Dr. LS16: Leeds 5H 49
Oak Pk. Grn. LS16: Leeds 4H 49
Oak Pk. La. LS16: Leeds 5H 49
Oak Pk. M. LS16: Leeds 4H 49
Oak Pk. Mt. LS16: Leeds 5H 49
Oak Pk. Ter. LS16: Leeds 5H 49
Oak Pl. BD17: Bail 3D 46
HX1: Hal 5N 97
HX6: Sow B 7H 97
LS25: Gar 7M 71
Oak Ridge LS22: Weth 4K 23
Oakridge Av. LS29: Men 4F 30
Oakridge Ct. BD16: Bgly 3F 44
Oak Ri. BD19: Hun 2H 101
WF8: Pon 1L 129
Oak Rd. HD2: Hud 6E 120
LS7: Leeds 1F 68
LS12: Leeds 7A 68
LS15: Leeds 6A 70
LS25: Gar 7M 71
LS27: Morl 2J 103
S72: Shaf 7L 161
OAKROYD 3L 155
Oak Royd LS25: Gar 7N 71
Oakroyd LS26: Rothw 9A 88
Oakroyd Av. BD6: B'frd 4A 82
Oakroyd Cl. BD11: B'haw 8L 83
HD6: Brigh 7N 99
Oak Royd Cotts. HX3: Hal 1A 118
Oakroyd Dr. BD11: B'haw 9L 83
HD6: Brigh 7N 99
Oakroyd Fold LS27: Chur 5M 85
Oakroyd Mt. LS28: Stan 6B 66
Oakroyd Rd. BD6: B'frd 4N 81
Oakroyd Ter. BD8: B'frd 4B 64
BD17: Bail 5B 46
LS27: Chur 5M 85
LS28: Stan 6B 66
Oakroyd Vs. BD8: B'frd 4B 64
Oaks, The BD15: Wils 9A 44
HD3: Hud 9D 118
LS10: Leeds 9G 86
LS20: Guis 6J 31
LS27: Chur 6L 85
WF4: S Comn 7J 127
Oak Scar La. HD9: Scho 6A 170
Oaks Dr. BD15: All 6H 63
Oaks Farm Cl. S75: Dart 8H 159
Oaks Farm Dr. S75: Dart 8H 159
Oaksfield LS26: Meth 2L 107
Oaks Fold BD5: B'frd 2C 82
Oaks Grn. Mt. HD6: Ras 4L 119
Oakshaw Ct. BD4: B'frd 8F 6 (1E 82)
Oaks Hill Ct. HD5: Hud 5F 138
Oaks La. BD8: B'frd 7J 63
BD15: All, B'frd 6H 63
LS23: B Spa 9C 24
Oaks Rd. WF17: Bat 8H 103
Oak St. BD14: Clay 1G 81
BD22: Haw 8D 42
BD22: Oxen 3C 60
HX5: Ell 5E 118
HX6: Sow B 7H 97
Oak St. HX7: Heb B 9H 77
LS27: Chur 6L 85
LS28: Pud 6N 65
OL12: Whit 6A 112
OL14: Tod 8J 93
WF1: Out 8L 105
WF4: N Cro 3H 145
WF9: S Elm 8M 163
WF16: Heck 8A 102
Oaks Wood Dr. S75: Dart 9H 159
Oak Ter. *HX1: Hal 5N 97*
(off Battinson Rd.)
HX4: Holy 7N 117
HX6: Sow B 7H 97
(off Oak Pl.)
LS15: Leeds 3E 70
(off Church La.)
OL15: Lit 9M 113
Oak Tree Av. HD8: Fen B 7H 139
HD9: Scho 5B 170
S72: Cud 9J 161
Oak Tree Bus. Pk. LS14: Leeds 8B 52
Oak Tree Cl. LS9: Leeds 3L 69
S75: Kex 9F 158
Oak Tree Ct. BD20: Sils 7D 12
LS9: Leeds 3L 69
(off Oak Tree Pl.)
WF1: Out 8K 105
Oak Tree Cres. LS9: Leeds 3L 69
Oak Tree Dr. LS8: Leeds 3L 69
Oak Tree Gro. LS9: Leeds 3L 69
WF9: Hems 3F 162
Oak Tree La. LS14: Leeds 4N 69
Oaktree La. HD3: Hud 1F 136
WF9: Bads 5J 147
Oak Tree Mdw. WF2: W'ton 4B 144
Oak Tree Mt. LS9: Leeds 3L 69
Oak Tree Pl. LS9: Leeds 3L 69
Oak Tree Rd. HD8: Fen B 7H 139
Oak Tree Ter. HD8: Fen B 7H 139
Oak Tree Wlk. LS9: Leeds 3L 69
Oak Vw. BD20: Sils 7E 12
LS16: Leeds 2M 49
Oak Vw. Ter. WF17: Bat 4C 102
Oak Vs. BD8: B'frd 4B 64
HX7: Heb B 2E 94
Oakville Rd. HX7: Heb B 2E 94
Oakway BD11: B'haw 9M 83
OAKWELL 1A 102
Oakwell Av. LS8: Leeds 9J 51
LS12: Leeds 7N 67
WF8: Pon 5J 129
WF17: Bat 6B 102
Oakwell Cl. BD7: B'frd 2N 81
BD11: Drig 8D 84
Oakwell Ct. LS13: Leeds 3E 66
LS28: Fars 3A 66
(off Water La.)
WF17: Birs 1C 102
(not continuous)
Oakwell Cres. LS8: Leeds 9J 51
Oakwell Dr. LS8: Leeds 9J 51
Oakwell Gdns. LS8: Leeds 9J 51
Oakwell Gro. LS13: Leeds 3F 66
Oakwell Hall 1A 102
Oakwell Hall Country Pk. 1N 101
Oakwell Ind. Est. WF17: Birs 1D 102
Oakwell Ind. Pk. WF17: Birs 1C 102
Oakwell Mt. LS8: Leeds 9J 51
Oakwell Oval LS8: Leeds 9J 51
Oakwell Rd. BD11: Drig 8D 84
WF9: Kins 8A 146
Oakwell Ter. LS28: Fars 3A 66
Oakwell Way WF17: Birs 1D 102
OAKWOOD 9K 51
Oakwood HD6: Brigh 9L 99
WF2: Wake 8F 124
Oakwood Av. BD2: B'frd 2B 64
BD11: B'haw 9L 83
LS8: Leeds 9K 51
S71: Roys 5D 160
WF2: Wake 6F 124
Oakwood Boundary Rd. LS8: Leeds 9K 51
Oakwood Cl. WF6: Alt 8G 106
WF11: Ferr 5M 109
Oakwood Cotts. BD16: Bgly 1F 44
WF5: Oss 6N 123
(off Prospect Rd.)
Oakwood Ct. BD8: B'frd 6A 64
LS8: Leeds 9L 51
Oakwood Cres. S71: Roys 5C 160
Oakwood Dr. BD16: Bgly 2E 44
LS8: Leeds 9K 51
LS26: Rothw 6M 87
WF6: Alt 8G 106
WF9: Hems 4E 162
Oakwood Gdns. HX2: Hal 9M 79
LS8: Leeds 9K 51
LS28: Pud 8B 66
WF4: Cal G 4F 142
Oakwood Gth. LS8: Leeds 9L 51
Oakwood Grange LS8: Leeds 9L 51
Oakwood Grange La. LS8: Leeds 9L 51
Oakwood Grn. LS8: Leeds 9L 51
Oakwood Gro. BD8: B'frd 5M 63
LS8: Leeds 9K 51
WF4: Horb 9E 124
Oakwood Ho. *LS13: Leeds 9A 48*
(off Rodley La.)
Oakwood La. LS8: Leeds 9K 51
LS9: Leeds 3M 69
Oakwood M. WF17: Bat 7H 103
Oakwood Mt. LS8: Leeds 9K 51
Oakwood Nook LS8: Leeds 9K 51
Oakwood Pk. LS8: Leeds 1L 69
Oakwood Pl. LS8: Leeds 9K 51
Oakwood Ri. LS8: Leeds 9L 51
Oak Wood Rd. LS22: Weth 2L 23
Oakwood Rd. S71: Roys 5C 160
WF17: Bat 7H 103
Oakwood Sq. S75: Kex 9D 158
Oakwood Ter. LS28: Pud 8B 66
Oakwood Vw. LS8: Leeds 9L 51
Oakwood Wlk. LS8: Leeds 9L 51
OAKWORTH 5C 42
Oakworth Crematorium BD22: Oak 4A 42
Oakworth Hall BD22: Oak 5C 42
Oakworth Rd. BD21: Keigh 2F 42
BD22: Keigh 2F 42
Oakworth Station
Keighley & Worth Valley Railway 6D 42
Oakworth Ter. *BD22: Oak 5C 42*
(off Dockroyd La.)
Oasby Cft. BD4: B'frd 4J 83
Oasis, The 8A 126
(off Doncaster Rd.)
Oast Ho. Cft. WF3: Rob H 1K 105
Oastler Av. HD1: Hud 5L 137
Oastler Gro. WF14: Mir 5L 121
Oastler Pl. BD12: Low M 7B 82
Oastler Rd. BD18: Ship 7L 45
LS28: Cal 9M 47
Oastler Shop. Cen. BD1: B'frd 3A 6 (7C 64)
Oastler St. WF13: Dew 3E 122
Oates St. WF13: Dew 3F 122
Oatland Cl. LS7: Leeds 1G 5 (4E 68)
Oatland Ct. LS7: Leeds 2G 5 (4E 68)
(not continuous)
Oatland Dr. LS7: Leeds 2G 5 (4E 68)
Oatland Gdns. LS7: Leeds 2G 5 (4E 68)
Oatland Grn. LS7: Leeds 1G 5 (4E 68)
Oatland Hgts. LS7: Leeds 2G 5
Oatland La. LS7: Leeds 1F 4 (4E 68)
Oatland Pl. LS7: Leeds 1F 4 (3E 68)
Oatland Rd. LS7: Leeds 1F 4 (4E 68)
Oatlands Dr. LS21: Otley 8L 17
Oatland Towers LS7: Leeds 2G 5 (4E 68)
Oats St. BD22: Keigh 3G 43
Oban Cl. WF3: Ting 3N 103
Oban Pl. LS12: Leeds 6K 67
Oban St. LS12: Leeds 6L 67
Oban Ter. LS12: Leeds 6L 67
WF3: Ting 3N 103
Oberon Way BD16: Cot 9G 44
Occupation La. BD22: Oak 3D 42
HD4: Thurs 8B 154
HX2: Illing 7L 79
LS16: B'hpe 5E 32
LS24: Tad 3D 54
LS28: Pud 8N 65
WF12: Dew 4K 123
WF13: Dew 9C 102
Occupation Rd. HD2: Hud 8A 120
HD3: Hud 2H 137
HD4: Hud 8M 137
Ochrewell Av. HD2: Hud 8C 120
O'cot La. HD3: Scam 5H 135
Octagon Ter. HX2: Hal 8L 97
Octavia Ct. BD3: B'frd 2D 6 (6D 64)
Odda La. LS20: Hawk 7C 30
Oddfellows Club Houses WF7: Ackw 5D 146
Oddfellows St. BD19: Scho 4D 100
HD6: Brigh 8N 99
WF14: Mir 6L 121
Oddfellow St. LS27: Morl 9K 85
Oddfellows Vs. *HD5: K'htn 2G 138*
(off New St.)
Oddy Fold HX3: Hal 3A 98
Oddy Pl. BD6: B'frd 4N 81
LS6: Leeds 9N 49
Oddy's Fold LS6: Leeds 7A 50
Oddy St. BD4: B'frd 4J 83
Odeon Cinema
Bradford 6K 65
Huddersfield 2B 138
Odette Ct. BD16: Bgly 3H 45
Odile M. BD16: Bgly 3H 45
ODSAL 5B 82
Odsal Rd. BD6: B'frd 4A 82
(not continuous)
Odsal Stadium 5C 82
ODSAL TOP 6C 82
Office Row BD22: Haw 7C 42
Office Village, The WF5: Oss 5D 124
Offley La. WF4: Wrag 4B 146
OGDEN 3K 79
Ogden Cres. BD13: Denh 4K 61
Ogden Ho. BD4: B'frd 1K 83
Ogden La. BD13: Denh 4K 61
HD6: Ras 3L 119
HX2: Ogd 3K 79
Ogden St. HX6: Sow B 9G 97
Ogden Vw. Cl. HX2: Illing 6K 79
Ogden Water Country Pk. 3H 79
Ogden Water Vis. Cen. 3J 79
Ogilby Ct. LS26: W'frd 6C 88
Ogilby M. LS26: W'frd 6C 88
O'Grady Sq. LS9: Leeds 8M 5 (7H 69)
Old Acre La. DN6: Nort 7N 149
Old Allen Rd. BD13: Thorn, Wils 4N 61
BD15: Wils 3N 61
Old Apple Tree La. BD15: All 5F 62
Old Arcade, The HX1: Hal 4L 7
Old Bank HD7: Slait 1M 151
HX3: Hal 5C 98
(not continuous)
HX6: Ripp 7E 116
Old Bank Bottom HD7: Mars 3J 151
Old Bank Fold HD5: Hud 5B 138
Old Bank Rd. WF12: Dew 3H 123
WF14: Mir 4L 121
Old Bar La. HD9: H'wth 8F 170
Old Barn Cl. LS17: Leeds 2C 50
Old Bell Ct. HX1: Hal 5K 7
Old Boston Rd. LS22: Weth 6N 23
Old Boyne Hill Farm WF4: Chap 7J 143
OLD BRAMHOPE 5D 32
Old Brandon La. LS17: Shad 3N 51
Old Bridge Ri. LS29: I'ly 4F 14
Old Canal Rd. BD1: B'frd 1B 6 (6C 64)
Old Cawsey HX6: Sow B 8J 97
(not continuous)
Old Chamber HX7: Heb B 2H 95
Old Church St. WF5: Oss 6N 123
Old Clock Mill Ct. BD13: Denh 6K 61
Old Cl. LS11: Leeds 5N 85
Old Cock Yd. HX1: Hal 4L 7 (5B 98)
Old Corn Mill La. BD7: B'frd 1M 81
Old Cottage Cl. HX3: Hip 5H 99
Old Cross Stone Rd. OL14: Tod 7L 93

Oval, The—Parkhome Est.

Oval, The WF4: Not 3C 160
WF13: Dew 1D 122
WF15: Liv 7G 101
Ovendale Hall *HX3: Hal* *2N 97*
(off Ovenden Rd.)
OVENDEN 2M 97
Ovenden Av. HX3: Hal 3N 97
Ovenden Cl. HX3: Hal 3N 97
Ovenden Cres. HX3: Hal 2N 97
Ovenden Grn. HX3: Hal 2N 97
Ovenden Rd. HX1: Hal 2K 7 (1N 97)
HX3: Hal 1H 7 (1N 97)
Ovenden Rd. Ter. HX3: Hal 2N 97
Ovenden Ter. HX3: Hal 2N 97
Ovenden Way HX3: Hal 2L 97
OVENDEN WOOD 2J 97
Ovenden Wood Rd. HX2: Hal 2J 97
Overcroft, The WF4: Horb 1C 142
Overdale HX6: Ripp 4E 116
Overdale Av. LS17: Leeds 2J 51
Overdale Cl. LS22: Weth 3L 23
Overdale Dr. BD18: Ship 6D 46
Overdale Mt. HX6: Sow B 7J 97
Overdale Ter. BD22: Haw 8C 42
LS15: Leeds 6B 70
Overend St. BD6: B'frd 4M 81
Overgreen Royd HX2: Mt T 9G 79
Over Hall Cl. WF14: Mir 5M 121
Over Hall Pk. WF14: Mir 5M 121
Overhall Rd. WF14: Mir 5M 121
Overland Cres. BD10: B'frd 7H 47
Overland Pk. LS27: Gil 8F 84
Overland Trad. Est. LS27: Gil 8F 84
Over La. LS19: Raw 4N 47
Overmoor Fold BD10: B'frd 8E 46
OVERTHORPE 9F 122
Overthorpe Av. WF12: T'hill 1F 140
Overthorpe Rd. WF12: T'hill 9G 123
Overthorpe Vs. WF12: T'hill 9G 122
OVERTON 4J 141
Overton Dr. BD6: B'frd 3J 81
OVERTOWN 5B 144
Over Wood HX2: Hal 6L 97
Ovington Dr. BD4: B'frd 4J 83
Owen Ct. BD16: Bgly 1F 44
Owens Quay BD16: Bgly 4E 44
Owen's Ter. HD9: Hon 6K 153
Owlcotes Dr. LS28: Pud 6N 65
Owlcotes Gdns. LS28: Pud 6N 65
Owlcotes Gth. LS28: Pud 6M 65
Owlcotes La. LS28: Pud 6N 65
LS28: Stan 5N 65
(not continuous)
Owlcotes Rd. LS28: Pud 6M 65
Owlcotes Shop. Cen. LS28: Stan 5A 66
Owlcotes Ter. LS28: Pud 6N 65
Owler Bars Rd. HD9: Mel 7B 152
Owler Ings Rd. HD6: Brigh 1M 119
Owler La. WF17: Birs 1B 102
Owler Mdws. WF16: Heck 7N 101
Owler Pk. Rd. LS29: I'ly 2D 14
Owlers Cl. HD2: Hud 6D 120
Owler's La. WF9: Bads 6M 147
Owlers Wlk. OL14: Tod 4H 93
OWLET 2B 64
Owlet Grange BD18: Ship 9A 46
Owlet Hurst La. WF15: Liv 1M 121
Owlet Rd. BD18: Ship 8A 46
Owlett Mead WF3: Thpe H 3G 105
Owlett Mead Cl. WF3: Thpe H 3G 105
Owl La. WF5: Oss 1K 123
WF12: Dew 9K 103
(not continuous)
Owl M. HD5: K'htn 4G 139
Owl Ridge LS27: Morl 1M 103
Owl St. *BD21: Keigh* *8K 27*
(off Parson St.)
Owlwood Cotts. WF10: All B 7A 90
Owlwood Ho's. WF10: All B 7A 90
Oxclose Rd. LS23: B Spa 9D 24
Oxclose Wlk. LS23: B Spa 8D 24
Oxendale Cl. LS26: W'frd 7C 88
Oxenford Ct. LS16: Leeds 4K 49
OXENHOPE 4C 60
Oxenhope Station
Keighley & Worth Valley Railway 3C 60
Oxfield Ct. HD5: Hud 4E 138
Oxford Av. LS20: Guis 6H 31
Oxford Cl. BD13: Que 5B 80
BD19: Gom 4M 101
Oxford Ct. Gdns. WF10: C'frd 5C 108
Oxford Cres. BD14: Clay 1G 80
HX3: Hal 8C 98
Oxford Dr. BD19: Gom 4M 101
LS25: Kip 4N 89
Oxford Grange *BD19: Gom* *4N 101*
(off Oxford Cl.)
Oxford La. HX3: Hal 8C 98
Oxford Pl. BD3: B'frd 1D 6 (6D 64)
BD17: Bail 5C 46
HD1: Hud 7K 137
LS1: Leeds 5D 4 (6D 68)
LS28: Stan 5B 66
Oxford Rd. BD2: B'frd 4E 64
BD13: Que 5B 80
BD19: Gom 2M 101
HX1: Hal 6K 7 (6B 98)
LS7: Leeds 3E 68
LS20: Guis 7H 31
WF1: Wake 1H 9 (3K 125)
WF13: Dew 2D 122
WF17: Birs 3B 102
Oxford Row LS1: Leeds 5D 4 (6D 68)
(not continuous)
Oxford St. BD14: Clay 1G 80
BD21: Keigh 1G 43
HD1: Hud 2B 8 (3M 137)
HX6: Sow B 7K 97
HX7: Heb B 1G 94
LS20: Guis 7J 31
LS27: Morl 2J 103
OL14: Tod 7K 93
WF1: Wake 8N 125
WF3: E Ard 4G 104
WF6: Norm 9K 107
Oxford St. WF7: F'stne 6C 128
WF9: S Elm 7M 163
WF17: Bat 8E 102
Oxford Ter. *BD17: Bail* *5C 46*
(off Otley Rd.)
HX7: Myth *4M 95*
(off Scout Rd.)
WF17: Bat 8G 103
Oxford Vs. LS20: Guis 7J 31
Oxford Wlk. BD19: Gom 4M 101
Ox Heys Mdws. BD13: Thorn 8F 62
Ox La. HD9: Nether 1K 169
Ox Lee La. HD9: H'wth 8B 170
Oxley Gdns. BD12: Low M 6A 82
Oxley Rd. HD2: Hud 7A 120
Oxleys Sq. HD3: Hud 1C 136
Oxley St. BD8: B'frd 6A 64
BD12: Low M 7A 82
LS9: Leeds 8M 5 (7H 69)
Oxton Mt. LS9: Leeds 6H 69
Oxton Rd. S71: Ath 9A 160
Oxton Way LS9: Leeds 6M 5 (6H 69)
Oxygrains Packhorse Bridge 6K 133
Oyster Cl. LS27: Morl 1M 103

P

Pacaholme Rd. WF2: Wake 3F 124
Pack Horse Cen. HD1: Hud 5C 8 (4N 137)
Pack Horse Cl. HD8: Clay W 5K 157
Packhorse Ct. HD7: Mars 5F 150
Pack Horse Wlk. HD1: Hud 5C 8
Pack Horse Yd. LS1: Leeds 6F 4
Packington St. BD13: Thorn 6B 62
Padan St. HX3: Hal 8C 98
PADDOCK 5J 137
Paddock BD9: B'frd 2A 64
HX3: North 8D 80
WF1: Wake 5M 9 (5M 125)
Paddock, The *BD4: B'frd* *4J 83*
(off Tennis Av.)
BD13: Cull 9K 43
BD17: Bail 3D 46
BD19: Scho 4D 100
DN14: Beal 5M 111
HD5: K'htn 3G 138
LS6: Leeds 8B 50
LS14: T'ner 2G 52
LS17: E Kes 2D 36
LS25: Bur S 1D 110
LS26: Rothw 8N 87
WF1: Wake 1J 125
WF4: Wool 2J 159
WF5: Oss 1L 123
WF6: Norm 2J 127
WF10: C'frd 6J 109
WF11: Knot 9E 110
WF12: Dew 5J 123
Paddock, The (Caravan Pk.) LS29: Add 9N 11
Paddock Cl. BD11: Drig 8B 84
BD12: Wyke 3A 100
HD8: Skelm 7E 156
LS25: Gar 8A 72
S75: S'ross 8L 159
WF7: Ackw 5D 146
Paddock Dr. BD11: Drig 8B 84
PADDOCK FOOT 5K 137
Paddock Foot HD1: Hud 5K 137
Paddock Grn. LS17: E Kes 3D 36
Paddock Ho. La. LS22: Sick 4B 22
Paddock La. BD16: Bgly 1J 45
HX2: Hal 4J 97
Paddock Rd. HD8: Kbtn 2L 155
HX3: North 8D 80
S75: S'ross 8L 159
Paddocks, The WF4: Flock 7F 140
WF8: D'ton 7C 130
WF14: Mir 8L 121
Paddock Vw. LS17: Bard 3E 36
WF10: C'frd 6H 109
Paddy Bri. Rd. HX7: Myth 3L 95
Padgett Way WF2: Wake 4F 124
Padgum BD17: Bail 3A 46
Padma Cl. BD7: B'frd 7N 63
Padmans La. LS23: B Spa 9D 24
Padstow Av. LS10: Leeds 8C 86
Padstow Gdns. LS10: Leeds 8C 86
Padstow Pl. LS10: Leeds 9C 86
Padstow Row LS10: Leeds 9C 86
Page Hill HX2: Illing 1L 97
Page St. HD1: Hud 6C 8 (5N 137)
Paget Cres. HD2: Hud 1J 137
Paget St. BD21: Keigh 9G 27
Pagewood Ct. BD10: B'frd 6E 46
Paignton Ct. LS13: Leeds 5G 66
PAINTHORPE 6G 142
Painthorpe La. WF4: Crig, Hol 5F 142
Painthorpe Ter. WF4: Crig 6G 142
Paisley Gro. LS12: Leeds 6K 67
Paisley Pl. LS12: Leeds 6K 67
Paisley Rd. LS12: Leeds 6K 67
Paisley St. LS12: Leeds 6K 67
Paisley Ter. LS12: Leeds 6K 67
Paisley Vw. LS12: Leeds 6K 67
Pakington St. BD5: B'frd 1B 82
Palace Ho. Rd. HX7: Heb B 2H 95
PALESIDE 4N 123
Paleside La. WF5: Oss 4N 123
Palesides Av. WF5: Oss 3N 123
Palestine Rd. HX7: Heb B 9H 77
Paley Rd. BD4: B'frd 8E 6 (1E 82)
Paley Ter. BD4: B'frd 8F 6 (1E 82)
Palin Av. BD3: B'frd 5H 65
Palma St. OL14: Tod 3D 92
Palm Cl. BD6: B'frd 5N 81
Palmer Rd. BD3: B'frd 6F 64
Palmer's Av. WF9: S Elm 7A 164
Palmerston Ho. *BD4: B'frd* *1J 83*
(off Tyersal La.)
Palmerston St. BD2: B'frd 4F 64
Palm St. HD4: Hud 8C 8 (6N 137)
HX3: Hal 2A 98
Pannal Av. WF1: Wake 3N 125
Pannal St. BD7: B'frd 2M 81
Pannel Hill WF10: All B 6D 90
Panorama Dr. LS29: I'ly 7D 14
Paper Hall, The
Bradford 3D 6
Papyrus Vs. LS24: N Kym 2J 39
Parade, The BD4: B'frd 2J 83
BD16: Cot 8F 44
LS6: Leeds *1N 67*
(off North La.)
LS16: B'hpe 5H 33
LS19: Yead *1K 47*
(off Westfield Dr.)
LS21: Otley 8J 17
WF17: Bat 8D 102
Paradise HX2: Midg 4C 96
Paradise Flds. WF8: Pon 2K 129
Paradise Fold BD7: B'frd 1K 81
PARADISE GREEN 1K 81
Paradise Gro. *LS18: Hors* *7H 49*
(off Low La.)
Paradise La. HX2: Hal 6H 97
LS24: Stut 2H 55
Paradise Pl. LS18: Hors 7H 49
Paradise Rd. BD9: B'frd 2L 63
Paradise St. BD1: B'frd 7B 64
(not continuous)
HX1: Hal 5J 7 (6A 98)
Paradise Vw. BD15: Wils 9A 44
Paradise Way LS23: B'ham 6C 38
LS24: Tad 6C 38
Paragon Av. WF1: Wake 1K 125
Paragon Bus. Village WF1: Wake 1J 125
Parc Mont LS8: Leeds 7L 51
Paris HD9: Scho 5B 170
Paris Gates HX3: Hal 8M 7
Parish Gate *LS29: Burl W* *8C 16*
(off Main St.)
Parish Ghyll Dr. LS29: I'ly 6E 14
Parish Ghyll La. LS29: I'ly 6E 14
Parish Ghyll Rd. LS29: I'ly 6F 14
Parish Ghyll Wlk. LS29: I'ly 6F 14
Paris M. HD9: Scho 6A 170
Parison Ct. WF10: C'frd 7E 108
Paris Rd. HD9: Scho 4B 170
PARK 3D 46
Park, The HD8: Clay W 7K 157
HD8: Kbtn 3J 155
HX3: Sou 8F 98
S75: Caw 4N 173
Park & Ride
King Lane 4D 50
Thornton Road 7B 64
Park App. LS15: Leeds 6G 70
Park Av. BD10: B'frd 5F 46
BD11: Drig 7B 84
BD16: Bgly 5E 44
BD18: Ship 7M 45
BD21: Keigh 1H 43
BD22: Oak 5D 42
DN6: Carc 9N 165
HD1: Hud 5A 8 (4L 137)
HD8: Clay W 6J 157
HD8: Shel 6K 155
HX5: Ell 5D 118
LS8: Leeds 7L 51
LS12: Leeds 6L 67
LS15: Leeds 4E 70
LS19: Raw 3N 47
LS19: Yead 9L 31
LS25: Kip 4C 90
LS26: Swil 4H 89
LS27: Morl 1J 103
LS28: Pud 7B 66
S71: Roys 6E 160
S72: B'ley 6B 162
S72: Cud 9J 161
S72: Grim 9A 162
WF1: K'thpe 4E 126
WF1: Out 8J 105
WF2: Wake 8H 9 (7K 125)
WF3: Loft 6L 105
WF4: Flock 7F 140
WF6: Norm 1J 127
WF8: D'ton 6B 130
WF8: Pon 3H 129
WF9: S Kirk 7H 163
WF10: All B 9C 90
WF10: C'frd 5F 108
WF13: Dew 4E 122
WF14: Mir 7M 121
WF15: Liv 1L 121
WF17: Bat 6G 103
Park Bottom BD12: Low M 8A 82
Park Bldgs. LS21: Pool 1G 32
Park Cir. LS10: Leeds 8D 86
Park Cliffe Rd. BD2: B'frd 4E 64
Park Cl. BD10: B'frd 1G 65
BD11: Drig 7B 84
BD13: Que 4C 80
BD16: Bgly 3F 44
BD21: Keigh 2J 43
HD8: Shel 6K 155
HX2: Hal 2H 97
HX3: Hip 5K 99
LS13: Leeds 3F 66
S75: S'ross 9L 159
WF4: Ryh 9J 145
WF6: Norm 1H 127
WF8: D'ton 6B 130
WF17: Bat 9E 102
Park Copse LS18: Hors 6D 48
Park Cotts. LS8: Leeds 6K 51
Park Ct. BD9: B'frd 4A 64
LS21: Pool 2G 33
OL14: Tod *5H 93*
(off Newton Gro.)
WF5: Oss 7B 124
WF7: F'stne 2D 128
Park Cres. BD3: B'frd 4E 64
HX3: Hal 3N 97
HX6: Sow B *8K 97*
(off Grove St.)
LS8: Leeds 5J 51
LS12: Leeds 6L 67
LS20: Guis 9G 31
Park Cres. LS26: Rothw 7B 88
LS27: Gil 7G 84
LS29: Add 1N 13
S71: Roys 6E 160
WF10: C'frd 5J 109
Park Crest WF9: Hems 2D 162
Park Cft. WF13: Dew 3D 122
WF17: Bat 8E 102
Parkcroft LS28: Fars 4A 66
Park Cross St. LS1: Leeds 6D 4 (6D 68)
Park Dale LS29: Men 4E 30
WF10: C'frd 3J 109
(Elizabeth Dr.)
WF10: C'frd 3J 109
(Well Wood Vw.)
Parkdale Dr. HX6: Ripp 4E 116
Park Dr. BD9: B'frd 2M 63
BD16: Bgly 2G 44
HD1: Hud 3K 137
HD8: Shel 6K 155
HX1: Hal 6N 97
HX2: Hal 7K 97
LS12: N Far 2K 85
LS18: Hors 7C 48
WF3: Loft 5L 105
WF14: Mir 6M 121
WF17: Bat 5D 102
Park Dr. Rd. BD21: Keigh 2J 43
Park Dr. Sth. HD1: Hud 4K 137
Park Edge Cl. LS8: Leeds 8L 51
Parker Av. WF6: Alt 8F 106
Parker La. WF14: Mir 6M 121
Parker Rd. WF4: Horb 1E 142
WF12: Dew 8F 122
Parker's La. BD20: Keigh 5G 27
Parker St. WF3: E Ard 5E 104
WF15: Liv 9N 101
WF16: Heck 8A 102
Park Est. WF9: S Kirk 7J 163
Park Farm Gdns. WF9: S Kirk 6J 163
Park Farm Ind. Est. LS11: Leeds 5D 86
Park Fld. LS29: Men 4E 30
Parkfield Av. HX5: Ell 5E 118
LS11: Leeds 2C 86
WF14: Mir 7N 121
Parkfield Cl. LS25: Kip 3B 90
LS28: Pud 7A 66
Parkfield Ct. LS14: Leeds 3N 69
LS27: Morl 1J 103
Parkfield Cres. WF14: Mir 7M 121
Parkfield Cft. WF14: Mir 7N 121
Parkfield Dr. BD13: Que 4C 80
HX6: Tri 1G 116
LS23: B Spa 9C 24
WF5: Oss 6C 124
Parkfield Gro. LS11: Leeds 2C 86
Parkfield La. HX6: Norl 9K 97
WF7: F'stne 2C 128
WF8: F'stne, Pon 9D 108
Parkfield Mt. LS11: Leeds 2C 86
LS28: Pud 7B 66
Parkfield Pl. LS11: Leeds 2C 86
Parkfield Rd. BD8: B'frd 4B 64
BD18: Ship 7K 45
LS11: Leeds 2C 86
Parkfield Row LS11: Leeds 2C 86
Park Flds. HX2: Hal 2H 97
Parkfield St. LS11: Leeds 9E 68
Parkfield Ter. LS28: Pud 7B 66
LS28: Stan 5B 66
(not continuous)
Parkfield Vw. LS11: Leeds 2C 86
WF5: Oss 6C 124
Parkfield Way LS14: Leeds 3N 69
WF14: Mir 7M 121
Park Gdns. HX2: Hal 7K 97
WF5: Oss 7B 124
WF11: Byram 4C 110
PARK GATE 6D 156
Park Gate BD1: B'frd 3D 6 (7D 64)
HD8: Skelm 6D 156
Parkgate HD4: Hud 1L 153
WF9: S Kirk 8H 163
Parkgate Av. WF1: Wake 5N 125
Park Ga. Cl. LS18: Hors 7E 48
Park Ga. Cres. LS20: Guis 8H 31
Park Ga. Rd. HD7: Slait 3H 151
Park Grn. BD20: Sils 8C 12
WF6: Norm 2G 127
(not continuous)
Park Gro. BD9: B'frd 2A 64
BD13: Que 4C 80
BD18: Ship 7L 45
BD21: Keigh 8J 27
HD1: Hud 4L 137
HX3: North 3E 98
LS6: Leeds 9N 49
LS10: Leeds 9E 86
LS18: Hors 7C 48
LS19: Yead 9L 31
LS26: Swil 5H 89
LS27: Gil 7G 84
WF4: Horb 9B 124
WF14: Mir 7N 121
Park Gro. Ct. BD9: B'frd 2A 64
Park Gro. Rd. WF2: Wake 6J 125
Park Halt Station
Middleton Railway 5F 86
PARK HEAD 3K 171
Parkhead Cl. BD6: B'frd 7L 81
S71: Roys 5B 160
Park Head La. HD8: Bird E, Cumb 3J 171
HD9: H'frth 3K 169
Park Hill HD2: Hud 5D 120
Park Hill Cl. BD8: B'frd 5J 63
Parkhill Cres. WF1: Wake 5N 125
Park Hill Dr. BD8: B'frd 5J 63
Park Hill Gro. *BD16: Bgly* *3F 44*
(off Staveley Rd.)
Parkhill Gro. OL14: Tod 3D 92
WF1: Wake 5A 126
Park Hill La. WF1: Wake 5M 9 (5N 125)
Park Hill Wlk. WF1: Wake 5M 9 (5M 125)
Park Holme LS7: Leeds 2G 69
Parkhome Est. LS26: Swil 4J 89

Park Ho. Cl.—Paw La.

Park Ho. Cl. BD12: Low M 6C 82
Park Ho. Ct. S36: Ing 8B 172
Park Ho. Cres. BD12: Low M 6C 82
Park Ho. Dr. WF12: Dew 7G 123
Park Ho. Gro. BD12: Low M 6C 82
Park Ho. Rd. BD12: Low M 7B 82
Park Ho. Wlk. BD12: Low M 6C 82
Parkin Hall La. HX6: Sow B 2B 116
Parkin La. BD10: B'frd 7K 47
HD9: Mel 7D 152
OL14: Tod 6F 92
Parkinson App. LS25: Gar 6N 71
Parkinson Cl. WF1: Wake 4N 125
Parkinson Fold LS29: Add 1N 13
(off Church St.)
Parkinson La. HX1: Hal 6G 7 (6L 97)
Parkinson Rd. BD13: Denh 6L 61
Parkinson St. BD5: B'frd 1B 82
Parkinson Way LS20: Guis 6H 31
Parkin Sq. HD7: Golc 5A 136
Parkland Av. HD3: Hud 4D 136
LS27: Morl 1H 103
Parkland Bus. Cen. BD10: B'frd 8H 47
Parkland Cres. LS6: Leeds 6C 50
Parkland Dr. BD10: B'frd 8G 46
LS6: Leeds 6C 50
Parkland Gdns. LS6: Leeds 7C 50
PARKLANDS 2B 70
Parklands BD16: Bgly 2G 45
HD9: H'frth 3K 169
LS16: B'hpe 5G 33
LS29: I'ly 5J 15
WF5: Oss 7B 124
WF10: C'frd 5E 108
Parklands Av. WF4: Horb 1A 142
Parklands Ct. WF4: Horb 1A 142
Parklands Cres. LS16: B'hpe 5H 33
WF4: Horb 1A 142
Parklands Dr. HX6: Tri 2E 116
WF4: Horb 1A 142
Parklands Ga. LS16: B'hpe 5H 33
Parklands Mnr. WF1: Wake 1M 9 (3M 125)
Parklands M. WF4: Horb 1A 142
Parklands Wlk. HD8: Shel 6K 155
LS16: B'hpe 6G 33
Parkland Ter. LS6: Leeds 7C 50
Parkland Vw. LS19: Yead 1M 47
Park La. BD5: B'frd 8A 6 (1B 82)
BD13: Que 4E 80
BD14: Clay 1G 81
BD17: Bail 3D 46
BD21: Keigh 1J 43
DN6: Wome 8M 131
HD4: Hud 2L 153
HD7: Golc 6C 136
HD8: Bird E, Up C 3L 171
HD8: Eml, Skelm 6D 156
HD9: Mel 7D 152
HG3: Spof 1A 22
HX3: Hal 1C 118
HX4: Sow 1M 135
HX7: Hept 6N 75
HX7: Myth 4J 95
LS1: Leeds 5C 4 (6C 68)
LS3: Leeds 5A 4 (6B 68)
LS8: Leeds 5K 51
LS20: Guis 9G 31
LS22: Sick 4C 22
LS25: Kip 5C 90
LS25: Led 4J 91
(not continuous)
LS26: Meth 3H 107
LS26: Rothw 8A 88
WF4: W Bret 2A 158
WF7: F'stne 2D 128
WF8: Pon 2D 128
WF10: All B 9B 90
Park La. Central LS6: Leeds 1N 67
(off Bennett Rd.)
Park La. Cl. DN6: Wome 8M 131
Park La. Ct. LS17: Shad 2L 51
Park La. Ends HX2: Ogd 5K 79
Park La. M. LS17: Leeds 3K 51
Park Lea HD2: Hud 5D 120
LS10: Leeds 8E 86
Parklee Ct. BD21: Keigh 1K 43
Park Lodge BD15: Wils 1B 62
Park Lodge Ct. WF1: Wake 5N 125
Park Lodge Cres. WF1: Wake 5N 125
Park Lodge Gro. WF1: Wake 4M 9 (5M 125)
Park Lodge La. WF1: Wake 4M 9 (5M 125)
Park Lodge Vw. HD8: Skelm 8D 156
Park Mead BD10: B'frd 5F 46
Park Mdws. S72: Shaf 6L 161
Parkmere Cl. BD4: B'frd 6F 82
Park M. LS21: Pool 2G 32
PARK MILL 5J 157
Park Mill La. WF5: Oss, Wake 3B 124
Park Mill Way HD8: Clay W 6J 157
Park Mt. LS5: Leeds 2K 67
LS12: Leeds 6K 67
LS21: Pool 3E 32
Park Mt. Av. BD17: Bail 4C 46
Park Nook HX3: Sou 1E 118
Park Pde. LS9: Leeds 8J 69
LS27: Morl 1J 103
WF13: Dew 4E 122
Park Pl. BD10: B'frd 5G 46
HX1: Hal 6N 97
(off Warley St.)
LS1: Leeds 6D 4 (6D 68)
LS8: Leeds 1M 69
WF8: Pon 3H 129
Park Pl. E. HX3: Hip 5K 99
Park Pl. W. HX3: Hip 5K 99
Park Ri. LS13: Leeds 2F 66
WF10: C'frd 5F 108
Park Rd. BD5: B'frd 8A 6 (9C 64)
BD10: B'frd 5F 46
(Ainsbury Av.)
BD10: B'frd 1G 65
(Victoria Rd.)
BD12: Low M 6A 82
BD16: Bgly 4E 44
BD18: Ship 8A 46
Park Rd. HD4: Hud 6J 137
(College St.)
HD4: Hud 6G 136
(Queens Rd. W.)
HD8: Clay W 6J 157
HX1: Hal 5H 7 (6A 98)
HX5: Ell, Hal 3E 118
HX6: Sow B 7J 97
LS12: Leeds 6K 67
LS13: Leeds 3F 66
LS15: Leeds 8E 70
LS19: Raw 3M 47
LS19: Yead 9L 31
LS20: Guis 9G 31
LS23: B Spa 9C 24
LS29: Men 4E 30
OL14: Tod 6K 93
S72: B'ley 6B 162
S72: Grim 9A 162
WF8: Pon 8G 109
WF10: C'frd 7G 108
WF12: Dew 4J 123
(Frances Rd.)
WF12: Dew 5F 122
(South St.)
WF13: Dew 2D 122
WF13: Raven 5C 122
WF16: Heck 8A 102
WF17: Bat 7G 102
Park Rd. Retail Pk. WF8: Pon 1H 129
Park Rd. W. HD4: Hud 6H 137
Park Row HD6: Brigh 1N 119
LS1: Leeds 6E 4 (6D 68)
LS21: Otley 9M 17
(off Cross Grn.)
LS28: Stan 5B 66
LS29: Burl W 7D 16
Park Row Apartments LS1: Leeds 6E 4
Park School M. BD16: Bgly 4E 44
(off Lime St.)
PARKSIDE 3D 82
Park Side BD14: Clay 1G 81
BD19: Gom 5L 101
HD5: K'htn 1G 138
HD9: Jack B 4C 170
WF14: Flock 7F 140
Parkside BD16: Bgly 3F 44
BD19: Cleck 5J 101
HX3: Hal 8A 98
LS18: Hors 7D 48
S71: Carl 8E 160
WF4: M'twn 4L 141
Parkside Av. BD13: Que 4C 80
LS6: Leeds 8B 50
Parkside Cl. LS4: Leeds 3L 67
LS6: Leeds 7B 50
OL14: Tod 3D 92
Parkside Ct. BD22: Cros R 7E 42
LS14: Leeds 2B 70
Parkside Cres. LS6: Leeds 7B 50
LS14: Leeds 2B 70
Parkside Dr. BD9: B'frd 3M 63
LS14: Leeds 2B 70
Parkside Gdns. LS6: Leeds 8B 50
Parkside Grn. LS6: Leeds 8B 50
Parkside Gro. BD9: B'frd 3M 63
LS11: Leeds 4C 86
Parkside Hgts. LS4: Leeds 3L 67
Parkside Ind. Est. LS11: Leeds 4E 86
Parkside La. LS11: Leeds 3E 86
WF3: S'ley 1N 125
Parkside Lawns LS6: Leeds 8B 50
Parkside Mt. LS11: Leeds 4C 86
Parkside Pde. LS11: Leeds 4C 86
Parkside Pl. LS6: Leeds 7B 50
Parkside Rd. BD5: B'frd 3B 82
LS6: Leeds 7B 50
LS16: Leeds 6N 49
LS28: Fars 4A 66
OL14: Tod 3C 92
Parkside Row LS11: Leeds 4C 86
Parkside Ter. BD13: Cull 9K 43
Parkside Vw. LS6: Leeds 7B 50
LS14: Leeds 2B 70
Parkside Wlk. LS28: Fars 4B 66
Parkside Way S75: Kex 8F 158
Parks La. LS29: Midd 1F 14
PARK SPRING 7G 66
Park Spring Gdns. LS13: Leeds 5E 66
Park Spring Ri. LS13: Leeds 6E 66
Park Sq. BD6: B'frd 5L 81
HX3: North 2F 98
(off Hough)
LS19: Raw 3N 47
(off Batter La.)
LS21: Pool 2G 33
LS28: Pud 7B 66
WF3: Loft 6L 105
WF5: Oss 7B 124
Park Sq. E. LS1: Leeds 6D 4 (6D 68)
Park Sq. Nth. LS1: Leeds 6D 4 (6D 68)
Park Sq. Sth. LS1: Leeds 6D 4 (6D 68)
Park Sq. W. LS1: Leeds 6D 4 (6D 68)
Parkstone HD2: Hud 5D 120
Parkstone Av. LS16: Leeds 6K 49
Parkstone Dr. BD10: B'frd 1G 65
Parkstone Grn. LS16: Leeds 6K 49
Parkstone Gro. LS16: Leeds 6K 49
Parkstone Mt. LS16: Leeds 6K 49
Parkstone Pl. LS16: Leeds 6K 49
Park Stone Ri. HX3: She 7G 81
Park St. BD18: Ship 7M 45
BD19: Cleck 6F 100
BD19: Gom 4N 101
BD22: Haw 8D 42
HD6: Brigh 1N 119
HD7: Golc 4B 136
HX6: Sow B 8K 97
LS1: Leeds 5D 4 (6D 68)
LS12: Leeds 6K 67
LS15: Leeds 6C 70
LS19: Yead 9L 31
LS27: Chur 5M 85
WF1: Wake 6L 9 (6M 125)
WF4: Horb 1C 142
Park St. WF5: Oss 7B 124
WF13: Dew 2G 122
WF16: Heck 8A 102
WF17: Bat 4B 102
Park Ter. BD12: Low M 7A 82
(off Fountain St.)
BD18: Ship 7M 45
BD21: Keigh 1M 43
(off Bank Top Way)
BD21: Keigh 9K 27
(Frederick St.)
HX1: Hal 6N 97
(not continuous)
HX3: Hal 3F 98
HX3: Hip 5J 99
LS6: Leeds 9N 49
LS21: Otley 9M 17
(off Cross Grn.)
LS21: Pool 3D 32
WF9: S Elm 7A 164
Park Top LS28: Stan 5B 66
Park Top Cotts. BD16: Bgly 2G 45
Park Top Row BD22: Haw 8C 42
Park Vw. BD11: B'haw 8L 83
BD13: Que 3C 80
BD19: Cleck 4G 100
HD7: Mars 5G 150
HD8: Clay W 7K 157
HD9: H'frth 3M 169
HG3: Kirkby 2K 21
HX1: Hal 6N 97
HX3: Hip 5K 99
HX4: Sow 2N 135
HX6: Sow B 7H 97
(off Tuel La.)
HX7: Heb B 1H 95
LS11: Leeds 2C 86
LS13: Leeds 3F 66
(not continuous)
LS16: Leeds 3M 49
LS19: Yead 9K 31
(off South Vw.)
LS25: Kip 4B 90
(off Roger Fold)
LS26: Swil 4H 89
LS28: Pud 7B 66
S71: Roys 5E 160
S72: B'ley 6B 162
S72: Shaf 7K 161
WF2: Wake 5G 124
WF3: Loft 6L 105
WF4: Flock 7F 140
WF6: Alt 7H 107
WF9: Kins 9B 146
WF9: S Kirk 6K 163
WF10: C'frd 6H 109
WF12: Dew 6F 122
(Thornie Vw.)
WF12: Dew 3J 123
(Wakefield Cres.)
WF12: T'hill 9H 123
WF14: Mir 7N 121
Park Vw. Av. BD22: Cros R 7E 42
HX3: North 3F 98
LS4: Leeds 3N 67
LS19: Raw 3N 47
Parkview Ct. BD18: Ship 8M 45
LS8: Leeds 5K 51
Park Vw. Cres. LS8: Leeds 6K 51
Park Vw. Gro. LS4: Leeds 3N 67
Park Vw. Rd. BD9: B'frd 3N 63
LS4: Leeds 4N 67
S75: S'ross 8M 159
Park Vw. Ter. BD9: B'frd 3N 63
BD16: Har 5A 44
LS15: Leeds 6B 70
(off Primrose La.)
LS19: Raw 3M 47
Park Villa Ct. LS8: Leeds 6J 51
PARK VILLAS 5J 51
Park Vs. HX6: Sow B 8K 97
(off Grove St.)
LS8: Leeds 6J 51
WF8: Pon 2H 129
Park Vs. Dr. WF8: Pon 2H 129
Parkville Pl. LS13: Leeds 2F 66
Parkville Rd. LS13: Leeds 3F 66
Park Wlk. WF4: H'cft 9K 145
Park Way BD21: Keigh 2J 43
LS21: Pool 1G 33
LS29: Men 4E 30
Parkway BD5: B'frd 3D 82
BD13: Que 4C 80
BD17: Bail 6L 45
BD20: Stee 3B 26
(Pot La.)
BD20: Stee 2C 26
(Stone Gro.)
LS27: Gil 7F 84
WF4: Croft 9G 126
Parkway Cl. LS14: Leeds 2N 69
Parkway Ct. LS14: Leeds 3N 69
Parkway Grange LS14: Leeds 3N 69
Parkways LS26: Oul 7C 88
Parkways Av. LS26: Oul 8C 88
Parkways Cl. LS26: Oul 7C 88
Parkways Ct. LS26: Oul 7C 88
Parkways Dr. LS26: Oul 7C 88
Parkways Gth. LS26: Oul 8C 88
Parkways Gro. LS26: Oul 7C 88
Parkway Towers LS14: Leeds 2N 69
Parkway Va. LS14: Leeds 2C 70
(Harewood Ct.)
LS14: Leeds 3N 69
(South Parkway)
Park West LS26: Rothw 8N 87
PARKWOOD 1J 43
Park Wood Av. LS11: Leeds 6B 86
Parkwood Av. LS8: Leeds 8J 51
PARK WOOD BOTTOM 1K 43
Park Wood Cl. LS11: Leeds 6B 86
Parkwood Cl. HD8: Shel 6K 155
Parkwood Ct. HD3: Hud 4D 136
LS8: Leeds 7J 51
Park Wood Crematorium HX5: Ell 2E 118
Park Wood Cres. LS11: Leeds 6B 86
Park Wood Dr. LS11: Leeds 5B 86
Parkwood Gdns. LS8: Leeds 8J 51
LS28: Cal 9L 47
Parkwood M. LS8: Leeds 8J 51
Parkwood Ri. BD21: Keigh 1J 43
Parkwood Rd. BD18: Ship 8L 45
HD3: Hud 4D 136
HD7: Golc 4D 136
LS11: Leeds 6B 86
LS28: Cal 9M 47
Parkwood St. BD21: Keigh 1J 43
Park Wood Top BD21: Keigh 1K 43
Parkwood Vw. LS8: Leeds 7J 51
Parkwood Way LS8: Leeds 8J 51
Parliament Pl. LS12: Leeds 6N 67
Parliament Rd. LS12: Leeds 7N 67
Parliament St. WF2: Wake 5G 9 (5K 125)
Parlington Ct. LS15: Bar E 8M 53
Parlington Dr. LS25: Aber 8E 54
Parlington La. LS25: Aber, Gar 3N 71
Parlington Mdw. LS15: Bar E 9M 53
Parlington Vs. LS25: Aber 8E 54
Parma St. BD5: B'frd 8B 6 (9C 64)
Parnaby Av. LS10: Leeds 4H 87
Parnaby Rd. LS10: Leeds 4H 87
Parnaby St. LS10: Leeds 4H 87
Parnaby Ter. LS10: Leeds 4H 87
Parratt Row BD3: B'frd 7H 65
Parrock La. HX7: Wads 7J 77
Parrott St. BD4: B'frd 4H 83
Parry Cl. BD16: Har 6N 43
Parry La. BD4: B'frd 9G 64
Parsley M. LS26: Meth 1K 107
Parsonage La. HD6: Brigh 9M 99
(not continuous)
Parsonage Rd. BD4: B'frd 9H 65
BD5: B'frd 2C 82
LS26: Meth 1L 107
Parsonage St. HX3: Hal 1M 7 (3C 98)
Parson La. WF4: Wool 1J 159
Parsons Grn. LS22: Weth 4N 23
Parson's La. BD20: Sils 2F 12
LS29: Add 1G 13
(not continuous)
Parsons Rd. BD9: B'frd 2M 63
Parson St. BD21: Keigh 8J 27
Partons Pl. WF3: Loft 6L 105
Partridge Cl. LS27: Morl 9N 85
Partridge Cres. WF12: T'hill 1J 141
Partridge Dr. BD6: B'frd 4H 81
Paslew Ct. BD20: E Mor 7A 28
Pasture Av. BD22: Oak 6C 42
LS7: Leeds 8F 50
Pasture Cl. BD14: Clay 1J 81
Pasture Cres. LS7: Leeds 8F 50
Pasture Dr. WF10: C'frd 6A 108
Pasture Fold LS29: Burl W 7C 16
Pasture Gro. LS7: Leeds 8F 50
Pasture La. BD7: B'frd 1H 81
BD14: Clay 1H 81
LS7: Leeds 8F 50
LS22: Kear 8N 21
WF8: K S'ton 4J 149
WF9: S Elm 6C 164
WF11: B'ton 3A 110
Pasture Mt. LS12: Leeds 6L 67
Pasture Pde. LS7: Leeds 8F 50
Pasture Pl. LS7: Leeds 8F 50
Pasture Ri. BD14: Clay 1J 81
Pasture Rd. BD17: Bail 5B 46
LS8: Leeds 2G 69
Pastures, The S71: Roys 6B 160
Pastureside Ter. E. BD14: Clay 1J 81
Pastureside Ter. W. BD14: Clay 1H 81
Pasture St. LS7: Leeds 8F 50
Pastures Way HD7: Golc 5C 136
Pasture Ter. LS7: Leeds 8F 50
Pasture Vw. LS12: Leeds 6L 67
WF7: Ackw 5D 146
Pasture Vw. Rd. LS26: Rothw 8N 87
Pasture Wlk. BD14: Clay 1H 81
Pasture Way WF10: C'frd 7A 108
Patchett Sq. BD13: Que 4G 80
(off Highgate Rd.)
Pateley Cres. HD2: Hud 9M 119
Patent St. BD9: B'frd 4N 63
Paternoster La. BD7: B'frd 1M 81
Paterson Av. WF2: Wake 5J 125
Patience La. WF6: Alt 9F 106
Patricia Gdns. HX6: Sow B 7G 96
Patrick Grn. LS26: Oul 4A 106
Patterdale App. LS22: Weth 4J 23
Patterdale Cl. DN6: Carc 8N 165
Patterdale Dr. HD5: Hud 4B 138
Patterdale Rd. WF12: Dew 1H 123
Patterson Ct. WF2: Wren 9H 105
Pattie St. BD20: Keigh 7H 27
Paulena Ter. LS27: Morl 2L 103
(off Britannia Rd.)
Pauline M. WF10: C'frd 5C 108
(off Pauline Ter.)
Pauline Ter. WF10: C'frd 5C 108
Paul La. HD5: Hud 7G 120
WF4: Flock 7N 139
Pavement La. HX2: Illing 5L 79
Pavement St. BD19: Cleck 5J 101
(off Bradford Rd.)
Pavilion Bus. Pk. LS12: Leeds 2M 85
Pavilion Cl. HX1: Hal 5M 97
LS28: Stan 4B 66
S72: B'ley 6A 162
WF12: Dew 5F 122
Pavilion Ct. BD4: B'frd 5G 82
WF12: Dew 5K 123
Pavilion Gdns. BD4: B'frd 2G 82
LS26: W'frd 7D 88
LS28: Fars 4B 66
Pavilion Ho. LS14: Leeds 2C 70
(off York Rd.)
Pavilion M. LS6: Leeds 3N 67
Pavilion Way HD9: Mel 7D 152
LS28: Pud 7A 66
WF1: Wake 2L 125
Paw La. BD13: Que 6E 80

Pawson St.—Pinfold Gro.

Pawson St. BD4: B'frd 8H 65
LS27: Morl 1J 103
WF3: E Ard 4G 104
WF3: Loft 2K 105
Paxton Ct. LS12: Leeds 4J 67
Peabody St. HX3: Hal 3N 97
Peace Hall HD8: Fen B 5G 139
Peace Hall Dr. HD8: Fen B 5G 138
Peace Museum, The
Bradford 4B 6
Peace St. BD4: B'frd 9G 65
Peach Tree Cl. WF8: Pon 4H 129
Peach Wlk. BD4: B'frd 1F 82
Peacock Av. WF2: Wake 3H 125
Peacock Cl. WF2: Wake 4H 125
Peacock Ct. LS19: Yead 1A 48
Peacock Grn. LS27: Morl 1M 103
Peacock Gro. WF2: Wake 4H 125
Peacock La. OL14: W'den 5K 113
Peak Chase S72: B'ley 7N 161
Peak District National Pk. 8J 151
Peak Vw. WF13: Dew 1C 122
Pearl St. BD22: Keigh 3G 42
WF17: Bat 6D 102
Pear Pl. OL14: Tod 3D 92
Pearson Av. LS6: Leeds 3A 68
Pearson Fold BD12: O'haw 9D 82
Pearson Gro. LS6: Leeds 3A 68
Pearson La. BD9: B'frd 5J 63
Pearson Rd. BD6: B'frd 5B 82
Pearson Rd. W. BD6: B'frd 5B 82
Pearson Row BD12: Wyke 1B 100
Pearsons Bldgs. LS21: Otley 1M 31
Pearsons Cl. LS14: Leeds 2B 70
Pearsons Ct. LS14: Leeds 2B 70
Pearsons Dr. LS14: Leeds 2B 70
Pearsons Fold LS14: Leeds 2B 70
Pearson's La. WF12: Bries 3C 140
Pearson St. BD3: B'frd 8G 65
BD19: Cleck 6J 101
(Bradford Rd.)
BD19: Cleck 6F 100
(Moorland Mt.)
LS10: Leeds 9F 68
LS28: Cal 8M 47
WF6: Alt 7H 107
Pearsons Vw. LS14: Leeds 2B 70
Pearsons Way LS14: Leeds 2B 70
Pearson Ter. LS6: Leeds 3A 68
Pear St. BD21: Keigh 4G 43
BD22: Oxen 4C 60
HD4: Hud 6K 137
HX1: Hal 6M 97
OL14: Tod 3D 92
Peart Pl. LS10: Leeds 9F 86
Pear Tree Acre LS23: T Arch 8E 24
Pear Tree Cl. HX3: Hip 5L 99
WF8: Pon 5H 129
Pear Tree Ct. BD20: Sils 7E 12
Peartree Fld. La. WF8: Thpe A. Went 6B 148
Pear Tree Gdns. LS15: Bar E 9M 53
Pear Tree La. WF9: Hems 2D 162
Pear Tree M. HD4: Hud 6K 137
Peartree Orchard S71: Roys 4E 160
Pear Tree Wlk. WF2: Wake 3J 125
Peas Acre BD16: Bgly 8D 28
Peasborough Vw. LS29: Burl W 9D 16
Pease Cl. WF8: Pon 5K 129
Peasefold LS25: Kip 4B 90
Peasehill Cl. LS19: Raw 3N 47
Peasehill Pk. LS19: Raw 3N 47
Peaseland Av. BD19: Cleck 5G 101
Peaseland Cl. BD19: Cleck 5H 101
Peaseland Rd. BD19: Cleck 5H 101
Peaselands BD18: Ship 8M 45
Peat Ponds HD3: Hud 1D 136
Pecket Bar HX7: Wads 6J 77
Peckett Cl. HD3: Hud 3H 137
PECKET WELL 5J 77
Peckfield Bus. Pk. LS25: M'fld 8E 72
Peckfield Cotts. LS25: M'fld 1D 90
Peckover Dr. LS28: Pud 5K 65
Peckover St. BD1: B'frd 3D 6 (7D 64)
Peebles Cl. HD3: Hud 1F 136
Peel Av. WF2: Wake 2G 143
WF17: Bat 7F 102
Peel Cl. BD4: B'frd 8J 65
WF4: Horb 1D 142
Peel Cott. Rd. OL14: W'den 2J 113
Peel Cott. St. OL14: W'den 3J 113
Peel Ct. BD2: B'frd 4D 64
Peel Ho. BD16: Bgly 5G 44
Peel Mills LS27: Morl 9L 85
(off Commercial St.)
Peel Mills Bus. Cen. LS27: Morl 9L 85
Peel Pk. Dr. BD2: B'frd 4F 64
Peel Pk. Ter. BD2: B'frd 4F 64
Peel Pk. Vw. BD3: B'frd 5E 64
Peel Pl. LS29: Burl W 7C 16
Peel Row BD7: B'frd 1M 81
Peel Sq. BD8: B'frd 6B 64
LS5: Leeds 2K 67
Peel St. BD13: Que 4E 80
BD13: Thorn 8C 62
BD15: Wils 2B 62
BD16: Bgly 4G 44
HD1: Hud 6B 8 (5M 137)
HD7: Mars 5F 150
HX6: Sow B 8H 97
LS27: Morl 9L 85
WF4: Horb 1C 142
WF16: Heck 8N 101
Peel Vs. LS27: Morl 9L 85
(off Commercial St.)
Peep Grn. La. WF15: Liv 1G 120
Peep Grn. Rd. WF15: Liv 1G 121
Pegholme Dr. LS21: Otley 2H 31
Pelham Ct. BD2: B'frd 3F 64
LS10: Leeds 1F 104
Pelham Pl. LS7: Leeds 8E 50
Pelham Rd. BD2: B'frd 3F 64
Pelican Works LS26: Rothw 6K 87
Pell Ct. HD9: H'frth 1A 170
Pell La. HD9: H'frth 2A 170
PELLON 4L 97
Pellon Ind. Est. HX1: Hal 4M 97
(off Queen's Rd.)
Pellon La. HX1: Hal 2G 7 (4M 97)
Pellon La. Retail Pk. HX1: Hal 2H 7
Pellon New Rd. HX1: Hal 4M 97
HX2: Hal 4L 97
Pellon St. OL14: W'den 1H 113
Pellon Ter. BD10: B'frd 6F 46
Pellon Wlk. BD10: B'frd 6F 46
Pemberley Ct. HX6: Ripp 9C 116
Pemberton Dr. BD7: B'frd 8B 64
Pemberton Rd. WF10: C'frd 4H 109
(Ruskin Dr.)
WF10: C'frd 3G 109
(Stansfield Rd.)
Pembridge Ct. S71: Roys 5D 160
(off Strawberry Gdns.)
Pembroke Cl. LS27: Morl 8J 85
Pembroke Ct. BD8: B'frd 6L 63
(off St Leonard's Rd.)
HD4: Hud 8G 137
Pembroke Dr. LS27: Morl 8J 85
LS28: Pud 6B 66
Pembroke Grange LS9: Leeds 4M 69
Pembroke Ri. LS25: Kip 3C 90
Pembroke Rd. LS28: Pud 6B 66
Pembroke St. BD5: B'frd 1C 82
Pembroke Towers LS9: Leeds 3M 69
Pembury Mt. LS15: Leeds 3G 70
Penarth Av. WF9: Upt 2N 163
Penarth Rd. LS15: Leeds 4C 70
Penarth Ter. WF9: Upt 2M 163
Pendas Dr. LS15: Leeds 4E 70
PENDAS FIELDS 3G 70
Pendas Gro. LS15: Leeds 3E 70
Pendas Wlk. LS15: Leeds 4E 70
Pendas Way LS15: Leeds 4E 70
Pendennis Av. WF9: S Elm 5L 163
Pendil Cl. LS15: Leeds 6D 70
Pendle Ct. BD13: Que 6D 80
Pendle Rd. BD16: Bgly 4G 45
Pendragon BD2: B'frd 3E 64
Pendragon La. BD2: B'frd 3F 64
Pendragon Pl. WF9: S Elm 7N 163
Pendragon Ter. LS20: Guis 7H 31
Penfield Gro. BD14: Clay 1H 81
Penfield Rd. BD11: Drig 7C 84
Pengarth BD16: Bgly 2G 45
Penistone Hill Country Pk. 9A 42
Penistone M. BD22: Haw 8C 42
Penistone Rd. HD5: Hud 5F 138
HD8: Bird E, H Flat 2K 171
HD8: Fen B, Kbtn, Shel 5F 138
HD9: Had E, H'wth 8N 169
HD9: New M 2C 170
Penlands Cres. LS15: Leeds 7E 70
Penlands Lawn LS15: Leeds 7E 70
Penlands Wlk. LS15: Leeds 7E 70
Penlington Cl. WF9: Hems 4D 162
Penn Cl. BD2: B'frd 2F 64
Penn Dr. WF15: Liv 6H 101
Penn Gro. WF15: Liv 6H 101
Pennine Cl. BD13: Que 6C 80
HD9: U'thng 3J 169
S75: Dart 7J 159
WF2: Wake 8G 124
Pennine Cres. HD3: Hud 2D 136
Pennine Dr. HD8: Clay W 7G 157
Pennine Gdns. HD7: Linth 9C 136
Pennine Gro. OL14: Tod 6L 93
Pennine Ind. Est. LS12: Leeds 6K 67
Pennine Ind. Pk. HX7: Heb B 9H 77
Pennine Ri. HD8: Clay W 7G 157
Pennine Rd. WF12: Dew 3H 123
Pennine Sailing Club 6N 175
Pennine Vw. HD5: K'htn 9G 121
HD7: Linth 9C 136
HX7: Blac H 9A 76
OL15: Lit 9M 113
S75: Dart 7J 159
WF9: Upt 1N 163
WF17: Birs 1D 102
Pennine Way HD8: Clay W 7G 157
WF9: Hems 2F 162
Pennington Ct. LS6: Leeds 3C 68
Pennington Gro. LS6: Leeds 2C 68
Pennington La. LS26: Oul 2C 106
Pennington Pl. LS6: Leeds 3C 68
Pennington St. LS6: Leeds 3C 68
Pennington Ter. BD5: B'frd 1A 82
LS6: Leeds 2C 68
Pennithorne Av. BD17: Bail 3A 46
Penn St. HX1: Hal 4N 97
Pennwell Dean LS14: Leeds 1E 70
Pennwell Fold LS14: Leeds 1E 70
Pennwell Gth. LS14: Leeds 1E 70
Pennwell Ga. LS14: Leeds 1E 70
Pennwell Grn. LS14: Leeds 1E 70
Pennwell Lawn LS14: Leeds 1E 70
Pennyfield Cl. LS6: Leeds 6B 50
Pennygate BD16: Bgly 2J 45
Penny Hill Centre, The LS10: Leeds 1G 86
Penny Hill Dr. BD14: Clay 1J 81
Penny La. HD5: Hud 5F 138
Penny La. Way LS10: Leeds 1F 86
Penny Spring HD5: Hud 7C 138
Pennythorne Ct. LS19: Yead 2L 47
Pennythorne Dr. LS19: Yead 2L 47
Penraevon 1 Light Ind. Est. LS7: Leeds 3E 68
Penraevon Av. LS7: Leeds 3E 68
Penraevon Ind. Est. LS7: Leeds 3E 68
(off Jackson Rd.)
Penraevon St. LS7: Leeds 3E 68
Penrhyn Av. HD5: K'htn 2G 138
Penrhyn Gdns. HD4: Hud 6H 137
Penrith Cres. WF10: C'frd 2L 109
Penrith Gro. LS12: Leeds 8M 67
Penrose Beck Dr. WF7: Ackw 5E 146
Penrose Dr. BD7: B'frd 2L 81
Penrose Pl. HX3: North 2F 98
WF2: Wake 5H 143
Pentland Av. BD14: Clay 1H 81
WF11: Knot 8D 110
Pentland Cl. BD22: Keigh 1G 43
Pentland Dr. LS25: Gar 9N 71
Pentland Gro. WF2: Wake 8G 124
Pentland Rd. WF12: Dew 5G 122
Pentland Way LS27: Morl 1K 103
Penuel Pl. HX3: Hal 9C 98
Penzance Ct. BD8: B'frd 6N 63
(off Fearnsides St.)
Peplow Cl. LS25: Bur S 1D 110
Pepper Gdns. LS13: Leeds 2H 67
PEPPER HILL
BD16 6M 43
HX3 7F 80
Pepper Hill BD19: Cleck 4H 101
Pepper Hill Lea BD22: Keigh 5F 42
Pepper Hills LS17: Leeds 3F 50
Pepper La. LS10: Leeds 2H 87
LS13: Leeds 2G 67
Pepper Rd. LS10: Leeds 3H 87
Pepper Royd St. WF13: Dew 2G 123
Percival St. BD3: B'frd 4F 6 (7E 64)
HD3: Hud 4E 136
LS2: Leeds 4E 4 (5D 68)
Percy St. BD16: Bgly 4F 44
BD21: Keigh 3H 43
HD2: Hud 1M 137
LS12: Leeds 8N 67
OL12: Whit 5A 112
Peregrine Av. LS27: Morl 9N 85
Peregrine Ct. HD4: Neth 2K 153
Peregrine Way BD6: B'frd 4H 81
Peridot Fold HD2: Hud 9A 120
Perkin La. BD10: B'frd 6D 46
(off W. Cote Dr.)
Per La. HX2: Illing 6K 79
Permain Ct. HD4: Hud 8D 8 (6N 137)
Perry Cl. BD22: Keigh 3G 43
Perserverence St. HD4: Hud 7E 136
Perseverance La. BD7: B'frd 2M 81
Perseverance Mill LS6: Leeds 3D 68
(off Cross Chancellor St.)
Perseverance Mills BD6: B'frd 4M 81
Perseverance Pl. HD9: H'frth 4L 169
Perseverance Rd. BD13: Que 2N 79
HX2: Ogd 2N 79
Perseverance St. BD12: Wyke 9A 82
BD17: Bail 3B 46
HD4: Hud 7M 137
HX6: Sow B 7H 97
LS28: Pud 7N 65
WF10: C'frd 4C 108
Perseverance Ter. HX1: Hal 8G 7 (7N 97)
LS26: Rothw 9N 87
WF17: Bat 9F 102
Perth Av. BD2: B'frd 3C 64
Perth Dr. WF3: Ting 4B 104
Perth Ho. BD4: B'frd 9H 65
(off Parsonage Rd.)
Perth Mt. LS18: Hors 3E 48
Peterborough Pl. BD2: B'frd 3F 64
Peterborough Rd. BD2: B'frd 4F 64
Peterborough Ter. BD2: B'frd 3F 64
Peterfoot Way S71: Carl 8C 160
Peter Hill WF17: Bat 1G 122
Peterhouse Dr. LS21: Otley 1N 31
Peter La. HX2: Hal 5H 97
LS27: Morl 8N 85
Peter Laylock Ind. Est. LS7: Leeds 3E 68
Peter Row HX7: Crag V 8L 95
Peters Cl. WF9: Upt 1C 164
Petersfield Av. LS10: Leeds 6G 86
Petersgarth BD18: Ship 7K 45
Peterson Rd. WF1: Wake 5L 9 (5M 125)
Pether Hill HX4: Stainl 8M 117
Petrel Cl. BD6: B'frd 4H 81
Petrel Way LS27: Morl 1M 103
Petrie Cres. LS13: Leeds 1A 66
Petrie Gro. BD3: B'frd 7J 65
Petrie Rd. BD3: B'frd 7J 65
Petrie St. LS13: Leeds 1A 66
Petworth Cft. S71: Roys 5C 160
Pevensey Gth. BD10: B'frd 9G 47
(off Rowantree Dr.)
Peverell Cl. BD4: B'frd 2J 83
Peveril Cres. S71: Ath 9B 160
Peveril Mt. BD2: B'frd 3G 64
Pexwood Pl. OL14: Tod 9H 93
Pexwood Rd. OL14: Tod 9H 93
Pheasant Dr. WF17: Birs 1D 102
Pheasant St. BD21: Keigh 8K 27
Philip Gth. WF1: Out 7K 105
Philippa Way LS12: Leeds 2M 85
Philip's Gro. WF3: Loft 6L 105
Philip's La. WF8: D'ton 6B 130
Phillips Cl. LS18: Hors 6F 48
(off Broadgate La.)
Phillips St. WF10: C'frd 4B 108
Phil May Ct. LS12: Leeds 8A 68
(off Holdforth Grn.)
Phoebe La. HX3: Hal 8C 98
Phoebe La. Ind. Est. HX3: Hal 8M 7 (8C 98)
Phoenix Av. HD8: Eml 3G 156
LS25: M'fld 8E 72
WF7: F'stne 5B 128
Phoenix Cl. LS14: Leeds 3B 70
Phoenix Ct. OL14: Tod 6M 93
WF2: Wake 5J 125
WF17: Bat 7J 103
Phoenix Pastures BD22: Keigh 4F 42
Phoenix St. HD6: Brigh 1N 119
OL14: Tod 6M 93
Phoenix Way BD4: B'frd 8J 65
Phoenix Works Est. WF4: Horb 1A 142
Piazza Centre, The
HD1: Hud 5C 8 (4N 137)
Piccadilly BD1: B'frd 3A 6 (7C 64)
WF2: Wake 5H 9 (5K 125)
Piccadilly Chambers BD1: B'frd 3A 6
Pickard Bank LS6: Leeds 1B 68
Pickard Ct. LS15: Leeds 6D 70
Pickard La. BD20: Sils 7E 12
Pickard Way WF13: Dew 2E 122
Pickering Av. LS25: Gar 6B 72
Pickering Ct. HD2: Hud 1N 137
Pickering Dr. WF5: Oss 2M 123
Pickering La. WF5: Oss 2M 123
Pickering Mt. LS12: Leeds 6N 67
Pickerings, The BD13: Que 5D 80
Pickering St. LS12: Leeds 6N 67
Pickersgill St. WF5: Oss 3M 123
Picker St. OL14: Tod 4G 92
Pickford Sq. HD3: Hud 6F 136
(off Pickford St.)
Pickford St. HD3: Hud 6F 136
Pick Hill Rd. HD9: Mel 6C 152
Pickles Ct. OL14: Tod 6K 93
Picklesfield WF17: Bat 1E 122
PICKLES HILL 3L 81
Pickles Hill BD22: Old 6N 41
Pickles La. BD7: B'frd 3L 81
HD8: Skelm 8E 156
Pickles St. BD21: Keigh 2H 43
WF17: Bat 1E 122
Pickle Top HD7: Slait 8L 135
Pickpocket La. LS26: Rothw, W'frd 6B 88
Pickthall Ter. OL14: Tod 7M 93
Pickup Bus. Pk. LS28: Stan 4C 66
Pickwood La. HX6: Norl 1L 117
PICKWOOD SCAR 1L 117
Picton Ho. BD8: B'frd 5A 64
(off Green La.)
Picton St. BD8: B'frd 5B 64
Picton Way HD5: Hud 3E 138
Picture House, The
Keighley 8J 27
(off North St.)
Picture House, The HD7: Golc 5C 136
Pictureville BD5: B'frd 5A 6 (8C 64)
Piece Hall, The
Halifax 4M 7 (5C 98)
Piece Hall Art Gallery
Halifax 4M 7
Piece Hall Yd. BD1: B'frd 4B 6 (7C 64)
Piece Wood Rd. LS16: Leeds 4G 48
Pigeon Cote Cl. LS14: Leeds 9B 52
Pigeon Cote Rd. LS14: Leeds 9B 52
Pigginer La. HD9: H'frth 3N 169
Piggott St. HD6: Brigh 9M 99
Pighill Top La. HD7: Slait 8L 135
Pigman La. HX2: Hal 6G 96
Pike End Ga. HX6: Rish 4M 133
Pike End Rd. HX6: Rish 2B 134
Pike Law La. HD7: Golc 5A 136
Pike Law Rd. HD7: Golc 5N 135
Pike Lowe Gro. S75: S'ross 9M 159
Pildacre Brow WF5: Oss 5M 123
Pildacre Cft. WF5: Oss 5M 123
Pildacre Hill WF12: Dew 5L 123
Pildacre La. WF5: Oss 5K 123
WF12: Dew 5K 123
Pilden La. WF3: E Ard 6E 104
Pilgrim Av. WF13: Dew 4C 122
Pilgrim Cres. WF13: Dew 4C 122
Pilgrim Dr. WF13: Dew 4C 122
Pilgrim Way LS28: Stan 4D 66
Pilkington St. WF2: Wake 7L 125
Pilling La. HD8: Clay W, Skelm 7F 156
Pilling Top La. HD8: Shel 5M 155
Pill White La. LS21: Lind, Stainb 4C 18
Pilmer Ct. WF2: Wake 7F 124
Pilot St. LS9: Leeds 3K 5 (5G 68)
Pincheon St. WF1: Wake 4L 9 (5M 125)
Pinder Av. LS12: Leeds 1J 85
Pinderfields Rd. WF1: Wake 3K 9 (4L 125)
PINDER GREEN 3K 107
Pinder Gro. LS12: Leeds 1J 85
Pinders Cres. WF11: Ferr 7B 110
Pinders Gth. WF11: Ferr 7B 110
Pinders Grn. Ct. LS26: Meth 3K 107
Pinders Grn. Dr. LS26: Meth 3K 107
Pinders Grn. Fold LS26: Meth 3K 107
Pinders Grn. Wlk. LS26: Meth 4K 107
Pinder's Gro. WF1: Wake 1M 9 (3N 125)
Pinders Sq. WF1: Wake 1L 9 (3M 125)
Pinder St. LS12: Leeds 1J 85
Pinder Vw. LS12: Leeds 1J 85
Pineapple Cotts. WF1: Warm 5F 126
Pinebury Dr. BD13: Que 4B 80
Pine Cl. LS22: Weth 2M 23
WF10: C'frd 6E 108
Pine Ct. HD4: Neth 3J 153
LS2: Leeds 7H 5 (7F 68)
Pine Ct. M. HD4: Neth 3J 153
Pine Cft. BD20: Keigh 7G 26
Pinedale BD16: Bgly 2E 44
Pinefield Pl. WF9: Kins 8B 146
Pine Gro. WF17: Bat 8E 102
Pinehurst Ct. HD3: Hud 1G 137
(off Lidget St.)
Pine Rd. OL14: Tod 5H 93
Pines, The LS10: Leeds 9G 86
LS17: Huby 6M 19
LS17: Leeds 4K 51
WF12: Dew 5H 123
Pines Gdns. LS29: I'ly 6E 14
Pine St. BD1: B'frd 3D 6 (7D 64)
BD22: Haw 9C 42
HD1: Hud 3D 8 (3N 137)
HX1: Hal 5K 7 (6B 98)
WF9: S Elm 8L 163
Pine Tree Av. LS23: B Spa 9E 24
WF8: Pon 5H 129
Pine Tree Ct. WF7: F'stne 7C 128
Pinewood HD6: Brigh 9L 99
(off Elmwood Dr.)
Pinewood Av. WF2: Wake 5F 124
Pinewood Cl. LS29: I'ly 6F 14
Pinewood Gdns. HX4: Holy 7A 118
WF14: Mir 6M 121
Pinewood Pl. WF11: Knot 9C 110
Pinfold BD14: Clay 1H 81
Pinfold Cl. HX4: Bark 6G 117
LS26: Meth 1L 107
WF4: Flock 8F 140
WF11: Ferr 7B 110
WF12: T'hill 9H 123
WF14: Mir 6M 121
Pinfold Cotts. WF11: Fair 9M 91
Pinfold Ct. LS15: Leeds 6C 70
Pinfold Dr. WF4: Croft 1H 145
Pinfold Grn. HX6: Sow B 9E 96
Pinfold Gro. LS15: Leeds 6B 70
WF2: Wake 1M 143

Pinfold Hill—Premier Way

Pinfold Hill LS15: Leeds .6C 70
WF13: Dew .3E 122
Pinfold La. HD2: Fix .5J 119
HD3: Scam .5J 135
HD7: Golc .6N 135
HD8: Lept .7L 139
HX6: Sow B .8D 96
LS12: Leeds .7L 67
LS15: Leeds .6B 70
LS16: Leeds .1H 49
LS25: Gar .7N 71
LS26: Meth .1M 107
S71: Roys .6D 160
WF2: Wake .1N 143
WF4: Flock .8F 140
WF8: K S'ton .5J 149
WF14: Mir .6M 121
Pinfold Mt. LS15: Leeds .7C 70
Pinfold Ri. LS25: Aber .7E 54
Pinfold Rd. LS15: Leeds .7C 70
Pinfold Sq. LS15: Leeds .6B 70
Pingle Ri. HD8: Den D .1D 172
Pin Hill La. HX2: Midg .3D 96
Pink St. BD22: Haw .1C 60
Pinnacle BD14: Clay .9H 63
(off Bradford Rd.)
Pinnacle, The WF1: Wake .6J 9 (6L 125)
Pinnacle La. HX7: Heb B .4F 94
Pinnar Cft. HX3: Sou .8F 98
Pinnar La. HX3: Sou .7E 98
Pintail Av. BD6: B'frd .4H 81
Pioneer Bus. Pk. WF10: C'frd .8N 107
Pioneer Ct. WF10: C'frd .7M 107
Pioneer St. OL14: W'den .4J 113
WF12: Dew .8F 122
Pioneer Way WF10: C'frd .7M 107
Pipe & Nook La. LS12: Leeds .7J 67
Pipercroft BD6: B'frd .7K 81
Piper Hill WF11: Fair .9N 91
Piper La. LS21: Otley .1K 31
Pipers Cl. WF2: Wren .2F 124
Piperwell Cl. WF16: Heck .7A 102
Piper Wells La. HD8: Cumb, Shep .2J 171
Pipit Mdw. LS27: Morl .1M 103
Pippin Ct. HX2: Hal .1M 97
Pippin's App. WF6: Norm .9J 107
Pippins Grn. Av. WF2: Kirk .1D 124
Pirie Cl. BD2: B'frd .3D 64
Pitchstone Ct. LS12: Leeds .7G 66
Pitcliffe Way BD5: B'frd .8B 6 (1D 82)
Pitfall St. LS1: Leeds .8G 5 (7E 68)
Pit Fld. Rd. WF3: Carl .2M 105
Pit Hill HX3: Hal .6C 98
Pit La. BD3: B'frd .3F 6 (7E 64)
BD6: B'frd .6L 81
BD13: Denh .6H 61
BD13: Que, Thorn .2B 80
BD19: Gom .2M 101
LS25: M'fld .1E 90
(not continuous)
LS26: Meth .9L 89
WF13: Dew .1C 122
Pits La. BD19: Scho .6C 100
Pitt Hill La. HX4: Holy .9J 117
Pit La. S75: Map .8J 159
Pitt Row LS1: Leeds .8F 4 (7E 68)
Pitts St. BD4: B'frd .1H 83
Pitt St. BD21: Keigh .9K 27
OL14: Tod .7M 93
WF15: Liv .1M 121
Pitt St. Bus. Cen. BD21: Keigh .9K 27
Pitty Beck Vw. BD15: All .7G 63
Place, The LS17: Leeds .3F 50
Place's Rd. LS9: Leeds .8L 5 (7G 69)
Plaid Row LS9: Leeds .6L 5 (6G 69)
Plainfield HX6: Sow B .7K 97
Plain La. HX6: Sow B .1C 116
Plains HD7: Mars .4G 150
Plains La. HD7: Mars .4G 150
HX5: Ell .2E 118
Plane Grn. WF8: Pon .2M 129
Plane St. HD4: Hud .7N 137
OL14: Tod .5G 93
Plane Tree Av. LS17: Leeds .3H 51
Plane Tree Cl. LS17: Leeds .3H 51
Plane Tree Cft. LS17: Leeds .3H 51
Plane Tree Gdns. LS17: Leeds .3H 51
Plane Tree Gro. LS19: Yead .1A 48
Plane Tree Nest HX2: Hal .6L 97
Plane Tree Nest La. HX2: Hal .6L 97
Plane Tree Ri. LS17: Leeds .3H 51
Plane Tree Rd. HX6: Sow B .7H 97
Plane Trees HX2: Hal .4K 97
HX2: Wain .5F 78
Plane Trees Cl. BD19: Hun .1H 101
Planetrees Rd. BD4: B'frd .8G 65
Planetrees St. BD15: All .5F 62
Plane Tree Vw. LS17: Leeds .3H 51
Plantation Av. LS15: Leeds .7A 70
LS17: Leeds .2J 51
S71: Roys .6E 160
Plantation Dr. HD4: Hud .9M 137
Plantation Fold BD22: Keigh .3F 42
Plantation Gdns. LS17: Leeds .2J 51
Plantation M. BD9: B'frd .1J 63
Plantation Pl. BD4: B'frd .1G 83
Plantations, The
BD12: Low M .7A 82
Plantation Way BD17: Bail .4B 46
Platform 1 Art Gallery .7J 93
Platform One LS5: Leeds .2L 67
(off Station App.)
Platnam Gro. HD2: Hud .2L 137
Platt Ct. BD18: Ship .7C 46
Platt La. HD7: Slait .9N 135
Platt Sq. BD19: Cleck .5H 101
(off Westgate)
Playfair Rd. LS10: Leeds .3F 86
Playground LS12: N Far .2G 84
Playhouse Sq. LS2: Leeds .6H 5 (6F 68)
Plaza, The LS2: Leeds .3F 4
Pleasance, The LS26: Swil .4H 89
Pleasant Ct. LS6: Leeds .3C 68
(off Woodhouse St.)
Pleasant Mt. LS11: Leeds .9C 68
Pleasant Pl. BD15: All .5F 62
LS11: Leeds .9C 68
Pleasant Row BD13: Que .5B 80
(off Moor Cl. La.)
Pleasant St. BD7: B'frd .1M 81
HX6: Sow B .8J 97
LS11: Leeds .9C 68
Pleasant Ter. LS11: Leeds .9C 68
Pleasant Vw. HX2: Midg .3C 96
OL14: Tod .7K 93
(off Mt. Pleasant)
WF3: Loft .5H 105
Pleasant Views BD13: Denh .5L 61
Pleasant Vw. Ter. WF3: Rob H .9K 87
(off Copley La.)
PLEDWICK .5M 143
Pledwick Cres. WF2: Wake .4M 143
Pledwick Dr. WF2: Wake .5M 143
Pledwick Gro. WF2: Wake .5L 143
Pledwick La. WF2: Wake .5M 143
Pledwick Ri. WF2: Wake .5M 143
Plevna St. LS10: Leeds .3J 87
Plevna Ter. BD16: Bgly .3E 44
Plimsoll St. BD4: B'frd .1E 82
WF9: Hems .2D 162
Plockwood Cotts. LS25: M'fld .1C 90
Ploughcroft La. HX3: Hal .2A 98
Ploughman's Cft. BD2: B'frd .2C 64
Plover Dr. WF17: Bat .7C 102
Plover Mills HD3: Hud .2G 137
Plover Rd. HD3: Hud .2G 136
Plover St. BD5: B'frd .2A 82
BD21: Keigh .8J 27
Plover Way LS27: Morl .1M 103
Plowmans Wlk. LS19: Yead .1K 47
Plumpton Av. BD2: B'frd .9D 46
Plumpton Cl. BD2: B'frd .1E 64
Plumpton Dr. BD2: B'frd .9D 46
Plumpton End BD2: B'frd .9E 46
Plumpton Gdns. BD2: B'frd .9C 46
Plumpton Lea BD2: B'frd .9D 46
Plumpton Mead BD2: B'frd .9D 46
Plumpton Pk. S72: Shaf .7K 161
Plumpton Pl. WF2: Wake .5J 125
Plumpton Rd. WF2: Wake .5J 125
Plumpton St. WF2: Wake .5J 125
Plumpton Ter. WF2: Wake .6J 125
Plumpton Wlk. BD2: B'frd .9D 46
Plum St. BD21: Keigh .4G 43
HX1: Hal .6M 97
Plum Tree Cl. WF8: Pon .5H 129
Plumtree Hill LS29: Add .1M 13
(off Main St.)
Plymouth Gro. HX1: Hal .4N 97
(off Pellon La.)
Pochard Cl. BD6: B'frd .4H 81
Pockets Leisure Cen. .2J 113
Poets Pl. LS18: Hors .5F 48
Pogson's Cotts. LS14: Leeds .1C 70
(off York Rd.)
Pohlman St. HX1: Hal .7M 97
Point, The LS12: Leeds .8A 4
WF2: Wake .5H 125
Pole Ga. HD3: Scam .7K 135
HD7: Slait .7K 135
Pole Ga. Branch HD3: Scam .6K 135
POLE MOOR .6K 135
Pole Position Indoor Karting
Leeds .9F 68
Pole Rd. BD22: Oak .8A 26
Police Flats OL14: Tod .7K 93
Pollard Av. BD16: Bgly .2G 44
BD19: Gom .3M 101
Pollard Cl. BD19: Gom .3M 101
Pollard La. BD2: B'frd .5F 64
LS13: Leeds .9E 48
POLLARD PARK .2F 6 (6E 64)
Pollards Flds. WF11: Ferr .7A 110
Pollard St. BD4: B'frd .7C 6 (9D 64)
BD16: Cot .9G 44
HD2: Hud .9N 119
OL14: Tod .5G 92
WF3: Loft .6L 105
Pollard St. Nth. HX3: Hal .2L 7 (4C 98)
Pollard St. Sth. HD3: Hud .6G 137
Pollard Way BD19: Gom .3M 101
Pollit Av. HX6: Sow B .9E 96
Polperro Cl. WF6: Norm .9J 107
Pomfret Ct. WF8: Pon .3N 129
Pomfret Pl. LS25: Gar .6B 72
Pond, The HX6: Tri .2E 116
Pond Cl. HD4: Hud .9L 137
Ponden Cl. WF9: Hems .2E 162
Ponden La. BD22: S'bury .8H 41
Ponderosa Cl. LS8: Leeds .3H 69
Ponderosa Rural Therapeutic Cen. .3A 122
Pond Farm Dr. HD6: Brigh .7K 99
Pondfields Cl. LS25: Kip .3B 90
Pondfields Crest LS25: Kip .3B 90
Pondfields Dr. LS25: Kip .3B 90
Pondfields Pl. LS25: Kip .3B 90
Pondfields Ri. LS25: Kip .3B 90
Pond La. HD8: Lept .8L 139
Pond St. BD21: Keigh .8J 27
Pond Ter. HD6: Brigh .7K 99
Ponker La. HD8: Lwr C .9B 156
Ponker Nook La. HD8: Skelm .8C 156
PONTEFRACT .3J 129
Pontefract & District Golf Course .2F 128
Pontefract Av. LS9: Leeds .8M 5 (7H 69)
Pontefract Baghill Station (Rail) .3L 129
Pontefract Castle .2K 129
Pontefract Crematorium WF8: Pon .5G 128
Pontefract La. LS9: Leeds, Swil .6M 5 (6H 69)
(not continuous)
LS15: Leeds .2B 88
WF9: Upt .9N 147
Pontefract La. Cl. LS9: Leeds .7M 5 (7H 69)
Pontefract Monkhill Station (Rail) .1L 129
Pontefract Mus. .3J 129
Pontefract Pk. Golf Course .2H 129
Pontefract Pk. (Racecourse) .9F 108
Pontefract Rd. LS10: Leeds .3J 87
LS26: Rothw .5M 87
S72: Cud, Shaf .9J 161
Pontefract Rd. WF4: Croft .9G 126
WF6: Norm .8L 107
(not continuous)
WF7: Ackw .2G 146
WF7: F'stne .7D 128
WF8: Pon .9M 109
WF9: Hems .9F 146
WF10: C'frd .4E 108
WF11: Ferr .7A 110
WF11: Knot .9B 110
Pontefract Squash & Leisure Club .2J 129
Pontefract St. LS9: Leeds .8M 5 (7H 69)
Pontefract Swimming Pool .2K 129
Pontefract Tanshelf Station (Rail) .2J 129
Pontefract Ter. WF9: Hems .3E 162
Pontey Caravan Pk. HD9: Hon .6J 153
Pontey Dr. HD5: Hud .5F 138
Pontey Mt. HD5: Hud .5F 138
Ponyfield Cl. HD2: Hud .1K 137
POOL .1F 32
Pool Bank Cl. LS21: Pool .1G 32
Pool Bank Ct. LS21: Pool .2G 32
Pool Bank New Rd. LS21: Pool .4E 32
Pool Bus. Pk. LS21: Otley .9C 18
Pool Ct. BD3: B'frd .3F 6 (7E 64)
POOLE .1D 110
Poole Cres. LS15: Leeds .4C 70
Poole La. LS25: Bur S .1D 110
Poole Mt. LS15: Leeds .5C 70
Poole Rd. LS15: Leeds .4C 70
Poole Row LS25: Bur S .1D 110
Poole Sq. LS15: Leeds .5C 70
Pool Hill La. HD8: Den D .3F 172
Pool Rd. LS21: Otley, Pool .9N 17
Pools La. S71: Roys .6F 160
Pool St. BD21: Keigh .7L 27
Popeley Ri. BD19: Gom .4N 101
Popeley Rd. WF16: Heck .6N 101
Pope St. BD21: Keigh .8K 27
WF6: Alt .7J 107
Poplar Av. BD7: B'frd .3L 81
BD18: Ship .1A 64
HD9: T'bdge .8A 154
HX6: Sow B .7J 97
LS15: Leeds .4E 70
LS22: Weth .2L 23
LS25: Gar .7M 71
OL14: Tod .5J 93
S72: Shaf .7K 161
WF2: Wake .6F 124
WF10: C'frd .5J 109
Poplar Bank HD8: Fen B .7G 139
Poplar Cl. LS13: Leeds .6J 67
LS29: Burl W .9D 16
Poplar Ct. BD7: B'frd .8N 63
LS13: Leeds .6H 67
Poplar Cres. BD18: Ship .9A 46
HX2: Illing .6M 79
WF3: Ting .3M 103
Poplar Cft. LS13: Leeds .6H 67
Poplar Dr. BD18: Ship .1A 64
BD20: Rid .9B 28
LS18: Hors .7C 48
WF6: Alt .7H 107
Poplar Farm La. LS28: Fars .2B 66
Poplar Gdns. LS13: Leeds .6H 67
Poplar Gth. LS13: Leeds .6H 67
Poplar Ga. LS13: Leeds .6H 67
Poplar Grn. LS13: Leeds .6H 67
WF8: Pon .2M 129
Poplar Gro. BD7: B'frd .3K 81
BD16: Har .6N 43
BD17: Bail .6K 45
BD18: Ship .1A 64
BD19: Cleck .6F 100
WF8: Pon .3H 129
WF11: Knot .1D 130
Poplar Ho. WF10: C'frd .5E 108
(off Parklands)
Poplar Mt. LS13: Leeds .6H 67
Poplar Pl. LS28: Pud .7M 65
Poplar Ri. HD8: Skelm .8E 156
LS13: Leeds .5H 67
Poplar Rd. BD7: B'frd .3M 81
BD18: Ship .9A 46
DN6: Skel .8N 165
Poplars, The HX3: Nor G .2M 99
LS6: Leeds .2A 68
LS16: B'hpe .6J 33
LS20: Guis .6J 31
WF3: Loft .4L 105
WF9: Kins .9B 146
WF11: Knot .1G 130
Poplars Pk. Rd. BD2: B'frd .2C 64
Poplar Sq. LS28: Fars .4A 66
Poplar St. HD2: Hud .1M 137
HD5: Hud .7F 8 (5A 138)
HX3: Hal .1K 7 (4B 98)
WF3: Loft .6L 105
Poplar Ter. BD16: Bgly .5F 44
BD20: Rid .9C 28
BD21: Keigh .9G 27
(off Lustre St.)
HD5: Hud .4B 138
S71: Roys .5E 160
WF4: Horb .2E 142
WF9: S Elm .7N 163
Poplar Vw. BD7: B'frd .3K 81
HX3: Hip .6M 99
LS12: N Far .2K 85
LS13: Leeds .6H 67
LS17: Shad .4A 52
WF4: Horb .2E 142
Poplar Way LS13: Leeds .6H 67
Poplarwood Gdns. BD10: B'frd .1J 65
Popley Butts HD9: Mel .8C 152
Popley Dr. HD9: Mel .8C 152
Popples HX2: Illing .6M 79
HX7: Wads .8L 77
Popples Dr. HX2: Illing .6M 79
Popples La. HX7: Wads .8L 77
Popples Side HX7: Hept .7E 76
Poppleton Ct. WF3: Ting .3A 104
Poppleton Cft. WF3: Ting .4A 104
(off Lowry Rd.)
Poppleton Dr. WF3: Ting .3A 104
Poppleton Ri. WF3: Ting .4A 104
Poppleton Rd. WF3: Ting .3A 104
Poppleton Way WF3: Ting .3A 104
Popple Wells La. HX2: Hal .5F 96
Poppy Ct. BD6: B'frd .7L 81
Poppyfield Ct. LS22: Weth .3N 23
Poppy La. WF3: E Ard .4G 105
Porritt St. BD19: Cleck .3H 101
Portage Av. LS15: Leeds .7A 70
Portage Cres. LS15: Leeds .7N 69
Portal Cres. WF14: Mir .3L 121
(not continuous)
Portal Dr. WF14: Mir .3L 121
Porter Wing HX1: Hal .8J 7
Portland Av. WF8: Pon .2H 129
Portland Cl. HD3: Hud .3H 137
Portland Ct. BD21: Keigh .1H 43
Portland Cres. LS1: Leeds .4E 4 (5D 68)
Portland Cft. WF8: Pon .2H 129
Portland Gate LS1: Leeds .4E 4 (5D 68)
(not continuous)
LS2: Leeds .4E 4 (5D 68)
Portland Ho. BD4: B'frd .8H 65
(off Fearnville Dr.)
HX5: Ell .4E 118
(off Crown St.)
Portland Pl. BD16: Bgly .5F 44
HD1: Hud .4A 8
HX1: Hal .5L 7 (6B 98)
WF9: Upt .2N 163
Portland Rd. HX3: Hal .1M 7 (4C 98)
LS12: Leeds .8M 67
Portland St. BD5: B'frd .6B 6 (8C 64)
BD22: Haw .8D 42
HD1: Hud .3A 8 (3L 137)
HX1: Hal .3L 7 (5B 98)
LS1: Leeds .5D 4 (6D 68)
LS28: Pud .6D 66
WF1: Wake .8A 126
Portland Way LS1: Leeds .4E 4 (5D 68)
Portman Cl. HX4: Stainl .7M 117
Portman St. LS28: Cal .9M 47
PORTOBELLO .9M 125
Portobello Gro. WF2: Wake .8M 125
Portobello Rd. WF1: Wake .8M 125
WF2: Wake .8M 125
Portree Dr. BD6: B'frd .4K 81
Portslade Ho. BD8: B'frd .5A 64
(off Green La.)
PORTSMOUTH .3B 92
Portsmouth Av. BD3: B'frd .5E 64
Portwood St. BD9: B'frd .4J 63
Post Hill Ct. LS12: Leeds .7G 66
Post Hill Gdns. LS28: Pud .7D 66
Post Hill Vw. LS28: Pud .7D 66
Post Office Bldgs. HX4: Bark .7G 117
Post Office Rd. BD2: B'frd .1G 64
WF7: F'stne .6D 128
Post Office Row HD8: Clay W .7H 157
(off Chapel Hill)
Post Office St. BD19: Cleck .6K 101
Post Office Yd. LS29: Burl W .8E 16
Pothill La. WF9: Upt .1A 164
Pot Ho. Rd. BD6: B'frd .5N 81
Pot La. BD20: Stee .2C 26
Potovens Ct. WF3: Loft .6L 105
Potovens La. WF1: Out .7K 105
WF2: Carr G, Wren .9H 105
WF3: Loft .7K 105
Potter Av. WF2: Wake .7G 125
Potter Brow Rd. BD17: Bail .9A 30
Potter Cl. BD12: Low M .8C 82
POTTERNEWTON .2F 68
Potternewton Av. LS7: Leeds .9D 50
Potternewton Ct. LS7: Leeds .9E 50
Potternewton Cres. LS7: Leeds .1D 68
Potternewton Gdns. LS7: Leeds .9E 50
Potternewton Gro. LS7: Leeds .9D 50
Potternewton Hgts. LS7: Leeds .9E 50
Potternewton La. LS7: Leeds .9C 50
Potternewton Mt. LS7: Leeds .9D 50
Potternewton Vw. LS7: Leeds .9D 50
Potters Cft. WF3: Loft .6L 105
Potters Ga. HD8: Cumb .8H 171
Potters Wlk. HD7: Golc .6D 136
POTTERTON .5M 53
Potterton Cl. LS15: Bar E .7M 53
Potterton Ct. LS15: Bar E .7M 53
(off Potterton Cl.)
Potterton La. LS15: Bar E, Pott .5M 53
Pottery Ct. WF11: Knot .8C 110
POTTERY FIELD .8F 68
Pottery La. LS26: W'frd .6E 88
WF11: Knot .7C 110
Pottery Rd. LS10: Leeds .1F 86
Pottery St. HD3: Hud .2D 136
WF10: C'frd .4B 108
Pott's Ter. WF6: Norm .3J 127
Poulton Pl. LS11: Leeds .2E 86
Poverty La. HX6: Tri .2A 116
Powell Av. BD5: B'frd .1A 82
Powell Rd. BD16: Bgly .4G 44
BD18: Ship .1B 64
Powell St. HX1: Hal .4K 7 (5B 98)
(not continuous)
WF9: S Kirk .6K 163
WF10: C'frd .4D 108
WF16: Heck .9B 102
Powerhouse 1 Showcase Theatre
Wakefield .5H 9
Powerleague
Leeds, Limewood App. .8B 52
Leeds, Wellington Bri. St. .6A 4 (6B 68)
Poxton Gro. WF9: S Elm .8L 163
Prail Cl. WF8: Pon .2M 129
Prail La. WF8: Pon .2M 129
Pratt La. BD18: Ship .9A 46
WF14: Mir .5L 121
Preachers M. BD16: Bgly .4F 44
(off Priestthorpe Rd.)
Precinct, The WF7: F'stne .6C 128
Premiere Pk. LS29: I'ly .6D 14
Premier Way HX5: Ell .3F 118
LS26: Oul .4A 106

Premier Way Nth. WF6: Norm 1N 127
Premier Way Sth. WF7: A'ton 2N 127
Prescott Pl. HX4: Stainl 7M 117
Prescott St. HX1: Hal 6K 7 (6B 98)
Prescott Ter. BD15: All 5G 63
Preston Bldgs. *BD19: Scho* *3D 100*
(off Tabbs La.)
Preston La. HX2: Hal 2J 97
(not continuous)
LS26: Gt P 6M 89
WF10: All B 6M 89
Preston Pde. LS11: Leeds 3C 86
Preston Pl. HX1: Hal 4G 7 (5N 97)
Preston St. BD7: B'frd 7A 64
WF12: Dew 5H 123
WF17: Bat 8F 102
Preston Ter. *BD16: Bgly* *2E 44*
(off Sleningford Rd.)
Preston Vw. LS26: Swil 4J 89
Prestwich Dr. HD2: Fix 8L 119
Prestwick Cl. LS21: Otley 2H 31
Prestwick Fold WF5: Oss 4N 123
Pretoria Rd. BD3: B'frd 7H 65
Pretoria St. HD7: Slait 9M 135
WF1: Wake 8M 125
WF7: F'stne 5C 128
WF10: C'frd 5E 108
Pretoria Ter. HX2: Hal 4K 97
PRICKLEDEN 4L 169
PRIEST HILL 1L 23
Priest Hill Gdns. LS22: Weth 2L 23
PRIESTHORPE 2M 65
Priesthorpe Av. LS28: Stan 4M 65
Priesthorpe Ct. LS28: Fars 2A 66
Priesthorpe La. LS28: Fars 3M 65
Priesthorpe Rd. LS28: Cal, Fars 2L 65
(not continuous)
Priest La. HX6: Ripp 7E 116
Priestley Av. BD6: B'frd 5A 82
S75: Kex 9E 158
WF16: Heck 6A 102
Priestley Centre for the Arts
Bradford 4D 6
Priestley Cl. LS28: Pud 6C 66
Priestley Ct. LS18: Hors 7H 49
LS28: Pud 6C 66
Priestley Dr. LS28: Pud 5C 66
Priestley Gdns. LS28: Pud 6C 66
WF16: Heck 7N 101
PRIESTLEY GREEN 3K 99
Priestley Gro. HD4: Hud 9L 137
Priestley Hill BD13: Que 6B 80
Priestley Pl. HX6: Sow B 9G 96
Priestley Sq. WF17: Birs 2B 102
Priestley St. BD1: B'frd 2C 6 (6D 64)
BD13: Thorn 8C 62
Priestley Ter. BD6: B'frd 4A 82
Priestley Vw. LS28: Pud 6C 66
Priestley Wlk. LS28: Pud 6C 66
Priestman Cl. BD8: B'frd 5A 64
Priestman St. BD8: B'frd 5A 64
Priest Royd S75: Dart 8J 159
PRIESTTHORPE 3F 44
Priestthorpe Cl. BD16: Bgly 3F 44
Priestthorpe La. BD16: Bgly 3F 44
Priestthorpe Rd. BD16: Bgly 4F 44
PRIESTWELL 6L 93
Priestwell St. OL14: Tod 6L 93
Primary Cl. HX2: Illing 7M 79
Primary Way BD2: B'frd 5F 64
Primitive St. HD1: Hud 4C 8 (4N 137)
WF3: Carl 1M 105
Primley Gdns. LS17: Leeds 3E 50
Primley Pk. Av. LS17: Leeds 3E 50
Primley Pk. Cl. LS17: Leeds 3F 50
Primley Pk. Ct. LS17: Leeds 2E 50
Primley Pk. Cres. LS17: Leeds 3E 50
Primley Pk. Dr. LS17: Leeds 3E 50
Primley Pk. Gth. LS17: Leeds 2F 50
Primley Pk. Grn. LS17: Leeds 2F 50
Primley Pk. Gro. LS17: Leeds 3E 50
Primley Pk. La. LS17: Leeds 3E 50
Primley Pk. Mt. LS17: Leeds 3F 50
Primley Pk. Ri. LS17: Leeds 3F 50
Primley Pk. Rd. LS17: Leeds 3E 50
Primley Pk. Vw. LS17: Leeds 2E 50
Primley Pk. Wlk. LS17: Leeds 2F 50
Primley Pk. Way LS17: Leeds 2E 50
Primo Pl. LS8: Leeds 3M 69
Primrose Av. LS15: Leeds 6B 70
LS26: Swil 4J 89
Primrose Bank BD16: Bgly 5G 45
Primrose Cl. LS15: Leeds 6B 70
WF8: Pon 4K 129
Primrose Ct. LS17: Leeds 2F 50
LS20: Guis *7J 31*
(off Orchard Way)
Primrose Cres. LS15: Leeds 5B 70
Primrose Dene WF11: Byram 5C 110
Primrose Dr. BD16: Bgly 5G 45
LS15: Leeds 6B 70
WF10: C'frd 6H 109
Primrose Gdns. LS15: Leeds 5B 70
WF17: Bat 6H 103
Primrose Gth. LS15: Leeds 6A 70
Primrose Gro. BD21: Keigh 9L 27
HD4: Hud 7M 137
LS15: Leeds 5B 70
PRIMROSE HILL 8B 8 (6M 137)
Primrose Hill *BD7: B'frd* *9A 64*
(off Gt. Horton Rd.)
BD16: Bgly 6H 45
LS28: Stan 5B 66
WF11: Knot 7F 110
WF17: Bat 6G 103
Primrose Hill Cl. LS26: Swil 4J 89
Primrose Hill Dr. LS26: Swil 4J 89
Primrose Hill Gdns. LS26: Swil 4J 89
Primrose Hill Gth. LS26: Swil 5J 89
Primrose Hill Grn. LS26: Swil 4J 89
Primrose Hill Gro. LS26: Swil 4J 89
Primrose Hill Rd. HD4: Hud 6M 137
Primrose Ho. WF1: Wake 6L 9
Primrose La. BD2: B'frd 2B 64
BD16: Bgly 4H 45
Primrose La. HD8: Kbtn 1H 155
LS11: Leeds 2E 86
LS15: Leeds 6A 70
(not continuous)
LS23: B Spa 1C 38
WF4: Cal G 4F 142
WF14: Mir 4N 121
WF15: Liv 7K 101
Primrose Rd. LS15: Leeds 6B 70
Primrose Row BD17: Bail 3D 46
Primrose St. BD8: B'frd 6A 64
BD21: Keigh 9L 27
HD4: Hud 8B 8 (6M 137)
Primrose Ter. HX7: Heb B 1H 95
HX7: Myth *4M 95*
(off Scout Rd.)
Primrose Va. WF11: Knot 8F 110
Primrose Wlk. LS27: Chur 5M 85
Primrose Way HX3: She 6J 81
WF4: Horb 9B 124
Primrose Yd. LS26: Oul 8D 88
Prince Albert Sq. BD13: Que 3G 80
Prince Edward Gro. LS12: Leeds 1K 85
Prince Edward Rd. LS12: Leeds 1K 85
Prince Henry Rd. LS21: Otley 7L 17
Prince Henrys Ct. LS21: Otley 8L 17
PRINCE ROYD 9H 119
Princeroyd Way BD7: B'frd 7M 63
Princes Av. LS8: Leeds 8K 51
Prince's Ct. BD18: Ship 9N 45
LS17: Leeds 6E 50
Prince's Cres. BD2: B'frd 3C 64
Princes Ga. HX3: Hal 8A 98
WF4: Horb 9F 124
Prince's Gro. LS6: Leeds 1N 67
Princess Alexandra Wlk. HD1: Hud 6C 8
Princess Av. WF9: S Elm 7M 163
WF12: Dew 3K 123
Princess Cl. WF12: Dew 3K 123
Princess Ct. LS15: Leeds 8E 70
LS17: Leeds 4F 50
WF6: Norm 2K 127
Princess Cres. WF12: Dew 4K 123
Princess Flds. LS15: Leeds 8E 70
Princess Gdns. *WF13: Dew* *3E 122*
(off Halliley St.)
Princess La. WF12: Dew 3K 123
Princess Mary Stadium 7K 101
Princess of Wales Precinct, The
WF13: Dew *3G 122*
(off Long Causeway)
Princes Sq. LS1: Leeds 8D 4 (7D 68)
Princess Rd. LS29: I'ly 6F 14
WF12: Dew 3K 123
Princess St. HD1: Hud 6B 8 (5M 137)
(not continuous)
HD6: Brigh 1N 119
HX1: Hal 3L 7 (5B 98)
HX4: Gree 4C 118
HX6: Sow B 8J 97
HX7: Heb B *9H 77*
(off Foster La.)
LS19: Raw 3L 47
S72: Cud 8K 161
S75: Map 8J 159
WF1: Out 8K 105
WF1: Wake 9M 125
WF6: Norm 1J 127
WF10: C'frd 3E 108
WF12: Dew 3K 123
WF14: Mir 7L 121
WF17: Bat 6F 102
Princess Ter. HX1: Hal 8J 7
Princes St. BD6: B'frd 5N 81
(Alexander St.)
BD6: B'frd 6K 81
(School St.)
WF16: Heck 8B 102
Prince St. BD4: B'frd 4G 83
BD20: Sils 8D 12
BD22: Haw 8D 42
HD4: Hud 6N 137
WF10: All B 6N 89
WF13: Dew 3G 122
WF17: Bat 6F 102
Princes Vw. HD2: Hud 9H 119
Prince's Way BD1: B'frd 5A 6 (8C 64)
Princeton Cl. HX2: Hal 3L 97
PRINCEVILLE 7N 63
Princeville Rd. BD7: B'frd 7M 63
Princeville St. BD7: B'frd 7N 63
(not continuous)
Prince William Ct. *WF7: F'stne* *7C 128*
(off Granville St.)
Prince Wood La. HD2: Hud 9H 119
Priordale Rd. WF7: F'stne 7B 128
Prior's La. BD23: Drau 3E 10
Prior St. BD21: Keigh 8L 27
Priory Bus. Pk. WF9: Fitz 6B 146
Priory Chase WF8: Pon 3K 129
Priory Cl. BD16: Bgly 3F 44
LS22: Weth 2N 23
WF5: Oss 7N 123
WF6: Alt 8G 107
WF14: Mir 5J 121
Priory Ct. BD8: B'frd 6B 64
BD16: Bgly 3F 44
BD19: Gom 3L 101
HD3: Hud 9G 119
Priory Cft. WF5: Oss 6N 123
Priory Est. WF9: S Elm 6A 164
Priory Grange WF8: Pon 1L 129
Priory Gro. BD16: Bgly 3F 44
Priory Ho. *BD10: B'frd* *8G 46*
(off Cavendish Rd.)
Priory M. WF3: S'ley 6A 106
Priory Pl. HD2: Hud 6D 120
Priory Ridge WF4: Croft 2H 145
Priory Rd. HD6: Brigh 1A 120
WF5: Oss 6N 123
WF7: F'stne 7B 128
Priory Sq. WF2: W'ton 4B 144
Priory Vw. *OL14: Tod* *6K 93*
(off Garden St.)
Priory Wlk. WF14: Mir 5J 121
Priory Way WF14: Mir 5J 121
Privas Way LS22: Weth 5N 23
Privet Dr. BD22: Oak 5D 42
Privilege St. LS12: Leeds 7L 67
PROBIZ Coliseum, The 3F 108
Proctor St. BD4: B'frd 3H 83
Prod La. BD17: Bail 5K 45
Progress Av. HD16: Har 6N 43
Prologis Pk. BD5: B'frd 4E 82
Prospect Av. BD18: Ship 8A 46
HX2: Hal 8L 97
LS13: Leeds 3F 66
LS28: Pud 6A 66
WF6: Norm 9J 107
Prospect Bank LS23: B'ham 5D 38
Prospect Bldgs. *WF3: E Ard* *5E 104*
(off Bradford Rd.)
Prospect Bus. Pk. *BD16: Bgly* *5F 44*
(off Bradford Rd.)
HD1: Hud *5M 137*
(off Prospect Ho.)
Prospect Cl. BD18: Ship 8A 46
HX2: Hal 8L 97
Prospect Cotts. HD5: K'htn 2G 138
WF9: S Elm 6L 163
Prospect Ct. HX2: Hal 4H 97
LS14: T'ner 2G 52
LS27: Morl *8K 85*
(off Prospect Pl.)
WF17: Bat 6F 102
Prospect Cres. BD22: Keigh 2E 42
LS10: Leeds 2F 86
Prospect Dr. BD22: Keigh 2E 42
Prospect Gdns.
LS15: Leeds 6C 70
Prospect Gro. BD18: Ship 8A 46
LS28: Pud 6A 66
Prospect Ho. HD1: Hud 7A 8
Prospect La. BD11: B'haw 8M 83
Prospect M. *LS27: Morl* *8K 85*
(off Prospect Pl.)
Prospect Mt. BD18: Ship 8A 46
BD22: Keigh 2E 42
Prospect Pl. BD2: B'frd 4G 65
BD9: B'frd 5L 63
BD13: Que 4D 80
HD3: Outl 2M 135
HD6: Brigh 1M 119
HD7: Golc 3B 136
HD9: H'frth 4M 169
HX2: Hal 1M 97
HX2: Mt T 1G 96
HX3: Nor G *2M 99*
(off Village St.)
LS13: Leeds 3F 66
LS18: Hors 7E 48
LS26: Rothw 9A 88
LS27: Morl 8K 85
WF3: Loft 2K 105
WF5: Oss 6A 124
Prospect Rd. BD3: B'frd 1D 6 (6D 64)
(not continuous)
BD16: Bgly 2H 45
BD19: Cleck 4H 101
HD3: Hud 4E 136
LS29: Burl W 9C 16
WF5: Oss 5N 123
WF15: Liv 2H 121
WF16: Heck 6N 101
Prospect Row HX2: Hal 1M 97
HX2: Mix 6J 79
LS29: Burl W 2A 30
Prospect Sq. HD8: Skelm 7D 156
LS28: Fars 4A 66
Prospect St. BD4: B'frd 7D 6 (9D 64)
BD6: B'frd 6L 81
BD10: B'frd 1G 64
BD13: Thorn 8D 62
BD18: Ship 8A 46
BD19: Cleck 4H 101
BD22: Haw 9C 42
BD22: Keigh 1F 42
DN6: Nort 7N 149
HD1: Hud 6A 8 (5M 137)
HX3: Hal 1M 7 (4C 98)
LS19: Raw 4N 47
LS28: Fars 3A 66
LS28: Pud 6N 65
WF4: Horb 2E 142
WF17: Bat 6F 102
Prospect Ter. BD15: All 5H 63
BD19: Cleck 4H 101
BD20: Rid 6M 27
HX2: Lud F 7E 96
HX4: Bark 7G 117
HX6: Norl 1H 117
LS9: Leeds 7M 5
LS13: Leeds 1B 66
(Airedale Mt.)
LS13: Leeds 3F 66
(Prospect Vw.)
LS18: Hors 6F 48
LS25: M'fld 8G 73
LS26: Rothw 9A 88
LS28: Fars 3A 66
WF9: S Kirk 7H 163
WF11: Knot 8F 110
WF15: Liv 8K 101
Prospect Vw. BD13: Que 6B 80
DN6: Nort 7N 149
LS13: Leeds 3F 66
WF15: Liv 1H 121
Prospect Vs. *BD19: Cleck* *4H 101*
(off Prospect St.)
HX2: Illing 7M 79
LS22: Weth 3M 23
Prospect Wlk. BD18: Ship 8A 46
Prospect Way
HD6: B Bri 6N 99
Prospect Yd. WF1: Wake 4H 9
Prosper St. LS10: Leeds 1G 86
Providence Av. BD17: Bail 3A 46
LS6: Leeds 2C 68
Providence Bldgs. *HX3: Sou* *8F 98*
(off New St.)
Providence Ct. BD22: Oak 5C 42
LS27: Morl 8K 85
(Bank St.)
LS27: Morl 1L 103
(Wide La.)
WF12: Dew 7E 122
Providence Cres. BD22: Oak 5C 42
Providence Grn. WF8: Pon 9L 109
Providence Hill HX4: Stainl 8L 117
Providence La. BD22: Haw, Oak 5C 42
Providence Mt. *LS27: Morl* *8K 85*
(off Bank St.)
Providence Pl. BD12: Wyke 9A 82
HD6: Brigh 2A 120
HX6: Sow B 9F 96
LS2: Leeds 3F 4 (5E 68)
LS15: Swil C 8H 71
LS25: Gar 7M 71
LS27: Morl 9H 85
LS28: Stan 5B 66
WF10: All B 1B 108
Providence Rd. LS6: Leeds 2C 68
Providence Row BD2: B'frd 3F 64
BD17: Bail 3A 46
BD20: E Mor 6D 28
HX2: Hal 1M 97
HX2: Mix 6J 79
Providence St. BD1: B'frd 4A 6 (7B 64)
BD19: Cleck 4J 101
BD19: Scho 3C 100
HX5: Ell 4E 118
LS28: Fars 4A 66
OL14: W'den 4J 113
WF1: Wake 3J 9 (4L 125)
WF12: Dew 4J 123
WF17: Bat 7F 102
Providence Ter. BD13: Thorn 8C 62
LS2: Leeds 1C 4 (3C 68)
Providence Vs. *BD19: Scho* *3C 100*
(off Providence St.)
LS23: Cliff 3D 38
Providence Works *LS27: Morl* *9G 85*
(off Howden Clough Rd.)
Providential St. WF4: Flock 7E 140
Prune Pk. La. BD15: All 3D 62
Pudding La. OL14: Tod 2E 92
PUDSEY
LS28 .... 6C 66
OL14 .... 2D 92
Pudsey Bus. Cen. LS28: Pud 7C 66
Pudsey Leisure Cen. 7B 66
Pudsey Rd. LS12: Leeds 7E 66
LS13: Leeds, Pud 7E 66
OL14: Tod 3D 92
Puffin Cl. BD6: B'frd 4H 81
Pugneys Country Pk. 2K 143
Pugneys Light Railway 2K 143
Pugneys Nature Reserve 2K 143
Pugneys Rd. WF2: Wake 9L 125
Pule Grn. La. HX3: Hal 1A 98
PULE HILL 1A 98
Pullan Av. BD2: B'frd 2F 64
Pullan Dr. BD2: B'frd 2G 65
Pullan Gro. BD2: B'frd 2G 65
Pullan La. BD17: Esh 2G 47
Pullan St. BD5: B'frd 9B 64
Pullan Way LS27: Morl 3J 103
Pullman Ct. LS11: Leeds 4A 86
LS27: Morl 8L 85
Pullman Ho. LS11: Leeds 4A 86
Pulmans Pl. *HX3: Hal* *1B 118*
(off Skircoat Grn.)
Pulmans Yd. HX3: Hal 1B 118
Pulse Sports & Fitness
Bradford 2D 64
Pumphouse La. WF14: Mir 5M 121
Pump La. HD8: Kbtn 2N 155
HX3: Hal 4E 98
WF3: W Ard 7A 104
WF4: Wrag 2A 146
WF13: Dew 3C 122
Pump St. HD8: H Flat 5M 171
Punch Bowl Yd. BD19: Cleck 5G 100
WF11: B'ton 4B 110
Pundles HX2: Illing 5L 79
Purbeck Ct. BD4: B'frd 3J 83
Purbeck Gro. LS25: Gar 8N 71
Purcell Dr. BD20: Sils 7D 12
Purley Wlk. BD6: B'frd 5N 81
Purlwell Av. WF17: Bat 9E 102
Purlwell Cres. WF17: Bat 9E 102
Purlwell Hall Rd. WF17: Bat 9F 102
Purlwell La. WF17: Bat 8F 102
Purprise La. HX7: P Wel 4H 77
PURSTON JAGLIN 7E 128
Purston La. WF7: Ackw 1F 146
Purston Pk. Ct. WF7: F'stne 7D 128
Pussy La. HD8: Shel 6L 155
Putting Mill Wlk.
HD8: Den D 2E 172
Pye Av. S75: Map 9J 159
Pyebank BD15: Wils 9A 44
PYE NEST 7M 97
Pye Nest Av. HX2: Hal 7K 97
Pye Nest Ct. WF15: Liv 8H 101
Pye Nest Dr. HX2: Hal 8L 97
Pye Nest Gdns. HX2: Hal 7L 97
Pye Nest Gro. HX2: Hal 7L 97
Pye Nest Ri. HX2: Hal 8L 97
Pye Nest Rd. HX2: Hal 8K 97
HX6: Sow B 8K 97
Pye Nook BD12: Low M 6B 82
Pyenot Av. BD19: Cleck 5J 101
Pyenot Dr. BD19: Cleck 6J 101
Pyenot Gdns. BD19: Cleck 6J 101
Pyenot Hall La. BD19: Cleck 5J 101
Pymont Ct. WF3: Loft 3L 105
Pymont Dr. LS26: W'frd 6B 88
Pymont Gro. LS26: W'frd 6C 88
Pymroyd La. HD4: Hud 6F 136
(not continuous)
Pym St. LS10: Leeds 9F 68
Pynate Rd. WF17: Bat 6D 102
Pyrah Fold BD12: Wyke 9A 82
Pyrah Rd. BD12: Low M 6B 82

Pyrah St.—Rathmell St.

Pyrah St. BD12: Wyke 9B 82
WF13: Dew 2F 122

Q

QBM Bus. Pk. WF17: Birs 2C 102
Q F Ind. Est. BD4: B'frd 1F 82
QM Ind. Pk. HD2: Hud 9B 120
Quail Av. BD6: B'frd 4H 81
Quail St. BD21: Keigh 8K 27
Quaker Ga. HD8: Skelm 6B 156
Quaker Ho. LS2: Leeds 1C 4 (3C 68)
Quaker Ho. Yd. WF1: Wake 7N 125
Quaker La. BD5: B'frd 2N 81
BD19: Cleck 5H 101
HD1: Hud 5K 137
WF15: Liv 6H 101
Quakers La. HX6: Ripp 9D 116
LS19: Raw 2M 47
Quaker St. BD3: B'frd 5F 64
QUARMBY 4G 136
Quarmby Clough HD3: Hud 4F 136
Quarmby Cft. HD3: Hud 3F 136
Quarmby Fold HD3: Hud 3F 136
Quarmby Rd. HD3: Hud 3G 136
Quarrie Dene Ct. LS7: Leeds 9E 50
Quarry, The LS17: Leeds 1C 50
LS22: Weth 3M 23
Quarry Av. WF11: Knot 9F 110
Quarry Bank Ct. LS5: Leeds 9J 49
Quarry Bldgs. WF4: Horb 1B 142
Quarry Cl. HD9: Brock 7A 154
S75: Kex 9F 158
Quarry Cotts. BD20: Stee 3D 26
LS18: Hors 6E 48
WF5: Oss 6N 123
Quarry Ct. HD3: Hud 3E 136
HX3: Hal 5D 98
WF10: C'frd 6D 108
Quarry Dene LS16: Leeds 7M 49
Quarrydene Dr. WF10: C'frd 6H 109
Quarry Dene Pk. LS16: Leeds 6M 49
Quarry Dr. HD5: K'htn 4F 138
Quarry Farm Rd. LS21: Pool 3D 32
Quarryfields WF14: Mir 4M 121
Quarryfield Ter. WF3: E Ard 5F 104
Quarry Gap Row BD4: B'frd 8J 65
Quarry Gdns. LS17: Leeds 1C 50
QUARRY HILL 6J 5 (6F 68)
Quarry Hill HD5: Hud 6F 138
HX6: Sow B 9H 97
LS26: Oul 8D 88
LS28: Fars *3A 66*
(off Wesley St.)
WF4: Horb 1B 142
Quarry Hill Ind. Est. WF4: Horb 1A 142
Quarry Hill La. LS22: Weth 2L 23
(not continuous)
Quarry Ho. LS2: Leeds 6J 5 (6G 68)
Quarry La. HD4: Neth 2H 153
HD5: K'htn 5G 138
LS27: Morl 2L 103
WF8: Lit S 4K 149
WF9: Upt 1N 163
WF12: Dew, Morl 5K 103
WF15: Liv 7G 101
WF17: Bat 4C 102
Quarry Mt. HD9: H'frth 3M 169
LS6: Leeds 2C 68
LS19: Yead *9N 31*
(off King St.)
WF4: Ryh 9J 145
Quarry Mt. Pl. LS6: Leeds 2C 68
Quarry Mt. St. LS6: Leeds 2C 68
Quarry Mt. Ter. LS6: Leeds 2C 68
Quarry Pl. BD2: B'frd 4F 64
LS6: Leeds 3C 68
WF14: Mir 5H 121
Quarry Rd. BD19: Cleck 5G 101
BD19: Gom 5M 101
HD1: Hud 4K 137
HD4: Hud 7G 136
HD6: Ras 4M 119
HX3: Hal 2L 97
LS21: Pool 3D 32
LS26: W'frd 7E 88
WF13: Dew 4E 122
WF15: Liv 8L 101
Quarryside Rd. WF14: Mir 5J 121
Quarry St. BD9: B'frd 2M 63
BD21: Keigh 9K 27
LS6: Leeds 3C 68
OL12: Whit 6A 112
WF7: Ackw 5F 146
Quarry Ter. LS18: Hors 6E 48
Quarry Vw. WF7: Ackw 5E 146
WF13: Dew 2C 122
Quaver La. BD15: All 5G 62
Quay Cl. BD6: B'frd 5M 81
Quay One LS9: Leeds 8J 5
Quayside BD17: Ship 7N 45
Quayside, The BD10: B'frd 7J 47
Quayside Ho. LS11: Leeds 8E 4
Quay St. HD1: Hud 4D 8 (4N 137)
Quba Ct. BD8: B'frd 4A 64
Quebec BD16: Cot 9G 44
Quebec Ho. *BD21: Keigh* *1H 43*
(off Aireworth St.)
Quebec Rd. HD3: Outl 5L 135
Quebec St. BD1: B'frd 5A 6 (8C 64)
BD21: Keigh 1H 43
HX5: Ell 4F 118
LS1: Leeds 6E 4 (7D 68)
OL14: W'den 2J 113
WF2: Wake 5H 9 (5K 125)
Queen Elizabeth Dr. WF6: Norm 3H 127
Queen Elizabeth Gdns. HD1: Hud 4A 8 (4L 137)
Queen Elizabeth Gro. WF1: Wake 4N 125
Queen Elizabeth Ho. WF1: Wake 2M 9 (4N 125)
Queen Elizabeth Rd. WF1: Wake 2M 9 (4M 125)
Queen Elizabeth St. WF1: Out 8K 105
Queen Margarets Av. WF11: Byram 4C 110
Queen Margarets Cl. WF11: B'ton 4C 110
Queen Margarets Dr. WF11: B'ton 4C 110
Queen's Arc. LS1: Leeds 6F 4
Queen's Av. BD2: B'frd 3D 64
WF8: Pon 4G 129
QUEENSBURY 4D 80
Queensbury Av. WF1: Out 7L 105
Queensbury Ct. WF6: Norm 2K 127
Queensbury Golf Course 5E 80
Queensbury Rd. HX3: Hal 9A 80
Queensbury Sq. BD13: Que 4E 80
Queensbury Swimming Pool 4D 80
Queens Cl. BD16: Bgly 4G 45
LS7: Leeds 7E 50
LS26: W'frd 7M 89
Queens Ct. BD16: Bgly 4E 44
BD18: Ship 7L 45
BD19: Gom *2M 101*
(off Queen St.)
LS1: Leeds 7G 5
LS17: Leeds 6E 50
LS26: W'frd 7M 89
LS28: Pud 6B 66
Queenscourt LS27: Morl 9K 85
Queen's Cres. WF4: S Comn 7K 127
WF5: Oss 6N 123
Queens Dr. HX3: Sou 8F 98
LS28: Pud 6A 66
LS29: I'ly 6E 14
S72: Cud 8K 161
S72: Shaf 6J 161
WF2: Wren 2G 124
WF3: Carl 1M 105
WF5: Oss, Wake 7A 124
Queens Dr. Cl. WF5: Oss 6B 124
Queen's Dr. La. LS29: I'ly 6E 14
Queensfield Dr. BD5: B'frd 1B 82
Queen's Gdns. LS29: I'ly 6F 14
WF5: Oss 6N 123
Queen's Ga. HX3: Hal 8H 7 (8A 98)
Queensgate BD1: B'frd 4B 6 (7C 64)
HD1: Hud 7B 8 (5M 137)
Queensgate Mkt. HD1: Hud 6C 8 (5N 137)
Queen's Gro. BD21: Keigh 2H 43
LS27: Morl 1J 103
Queens Hall LS27: Morl 1J 103
Queenshill App. LS17: Leeds 5E 50
Queenshill Av. LS17: Leeds 5E 50
Queenshill Cl. LS17: Leeds 5E 50
Queenshill Cres. LS17: Leeds 4E 50
Queenshill Dr. LS17: Leeds 5D 50
Queenshill Gdns. LS17: Leeds 5D 50
Queenshill Gth. LS17: Leeds 5E 50
Queenshill Lawn *LS17: Leeds* *5E 50*
(off Queenshill App.)
Queenshill Rd. LS17: Leeds 5E 50
Queenshill Vw. LS17: Leeds 5E 50
Queenshill Wlk. LS17: Leeds 5E 50
Queens Mead HX3: North 1F 98
Queens Mill Rd. HD1: Hud 8A 8 (6M 137)
HD4: Hud 8A 8 (6M 137)
Queens Mill Rd. Ind. Est.
HD1: Hud 8B 8 (6M 137)
Queen's Pk. Cl. WF10: C'frd 4H 109
Queen's Pk. Dr. WF10: C'frd 5G 108
Queen's Pl. BD18: Ship 7L 45
LS21: Otley 1L 31
LS27: Morl 9L 85
Queen's Prom. LS27: Morl 8K 85
Queen Sq. LS2: Leeds 4F 4 (5E 68)
Queen Sq. Ct.
LS2: Leeds 4E 4 (5D 68)
Queen's Ri. BD2: B'frd 3D 64
Queen's Rd. BD2: B'frd 4B 64
BD8: B'frd 4B 64
BD16: Bgly 1D 44
BD18: Ship 7L 45
BD21: Keigh 3G 43
HD2: Hud 2K 137
HX1: Hal 5M 97
HX3: Nor G 2L 99
LS6: Leeds 4A 68
LS23: B Spa 9C 24
LS27: Morl 1J 103
LS29: I'ly 6F 14
S72: Cud 8K 161
WF8: Pon 4G 129
WF10: C'frd 5H 109
Queens Rd. W. HD4: Hud 6G 136
Queens Sports Club 8H 7 (7A 98)
Queens Sq. HD1: Hud 5C 8 (4N 137)
HD2: Hud 1B 138
WF8: Pon 4G 129
Queens Sq. Bus. Pk. HD9: Hon 3M 153
Queens St. BD13: Cull 9K 43
Queens Tap Yd. HD1: Hud 5B 8 (4M 137)
Queens Ter. HX7: Heb B 1G 95
LS20: Guis 7H 31
LS21: Otley 1L 31
WF5: Oss 6N 123
WF8: Pon 3H 129
Queensthorpe Av. LS13: Leeds 6G 67
Queensthorpe Cl. LS13: Leeds 6H 67
Queensthorpe Ri. LS13: Leeds 6G 67
Queen St. BD6: B'frd 6K 81
BD10: B'frd 8H 47
BD15: Wils 2B 62
BD16: Bgly 4E 44
BD17: Bail 6A 46
BD19: Cleck 6J 101
BD19: Gom 2M 101
BD20: Sils 8E 12
BD20: Stee 3C 26
BD22: Haw 9C 42
HD1: Hud 5C 8 (4N 137)
HD8: Skelm 7D 156
HX4: Gree 5B 118
HX6: Sow B 9E 96
HX7: Myth 4M 95
LS1: Leeds 7C 4 (7C 68)
LS10: Leeds 3J 87
LS19: Raw 3M 47
LS26: W'frd 7M 89
LS27: Morl 8K 85
OL14: Tod 7K 93
WF1: Out 8K 105
WF1: Wake 5J 9 (5L 125)
WF3: Carl 1M 105
Queen St. WF3: E Ard 4F 104
WF4: Horb 1C 142
WF5: Oss 6N 123
WF6: Norm 1H 127
WF8: Pon 3J 129
WF9: S Elm 7M 163
WF10: C'frd 4E 108
WF12: Dew 4L 123
WF13: Raven 5B 122
WF14: Mir 7L 121
WF16: Heck 9N 101
Queen St. Sth. HD1: Hud 8C 8 (5N 137)
Queensview LS14: Leeds 1B 70
Queen's Wlk. LS6: Leeds 9K 49
WF5: Oss 6B 124
Queens Way HD8: Kbtn 4K 155
Queensway BD16: Bgly 5G 45
BD21: Keigh *9J 27*
(within Airedale Shop. Cen.)
HD8: Kbtn 4L 155
HX1: Hal 4M 97
LS15: Leeds 6D 70
LS19: Yead 7J 31
LS20: Guis, Yead 7J 31
LS25: Gar 7L 71
LS26: Rothw 7N 87
LS27: Morl 9K 85
S71: Roys 5D 160
WF6: Norm 4H 127
(not continuous)
WF8: Pon 9M 109
WF13: Dew *3G 122*
(off Foundry St.)
Queensway Pl. WF8: Pon 9M 109
Queenswood Cl. LS6: Leeds 9K 49
Queenswood Ct. LS6: Leeds 2M 67
Queenswood Dr. LS6: Leeds 8K 49
Queenswood Gdns. LS6: Leeds 2M 67
Queenswood Grn. LS6: Leeds 8K 49
Queenswood Hgts. LS6: Leeds 1M 67
Queenswood Mt. LS6: Leeds 1L 67
Queenswood Ri. LS6: Leeds 1L 67
Queenswood Rd. LS6: Leeds 1L 67
Queen Victoria Cres. HX3: North 1G 98
Queen Victoria St. LS1: Leeds 6G 5
Quincy Cl. BD2: B'frd 2G 64
Qureshi Vw. BD8: B'frd 5A 64

R

Raby Av. LS7: Leeds 3F 68
RABY PARK 3M 23
Raby Pk. LS22: Weth 3L 23
Raby St. LS7: Leeds 3F 68
Raby Ter. LS7: Leeds 3F 68
Racca Av. WF11: Knot 8G 110
RACCA GREEN 8G 110
Racca Grn. WF11: Knot 8F 110
Racecourse App. LS22: Weth 1A 24
Race Moor La. BD22: Oak 4B 42
Racemoor La. BD22: Oak 4D 42
Rachael Ct. WF4: Horb 1B 142
Rachael St. WF4: Horb 1B 142
Rachel Ct. LS9: Leeds 4K 69
Racton St. HD7: Slait 9M 135
Radcliffe Av. BD2: B'frd 1E 64
Radcliffe Gdns. LS28: Pud 8B 66
Radcliffe Gro. LS28: Pud 8B 66
Radcliffe La. HX2: Midg 2C 96
LS28: Pud 7B 66
Radcliffe Pl. WF1: Wake 4J 9 (5L 125)
Radcliffe Rd. HD3: Hud 6G 136
(not continuous)
HD7: Golc 9N 135
S71: Ath 9A 160
WF2: Wake 7F 124
Radcliffe St. HD8: Skelm 7C 156
Radcliffe Ter. LS28: Pud 8B 66
Radfield Dr. BD6: B'frd 4C 82
Radfield Rd. BD6: B'frd 4C 82
Radford Pk. Av.
WF9: S Kirk 8H 163
Radiant Works HD1: Hud 3C 8
Radnor St. BD3: B'frd 7G 65
LS12: Leeds 8A 68
Radulf Gdns. WF15: Liv 7L 101
Radwell Dr. BD5: B'frd 7A 6 (9C 64)
Raeburn Dr. BD6: B'frd 6M 81
Rae Ct. WF3: S'ley 7N 105
Rae Rd. BD18: Ship 9N 45
Rafborn Av. HD3: Hud 1D 136
Rafborn Gro. HD3: Hud 1D 136
Raglan Av. BD22: Keigh 1F 42
Raglan Cl. WF10: C'frd 4A 108
Raglan Ct. HX1: Hal 3G 7
Ragland Ind. Est. WF10: C'frd 4A 108
Raglan Gdns. HX1: Hal 3G 7
Raglan Ind. Est.
WF10: C'frd 4B 108
Raglan Rd. LS2: Leeds 3C 68
LS6: Leeds 1C 4 (3C 68)
Raglan St. BD3: B'frd 7H 65
BD13: Que 4E 80
BD22: Keigh 1F 42
HX1: Hal 3G 7 (5N 97)
OL14: Tod 7K 93
Raglan Ter. BD3: B'frd 7J 65
Ragley Vw. HX7: Heb B 9F 76
Raikes Av. BD4: B'frd 2K 83
Raikes La. BD4: B'frd 3L 83
BD4: E Bier 5J 83
WF17: Birs 2B 102
Raikes Wood Dr. BD4: E Bier 6J 83
Rail Balk La. LS22: Weth 2L 23
(not continuous)
Railes Cl. HX2: Lud 3D 96
Railes Cotts. HX2: Lud 3D 96
Railsfield Cliff *LS13: Leeds* *4F 66*
(off Bath La.)
Railsfield Mt. LS13: Leeds 5F 66
Railsfield Ri. LS13: Leeds 5F 66
Railsfield Way LS13: Leeds 4G 66
Railway Arches HD1: Hud 3B 8
Railway Av. WF8: Pon 2J 129
Railway Cotts. BD23: Bolt A 3J 11
LS25: M'fld 8G 72
WF7: Ackw *5G 146*
(off Millgate)
WF9: S Elm 6N 163
WF9: Upt 2D 164
Railway Ct. HD8: Clay W 6J 157
Railway Rd. BD10: B'frd 7F 46
LS15: Leeds 4D 70
(not continuous)
LS29: I'ly 5G 14
Railway St. BD4: B'frd 3G 83
BD19: Cleck 5H 101
BD20: Keigh 7J 27
HD1: Hud 4B 8 (4M 137)
HD6: Ras 2N 119
LS9: Leeds 7K 5 (7G 68)
OL14: Tod 6K 93
WF12: Dew 3G 123
WF13: Dew 5D 122
WF16: Heck 9A 102
Railway Ter. BD12: Low M 8C 82
HD6: Clift *1A 120*
(off Clifton Comn.)
HX3: Hal 1N 117
LS29: I'ly 5H 15
S71: Roys *5B 160*
(off High St.)
WF1: Out 7K 105
WF3: E Ard 3E 104
WF6: Norm 1H 127
WF7: F'stne 6D 128
WF9: Fitz 7A 146
Railway Vw. HX7: Heb B 2H 95
OL14: W'den *2J 113*
(off Winterbutlee Rd.)
WF10: C'frd 5B 108
Rainbow M. BD6: B'frd 7L 81
Raincliffe Gro. LS9: Leeds 6J 69
Raincliffe Mt. LS9: Leeds 7J 69
Raincliffe Rd. LS9: Leeds 6J 69
Raincliffe St. LS9: Leeds 6J 69
Raincliffe Ter. LS9: Leeds 7J 69
Raines Ho. WF1: Wake 6J 9 (6L 125)
Rainsborough Av. WF11: Knot 9B 110
Raistrick Way BD18: Ship 7B 46
Rake HX7: Heb B 3G 95
Rake Bank HX2: Mix 9K 79
Rake Head Barn La. OL14: W'den 3H 113
Rake Head Rd. HD9: H'lm 9D 168
Rakehill Rd. LS15: Bar E, Scho 8G 52
Raleigh St. HX1: Hal 7M 97
Rampart Rd. LS6: Leeds 3C 68
Ramsden Av. BD7: B'frd 9K 63
Ramsden Cl. WF11: B'ton 4B 110
Ramsden Ct. BD7: B'frd 1M 81
HD1: Hud 7B 8
Ramsden La. HD9: Holm 9G 168
OL14: W'den 4G 113
Ramsden Mill La. HD7: Golc 7D 136
(not continuous)
HD7: Linth 7E 136
Ramsden Pl. BD14: Clay 9G 63
Ramsden Rd. HD9: Holm 9G 169
OL12: Ward 9E 112
(not continuous)
Ramsden St. HD1: Hud 6B 8 (5M 137)
HD7: Golc 6D 136
HX3: Hal 2L 97
LS25: Kip 5N 89
OL14: W'den 4J 113
WF10: C'frd 7C 108
Ramsden Wood Rd. OL14: W'den 4H 113
Ramsey Ct. WF4: M'twn 3L 141
Ramsey Cres. WF4: M'twn 3L 141
Ramsey Rd. WF4: M'twn 3K 141
Ramsey St. BD5: B'frd 2B 82
Ramsey Ter. LS21: Otley 9L 17
Ramsey Vw. WF4: M'twn 3K 141
Ramsgate WF3: Loft 3K 105
Ramsgate Cres. WF3: Loft 3K 105
Ramsgate St. HX1: Hal 5M 97
Ramsgill Cl. BD6: B'frd 5K 81
Ramshead App. LS14: Leeds 9B 52
Ramshead Cl. LS14: Leeds 8B 52
Ramshead Cres. LS14: Leeds 8A 52
Ramshead Dr. LS14: Leeds 8A 52
Ramshead Gdns. LS14: Leeds 8A 52
Ramshead Gro. LS14: Leeds 9B 52
Ramshead Hgts. LS14: Leeds 1B 70
(Bailey's La.)
LS14: Leeds 9B 52
(Eastdean Rd.)
Ramshead Hill LS14: Leeds 9B 52
Ramshead Pl. LS14: Leeds 9B 52
Ramshead Vw. LS14: Leeds 9B 52
Randall Pl. BD9: B'frd 3M 63
Randall Well St. BD7: B'frd 5A 6 (8B 64)
Randolph St. BD3: B'frd 6J 65
HX3: Hal 1K 7 (3B 98)
LS13: Leeds 4D 66
Random Cl. BD22: Keigh 2F 42
Rand Pl. BD7: B'frd 9A 64
Rand St. BD7: B'frd 9A 64
Ranelagh Av. BD10: B'frd 1H 65
Range Bank HX3: Hal 1L 7 (3B 98)
Range Bank Top *HX3: Hal* *3B 98*
(off Range La.)
Range Ct. HX3: Hal 1L 7
Range Gdns. HX3: Hal 3B 98
Range La. HX3: Hal 1L 7 (4B 98)
Ranger's Wlk. LS25: Aber 4J 73
Range St. HX3: Hal 1L 7 (3B 98)
Ransdale Dr. BD5: B'frd 2B 82
Ransdale Gro. BD5: B'frd 2B 82
Ransdale Rd. BD5: B'frd 2B 82
Ranter's Fold WF4: Horb 1C 142
Raper Vw. LS25: Aber 7E 54
Rapid Solicitors 8N 125
Rashcliffe Hill Rd. HD1: Hud 8A 8 (6L 137)
RASTRICK 3L 119
Rastrick Comn. HD6: Ras 3M 119
Rathlin Rd. WF12: Dew 1J 123
Rathmell Rd. LS15: Leeds 7N 69
Rathmell St. BD5: B'frd 4B 82

Ratten Row—Rhondda Pl.

Ratten Row WF8: Pon 2K 129
Ratten Row Rd. HX6: Sow B 2C 116
Rattle Row HD9: H'frth 3M 169
(off Bunkers Hill)
Raven Bank HX2: Lud F 6D 96
Raven Cl. WF7: A'ton 2A 128
Raven La. S72: S Hien 3H 161
Raven Rd. LS6: Leeds 2A 68
Raven Royd S71: Ath 8A 160
Ravens Av. HD5: Hud 5C 138
WF13: Dew 5D 122
Ravenscar Av. LS8: Leeds 9J 51
Ravenscar Mt. LS8: Leeds 9J 51
Ravenscar Ter. LS8: Leeds 9J 51
Ravenscar Vw. LS8: Leeds 9J 51
Ravenscar Wlk. LS8: Leeds 9J 51
RAVENSCLIFFE 2J 65
Ravenscliffe Av. BD10: B'frd 1H 65
Ravenscliffe Cl. HX3: Hal 1A 118
Ravenscliffe Rd. LS28: Cal 9K 47
Ravens Cl. S75: Map 9K 159
Ravens Cres. WF13: Dew 5D 122
(not continuous)
Ravens Cft. WF13: Dew 5D 122
Ravenscroft Rd. HX3: Hal 9A 98
Ravensdene HD3: Hud 2J 137
Ravensfield Rd. WF13: Dew 5D 122
Ravens Gro. WF13: Dew 5D 122
Ravenshouse Rd. WF13: Dew 4C 122
Ravensknowle Rd. HD5: Hud 5C 138
Ravens Lodge Ter. WF13: Dew 5D 122
Ravensmead WF7: F'stne 6F 128
Ravens Mt. LS28: Pud 7C 66
Ravens St. WF13: Raven 5C 122
RAVENSTHORPE 6B 122
Ravensthorpe Ind. Est. WF13: Raven 6B 122
Ravensthorpe Rd. WF12: Dew 7C 122
Ravensthorpe Shop. Pk.
WF13: Raven 6B 122
Ravensthorpe Station (Rail) 7C 122
Ravenstone Dr. HX4: Gree 5B 118
Raven St. BD16: Bgly 4E 44
BD21: Keigh 9H 27
HD1: Hud 5J 137
HX1: Hal 5M 97
Ravens Wlk. WF13: Dew 5D 122
Ravens Way HD9: Scho 4C 170
Ravenswharf Rd. WF13: Dew 5D 122
Ravensworth Cl. LS15: Leeds 3G 70
Ravensworth Way LS15: Leeds 3G 70
Raven Ter. BD8: B'frd 7H 63
Rawden Hill LS21: Arth 2A 34
RAWDON 4A 48
Rawdon Crematorium LS19: Raw 6B 48
Rawdon Dr. LS19: Raw 4M 47
Rawdon Golf Course 4M 47
Rawdon Hall Dr. LS19: Raw 4M 47
Rawdon Pk. LS19: Raw 2M 47
Rawdon Rd. BD22: Haw 8C 42
LS18: Hors, Yead 5B 48
Rawdon St. BD22: Keigh 1G 42
Raw End Rd. HX2: Hal 3F 96
Rawfield La. WF11: Fair 8N 91
RAWFOLDS 6K 101
Rawfolds Av. WF17: Birs 2C 102
Rawfolds Ind. Est. BD19: Cleck 6K 101
Rawfolds Way BD19: Cleck 6K 101
Rawgate Av. WF10: C'frd 4A 108
RAW GREEN 5N 173
Raw Hill HD6: Ras 3L 119
Raw La. HX2: Illing 8K 79
HX7: Heb B, Myth 1L 95
Raw La. Bottom HX6: Sow B 9D 96
Rawling St. BD21: Keigh 2H 43
Rawling Way LS6: Leeds 1C 68
RAW NOOK 7C 82
Rawnook BD12: Low M 8C 82
Raw Nook Rd. HD3: Hud 2D 136
Rawroyds HX4: Gree, Holy 6B 118
Rawson Av. BD3: B'frd 6H 65
HX3: Hal 9A 98
Rawson Pl. BD1: B'frd 3A 6 (7C 64)
HX6: Sow B 9G 96
LS11: Leeds 2E 86
Rawson Quarter Shop. Complex BD1: B'frd 3A 6
Rawson Rd. BD1: B'frd 3A 6 (7C 64)
Rawson Sq. BD1: B'frd 3A 6 (7C 64)
(not continuous)
BD10: B'frd 6F 46
Rawson St. BD12: Wyke 9B 82
HX1: Hal 4K 7 (5B 98)
Rawson St. Nth. HX3: Hal 3A 98
Rawson Ter. LS11: Leeds 2E 86
Rawson Wing HX1: Hal 8K 7
Rawson Wood HX6: Sow B 1E 116
RAWTHORPE 2C 138
Rawthorpe Cres. HD5: Hud 2C 138
Rawthorpe La. HD5: Hud 3B 138
Rawthorpe Ter. HD5: Hud 2C 138
Rawtonstall Bank HX7: Blac H 9E 76
Rayfield WF2: Wake 6H 125
Ray Ga. HD3: Hud 2C 136
HD9: New M 9B 154
HX2: Midg 6N 77
Raygill Cl. LS17: Leeds 2K 51
Raylands Cl. LS10: Leeds 7H 87
Raylands Ct. LS10: Leeds 7H 87
Raylands Fold LS10: Leeds 7H 87
Raylands Gth. LS10: Leeds 7H 87
Raylands La. LS10: Leeds 7H 87
Raylands Pl. LS10: Leeds 7H 87
Raylands Rd. LS10: Leeds 7H 87
Raylands Way LS10: Leeds 8G 87
Rayleigh St. BD4: B'frd 8F 6 (1E 82)
Raymond Dr. BD5: B'frd 3C 82
Raymond St. BD5: B'frd 3C 82
Raynbron Cres. BD5: B'frd 3D 82
Raynel App. LS16: Leeds 4K 49
Raynel Cl. LS16: Leeds 3J 49
Raynel Dr. LS16: Leeds 4K 49
Raynel Gdns. LS16: Leeds 3K 49
Raynel Gth. LS16: Leeds 4K 49
Raynel Grn. LS16: Leeds 4K 49
Raynel Mt. LS16: Leeds 3K 49
Raynel Way LS16: Leeds 3J 49
Rayner Av. BD8: B'frd 5L 63
WF16: Heck 6A 102
Rayner Dr. HD6: Brigh 8M 99
Rayner Gdns. LS28: Fars 3B 66
Rayner Mt. BD15: All 6G 62
Rayner Rd. HD6: Brigh 8M 99
Rayners Av. WF15: Liv 8G 101
Rayner St. WF4: Horb 1C 142
Raynham Cres. BD21: Keigh 8E 26
Raynor Cl. HD3: Hud 3H 137
Raynor Ter. LS28: Pud 6C 66
Raynville App. LS13: Leeds 4H 67
Raynville Av. LS13: Leeds 3H 67
Raynville Cl. LS13: Leeds 3H 67
Raynville Ct. LS13: Leeds 4H 67
Raynville Cres. LS12: Leeds 4J 67
Raynville Dene LS12: Leeds 3J 67
Raynville Dr. LS13: Leeds 3H 67
Raynville Gdns. LS12: Leeds 4J 67
Raynville Gth. LS12: Leeds 4J 67
Raynville Grange
LS13: Leeds 4H 67
(off Raynville Rd.)
Raynville Grn. LS13: Leeds 4H 67
Raynville Gro. LS13: Leeds 3H 67
Raynville Mt. LS13: Leeds 3H 67
Raynville Pl. LS13: Leeds 4H 67
Raynville Ri. LS13: Leeds 4H 67
Raynville Rd. LS12: Leeds 3H 67
LS13: Leeds 3G 67
Raynville St. LS13: Leeds 3H 67
Raynville Ter. LS13: Leeds 3H 67
Raynville Wlk. LS13: Leeds 4H 67
Raynville Way LS12: Leeds 4J 67
Ray St. HD1: Hud 2C 8 (3N 137)
Ray St. Ent. Cen. HD1: Hud 2C 8 (3N 137)
Raywood Cl. LS19: Yead 8L 31
Reade St. HX3: Hal 1B 118
(off St Anne's Rd.)
Reap Hirst Rd. HD2: Hud 9J 119
Rebecca St. BD1: B'frd 6B 64
Recreation Av. LS11: Leeds 1C 86
Recreation Cres. LS11: Leeds 1B 86
Recreation Gro. LS11: Leeds 1B 86
Recreation La. HX5: Ell 5D 118
Recreation Mt. LS11: Leeds 1B 86
Recreation Pl. LS11: Leeds 1B 86
Recreation Rd. HX6: Sow B 8J 97
LS11: Leeds 3B 86
Recreation Row LS11: Leeds 1B 86
Recreation St. LS11: Leeds 1B 86
Recreation Ter. LS11: Leeds 1B 86
Recreation Vw. LS11: Leeds 1B 86
Rectory Av. WF10: C'frd 4D 108
Rectory Cl. DN6: S'brk 4G 165
HD7: Mars 5F 150
LS25: Gar 7N 71
S71: Carl 8E 160
Rectory Ct. WF8: D'ton 7D 130
WF8: K S'ton 4J 149
Rectory Cres. WF4: Croft 2G 145
Rectory Dr. HD5: K'htn 3F 138
WF17: Bat 3D 102
Rectory Farm La. HD8: Up C 2N 171
Rectory Gdns. HD8: Eml 2G 156
Rectory Gth. WF9: Hems 2D 162
Rectory La. HD8: Eml 2G 156
Rectory Row BD21: Keigh 9H 27
Rectory St. LS9: Leeds 3L 5 (5G 69)
WF10: C'frd 4D 108
Rectory Vw. WF12: T'hill 8H 123
Red Acre HX7: Myth 3M 95
Redbarn Cl. LS10: Leeds 2E 104
Redbarn Ct. LS10: Leeds 2E 104
Redbeck Cotts. LS18: Hors 7B 48
Red Beck Rd. HX3: Hal 3E 98
Red Beck Va. BD18: Ship 1M 63
Redberry Av. WF16: Heck 7B 102
Red Brick La. HX6: Sow B 1C 116
Redbrick Mill WF17: Bat 1G 122
Red Brink La. HX6: Sow B 1B 116
Red Brink Rd. HX6: Sow B 1B 116
Redbrook Way BD9: B'frd 1J 63
Redburn Av. BD18: Ship 1M 63
Redburn Dr. BD18: Ship 1M 63
Redburn Rd. BD18: Ship 1N 63
Redcar La. BD20: Keigh, Stee 5B 26
Redcar Rd. BD10: B'frd 9J 47
Redcar St. HX1: Hal 5M 97
Redcliffe Av. BD21: Keigh 9G 27
Redcliffe Gro. BD21: Keigh 9G 26
Redcliffe St. BD21: Keigh 9G 26
(not continuous)
Redcote La. LS4: Leeds 5L 67
LS12: Leeds 6L 67
Redcourt LS12: Leeds 7M 67
(off Athone Gro.)
Red Deer Pk. La. WF4: G Moor 5B 140
Red Delph Gdns. BD13: Que 4C 80
Redding Mill BD20: Stee 3C 26
Redding Wood La. BD20: Stee 4C 26
Reddisher Rd. HD7: Mars 4E 150
Red Doles Ind. Est. HD2: Hud 1A 138
Red Doles La. HD2: Hud 1A 138
Red Doles Rd. HD2: Hud 9A 120
Reddyshore Scout Ga.
OL14: W'den 6K 113
Redesdale Gdns. LS16: Leeds 4K 49
Redfearn Av. WF16: Heck 7A 102
Redgate La. HD3: Scam 7F 134
Red Hall App. LS14: Leeds 6B 52
Red Hall Av. LS17: Leeds 6A 52
WF1: Wake 1K 125
Red Hall Chase LS14: Leeds 6B 52
Redhall Cl. LS11: Leeds 4A 86
Red Hall Ct. LS14: Leeds 6B 52
WF1: Wake 1J 125
Red Hall Cres. WF1: Wake 1K 125
Redhall Cres. LS11: Leeds 4A 86
Red Hall Cft. LS14: Leeds 6B 52
Red Hall Dr. LS14: Leeds 6B 52
Red Hall Gdns. LS17: Leeds 6A 52
Red Hall Gth. LS14: Leeds 6B 52
Redhall Ga. LS11: Leeds 4A 86
Red Hall Grn. LS14: Leeds 6B 52
Red Hall La. LS14: Leeds 6B 52
LS17: Leeds 6A 52
WF1: Wake 2J 125
Red Hall Va. LS14: Leeds 7B 52
Red Hall Vw. LS14: Leeds 6B 52
Red Hall Wlk. LS14: Leeds 6B 52
Red Hall Way LS14: Leeds 6B 52
RED HILL 5G 109
Redhill Av. WF3: W Ard 7A 104
WF10: C'frd 6F 108
Redhill Chase WF10: C'frd 6G 108
Redhill Cl. BD4: B'frd 5K 83
WF3: W Ard 7A 104
Redhill Cres. WF3: W Ard 7A 104
Redhill Dr. WF3: W Ard 7A 104
WF10: C'frd 5G 109
Redhill Gdns. WF10: C'frd 6G 109
Redhill Hgts. WF10: C'frd 6G 108
Redhill La. LS25: S Mil 4N 91
Redhill Mt. WF10: C'frd 5G 108
Redhill Rd. WF10: C'frd 5G 108
Redhill Vw. WF10: C'frd 6G 109
Redhill Wlk. WF10: C'frd 6G 108
Red Holt Av. BD21: Keigh 3G 43
Red Holt Cres. BD21: Keigh 3G 43
Red Holt Dr. BD21: Keigh 3G 43
Red Ho. Gdns. LS29: Men 5E 30
Redhouse Interchange
DN6: Wood 9K 165
Redhouse La. LS7: Leeds 8G 50
Red House Mus. 3M 101
Red Laithes Ct. WF13: Raven 5B 122
Red Laithes La. WF13: Raven 5B 122
Redland Cres. WF9: Kins 8B 146
Redland Dr. HD8: Kbtn 2J 155
Redland Gro. S75: S'ross 7K 159
Redlands Cl. WF14: Mir 4L 121
Red La. HD9: Mel 7N 151
LS28: Fars 3N 65
WF1: Warm 6F 126
WF4: N Sha 6F 126
WF7: Street 6M 127
Red Lodge Cl. LS8: Leeds 2M 69
Redman Cl. BD22: Haw 8B 42
Redman Gth. BD22: Haw 8B 42
Redmayne Gro. WF11: Knot 8C 110
Redmire Ct. LS14: Leeds 2C 70
Redmire Dr. LS14: Leeds 2B 70
Redmire Gro. LS14: Leeds 2B 70
Redmire St. BD3: B'frd 7J 65
Redmire Vw. LS14: Leeds 2B 70
Redpoll Dr. WF10: All B 9B 90
Redpoll Way BD6: B'frd 4H 81
Redruth Dr. WF6: Norm 9J 107
Redshank Cl. BD6: B'frd 4H 81
Redshank Pl. WF4: Neth 2N 141
Redshaw Rd. LS12: Leeds 8N 67
Redthorne Way S72: Shaf 6J 161
Red Va. BD19: Gom 2M 101
Redvers Cl. LS16: Leeds 6K 49
Redwald Dr. LS20: Guis 7H 31
Redwing Cres. HD3: Hud 5E 136
Redwing Dr. BD6: B'frd 4H 81
Redwing Pk. WF14: Mir 5L 121
Redwood Av. S71: Roys 6D 160
WF3: Ting 4C 104
Redwood Cl. BD10: B'frd 8G 47
BD21: Keigh 2L 43
LS19: Yead 9K 31
LS26: W'frd 7F 88
Redwood Cres. BD4: B'frd 5F 82
Redwood Dr. HD2: Hud 6B 120
Redwood Gro. HD5: Hud 4B 138
(off Highroyd La.)
LS19: Yead 9K 31
WF4: S Comn 7K 127
Redwood Way LS19: Yead 9K 31
Reedling Dr. LS27: Morl 1M 103
Reed Rd. LS12: Leeds 8N 67
Reedsdale Av. LS27: Gil 6F 84
Reedsdale Dr. LS27: Gil 6F 84
Reedsdale Gdns.
LS27: Gil 6F 84
Reed St. HD3: Hud 3J 137
Rees Way BD3: B'frd 1D 6 (6D 64)
Reeth Rd. HD6: Ras 3K 119
Reevy Av. BD6: B'frd 5L 81
Reevy Cres. BD6: B'frd 6K 81
Reevy Dr. BD6: B'frd 5M 81
Reevylands Dr. BD6: B'frd 5M 81
Reevy Pk. Ct. BD6: B'frd 5K 81
Reevy Rd. BD6: B'frd 5L 81
Reevy Rd. W. BD6: B'frd 5J 81
Reevy St. BD6: B'frd 4M 81
Reevy Yd. BD6: B'frd 5N 81
(off Green End Rd.)
Reform St. BD19: Gom 3M 101
WF13: Dew 2D 122
Regal Cl. HX6: Rish 1C 134
Regal Ct. WF12: Dew 3H 123
Regal Dr. HX6: Rish 1C 134
Regal Pde. LS15: Leeds 4C 70
Regency Ct. BD8: B'frd 6N 63
LS6: Leeds 2A 68
LS29: I'ly 6F 14
Regency Gdns. WF3: W Ard 4C 104
Regency Pk. Gro. LS28: Pud 9B 66
Regency Pk. Rd.
LS28: Pud 9B 66
Regency Rd. WF14: Mir 7L 121
Regency Vw. BD3: B'frd 4E 64
Regent Av. LS18: Hors 8F 48
Regent Cl. HD6: Ras 5K 119
LS18: Hors 8F 48
Regent Ct. HX3: Hal 8N 97
LS1: Leeds 7G 5
LS18: Hors 8F 48
Regent Cres. LS18: Hors 8E 48
S72: S Hien 4M 161
Regent Ho. HX5: Ell 4E 118
Regent M. WF17: Bat 8J 103
Regent Pde. HX6: Sow B 8J 97
(off Wharf St.)
Regent Pk. Av. LS6: Leeds 2B 68
Regent Pk. Ter. LS6: Leeds 2B 68
Regent Pl. BD10: B'frd 6E 46
HX6: Sow B 7H 97
HX7: Heb B 9H 77
WF3: Thpe H 2H 105
Regent Rd. HD1: Hud 3K 137
HD5: K'htn 9G 120
LS18: Hors 8E 48
LS29: I'ly 5F 14
Regents Pk. WF1: Wake 5N 125
Regent St. BD10: B'frd 8H 47
(Haigh Hall Rd.)
BD10: B'frd 6E 46
(Northlea Av.)
BD13: Que 4E 80
BD22: Haw 8D 42
HX1: Hal 5J 7 (6B 98)
HX7: Heb B 1H 95
LS2: Leeds 5J 5 (6F 68)
LS7: Leeds 5J 5 (6F 68)
(New York Rd.)
LS7: Leeds 8F 50
(Well La.)
OL14: W'den 2J 113
S72: S Hien 4M 161
WF1: Wake 7N 125
WF4: Horb 1B 142
WF6: Norm 8K 107
WF7: F'stne 6C 128
WF9: Hems 2C 162
WF9: S Elm 6L 163
WF10: C'frd 5C 108
WF14: Mir 8L 121
WF16: Heck 9N 101
Regent Ter. LS6: Leeds 4B 68
LS7: Leeds 8F 50
Regina Cres. S72: B'ley 7M 161
WF4: H'cft 9K 145
Regina Dr. LS7: Leeds 9F 50
Regina Ho. LS13: Leeds 6G 66
Reginald Mt. LS7: Leeds 2F 68
Reginald Pl. LS7: Leeds 2F 68
Reginald Row LS7: Leeds 2F 68
Reginald St. BD5: B'frd 2B 82
LS7: Leeds 2F 68
Reginald Ter. LS7: Leeds 2F 68
Reginald Vw. LS7: Leeds 2F 68
Reginald Vs. LS17: N Rig 4N 19
Reid Pk. Av. WF4: Horb 1A 142
Reighton Cft. BD10: B'frd 9J 47
Rein, The LS14: Leeds 9A 52
Rein Ct. LS25: Aber 7E 54
Rein Gdns. WF3: Ting 4M 103
Rein M. WF3: Ting 4M 103
Rein Rd. LS18: Hors 8E 48
LS27: Morl 2L 103
WF3: Ting 2L 103
Reins Av. BD17: Bail 6N 45
Reins Hill HD9: Hon 4M 153
Reins Rd. HD6: Ras 3K 119
Reins Ter. HD9: Hon 3M 153
Rein St. LS27: Morl 3M 103
Reinwood Av. HD3: Hud 4G 137
LS8: Leeds 1M 69
Reinwood Rd. HD3: Hud 4G 136
Rembrandt Av. WF3: Ting 4B 104
Renaissance Ct. LS27: Chur 5M 85
Renaissance Dr. LS27: Chur 5M 85
Renald La. S36: Hoy 9H 173
Renee Cl. BD4: B'frd 5G 82
Renfield Gro. WF6: Norm 9L 107
Renshaw St. BD10: B'frd 6F 46
Renton Av. LS20: Guis 7H 31
Renton Dr. LS20: Guis 8H 31
Renton Lea LS20: Guis 8H 31
Repton Rd. DN6: Skel 9N 165
Reservoir Ct. LS28: Cal 9L 47
Reservoir Farm Ct. WF4: Wint 6H 145
Reservoir Pl. BD13: Que 3B 80
WF13: Dew 2D 122
Reservoir Rd. BD22: Haw 8M 41
HX2: Hal 4L 97
HX6: Tri 3M 115
WF17: Bat 8C 102
Reservoir Side Rd. HD7: Linth 2D 152
Reservoir St. WF13: Dew 2D 122
Reservoir Vw. BD13: Thorn 8B 62
HD8: Skelm 7B 156
Restmore Av. LS20: Guis 6H 31
Retford Pl. BD7: B'frd 9A 64
Reuben St. WF15: Liv 7L 101
Reva Cl. BD16: Bgly 3G 45
Reva Syke Rd. BD14: Clay 2G 81
Revel Gth. HD8: Den D 3D 172
Revie Rd. LS11: Leeds 2B 86
Revie Rd. Ind. Est. LS11: Leeds 2B 86
Revis Barber Hall BD5: B'frd 9A 64
Rex Cinema
Elland 4E 118
Reyden M. LS12: Leeds 8M 67
Reydon Wlk. BD6: B'frd 4L 81
Reyhill Gro. BD5: B'frd 7B 6 (9C 64)
Reynards, The WF14: Mir 5L 121
Reynolds Av. BD7: B'frd 9K 63
Rhine St. BD4: B'frd 8F 6 (9E 64)
Rhodes Av. WF16: Heck 6A 102
Rhodes Ct. LS27: Morl 1L 103
(off High St.)
Rhodes Cres. WF8: Pon 5K 129
Rhodes Gdns. WF3: Loft 6L 105
Rhode's Hill La. LS23: B'ham 5E 38
Rhodesia Av. BD15: All 6H 63
HX3: Hal 9B 98
Rhodes La. LS23: Cliff 2B 38
Rhodes Pl. BD17: Ship 7N 45
Rhodes St. BD18: Ship 7M 45
HX1: Hal 4H 7 (5A 98)
WF10: C'frd 5B 108
(Lumley St.)
WF10: C'frd 4C 108
(Wilson St.)
WF15: Liv 8N 101
Rhodes Ter. BD2: B'frd 2F 64
LS12: Leeds 8A 68
Rhodesway BD8: B'frd 7J 63
Rhondda Pl. HX1: Hal 6L 97

Rhum Cl.—Robinwood Ct.

Rhum Cl. BD6: B'frd 7L 81
Rhyddings Av. WF7: Ackw 5F 146
Rhyddings Dr. WF7: Ackw 5F 146
Rhyddings Gdns. LS29: I'ly 5J 15
Rhyddings Vw. LS21: Askw 3E 16
Rhylstone Mt. BD7: B'frd 8L 63
Rhyl St. WF7: F'stne 5D 128
Rialto Ct. LS13: Leeds 1B 66
Ribble Ct. *BD20: Sils* *8E 12*
(off Wharfe Ct.)
Ribblesdale Av. LS25: Gar 8B 72
Ribble St. BD21: Keigh 8L 27
Ribbleton Gro. BD3: B'frd 2F 6 (6E 64)
Riber Av. S71: Ath 9B 160
Ribstone St. HX7: Myth 3M 95
Riccall Nook BD10: B'frd 9H 47
Rice St. HD1: Hud 6C 8 (4N 137)
Richard Dunn Sports Cen. 4B 82
Richard Gossop Ct. LS29: Burl W 8C 16
Richard Pl. *HD6: Brigh* *8M 99*
(off Richard St.)
Richard Rd. S75: Dart 9F 158
Richardshaw Dr. LS28: Stan 5B 66
Richardshaw La. LS28: Pud, Stan 5B 66
Richardshaw Rd. LS28: Stan 5B 66
Richardson Av. BD6: B'frd 5A 82
Richardson Cres. LS9: Leeds 7K 69
Richardson Rd. LS9: Leeds 7K 69
Richardson Sq. HD1: Hud 5A 8
Richardson St. BD12: O'haw 9E 82
Richard St. BD3: B'frd 4E 6 (7E 64)
HD6: Brigh 8M 99
WF1: Wake 2K 9 (4L 125)
Richard Thorpe Av. WF14: Mir 6M 121
Richmond Av. HD2: Hud 9M 119
HX6: Sow B 9F 96
LS6: Leeds 2A 68
S75: Dart 9F 158
WF8: Pon *2K 129*
(off Richmond Ct.)
WF11: Ferr 7A 110
Richmond Cl. HX1: Hal 2K 7 (4B 98)
LS13: Leeds 4D 66
LS26: Rothw 7A 88
LS27: Morl 1K 103
Richmond Ct. HD4: Hud 7E 136
LS9: Leeds 7M 5 (7H 69)
LS13: Leeds 1B 66
LS26: Rothw 7A 88
LS29: I'ly *6H 15*
(off Richmond Pl.)
WF4: Croft 2H 145
WF8: Pon 2K 129
Richmond Cft. LS9: Leeds 8M 5 (7H 69)
Richmondfield Av. LS15: Bar E 9M 53
Richmondfield Cl. LS15: Bar E 9M 53
Richmondfield Cres. LS15: Bar E 9M 53
Richmondfield Cross LS15: Bar E 9M 53
Richmondfield Dr. LS15: Bar E 9M 53
Richmondfield Gth. LS15: Bar E 8M 53
Richmondfield Gro. LS15: Bar E 9M 53
Richmondfield La. LS15: Bar E 9M 53
Richmondfield Mt. LS15: Bar E 9M 53
Richmondfield Wlk. LS15: Bar E 9M 53
Richmondfield Way LS15: Bar E 9M 53
Richmond Flats HD1: Hud 3C 8
Richmond Gdns. HX6: Sow B 9F 96
LS28: Pud 7D 66
Richmond Gth. WF5: Oss 7B 124
Richmond Grn. St. LS9: Leeds 7L 5
Richmond Gro. BD19: Gom 2M 101
RICHMOND HILL 8M 5 (7H 69)
Richmond Hill App. LS9: Leeds 8L 5 (7G 69)
Richmond Hill Cl. LS9: Leeds 8L 5 (7G 69)
Richmond Ho. HX1: Hal 8J 7
LS8: Leeds *5K 51*
(off Street La.)
Richmond Lea WF14: Mir 5L 121
Richmond M. BD18: Ship 7L 45
Richmond Mt. LS6: Leeds 2A 68
Richmond Pk. Av. WF15: Liv 9L 101
Richmond Pl. BD18: Ship 7L 45
LS29: I'ly 6H 15
Richmond Rd. BD7: B'frd 7A 64
(not continuous)
BD18: Ship 7L 45
HX1: Hal 2H 7 (4A 98)
LS6: Leeds 2A 68
LS28: Fars 4N 65
WF1: Wake 1H 9 (3K 125)
WF9: Upt 2N 163
WF16: Heck 6B 102
WF17: Bat 1G 123
Richmond St. BD19: Cleck 5H 101
BD21: Keigh 8H 27
HX1: Hal 2J 7 (4A 98)
LS9: Leeds 8K 5 (7G 68)
OL14: Tod 7L 93
WF10: C'frd 5D 108
Richmond Ter. *HX2: Lud* *3E 96*
(off High St.)
LS20: Guis 7H 31
LS21: Otley 1K 31
LS28: Pud 7D 66
WF8: Pon *2K 129*
(off Finkle St.)
Richmond Way LS25: Gar 9N 71
Rickard St. LS12: Leeds 8A 4 (8B 68)
Ridding Ga. LS21: Otley 8J 17
RIDDINGS 8B 120
Riddings, The LS29: Add 8L 11
Riddings Cl. HD2: Hud 8B 120
WF9: Hems 4D 162
Riddings Ri. HD2: Hud 8B 120
Riddings Rd. HD2: Hud 8B 120
LS29: I'ly 6G 14
RIDDLESDEN 7M 27
Riddlesden Golf Course 4H 27
Riddlesden St. BD20: Rid 7M 27
Riddlesden Vw. BD21: Keigh 9M 27
Ridehalgh La. BB10: B'clif 3B 56
Rider Rd. LS6: Leeds 2D 68
Rider St. LS9: Leeds 5K 5 (6G 68)
Ridge, The LS22: Lin 6K 23
Ridge Av. WF4: M'twn 3K 141
Ridge Bank OL14: Tod 7K 93
Ridge Cl. HD4: Hud 7M 137
HD8: Skelm 8D 156
LS20: Guis 8G 30
Ridge Cres. WF4: M'twn 4K 141
Ridgedale Mt. WF8: Pon 8K 109
Ridgefield St. WF10: C'frd 5C 108
Ridgefoot *OL14: Tod* *7K 93*
(off Queen St.)
Ridge Gro. LS7: Leeds 1C 68
Ridge Hill HD6: Ras 2K 119
Ridge La. BD20: Sils 1C 12
Ridge Lea HD6: Ras 2L 119
Ridge Mt. LS6: Leeds 2C 68
Ridgemount Rd. BD20: Rid 6L 27
Ridge Rd. LS7: Leeds 2D 68
LS25: Aber, Kip, Leds 5D 90
OL14: Tod 7K 93
WF4: M'twn 3K 141
Ridge Steps *OL14: Tod* *7K 93*
(off Ridge Bank)
Ridgestone Av. WF9: Hems 2E 162
Ridge St. HD4: Hud 7M 137
Ridge Ter. LS6: Leeds 1A 68
Ridge Vw. LS13: Leeds 6F 66
Ridgeview HX5: Ell 5H 119
Ridge Vw. Dr. HD2: Hud 9J 119
Ridge Vw. Gdns.
BD10: B'frd 8G 46
Ridge Vw. Rd. HD6: Ras 2M 119
Ridgeway BD13: Que 5E 80
BD15: All 6F 62
BD18: Ship 9C 46
HD5: Hud 3C 138
LS8: Leeds 9H 51
LS20: Guis 8F 30
Ridgeway, The WF11: Knot 9E 110
Ridgeway Cl. HD5: Hud 3C 138
LS8: Leeds 9H 51
Ridgeway Cres. S71: Carl 8D 160
Ridgeway Dr. WF17: Bat 3D 102
Ridgeway Gdns. HD6: Brigh 7K 99
Ridgeway Mt. BD22: Keigh 2F 42
Ridgeways, The HD7: Linth 9C 136
Ridgeway Sq. WF11: Knot 9E 110
Ridgeway Ter. *LS6: Leeds* *2C 68*
(off Delph La.)
Ridgewood Cl. BD17: Bail 4C 46
Ridgill Av. DN6: Skel 8M 165
Riding Head La. HX2: Lud 3E 96
Riding Hill HX3: She 7K 81
Riding La. HX2: Hal 1J 97
Ridings, The BD20: Keigh 5H 27
Ridings Bus. Pk. HX1: Hal 6M 97
Ridings Cl. WF3: Loft 6K 105
Ridings Ct. WF3: Loft 6K 105
Ridings Cft. BD5: B'frd 4F 82
Ridings Flds. HD9: Brock 6A 154
Ridings Gdns. WF3: Loft 6K 105
Ridings La. HD7: Golc 6B 136
HD9: T'bdge 1A 170
WF3: Loft 6K 105
Ridings M. WF3: Loft 6K 105
Ridings Rd. WF12: Dew 3G 123
Ridings Shop. Cen. WF1: Wake 5K 9 (5L 125)
Ridings Sports Centre, The 1M 97
Riding St. WF17: Bat 6B 102
Ridings Way BD6: B'frd 4K 81
WF3: Loft 6K 105
Ridings Wood HD5: Hud 4F 138
Ridingwood Ri. HD8: Clay W 7H 157
Ridleys Fold LS29: Add 1M 13
Rievaulx Av. BD8: B'frd 6A 64
Rievaulx Cl. LS23: B Spa 1C 38
Riffa Bus. Pk. LS21: Cast 7J 19
Riffa La. LS21: Leat 6F 18
Rifle Flds. HD1: Hud 5A 8 (4L 137)
Rifle St. HD1: Hud 6C 8 (5N 137)
Rigg La. WF7: Ackw 2J 147
WF8: E Hard 3J 147
Rightox Rd. HD9: Brock 6A 154
Riglet La. WF4: W Har 9A 128
Rigton App. LS9: Leeds 5L 5 (6G 69)
Rigton Bank LS17: Bard 4E 36
Rigton Cl. LS9: Leeds 5M 5 (6H 69)
Rigton Dr. LS9: Leeds 5L 5 (6G 69)
Rigton Grn. LS9: Leeds 5L 5 (6G 69)
LS17: Bard 4F 36
RIGTON HILL 2F 36
Rigton Hill LS17: N Rig 2N 19
Rigton Lawn LS9: Leeds 5L 5 (6G 69)
Rigton M. LS9: Leeds 5L 5 (6G 69)
Rigton St. BD5: B'frd 2B 82
RILEY 3J 155
Riley La. HD8: Kbtn 4J 155
HX2: Illing 5M 79
Riley Pk. HD8: Kbtn 3K 155
Riley St. HD4: Hud 8C 8 (6N 137)
Rillbank La. LS3: Leeds 5B 68
Rillbank St. *LS3: Leeds* *5B 68*
(off Woodsley Rd.)
Rill Ct. WF9: Hems 2D 162
Rillington Mead BD10: B'frd 9H 47
Rillside HD8: Shep 8K 155
Rills Mead LS21: Otley 1L 31
Rilston St. BD7: B'frd 8N 63
Rimswell Holt BD10: B'frd 9J 47
Ringby La. HX3: Hal 9A 80
Ring Hay Rd. BD4: B'frd 4L 83
Ring O' Bells Yd. WF4: Horb 1C 142
Ring Rd. Adel LS16: Leeds 5N 49
Ring Rd. Beeston LS11: Leeds 4A 86
LS12: Leeds 1M 85
Ring Rd. Beeston Pk. LS10: Leeds 5C 86
LS11: Leeds 5C 86
Ring Rd. Bramley LS13: Leeds 6G 66
Ring Rd. Cross Gates LS15: Leeds 3D 70
Ring Rd. Farnley LS12: Leeds 6G 66
Ring Rd. Farsley LS13: Leeds, Pud 4M 65
LS28: Fars 4M 65
Ring Rd. Halton LS15: Leeds 5D 70
Ring Rd. Horsforth LS16: Leeds 7J 49
LS18: Hors, Leeds 7H 49
Ring Rd. Lwr. Wortley
LS12: Leeds 8J 67
Ring Rd. Meanwood LS6: Leeds 5A 50
LS16: Leeds 5A 50
LS17: Leeds 5A 50
Ring Rd. Middleton LS10: Leeds 8F 86
Ring Rd. Moortown LS6: Leeds 5C 50
LS17: Leeds 5C 50
Ring Rd. Seacroft LS14: Leeds 7A 52
Ring Rd. Shadwell LS17: Leeds 4L 51
Ring Rd. Weetwood LS16: Leeds 6L 49
Ring Rd. West Pk. LS16: Leeds 6J 49
Ringshaw Dr. BD19: Gom 3L 101
Ringstone HX4: Bark 1G 135
Ringstone Gro. S72: B'ley 6A 162
Rington Rd. LS11: Leeds 2D 86
Ringway LS25: Gar 8L 71
Ringway Centre, The HD1: Hud 1A 8 (2M 137)
Ringwood Av. LS14: Leeds 7A 52
Ringwood Ct. WF1: Out 7M 105
Ringwood Cres. LS14: Leeds 6B 52
Ringwood Dr. LS14: Leeds 7B 52
Ringwood Edge HX5: Ell 5C 118
Ringwood Gdns. LS14: Leeds 7B 52
Ringwood Mt. LS14: Leeds 7B 52
Ringwood Rd. BD5: B'frd 2N 81
Ringwood Way WF9: Hems 2E 162
Rink Pde. *WF17: Bat* *9G 102*
(off Rink St.)
Rink St. WF17: Bat 9G 102
Rink Ter. WF17: Bat 9G 102
Ripley Cl. WF3: E Ard 3F 104
WF6: Norm 1L 127
Ripley Ct. WF6: Norm 3J 127
Ripley Dr. WF6: Norm 9L 107
Ripley La. LS20: Guis 5J 31
Ripley Rd. BD4: B'frd 2D 82
(Bowling Pk. Dr.)
BD4: B'frd 1D 82
(St Dunstans Technology Pk.)
WF15: Liv 8K 101
Ripley St. BD5: B'frd 8C 6 (1C 82)
(not continuous)
BD15: All 4F 62
BD20: Rid 7M 27
HX3: Hip 5M 99
Ripley Ter. HX2: Lud F 5D 96
Ripon Av. HD2: Hud 9M 119
Ripon Ho. HX5: Ell 4E 118
LS28: Fars 3A 66
Ripon Rd. WF12: Dew 2J 123
Ripon St. HX1: Hal 6L 97
Ripon Ter. HX3: Hal 3A 98
RIPPONDEN 7D 116
Ripponden Old Bank HX6: Ripp 7E 116
Ripponden Old La. HX6: Ripp 7N 115
Ripponden Packhorse Bridge *7E 116*
(off Priest La.)
Ripponden Rd. HX6: Rish 9F 132
OL3: Dens 9F 132
RIPPONDEN WOOD 5E 116
Rise, The HX3: North 2F 98
LS5: Leeds 1K 67
LS25: Kip 4A 90
S72: B'ley 7A 162
WF8: Pon 4L 129
WF11: B'ton 4B 110
Risedale Av. WF17: Birs 2E 102
Risedale Cl. WF17: Birs 2E 102
Rise La. OL14: Tod 7J 93
(Rose Bank Rd.)
OL14: Tod 7K 93
(Station App.)
Rise La. Ho. *OL14: Tod* *7K 93*
(off Rise La.)
RISHWORTH 1C 134
Rishworth Av. HD8: Eml 3G 156
Rishworth Bus. Complex HX6: Rish 9C 116
Rishworth Church Footway *HX6: Rish* *2C 134*
(off Oldham Rd.)
Rishworth Cl. WF2: Wren 1G 125
Rishworth Hall Cl. HX6: Rish 1B 134
Rishworthian Ct. HX3: Hal 2N 117
Rishworth Mill La. HX6: Rish 2D 134
Rishworth New Rd. HX6: Rish 1B 134
Rishworth Pal. HX6: Rish 2D 134
Rishworth Rd. HX4: Bark 7G 116
WF12: Dew 3G 122
Rishworth St. BD22: Keigh 2F 42
WF1: Wake 3J 9 (4L 125)
WF12: Dew 3G 123
Rivadale Vw. LS29: I'ly 4G 15
Rivelin Rd. WF10: C'frd 6C 108
Rivendale LS10: Leeds 9G 86
Riverbank Ent. Cen. WF13: Dew 5D 122
River Bank Way HX5: Ell 2G 118
Riverdale DN14: Beal 5M 111
LS22: Weth 5N 23
Riverdale Av. WF3: S'ley 1A 126
Riverdale Cl. WF3: S'ley 1A 126
Riverdale Ct. LS21: Otley 9L 17
Riverdale Cres. WF3: S'ley 1A 126
Riverdale Dr. WF3: S'ley 1A 126
Riverdale Gdns. LS21: Otley 9L 17
LS23: B Spa 1F 38
Riverdale Ho. *HX7: Heb B* *1G 94*
(off Mytholm Cl.)
Riverdale Rd. LS21: Otley 9L 17
WF3: S'ley 1A 126
River Holme Vw. HD9: Brock 7A 154
Riverine HX6: Sow B 8K 97
Rivermead WF2: Wake 8M 125
Rivermead Ct. *WF2: Wake* *8M 125*
(off Rivermead)
River Mt. BD21: Rid 7L 27
River Pk. HD9: Hon 4L 153
Riverside BD16: Bgly 2C 44
BD21: Keigh 9L 27
HD8: Clay W 7H 157
LS22: Weth 4L 23
Riverside, The HD7: Linth 8C 136
Riverside Av. LS21: Otley 7M 17
Riverside Bus. Pk. LS29: I'ly 4H 15
Riverside Cl. LS21: Otley 8M 17
Riverside Ct. BD17: Ship 6M 45
HD1: Hud 8B 8 (6M 137)
HD8: Den D 2D 172
Riverside Ct. HD9: Holm 6H 169
HX3: Hal 9C 98
LS1: Leeds 8G 5 (7E 68)
WF7: F'stne 5C 128
Riverside Cres. LS21: Otley 7M 17
Riverside Dr. BD19: Cleck 3H 101
LS21: Otley 7M 17
Riverside Est. BD17: Ship 7M 45
Riverside Ind. Est. WF4: Horb 2A 142
WF12: Dew 4F 122
Riverside Landings *BD16: Bgly* *4E 44*
(off Ferrand La.)
Riverside Pk. LS21: Otley 8M 17
Riverside Vs. WF2: Wake 8L 125
Riverside Wlk. LS23: B Spa 9D 24
LS29: I'ly 4E 14
Riverside Way LS1: Leeds 8C 4 (7C 68)
WF13: Raven 6B 122
Riverside W. LS1: Leeds 8B 4 (7C 68)
River St. BD21: Keigh 7L 27
BD22: Haw 8D 42
HD3: Hud 6F 136
HD6: Brigh 2A 120
HX7: Heb B *1G 95*
(off Bridges La.)
OL14: Tod 7L 93
River Valley Vw. *HD8: Den D* *2D 172*
(off Miller Hill)
River Vw. LS18: Hors 6E 48
LS23: B Spa 1F 38
LS29: I'ly 4K 15
S75: W Gran 6G 158
WF10: C'frd 4B 108
WF14: Mir 5H 121
River Wlk. BD16: Bgly 4E 44
HX6: Sow B 9H 97
Riverwood Dr. HX3: Hal 1A 118
Riviera Gdns. LS7: Leeds 9E 50
Rivock Av. BD20: Keigh 5F 26
BD20: Stee 2D 26
Rivock Gro. BD20: Keigh 5F 26
Roach Grange Av. LS25: Kip 2A 90
Road End HX4: Gree 4B 118
Roaine Dr. HD9: H'frth 4N 169
Roans Brae BD10: B'frd 9J 47
Robb Av. LS11: Leeds 4C 86
Robbins Ter. WF7: F'stne 5D 128
Robb St. LS11: Leeds 4C 86
Roberson Ter. BD19: Gom 4L 101
Robert Ct. WF15: Liv 9K 101
Robert Ho. *LS27: Morl* *8L 85*
(off Pullman Ct.)
Robert La. HD9: H'frth 1A 170
Roberts Av. LS9: Leeds 4K 69
Roberts Bldgs. *HX2: Hal* *5K 97*
(off Gibbet St.)
Roberts Ct. LS9: Leeds 4K 69
Robertsgate WF3: Loft 3K 105
Robertsgate Sq. *WF3: Loft* *3K 105*
(off Robertsgate)
Robertshaw Pl. BD16: Bgly 5F 44
Robertshaw Rd. HX7: Heb B 1G 94
Robertson Av. HD6: Ras 3M 119
Roberts Pas. OL15: Lit 9M 113
Roberts Pl. BD1: B'frd 2A 6 (6B 64)
LS9: Leeds 5K 69
Roberts St. BD19: Cleck 5G 101
BD22: Lay 1C 42
LS26: W'frd 7D 88
Robert St. BD3: B'frd 5E 6 (8E 64)
BD22: Cros R 7F 42
HX3: Hal 2N 97
Robert St. Nth. HX3: Hal 2B 98
Roberts Way WF2: Wake 1A 144
Roberts Wharf LS9: Leeds 8K 5 (8G 68)
ROBERTTOWN 1K 121
Roberttown Grange *WF15: Liv* *1J 121*
(off School St.)
Roberttown La. WF15: Liv 2J 121
Robina Cl. LS23: B Spa 1C 38
Robin Chase LS28: Pud 7C 66
Robin Cl. BD2: B'frd 2G 64
WF8: Pon 9K 109
Robin Dr. BD2: B'frd 2G 64
BD20: Stee 2B 26
Robin Hill WF17: Bat 4D 102
ROBIN HOOD 1K 105
Robin Hood Av. S71: Roys 5E 160
Robin Hood Cres. WF2: Wake 7F 124
Robin Hood Gro. HD2: Hud 7A 120
Robin Hood Hill HD4: Hud 2L 153
Robin Hood Rd. HD2: Hud 7A 120
Robin Hood St. WF10: C'frd 5E 108
Robin Hood Way HD6: Clift 1C 120
Robinia Wlk. WF2: Wake 3J 125
Robin La. LS28: Pud 7B 66
S71: Roys 5E 160
WF9: Hems 4N 161
WF13: Dew 9C 102
(Kilpin Hill La.)
WF13: Dew 1E 122
(Upper Rd.)
Robin Rocks HD9: Brock 7A 154
Robin Royd Av. WF14: Mir 3L 121
Robin Royd Cft. WF14: Mir 3L 121
Robin Royd Dr. WF14: Mir 3L 121
Robin Royd Gth. WF14: Mir 3L 121
Robin Royd Gro. WF14: Mir 3L 121
Robin Royd La. WF14: Mir 4L 121
Robins, The LS29: Burl W 9C 16
Robins Ct. BD12: O'haw 9E 82
Robin's Gro. LS26: Rothw 8A 88
Robinson Cl. WF10: C'frd 5B 108
Robinson Ct. BD7: B'frd 8L 63
Robinson La. HD9: Brock 6N 153
LS25: Kip 4B 90
Robinson's Row LS17: N Rig 2N 19
Robinson St. HD1: Hud 6D 8 (5N 137)
WF8: Pon 2K 129
WF10: All B 9B 90
Robin St. BD5: B'frd 1A 82
HD1: Hud 5J 137
Robin Wlk. BD18: Ship 9B 46
Robinwood Activity Cen. 4G 92
Robinwood Ct. LS8: Leeds 6J 51

Robinwood Ter. OL14: Tod . . . 4G 92
Robson Cl. WF8: Pon . . . 5K 129
Robsons Dr. HD5: Hud . . . 4B 138
Robsons Rd. WF1: Wake . . . 5H 9 (5K 125)
Roby Ho. BD1: B'frd . . . 7B 64
Rochdale Dr. HX6: Tri . . . 1F 116
Rochdale Rd. HD7: Golc . . . 6M 135
HX2: Hal . . . 7K 97
HX4: Gree . . . 4K 117
HX6: Ripp . . . 1E 132
HX6: Sow B, Tri . . . 3E 116
OL14: Tod, W'den . . . 9J 93
Rocheford Cl. LS10: Leeds . . . 2H 87
Rocheford Ct. LS10: Leeds . . . 2H 87
Rocheford Gdns. LS10: Leeds . . . 2H 87
Rocheford Gro. LS10: Leeds . . . 2H 87
Rocheford Wlk. LS10: Leeds . . . 2H 87
Rochester Ct. WF4: Horb . . . 8E 124
Rochester Dr. WF4: Horb . . . 8E 124
Rochester Gdns. LS13: Leeds . . . 2C 66
Rochester Pl. *HX5: Ell* . . . *5E 118*
(off Savile Rd.)
Rochester Rd. WF17: Birs . . . 1B 102
Rochester St. BD3: B'frd . . . 7G 64
BD18: Ship . . . 9A 46
Rochester Ter. LS6: Leeds . . . 2N 67
Rochester Wynd LS17: Leeds . . . 3J 51
Rock, The HD7: Linth . . . 9D 136
Rockcliffe Av. BD17: Bail . . . 6A 46
Rock Cliffe Mt. HX2: Lud F . . . 5D 96
Rock Cotts. HD9: New M . . . 1C 170
Rock Ct. LS27: Morl . . . 8L 85
Rock Edge WF15: Liv . . . 7L 101
Rockery Cft. LS18: Hors . . . 5F 48
Rockery Rd. LS18: Hors . . . 5F 48
Rockfield *LS19: Yead* . . . *9N 31*
(off Rockfield Ter.)
Rockfield Ter. LS19: Yead . . . 9N 31
Rock Fold HD7: Golc . . . 6C 136
Rock Hill WF10: C'frd . . . 6F 108
Rockhill Cl. WF17: Bat . . . 3C 102
Rockhill La. BD4: B'frd . . . 6E 82
(not continuous)
Rock Ho. Dr. WF13: Dew . . . 1F 122
Rockingham Cl. LS15: Leeds . . . 3G 70
Rockingham La. WF9: Bads . . . 5L 147
Rockingham Rd. LS15: Leeds . . . 3G 70
Rockingham St. WF9: Fitz . . . 7B 146
Rockingham Way LS15: Leeds . . . 3G 70
Rocking Stones HD3: Outl . . . 5M 135
Rockland Cres. BD7: B'frd . . . 9K 63
Rocklands Av. BD17: Bail . . . 3A 46
Rocklands Pl. BD17: Bail . . . 3A 46
Rock La. BD13: Thorn . . . 6B 62
HD7: Slait . . . 7M 135
LS13: Leeds . . . 2E 66
Rock Lea BD13: Que . . . 4E 80
Rockley Cl. HD5: Hud . . . 6C 138
Rockley Dr. WF2: Wake . . . 5K 143
Rockley Grange Gdns. LS25: Gar . . . 9L 71
Rockley Hall Yd. LS1: Leeds . . . 6G 5
Rockley St. WF13: Dew . . . 3G 123
Rockmill Rd. HD9: Brock . . . 7A 154
Rock Rd. HD3: Hud . . . 9G 119
Rocks La. HX2: Ogd . . . 5K 79
Rocks Rd. HX3: Hal . . . 9N 97
Rock St. HD3: Hud . . . 3E 136
HD6: Brigh . . . 9M 99
Rocks Vw. HX2: Hal . . . 8N 97
Rock Ter. BD8: B'frd . . . 5B 64
BD13: Thorn . . . 8C 62
BD22: Oak . . . 1B 42
HD3: Hud . . . 1G 136
HX3: Hip . . . 4J 99
LS15: Leeds . . . 6A 70
LS27: Morl . . . 8L 85
OL14: Tod . . . 1J 113
WF10: C'frd . . . 6G 108
WF12: Dew . . . 6L 103
Rock Vw. HD7: Mars . . . 6F 150
HX4: Holy . . . 7B 118
OL12: Whit . . . 4A 112
Rockville Ter. HX1: Hal . . . 7N 97
LS19: Yead . . . *1N 47*
(off Rufford Ridge)
Rockwell La. BD10: B'frd . . . 9G 46
Rockwood Cl. HD2: Hud . . . 5C 120
S75: Dart . . . 8H 159
WF11: Knot . . . 7D 110
Rockwood Cres. LS28: Cal . . . 4L 65
WF4: Cal G . . . 4F 142
Rockwood Gro. LS28: Cal . . . 3M 65
Rockwood Hill Ct. LS28: Cal . . . 4L 65
Rockwood Ri. HD8: Den D . . . 1D 172
Rockwood Rd. LS28: Cal . . . 4L 65
Roderick St. LS12: Leeds . . . 7L 67
Rodger La. WF2: Wren . . . 1H 125
Rodin Av. BD8: B'frd . . . 7J 63
RODLEY . . . 1B 66
Rodley Hall *LS13: Leeds* . . . *1C 66*
(off Club La.)
Rodley La. HD8: Eml . . . 2G 156
LS13: Leeds . . . 2D 66
(Airedale Quay)
LS13: Leeds . . . 9N 47
(Calverley La.)
LS28: Cal . . . 9N 47
Rodley Nature Reserve . . . 1D 66
Rodney Yd. WF1: Wake . . . 5J 9 (5L 125)
Rods Mills La. LS27: Morl . . . 1L 103
Rods Vw. LS27: Morl . . . 1L 103
Rodwell End OL14: Tod . . . 5A 94
Rodwell End La. OL14: Tod . . . 6A 94
Roebuck La. LS21: Clift . . . 5K 17
Roebucks Homes HD5: Hud . . . 4D 138
Roebuck St. WF17: Birs . . . 3C 102
Roebuck Ter. LS21: Clift . . . 5K 17
Roeburn Cl. BD6: B'frd . . . 4K 81
S75: Map . . . 7J 159
Roedhelm Rd. BD20: E Mor . . . 7A 28
Roe Ho. *BD17: Bail* . . . *6N 45*
(off Greenwood Rd.)
Roe La. WF11: Birk . . . 2M 111
Roger Ct. BD2: B'frd . . . 4F 64
Roger Dr. WF2: Wake . . . 1M 143
Roger Fold LS25: Kip . . . 4B 90
Roger Ga. HX7: Myth . . . 3K 95
Roger La. HD4: Hud . . . 7N 137
Rogers Ct. WF3: S'ley . . . 6A 106
Rogerson Sq. HD6: Brigh . . . 9M 99
Rogers Pl. LS28: Pud . . . 6C 66
Roils Head Rd. HX2: Hal . . . 5H 97
Rokeby Gdns. BD10: B'frd . . . 9J 47
LS6: Leeds . . . 1M 67
Roker La. LS28: Pud . . . 9C 66
ROKER LANE BOTTOM . . . 1D 84
Rolleston Rd. DN6: Carc . . . 9N 165
Roman Av. HD3: Hud . . . 1C 136
LS8: Leeds . . . 5J 51
Romanby Shaw BD10: B'frd . . . 9H 47
Roman Cl. HD3: Hud . . . 1C 136
Roman Ct. LS8: Leeds . . . 5K 51
Roman Cres. LS8: Leeds . . . 5K 51
Roman Dr. HD3: Hud . . . 1C 136
LS8: Leeds . . . 5K 51
Roman Gdns. LS8: Leeds . . . 5J 51
Roman Gro. LS8: Leeds . . . 5J 51
Roman Mt. LS8: Leeds . . . 5K 51
Roman Pl. LS8: Leeds . . . 5K 51
Roman Ri. WF8: Pon . . . 6J 129
Roman Rd. S75: Kex . . . 9F 158
WF17: Bat . . . 4C 102
Roman Ter. LS8: Leeds . . . 5J 51
Roman Vw. LS8: Leeds . . . 5K 51
WF10: C'frd . . . 6H 109
Rombald Grange LS29: I'ly . . . 6H 15
Rombalds Av. LS12: Leeds . . . 6M 67
Rombalds Ct. LS29: Men . . . 4D 30
Rombalds Cres. BD20: Sils . . . 9F 12
LS12: Leeds . . . 5M 67
Rombalds Cft. LS19: Yead . . . 9M 31
Rombalds Dr. BD16: Bgly . . . 4G 45
Rombalds Gro. LS12: Leeds . . . 6M 67
Rombalds La. LS29: I'ly . . . 6K 15
Rombalds Pl. LS12: Leeds . . . 5M 67
Rombalds St. LS12: Leeds . . . 5M 67
Rombalds Ter. LS12: Leeds . . . 6M 67
Rombalds Vw. LS12: Leeds . . . 5M 67
LS21: Otley . . . 7H 17
LS29: I'ly . . . 4J 15
Romford Av. LS27: Morl . . . 1K 103
Romford Ct. BD6: B'frd . . . 7L 81
Romney Mt. LS28: Pud . . . 9D 66
Romsey Cl. HD3: Hud . . . 1E 136
Romsey Gdns. BD4: B'frd . . . 2H 83
Romsey M. BD4: B'frd . . . 2H 83
Romwood Cl. WF9: Kins . . . 8B 146
Rona Cft. LS26: Rothw . . . 8B 88
Ronald Dr. BD7: B'frd . . . 8M 63
Ron Lawton Cres. LS29: Burl W . . . 9B 16
Roods Footpath HD9: Mel . . . 7D 152
Roods La. HD9: Holm . . . 5F 168
Rookery HX3: Hal . . . 9C 98
Rookery, The LS29: Add . . . 1M 13
Rookery La. HX3: Hal . . . 9C 98
Rookery Pl. HD6: Brigh . . . 9N 99
Rookes Av. BD6: B'frd . . . 5A 82
Rookes La. HX3: Hip, Nor G . . . 3M 99
Rookes La. Top HX3: Nor G . . . 2M 99
Rookes Vw. HX3: Nor G . . . 2M 99
Rookhill Dr. WF8: Pon . . . 4L 129
Rookhill Mt. WF8: Pon . . . 4M 129
Rookhill Rd. WF8: Pon . . . 4M 129
Rook La. BD4: B'frd . . . 3F 82
Rooks Av. BD19: Cleck . . . 4G 101
Rooks Cl. BD12: Wyke . . . 3B 100
Rook's Nest Rd. WF1: Out . . . 8L 105
WF3: S'ley . . . 8L 105
Rook St. BD16: Bgly . . . 4E 44
HD1: Hud . . . 3A 8 (3M 137)
(not continuous)
Rookwith Pde. BD10: B'frd . . . 9H 47
Rookwood Av. LS9: Leeds . . . 6L 69
LS25: Kip . . . 5A 90
Rookwood Cres. LS9: Leeds . . . 6L 69
Rookwood Cft. LS9: Leeds . . . 7L 69
Rookwood Gdns. LS9: Leeds . . . 6L 69
Rookwood Hill LS9: Leeds . . . 6L 69
Rookwood Mt. LS9: Leeds . . . 6L 69
Rookwood Pde. LS9: Leeds . . . 6M 69
Rookwood Pl. LS9: Leeds . . . 6L 69
Rookwood Rd. LS9: Leeds . . . 6L 69
Rookwood Sq. LS9: Leeds . . . 6M 69
Rookwood St. LS9: Leeds . . . 7L 69
Rookwood Ter. LS9: Leeds . . . 6L 69
Rookwood Va. LS9: Leeds . . . 7L 69
Rookwood Vw. LS9: Leeds . . . 6L 69
Rookwood Wlk. LS9: Leeds . . . 6L 69
Rooley Av. BD6: B'frd . . . 5B 82
Rooley Banks HX6: Sow B . . . 9E 96
Rooley Cl. BD5: B'frd . . . 4C 82
Rooley Ct. HX6: Sow B . . . 9D 96
Rooley Cres. BD6: B'frd . . . 4C 82
Rooley Hgts. HX6: Sow B . . . 9D 96
ROOLEY HILL . . . 9D 96
Rooley La. BD4: B'frd . . . 4D 82
BD5: B'frd . . . 4B 82
HX6: Sow B . . . 1D 116
Roomfield Ct. *OL14: Tod* . . . *7K 93*
(off Halifax Rd.)
Roomfield Ho. OL14: Tod . . . 7K 93
Roomfield St. OL14: Tod . . . 7K 93
ROOMS . . . 5J 85
Rooms Fold LS27: Morl . . . 7K 85
Rooms La. LS27: Gil, Morl . . . 5J 85
Rooms Way LS27: Morl . . . 6J 85
Roper Av. LS8: Leeds . . . 7H 51
Roper Gdns. HX2: Mix . . . 9K 79
Ropergate WF8: Pon . . . 3J 129
Ropergate End *WF8: Pon* . . . *3J 129*
(off Ropergate)
Ropergate Service Rd. WF8: Pon . . . 3J 129
Roper Grn. HX2: Mix . . . 9K 79
Roper Gro. LS8: Leeds . . . 7H 51
Roper Ho. HX2: Mix . . . 9K 79
Roper La. BD13: Que . . . 2A 80
HX2: Brad . . . 5M 79
Ropers Flats WF11: Knot . . . 8G 110
Roper St. BD21: Keigh . . . 9H 27
Rope Wlk. HX2: Wain . . . 6F 78
Ropewalk WF11: Knot . . . 8F 110
Rordin Hgts. HD2: Hud . . . 7A 120
Rosa Ct. WF8: Pon . . . 3M 129
Roscoe St. LS7: Leeds . . . 1J 5 (4F 68)
Roscoe Ter. LS12: Leeds . . . 7L 67
Roseate Grn. LS27: Morl . . . 1M 103
Rose Av. HD3: Hud . . . 4H 137
HD4: Hud . . . 7E 136
LS18: Hors . . . 8E 48
WF9: Upt . . . 2M 163
Rose Bank *BD8: B'frd* . . . *5A 64*
(off E. Squire La.)
BD12: Wyke . . . 9B 82
HX2: Hal . . . 7M 97
LS29: Burl W . . . 9C 16
Rosebank Cl. LS17: Leeds . . . 6A 52
Rosebank Cres.
LS3: Leeds . . . 2A 4 (4B 68)
Rosebank Gdns. LS3: Leeds . . . 5B 68
Rosebank Ho. LS3: Leeds . . . 2A 4 (4B 68)
Rose Bank Pl. BD8: B'frd . . . 7K 63
Rose Bank Rd. OL14: Tod . . . 7J 93
Rosebank Rd. LS3: Leeds . . . 3A 4 (5B 68)
Rosebank Row
LS3: Leeds . . . 3A 4 (5B 68)
Rosebank St. WF17: Bat . . . 6D 102
Roseberry St. BD22: Oak . . . 5D 42
Rosebery Av. BD18: Ship . . . 8A 46
HX3: Hal . . . 8C 98
Rosebery Mt. BD18: Ship . . . 8B 46
Rosebery Rd. BD8: B'frd . . . 4A 64
Rosebery St. HD2: Hud . . . 1L 137
HX5: Ell . . . 5E 118
LS28: Pud . . . 6N 65
OL14: Tod . . . 3E 92
Rosebery Ter. HX1: Hal . . . 4N 97
LS28: Stan . . . 4C 66
Rose Bowl, The
Leeds Metropolitan University . . . 4E 4
Rosebud Wlk. LS8: Leeds . . . 1K 5 (4G 69)
Rosechapel Cl. BD6: B'frd . . . 7L 81
Rosecliffe Mt. LS13: Leeds . . . 3E 66
Rosecliffe Ter. LS13: Leeds . . . 4F 66
Rose Cl. WF9: Upt . . . 2N 163
Rose Ct. LS25: Gar . . . 7A 72
Rose Cft. LS17: E Kes . . . 2D 36
Rosedale LS26: Rothw . . . 7A 88
Rosedale Av. BD15: All . . . 4E 62
HD5: Hud . . . 5C 138
WF2: Wake . . . 2N 143
WF15: Liv . . . 1H 121
Rosedale Bank LS10: Leeds . . . 4F 86
Rosedale Cl. BD17: Bail . . . 5M 45
WF6: Norm . . . 2L 127
WF9: Upt . . . 2A 164
Rosedale Ct. BD4: E Bier . . . 6J 83
WF3: W Ard . . . 6A 104
Rosedale Dr. WF3: W Ard . . . 6A 104
Rosedale Fold BD10: B'frd . . . 9G 47
Rosedale Gdns. LS10: Leeds . . . 4F 86
(not continuous)
WF3: Ting . . . 4D 104
Rosedale Grn. LS10: Leeds . . . 4F 86
Rosedale Ri. LS23: B Spa . . . 1C 38
Rosedale Wlk. LS10: Leeds . . . 4F 86
Rose Farm App. WF6: Alt . . . 8G 106
Rose Farm Cl. WF6: Alt . . . 7G 107
Rose Farm Fold WF6: Alt . . . 7G 106
Rose Farm Mdws. WF6: Alt . . . 8G 106
Rose Farm Ri. WF6: Alt . . . 7G 106
Rosefield Av. S75: W Gran . . . 6G 158
Rose Gth. WF4: Croft . . . 1G 145
Rosegarth Av. HD9: H'frth . . . 1A 170
Rose Gro. HX2: Lud . . . 1E 96
HX6: Sow B . . . 7G 96
HX7: Heb B . . . 9H 77
HX7: Myth . . . 4M 95
LS26: Rothw . . . 7M 87
WF9: Upt . . . 2N 163
Rose Gro. La. HX6: Sow B . . . 7F 96
Rose Heath HX2: Illing . . . 6K 79
Rose Hill HD7: Mars . . . 5G 151
HX6: Sow B . . . *8J 97*
(off Tuel La.)
Rosehill Av. WF9: Hems . . . 3C 162
Rosehill Cres.
BD12: Low M . . . 8A 82
Rosehill Dr. HD2: Hud . . . 1K 137
Rosehip Ri. BD14: Clay . . . 2G 81
Rosehip Wlk. WF10: C'frd . . . 7B 108
Rose La. WF7: Ackw . . . 5D 146
Roselee Cl. HX3: Hal . . . 9D 98
Rose Lynn Ter. *BD6: B'frd* . . . *6L 81*
(off Halifax Rd.)
Rosemary Av. *LS12: Leeds* . . . *7N 67*
(off Armley Gro. Pl.)
Rosemary Cl. HD6: Ras . . . 2M 119
Rosemary Gdns. BD15: All . . . 5F 62
Rosemary Gro. HX3: Hal . . . 9D 98
(not continuous)
Rosemary Hill HX3: Hal . . . 1D 118
Rosemary La. HD6: Ras . . . 3M 119
HX3: Hal . . . 9D 98
Rosemary Pl. *HD6: Ras* . . . *3M 119*
(off Rosemary La.)
Rosemary Ter. HX3: Hal . . . 9D 98
Rosemead S36: Ing . . . 8C 172
Rose Mdws. BD22: Keigh . . . 2E 42
Rosemont *LS16: B'hpe* . . . *5G 33*
(off Breary La.)
Rosemont Av. LS13: Leeds . . . 4F 66
LS28: Pud . . . 6C 66
Rosemont Dr. LS28: Pud . . . 6C 66
Rosemont Gro. LS13: Leeds . . . 4E 66
Rosemont La. BD17: Bail . . . 5C 46
Rosemont Pl. LS13: Leeds . . . 4F 66
Rosemont Rd. LS13: Leeds . . . 4F 66
Rosemont St. LS13: Leeds . . . 4F 66
LS28: Pud . . . 6C 66
Rosemont Ter. LS13: Leeds . . . 4F 66
LS28: Pud . . . 6C 66
Rosemont Vw. LS13: Leeds . . . 4E 66
Rosemont Vs. LS28: Pud . . . 6C 66
Rosemont Wlk. LS13: Leeds . . . 4F 66
ROSEMOUNT . . . 5F 118
Rose Mt. BD2: B'frd . . . 3E 64
BD4: B'frd . . . 5L 83
HD2: Hud . . . 1J 137
HX2: Hal . . . 8N 97
Rosemount *LS7: Leeds* . . . *9E 50*
(off School La.)
Rosemount Av. HX5: Ell . . . 5F 118
Rosemount Cl. *BD21: Keigh* . . . *9H 27*
(off Well St.)
Rosemount Dr. WF6: Norm . . . 2L 127
Rosemount Gdns. BD8: B'frd . . . 4B 64
Rose Mt. Pl. LS12: Leeds . . . 8N 67
Rosemount Ter. HX5: Ell . . . 5F 118
Rosemount Wlk. *BD21: Keigh* . . . *9H 27*
(off Well St.)
Roseneath Pl. LS12: Leeds . . . 8N 67
Roseneath St. LS12: Leeds . . . 8N 67
Roseneath Ter. LS12: Leeds . . . 8N 67
Rose Pl. HX2: Lud F . . . 7E 96
Rose St. BD8: B'frd . . . 5N 63
BD21: Keigh . . . 9M 27
BD22: Haw . . . 9C 42
HX1: Hal . . . 6M 97
LS18: Hors . . . 7E 48
OL14: Tod . . . 7K 93
Rose Ter. HD1: Hud . . . 1C 8
HX1: Hal . . . *5N 97*
(off Battinson Rd.)
HX2: Hal . . . 8N 97
LS18: Hors . . . 7D 48
LS29: Add . . . 1M 13
Rose Tree Av. S72: Cud . . . 9J 161
Rose Tree Ct. S72: Cud . . . 9J 161
Rosetta Dr. BD8: B'frd . . . 6L 63
Rosevale Vw. HX6: Sow B . . . 7J 97
Rose Vs. HX7: Heb B . . . 1G 95
HX7: Myth . . . 4L 95
Roseville Bus. Pk. LS8: Leeds . . . 1L 5 (4G 69)
Roseville Rd. LS8: Leeds . . . 2K 5 (4G 68)
Roseville St. LS8: Leeds . . . 1L 5 (4G 69)
Roseville Ter. *LS15: Leeds* . . . *3E 70*
(off Church La.)
WF12: Dew . . . *3J 123*
(off Old Bank Rd.)
Roseville Way LS8: Leeds . . . 2K 5 (4G 68)
Rosewood Av. BD20: Rid . . . 7M 27
LS25: Kip . . . 2N 89
Rosewood Ct. *LS17: Leeds* . . . *4C 50*
(off Cranmer Cl.)
LS26: Rothw . . . 6A 88
Rosewood Gro. BD4: B'frd . . . 9H 65
Rosgill Dr. LS14: Leeds . . . 1A 70
Rosgill Grn. LS14: Leeds . . . 1B 70
Rosgill Wlk. LS14: Leeds . . . 1A 70
Rosie Rd. WF6: Norm . . . 1N 127
Rosley Mt. BD6: B'frd . . . 7L 81
Roslyn Av. HD4: Neth . . . 2H 153
Roslyn Pl. BD7: B'frd . . . 8N 63
Rossall Rd. LS8: Leeds . . . 2H 69
Rossefield App. LS13: Leeds . . . 5G 66
Rossefield Av. HD2: Hud . . . 1K 137
LS13: Leeds . . . 4G 67
Rossefield Chase LS13: Leeds . . . 4G 66
Rossefield Cl. LS13: Leeds . . . 4G 66
Rossefield Dr. LS13: Leeds . . . 4G 66
Rossefield Gdns. LS13: Leeds . . . 4G 66
Rossefield Gth. LS13: Leeds . . . 4G 66
Rossefield Grn. *LS13: Leeds* . . . *4G 66*
(off Rossefield Dr.)
Rossefield Gro. LS13: Leeds . . . 4G 66
Rossefield Lawn LS13: Leeds . . . 4G 66
Rossefield Pde. *LS13: Leeds* . . . *4G 66*
(off Rossefield Wlk.)
Rosse Fld. Pk. BD9: B'frd . . . 2N 63
Rossefield Pl. LS13: Leeds . . . 4G 66
Rossefield Rd. BD9: B'frd . . . 2M 63
Rossefield Ter. LS13: Leeds . . . 4G 66
Rossefield Vw. LS13: Leeds . . . 4G 66
Rossefield Wlk. LS13: Leeds . . . 4G 66
Rossefield Way LS13: Leeds . . . 4G 66
Rossendale Pl. BD18: Ship . . . 8M 45
Rossendale Vw. OL14: Tod . . . 8B 94
Rosse St. BD8: B'frd . . . 7M 63
BD18: Ship . . . 7N 45
Rossett Bus. Pk. LS13: Leeds . . . 2E 66
Rossett Ho. BD3: B'frd . . . 2D 6
Ross Gro. LS13: Leeds . . . 2D 66
Rossington Gro. LS8: Leeds . . . 2G 69
Rossington Pl. LS8: Leeds . . . 2G 69
Rossington Rd. LS8: Leeds . . . 1J 69
Rossington St. LS2: Leeds . . . 5E 4 (6D 68)
Rossiter Dr. WF11: Knot . . . 9C 110
Rosslyn Av. WF7: Ackw . . . 5F 146
Rosslyn Cl. WF7: Ackw . . . 5F 146
Rosslyn Ct. WF7: Ackw . . . 5F 146
WF12: Dew . . . 4J 123
Rosslyn Gro. BD22: Haw . . . 9C 42
WF7: Ackw . . . 5F 146
Rossmore Dr. BD15: All . . . 5H 63
Ross Ter. LS13: Leeds . . . 2D 66
Rotary Cl. WF13: Dew . . . 1F 122
ROTCHER . . . 1L 151
Rotcher La. HD7: Slait . . . 1L 151
Rotcher Rd. HD9: H'frth . . . 3M 169
Rothbart Gdns. BD16: Bgly . . . 3H 45
Rothbury Gdns. LS16: Leeds . . . 4L 49
Rother Gth. WF9: S Elm . . . 7A 164
Rother M. WF9: S Elm . . . 7A 164
Rothery Ct. HX1: Hal . . . 2G 7
Rothesay Ter. BD7: B'frd . . . 8A 64
ROTHWELL . . . 8N 87
Rothwell Country Pk. . . . 5B 88
Rothwell Dr. HX1: Hal . . . 7H 7 (7A 98)
ROTHWELL HAIGH . . . 7M 87
Rothwell La. LS26: Rothw . . . 7B 88
Rothwell Mt. HX1: Hal . . . 7H 7 (7A 98)
Rothwell Rd. HX1: Hal . . . 7H 7 (7A 98)
Rothwell Sports Cen. . . . 9D 88
Rothwell St. HD5: Hud . . . 4C 138
Rough Bottom HX7: Myth . . . 1N 95
Rough Hall La. HX2: Wain . . . 8F 78
Rough Hey La. HX7: Hept . . . 5L 75
OL14: W'den . . . 2H 113
Rough Hey Wood HX6: Tri . . . 3F 116
Rough Side La. OL14: Tod . . . 8L 93

Round Cl. Rd.—Ryecroft

Round Cl. Rd. HD9: Had E 2M 175
Roundell Av. BD4: B'frd 5F 82
Roundfield Pl. *BD13: Thorn* 7C 62
(off West La.)
ROUNDHAY 6J 51
Roundhay Av. LS8: Leeds 1H 69
Roundhay Ct. LS8: Leeds 6J 51
Roundhay Cres. LS8: Leeds 1H 69
Roundhay Gdns. LS8: Leeds 1H 69
Roundhay Golf Course 5L 51
Roundhay Gro. LS8: Leeds 1H 69
Roundhay Mt. LS8: Leeds 1H 69
Roundhay Park 6K 51
Roundhay Pk. La. LS17: Leeds 2K 51
Roundhay Pl. LS8: Leeds 1H 69
Roundhay Rd. LS7: Leeds 1J 5 (4F 68)
LS8: Leeds 1J 5 (4F 68)
Roundhay Vw. LS8: Leeds 1H 69
Roundhead Fold BD10: B'frd 7J 47
ROUND HILL 6D 108
Round Hill *BD13: Que* 5B 80
(off Rope La.)
HX2: Illing 7M 79
S75: Dart 8J 159
Roundhill Av. BD16: Cot 7G 44
Round Hill Cl. HD8: Skelm 7B 156
HX2: Illing 7M 79
Roundhill Cl. BD13: Que 3G 81
Round Hill La. HD5: Hud 7E 120
Roundhill Mt. BD16: Cot 8G 44
Round Hill Pl. BD13: Que 3G 80
Roundhill Pl. BD1: B'frd 7B 64
Round Hill Rd. LS28: Pud 7N 65
Roundhill Rd. WF10: C'frd 5D 108
Roundhill St. BD5: B'frd 1B 82
Roundhouse Bus. Pk. LS12: Leeds 8A 4 (7B 68)
Round Ings Rd. HD3: Outl 3M 135
Round St. BD5: B'frd 2C 82
(not continuous)
WF1: Wake 7N 125
Round Thorn Pl. BD8: B'frd 6M 63
Roundway HD9: Hon 5L 153
Roundway, The LS27: Morl 9H 85
Roundwell Rd. WF15: Liv 7G 101
Roundwood BD18: Ship 8K 45
Round Wood Av. HD5: Hud 4E 138
Roundwood Av. BD10: B'frd 1J 65
BD17: Bail 4D 46
Roundwood Crest WF2: Wake 6E 124
Roundwood Glen BD10: B'frd 8J 47
Roundwood Ind. Est. WF5: Oss 6D 124
Roundwood Ri. WF2: Wake 7F 124
Roundwood Rd. BD17: Bail 4C 46
WF5: Oss 7C 124
Roundwood Vw. BD10: B'frd 9J 47
Rouse Fold BD4: B'frd 7D 6 (9D 64)
Rouse Mill La. WF17: Bat 8G 103
Rouse St. WF15: Liv 8L 101
ROW 1J 151
Row, The *LS19: Raw* 3L 47
(off Apperley La.)
Rowan Av. BD3: B'frd 7J 65
HD4: Neth 3J 153
LS16: Leeds 2M 49
WF6: Norm 3H 127
Rowan Av. M. HD4: Neth 3J 153
Rowanberries BD14: Clay 2G 80
Rowanberry Cl. BD2: B'frd 2F 64
Rowan Cl. LS21: Pool 2H 33
WF11: Knot 1C 130
WF17: Birs 2D 102
Rowan Ct. BD2: B'frd 5G 65
LS19: Raw 2M 47
LS26: W'frd 7F 88
WF2: Wake 3H 125
Rowan Dr. HD6: Clift 9A 100
Rowan Grn. WF8: Pon 2M 129
Rowan La. S72: S Hien 3M 161
Rowan M. WF3: Rob H 2J 105
Rowan Pl. LS25: Gar 8B 72
Rowans, The BD17: Bail 4L 45
LS13: Leeds 3C 66
LS16: B'hpe 6J 33
LS22: Weth 3A 24
WF3: Rob H 2J 105
Rowan St. BD20: Keigh 6G 27
Rowan Trade Pk. BD4: B'frd 1F 82
Rowantree Av. BD17: Bail 3N 45
Rowan Tree Ct. WF1: Out 7K 105
Rowantree Dr. BD10: B'frd 9F 46
Rowan Way HX3: North 9F 80
Rowanwood Gdns. BD10: B'frd 1J 65
Rowany Gdns. LS29: I'ly 6J 15
Row Bottom Ter. HX6: Sow B 8D 96
Rowe Cl. WF9: S Elm 5N 163
Row Ga. HD8: Shep 1H 171
Rowgate HD8: Up C 2L 171
Rowick, The WF2: Wake 6J 125
Rowland La. HX7: Heb B, Wads 1K 95
Rowland Meyrick Way LS22: Weth 3A 24
Rowland Pl. LS11: Leeds 2D 86
Rowland Rd. LS11: Leeds 2D 86
Rowlands Av. HD5: Hud 4D 138
WF9: Upt 2N 163
Rowlands Cl. BD13: Thorn 8A 62
Rowland St. S71: Roys 5E 160
Rowland Ter. LS11: Leeds 2D 86
Row La. HD7: Slait 1J 151
HX6: Sow B 9D 96
Rowlestone Ri. BD10: B'frd 9J 47
Rowley Ct. HD8: Lept 7K 139
Rowley Cft. WF9: S Elm 7N 163
Rowley Dr. HD8: Fen B 7H 139
LS29: I'ly 6L 15
ROWLEY HILL 8J 139
Rowley La. HD8: Fen B, Lept 8H 139
WF9: S Elm 8N 163
Rowsley St. BD21: Keigh 9K 27
Row St. HD4: Hud 6K 137
Rowton Thorpe BD10: B'frd 9J 47
Roxburghe Dale WF6: Norm 2L 127
Roxburgh Gro. BD15: All 6G 62
Roxburgh M. LS12: Leeds 4J 67
Roxby Cl. LS9: Leeds 4L 5 (5G 69)
Roxby St. BD5: B'frd 2B 82
Roxholme Av. LS7: Leeds 1G 69
Roxholme Gro. LS7: Leeds 1G 69
Roxholme Pl. LS7: Leeds 1G 69
Roxholme Rd. LS7: Leeds 1G 69
Roxholme Ter. LS7: Leeds 1G 69
Royal Acre HD7: Golc 5A 136
Royal Arc. BD21: Keigh 9J 27
Royal Armouries Museum, The 8J 5 (8F 68)
Royal Armouries Sq. LS10: Leeds 8J 5
Royal Birkdale Way WF6: Norm 2L 127
Royal Cl. BD7: B'frd 2L 81
LS10: Leeds 3F 86
Royal Ct. LS10: Leeds 3F 86
WF8: Pon 6H 129
Royal Dr. LS10: Leeds 3F 86
Royal Gdns. BD9: B'frd 3J 63
LS10: Leeds 3F 86
Royal Gro. LS10: Leeds 3F 86
Royal Ind. Pk. HX1: Hal 4H 7 (5A 98)
Royal Lofts, The *HX6: Sow B* 9H 97
(off Sowerby St.)
Royal London Ind. Estate, The
LS11: Leeds 4B 86
Royal Pk. Av. LS6: Leeds 1A 4 (4B 68)
Royal Pk. Gro. LS6: Leeds 1A 4 (3B 68)
Royal Pk. Mt. LS6: Leeds 3B 68
Royal Pk. Rd. LS6: Leeds 1A 4 (4A 68)
Royal Pk. Ter. LS6: Leeds 1A 4 (4B 68)
Royal Pk. Vw. LS6: Leeds 3B 68
Royal Pl. LS10: Leeds 3F 86
Royal Ter. HD3: Hud 5F 136
LS23: B Spa 9D 24
Royal Troon Dr. WF1: Wake 2N 125
Royal Troon M. WF1: Wake 2M 125
Royd HX6: Sow B 9E 96
OL14: Tod 5K 93
Royd, The HX6: Ripp 7D 116
Royd Av. BD16: Bgly 4H 45
HD3: Hud 8F 118
S75: Map 8K 159
WF16: Heck 6A 102
Royd Ct. WF14: Mir 7L 121
Royd Cres. HX1: Hal 4L 97
HX7: Myth 3N 95
Royd Cft. HD3: Hud 4G 137
ROYD EDGE 9C 152
Royd End BD15: Wils 1B 62
Royd Farm *HX2: Illing* 6L 79
(off Keighley Rd.)
Roydfield St. HD2: Hud 9N 119
Royd Head Farm WF5: Oss 6M 123
ROYDHOUSE 4A 156
Royd Ho. HD7: Linth 9C 136
Royd Ho. Gro. BD21: Keigh 2L 43
Royd Ho. La. HD7: Linth 9C 136
Royd Ho. Rd. BD21: Keigh 2L 43
Royd Ho. Wlk. BD21: Keigh 2L 43
Royd Ho. Way BD21: Keigh 2L 43
Royd Ings Av. BD21: Keigh 7J 27
Roydlands St. HX3: Hip 4J 99
Roydlands Ter. HX3: Hip 5J 99
Royd La. BD20: Keigh 7H 27
HD9: H'frth 6K 169
HX2: Illing 6L 79
HX3: Hal 9N 79
(not continuous)
HX6: Ripp 7C 116
OL14: Tod 5K 93
Royd Mill Bus. Pk. HD6: Brigh 2A 120
ROYD MOOR 2H 163
Royd Moor La. WF9: Bads, Hems 9F 146
(not continuous)
Royd Moor Rd. BD4: B'frd 4K 83
Royd Mt. HD9: H'frth 4M 169
HX3: Hal 2B 98
Roydon Gro. BD9: B'frd 4M 63
Royd Pk. HX6: Ripp 7D 116
Royd Pl. HX3: Hal 2B 98
Royd Rd. HD9: Mel 9D 152
OL14: Tod 5J 93
Royds, The HD8: Clay W 6K 157
HD9: H'frth 4M 169
HX3: Hal 9A 98
Royds Av. BD11: B'haw 8M 83
HD3: Hud 4H 137
HD6: B Bri 4N 99
HD7: Linth 8C 136
HD9: New M 2B 170
WF5: Oss 3M 123
WF10: C'frd 4J 109
Roydscliffe Dr. BD9: B'frd 2L 63
Roydscliffe Rd. BD9: B'frd 3L 63
Royds Cl. HD9: New M 2B 170
LS12: Leeds 1M 85
Royds Ct. *LS26: Rothw* 8A 88
(off Royds La.)
Royds Cres. HD6: B Bri 5N 99
Roydsdale Way BD4: B'frd 7E 82
Royds Dr. HD9: New M 2B 170
Royds Edge HD9: Mel 8D 152
Royds Ent. Pk. BD6: B'frd 4K 81
Royds Farm Rd. LS12: Leeds 3M 85
ROYDS GREEN 2B 106
Royds Gro. WF1: Out 7L 105
ROYDS HALL 5H 137
Royds Hall Av. BD6: B'frd 5A 82
Royds Hall La. BD6: B'frd 7M 81
(Alderholt Dr.)
BD6: B'frd, Low M 8M 81
(Lingdale Rd.)
BD12: Low M, Wyke 1M 99
Royds Hall Rd. LS12: Leeds 1M 85
Royds Hall Sports Cen. 4H 137
Royds La. LS12: Leeds 1M 85
LS26: Oul, Rothw 9A 88
Royds Mill WF5: Oss 3M 123
Royds Mt. HD8: Kbtn 2L 155
Royds Pk. HD8: Den D 2D 172
LS12: Leeds 1M 85
Royds Pk. Cres. BD12: Wyke 9B 82
Royd Sq. *HX7: Heb B* 1H 95
(off Bond St.)
Royds St. HD7: Mars 6F 150
Roydstone Rd. BD3: B'frd 6H 65
Roydstone Ter. BD3: B'frd 6H 65
Royd St. BD12: Wyke 9A 82
BD13: Thorn 8B 62
BD15: Wils 2B 62
BD20: Keigh 6H 27
(not continuous)
HD3: Hud 5E 136
HD7: Slait 9M 135
OL14: Tod 6J 93
WF17: Bat 9H 103
Royd St. Av. HD3: Hud 5F 136
Royds Vw. HD7: Linth 9C 136
Royds Wood BD18: Ship 1M 63
Royd Ter. HD4: Arm B 1K 153
HX3: Hal 8N 97
HX7: Heb B 1H 95
Royd Vw. HX7: Myth 3M 95
LS28: Pud 8N 65
S72: B'ley 6A 162
Royd Vs. HX7: Heb B 1H 95
Royd Way BD21: Keigh 7J 27
Royd Well BD11: B'haw 8M 83
Royd Wells WF14: Mir 5L 121
Royd Wood BD19: Cleck 6H 101
BD22: Oxen 2D 60
Roydwood Ter. BD13: Cull 9K 43
Royle Fold WF16: Heck 8A 102
Royles Cl. WF9: S Kirk 7J 163
Royles Head La. HD3: Hud 4D 136
Roy Rd. BD6: B'frd 4J 81
ROYSTON 6D 160
Royston Cl. WF3: E Ard 6F 104
Royston Hill WF3: E Ard 6F 104
Royston La. S71: Carl, Roys 7D 160
Royston Leisure Cen. 5D 160
Royston Rd. S72: Cud 8H 161
Roy St. OL14: Tod 3C 92
Ruby St. BD22: Keigh 3G 42
LS9: Leeds 3K 5 (5G 68)
WF17: Bat 5D 102
Rudding Av. BD15: All 5F 62
Rudding Cres. BD15: All 5F 62
Rudding Dr. WF17: Bat 6C 102
Rudding St. HD4: Hud 6J 137
Rudd St. BD7: B'frd 1M 81
Rudgate LS23: T Arch 7J 25
LS24: N Kym, Tad 2K 39
LS24: Wig 6J 25
YO26: B Ain 2K 25
Rudgate Ct. LS23: T Arch 7J 25
Rudgate M. LS23: T Arch 6G 24
Rudgate Pk. LS23: T Arch 6G 24
(not continuous)
Rud La. HX7: Crag V 9G 95
Ruffield Side BD12: Wyke 8A 82
Rufford Av. LS19: Yead 1M 47
S71: Ath 9B 160
Rufford Bank LS19: Yead 1N 47
Rufford Cl. LS19: Yead 1N 47
WF4: Ryh 9H 145
Rufford Cres. LS19: Yead 1N 47
Rufford Dr. LS19: Yead 1N 47
Rufford Gdns. LS19: Yead 1M 47
RUFFORD PARK 1M 47
Rufford Pl. HX3: Hal 8J 7 (8A 98)
Rufford Ridge LS19: Yead 1N 47
Rufford Ri. LS19: Yead 1M 47
Rufford Rd. HD3: Hud 5E 136
HX3: Hal 8J 7 (8A 98)
HX5: Ell 5E 118
Rufford St. BD3: B'frd 7G 64
WF2: Wake 5H 125
Rufford Vs. HX3: Hal 8J 7 (8A 98)
Rufus St. BD5: B'frd 2N 81
BD21: Keigh 8J 27
Rugby Av. HX3: Hal 1M 97
Rugby Dr. HX3: Hal 1M 97
Rugby Gdns. HX3: Hal 1M 97
Rugby League Heritage Mus. 4B 8 (4M 137)
Rugby Mt. HX3: Hal 1M 97
Rugby Pl. BD7: B'frd 8N 63
Rugby Ter. HX3: Hal 1M 97
Rumble Rd. WF12: Dew 2J 123
Rumbold Rd. HD3: Hud 3J 137
Rumple Cft. LS21: Otley 7J 17
Runnymede Ct. *BD10: B'frd* 8F 46
(off Cobden St.)
Runswick Av. LS11: Leeds 9B 68
Runswick Gro. BD5: B'frd 4B 82
Runswick Pl. LS11: Leeds 9B 68
Runswick St. BD5: B'frd 4B 82
LS11: Leeds 9B 68
Runswick Ter. BD5: B'frd 4B 82
LS11: Leeds 9C 68
RUNTLINGS 6M 123
Runtlings WF5: Oss 6M 123
Runtlings, The WF5: Oss 6L 123
Runtlings La. WF5: Oss 7M 123
Runtlings Ter. *WF5: Oss* 6M 123
(off W. Wells Rd.)
Rupert Rd. LS29: I'ly 4F 14
Rupert St. BD21: Keigh 8J 27
BD22: Cros R 7F 42
Ruscombe Pl. S71: Carl 8D 160
Rushbearers Wlk. HD5: Hud 7C 138
Rush Cft. BD10: B'frd 6D 46
Rushcroft Ter. BD17: Bail 4A 46
Rushdene Ct. BD12: Wyke 3A 100
Rushfield Va. HD8: Fen B 6G 139
Rushmead Ct. WF5: Oss 6C 124
Rushmoor Rd. BD4: B'frd 3H 83
Rusholme Dr. LS28: Fars 3N 65
Rushton Av. BD3: B'frd 6J 65
Rushton Hill HX2: Hal 3J 97
Rushton Hill Cl. HX2: Hal 3J 97
Rushton Rd. BD3: B'frd 6J 65
Rushton St. HX1: Hal 4M 97
LS28: Cal 9M 47
Rushton Ter. BD3: B'frd 7J 65
Rushworth Cl. S75: Kex 9E 158
WF3: S'ley 7N 105
Rushworth St. HX3: Hal 3N 97
Rushy Fall Mdw. BD22: Keigh 5G 42
Ruskin Av. BD9: B'frd 3J 63
WF1: Wake 1H 125
Ruskin Cl. WF10: C'frd 4H 109
Ruskin Ct. WF1: Wake 1H 125
Ruskin Cres. LS20: Guis 8K 31
Ruskin Dr. WF10: C'frd 4G 109
Ruskin Gro. HD2: Hud 8B 120
Ruskin Pl. WF10: C'frd 4H 109
Ruskin St. LS28: Stan 5N 65
Ruskin Ter. HX3: Hal 3N 97
Russell Av. BD13: Que 5D 80
WF4: Hol 7H 143
Russell Cl. WF16: Heck 9B 102
WF17: Bat 7F 102
Russell Ct. LS17: Bard 5E 36
Russell Gro. BD11: B'haw 7M 83
LS8: Leeds 2H 69
Russell Hall La. BD13: Que 4D 80
Russell Rd. BD13: Que 5C 80
Russell Sq. BD11: B'haw 8M 83
Russell St. BD5: B'frd 7A 6 (9B 64)
BD13: Que 4D 80
BD18: Ship 1A 64
BD21: Keigh 9H 27
HX1: Hal 4L 7 (5B 98)
LS1: Leeds 6E 4 (6D 68)
OL14: Tod 7L 93
WF1: Wake 8K 9 (7L 125)
WF13: Dew 2D 122
Russell Way HD6: Brigh 8N 99
Russet Fold WF15: Liv 8L 101
Russets, The WF2: Wake 4N 143
WF4: Flock 8E 140
Russett Gro. HD4: Hud 7N 137
Russetts, The HX3: Hal 4D 98
Rustic Av. HX3: Sou 8F 98
Rustless Cl. BD19: Cleck 6E 100
Ruston Dr. S71: Roys 5D 160
Ruswarp Cres. BD10: B'frd 9H 47
Ruth Ho. BD3: B'frd 3E 6
Ruth St. BD22: Cros R 7E 42
HD4: Hud 8M 137
Ruthven Vw. LS8: Leeds 3J 69
Rutland Av. WF2: Wake 9L 125
WF8: Pon 6K 129
Rutland Cl. LS25: Kip 3B 90
LS26: W'frd 7E 88
Rutland Ct. *LS28: Pud* 6B 66
(off Richardshaw La.)
Rutland Dr. LS25: Kip 3B 90
WF4: Croft 9D 126
Rutland Ho. *BD16: Bgly* 4F 44
(off Clyde St.)
Rutland Ind. Est.
WF1: Wake 7L 9 (6M 125)
Rutland Mt. LS3: Leeds 5A 4 (6B 68)
Rutland Rd. HD3: Hud 5F 136
WF4: Flock 7F 140
WF17: Bat 6G 102
Rutland St. BD4: B'frd 8E 6 (1E 82)
BD21: Keigh 2H 43
LS3: Leeds 5B 4 (6C 68)
Rutland Ter. LS3: Leeds 5A 4 (6B 68)
Rutland Wlk. *WF13: Dew* 3E 122
(off Lacey St.)
Ryan Gro. BD22: Keigh 8D 26
Ryan Pl. LS8: Leeds 2J 69
Ryan St. BD5: B'frd 2B 82
Ryburn HX4: Bark 7K 117
Ryburn Bldgs. *HX6: Sow B* 9H 97
(off Town Hall St.)
Ryburn Ct. *HX1: Hal* 5M 97
(off Hanson La.)
Ryburndale HX6: Ripp 9B 116
Ryburn Golf Course 2J 117
Ryburn Ho. *HX1: Hal* 5M 97
(off Clay St.)
Ryburn La. HX6: Ripp 6E 116
Ryburn Pl. WF2: Wake 7H 9 (6K 125)
Ryburn Rd. HD3: Hud 3G 136
Ryburn St. HX6: Sow B 9H 97
Ryburn Ter. HX1: Hal 5M 97
HX6: Ripp 9C 116
Ryburn Vw. HX2: Hal 7L 97
HX6: Ripp 8C 116
Rycroft Av. BD16: Cot 9F 44
LS13: Leeds 5D 66
Rycroft Cl. LS13: Leeds 5E 66
Rycroft Ct. LS13: Leeds 5E 66
Rycroft Dr. LS13: Leeds 5E 66
Rycroft Gdns. LS13: Leeds 5D 66
Rycroft Grn. LS13: Leeds 5E 66
Rycroft Pl. LS13: Leeds 5E 66
Rycroft St. BD18: Ship 1B 64
Rycroft Towers LS13: Leeds 5D 66
Rydal Av. BD9: B'frd 2A 64
BD17: Bail 6K 45
LS25: Gar 8N 71
Rydal Cres. LS27: Morl 8N 85
WF2: Wake 4G 125
Rydal Dr. HD5: Hud 4B 138
LS27: Morl 8N 85
WF2: Wake 4G 125
Rydale Ct. WF5: Oss 7N 123
WF15: Liv 8H 101
Rydale Ho. HX6: Sow B 9H 97
Rydale M. WF5: Oss 7N 123
Rydal Gro. WF15: Liv 2L 121
Rydall Pl. LS11: Leeds 9B 68
Rydall St. LS11: Leeds 9B 68
Rydall Ter. LS11: Leeds 9B 68
Rydal Rd. DN6: Carc 8N 165
Rydal St. BD21: Keigh 1G 43
WF10: C'frd 4K 109
Ryder Cl. WF8: Pon 3H 129
Ryder Gdns. LS8: Leeds 8J 51
Ryder M. WF9: Hems 3D 162
Rydings, The HD6: Brigh 9M 99
Rydings Av. HD6: Brigh 9M 99
Rydings Cl. HD6: Brigh 9L 99
Rydings Dr. HD6: Brigh 9L 99
Rydings Wlk. HD6: Brigh 9L 99
Ryebank HD9: H'frth 4N 169
Ryebread WF10: C'frd 3E 108
Rye Cl. La. HD9: H'lm 4C 168
Rye Cft. HX2: Illing 7M 79
Ryecroft BD16: Har 6M 43
HD9: Hon 5M 153

Ryecroft Av.—St Margaret's Pl.

Ryecroft Av. DN6: Nort 7N 149
WF4: H'cft 8K 145
Ryecroft Cl. BD4: B'frd 3K 83
HX3: Hip 5M 99
WF1: Out 7L 105
Ryecroft Cres. HX2: Hal 3K 97
Ryecroft Dr. HD3: Hud 1G 136
Ryecroft Farm Cl.
S72: S Hien 2L 161
Ryecroft La. HD6: Ras 3A 120
HD9: Scho 5A 170
HX2: Hal 4K 97
Ryecroft Rd. BD16: Har 5K 43
DN6: Nort 7N 149
Ryecroft St. WF5: Oss 5M 123
Ryecroft Ter. HX2: Hal 3K 97
Ryedale HD5: K'htn 9F 120
Ryedale Av. LS12: Leeds 1L 85
WF11: Knot 1D 130
Ryedale Cl. WF6: Alt 7H 107
Ryedale Ct. LS14: Leeds 1A 70
Ryedale Holt LS12: Leeds 9M 67
Ryedale Pk. LS29: I'ly 6J 15
Ryedale Pl. WF6: Alt 7H 107
Ryedale Way BD15: All 4F 62
WF3: W Ard 4N 103
Ryefield Av. BD14: Clay 9G 63
Rye Fld. La. HX4: Bark 4F 134
Rye Fld. La. W. HX4: Bark 4F 134
Ryefields HD9: Scho 4B 170
Ryefields Av. HD3: Hud 3F 136
Ryefields Rd. HD7: Golc 6D 136
Ryefield Way BD20: Sils 9E 12
Rye Gth. LS22: Weth 1L 23
Ryegrass Gdns. WF10: C'frd 7A 108
Ryelands Gro. BD9: B'frd 2J 63
Rye La. HX2: Hal 3H 97
Rye Pl. LS14: Leeds 5A 70
Ryestone Dr. HX6: Ripp 9C 116
Rye St. BD21: Keigh 3H 43
Rye Way WF10: C'frd 4H 109
RYHILL 9J 145
Ryhill Ind. Est. WF4: Ryh 9J 145
Ryhill Pits La. WF4: Col H 9E 144
Rylands Av. BD16: Bgly 4G 45
Rylands Mdw. BD22: Haw 7E 42
Rylands Pk. HX6: Ripp 9C 116
Rylstone Gdns. BD3: B'frd 4E 64
Rylstone Gro. WF1: Wake 3N 125
Rylstone Rd. BD17: Bail 5L 45
Rylstone St. BD21: Keigh 8K 27
Rylston Gdns. HX3: Hal 9A 98
Ryndleside HD3: Hud 1E 136
Ryshworth Av. BD16: Bgly 9C 28
Ryshworth Bri. BD16: Bgly 1C 44
Ryshworth Cres. BD16: Bgly 9C 28
Ryton Dale BD10: B'frd 9J 47

S

Sabine Fold WF4: Horb 1A 142
Sable Crest BD2: B'frd 2D 64
Sackup La. S75: Dart, S'ross 8H 159
Sackville App. LS7: Leeds 1G 5 (3E 68)
Sackville Rd. BD20: Sils 7E 12
Sackville St. BD1: B'frd 4A 6 (7C 64)
HX7: Heb B 9H 77
LS7: Leeds 1G 5 (3E 68)
OL14: Tod 7K 93
WF13: Raven 5B 122
Saddlers Cft. LS29: I'ly 5F 14
WF10: C'frd 6H 109
Saddlers Gro. WF9: Bads 7L 147
Saddler's La. WF11: B'ton 3B 110
Saddler St. BD12: Wyke 9A 82
Saddleworth Rd. HD3: Bark, Scam 9N 133
HX4: Bark, Gree 8G 116
HX5: Ell 4C 118
Sadler Cl. LS16: Leeds 3M 49
Sadler Copse LS16: Leeds 3M 49
Sadlers Wlk. LS22: Weth 3N 23
Sadler Way LS16: Leeds 3M 49
Saffron Cl. HX6: Sow B 7J 97
Saffron Ct. WF2: Wake 3G 124
Saffron Dr. BD15: All 5G 62
Sagar La. OL14: Tod 2F 92
Sagar Pl. LS6: Leeds 2N 67
Sagar St. WF10: C'frd 4D 108
Sage Gro. HD6: Ras 4K 119
Sage St. BD5: B'frd 1A 82
Sahara Ct. BD8: B'frd 4B 64
St Abbs Cl. BD6: B'frd 6A 82
St Abbs Dr. BD6: B'frd 6A 82
St Abbs Fold BD6: B'frd 6A 82
St Abbs Ga. BD6: B'frd 6A 82
St Abbs Wlk. BD6: B'frd 6A 82
St Abbs Way BD6: B'frd 6A 82
St Aidans Rd. BD17: Bail 5B 46
LS26: Gt P 5M 89
St Aidans Sq. *BD16: Bgly* 1D 44
(off Old Souls Way)
St Aiden's Wlk. WF5: Oss 7C 124
St Alban App. LS9: Leeds 5L 69
St Alban Cl. LS9: Leeds 5L 69
St Alban Ct. LS9: Leeds 5L 69
St Alban Cres. LS9: Leeds 5L 69
St Alban Gro. LS9: Leeds 5L 69
St Alban Mt. LS9: Leeds 5L 69
St Alban Rd. LS9: Leeds 5L 69
St Albans Av. HD3: Hud 8F 118
HX3: Hal 9B 98
St Albans Ct. HX3: Hal 8C 98
St Alban's Pl.
LS2: Leeds 4G 5 (5E 68)
St Albans Rd. HX3: Hal 9B 98
St Alban Vw. LS9: Leeds 5L 69
St Andrew's Av. LS27: Morl 1H 103
St Andrews Cl. HX2: Hal 8N 79
LS13: Leeds 1B 66
LS19: Yead 8N 31
LS27: Morl 1H 103
WF1: Wake 1M 125
St Andrews Ct. *HD6: Brigh* 8M 99
(off Mary St.)
St Andrews Ct. HD7: Slait 9K 135
LS3: Leeds 5A 4
LS19: Yead 8M 31
(off Haw La.)
St Andrews Cres. BD12: O'haw 9E 82
St Andrew's Cft. LS17: Leeds 3D 50
St Andrews Dr. HD5: K'htn 2G 138
HD6: Brigh 8M 99
LS17: Leeds 3E 50
S75: Dart 8J 159
WF7: F'stne 2D 128
WF11: Ferr 7B 110
St Andrew's Gro. LS27: Morl 1J 103
St Andrews Pl. BD7: B'frd 8A 64
LS3: Leeds 5A 4 (6B 68)
WF6: Norm 2L 127
St Andrew's Rd. HD1: Hud 6E 8 (4A 138)
LS19: Yead 9N 31
WF10: C'frd 3K 109
St Andrew's St. LS3: Leeds 5A 4 (6B 68)
St Andrews Ter. LS27: Morl 2H 103
St Andrew's Vs. BD7: B'frd 7A 64
St Andrew's Wlk. LS17: Leeds 3E 50
St Anne's Av. HD3: Hud 8F 118
St Anne's Cl. WF12: Dew 7G 122
St Annes Ct. LS5: Leeds 2M 67
St Annes Dr. LS4: Leeds 2M 67
WF1: Wake 2N 125
St Annes Pl. HX4: Holy 7L 117
LS5: Leeds 2L 67
St Anne's Rd. HX3: Hal 1B 118
LS6: Leeds 1M 67
St Anne's Roman Catholic Cathedral 5E 4 (6D 68)
St Annes Sq. *HD9: H'frth* 3M 169
(off Holmfirth Town Ga.)
HD9: Nether 9L 153
(off Out La.)
St Anne's St. LS2: Leeds 5E 4 (6D 68)
WF4: Ryh 9J 145
St Annes Ter. BD17: Bail 5B 46
St Annes Vs. WF8: Pon 1L 129
St Ann's Av. LS4: Leeds 4N 67
St Ann's Cl. LS4: Leeds 3M 67
St Ann's Gdns. LS4: Leeds 3M 67
St Ann's Grn. LS4: Leeds 2M 67
St Ann's La. LS4: Leeds 2M 67
St Ann's Mt. LS4: Leeds 3N 67
St Ann's Pl. HX1: Hal 2G 7 (4N 97)
St Ann's Ri. LS4: Leeds 3L 67
St Anns Sq. HX6: Sow B 8J 97
LS4: Leeds 3M 67
St Ann's Way LS4: Leeds 3M 67
St Anthony's Dr. LS11: Leeds 3B 86
St Anthonys Gdns. *BD18: Ship* 9B 46
(off Wrose Rd.)
St Anthony's Rd. LS11: Leeds 3A 86
St Anthony's Ter. LS11: Leeds 4A 86
St Armands Ct. LS25: Gar 7N 71
St Augustines Ct. *LS8: Leeds* 3H 69
(off Harehills Pl.)
St Augustine's Ter. BD3: B'frd 1E 6 (5E 64)
HX1: Hal 5N 97
St Barnabas Rd. LS11: Leeds 8D 68
WF15: Liv 7G 101
St Bartholomews Ct. *HD9: Mel* 7C 152
(off Greens End Rd.)
St Bartholomews Cl. LS12: Leeds 7M 67
St Bartholomews Cl. WF2: Wake 7E 124
St Benedicts Chase LS13: Leeds 1G 67
St Benedicts Dr. LS13: Leeds 1H 67
St Benedicts Gdns. LS13: Leeds 1H 67
St Bernard's Av. WF8: Pon 3H 129
St Bevan's Rd. HX3: Hal 9B 98
St Blaise Ct. BD5: B'frd 6B 6 (9C 64)
St Blaise Sq. BD1: B'frd 3B 6 (7C 64)
St Blaise Way BD1: B'frd 3B 6 (6C 64)
St Botolphs Cl. WF11: Knot 8F 110
St Catherine's Bus. Complex *LS13: Leeds* 2G 67
(off Broad La.)
St Catherines Cres. LS13: Leeds 2G 67
St Catherine's Dr. LS13: Leeds 2G 66
St Catherines Grn. LS13: Leeds 2G 67
St Catherine's Hill LS13: Leeds 2G 66
St Catherine St. WF1: Wake 8A 126
St Catherine's Vs. WF1: Wake 8A 126
St Catherines Wlk. LS8: Leeds 9J 51
St Cecilia St. LS2: Leeds 6J 5 (6F 68)
St Chad's Av. HD6: Brigh 7K 99
LS6: Leeds 9M 49
St Chad's Dr. LS6: Leeds 9M 49
St Chad's Gro. LS6: Leeds 9M 49
St Chads Pde. LS16: Leeds 9N 49
St Chad's Ri. LS6: Leeds 9M 49
St Chads Rd. BD8: B'frd 5N 63
LS16: Leeds 9N 49
St Chad's Vw. LS6: Leeds 1M 67
St Christopher's Av. LS26: Rothw 8A 88
St Christophers Dr. LS29: Add 1M 13
St Christopher's Wlk. WF1: Wake 3G 9 (4K 125)
St Clair Grn. WF2: Wake 3F 124
St Clair Rd. LS21: Otley 9M 17
(not continuous)
St Clair St. LS21: Otley 9M 17
WF1: Wake 5L 9 (5M 125)
St Clair Ter. *LS21: Otley* 9M 17
(off St Clair St.)
St Clare's Av. BD2: B'frd 4H 65
St Clements Av. LS26: Rothw 8N 87
St Clements Cl. LS26: Rothw 9M 87
St Clements Ct. WF7: Ackw 5E 146
WF9: S Kirk 6H 163
St Clements Ri. LS26: Rothw 8M 87
St Cuthberts Ct. WF7: Ackw 1G 146
St Cyprian's Gdns. LS9: Leeds 4K 69
St Davids Cl. WF3: Rob H 2K 105
St Davids Ct. HX3: Hal 3A 98
LS11: Leeds 8D 4
St Davids Gth. WF3: Rob H 2K 105
St Davids Rd. LS21: Otley 7J 17
WF3: Rob H 2K 105
St Dunstans Technology Pk.
BD4: B'frd 8C 6 (1D 82)
St Edmund's Cl. WF10: C'frd 4J 109
St Edmunds Ct. LS8: Leeds 5J 51
St Edwards Cl. WF11: Byram 5D 110
St Edward's Ter. *LS23: Cliff* 3D 38
(off High St.)
St Elmo BD13: Que 6B 80
St Elmo Gro. LS9: Leeds 6J 69
St Eloi Av. BD17: Bail 3A 46
St Enoch's Rd. BD6: B'frd 4N 81
St Francis Cl. LS11: Leeds 2D 86
St Francis Gdns. HD2: Fix 6M 119
St Francis Pl. LS11: Leeds 8D 68
St Gabriel Ct. LS14: Leeds 1E 70
St Gabriels Ct. LS18: Hors 3E 48
St George Bldg. *LS1: Leeds* 5C 68
(off Gt. George St.)
St George's Av. HD3: Hud 8F 118
LS26: Rothw 6L 87
St George's Concert Hall
Bradford 5C 6
St Georges Ct. WF4: H'cft 8L 145
St Georges Cres. HX3: Hal 1H 7 (3A 98)
LS26: Rothw 6L 87
St George's Fold HX7: Myth 4M 95
St Georges M. WF2: Wake 5J 143
St George's Pl. BD4: B'frd 1F 82
BD5: B'frd 7A 6 (9C 64)
St Georges Rd. HD9: Scho 4B 170
HX3: Hal 1G 7 (3N 97)
LS1: Leeds 4D 4 (5D 68)
LS10: Leeds 8F 86
WF2: Wake 8F 124
St Georges Sq. HD1: Hud 4B 8 (4M 137)
HD3: Outl 2A 136
HX3: Hal 3A 98
HX7: Heb B 1H 95
(off Bridge Ga.)
St Georges St. BD3: B'frd 8F 64
HD1: Hud 4B 8 (4M 137)
HX7: Heb B 1H 95
St George's Ter. HX3: Hal 3A 98
St George's Wlk. WF2: Wake 4L 143
St Giles Av. WF8: Pon 3H 129
St Giles Cl. HD6: Brigh 7K 99
St Giles Ct. HX3: Hip 5K 99
St Giles Gth. LS16: B'hpe 5G 33
St Giles Mt. WF8: Pon 3H 129
St Giles Rd. HD6: Brigh 6K 99
HX3: Hip 5K 99
St Giles Vw. WF8: Pon 4K 129
St Helena BD13: Denh 5L 61
St Helena Rd. BD6: B'frd 4N 81
St Helenas Caravan Pk.
LS18: Hors 7F 32
St Helens HX4: Holy 7B 118
St Helens Av. LS16: Leeds 4N 49
WF9: Hems 2C 162
St Helens Cl. LS16: Leeds 4N 49
(not continuous)
St Helens Cft. LS16: Leeds 4M 49
St Helen's Dr. LS25: M'fld 6F 72
St Helen's Fld. HD4: Hud 8E 138
St Helens Gdns. LS16: Leeds 4M 49
St Helens Ga. HD4: Hud 8E 138
St Helens Gro. LS16: Leeds 4M 49
WF2: Wake 1A 144
St Helens La. LS16: Leeds 4L 49
St Helens M. LS24: N Kym 2L 39
St Helens Pl. WF10: C'frd 5E 108
St Helen's St. LS10: Leeds 9F 68
St Helens Way LS16: Leeds 4N 49
LS29: I'ly 5J 15
St Helier Gro. BD17: Bail 3B 46
St Hilaire Wlk. *LS10: Leeds* 9G 86
(off Topliss Way)
St Hilda's Av. LS9: Leeds 8H 69
St Hilda's Cres. LS9: Leeds 8H 69
St Hilda's Mt. LS9: Leeds 8H 69
St Hilda's Pl. LS9: Leeds 8H 69
St Hilda's Rd. LS9: Leeds 8H 69
St Hilda's Ter. BD3: B'frd 6J 65
St Hughes Lodge *LS12: Leeds* 6M 67
(off Armley Lodge Rd.)
St Ians Cft. LS29: Add 2M 13
St Ives Cl. WF8: Pon 9K 109
St Ives Cres. WF10: C'frd 7J 109
St Ives Est. BD16: Har 5B 44
St Ives Gdns. HX3: Hal 9B 98
St Ives Gro. BD16: Har 5B 44
LS12: Leeds 6K 67
St Ives Mt. LS12: Leeds 6K 67
St Ives Pl. BD16: Har 5B 44
St Ives Rd. BD16: Har 4C 44
(Cross Gates La.)
BD16: Har 5B 44
(St Ives Pl.)
HX3: Hal 9B 98
St James App. LS14: Leeds 2B 70
St James Av. LS18: Hors 6F 48
St James Bus. Pk. BD1: B'frd 5D 6 (8D 64)
St James Cl. BD17: Bail 4C 46
LS12: Leeds 6J 67
St James Ct. HD6: Brigh 9N 99
HX1: Hal 3K 7
WF4: H'cft 9K 145
St James Cres. LS28: Pud 7M 65
St James Dr. LS18: Hors 6G 48
St James M. LS12: Leeds 6J 67
LS15: Leeds 3E 70
St James Pl. *BD17: Bail* 3D 46
(off Otley Rd.)
St James Ri. WF2: Wake 7E 124
St James Rd. BD17: Bail 3D 46
HX1: Hal 3K 7 (5B 98)
LS29: I'ly 6F 14
St James's Ct. LS9: Leeds 1L 5 (4G 69)
WF2: Wake 8H 9 (7K 125)
St James's Mkt. BD4: B'frd 6E 6 (8E 64)
St James's Pk. WF1: Wake 5N 125
St James Sq. HX3: North 2F 98
St James's Rd. HD1: Hud 3J 137
St James's Sq. BD5: B'frd 8B 6 (9C 64)
St James's St. LS22: Weth 4M 23
St James St. HX1: Hal 3K 7 (5B 98)
WF16: Heck 9A 102
WF17: Bat 7F 102
St James Ter. LS18: Hors 6G 48
St James Wlk. LS18: Hors 6G 48
St James Way HD5: Hud 2C 138
WF4: Crig 4H 143
St John Pde. WF13: Dew 3E 122
ST JOHNS
LS25 6E 54
WF1 1G 9 (4K 125)
St Johns LS29: I'ly 6F 14
S36: Hoy 9J 173
St Johns Av. HD4: Hud 8M 137
HD5: K'htn 1G 138
LS6: Leeds 2A 4 (4B 68)
LS14: T'ner 2G 52
LS28: Fars 4A 66
LS29: Add 1M 13
WF1: Wake 1G 9 (3K 125)
WF5: Oss 6C 124
WF17: Bat 6D 102
St John's Cen. LS2: Leeds 5F 4 (6E 68)
St John's Chase WF1: Wake 2G 9 (4K 125)
St John's Church
Leeds 5F 4 (6E 68)
St Johns Cl. BD4: B'frd 3G 82
BD19: Cleck 5J 101
BD20: Sils 8E 12
HX6: Rish 1C 134
HX7: Heb B 1H 95
(off Birchcliffe Rd.)
LS6: Leeds 2A 4 (4B 68)
LS25: Aber 6E 54
WF5: Oss 6C 124
WF13: Dew 3E 122
St John's Ct. BD17: Bail 5C 46
BD20: Keigh 6G 27
(off St John's Rd.)
HD8: Lept 7K 139
HD9: H'frth 4K 169
LS7: Leeds 2F 68
LS14: T'ner 2G 52
LS19: Yead 1L 47
WF1: Wake 2G 9 (4K 125)
St Johns Cres. BD8: B'frd 6K 63
HD1: Hud 1A 8 (2M 137)
WF5: Oss 6B 124
WF6: Norm 4H 127
St John's Cft. WF1: Wake 2G 9 & 1G 9 (4K 125)
St John's Cross HX2: Brad 5N 79
St John's Dr. HD1: Hud 1A 8 (2M 137)
LS17: N Rig 2N 19
LS19: Yead 1L 47
St John's Gth. LS25: Aber 7E 54
St John's Gro. LS6: Leeds 1A 4 (4B 68)
WF1: Wake 1K 9 (3L 125)
St John's La. HX1: Hal 6K 7 (6B 98)
St Johns M. *BD13: Cull* 9K 43
(off Station Rd.)
WF1: Wake 2G 9 (4K 125)
St John's Mt. WF1: Wake 1G 9 (3J 125)
St John's Nth. WF1: Wake 2H 9 (4K 125)
St John's Pk. LS29: Men 3D 30
St Johns Pl. BD11: B'haw 7L 83
BD19: Cleck 5J 101
HX1: Hal 5K 7
LS5: Leeds 2L 67
(off Vicarage Ter.)
St John's Rd. BD20: Keigh 6G 27
HD1: Hud 1A 8 (2M 137)
HD5: K'htn 1G 138
LS3: Leeds 3A 4 (5B 68)
LS19: Yead 1L 47
LS23: Cliff 1D 38
LS29: I'ly 5K 15
St John's Sq. WF1: Wake 2G 9 (4K 125)
St John's St. BD20: Sils 8E 12
LS26: Oul 8D 88
WF4: Horb 1A 142
St John's Ter. LS3: Leeds 2A 4 (4B 68)
St John St. HD6: Ras 2M 119
WF13: Dew 3E 122
St John's Vw. LS23: B Spa 1C 38
WF17: Bat 6D 102
St Johns Wlk. LS26: Swil 4J 89
S71: Roys 6E 160
St Johns Way BD22: Keigh 1F 42
LS19: Yead 1L 47
St John's Yd. LS26: Oul 8D 88
St John Wlk. WF13: Dew 3E 122
St Josephs Ct. LS19: Raw 5M 47
LS25: Gar 7M 71
St Josephs Mt. WF8: Pon 4H 129
St Jude's Pl. BD1: B'frd 1A 6 (6B 64)
St Jude's St. BD8: B'frd 6B 64
HX1: Hal 8H 7 (7A 98)
St Laurence's Cl. BD2: B'frd 1B 64
St Lawrence Cl. LS28: Pud 7A 66
St Lawrence St. LS7: Leeds 9F 50
St Lawrence Ter. LS28: Pud 7B 66
St Leonards Cl. LS29: Add 2M 13
St Leonards Ct. BD8: B'frd 5L 63
St Leonard's Farm Pk. 2G 46
St Leonard's Gro. BD8: B'frd 5L 63
St Leonard's Rd. BD8: B'frd 5L 63
St Leonards Yd. WF4: Horb 1C 142
St Lucius's Cl. HD4: Farn T 3C 154
St Lukes Cl. BD5: B'frd 8A 6 (9B 64)
BD19: Cleck 5F 100
LS23: Cliff 3D 38
WF4: M'twn 3L 141
WF17: Bat 8H 103
St Luke's Cres. LS11: Leeds 1C 86
St Luke's Grn. LS11: Leeds 1C 86
St Luke's Rd. LS11: Leeds 1C 86
St Luke's St. LS11: Leeds 1C 86
St Luke's Ter. BD19: Cleck 5F 100
BD20: E Mor 8C 28
St Luke's Vw. LS11: Leeds 1C 86
St Margaret's Av. BD4: B'frd 3H 83
LS8: Leeds 9J 51
LS18: Hors 6E 48
LS26: Meth 1L 107
St Margaret's Cl. LS18: Hors 5E 48
St Margaret's Ct. WF9: S Elm 3N 163
St Margaret's Dr. LS8: Leeds 9J 51
LS18: Hors 5E 48
St Margaret's Gro. LS8: Leeds 9J 51
St Margaret's Pl. BD7: B'frd 9N 63

St Margaret's Rd.—Sands Ho. La.

St Margaret's Rd. BD7: B'frd ... 8N 63
LS18: Hors ... 5E 48
LS26: Meth ... 1L 107
St Margaret's Ter. BD7: B'frd ... 9N 63
LS29: I'ly ... 6G 14
St Margaret's Vw. LS8: Leeds ... 9J 51
St Mark's Av. BD12: Low M ... 8A 82
LS2: Leeds ... 1C 4 (3D 68)
St Marks Ct. HD8: Shep ... 2J 171
LS6: Leeds ... 1D 4 (3D 68)
St Mark's Flats LS2: Leeds ... 1C 4
St Mark's Ho. LS2: Leeds ... 1D 4
St Mark's Pl. BD12: Low M ... 8A 82
St Mark's Rd. HD3: Hud ... 4F 136
LS2: Leeds ... 1D 4 (4D 68)
LS6: Leeds ... 1C 4 (3C 68)
(not continuous)
St Mark's St. LS2: Leeds ... 1C 4 (4C 68)
WF1: Wake ... 1L 9 (3M 125)
St Mark's Ter. BD12: Low M ... 8A 82
St Mark's Vw. HD3: Hud ... 4F 136
St Martins Av. BD7: B'frd ... 7A 64
LS7: Leeds ... 1E 68
LS21: Otley ... 7K 17
St Martins Cl. WF7: F'stne ... 7C 128
St Martins Ct. WF3: Rob H ... 2K 105
St Martin's Cres. LS7: Leeds ... 1F 68
St Martin's Dr. LS7: Leeds ... 9F 50
St Martin's Fld. LS21: Otley ... 8K 17
St Martins Fold WF3: Rob H ... 2K 105
St Martin's Gdns. LS7: Leeds ... 1E 68
St Martin's Gro. LS7: Leeds ... 1F 68
WF10: C'frd ... 6B 108
St Martin's Rd. LS7: Leeds ... 9F 50
St Martin's Ter. LS7: Leeds ... 1F 68
St Martin's Vw. HD6: Brigh ... 9M 99
LS7: Leeds ... 1F 68
St Mary Magdalenes Cl. BD8: B'frd ... 6B 64
St Mary's Av. BD12: Wyke ... 2A 100
HD9: Nether ... 9L 153
LS26: Swil ... 4H 89
WF6: Alt ... 8G 107
WF14: Mir ... 5N 121
WF17: Bat ... 9D 102
St Marys Cl. BD12: Wyke ... 2N 99
LS7: Leeds ... 1F 68
LS12: Leeds ... 8N 67
LS25: Gar ... 8N 71
LS29: I'ly ... 5H 15
WF3: W Ard ... 5M 103
WF9: S Elm ... 7N 163
St Mary's Ct. LS7: Leeds ... 1F 68
WF10: All B ... 9B 90
St Mary's Cres. BD12: Wyke ... 3N 99
HD9: Nether ... 9L 153
St Mary's Dr. BD12: Wyke ... 2A 100
St Marys Fold HD5: K'htn ... 2G 138
St Mary's Gdns. BD12: Wyke ... 2A 100
St Mary's Gth. LS17: E Kes ... 3C 36
St Mary's Ga. HX5: Ell ... 4E 118
St Mary's Hall LS9: Leeds ... 5K 5
St Mary's La. HD5: K'htn ... 3F 138
LS9: Leeds ... 5K 5 (6G 68)
St Mary's M. HD9: Hon ... 4L 153
St Mary's Mt. BD12: Wyke ... 2N 99
St Mary's Pk. App. LS12: Leeds ... 6J 67
St Mary's Pk. Ct. LS12: Leeds ... 6J 67
St Mary's Pk. Cres. LS12: Leeds ... 6J 67
St Mary's Pk. Grn. LS12: Leeds ... 6J 67
St Mary's Pl. WF10: C'frd ... 4D 108
WF12: Dew ... 5G 122
St Mary's Ri. HD9: Nether ... 9L 153
St Mary's Rd. BD4: B'frd ... 9H 65
BD8: B'frd ... 4A 64
BD9: B'frd ... 4A 64
BD20: Rid ... 6M 27
HD9: Hon ... 4L 153
HD9: Nether ... 9L 153
LS7: Leeds ... 1F 68
WF6: Alt ... 9G 107
St Mary's Sq. BD12: Wyke ... 2A 100
HD9: Hon ... 4L 153
LS27: Morl ... 9K 85
St Mary's St. LS9: Leeds ... 5J 5 (6F 68)
LS23: B Spa ... 9D 24
St Mary St. HX1: Hal ... 5H 7 (6A 98)
St Mary's Vw. WF9: Bads ... 8L 147
St Mary's Wlk. LS25: M'fld ... 7F 72
WF14: Mir ... 5N 121
St Mary's Way HD9: Nether ... 9L 153
St Mathew Way LS14: Leeds ... 1F 70
St Matthew Rd. WF13: Dew ... 3E 122
St Matthews Cl. BD15: Wils ... 2A 62
St Matthews Ct. HX3: North ... 2F 98
St Matthew's Dr. HX3: North ... 1F 98
St Matthews Gro. BD15: Wils ... 2B 62
St Matthews Rd. BD5: B'frd ... 4B 82
St Matthew's St. LS11: Leeds ... 9C 68
St Matthews Wlk. LS7: Leeds ... 7E 50
St Matthias Ct. LS4: Leeds ... 4N 67
St Matthias Gro. LS4: Leeds ... 4N 67
St Matthias St. LS4: Leeds ... 5N 67
(not continuous)
St Matthias Ter. LS4: Leeds ... 4N 67
St Mellion Ct. WF6: Norm ... 2L 127
St Michael Ct. LS13: Leeds ... 3F 66
St Michael's Av. WF8: Pon ... 3H 129
St Michaels Cl. BD16: Cot ... 9G 45
HD8: Eml ... 2G 157
WF2: Wake ... 6J 125
WF10: C'frd ... 5D 108
WF12: T'hill ... 1H 141
St Michael's Ct. LS6: Leeds ... 1N 67
St Michael's Cres. LS6: Leeds ... 2N 67
St Michael's Gdns. HD8: Eml ... 2G 156
St Michael's Grn. WF6: Norm ... 2H 127
St Michael's Gro. LS6: Leeds ... 2N 67
St Michael's Ho. *WF2: Wake* ... *6J 125*
(off Horbury Rd.)
St Michael's La. LS4: Leeds ... 3M 67
LS6: Leeds ... 2N 67
St Michael's Mt. WF12: T'hill ... 9H 123
St Michael's Rd. BD8: B'frd ... 6A 64
LS6: Leeds ... 2N 67
St Michael's Ter. LS6: Leeds ... 2N 67
St Michael's Vs. *LS6: Leeds* ... *2N 67*
(off St Michael's Cres.)
St Michaels Way LS29: Add ... 2M 13
LS29: Burl W ... 9D 16
St Nicholas Rd. LS29: I'ly ... 4F 14
St Nicholas St. WF10: C'frd ... 5D 108
St Oswald Av. WF8: Pon ... 3H 129
St Oswald Ct. *WF9: Hems* ... *3E 162*
(off Baylee St.)
St Oswald Rd. WF2: Wake ... 6E 124
St Oswalds Cl. LS26: Meth ... 2K 107
St Oswald's Gth. LS20: Guis ... 7K 31
St Oswalds Pl. WF5: Oss ... 4A 124
St Oswald's Ter. LS20: Guis ... 7J 31
St Oswald St. WF10: C'frd ... 4D 108
St Paulinus Cl. WF13: Dew ... 3E 122
St Paul's Av. BD6: B'frd ... 5N 81
BD11: B'haw ... 8M 83
St Pauls Bldgs. *HX5: Ell* ... *5E 118*
(off Langdale St.)
St Paul's Cl. *BD8: B'frd* ... *5A 64*
(off Church St.)
WF9: Upt ... 1C 164
St Pauls Ct. WF8: Pon ... 9L 109
St Paul's Dr. WF2: Wake ... 3F 124
St Paul's Gro. BD6: B'frd ... 5N 81
LS29: I'ly ... 5J 15
St Paul's Pl. LS1: Leeds ... 6D 4 (6D 68)
St Pauls Ri. LS29: Add ... 2M 13
St Pauls Rd. BD6: B'frd ... 5N 81
BD8: B'frd ... 4A 64
(not continuous)
BD11: B'haw ... 8M 83
BD18: Ship ... 8M 45
BD21: Keigh ... 1K 43
HD5: K'htn ... 2F 138
HX1: Hal ... 7M 97
WF14: Mir ... 7L 121
St Paul's St. HD1: Hud ... 7C 8 (5N 137)
LS1: Leeds ... 6C 4 (6C 68)
LS27: Morl ... 1L 103
St Paul's Ter. WF14: Mir ... 7L 121
St Paul's Wlk. WF2: Wake ... 3F 124
St Peg Cl. BD19: Cleck ... 5J 101
St Peg La. BD19: Cleck ... 5J 101
St Peter's Av. HX6: Sow B ... 9E 96
LS26: Rothw ... 8A 88
St Peter's Bldgs. LS9: Leeds ... 6J 5
St Peters Cl. LS21: Otley ... 9M 17
WF14: Mir ... 6K 121
WF17: Birs ... 3A 102
St Peters Ct. LS11: Leeds ... 1E 86
LS13: Leeds ... 3G 66
LS29: Add ... 2M 13
WF4: Horb ... 9C 124
St Peters Cres. HD5: K'htn ... 2F 138
LS27: Morl ... 7K 85
WF3: S'ley ... 6C 106
St Peter's Gdns. LS13: Leeds ... 3F 66
WF12: Dew ... 4J 123
St Peter's Gth. LS14: T'ner ... 1H 53
St Peters Ga. OL14: W'den ... 3J 113
WF5: Oss ... 4N 123
St Peter's Gro. WF4: Horb ... 1D 142
St Peter's Mt. LS13: Leeds ... 4G 66
St Peter's Pde. WF12: Dew ... 4J 123
St Peter's Pl. LS9: Leeds ... 6J 5 (6F 68)
St Peters Sq. HX6: Sow B ... 9E 96
LS9: Leeds ... 6J 5 (6F 68)
St Peter's St. HD1: Hud ... 4B 8 (4M 137)
LS2: Leeds ... 6H 5 (6F 68)
St Peters Vw. *LS27: Morl* ... *7K 85*
(off Rooms La.)
St Peter's Way LS29: Men ... 4D 30
St Philip's Av. LS10: Leeds ... 8D 86
St Philip's Cl. LS10: Leeds ... 8D 86
LS29: Burl W ... 8D 16
WF13: Dew ... 2G 123
St Philips Ct. HD3: Hud ... 9G 119
St Philip's Dr. LS29: Burl W ... 9D 16
St Philip's Way LS29: Burl W ... 8D 16
St Phillips Ct. *BD8: B'frd* ... *5M 63*
(off Thorn St.)
St Richard's Rd. LS21: Otley ... 7J 17
St Stephen's Ct. BD20: Stee ... 2C 26
HX3: Hal ... 1N 117
LS9: Leeds ... 5M 5 (6H 69)
St Stephens Fold HD3: Hud ... 1G 136
St Stephen's Rd. BD5: B'frd ... 2B 82
BD20: Stee ... 3C 26
HD1: Hud ... 8A 8 (6L 137)
LS9: Leeds ... 5M 5 (6H 69)
LS28: Cal ... 8L 47
St Stephen's St. HX3: Hal ... 1N 117
St Stephen's Ter. BD5: B'frd ... 2C 82
HX3: Hal ... 1N 117
Saint St. BD7: B'frd ... 1M 81
St Swithins Ct. WF3: S'ley ... 1A 126
St Swithins Dr. WF3: S'ley ... 1A 126
St Swithins Gro. WF3: S'ley ... 1A 126
St Thomas Gdns. HD2: Hud ... 5D 120
St Thomas Rd. HD1: Hud ... 8A 8 (5L 137)
WF7: F'stne ... 6D 128
St Thomas Row LS2: Leeds ... 4H 5 (5F 68)
St Thomas's Rd. BD1: B'frd ... 7B 64
St Thomas's Ter. WF8: Pon ... 9M 109
St Vincent Ct. *LS28: Pud* ... *8B 66*
(off Littlemoor Rd.)
St Vincent Rd. LS28: Pud ... 8B 66
St Wilfrid's Av. LS8: Leeds ... 2J 69
(not continuous)
St Wilfrid's Cir. LS8: Leeds ... 3K 69
St Wilfrid's Cl. BD7: B'frd ... 9L 63
St Wilfrid's Cres. BD7: B'frd ... 9L 63
LS8: Leeds ... 2K 69
St Wilfrid's Dr. LS8: Leeds ... 2J 69
St Wilfrid's Gth. LS8: Leeds ... 3K 69
St Wilfrid's Gro. LS8: Leeds ... 2J 69
St Wilfrid's Rd. BD7: B'frd ... 9L 63
St Wilfrid's St. LS28: Cal ... 8M 47
St Wilfrids Ter. *LS21: Pool* ... *1F 32*
(off Main St.)
St Winifred's Cl. HX2: Illing ... 8K 79
Salamanca Cres. LS10: Leeds ... 9G 87
Salcombe Cl. S75: Map ... 9L 159
Salcombe Pl. BD4: B'frd ... 3J 83
Salem Pl. LS10: Leeds ... 8G 5 (8E 68)
LS25: Gar ... 7M 71
Salem St. BD1: B'frd ... 2A 6 (6C 64)
BD13: Que ... 4C 80
HX7: Heb B ... 1G 95
SALENDINE NOOK ... 2D 136
SALFORD
HD4 ... 8L 137
OL14 ... 8K 93
Salford OL14: Tod ... 7J 93
Salford Way OL14: Tod ... 7J 93
Salisbury Av. BD17: Bail ... 4A 46
LS12: Leeds ... 6M 67
Salisbury Cl. WF6: Norm ... 9J 107
WF12: Dew ... 3J 123
Salisbury Ct. LS18: Hors ... 6G 48
Salisbury Gro. LS12: Leeds ... 6M 67
Salisbury M. LS18: Hors ... 6G 49
WF3: Ting ... 3N 103
Salisbury Pl. HX3: Hal ... 3A 98
HX3: Hip ... 4H 99
LS28: Cal ... 9L 47
Salisbury Rd. BD9: B'frd ... 1A 64
BD12: Low M ... 7A 82
BD19: Scho ... 4D 100
BD22: Keigh ... 1G 43
LS12: Leeds ... 6M 67
Salisbury St. HX6: Sow B ... 9G 97
LS19: Raw ... 3M 47
LS28: Cal ... 9L 47
Salisbury Ter. HX3: Hal ... 3A 98
LS12: Leeds ... 6M 67
Salisbury Vw. LS12: Leeds ... 6M 67
LS18: Hors ... 6G 49
Salley St. OL15: Lit ... 9L 113
Salmon Cres. LS18: Hors ... 6F 48
Sal Nook Cl. BD12: Low M ... 6B 82
Sal Royd Rd. BD12: Low M ... 8C 82
SALTAIRE ... 7L 45
Saltaire BD22: Cros R ... 7F 42
Saltaire Brewery ... 6A 46
Saltaire Rd. BD16: Bgly ... 2J 45
BD18: Ship ... 7L 45
Saltaire Station (Rail) ... 6L 45
Saltburn Pl. BD9: B'frd ... 4L 63
Saltburn St. HX1: Hal ... 5M 97
Salt Drake HX6: Hal, Ripp ... 3B 116
SALTERHEBBLE ... 9C 98
Salterhebble Hill HX3: Hal ... 1C 118
Salterhebble Ter. *HX3: Hal* ... *9C 98*
(off Huddersfield Rd.)
Salterlee HX3: North ... 2D 98
Salter Oak Cft. S71: Carl ... 8D 160
Salter Rake Ga. OL14: W'den ... 1K 113
Salter Row WF8: Pon ... 3K 129
Salters Gdn. *LS28: Pud* ... *7B 66*
(off Crawshaw Rd.)
Saltersgate Av. WF11: Knot ... 7D 110
Salter St. WF17: Bat ... 1E 122
Salt Horn Cl. BD12: O'haw ... 8D 82
Saltonstall La. HX2: Wain ... 8D 78
Salt Pie All. WF2: Wake ... 5G 9 (6K 125)
Salts Mill BD18: Ship ... 6M 45
Salts Mill Rd. BD18: Ship ... 7M 45
Salt St. BD8: B'frd ... 5A 64
HX1: Hal ... 2G 7 (4N 97)
Samara West Mt. LS2: Leeds ... 4A 4
Sampson St. WF15: Liv ... 8L 101
Sams Yd. *LS15: Bar E* ... *8L 53*
(off Elmwood La.)
Samuel Ct. S72: Cud ... 9K 161
Samuel Dr. WF3: S'ley ... 7N 105
Samuel St. BD21: Keigh ... 8H 27
Samuel Way BD18: Ship ... 7B 46
Sanctuary Way BD16: Bgly ... 9J 29
Sandacre Cl. BD10: B'frd ... 3J 65
SANDAL ... 1N 143
Sandal Av. WF2: Wake ... 1N 143
Sandal Bus. Cen. WF2: Wake ... 3L 143
Sandal Castle Cen. WF2: Wake ... 3L 143
Sandal Castle (remains of) ... 1M 143
Sandal Castle Vis. Cen. ... 1M 143
Sandal Cliff WF2: Wake ... 2N 143
Sandale Wlk. BD6: B'frd ... 6L 81
Sandal Grange Gdns. WF2: Wake ... 2A 144
Sandal Hall Cl. WF2: Wake ... 1A 144
Sandal Hall M. WF2: Wake ... 1N 143
Sandall Cl. LS25: Kip ... 3B 90
SANDAL MAGNA ... 1N 143
Sandal Magna HX3: She ... 6K 81
Sandal Ri. WF8: Thpe A ... 5N 147
Sandals Mt. BD17: Bail ... 4A 46
Sandals Rd. BD17: Bail ... 4A 46
Sandal St. *HX7: Heb B* ... *1J 95*
(off Sandy Ga.)
Sandal Ter. HX6: Sow B ... 9J 97
Sandal Way WF17: Birs ... 3C 102
Sandalwood M. BD15: All ... 7F 62
Sandbeck App. LS22: Weth ... 1M 23
Sandbeck Ct. LS22: Weth ... 2N 23
Sandbeck Ind. Est. LS22: Weth ... 2N 23
Sandbeck La. LS22: Weth ... 2N 23
(not continuous)
Sandbeck Pk. LS22: Weth ... 2N 23
Sandbeck Way LS22: Weth ... 2N 23
Sand Bed HX7: Heb B ... 3D 94
Sandbed HX4: Sow ... 9M 117
Sandbed Ct. LS15: Leeds ... 3E 70
Sandbed La. LS15: Leeds ... 3E 70
Sandbed Lawns LS15: Leeds ... 3E 70
Sandbeds BD13: Cull ... 1J 61
BD13: Que ... 4D 80
HD9: Hon ... 3L 153
Sandbeds Ct. WF5: Oss ... 4A 124
Sandbeds Cres. HX2: Hal ... 3L 97
Sandbeds Rd. HX2: Hal ... 4K 97
Sandbeds Ter. HX2: Hal ... 3L 97
Sandbeds Trad. Est. WF5: Oss ... 4A 124
Sand Bed Vs. HX7: Heb B ... 3D 94
Sandene Av. HD4: Hud ... 8G 137
Sandene Dr. HD4: Hud ... 8H 137
Sanderling Ct. BD8: B'frd ... 7H 63
Sanderling Gth. LS10: Leeds ... 8F 86
Sanderling Way LS10: Leeds ... 8F 86
Sanderson Av. BD6: B'frd ... 4A 82
WF6: Norm ... 2H 127
Sanderson La. LS26: Oul ... 2B 106
(not continuous)
Sanderson St. WF1: Wake ... 5M 9 (5M 125)
Sandfield Av. LS6: Leeds ... 9A 50
Sandfield Gth. LS6: Leeds ... 9A 50
Sandfield Rd. BD10: B'frd ... 9F 46
Sandfield Vw. *LS6: Leeds* ... *9A 50*
(off Highbury Mt.)
SANDFORD ... 2H 67
Sandford Pl. LS5: Leeds ... 2K 67
Sandford Rd. BD3: B'frd ... 7G 64
(not continuous)
LS5: Leeds ... 3L 67
WF9: S Elm ... 4N 163
Sandforth Av. HX3: Hal ... 2B 98
Sandgate Dr. LS25: Kip ... 2B 90
Sandgate La. LS25: Gar, Kip ... 2C 90
LS25: Kip ... 4C 90
(not continuous)
Sandgate Ri. LS25: Kip ... 3C 90
Sandgate Ter. LS25: Kip ... 4C 90
Sandgate Wlk. BD4: B'frd ... 3K 83
Sandhall Av. HX2: Hal ... 5K 97
Sandhall Cres. *HX2: Hal* ... *4K 97*
(off Sandhall Grn.)
Sandhall Dr. HX2: Hal ... 5K 97
Sandhall Grn. HX2: Hal ... 5K 97
(not continuous)
Sandhall La. HX2: Hal ... 5K 97
Sandhill Cl. BD8: B'frd ... 6J 63
WF8: Pon ... 8K 109
Sandhill Ct. LS17: Leeds ... 4F 50
Sandhill Cres. LS17: Leeds ... 3G 50
Sandhill Dr. LS17: Leeds ... 3F 50
Sandhill Fold BD10: B'frd ... 8E 46
Sandhill Gro. LS17: Leeds ... 2G 51
S72: Grim ... 8A 162
Sandhill La. LS17: Leeds ... 4F 50
Sandhill Lawn WF8: Pon ... 4J 129
Sandhill Lawns LS17: Leeds ... 4F 50
Sandhill Mt. BD10: B'frd ... 9F 46
LS17: Leeds ... 2G 50
Sandhill Oval LS17: Leeds ... 2G 50
Sandhill Ri. WF8: Pon ... 9K 109
SANDHILLS ... 4F 52
Sandhills Cotts. HD7: Slait ... 3H 151
Sandhill Vs. LS14: T'ner ... 4F 52
Sandholme Cres. HX3: Hip ... 5J 99
Sandholme Dr. BD10: B'frd ... 9F 46
LS29: Burl W ... 9D 16
WF5: Oss ... 6N 123
Sandholme Fold HX3: Hip ... 5J 99
Sandhurst Av. LS8: Leeds ... 3J 69
Sandhurst Gro. LS8: Leeds ... 3J 69
Sandhurst Mt. LS8: Leeds ... 2J 69
Sandhurst Pl. LS8: Leeds ... 3J 69
Sandhurst Rd. LS8: Leeds ... 3J 69
Sandhurst St. LS28: Cal ... 8L 47
Sandhurst Ter. LS8: Leeds ... 3J 69
Sandiford Cl. LS15: Leeds ... 3E 70
Sandiford Ter. LS15: Leeds ... 3E 70
Sandiway Bank WF12: T'hill ... 8G 123
Sand La. WF9: Upt ... 2A 164
Sandleas Way LS15: Leeds ... 4G 70
Sandlewood Cl. LS11: Leeds ... 9C 68
Sandlewood Ct. LS6: Leeds ... 6B 50
Sandlewood Cres. LS6: Leeds ... 6B 50
Sandlewood Grn. LS11: Leeds ... 9D 68
Sandmead Cl. BD4: B'frd ... 2J 83
LS27: Morl ... 7K 85
Sandmead Cft. LS27: Morl ... 7K 85
Sandmead Way LS27: Morl ... 7K 85
Sandmoor Av. LS17: Leeds ... 1F 50
Sandmoor Chase LS17: Leeds ... 2F 50
Sandmoor Cl. BD13: Thorn ... 8D 62
LS17: Leeds ... 2F 50
Sandmoor Ct. LS17: Leeds ... 2F 50
Sandmoor Dr. HD3: Hud ... 1G 136
LS17: Leeds ... 1F 50
Sandmoor Gdns. HX3: She ... 8G 80
Sandmoor Gth. BD10: B'frd ... 6F 46
Sand Moor Golf Course ... 1E 50
Sandmoor Grn. LS17: Leeds ... 1E 50
Sandmoor La. LS17: Leeds ... 1F 50
Sandmoor M. LS17: Leeds ... 2F 50
Sandon Gro. LS10: Leeds ... 3G 86
Sandon Mt. LS10: Leeds ... 3G 86
Sandon Pl. LS10: Leeds ... 3G 86
Sandown Av. HX2: Illing ... 9L 79
WF4: Croft ... 1G 145
Sandown Rd. HX2: Illing ... 9L 79
Sandpiper App. LS27: Morl ... 1M 103
Sandpiper Ct. WF4: Cal G ... 4F 142
WF10: C'frd ... 6B 108
Sandpiper M. BD8: B'frd ... 7H 63
WF4: Cal G ... 4F 142
Sandpiper Rd. WF4: Cal G ... 4F 142
Sandringham App. LS17: Leeds ... 4G 50
Sandringham Av. LS28: Pud ... 8B 66
WF11: Ferr ... 8B 110
Sandringham Cl. BD14: Clay ... 9J 63
LS27: Morl ... 8M 85
WF8: Pon ... 6J 129
Sandringham Ct. BD14: Clay ... 9J 63
HD2: Hud ... 6B 120
LS17: Leeds ... 3F 50
WF7: Street ... *6L 127*
(off Thistle Hill Dr.)
Sandringham Cres. LS17: Leeds ... 4F 50
Sandringham Dr. LS17: Leeds ... 4F 50
WF3: W Ard ... 5B 104
Sandringham Fold LS27: Morl ... 8M 85
Sandringham Gdns. LS17: Leeds ... 4F 50
Sandringham Grn. LS17: Leeds ... 3G 50
Sandringham Ho. LS17: Leeds ... 2F 50
Sandringham Mt. LS17: Leeds ... 4G 50
Sandringham Rd. BD14: Clay ... 9J 63
LS22: Weth ... 3M 23
WF11: Byram ... 5C 110
Sandringham Way LS17: Leeds ... 4F 50
Sandrock Rd. WF8: Pon ... 1L 129
Sandsend Cl. BD9: B'frd ... 3J 63
Sands Ho. La. HD4: Hud ... 9G 136

Sandside Cl.—Scott La.

Sandside Cl. BD5: B'frd . . . 3D 82
Sands La. HD8: Lept . . . 4K 139
WF12: Dew . . . 4G 123
WF14: Mir . . . 7A 122
Sands Rd. WF12: Dew . . . 5H 123
Sands Ter. HD2: Hud . . . 9C 120
Sandstone Cl. HD9: Hon . . . 6L 153
Sandstone Dr. LS12: Leeds . . . 7F 66
Sandstone La. HD4: Hud . . . 7G 136
Sand St. BD21: Keigh . . . 8J 27
BD22: Haw . . . 9C 42
HD1: Hud . . . 6D 8 (5N 137)
Sandway LS15: Leeds . . . 4C 70
Sandway Gdns. LS15: Leeds . . . 4C 70
Sandway Gro. LS15: Leeds . . . 4C 70
Sandwell St. HD7: Slait . . . 9M 135
Sandwich Cres. HD2: Fix . . . 8L 119
Sandyacres LS26: Rothw . . . 7A 88
Sandyacres Cres. LS26: Rothw . . . 7A 88
Sandyacres Dr. LS26: Rothw . . . 7A 88
Sandy Bank Av. LS26: Rothw . . . 7A 88
Sandy Banks BD16: Har . . . 7A 44
Sandy Beck BD15: All . . . 3E 62
Sandybridge La. S72: Shaf . . . 4H 161
Sandybridge La. Ind. Est. S72: Shaf . . . 5J 161
Sandy Dyke La. HX6: Tri . . . 3E 116
Sandyfields Vw. DN6: Skel . . . 8N 165
Sandyfield Ter. WF17: Bat . . . 6E 102
(off Bradford Rd.)
Sandyfoot HX4: Bark . . . 7H 117
Sandy Fore HX2: Mt T . . . 9F 78
Sandy Ga. BD20: Keigh . . . 8G 26
HD9: Scho . . . 4A 170
HX7: Heb B . . . 1J 95
LS17: Hare . . . 1F 34
Sandy Ga. La. HX7: Heb B . . . 9J 77
Sandygate La. WF7: Ackw . . . 8H 129
WF8: E Hard . . . 8H 129
WF9: Hems . . . 2C 162
Sandygate Ter. BD4: B'frd . . . 9H 65
Sandy Gro. LS26: Rothw . . . 7A 88
Sandylands HD4: Neth . . . 3J 153
SANDY LANE . . . 2F 62
Sandy La. HD4: S Cros . . . 2F 152
WF4: M'twn . . . 3L 141
Sandy Lobby LS21: Pool . . . 2F 32
Sandymoor BD15: All . . . 2F 62
Sandy Wlk. LS16: B'hpe . . . 6J 33
WF1: Wake . . . 3G 9 (4K 125)
Sandy Way LS19: Yead . . . 9M 31
Sandywood Ct. LS18: Hors . . . 8F 48
Sandywood St. BD21: Keigh . . . 8J 27
Sanford Ct. WF5: Oss . . . 6N 123
Sangster Way BD5: B'frd . . . 4E 82
Sanquah Ter. WF6: Norm . . . 9K 107
Santa Monica Cres. BD10: B'frd . . . 8E 46
Santa Monica Gro. BD10: B'frd . . . 8E 46
Santa Monica Rd. BD10: B'frd . . . 8E 46
Santingley La. WF4: N Cro . . . 3H 145
Santorini LS12: Leeds . . . 7B 4 (7C 68)
Sanworth St. OL14: Tod . . . 7L 93
Sapgate La. BD13: Thorn . . . 8D 62
Sapling Gro. Cotts. HX2: Hal . . . 8M 97
Saplin St. BD8: B'frd . . . 5N 63
Sapphire Ct. WF17: Bat . . . 6D 102
Sarah St. WF3: E Ard . . . 4F 104
Sardinia St. LS10: Leeds . . . 9F 68
Saughes Cotts. HX7: Heb B . . . 1K 95
Saunders Cl. HD3: Hud . . . 3H 137
Saunters Way WF6: Alt . . . 8H 107
Savannah Way LS10: Leeds . . . 5K 87
Savile Av. HD8: Eml . . . 2G 156
LS7: Leeds . . . 3F 68
Savile Bus. Cen. WF12: Dew . . . 4G 122
Savile Cen. WF12: T'hill . . . 9G 123
Savile Cl. HD6: Clift . . . 9B 100
HD8: Eml . . . 2G 156
Savile Ct. HD3: Hud . . . 5F 136
WF13: Raven . . . 6B 122
WF14: Mir . . . 5L 121
Savile Cres. HX1: Hal . . . 6J 7 (6A 98)
Savile Dr. HX1: Hal . . . 7H 7 (7A 98)
LS7: Leeds . . . 2F 68
WF4: Horb . . . 9C 124
Savile Glen HX1: Hal . . . 6J 7 (6A 98)
Savile Grn. HX1: Hal . . . 6K 7 (6B 98)
Savile Gro. WF12: Dew . . . 4F 122
Savile La. HD6: Clift . . . 9B 100
Savile Lea HX1: Hal . . . 6J 7 (6A 98)
Savile M. HX1: Hal . . . 7J 7 (7A 98)
WF12: Dew . . . 6F 122
Savile Mt. HX1: Hal . . . 7H 7 (7A 98)
LS7: Leeds . . . 3F 68
Savile Pde. HX1: Hal . . . 8H 7 (7A 98)
SAVILE PARK . . . 7H 7 (7N 97)
Savile Pk. HX1: Hal . . . 8G 7 (7N 97)
HX3: Hal . . . 8H 7 (8A 98)
Savile Pk. Gdns. HX1: Hal . . . 8H 7 (7A 98)
Savile Pk. Mills HX1: Hal . . . 8G 7
Savile Pk. Rd. BD19: Hun . . . 1H 101
HX1: Hal . . . 7H 7 (7A 98)
Savile Pk. St. HX1: Hal . . . 8G 7 (7N 97)
Savile Pk. Ter. HX1: Hal . . . 7N 97
(off Moorfield St.)
Savile Pit La. WF12: Dew . . . 2K 123
Savile Pl. LS7: Leeds . . . 3F 68
WF14: Mir . . . 4L 121
Savile Pct. WF10: C'frd . . . 4C 108
Savile Rd. HD3: Hud . . . 2H 137
HX1: Hal . . . 6J 7 (6A 98)
HX5: Ell . . . 5E 118
HX7: Heb B . . . 1F 94
LS7: Leeds . . . 3F 68
LS26: Meth . . . 1L 107
WF10: C'frd . . . 4C 108
WF12: Dew . . . 6F 122
Savile Row HX1: Hal . . . 5J 7 (6A 98)
Savile Royd HX1: Hal . . . 7H 7 (7A 98)
Savile Sq. WF14: Mir . . . 6L 121
(off Beech St.)
Savile St. BD19: Cleck . . . 3H 101
HD3: Hud . . . 5F 136
HD8: Eml . . . 2G 156
WF13: Dew . . . 1G 122
WF17: Bat . . . 1G 122
Savile Ter. HX1: Hal . . . 7G 7
SAVILE TOWN . . . 5G 122
Savile Wlk. S72: B'ley . . . 6B 162
Savile Way HX5: Ell . . . 3F 118
Saville Cl. WF3: Loft . . . 3L 105
Saville Ct. HD8: Kbtn . . . 3G 154
LS21: Otley . . . 1K 31
Saville Grange HX3: Hal . . . 8J 7 (8A 98)
Saville Grn. LS9: Leeds . . . 6H 69
Saville Pk. HX1: Hal . . . 7M 97
WF5: Oss . . . 7B 124
Saville Rd. HD8: Skelm . . . 7D 156
Saville's Sq. LS27: Morl . . . 9K 85
(off Queen St.)
Saville St. HD8: Clay W . . . 8G 157
WF1: Wake . . . 2J 9 (4L 125)
WF5: Oss . . . 7B 124
Saville Wlk. WF13: Dew . . . 3F 122
(off Eightlands Rd.)
Savins Mill Way LS5: Leeds . . . 2K 67
Savoy Ct. LS28: Stan . . . 5A 66
Saw Hill HX6: Tri . . . 3E 116
Sawley Cl. WF1: Wake . . . 3N 125
Sawley St. BD21: Keigh . . . 1H 43
Saw Mill La. LS29: Add . . . 1N 13
Saw Mill St. LS11: Leeds . . . 8D 4 (8D 68)
Saw Mill Yd. LS11: Leeds . . . 8D 4 (8D 68)
SAWOOD . . . 5F 60
Sawood La. BD22: Oxen . . . 5F 60
Sawrey Pl. BD5: B'frd . . . 6A 6 (8B 64)
Saw Yd. WF1: Wake . . . 4J 9 (5L 125)
Sawyers Gth. LS29: Add . . . 1N 13
Saxilby Rd. BD20: E Mor, Rid . . . 7A 28
Saxon Av. WF9: S Kirk . . . 7F 162
Saxon Cl. HD8: Eml . . . 3F 156
WF9: Upt . . . 2D 164
Saxon Ct. BD12: Wyke . . . 1N 99
LS17: Leeds . . . 4D 50
Saxondale Ct. WF4: Horb . . . 9D 124
Saxon Ga. LS17: Leeds . . . 5D 50
Saxon Grn. LS17: Leeds . . . 5C 50
Saxon Gro. LS17: Leeds . . . 4C 50
WF9: S Kirk . . . 8G 162
Saxon Mt. LS17: Leeds . . . 4D 50
WF9: S Kirk . . . 7F 162
Saxon Rd. LS17: Leeds . . . 5C 50
Saxon St. BD8: B'frd . . . 6A 64
HX1: Hal . . . 5M 97
OL14: W'den . . . 2J 113
Saxstead Ri. LS12: Leeds . . . 8M 67
SAXTON . . . 9N 55
Saxton LS9: Leeds . . . 7K 5 (7G 68)
Saxton Av. BD6: B'frd . . . 4K 81
Saxton Ct. LS25: Gar . . . 6N 71
Saxton Gdns. LS9: Leeds . . . 7G 68
(off The Avenue)
Saxton Ho. LS19: Yead . . . 1M 47
Saxton La. LS9: Leeds . . . 7K 5 (7G 68)
LS24: Saxt . . . 9N 55
Saxton Pl. HD5: Hud . . . 6E 138
Saxton St. WF15: Liv . . . 7N 101
Sayers Cl. LS5: Leeds . . . 2L 67
Sayle Av. BD4: B'frd . . . 4F 82
Sayner La. LS10: Leeds . . . 8F 68
Sayner Rd. LS10: Leeds . . . 8F 68
Scafell Ct. WF12: Dew . . . 1H 123
SCAITCLIFFE . . . 5H 93
Scaitcliffe Vw. OL14: Tod . . . 5H 93
Scala Ct. LS10: Leeds . . . 9F 68
Scalebor Pk. Cl. LS29: Burl W . . . 9C 16
Scalebor Sq. LS29: Burl W . . . 9B 16
Scale Hill HD2: Hud . . . 9M 119
HD9: Hon . . . 3N 153
Scales La. BD4: B'frd . . . 6G 82
Scaley St. BD3: B'frd . . . 7H 65
Scaly Ga. HD9: Jack B . . . 6E 170
HD9: New M . . . 3E 170
Scammonden Rd. HX4: Bark . . . 5G 117
Scampston Dr. WF3: E Ard . . . 3F 104
Scandinavia Ter. BD19: Cleck . . . 3H 101
SCAPEGOAT HILL . . . 4A 136
Scape Vw. HD7: Golc . . . 6C 136
Scarboro Mdws. WF14: Mir . . . 6L 121
Scarborough Gro. BD18: Ship . . . 8M 45
Scarborough Junc. LS13: Leeds . . . 5F 66
Scarborough La. WF3: Ting . . . 4N 103
Scarborough Rd. BD18: Ship . . . 8M 45
LS21: Otley . . . 1K 31
Scarborough St. WF3: Ting . . . 3N 103
WF12: Dew . . . 5G 123
Scarborough Ter. HX5: Ell . . . 5E 118
SCAR BOTTOM . . . 8M 97
Scar Bottom HX7: Myth . . . 4L 95
Scar Bottom Cotts. HX7: Myth . . . 4M 95
(off The Brook)
Scar Bottom La. HX4: Gree . . . 4M 117
SCARCROFT . . . 8D 36
Scarcroft Ct. LS14: S'cft . . . 8E 36
Scarcroft Golf Course . . . 8C 36
SCARCROFT HILL . . . 9F 36
Scarcroft Vw. LS17: Leeds . . . 1A 52
Scar End La. HD9: New M . . . 4E 170
Scar Fold HD9: H'frth . . . 3M 169
Scargill Bldgs. LS27: Morl . . . 9N 85
Scargill Cl. LS9: Leeds . . . 4M 5
Scargill Grange LS9: Leeds . . . 5M 5 (6H 69)
Scar Gro. HD4: Hud . . . 8L 137
Scar Head HX6: Sow B . . . 1H 117
Scar Head Rd. HX6: Sow B . . . 9H 97
Scar Hole La. HD8: Cumb . . . 4D 170
HD9: New M . . . 4D 170
Scarhouse La. HD7: Golc . . . 6D 136
Scar La. HD3: Hud . . . 6D 136
HD7: Golc . . . 6D 136
SCARLET HEIGHTS . . . 4E 80
Scarlet Hgts. BD13: Que . . . 4E 80
Scarr & Long Wood Nature Reserve . . . 9N 97
Scarr Bottom Rd. HX2: Hal . . . 8M 97
Scarr End La. WF12: Dew . . . 6J 123
WF13: Dew . . . 1C 122
Scarr End Vw. WF13: Dew . . . 1C 122
Scarr Grn. Cl. HD9: Mel . . . 7C 152
Scarsdale La. LS17: Bard . . . 2F 36
Scarsdale Ridge LS17: Bard . . . 2F 36
Scarth Av. LS9: Leeds . . . 4J 69
Scarth Ter. WF3: S'ley . . . 6C 106
SCAR TOP . . . 8J 41
Scar Top HD7: Golc . . . 6D 136
HX4: Gree . . . 4M 117
(not continuous)
Scar Top La. HD4: Neth . . . 3J 153
Scar Top Rd. BD22: Old . . . 8G 41
Scarwood Cl. BD16: Bgly . . . 3F 44
Scarwood Ter. HD3: Hud . . . 6F 136
Scatcherd Gro. LS27: Morl . . . 9J 85
Scatcherd La. LS27: Morl . . . 1J 103
Scatcherd Pk. Av. LS27: Morl . . . 8K 85
Scatcherd's Bldgs. LS27: Morl . . . 7K 85
Scawthorpe Cl. WF8: Pon . . . 2M 129
Sceptone Gro. S72: Shaf . . . 6K 161
Schofield Ct. LS27: Morl . . . 9K 85
(off Queenscourt)
Schofield La. HD5: Hud . . . 4B 138
Schofield Pl. OL15: Lit . . . 9M 113
Schofield St. OL14: Tod . . . 6K 93
OL15: Lit . . . 9M 113
Scholars Ga. LS25: Gar . . . 9M 71
S72: Cud . . . 9J 161
Scholars Wlk. BD2: B'frd . . . 3F 64
Scholars Way BD20: Rid . . . 6M 27
LS15: Leeds . . . 8F 70
Scholebroke La. LS28: Pud . . . 2N 83
SCHOLEBROOK . . . 2N 83
Scholebrook Ct. BD4: B'frd . . . 4J 83
(off Broadfield Cl.)
Scholebrook La. BD4: B'frd . . . 2N 83
SCHOLEMOOR . . . 9L 63
Scholemoor Av. BD7: B'frd . . . 9K 63
Scholemoor Crematorium
BD7: B'frd . . . 8K 63
Scholemoor La. BD7: B'frd . . . 9K 63
Scholemoor Rd. BD7: B'frd . . . 9L 63
SCHOLES
BD19 . . . 4D 100
BD22 . . . 6N 41
HD9 . . . 5B 170
LS15 . . . 9G 52
Scholes Fld. La. WF8: Thpe A . . . 5N 147
Scholes La. BD19: Scho . . . 4D 100
BD22: Oak . . . 6N 41
HX4: Gree . . . 2N 117
LS15: Leeds . . . 7F 52
Scholes Lodge La. LS15: Scho . . . 1H 71
Scholes Moor Rd. HD9: Scho . . . 8N 169
Scholes Rd. HD2: Hud . . . 9M 119
HD9: Jack B . . . 4C 170
WF10: C'frd . . . 3K 109
Scholes St. BD5: B'frd . . . 3B 82
Scholey Av. HD6: Ras . . . 3M 119
SCHOLEY HILL . . . 4H 107
Scholey Rd. HD6: Ras . . . 3M 119
Schoolaboards La. WF8: Pon . . . 3M 129
School Av. WF13: Dew . . . 2C 122
School Cl. HX2: Illing . . . 6M 79
HX6: Ripp . . . 7E 116
LS12: N Far . . . 2G 85
WF4: S Comn . . . 7J 127
School Cote Brow HX3: Hal . . . 7A 80
School Cote Ter. HX3: Hal . . . 7A 80
School Ct. WF6: Norm . . . 9L 107
School Cres. HX2: Illing . . . 6M 79
WF2: Wake . . . 7F 124
WF13: Dew . . . 2C 122
School Cft. LS26: Rothw . . . 7N 87
WF11: B'ton . . . 4B 110
School Dr. WF11: Ferr . . . 7B 110
School Farm La. WF7: Ackw . . . 3F 146
School Fold BD12: Low M . . . 7N 81
Schoolgate LS15: Bar E . . . 8M 53
SCHOOL GREEN . . . 8F 62
School Grn. BD13: Thorn . . . 8F 62
HD6: Ras . . . 3M 119
LS16: B'hpe . . . 6H 33
School Grn. Av. BD13: Thorn . . . 8E 62
School Gro. WF13: Dew . . . 2C 122
SCHOOL HILL . . . 3K 155
School Hill HD4: S Cros . . . 2F 152
HD8: Kbtn . . . 3K 155
WF2: New . . . 6K 143
School Ho. HX3: North . . . 1F 98
School Ho. Fold BD20: Rid . . . 6M 27
School Land La. HX7: Hept . . . 7A 76
School La. BD5: B'frd . . . 3A 82
BD6: B'frd . . . 4N 81
BD21: Keigh . . . 9K 27
HD1: Hud . . . 5K 137
HD4: Hud . . . 1L 153
HD5: K'htn . . . 3F 138
HD7: Golc . . . 4A 136
HD7: Mars . . . 3J 151
HD8: Den D . . . 2D 172
HD8: Eml . . . 2G 156
HX2: Brad, Illing . . . 7M 79
HX3: Sou . . . 9F 98
(not continuous)
LS6: Leeds . . . 9A 50
LS7: Leeds . . . 8E 50
LS15: Leeds . . . 8F 70
(Colton Rd. E.)
LS15: Leeds . . . 6B 70
(Pinfold Gro.)
LS17: E Kes . . . 3D 36
LS17: Wike . . . 8K 35
LS22: Coll . . . 9J 23
LS23: W'ton . . . 5F 24
LS25: Aber . . . 8E 54
LS29: Add . . . 9L 11
OL14: Tod . . . 7K 93
WF2: Wren . . . 1G 125
WF2: W'ton . . . 3B 144
WF4: Horb . . . 1C 142
WF4: Ryh . . . 9J 145
WF10: C'frd . . . 6F 108
WF13: Dew . . . 2C 122
WF15: Liv . . . 1H 121
School M. LS12: Leeds . . . 7M 67
School Pl. BD12: Wyke . . . 9A 82
School Ridge BD13: Thorn . . . 6B 62
School Rd. BD22: Keigh . . . 9F 26
HD7: Golc . . . 4A 136
School Rd. LS22: Weth . . . 3N 23
WF2: Wake . . . 7F 124
WF8: Pon . . . 4L 129
School Row LS29: Den . . . 2M 15
School Sq. BD3: B'frd . . . 7H 65
School St. BD1: B'frd . . . 3B 6 (7C 64)
BD4: B'frd . . . 2G 83
(Cutler Hgts. La.)
BD4: B'frd . . . 5F 82
(Shetcliffe Rd.)
BD6: B'frd . . . 6K 81
BD12: Low M . . . 7A 82
BD12: O'haw . . . 9E 82
BD13: Cull . . . 9K 43
BD13: Denh . . . 6L 61
BD14: Clay . . . 1G 81
BD15: Wils . . . 1B 62
BD16: Cot . . . 8G 44
BD19: Cleck . . . 6F 100
BD20: Keigh . . . 6G 27
BD20: Stee . . . 3C 26
HD5: Hud . . . 5B 138
HD9: H'frth . . . 3M 169
HD9: Hon . . . 5L 153
HD9: Nether . . . 9M 153
HX1: Hal . . . 5M 7 (6C 98)
HX4: Gree . . . 3A 118
HX7: Heb B . . . 1H 95
(off Birchcliffe Rd.)
LS27: Chur . . . 5M 85
LS27: Morl . . . 9L 85
LS28: Fars . . . 3A 66
LS28: Pud . . . 8A 66
S72: Cud . . . 9J 161
S75: Dart . . . 8G 159
S75: S'ross . . . 8L 159
WF3: W Ard . . . 7N 103
WF5: Oss . . . 2M 123
WF9: Upt . . . 9C 148
WF10: C'frd . . . 4C 108
(Savile Rd.)
WF10: C'frd . . . 3E 108
(Wheldon Rd.)
WF12: Dew . . . 3L 123
WF13: Dew . . . 3F 122
WF13: Raven . . . 6B 122
WF15: Liv . . . 1J 121
(Church Pk.)
WF15: Liv . . . 1M 121
(Grove St.)
WF17: Birs . . . 3C 102
School St. W. HD3: Hud . . . 2G 137
School Ter. BD19: Scho . . . 4D 100
HD3: Hud . . . 6F 136
HD7: Slait . . . 1M 151
HD8: Clay W . . . 7J 157
(off Holmfield)
HD8: Shel . . . 6L 155
LS25: Gar . . . 6A 72
WF11: Fair . . . 9N 91
(off Gauk St.)
School Vw. LS6: Leeds . . . 3A 68
School Wlk. BD22: Keigh . . . 9F 26
School Yd. WF4: Horb . . . 1D 142
School Yd. Vw. HX3: Hal . . . 1L 7 (3B 98)
SCISSETT . . . 8G 157
Scissett Baths . . . 7H 157
Sconce La. BD16: Bgly . . . 8M 29
BD17: Bail . . . 8M 29
Scopsley Grn. WF12: W'ley . . . 2B 140
Scopsley La. WF12: W'ley . . . 1A 140
Scorcher Hills La. DN6: Burg . . . 4J 165
Score Cft. HD8: Skelm . . . 7D 156
Score Hill HX3: North . . . 9F 80
Scoresby St. BD1: B'frd . . . 4D 6 (7D 64)
Scotchman Cl. LS27: Morl . . . 2J 103
Scotchman La. LS27: Morl . . . 4G 103
Scotchman Rd. BD9: B'frd . . . 4L 63
Scotch Pk. Trad. Est.
LS12: Leeds . . . 6N 67
Scotgate Fold HD9: Hon . . . 5K 153
Scotgate Rd. HD9: Hon . . . 4J 153
SCOTLAND . . . 2E 48
Scotland HX2: Midg . . . 2C 96
Scotland Cl. LS18: Hors . . . 4E 48
Scotland La. HX2: Midg . . . 2B 96
LS18: Hors . . . 8D 32
Scotland Mill La. LS6: Leeds . . . 5B 50
LS17: Leeds . . . 5B 50
Scotland St. WF17: Birs . . . 2N 101
Scotland Way LS18: Hors . . . 3D 48
Scotland Wood Rd. LS17: Leeds . . . 5B 50
Scott Av. WF16: Heck . . . 6A 102
Scott Cl. LS26: Swil . . . 4H 89
WF16: Heck . . . 8B 102
Scott Dr. WF4: Croft . . . 2J 145
SCOTT GREEN . . . 6E 84
Scott Grn. LS27: Gil . . . 5E 84
Scott Grn. Cres. LS27: Gil . . . 5E 84
Scott Grn. Dr. LS27: Gil . . . 5E 84
Scott Grn. Gro. LS27: Gil . . . 5F 84
Scott Grn. Mt. LS27: Gil . . . 5E 84
Scott Grn. Vw. LS27: Gil . . . 5F 84
SCOTT HALL . . . 1E 68
Scott Hall Av. LS7: Leeds . . . 1E 68
Scott Hall Cres. LS7: Leeds . . . 9D 50
Scott Hall Dr. LS7: Leeds . . . 2E 68
Scott Hall Grn. LS7: Leeds . . . 1E 68
Scott Hall Gro. LS7: Leeds . . . 1E 68
Scott Hall Pl. LS7: Leeds . . . 1E 68
Scott Hall Rd. LS7: Leeds . . . 8D 50
LS17: Leeds . . . 8D 50
Scott Hall Row LS7: Leeds . . . 2F 68
Scott Hall Sports Cen. . . . 9E 50
Scott Hall Sq. LS7: Leeds . . . 1E 68
Scott Hall St. LS7: Leeds . . . 2E 68
Scott Hall Ter. LS7: Leeds . . . 1E 68
Scott Hall Wlk. LS7: Leeds . . . 2E 68
Scott Hall Way LS7: Leeds . . . 9E 50
Scott Hill HD8: Clay W . . . 6J 157
Scott La. BD19: Cleck . . . 4J 101
BD19: Gom . . . 3M 101
BD20: Rid . . . 6L 27
LS22: Weth . . . 4M 23
LS27: Morl . . . 2G 102

Scott La. W.—Shibden Head La.

Scott La. W. BD20: Rid 6K 27
Scott M. LS22: Weth 4M 23
Scotts Almshouse's LS10: Leeds 4G 87
Scotts Bldgs. *LS6: Leeds* *9N 49*
(off Mansfield Pl.)
Scott's Cotts. HD8: Clay W 6J 157
Scotts Hill Cl. LS14: T'ner 2G 52
Scott St. BD6: B'frd 5B 82
BD21: Keigh 9H 27
LS28: Pud 8C 66
OL14: W'den 3J 113
Scott Va. HD2: Hud 8B 120
Scott Wood La. LS7: Leeds 1D 68
Scotty Bank HD6: Ras 1M 119
Scotty Cft. La. *HD6: Ras* *2M 119*
(off Bramston St.)
Scotty La. *BD8: B'frd* *5A 64*
(off Carlisle Rd.)
SCOUT 6H 151
Scout Bottom La. HX7: Myth 4N 95
Scout Cl. HX7: Myth 4N 95
SCOUT DIKE 9E 172
Scout End HX7: Myth 4N 95
SCOUT HILL 5D 122
Scout Hill Rd. WF13: Dew 5D 122
Scout Hill Ter. *WF13: Dew* *5D 122*
(off Scout Hill Rd.)
Scout Hill Vw. *WF13: Dew* *5D 122*
(off Scout Hill Rd.)
Scout La. HD7: Slait 9H 135
Scout Rd. HX2: Lud F 4M 95
HX7: Myth 4M 95
Scout Vw. HX7: Myth 4M 95
Scrapers La. OL14: Tod 4K 93
Scriftain La. LS22: K Dei 1M 23
Sculptor Pl. *HD6: Brigh* *9M 99*
(off Waterloo Rd.)
SDH Ind. Est. HX6: Sow B 9H 97
SEACROFT 1B 70
Seacroft Av. LS14: Leeds 1C 70
Seacroft Cres. LS14: Leeds 1C 70
Seacroft Ga. LS14: Leeds 1C 70
(not continuous)
Seacroft Ind. Est. LS14: Leeds 7C 52
(not continuous)
Seaforth Av. LS9: Leeds 3J 69
Seaforth Gro. LS9: Leeds 3J 69
Seaforth Mt. LS9: Leeds 3J 69
Seaforth Pl. LS9: Leeds 3J 69
Seaforth Rd. LS9: Leeds 3J 69
Seaforth Ter. LS9: Leeds 3J 69
Seagrave Rd. HD4: Hud 7H 137
Seamers Cl. WF1: Wake 2L 125
Seaton St. BD3: B'frd 7F 64
Seckar La. WF4: Wool 1J 159
Seckar Wood Local Nature Reserve 9K 143
Secker St. WF2: Wake 8K 125
Second Av. BD3: B'frd 5G 65
BD21: Keigh 1H 43
HD5: Hud 3D 138
HD7: Golc 6C 136
HX3: Hal 8J 7 (8A 98)
LS12: Leeds 7A 68
LS17: Bard 3F 36
LS19: Raw 2N 47
LS22: Weth 4N 23
LS26: Rothw 6A 88
WF1: Wake 1K 125
WF4: Horb 1B 142
WF9: Fitz 6A 146
WF9: S Kirk 8F 162
WF9: Upt 1N 163
WF15: Liv 8F 100
Second St. BD12: Low M 7C 82
Sedan St. HX1: Hal 5K 7
Sedbergh Cl. BD10: B'frd 9H 47
LS15: Leeds 7N 69
Sedbergh Dr. LS29: I'ly 6H 15
Sedbergh Pk. LS29: I'ly 6G 15
Sedburgh Rd. HX1: Hal 7M 7 (7C 98)
HX3: Hal 7M 7 (7C 98)
Sedgegarth LS14: T'ner 1G 53
Sedge Gro. BD22: Haw 7C 42
Sedge Ri. LS24: Tad 6N 39
Sedgewick St. WF17: Birs 3B 102
Sedgfield Ter. BD1: B'frd 7B 64
Sedgwick Cl. BD8: B'frd 6B 64
Seedhill La. *OL14: Tod* *7M 93*
(off Millwood La.)
Seed Hill Ter. BD20: Stee 3D 26
HX2: Mix 7J 79
Seed Row BD4: B'frd 5F 82
Seed St. BD12: Low M 7B 82
See Mill La. HX3: Hal 2A 98
Seemore Arc. *WF5: Oss* *6N 123*
(off Towngate)
Seemore Shop. Cen. WF5: Oss 5N 123
Sefton Av. HD6: Brigh 7L 99
LS11: Leeds 2C 86
Sefton Ct. LS6: Leeds 9N 49
Sefton Cres. HD6: Brigh 7L 99
Sefton Dr. HD6: Brigh 7L 99
LS29: I'ly 6G 15
Sefton Gro. BD2: B'frd 3F 64
Sefton La. HD9: Mel 7C 152
Sefton Pl. BD2: B'frd 3F 64
BD21: Keigh 8J 27
Sefton Ri. WF12: Dew 7G 122
Sefton St. BD21: Keigh 8J 27
HX1: Hal 2G 7 (4N 97)
LS11: Leeds 2D 86
Sefton Ter. HX1: Hal 2G 7 (4N 97)
LS11: Leeds 2C 86
Selborne Gro. BD9: B'frd 3N 63
BD21: Keigh 2G 43
Selborne Mt. BD9: B'frd 4A 64
Selborne Ter. BD9: B'frd 4N 63
BD18: Ship 9N 45
Selborne Vs. *BD9: B'frd* *4N 63*
(off Selborne Gro.)
BD14: Clay 2H 81
Selbourne Av. WF12: Dew 5F 122
Selbourne Dr. WF12: Dew 6F 122
Selbourne Rd. WF12: Dew 6F 122
Selby HX2: Illing 7K 79
Selby Av. LS9: Leeds 6N 69
Selby Fork Junction
LS25: S Mil 5M 91
SELBY FORK SERVICE AREA 4M 91
Selby Rd. LS9: Leeds 6N 69
LS15: Leeds, Swil C 6B 70
LS25: Gar, M'fld 9L 71
Selby St. WF1: Wake 2K 9 (4M 125)
Seldon St. BD5: B'frd 2N 81
Select Ct. LS28: Fars 2A 66
Selene Cl. BD19: Gom 2N 101
SELLARS FOLD 1M 81
Sellerdale Av. BD12: Wyke 3B 100
Sellerdale Dr. BD12: Wyke 2B 100
Sellerdale Ri. BD12: Wyke 3B 100
Sellerdale Way BD12: Wyke 3B 100
Sellers Fold BD7: B'frd 1M 81
Selside Ho. *BD10: B'frd* *7G 46*
(off Woodfield Cl.)
Selso Rd. WF12: Dew 2J 123
Seminary St. LS2: Leeds 3C 4 (5C 68)
Semon Av. BD2: B'frd 1D 64
Senior St. HD5: Hud 5C 138
WF13: Dew 4E 122
Senior Way BD5: B'frd 6A 6 (8C 64)
(not continuous)
Sentry HD9: Hon 4K 153
Sergeantson St. HD1: Hud 5B 8 (4M 137)
Serin Wlk. BD6: B'frd 4J 81
Serpentine Rd. BD19: Cleck 4H 101
Servia Dr. LS7: Leeds 1E 4 (3E 68)
Servia Gdns. LS7: Leeds 1F 4 (3E 68)
Servia Hill LS6: Leeds 1E 4 (3D 68)
LS7: Leeds 1E 4 (3D 68)
Servia Rd. LS7: Leeds 1E 4 (3D 68)
Service Rd. LS9: Leeds 3L 87
Sessions Ho. Yd. WF8: Pon 2J 129
Seven Acres BD13: Denh 6K 61
Seven Hills Point LS27: Morl 8L 85
Sevenoaks Mead BD15: All 5G 62
Seventh Av. LS26: Rothw 6B 88
WF15: Liv 7F 100
Severn Dr. LS25: Gar 9B 72
Severn Rd. BD2: B'frd 3E 64
LS10: Leeds 2H 87
Severn Way LS10: Leeds 1H 87
Sewage Works Rd. LS9: Leeds 2L 87
Sewell Rd. BD3: B'frd 8F 64
Sewerbridge La. WF7: A'ton 2N 127
Seymour St. BD3: B'frd 5F 6 (8E 64)
WF2: Wake 8K 9 (7L 125)
Seymour Wlk. HD9: Mel 7D 152
SHACKLETON 5F 76
Shackleton Hill HX7: Heb B 4D 76
Shackleton St. OL14: Tod 3E 92
Shackleton Ter. BD16: Har 6N 43
SHADE 9J 93
Shade St. OL14: Tod 9J 93
SHADWELL 3A 52
Shadwell La. LS17: Leeds 5F 50
Shadwell Pk. Av. LS17: Leeds 2L 51
Shadwell Pk. Cl. LS17: Shad 2L 51
Shadwell Pk. Ct. LS17: Shad 3L 51
Shadwell Pk. Dr. LS17: Shad 3L 51
Shadwell Pk. Gdns. LS17: Shad 2L 51
Shadwell Pk. Gro. LS17: Shad 2L 51
Shadwell Wlk. LS17: Leeds 4G 51
Shaftesbury Av. BD9: B'frd 4J 63
BD18: Ship 8A 46
DN14: Beal 7L 111
HD6: Ras 4N 119
LS8: Leeds 6J 51
Shaftesbury Ct. BD9: B'frd 5J 63
Shaftesbury Pde. LS9: Leeds 5L 69
Shaftesbury Rd. LS8: Leeds 5J 51
SHAFTON 6K 161
Shafton Hall Dr. S72: Shaf 6J 161
Shafton La. LS11: Leeds 9B 68
Shafton Pl. LS11: Leeds 9B 68
Shafton St. LS11: Leeds 9B 68
SHAFTON TWO GATES 8K 161
Shafton Vw. LS11: Leeds 9B 68
Shakespeare App. LS9: Leeds 3M 5 (5H 69)
Shakespeare Av. LS9: Leeds 3M 5 (5H 69)
OL14: Tod 6M 93
WF6: Norm 4H 127
Shakespeare Bldgs. *HD1: Hud* *4J 137*
(off Mount Rd.)
Shakespeare Cl. BD3: B'frd 2F 6 (6E 64)
LS9: Leeds 5H 69
LS20: Guis 8K 31
Shakespeare Ct. LS9: Leeds 3M 5
Shakespeare Cres. WF10: C'frd 7K 109
Shakespeare Gdns. LS9: Leeds 3M 5 (5H 69)
Shakespeare Grange LS9: Leeds 3M 5 (5H 69)
Shakespeare Lawn LS9: Leeds 3M 5 (5H 69)
Shakespeare Rd. LS20: Guis 8J 31
Shakespeare St. HX1: Hal 4L 7 (6B 98)
LS9: Leeds 2M 5 (4H 69)
Shakespeare Towers LS9: Leeds 2M 5 (5H 69)
Shakespeare Va. LS9: Leeds 3M 5 (5H 69)
Shakespeare Wlk. LS9: Leeds 3M 5 (5H 69)
Shalimar St. HX1: Hal 5M 97
Shambles, The HD1: Hud 5C 8
LS22: Weth 4M 23
Shancara Ct. WF3: Ting 3A 104
Shann Av. BD21: Keigh 8F 26
Shann Cres. BD21: Keigh 8F 26
Shann La. BD20: Keigh 8F 26
Shannon Cl. HD6: Ras 4K 119
LS29: I'ly 6E 14
Shannon Dr. HD3: Hud 1C 136
Shannon Rd. HD6: Ras 4K 119
LS9: Leeds 6L 5 (6G 69)
Shannon St. LS9: Leeds 6K 5 (6G 69)
Shann St. BD2: B'frd 2B 64
Shanter Cl. OL12: Whit 5A 112
Shapla Cl. BD22: Keigh 1G 42
Share Hill HD7: Golc 6B 136
Sharket Head Cl. BD13: Que 4D 80
SHARLSTON 9J 127
SHARLSTON COMMON 8J 127
Sharon Cotts. *WF5: Oss* *4N 123*
(off Northfield Rd.)
Sharp Av. BD6: B'frd 5A 82
Sharpe St. BD5: B'frd 6A 6 (8C 64)
WF16: Heck 9A 102
Sharp Ho. Pl. LS10: Leeds 9H 87
Sharp Ho. Rd. LS10: Leeds 9G 87
Sharp La. HD4: Hud 8D 138
HD5: Hud 8D 138
LS10: Leeds 8G 87
(Dolphin Rd.)
LS10: Leeds 8F 86
(Dunlin Dr.)
WF3: Rob H, Thpe H 8G 87
Sharp M. LS6: Leeds 1B 68
Sharp Row LS28: Pud 8B 66
Sharp Royd HD5: Hud 6E 138
Sharp St. BD6: B'frd 4A 82
WF13: Dew 2G 122
SHAW 4B 60
Shaw Av. WF6: Norm 1K 127
Shaw Barn Cft. LS22: Weth 4K 23
Shaw Barn La. LS22: Weth 4K 23
Shaw Booth La. HX2: Wain 9F 78
Shaw Bri. OL14: Tod 6A 94
Shaw Bus. Pk. HD5: Hud 6F 8 (4A 138)
Shaw Cl. HX4: Holy 7B 118
LS20: Guis 8K 31
LS25: Gar 9A 72
WF6: Norm 1K 127
WF9: S Elm 5N 163
Shawcroft Hill HX7: Wads 6J 77
SHAW CROSS 1K 123
Shawcross Bus. Pk. WF12: Dew 1K 123
Shawfield Av. HD9: H'frth 4J 169
Shaw Flds. La. HD7: Slait 1J 151
Shaw Fold WF2: Wake 1N 143
SHAWFORTH 5A 112
Shaw Ga. HD7: Slait 3L 151
Shaw Gro. HD9: Hon 5K 153
Shaw Hill HX1: Hal 8L 7 (7B 98)
Shaw Hill La. HX3: Hal 7M 7 (7C 98)
SHAW LANE 8L 31
Shaw La. BD13: North 7E 80
BD21: Keigh 5K 43
BD22: Oxen 4B 60
HD3: Hud 2B 136
(Ray Ga.)
HD3: Hud 6G 136
(Whiteley St.)
HD7: Golc 3A 136
HD7: Slait 2F 150
HD8: Kbtn 4J 155
HD9: H'frth 4J 169
HX3: Hal 7M 7 (7C 98)
HX4: Holy 7A 118
HX5: Ell 3H 119
HX6: Norl 2H 117
HX6: Rish 1C 134
LS6: Leeds 9N 49
LS20: Guis 7K 31
OL14: Tod 1D 92
S71: Carl 8E 160
S75: S'ross 7L 159
Shaw La. Gdns. LS20: Guis 7K 31
Shaw Leys LS19: Yead 8L 31
Shaw Lodge HX1: Hal 7M 7 (7C 98)
Shaw Mt. HX2: Lud F 4E 96
Shaw Plains OL14: Tod 7A 94
Shaw Ri. WF6: Norm 1K 127
Shaw Royd LS19: Yead 8L 31
Shaw Royd Ct. *LS19: Yead* *8L 31*
(off Shaw Royd)
Shaws La. HX6: Tri 2A 116
LS15: Bar E 9K 53
Shaws Ter. HD7: Mars 5F 150
Shaw St. BD12: Low M 7N 81
BD19: Cleck 5F 100
HX4: Holy 7B 118
WF14: Mir 6L 121
Shaw Vs. *LS20: Guis* *7K 31*
(off Queensway)
Shaw Wood Av. OL14: Tod 6B 94
Shaw Wood Rd. OL14: Tod 6A 94
Shay, The 7L 7 (7B 98)
SHAY BROW 3E 62
Shay Cl. BD9: B'frd 2L 63
Shay Ct. LS6: Leeds 1D 4 (3D 68)
WF4: Croft 1F 144
Shay Cres. BD9: B'frd 2K 63
Shay Dr. BD9: B'frd 2K 63
Shayfield La. WF3: Carl, Loft 2L 105
Shay Fold BD9: B'frd 2K 63
Shay Gap Rd. BD22: Lay 1C 42
Shay Ga. BD15: Wils 2D 62
Shay Grange BD9: B'frd 1K 63
Shay Grange Golf Course 2K 63
Shay Gro. BD9: B'frd 2L 63
Shay La. BD4: B'frd 2K 83
BD9: B'frd 1K 63
BD15: Wils 1C 62
HD9: H'lm 5D 168
HX2: Hal 1N 97
HX3: Hal 1N 97
WF2: W'ton 4B 144
WF4: Croft, W'ton 2E 144
Shay St. LS6: Leeds 1D 4 (3D 68)
Shay Syke HX1: Hal 6M 7 (6C 98)
Sheaf St. LS10: Leeds 8H 5 (8F 68)
SHEARBRIDGE 8N 63
Shearbridge Pl. BD7: B'frd 8A 64
Shearbridge Rd. BD7: B'frd 8A 64
Shearbridge Ter. BD7: B'frd 9A 64
Shearburn Cl. WF5: Oss 3N 123
Sheardale HD9: Hon 5K 153
Shearers Ho. LS9: Leeds 8K 5
SHEARING CROSS 1B 8 (2M 137)
Shearing Path LS29: Add 9L 11
Shearings, The WF15: Liv 7G 101
Shearings Cross Gdns. HD1: Hud 2N 137
Shear's Yd. LS2: Leeds 7H 5 (7F 68)
Shed St. BD21: Keigh 9J 27
Sheep Hill La. BD13: Que 3G 80
Sheepridge Gro. HD2: Hud 8A 120
Sheepridge Rd. HD2: Hud 8A 120
SHEEPSCAR 1J 5 (3F 68)
Sheepscar Ct. LS7: Leeds 1H 5 (4F 68)
Sheepscar Gro. LS7: Leeds 3H 5 (5F 68)
Sheepscar Row LS7: Leeds 2J 5 (4F 68)
Sheepscar St. Nth. LS7: Leeds 1H 5 (3E 68)
Sheepscar St. Sth. LS7: Leeds 2J 5 (4F 68)
Sheepscar Way LS7: Leeds 1H 5 (3F 68)
Sheepwalk La. WF9: Upt 9D 148
WF10: C'frd 6J 109
Sheerien Cl. S71: Ath 9N 159
Sheffield Rd. HD9: H'wth, Jack B, New M 2C 170
Sheila Henry Dr. BD6: B'frd 3H 81
Sheila Ter. WF16: Heck 9N 101
Shelby Grange BD10: B'frd 9G 46
Sheldon Ridge BD4: B'frd 6F 82
Sheldrake Av. BD8: B'frd 7H 63
Sheldrake Rd. WF10: C'frd 6D 108
SHELF 8H 81
Shelf Hall La. HX3: She 8G 81
Shelf Moor HX3: She 6H 81
Shelf Moor Rd. HX3: She 6H 81
Shelf Rd. HX7: Heb B 1G 95
Shelldrake Dr. LS10: Leeds 8F 86
SHELLEY 6L 155
Shelley Av. WF16: Heck 1B 122
SHELLEY BANK BOTTOM 7L 155
Shelley Cl. LS26: Oul 1D 106
Shelley Ct. BD16: Bgly 3F 44
WF4: Horb 9E 124
Shelley Cres. LS26: Oul 1D 106
Shelley Dr. WF11: Ferr 8A 110
SHELLEY FAR BANK 6L 155
Shelley Gro. BD8: B'frd 6K 63
Shelley La. HD8: Kbtn 4K 155
Shelley Station
Kirklees Light Railway 8M 155
Shelley Wlk. WF3: S'ley 6N 105
SHELLEY WOODHOUSE 7A 156
Shelley Woodhouse La. HD8: Lwr C, Shel 7A 156
Shell La. LS28: Cal 9M 47
Shelton Ct. BD13: Denh 5L 61
Shepcote Cl. LS16: Leeds 4J 49
Shepcote Cres. LS16: Leeds 4J 49
SHEPHERD HILL 5C 124
Shepherds Cft. BD22: Haw 8D 42
Shepherds Fold HX3: North 1E 98
Shepherds Gro. HD2: Hud 8C 120
LS7: Leeds 2G 69
Shepherd's La. LS7: Leeds 2G 69
LS8: Leeds 2G 69
Shepherd's Pl. LS8: Leeds 2H 69
Shepherds Thorn La. HD2: Brigh, Hud 4N 119
HD6: Ras 4N 119
Shepherd St. BD7: B'frd 1M 81
SHEPLEY 9J 155
Shepley Mt. WF14: Mir 4M 121
Shepley Rd. HD4: Stock 7G 155
Shepley Station (Rail) 8K 155
Shepley St. WF1: Wake 4M 9 (5N 125)
Shepstye Rd. WF4: Horb 1C 142
Shepton Apartments BD5: B'frd 7A 6
Sherborne Dr. BD22: Keigh 2E 42
Sherborne Rd. BD7: B'frd 8B 64
BD10: B'frd 6F 46
Sherbourne Dr. LS6: Leeds 6A 50
Sherbrooke Av. LS15: Leeds 7A 70
Sherburn App. LS14: Leeds 9D 52
Sherburn Cl. BD11: B'haw 7M 83
DN6: Skel 7K 165
LS14: Leeds *9D 52*
(off Sherburn App.)
Sherburn Ct. *LS14: Leeds* *9D 52*
(off Sherburn App.)
Sherburn Gro. BD11: B'haw 7M 83
Sherburn Pl. LS14: Leeds 9D 52
Sherburn Rd. HD6: Ras 3J 119
LS14: Leeds 9D 52
Sherburn Rd. Nth. LS14: Leeds 7C 52
Sherburn Row *LS14: Leeds* *9D 52*
(off Sherburn App.)
Sherburn Sq. *LS14: Leeds* *9D 52*
(off Sherburn Pl.)
Sherburn Wlk. *LS14: Leeds* *9D 52*
(off Sherburn App.)
Sheridan Cl. LS28: Pud 8C 66
Sheridan Ct. LS28: Pud 8C 66
Sheridan Ho. LS27: Gil 7F 84
Sheridan St. BD4: B'frd 1E 82
WF1: Out 7L 105
Sheridan Way LS28: Pud 8C 66
Sheriff Ct. BD16: Bgly 2H 45
Sheriff La. BD16: Bgly 2H 45
Sherwell Gro. BD15: All 5H 63
Sherwell Ri. BD15: All 5H 63
Sherwood Av. BD19: Gom 4M 101
HD2: Hud 6D 120
Sherwood Cl. BD16: Bgly 2H 45
BD19: Gom 4M 101
WF13: Dew 9C 102
Sherwood Ct. WF2: Wake 5J 143
Sherwood Dr. DN6: Skel 7K 165
HD4: Neth 2H 153
WF2: Wake 5H 143
Sherwood Gdns. WF3: Loft 2K 105
Sherwood Grn. WF3: Rob H 1J 105
Sherwood Gro. BD18: Ship 7K 45
WF2: Wake 7G 124
Sherwood Ind. Est. WF3: Rob H 1K 105
Sherwood Pl. BD2: B'frd 4F 64
Sherwood Rd. HD6: Brigh 1A 120
Sherwood Wlk. LS10: Leeds 9G 86
Sherwood Way LS26: W'frd 6C 88
S72: Cud 8H 161
Sherwood Works HD6: Brigh 2B 120
Shetcliffe La. BD4: B'frd 5F 82
Shetcliffe Rd. BD4: B'frd 5F 82
Shetland Cl. BD2: B'frd 2D 64
Shibden Dr. WF17: Bat 6C 102
Shibden Fold HX3: Hal 3D 98
Shibden Gth. HX3: Hip 5F 98
Shibden Grange Dr. HX3: Hal 3E 98
Shibden Hall 4E 98
Shibden Hall Cft. HX3: Hal 4F 98
Shibden Hall Folk Mus. 4E 98
Shibden Hall Rd. HX3: Hal 4D 98
SHIBDEN HEAD 7B 80
Shibden Head Ct. BD13: Que 6B 80
Shibden Head La. BD13: Que 6B 80

Shibden Mill Fold—Smawthorne Av.

Shibden Mill Fold HX3: North 1D 98
Shibden Park 4E 98
Shibden Pk. & Cunnery Wood Nature Reserve 4E 98
Shibden Vw. BD13: Que 6C 80
Shield Cl. LS15: Leeds 3F 70
Shield Hall La. HX6: Sow B 8C 96
Shill Bank Av. WF14: Mir 5A 122
Shill Bank La. WF14: Mir 5N 121
Shill Bank Vw. WF14: Mir 5N 121
Shillinghill WF8: Pon 1A 130
Shillinghill La. WF11: Knot 1B 130
Shilling St. WF1: Wake 1L 9 (3M 125)
Shinwell Dr. WF9: Upt 1C 164
SHIPLEY 8N 45
Shipley Airedale Rd. BD1: B'frd 5D 6 (8D 64)
BD3: B'frd 2C 6 (6D 64)
Shipley Flds. Rd. BD18: Ship 1N 63
(not continuous)
Shipley Glen Cable Tramway 5L 45
Shipley Golf Course 6E 44
Shipley Lanes 8N 45
Shipley Station (Rail) 8N 45
Shipley Swimming Pool 8M 45
Ship St. HD6: Brigh 1N 119
Shipton M. LS27: Morl 1L 103
Ship Yd. LS1: Leeds 6F 4
WF1: Wake 6L 9 (6M 125)
Shire Cl. BD6: B'frd 6L 81
LS27: Morl 2L 103
Shire Ct. LS27: Morl 3L 103
Shiredene LS6: Leeds 1A 68
Shire Gro. LS27: Morl 3K 103
Shire Oak Rd. LS6: Leeds 1A 68
Shire Oak St. LS6: Leeds 1N 67
Shireoaks Way S72: Grim 9N 161
Shire Rd. LS27: Morl 2L 103
Shires Bus. Pk. BD7: B'frd 9M 63
Shires Ct. LS23: B Spa 9E 24
Shires Fold HD3: Hud 3J 137
Shires Gro. WF3: S'ley 7A 106
Shires Hill HD1: Hud 5K 137
Shires Rd. LS20: Guis 8J 31
Shire Yd. WF4: Horb 1C 142
Shirley Av. BD12: Wyke 3N 99
BD19: Gom 4M 101
WF17: Birs 2A 102
Shirley Cl. LS21: Otley 1M 31
Shirley Cres. BD12: Wyke 3N 99
Shirley Dr. LS13: Leeds 2F 66
Shirley Gro. BD19: Gom 4M 101
HX3: Hip 5M 99
Shirley Mnr. Gdns. BD12: Wyke 3N 99
Shirley Mt. BD19: Gom 4M 101
Shirley Pde. BD19: Gom 4L 101
Shirley Pl. BD12: Wyke 3A 100
BD19: Gom 4M 101
Shirley Rd. BD4: B'frd 4H 83
BD7: B'frd 8N 63
BD19: Gom 5M 101
Shirley Sq. BD19: Gom 4M 101
Shirley St. BD13: Denh 5L 61
BD18: Ship 7L 45
BD22: Haw 8B 42
Shirley Ter. BD19: Gom 4M 101
Shirley Vs. BD19: Cleck 6K 101
Shirley Wlk. BD19: Gom 4M 101
Shoebridge Av. BD20: East 2A 26
Shoebroad La. OL14: Tod 8K 93
Shoemarket WF8: Pon 3K 129
Sholebroke Av. LS7: Leeds 2F 68
Sholebroke Ct. LS7: Leeds 2F 68
Sholebroke Mt. LS7: Leeds 2E 68
Sholebroke Pl. LS7: Leeds 2F 68
Sholebroke St. LS7: Leeds 2E 68
Sholebroke Ter. LS7: Leeds 1F 68
Sholebroke Vw. LS7: Leeds 2F 68
Shone Ct. LS27: Morl 2L 103
Shop La. HD5: K'htn 2G 138
WF3: Loft 4K 105
SHORE 2E 92
Shore End La. HX2: Midg 4A 78
Shore Grn. OL14: Tod 2E 92
Shoreham Rd. LS12: Leeds 7M 67
SHOREHEAD 5D 8 (4N 137)
Shore New Rd. OL14: Tod 3D 92
Shore Rd. OL14: Tod 3E 92
Short Cl. BD12: Wyke 8N 81
Shortfield Ct. S71: Ath 9N 159
Short La. LS7: Leeds 8E 50
Short Row BD12: Low M 7B 82
Short St. *OL14: Tod* 7K 93
(off Dalton St.)
WF7: F'stne 6C 128
WF12: Dew 4K 123
Shortway BD13: Thorn 8F 62
LS28: Stan 5L 65
Showcase Cinema
Birstall 9E 84
Shrike Cl. BD6: B'frd 4H 81
Shroggs HX7: Heb B 3J 95
Shroggs, The BD20: Stee 3C 26
Shroggs Rd. HX3: Hal 1G 7 (2M 97)
Shroggs St. HX1: Hal 2G 7 (4N 97)
Shroggs Vue Ter. HX1: Hal 2G 7 (4N 97)
Shutt, The WF4: Horb 2D 142
Shuttle Eye Way WF4: G Moor 6B 140
Shuttle Fold BD22: Haw 7D 42
Shuttleworth La. BD8: B'frd 6K 63
Shuttocks Cl. LS25: Kip 2A 90
Shuttocks Fold LS25: Kip 2B 90
Shutts, The LS26: Rothw 8L 87
Shutts La. HX3: Nor G 2K 99
Sickleholme Ct. HD2: Hud 6C 120
Sickle St. BD19: Cleck 4J 101
SICKLINGHALL 4D 22
Sicklinghall Rd. LS22: Weth 4G 22
Sidcop Rd. S72: Cud 8H 161
SIDDAL 9D 98
Siddal Gro. HX3: Hal 8C 98
Siddal La. HX3: Hal 8D 98
Siddall St. LS11: Leeds 8D 68
Siddal New Rd. HX3: Hal 8M 7 (7C 98)
Siddal Pl. HX3: Hal 9D 98
Siddal St. HX3: Hal 9D 98
Siddal Top La. HX3: Hal 8D 98
Siddal Vw. HX3: Hal 8D 98
Siddon Dr. HD5: Hud 7E 138
Side Copse LS21: Otley 9M 17
Side La. HD3: Hud 4E 136
Sides Cl. WF8: Pon 5K 129
Sides Rd. WF8: Pon 5K 129
Sidings, The BD18: Ship 7A 46
LS20: Guis 7H 31
WF12: Dew 5F 122
Sidings Cl. BD2: B'frd 3B 64
Sidney St. LS1: Leeds 6G 5 (6E 68)
Sid's Café 3M 169
Siegen Cl. LS27: Morl 9K 85
Siegen Mnr. *LS27: Morl* 9K 85
(off Wesley St.)
Siegfried Wlk. BD16: Bgly 3H 45
Sigget La. OL14: Tod 6H 93
Sigott St. HD3: Hud 4E 136
Sike Cl. HD9: H'frth 3B 170
S75: Kex 8E 158
Sike La. HD9: H'frth 4A 170
WF2: W'ton 5C 144
Sikes Cl. HD5: Hud 7D 138
Sikh Leisure Cen.
Huddersfield 6A 8
Silcoates Av. WF2: Wren 2G 124
Silcoates Ct. WF2: Wake 3F 124
Silcoates Dr. WF2: Wren 2G 124
Silcoates La. WF2: Wren 2F 124
Silcoates St. WF2: Wake 3H 125
Silk Mill App. LS16: Leeds 5H 49
Silk Mill Av. LS16: Leeds 4G 49
Silk Mill Bank LS16: Leeds 5G 49
Silk Mill Chase HX6: Ripp 8C 116
Silk Mill Cl. LS16: Leeds 4G 49
Silk Mill Dr. BD20: E Mor 7D 28
LS16: Leeds 5G 49
Silk Mill Gdns. LS16: Leeds 5G 48
Silk Mill Grn. LS16: Leeds 5H 49
Silk Mill M. LS16: Leeds 5J 49
Silk Mill Rd. LS16: Leeds 5G 49
Silk Mill Way LS16: Leeds 5H 49
Silkstone Cl. LS25: Gar 5B 72
Silkstone Ct. LS15: Leeds 5D 70
WF6: Alt 8G 107
Silkstone Cres. WF2: Wake 4L 143
Silkstone Crest WF6: Alt 8G 107
Silkstone Ho. WF8: Pon 2K 129
Silkstone Rd. BD3: B'frd 7F 64
Silkstone Sq. WF10: All B 9C 90
Silkstone Way LS15: Leeds 5D 70
Silk St. BD9: B'frd 4M 63
Silk Warehouse BD9: B'frd 4N 63
Silkwood Ct. WF5: Oss 4E 124
Silkwood Pk. WF5: Oss 5D 124
Silsbridge St. *BD1: B'frd* 7B 64
(off Grattan Rd.)
SILSDEN 8E 12
Silsden Driving Range 1D 26
Silsden Golf Course 9G 13
Silsden Ho. Gdns. BD20: Sils 7C 12
Silsden Rd. BD20: Rid 4L 27
LS29: Add 2H 13
Silson La. BD17: Bail 3C 46
Silver Birch HD9: Brock 6A 154
Silver Birch Av. BD12: Wyke 2B 100
Silver Birch Cl. BD12: Wyke 2B 100
Silver Birch Dr. BD12: Wyke 2B 100
Silver Birch Gro. BD12: Wyke 2B 100
Silver Ct. LS13: Leeds 5C 66
Silver Ct. Ind. Est. HD5: Hud 6E 8 (5A 138)
Silver Cross Way LS20: Guis 7H 31
Silverdale Av. BD20: Rid 7L 27
LS17: Leeds 2K 51
LS20: Guis 8J 31
Silverdale Cl. LS20: Guis 9J 31
Silverdale Cres. LS20: Guis 8J 31
Silverdale Dr. LS20: Guis 9J 31
Silverdale Grange LS20: Guis 9J 31
Silverdale Gro. LS20: Guis 9H 31
Silverdale Mt. LS20: Guis 9J 31
Silverdale Rd. BD5: B'frd 3C 82
LS20: Guis 9H 31
Silverdale Ter. HX4: Gree 5N 117
Silverhill Av. BD3: B'frd 5H 65
Silverhill Dr. BD3: B'frd 5H 65
Silverhill Rd. BD3: B'frd 5G 65
Silver Ho. LS2: Leeds 3F 4
Silver La. LS19: Yead 9M 31
Silver Mill Hill LS21: Otley 2M 31
Silver Royd Av. LS12: Leeds 8J 67
Silver Royd Cl. LS12: Leeds 8J 67
Silver Royd Dr. LS12: Leeds 8J 67
Silver Royd Gth. LS12: Leeds 8J 67
Silver Royd Gro. LS12: Leeds 8J 67
SILVER ROYD HILL 8J 67
Silver Royd Hill LS12: Leeds 8J 67
Silver Royd Pl. LS12: Leeds 8J 67
Silver Royd Rd. LS12: Leeds 8J 67
Silver Royd St. LS12: Leeds 8J 67
Silver Royd Ter. LS12: Leeds 8J 67
Silver Royd Way LS12: Leeds 8J 67
Silverstone Av. S72: Cud 9K 161
Silver St. BD8: B'frd 5N 63
HD5: Hud 5A 138
HX1: Hal 4K 7 (5B 98)
HX7: Hept 8G 76
LS11: Leeds 8C 4 (8C 68)
OL14: W'den 4J 113
WF1: Wake 9K 105
(Leeds Rd.)
WF1: Wake 4J 9 (5L 125)
(Westgate)
WF11: Fair 9N 91
Silver St. E. HD5: Hud 6F 8 (5A 138)
Silver St. W. HD5: Hud 6F 8 (5A 138)
Silvertrees LS16: B'hpe 5G 33
Silverwood Av. HX2: Hal 3J 97
(not continuous)
Silverwood Grange WF5: Oss 6L 123
Silverwood Rd. S75: W Gran 7G 158
Silverwood Wlk. HX2: Hal 3J 97
Silverwood Way WF9: Kins 8B 146
Silwood Dr. BD2: B'frd 3G 64
Simeon St. OL14: W'den 3J 113
Simes St. BD1: B'frd 3A 6 (7B 64)
Simm Carr HX3: North 9C 80
Simm Carr La. HX3: North 9C 80
Simmonds La. HX1: Hal 7M 7 (7C 98)
Simmons Ct. LS9: Leeds 8M 5 (8H 69)
Simmons Way LS8: Leeds 2K 69
Simms Dene BD15: All 2F 62
Simon Cl. BD4: B'frd 3K 83
Simon Fold BD12: Wyke 2A 100
Simon Grn. HD7: Golc 8A 136
Simon Grn. Rd. HD7: Golc 7A 136
Simon Marks Ct. *LS12: Leeds* 9M 67
(off Lynwood Gth.)
SIMPSON GREEN 6G 46
Simpson Gro. BD10: B'frd 6G 47
LS12: Leeds 7N 67
Simpson Rd. HX7: Myth 4L 95
WF9: S Elm 5A 164
Simpsons Fold E. LS10: Leeds 8G 5 (7E 68)
Simpsons Fold W. LS10: Leeds 8G 5
Simpsons La. WF11: Knot 9C 110
Simpson St. BD21: Keigh 9G 27
HX3: Hal 2A 98
WF3: E Ard 4G 104
Simpson Ter. HX1: Hal 8J 7
Sim Royd La. HD8: Den D, Pen 5G 173
Sinclair Gth. WF2: Wake 3N 143
Sinclair Rd. BD2: B'frd 1D 64
Sinden M. BD10: B'frd 5F 46
Sinderhill Ct. HX3: North 9F 80
Singleton St. BD1: B'frd 1B 6 (6C 64)
Sion Hill HX3: Hal 9D 98
Sirdar Bus. Pk. WF2: Wake 4F 124
Sir Francis Crossley's Almshouses HX1: Hal 4G 7
Sir George Martin Dr. LS16: Leeds 3N 49
Sir Isaac Holden Pl. BD7: B'frd 7N 63
Sir John Lewis Cotts. LS25: Led 5K 91
Sir Karl Cohen Sq. LS12: Leeds 7L 67
Sirocco Av. WF10: All B 9C 90
Sir Wilfred Pl. BD10: B'frd 7F 46
Siskin Ct. LS27: Morl 1L 103
Siskin Dr. BD6: B'frd 4H 81
Siskin Way WF10: All B 9B 90
Sisley La. OL14: Tod 8B 94
Sissons Av. LS10: Leeds 9D 86
Sissons Cres. LS10: Leeds 9D 86
Sissons Dr. LS10: Leeds 9D 86
Sissons Grn. LS10: Leeds 9D 86
Sissons Gro. LS10: Leeds 9D 86
Sissons La. LS10: Leeds 9D 86
Sissons Mt. LS10: Leeds 1C 104
Sissons Pl. LS10: Leeds 8D 86
Sissons Rd. LS10: Leeds 9C 86
Sissons Row LS10: Leeds 9D 86
Sissons St. LS10: Leeds 9D 86
Sissons Ter. LS10: Leeds 9C 86
Sissons Vw. LS10: Leeds 1C 104
Sitka Cl. S71: Roys 7C 160
Siward St. WF9: Fitz 6A 146
Sixrood La. DN6: Burg 3L 165
Sixth Av. BD3: B'frd 5G 64
LS26: Rothw 6B 88
WF15: Liv 7F 100
Sizers Ct. LS19: Yead 2L 47
SKELBROOKE 5G 165
Skelbrooke Dr. WF8: Pon 6K 129
Skelda Ri. LS29: I'ly 6G 15
SKELLOW 8M 165
Skellow Dr. BD4: B'frd 4L 83
Skellow Hall Gdns. DN6: Skel 8L 165
Skellow Rd. DN6: Carc, Skel 8L 165
SKELMANTHORPE 7D 156
Skelmanthorpe Bus. Pk. HD8: Skelm 7D 156
Skelmanthorpe Station
Kirklees Light Railway 6D 156
Skelmanthorpe Technology Pk.
HD8: Skelm 6C 156
Skelton Av. LS9: Leeds 6K 69
S75: Map 8K 159
Skelton Cres. HD4: Hud 7G 137
LS9: Leeds 6K 69
Skelton Grange Cotts. LS9: Leeds 2L 87
Skelton Grange Rd. LS10: Leeds 3K 87
Skelton Mt. LS9: Leeds 6K 69
Skelton Pl. *LS9: Leeds* 6K 69
(off Ivy Av.)
Skelton Rd. LS9: Leeds 6K 69
Skeltons La. LS14: Leeds, T'ner 6C 52
Skelton St. LS9: Leeds 6K 69
Skelton Ter. LS9: Leeds 6K 69
Skelton Wlk. BD10: B'frd 8H 47
Skelwith App. LS14: Leeds 4B 70
Skelwith Wlk. LS14: Leeds 4B 70
Skinner La. BD8: B'frd 4A 64
LS7: Leeds 3H 5 (5F 68)
WF8: Pon 1K 129
Skinner St. LS1: Leeds 6B 4
Skippon Ter. LS14: T'ner 2G 52
Skipton Av. HD2: Hud 9M 119
Skipton Cl. WF3: E Ard 3F 104
Skipton Ri. LS25: Gar 7B 72
Skipton Rd. BD20: Keigh 5F 26
BD20: Sils 8B 12
BD20: Stee 3B 26
BD21: Keigh 8J 27
LS29: Add 8K 11
LS29: I'ly 4B 14
Skipton St. WF17: Bat 9F 102
SKIRCOAT GREEN 1A 118
Skircoat Grn. HX3: Hal 1B 118
Skircoat Grn. Rd. HX3: Hal 8L 7 (9B 98)
Skircoat Lodge HX3: Hal 9A 98
Skircoat Moor Cl. HX3: Hal 8N 97
Skircoat Moor Rd. HX1: Hal 7M 97
HX3: Hal 7M 97
Skircoat Rd. HX1: Hal 6L 7 (6B 98)
Skirdon Ct. HX2: Illing 6L 79
Skirrow St. BD16: Cot 9G 44
Skopos Motor Mus. 8G 103
Skye Cft. S71: Roys 4D 160
Skye Vw. LS26: Rothw 8A 88
Skylark Av. BD6: B'frd 4H 81
Skyline LS9: Leeds 6J 5 (6F 68)
Sky Plaza LS2: Leeds 3F 4
SLACK
HD3 3N 135
HX7 7E 76
Slack Bottom HX7: Hept 7F 76
Slack Bottom Rd. BD6: B'frd 5M 81
Slack Cotts. HX4: Bark 8F 116
Slack End BD6: B'frd 6L 81
Slack Ho. La. HX7: Wads 7J 77
Slack La. BD22: Oak 4A 42
HD3: Outl 2N 135
HD9: H'frth 3N 169
HX2: Midg 9B 78
HX4: Bark 8G 116
HX6: Ripp 6N 115
HX6: Tri 2N 115
S72: S Hien 4J 161
WF2: New 6K 143
WF4: Croft 2G 145
SLACK SIDE 4L 81
Slacks La. HD7: Slait 1G 151
(Cop Hill Side)
HD7: Slait 4L 151
(Krives La.)
Slack Ter. HD8: Cumb 6F 170
Slack Top HX7: Hept 7E 76
Slack Top La. HD8: Cumb 7G 171
Sladdin Row BD13: Que 5B 80
Slade Cl. LS23: B Spa 1D 38
Slade Ct. HD8: Kbtn 3F 154
Slade Ho. *BD2: B'frd* 4H 65
(off St Clare's Av.)
Slade La. BD20: Rid 6L 27
HD6: Ras 5K 119
Sladen Bri. BD22: S'bury 8N 41
Sladen St. BD21: Keigh 9G 27
Slades La. HD9: Mel 4C 152
Slades Rd. HD7: Golc 6A 136
Slade Wlk. WF17: Bat 3C 102
SLAID HILL 2K 51
Slaid Hill Ct. LS17: Leeds 2K 51
Slaids HD7: Linth 9E 136
SLAITHWAITE 9N 135
Slaithwaite Av. WF12: Dew 7F 122
Slaithwaite Cl. WF12: Dew 7F 122
Slaithwaite Ga. HD7: Golc 6N 135
Slaithwaite Rd. HD7: Slait 4N 151
HD9: Mel 4N 151
WF12: Dew 7F 122
Slaithwaite Station (Rail) 9M 135
Slant Ga. HD7: Linth 8D 136
HD8: Kbtn 2J 155
Slant La. OL14: Tod 6M 93
Slate Quarry La. BD16: Bgly 3G 45
Slater Av. HX7: Heb B 9H 77
Slater Bank *HX7: Heb B* 9H 77
(off Lee Wood Rd.)
Slater Bank La. HX7: Heb B 9H 77
Slatering La. HX7: Hept 7D 76
Slaters Rd. LS28: Stan 5B 66
Slates La. LS29: I'ly 2F 14
Slawtree Ct. HD7: Slait 1M 151
Slaymaker La. BD22: Oak 4B 42
Slazenger Sports & Social Club 2C 142
Slead Av. HD6: Brigh 8L 99
Slead Ct. HD6: Brigh 8L 99
Slead Cres. HD6: Brigh 8L 99
Slead Gro. HD6: Brigh 8L 99
Slead Royd HD6: Brigh 8L 99
SLEAD SYKE 8K 99
Slead Syke Sports Cen. 7L 99
Slead Vw. HD6: Brigh 8L 99
Sledgate La. HD7: Slait 4L 151
Sledge Ga. HD3: Scam 7E 134
Sledmere Cft. LS14: Leeds 9D 52
Sledmere Gth. LS14: Leeds 9D 52
Sledmere Grn. *LS14: Leeds* 9D 52
(off Sledmere Pl.)
Sledmere La. LS14: Leeds 9D 52
(not continuous)
Sledmere Pl. LS14: Leeds 9D 52
Sledmere Sq. *LS14: Leeds* 9D 52
(off Sledmere Pl.)
Sleep Hill La. DN6: S'brk 3F 164
WF9: Upt 2D 164
Sleights, The LS17: Huby 6L 19
Sleights Bungalows
LS17: Huby 5L 19
Sleights La. LS17: Hare 2K 35
Sleningford Gro. BD18: Ship 7K 45
Sleningford Ri. BD16: Bgly 2E 44
Sleningford Rd. BD16: Bgly 2D 44
BD18: Ship 7K 45
Sleningford Ter. *BD16: Bgly* 2E 44
(off Sleningford Rd.)
Slicer's Yd. *BD16: Bgly* 4E 44
(off Busfeild St.)
Slingsby Cl. BD10: B'frd 7H 47
Slipper La. WF14: Liv, Mir 3J 121
Slippery Ford La. BD22: Oak 1K 41
Slippy La. HX2: Mix 8J 79
Sloane Pl. WF10: C'frd 3J 109
Slutwell La. WF8: Pon 3K 129
Smalewell Cl. LS28: Pud 8A 66
Smalewell Dr. LS28: Pud 8N 65
Smalewell Gdns. LS28: Pud 8N 65
Smalewell Grn. LS28: Pud 8A 66
Smalewell Rd. LS28: Pud 8N 65
(Smalewell Dr.)
LS28: Pud 8M 65
(Tyersal La.)
Small La. HD7: Golc 6C 136
S75: Caw 8L 173
Small Lees La. *HX6: Ripp* 8D 116
(off Small Lees Rd.)
Small Lees Rd. HX6: Ripp 8D 116
Smallpage *BD13: Que* 4D 80
(off Albert Rd.)
Small Page Fold BD13: Que 4D 80
Smallpage Yd. WF1: Wake 4K 9 (5L 125)
Small Shaw La. HX7: P Wel 3H 77
Smallwood Gdns. WF12: Dew 9L 103
Smallwood Rd. WF12: Dew 9K 103
(not continuous)
Smawell La. WF4: Not 2B 160
Smawthorne Av. WF10: C'frd 5D 108

South Vw.—Spring Hall Sports Facility

South Vw. LS20: Guis 7J 31
LS22: Coll 9G 23
LS22: Weth 1M 23
LS23: Cliff 3D 38
LS26: Rothw 7N 87
LS27: Chur 6L 85
LS28: Pud 7C 66
LS28: Stan 5N 65
LS29: Men 5E 30
WF3: W Ard 7N 103
WF4: Crig 6F 142
WF7: F'stne 5D 128
WF10: C'frd 7E 108
(Durham St.)
WF10: C'frd 2J 109
(William St.)
WF12: Dew 5G 122
WF17: Birs 3C 102
Southview Bus. Pk. LS20: Guis 9J 31
South Vw. Cl. BD4: E Bier 6J 83
LS19: Yead 9K 31
South Vw. Cotts. BD23: Drau 4D 10
LS17: Shad 4A 52
South Vw. Ct. HX3: Hip 6J 99
South Vw. Cres. LS19: Yead 9K 31
South Vw. Dr. BD4: E Bier 6K 83
South Vw. Fold S36: Ing 8B 172
South Vw. Gdns. WF8: Pon 3M 129
South Vw. Gro. BD19: Gom 5M 101
South Vw. Rd. BD4: E Bier 6K 83
LS19: Yead 9M 31
South Vw. St. OL14: Tod 3E 92
South Vw. Ter. BD16: Bgly 2H 45
BD17: Bail 4A 46
BD20: Sils 8D 12
HX1: Hal 4M 97
(off Kelsey St.)
LS19: Yead 1N 47
LS21: Otley 1M 31
(off Crow La.)
WF4: G Moor 6B 140
WF13: Dew 1E 122
(off Halifax Rd.)
Southwaite Cl. LS14: Leeds 2A 70
Southwaite Gth. LS14: Leeds 2A 70
Southwaite La. LS14: Leeds 2A 70
Southwaite Lawn LS14: Leeds 2A 70
Southwaite Pl. LS14: Leeds 2A 70
South Wlk. BD16: Har 6N 43
South Way BD4: E Bier 6J 83
BD18: Ship 8J 45
Southway BD16: Bgly 2H 45
HD3: Hud 1H 137
LS18: Hors 4D 48
LS20: Guis 8E 30
LS29: Burl W 6A 16
LS29: I'ly 6J 15
WF14: Mir 4K 121
Southwell Av. HD3: Hud 3G 136
Southwell La. WF4: Horb 1C 142
Southwood Av. HD9: Hon 4N 153
Southwood Cl. LS14: Leeds 2D 70
Southwood Cres. LS14: Leeds 2D 70
Southwood Ga. LS14: Leeds 2D 70
Southwood Rd. LS14: Leeds 2D 70
Sovereign Bus. Pk. LS10: Leeds 8F 68
Sovereign Cl. WF17: Birs 3C 102
Sovereign Ct. BD2: B'frd 2G 64
LS17: Leeds 1G 50
Sovereign Gdns. WF6: Norm 1H 127
Sovereign Ind. Est. HD8: Shep 2K 171
Sovereign Mill *LS27: Morl 1L 103*
(off Sth. Queen St.)
Sovereign Pk. BD17: Bail 3C 46
Sovereign Pl. LS1: Leeds 8E 4 (7D 68)
Sovereign Quay LS1: Leeds 8F 4
Sovereign Rd. WF1: Out 9K 105
Sovereign Sq. HD6: B Bri 5N 99
Sovereign St. HX1: Hal 4J 7 (5A 98)
LS1: Leeds 8E 4 (7E 68)
Sovereign's Way WF12: Dew 8E 122
Sowden Bldgs. BD2: B'frd 4F 64
Sowden Grange BD13: Thorn 8C 62
(James St.)
BD13: Thorn 8C 62
(Lane End)
Sowden La. BD12: Wyke 1M 99
HX3: Nor G 1L 99
Sowden Rd. BD9: B'frd 3J 63
Sowden St. BD7: B'frd 2N 81
Sowden's Yd. LS16: Leeds 9N 49
SOWERBY 9E 96
SOWERBY BRIDGE 8J 97
Sowerby Bridge Pool 9H 97
Sowerby Bridge Station (Rail) 9J 97
Sowerby Cft. HX6: Sow B 1J 117
Sowerby Cft. La. HX6: Norl, Sow B 9H 97
Sowerby Grn. HX6: Sow B 9D 96
Sowerby La. HX2: Lud F 5B 96
Sowerby New Rd. HX6: Sow B 9E 96
Sowerby St. HX6: Sow B 9H 97
Sowerby Town HX6: Sow B 9D 96
Sowgate La. WF8: Pon 1N 129
WF11: Ferr, Knot 9A 110
SOWOOD 1M 135
Sowood Av. WF5: Oss 8A 124
Sowood Ct. WF5: Oss 8B 124
Sowood Fold HX4: Sow 1N 135
Sowood Gdns. WF5: Oss 8B 124
Sowood Grange WF5: Oss 8A 124
SOWOOD GREEN 9M 117
SOWOOD HILL 1N 135
Sowood Hill Vw. HX3: Hal 1M 7
Sowood La. WF4: G Moor 5C 140
WF5: Oss 8B 124
WF12: Bries 3E 140
Sowood St. LS4: Leeds 4M 67
Sowood Vw. WF5: Oss 7B 124
SOYLAND TOWN 5D 116
Soyland Town Rd. HX6: Ripp 5D 116
Spa Bottom HD8: Fen B 6G 138
Spa Bldgs. *LS29: I'ly 5G 14*
(off The Grove)
Spa Courtyard HD8: Fen B 6G 138
Spa Cft. Rd. WF5: Oss 7C 124
Spa Flds. HD7: Slait 9N 135
Spa Flds. Ind. Est. HD7: Slait 9A 136
Spa Fld. Ter. *HD7: Slait 9N 135*
(off New St.)
Spa Fold WF3: S'ley 8A 106
Spa Grn. La. HX6: Ripp 8B 116
Spa Gro. WF2: Wake 8G 124
Spa Hill WF17: Bat 7F 102
Spa Ind. Est. LS7: Leeds 2E 68
Spaines Rd. HD2: Hud 1M 137
Spa La. BD16: Bgly 2F 44
HD7: Linth 9A 136
LS23: B Spa 1E 38
WF5: Oss 7C 124
Spalding Towers LS9: Leeds 4L 5
Spa M. LS23: B Spa 1E 38
Spa Mill Ter. HD7: Slait 9N 135
Spandola Ct. BD21: Keigh 8F 26
Spanefield La. HX2: Wain 9F 78
Sparable La. BD16: Bgly 4H 45
WF1: Wake 8N 125
Sparkfields S75: Map 9K 159
Spark Hall Cl. HD3: Hud 3E 136
Spark Ho. La. HX6: Sow B 9J 97
Spark La. S75: Map 9J 159
Sparks Rd. HD3: Hud 3G 136
Spark St. HD3: Hud 4E 136
Sparrow Ri. HD9: Mel 7C 152
Spartal La. WF10: Leds 5E 90
Spartan Rd. BD12: Low M 8B 82
Sparth La. HD9: H'frth 4G 168
Spa St. WF5: Oss 7D 124
WF17: Bat 7F 102
Spa Ter. HD1: Hud 7L 137
HD8: Fen B 5G 138
Spawd Bone La. WF11: Knot 9D 110
Spa Well Gro. S72: B'ley 6A 162
Spa Wood Top HD4: Hud 7L 137
Speak Cl. WF1: Wake 3A 126
Speakers Ct. WF13: Dew 3E 122
Spear Fir LS17: Bard 6B 36
Spearhead Way BD21: Keigh 8J 27
Speedwell Mt. LS6: Leeds 3D 68
Speedwell Rd. WF10: C'frd 6M 107
Speedwell St. HD1: Hud 5J 137
LS6: Leeds 3D 68
Speeton Av. BD7: B'frd 3K 81
Speeton Gro. BD7: B'frd 3J 81
Speights Pl. *BD4: B'frd 3G 83*
(off Dawson La.)
Spen App. LS16: Leeds 8J 49
Spen Bank BD19: Cleck 5K 101
LS16: Leeds 8J 49
Spenborough Ind. Est. WF15: Liv 9N 101
Spenborough Pool & Sports Complex 7K 101
Spence La. LS12: Leeds 8A 4 (8B 68)
Spenceley St. LS2: Leeds 1C 4 (3C 68)
(not continuous)
Spencer Av. BD7: B'frd 9M 63
BD20: Sils 7E 12
LS27: Morl 2K 103
Spencer Bus. Factory BD4: B'frd 3G 82
Spencer La. HX7: Heb B 3H 95
Spencer Mt. LS8: Leeds 3G 69
Spencer Pl. LS7: Leeds 1L 5 (3G 69)
Spencer Rd. BD7: B'frd 9L 63
(not continuous)
Spencers Ct. *HX1: Hal 5L 7*
(off Wellington Pl.)
Spencer St. BD21: Keigh 9G 27
(not continuous)
HD8: Skelm 7D 156
WF14: Mir 8L 121
Spencer Ter. HD2: Hud 8B 120
Spen Cl. BD4: B'frd 6F 82
Spen Comn. La. LS24: Tad 1E 54
Spen Cres. LS16: Leeds 8J 49
Spen Dr. LS16: Leeds 7K 49
Spenfield Ct. WF15: Liv 1L 121
Spen Gdns. LS16: Leeds 7L 49
Spen Grn. LS16: Leeds 8J 49
Spen La. BD19: Cleck, Gom 4K 101
LS5: Leeds 1K 67
LS6: Leeds 9K 49
LS16: Leeds 6K 49
(not continuous)
Spen Lawn LS16: Leeds 8J 49
SPEN LOWER 5K 101
Spen M. LS16: Leeds 8K 49
Spennithorne Av. LS16: Leeds 5K 49
Spennithorne Dr. LS16: Leeds 6K 49
Spennithorne Rd. DN6: Skel 7L 165
Spen Rd. LS16: Leeds 7K 49
Spenser Ri. LS20: Guis 8K 31
Spenser Rd. LS20: Guis 8K 31
Spens Ho. LS2: Leeds 2E 4
Spenslea Gro. LS27: Morl 2K 103
Spen Trad. Est. BD19: Cleck 4K 101
Spen Va. St. WF16: Heck 9A 102
Spen Valley Ind. Pk. BD19: Cleck 6J 101
Spen Valley Rd. WF13: Raven 5B 122
Spen Vw. WF13: Dew 3C 122
Spen Vw. La. BD4: B'frd 6F 82
Spen Wlk. LS16: Leeds 8J 49
Spen Way LS16: Leeds 9K 49
Spey Cl. S75: Map 9L 159
Spibey Cres. LS26: Rothw 6M 87
Spibey La. LS26: Rothw 6M 87
Spicer Ho. La. S36: Ing, M Grn 8L 171
Spicer St. BD5: B'frd 2A 82
Spiers Gth. BD6: B'frd 4B 82
Spiggs HX3: North 1E 98
Spindle Cl. WF12: Dew 4K 123
Spindle La. HD3: Hud 4E 136
Spindle Point HX2: Hal 8N 79
Spindles, The LS10: Leeds 5F 86
Spindle St. HX2: Hal 8N 79
Spinkfield Rd. HD2: Hud 2L 137
Spink La. WF8: Pon 2K 129
Spink Pl. BD8: B'frd 6B 64
Spinks Gdns. LS14: Leeds 2C 70
Spink St. BD8: B'frd 6B 64
Spinkwell Cl. BD3: B'frd 1C 6 (5D 64)
Spink Well La. WF3: Ting 3B 104
Spinkwell Rd. WF13: Dew 2F 122
Spinners Av. WF1: Wake 2L 125
Spinners Chase LS28: Pud 7B 66
Spinners Cl. HX1: Hal 4M 97
Spinners Fold WF13: Dew 9C 102
Spinners Ga. BD4: B'frd 8J 65
Spinners Hollow HX6: Ripp 8D 116
Spinners Way BD19: Scho 4D 100
BD22: Haw 9C 42
WF14: Mir 8K 121
Spinney, The BD20: E Mor 8C 28
BD23: Drau 5D 10
HD6: Brigh 7M 99
HX7: Heb B 2J 95
LS9: Leeds 8L 5 (7G 69)
LS17: Leeds 5G 50
LS19: Raw 5L 47
LS22: Weth 3L 23
WF2: Wake 3N 143
Spinneyfield HD2: Fix 7M 119
Spinneyfield Ct. LS9: Leeds 8L 5 (7G 69)
Spinney Ri. BD4: B'frd 4K 83
Spinning Mill, The BD22: Haw 7B 42
Spinning Mill Ct. BD18: Ship 6K 45
(Hirst La.)
BD18: Ship 7K 45
(Sherwood Gro.)
Spion Kop LS14: T'ner 2G 53
Spire Ct. HD1: Hud 3K 137
Spire Hgts. BD16: Bgly 4J 45
Spitalgap La. WF8: Pon 4A 130
Spittal Hardwick La. WF8: Pon 6J 109
WF10: C'frd 6J 109
Spittlerush La. DN6: Nort 6M 149
Spofforth Hill LS22: Weth 3K 23
Spofforth Wlk. LS25: Gar 7B 72
Spool Ct. HD6: B Bri 5A 100
Spout Fold WF2: Wake 5F 124
Spout Hill HD6: Ras 5K 119
Spout Ho. La. HD6: Brigh 6K 99
Spring Av. BD21: Keigh 1L 43
LS27: Gil 6F 84
SPRING BANK 3J 43
Spring Bank BD13: Cull 1J 61
HD1: Hud 3A 8
HD8: Kbtn 2J 155
HD9: H'frth 4J 169
HX2: Lud 3E 96
HX6: Sow B 7G 97
LS5: Leeds 2K 67
WF8: Pon 4K 129
WF15: Liv 1N 121
Springbank LS19: Raw 4L 47
LS21: Askw 4E 16
LS25: Gar 9K 71
Springbank Av. LS27: Gil 6F 84
LS28: Fars 3B 66
Springbank Cl. LS28: Fars 3A 66
S71: Carl 9D 160
Spring Bank Cres. LS6: Leeds 2A 68
Springbank Cres. HD2: Hud 1B 138
LS25: Gar 8K 71
LS27: Gil 5F 84
Spring Bank Cft. HD9: H'frth 4J 169
Spring Bank Dr. WF15: Liv 1M 121
Springbank Dr. LS28: Fars 3B 66
Springbank Gro. LS28: Fars 3B 66
Spring Bank Ind. Est.
HX6: Sow B 1H 117
Springbank M. WF3: Loft 5H 105
Spring Bank Pl. BD8: B'frd 5B 64
Spring Bank Ri. BD21: Keigh 3J 43
Springbank Ri. LS28: Fars 3B 66
Springbank Rd. HD2: Hud 1B 138
LS27: Gil 5F 84
LS28: Fars 3A 66
Spring Bank Ter. LS20: Guis 7J 31
Spring Bottom OL14: W'den 4H 113
Springcliffe BD8: B'frd 5N 63
Springcliffe St. BD8: B'frd 5N 63
Spring Cl. BD16: Bgly 5G 45
BD21: Keigh 1L 43
LS25: Gar 8B 72
(Firtree Av.)
LS25: Gar 6A 72
(Newhold Ind. Est.)
WF9: Kins 8B 146
Spring Cl. Av. LS9: Leeds 8M 5 (8H 69)
Spring Cl. Gdns. LS9: Leeds 8M 5 (8H 69)
Spring Cl. St. LS9: Leeds 8L 5 (8G 69)
Spring Cl. Wlk. LS9: Leeds 8M 5 (8H 69)
Spring Dale HD9: Hon 4L 153
Springdale Av. HD1: Hud 6L 137
Springdale Cres. BD10: B'frd 7G 47
Springdale St. HD1: Hud 6L 137
Spring Dr. BD21: Keigh 1L 43
Spring Edge Nth. HX1: Hal 7N 97
Spring Edge Sth. HX1: Hal 7N 97
Spring Edge W. HX1: Hal 7M 97
SPRING END 8D 124
Spring End Rd. WF4: Horb 8D 124
Spring Farm WF4: Not 3B 160
Spring Farm La. BD16: Har 6N 43
Spring Farm M. BD15: Wils 1B 62
SPRINGFIELD
BD10 9F 46
WF13 2F 122
Springfield BD13: Que 4C 80
HD3: Outl 2A 136
HX2: Midg 3C 96
HX3: Hip 4H 99
HX3: North 1D 98
HX6: Sow B 9G 97
LS23: B Spa 9D 24
LS23: Cliff 3D 38
Springfield Av. BD7: B'frd 9L 63
HD7: Slait 2L 151
HD8: Clay W 7H 157
HD9: Hon 6L 153
LS27: Morl 7J 85
LS29: I'ly 5H 15
WF3: Loft 5L 105
WF8: Pon 2M 129
WF9: Hems 3E 162
WF11: Knot 8G 110
WF17: Bat 7E 102
Springfield Cl. HD8: Clay W 7H 157
LS18: Hors 6H 49
WF3: Loft 5L 105
Springfield Commercial Cen. LS28: Fars 2B 66
Springfield Cotts. HX6: Ripp 9D 116
Springfield Ct. BD20: Keigh 8G 27
LS17: Leeds 3J 51
LS19: Yead 8L 31
LS20: Guis 7J 31
(off West St.)
WF6: Norm 3J 127
WF15: Liv 2J 121
Springfield Cres. LS27: Morl 7K 85
WF8: K S'ton 5K 149
Springfield Dr. HD8: Bird E 4L 171
WF15: Liv 7G 100
Springfield Footpath HD1: Hud 5K 137
Springfield Gdns. BD20: Keigh 8G 27
LS18: Hors 6G 49
LS28: Pud 8C 66
Springfield Grange WF2: Wake 5F 124
Springfield Grn. LS10: Leeds 3G 87
Springfield Gro. BD16: Bgly 3E 44
HD6: Brigh 7M 99
Springfield La. BD4: B'frd 3B 84
HD8: Kbtn 2J 155
LS27: Morl 7K 85
WF15: Liv 7J 101
Springfield M. LS20: Guis 7J 31
LS27: Morl 7K 85
Springfield Mills HD8: Kbtn 2H 155
Springfield Mt. LS2: Leeds 3B 4 (5C 68)
LS12: Leeds 6K 67
LS18: Hors 6G 48
LS29: Add 9M 11
WF9: S Elm 9L 163
Springfield Pk. WF14: Mir 6M 121
Springfield Pl. BD1: B'frd 1A 6 (6B 64)
BD10: B'frd 8F 46
LS10: Leeds 3G 87
(Leasowe Rd.)
LS10: Leeds 3J 87
(Pontefract Rd.)
LS20: Guis 7J 31
LS21: Otley 1K 31
LS25: Gar 8K 71
Springfield Ri. LS18: Hors 6G 49
LS26: Rothw 9A 88
Springfield Rd. BD17: Bail 3N 45
BD20: Keigh 8G 26
HX5: Ell 4G 118
LS20: Guis 8J 31
LS27: Morl 7J 85
S72: Grim 9A 162
WF3: Loft 5L 105
SPRINGFIELDS 8G 110
Springfields WF10: C'frd 4E 108
WF11: Knot 8G 110
Springfield St. BD8: B'frd 6A 64
BD13: Thorn 8D 62
LS26: Rothw 9A 88
Springfields Vw. HX4: Gree 4A 118
Springfield Ter. BD8: B'frd 6A 64
BD13: Cull 1L 61
BD19: Scho 3D 100
HD3: Outl 1A 136
(off Mulehouse La.)
HD8: Eml 2D 156
HX2: Midg 3C 96
HX3: Hip 4H 99
HX7: Crag V 8K 95
LS17: Leeds 3J 51
(off Springfield Ct.)
LS20: Guis 8J 31
LS28: Stan 5A 66
WF13: Dew 2F 122
WF15: Liv 7G 101
Springfield Vw. *LS25: Kip 4B 90*
(off Hanover Pl.)
WF7: A'ton 3A 128
Springfield Vs. LS27: Gil 5E 84
Springfield Wlk. LS18: Hors 6G 49
Spring Gdn. Cotts. *BD20: Sils 8D 12*
(off South Vw. Ter.)
SPRING GARDENS 7C 84
Spring Gdns. BD1: B'frd 1A 6 (6C 64)
BD11: Drig 7C 84
BD20: Sils 8D 12
(off Elliott St.)
HD9: U'thng 3K 169
HX2: Mix 1L 97
HX3: Nor G 2L 99
HX6: Sow B 7H 97
HX7: Myth 3N 95
(off Orchard Wlk.)
LS17: Hare 1J 35
LS27: Chur 6M 85
LS29: Burl W 8D 16
WF17: Bat 7E 102
Spring Gdns. La. BD20: Keigh 6G 26
Spring Gdns. Mt. BD20: Keigh 7H 27
Spring Gdns. Rd. BD9: B'frd 3M 63
Spring Gdn. St. BD13: Que 4D 80
Spring Gro. BD10: B'frd 8F 46
HD7: Linth 1A 152
HD7: Mars 3J 151
HD8: Clay W 7H 157
HD8: Kbtn 2H 155
HX1: Hal 5L 97
HX7: Heb B 9H 77
S71: Carl 8E 160
Spring Gro. Av. LS6: Leeds 4A 68
Spring Gro. Cotts. HX4: Bark 3F 134
Spring Gro. St.
HD1: Hud 6A 8 (5M 137)
Spring Gro. Vw. LS6: Leeds 4A 68
Spring Gro. Wlk. LS6: Leeds 4A 68
Spring Hall Cl. HX3: She 8G 80
Spring Hall Ct. HX1: Hal 4L 97
Spring Hall Dr. HX2: Hal 6L 97
Spring Hall Gdns. HX2: Hal 5L 97
Spring Hall Gro. HX2: Hal 5L 97
Spring Hall La. HX1: Hal 6L 97
Spring Hall Pl. HX1: Hal 5L 97
Spring Hall Sports Facility 8L 7 (7C 98)

Spring Head—Stansfield Rd.

Spring Head HX2: Hal .3L 97
HX3: She .8H 81
Springhead BD22: Oak .7B 42
Spring Head La. HD7: Mars .5F 150
Springhead Mills BD22: Haw .7C 42
Spring Head Rd. BD13: Thorn .8D 62
BD22: Haw .7B 42
Springhead Rd. LS26: Rothw .7B 88
Spring Head Ter. BD13: Thorn .7B 62
SPRING HILL .1G 145
Spring Hill BD15: Wils .1B 62
BD17: Bail .4L 45
BD18: Ship .8C 46
LS7: Leeds .2E 68
LS16: Leeds .3A 50
S75: W Gran .6G 158
Springhill Av. WF4: Croft .1H 145
Springhill Cl. WF1: Out .7J 105
Spring Hill Cotts. LS6: Leeds .9A 50
(off Monk Bri. Rd.)
Springhill Dr. WF4: Croft .1H 145
Springhill Gro. WF4: Croft .1H 145
Springhill Mt. WF4: Croft .2H 145
Spring Hill Pl. BD15: Wils .1B 62
Springhills WF1: Out .7J 105
Spring Hill Ter. LS6: Leeds .9A 50
(off Monk Bri. Rd.)
Spring Holes La. BD13: Thorn .7B 62
Springhouses HD8: Den D .3C 172
(off Dearneside Rd.)
Springhurst Rd. BD18: Ship .8M 45
Spring La. BD16: Bgly .1J 45
HD9: H'frth .4K 169
HD9: Holm .6J 169
HD9: New M .3C 170
HG3: Kirkby .5H 21
HX4: Gree .4N 117
LS22: Weth .4C 24
S71: Carl .9E 160
WF4: N Cro .3J 145
WF4: Wool .5L 159
WF17: Bat .5E 102
Spring Life Health Club for Ladies
Castleford .4C 108
Springlodge Pl. BD8: B'frd .5B 64
Springmead Dr. LS25: Gar .8N 71
Spring Mill Fold HX2: Wain .5F 78
Spring Mill Golf Course .5B 124
Spring Mill Gro. WF17: Bat .6D 102
Spring Mill La. WF5: Oss .4B 124
Spring Mill St. BD5: B'frd .8B 6 (9C 64)
Spring Mt. BD21: Keigh .2L 43
Spring Pk. Rd. BD15: Wils .9B 44
Spring Pl. BD7: B'frd .9A 64
BD21: Keigh .2L 43
Spring Pl. Ct. WF14: Mir .5A 122
Spring Pl. Gdns. WF14: Raven .5A 122
Spring Ram Bus. Pk. S75: Kex .7E 158
Spring Ri. BD21: Keigh .1L 43
BD23: Drau .5D 10
Spring Rd. LS6: Leeds .2N 67
Springrove Ter. LS6: Leeds .4A 68
Spring Row BD13: Que .4D 80
BD16: Har .6A 44
BD21: Keigh .1H 43
(not continuous)
BD22: Cros R .7F 42
BD22: Oxen .5E 60
HX2: Mix .6J 79
Spring Royd HX2: Lud F .4C 96
Springroyd Ter. BD8: B'frd .6L 63
Springs, The WF1: Wake .4K 9 (5L 125)
Spring Side OL12: Whit .7A 112
Spring Side Ri. HD7: Golc .5C 136
Springs La. LS22: Bick .2F 24
LS23: W'ton .2F 24
LS29: I'ly .5H 15
Springs Rd. HD9: H'lm .5A 168
LS19: Yead .1J 47
Springs Ter. LS29: I'ly .5H 15
Springstone Av. WF5: Oss .4N 123
WF9: Hems .2E 162
Spring St. BD10: B'frd .8F 46
BD15: All .3F 62
BD21: Keigh .8J 27
BD22: Cros R .7F 42
(off Bingley Rd.)
HD1: Hud .5A 8 (4M 137)
HD6: Brigh .1M 119
HD7: Mars .6F 150
HD7: Slait .1M 151
HX6: Ripp .7D 116
OL14: Tod .3E 92
WF13: Dew .2F 122
WF15: Liv .8M 101
Springswood Av. BD18: Ship .8M 45
Springswood Pl. BD18: Ship .8M 45
Springswood Rd. BD18: Ship .8M 45
Spring Ter. BD21: Keigh .1L 43
HX2: Wain .5F 78
HX3: Hal .2M 7 (4C 98)
HX4: Holy .9L 117
HX6: Sow B .1J 117
WF9: S Elm .7M 163
Springvale Cl. WF4: S Comn .8K 127
Springvale Ri. WF9: Hems .1D 162
Springvale Rd. WF9: S Kirk .6J 163
Springvale Works HD6: Brigh .8K 99
Spring Valley LS28: Stan .5B 66
Spring Valley Av. LS13: Leeds .5F 66
Spring Valley Cl. LS13: Leeds .5F 66
WF15: Liv .7L 101
(off Spring Valley St.)
Spring Valley Ct. LS13: Leeds .5F 66
Spring Valley Cres. LS13: Leeds .5F 66
Spring Valley Cft. LS13: Leeds .5F 66
Spring Valley Dr. LS13: Leeds .5F 66
Spring Valley Sq. WF15: Liv .7L 101
(off Well St.)
Spring Valley St. WF15: Liv .7L 101
Spring Valley Vw. LS13: Leeds .5F 66
Spring Valley Wlk. LS13: Leeds .5F 66
Spring Vw. BD13: Thorn .6B 62
(off Lower Hgts. Rd.)
HX2: Lud F .6D 96
Spring Vw. LS27: Gil .5G 84
WF5: Oss .5B 124
Spring Vw. Rd. HX2: Lud F .6D 96
Spring Vs. HX7: Myth .3N 95
OL14: Tod .3D 92
Springville Gdns. WF9: Upt .2A 164
Springville Ter. BD10: B'frd .8F 46
Spring Way BD21: Keigh .1L 43
Springwell Av. LS26: Swil .4H 89
Springwell Cl. LS19: Yead .1N 47
WF15: Liv .1N 121
Springwell Ct. LS12: Leeds .8B 68
WF3: Ting .3A 104
WF9: Hems .3E 162
Springwell Dr. BD5: B'frd .1C 82
Springwell Rd. LS12: Leeds .8A 4 (8B 68)
LS26: Swil .4H 89
WF5: Oss .6A 124
Spring Wells BD22: Oak .3C 42
Springwell St. LS12: Leeds .8A 4 (8B 68)
Springwell Ter. BD6: B'frd .4M 81
LS19: Yead .1N 47
Springwell Vw. LS12: Leeds .8C 68
WF17: Birs .3C 102
(off South Vw.)
Springwood Av. BD5: B'frd .2D 82
HD1: Hud .6A 8 (5L 137)
HX3: Hal .1A 118
Springwood Bus. Pk. HX4: Holy .7B 118
Springwood Cl. WF3: Thpe H .3G 105
Springwood Ct. LS8: Leeds .9K 51
(off Bk. Wetherby Rd.)
LS27: Morl .3L 103
Springwood Dr. HX3: Hal .1A 118
Spring Wood Gdns. BD5: B'frd .3D 82
HX3: Hal .2A 118
Springwood Gdns. LS8: Leeds .9K 51
Springwood Gro. LS8: Leeds .9L 51
Springwood Hall Cl. HD1: Hud .4K 137
Springwood Hall Gdns. HD1: Hud .5K 137
Springwood M. LS8: Leeds .9L 51
Springwood Pl. BD2: B'frd .4C 64
(off Bolton Rd.)
Springwood Rd. HD9: T'bdge .9A 154
LS8: Leeds .9K 51
LS19: Raw .4L 47
Springwood Sq. HD1: Hud .5A 8
Springwood St. HD1: Hud .6A 8 (5M 137)
Springwood Ter. BD2: B'frd .4C 64
(off Bolton La.)
HX4: Holy .7B 118
HX7: Heb B .8H 77
Spruce Av. S71: Roys .6C 160
Spruce Cl. WF2: Wake .9J 125
Spruce Dr. HD4: Neth .3J 153
HX3: North .9F 80
Spruce Dr. M. HD4: Neth .3J 153
Spruce Hgts. HD6: Brigh .6M 99
Spruce St. BD21: Keigh .8K 27
Spruce Wlk. OL14: W'den .3J 113
Sprutts La. HX7: P Wel .6J 77
Spur Dr. LS15: Leeds .3F 70
Spurr Gro. WF2: W'ton .4C 144
Spurrier's Av. WF11: Knot .9B 110
Spurr St. WF17: Bat .8G 103
Square HX1: Hal .4L 7 (5B 98)
HX2: Wain .6F 78
HX3: North .1F 98
HX7: Myth .4M 95
Square, The BD8: B'frd .7H 63
BD20: E Mor .7C 28
(off Hartley's Sq.)
HD8: Shep .9J 155
HX3: Sou .7D 98
HX7: Heb B .3L 95
(off Burnley Rd.)
LS17: Hare .1J 35
LS18: Hors .7E 48
LS21: F'ley .6A 18
LS23: B Spa .1E 38
LS25: Kip .4A 90
WF10: C'frd .5J 109
WF11: Ferr .6B 110
WF17: Bat .6C 102
Square Chapel Centre for the Arts
.4M 7 (5C 98)
Square Hill HD5: K'htn .2F 138
Square Rd. HX1: Hal .4M 7 (5C 98)
OL14: W'den .3J 113
Square St. BD4: B'frd .8F 6 (9E 64)
Square Vw. OL14: W'den .3K 113
Squire Grn. BD8: B'frd .5L 63
Squire La. BD8: B'frd .5L 63
BD9: B'frd .5L 63
Squirrel Cl. WF13: Dew .9D 102
Squirrel Ct. HD2: Hud .9H 119
Squirrel Ditch HD4: Hud .7A 138
Squirrel End WF13: Dew .1C 122
Squirrel Hall Dr.
WF13: Dew .9C 102
Squirrel La. BD13: Thorn .9A 62
Squirrels Drey WF4: Dur .3H 143
Squirrel Wlk. WF13: Dew .9D 102
Squirrel Way LS17: Leeds .3H 51
Stable Ct. LS28: Cal .9M 47
(off Bk. Thornhill St.)
Stable Fold BD12: Wyke .2B 100
Stableford Gdns. HD2: Hud .9J 119
Stableford Mnr. HD7: Golc .5D 136
Stable La. HX3: Hal .3A 98
Stable M. BD16: Cot .8D 44
Stablers Wlk. WF6: Alt .8H 107
Stables, The LS21: Otley .9L 17
(off Wesley St.)
LS22: Weth .4M 23
(off High Cliffe Ter.)
WF2: W'ton .3B 144
Stables La. LS23: B Spa .1E 38
Stacey Cres. S72: Grim .9N 161
Stackgarth HD6: Ras .3M 119
Stackhills Rd. OL14: Tod .7L 93
Stacks La. HX7: Crag V .7M 95
Stadium Health & Fitness Club
Huddersfield .1F 8 (2A 138)
Stadium Rd. BD6: B'frd .5C 82
Stadium Way HD1: Hud .2E 8 (3A 138)
LS11: Leeds .2A 86
WF9: S Elm .4A 164
Stafford Av. HX3: Hal .8B 98
Stafford Grn. HX3: Hal .9B 98
STAFFORD HILL .3G 139
Stafford Hill La. HD5: K'htn .2G 138
Stafford Pde. HX3: Hal .9B 98
Stafford Pl. HX3: Hal .8B 98
Stafford Rd. HX3: Hal .9B 98
Stafford Sq. HX3: Hal .9C 98
Stafford St. BD4: B'frd .1F 82
LS10: Leeds .1G 86
LS27: Morl .2J 103
WF10: C'frd .4C 108
Stafford Ter. WF2: Wake .5H 125
Stainbeck Av. LS7: Leeds .9B 50
Stainbeck Cnr. LS7: Leeds .8E 50
(off Harrogate Rd.)
Stainbeck Gdns. BD6: B'frd .5J 81
LS7: Leeds .8D 50
Stainbeck La. LS7: Leeds .8C 50
Stainbeck Rd. LS7: Leeds .9B 50
Stainbeck Wlk. LS7: Leeds .9D 50
STAINBURN .4G 19
Stainburn Av. LS17: Leeds .6G 50
WF10: C'frd .7G 108
Stainburn Cres. LS17: Leeds .6F 50
Stainburn Dr. LS17: Leeds .6F 50
Stainburn Gdns. LS17: Leeds .6G 50
Stainburn La. LS21: Leat .6D 18
Stainburn Mt. LS17: Leeds .7G 50
Stainburn Pde. LS17: Leeds .6F 50
Stainburn Rd. LS17: Leeds .7F 50
Stainburn Ter. LS17: Leeds .7F 50
Stainburn Vw. LS17: Leeds .6G 50
STAINCLIFFE .8E 102
Staincliffe Cl. WF13: Dew .2D 122
Staincliffe Ct. BD20: Sils .8D 12
Staincliffe Cres. WF13: Dew .1C 122
Staincliffe Hall Rd. WF17: Bat .9C 102
Staincliffe Rd. WF13: Dew .9C 102
Staincliffe Vw. WF13: Dew .1C 122
STAINCROSS .7K 159
Staincross Comn. S75: S'ross .6K 159
Stainecross Av. HD4: Hud .8H 137
Staines Cft. HD5: Hud .4C 138
STAINLAND .7M 117
Stainland Dean HX4: Holy .1K 135
Stainland Rd. HD3: Outl .2N 135
HX4: Bark .7G 116
HX4: Gree .2C 118
HX4: Holy, Sow, Stainl .8M 117
Stainmore Cl. LS14: Leeds .3B 70
Stainmore Pl. LS14: Leeds .3B 70
Stainton Cl. BD6: B'frd .5K 81
Stainton La. WF3: Carl .9M 87
Staircase La. LS16: B'hpe .2G 33
LS21: Pool .2G 33
Stairfoot Cl. LS16: Leeds .2N 49
Stairfoot La. LS16: Leeds .2N 49
LS17: Leeds .2N 49
Stairfoot Vw. LS16: Leeds .2N 49
Stairfoot Wlk. LS16: Leeds .2N 49
STAIRS .4M 59
Stairs La. BD22: Oxen .6K 59
Staithe Av. LS10: Leeds .8F 86
Staithe Cl. LS10: Leeds .8F 86
Staithe Gdns. LS10: Leeds .8F 86
Staithes, The BD17: Bail .4A 46
(off Baildon Rd.)
Staithgate La. BD4: B'frd .4D 82
BD6: B'frd .4D 82
Stake La. HX7: Crag V .5N 95
Stake La. Bank HD9: H'frth .3N 169
Stakes Fold WF16: Heck .8B 102
Staley Royd La. HD9: Jack B .4D 170
Stallabrass St. BD8: B'frd .6A 64
Stamford Av. WF10: C'frd .6A 108
Stamford St. BD4: B'frd .9F 64
Stamford Way S75: S'ross .7K 159
Stammergate La. LS22: Lin .8J 23
Stamp Hill Cl. LS29: Add .1K 13
Stanacre Pl. BD3: B'frd .1D 6 (6D 64)
Stanage La. HX3: She .6H 81
Stanbeck Ct. LS7: Leeds .7E 50
STANBURY .8L 41
Stancliffe Way HD5: K'htn .1F 138
Standale Av. LS28: Pud .6A 66
Standale Cres. LS28: Pud .6A 66
Standale Ri. LS28: Pud .6A 66
Standard Dr. HD4: Hud .8G 136
Standard Vs. LS12: Leeds .1L 85
Standback Way HD8: Skelm .6C 156
STAND BRIDGE .4L 143
Standbridge Cl. WF2: Wake .5J 143
Standbridge Gth. WF4: Crig .4H 143
Standbridge La. WF2: Wake .4L 143
WF4: Crig .5H 143
Standedge Tunnel Vis. Cen. .5D 150
Standhill Cres. S71: Smit .9N 159
Standiforth La. HD5: Hud .3C 138
Standiforth Pl. HD5: Hud .4D 138
Standiforth Rd. HD5: Hud .4B 138
Standinghurst HD8: Shel .4M 155
Standish Cres. WF9: S Kirk .5J 163
Stanhall Av. LS28: Stan .5A 66
Stanhall M. LS28: Stan .5A 66
Stanhope Av. LS18: Hors .5F 48
Stanhope Cl. LS18: Hors .5F 48
Stanhope Cotts. LS21: Pool .1F 32
(off The Old Orchard)
Stanhope Ct. LS18: Hors .4E 48
Stanhope Dr. LS18: Hors .7E 48
Stanhope Gdns. WF3: Thpe H .3G 105
Stanhope Gro. WF3: Thpe H .3G 105
Stanhope Rd. WF3: Thpe H .3G 104
Stanhope St. HD8: Clay W .8G 157
STANK .2F 34
STANKS .1E 70
Stanks App. LS14: Leeds .2E 70
Stanks Av. LS14: Leeds .2E 70
Stanks Cl. LS14: Leeds .2F 70
Stanks Cross LS14: Leeds .2F 70
Stanks Dr. LS14: Leeds .9D 52
Stanks Gdns. LS14: Leeds .1E 70
Stanks Gth. LS14: Leeds .2F 70
Stanks Grn. LS14: Leeds .2F 70
Stanks Gro. LS14: Leeds .2E 70
Stanks La. Nth. LS14: Leeds .9D 52
Stanks La. Sth. LS14: Leeds .2E 70
Stanks Pde. LS14: Leeds .2E 70
Stanks Ri. LS14: Leeds .2F 70
Stanks Rd. LS14: Leeds .2E 70
Stanks Way LS14: Leeds .2E 70
Stanleigh Cft. HX7: Heb B .1G 95
STANLEY .7A 106
Stanley Av. LS9: Leeds .4H 69
Stanley Cotts. WF6: Norm .1H 127
Stanley Ct. HD3: Hud .3J 137
(off Shires Fold)
HX1: Hal .5M 97
(off Walsh St.)
Stanley Cryer Ct. OL14: Tod .6M 93
(off Dover St.)
Stanley Dr. LS8: Leeds .5K 51
STANLEY FERRY .9C 106
Stanley Ferry Aqueduct .9C 106
Stanley Gth. WF16: Heck .8B 102
Stanley Gro. LS20: Guis .8J 31
Stanley Ho. LS10: Leeds .8F 68
Stanley La. HX4: Stainl .8M 117
WF1: Out .8M 105
WF15: Liv .7L 101
Stanley Marsh Nature Reserve .8N 105
Stanley Mills Bus. Pk. HD3: Hud .6E 136
Stanley Pl. HD7: Golc .6C 136
LS9: Leeds .4J 69
WF17: Bat .7G 102
Stanley Rd. BD2: B'frd .2B 64
BD22: Keigh .3G 42
HD3: Hud .1H 137
(Holly Bank Rd.)
HD3: Hud .7F 118
(Lindley Moor Rd.)
HD7: Slait .3K 151
HX1: Hal .6M 97
LS7: Leeds .3F 68
LS9: Leeds .4H 69
WF1: Wake .4M 9 (5M 125)
WF15: Liv .1L 121
Stanley St. BD10: B'frd .8H 47
(Fieldgate Rd.)
BD10: B'frd .7F 46
(Moorfield Pl.)
BD16: Bgly .4F 44
BD18: Ship .1A 64
BD19: Cleck .4H 101
BD21: Keigh .8H 27
BD22: Cros R .7E 42
HD1: Hud .7K 137
HD6: Brigh .9N 99
HD9: Holm .6J 169
HX6: Sow B .8J 97
WF1: Wake .3M 9 (5M 125)
WF7: F'stne .4D 128
WF10: C'frd .4E 108
Stanley St. Nth. HX2: Hal .8N 79
(off Shay La.)
Stanley St. W. HX6: Sow B .9H 97
(off Salisbury St.)
Stanley Ter. LS9: Leeds .4J 69
(not continuous)
LS12: Leeds .7M 67
WF17: Bat .6G 102
(off Stanley Pl.)
Stanley Vw. LS12: Leeds .7M 67
Stanley Vs. HD5: K'htn .1G 138
Stanmoor Dr. WF3: S'ley .6N 105
Stanmore Av. LS4: Leeds .3M 67
Stanmore Cres. LS4: Leeds .3M 67
Stanmore Gro. LS4: Leeds .3M 67
Stanmore Hill LS4: Leeds .3N 67
Stanmore Mt. LS4: Leeds .3M 67
Stanmore Pl. BD7: B'frd .9M 63
LS4: Leeds .3M 67
Stanmore Rd. LS4: Leeds .3M 67
Stanmore St. LS4: Leeds .3M 67
Stanmore Ter. LS4: Leeds .3M 67
Stanmore Vw. LS4: Leeds .3M 67
Stannally St. OL14: Tod .4G 93
Stannard Well Dr. WF4: Horb .9D 124
Stannard Well La. WF4: Horb .9D 124
Stannary HX4: Stainl .7N 117
Stannary Pl. HX1: Hal .2J 7 (4A 98)
Stannery End La. HX7: Crag V .5N 95
Stanningden Ri. HX6: Ripp .9C 116
STANNINGLEY .4C 66
Stanningley Av. HX2: Mix .8H 79
Stanningley By-Pass LS13: Leeds .5M 65
LS28: Stan .5M 65
Stanningley Ct. LS28: Stan .4C 66
(off Leeds & Bradford Rd.)
Stanningley Dr. HX2: Mix .8H 79
Stanningley Fld. Cl. LS13: Leeds .5D 66
Stanningley Grn. HX2: Mix .7J 79
Stanningley Gro. WF16: Heck .9A 102
Stanningley Ind. Est. LS28: Stan .5A 66
Stanningley Loft LS28: Stan .5B 66
(off Town St.)
Stanningley Rd. HX2: Mix .8H 79
LS12: Leeds .5H 67
LS13: Leeds .4D 66
LS28: Stan .4C 66
Stansfield Cl. HX1: Hal .3G 7 (5N 97)
WF10: C'frd .3H 109
Stansfield Ct. HX6: Sow B .9H 97
OL14: Tod .6K 93
(off Stansfield Hall Rd.)
Stansfield Dr. WF10: C'frd .4J 109
Stansfield Fold LS18: Hors .5F 48
(off Rockery Rd.)
Stansfield Grange HX6: Tri .2E 116
Stansfield Hall OL15: Lit .9L 113
Stansfield Hall Rd. OL14: Tod .6K 93
Stansfield Hey HX6: Ripp .9A 116
Stansfield Mill La. HX6: Norl, Tri .2E 116
Stansfield Pl. BD10: B'frd .6F 46
Stansfield Rd. OL14: Tod .7K 93
WF10: C'frd .3G 109

Stansfield St.—Stoney Bank Rd.

Stansfield St. OL14: Tod 6K **93**
Stansfield Ter. *OL14: Tod* *3D* ***92***
(off Parkside Rd.)
Stan Valley WF8: Lit S 4K **149**
Stanwell Av. HD2: Hud 1J **137**
Stanwell La. DN6: Moor 8D **164**
(not continuous)
Stanwick Ho. BD2: B'frd 2B **64**
Staples La. BD21: Keigh 8G **43**
STAPLETON 7H **131**
Stapleton Ho. BD2: B'frd 2B **64**
Stapleton Pk. Cotts. WF8: Stap 7G **130**
Stapper Grn. BD15: Wils 9A **44**
Starbeck Rd. WF1: Wake 3N **125**
Starkie St. BD21: Keigh 1H **43**
Starling Ho. *WF9: Hems* *3D* ***162***
(off Lilley St.)
Starling M. *BD15: All* *7G* ***62***
(off Greenway Dr.)
Star St. BD5: B'frd 2A **82**
Star Ter. HD6: Ras 4K **119**
Starting Post BD10: B'frd 8D **46**
Starwort Cl. WF8: Pon 4K **129**
Station Apartments *LS15: Leeds* *4D* ***70***
(off Station Rd.)
Station App. HD9: Hon 4M **153**
HX1: Hal 5M **7** (6C **98**)
LS5: Leeds 2L **67**
LS29: Burl W 9C **16**
OL14: Tod 7K **93**
WF11: Knot *8D* ***110***
(off Pontefract Rd.)
Station Av. LS13: Leeds 4E **66**
Station Bri. *BD21: Keigh* *9K* ***27***
(off Bradford Rd.)
Station Cl. LS25: Gar 7N **71**
Station Cotts. LS14: T'ner 1G **53**
LS17: Huby 5N **19**
LS24: N Kym 2J **39**
S75: Dart 8G **158**
WF4: Wrag 5L **145**
Station Ct. BD1: B'frd 4C **6** (7D **64**)
HD8: Clay W 6J **157**
HD8: Fen B 7G **139**
LS15: Leeds 5D **70**
LS25: Gar 6N **71**
Station Cres. LS12: Leeds 7L **67**
Station Flds. LS25: Gar 7N **71**
Station Gdns. LS15: Scho 8G **52**
LS22: Weth 4L **23**
Station Ho. *LS25: M'fld* *8G* ***73***
(off Old Great Nth. Rd.)
Station Ind. Pk. HX2: Lud F 5D **96**
Station La. BD11: B'haw 7L **83**
HD4: Hud 1L **153**
HD7: Golc 7C **136**
HD8: Shep 8K **155**
HX4: Gree 3C **118**
LS14: T'ner 1G **53**
LS22: Coll 8J **23**
LS26: W'frd 6E **88**
WF3: E Ard 3F **104**
WF3: Ting 2A **104**
(not continuous)
WF7: F'stne 5C **128**
WF8: Pon 3K **129**
WF16: Heck 1N **121**
Station Mt. LS13: Leeds 4E **66**
Station Pde. LS5: Leeds 2L **67**
OL14: Tod 3B **92**
Station Pas. WF1: Wake 6L **9** (6M **125**)
Station Pl. LS13: Leeds 4F **66**
Station Plaza *LS29: I'ly* *5G* ***15***
(off Railway Rd.)
Station Rd. BD1: B'frd 4C **64**
BD11: Drig 8B **84**
BD12: Low M 8C **82**
BD12: Wyke 2M **99**
BD13: Cull 9J **43**
BD13: Denh 6K **61**
BD13: Que 3E **80**
BD14: Clay 1H **81**
BD15: Wils 3M **61**
BD17: Bail 4A **46**
BD17: Esh 1F **46**
BD18: Ship 7N **45**
BD20: Stee 3D **26**
BD22: Haw 8C **42**
BD22: Oak 5D **42**
BD22: Oxen 3C **60**
DN6: Wome 9N **131**
HD2: Hud 6E **120**
HD4: Stock 7G **155**
HD6: Clift 1A **120**
HD7: Golc 6C **136**
HD7: Mars 5F **150**
HD7: Slait 9M **135**
HD8: Fen B 7G **139**
HD8: Shep 9J **155**
HD8: Skelm 7D **156**
HD9: H'frth 3M **169**
HD9: Hon 4M **153**
HD9: Mel 7D **152**
HX2: Lud F 5D **96**
HX3: Hal 8N **79**
HX3: Hip 5H **99**
HX3: Nor G 2M **99**
HX4: Holy 7A **118**
HX6: Sow B 9H **97**
HX7: Heb B 2H **95**
LS12: Leeds 7L **67**
LS15: Leeds 4D **70**
LS15: Scho 8G **52**
LS18: Hors 5F **48**
LS20: Guis 7H **31**
LS21: Arth 2J **33**
LS21: Otley 1L **31**
LS25: Gar 7N **71**
LS25: Kip 5N **89**
LS26: Meth 1J **107**
LS27: Morl 8K **85**
LS29: Burl W 9C **16**
LS29: I'ly 5G **14**
LS29: Men 4F **30**
OL14: Tod 3E **92**
Station Rd. S71: Roys 4C **160**
S75: Dart 8G **159**
WF4: Ryh 9H **145**
WF5: Oss 6N **123**
(not continuous)
WF6: Alt 9G **107**
WF7: Ackw 3G **147**
WF8: E Hard 2J **147**
WF9: Hems 2D **162**
WF9: S Elm 6N **163**
WF10: All B 9B **90**
WF10: C'frd 4D **108**
WF11: Ferr 7B **110**
WF12: Dew 5J **123**
(Becks Ct., not continuous)
WF12: Dew 6F **122**
(Lees Ho. Rd.)
WF14: Mir 7L **121**
WF16: Heck 9A **102**
WF17: Bat 8G **103**
Station Rd. Ind. Est.
LS25: Kip 6N **89**
Station Sq. LS28: Stan 5N **65**
Station St. HD1: Hud 4B **8** (4M **137**)
HD9: Mel 7C **152**
LS28: Pud 8A **66**
WF1: Wake 9N **125**
Station Ter. HD8: Skelm 7C **156**
LS13: Leeds 4F **66**
S71: Roys 5F **160**
WF10: All B 9C **90**
Station Vw. BD20: Stee 3D **26**
BD22: Oxen 3C **60**
HX7: Heb B 2J **95**
LS15: Leeds 5D **70**
Station Wlk. LS27: Morl 8L **85**
Station Way LS12: Leeds 7L **67**
Station Works Ind. Pk.
BD21: Keigh 9L **27**
Staups La. HX3: North 2E **98**
OL14: Tod 1A **94**
Staveley Ct. BD16: Bgly 3F **44**
BD18: Ship 7J **45**
BD22: Keigh 3G **42**
Staveley Dr. BD18: Ship 8J **45**
Staveley Gro. BD22: Keigh 4G **42**
Staveley M. BD16: Bgly 3F **44**
Staveley Rd. BD7: B'frd 8N **63**
BD16: Bgly 3F **44**
BD18: Ship 7J **45**
BD22: Keigh 4G **42**
Staveley Way BD22: Keigh 3G **42**
Staverton Gro. BD13: Thorn 7D **62**
Staverton St. HX2: Hal 5L **97**
Stax Trade Cen. LS27: Morl 3K **103**
Staybrite Av. BD16: Cot 8F **44**
STAYGATE 3C **82**
Staygate Grn. BD6: B'frd 4C **82**
Staynton Cres. HD2: Hud 6D **120**
(not continuous)
STEAD 8M **15**
Stead Ga. HD8: Shel 7A **156**
Stead Hill Way BD10: B'frd 6D **46**
Steadings Way BD22: Keigh 2E **42**
Stead La. BD16: Bgly 1J **45**
HD5: K'htn 2F **138**
HX6: Ripp 9C **116**
LS14: T'ner 2G **53**
LS29: Burl W 9N **15**
Steadman St. BD3: B'frd 8F **64**
Steadman Ter. BD3: B'frd 8F **64**
Stead Rd. BD4: B'frd 5J **83**
Stead St. BD17: Ship 7N **45**
HX1: Hal 4J **7** (5A **98**)
(not continuous)
Steads Yd. LS18: Hors 5F **48**
Steanard La. WF14: Mir 8M **121**
Steed Ct. Bus. Pk. WF9: Upt 2B **164**
Steele La. HX4: Holy 9H **117**
Steel Grn. LS12: N Far 2K **85**
STEEL LANE HEAD 9H **117**
Steel Ter. *LS26: Rothw* *8A* ***88***
(off Bk. Gillett La.)
Steep Bank Side HX3: Hal 6D **98**
Steep Fields Footpath *HX7: Heb B* *9H* ***77***
(off Foster La.)
Steeplands HD2: Hud 5D **120**
STEEP LANE 8B **96**
Steep La. HD2: Hud 5D **120**
HX6: Sow B 8A **96**
Steeple Av. WF4: G Moor 6B **140**
Steeple Cl. LS27: Morl 3L **103**
Steeple Vw. HD7: Golc 6C **136**
Steep Riding HD9: Brock 6A **154**
Steerforth Cl. *BD5: B'frd* *2C* ***82***
(off Mumford St.)
STEETON 3C **26**
Steeton & Silsden Station (Rail) 2D **26**
Steeton Gro. BD20: Stee 2C **26**
Steeton Hall Gdns. BD20: Stee 2C **26**
Stella Gdns. WF8: Pon 1M **129**
Stell Hill BD22: Keigh 2D **42**
Stennard Island WF1: Wake 7M **9** (6M **125**)
Stephen Cl. HX3: North 3F **98**
Stephen Cres. BD2: B'frd 3C **64**
Stephen G Beaumont Mus. 2M **125**
Stephen Rd. BD6: B'frd 3L **81**
Stephen Row *HX3: North* *2F* ***98***
(off Towngate)
Stephenson Cl. WF12: Dew 2H **123**
Stephenson Dr. LS12: N Far 2G **85**
Stephenson Ho. *LS27: Morl* *8L* ***85***
(off Pullman Ct.)
Stephenson Rd. BD15: All 4C **62**
Stephenson St. BD7: B'frd 2N **81**
Stephensons Way LS29: I'ly 5G **15**
Stephenson Way LS12: N Far 2G **85**
WF2: Carr G 7H **105**
Stephen St. HX7: Heb B 1H **95**
Stepping Stones BD20: E Mor 8D **28**
HX6: Ripp 8D **116**
STEPS 3L **153**
Steps, The HX6: Sow B 7J **97**
Steps Ind. Pk. HD9: Hon 3L **153**
Steps La. HX6: Sow B 7J **97**
Sterling Ct. WF3: Ting 2A **104**
WF8: Pon *3J* ***129***
(off Halfpenny La.)
Sterling Ind. Pk. WF10: C'frd 7F **108**
Sterling Way WF3: Ting 2N **103**
Stevenson Av. WF10: C'frd 7J **109**
Stewart Cl. BD2: B'frd 1G **65**
LS15: Leeds 7D **70**
Stewart Ho. *HD1: Hud* *5C* ***8***
(off Oldgate)
Stewart Royd WF16: Heck 8B **102**
Stewart St. BD22: Cros R 7E **42**
Sticker La. BD4: B'frd 2G **82**
STILE 1E **116**
STILE COMMON 7N **137**
Stile Comn. Rd. HD4: Hud 6N **137**
Stile Hill Way LS15: Leeds 7G **70**
Stile Moor Ri. OL14: Tod 5J **93**
Stile Rd. OL14: Tod 5J **93**
Stile Ter. HX6: Tri 2E **116**
Stile Way BD9: B'frd 3N **63**
Stillington Ho. BD2: B'frd 2B **64**
Stillwell Dr. WF2: Wake 2N **143**
Stillwell Gth. WF2: Wake 2N **143**
Stillwell Gro. WF2: Wake 2N **143**
Stirley Hill HD4: Hud 2N **153**
Stirling Cres. BD4: B'frd 2J **83**
LS18: Hors 3D **48**
Stirling Rd. LS29: Burl W 8B **16**
Stirling St. BD20: Sils 7E **12**
HX1: Hal 5H **7** (6A **98**)
Stirling Way LS25: Gar 7B **72**
Stirrup Gro. BD2: B'frd 2D **64**
Stirton St. BD5: B'frd 2B **82**
Stithy St. WF5: Oss 3M **123**
(not continuous)
Stock A Ho's. BD16: Cot 9E **44**
STOCKBRIDGE 7L **27**
Stockbridge Wharf BD20: Rid 7M **27**
Stockeld La. LS22: Sick 3E **22**
Stockeld Pk. House 2F **22**
Stockeld Rd. LS29: I'ly 5F **14**
Stockeld Way LS29: I'ly 4F **14**
Stockerhead HD7: Slait 2N **151**
Stockerhead La. HD7: Slait 1N **151**
Stockheld La. LS15: Leeds, Scho 6G **53**
Stock Hey La. OL14: Tod 6C **94**
Stockhill Fold BD10: B'frd 7H **47**
(not continuous)
Stockhill Rd. BD10: B'frd 8H **47**
Stockhill St. WF13: Dew 3D **122**
Stockingate WF9: S Kirk 8H **163**
Stockinger La. LS29: Add 1M **13**
Stocking La. LS25: Aber 9F **54**
WF11: Knot 8H **111**
Stock La. HX2: Hal 6H **97**
Stocks App. LS14: Leeds 2C **70**
Stocks Av. HX7: Myth 4L **95**
STOCKS BANK 6J **121**
Stocks Bank Dr. WF14: Mir 5H **121**
Stocks Bank Rd. WF14: Mir 4H **121**
Stocks Cres. HX7: Myth 4L **95**
Stocks Dr. HD8: Shep 9H **155**
HX7: Myth 4L **95**
Stocksfield Vw. BD13: Que 4G **80**
Stocks Gdns. HX7: Myth 4L **95**
Stocks Hill LS11: Leeds 9C **68**
LS12: Leeds 6M **67**
LS26: Meth *1L* ***107***
(off Hicks La.)
LS29: Men 4D **30**
Stocks Hill Cl. BD20: E Mor 7C **28**
Stockshill Cl. S71: Carl 8D **160**
Stocks Hill Gth. *LS29: Men* *4D* ***30***
(off Stocks Hill)
Stocks La. BD13: Que 4G **81**
HD4: Stock 8F **154**
HX2: Lud, Mt T 3E **96**
HX6: Sow B 9E **96**
HX7: Myth 4L **95**
WF17: Bat 7F **102**
STOCKSMOOR 7G **154**
Stocksmoor Common Nature Reserve 7M **141**
Stocksmoor La. WF4: Midg 8N **141**
Stocks Moor Rd. HD4: Stock 7E **154**
Stocksmoor Rd. WF4: Midg 8M **141**
Stocksmoor Station (Rail) 7G **155**
Stocks Ri. LS14: Leeds 2C **70**
Stocks Rd. LS14: Leeds 2D **70**
Stocks St. LS7: Leeds 3E **68**
Stocks Vs. HX7: Hept 8G **77**
Stocks Wlk. HD5: Hud 7D **138**
Stocks Way HD8: Shep 9H **155**
Stockwell Ct. S75: W Gran 6F **158**
Stockwell Dr. WF17: Bat 6F **102**
Stockwell Hill HD4: Hud 1L **153**
Stockwell Va. HD4: Arm B 1L **153**
Stod Fold HX2: Ogd 5J **79**
Stogden Hill BD13: Que 4G **80**
Stone Acre Ct. BD5: B'frd 3C **82**
Stone Acre Hgts. HD9: Mel 8E **152**
Stonebank Gdns. LS17: Bard 4E **36**
Stonebridge App. LS12: Leeds 8H **67**
Stonebridge Av. LS12: Leeds 8J **67**
Stone Bri. Ct. *LS12: Leeds* *8H* ***67***
(off Farnley Cres.)
Stonebridge Gro. LS12: Leeds 8H **67**
Stonebridge Idlecroft Rd. *BD10: B'frd* *7F* ***46***
(off Idlecroft Rd.)
Stonebridge La. LS12: Leeds 9H **67**
Stone Bri. Lea *LS12: Leeds* *8H* ***67***
(off Farnley Cres.)
Stonebridge Wlk. HD8: Shep 8K **155**
Stone Brig Grn. LS26: Rothw 9M **87**
Stone Brig La. LS26: Rothw 9M **87**
STONE CHAIR 9G **81**
Stonechat Ri. LS27: Morl 9M **85**
Stone Cliffe *HX3: Hal* *8N* ***97***
(off Skircoat Moor Cl.)
Stonecliffe Bank LS12: Leeds 8H **67**
Stonecliffe Cl. LS12: Leeds 8H **67**
Stonecliffe Cres. LS12: Leeds 8H **67**
Stonecliffe Dr. LS12: Leeds 8H **67**
WF4: M'twn 3L **141**
Stonecliffe Gdns. LS12: Leeds 8H **67**
Stonecliffe Gth. LS12: Leeds 8H **67**
Stonecliffe Grn. LS12: Leeds 8H **67**
Stonecliffe Gro. LS12: Leeds 8H **67**
Stonecliffe Lawn LS12: Leeds 8H **67**
Stonecliffe Mt. LS12: Leeds 8H **67**
Stonecliffe Pl. *LS12: Leeds* *8H* ***67***
(off Stonebridge La.)
Stonecliffe Ter. LS12: Leeds 8H **67**
Stonecliffe Vw. LS12: Leeds 8H **67**
Stonecliffe Wlk. LS12: N Far 9H **67**
Stonecliffe Way LS12: Leeds 8H **67**
Stone Ct. BD20: E Mor 8C **28**
S72: S Hien 4M **161**
Stonecroft BD2: B'frd 2G **64**
WF3: S'ley 7N **105**
Stone Cft. Ct. LS26: Oul 8D **88**
Stonecroft Fold HX2: Lud F 7D **96**
Stonecroft Gdns. HD8: Shep 9K **155**
Stonecroft Mt. HX6: Sow B 6J **97**
Stonecrop Dr. WF10: C'frd 7A **108**
Stonecross BD15: Wils 1B **62**
Stonedale Cl. LS21: Pool 2H **33**
Stonedene LS6: Leeds 7B **50**
Stonedene Ct. WF16: Heck 7B **102**
Stonedene Pk. LS22: Weth 3N **23**
Stonefield LS14: S'cft 8E **36**
Stonefield Av. HD4: Hud 7G **137**
Stonefield Cl. BD2: B'frd 1F **64**
Stonefield Pl. WF17: Birs 3C **102**
Stonefield Rd. HD4: Hud 7G **137**
Stonefield St. BD19: Cleck 6E **100**
WF13: Dew 2F **122**
Stonefield Ter. LS27: Chur 5M **85**
Stonefleece Ct. HD9: Hon 6L **153**
Stone Fold BD17: Bail 5M **45**
HD9: Hon 5L **153**
Stone Folds La. HD7: Mars 3E **150**
Stonegate BD16: Bgly 2F **44**
LS7: Leeds 3E **68**
(not continuous)
WF5: Oss 8A **124**
Stonegate App. LS7: Leeds 9B **50**
Stonegate Chase LS7: Leeds 8B **50**
Stonegate Cl. LS17: Leeds 4F **50**
Stone Ga. Ct. HD4: Hud 8K **137**
Stonegate Cres. LS7: Leeds 8C **50**
Stonegate Dr. LS7: Leeds 8C **50**
WF8: Pon 5J **129**
Stonegate Edge LS7: Leeds 8C **50**
Stonegate Farm Cl. LS7: Leeds 8B **50**
Stonegate Gdns. LS7: Leeds 8B **50**
Stonegate Grn. LS7: Leeds 9B **50**
Stonegate Gro. LS7: Leeds 8C **50**
Stone Ga. Ho. BD1: B'frd 2B **6**
Stonegate La. LS7: Leeds 8B **50**
WF7: Ackw 5E **146**
Stonegate M. LS7: Leeds 9B **50**
Stonegate Pl. LS7: Leeds 9B **50**
Stonegate Rd. BD10: B'frd 9F **46**
LS6: Leeds 8B **50**
LS17: Leeds 8B **50**
Stonegate Vw. LS7: Leeds 8B **50**
Stonegate Wlk. LS7: Leeds 9C **50**
Stonegate Way LS17: Leeds 5E **50**
Stone Gro. BD20: Stee 3C **26**
(not continuous)
Stone Hall M. BD2: B'frd 2G **64**
Stone Hall Rd. BD2: B'frd 2F **64**
Stonehaven Ct. BD21: Keigh 2L **43**
Stone Hill BD16: Bgly 3G **45**
Stonehouse Dr. BD13: Que 5B **80**
Stone Ho. Fold BD22: Oak 5B **42**
Stonehurst LS14: Leeds 2E **70**
Stonehurst Rd. WF14: Mir 5L **121**
Stonehyrst Av. WF13: Dew 2G **122**
Stone La. BD22: Oxen 4A **60**
Stonelea BD4: B'frd 5L **83**
HX4: Bark 6G **117**
Stonelea Ct. LS6: Leeds 1N **67**
LS7: Leeds 8C **50**
Stonelea Dr. HD6: Ras 4L **119**
Stone Lea Gro. WF9: S Elm 7N **163**
Stoneleigh BD13: Que 4E **80**
Stoneleigh Av. LS17: Leeds 3H **51**
Stoneleigh Cl. LS17: Leeds 3H **51**
Stoneleigh Cotts. WF4: Wint 6H **145**
Stoneleigh Ct. BD19: Scho 3C **100**
HD8: Shel 6L **155**
LS17: Leeds 3H **51**
Stoneleigh Gth. LS17: Leeds 4H **51**
Stoneleigh Gro. WF5: Oss 6N **123**
Stoneleigh La. LS17: Leeds 4H **51**
Stoneleigh Way LS17: Leeds 4H **51**
Stonely Dr. OL14: W'den 4J **113**
Stonemere Av. OL14: Tod 6N **93**
Stone Mill App. LS6: Leeds 8A **50**
Stone Mill Ct. LS6: Leeds 8A **50**
Stone Mill Way LS6: Leeds 8A **50**
Stone Pits La. LS27: Gil 7G **85**
Stoneroyd WF4: G Moor 5B **140**
Stoneroyd Farm WF4: Flock 7G **141**
Stones Bank HX6: Ripp 9C **116**
Stones Dr. HX6: Ripp 9B **116**
Stones Hey Ga. HX7: Hept 7E **76**
Stones La. HD7: Golc 7C **136**
HD7: Linth 1B **152**
OL14: Tod 7G **92**
Stones Rd. OL14: Tod 8H **93**
Stone Stay Fold LS29: Add 1L **13**
Stones Ter. OL14: W'den 1H **113**
Stone St. BD1: B'frd 3B **6** (7C **64**)
BD13: Que *3B* ***80***
(off Derwent Pl.)
BD15: All 3F **62**
BD17: Bail 5C **46**
BD19: Cleck 5G **101**
BD22: Haw *9C* ***42***
(off Jacky La.)
Stone Ter. BD16: Har 5A **44**
Stone Vs. LS6: Leeds 9N **49**
Stonewaite Ct. LS26: W'frd 7C **88**
Stone Wood La. HD4: Stock 8G **155**
HD8: Shep 8G **155**
Stoney Bank La. HD9: New M 9B **154**
Stoney Bank Rd. HD9: New M, T'bdge 9A **154**

Stoney Bank St.—Sunnybank Rd.

Stoney Bank St. WF13: Dew 5D 122
Stoney Battery HX3: Hal 1L 7 (4B 98)
Stoney Battery Rd. HD1: Hud 6J 137
Stoneybrook Cl. WF4: W Bret 1B 158
Stoney Brow HX3: Hal 8D 98
Stoneybutts La. HX4: Bark 6H 117
Stoney Cft. BD19: Gom 5M 101
Stoneycroft LS18: Hors 7E 48
LS19: Raw 3N 47
(off Batter La.)
Stoneycroft La. BD20: Keigh 6H 27
Stoney Cross St. HD4: Hud 8L 137
Stoney Ford La. HD5: K'htn 1F 138
Stoney Gth. WF4: Hol 7H 143
Stoney Hill HD6: Ras 1M 119
Stoneyhurst Sq. BD4: B'frd 2J 83
Stoneyhurst Way BD4: B'frd 2J 83
Stoney La. HD3: Hud 4D 136
HD4: Hud 8L 137
HX2: Hal 7M 97
HX3: Hal 1N 97
HX3: Hip 5M 99
HX3: Sou 7H 99
HX7: Heb B 1G 95
(off Bridges La.)
HX7: Myth 2A 96
HX7: P Wel 5J 77
LS17: Shad 2B 52
LS18: Hors 7E 48
LS26: Meth 4F 106
LS29: Burl W 2A 30
WF2: Kirk 7F 104
WF3: E Ard 7E 104
WF4: Chap, Hol 8H 143
WF14: Mir 4A 122
WF17: Bat 6G 102
Stoney Ridge Av. BD9: B'frd 2G 63
Stoney Ridge Rd. BD16: Cot 2G 63
Stoney Ri. LS18: Hors 7E 48
Stoney Rock Ct. LS9: Leeds 4M 5 (5H 69)
Stoney Rock Gro. LS9: Leeds 4M 5 (5H 69)
Stoney Rock La. LS9: Leeds 4M 5 (5H 69)
STONEY ROYD 8M 7 (7C 98)
Stoney Royd LS29: Burl W 7C 16
(off Main St.)
S71: Ath 8A 160
Stoney Royd La. OL14: Tod 4H 93
Stoney Royd Ter. HD7: Linth 1B 152
(off Holyoake Av.)
HX3: Hal 8M 7 (8C 98)
Stoneys Fold BD15: Wils 9A 44
Stoney Springs Ho. HX2: Lud F 4B 96
Stoney Springs Ind. Units HX2: Lud F 4B 96
Stoney St. BD20: Keigh 6H 27
Stoneythorpe LS18: Hors 7E 48
Stony Cliffe Wood (Nature Reserve) 6M 141
Stony Cft. La. DN6: Burg, Skel 6M 165
HX4: Bark 6H 117
Stony Ga. HD9: H'frth 6K 169
Stony Head OL15: Lit 9L 113
(off Higher Calderbrook Rd.)
Stony Hill WF8: Pon 2L 129
(off Southgate)
Stony La. BD2: B'frd 1G 64
BD15: All 4E 62
BD22: Oak 1A 42
HD8: Clay W 9G 157
HD9: Hon 5L 153
HX4: Gree 3N 117
HX6: Ripp 6D 116
HX7: Heb B 2D 94
HX7: Hept 7B 76
OL14: Tod 2G 92
Stony Royd LS28: Fars 3N 65
Stony Royd La. HX7: Crag V 8H 95
Stoodley Cl. OL14: Tod 7B 94
Stoodley Glen OL14: Tod 5B 94
Stoodley Grange OL14: Tod 7C 94
Stoodley La. OL14: Tod 5B 94
Stoodley Pike Monument 7D 94
Stoodley Ter. HX2: Hal 6L 97
Stoodley Vw. HX7: Heb B 9J 77
Stopford Av. WF2: Wake 2N 143
Stopford Gth. WF2: Wake 2N 143
Storey Pl. LS14: Leeds 5N 69
Storie Cres. WF2: Wake 7G 125
STORITHS 1N 11
Storiths Ct. LS29: Add 2M 13
Storiths La. BD23: Haz, Stor 1N 11
Stormer Hill HX6: Norl 1K 117
Stormer Hill La. HX6: Norl 1K 117
Storr Hill BD12: Wyke 9A 82
Storr Hill Ter. BD12: Wyke 9A 82
Storrs Hill Rd. WF4: Horb 1A 142
WF5: Oss 1A 142
Storth Av. HD4: Hud 7E 136
Storthes Hall La. HD8: Kbtn 4F 154
Storth La. HD2: Hud 9K 119
Storth Lea HX5: Ell 6G 118
Storth Pl. HD2: Hud 1L 137
Storths Rd. HD2: Hud 1K 137
Storth Vw. HX5: Ell 6G 118
Story Stones BD16: Bgly 2J 45
Stott Cl. HX1: Hal 4M 97
Stott Gap BD13: Thorn 7C 62
Stott Hill BD1: B'frd 3C 6 (7D 64)
Stott Rd. LS6: Leeds 3A 68
Stott St. LS12: Leeds 7N 67
Stott Ter. BD2: B'frd 2H 65
STOURTON 4K 87
Stourton Bus. Pk. LS10: Leeds 3J 87
Stourton Rd. LS29: I'ly 4E 14
Stowe Gro. LS9: Leeds 6L 69
Stowell Mill St. BD5: B'frd 1B 82
Stradbroke Ct. HX6: Sow B 6J 97
Stradbroke Way LS12: Leeds 8M 67
Stradmore Rd. BD13: Denh 6L 61
Strafford St. S75: Kex 9E 158
Strafford Way BD10: B'frd 7J 47
Straightacres La. BD10: B'frd 1H 65
Straight La. DN6: S'brk 6F 164
HX2: Mix 8K 79
LS29: Add 4J 13
Strait La. LS17: Huby 5M 19
Straits BD17: Bail 3A 46
Stralau St. WF17: Bat 6F 102
Strand BD16: Cot 9G 45
Strands Ct. WF4: Neth 4A 142
Strangford Ct. BD10: B'frd 7H 47
Stranglands La. WF11: Ferr 6M 109
Stratford Av. LS11: Leeds 2C 86
Stratford Cl. HD7: Golc 5D 136
Stratford Ct. LS7: Leeds 9E 50
Stratford Rd. BD7: B'frd 9N 63
Stratford St. LS11: Leeds 3D 86
Stratford Ter. LS11: Leeds 2D 86
Strathallan Dr. BD17: Bail 4B 46
Stratheden Rd. WF2: Wake 4J 125
Strathmore Av. LS9: Leeds 4J 69
Strathmore Cl. BD2: B'frd 3F 64
Strathmore Dr. BD17: Bail 3N 45
LS9: Leeds 3J 69
Strathmore Gdns. WF9: S Elm 5A 164
Strathmore Rd. LS29: I'ly 5K 15
Strathmore St. LS9: Leeds 4K 69
Strathmore Ter. LS9: Leeds 4J 69
Strathmore Vw. LS9: Leeds 4J 69
Stratton Cl. HD6: Ras 2N 119
Stratton Pk. HD6: Ras 2N 119
Stratton Rd. HD6: Ras 2N 119
Stratton Vw. BD4: B'frd 1J 83
Stratton Wlk. BD15: All 6F 62
Stratus Cl. WF7: Ackw 6F 146
Strawberry Av. LS25: Gar 8M 71
WF15: Liv 8L 101
Strawberry Bank WF15: Liv 8L 101
Strawberry Flds. BD21: Keigh 8J 27
Strawberry Gdns. S71: Roys 5D 160
Strawberry La. LS12: Leeds 7M 67
(not continuous)
Strawberry Rd. LS12: Leeds 7M 67
Strawberry Sq. WF16: Heck 9A 102
(off St James St.)
Strawberry St. BD20: Sils 8D 12
BD21: Keigh 8J 27
Straw Vw. BD10: B'frd 7D 46
Stray, The BD10: B'frd 9E 46
Stray Vw. LS24: Saxt 8N 55
Stream Head BD13: Thorn 5A 62
Stream Head Rd. BD13: Thorn 4A 62
Streamside LS6: Leeds 9A 50
Streamside Fold HX7: Myth 4M 95
Streamside Ho. HX7: Heb B 1G 94
(off Bankfoot)
Street, The LS29: Add 2L 13
(Hart Rhydding La.)
LS29: Add 1K 13
(Stamp Hill Cl.)
Street 1 LS23: T Arch 9G 25
Street 2 LS23: T Arch 9H 25
Street 3 LS23: T Arch 8H 25
(not continuous)
Street 4 LS23: T Arch 8H 25
Street 5 LS23: T Arch 7H 25
Street 6 LS23: T Arch 6H 25
(not continuous)
Street 7 LS23: T Arch 6H 25
Street 8 LS23: T Arch 7J 25
(not continuous)
Street Furlong La. WF8: Pon 4A 130
Street Head La. BD22: Old 6M 41
STREETHOUSE 6L 127
Streethouse Station (Rail) 6L 127
Street La. BD20: E Mor, W Mor 5A 28
LS8: Leeds 5J 51
LS17: Leeds 5E 50
LS27: Gil 8F 84
Strelley Rd. S71: Ath 9N 159
Strensall Grn. BD6: B'frd 5K 81
Stretch Ga. HD8: Shep 8K 155
Stretchgate La. HX2: Hal 4L 97
Stretton Av. LS6: Leeds 6A 50
Stretton Cl. WF7: A'ton 2A 128
Strickland Av. LS17: Shad 3A 52
Strickland Cl. LS17: Shad 3A 52
Strickland Cres. LS17: Shad 3A 52
Strickland Rd. WF9: Upt 1C 164
Strike La. HD8: Skelm 6C 156
Strines OL14: W'den 4J 113
Strines La. OL14: W'den 4H 113
Strines Moor Rd. HD9: Had E 9A 170
Strines St. OL14: W'den 4J 113
Stringer Cl. BD4: B'frd 5G 82
Stringer Ho. La. HD8: Eml 2D 156
Stringer La. WF4: Horb 1D 142
Stringer's Yd. WF4: Horb 1C 142
Strone, The BD10: B'frd 6K 47
STRONG CLOSE 9L 27
Strong Cl. Gro. BD21: Keigh 9L 27
Strong Cl. Rd. BD21: Keigh 9L 27
Strong Cl. Way BD21: Keigh 9L 27
(off Strong Cl. Gro.)
Stuart Ct. BD5: B'frd 8A 6
Stuart Gro. HD7: Slait 1N 151
WF6: Alt 8H 107
Stuart Pl. HD2: Hud 6D 120
Stuart Rd. WF8: Pon 2J 129
Stuart St. WF8: Pon 2J 129
WF10: C'frd 4E 108
Stubb HX7: Myth 3K 95
Stubbin Fold HD9: Holm 5H 169
Stubbing Brink HX7: Heb B 1F 94
Stubbing Dr. HX7: Heb B 1F 94
Stubbing Footpath HX7: Heb B 1H 95
(off Cliffe St.)
Stubbing Holme Rd. HX7: Heb B 1G 94
Stubbing La. HX4: Gree, Holy 6L 117
HX6: Tri 3E 116
Stubbings Cl. HX7: Myth 4M 95
Stubbings Farm (Caravan Site) LS21: Otley 2B 32
Stubbing Sq. HX7: Heb B 1F 94
Stubbings Rd. BD17: Bail 5L 45
Stubbings St. HX7: Myth 4M 95
Stubbing Way BD18: Ship 9A 46
(not continuous)
Stubbin La. HD8: Den D 2E 172
HD9: Holm 5H 169
Stubbin Rd. HD7: Mars 5H 151
Stubbs La. WF3: E Ard 5G 104
WF11: Wome, Cri S 4F 130
Stubbs Rd. DN6: Wal S 5M 149
WF8: Wal S 5M 149
Stubham Ri. LS29: I'ly 4F 14
Stubley Farm M. LS27: Morl 8K 85
Stubley Farm Rd. WF16: Heck 6A 102
Stubley Holme OL14: Tod 3C 92
Stubley La. OL14: Tod 3C 92
Stubley Rd. WF16: Heck 6N 101
Stubley St. WF1: Wake 5H 9 (5K 125)
Stubs Beck La. BD19: Cleck 2H 101
Stub Thorn La. HX3: Sou 6E 98
Studdards Fold BD7: B'frd 1M 81
Studd Brow OL12: Whit 8A 112
Studdley Cres. BD16: Bgly 4G 45
Studfold Vw. LS14: Leeds 4B 70
Studio Rd. LS3: Leeds 5A 68
Studleigh Ter. HD6: Brigh 7K 99
(off Brooklyn Ter.)
Studley Av. BD6: B'frd 6N 81
Studley Cl. BD20: E Mor 7C 28
Studley Rd. BD3: B'frd 4D 64
Studley Ter. LS28: Pud 6B 66
STUMP CROSS 3E 98
Stumpcross Cl. WF8: Pon 9M 109
Stumpcross Ct. WF8: Pon 9M 109
Stumpcross La. WF8: Pon 9M 109
Stumpcross Mdws. WF8: Pon 1M 129
Stumpcross Way WF8: Pon 9M 109
Stumps, The BD18: Ship 6C 46
Stumps Cl. WF1: Wake 2L 125
Stunsteads Rd. BD19: Cleck 4H 101
Sturges Gro. BD2: B'frd 4F 64
Sturton Av. LS25: Gar 6A 72
Sturton Grange La. LS25: Gar 7B 72
Sturton Gro. HX2: Illing 6L 79
Sturton La. HX2: Illing 6L 79
LS25: Gar 6A 72
Stutely Gro. HD2: Hud 6C 120
STUTTON 9N 39
Stutton Rd. LS24: Stut, Tad 8N 39
Styebank La. LS26: Rothw 7A 88
Styes La. HX6: Sow B 8D 96
Sty La. BD16: Bgly 1D 44
Styveton Way BD20: Stee 2B 26
Sude Hill HD9: New M 2C 170
Sude Hill Ter. HD9: New M 2D 170
Sudforth La. DN14: Beal 7L 111
Suffield Cl. LS27: Gil 5E 84
Suffield Cres. LS27: Gil 5E 84
Suffield Dr. LS27: Gil 5E 84
Suffield Rd. LS27: Gil 5E 84
Suffolk Av. WF17: Bat 9D 102
Suffolk Cl. WF5: Oss 7M 123
Suffolk Ct. LS19: Yead 9M 31
Suffolk Ho. WF1: Wake 8A 126
Suffolk Pl. BD2: B'frd 2D 64
Suffolk Ri. HD2: Hud 7A 120
Suffolk St. WF17: Bat 8E 102
Sufton St. HD2: Hud 1L 137
SUGAR HILL 4D 102
Sugar Hill LS29: Add 1M 13
Sugar Hill Cl. LS26: Oul 1D 106
Sugar La. WF1: Wake 8M 9 (7N 125)
WF12: Dew 2H 123
Sugar Well App. LS7: Leeds 1C 68
Sugar Well Ct. LS7: Leeds 2D 68
Sugar Well Mt. LS7: Leeds 1C 68
Sugar Well Rd. LS7: Leeds 1C 68
Sugden Cl. HD6: Ras 3M 119
Sugden End BD22: Cros R 8F 42
Sugden Ho. Farm BD21: Keigh 8H 43
Sugden Pl. BD6: B'frd 6K 81
(off Beck Hill)
Sugden's Almshouses BD22: Oak 4D 42
Sugden St. BD1: B'frd 7A 64
BD12: O'haw 9D 82
Sulby Gro. BD10: B'frd 8J 47
Sullivan Cl. HD4: Hud 7J 137
Sullivan Gro. WF9: S Kirk 8H 163
Summerbank Cl. BD11: Drig 6C 84
Summerbridge Cl. WF17: Bat 6D 102
Summerbridge Cres. BD10: B'frd 1H 65
BD19: Gom 2N 101
Summerbridge Dr. BD10: B'frd 1H 65
Summerdale BD19: Gom 2M 101
Summerfield Av. HD6: B Bri 6N 99
LS13: Leeds 3D 66
Summerfield Cl. BD17: Bail 4N 45
WF11: B'ton 4D 110
Summerfield Ct. HX2: Hal 8N 79
Summerfield Dr. BD17: Bail 4N 45
LS13: Leeds 3D 66
WF11: B'ton 4D 110
Summerfield Gdns. LS13: Leeds 3D 66
Summerfield Grn. BD17: Bail 4N 45
LS13: Leeds 3D 66
Summerfield Gro. BD17: Bail 4N 45
HD8: Lept 8H 139
Summerfield Pk. BD17: Bail 4N 45
Summerfield Pl. LS13: Leeds 3D 66
LS28: Stan 6B 66
(off Richardshaw La.)
Summerfield Rd. BD10: B'frd 9G 46
LS13: Leeds 3D 66
OL14: Tod 7L 93
Summerfield Rd. W. OL14: Tod 7L 93
Summerfield Wlk. LS13: Leeds 3D 66
Summer Ford Cft. S36: Ing 7A 172
Summergate Pl. HX1: Hal 6M 97
Summergate St. HX1: Hal 6M 97
Summer Hall Ing BD12: Wyke 9N 81
Summerhill Av. BD20: Stee 2D 26
Summerhill Dr. BD20: Stee 2D 26
Summerhill Gdns. LS8: Leeds 5K 51
Summerhill Gro. LS25: Gar 7L 71
Summerhill La. BD20: Stee 2D 26
Summerhill Pl. LS8: Leeds 5K 51
Summerhill Rd. LS25: Gar 7L 71
LS26: Meth 1L 107
Summer Hill St. BD7: B'frd 9M 63
Summerlands Gro. BD5: B'frd 3E 82
Summerland Ter. HX6: Sow B 8K 97
Summer La. HD8: Eml 3G 157
S71: Roys 5C 160
Summer Lea BD10: B'frd 7E 46
Summerley Ct. BD10: B'frd 8F 46
Summer Mdw. WF8: Pon 4J 129
Summer Rd. S71: Roys 5C 160
Summerscale St. HX1: Hal 4N 97
Summerseat LS19: Raw 4A 48
Summerseat Pl. BD7: B'frd 9A 64
Summerset Pl. BD2: B'frd 4F 64
(off Green Pl.)
Summersgill Sq. LS18: Hors 7E 48
Summer St. HD1: Hud 6L 137
HD4: Neth 3J 153
HX1: Hal 7M 97
Summervale HD9: H'frth 2M 169
Summer Vw. S71: Roys 6C 160
Summerville Rd. BD7: B'frd 8A 64
LS28: Stan 5N 65
SUMMIT 9M 113
Summit St. BD21: Keigh 8H 27
Sunbeam Av. LS11: Leeds 2D 86
Sunbeam Gro. LS11: Leeds 2D 86
Sunbeam Pl. LS11: Leeds 2D 86
Sunbeam Ter. LS11: Leeds 2D 86
WF3: Ting 3A 104
Sunbridge Rd. BD1: B'frd 4A 6 (7B 64)
Sun Bldgs. HX2: Wain 8E 78
Sunbury Gro. HD5: Hud 4C 138
Sun Ct. WF7: F'stne 3C 128
Sunderland Cl. HD6: Brigh 9M 99
(off Thornhill Bri. La.)
Sunderland Rd. BD9: B'frd 4N 63
Sunderland St. BD21: Keigh 1H 43
BD22: Cros R 7F 42
HX1: Hal 4J 7 (5A 98)
Sundown Av. BD7: B'frd 1K 81
Sun Field LS28: Stan 5A 66
Sunfield Cl. LS28: Stan 4A 66
Sunfield Dr. LS28: Stan 4A 66
Sunfield Gdns. LS28: Stan 4A 66
Sunfield Pl. LS28: Stan 5A 66
Sunfield Ter. BD19: Cleck 5J 101
(off Neville St.)
Sun Fold HX1: Hal 6M 7 (6C 98)
Sunhill Dr. BD17: Bail 5K 45
Sunhurst Cl. BD22: Oak 5C 42
Sunhurst Dr. BD22: Oak 5C 42
Sun Inn Yd. HD1: Hud 5C 8
Sun La. BD22: Haw, S'bury 8M 41
LS29: Burl W 7B 16
WF1: Wake 5L 9 (5M 125)
Sun Lane Swimming Pool
Wakefield 4L 9 (5M 125)
Sunningdale BD8: B'frd 6J 63
LS25: M'fld 6F 72
Sunningdale Av. LS17: Leeds 3C 50
S75: Dart 8J 159
Sunningdale Cl. LS17: Leeds 3C 50
Sunningdale Cres. BD13: Cull 1L 61
Sunningdale Cft. HD2: Fix 8L 119
Sunningdale Dr. LS17: Leeds 3C 50
S72: Cud 9K 161
Sunningdale Grn. LS17: Leeds 3C 50
Sunningdale Rd. HD4: Hud 7J 137
Sunningdales WF6: Norm 2L 127
Sunningdale Wlk. LS17: Leeds 3C 50
Sunningdale Way LS17: Leeds 3C 50
Sunny Av. WF9: S Elm 7A 164
WF9: Upt 2N 163
SUNNYBANK 4A 118
Sunny Bank BD9: B'frd 4J 63
BD12: Wyke 9C 82
BD13: Que 4E 80
BD18: Ship 8N 45
HD7: Golc 7A 136
HX3: Nor G 2L 99
HX7: Crag V 8K 95
HX7: Myth 3M 95
LS8: Leeds 1H 69
LS27: Chur 5M 85
(off Sunny Gro.)
WF4: Ryh 9H 145
WF6: Norm 3J 127
WF9: Fitz 7A 146
WF11: Knot 8F 110
(not continuous)
Sunnybank HD8: Den D 3C 172
HX7: Hept 7D 76
LS21: Clift 5K 17
LS25: M'fld 8H 73
Sunny Bank Av. BD5: B'frd 4B 82
WF14: Mir 3L 121
Sunnybank Av. BD3: B'frd 5K 65
LS18: Hors 8E 48
Sunnybank Cl. BD19: Scho 5D 100
Sunnybank Ct. LS19: Yead 9A 32
Sunnybank Cres. HX4: Gree 4N 117
HX6: Sow B 8J 97
(off Beech Rd.)
LS19: Yead 9A 32
Sunny Bank Dr. WF14: Mir 3K 121
Sunnybank Dr. HX4: Gree 4A 118
HX6: Sow B 8J 97
Sunnybank Grange HD6: Brigh 1L 119
Sunny Bank Gro. LS8: Leeds 1H 69
WF14: Mir 4L 121
Sunnybank Gro. BD3: B'frd 5K 65
Sunny Bank Ho. LS28: Fars 3A 66
Sunny Bank La. HX3: Sou 7G 98
(not continuous)
HX7: Crag V 8K 95
WF17: Bat 5G 102
Sunnybank La. BD3: B'frd 5K 65
HX4: Gree 4A 118
Sunny Bank Mills LS28: Fars 3A 66
Sunny Bank Pde. WF14: Mir 3K 121
Sunny Bank Rd. BD5: B'frd 4B 82
HD6: Brigh 1M 119
HD7: Golc 7A 136
HD9: Mel 7B 152
HX2: Mix 8H 79
HX7: P Wel 2G 77
WF14: Mir 2K 121
Sunnybank Rd. HD3: Hud 2J 137
HX4: Gree 4N 117
LS18: Hors 8E 48
WF17: Bat 6G 102

Thorn Dr.—Tom Dando Cl.

Thorn Dr. BD9: B'frd 2J 63
BD13: Que 6B 80
LS8: Leeds 3K 69
Thorne Cl. LS28: Pud 6M 65
S71: Smit 9N 159
WF6: Norm 2K 127
Thorne End Rd. S75: S'ross 7K 159
Thornefield Cres. WF3: Ting 4N 103
Thorne Gro. LS26: Rothw 7A 88
THORNER 2G 53
Thorner La. LS14: S'cft 8E 36
LS14: T'ner 5F 52
LS23: B'ham, Coll 6K 37
Thorne Rd. HD1: Hud 6K 137
Thorner Rd. LS23: B'ham 8L 37
THORNES 8K 125
Thornes Farm App. LS9: Leeds 9M 69
Thornes Farm Way LS9: Leeds 9M 69
Thornes Fold HD8: Lept 7K 139
Thornes Ind. Est. WF1: Wake 8K 9 (6L 125)
Thornes La. WF1: Wake 8L 9 (7M 125)
WF2: Wake 8J 9 (7K 125)
Thornes La. Wharf WF1: Wake 8L 9 (7M 125)
Thornes Moor Av. WF2: Wake 8J 125
Thornes Moor Cl. WF2: Wake 8J 125
Thornes Moor Dr. WF2: Wake 8J 125
Thornes Moor Rd. WF2: Wake 9J 125
Thornes Office Pk. WF2: Wake 8K 125
Thornes Pk. 7J 125
Thornes Pk. BD18: Ship 1B 64
HD6: Ras 2M 119
Thornes Park Athletics Stadium 6J 125
Thornes Pk. Ct. WF2: Wake 8K 125
Thornes Rd. WF2: Wake 8H 125
Thorne St. HX4: Holy 7N 117
Thorneycroft Rd. BD20: E Mor 7A 28
Thorney La. HX2: Midg 3C 96
Thornfield BD16: Bgly 3D 44
BD22: Haw 8D 42
WF12: Dew 5G 122
Thornfield Av. BD6: B'frd 5B 82
HD4: Hud 7K 137
LS28: Fars 3N 65
Thornfield Cl. HD4: Hud 7K 137
Thornfield Ct. LS15: Leeds 4C 70
Thornfield Dr. LS15: Leeds 4C 70
Thornfield Hall BD13: Thorn 8D 62
(off Thornton Rd.)
Thornfield M. BD16: Bgly 9D 28
LS15: Leeds 4C 70
Thornfield Mt. WF17: Birs 3D 102
Thornfield Pl. BD2: B'frd 3G 64
Thornfield Ri. HX4: Gree 4A 118
Thornfield Rd. HD4: Hud 8K 137
LS16: Leeds 7L 49
Thornfield Sq. BD2: B'frd 3G 64
Thornfield St. HX4: Gree 4A 118
Thornfield Ter. BD15: Wils 2A 62
Thornfield Way LS15: Leeds 4C 70
Thorn Gth. BD19: Cleck 6G 100
BD20: Keigh 7G 26
Thorngate BD13: Denh 4M 61
Thorn Gro. BD9: B'frd 2J 63
LS8: Leeds 3K 69
THORNHILL 9H 123
Thorn Hill HX4: Sow 9M 117
Thornhill Av. BD18: Ship 1B 64
BD22: Oak 4E 42
HD3: Hud 3H 137
Thornhill Beck La. HD6: Brigh, Clift 8N 99
Thornhill Bri. La. HD6: Brigh 9M 99
Thornhill Cl. HX4: Sow 9M 117
(off Thorn Hill)
LS28: Cal 8M 47
WF2: W'ton 4B 144
WF4: M'twn 3L 141
Thornhill Ct. LS12: Leeds 8M 67
Thornhill Cft. LS12: Leeds 8L 67
WF2: W'ton 3B 144
Thornhill Dr. BD10: Cal 7K 47
BD18: Ship 1B 64
LS28: Cal 7M 47
WF2: W'ton 4B 144
THORNHILL EDGE 1H 141
Thornhill Gro. BD18: Ship 1B 64
BD20: Stee 2B 26
LS28: Cal 8M 47
Thornhill Hey HX4: Sow 9M 117
Thornhill Ho. BD3: B'frd 6J 65
(off Thornhill Pl.)
THORNHILL LEES 7F 122
Thornhill Pk. Av. WF12: Dew 7G 123
Thornhill Pl. BD3: B'frd 6J 65
HD6: Ras 2M 119
LS12: Leeds 8L 67
Thornhill Rd. BD20: Stee 1B 26
HD3: Hud 4F 136
(Bk. Thornhill Rd.)
HD3: Hud 3J 137
(Rumbold Rd.)
HD6: Ras 3L 119
LS12: Leeds 8L 67
WF4: M'twn 2K 141
WF10: C'frd 6E 108
WF12: Dew 5E 122
WF13: Dew 4E 122
Thornhill Rd. Bus. Pk. WF12: Dew 5E 122
THORNHILLS 8A 100
Thornhills La. HD6: Clift 8A 100
Thornhill St. LS12: Leeds 8L 67
LS28: Cal 8M 47
WF1: Wake 5K 9 (5L 125)
WF12: Dew 5G 122
Thornhill St. Bungs. WF1: Wake 6K 9 (6L 125)
Thornhill Ter. BD3: B'frd 6H 65
THORNHURST 3F 36
Thornie Bank WF12: Dew 5G 123
Thornie Vw. WF12: Dew 6F 122
Thorn La. BD9: B'frd 2J 63
(not continuous)
LS8: Leeds 8H 51
Thornlea Cl. LS19: Yead 2K 47
Thorn Lee HX2: Lud 3E 96
Thornleigh WF12: Dew 5G 122
Thornleigh Av. WF2: Wake 7L 125
Thornleigh Cres. WF2: Wake 8L 125
Thornleigh Cft. WF2: Wake 8J 9 (7L 125)
Thornleigh Dr. WF2: Wake 7L 125
WF15: Liv 7M 101
Thornleigh Gdns. LS9: Leeds 8M 5 (8H 69)
Thornleigh Gth. WF2: Wake 8L 125
Thornleigh Gro. LS9: Leeds 8H 69
WF2: Wake 8L 125
Thornleigh Mt. LS9: Leeds 8H 69
Thornleigh Rd. HD4: Hud 7G 137
WF2: Wake 8J 9 (7L 125)
Thornleigh St. LS9: Leeds 8H 69
Thornleigh Vw. LS9: Leeds 8H 69
Thornmead Rd. BD17: Bail 5B 46
Thorn Mt. LS8: Leeds 2L 69
Thorn Pl. OL14: Tod 7L 93
(off Beaconsfield St.)
Thorn Rd. WF12: T'hill 1F 140
Thorn Royd Dr. BD4: B'frd 3K 83
Thornsgill Av. BD4: B'frd 2G 83
Thorn St. BD8: B'frd 5L 63
BD22: Haw 7E 42
WF17: Birs 3B 102
Thorn Ter. HX2: Lud 3E 96
LS8: Leeds 2K 69
THORNTON 8C 62
Thornton Av. LS12: Leeds 7K 67
Thornton Cl. WF9: Hems 4D 162
WF17: Birs 1C 102
Thornton Ct. BD8: B'frd 6L 63
(off Lane Ends Cl.)
WF9: Upt 1C 164
Thornton Gdns. LS12: Leeds 7K 67
Thornton Gro. LS12: Leeds 7K 67
Thornton La. BD5: B'frd 2A 82
Thornton Lodge Rd. HD1: Hud 6K 137
Thornton Moor Rd. BD13: Denh 6G 60
BD22: Oxen 6G 60
Thornton Old Rd. BD8: B'frd 7J 63
Thornton Recreation Cen. 8G 63
Thornton Rd. BD1: B'frd 5A 6 (6M 63)
BD7: B'frd 6M 63
BD8: B'frd 6M 63
BD13: Denh, Thorn 9L 61
BD13: Que 3C 80
HD6: Ras 3K 119
WF12: Dew 7F 122
Thornton Road (Park & Ride) 7B 64
Thornton Rd. Ind. Est. BD8: B'frd 6M 63
Thornton's Arc. LS1: Leeds 6F 4 (6E 68)
Thorntons Dale LS18: Hors 9E 48
Thornton Sq. HD6: Brigh 1M 119
(off Briggate)
Thornton St. BD1: B'frd 7A 64
BD19: Cleck 5K 101
(Bradford Rd.)
BD19: Cleck 6E 100
(Moorside)
HX1: Hal 7M 97
LS29: Burl W 7C 16
WF13: Dew 3E 122
Thornton Ter. HX1: Hal 7M 97
Thornton Vw. Rd. BD14: Clay 2H 81
Thorntonville BD19: Cleck 6K 101
Thorntree Av. WF4: Croft 1F 144
Thorntree Cl. WF8: D'ton 7C 130
Thorn Tree Cotts. HX3: Sou 8J 99
Thorntree Ct. WF4: Croft 1F 144
Thorn Tree St. HX1: Hal 7M 97
Thorn Vw. HX2: Lud 3E 96
HX3: Hal 2B 98
HX5: Ell 5F 118
HX7: Myth 4M 95
LS8: Leeds 3L 69
Thornville LS27: Chur 6L 85
Thornville Av. LS6: Leeds 4A 68
Thornville Ct. BD8: B'frd 4A 64
LS6: Leeds 4A 68
(off Thornville Rd.)
Thornville Cres. LS6: Leeds 3A 68
Thornville Gro. LS6: Leeds 4A 68
Thornville Mt. LS6: Leeds 4A 68
WF13: Dew 5D 122
Thornville Pl. LS6: Leeds 4A 68
WF13: Dew 5D 122
Thornville Rd. LS6: Leeds 4A 68
Thornville Row LS6: Leeds 4A 68
Thornville St. LS6: Leeds 4A 68
WF13: Dew 5D 122
Thornville Ter. LS6: Leeds 4A 68
WF13: Dew 5E 122
Thornville Vw. LS6: Leeds 4A 68
Thornville Wlk. WF13: Dew 5D 122
Thorn Wlk. LS8: Leeds 3L 69
Thorny Bank HX6: Norl 1K 117
Thorold Ho. BD10: B'frd 8G 47
(off Haigh Beck Vw.)
THORP ARCH 8E 24
Thorp Arch Est. LS23: T Arch 7H 25
Thorp Arch Grange LS23: T Arch 6F 24
Thorp Arch Pk. LS23: T Arch 8E 24
Thorp Arch Retail Pk. LS23: T Arch 8H 25
Thorp Av. HD9: H'frth 4N 169
THORPE 8G 47
THORPE AUDLIN 5N 147
Thorpe Av. BD13: Thorn 8F 62
Thorpe Cl. LS20: Guis 8F 30
Thorpe Ct. LS10: Leeds 1E 104
Thorpe Cres. LS10: Leeds 9E 86
Thorpe Dr. LS20: Guis 7G 30
THORPE EDGE 8G 47
Thorpe Gdns. LS10: Leeds 9E 86
Thorpe Gth. LS10: Leeds 1D 104
Thorpe Ga. Est. WF9: Bads 6N 147
Thorpe Grange Gdns. HD5: Hud 7D 138
Thorpe Grn. Dr. HD7: Golc 4D 136
Thorpe Gro. BD13: Thorn 8G 62
LS10: Leeds 9E 86
Thorpe La. HD5: Hud 7D 138
HD8: Den D, Skelm 8D 156
LS10: Leeds 3B 104
LS20: Guis 8E 30
WF3: Ting 3B 104
WF8: Thpe A 8M 147
WF9: Bads, Thpe A 8M 147
Thorpe Lodge WF3: Loft 3L 105
(off Long Thorpe La.)
Thorpe Lwr. La. WF3: Rothw, Thpe H 2H 105
Thorpe Mill Ct. HX6: Tri 3E 116
Thorpe Mt. LS10: Leeds 1D 104
THORPE ON THE HILL 2F 104
Thorpe Pk. LS15: Leeds 7G 71
Thorpe Pl. HX6: Sow B 1C 116
Thorpe Rd. BD13: Thorn 8F 62
LS10: Leeds 8E 86
LS28: Pud 6A 66
WF3: E Ard 5E 104
Thorpes Av. HD8: Den D 1D 172
Thorpes Cres. HD8: Skelm 8D 156
Thorpe Sq. LS10: Leeds 9F 86
Thorpe St. BD21: Keigh 8J 27
HX3: Hal 2A 98
LS10: Leeds 9E 86
LS15: Leeds 6B 70
Thorpe Ter. HX2: Lud 3D 96
(Solomon Hill)
HX2: Lud 3D 96
(South Carr)
Thorpe Vw. LS10: Leeds 1E 104
WF2: Wake 5H 125
WF5: Oss 3N 123
Thorp Gth. BD10: B'frd 8F 46
Thorp Pyn Cft. HD5: Hud 3C 138
Thorverton Dr. BD4: B'frd 5J 83
Thorverton Gro. BD4: B'frd 5J 83
Threadneedle St. HD1: Hud 5A 8 (4M 137)
HX1: Hal 7M 97
(off Thorn Tree St.)
Threap Cft. HX2: Illing 7M 79
Threelands BD11: B'haw 7L 83
Three La. Ends Bus. Cen. WF10: C'frd 4A 108
Three Nooked M. BD10: B'frd 7H 47
(off Albion Rd.)
Three Nooks La. S72: Cud 8J 161
Three Sisters Sq. HD1: Hud 1M 137
Threshfield BD17: Bail 4A 46
Threshfield Cres. BD11: B'haw 7L 83
Thrice Fold BD10: B'frd 7D 46
Thrift Way BD16: Bgly 5E 44
Throstle Av. LS10: Leeds 1D 104
Throstle Bank HX2: Hal 7M 97
(off Gainest)
Throstle Bower HX7: Heb B 2E 94
(off Turrett Hall Rd.)
Throstle Crest WF7: A'ton 3A 128
Throstle Dr. LS10: Leeds 1C 104
Throstle Hill LS10: Leeds 1D 104
Throstle La. LS10: Leeds 1D 104
Throstle Mt. HX2: Lud F 7F 96
LS10: Leeds 1D 104
Throstle Nest HD7: Mars 6F 150
HX7: Myth 4L 95
WF17: Bat 8D 102
Throstle Nest Cl. LS21: Otley 7H 17
Throstle Nest Rd. BD20: Sils 7D 12
Throstle Nest Vw. LS18: Hors 8F 48
Throstle Pde. LS10: Leeds 1D 104
Throstle Pl. LS10: Leeds 1D 104
Throstle Rd. LS10: Leeds 1E 104
Throstle Rd. Nth. LS10: Leeds 8G 87
Throstle Row LS10: Leeds 1D 104
WF11: Knot 1D 130
Throstle Sq. LS10: Leeds 1F 104
Throstle St. LS10: Leeds 1D 104
OL14: W'den 5K 113
Throstle Ter. LS10: Leeds 1E 104
Throstle Vw. LS10: Leeds 1F 104
Throstle Wlk. LS10: Leeds 1D 104
Throxenby Way BD14: Clay 1H 81
Thrum Hall Cl. HX1: Hal 5M 97
Thrum Hall Dr. HX1: Hal 5M 97
Thrum Hall Ind. Pk. HX2: Hal 4L 97
Thrum Hall La. HX1: Hal 5M 97
Thrush Hill Rd. HX7: Myth 4L 95
Thrush St. BD21: Keigh 8K 27
Thruxton Cl. S72: Cud 9K 161
Thryberg St. BD3: B'frd 4F 6 (7E 64)
THUNDER BRIDGE 5H 155
Thunder Bri. La. HD8: Kbtn 6H 155
Thunderhead Ridge WF10: C'frd 7E 108
Thunderton La. HX6: Sow B 1B 116
Thurgory Ga. HD8: Lept 7J 139
Thurgory La. HD8: Lept 6H 139
Thurlestone Ct. BD20: E Mor 8A 28
Thurley Dr. BD4: B'frd 3F 82
Thurley Rd. BD4: B'frd 3F 82
Thurnscoe Rd. BD1: B'frd 1A 6 (6B 64)
(not continuous)
Thurrish La. HX7: P Wel 8J 59
Thursby St. BD3: B'frd 7F 64
Thurston Gdns. BD15: All 6G 63
THURSTONLAND 8D 154
Thurstonland Bank Rd. HD4: Thurs 8A 154
HD9: Brock 8A 154
Thurstonland Rd. HD4: Farn T 4C 154
Thwaite Ct. LS18: Hors 7H 49
THWAITE GATE 2H 87
Thwaite Ga. LS10: Leeds 2H 87
Thwaite La. LS10: Leeds 2J 87
Thwaite Mills Watermill Mus. 2K 87
THWAITES 9M 27
Thwaites Almshouses WF8: Pon 3H 129
(off Hartley Pk. Av.)
Thwaites Av. LS29: I'ly 5H 15
Thwaites Bank BD21: Keigh 9M 27
Thwaites Bri. BD21: Keigh 9L 27
THWAITES BROW 1M 43
Thwaites Brow Rd. BD21: Keigh 9M 27
Thwaites La. BD21: Keigh 9L 27
Tibgarth LS22: Lin 6J 23
Tichborne Rd. BD5: B'frd 2C 82
Tichborne Rd. W. BD5: B'frd 2C 82
Tichborne St. WF15: Liv 8J 101
Tichbourne St. WF17: Bat 8C 102
Tickhill St. BD3: B'frd 8F 64
Tiding Fld. HD7: Slait 8K 135
Tiding Fld. La. HD7: Slait 8K 135
Tidswell St. WF16: Heck 8B 102
Tilbury Av. LS11: Leeds 1B 86
Tilbury Gro. LS11: Leeds 1B 86
Tilbury Mt. LS11: Leeds 1B 86
Tilbury Pde. LS11: Leeds 1B 86
Tilbury Rd. LS11: Leeds 1B 86
Tilbury Row LS11: Leeds 1B 86
Tilbury Ter. LS11: Leeds 1B 86
Tilbury Vw. LS11: Leeds 1B 86
Tile La. LS16: Leeds 4N 49
Tile St. BD8: B'frd 5N 63
Tile Ter. HD6: Ras 2M 119
Tiley Sq. BD5: B'frd 1C 82
Till Carr La. HX3: Hip 5M 99
Tillotson Av. HX6: Sow B 9G 96
Tillotson's Bldgs. HX2: Lud F 5D 96
Tillotson St. BD20: Sils 7D 12
Timber St. BD21: Keigh 8L 27
HX5: Ell 5E 118
Timberwood HD8: Kbtn 5H 155
Timble Dr. BD16: Bgly 3G 45
Tim La. BD22: Oak 5B 42
Timmey La. HX6: Sow B 7G 96
Timothy La. WF17: Bat 5F 102
Timothy Taylor Brewery 2H 43
Tinderley Gro. HD5: Hud 6C 138
Tingle Vw. LS12: N Far 2K 85
TINGLEY 3A 104
Tingley Av. WF3: Ting 3A 104
Tingley Comn. LS27: Morl 2L 103
Tingley Cres. WF3: Ting 3M 103
Tingley Hall Ri. WF3: Ting 3A 104
Tinker Bank La. HX7: Hept 8G 77
Tinker La. HD8: Lept 8L 139
HD9: Mel 8C 152
Tinkingfield La. LS22: Bick 1J 25
Tinkler's La. WF11: Birk 1M 111
Tinkler Stile BD10: B'frd 7D 46
Tinsel Rd. WF12: Dew 2J 123
TINSHILL 3G 49
Tinshill Av. LS16: Leeds 4H 49
Tinshill Cl. LS16: Leeds 4H 49
Tinshill Cres. LS16: Leeds 3H 49
Tinshill Dr. LS16: Leeds 2H 49
Tinshill Gth. LS16: Leeds 3H 49
Tinshill Gro. LS16: Leeds 3H 49
Tinshill La. LS16: Leeds 4G 48
TINSHILL MOOR 2H 49
Tinshill Mt. LS16: Leeds 3H 49
Tinshill Rd. LS16: Leeds 4G 48
Tinshill Vw. LS16: Leeds 3H 49
Tinshill Wlk. LS16: Leeds 2H 49
Tinsworth Rd. WF2: Wake 6J 143
Tintagel Ct. WF6: Norm 9J 107
Tintern Av. BD8: B'frd 7J 63
HD3: Hud 5E 136
Tippaty La. WF11: Byram 5F 110
Tipping La. HD8: Eml 2G 157
Tipsey Ct. S75: S'ross 8M 159
Tipsey Hill S75: S'ross 8M 159
Tisma Dr. BD4: B'frd 5G 82
Titan Cen. BD12: Wyke 2A 100
Titania Cl. BD16: Cot 9G 44
Titanic M. HD7: Linth 8C 136
Tithe Barn Fold LS15: Bar E 8L 53
Tithe Barn La. LS17: Bard 6C 36
Tithe Barn Rd. WF11: Knot 8F 110
Tithe Barn St. WF4: Horb 1C 142
WF13: Dew 3G 122
Tithe Barn Vw. HD6: Ras 3A 120
Tithefields HD8: Fen B 6G 139
Tithe Ho. Way HD2: Hud 5C 120
Titus La. HD8: Eml 3A 156
Titus St. BD18: Ship 7L 45
Tiverton Wlk. BD4: B'frd 3J 83
Tivoli Pl. BD5: B'frd 2A 82
LS29: I'ly 6H 15
TIVY DALE 4N 173
Tivy Dale S75: Caw 4N 173
Tivy Dale Dr. S75: Caw 4N 173
Toad La. OL15: Lit 1C 132
Toby La. BD7: B'frd 9M 63
Toby Wood La. HD8: Den D 4A 172
Todd Ter. BD7: B'frd 1N 81
Todley Hall Rd. BD22: Oak 1M 41
TODMORDEN 7K 93
Todmorden Golf Course 6L 93
Todmorden Rd. OL15: Lit 8L 113
Todmorden Sports Cen. 6H 93
Todmorden Station (Rail) 7K 93
Todmorden Toy & Model Mus. 7K 93
Todwell La. BD5: B'frd 2A 82
Toft La. HD4: Farn T 3D 154
Tofts Av. BD12: Wyke 2A 100
Tofts Gro. HD6: Ras 4K 119
Tofts Gro. Fold HD6: Ras 4L 119
Tofts Gro. Gdns. HD6: Ras 4L 119
Tofts Gro. Pl. HD6: Ras 4L 119
(off Tofts Gro.)
TOFTSHAW 5H 83
Toftshaw Fold BD4: B'frd 5H 83
Toftshaw La. BD4: B'frd 5J 83
Toftshaw New Rd. BD4: B'frd 5H 83
Tofts Ho. Cl. LS28: Pud 7B 66
Tofts Rd. BD19: Cleck 5H 101
LS28: Pud 7A 66
Toft St. LS12: Leeds 8N 67
Toll Bar La. WF2: Wren 2G 124
Toll Bar Rd. WF10: C'frd 5N 107
Toller Dr. BD9: B'frd 3K 63
Toller Gro. BD9: B'frd 3L 63
Toller La. BD8: B'frd 4L 63
BD9: B'frd 3K 63
Toller Pk. BD9: B'frd 3L 63
Tollgate Cl. S72: Shaf 7L 161
Tollgate Ct. BD8: B'frd 5M 63
Toll Hill Ct. WF10: C'frd 6J 109
Toll Hill Dr. WF10: C'frd 6H 109
Tolson Cres. HD5: Hud 3D 138
Tolson Grange HD5: Hud 5D 138
Tolson Memorial Mus. 4C 138
Tolson St. WF5: Oss 3L 123
WF13: Dew 2F 122
Tolsons Yd. HD5: Hud 5B 138
Tolworth Fold BD15: All 6G 62
Tomahawk Trail WF10: C'frd 7E 108
Tombridge Cres. WF9: Kins 8B 146
Tom Dando Cl. WF6: Norm 1M 127

Tom La.—Tudor Ct.

Tom La. HD4: Hud 7G 136
Tomling Cote La. BD20: Sils 9G 13
Tomlinson Bldgs. BD10: B'frd 6E 46
Tomlinson Yd. HD1: Hud 4C 8
Tommy La. HD7: Linth 9D 136
Tomroyds La. WF14: Mir 3A 122
Tom Wood Ash La. WF9: Upt 2C 164
Tonbridge Cl. BD6: B'frd 5L 81
TONG 3A 84
Tong App. LS12: Leeds 8G 67
Tong Dr. LS12: Leeds 7G 66
Tonge Brink OL14: Tod 2E 92
Tong Ga. LS12: Leeds 7G 67
Tong Grn. LS12: Leeds 7G 67
Tong Hall Bus. Pk. BD4: B'frd 3A 84
Tong La. BD4: B'frd 5N 83
Tong Moor Side BD11: B'haw 6L 83
TONG PARK 2D 46
Tong Pk. BD17: Bail 2D 46
Tong Rd. LS12: Leeds, N Far 1E 84
Tong Rd. Bus. Pk. LS12: Leeds 7M 67
Tong Sports Centre & Pool 5K 83
TONG STREET 4J 83
Tong St. BD4: B'frd 3G 82
Tongue La. LS6: Leeds 7B 50
Tong Wlk. LS12: Leeds 7G 67
Tong Way LS12: Leeds 7G 66
Tonson Ct. BD21: Keigh 8J 27
Tony Miller App. BD17: Ship 7A 46
Tootal St. WF1: Wake 7L 9 (6M 125)
TOOTHILL 4M 119
Toothill Av. HD6: Ras 4M 119
Toothill Bank HD6: Ras 3M 119
Toot Hill La. HX6: Sow B 1B 116
Toothill La. HD6: Ras 5M 119
Toothill La. Sth. HD6: Ras 6L 119
Topaz Cl. HD2: Hud 9A 120
TOPCLIFFE 2M 103
Topcliffe Av. LS27: Morl 9N 85
Topcliffe Cl. WF3: Ting 2N 103
Topcliffe Ct. LS27: Morl 9A 86
Topcliffe Fold LS27: Morl 2M 103
Topcliffe Grn. LS27: Morl 9N 85
Topcliffe Gro. LS27: Morl 2M 103
Topcliffe La. LS27: Morl 2M 103
WF3: Ting 1N 103
Topcliffe Mead LS27: Morl 9N 85
Topcliffe M. LS27: Morl 9N 85
Top Fold LS12: Leeds 8L 67
WF11: Fair 9N 91
Top Headlands WF5: Oss 6M 123
Top Ho. Ct. WF8: K S'ton 4J 149
Top Ho. Farm M. WF11: Fair 8N 91
Topland Country Bus. Pk.
HX7: Myth 4M 95
Top La. WF4: Midg 9N 141
Topliss Way LS10: Leeds 9G 86
Top Meadow WF14: Up H 9K 121
Top Moor Side LS11: Leeds 9C 68
Top of Carr *WF17: Bat* 1E 122
(off Upper Rd.)
TOP OF COWCLIFFE 8L 119
Top of the Hill HD4: Thurs 7C 154
HD7: Slait 2L 151
Top Orchard WF4: Ryh 9J 145
Top o' th' Bank HD4: Thurs 8C 154
Top o' th' Cl. Rd. OL14: W'den 5L 113
Top o' th' Hill HX7: Wads 8K 77
OL14: W'den 2J 113
Top o' th' Hill Rd.
OL14: W'den 2J 113
Top o' th' Moor HD4: Stock 7G 154
Top o' th' Town *HX7: Hept* 8G 76
(off Smithwell La.)
Top Rd. HD8: Lwr C 1B 172
Top Row HD4: Arm B 1K 153
LS21: Clift 4J 17
S75: Dart 6G 159
Tops Health Club
Outwood 8K 105
(off Cobham Pde.)
Top Stone Cl. LS25: Bur S 1D 110
Top St. OL14: W'den 4J 113
WF9: Hems 2C 162
Tor Av. BD12: Wyke 3A 100
Torcote Cres. HD2: Hud 6A 120
Tordoff Av. BD7: B'frd 9K 63
Tordoff Grn. BD6: B'frd 5N 81
Tordoff Pl. LS5: Leeds 2K 67
Tordoff Rd. BD12: Low M 7C 82
Tordoff Ter. LS5: Leeds 2K 67
Tornwood Cl. BD22: Oak 5B 42
Toronto Pl. LS7: Leeds 9F 50
Toronto Sq. LS1: Leeds 6E 4
Toronto St. LS1: Leeds 6E 4 (6D 68)
LS6: Leeds 4A 68
(off Queen's Rd.)
Torre Cl. LS9: Leeds 6J 69
Torre Cres. BD6: B'frd 4J 81
LS9: Leeds 6K 69
Torre Dr. LS9: Leeds 5J 69
Torre Gdns. LS9: Leeds 5M 5 (6H 69)
Torre Grn. LS9: Leeds 5M 5 (6H 69)
Torre Gro. BD6: B'frd 4J 81
LS9: Leeds 5J 69
Torre Hill LS9: Leeds 6K 69
Torre La. LS9: Leeds 6K 69
Torre Mt. LS9: Leeds 5J 69
Torre Pl. LS9: Leeds 6J 69
Torre Rd. BD6: B'frd 4J 81
LS9: Leeds 5M 5 (6H 69)
Torre Sq. LS9: Leeds 5J 69
Torre Vw. LS9: Leeds 5K 69
Torre Wlk. LS9: Leeds 5K 69
Torridon Cres. BD6: B'frd 7K 81
Torridon Rd. WF12: Dew 1H 123
Tor Vw. HD9: Brock 7A 154
Total Fitness
Huddersfield 5F 138
Totley Cl. S71: Ath 9C 160
TOTTIES 3B 170
Totties La. HD9: H'frth 3B 170
Toulson La. LS24: B'ham, Tad 6E 38
TOULSTON 3J 39
Toulston La. LS23: B'ham, Tad 6E 38
Tourist Info. Cen.
Bradford 5B 6 (8C 64)
Halifax 4M 7 (5C 98)
Haworth 8B 42
Hebden Bridge 1H 95
Holmfirth 3M 169
Huddersfield 6B 8 (5M 137)
Ilkley 5G 15
Leeds Station 7E 4 (7D 68)
Otley 1L 31
Todmorden 7K 93
Wakefield 4J 9 (5L 125)
Wetherby 4M 23
Tow Bank Cl. LS23: B Spa 9D 24
Towcester Av. LS10: Leeds 1F 104
Tower Av. WF9: Upt 1N 163
Tower Bldgs. *WF16: Heck* 9A 102
(off Church La.)
Tower C'way. OL14: Tod 4D 92
Tower Ct. LS12: Leeds 6N 67
LS29: I'ly 5G 15
(off Wharfe Vw. Rd.)
Tower Drive, The LS21: Pool 2H 33
Tower Gdns. HX2: Hal 8M 97
Tower Gro. LS12: Leeds 6K 67
Tower Hill HX6: Sow B 8H 97
Tower Ho. St. LS2: Leeds 4G 5 (5E 68)
Tower La. LS12: Leeds 6J 67
(not continuous)
Tower Pl. LS12: Leeds 6J 67
Tower Rd. BD18: Ship 7K 45
Towers, The LS12: Leeds 6J 67
Towers Cl. WF4: Croft 2H 145
Towers La. WF4: Croft 1J 145
Towers Paddock WF10: C'frd 5G 109
Towers Sq. LS6: Leeds 7C 50
Tower St. BD2: B'frd 4F 64
OL14: Tod 3C 92
Towers Way LS6: Leeds 7C 50
Tower Vw. *HX2: Hal* 7L 97
(off Plane Tree Nest La.)
Tower Works LS11: Leeds 8D 4 (7D 68)
Towler Dr. LS13: Leeds 1B 66
Towlerton La. WF2: Wren 1G 125
Town, The WF12: T'hill 9G 123
Town Av. HD1: Hud 1E 8 (2A 138)
Town Cl. LS18: Hors 6E 48
Townclose Vw. LS25: Kip 5N 89
Town Cres. HD1: Hud 1E 8 (2A 138)
TOWN END
BD14 9G 63
HD7 6B 136
HD8 6L 155
HD9 2A 170
LS12 9L 67
LS13 4H 67
LS27 9K 85
WF3 3L 105
WF5 5N 123
Town End BD7: B'frd 1M 81
HD5: Hud 6C 138
HD7: Golc 6C 136
LS25: Gar 6M 71
LS27: Gil 6G 84
LS27: Morl 9L 85
(off Middleton Rd.)
WF5: Oss 6N 123
Town End Av. HD9: H'frth 1A 170
WF7: Ackw 3J 147
Town End Cl. LS13: Leeds 5H 67
Town End Cres. HD9: H'frth 1A 170
Town End Rd. HD8: Lept 6L 139
Townend Pl. LS28: Pud 6C 66
Town End Rd. BD14: Clay 9G 63
HD9: H'frth 2N 169
Townend Rd. LS12: Leeds 9L 67
Town End Vw. HD9: H'frth 2N 169
Town End Yd. LS13: Leeds 5G 67
Townfield BD15: Wils 1B 62
HX7: Hept 8G 76
Townfield La. HX7: Hept 8G 76
Town Flds. Rd. HX5: Ell 5D 118
Townfield Vw. *HX7: Hept* 8G 76
(off Townfield La.)
Townfold WF5: Oss 5A 124
TOWN GATE 8C 152
TOWNGATE 6M 121
Town Ga. BD10: B'frd 7F 46
BD12: Wyke 2A 100
BD19: Scho 4D 100
HD8: Kbtn 1J 155
HD8: Lept 6L 139
HD9: H'wth 6C 170
HD9: Nether 9L 153
LS20: Guis 7J 31
LS28: Cal 8M 47
Towngate *BD17: Bail* 3B 46
(off Northgate)
BD18: Ship 8B 46
BD21: Keigh 9J 27
HD4: Hud 8M 137
HD6: Clift 9B 100
HD7: Mars 5F 150
HD9: U'thng 3J 169
HX2: Midg 3B 96
HX3: Hip 4H 99
HX3: North 2F 98
HX3: Sou 8F 98
HX6: Sow B 9D 96
HX7: Hept 8G 76
S75: Map 8K 159
WF5: Oss 6N 123
(not continuous)
WF14: Mir 5M 121
Towngate Av. HD6: Clift 9B 100
Town Ga. Cl. LS20: Guis 7J 31
Towngate Fold HD9: Mel 7D 152
Towngate Gro. WF14: Mir 5M 121
Towngate Ho. HX5: Ell 5E 118
Towngate Rd. WF17: Bat 7D 102
Town Grn. WF12: Dew 4H 123
Town Hall Bldgs. *HX5: Ell* 5E 118
(off Southgate)
Town Hall Ct. HX6: Sow B 8H 97
Town Hall Sq. LS19: Yead 9M 31
Town Hall St. BD21: Keigh 9J 27
HD9: H'frth 3M 169
HX5: Ell 5E 118
Town Hall St.HX6: Sow B 9H 97
WF14: Mir 7L 121
Town Hall St. E. HX1: Hal 3L 7 (5B 98)
Town Hall Way WF12: Dew 3G 122
TOWN HEAD 7F 12
Town Head HD9: Hon 4L 153
Town Head Fold LS29: Add 1L 13
Town Hill LS23: B'ham 6D 38
Town Hill St. BD16: Cot 9G 45
Town Ing Mills HX4: Stainl 8N 117
Town Ing Way HX4: Stainl 8M 117
Town La. BD10: B'frd 6F 46
Townley Av. HX3: Sou 8F 98
Townley Rd. WF2: Wake 6F 124
Town Moor HD4: Thurs 7D 154
Town Pl. HD1: Hud 1E 8 (2A 138)
Town Rd. HD5: K'htn 1G 138
Town Sq. *LS18: Hors* 6E 48
(off Kerry Gth.)
Town St. BD11: B'haw 7L 83
LS7: Leeds 8F 50
LS10: Leeds 8D 86
LS11: Leeds 4A 86
LS12: Leeds 6K 67
LS13: Leeds 3F 66
(Bell La.)
LS13: Leeds 1B 66
(St Andrew's Cl.)
LS18: Hors 7E 48
LS19: Raw 4A 48
LS19: Yead 9M 31
LS20: Guis 7J 31
LS27: Gil 6F 84
LS28: Fars 3A 66
LS28: Stan 5B 66
WF3: Carl 1M 105
WF9: Hems 2C 162
WF12: Dew 4J 123
WF13: Dew 1F 122
WF17: Bat 1F 122
Town St. Ct. LS18: Hors 6E 48
Town St. M. LS7: Leeds 8F 50
Town St. Wlk. LS7: Leeds 8F 50
Town Ter. HD1: Hud 1E 8 (2A 138)
Town Top HD5: K'htn 1G 138
TOWNVILLE 6K 109
Town Wells Dr. LS28: Cal 9M 47
Towton Dr. WF10: C'frd 6A 108
Track Mt. WF17: Bat 1E 122
Track Rd. WF17: Bat 1E 122
Trackside BD12: O'haw 8D 82
Trafalgar Cl. HD2: Hud 7N 119
Trafalgar Gdns. LS27: Morl 1K 103
Trafalgar Rd. LS29: I'ly 5G 15
WF13: Dew 2E 122
Trafalgar Sq. HX1: Hal 7N 97
Trafalgar St. BD1: B'frd 2A 6 (6C 64)
DN6: Carc 8N 165
HX1: Hal 7N 97
LS2: Leeds 5H 5 (6F 68)
WF17: Bat 8D 102
Trafalgar Way DN6: Carc 8N 165
Trafford Av. LS9: Leeds 4K 69
Trafford Gro. LS9: Leeds 3J 69
Trafford Ter. LS9: Leeds 4K 69
Train Fix Health Club 8H 25
Tramways BD12: O'haw 8D 82
LS20: Guis 7G 30
Tranbeck Rd. LS20: Guis 7F 30
Tranfield Av. LS20: Guis 7G 31
Tranfield Cl. LS20: Guis 7G 31
Tranfield Ct. LS20: Guis 7G 31
Tranfield Gdns. LS20: Guis 7G 31
Tranmere Ct. LS20: Guis 7G 30
Tranmere Dr. LS20: Guis 7G 30
Tranmere Pde. *LS20: Guis* 7G 30
(off Tranmere Ct.)
TRANMERE PARK 8F 30
Tranquility LS15: Leeds 4D 70
Tranquility Av. LS15: Leeds 4D 70
Tranquility Ct. *LS15: Leeds* 4D 70
(off Tranquility Av.)
Tranquility Wlk. LS15: Leeds 4D 70
Transvaal Ter. WF17: Bat 5E 102
Tranter Gro. BD4: B'frd 9J 65
Tranter Pl. LS15: Leeds 6N 69
Travis Ho. *OL14: W'den* 4J 113
(off Beswick St.)
Travis Lacey Ter. WF13: Dew 3E 122
Tray Royd HX2: Midg 2C 96
Treadwells Mills BD1: B'frd 3D 6
Treasurers Ho. *WF8: Pon* 1K 129
(off Cromwell Mt.)
Tredgold Av. LS16: B'hpe 6H 33
Tredgold Cl. LS16: B'hpe 6H 33
Tredgold Cres. LS16: B'hpe 6H 33
Tredgold Gth. LS16: B'hpe 6H 33
Treefield Ind. Est. LS27: Gil 7G 84
Tree La. HX2: Wain 8F 78
Trees St. BD8: B'frd 5A 64
Tree Tops Ct. LS8: Leeds 8L 51
Tree Top Vw. BD13: Que 3B 80
Trelawn Av. LS6: Leeds 1N 67
Trelawn Cres. LS6: Leeds 1N 67
Trelawn Pl. LS6: Leeds 1N 67
Trelawn St. LS6: Leeds 1N 67
Trelawn Ter. LS6: Leeds 1N 67
Tremont Gdns. LS10: Leeds 3G 87
Trenam Pk. Dr. BD10: B'frd 5E 46
Trenance Dr. BD18: Ship 8L 45
Trenance Gdns. HX4: Gree 4M 117
Trenholme Av. BD6: B'frd 7N 81
Trenic Cres. LS6: Leeds 3N 67
Trenic Dr. LS6: Leeds 3N 67
Trent Av. LS25: Gar 8B 72
WF6: Alt 8H 107
Trent Bri. Way WF1: Wake 2L 125
Trentham Av. LS11: Leeds 2D 86
Trentham Gro. LS11: Leeds 2D 86
Trentham Pl. LS11: Leeds 2D 86
Trentham Row LS11: Leeds 2D 86
Trentham St. LS11: Leeds 3D 86
Trentham Ter. LS11: Leeds 2D 86
Trenton Dr. BD8: B'frd 5A 64
Trenton Rd. WF17: Bat 9J 103
Trent Rd. LS9: Leeds 6H 69
Trent St. LS11: Leeds 9D 68
Trescoe Av. LS13: Leeds 5H 67
Tresham Ct. WF12: Dew 1J 123
Trevelyan Sq. LS1: Leeds 7F 4 (7E 68)
Trevelyan St. HD5: Hud 5B 138
HD6: Brigh 7M 99
Trevithick Rd. WF10: All B 9C 90
Trevor Foster Way BD5: B'frd 3D 82
Trevor Ter. WF2: Carr G 6G 105
TRIANGLE 2E 116
Triangle *BD6: B'frd* 5B 82
(off Odsal Rd.)
Triangle, The HD1: Hud 5K 137
LS3: Leeds 5B 68
(off Burley Rd.)
Triangle Bus. Pk. WF17: Birs 1D 102
Triath Ct. WF17: Bat 6B 102
Trident Bus. Pk. HD2: Hud 8D 120
Trigot Ct. WF9: S Kirk 6J 163
Trilby St. WF1: Wake 3L 9 (4M 125)
Trimmer La. HX7: Blac H 9M 75
Trimmingham La. HX2: Hal 6K 97
Trimmingham Rd. HX2: Hal 6K 97
Trimmingham Vs. HX2: Hal 6L 97
Trinity Bus. Cen. HX1: Hal 6L 7
WF1: Wake 6M 9 (6N 125)
(not continuous)
Trinity Bus. Pk. WF1: Wake 7K 9 (6L 125)
Trinity Chapel *LS28: Pud* 6B 66
(off Wesley Sq.)
Trinity Chu. Ga. WF1: Wake 5L 9 (5M 125)
Trinity Cl. HX2: Illing 7N 79
LS18: Hors 4E 48
Trinity Ct. HD9: Hon 5L 153
LS8: Leeds 8G 51
WF9: S Elm 5N 163
Trinity Dr. HD8: Den D 3C 172
Trinity Fold HX1: Hal 5K 7
Trinity Ho. WF1: Wake 5L 9
Trinity Leeds LS1: Leeds 7F 4 (7E 68)
Trinity One LS9: Leeds 8J 5 (7F 68)
Trinity Pl. BD16: Bgly 5F 44
HX1: Hal 5K 7 (6B 98)
HX3: Hip 5H 99
(off Barfield Rd.)
Trinity Ri. LS21: Otley 1M 31
Trinity Rd. BD5: B'frd 7A 6 (9B 64)
HX1: Hal 5K 7 (6B 98)
Trinity Row HX1: Hal 5K 7 (6B 98)
Trinity St. *BD21: Keigh* 8J 27
(off Spring St.)
HD1: Hud 4A 8 (3K 137)
HX1: Hal 5K 7
HX7: Heb B 1G 94
LS1: Leeds 6F 4 (6E 68)
WF1: Wake 8A 126
WF8: Pon 2K 129
WF14: Mir 7L 121
WF17: Bat 1F 122
Trinity Ter. WF17: Birs 3A 102
Trinity Vw. BD12: Low M 6C 82
HX3: Hal 6M 7 (6C 98)
LS28: Fars 2A 66
(off Bryan St.)
WF5: Oss 4N 123
Trinity Wlk. BD12: Low M 6C 82
WF1: Wake 3K 9 (5L 125)
WF9: S Elm 5N 163
Trinity Wlk. Shop. Cen. WF1: Wake 3K 9 (4L 125)
Trip Gth. LS22: Lin 7J 23
Trip La. LS22: Lin 7G 22
Tristram Av. BD5: B'frd 3E 82
Tristram Centre, The LS12: Leeds 1A 86
Triumph Cl. LS11: Leeds 8C 68
Trojan Ct. *LS27: Morl* 8K 85
(off Troy Hill)
Troon Cl. WF6: Norm 2L 127
Troon Dr. HD2: Fix 8L 119
Troon Way WF2: Wake 9J 125
Trooper La. HX3: Hal 7C 98
Trooper Ter. HX3: Hal 7C 98
Tropical World 6K 51
Trough La. BD13: Denh 5F 60
WF9: S Elm 6B 164
Troughton St. LS28: Pud 9C 66
Trough Well La. WF2: Wren 8G 104
Troutbeck Av. BD17: Bail 6K 45
(not continuous)
Trowell Way S71: Ath 9A 160
TROY 5F 48
TROYDALE 8E 66
Troydale Gdns. LS28: Pud 9E 66
Troydale Gro. LS28: Pud 9E 66
Troydale La. LS12: Pud 8D 66
LS28: Pud 8D 66
Troydale Pk. LS28: Pud 9E 66
TROY HILL 8K 85
Troy Hill LS18: Hors 5F 48
LS27: Morl 8K 85
Troy Mills LS18: Hors 5F 48
Troy Ri. LS27: Morl 8L 85
Troy Rd. LS18: Hors 5F 48
LS27: Morl 8K 85
Trueman Av. WF16: Heck 8B 102
Trueman Ct. BD12: Low M 7C 82
Trueman Way WF9: S Elm 5N 163
TRUNCLIFFE 4B 82
Truncliffe BD5: B'frd 4B 82
Truncliffe Ho. *BD5: B'frd* 4B 82
(off Truncliffe)
Trundles La. WF11: Knot 8G 111
Truro Dr. WF6: Norm 9J 107
Truro St. LS12: Leeds 6M 67
Truro Wlk. WF6: Norm 9J 107
Trust Fold LS25: Bur S 1C 110
Tubby La. HD2: Hud 1N 137
Tudor Barn Ct. BD18: Ship 8B 46
Tudor Cl. LS28: Fars 4N 65
WF8: Pon 6J 129
Tudor Ct. BD5: B'frd 8A 6
WF9: S Elm 6M 163

Tudor Cft.—Upper Warrengate

Tudor Cft. HD2: Hud 6D 120
Tudor Gdns. LS11: Leeds 3A 86
Tudor Ho. HD1: Hud 5C 8
WF1: Wake 5K 9 (5L 125)
Tudor Lawns LS8: Leeds 8L 51
WF2: Carr G 7G 105
Tudor St. BD5: B'frd 8A 6 (1B 82)
HD7: Linth 1N 151
Tudor Way LS11: Leeds 4A 86
WF12: Dew 8E 122
Tuel La. HX6: Sow B 7H 97
Tufters Fold HD6: B Bri 5N 99
Tufton St. BD20: Sils 8D 12
Tuke Gro. WF1: Wake 1L 9 (3M 125)
Tulip Retail Pk. LS10: Leeds 2F 86
Tulip St. BD22: Haw 1C 60
LS10: Leeds 2F 86
Tulyar Ct. BD16: Bgly 4G 45
Tumbling Cl. WF5: Oss 5A 124
Tumbling Hill WF8: Pon 6N 129
Tumbling Hill St. BD7: B'frd 8B 64
Tundra Gro. BD16: Bgly 3H 45
Tun La. S72: S Hien 3L 161
Tunnacliffe Rd. HD4: Hud 7N 137
TUNNEL END 4E 150
Tunnel St. BD13: Denh 6K 61
HD4: Neth 2H 153
Tunnicliffe Pl. BD20: Sils 8D 12
Tunnicliffe Way BD3: B'frd 7K 65
Tunstall Grn. BD4: B'frd 2J 83
Tunstall Rd. LS11: Leeds 2E 86
Tunwell La. BD2: B'frd 2G 64
Tunwell St. BD2: B'frd 2G 65
Tup La. WF4: H'cft 1K 161
Turbary Av. LS28: Fars 4B 66
Turbid La. HD4: S Cros 2F 152
Turbury La. HX4: Gree 3L 117
Turf Ct. BD13: Cull 1J 61
Turf La. BD13: Cull 9J 43
Turf Moor La. LS21: Stainb 1H 19
(not continuous)
Turgate HX7: Myth 4J 95
Turgate La. HX6: Tri 2N 115
Turkey Hill LS28: Pud 8C 66
(not continuous)
Turks Head Yd. LS1: Leeds 6F 4
Turley Cote La. HD3: Outl 1A 136
Turlow Ct. LS9: Leeds 8J 5 (7F 68)
Turnberry Av. LS17: Leeds 3D 50
Turnberry Cl. LS17: Leeds 3D 50
WF3: Ting 4N 103
Turnberry Ct. BD20: Keigh 5G 27
WF6: Norm 2L 127
Turnberry Dr. LS17: Leeds 3D 50
WF3: Ting 4N 103
Turnberry Fold LS17: Leeds 3D 50
Turnberry Gdns. WF3: Ting 4N 103
Turnberry Gro. LS17: Leeds 3D 50
S72: Cud 9K 161
Turnberry Pk. Rd. LS27: Gil 9G 84
Turnberry Pl. LS17: Leeds 3D 50
Turnberry Ri. LS17: Leeds 3D 50
Turnberry Vw. LS17: Leeds 3D 50
Turnbridge Mills HD1: Hud 4D 8 (4N 137)
(not continuous)
Turnbridge Rd. HD1: Hud 4D 8 (4N 137)
Turnbull Ct. LS8: Leeds 1M 69
Turner Av. BD7: B'frd 9L 63
WF17: Bat 7F 102
Turner Av. Nth. HX2: Illing 8K 79
Turner Av. Sth. HX2: Illing 8L 79
Turner Cl. WF3: Ting 4A 104
WF5: Oss 5N 123
Turner Cres. LS21: Otley 8M 17
Turner Dr. WF3: Ting 4A 104
Turner Farm *HX2: Illing* *6L 79*
(off Keighley Rd.)
Turner Ho. LS5: Leeds 2J 67
Turner La. HX3: Hal 1M 7 (3C 98)
(not continuous)
LS29: Add 1J 13
(Addingham Wharfedale Rd.)
LS29: Add 3J 13
(Straight La.)
Turner Pl. BD7: B'frd 9N 63
HX2: Illing 8L 79
Turners Ct. HX3: Hal 2A 98
Turner St. LS28: Fars 3A 66
Turner's Yd. LS13: Leeds 4G 66
LS28: Fars 3A 66
Turner Vw. *HX2: Illing* *9L 79*
(off Bank Edge Rd.)
Turner Way WF2: Wake 7K 9 (6L 125)
Turney St. HX3: Hal 2N 97
(not continuous)
Turnip La. WF12: T'hill 9G 122
Turn Lea HX2: Lud 3C 96
Turn o the Nook WF5: Oss 5M 123
Turnpike Cl. BD11: B'haw 9L 83
Turnpike St. HX5: Ell 4F 118
Turnshaw Rd. BD22: Oak 5N 41
HD8: Kbtn 3K 155
Turnshaws Av. HD8: Kbtn 3L 155
Turnshaws Cl. HD8: Kbtn 2L 155
Turnsteads Av. BD19: Cleck 4F 100
Turnsteads Cl. BD19: Cleck 4G 100
Turnsteads Cres. BD19: Cleck 4G 100
Turnsteads Dr. BD19: Cleck 4G 100
Turnsteads Mt. BD19: Cleck 4G 100
Turnstone Ct. LS10: Leeds 8F 86
Turnways, The LS6: Leeds 2M 67
Turret Hall Rd. HX7: Heb B 2D 94
Turret Royd HX7: Heb B 2D 94
Turret Royd Rd. HX7: Heb B 2D 94
Turton Grn. LS27: Gil 6G 84
Turton St. WF1: Wake 5L 9 (5M 125)
Turton Va. LS27: Gil 7G 84
Turver's La. WF11: Kell 8K 111
Turvin Cotts. HX7: Crag V 2K 115
Turvin Rd. HX6: Ripp 1E 132
Tuscany Way WF6: Alt 6J 107
Twain Cres. WF10: C'frd 7J 109
Tweedale Gdns. WF13: Dew 3E 122
Tweedale St. WF13: Dew 3E 122
Tweed Cl. WF17: Birs 3D 102
Tweedy St. BD15: Wils 1B 62
Twelfth Av. WF15: Liv 7F 100
Twentyman Wlk. LS10: Leeds 9F 86
Twenty Twenty LS2: Leeds 4J 5 (5F 68)
Twickenham Ct. BD8: B'frd 4B 64
Twill Cl. WF2: Wake 4F 124
Twine Cotts. HX7: Heb B 1L 95
Twine La. HX7: Myth 3A 96
Twine St. LS10: Leeds 9G 69
Twinge La. HX3: Sou 6E 98
Twist Clough HX7: Crag V 8L 95
Twitch Hill WF4: Horb 1D 142
Twivey Ct. *WF10: C'frd* *5C 108*
(off Pauline Ter.)
Twivey St. WF10: C'frd 5C 108
Two Gates HD7: Slait 9L 135
Two Gates Way S72: Shaf 7K 161
Two Laws BD22: Old 7F 40
Two Laws Rd. BD22: Old 6D 40
Tyas Gro. LS9: Leeds 7K 69
Tyas La. HD7: Slait 9H 135
Tyburn La. HD8: Eml 3E 156
TYERSAL 8J 65
Tyersal Av. BD4: B'frd 7K 65
Tyersal Cl. BD4: B'frd 8K 65
Tyersal Ct. BD4: B'frd 8J 65
Tyersal Cres. BD4: B'frd 8K 65
Tyersal Dr. BD4: B'frd 8K 65
Tyersal Gth. BD4: B'frd 8K 65
TYERSAL GATE 1J 83
Tyersal Grn. BD4: B'frd 8K 65
Tyersal Gro. BD4: B'frd 8K 65
Tyersal La. BD4: B'frd, Pud 1J 83
LS28: Pud 8N 65
Tyersal M. BD4: B'frd 8K 65
Tyersal Pk. BD4: B'frd 8K 65
Tyersal Rd. BD4: B'frd 8J 65
Tyersal Ter. BD4: B'frd 8J 65
Tyersal Vw. BD4: B'frd 8J 65
Tyersal Wlk. BD4: B'frd 8K 65
Tyler Cl. WF6: Norm 1M 127
Tyler Ct. BD10: B'frd 7G 46
Tyndale Av. WF4: Horb 9E 124
Tyndale Wlk. WF17: Bat 7B 102
Tynedale Ct. LS7: Leeds 9C 50
Tyne St. BD3: B'frd 2D 6 (6D 64)
BD21: Keigh 9K 27
BD22: Haw 8D 42
Tynwald Cl. LS17: Leeds 5C 50
Tynwald Dr. LS17: Leeds 4C 50
Tynwald Gdns. LS17: Leeds 5C 50
Tynwald Grn. LS17: Leeds 4C 50
Tynwald Hill LS17: Leeds 5C 50
Tynwald Mt. LS17: Leeds 4C 50
Tynwald Rd. LS17: Leeds 5C 50
Tynwald Wlk. LS17: Leeds 4C 50
Tyrls, The BD1: B'frd 5B 6 (8C 64)
Tyrrell Ct. WF2: Wake 4F 124
Tyrrel St. BD1: B'frd 4B 6 (7C 64)
Tyson St. BD1: B'frd 2A 6 (6B 64)
HX1: Hal 6L 97

U

UK Superbowl
Huddersfield 1B 138
Ullswater Av. WF12: Dew 1H 123
Ullswater Cl. HX5: Ell 4G 119
WF11: Knot 2D 130
WF12: Dew 1H 123
Ullswater Cres. LS15: Leeds 7N 69
LS26: W'frd 7D 88
Ullswater Dr. BD6: B'frd 7L 81
LS22: Weth 3K 23
Ullswater Ri. LS22: Weth 3K 23
Ullswater Rd. WF12: Dew 1H 123
Umpire Cl. WF1: Wake 1L 125
Una Pl. HD2: Hud 2K 137
UNDER BANK 4M 169
Underbank Av. HX7: Heb B 3D 94
Underbank End Rd. HD9: H'frth 5N 169
Underbank Hoe HX7: Heb B 2D 94
Underbank Old Rd. HD9: H'frth 4N 169
UNDERCLIFFE 4E 64
Undercliffe La. BD3: B'frd 1E 6 (5E 64)
Undercliffe Old Rd. BD2: B'frd 5F 64
Undercliffe Ri. LS29: I'ly 7K 15
Undercliffe Rd. BD2: B'frd 3F 64
Undercliffe St. BD3: B'frd 5F 64
Undercliffe Ter. *HX2: Hal* *8M 97*
(off Scarr Bottom Rd.)
Under Cragg HX7: Heb B 2E 94
Underwood Dr. LS19: Raw 5M 47
Underwood Ho. BD3: B'frd 2D 6
Union Bank Yd. HD1: Hud 5B 8 (4M 137)
Union Bri. Mill LS28: Pud 1E 84
Union Ct. LS21: Otley 1K 31
Union Cross Yd. HX1: Hal 3L 7 (5B 98)
Union Gro. WF15: Liv 9M 101
Union Ho. Ct. BD13: Que 3H 81
Union Ho. La. BD13: Que 3H 81
Union La. HX2: Ogd 5K 79
Union Pl. LS11: Leeds 8D 68
Union Rd. BD7: B'frd 9N 63
BD12: Low M 6A 82
WF15: Liv 9M 101
Union Sq. WF1: Wake 5K 9 (5L 125)
Union St. BD13: Que 4D 80
BD16: Bgly 9D 28
BD17: Bail 5C 46
HD1: Hud 3C 8 (3N 137)
HD3: Hud 2G 137
HD7: Slait 9M 135
HX1: Hal 4L 7 (5B 98)
HX4: Gree 4C 118
HX6: Sow B 7J 97
HX6: Tri 2E 116
HX7: Heb B *1H 95*
(off Commercial St.)
LS2: Leeds 6G 5 (6F 68)
LS21: Otley 1K 31
LS27: Chur 5M 85
OL14: Tod *7K 93*
(off Halifax Rd.)
Union St. WF1: Wake 3K 9 (4L 125)
WF5: Oss 5N 123
WF9: Hems 3E 162
WF13: Dew 3G 122
WF16: Heck 9N 101
WF17: Birs 3B 102
Union St. Sth. HX1: Hal 6B 98
OL14: Tod 7K 93
Union Ter. LS7: Leeds 9E 50
Union Yd. BD10: B'frd 7F 46
United Bus. Pk. LS12: Leeds 1A 86
Unity Cl. LS6: Leeds 2D 68
Unity Ct. HD6: Ras 3L 119
WF13: Dew 3E 122
Unity Hall Ct. WF3: W Ard 5B 104
Unity St. BD20: Rid 6M 27
HX7: Heb B 9H 77
OL14: W'den 3J 113
WF3: Carl 1M 105
Unity St. Nth. BD16: Bgly 5E 44
Unity St. Sth. BD16: Bgly 5E 44
Unity Ter. HX1: Hal 6L 97
University Academy Keighley Athletics Track 7H 27
University of Bradford
Cobden & Forster Buildings *8A 64*
(off Campus Rd.)
Laisteridge Lane Campus 9A 64
School of Health Studies 9B 64
School of Management 2N 63
Tumbling Hill St. 8A 64
University of Bradford Sports Cen. 8A 64
University of Huddersfield, The
Firth St. 7C 8 (5N 137)
Queensgate Campus 6C 8 (5N 137)
Storthes Hall Park Campus 3F 154
University of Leeds
Bretton Hall Campus 3A 158
Woodhouse Lane 2C 4 (5C 68)
University Rd. LS2: Leeds 2B 4 (4C 68)
University St. WF10: C'frd 5D 108
Unna Way HD1: Hud 3B 8 (3M 137)
Unwin Pl. BD9: B'frd 4K 63
Upcroft Ct. BD13: Que 3B 80
Upland Cres. LS8: Leeds 1J 69
Upland Gdns. LS8: Leeds 2J 69
Upland Gro. LS8: Leeds 1J 69
Upland Rd. LS8: Leeds 2J 69
Uplands BD20: Keigh 7G 26
HD2: Hud 1K 137
Uplands, The WF8: Pon 4J 129
Uplands Av. BD13: Que 3G 80
S75: Kex 9E 158
Uplands Cl. BD13: Que 3G 81
Uplands Cres. BD13: Que 3G 80
Uplands Dr. WF14: Mir 5L 121
Uplands Gro. BD13: Que 3G 80
Up. Abbots Royd Caravan Site HX4: Bark 5H 117
Up. Accommodation Rd. LS9: Leeds 6L 5 (6G 69)
Up. Ada St. BD18: Ship 7L 45
Up. Addison St. BD4: B'frd 7D 6 (9D 64)
Up. Allerton La. BD15: All 6D 62
UPPER ARMLEY 5J 67
Up. Ash Gro. WF9: S Elm 6N 163
Up. Ashley La. BD17: Ship 7N 45
Up. Bank End Rd. HD9: H'frth 5N 169
Up. Bank Hey Bottom HX6: Ripp 8E 116
Upper Bankhouse HX2: Mt T 9H 79
Up. Bank St. *WF12: Dew* *3G 123*
(off Cross Bank St.)
Up. Barker St. WF15: Liv 8L 101
Up. Basinghall St. LS1: Leeds 5E 4 (6D 68)
UPPER BATLEY 5F 102
Up. Batley La. WF17: Bat 3C 102
Up. Batley Low La. WF17: Bat 2E 102
Up. Battye St. WF16: Heck 7A 102
Up. Bell Cft. HX3: Sou 8F 98
Up. Bell Hall HX1: Hal 8G 7 (7N 97)
Up. Bentley Royd HX6: Sow B 9G 96
(not continuous)
Up. Birks HX7: Crag V 7L 95
Up. Bolton Brow HX6: Sow B 7K 97
Upper Bonegate HD6: Brigh 9N 99
Up. Brig Royd HX6: Ripp 7D 116
UPPER BROCKHOLES 5K 79
Up. Brow Rd. HD1: Hud 5J 137
Upper Butts BD19: Cleck 5H 101
Up. Calton St. BD21: Keigh 2H 43
Up. Camroyd St. WF13: Dew 2G 123
Up. Carr La. LS28: Cal 9L 47
Up. Carr St. WF15: Liv 7L 101
Up. Castle HX7: Crag V 8K 95
Up. Castle St. BD5: B'frd 8B 6 (9C 64)
Up. Chelsea St. BD21: Keigh 2H 43
UPPER CLOUGH 1B 152
Up. Clough Rd. HD7: Linth 1B 152
Up. Commercial St. WF17: Bat 7F 102
UPPER COMMON
BD12 9B 82
HD8 9H 157
Upper Comn. La. HD8: Clay W 9J 157
Up. Croft Rd. WF17: Bat 8E 102
Up. Cross St. WF13: Dew 2G 122
UPPER CUDWORTH 9J 161
UPPER CUMBERWORTH 2M 171
Up. Deer Play HX6: Mill B 3D 116
UPPER DENBY 5C 172
UPPER EASTWOOD 4B 94
Upper Ellistones *HX4: Gree* *4N 117*
(off Martin Grn. La.)
Up. Ellistones Ct. HX4: Gree 4N 117
UPPER EXLEY 2D 118
UPPER FAGLEY 4J 65
Up. Fawth Cl. BD13: Que 4F 80
Up. Ferndown Grn. BD15: All 5F 62
Upperfield Dr. HD7: Golc 6B 136
Upper Field Ho. La. HX6: Sow B 1D 116
Upperfield La. S75: H Hoy, Kex 8M 157
Upper Fold *HD9: Hon* *5L 153*
(off Southgate)
HD9: New M 2C 170
Up. Forest Rd. S71: Ath 9A 160
Up. Fountain St. HX6: Sow B 8H 97
Up. Fyfe La. BD17: Bail 4C 46
Upper Ga. HD9: H'wth 6C 170
Upper Gaukroger HX6: Sow B 9F 96
Up. George St. BD6: B'frd 4N 81
HD1: Hud 5A 8 (4L 137)
HX1: Hal 4K 7
WF16: Heck 8A 102
Up. Gilbert Flds. HX4: Bark 5J 117
Up. Grange Av. BD15: All 6G 63
UPPER GREEN
BD7 1K 81
WF3 5N 103
Upper Grn. BD7: B'frd 2L 81
BD17: Bail 5N 45
Up. Green Av. BD19: Scho 4D 100
WF3: W Ard 5N 103
Up. Green Cl. WF3: W Ard 5A 104
Up. Green Dr. WF3: W Ard 5A 104
Up. Green La. HD6: Brigh 7K 99
Up. Green Royd HX2: Mt T 9G 79
Up. Greenside HD4: Thurs 6E 154
Up. Green Way WF3: W Ard 5N 103
Up. Hagg Rd. HD9: T'bdge 7N 153
Upper Haley BD22: Oxen 3D 60
Up. Hall Fold HX4: Bark 7H 117
Up. Hall Vw. HX3: North 1F 98
Up. Hatfield Pl. WF4: H'cft 8L 145
Upper Haughs HD7: Golc 5B 136
Up. Haugh Shaw HX1: Hal 7G 7 (7N 97)
Upper Headley BD13: Thorn 9C 62
Upperhead Row HD1: Hud 5A 8 (4M 137)
UPPER HEATON 8F 120
Up. Heaton La. HD5: K'thn 9F 120
Up. Heights Rd. BD13: Thorn 6B 62
Upper Highfield HD7: Slait 7M 135
Up. High Lees HX2: Midg 2C 96
Up. High Royds S75: Dart 9J 159
Up. Hird St. BD21: Keigh 2G 43
Upper Hirst HD3: Hud 2C 136
UPPER HOLME 1K 151
UPPER HOPTON 9K 121
Up. House Cotts. BD13: Que 3F 80
Up. House Fold HD8: Up D 5C 172
Up. House La. WF15: Liv 8G 101
Up. House Rd. HD9: Had E 8A 170
Up. House St. BD4: B'frd 9F 64
Up. Hoyle Ing BD13: Thorn 7E 62
Upper Jackroyd HX3: Hal 3M 97
Upper Kell HX2: Wain 7F 78
Upper Kingston HX1: Hal 6L 97
Up. Kipping Cl. BD13: Thorn 8C 62
Upper Kirkgate HX1: Hal 4M 7 (5C 98)
Upper La. BD19: Gom 5M 101
HD8: Eml 2F 156
HX3: North 9E 80
OL14: Tod 3M 93
WF4: Neth 7M 141
Upper Langley HD8: Clay W 6H 157
Upper Langwith LS22: Coll 9F 22
Up. Lombard St. LS19: Raw 3L 47
Up. Lumb La. HX7: Crag V 8J 95
Up. Lunns Cl. S71: Roys 6F 160
UPPER MARSH 1A 60
Upper Marsh HX3: Sou 7E 98
Up. Marsh La. BD22: Oxen 1N 59
Up. Martin Grn. HX4: Gree 4N 117
Up. Mary St. BD18: Ship 7L 45
Up. Maythorn La. HD9: H'wth 8H 171
Upper Mdws. BD13: Que 5D 80
HD9: U'thng 3J 169
Up. Mill Cotts. BD17: Esh 2F 46
Upper Millergate BD1: B'frd 4A 6
Up. Mill Row BD20: E Mor 6D 28
Upper Mills HD7: Slait 1M 151
Up. Mills Vw. HD9: Mel 7B 152
Uppermoor LS28: Pud 7N 65
Uppermoor Cl. LS28: Pud 8A 66
UPPER MOOR SIDE 3F 84
Up. Mosscar St. BD3: B'frd 4F 6 (7E 64)
Upper Mt. HD9: Mel 8E 152
Up. Mount St. HD1: Hud 6L 137
WF17: Bat 9F 102
Up. Nidd St. BD3: B'frd 8F 64
Upper Nth. St. WF17: Bat 8E 102
UPPER OLDFIELD 8K 153
Upper Ozzings HD8: Shel 9M 155
Up. Parish Ghyll La. LS29: I'ly 6E 14
Up. Park Ga. BD1: B'frd 3D 6 (7D 64)
Up. Peel St. WF13: Dew 2G 122
Upper Piccadilly BD1: B'frd 3A 6 (7C 64)
Up. Pierce Cl. BD22: Cros R 6F 42
Up. Pike Law HD7: Golc 5A 136
Upper Pikeley BD15: All 6C 62
Upper Prospect HD7: Golc 3B 136
Up. Putting Hill HD8: Den D 1E 172
Up. Quarry Rd. HD2: Hud 5E 120
Up. Raglan St. OL14: Tod 6K 93
Upper Range *HX3: Hal* *3B 98*
(off Woodlands Gro.)
Up. Reap Hurst HX2: Mt T 9G 78
Upper Reins HD9: Hon 4M 153
Upper Rd. WF13: Dew 1E 122
WF17: Bat 1E 122
Upper Rotcher HD7: Slait 1L 151
Upper Row *HD9: Holm* *6H 169*
(off Old Rd.)
WF4: G Moor 5B 140
Up. Rushton Rd. BD3: B'frd 5H 65
Up. School St. BD20: Stee 3C 26
Up. Seymour St. BD3: B'frd 7F 64
Upper Slack HX2: Wain 7F 78
Up. South St. WF13: Dew 2F 122
Up. Station Rd. WF17: Bat 8G 103
Upper St. *WF3: Ting* *3B 104*
(off Bradford Rd.)
Upper Stubbins HX6: Tri 3E 116
Up. Sunnybank M. HD9: Mel 7B 152
Up. Sutherland Rd. HX3: Hip 4K 99
UPPER SWITHEN 6D 158
Upper Tewit HX2: Illing 6M 79
UPPERTHONG 3J 169
Upperthong La. HD9: U'thng, H'frth 3K 169
(not continuous)
UPPER TOWN 4C 60
Upper Town BD22: Oxen 4C 60
Up. Town St. LS13: Leeds 3F 66
Upper Warrengate WF1: Wake 4L 9 (5M 125)

Up. Washer La.—Victoria Ter.

Up. Washer La. HX2: Hal 7M 97
Upper Watroyd HD7: Golc 8B 136
Upper Wellhouse HD7: Golc 7B 136
Up. Wellhouse Rd. HD7: Golc 7B 136
Up. Well Royd HX2: Hal 5J 97
Up. Westlock Av. LS9: Leeds 5J 69
Up. West Scausby HX2: Illing 5M 79
Up. West St. WF17: Bat 7H 103
Up. White Lees HX7: Myth 3N 95
Up. Willow Hall HX2: Hal 6K 97
Upper Wilshaw HD9: Mel 9G 152
Up. Woodlands Rd. BD8: B'frd 5M 63
Up. Wood Nook HX6: Sow B 1G 116
Up. Woodview Pl. *LS11: Leeds* *3D 86*
(off Woodview St.)
UPPER WORTLEY 8L 67
Up. Wortley Ct. *LS12: Leeds* *7L 67*
(off Up. Wortley Dr.)
Up. Wortley Dr. LS12: Leeds 7L 67
Up. Wortley Rd. LS12: Leeds 7L 67
UPPER WYKE 1B 100
Up. York St. WF1: Wake 3J 9 (4L 125)
UPTON 2A 164
UPTON BEACON 1N 163
Upton St. WF17: Bat 6E 102
Upton's Yd. LS1: Leeds 6F 4
Upton Wlk. BD15: All 6G 63
Upwood BD20: W Mor 4B 28
Upwood Holiday Pk. BD22: Oxen 3E 60
Upwood La. BD20: E Mor 6C 28
Urban Ter. WF4: G Moor 5B 140
Ure Cres. BD8: B'frd 6A 64
Ure Gro. LS22: Weth 1L 23
Usher St. BD4: B'frd 8D 6 (9E 64)
Uttley St. HX3: Hal 2A 98

V

VALE 3E 92
Vale, The LS6: Leeds 1B 68
LS22: Coll 9H 23
Vale Av. LS8: Leeds 5J 51
WF11: Knot 8C 110
Vale Bower HX7: Myth 4L 95
Vale Cl. HD5: Hud 7D 138
Vale Cres. WF11: Knot 8C 110
Vale Gro. BD13: Que 4E 80
BD20: Sils 8D 12
Vale Head Gro. WF11: Knot 8C 110
Vale Head Mt. WF11: Knot 8C 110
Vale Head Pk. Golf Course 9C 146
Vale Mill La. BD22: Haw 6D 42
Valentine Ct. BD13: Thorn 7D 62
Valentine M. WF3: Loft 4L 105
Vale Rd. WF9: Kins 9B 146
Vales, The BD22: Oxen 4C 60
Valestone Av. WF9: Hems 2E 162
Vale St. BD21: Keigh 7L 27
HD6: Brigh 9M 99
OL14: Tod 7K 93
Vale Ter. BD22: Oak 6D 42
HX7: Myth 4L 95
WF11: Knot 7C 110
Vale Vw. BD20: Sils 8D 12
WF7: Ackw 3H 147
Vale Wlk. WF11: Knot 8C 110
Valley, The LS17: Leeds 1C 50
Valley Av. HX3: Hip 4M 99
WF9: S Elm 6A 164
Valley Cl. LS17: Leeds 1C 50
Valley Ct. BD1: B'frd 5C 64
BD11: Drig 5D 84
LS6: Leeds 2N 67
LS17: Leeds *7F 50*
(off Allerton Grange Gdns.)
WF10: C'frd 7A 108
WF15: Liv 7M 101
Valley Cres. WF2: Wren 1H 125
Valley Dr. LS15: Leeds 5B 70
LS26: Gt P 5M 89
LS29: I'ly 5J 15
WF2: Wren 2H 125
WF12: T'hill 1H 141
Valley Farm Rd. LS10: Leeds 4J 87
Valley Farm Way LS10: Leeds 4J 87
Valley Fold BD13: Que 5D 80
Valley Gdns. LS7: Leeds 7E 50
WF8: D'ton 7D 130
Valley Grn. LS28: Pud 8C 66
Valley Gro. HX2: Illing 6M 79
LS28: Pud 8C 66
Valley Head HD2: Hud 9H 119
Valley Hgts. BD13: Denh 5K 61
Valley Mills LS27: Drig 5E 84
Valley Mt. LS13: Leeds 6D 66
LS25: Kip 3N 89
Valley Pde. BD8: B'frd 5B 64
Valley Pl. BD1: B'frd 5C 64
Valley Ridge LS25: Kip 2N 89
(not continuous)
Valley Ri. *HX6: Mill B* *4D 116*
(off Lumb La.)
LS13: Leeds 1F 66
Valley Rd. BD1: B'frd 1A 6 (4B 64)
BD18: Ship 8N 45
BD19: Cleck 4J 101
BD21: Keigh 9M 27
HX7: Heb B 1H 95
LS13: Leeds 1F 66
LS25: Kip 2N 89
LS27: Morl 8L 85
LS28: Pud 8B 66
LS29: I'ly 4J 15
S75: Map 8J 159
WF5: Oss 7N 123
WF8: D'ton 7D 130
WF8: Pon 3K 129
WF12: T'hill 9J 123
WF15: Liv 8L 101
Valley Rd. Retail Pk.
BD1: B'frd 1B 6 (6C 64)
Valley Sq. LS28: Pud 8C 66
Valley St. WF9: S Elm 7M 163
Valley Ter. LS17: Leeds 4H 51
Valley Vw. BD16: Har 6N 43
BD17: Bail 6N 45
HX2: Illing 6M 79
HX3: Nor G 2L 99
HX7: Hept 9G 76
LS21: Arth 2J 33
LS21: Pool 3E 32
LS28: Pud 7D 66
OL14: Tod 7K 93
WF9: S Elm 6A 164
Valley Vw. Cl. BD22: Oak 4E 42
Valley Vw. Gdns. BD22: Cros R 7E 42
Valley Vw. Gro. BD2: B'frd 3E 64
Valley Vw. Rd. HX7: Hept 9G 77
WF5: Oss 7N 123
Valley Way HX2: Illing 6M 79
Vancouver Pl. LS7: Leeds 9G 50
Vantage Point LS27: Morl 3J 103
Varley Rd. HD7: Slait 4M 151
Varleys Bldgs. *WF4: Horb* *1C 142*
(off High St.)
Varley St. LS28: Stan 5A 66
(not continuous)
Varleys Yd. LS28: Pud 7C 66
Vaughan St. BD1: B'frd 7B 64
HX1: Hal 7M 97
Vaughan Way WF2: Wake 5J 143
Vaux Yd. WF8: Pon 3K 129
Vegal Cres. HX3: Hal 2M 97
Venice M. BD17: Bail 5B 46
Venn St. HD1: Hud 5C 8 (4N 137)
Ventnor Cl. BD19: Gom 2M 101
WF5: Oss 6N 123
Ventnor Dr. WF5: Oss 6N 123
Ventnor St. BD3: B'frd 4F 6 (7E 64)
Ventnor Ter. HX3: Hal 8A 98
Ventnor Way WF5: Oss 6N 123
Vento Cl. BD6: B'frd 5N 81
Verandah Cotts. WF1: Hea 6C 126
Verdun Rd. BD6: B'frd 5M 81
Vere Sq. BD5: B'frd 1C 82
Veritys Pl. LS28: Pud 6C 66
Verity Spur LS9: Leeds 6N 69
Verity St. BD4: E Bier 6K 83
Verity Vw. LS9: Leeds 5N 69
Vermont Cl. HD7: Golc 5B 136
Vermont St. LS13: Leeds 4D 66
Verner St. WF7: F'stne 7C 128
Vernon Av. HD1: Hud 3L 137
Vernon Cl. HD1: Hud 3L 137
Vernon Ct. BD20: Keigh 8H 27
Vernon Pl. BD2: B'frd 4F 64
BD13: Que 6B 80
LS28: Stan 5B 66
OL14: Tod *9J 93*
(off Rochdale Rd.)
WF2: Wake 8K 125
Vernon Rd. LS1: Leeds 3D 4 (5D 68)
WF15: Liv 8M 101
WF16: Heck 8M 101
Vernon St. BD22: Cros R 7F 42
LS2: Leeds 4E 4 (5D 68)
OL14: Tod 9J 93
Vesper Cl. LS5: Leeds 9J 49
Vesper Ct. LS5: Leeds 9H 49
Vesper Ct. Dr. LS5: Leeds 9H 49
Vesper Gdns. LS5: Leeds 1J 67
Vesper Ga. Cres. LS5: Leeds 1J 67
Vesper Ga. Dr. LS5: Leeds 9H 49
Vesper Ga. Mt. LS5: Leeds 9J 49
Vesper Gro. LS5: Leeds 2K 67
Vesper La. LS5: Leeds 1J 67
Vesper Mt. LS5: Leeds 2K 67
Vesper Pl. LS5: Leeds 2K 67
LS27: Morl *2K 103*
(off High St.)
Vesper Ri. LS5: Leeds 9H 49
Vesper Rd. LS5: Leeds 9G 49
Vesper Ter. LS5: Leeds 2K 67
Vesper Wlk. LS5: Leeds 1H 67
Vesper Way LS5: Leeds 9H 49
Vestry St. BD4: B'frd 2F 82
Viaduct Cotts. HD8: Den D 3C 172
Viaduct Rd. LS4: Leeds 5N 67
Viaduct St. HD1: Hud 3B 8 (3M 137)
(not continuous)
HD7: Slait 9N 135
LS28: Stan 5A 66
Viaduct Theatre
Halifax *1K 7*
(within Dean Clough)
Vicarage Av. LS5: Leeds 2L 67
LS27: Gil 7F 84
Vicarage Cl. BD12: Wyke 2A 100
WF1: Out 7K 105
WF9: S Kirk 6J 163
Vicarage Ct. BD19: Cleck 4H 101
Vicarage Dr. HD9: Mel 8C 152
LS28: Pud 7A 66
Vicarage Gdns. BD11: B'haw 8L 83
HD6: Ras 3L 119
LS21: Otley 1L 31
WF7: F'stne 3D 128
Vicarage La. LS23: B'ham 6D 38
S71: Roys 6D 160
WF7: F'stne 6D 128
Vicarage Mdw. WF14: Mir 6N 121
Vicarage Mdws. HD9: H'frth 4N 169
Vicarage M. BD2: B'frd 3E 64
LS5: Leeds *2L 67*
(off Vicarage Ter.)
WF4: Wool 2J 159
Vicarage Pl. LS5: Leeds 2L 67
Vicarage Rd. BD18: Ship 7C 46
HD3: Hud 4F 136
LS6: Leeds 4B 68
WF12: Dew 3G 122
(Longcauseway)
WF12: Dew 6F 122
(Savile Rd.)
Vicarage St. LS5: Leeds 2L 67
Vicarage St. Sth. WF1: Wake 4L 9 (5M 125)
Vicarage Ter. LS5: Leeds 2L 67
WF17: Bat 5D 102
Vicarage Vw. LS5: Leeds 2L 67
Vicar La. BD1: B'frd 4C 6 (7D 64)
(not continuous)
LS1: Leeds 6G 5 (6E 68)
LS2: Leeds 6G 5 (6E 68)
WF4: Horb *1D 142*
(off Church St.)
WF5: Oss 8A 124
Vicar Pk. Dr. HX2: Hal 4H 97
Vicar Pk. Rd. HX2: Hal 5H 97
Vicars Cft. WF11: B'ton 4B 110
Vicars M. WF11: B'ton 4B 110
Vicars Rd. LS8: Leeds 2H 69
Vicars Ter. LS8: Leeds 2H 69
WF10: All B 9B 90
Vicar St. *WF15: Liv* *7L 101*
(off Knowler Hill)
Vickerman Cres. HD4: Hud 9L 137
Vickerman St. HX1: Hal 6M 97
(not continuous)
Vickers Av. LS5: Leeds 3J 67
WF9: S Elm 8L 163
Vickersdale LS28: Stan 4B 66
Vickersdale Ct. LS28: Stan 4B 66
Vickersdale Gro. *LS28: Stan* *4B 66*
(off Arthur St.)
Vickers Pl. LS28: Stan 4B 66
Vickers St. LS27: Morl 2J 103
WF10: C'frd 4D 108
Victor Dr. LS20: Guis 8J 31
VICTORIA
HD9, Hepworth 9F 170
HD9, Holmfirth 4K 169
Victoria Av. BD2: B'frd 2H 65
BD18: Ship 7L 45
BD19: Cleck 5H 101
BD21: Keigh 8J 27
BD22: Haw 7C 42
HD6: Clift 9A 100
HX1: Hal 6M 97
HX5: Ell 5D 118
HX6: Sow B 8J 97
LS9: Leeds 6J 69
LS18: Hors 8D 48
LS19: Yead 1A 48
LS26: Rothw 9N 87
LS27: Morl 8K 85
LS29: I'ly 5E 14
LS29: Men 3D 30
WF1: Out 9K 105
WF2: Wake 5J 125
WF17: Bat 8F 102
Victoria Bldgs. HX7: Crag V 1K 115
WF12: Dew 2H 123
Victoria Chase HD6: B Bri 4N 99
Victoria Cl. HD4: Hud 1L 153
LS18: Hors 8D 48
LS19: Yead 9A 32
LS29: I'ly 5F 14
WF10: All B 9B 90
Victoria Ct. *BD18: Ship* *7L 45*
(off Victoria Av.)
BD21: Keigh 8H 27
HD1: Hud 8A 8 (6M 137)
HD3: Hud 4F 136
LS6: Leeds 2M 67
LS15: Leeds 2E 70
LS21: Otley *1L 31*
(off Station Rd.)
LS22: Weth *4N 23*
(off Horsefair)
LS27: Morl *8K 85*
(off Victoria M.)
WF9: Upt 2N 163
WF10: C'frd 6D 108
WF17: Birs 3C 102
Victoria Ct. M. LS6: Leeds 3A 68
Victoria Cres. HX5: Ell 5E 118
LS18: Hors 8D 48
LS28: Pud 7N 65
WF13: Dew 1E 122
Victoria Dr. BD2: B'frd 2H 65
HX3: North 1G 98
LS18: Hors 8D 48
LS27: Morl 7L 85
LS29: I'ly 5E 14
WF12: Dew 7F 122
Victoria Gdns. LS18: Hors 8E 48
LS28: Pud 7N 65
LS29: I'ly 5E 14
Victoria Grange Dr. LS27: Morl 8K 85
Victoria Grange Way LS27: Morl 8K 85
Victoria Gro. LS9: Leeds 6K 69
LS18: Hors 9D 48
LS28: Pud 7N 65
LS29: I'ly 5E 14
WF2: Wake 8F 124
Victoria Hall
Keighley 8K 27
Victoria Ho's. *LS5: Leeds* *2K 67*
(off Church St.)
Victoria Ind. Est. BD2: B'frd 2G 65
Victoria Ind. Pk. LS14: Leeds 8C 52
Victoria La. HD1: Hud 6C 8 (5N 137)
HD7: Golc 6B 136
LS18: Hors 8D 48
Victoria M. *BD21: Keigh* *9H 27*
(off Cartmel Rd.)
HX5: Ell *5E 118*
(off John St.)
LS18: Hors 8D 48
LS27: Morl 8K 85
Victoria Mills HD9: H'frth 4K 169
WF17: Bat 6E 102
Victoria Mills 1 BD17: Ship 6N 45
Victoria Mills 2 BD17: Ship 6N 45
Victoria Mt. LS18: Hors 7D 48
Victorian Arc. *LS29: I'ly* *5G 14*
(off Church St.)
Victoria Pk. BD18: Ship 8L 45
HX1: Hal 5N 97
Victoria Pk. Av. LS5: Leeds 3H 67
LS13: Leeds 3H 67
Victoria Pk. Gro. LS5: Leeds 3J 67
LS13: Leeds 3H 67
Victoria Pk. St. BD21: Keigh 8K 27
Victoria Pk. Vw. BD21: Keigh 8K 27
Victoria Pl. BD10: B'frd 1G 65
HD4: Hud 9F 136
HD5: Hud 5B 138
HD6: Ras 2N 119
HD9: Hon 5L 153
HX2: Lud F 7E 96
HX3: North 1G 98
LS11: Leeds 8D 68
LS19: Yead 9L 31
LS23: Cliff 4D 38
LS26: Meth 1K 107
WF10: C'frd 4D 108
WF14: Mir 6K 121
Victoria Quarter LS1: Leeds 6G 5 (6E 68)
Victoria Ri. LS28: Pud 7N 65
Victoria Rd. BD2: B'frd 1G 65
BD6: B'frd 5M 81
BD10: B'frd 1G 65
BD18: Ship 7L 45
BD19: Gom 4N 101
BD21: Keigh 1H 43
BD22: Haw 8D 42
BD22: Oak 5D 42
DN6: Nort 7N 149
HD1: Hud 8A 8 (7L 137)
HD6: B Bri 4N 99
HD9: Mel 7C 152
HX1: Hal 5N 97
HX3: Hip 5J 99
HX5: Ell 5C 118
HX6: Sow B 9H 97
HX7: Heb B 9H 77
LS5: Leeds 2K 67
LS6: Leeds 3A 68
LS11: Leeds 8E 4 (8D 68)
LS14: Leeds 8C 52
LS20: Guis 8H 31
LS26: Rothw 7M 87
LS27: Chur, Morl 8K 85
LS28: Fars 4A 66
LS28: Pud 7N 65
LS29: Burl W 8C 16
LS29: I'ly 5E 14
OL14: Tod 6K 93
S71: Roys 5E 160
WF12: Dew 7F 122
WF13: Dew 2F 122
WF15: Liv 9L 101
Victoria Spring Bus. Pk. WF15: Liv 8M 101
Victoria Springs HD9: H'frth 4K 169
Victoria Sq. HD9: H'frth 3M 169
HX6: Ripp 7D 116
LS1: Leeds 5D 4 (6D 68)
Victoria St. BD1: B'frd 1A 6 (6B 64)
BD2: B'frd 4G 65
BD10: B'frd 5F 46
BD13: Cull 9L 43
BD13: Que 4E 80
BD14: Clay 1G 81
BD15: All 3F 62
BD15: Wils 2B 62
BD16: Bgly 9D 28
(New St.)
BD16: Bgly 5E 44
(York Cres.)
BD17: Bail 6A 46
BD17: Ship 7N 45
BD19: Cleck 4H 101
BD22: Oak *5D 42*
(off Victoria Rd.)
HD1: Hud 8A 8 (6M 137)
HD2: Hud 8C 120
HD3: Hud 2H 137
HD5: Hud 5B 138
HD6: Clift 9A 100
HD6: Ras 2N 119
HD7: Mars 5F 150
HD8: Clay W 7H 157
HD9: H'frth 3M 169
HX1: Hal 3K 7 (5B 98)
HX4: Gree 4C 118
HX6: Sow B 9H 97
LS3: Leeds 4A 4 (5B 68)
LS7: Leeds 8F 50
LS22: Weth 4M 23
LS27: Chur 6M 85
LS27: Morl 8J 85
LS28: Cal 9L 47
OL14: Tod 3E 92
S72: Cud 9J 161
WF1: Out 8K 105
WF2: Wake 4J 125
WF4: Horb 1B 142
WF7: Ackw 5D 146
WF7: F'stne 6D 128
WF8: Pon 9K 109
WF9: Hems 3E 162
WF10: All B 9B 90
WF10: C'frd 4B 108
WF13: Raven 5B 122
WF16: Heck 8A 102
WF17: Bat 6E 102
WF17: Birs 3C 102
Victoria Ter. BD18: Ship 6L 45
BD19: Cleck *5H 101*
(off Victoria Av.)
BD21: Keigh *9K 27*
(off Berry St.)
HD8: Clay W 7J 157
HX1: Hal *6N 97*
(off Hopwood La.)
HX2: Hal 8N 97
HX2: Lud F 7E 96
HX3: Hip 5J 99
HX6: Mill B 4D 116
LS3: Leeds 4A 4 (5B 68)
LS5: Leeds 2K 67
LS6: Leeds 9N 49
LS19: Yead 9N 31
LS20: Guis *7J 31*
(off West Pde.)
LS28: Stan 4C 66
LS29: Add *1M 13*
(off Main St.)

Victoria Ter.—Warley Wood

Victoria Ter. OL14: Tod 5B 94
WF4: Horb 1N 141
Victoria Theatre, The
Halifax 5K 7
Victoria Vs. LS28: Stan 5B 66
Victoria Wlk. *LS1: Leeds* 6F 4
(within The Core Shop. Cen.)
LS18: Hors 8D 48
Victoria Way WF1: Out 9K 105
Victoria Works HX2: Hal 6N 79
Victor Rd. BD9: B'frd 4N 63
WF9: S Kirk 7J 163
Victor St. BD3: B'frd 7J 65
BD9: B'frd 4N 63
DN6: Carc 9N 165
WF9: S Elm 7M 163
WF10: C'frd 7C 108
WF17: Bat 7G 103
Victor Ter. BD9: B'frd 4N 63
HX1: Hal 4N 97
Victory Av. HD3: Hud 5G 137
WF3: S'ley 1B 126
Victory Rd. LS29: I'ly 5G 15
Vienna Ct. LS27: Chur 5M 85
View, The HD9: Hon 6J 153
LS8: Leeds 7H 51
LS17: Leeds 1B 50
View Cft. Rd. BD17: Ship 7A 46
Viewlands HD2: Fix 7M 119
LS29: Midd 2H 15
WF8: Lit S 3K 149
Viewlands Cres. LS29: Men 3H 31
Viewlands Mt. LS29: Men 3H 31
Viewlands Ri. LS29: Men 4H 31
View Pl. BD13: Que 3B 80
View Rd. BD20: Keigh 8G 27
View Row BD15: All 6H 63
Views, The S75: Map 8K 159
View St. HD5: Hud 5B 138
Vignola Ter. BD14: Clay 9H 63
Viking Av. HD8: Eml 3G 156
Viking Rd. WF8: Pon 3L 129
Villa Cl. WF7: Ackw 2H 147
Villa Gdns. HX3: She 7J 81
WF17: Bat 9G 102
Village, The HD4: Farn T 3D 154
HD4: Thurs 8C 154
HD9: H'lm 8E 168
LS23: T Arch 8E 24
Village Av. LS4: Leeds 4N 67
Village Ct. S72: Cud 9K 161
Village Farm Cl. DN14: Beal 5N 111
Village Farm Ct. DN14: Beal 5N 111
Village Gdns. LS15: Leeds 8E 70
(not continuous)
Village Golf Course, The 7N 35
Village Hotel & Leisure Club
Leeds 7M 49
Village M. BD15: Wils 1B 62
Village Pl. LS4: Leeds 4N 67
Village Rd. LS16: Ecc 6B 34
Village St. HX3: Nor G 1L 99
Village Street, The LS4: Leeds 4N 67
Village Ter. LS4: Leeds 3N 67
Villa Gro. BD16: Bgly 3F 44
Villa Mt. BD12: Wyke 3A 100
Villa Rd. BD16: Bgly 3F 44
Villas, The BD19: Cleck 5J 101
Villa St. HX6: Sow B 8J 97
Villa Ter. HX4: Bark 9H 117
Villier Ct. BD15: All 5G 63
Vincent Av. BD20: East 3A 26
Vincent St. BD1: B'frd 4A 6 (7B 64)
HX1: Hal 6M 97
Vine Av. BD19: Cleck 4G 101
Vine Cl. HD6: Clift 1B 120
Vine Cotts. LS25: Aber 7E 54
Vine Ct. HD6: Clift 1B 120
LS20: Guis 8J 31
Vine Cres. BD19: Cleck 4G 101
Vine Gth. HD6: Clift 9B 100
Vine Gro. HD6: Clift 1B 120
Vine Ind. Est. HD6: Brigh 9L 99
Vine Pl. BD2: B'frd 3F 64
Vinery Av. LS9: Leeds 6J 69
Vinery Cl. HD8: Clay W 7J 157
Vinery Gro. LS9: Leeds 6J 69
Vinery Mt. LS9: Leeds 7J 69
Vinery Pl. LS9: Leeds 7J 69
Vinery Rd. LS4: Leeds 4N 67
Vinery St. LS9: Leeds 6J 69
Vinery Ter. LS9: Leeds 7J 69
Vinery Vw. LS9: Leeds 7J 69
Vine St. BD7: B'frd 9N 63
BD19: Cleck 4H 101
HD1: Hud 1D 8 (2N 137)
Vine Ter. BD13: Thorn 8C 62
HX1: Hal 6J 7 (6A 98)
LS21: Askw 4D 16
Vine Ter. E. BD8: B'frd 6K 63
Vine Ter. W. BD8: B'frd 6K 63
Vineyard HD7: Golc 5C 136
OL12: Whit 6A 112
Vintage Carriages Trust Museum of Rail Travel
3H 43
(off Halifax Rd.)
Vint Ri. BD10: B'frd 8E 46
Violet Cl. WF10: C'frd 7B 108
Violet Farm Ct. S72: B'ley 7A 162
Violet Pritchard Ho. *WF8: Pon* 2K 129
(off Horsefair)
Violet Rd. WF3: E Ard 4H 105
Violet St. BD22: Haw 1C 60
HX1: Hal 5N 97
Violet St. Nth. HX1: Hal 4N 97
Violet Ter. HX6: Sow B 8J 97
Virgin Active
Bradford 6K 65
Leeds, Cardigan Flds. Rd. 5M 67
Leeds, Centaur Ho. 5C 4
Leeds, The Headrow 5E 4
Virginia Cl. WF3: Loft 6J 105
Virginia Ct. WF3: Loft 6J 105
WF5: Oss 6A 124
Virginia Dr. WF3: Loft 6J 105
Virginia Gdns. WF3: Loft 6J 105
Virginia Rd. HD3: Hud 3H 137
Virginia St. BD14: Clay 2H 81
Virginia Ter. *BD14: Clay* 2H 81
(off Virginia St.)
LS14: T'ner 2G 52
Vissett Cl. WF9: Hems 3B 162
Vissitt La. WF9: Hems 3A 162
Vivian Pl. BD7: B'frd 2M 81
Vivien Rd. BD8: B'frd 6H 63
Vollan's Ct. LS14: Leeds 1B 70
Vue Cinema
Halifax 3L 7 (5B 98)
Leeds, Cardigan Flds. Rd. 5N 67
Leeds, The Headrow 5F 4 (6E 68)
Vulcan Cl. WF13: Dew 3F 122
Vulcan Gdns. WF13: Dew 3F 122
Vulcan Rd. WF13: Dew 3E 122
Vulcan St. BD4: B'frd 4H 83
HD6: Brigh 2A 120
OL14: W'den 2J 113

W

Waddington St. BD21: Keigh 1J 43
Wade Ho. Av. HX3: She 7H 81
Wade Ho. Rd. HX3: She 8H 81
Wade La. LS2: Leeds 5F 4 (6E 68)
Wade St. HX1: Hal 3L 7 (5B 98)
LS28: Fars 3A 66
Wadhouse La. WF2: Wake 2H 143
WF4: Dur 2H 143
Wadlands Cl. LS28: Fars 2A 66
Wadlands Dr. LS28: Fars 3N 65
Wadlands Gro. LS28: Fars 2N 65
Wadlands Ri. LS28: Fars 3N 65
Wadman Rd. HD9: Scho 5B 170
WADSWORTH 7J 77
Wadsworth BD22: Oxen 5C 60
Wadsworth Av. *OL14: Tod* 9J 93
(off Weir St.)
Wadsworth Ct. BD19: Cleck 4G 100
HX1: Hal 4N 97
Wadsworth La. HX7: Heb B 1J 95
Wadsworth St. HX1: Hal 4M 97
(not continuous)
Wadsworth Vw. *HX7: Hept* 8G 77
(off Northgate)
Wager La. S72: B'ley 6A 162
Waggon La. WF9: Upt 2A 164
Waggon Rd. LS10: Leeds 9F 86
Wagon La. BD16: Bgly 6F 44
Wagtail Cl. BD6: B'frd 4H 81
Waides Bldgs. LS26: Meth 1M 107
Wain Brow HD4: Hud 1L 153
Waincliffe Cres. LS11: Leeds 4B 86
Waincliffe Dr. LS11: Leeds 5B 86
Waincliffe Gth. LS11: Leeds 4B 86
Waincliffe Ho. *BD4: B'frd* 8H 65
(off Fearnville Dr.)
Waincliffe Mt. LS11: Leeds 4B 86
Waincliffe Pl. LS11: Leeds 4B 86
Waincliffe Sq. LS11: Leeds 4B 86
Waincliffe Ter. LS11: Leeds 5B 86
Wain Ct. HD4: Hud 1L 153
Waindale Cl. HX2: Mt T 1G 97
Waindale Cres. HX2: Mt T 1G 97
Wain Dyke Cl. WF6: Norm 9K 107
Waindyke Way WF6: Norm 1L 127
Wainfleet Ho. *BD3: B'frd* 6J 65
(off Rushton Rd.)
Waingate HD4: Hud 1L 153
HD7: Linth 1C 152
Waingate Pk. HD7: Linth 9C 136
Wainhouse Rd. HX1: Hal 7M 97
Wainhouse Ter. *HX2: Hal* 7M 97
(off Burnley Rd.)
Wainhouse Tower 7M 97
Wainman Sq. BD12: Wyke 1A 100
Wainman St. BD12: Wyke 1A 100
BD17: Bail 3B 46
BD17: Ship 7N 45
HX1: Hal 5M 97
Wain Pk. HD4: Hud 1L 153
Wainscot Cl. HX7: Wads 7J 77
Wainscot Pl. DN6: Skel 7M 165
Wainsgate HX7: Wads 7J 77
Wainsgate La. HX7: Wads 7J 77
WAINSTALLS 7F 78
Wainstalls La. HX2: Wain 8E 78
Wainstalls Lodge La. HX2: Wain 8E 78
Wainstalls Rd. HX2: Wain 7F 78
Waites Cft. WF2: Kirk 1D 124
Waites Ter. LS21: Otley 1M 31
Waite St. WF2: Wake 5G 124
WAKEFIELD 4K 9 (4L 125)
Wakefield 41 Ind. Pk. WF2: Carr G 7H 105
(Telford Way)
WF2: Carr G 6H 105
(Trevor Ter.)
Wakefield Av. LS14: Leeds 5A 70
Wakefield Commercial Pk. WF4: Horb 2A 142
Wakefield Crematorium WF4: Crig 4J 143
Wakefield Cres. WF12: Dew 3J 123
Wakefield Europort WF6: Alt 7K 107
(Pope St.)
WF6: Alt 6J 107
(Tuscany Way)
Wakefield FC
College Grove 1K 9 (3L 125)
Wakefield Ga. HX3: Hal 8M 97
Wakefield Golf Course 4M 143
Wakefield Kirkgate Station (Rail) 6M 9 (6M 125)
Wakefield Mus. 4H 9 (5K 125)
Wakefield Old Rd. WF12: Dew 3G 122
Wakefield One WF1: Wake 4H 9
Wakefield Rd. BD4: B'frd 6D 6 (8D 64)
(not continuous)
BD11: Drig 7C 84
(not continuous)
DN6: Hamp 5D 164
HD1: Hud 6D 8 (5N 137)
HD5: Fen B 6D 8 (4F 138)
HD5: Hud 5A 138
Wakefield Rd. HD6: B Bri 5J 99
HD6: Brigh, Hud 1N 119
(not continuous)
HD8: Clay W, Den D, Eml 3B 172
HD8: Fen B, Lept 7L 139
HX3: Hal 8K 97
HX3: Hip 5J 99
HX6: Sow B 8K 97
LS10: Leeds 3H 87
LS24: Saxt 9J 55
LS25: Aber 9J 55
LS25: Gar 8K 71
LS26: Gar, Kip, Swil 5F 88
LS26: Leeds, Rothw 8K 87
LS26: Oul 3C 106
LS27: Gil, Morl 8F 84
S71: Ath, Smit 6L 159
(not continuous)
S75: S'ross 6L 159
WF1: Warm 5F 126
WF4: G Moor 7A 140
WF4: Horb 1D 142
WF5: Oss 4A 124
(Dewsbury Rd., not continuous)
WF5: Oss 3L 123
(Co-operative St.)
WF6: Norm 4G 127
WF7: Ackw 5D 146
WF7: Street 6M 127
WF8: F'stne, Pon 5G 128
WF9: Fitz, Hems, Kins 6A 146
WF12: Dew, Oss 3G 123
(not continuous)
WF14: Mir 2D 120
WF15: Liv 8M 101
Wakefield Sports Club 1K 9 (3L 125)
Wakefield Theatre Royal & Opera House 4H 9
Wakefield Trinity Wildcats RLFC 8N 125
Wakefield Westgate Station (Rail) 4G 9 (5K 125)
Walden Dr. BD9: B'frd 3H 63
Walden Howe Cl. WF7: F'stne 3C 128
Walden St. WF10: C'frd 5D 108
Waldorf Way WF2: Wake 7J 9 (6L 125)
Walesby Ct. LS16: Leeds 5H 49
Walford Av. LS9: Leeds 6J 69
Walford Gro. LS9: Leeds 6J 69
Walford Mt. LS9: Leeds 6J 69
Walford Rd. LS9: Leeds 6J 69
Walford Ter. LS9: Leeds 6J 69
Walk, The BD21: Keigh 1J 43
LS28: Fars 4N 65
Walker Av. BD7: B'frd 9K 63
(not continuous)
WF2: Wake 4H 125
Walker Dr. BD8: B'frd 6N 63
Walkergate LS21: Otley 9L 17
WF8: Pon 2L 129
Walker Grn. WF12: T'hill 9H 123
Walker Ho. LS5: Leeds 2J 67
Walker La. HX6: Sow B 8K 97
HX7: Chis 8K 77
WF4: Horb 1D 142
Walker Pl. BD18: Ship 7B 46
LS27: Chur 6L 85
Walker Rd. BD12: O'haw 9D 82
LS18: Hors 6E 48
LS29: Men 4D 30
Walkers Bldgs. *LS28: Pud* 6B 66
(off Clifton Hill)
Walker's Grn. LS12: Leeds 1M 85
Walker's La. BD20: Sils 2D 12
LS12: Leeds 1M 85
(not continuous)
Walkers Mt. LS6: Leeds 1B 68
WF17: Bat 9F 102
Walker's Pl. BD20: Sils 9E 12
Walkers Row LS19: Yead 9L 31
Walkers Ter. WF1: Wake 4H 9 (5K 125)
Walker St. BD4: B'frd 5F 82
BD19: Cleck 4H 101
BD19: Scho 4D 100
WF12: Dew 7G 122
(Ingham Rd.)
WF12: Dew 5J 123
(Long La.)
WF13: Raven 7A 122
Walker Ter. BD4: B'frd 1F 82
BD13: Cull 1K 61
Walker Vw. LS10: Leeds 9F 86
Walker Wood BD17: Bail 5L 45
Walkley Av. WF16: Heck 9A 102
Walkley Clogs *3M 95*
(off Midgley Rd.)
Walkley Gro. WF16: Heck 9A 102
Walkley La. WF16: Heck 9A 102
Walkley Ter. WF16: Heck 1B 122
Walkley Vs. WF16: Heck 1B 122
Wallace Gdns. WF3: Loft 6K 105
Wallace St. HX1: Hal 6M 97
Wallbank Dr. BD18: Ship 9A 46
Walled Garden, The WF4: Wool 2J 159
Waller Clough HD7: Golc 6M 135
Waller Clough Rd. HD7: Golc 6M 135
Wallingford Mt. BD15: All 7G 63
Wallis St. BD8: B'frd 7L 63
(Greenside La.)
BD8: B'frd 7M 63
(Waterside Rd.)
HX6: Sow B 8H 97
Wall Nook La. HD8: Cumb 2H 171
Wallroyds HD8: Den D 3B 172
Wall St. BD22: Keigh 1F 42
Walmer Gro. LS28: Pud 9C 66
Walmer Vs. BD8: B'frd 5B 64
Walmsley Dr. WF9: Upt 2A 164
Walmsley Rd. LS6: Leeds 3A 68
Walnut Av. WF2: Wake 4H 125
WF12: Dew 4K 123
Walnut Bus. Pk. HX1: Hal 5N 97
Walnut Cl. LS14: Leeds 7D 52
LS24: Saxt 9N 55
(not continuous)
WF12: Dew 5K 123
Walnut Cres. WF2: Wake 4H 125
WF12: Dew 4K 123
Walnut Dr. WF6: Norm 4H 127
WF8: Pon 5J 129
WF12: Dew 4L 123
Walnut Gro. WF12: Dew 4L 123
Walnut La. WF12: Dew 4K 123
Walnut Pl. WF12: Dew 4K 123
Walnut Rd. WF12: Dew 4K 123
Walnut St. BD3: B'frd 8G 64
BD21: Keigh 3H 43
HX1: Hal 5N 97
WF9: S Elm 8M 163
WALPOLE 7H 137
Walpole Rd. HD4: Hud 7H 137
WALSDEN 3K 113
Walsden Ind. Est. OL14: W'den 4K 113
Walsden Station (Rail) 2J 113
Walsham Dr. HD3: Hud 1D 136
Walshaw La. HX7: Heb B 2D 76
Walshaw St. BD7: B'frd 1M 81
Walsh La. BD16: Bgly 1E 44
HX3: Hal 1H 7 (3A 98)
LS12: N Far 3F 84
Walsh's Sq. HX1: Hal 8G 7
Walsh St. HX1: Hal 5M 97
Walter Clough La. HX3: Sou 7G 98
Walter Cres. LS9: Leeds 8M 5 (7H 69)
Walter St. BD2: B'frd 2B 64
BD10: B'frd 7F 46
LS4: Leeds 5N 67
Waltham Dr. DN6: Skel 7K 165
Waltin Rd. HD9: H'frth 7L 169
WALTON
LS23 5G 24
WF2 3B 144
Walton Chase LS23: T Arch 6F 24
Walton Colliery Nature Pk. 1D 144
Walton Cft. HD5: Hud 4C 138
LS28: Fars 3A 66
(off Water La.)
Walton Dr. BD11: Drig 7C 84
Walton Fold *OL14: Tod* 6M 93
(off Cross Stone Rd.)
Walton Gdns. LS23: T Arch 6F 24
Walton Gth. BD11: Drig 8C 84
Walton Gates LS23: T Arch 5D 24
Walton Golf Cen. (Driving Range) 5A 144
Walton Head La. HG3: Kirkby 1E 20
Walton La. BD19: Scho 7C 100
WF2: Wake 1N 143
Walton Locks WF2: W'ton 3C 144
Walton Rd. LS22: Weth 4N 23
LS23: T Arch 5A 24
(Watersole La.)
LS23: T Arch 8F 24
(Church C'way)
WF9: Upt 1C 164
Waltons Bldgs. HX2: Hal 9M 79
Waltons Hgts. WF15: Liv 8F 100
Walton Sta. La. WF2: Wake 3N 143
Walton St. BD4: B'frd 7D 6 (9D 64)
HX6: Sow B 8H 97
LS10: Leeds 1G 86
LS11: Leeds 8D 68
Walton Vw. WF4: Croft 2G 145
Walton Wood M. WF9: Upt 9C 148
Walt Royd HX2: Mix 1K 97
Waltroyd Rd. BD19: Cleck 5G 100
Wand La. HX3: Hip 4H 99
Wansford Cl. BD4: B'frd 3J 83
LS15: Leeds 6F 70
Wanstead Cres. BD15: All 6G 63
WAPPING 2D 6 (6D 64)
Wapping Nick La. HD3: Hud 9D 118
(not continuous)
Wapping Rd. BD3: B'frd 1C 6 (6D 64)
Warburton HD8: Eml 3F 156
Warburton Pl. BD6: B'frd 4A 82
Warcock La. HX7: Blac H 9M 75
Ward Bank Rd. HD9: H'frth 5L 169
Ward Ct. HD6: Ras 4L 119
Ward Fall WF4: Hol 7H 143
Ward La. LS10: Leeds 4F 86
WF3: S'ley 1B 126
Wardle Cres. BD21: Keigh 8F 26
Wardman St. BD21: Keigh 8L 27
Ward Pl. La. HD9: H'frth 5L 169
Wards End BD13: Thorn 6C 62
HX1: Hal 4L 7 (6B 98)
Wards Hill WF17: Bat 7F 102
Wards Hill Ct. WF17: Bat 7F 102
Wards Pl. WF17: Bat 7D 102
Ward Sq. HD1: Hud 5A 8
Ward St. BD7: B'frd 2M 81
BD21: Keigh 1H 43
WF13: Dew 2G 122
(Caulms Wood Rd.)
WF13: Dew 2F 122
(Bradford Rd., not continuous)
Wareham Cnr. BD4: B'frd 3J 83
Warehouse, The *LS5: Leeds* 2J 67
(off Broad La.)
Warehouse Hill Rd. HD7: Mars 5F 150
Warehouse St. WF17: Bat 8G 103
Warhurst Rd. HX5: Ell 3F 118
WARING GREEN 9M 99
Warings Bldgs. WF3: W Ard 5N 103
Waring Way WF12: Dew 2H 123
WARLAND 6M 113
Warland Ga. End OL14: W'den 6M 113
Warlbeck LS29: I'ly 5E 14
Warley Av. BD3: B'frd 6H 65
Warley Dene HX2: Hal 6H 97
Warley Dr. BD3: B'frd 7H 65
Warley Edge HX2: Hal 5J 97
Warley Edge La. HX2: Hal 5H 97
Warley Gro. BD3: B'frd 6H 65
HX2: Hal 5K 97
Warley Rd. HX1: Hal 5K 97
HX2: Hal 5K 97
Warley St. HX1: Hal 6N 97
WARLEY TOWN 6H 97
Warley Town La. HX2: Hal 5G 97
Warley Vw. HX2: Hal 5K 97
LS13: Leeds 2E 66
Warley Wood HX2: Lud F 7F 96

Well Ho. Cres.—Westerman St.

Well Ho. Cres. LS8: Leeds 1J 69
Well Ho. Dr. LS8: Leeds 1J 69
Wellhouse Flds. HD7: Golc 8C 136
Wellhouse Gdns. LS8: Leeds 1J 69
Wellhouse Grn. HD7: Golc 7C 136
Wellhouse La. HD5: Hud 1E 138
WF14: Mir 3L 121
Well Ho. Rd. LS8: Leeds 1J 69
Wellhouse Rd. HD7: Golc 7C 136
Well Houses HD9: H'frth 6L 169
Well Ings Cl. HD8: Shep 8K 155
Wellington Arc. HD6: Brigh 1N 119
(off Briggate)
Wellington Bri. St.
LS1: Leeds 7B 4 (7B 68)
LS3: Leeds 6A 4 (6B 68)
Wellington Bus. Cen. HX5: Ell 4F 118
Wellington Ct. BD11: B'haw 7L 83
HX2: Hal 4L 97
WF17: Bat 7E 102
Wellington Cres. BD18: Ship 8M 45
Wellington Gdns. LS13: Leeds 3G 67
Wellington Gth. LS13: Leeds 2G 66
Wellington Gro. BD2: B'frd 4F 64
LS13: Leeds 2G 66
LS28: Pud 7N 65
WELLINGTON HILL 7A 52
Wellington Hill LS17: Leeds 4B 52
Wellington Mt. LS13: Leeds 2G 66
Wellington Pl. BD2: B'frd 3G 64
HX1: Hal 5M 7 (6B 98)
LS1: Leeds 7B 4 (7C 68)
WF11: Knot 8C 110
Wellington Rd. BD2: B'frd 3F 64
BD15: Wils 2A 62
BD21: Keigh 1J 43
LS1: Leeds 7A 4 (7B 68)
LS12: Leeds 8A 4 (8A 68)
LS29: I'ly 5G 15
OL14: Tod 6K 93
WF13: Dew 3F 122
Wellington Rd. E. WF13: Dew 3F 122
Wellington Rd. Ind. Est. LS12: Leeds 7A 4 (7B 68)
Wellington St. BD1: B'frd 3C 6 (7D 64)
BD2: B'frd 3F 64
BD4: B'frd 8H 65
BD10: B'frd 8F 46
BD11: B'haw 7L 83
(off Wellington Ct.)
BD13: Que 4E 80
BD15: All 5H 63
BD15: Wils 2B 62
BD16: Bgly 4E 44
HD3: Hud 2G 136
LS1: Leeds 6A 4 (6B 68)
LS27: Morl 9K 85
WF2: Wake 4G 124
WF10: C'frd 4B 108
WF13: Dew 3F 122
WF15: Liv 9M 101
WF17: Bat 7E 102
(not continuous)
Wellington St. Sth. HX1: Hal 5M 7 (6C 98)
Wellington St. W. HX1: Hal 6H 7 (6A 98)
Wellington Ter. HD7: Mars 5G 150
LS13: Leeds 2G 66
Wellington Wlk. WF13: Dew 3F 122
Well La. BD19: Scho 3D 100
DN6: Burg 5M 165
HD6: Clift 1C 120
HD6: Ras 3L 119
HD7: Mars 7G 150
HX1: Hal 3M 7 (5C 98)
LS7: Leeds 8F 50
LS19: Raw 4N 47
LS19: Yead 1M 47
LS20: Guis 7J 31
LS25: Kip 4A 90
OL14: Tod 7K 93
WF13: Dew 3C 122
WF17: Bat 7G 102
Well Royd Av. HX2: Hal 5J 97
Well Royd Cl. HX2: Hal 5K 97
Wells, The HX2: Hal 7L 97
(Green La.)
HX2: Hal 5J 97
(Up. Well Royd)
Wells Ct. HX3: Hal 3A 98
LS19: Yead 9M 31
(off Well La.)
LS29: I'ly 6G 14
(off Wells Prom.)
S75: Map 9L 159
WF5: Oss 6M 123
Wells Cft. LS6: Leeds 8A 50
Wells Grn. Gdns. HD9: Nether 1L 169
Wells Gro. LS20: Guis 7J 31
Wells Ho. HX6: Sow B 8J 97
(off Church Vw.)
Wells M. LS29: I'ly 6G 14
(off Wells Prom.)
Wells Mt. HD8: Up C 2L 171
LS20: Guis 7J 31
Wells Prom. LS29: I'ly 5G 14
Wells Rd. LS20: Guis 7J 31
LS29: I'ly 7F 14
WF12: T'hill 9H 123
Well's St. S75: Dart 9G 158
Wells Ter. BD22: Lay 9C 26
HX3: Nor G 2M 99
(off Rookes La.)
Wellstone Av. LS13: Leeds 5E 66
Wellstone Dr. LS13: Leeds 5E 66
Wellstone Gdns. LS13: Leeds 6E 66
Wellstone Gth. LS13: Leeds 6E 66
Wellstone Grn. LS13: Leeds 5E 66
Wellstone Ri. LS13: Leeds 6E 66
Wellstone Rd. LS13: Leeds 6E 66
Wellstone Way LS13: Leeds 6E 66
Well St. BD1: B'frd 4C 6 (7D 64)
BD13: Denh 6K 61
BD15: Wils 1B 62
BD21: Keigh 9H 27
HD1: Hud 5L 137
HX4: Holy 7A 118
Well St. LS20: Guis 7J 31
(off Wells Rd.)
LS28: Fars 3A 66
OL14: Tod 8K 93
WF12: Dew 3H 123
WF15: Liv 7L 101
Wells Wlk. LS29: I'ly 6G 14
Wells Way WF5: Oss 4N 123
Well Ter. LS20: Guis 7J 31
Wellthorne Av. S36: Ing 7B 172
Wellthorne La. S36: Ing 7A 172
Well Vw. LS20: Guis 7J 31
Well Wood Vw. WF10: C'frd 3J 109
Welton Gro. LS6: Leeds 3A 68
Welton Mt. LS6: Leeds 3A 68
Welton Pl. LS6: Leeds 3A 68
Welton Rd. LS6: Leeds 3A 68
Welwyn Av. BD18: Ship 8D 46
WF17: Bat 6C 102
Welwyn Dr. BD17: Bail 5A 46
BD18: Ship 8D 46
Welwyn Rd. WF12: Dew 9J 103
Wembley Av. BD13: Thorn 8E 62
Wenborough La. BD4: B'frd 2K 83
Wendel Av. LS15: Bar E 8L 53
Wendover Ct. LS16: Leeds 4N 49
Wendron Cl. WF15: Liv 2K 121
Wendron Way BD10: B'frd 8F 46
Wenlock St. BD3: B'frd 5E 6 (8E 64)
Wenning St. BD21: Keigh 8L 27
Wensley Av. BD18: Ship 8M 45
LS7: Leeds 8E 50
Wensley Bank BD13: Thorn 8B 62
Wensley Bank Ter. BD13: Thorn 8B 62
Wensley Bank W. BD13: Thorn 8B 62
Wensley Cres. LS7: Leeds 8E 50
Wensleydale Av. LS12: Leeds 4J 67
Wensleydale Cl. LS12: Leeds 4J 67
Wensleydale Ct. LS7: Leeds 8E 50
(off Stainbeck La.)
Wensleydale Cres. LS12: Leeds 4J 67
Wensleydale Dr. LS12: Leeds 4J 67
Wensleydale Ho. WF17: Bat 1F 122
(off Dale Cl.)
Wensleydale M. LS12: Leeds 4J 67
Wensleydale Pde. WF17: Bat 4B 102
Wensleydale Ri. BD17: Bail 3C 46
LS12: Leeds 4J 67
Wensleydale Rd. BD3: B'frd 7J 65
Wensleydale Way BD20: Rid 7A 28
Wensley Dr. LS7: Leeds 7D 50
WF8: Pon 5L 129
Wensley Gdns. LS7: Leeds 7D 50
Wensley Grn. LS7: Leeds 8D 50
Wensley Gro. HD6: Ras 3K 119
LS7: Leeds 8E 50
Wensley Lawn LS10: Leeds 9E 86
Wensley Rd. LS7: Leeds 7D 50
Wensley St. WF4: Horb 1C 142
Wensley St. E. WF4: Horb 1B 142
Wensley Vw. LS7: Leeds 8E 50
WENTBRIDGE 3C 148
Wentbridge La. WF8: Thpe A, Went 5A 148
Wentbridge Rd. WF7: F'stne 7E 128
Wentcliffe Rd. WF11: Ferr 8A 110
Went Cft. WF8: Pon 6K 129
Wentdale WF8: Lit S 4K 149
Went Dale Rd. WF8: Pon 6J 129
Went Edge Rd. WF8: Went, K S'ton 4C 148
Went Fold WF8: Pon 6K 129
(not continuous)
Went Gth. WF8: Pon 6J 129
Went Hill Cl. WF7: Ackw 2G 146
Went La. WF4: W Har, Wrag 3B 146
WF7: F'stne 3B 146
Wentvale Ct. WF8: Went 3C 148
Went Vw. WF8: Thpe A 5N 147
Went Vw. Ct. WF8: E Hard 3M 147
Wentwell Rd. WF7: Street 6L 127
Wentworth Av. HD8: Eml 3F 156
LS17: Leeds 3D 50
Wentworth Cl. LS29: Men 4E 30
WF4: Wool 2H 159
Wentworth Ct. HD6: Ras 4L 119
Wentworth Cres. BD4: B'frd 3K 83
LS17: Leeds 3E 50
S75: Map 9M 159
Wentworth Dr. HD8: Eml 3F 156
HX2: Illing 6M 79
S75: Map 9L 159
WF4: Croft 2H 145
WF9: S Kirk 6J 163
Wentworth Farm Res. Pk. LS12: N Far 3G 84
Wentworth Ga. LS22: Weth 3J 23
Wentworth Gro. HX2: Illing 6M 79
Wentworth Lodge WF1: Wake 2H 9
Wentworth M. WF7: Ackw 5D 146
Wentworth Pk. Ri. WF8: D'ton 6C 130
Wentworth Rd. S75: Kex 9C 158
S75: Map 9L 159
WF7: F'stne 7B 128
Wentworth St. HD1: Hud 3L 137
WF1: Wake 1G 9 (3K 125)
Wentworth Ter. LS19: Raw 4A 48
(off Town St.)
WF1: Wake 2H 9 (4K 125)
WF9: Fitz 7B 146
Wentworth Way LS17: Leeds 3E 50
WF2: Wake 1N 143
Wepener Mt. LS9: Leeds 5K 69
Wepener Pl. LS9: Leeds 5K 69
Werner Ct. WF10: C'frd 5E 108
Wescoe Hill LS17: Wee 7L 19
Wescoe Hill La. LS17: Wee 7M 19
Wesleyan St. BD4: B'frd 2G 82
Wesley App. LS11: Leeds 3B 86
Wesley Av. BD12: Low M 6C 82
HD9: Nether 9L 153
LS12: Leeds 7M 67
Wesley Av. Sth. BD12: Low M 7C 82
Wesley Cl. LS11: Leeds 2B 86
WF17: Birs 3B 102
Wesley Ct. HX1: Hal 3L 7 (5B 98)
LS6: Leeds 3C 68
(off Woodhouse St.)
Wesley Ct. LS11: Leeds 3B 86
LS19: Yead 9K 31
(off South Vw.)
WF5: Oss 5M 123
Wesley Cft. LS11: Leeds 2B 86
Wesley Dr. BD12: Low M 6C 82
Wesley Gth. LS11: Leeds 2B 86
Wesley Grn. LS11: Leeds 3B 86
Wesley Gro. BD10: B'frd 6G 46
Wesley Hall Ct. WF3: S'ley 1A 126
Wesley Ho. LS11: Leeds 3A 86
WESLEY PLACE 7B 82
Wesley Pl. BD12: Low M 7C 82
(off Breaks Rd.)
BD20: Sils 8E 12
BD21: Keigh 4G 43
HX6: Sow B 9D 96
LS9: Leeds 7L 5 (7G 69)
LS12: Leeds 7M 67
LS29: Add 9M 11
WF7: F'stne 7D 128
WF13: Dew 3F 122
Wesley Rd. LS12: Leeds 7M 67
LS28: Stan 5N 65
Wesley Row LS28: Pud 6B 66
Wesley Sq. LS28: Pud 7B 66
Wesley St. BD19: Cleck 4H 101
LS11: Leeds 2B 86
LS13: Leeds 1C 66
LS21: Otley 9L 17
LS27: Morl 9K 85
LS28: Fars 3A 66
LS28: Stan 4A 66
WF1: Wake 8N 125
WF5: Oss 5M 123
(not continuous)
WF9: S Elm 7L 163
WF10: C'frd 4D 108
(Aire St.)
WF10: C'frd 7C 108
(Leeds Rd.)
WF13: Dew 3F 122
Wesley Ter. HD8: Den D 2C 172
LS9: Leeds 7L 5
LS13: Leeds 3G 66
(Bellmount Vw.)
LS13: Leeds 1C 66
(Wesley St.)
LS25: Gar 7N 71
LS28: Pud 6B 66
Wesley Vw. LS13: Leeds 1C 66
LS28: Pud 7B 66
Wesley Way BD16: Bgly 8J 29
Wessen Ct. HD7: Mars 5F 150
Wessenden Head Rd. HD9: H'lm, Mel 5M 167
Wessenden Rd. HD7: Mars 8F 150
West 26 Ind. Est. BD19: Cleck 2G 101
W. Acre Dr. WF17: Bat 7H 103
(Broom Wlk.)
WF17: Bat 7G 103
(Lady Ann Rd.)
West Acres WF11: Byram 4C 110
Westacres HD6: Ras 3N 119
WEST ARDSLEY 4A 104
West Av. BD15: All 3E 62
BD17: Bail 4A 46
HD3: Hud 1H 137
HD9: Hon 5K 153
HX3: Hal 8H 7 (8A 98)
HX3: Hip 5M 99
LS8: Leeds 7L 51
LS23: B Spa 8C 24
S71: Roys 5E 160
WF4: Horb 1E 142
WF8: Pon 4G 129
WF9: S Elm 5A 164
WF9: Upt 2N 163
W. Av. Loop WF7: F'stne 8C 128
West Bank BD9: B'frd 2L 63
BD20: Sils 7D 12
BD22: Keigh 8F 26
(off W. Bank Ri.)
HX2: Illing 9K 79
(not continuous)
WF17: Bat 6E 102
W. Bank Cl. BD22: Keigh 8F 26
W. Bank Gro. BD20: Rid 6L 27
W. Bank Ri. BD22: Keigh 8F 26
W. Bank Rd. BD20: Rid 6K 27
WESTBOROUGH 2D 122
Westborough Dr. HX2: Hal 5K 97
West Bottom HX6: Norl 1H 117
Westbourne Av. LS11: Leeds 2D 86
LS25: Gar 8L 71
(not continuous)
WF8: Pon 4J 129
Westbourne Cl. LS21: Otley 1J 31
WF2: Wake 4L 143
Westbourne Cres. HX3: Hal 9C 98
LS25: Gar 8L 71
WF8: Pon 4H 129
Westbourne Dr. LS20: Guis 7G 31
LS25: Gar 8L 71
LS29: Men 3D 30
Westbourne Gdns. LS25: Gar 8L 71
Westbourne Gro. HX3: Hal 9C 98
LS21: Otley 1J 31
LS25: Gar 8L 71
Westbourne Mt. LS11: Leeds 2D 86
WF8: Pon 4J 129
Westbourne Pl. LS11: Leeds 2D 86
LS28: Stan 5A 66
Westbourne Rd. BD8: B'frd 4N 63
HD1: Hud 3J 137
WF8: Pon 4J 129
Westbourne St. LS11: Leeds 2D 86
Westbourne Ter. BD13: Que 4D 80
(off Albert Rd.)
HX3: Hal 9C 98
LS25: Gar 8L 71
Westbourne Vs. LS21: Otley 1J 31
WEST BOWLING 2C 82
West Bradford Golf Course 3H 63
WEST BREARY 5J 33
WEST BRETTON 1B 158
Westbrook Cl. LS18: Hors 5E 48
Westbrook Ct. HX1: Hal 2J 7
Westbrook Dr. HD5: Hud 4F 138
Westbrook La. LS18: Hors 5E 48
Westbrook Ter. WF17: Bat 6E 102
Westburn Av. BD22: Keigh 1F 42
Westburn Cres. BD22: Keigh 2F 42
Westburn Gro. BD22: Keigh 2F 42
Westburn Pl. BD19: Cleck 5G 100
Westburn Way BD22: Keigh 2F 42
Westbury Cl. BD4: B'frd 9H 65
Westbury Ct. HX1: Hal 6L 97
Westbury Gdns. LS16: Leeds 8K 49
Westbury Gro. LS10: Leeds 3H 87
Westbury Mt. LS10: Leeds 4H 87
Westbury Pl. HX1: Hal 6L 97
Westbury Pl. Nth. LS10: Leeds 3H 87
Westbury Pl. Sth.
LS10: Leeds 4H 87
Westbury Rd. BD6: B'frd 4J 81
Westbury St. BD4: B'frd 9H 65
HX5: Ell 4F 118
LS10: Leeds 4H 87
Westbury Ter. HX1: Hal 6L 97
LS10: Leeds 4H 87
W. Busk La. LS21: Otley 2G 31
West Byland HX2: Illing 6L 79
WEST CARLTON 5M 31
W. Carr La. HD3: Scam 8D 134
W. Chevin Rd. LS21: Otley 3H 31
LS29: Men 3H 31
Westcliffe Av. BD17: Bail 3N 45
Westcliffe Dr. HX2: Hal 5K 97
Westcliffe M. BD18: Ship 8N 45
(off Westcliffe Rd.)
Westcliffe Ri. BD19: Cleck 5G 101
Westcliffe Rd. BD18: Ship 8M 45
BD19: Cleck 4G 101
West Cl. HD2: Hud 9N 119
WF6: Alt 9H 107
WF8: Pon 6L 129
Westcombe Av. LS8: Leeds 5J 51
Westcombe Ct.
BD12: Wyke 9A 82
W. Cote Dr. BD10: B'frd 6D 46
Westcott Ho. BD8: B'frd 5A 64
(off Green La.)
West Ct. LS8: Leeds 7L 51
LS13: Leeds 5F 66
West Cft. BD12: Wyke 2A 100
LS29: Add 1M 13
Westcroft HD9: Hon 5K 153
Westcroft Av. HX3: She 9G 81
Westcroft Dr. WF5: Oss 2M 123
Westcroft Ho. WF10: C'frd 4C 108
(off West St.)
Westcroft Rd. BD7: B'frd 1M 81
WF9: Hems 2D 162
West Dale LS23: B Spa 8C 24
Westdale Dr. LS28: Pud 6A 66
Westdale Gdns. LS28: Pud 6A 66
Westdale Gro. LS28: Pud 6A 66
Westdale M. LS28: Pud 6A 66
(off Westdale Gro.)
Westdale Ri. LS28: Pud 6A 66
Westdale Rd. LS28: Pud 6A 66
W. Dean Cl. BD13: Que 5D 80
West Dene BD20: Sils 7E 12
LS17: Leeds 1H 51
West Dr. BD22: Oxen 3C 60
WF8: Pon 4L 129
WEST END
BD13 5C 80
BD19 4G 100
BD22 7E 40
LS18 6C 48
West End BD13: Que 5C 80
BD19: Cleck 4G 100
HD9: Nether 9L 153
HX1: Hal 6L 97
HX7: Heb B 1H 95
LS12: N Far 2G 85
LS23: B Spa 8C 24
LS27: Gil 6F 84
WF15: Liv 9M 101
West End App. LS27: Morl 1G 103
West End Av. HD9: H'frth 2A 170
S71: Roys 6B 160
WF7: A'ton 3A 128
West End Cl. LS18: Hors 6C 48
West End Cotts. WF4: Horb 1B 142
WF8: D'ton 6B 130
West End Cres. S71: Roys 6B 160
West End Dr. BD19: Cleck 6F 100
LS18: Hors 6C 48
West End Golf Course 4J 97
West End Gro. LS18: Hors 6C 48
West End La. LS18: Hors 6C 48
Westend La. BD1: B'frd 7B 64
(off Sunbridge Rd.)
West End Ri. LS18: Hors 6C 48
West End Rd. DN6: Nort 7N 149
HD7: Golc 6B 136
HX1: Hal 6L 97
LS28: Cal 9M 47
WF12: Dew 4E 122
Westend St. BD1: B'frd 7B 64
West End Ter. BD2: B'frd 1F 64
BD18: Ship 7M 45
HX7: Myth 3M 95
LS20: Guis 7G 31
Westercroft HX3: North 1G 98
Westercroft Gth. BD13: Que 5B 80
(off Moor Cl. La.)
Westercroft La. HX3: North 1G 98
Westercroft Vw. HX3: North 1G 98
Westerley Cl. HD8: Shel 6L 155
Westerley Cres. BD20: Sils 8C 12
Westerley La. HD8: Shel 6K 155
Westerley Way HD8: Shel 6L 155
Westerly Cft. LS12: Leeds 6M 67
Westerly Ri. LS12: Leeds 6M 67
(off Mistresses La.)
Westerman Cl. WF7: F'stne 5D 128
Westerman St. WF1: Wake 8N 125

Western Av.—West Vw. Av.

Western Av. BD20: Rid 5J 27
WF8: Pon 3M 129
WF17: Birs 3D 102
Western Cl. BD6: B'frd 6L 81
Western Ct. WF8: Pon 2M 129
WF9: S Kirk 7F 162
Western Fold BD6: B'frd 6L 81
Western Gales Way WF6: Norm 3L 127
Western Gro. LS12: Leeds 9L 67
Western Mt. LS12: Leeds 9L 67
Western Pl. BD13: Que 4G 80
HD1: Hud 5A 8
Western Rd. HD4: Hud 6F 136
LS12: Leeds 9L 67
Western St. LS12: Leeds 9L 67
Western Way BD6: B'frd 6L 81
WESTERTON 5B 104
Westerton Cl. WF3: W Ard 4D 104
Westerton Ct. BD12: O'haw 8F 82
Westerton Rd. WF3: W Ard 5N 103
Westerton Wlk. WF3: W Ard 4D 104
W. Farm Av. LS10: Leeds 8D 86
Westfell Cl. BD22: Keigh 1F 42
Westfell Rd. BD22: Keigh 1F 42
Westfell Way BD22: Keigh 1F 42
WESTFIELD
LS19 1K 47
WF16 7N 101
West Fld. HX6: Norl 1J 117
Westfield BD13: Thorn 8F 62
HX3: Sou 9E 98
HX7: Chis 8K 77
LS7: Leeds 8E 50
LS28: Stan 5A 66
WF5: Oss 6M 123
Westfield Av. HD3: Hud 3G 136
HD8: Skelm 8C 156
HD9: Mel 6B 152
HX3: Hip 5J 99
LS12: Leeds 6J 67
LS19: Yead 1K 47
LS25: Kip 4A 90
WF8: Pon 5J 129
WF10: All B 8A 90
WF10: C'frd 7C 108
WF11: Knot 9E 110
WF12: Dew 3K 123
Westfield Bldgs. *LS27: Morl* 3M 103
(off Tingley Comn.)
Westfield Bungs. WF9: S Elm 7M 163
(not continuous)
WF10: All B 8A 90
Westfield Cl. LS19: Yead 1K 47
LS26: Rothw 9L 87
WF6: Norm 2H 127
WF16: Heck 7N 101
Westfield Cotts. *LS25: Kip* 4B 90
(off High St.)
WF8: Pon 6J 129
Westfield Ct. HD5: Hud 4B 138
LS3: Leeds 5B 68
(off Westfield Ter.)
LS26: Rothw 9L 87
WF4: Horb 9B 124
WF14: Mir 6L 121
Westfield Cres. BD2: B'frd 5F 64
BD18: Ship 9C 46
BD20: Rid 6M 27
LS3: Leeds 2A 4 (4B 68)
(Bk. Rosebank Cres.)
LS3: Leeds 5B 68
(Westfield Rd.)
WF2: Kirk 1D 124
WF4: Ryh 9H 145
WF5: Oss 6M 123
Westfield Dr. BD20: Rid 7M 27
HD8: Skelm 8C 156
HX3: Hip 5J 99
LS19: Yead 1J 47
WF5: Oss 6M 123
Westfield Ent. Cen. WF9: S Elm 6N 163
Westfield Farm WF5: Oss 5M 123
Westfield Gdns. HX3: Hip 5J 99
LS25: Kip 3N 89
WF11: Knot 8G 110
(off Weeland Ct.)
Westfield Gro. BD10: B'frd 7E 46
BD18: Ship 9C 46
LS19: Yead 1K 47
S36: Ing 7A 172
WF1: Wake 1K 9 (3L 125)
WF7: Ackw 2H 147
WF10: All B 8A 90
WF10: C'frd 7C 108
WF13: Dew 3C 122
Westfield Ho. *BD10: B'frd* 8F 46
(off Garsdale Av.)
Westfield Ind. Est. LS19: Yead 1L 47
Westfield La. BD10: B'frd 7D 46
BD12: Wyke 2A 100
BD18: Ship 9C 46
BD19: Scho 2A 100
HD8: Eml 1B 156
HD9: H'frth 3N 169
LS14: T'ner 3F 52
LS23: Cliff 3D 38
LS25: Kip 3N 89
LS25: S Mil 3M 91
WF8: D'ton 7B 130
WF8: K S'ton 7K 149
WF9: S Elm 8M 163
Westfield M. BD13: Thorn 8F 62
Westfield Mills *LS12: Leeds* 6K 67
(off Greenock Rd.)
Westfield Mt. LS19: Yead 1K 47
Westfield Oval LS19: Yead 1J 47
Westfield Pk. WF1: Wake 1K 9 (3L 125)
Westfield Pl. BD19: Scho 3C 100
HX1: Hal 6N 97
LS27: Morl 9K 85
WF2: Kirk 9D 104
Westfield Rd. BD9: B'frd 4M 63
BD14: Clay 1G 80
BD20: Rid 7M 27
LS3: Leeds 4A 4 (5B 68)
Westfield Rd. LS26: Rothw 1L 105
LS27: Morl 9K 85
WF1: Wake 1H 9 (3L 125)
WF3: Carl 1L 105
WF4: Horb 9B 124
WF9: Hems 2C 162
WF11: Knot 9E 110
WF16: Heck 7N 101
Westfields S71: Roys 5B 160
WF10: C'frd 7C 108
Westfields Av. WF14: Mir 6L 121
Westfields Rd. WF14: Mir 6L 121
Westfield St. HX1: Hal 5H 7 (6A 98)
WF5: Oss 6M 123
WF16: Heck 7N 101
Westfield Ter. BD2: B'frd 5F 64
BD14: Clay 1G 80
BD17: Bail 3A 46
HX1: Hal 4N 97
HX7: Myth 3M 95
LS3: Leeds 5B 68
LS7: Leeds 8E 50
WF1: Wake 1J 9 (3L 125)
WF4: Horb 1C 142
WF10: All B 8A 90
Westfield Vw. WF1: Wake 2L 125
Westfield Villa WF1: Wake 1L 9 (3M 125)
Westfield Vs. WF4: Horb 1B 142
Westfield Yd. LS12: Leeds 9L 67
West Fold BD17: Bail 3A 46
WEST GARFORTH 9L 71
Westgarth LS22: Lin 6J 23
West Gth. M. BD17: Bail 5N 45
WESTGATE 4L 105
West Gate BD21: Keigh 9H 27
HD9: H'frth 8L 169
Westgate BD1: B'frd 3A 6 (7B 64)
BD2: B'frd 2G 65
BD17: Bail 3A 46
BD18: Ship 7N 45
BD19: Cleck 5G 101
HD1: Hud 5B 8 (4M 137)
HD5: Hud 8D 138
HD6: Clift 1C 120
HD9: Hon 5L 153
HD9: Mel 7C 152
HX1: Hal 4L 7 (5B 98)
HX4: Stainl 8M 117
HX5: Ell 4E 118
LS1: Leeds 6B 4 (6C 68)
(not continuous)
LS20: Guis 8E 30
LS21: Otley 1K 31
LS22: Weth 4M 23
WF1: Wake 4J 9 (5L 125)
WF2: Wake 5G 9 (5K 125)
WF9: Hems 2C 162
WF13: Dew 3G 122
WF16: Heck 8N 101
Westgate Cl. WF3: Loft 4L 105
WESTGATE COMMON 5J 125
Westgate Ct. *LS22: Weth* 4M 23
(off Westgate)
WF3: Loft 4L 105
WF5: Oss 5D 124
Westgate End WF2: Wake 5G 9 (6J 125)
Westgate Gdns. *BD21: Keigh* 1H 43
(off Aireworth St.)
Westgate Gro. WF3: Loft 4L 105
WESTGATE HILL 5L 83
Westgate Hill St. BD4: B'frd 5K 83
Westgate Ho. LS28: Pud 6N 65
Westgate La. WF3: Loft 4K 105
(not continuous)
Westgate Mall BD1: B'frd 4A 6
Westgate Mkt. HX1: Hal 4L 7 (5B 98)
Westgate Pl. BD4: B'frd 5L 83
Westgate Retail & Leisure Pk.
WF2: Wake 6G 9 (6K 125)
Westgate Ter. BD4: B'frd 5L 83
WF13: Dew 3F 122
(off Old Westgate)
W. Grange Cl. LS10: Leeds 4F 86
W. Grange Dr. LS10: Leeds 4F 86
W. Grange Fold LS10: Leeds 4F 86
W. Grange Gdns. LS10: Leeds 4F 86
W. Grange Gth. LS10: Leeds 4F 86
W. Grange Grn. LS10: Leeds 4F 86
W. Grange Rd. LS10: Leeds 5F 86
W. Grange Wlk. LS10: Leeds 4F 86
West Gro. BD17: Bail 3A 46
S71: Roys 5B 160
West Gro. Av. HD5: Hud 4B 138
Westgrove Ct. BD19: Cleck 4G 101
West Gro. St. LS28: Stan 5A 66
West Gro. Ter. HX1: Hal 4H 7 (5A 98)
West Hall LS19: Yead 1N 47
West Hall Ct. LS16: B'hpe 5H 33
West Hall La. LS29: Nes 8N 11 & 1A 14
WEST HARDWICK 1B 146
West Hill HX7: Heb B 1H 95
West Hill Av. LS7: Leeds 8E 50
Westhill Av. BD13: Cull 1L 61
West Hill St. HX1: Hal 3G 7 (5N 97)
West Hill Ter. LS7: Leeds 8E 50
Westholme Rd. HX1: Hal 5M 97
Westholme St. BD1: B'frd 4A 6 (8B 64)
West Ings Cl. WF11: Knot 7G 110
West Ings Ct. WF11: Knot 7G 110
West Ings Cres. WF11: Knot 7G 110
West Ings La. WF11: Knot 7G 110
West Ings M. WF11: Knot 7G 111
West Ings Way WF11: Knot 7G 110
West Laithe *HX7: Hept* 9G 76
(off Church La.)
Westland Ct. LS11: Leeds 5D 86
Westland Rd. LS11: Leeds 4D 86
Westlands Dr. BD15: All 5G 63
Westlands Gro. BD15: All 5H 63
Westland Sq. LS11: Leeds 5D 86
West La. BD13: Thorn 7C 62
BD17: Bail 4L 45
BD19: Gom 3M 101
BD21: Keigh 8F 26
BD22: Haw 8B 42
West La. HX3: Sou 9E 98
LS21: Askw 4B 16
LS23: B Spa 8C 24
WF4: S Comn 9J 127
Westlea WF7: Ackw 1E 146
Westlea Av. BD20: Rid 7M 27
W. Lea Cl. LS17: Leeds 6D 50
Westlea Cotts. WF11: Knot 9F 110
W. Lea Cres. LS19: Yead 1K 47
WF3: W Ard 5N 103
W. Lea Dr. LS17: Leeds 6D 50
WF3: W Ard 5N 103
W. Lea Gdns. LS17: Leeds 6D 50
W. Lea Gth. LS17: Leeds 6D 50
W. Lea Gro. LS19: Yead 1K 47
W. Leeds St. BD21: Keigh 9G 27
Westleigh BD16: Bgly 3F 44
WF5: Oss 6M 123
Westleigh Cl. BD17: Bail 5M 45
Westleigh Dr. BD17: Bail 5M 45
Westleigh Rd. BD17: Bail 4M 45
Westleigh Way BD17: Bail 4M 45
West Ley HD9: Hon 5K 153
Westlock Av. LS9: Leeds 5J 69
West Lodge LS29: Burl W 9C 16
W. Lodge Cres. HD2: Hud 7G 118
W. Lodge Gdns. LS7: Leeds 9E 50
West Mead WF10: C'frd 5G 108
Westmead LS28: Stan 5L 65
Westmeads S71: Roys 6C 160
West M. WF7: F'stne 7C 128
Westminster Av. BD14: Clay 1F 80
Westminster Cl. LS13: Leeds 2C 66
Westminster Cres. BD14: Clay 1F 80
LS15: Leeds 7N 69
Westminster Cft. LS13: Leeds 2C 66
Westminster Dr. BD14: Clay 1F 80
LS13: Leeds 2C 66
Westminster Gdns. BD14: Clay 1F 80
Westminster Pl. BD3: B'frd 1D 6 (5D 64)
Westminster Rd. BD3: B'frd 1D 6 (5D 64)
HX3: Hip 6J 99
Westminster Ter. BD3: B'frd 1D 6 (5D 64)
Westmoor Av. BD17: Bail 3N 45
Westmoor Cl. BD17: Bail 3N 45
Westmoor Pl. LS13: Leeds 3E 66
Westmoor Ri. LS13: Leeds 3E 66
W. Moor Rd. WF9: Kins 8A 146
Westmoor Rd. LS13: Leeds 3E 66
Westmoor St. LS13: Leeds 3E 66
W. Moor Vw. HD9: Hon 5K 153
Westmoreland Mt. LS13: Leeds 2G 67
Westmorland Ho. WF1: Wake 4K 9
Westmorland St. WF1: Wake 4K 9 (5L 125)
WEST MORTON 6B 28
West Mt. Pl. HX1: Hal 2G 7
West Mt. St. LS11: Leeds 2C 86
WF8: Pon 3J 129
Westoff La. S72: S Hien 1K 161
WESTON 6F 16
Weston Av. BD13: Que 4C 80
Weston Cres. LS21: Otley 8J 17
Weston Dr. LS21: Otley 7H 17
Weston La. LS21: Otley 8H 17
Weston Moor Rd. LS21: Askw, Clift 1F 16
Weston Pk. Vw. LS21: Otley 7H 17
Weston Ridge LS21: Otley 7J 17
Weston Rd. LS29: I'ly 5G 15
Weston St. BD22: Keigh 2F 42
Weston Va. Rd. BD13: Que 5C 80
Westover Av. LS13: Leeds 3F 66
Westover Cl. LS13: Leeds 3G 66
Westover Dr. LS28: Pud 7N 65
Westover Gdns. LS28: Pud 7N 65
Westover Grn. LS13: Leeds 3F 66
Westover Gro. LS13: Leeds 3F 66
Westover Mt. LS13: Leeds 3F 66
Westover Rd. LS13: Leeds 3F 66
Westover St. LS13: Leeds 3F 66
Westover Ter. LS13: Leeds 3F 66
Westover Vw. LS13: Leeds 3F 66
West Pde. HX1: Hal 5J 7 (6A 98)
HX6: Sow B 8K 97
LS16: Leeds 7K 49
LS20: Guis 7J 31
LS26: Rothw 8A 88
LS29: I'ly 5H 15
WF1: Wake 5K 9 (5L 125)
West Pde. Flats HX1: Hal 5J 7
West Pde. St. WF1: Wake 6K 9 (6L 125)
WEST PARK
LS16 7K 49
LS23 8C 24
West Pk. LS20: Guis 6G 31
LS28: Pud 7A 66
West Pk. Av. LS8: Leeds 4K 51
West Pk. Chase LS8: Leeds 4J 51
West Pk. Cl. LS8: Leeds 4J 51
West Pk. Ct. LS8: Leeds 4K 51
West Pk. Cres. LS8: Leeds 5K 51
West Pk. Dr. LS16: Leeds 7K 49
WF8: D'ton 9C 130
West Pk. Dr. E. LS8: Leeds 4J 51
West Pk. Dr. W. LS8: Leeds 4H 51
West Pk. Gdns. LS8: Leeds 5K 51
West Pk. Gro. LS8: Leeds 4J 51
WF17: Bat 7D 102
West Pk. Ind. Est. BD7: B'frd 1L 81
West Pk. Pl. LS8: Leeds 5K 51
West Pk. Residential Pk. WF8: D'ton 9C 130
West Pk. Rd. BD8: B'frd 6L 63
LS8: Leeds 5K 51
WF17: Bat 8C 102
West Pk. St. HD6: Brigh 1N 119
WF13: Dew 2E 122
West Pk. Ter. BD8: B'frd 6L 63
WF8: D'ton 9C 130
WF17: Bat 8D 102
West Pk. Vs. LS8: Leeds 4K 51
West Pk. Wlk. *LS16: Leeds* 8K 49
(off Old Oak Dr.)
W. Pasture Cl. LS18: Hors 6C 48
West Pinfold S71: Roys 6D 160
West Pl. HD5: Hud 4B 138
West Point LS1: Leeds 7C 4 (7D 68)
Westray LS12: Leeds 7B 4 (7B 68)
Westridge Dr. HD4: Hud 9H 137
West Rd. LS9: Leeds 2L 87
West Rd. Nth. LS9: Leeds 2L 87
WEST ROYD 7C 46
West Royd BD15: Wils 1B 62
HX3: Hip 4H 99
Westroyd *BD13: Que* 2B 80
(off Brighouse & Denholme Rd.)
LS21: Clift 6L 17
LS28: Pud 8N 65
W. Royd Av. BD2: B'frd 2F 64
BD18: Ship 7B 46
HX1: Hal 6N 97
WF14: Mir 6L 121
Westroyd Av. BD19: Hun 1H 101
LS28: Pud 8N 65
W. Royd Cl. BD18: Ship 7B 46
HX1: Hal 7N 97
W. Royd Cres. BD18: Ship 7C 46
Westroyd Cres. LS28: Pud 9N 65
(not continuous)
W. Royd Dr. BD18: Ship 7C 46
WF14: Mir 5L 121
Westroyd Gdns. LS28: Pud 8N 65
W. Royd Gro. BD18: Ship 7C 46
WF14: Mir 5L 121
WESTROYD HILL 8A 66
W. Royd Ho. LS28: Fars 4A 66
W. Royd Mt. BD18: Ship 7C 46
W. Royd Pk. WF14: Mir 5L 121
W. Royd Rd. BD18: Ship 7C 46
W. Royd Ter. BD18: Ship 7C 46
W. Royd Vs. *HX1: Hal* 7N 97
(off Kings Cross Rd.)
W. Royd Wlk. BD18: Ship 7C 46
W. Scausby Pk. HX2: Illing 6L 79
WEST SCHOLES 2C 80
West Shaw BD22: Oxen 3B 60
W. Shaw La. BD22: Oxen 3A 60
Westside Ct. *BD8: B'frd* 6M 63
(off Washington St.)
West Side Retail Pk. LS20: Guis 9K 31
Westside Vw. *BD11: Drig* 7B 84
(off West St.)
W. Slaithwaite Rd. HD7: Slait 2J 151
West St. BD1: B'frd 5D 6 (8D 64)
BD2: B'frd 3F 64
BD11: Drig 8B 84
BD17: Bail 3A 46
BD19: Cleck 5H 101
BD19: Gom 3M 101
HD3: Hud 1F 136
HD6: B Bri 5N 99
HD6: Brigh 9M 99
HX1: Hal 5N 97
HX3: She 9G 81
HX4: Holy 7A 118
HX6: Sow B 9H 97
LS1: Leeds 6A 4 (6B 68)
LS20: Guis 7J 31
LS27: Morl 1L 103
LS28: Stan 6B 66
LS29: I'ly 5G 14
OL14: Tod 6J 93
S71: Roys 5E 160
S72: S Hien 4M 161
WF2: Wake 6H 125
WF3: S'ley 1A 126
WF4: H'cft 9K 145
WF6: Norm 1H 127
WF9: Hems 2C 162
WF9: S Elm 5A 164
WF9: S Kirk 8F 162
WF10: C'frd 4C 108
WF12: Dew 4F 122
WF17: Bat 7G 103
(not continuous)
West Ter. LS29: Burl W 7C 16
West Ter. St. *LS28: Stan* 5A 66
(off West Gro. St.)
WEST TOWN 4E 122
WEST VALE 4C 118
West Vale LS12: Leeds 9A 68
WF12: Dew 5E 122
Westvale M. LS13: Leeds 5H 67
West Vw. BD4: B'frd 1E 82
BD11: B'haw 9M 83
BD16: Bgly 2H 45
BD17: Bail 3A 46
(off Newton Way)
BD19: Scho 3D 100
BD20: Sils 7E 12
BD23: Drau 5D 10
HD1: Hud 5J 137
HD8: Den D 2D 172
HX1: Hal 6M 97
(off Vickerman St.)
HX3: Hal 2A 98
HX3: Hip 4J 99
HX4: Holy 7N 117
HX6: Sow B 8J 97
HX7: Heb B 9F 76
HX7: Myth 5L 95
LS11: Leeds 1C 86
LS19: Yead 9K 31
LS21: Arth 2J 33
LS21: Otley 1M 31
LS25: Kip 3B 90
LS25: M'fld 8H 73
LS26: Oul 8D 88
LS28: Fars 4A 66
(off New St.)
LS29: I'ly 6G 15
OL14: Tod 6K 93
WF1: Hea 8D 126
WF2: Kirk 1D 124
WF4: Crig 6G 142
WF5: Oss 6M 123
WF6: Alt 7G 107
WF7: Ackw 5D 146
WF16: Heck 7A 102
WF17: Bat 1E 122
West Vw. Av. BD18: Ship 8C 46
HX2: Hal 5L 97

West Vw. Av.—White Laithe App.

West Vw. Av. LS29: Burl W 8C 16
WF10: C'frd 5G 109
Westview Av. BD20: Keigh 8G 27
West Vw. Cl. BD18: Ship 8C 46
West Vw. Ct. LS19: Yead 9K 31
Westview Ct. BD20: Keigh 8G 27
West Vw. Cres. HX2: Hal 5L 97
West Vw. Dr. HX2: Hal 5K 97
Westview Gro. BD20: Keigh 8G 27
West Vw. Ri. HD1: Hud 5J 137
West Vw. Rd. HX3: Hal 2A 98
LS29: Burl W 8C 16
West Vw. St. BD22: Cros R 7F 42
West Vw. Ter. HX2: Brad 4M 79
HX2: Hal 4L 97
WF2: Wake 3F 124
Westview Way BD20: Keigh 8H 27
W. Villa Rd. LS20: Guis 7J 31
West Ville BD13: Thorn 8C 62
Westville LS29: I'ly 5F 14
Westville Av. LS29: I'ly 5F 14
Westville Cl. LS29: I'ly 5F 14
Westville Rd. LS29: I'ly 5F 14
Westville Way BD13: Thorn 8C 62
Westward Cft. HD3: Hud 9H 119
Westward Ho. HX3: Hal 9N 79
West Way BD18: Ship 8J 45
LS1: Leeds 6B 4 (6C 68)
Westway BD9: B'frd 4H 63
BD16: Bgly 2G 45
BD20: Keigh 8F 26
LS20: Guis 8F 30
LS25: Gar 8L 71
LS28: Fars 3N 65
WF14: Mir 4K 121
WF17: Bat 9J 103
Westways WF2: Wren 9H 105
Westways Cl. WF2: Wren 1H 125
Westways Dr. LS8: Leeds 8L 51
Westways Ri. WF2: Wren 1H 125
W. Wells Cres. WF5: Oss 6M 123
W. Wells Rd. WF5: Oss 6M 123
West Winds LS29: Men 3C 30
Westwinds WF7: Ackw 1F 146
Westwinn Gth. LS14: Leeds 7D 52
Westwinn Vw. LS14: Leeds 6D 52
WESTWOOD 7N 135
Westwood BD9: B'frd 2L 63
Westwood Av. BD2: B'frd 1F 64
HD9: Hon 5A 154
Westwood Cl. LS27: Morl 7L 85
WF7: F'stne 4D 128
Westwood Cotts. LS23: Cliff 3E 38
Westwood Ct. HD4: Hud 7E 138
LS10: Leeds 8C 86
Westwood Cres. BD16: Cot 7F 44
Westwood Dr. LS29: I'ly 7E 14
Westwood Edge Rd. HD7: Golc 7N 135
Westwood Fold HD7: Golc 8A 136
Westwood Gro. BD2: B'frd 1F 64
Westwood Hall BD6: B'frd 4H 81
Westwood Ho. BD13: Que 4D 80
Westwood Ri. LS27: Morl 7L 85
LS29: I'ly 7E 14
West Wood Rd. LS10: Leeds 9B 86
LS27: Chur 9B 86
Westwood Rd. WF5: Oss 6B 124
WF10: C'frd 7B 108
Westwood Side LS27: Morl 6K 85
W. Woods Rd. LS22: Coll 9N 23
LS23: B Spa, B'ham, Cliff 9N 23
Westwood St. HD5: Hud 5E 120
Westwood Way LS23: B Spa 1D 38
Westy Bank Cft. BD20: Stee 6C 26
W. Yorkshire Ind. Est. BD4: B'frd 5H 83
West Yorkshire Playhouse, The 6J 5 (6F 68)
West Yorkshire Print Workshop 7L 121
W. Yorkshire Retail Pk. WF17: Birs 9D 84
WETHERBY 4M 23
Wetherby Bus. Pk. LS22: Weth 3N 23
Wetherby Golf Course 5K 23
Wetherby Grange LS22: Weth 7A 24
Wetherby Gro. LS4: Leeds 4M 67
Wetherby Leisure Cen. 5M 23
Wetherby Pl. LS4: Leeds 4N 67
Wetherby Racecourse 3B 24
Wetherby Rd. HG3: Spof 1F 22
LS8: Leeds 9K 51
LS14: Bard, Leeds, S'cft 8N 51
LS14: S'cft 6A 52
LS17: Bard 4E 36
LS17: Leeds 6A 52
LS22: K Dei 1L 23
LS22: Sick 4E 22
LS23: B'ham 5C 38
LS23: W'ton 5E 24
LS24: N Kym 2H 39
WETHERBY SERVICE AREA 1A 24
Wetherby Ter. LS4: Leeds 4M 67
Wetherhill St. WF17: Bat 7E 102
Wetherill Ter. WF13: Dew 9C 102
(off Bower La.)
Wetlands Rd. HD9: Mel 8D 152
Wet Shod La. HD6: Brigh 8K 99
Wetton Ct. BD3: B'frd 7H 65
Wetville BD22: Oxen 3C 60
Weybridge Ho. BD8: B'frd 5A 64
(off Trenton Dr.)
Weydale Av. HD3: Hud 2F 136
Weyhill Dr. BD15: All 6G 63
Weymouth Av. BD15: All 6F 62
HD3: Hud 3G 136
Weymouth St. HX1: Hal 3K 7 (5B 98)
Whack Ho. LS19: Yead 1K 47
(off Westfield Av.)
Whack Ho. Cl. LS19: Yead 1L 47
Whack Ho. La. LS19: Yead 1L 47
Whalley La. BD13: Denh 4K 61
Wham Leigh HX4: Sow 1M 135
Wharf, The WF11: Knot 7D 110
Wharf App. LS1: Leeds 8D 4
LS11: Leeds 8D 4 (7D 68)
Wharf Cl. WF12: Dew 4G 122
Wharfdale Av. LS29: Men 6F 30
Wharfdale Ct. LS29: Men 6E 30
Wharfdale Cft. LS29: Men 6E 30
Wharfdale Fold LS29: Men 6E 30
Wharfe Bank LS22: Coll 9F 22
Wharfebank Bus. Cen. LS21: Otley 1J 31
Wharfe Cl. LS16: Leeds 3N 49
Wharfe Ct. BD20: Sils 8E 12
LS29: Burl W 8D 16
Wharfe Cres. LS21: Pool 1G 32
Wharfedale Av. LS7: Leeds 2D 68
Wharfedale Bus. Pk. BD4: B'frd 4H 83
Wharfedale Cl. LS12: Leeds 4J 67
Wharfedale Ct. LS14: Leeds 1A 70
LS21: Otley 9L 17
LS21: Pool 1G 32
(off Main St.)
Wharfedale Cres. HD8: Skelm 8E 156
LS25: Gar 9N 71
Wharfedale Dr. LS29: I'ly 5H 15
WF6: Alt 8H 107
Wharfedale Gdns. BD17: Bail 3C 46
Wharfedale Gro. LS7: Leeds 2D 68
Wharfedale Lawns LS22: Weth 4M 23
Wharfedale M. LS21: Otley 9M 17
Wharfedale Mt. HX3: She 8G 80
LS7: Leeds 2D 68
Wharfedale Pl. LS7: Leeds 2D 68
Wharfedale Ri. BD9: B'frd 4H 63
WF3: W Ard 5N 103
Wharfedale Rd. BD4: B'frd 6E 82
Wharfedale St. LS7: Leeds 2D 68
Wharfedale Ter. LS22: Coll 8H 23
Wharfedale Vw. LS7: Leeds 2D 68
LS29: Add 1L 13
LS29: Men 4E 30
Wharfe Grange LS22: Weth 4L 23
Wharfe Gro. LS22: Weth 4L 23
Wharfe La. LS22: Kear 7L 21
Wharfe M. LS29: Men 4F 30
Wharfe Pk. LS29: Add 1N 13
Wharfe Rein LS22: Coll 9F 22
Wharfeside LS23: B Spa 1F 38
Wharfeside La. LS29: I'ly 4H 15
Wharfe St. LS21: Otley 9M 17
Wharfe Vw. HG3: Kirkby 2K 21
LS21: Pool 1F 32
LS22: Weth 4L 23
Wharfe Vw. Rd. LS29: I'ly 5G 15
Wharfe Way WF10: C'frd 4H 109
(not continuous)
Wharf St. BD3: B'frd 2C 6 (6D 64)
BD17: Ship 7N 45
HD6: Brigh 1N 119
HX6: Sow B 8J 97
LS2: Leeds 7H 5 (7F 68)
OL14: W'den 2J 113
WF12: Dew 4G 122
Wharncliffe Bus. Pk. S71: Ath 9C 160
Wharncliffe Cres. BD2: B'frd 2H 65
Wharncliffe Dr. BD2: B'frd 2H 65
Wharncliffe Gro. BD2: B'frd 2H 65
BD18: Ship 9N 45
Wharncliffe Rd. BD18: Ship 1N 63
WF2: Wake 5J 143
Wharncliffe St. S71: Carl 9E 160
Whartons, The LS21: Otley 7L 17
Wharton Sq. BD13: Que 4G 80
(off Highgate Rd.)
Wharton St. WF15: Liv 8M 101
Wharton Ter. WF16: Heck 9A 102
(off Church La.)
Wheat Cl. HD9: Holm 7G 168
WF13: Dew 3C 122
Wheatcroft WF10: C'frd 6H 109
WF17: Bat 7F 102
(off Hanover St.)
Wheatcroft Av. WF17: Bat 8F 102
Wheater Ho. WF1: Wake 5J 9 (5L 125)
Wheater Rd. BD7: B'frd 9M 63
Wheaters Fold LS28: Stan 5B 66
(off Woods Row)
Wheatfield Av. HD3: Hud 2F 136
Wheatfield Cl. LS28: Fars 2B 66
Wheatfield Ct. LS28: Pud 8A 66
Wheathead Cres. BD22: Keigh 2E 42
Wheathead Dr. BD22: Keigh 2F 42
Wheathead La. BD22: Keigh 2E 42
Wheathouse Gro. HD2: Hud 2L 137
Wheathouse Rd. HD2: Hud 1L 137
Wheathouse Ter. HD2: Hud 1L 137
Wheatings, The WF5: Oss 6B 124
Wheatlands LS28: Fars 3N 65
LS29: I'ly 5H 15
Wheatlands Av. BD9: B'frd 4K 63
Wheatlands Cres. BD9: B'frd 4K 63
Wheatlands Dr. BD9: B'frd 4K 63
WF15: Liv 1K 121
Wheatlands Gro. BD9: B'frd 4K 63
Wheatlands Sq. BD9: B'frd 4K 63
WHEATLEY 2L 97
Wheatley Av. LS29: I'ly 6K 15
WF6: Norm 2J 127
Wheatley City HX3: Hal 2L 97
(off City La.)
Wheatley Cl. HX3: Hal 3N 97
LS29: I'ly 5K 15
Wheatley Ct. HX2: Mix 9K 79
Wheatley Dr. S75: W Gran 6G 158
WF10: C'frd 2J 109
WF14: Mir 8L 121
Wheatley Gdns. LS29: I'ly 6K 15
Wheatley Gro. LS29: I'ly 6K 15
Wheatley Hill La. HD8: Clay W 9G 157
Wheatley La. HX3: Hal 3N 97
LS29: I'ly 6K 15
Wheatley Lane Ends HX3: Hal 2L 97
(off Wheatley Rd.)
Wheatley Ri. LS29: I'ly 6K 15
S75: S'ross 7K 159
Wheatley Rd. HX3: Hal 2L 97
(Denfield La.)
HX3: Hal 3M 97
(Greenwood's Ter.)
LS29: I'ly 6H 15
Wheatley Ter. HD5: Hud 6H 121
Wheaton Av. LS15: Leeds 6B 70
Wheaton Ct. LS15: Leeds 6B 70
(off Wheaton Av.)
Wheatroyd Cres. WF5: Oss 8N 123
Wheatroyd La. HD5: Hud 8C 138
Wheat St. BD22: Keigh 3G 43
Wheelwright Av. LS12: Leeds 9K 67
Wheelwright Cl. LS12: Leeds 9K 67
(not continuous)
Wheelwright Dr. WF13: Dew 1D 122
Wheelwright St. WF13: Dew 3F 122
WHELDALE 3K 109
Wheldale Ct. WF10: C'frd 3H 109
(off Stansfield Cl.)
Wheldale Farm Cotts. WF10: C'frd 2J 109
Wheldale La. WF10: C'frd 2K 109
Wheldon Rd. WF10: C'frd 4E 108
Whernside Ct. LS29: Men 5F 30
(off Jackson Wlk.)
Whernside Mt. BD7: B'frd 3K 81
Whernside Way HX2: Mt T 1G 97
Wherwell Rd. HD6: Ras 2N 119
Whetley Cl. BD8: B'frd 6A 64
Whetley Gro. BD8: B'frd 5M 63
Whetley Hill BD8: B'frd 5N 63
Whetley La. BD8: B'frd 6M 63
Whetley St. BD8: B'frd 6A 64
(off Denby St.)
Whetley Ter. BD8: B'frd 6A 64
Whewell St. WF17: Birs 3B 102
Whiddon Cft. LS29: Men 3D 30
Whimbrel Cl. BD8: B'frd 7H 63
Whimbrel M. LS27: Morl 1M 103
Whinbeck Av. WF6: Norm 2K 127
Whinberry Pl. WF17: Birs 1C 102
Whinbrook Ct. LS17: Leeds 6E 50
Whinbrook Cres. LS17: Leeds 6E 50
Whinbrook Gdns. LS17: Leeds 6E 50
Whinbrook Gro. LS17: Leeds 6E 50
Whin Cl. WF9: Hems 4D 162
Whincop Av. WF10: C'frd 5A 108
Whin Cnr. S72: Shaf 5J 161
Whincover Bank LS12: Leeds 9J 67
Whincover Cl. LS12: Leeds 9J 67
Whincover Cross LS12: Leeds 9J 67
Whincover Dr. LS12: Leeds 9H 67
Whincover Gdns. LS12: Leeds 9J 67
Whincover Grange LS12: Leeds 9J 67
Whincover Gro. LS12: Leeds 9J 67
Whincover Hill LS12: Leeds 9J 67
Whincover Mt. LS12: Leeds 9J 67
Whincover Rd. LS12: Leeds 9H 67
Whin Covert La. WF8: K S'ton 8K 149
Whincover Vw. LS12: Leeds 9J 67
S71: Roys 5F 160
Whincup Gdns. LS10: Leeds 3G 86
(off Telford Pl.)
Whinfield LS16: Leeds 3L 49
Whinfield Av. BD22: Keigh 8E 26
Whinfield Cl. BD22: Keigh 8F 26
Whinfield Dr. BD22: Keigh 8E 26
Whinfield Pl. WF5: Oss 7C 124
Whinfield Ter. WF5: Oss 7D 124
Whingate LS12: Leeds 6K 67
Whingate Av. LS12: Leeds 7K 67
Whingate Bus. Pk. LS12: Leeds 7L 67
Whingate Cl. LS12: Leeds 7K 67
Whingate Ct. LS12: Leeds 7L 67
Whingate Grn. LS12: Leeds 7K 67
Whingate Gro. LS12: Leeds 7K 67
Whingate Rd. LS12: Leeds 7K 67
Whingrove Av. HD9: Mel 8B 152
Whin Knoll Av. BD21: Keigh 8F 26
Whin La. LS25: S Mil 3N 91
S75: Silk 9N 173
WHINMOOR 7C 52
Whinmoor Ct. LS14: Leeds 6B 52
Whinmoor Cres. LS14: Leeds 6B 52
Whinmoor Dr. HD8: Clay W 5K 157
Whinmoor Gdns. LS14: Leeds 6A 52
Whin Moor La. S75: Silk 8M 173
Whinmoor Way LS14: Leeds 8D 52
(not continuous)
Whinmore Gdns. BD19: Gom 5N 101
Whin Mt. WF6: Norm 3K 127
Whinn Dale WF6: Norm 3J 127
Whinney Bank La. HD9: H'frth 3N 169
Whinney Brow BD10: B'frd 7D 46
Whinney Cl. WF7: Street 6L 127
Whinney Fld. HX3: Hal 8B 98
Whinney Hill BD4: B'frd 9J 65
BD13: Que 4E 80
(off Sandbeds)
Whinney Hill Pk. HD6: Brigh 7M 99
Whinney La. WF7: Street 6K 127
Whinney Moor Av. WF2: Wake 8F 124
Whinney Royd La. HX3: North 8F 80
Whinn Moor La. LS17: Leeds, Shad 4N 51
Whin Pk. LS21: Arth 3M 33
Whins La. HG3: Spof 2D 22
HX7: Hept 9G 76
LS23: T Arch 8F 24
Whin St. BD21: Keigh 9G 26
Whin Vw. Ct. WF4: H'cft 9K 145
Whin Wood Grange LS14: Leeds 7C 52
Whirlaw Av. OL14: Tod 5J 93
WHIRLAW COMMON 4K 93
Whirlaw La. OL14: Tod 4J 93
Whiskers La. HX3: North 1D 98
Whisperwood Cl. WF1: Out 7M 105
Whisperwood Rd. WF1: Out 7M 105
Whistler Dr. WF10: C'frd 8E 108
Whitacre Cl. HD2: Hud 8C 120
Whitacre St. HD2: Hud 8C 120
Whitaker Av. BD2: B'frd 3G 65
Whitaker Cl. BD2: B'frd 3G 65
Whitaker Ho. HX1: Hal 8J 7
Whitaker St. LS28: Fars 5A 66
WF17: Bat 8G 102
Whitaker Wlk. BD22: Oxen 4C 60
Whitburn Way BD15: All 6G 63
Whitby Av. HD2: Hud 9M 119
Whitby Ct. HD8: Shep 7K 155
Whitby Cres. WF12: Dew 3J 123
Whitby Rd. BD8: B'frd 5M 63
(not continuous)
Whitby Ter. BD8: B'frd 5M 63
Whitcliffe Mount Sports Cen. 4F 100
Whitcliffe Rd. BD19: Cleck 4G 100
Whitcliffe Sq. BD19: Cleck 4H 101
(off Whitecliffe Rd.)
White Abbey Rd. BD8: B'frd 6A 64
White Apron St. WF9: S Kirk 7H 163
Whitebeam Grn. WF8: Pon 2M 129
Whitebeam La. LS10: Leeds 5F 86
Whitebeam Pk. HD2: Hud 9J 119
Whitebeam Wlk. BD2: B'frd 1F 64
White Birch Ter. HX3: Hal 2L 97
Whitebridge Av. LS9: Leeds 6N 69
Whitebridge Cres. LS9: Leeds 5N 69
Whitebridge Spur LS9: Leeds 5N 69
Whitebridge Vw. LS9: Leeds 5N 69
White Castle Ct. BD13: Que 3A 80
Whitechapel Cl. LS8: Leeds 9K 51
Whitechapel Gro. BD19: Scho 3E 100
Whitechapel Rd. BD19: Cleck, Scho 3D 100
Whitechapel Way LS8: Leeds 9K 51
Whitecliffe Cres. LS26: Swil 3H 89
Whitecliffe Dr. LS26: Swil 3H 89
Whitecliffe La. LS26: Swil 3H 89
Whitecliffe Ri. LS26: Swil 3H 89
White Cl. La. HD8: Den D 2D 172
WHITECOTE 2F 66
Whitecote Gdns. LS13: Leeds 2E 66
Whitecote Hill LS13: Leeds 2E 66
Whitecote Ho. LS13: Leeds 1E 66
Whitecote La. LS13: Leeds 2E 66
LS25: S Mil 1M 91
Whitecote Ri. LS13: Leeds 2E 66
White Ct. WF4: Croft 2H 145
WHITE CROSS 6G 30
White Cross HD2: Hud 6C 120
White Cross Gdns. S72: S Hien 2L 161
White Cross Rd. WF12: Dew 2H 123
White Fld. La. HX7: Myth 4K 95
Whitefield Pl. BD8: B'frd 6M 63
White Ga. HD9: Hon 4L 153
Whitegate HX2: Ogd 6K 79
HX3: Hal 8M 7 (8C 98)
LS17: E Kes 2D 36
Whitegate Dr. HX3: Hal 8M 7 (8C 98)
Whitegate La. WF8: E Hard 2L 147
Whitegate Rd. HD4: Hud 8C 8 (6N 137)
HD9: Holm, H'frth 7J 169
HX3: Hal 7M 7 (7C 98)
Whitegates Cl. WF1: Wake 2J 125
Whitegates Gro. HD8: Fen B 8H 139
Whitegate Ter. HX3: Hal 8M 7 (8C 98)
Whitegate Top HX3: Hal 8D 98
White Gro. LS8: Leeds 7J 51
Whitehall LS12: Leeds 8B 4 (7C 68)
Whitehall Av. BD12: Wyke 3A 100
WF1: Wake 2J 125
WF14: Mir 4L 121
Whitehall Ct. LS12: N Far 1K 85
WF4: Horb 1D 142
Whitehall Cres. WF1: Wake 2J 125
Whitehall Cft. LS12: Leeds 1L 85
(off Whitehall Dr.)
LS26: Rothw 8A 88
Whitehall Cross LS12: N Far 1J 85
Whitehall Dr. LS12: Leeds 1L 85
Whitehall Grn. LS12: Leeds 1K 85
Whitehall Gro. BD11: B'haw 8M 83
BD11: Drig 7A 84
Whitehall Ind. Est. LS12: N Far 1J 85
White Hall La. HX2: Wain 7G 78
Whitehall Pk. LS12: N Far 1J 85
Whitehall Pl. LS12: Leeds 8A 4 (8B 68)
Whitehall Quay LS1: Leeds 7D 4 (7D 68)
Whitehall Ri. WF1: Wake 3J 125
Whitehall Rd. BD11: Drig, N Far 7A 84
(not continuous)
BD12: Scho, Wyke 3C 100
BD19: B'frd, Cleck 2G 101
HD7: Linth 1B 152
HX3: Hip 3L 99
LS1: Leeds 8A 4 (8B 68)
LS12: Leeds, N Far 8A 4 (4E 84)
Whitehall Rd. E. BD11: B'haw 9L 83
Whitehall Rd. W. BD11: B'haw 2J 101
BD19: Hun 2H 101
Whitehall St. HX3: Hip 5J 99
WF2: Wake 6H 125
Whitehall Vs. HX3: Hip 4K 99
Whitehall Waterfront LS1: Leeds 8C 4 (7C 68)
Whitehall Way WF13: Dew 2G 122
White Hart Dr. HD4: Hud 7M 137
White Hart Fold HX6: Ripp 8C 116
OL14: Tod 7K 93
(off Station App.)
WF9: S Elm 3A 164
Whitehaven Cl. BD6: B'frd 6L 81
Whitehead Cl. BD4: B'frd 8H 65
Whitehead Gro. BD2: B'frd 5G 64
Whitehead La. HD4: Hud 8B 8 (7L 137)
HD4: S Cros 3E 152
Whitehead Pl. BD2: B'frd 4G 64
Whitehead's Ter. HX1: Hal 5M 97
Whitehead St. BD3: B'frd 8F 64
White Hill HD7: Slait 2J 151
Whitehill Cotts. HX2: Illing 8L 79
Whitehill Cres. HX2: Illing 7L 79
Whitehill Dr. HX2: Illing 7L 79
Whitehill Grn. HX2: Illing 7M 79
Whitehill Rd. BD22: Oak 2L 41
HX2: Illing 8L 79
White Home Dr. LS21: Pool 2H 33
Whitehorn Rd. WF10: C'frd 8F 108
White Horse Cl. WF17: Birs 2E 102
White Horse Fold WF10: Leds 7E 90
White Horse Yd. WF1: Wake 5J 9 (5L 125)
Whitehouse Av. LS26: Gt P 5L 89
White Ho. Bungs. WF2: Wake 8K 125
Whitehouse Cres. LS26: Gt P 5M 89
Whitehouse Dr. LS26: Gt P 5L 89
Whitehouse La. LS19: Yead 8B 32
LS26: Swil, Kip 2K 89
White Ho's. HX7: Myth 3L 95
Whitehouse St. LS10: Leeds 9F 68
White Laithe App. LS14: Leeds 7C 52

A-Z West Yorkshire Atlas 275

White Laithe Av.—Windermere Rd.

White Laithe Av. LS14: Leeds 7C 52
White Laithe Cl. LS14: Leeds 7C 52
White Laithe Ct. LS14: Leeds 7C 52
White Laithe Cft. LS14: Leeds 7C 52
White Laithe Gdns. LS14: Leeds 7C 52
White Laithe Gth. LS14: Leeds 6C 52
White Laithe Grn. LS14: Leeds 7D 52
White Laithe Gro. LS14: Leeds 7D 52
White Laithe Rd. LS14: Leeds 7C 52
White Laithe Wlk. LS14: Leeds 7D 52
Whitelands LS19: Raw 3L 47
  LS28: Pud 6C 66
Whitelands Cres. BD17: Bail 4B 46
Whitelands Rd. BD17: Bail 4B 46
White La. BD6: B'frd 4B 82
  BD22: Oak 5N 41
White La. Top *BD6: B'frd* *5B 82*
  (off White La.)
WHITE LEE 5B 102
White Lee Cl. WF17: Bat 6B 102
White Lee Cft. HX7: Myth 3N 95
White Lee Gdns. HX7: Myth 3N 95
White Lee Rd. WF16: Heck 5B 102
  WF17: Bat 5B 102
White Lee Side WF16: Heck 6B 102
White Lee Ter. HX7: Myth 4N 95
Whiteley Av. HX6: Sow B 9F 96
White Ley Bank HD9: New M 1E 170
Whiteley Cft. LS21: Otley 1L 31
Whiteley Cft. Cl. LS21: Otley 1L 31
Whiteley Cft. Gth. LS21: Otley 1K 31
Whiteley Cft. Ri. LS21: Otley 1L 31
Whiteley Cft. Rd. LS21: Otley 1K 31
White Ley Rd. DN6: Nort 1J 165
  WF8: Went 1J 165
Whiteley St. HD3: Hud 6G 137
  HX1: Hal 5J 7 (6A 98)
  WF7: F'stne 6C 128
Whiteley Ter. HX6: Ripp 9C 116
White Lion Yd. HD1: Hud 5C 8
Whitelock St. LS7: Leeds 3H 5 (5F 68)
White Moor La. BD22: Oxen 7C 60
Whitemoor Way BD13: Denh 8L 61
White Moss Cl. WF7: Ackw 4F 146
Whiteplatts St. OL14: Tod 6K 93
White Rose Av. HD5: Hud 3D 138
  LS25: Gar 7N 71
White Rose Ct. WF2: Wake 6G 124
White Rose Mead LS25: Gar 7A 72
White Rose Shop. Centre, The
  LS11: Leeds 6A 86
White Rose Way LS25: Gar 7A 72
White's Bldgs. WF5: Oss 4N 123
Whites Cl. BD9: B'frd 3J 63
White Slack Ga. OL14: W'den 5H 113
White's Rd. WF1: Wake 4L 9 (5M 125)
White's Row WF4: Horb 1N 141
White's Ter. BD8: B'frd 5N 63
Whitestone Cres. LS19: Yead 9M 31
Whitestone Dr. BD20: E Mor 7C 28
Whitestone La. HD1: Hud 1C 8 (2N 137)
Whitestones HD4: Stock 7F 154
White St. LS26: W'frd 7E 88
White's Vw. BD8: B'frd 6N 63
White Walls La. HD9: Holm 4E 168
Whiteways BD2: B'frd 3C 64
White Wells Ct. HD9: Scho 5B 170
White Wells Gdns. HD9: Scho 5B 170
White Wells Rd. HD9: Scho 5B 170
White Wells Spa Cottage 7G 15
White Windows Cotts. HX6: Sow B 9G 97
Whitewood Cl. S71: Roys 7C 160
Whitfield Av. LS10: Leeds 1G 86
Whitfield Gdns. LS10: Leeds 1G 86
Whitfield Mill BD10: B'frd 7J 47
Whitfield Pl. LS10: Leeds 1G 86
Whitfield Sq. LS10: Leeds 1G 86
Whitfield St. BD19: Cleck 4H 101
  LS8: Leeds 3H 69
Whitfield Way LS10: Leeds 1G 86
Whitham Cl. LS23: B Spa 9D 24
Whitham Rd. BD18: Ship 7K 45
WHITKIRK 5D 70
Whitkirk Cl. LS15: Leeds 6E 70
Whitkirk La. LS15: Leeds 6E 70
WHITKIRK LANE END 6E 70
Whitlam St. BD18: Ship 7L 45
Whitley Dr. HX2: Illing 7M 79
Whitley Farm Dr. WF4: Neth 5A 142
Whitley Gdns. LS8: Leeds 1L 5
WHITLEY HEAD 4C 26
Whitley La. HX3: Sou 7F 98
WHITLEY LOWER 2B 140
Whitley Pl. WF10: All B 9B 90
Whitley Rd. BD21: Keigh 2G 42
  S36: M Grn 9J 171
  WF12: T'hill, W'ley 2A 140
Whitley Spring Cres.
  WF5: Oss 5B 124
Whitley Spring Rd. WF5: Oss 5B 124
Whitley St. BD3: B'frd 4E 6 (7E 64)
  BD16: Bgly 4E 44
Whitley Way WF4: G Moor 5B 140
Whitley Willows HD8: Lept 4J 139
Whitmore St. WF9: S Elm 6N 163
Whittaker Rd. HX7: Heb B 6F 94
Whitteron Cl. HD3: Hud 1G 137
Whittle Cres. BD14: Clay 9G 63
Whitton Cft. Rd. LS29: I'ly 5G 15
Whitty La. HX2: Hal 6H 97
Whitwams Bldgs. *HD7: Slait* *9N 135*
  (off Clay La.)
Whitwell Av. HX5: Ell 4G 118
Whitwell Dr. HX5: Ell 4G 118
  WF7: Street 6L 127
Whitwell Grn. La. HX5: Ell 5G 118
Whitwell Gro. HX5: Ell 4G 118
Whitwell Main WF7: Street 6L 127
Whitwell St. BD4: B'frd 8E 6 (9E 64)
WHITWOOD 6N 107
WHITWOOD COMMON 7N 107
Whitwood Comn. La. WF10: C'frd 8M 107
Whitwood Ent. Pk. WF10: C'frd 6N 107
Whitwood Freight Cen. WF10: C'frd 7M 107
Whitwood Golf Course 6M 107
Whitwood La. HD6: B Bri 5A 100
  (not continuous)
  WF10: C'frd 6L 107
WHITWOOD MERE 4A 108
Whitwood Ter. WF10: C'frd 7M 107
Whitworth Rd. WF13: Dew 4E 122
Whitworth Ter. HX1: Hal 8K 7
Wholestone Ga. HD7: Golc 5A 136
Whyment Cl. LS27: Chur 4M 85
Whytecote End BD12: Wyke 9A 82
WIBSEY 4N 81
Wibsey Bank BD6: B'frd 4B 82
Wibsey Pk. Av. BD6: B'frd 5L 81
Wicken Cl. BD10: B'frd 9G 47
Wicken La. BD13: Thorn 7C 62
Wicken Tree La. WF4: M'twn 3M 141
Wicket, The LS28: Cal 8M 47
Wicket Dr. WF1: Wake 2L 125
Wickets, The BD2: B'frd 4G 64
  LS6: Leeds 8B 50
  LS15: Leeds 7F 70
  WF2: Wake 1N 143
  WF17: Bat 1E 122
Wickets Cl. BD6: B'frd 5B 82
Wickham Av. BD6: B'frd 5A 82
  LS23: B Spa 1C 38
Wickham Cl. LS23: B Spa 9C 24
Wickham St. BD19: Scho 4D 100
  LS11: Leeds 2C 86
Wicking La. HX6: Ripp 3N 115
Wickins La. HD9: H'frth 2H 169
Wickleden Ga. HD9: Scho 5B 170
WIDDOP 7J 57
Widdop Cl. BD6: B'frd 3H 81
Widdop Rd. HX7: Hept 6D 76
Wide La. BD22: Oak 4A 42
  LS27: Morl 1L 103
Widow's Row LS25: Aber 9E 54
Wigan St. BD1: B'frd 7B 64
Wigeon App. LS27: Morl 9M 85
Wiggan La. HD2: Hud 7B 120
WIGHILL 7N 25
Wighill La.
  LS23: T Arch, W'ton 5G 24
  LS24: Tad 8N 25
Wightman St. BD3: B'frd 5E 64
Wignall St. BD20: Keigh 6H 27
Wigton Chase LS17: Leeds 2J 51
Wigton Ga. LS17: Leeds 1G 50
Wigton Grn. LS17: Leeds 1H 51
Wigton Gro. LS17: Leeds 1G 50
Wigton La. LS17: Leeds 1G 51
Wigton Pk. Cl. LS17: Leeds 1H 51
WIKE 7M 35
Wike La. LS17: Bard, E Kes 6A 36
  LS17: Hare, Wike 5K 35
Wike Ridge Av. LS17: Leeds 2J 51
Wike Ridge Cl. LS17: Leeds 1K 51
Wike Ridge Ct. LS17: Leeds 1K 51
Wike Ridge Fold LS17: Leeds 1J 51
Wike Ridge Gdns. LS17: Leeds 2K 51
Wike Ridge Gro. LS17: Leeds 2K 51
Wike Ridge La. LS17: Leeds, Wike 2K 51
Wike Ridge M. LS17: Leeds 2K 51
Wike Ridge Mt. LS17: Leeds 2K 51
Wike Ridge Vw. LS17: Leeds 2J 51
WILBERLEE 8K 135
Wilby St. BD19: Cleck 5H 101
Wilcock La. BD20: L Bra 4A 12
Wilcroft Ter. HX7: P Wel 5J 77
Wilday Cl. BD16: Bgly 1D 44
Wilderness Rd. HX5: Ell 5H 119
Wild Flower Way LS10: Leeds 9F 86
Wild Gro. LS28: Pud 7L 65
Wild Heather Cl. BD13: Cull 1J 61
Wild's Pas. OL15: Lit 9M 113
Wildspur Gro. HD9: New M 4C 170
Wildspur Mills HD9: New M 3C 170
Wild's Yd. WF1: Wake 6K 9 (6L 125)
Wild Wood Ri. *OL14: Tod* *3E 92*
  (off Burnley Rd.)
Wilford Rd. S71: Ath 8N 159
Wilfred, The WF5: Oss 4E 124
Wilfred Av. LS15: Leeds 6C 70
Wilfred St. BD14: Clay 1J 81
  LS15: Leeds 6C 70
Wilfred Ter. LS12: Leeds 1K 85
Wilkinson Fold BD12: Wyke 1A 100
Wilkinson Ho. *OL14: Tod* *4G 93*
  (off Harley Wood)
Wilkinson Ter. BD7: B'frd 8L 63
Wilkinson Way LS21: Otley 8J 17
Wilkin St. BD21: Keigh 9H 27
Willans Av. LS26: Rothw 6N 87
Willan's Rd. WF13: Dew 3F 122
Willerton Cl. WF12: Dew 9L 103
Willgutter La. BD22: Old 5N 41
William Av. LS15: Leeds 6N 69
  LS26: W'frd 7M 89
William Ct. WF9: S Kirk 7H 163
William Fison Ride LS29: Burl W 9B 16
William Foster Way LS29: Burl W 9B 16
William Henry St. BD18: Ship 6L 45
  HD6: Brigh 9M 99
William Hey Ct. LS9: Leeds 4K 69
William Horsfall St. HD4: Hud 7H 137
William La. LS28: Pud 7A 66
William Prince Gro. WF1: Wake 7N 125
William Ri. LS15: Leeds 6N 69
William Royd La. WF16: Heck 7B 102
Williams Ct. LS28: Fars 3A 66
Williams Dr. BD20: Stee 3B 26
Williamson St. HX1: Hal 4N 97
Williams Rd. BD20: Stee 3B 26
William St. BD4: B'frd 4H 83
  BD5: B'frd 6A 6 (8C 64)
  BD6: B'frd 6L 81
  BD13: Denh 5K 61
  HD1: Hud 2C 8 (3N 137)
  (not continuous)
  HD4: Hud 6H 137
  HD6: Ras 2M 119
  HX4: Gree 5C 118
  LS6: Leeds 3A 68
  LS27: Chur 5M 85
William St. LS28: Stan 4C 66
  (Milestone Ct.)
  LS28: Stan 5A 66
  (Sun Field)
  WF1: Wake 6L 9 (6M 125)
  WF10: C'frd 2J 109
  (Hope St.)
  WF10: C'frd 3D 108
  (Lock La.)
  WF10: C'frd 3E 108
  (Ryebread)
  WF12: Dew 2H 123
  WF13: Dew 9C 102
  WF13: Raven 6B 122
  WF15: Liv 8M 101
William Vw. LS15: Leeds 6N 69
Willington Rd. DN6: Skel 8M 165
Willis St. LS9: Leeds 8L 5 (7G 69)
Willoughby Ter. LS11: Leeds 9B 68
Willow App. LS4: Leeds 5A 68
Willow Av. BD2: B'frd 9E 46
  LS4: Leeds 5A 68
  LS23: Cliff 2D 38
Willow Bank BD20: Rid 6K 27
  HD2: Hud 1L 137
  HX1: Hal 7N 97
  HX2: Lud F 6D 96
  OL14: Tod 6K 93
Willow Bank Cl. BD15: All 7G 63
Willow Bank Dr. WF8: Pon 1L 129
Willowbank Gro. HD5: K'htn 1F 138
Willow Beck WF4: Not 3B 160
Willowbridge Cl. WF10: C'frd 7A 108
Willowbridge La. WF10: C'frd 6N 107
Willowbridge Rd.
  WF8: K S'ton, Lit S 6L 149
Willowbridge Way WF10: C'frd 6M 107
Willowbrook DN6: Skel 7L 165
Willow Brook Cl. S75: Dart 9J 159
Willow Cl. BD6: B'frd 6A 82
  BD19: Gom 5M 101
  HD8: Skelm 8C 156
  HX2: Hal 6K 97
  LS4: Leeds 5A 68
  LS20: Guis 7J 31
  LS29: Burl W 8C 16
  S72: Cud 9J 161
Willow Clough
  HX6: Ripp 9D 116
Willow Ct. HX5: Ell 5D 118
  LS21: Pool 2G 32
  WF2: Wake 4F 124
  WF7: F'stne 2C 128
  WF10: C'frd 6E 108
  WF17: Bat 6F 102
Willow Cres. BD2: B'frd 9E 46
  HX6: Sow B 7J 97
  LS15: Leeds 7A 70
  LS23: Cliff 2D 38
  WF6: Norm 3H 127
Willow Cft. LS29: Men 4E 30
Willowcroft BD19: Cleck 5G 100
Willowdale LS10: Leeds 9G 86
Willow Dene Av. HX2: Hal 7K 97
Willowdene La. WF8: Pon 9K 109
Willow Dene Rd. S72: Grim 9A 162
Willow Dr. BD6: B'frd 6A 82
  HX2: Hal 6K 97
  WF1: Wake 8N 125
  WF4: H'cft 1J 161
  WF9: Hems 4D 162
WILLOW FIELD 7J 97
Willowfield Av. HX2: Hal 7K 97
Willowfield Cl. HX2: Hal 6K 97
Willowfield Cres. BD2: B'frd 9E 46
  HX2: Hal 6K 97
Willowfield Dr. HX2: Hal 7K 97
Willowfield Lodge HD6: Ras 4K 119
Willowfield Rd. HX2: Hal 6K 97
Willow Flds. HD8: Lept 7L 139
Willowfield St. BD7: B'frd 8N 63
Willowfield Ter. HX2: Hal 7L 97
Willowfield Vw. HX2: Hal 6K 97
Willow Fold WF2: Wake 4F 124
Willow Gdns. BD2: B'frd 9E 46
  HX2: Hal 7L 97
  LS20: Guis 7J 31
  WF2: Wake 4F 124
  WF10: C'frd 7K 109
Willow Gth. LS4: Leeds 5A 68
  WF4: Dur 4G 143
  WF7: F'stne 2C 128
  WF9: S Elm 7A 164
Willow Gth. Av. LS14: Leeds 7C 52
Willow Gth. Cl. LS14: Leeds 7C 52
Willowgarth Cl. WF4: Ryh 1H 161
Willow Glade LS23: Cliff 3D 38
Willow Grn. WF1: Wake 9K 105
Willow Gro. BD2: B'frd 9E 46
  BD21: Keigh *4G 43*
  (off Halifax Rd.)
  HD7: Golc 5D 136
  LS23: Cliff 2D 38
  LS25: Kip 2N 89
  WF1: Wake 8N 125
  WF5: Oss 8A 124
Willow Hall Dr. HX6: Sow B 7K 97
Willow Hall Fold *HX6: Sow B* *7K 97*
  (off Willow Hall La.)
Willow Hall La. HX6: Sow B 7K 97
Willow Ho. LS7: Leeds 8F 50
Willow Ho's. *HX6: Sow B* *7K 97*
  (off Rochdale Rd.)
Willow Ind. Complex HX6: Sow B 9G 97
Willow La. HD1: Hud 1A 8 (2M 137)
  LS20: Bail, Guis 1D 46
  LS23: Cliff 2D 38
  WF2: Wake 4E 124
  WF6: Norm 4E 126
  WF7: F'stne 2C 128
  WF11: Ferr 5M 109
Willow La. E. HD1: Hud 1C 8 (2N 137)
  WF7: F'stne 2C 128
Willow M. WF2: Wake 4F 124
Willowmore Fold WF7: F'stne 4C 128
Willow Mt. *HX3: She* *7J 81*
  (off Witchfield Hill)
  WF2: Wake 4F 124
WILLOW PARK 3M 129
Willow Pk. WF1: Wake 1K 125
  WF8: Pon 3M 129
Willow Pk. Dr. HX3: She 7J 81
Willow Ri. HX2: Hal 6K 97
  LS24: Tad 6N 39
Willow Rd. LS4: Leeds 5A 68
  LS28: Fars 4N 65
  WF2: Wake 4F 124
  WF10: C'frd 6D 108
  WF11: Knot 7F 110
  WF17: Bat 8H 103
Willows, The BD16: Har 6A 44
  BD17: Bail 5K 45
  HX2: Illing 6L 79
  LS10: Leeds 9G 86
  LS17: Leeds 5E 50
  LS26: W'frd *7E 88*
  (off Aberford Rd.)
  WF4: Crig 5H 143
  WF4: Horb 1C 142
Willow Sq. LS26: Oul 8D 88
Willow St. BD8: B'frd 6L 63
  BD19: Cleck 3H 101
  HX1: Hal 6N 97
  HX6: Sow B 8K 97
Willow Ter. HX6: Sow B 7J 97
  LS1: Leeds 3C 4 (5C 68)
  WF17: Bat 8H 103
Willow Tree Cl. BD21: Keigh 2K 43
Willow Tree Gdns. LS29: Burl W 7D 16
Willowtree Gdns. BD16: Bgly 2H 45
Willow Va. LS22: Weth 2L 23
Willow Valley Golf Course 7D 100
Willow Vw. *HX6: Sow B* *7K 97*
  (off Bairstow Mt.)
  WF2: Wake 4F 124
Willow Vs. BD2: B'frd 9E 46
Willow Wlk. WF9: Kins 8B 146
  WF15: Liv 9L 101
Willow Well Rd. LS15: Leeds 6A 70
Wills Gill LS20: Guis 7K 31
Will St. BD4: B'frd 1H 83
Willwood Av. HD3: Hud 3G 136
Wilman Dr. WF5: Oss 5M 123
Wilman Hill BD6: B'frd 4N 81
  (not continuous)
Wilman Post WF5: Oss 5M 123
Wilmar Dr. HD3: Hud 2D 136
Wilmer Dr. BD9: B'frd 2M 63
  BD18: Ship 1M 63
Wilmer Rd. BD9: B'frd 3M 63
Wilmers OL15: Lit 9M 113
Wilmington Gro. LS7: Leeds 1G 5 (4E 68)
Wilmington St. LS7: Leeds 1H 5 (4F 68)
Wilmington Ter. LS7: Leeds 1G 5
Wilmot Rd. LS29: I'ly 5H 15
Wilmur Mt. HX2: Lud F 6E 96
WILSDEN 1B 62
WILSDEN HILL 9A 44
Wilsden Hill Rd. BD15: Wils 1A 62
Wilsden Old Rd. BD16: Har 6A 44
Wilsden Rd. BD15: All 2D 62
  BD16: Har 6A 44
WILSHAW 9G 152
Wilshaw Mill Rd. HD9: Mel 9F 152
Wilshaw Rd. HD9: Mel 9E 152
Wilson Av. BD20: Stee 2B 26
  WF5: Oss 7C 124
  WF14: Mir 6K 121
Wilson Cl. OL14: Tod 5J 93
Wilson Ct. WF1: Out 8L 105
Wilson Dr. WF1: Out 8K 105
Wilson Fold BD12: Low M 8B 82
Wilson Gdns. *HD3: Hud* *6F 136*
  (off New St.)
Wilson Rd. BD12: Wyke 9B 82
  BD16: Bgly 3E 44
  HX1: Hal 7M 97
  WF14: Mir 6K 121
Wilson's Row LS26: Meth 1N 107
Wilson St. BD8: B'frd 5A 64
  WF7: F'stne 6C 128
  WF8: Pon 2K 129
  WF10: C'frd 4C 108
Wilsons Yd. LS28: Stan 5A 66
Wilson Ter. WF14: Mir 6K 121
Wilson Wood St. WF17: Bat 1F 122
Wilton Av. HD2: Hud 5C 120
Wilton Gro. LS6: Leeds 9A 50
Wilton Ind. Ct. WF17: Bat 4C 102
Wilton Rd. LS29: I'ly 6F 14
Wilton St. BD5: B'frd 6A 6 (8B 64)
  HD6: Brigh 9L 99
  WF12: Dew 4G 122
Wilton Ter. BD19: Cleck 5H 101
Wimborne Dr. BD15: All 5H 63
  BD21: Keigh 8F 26
Winbrooke Ter. BD6: B'frd 4M 81
Winburg Rd. BD7: B'frd 9M 63
Winburn Ter. HX2: Hal 6H 97
Winchester Cl. WF2: Wren 2F 124
Winchester Gdns. BD4: B'frd 9H 65
Winchester Ho. *HX6: Sow B* *8J 97*
  (off Church Vw.)
Winchester St. LS12: Leeds 7N 67
Winchester Way WF9: S Elm 5N 163
Winden Cl. WF3: Loft 7L 105
  WF4: Cal G 4F 142
Winden Gro. WF3: Loft 7K 105
Windermere Av. LS29: Men 2E 30
Windermere Cl. DN6: Skel 8M 165
  HD9: Mel 8D 152
Windermere Dr. LS17: Leeds 1B 50
  LS25: Gar 8N 71
  WF11: Knot 1D 130
Windermere Ri. HD6: B Bri 6N 99
Windermere Rd. BD7: B'frd 2K 81
  BD17: Bail 6L 45
  WF2: Wake 4H 125
  WF10: C'frd 5K 109
  WF12: Dew 9H 103

Windermere Ter.—Woodland Dell

Windermere Ter. BD7: B'frd 2K 81
Winders Dale LS27: Morl 7J 85
Windgate BD20: Sils 9F 12
WINDHILL 8A 46
Windhill Av. S75: S'ross 6J 159
Windhill Ct. WF1: Wake 3A 126
Windhill Cres. S75: S'ross 6J 159
WF1: Wake 3N 125
Windhill Dr. S75: S'ross 6J 159
Windhill La. S75: S'ross 6J 159
Windhill Mt. S75: S'ross 6J 159
Windhill Old Rd.
BD10: B'frd 6D 46
BD18: Ship 6D 46
Windhill Ri. S75: W Gran 6G 158
Windhill Rd. WF1: Wake 3N 125
Windhill Vw. WF1: Wake 2M 9 (3N 125)
Winding Ri. HD6: B Bri 5N 99
Winding Rd. HX1: Hal 3L 7 (5B 98)
Winding Way LS17: Leeds 2D 50
Windle Edge S36: Dun B 9M 175
Windle Royd La. HX2: Hal 5J 97
Windmill App. LS10: Leeds 5G 87
Windmill Av. S72: Grim 9N 161
Windmill Chase LS26: Rothw 9N 87
Windmill Cl. LS10: Leeds 6G 87
Windmill Cotts. LS15: Leeds 8G 70
Windmill Ct. LS12: Leeds 8K 67
LS14: Leeds 9C 52
Windmill Cres. HD8: Skelm 8E 156
HX3: North 2F 98
Windmill Dr. HX3: North 2F 98
Windmill Fld. Rd. LS26: Rothw 9N 87
Windmill Fold *LS19: Yead* 9N 31
(off Windmill La.)
Windmill Gdns. LS15: Leeds 7E 70
Windmill Ga. LS12: Leeds 7K 67
Windmill Grn. LS26: Rothw 9N 87
Windmill Gro. BD19: Gom 6M 101
LS24: Tad 6N 39
Windmill Health & Strength Club 1N 81
(off Ebenezer Pl.)
WINDMILL HILL
LS28 8N 65
WF4 1J 145
Windmill Hill BD6: B'frd 4M 81
HX3: North 3F 98
LS28: Pud 8N 65
Windmill Hill La. HD8: Dew, Eml 1C 156
Windmill La. BD6: B'frd 4A 82
DN6: Nort 8N 149
HD8: Cumb, Bird E, H Flat 5F 170
HX3: North 2F 98
LS19: Yead 1N 47
LS26: Rothw 9N 87
LS27: Gil 7G 85
LS29: Men 4H 31
WF17: Bat 3D 102
Windmill Pl. *LS19: Yead* 1N 47
(off Windmill La.)
Windmill Ri. LS12: Leeds 8K 67
LS25: Aber 9E 54
Windmill Rd. LS10: Leeds 5G 86
LS23: B'ham 5D 38
Windmill Ter. HD4: Hud 1L 153
S71: Roys 4C 160
Windmill Vw. HD9: Scho 5A 170
Windross Cl. WF6: Alt 8H 107
Windrush Ct. *LS7: Leeds* 2F 68
(off Chapeltown Rd.)
Windsor Av. BD20: Sils 7D 12
LS15: Leeds 6C 70
S75: Kex 9E 158
WF7: Ackw 3J 147
Windsor Cl. LS25: Kip 3A 90
WF6: Norm 2K 127
WF12: Dew 9L 103
Windsor Ct. BD5: B'frd 8A 6
BD18: Ship 8N 45
(off Manor La.)
LS13: Leeds 4G 67
LS17: Leeds 5G 50
LS27: Morl 9K 85
WF12: Dew 1K 123
Windsor Cres. BD22: Oak 5B 42
HX2: Hal 3L 97
LS26: Rothw 7N 87
WF1: Wake 2J 125
Windsor Dr. HD5: Hud 4E 138
HD8: Skelm 8E 156
WF11: Ferr 7A 110
WF15: Liv 1M 121
Windsor Gdns. WF12: Dew 9L 103
Windsor Grn. LS25: Gar 7B 72
Windsor Gro. BD13: Thorn 8C 62
BD22: Oak 5B 42
Windsor Mt. LS15: Leeds 6C 70
Windsor Oval WF3: W Ard 7N 103
Windsor Pl. HD2: Hud 6C 120
HX7: Heb B 9H 77
(off Spring Gro.)
Windsor Ri. WF8: Pon 6H 129
Windsor Rd. BD18: Ship 8N 45
BD22: Oak 5B 42
HD4: Hud 7E 136
HX7: Heb B 9H 77
OL14: Tod 6J 93
WF1: Wake 1H 125
WF9: Hems 3F 162
WF12: Dew 1K 123
WF17: Bat 3D 102
Windsor St. BD4: B'frd 7E 6 (9E 64)
HX1: Hal 6K 7 (6B 98)
WF9: S Elm 7A 164
Windsor Ter. HX6: Sow B 1H 117
LS27: Gil 6G 84
Windsor Vw. HX7: Heb B 9H 77
WF12: Dew 1L 123
Windsor Vs. HX3: Nor G 2L 99
Windsor Wlk. HX3: Hip 6M 99
WF17: Bat 2E 102
Windy Bank La. BD13: Que 7A 80
HX3: Que 7A 80
WF15: Liv 7F 100
Windycroft HD9: Hon 6L 153
Windy Gro. BD15: Wils 2C 62
(not continuous)
Windy Harbour La. OL14: Tod 3K 93
Windy Ridge WF8: Lit S 4L 149
Windyridge St. WF4: Horb 9B 124
Wine Tavern La. HX6: Sow B 9B 96
Wine Tavern Rd. HX6: Sow B 9B 96
Winfield Dr. BD4: E Bier 7J 83
HD3: Hud 2E 136
Winfield Gro. LS2: Leeds 1D 4
Winfield Pl. LS2: Leeds 1E 4 (4D 68)
Winfield Ter. LS2: Leeds 1E 4
Wingate Av. BD22: Keigh 1F 42
Wingate Cft. WF2: Wake 2A 144
Wingate Gro. WF2: Wake 2A 144
Wingate Way BD22: Keigh 1F 42
Winget Av. HD4: Hud 7E 136
Wingfield Ct. BD16: Bgly 3F 44
Wingfield Mt. BD3: B'frd 6F 64
Wingfield Rd. S71: Ath 9B 160
Wingfield St. BD3: B'frd 6F 64
Winker Grn. Lodge *LS12: Leeds* 6M 67
(off Eyres Mill Side)
Winker Grn. Mills *LS12: Leeds* 6L 67
(off Eyres Mill Side)
Winmarith Ct. S71: Roys 6C 160
Winnan Ct. WF10: C'frd 3J 109
Winnard Row BD5: B'frd 3D 82
Winnipeg Pl. LS7: Leeds 9F 50
Winn Mt. LS13: Leeds 9E 48
Winnow La. LS23: B Spa 1A 38
Winrose App. LS10: Leeds 6G 86
Winrose Av. LS10: Leeds 5F 86
Winrose Cl. BD12: Wyke 9A 82
Winrose Cres. LS10: Leeds 5F 86
Winrose Dr. LS10: Leeds 5F 86
Winrose Gth. LS10: Leeds 5G 86
Winrose Gro. LS10: Leeds 5G 87
Winrose Hill LS10: Leeds 4G 86
Winscar Av. BD6: B'frd 4H 81
Winsford Dr. HD5: Hud 3F 138
Winslow Rd. BD10: B'frd 2J 65
Winstanley Ter. *LS6: Leeds* 3A 68
(off Victoria Rd.)
Winston Gdns. LS6: Leeds 1M 67
Winston Mt. LS6: Leeds 1M 67
Winston Ter. BD7: B'frd 9M 63
Winter Av. S71: Roys 4D 160
Winterbourne Av. LS27: Morl 7L 85
Winterburn Hill HX2: Hal 6G 97
Winterburn La. HX2: Hal 5G 97
Winterburn St. BD21: Keigh 8J 27
Winterbutlee Gro. OL14: W'den 2J 113
Winterbutlee Rd. OL14: W'den 2J 113
Winter Ct. BD15: All 3F 62
Winter Hill HD7: Linth 2A 152
HX3: Sou 9F 98
Winterneb HX2: Lud F 7E 96
Winter's Cotts. HX7: Blac H 2D 94
WINTERSETT 6H 145
Wintersett Cl. WF4: Ryh 9H 145
Wintersett La. WF4: Wint 6H 145
Winter's La. HX7: Blac H 2C 94
Winter St. HX1: Hal 7M 97
Winterton Dr. BD12: Low M 8A 82
Winthorpe Av. WF3: Thpe H 2F 104
Winthorpe Cres. WF3: Thpe H 2F 104
Winthorpe St. LS6: Leeds 9B 50
Winthorpe Vw. WF3: Thpe H 2G 104
Winton Grn. BD6: B'frd 7N 81
Winton Mill HX6: Sow B 8J 97
Winton St. HD1: Hud 7K 137
Wintoun St. LS7: Leeds 3H 5 (5F 68)
Wira Ho. LS16: Leeds 6J 49
Wirefield Rd. BD22: Keigh 3G 43
WIRING FIELD 7M 67
Wiseley Cft. S72: Grim 9A 162
Wiston Dr. WF8: Pon 9L 109
Wistons La. HX5: Ell 4F 118
(not continuous)
WITCHFIELD 7J 81
Witchfield Ct. *HX3: She* 7J 81
(off Burned Rd.)
Witchfield Grange HX3: She 7H 81
Witchfield Hill HX3: She 7J 81
Witham Way LS25: Gar 8A 72
Withens Ct. S75: Map 8J 159
Withens End La. HX6: Rish 3E 134
Withens Hill Cft. HX2: Illing 6K 79
Withens La. HX4: Bark 2F 134
HX7: Crag V 9G 95
Withens New Rd. HX2: Ogd, Wain 3F 78
HX7: Crag V 9D 94
OL14: Tod 9M 93
(not continuous)
Withens Rd. HX2: Wain 3F 78
WF17: Birs 2B 102
Withinfield Ct. HX3: Sou 8F 98
Within Flds. HX3: Sou 8F 98
Withins Cl. BD5: B'frd 3N 81
Withyside HD8: Den D 2D 172
Woburn Ct. WF5: Oss 6N 123
Woburn Dr. HD5: Hud 4F 138
Woburn Ter. BD14: Clay 1G 80
Woburn Way WF6: Norm 2L 127
Wold Cl. BD13: Thorn 8C 62
Wolfstones Rd. HD9: H'frth 1G 169
Wollaton Cl. S71: Ath 9N 159
Wolley Av. LS12: N Far 2G 84
Wolley Ct. LS12: N Far 2G 85
Wolley Dr. LS12: N Far 2G 85
Wolley Gdns. LS12: N Far 2G 85
Wolseley Rd. LS4: Leeds 5N 67
(not continuous)
Wolseley St. BD14: Clay 9H 63
Wolseley Ter. *HX1: Hal* 5M 97
(off Battinson Rd.)
Wolsey Av. WF8: Pon 3H 129
Wolston Cl. BD4: B'frd 3J 83
WOMERSLEY 8L 131
Womersley Ct. *LS28: Pud* 8A 66
(off Womersley Pl.)
Womersley Pk. Gdns. DN6: Wome 8M 131
Womersley Pl. LS28: Pud 8A 66
LS28: Stan 5M 65
Womersley Rd. WF11: Knot 8F 110
Womersley St. HX1: Hal 5M 97
Wonder St. WF1: Wake 6L 9 (6M 125)
Woodacre Cres. LS17: Bard 5D 36
Woodacre Grn. LS17: Bard 4D 36
Woodacre La. LS17: Bard 4D 36
Wodale Av. BD9: B'frd 3J 63
Woodalls Bldgs. *WF11: Knot* 8F 110
(off Foundry La.)
Wood Av. WF16: Heck 7A 102
Woodbank OL14: W'den 6M 113
Woodbine Av. WF8: Pon 3J 129
Woodbine Gro. BD10: B'frd 8F 46
Woodbine Pl. HX7: Heb B 1F 94
HX7: Myth 4N 95
Woodbine Rd. HD1: Hud 1N 137
Woodbine St. BD3: B'frd 3E 6 (7E 64)
HX1: Hal 7N 97
WF5: Oss 4N 123
Woodbine Ter. BD10: B'frd 8F 46
HD8: Clay W 6J 157
HX1: Hal 7G 7
LS6: Leeds 9A 50
LS13: Leeds 3F 66
LS18: Hors 8F 48
(off Wood La.)
OL14: Tod 3D 92
WOODBOTTOM 7A 48
Wood Bottom LS19: Raw 7A 48
Woodbottom WF14: Mir 9N 121
Woodbottom Cl. BD17: Bail 5B 46
Wood Bottom La. HD6: Brigh 7J 99
Wood Bottom Rd. HD4: Neth 4G 153
Woodbourne LS8: Leeds 8L 51
Woodbourne Av. LS17: Leeds 6E 50
Woodbridge Av. LS25: Gar 5C 72
Woodbridge Cl. LS6: Leeds 1L 67
WF1: Wake 5N 125
Woodbridge Cres. LS6: Leeds 9K 49
Woodbridge Fold LS6: Leeds 1K 67
Woodbridge Gdns. LS6: Leeds 1K 67
Woodbridge Gth. LS6: Leeds 1L 67
Woodbridge Grn. LS6: Leeds 1L 67
Woodbridge Lawn LS6: Leeds 1K 67
Woodbridge Pl. LS6: Leeds 1K 67
Woodbridge Rd. LS6: Leeds 1K 67
Woodbridge Va. LS6: Leeds 1K 67
Woodbrook Av. HX2: Mix 8J 79
Woodbrook Cl. HX2: Mix 8J 79
Woodbrook Pl. HX2: Mix 8J 79
Woodbrook Rd. HX2: Mix 8J 79
Woodburn Av. WF12: Dew 6J 123
Woodchurch Vw. HD9: T'bdge 9N 153
Wood Cl. BD17: Bail 5N 45
LS7: Leeds 8E 50
LS26: Rothw 7M 87
WF6: Alt 9F 106
WF9: Kins 8A 146
Wood Cl. Bottom HD7: Linth 1B 152
Woodcock St. WF1: Wake 8M 125
Woodcock Way WF9: S Elm 5N 163
Woodcot Av. BD17: Bail 5B 46
Wood Cote Fold BD22: Oak 1B 42
Wood Cotts. OL14: Tod 1J 113
Wood Cres. LS26: Rothw 7M 87
Wood Cft. HD6: Ras 2L 119
HX6: Sow B 9E 96
Woodcroft WF2: Wake 1N 143
Woodcroft Grange HX2: Hal 6K 97
Woodcross LS27: Morl 7K 85
Woodcross Ct. BD5: B'frd 1B 82
Woodcross End LS27: Morl 6K 85
Woodcross Fold LS27: Morl 7K 85
Woodcross Gdns. LS27: Morl 7K 85
Woodcross Gth. LS27: Morl 6K 85
Woodddle Hole La. WF8: K S'ton, Nort 8H 149
Wood Dr. LS26: Rothw 7L 87
Woodedge Av. HD5: Hud 4E 138
WOOD END 9H 77
WOODEND
BD18 8B 46
WF10 8N 89
Wood End HD4: Hud 7L 137
Woodend WF10: All B 7N 89
Wood End Cl. HX3: Hal 9A 98
Woodend Ct. BD5: B'frd 3D 82
Wood End Cres. BD18: Ship 7B 46
Woodend Cres. WF10: All B 8N 89
Wood End La. HD8: Shep 1G 170
HX4: Bark 5K 117
Wood End Rd. HD4: Arm B 1K 153
Woodend Rd. WF14: Mir 7K 121
Woodeson Ct. LS13: Leeds 1C 66
Woodeson Lea LS13: Leeds 1C 66
Wood Farm La. HD9: Brock 7A 154
Woodfield Av. HX4: Gree 4A 118
WF17: Bat 8D 102
Woodfield Cl. BD10: B'frd 7G 46
Woodfield Ct. HD2: Hud 2L 137
LS8: Leeds 2M 69
WF17: Bat 1E 122
Woodfield Dr. HX4: Gree 5A 118
Woodfield Pk. WF2: W'ton 4B 144
Woodfield Rd. BD13: Cull 8L 43
DN6: Cam 1H 165
WF8: Went 1H 165
Woodfield St. *OL14: Tod* 6J 93
(off Buckley Vw.)
Woodfield Ter. LS28: Pud 8C 66
Woodford Av. HX3: Hal 8M 7 (8C 98)
Woodford Cl. BD15: All 6F 62
Woodford Dr. HD5: Hud 3E 138
Woodgarth Gdns. BD4: B'frd 2K 83
Woodgate La. LS17: Wee 4N 19
Wood Grn. WF10: C'frd 7N 107
Wood Gro. LS12: Leeds 7G 66
WF5: Oss 3N 123
WOODHALL 4L 65
Woodhall Av. BD3: B'frd 5J 65
LS5: Leeds 9H 49
Woodhall Cl. LS28: Stan 4L 65
WF4: Dur 4H 143
WF4: Over 4K 141
Woodhall Ct. LS15: Leeds 8E 70
LS28: Cal 1L 65
Woodhall Cres. HX3: Hal 9N 97
Woodhall Cft. LS28: Stan 4L 65
Woodhall Dr. LS5: Leeds 9H 49
WF7: Ackw 4F 146
WF17: Bat 8D 102
Woodhall Gro. LS26: Meth 1L 107
(not continuous)
WOODHALL HILLS 3L 65
Woodhall Hills LS28: Cal 3K 65
Woodhall Hills Golf Course 2K 65
Woodhall La. DN6: Wome 7M 131
LS28: Cal, Stan 3L 65
WOODHALL PARK 4M 65
Woodhall Pk. HX3: North 1F 98
Woodhall Pk. Av. LS28: Stan 4L 65
Woodhall Pk. Cres. E. LS28: Stan 5M 65
Woodhall Pk. Cres. W. LS28: Stan 5L 65
Woodhall Pk. Dr. LS28: Stan 5L 65
Woodhall Pk. Gdns. LS28: Stan 5M 65
Woodhall Pk. Gro. LS28: Stan 5L 65
Woodhall Pk. Mt. LS28: Stan 4L 65
Woodhall Pl. BD3: B'frd 5J 65
Woodhall Retail Pk. BD3: B'frd 5J 65
Woodhall Rd. BD3: B'frd 6J 65
LS28: Cal 3J 65
Woodhall Ter. BD3: B'frd 5J 65
Woodhall Vw. BD3: B'frd 5K 65
Woodhead Cl. HD2: Hud 8A 120
WF5: Oss 5N 123
Woodhead La. HD6: Clift 2C 120
LS27: Gil 6F 84
Woodhead Rd. BD7: B'frd 8N 63
HD4: Hud 9K 137
(not continuous)
HD9: H'frth, Hon 5M 153
HD9: Holm, H'lm, H'frth 3C 174
WF17: Birs 1E 102
Woodhead St. BD19: Cleck 6J 101
HX2: Hal 4L 97
Wood Hey La. HX7: Heb B 3J 95
WOOD HILL 2E 122
Wood Hill LS26: Rothw 7M 87
Wood Hill Ct. LS16: Leeds 3G 48
Wood Hill Cres. LS16: Leeds 4F 48
Wood Hill Gdns. LS16: Leeds 3G 48
Wood Hill Gth. LS16: Leeds 3G 48
Wood Hill Gro. LS16: Leeds 4F 48
Wood Hill La. LS21: Clift 5J 17
Wood Hill Ri. LS16: Leeds 3G 48
Woodhill Ri. BD10: B'frd 7J 47
Wood Hill Rd. LS16: Leeds 4G 48
Woodhill Vw. LS22: Weth 3M 23
WOODHOUSE
BD21 2J 43
HD6 3A 120
LS2 1D 4 (4D 68)
WF6 3H 127
Woodhouse BD16: Bgly 5F 44
OL14: Tod 7N 93
Woodhouse Av. BD21: Keigh 2J 43
HD2: Hud 9N 119
Woodhouse Bus. Cen. WF6: Norm 3H 127
WOODHOUSE CARR 3D 68
WOODHOUSE CLIFF 2C 68
Woodhouse Cliff LS6: Leeds 2C 68
Woodhouse Cl. BD21: Keigh 2J 43
WF3: E Ard 6D 104
WOODHOUSE COMMON 4H 127
Woodhouse Ct. OL14: Tod 6N 93
Woodhouse Cres. WF6: Norm 3J 127
Woodhouse Dr. BD21: Keigh 2J 43
Woodhouse Flats LS2: Leeds 1C 4
Woodhouse Gdns. HD6: Ras 3A 120
Woodhouse Gro. BD15: All 2F 62
BD21: Keigh 2J 43
HD2: Hud 9A 120
HX7: Myth 4N 95
OL14: Tod 7M 93
Woodhouse Hall Rd. HD2: Hud 9A 120
WOODHOUSE HILL
HD2 9A 120
LS10 3G 87
Woodhouse Hill HD2: Hud 9A 120
Woodhouse Hill Av. LS10: Leeds 3G 86
Woodhouse Hill Gro. LS10: Leeds 3G 86
Woodhouse Hill Pl. LS10: Leeds 3G 86
Woodhouse Hill Rd. LS10: Leeds 3G 86
Woodhouse La. HD6: Ras 4N 119
HD8: Eml 2J 157
HD9: Holm 7J 169
HX3: Hal 9N 97
LS1: Leeds 3E 4 (5D 68)
LS2: Leeds 1B 4 (3C 68)
WF2: Kirk 9C 104
WF3: E Ard, Kirk 9C 104
WF4: Wool 3J 159
Woodhouse Mill OL14: Tod 7N 93
Woodhouse Mt. WF6: Norm 3H 127
Woodhouse Rd. BD21: Keigh 2J 43
OL14: Tod 7N 93
WF1: Wake 4M 9 (5N 125)
Woodhouse Sq.
LS3: Leeds 4C 4 (6C 68)
Woodhouse St. LS6: Leeds 3C 68
Woodhouse Ter. BD6: B'frd 5C 82
Woodhouse Wlk. BD21: Keigh 2J 43
Woodhouse Way BD21: Keigh 2K 43
WOODKIRK 5N 103
Woodkirk Av. WF3: Ting 4M 103
Woodkirk Gdns. WF12: Dew 6L 103
Woodkirk Gro. BD12: Wyke 3A 100
WF3: Ting 4N 103
Woodland Av. LS26: Swil 4H 89
WF1: K'thpe 4D 126
Woodland Cl. BD9: B'frd 2H 63
LS15: Leeds 6D 70
WF4: Hol 8H 143
Woodland Ct. LS8: Leeds 1H 69
LS23: T Arch 6F 24
Woodland Cres. BD9: B'frd 2G 63
LS26: Rothw 7M 87
LS26: Swil 4H 89
Woodland Cft. LS18: Hors 5F 48
LS23: T Arch 6G 24
Woodland Dell HX7: Heb B 2E 94

Woodland Dr.—Woodville Sq.

Woodland Dr. HD6: Brigh ... 9L **99**
HD8: Skelm ... 8E **156**
HX2: Hal ... 7K **97**
LS7: Leeds ... 8F **50**
LS10: Leeds ... 9H **87**
LS23: T Arch ... 6F **24**
LS26: Swil ... 4G **89**
WF2: Wake ... 4M **143**
Woodland Glade Sports & Leisure Cen. ... 6B **120**
Woodland Gro. BD9: B'frd ... 1H **63**
LS7: Leeds ... 2G **68**
LS26: Swil ... 4H **89**
WF7: Ackw ... 1G **147**
Woodland Hill LS15: Leeds ... 6C **70**
Woodland Ho. *BD10: B'frd ... 8G 46*
(off Fairhaven Grn.)
Woodland La. LS7: Leeds ... 8F **50**
Woodland Mdw. HD8: Kbtn ... 2K **155**
Woodland M. LS23: T Arch ... 6G **24**
Woodland Mt. LS7: Leeds ... 2G **69**
Woodland Pk. LS26: Oul ... 8D **88**
Woodland Pk. Rd. LS6: Leeds ... 1A **68**
Woodland Ri. HD2: Hud ... 1L **137**
LS15: Leeds ... 6D **70**
WF2: Wake ... 5F **124**
Woodland Rd. HD2: Hud ... 9D **120**
LS15: Leeds ... 6C **70**
WF2: Wake ... 5F **124**
WOODLANDS ... 2B **98**
Woodlands BD12: O'haw ... 8E **82**
BD17: Bail ... 3C **46**
HX6: Tri ... 1F **116**
LS17: Leeds ... 5G **50**
LS29: I'ly ... 5J **15**
WF3: E Ard ... 5E **104**
WF4: Croft ... 1G **144**
WF4: Horb ... 9E **124**
WF5: Oss ... 4N **123**
Woodlands, The HD9: Mel ... 4D **152**
HX7: Heb B ... 2H **95**
LS21: Pool ... 2H **33**
LS26: Oul ... 8D 88
(off Farrer La.)
WF8: Pon ... 5L **129**
Woodlands Av. BD13: Que ... 4G **80**
BD19: Gom ... 3L **101**
HD8: Lept ... 7J **139**
HD9: T'bdge ... 9A **154**
HX3: Hal ... 3B **98**
LS24: Tad ... 6N **39**
LS28: Stan ... 5N **65**
OL14: Tod ... 6K **93**
WF10: C'frd ... 6J **109**
Woodlands Cl. BD10: B'frd ... 6K **47**
BD13: Thorn ... 8C **62**
HD2: Hud ... 5E **120**
HD8: Den D ... 2D **172**
LS14: S'cft ... 8D **36**
LS29: I'ly ... 5E **14**
WF3: E Ard ... 5E **104**
Woodlands Ct. *BD8: B'frd ... 6A 64*
(off Woodlands St.)
BD16: Bgly ... 2C **44**
LS16: Leeds ... 6L **49**
LS25: Kip ... 5B **90**
LS28: Pud ... 9A **66**
S75: W Gran ... 6G **158**
Woodlands Cres. BD19: Gom ... 3L **101**
WF9: Hems ... 1E **162**
Woodlands Cft. LS25: Kip ... 5B **90**
WF2: Wake ... 1N **143**
Woodlands Dr. BD10: B'frd ... 6K **47**
BD19: Gom ... 3L **101**
HD8: Lept ... 8J **139**
LS19: Raw ... 5L **47**
LS25: Gar ... 8B **72**
LS27: Morl ... 7J **85**
WF3: E Ard ... 5D **104**
Woodlands End HD8: Lept ... 7J **139**
Woodlands Fold BD11: B'haw ... 8M **83**
Woodlands Gdns. LS14: S'cft ... 1D **52**
Woodlands Gro. BD13: Que ... 4F **80**
BD16: Cot ... 8G **44**
BD17: Bail ... 5L **45**
HX3: Hal ... 3B **98**
LS25: Kip ... 5C **90**
LS28: Stan ... 5N **65**
LS29: I'ly ... 5E **14**
WF13: Dew ... 3C **122**
Woodlands La. WF13: Dew ... 3C **122**
Woodlands Mill *BD20: Stee ... 3C 26*
(off Mulberry La.)
Woodlands Mt. HX3: Hal ... 2B **98**
(not continuous)
Woodlands Pk. BD19: Cleck ... 1F **100**
LS14: S'cft ... 8D **36**
Woodlands Pk. Gro. LS28: Pud ... 9A **66**
Woodlands Pk. Rd. LS28: Pud ... 9A **66**
Woodland Sq. HD6: Brigh ... 2A **120**
LS12: Leeds ... 6J **67**
Woodlands Ri. BD22: Haw ... 1C **60**
LS29: I'ly ... 5D **14**
Woodlands Rd. BD8: B'frd ... 6M **63**
BD13: Que ... 4F **80**
BD16: Bgly ... 3H **45**
BD19: Gom ... 3L **101**
HD8: Lept ... 7J **139**
HX3: Hal ... 3B **98**
HX5: Ell ... 3E **118**
WF17: Bat ... 4D **102**
Woodlands Rd. E. HD8: Fen B ... 7H **139**
Woodlands St. BD8: B'frd ... 6A **64**
Woodlands Ter. BD8: B'frd ... 5M **63**
BD12: O'haw ... 8F **82**
LS28: Stan ... 5N **65**
Woodlands Vw. BD19: Gom ... 4L **101**
BD22: Oak ... 5C **42**
HX3: Hal ... 3B 98
(off Range St.)
LS14: S'cft ... 9D **36**
LS24: Tad ... 6N **39**
LS25: Kip ... 5C **90**
Woodlands Village
WF1: Wake ... 8M **125**
Woodlands Way HD8: Lept ... 8J **139**
Woodland Ter. HX3: Hal ... 3B **98**
LS7: Leeds ... 8C **50**
Woodland Vw. HX7: Heb B ... 2E **94**
LS7: Leeds ... 8F **50**
LS28: Cal ... 8L **47**
WF1: Hea ... 7D **126**
WF3: W Ard ... 7N **103**
WF8: Pon ... 5L **129**
WF9: S Elm ... 6L 163
(off Minsthorpe La.)
Woodland Vs. LS14: Leeds ... 2E **70**
Woodland Way WF9: Upt ... 9C **148**
Wood La. BD2: B'frd ... 2C **64**
BD16: Bgly ... 9E **28**
HD4: Hud ... 7N **137**
HD5: Hud ... 6H **121**
HD6: Brigh ... 1J **119**
HD7: Slait ... 4M **151**
HD8: Den D ... 2B **172**
HD8: Kbtn ... 5F **154**
HD9: H'frth ... 2M **169**
HX2: Hal ... 3K **97**
HX2: Midg ... 7B **78**
HX3: Hip ... 3G **99**
HX3: Sou ... 9G **99**
HX6: Sow B ... 9E **96**
LS6: Leeds ... 1N **67**
LS7: Leeds ... 8E **50**
(not continuous)
LS12: Leeds ... 6G **66**
LS12: N Far ... 3G **85**
LS13: Leeds ... 2F **66**
(Bellmount Pl.)
LS13: Leeds ... 6G **66**
(Ring Rd. Farnley)
LS15: Leeds, Scho ... 1F **70**
LS17: Bard ... 5E **36**
LS18: Hors ... 8F **48**
LS23: T Arch ... 5E **24**
LS26: Gt P, Swil ... 7M **89**
LS26: Rothw ... 6K **87**
LS28: Cal ... 8M **47**
S71: Carl ... 7B **160**
(Ruscombe Pl.)
S71: Carl ... 8D **160**
(Woodroyd Av.)
S71: S'ross ... 7N **159**
WF2: New ... 7J **143**
WF4: Chap ... 7J **143**
WF4: Over ... 2G **141**
WF10: C'frd ... 7N **107**
WF11: Birk ... 1N **111**
WF12: Bries ... 2G **141**
WF13: Dew ... 1G **122**
WF14: Hud ... 6H **121**
WF14: Up H ... 8J **121**
WF17: Bat ... 9G **103**
Wood La. Ct. LS6: Leeds ... 1A **68**
Woodlark Cl. BD6: B'frd ... 4J **81**
Wood Lea OL14: Tod ... 4G **93**
WF11: Byram ... 4C **110**
Woodlea LS23: B Spa ... 9D **24**
WF9: S Elm ... 7M **163**
Woodlea App. LS6: Leeds ... 6B **50**
LS19: Yead ... 1K **47**
Woodlea Av. HD3: Hud ... 4H **137**
LS6: Leeds ... 6B **50**
Woodlea Chase LS6: Leeds ... 7B **50**
Woodlea Cl. LS19: Yead ... 2K **47**
Woodlea Ct. LS6: Leeds ... 7B **50**
LS17: Leeds ... 3K **51**
Woodlea Cft. LS6: Leeds ... 6B **50**
Woodlea Dr. LS6: Leeds ... 6B **50**
LS19: Yead ... 2K **47**
Woodlea Farm HD8: Shep ... 7K **155**
Woodlea Fold LS6: Leeds ... 6B **50**
Woodlea Gdns. LS6: Leeds ... 6B **50**
Woodlea Gth. LS6: Leeds ... 6B **50**
Woodlea Ga. LS6: Leeds ... 7B **50**
Woodlea Grn. LS6: Leeds ... 6B **50**
Woodlea Gro. LS6: Leeds ... 7B **50**
LS11: Leeds ... 2B 86
(off Woodlea Mt.)
LS19: Yead ... 1K **47**
Woodlea Hall LS6: Leeds ... 6B **50**
Woodlea Holt LS6: Leeds ... 6B **50**
Woodlea La. LS6: Leeds ... 6B **50**
Woodlea Lawn LS6: Leeds ... 6B **50**
Woodlea Mt. LS11: Leeds ... 2B **86**
LS19: Yead ... 1K **47**
Woodlea Pk. LS6: Leeds ... 7B **50**
Woodlea Pl. LS6: Leeds ... 6B **50**
LS11: Leeds ... 2C **86**
Woodlea Rd. LS19: Yead ... 1K **47**
Woodlea Sq. LS6: Leeds ... 7B **50**
Woodlea St. LS11: Leeds ... 2B **86**
Woodlea Vw. LS6: Leeds ... 7B **50**
LS19: Yead ... 2K **47**
Woodleigh HX7: Heb B ... 1F **94**
Woodleigh Av. BD5: B'frd ... 4C **82**
LS25: Gar ... 7M 71
(off Providence Pl.)
Woodleigh Cres. WF7: Ackw ... 4F **146**
Woodleigh Gro. HD4: Hud ... 9H **137**
Woodleigh Hall M. LS19: Raw ... 6A **48**
Woodleigh Hall Vw. LS19: Raw ... 6B **48**
WOODLESFORD ... 6D **88**
Woodlesford HX2: Hal ... 2J **97**
Woodlesford Cres. HX2: Hal ... 2H **97**
Woodlesford Station (Rail) ... 6E **88**
Woodliffe Ct. LS7: Leeds ... 8E **50**
Woodliffe Cres. LS7: Leeds ... 8E **50**
Woodliffe Dr. LS7: Leeds ... 8E **50**
Woodlock Cl. HD2: Hud ... 7A **120**
Woodman Av. HD2: Hud ... 6D **120**
HX5: Ell ... 6E **118**
Woodman Ct. BD6: B'frd ... 7K **81**
Woodman St. LS15: Leeds ... 6B **70**
Woodman Works HX5: Ell ... 6E **118**
Woodman Yd. *LS16: Leeds ... 9N 49*
(off Otley Rd.)
Woodmoor Cl. WF4: Crig ... 6G **142**
Wood Moor Ct. LS17: Leeds ... 1G **50**
Woodmoor Dr. WF4: Crig ... 6G **142**
Woodmoor Ri. WF4: Crig ... 5F **142**
Wood Moor Rd. WF9: Hems ... 2F **162**
Woodmoor Rd. WF2: Wake ... 5J **143**
Woodmoor St. S71: Carl ... 9E **160**
Wood Mt. HX2: Hal ... 8M **97**
LS26: Rothw ... 7L **87**
WF4: Over ... 4J **141**
WOOD NOOK ... 7B **140**
Wood Nook BD13: Denh ... 3M **61**
HD8: Den D ... 2C **172**
HD9: Mel ... 7H **153**
HX6: Sow B ... 2G **116**
Woodnook Cl. LS16: Leeds ... 5G **48**
Woodnook Dr. LS16: Leeds ... 5G **48**
Woodnook Gth. LS16: Leeds ... 5G **48**
Wood Nook La. HD9: Hon, Mel ... 7G **153**
HX6: Sow B ... 7J **97**
Woodnook Rd. LS16: Leeds ... 4G **49**
Wood Nook Ter. LS28: Stan ... 5N **65**
Wood Pk. Vw. S71: Ath ... 8A **160**
Woodpecker Cl. BD15: All ... 7G **62**
Woodpecker Rd. LS29: Burl W ... 7C **16**
Wood Pl. BD8: B'frd ... 6A **64**
BD9: B'frd ... 2A **64**
Wood Rd. BD5: B'frd ... 1C **82**
BD9: B'frd ... 2A **64**
WOOD ROW ... 1J **107**
Wood Row LS26: Meth ... 1J **107**
Woodrow Cres.
LS26: Meth ... 1H **107**
Woodrow Dr. BD12: Low M ... 7C **82**
Woodroyd HD7: Golc ... 5B **136**
HX2: Lud F ... 7F **96**
Woodroyd Av. BD5: B'frd ... 3D **82**
HD9: Hon ... 4N **153**
S71: Carl ... 8D **160**
Woodroyd Cl. S71: Carl ... 8D **160**
Woodroyd Cres. HX6: Lud F ... 7G **96**
Woodroyd Dr. HX3: Hal ... 2M **97**
Woodroyd Gdns. HX2: Lud F ... 7F **96**
LS29: I'ly ... 6L **15**
Woodroyd Hill La. HD9: H'wth ... 9F **170**
Woodroyd Rd. BD5: B'frd ... 2C **82**
(not continuous)
Woodroyd Ter. BD5: B'frd ... 3D **82**
Woods Av. HD7: Mars ... 5H **151**
WOODSIDE
BD6 ... 6M **81**
HX3 ... 1K **7 (4B 98)**
Wood Side HX4: Bark ... 6K **117**
Woodside BD18: Ship ... 7B **46**
BD20: Keigh ... 7G **26**
HD8: Den D ... 2D **172**
HX4: Gree ... 5C **118**
HX7: Heb B ... 2K **95**
LS26: Meth ... 1H **107**
WF2: Wren ... 1G **125**
WF10: C'frd ... 3J **109**
Woodside Av. BD16: Cot ... 8E **44**
BD18: Ship ... 7K **45**
LS4: Leeds ... 4M **67**
LS7: Leeds ... 8B **50**
WF2: Wren ... 1G **125**
WF4: S Comn ... 8K **127**
Woodside Cl. LS27: Morl ... 7K **85**
Woodside Cotts. HD3: Hud ... 6F **136**
Woodside Ct. BD13: Cull ... 9K **43**
LS16: Leeds ... 6J **49**
LS18: Hors ... 7H 49
(off Broadgate La.)
LS18: Hors ... 7H **49**
(Tanhouse Hill)
LS29: I'ly ... 3F **14**
WF6: Norm ... 8L 107
(off Pontefract Rd.)
Woodside Cres. BD16: Cot ... 8E **44**
HX3: Hal ... 1J **7 (3A 98)**
WF4: S Comn ... 7K **127**
WF17: Bat ... 8D **102**
Woodside Dr. BD16: Cot ... 8E **44**
LS27: Morl ... 6K **85**
WF2: Wren ... 1G **125**
Woodside Gdns. LS27: Morl ... 6K **85**
Woodside Gro. HX3: Hal ... 1K **7 (3B 98)**
HX4: Gree ... 5B **118**
WF10: All B ... 7N **89**
Woodside Hill Cl. LS18: Hors ... 7H **49**
Woodside La. HD2: Fix ... 7N **119**
LS27: Morl ... 6K **85**
Woodside Lawn LS12: Leeds ... 7G **66**
Woodside Lodge HD8: Kbtn ... 3F **154**
Woodside M. LS7: Leeds ... 8B **50**
Woodside Mt. HX3: Hal ... 1J **7 (4A 98)**
Woodside Pk. Av. LS18: Hors ... 7G **48**
Woodside Pk. Dr. LS18: Hors ... 7G **48**
Woodside Pl. HX3: Hal ... 1J **7 (3A 98)**
LS4: Leeds ... 4M **67**
Woodside Rd. BD12: Low M, Wyke ... 1A **100**
BD20: Sils ... 8C **12**
HD4: Hud ... 9H **137**
HX3: Hal ... 1J **7 (4A 98)**
LS23: B Spa ... 1B **38**
Woodside St. WF10: All B ... 7N **89**
Woodside Ter. HX3: Hal ... 1K **7 (3B 98)**
HX4: Gree ... 5C **118**
LS4: Leeds ... 4M **67**
Woodside Vw. BD16: Cot ... 8E **44**
HD4: Hud ... 7E **136**
HD9: H'frth ... 4J **169**
HX3: Hal ... 1J **7 (3A 98)**
HX4: Gree ... 5C 118
(off Workhouse La.)
LS4: Leeds ... 3M **67**
LS10: Leeds ... 9G **86**
WF3: Loft ... 4K **105**
WF7: Street ... 6K **127**
Woodsley Fold BD13: Thorn ... 8A **62**
Woodsley Grn. LS6: Leeds ... 2A **4 (4B 68)**
Woodsley Rd. BD10: B'frd ... 9E **46**
LS2: Leeds ... 2A **4 (5A 68)**
LS3: Leeds ... 5A **68**
LS6: Leeds ... 2A **4 (5A 68)**
Woodsley Ter. LS2: Leeds ... 3B **4 (5C 68)**
Woods M. LS29: I'ly ... 5H **15**
Woods Mt. HD7: Mars ... 5H **151**
Woodsome Av. WF14: Mir ... 5J **121**
Woodsome Dr. HD8: Fen B ... 8H **139**
WF14: Mir ... 5K **121**
Woodsome Est. WF17: Bat ... 8D **102**
Woodsome Hall Golf Course ... 9G **138**
Woodsome Hall La. HD8: Kbtn ... 9G **138**
Woodsome Lees HD8: Kbtn ... 1H **155**
Woodsome Lees La.
HD8: Kbtn ... 2G **155**
Woodsome Pk. HD8: Fen B ... 8H **139**
Woodsome Rd. HD4: Farn T ... 3D **154**
HD8: Fen B ... 8E **138**
Wood Sq. HX3: Hal ... 2A **98**
Woods Row LS28: Stan ... 5B **66**
Woods Ter. HD7: Mars ... 5H **151**
Woodstock Cl. LS16: Leeds ... 4N **49**
Woodstock Cres. HD3: Hud ... 2G **137**
Woodstock Wlk. BD5: B'frd ... 8A **6**
(not continuous)
Wood St. BD8: B'frd ... 6A **64**
BD12: Low M ... 7B **82**
BD15: All ... 5H **63**
BD16: Bgly ... 1D **44**
BD17: Bail ... 6A **46**
BD19: Cleck ... 5G **100**
BD20: Stee ... 3C **26**
BD21: Keigh ... 1J **43**
BD22: Haw ... 9C **42**
HD1: Hud ... 4B **8 (4M 137)**
HD3: Hud ... 4E **136**
HD5: Hud ... 4B **138**
HD6: Brigh ... 1N **119**
HD7: Slait ... 9M **135**
HD8: Clay W ... 8G **157**
HD8: Skelm ... 7C **156**
HD9: H'frth ... 2M **169**
HX5: Ell ... 5F **118**
LS18: Hors ... 5F **48**
LS27: Morl ... 8J **85**
OL14: Tod ... 6K **93**
S72: S Hien ... 3M **161**
WF1: Wake ... 4J **9 (5L 125)**
WF3: E Ard ... 4F **104**
WF4: S Comn ... 7J **127**
WF5: Oss ... 3N **123**
WF10: C'frd ... 4C **108**
WF13: Dew ... 2G **122**
WF17: Bat ... 7F **102**
Wood Ter. HD4: Hud ... 7M **137**
Woodthorne Cft. LS17: Leeds ... 3J **51**
WOODTHORPE ... 3N **143**
Woodthorpe BD13: Denh ... 6K **61**
Woodthorpe Cl. WF2: Wake ... 3N **143**
Woodthorpe Dr. WF2: Wake ... 3N **143**
Woodthorpe Gdns. WF2: Wake ... 3M **143**
Woodthorpe Glades WF2: Wake ... 3N **143**
Woodthorpe La. WF2: Wake ... 3M **143**
Woodthorpe Mnr. WF2: Wake ... 4N **143**
Woodthorpe Pk. Dr. WF2: Wake ... 3M **143**
Woodthorpe Ter. HD1: Hud ... 5L **137**
WOOD TOP ... 3J **95**
Wood Top BD18: Ship ... 7B **46**
HD6: Brigh ... 7K **99**
HD7: Mars ... 6F **150**
Wood Top Rd. HX7: Heb B ... 2J **95**
Woodvale Cl. BD4: B'frd ... 9J **65**
Woodvale Cres. BD16: Bgly ... 2F **44**
Woodvale Gro. BD7: B'frd ... 9K **63**
Woodvale Office Pk. HD6: Brigh ... 8N **99**
Woodvale Rd. HD6: Brigh ... 9N **99**
Woodvale Ter. LS18: Hors ... 8G **49**
Woodvale Way BD7: B'frd ... 9K **63**
Wood Vw. BD12: O'haw ... 9E **82**
BD13: Cull ... 9L **43**
BD13: Denh ... 8L **61**
BD17: Bail ... 6M **45**
HD2: Hud ... 1J **137**
(Broombank)
HD2: Hud ... 8B **120**
(Wiggan La.)
HX3: Hal ... 8N **97**
LS27: Chur ... 5N **85**
LS29: I'ly ... 4J **15**
WF10: C'frd ... 4A **108**
Woodview BD8: B'frd ... 3B **64**
BD11: Drig ... 6A **84**
BD13: Denh ... 3J **61**
BD22: Oak ... 3E **42**
Wood Vw. Av. WF10: C'frd ... 4A **108**
Woodview Av. BD17: Bail ... 3D **46**
Wood Vw. Bungs. WF10: C'frd ... 5A **108**
Wood Vw. Cl. WF10: C'frd ... 5A **108**
Woodview Cl. LS18: Hors ... 5F **48**
Woodview Ct. LS14: Leeds ... 2E **70**
Wood Vw. Cres. WF10: C'frd ... 4A **108**
Wood Vw. Dr. BD2: B'frd ... 4G **65**
Wood Vw. Gro. HD6: Brigh ... 8L **99**
Woodview Gro. LS11: Leeds ... 3D **86**
Woodview M. LS14: Leeds ... 1E **70**
Woodview Mt. LS11: Leeds ... 3D **86**
Woodview Pl. LS11: Leeds ... 3D **86**
Woodview Rd. BD22: Oak ... 3F **42**
LS11: Leeds ... 3D **86**
Woodview St. LS11: Leeds ... 3D **86**
Wood Vw. Ter. LS27: Chur ... 5N **85**
WF12: Dew ... 6L **103**
Woodview Ter. BD8: B'frd ... 3B **64**
BD21: Keigh ... 3H 43
(off Hainworth La.)
LS11: Leeds ... 3D **86**
Wood Vs. HX7: Heb B ... 3D **94**
Woodville Av. HD7: Golc ... 6D **136**
LS18: Hors ... 7G **49**
Woodville Ct. LS8: Leeds ... 6K **51**
WF2: Wake ... 9L **125**
Woodville Cres. LS18: Hors ... 6H **49**
Woodville Gro. BD22: Cros R ... 7F **42**
LS10: Leeds ... 4G **86**
LS18: Hors ... 7G **49**
Woodville Mt. LS10: Leeds ... 4G **86**
Woodville Pl. BD9: B'frd ... 2L **63**
HD2: Hud ... 5C **120**
LS18: Hors ... 6H **49**
Woodville Rd. BD20: Keigh ... 8H **27**
WF12: Dew ... 3G **123**
Woodville Sq. LS10: Leeds ... 4G **86**

Woodville St.—Zoar St.

Woodville St. BD18: Ship 7B 46
HX3: Hal 3N 97
LS18: Hors 7H 49
Woodville Ter. BD5: B'frd 7A 6 (9B 64)
BD18: Ship 7B 46
BD22: Cros R 7F 42
(off Gott St.)
LS18: Hors 6G 49
Wood Vine St. LS28: Stan 5N 65
Wood Wlk. S71: Roys 4D 160
Woodward Ct. WF14: Mir 4M 121
Woodway BD16: Cot 8E 44
LS18: Hors 8F 48
Woodway Dr. LS18: Hors 8F 48
Woodworth Gro. BD21: Keigh 4H 43
Wood Yd. Cotts. WF1: W'ton 2C 144
Woolcomb Ct. BD9: B'frd 4N 63
Woolcombers Way BD4: B'frd 9H 65
Woolcroft Dr. HD9: H'frth 2A 170
WOOLDALE 1B 170
Wooldale Cliff Rd. HD9: H'frth 3N 169
(not continuous)
Wooldale Rd. HD9: H'frth 1A 170
Wooler Av. LS11: Leeds 3C 86
Wooler Dr. LS11: Leeds 3C 86
Wooler Gro. LS11: Leeds 3C 86
Wooler Pl. LS11: Leeds 3B 86
Wooler Rd. LS11: Leeds 3B 86
Wooler St. LS11: Leeds 3B 86
Wool Exchange, The
Bradford 4B 6
Wooley Edge La. S75: W Gran 6G 158
Woolford Way WF3: Loft 6M 105
Wool Ga. BD16: Cot 8G 45
WOOLGREAVES 4M 143
Woolgreaves Av. WF2: Wake 4M 143
Woolgreaves Cl. WF2: Wake 3M 143
Woolgreaves Cft. WF2: Wake 4M 143
Woolgreaves Dr. WF2: Wake 4M 143
Woolgreaves Gth. WF2: Wake 4M 143
Wooller Rd. BD12: Low M 8B 82
WOOLLEY 2J 159
Woolley Colliery Rd. S75: Dart 8G 158
Woolley Edge La. WF4: Wool 1F 158
WOOLLEY EDGE SERVICE AREA 9D 142
WOOLLEY GRANGE 6G 158
Woolley Hall Gdns. WF4: Wool 2J 159
Woolley Low Moor La. WF4: Wool 8F 142
Woolley Mill La. WF4: Not 1M 159
Woolley Park 2K 159
Woolley Pk. Gdns. WF4: Wool 2J 159
Woolley Park Golf Course 3K 159
Woolley Vw. WF4: Hol 8H 143
Woollin Av. WF3: W Ard 7A 104
Woollin Cres. WF3: W Ard 6A 104
Woolmarket WF8: Pon 3K 129
Woolpack HX1: Hal 3L 7 (5B 98)
(not continuous)
Woolpacks' Yd. WF1: Wake 4H 9 (5K 125)
Wool Pl. HD8: Skelm 8E 156
Wool Row La. HD8: Shel 4N 155
Woolrow La. HD6: B Bri 6A 100
Woolshops HX1: Hal 4L 7 (5B 98)
Woolstocks La. S75: Caw 5N 173
Wool St. WF16: Heck 9A 102
WF17: Bat 7G 102
Wootton St. BD5: B'frd 1C 82
Worcester Av. LS10: Leeds 9H 87
Worcester Cl. WF3: E Ard 3E 104
Worcester Dr. LS10: Leeds 9H 87
Worcester Gro. HD4: Hud 7N 137
Worcester Pl. BD4: B'frd 1E 82
Worden Gro. BD7: B'frd 1K 81
Wordsworth App. WF8: Pon 1K 129
Wordsworth Ct. LS26: Oul 1D 106
Wordsworth Dr. LS26: Oul 1D 106
WF11: Ferr 8A 110
Wordsworth Gro. WF3: S'ley 7N 105
Wordsworth Ho. *LS29: I'ly 4K 15*
(off Blackthorn Rd.)
Wordsworth Way BD16: Bgly 2F 44
Workhouse La. HX2: Hal 5G 97
HX2: Midg 2B 96
HX4: Gree 5C 118
Workouts Health & Fitness Cen.
Keighley *1G 43*
(off Oakworth Rd.)
Workout Warehouse Health & Fitness Cen.
Halifax 4M 7
Works Skatepark, The 9F 68
World's End LS19: Yead 9N 31
Wormald Lea *BD4: B'frd 2J 83*
(off Kirkwall Dr.)
Wormald Row LS2: Leeds 5F 4 (6E 68)
Wormalds Bldgs. HD1: Hud 1B 8
Wormald St. HD5: Hud 7D 138
WF13: Dew 3F 122
WF15: Liv 9N 101
Wormalds Vw. WF12: Dew 5E 122
Wormald's Yd. HD1: Hud 5C 8
Worrall Rd. WF2: Wake 6J 143
Worrall St. LS27: Morl 1J 103
Worsley Pl. DN6: Skel 7L 165
Worsnop Bldgs. BD12: Wyke 9A 82
Worsnop St. BD12: Low M 7B 82
Worstead Rd. BD22: Cros R 6F 42
Worsted Cl. HX1: Hal 4M 97
Worsted Ho. LS9: Leeds 8K 5
Worth Av. BD21: Keigh 7L 27
Worth Bri. Rd. BD21: Keigh 8L 27
Worthing Head Cl. BD12: Wyke 1B 100
Worthing Head Rd. BD12: Wyke 1A 100
Worthing St. BD12: Wyke 1B 100
Worthington Ct. *BD8: B'frd 6A 64*
(off Worthington St.)
Worthington St. BD8: B'frd 6A 64
Worth Valley Vw. BD22: Oak 5D 42
Worth Vw. BD22: Oak 4E 42
WORTH VILLAGE 8L 27
Worthville Cl. BD21: Keigh 2J 43
Worth Way BD21: Keigh 1J 43
WORTLEY 8M 67
Wortley Hgts. LS12: Leeds 8N 67
Wortley La. LS11: Leeds 8B 68
LS12: Leeds 8B 68
Wortley Moor La. LS12: Leeds 8L 67
Wortley Moor La. Trad. Est. LS12: Leeds 8K 67
Wortley Moor Pde. LS12: Leeds 7K 67
Wortley Moor Rd. LS12: Leeds 7K 67
Wortley Pk. LS12: Leeds 8N 67
Wortley Pl. WF9: Hems 2C 162
Wortley Rd. LS12: Leeds 7K 67
Wortley St. BD16: Bgly 4G 44
Wortley Towers LS12: Leeds 8A 68
WORTS HILL 6J 135
Worts Hill La. HD3: Scam 6H 135
Worts Hill Side HD7: Slait 6J 135
WRAGBY 3A 146
Wragby Cotts. WF4: Wrag 3A 146
WRANGBROOK 2D 164
Wrangbrook La. WF8: Went 3B 164
WF9: S Elm, Upt, Went 3B 164
Wrangbrook Rd. WF9: Upt 1C 164
Wrangthorn Av. LS6: Leeds 1A 4 (3B 68)
Wrangthorn Pl. LS6: Leeds 3B 68
Wrangthorn Ter. LS6: Leeds 3B 68
Wray's Bldgs. WF4: Horb 1C 142
Wrelton Cl. S71: Roys 6C 160
Wren Av. BD7: B'frd 9K 63
Wrenbeck Av. LS21: Otley 7L 17
Wrenbeck Cl. LS21: Otley 7L 17
Wrenbeck Dr. LS21: Otley 7L 17
Wrenbury Av. LS16: Leeds 2G 49
Wrenbury Cres. LS16: Leeds 2G 49
Wrenbury Gro. LS16: Leeds 2H 49
Wren Cft. WF8: Pon 9K 109
Wren Dr. LS27: Morl 1N 103
Wren Gth. WF2: Wake 5M 143
Wren Hill WF17: Bat 4D 102
Wren Nest Rd. HX6: Ripp 7A 116
Wren St. BD21: Keigh 8J 27
BD22: Haw 8D 42
HD1: Hud 5J 137
WRENTHORPE 2H 125
Wrenthorpe La. WF2: Wren 2E 124
Wrenthorpe Rd. WF1: Wake 2H 125
WF2: Wren 1G 125
Wrexhall Rd. WF12: Dew 1H 123
Wrexham Rd. LS29: Burl W 8B 16
Wright Av. BD22: Oak 4D 42
Wrights La. WF11: Wome, Cri S 4J 131
Wright St. BD22: Oak 5D 42
Wrigley HX2: Illing 7L 79
Wrigley Av. BD4: B'frd 4F 82
Wrigley Ct. HD4: Neth 4J 153
Wrigley Hill HX2: Illing 8L 79
Wroe Cres. BD12: Wyke 1A 100
Wroe Pl. BD12: Wyke 1A 100
Wroe St. WF13: Dew 2C 122
Wroe Ter. BD12: Wyke 1A 100
WROSE 9B 46
Wrose Av. BD2: B'frd 1E 64
BD18: Ship 9B 46
Wrose Brow Rd. BD18: Ship 7B 46
Wrosecliffe Gro. BD10: B'frd 7D 46
Wrose Dr. BD18: Ship 9B 46
Wrose Gro. BD2: B'frd 9D 46
BD18: Ship 9B 46
Wrose Hill Pl. BD2: B'frd 1B 64
Wrose Mt. BD18: Ship 9C 46
Wrose Rd. BD2: B'frd 9D 46
BD18: Ship 9B 46
Wrose Vw. BD17: Bail 3A 46
BD18: Ship 9B 46
Wycliffe Cl. LS13: Leeds 1A 66
Wycliffe Dr. LS17: Leeds 5F 50
Wycliffe Gdns. BD18: Ship 7M 45
Wycliffe Rd. BD18: Ship 7M 45
LS13: Leeds 1A 66
Wycliffe St. WF5: Oss 4M 123
Wycoller Rd. BD12: Wyke 9A 82
Wycombe Grn. BD4: B'frd 2J 83
WYKE 1A 100
Wykebeck Av. LS9: Leeds 7M 69
Wykebeck Cres. LS9: Leeds 6M 69
Wykebeck Gdns. LS9: Leeds 6M 69
Wykebeck Gro. LS9: Leeds 6M 69
Wykebeck Mt. LS9: Leeds 7M 69
Wykebeck Pl. LS9: Leeds 6N 69
Wykebeck Rd. LS9: Leeds 6M 69
Wykebeck Sq. LS9: Leeds 6M 69
Wykebeck St. LS9: Leeds 6M 69
Wykebeck Ter. LS9: Leeds 6M 69
Wykebeck Valley Rd. LS9: Leeds 4M 69
Wykebeck Vw. LS9: Leeds 6M 69
Wyke Bottoms BD12: O'haw 9D 82
WYKE COMMON 2B 100
Wyke Cres. BD12: Wyke 2B 100
Wyke La. BD12: O'haw, Wyke 2A 100
Wykelea Cl. BD12: Wyke 1B 100
Wyke Old La. HD6: B Bri 5N 99
Wyncliffe Ct. LS17: Leeds 5E 50
Wyncliffe Gdns. LS17: Leeds 5F 50
Wyncroft Ct. LS15: Bar E 9M 53
Wyncroft Gro. LS16: B'hpe 6J 33
Wyncroft Ri. BD18: Ship 1B 64
Wyndham Av. BD2: B'frd 3D 64
Wyndy Ridge BD13: Thorn 7B 62
Wynford Av. LS16: Leeds 6L 49
Wynford Dr. WF9: S Elm 6N 163
Wynford Gro. LS16: Leeds 6L 49
Wynford Mt. LS16: Leeds 6K 49
Wynford Ri. LS16: Leeds 6K 49
Wynford Ter. LS16: Leeds 6K 49
Wynford Way BD12: Low M 5C 82
Wynmore Av. LS16: B'hpe 6H 33
Wynmore Cres. LS16: B'hpe 6J 33
Wynmore Dr. HD3: Hud 1E 136
LS16: B'hpe 6J 33
Wynne St. BD1: B'frd 6B 64
Wynthorpe Rd. WF4: Horb 1D 142
Wynyard Dr. LS27: Morl 9J 85
Wyre Cl. BD6: B'frd 4K 81
Wytehill Chase HX3: North 9F 80
Wyther Av. LS5: Leeds 3J 67
Wyther Dr. LS5: Leeds 3K 67
Wyther Grn. LS5: Leeds 3K 67
Wyther La. LS5: Leeds 3J 67
Wyther La. Ind. Est. LS5: Leeds 3K 67
Wyther Pk. Av. LS12: Leeds 5J 67
Wyther Pk. Cl. LS12: Leeds 5J 67
Wyther Pk. Cres. LS12: Leeds 5J 67
Wyther Pk. Gro. LS12: Leeds 4J 67
Wyther Pk. Hill LS12: Leeds 4J 67
Wyther Pk. Mt. LS12: Leeds 5J 67
Wyther Pk. Pl. LS12: Leeds 4J 67
Wyther Pk. Rd. LS12: Leeds 5H 67
Wyther Pk. Sq. LS12: Leeds 4H 67
Wyther Pk. St. LS12: Leeds 5J 67
Wyther Pk. Ter. LS12: Leeds 5J 67
Wyther Pk. Vw. LS12: Leeds 4J 67
Wyvern Av. HD3: Hud 4H 137
Wyvern Cl. BD7: B'frd 9L 63
WF17: Bat 6F 102
Wyverne Rd. HD7: Golc 6D 136
Wyvern Pl. HX2: Hal 4L 97
Wyvern Ter. HX2: Hal 4L 97
Wyvil Cres. LS29: I'ly 5K 15
Wyvil Rd. LS29: I'ly 4K 15

X

Xscape 8F 108

Y

Yarborough Cft. HX3: North 9F 80
Yardley Way BD12: Low M 7C 82
Yard No. 1 WF17: Bat 8E 102
Yard No. 4 WF16: Heck 8C 102
WF17: Bat 4C 102
Yarn Cl. HX1: Hal 4M 97
Yarn Cft. HD6: B Bri 5A 100
Yarn St. LS10: Leeds 9G 69
Yarra Ct. LS27: Gil 6G 85
Yarwood Gro. BD7: B'frd 2K 81
Yateholm Dr. BD6: B'frd 4H 81
Yate La. BD22: Oxen 4C 60
Yates Flat BD18: Ship 9B 46
Yates La. HD3: Hud 6G 136
YEADON 9N 31
Yeadon Airport Ind. Est. LS19: Yead 7B 32
Yeadon Dr. HX3: Sou 8F 98
Yeadon Moor Rd. LS19: Yead 1B 48
(Bayton La.)
LS19: Yead 8D 32
(Scotland La.)
Yeadon Row *LS18: Hors 8F 48*
(off Regent Av.)
Yeadon Stoops *LS19: Yead 1A 48*
(off Bayton La.)
Ye Farre Cl. HD6: Brigh 8M 99
Yeoman Ct. BD6: B'frd 3H 81
Yewbank Cl. LS29: I'ly 5F 14
Yewbank Ter. LS29: I'ly 5F 14
Yew Cft. *LS29: I'ly 5F 14*
(off Westville Rd.)
Yewdall Rd. LS13: Leeds 1A 66
Yewdall Way BD10: B'frd 9G 47
Yew Grn. Av. HD4: Hud 7K 137
Yew Grn. Rd. HD4: Hud 7K 137
Yew Gro. HD4: Hud 7E 136
Yew La. LS25: Gar 8B 72
Yew Pk. HD6: Brigh 7K 99
YEWS GREEN 2D 80
Yews Hill Rd. HD1: Hud 6K 137
HD4: Hud 6K 137
Yews Mt. HD1: Hud 6L 137
Yew St. HD2: Hud 1M 137
Yew Tree HD7: Slait 2M 151
Yew Tree Av. BD8: B'frd 5J 63
Yew Tree Cl. BD18: Ship 9B 46
Yew Tree Cotts. HX2: Midg 3C 96
Yew Tree Ct. LS17: Leeds 4C 50
OL14: W'den 3J 113
Yew Tree Ct. *WF15: Liv 7L 101*
(off Carr St.)
Yew Tree Cres. BD8: B'frd 5K 63
Yew Tree Cft. HX2: Midg 3C 96
Yew Tree Dr. LS26: W'frd 7F 88
Yew Tree Gro. BD8: B'frd 5K 63
Yew Tree La. BD15: All 6C 62
HD4: Hud 7E 136
HD7: Slait 1M 151
HD9: Holm 5H 169
LS15: Leeds 7F 70
Yew Tree Rd. HD2: Hud 9F 118
HD3: Hud 9F 118
HD8: Shep 8K 155
Yew Trees HX3: Sou 8F 98
Yew Trees Av. HX3: North 1F 98
Yew Tree St. WF1: Wake 7A 126
Yew Tree Ter. OL12: Whit 5A 112
Yew Tree Wlk. WF11: Knot 1D 130
York Av. HD2: Hud 9M 119
York Cl. WF9: S Elm 5N 163
York Ct. WF17: Bat 6F 102
York Cres. BD16: Bgly 5F 44
York Dr. WF16: Heck 6A 102
WF17: Bat 6G 102
York Ga. LS21: Otley 3J 31
York Gate Garden 2N 49
York Gro. WF14: Mir 6K 121
WF17: Bat 6G 102
York Ho. BD10: B'frd 8G 47
HD1: Hud 5C 8
(off Oldgate)
HX5: Ell 4E 118
(off Westgate)
HX6: Sow B 8J 97
(off Beech Rd.)
LS28: Fars 4A 66
(off Cotefields Av.)
York Pl. BD19: Cleck 4H 101
LS1: Leeds 6D 4 (6D 68)
LS22: Weth 3M 23
OL14: Tod 7K 93
(off Bond St.)
WF7: Ackw 3H 147
York Rd. DN6: Skel 7K 165
LS9: Leeds 6L 5 (6G 69)
(not continuous)
LS14: Leeds 5N 69
LS15: Leeds, T'ner 9D 52
LS22: Weth 3N 23
LS25: Bur S 1C 110
LS29: Burl W 8D 16
WF12: Dew 2J 123
WF14: Mir 6K 121
WF17: Bat 6F 102
York Rd. Ind. Est. LS22: Weth 3N 23
Yorkshire County Cricket Club 2N 67
Yorkshire Dales National Pk. 2M 11
Yorkshire Dr. BD5: B'frd 4E 82
Yorkshire Indoor Cricket Centre, The 2N 67
Yorkshire Mill WF17: Bat 7G 103
Yorkshire Sculpture Pk. 2A 158
Yorkshire Sculpture Pk. Vis. Cen. 2B 158
Yorkshire Technology Pk. HD4: Arm B 1K 153
Yorkshire Way BD7: B'frd 2N 81
Yorkstone HD4: Hud 7G 136
York St. BD8: B'frd 7K 63
BD13: Que 4C 80
BD16: Bgly 5F 44
HD6: Ras 2M 119
(off Thomas St.)
HD6: Ras 2M 119
(Capel St.)
HX1: Hal 5J 7 (6A 98)
HX7: Heb B 2H 95
LS2: Leeds 7H 5 (7F 68)
LS9: Leeds 7H 5 (7F 68)
OL14: Tod 6K 93
WF6: Alt 9G 106
WF9: Hems 4E 162
WF10: C'frd 4D 108
York Ter. HX3: Hal 3A 98
LS29: Burl W 8D 16
York Towers LS9: Leeds 6J 69
York Towers Pde. *LS9: Leeds 6J 69*
(off York Towers)
York Vs. WF6: Norm 1J 127
Young's Ct. LS25: Aber 9E 54
Young St. BD8: B'frd 6L 63
Young St. Ind. Est. BD8: B'frd 6L 63

Z

Zara Sports Centre, The 2J 63
Zealand St. BD4: B'frd 1H 83
Zermatt Gro. LS7: Leeds 9E 50
Zermatt Mt. LS7: Leeds 9E 50
Zermatt St. LS7: Leeds 9F 50
Zermatt Ter. LS7: Leeds 9F 50
Zetland Pl. LS8: Leeds 3H 69
Zetland St. HD1: Hud 6C 8 (4N 137)
WF1: Wake 4K 9 (5L 125)
Zion Cl. HD3: Hud 1G 137
Zion Dr. S75: Map 8K 159
Zion St. WF5: Oss 2M 123
Zion Ter. HX7: Heb B 1H 95
HX7: Myth 3M 95
Zoar St. LS27: Morl 9K 85

HOSPITALS, HOSPICES and selected HEALTHCARE FACILITIES covered by this atlas.

N.B. Where it is not possible to name these facilities on the map,
the reference given is for the road in which they are situated.

AIREDALE GENERAL HOSPITAL 2A **26**
Skipton Road
Steeton
KEIGHLEY
BD20 6TD
Tel: 01535 652511

BIERLEY CYGNET HOSPITAL 4F **82**
Bierley Lane
BRADFORD
BD4 6AD
Tel: 01274 686767

BRADFORD ROYAL INFIRMARY 5K **63**
Duckworth Lane
BRADFORD
BD9 6RJ
Tel: 01274 542200

CALDERDALE ROYAL HOSPITAL 9C **98**
Huddersfield Road
Salterhebble
HALIFAX
HX3 0PW
Tel: 01422 357171

CASTLEFORD, NORMANTON & DISTRICT HOSPITAL
. . . . .6B **108**
Lumley Street
CASTLEFORD
WF10 5LT
Tel: 01977 605500

CHAPEL ALLERTON HOSPITAL 1G **68**
Chapeltown Road
LEEDS
LS7 4SA
Tel: 0113 2623404

CORONATION HOSPITAL (ILKLEY) 6H **15**
Springs Lane
ILKLEY
LS29 8TG
Tel: 01943 609666

DEWSBURY & DISTRICT HOSPITAL 1D **122**
Halifax Road
DEWSBURY
WF13 4HS
Tel: 0844 8118110

ECCLESHILL COMMUNITY HOSPITAL 1H **65**
Harrogate Road
BRADFORD
BD10 0JE
Tel: 01274 323200

ECCLESHILL NHS TREATMENT CENTRE 1J **65**
Harrogate Road
BRADFORD
BD10 0EP
Tel: 01274 623000

ELLAND SPIRE HOSPITAL 4F **118**
Elland Lane
ELLAND
HX5 9EB
Tel: 01422 324000

FIELDHEAD HOSPITAL .2L **125**
Ouchthorpe Lane
WAKEFIELD
WF1 3SP
Tel: 01924 327000

HOLME VALLEY MEMORIAL HOSPITAL 1M **169**
Huddersfield Road
HUDDERSFIELD
HD9 3TS
Tel: 01484 345627

HUDDERSFIELD BMI HOSPITAL 1K **137**
Birkby Hall Road
HUDDERSFIELD
HD2 2BL
Tel: 01484 533131

HUDDERSFIELD ROYAL INFIRMARY 2H **137**
Acre Street
HUDDERSFIELD
HD3 3EA
Tel: 01484 342000

KIRKWOOD HOSPICE .3E **138**
21 Albany Road
Dalton
HUDDERSFIELD
HD5 9UY
Tel: 01484 557900

LEEDS CHILDREN'S INFIRMARY 4C **4**
Leeds General Infirmary
Clarendon Wing, Great George Street
LEEDS
LS1 3EX
Tel: 0113 2432799

LEEDS DENTAL INSTITUTE 4C **4** (5C **68**)
Clarendon Way
LEEDS
LS2 9LU
Tel: 0113 2440111

LEEDS GENERAL INFIRMARY 4D **4** (5D **68**)
Great George Street
LEEDS
LS1 3EX
Tel: 0113 2432799

LEEDS NUFFIELD HEALTH HOSPITAL . . .5C **4** (6C **68**)
2 Leighton Street
LEEDS
LS1 3EB
Tel: 0113 507543

LEEDS SPIRE HOSPITAL 8J **51**
Jackson Avenue
LEEDS
LS8 1NT
Tel: 0113 2693939

LONGLANDS CLASSIC CONSULTING ROOMS
. . . . .9D **102**
Cullingworth Street
DEWSBURY
WF13 4AN
Tel: 01924 410610

LYNFIELD MOUNT HOSPITAL 4J **63**
Heights Lane
BRADFORD
BD9 6DP
Tel: 01274 494194

MALHAM HOUSE DAY HOSPITAL 4B **4** (5C **68**)
25 Hyde Terrace
LEEDS
LS2 9LN
Tel: 0113 3055000

MANORLANDS (SUE RYDER) HOSPICE 3C **60**
Keighley Road
Oxenhope
KEIGHLEY
BD22 9HJ
Tel: 01535 642308

MARIE CURIE HOSPICE (BRADFORD) 7F **64**
Maudsley Street
BRADFORD
BD3 9LE
Tel: 01274 337000

MARTIN HOUSE CHILDREN'S HOSPICE 1E **38**
Grove Road
Boston Spa
WETHERBY
LS23 6TX
Tel: 01937 845045

METHLEY PARK SPIRE HOSPITAL 1H **107**
Methley Lane
Methley
LEEDS
LS26 9HG
Tel: 01977 518518

NHS WALK-IN CENTRE (HALIFAX) 5A **98**
within Horne St. Health Centre
Horne Street
HALIFAX
HX1 5UA
Tel: 01422 399858

NHS WALK-IN CENTRE
(LEEDS GENERAL INFIRMARY) 4D **4**
Great George Street
LEEDS
LS1 3EX
Tel: 0113 2432799

NHS WALK-IN CENTRE (NORTH KIRKLEES)
. . . . .1D **122**
Dewsbury & District Hospital
Halifax Road
DEWSBURY
WF13 4HS
Tel: 01924 816200

NHS WALK-IN CENTRE (SHAKESPEARE) 5G **69**
Cromwell Mount .
LEEDS
LS9 7TA
Tel: 0113 2951132

NHS WALK-IN CENTRE (TODMORDEN) 7L **93**
82 Halifax Road
Lwr. George Street
TODMORDEN
OL14 5QJ
Tel: 01706 811106

NHS WALK-IN CENTRE (WAKEFIELD) 4H **9**
47 King Street
WAKEFIELD
WF1 2SY
Tel: 0845 1211023

OVERGATE HOSPICE 5C **118**
30 Hullenedge Road
ELLAND
HX5 0QY
Tel: 01422 379151

PINDERFIELDS HOSPITAL 3M **125**
Aberford Road
WAKEFIELD
WF1 4DG
Tel: 0844 8118110

PONTEFRACT GENERAL INFIRMARY 3K **129**
Friarwood Lane
PONTEFRACT
WF8 1PL
Tel: 08448 118110

PRINCE OF WALES HOSPICE 3G **129**
Halfpenny Lane
PONTEFRACT
WF8 4BG
Tel: 01977 708868

ST GEMMA'S HOSPICE .6F **50**
329 Harrogate Road
LEEDS
LS17 6QD
Tel: 0113 2185500

ST JAMES'S UNIVERSITY HOSPITAL . . .2M **5** (4H **69**)
Beckett Street
LEEDS
LS9 7TF
Tel: 0113 2433144

ST LUKE'S HOSPITAL (BRADFORD) 8A **6** (1B **82**)
Little Horton Lane
BRADFORD
BD5 0NA
Tel: 01274 734744

ST MARY'S HOSPITAL 6J **67**
Green Hill Road
LEEDS
LS12 3QE
Tel: 0113 2790121

SEACROFT HOSPITAL 5B **70**
York Road
LEEDS
LS14 6UH
Tel: 0113 2648164

SHIPLEY HOSPITAL 8M **45**
98 Kirkgate
SHIPLEY
BD18 3LT
Tel: 01274 773390

WAKEFIELD HOSPICE .2N **125**
Aberford Road
WAKEFIELD
WF1 4TS
Tel: 01924 213900

WESTBOURNE GREEN
COMMUNITY HEALTH CARE CENTRE 4N **63**
50 Heaton Road
BRADFORD
BD8 8RA
Tel: 01274 202485

WESTWOOD PARK DIAGNOSTIC
TREATMENT CENTRE 4H **81**
Swift Drive
Cooper Lane
BRADFORD
BD6 3NL
Tel: 01274 425990

WHARFEDALE HOSPITAL 7K **17**
Newall Carr Road
OTLEY
LS21 2LY
Tel: 01943 465522

WHEATFIELDS SUE RYDER HOSPICE 1A **68**
Grove Road
Headingley
LEEDS
LS6 2AE
Tel: 0113 2787249

WYKE CYGNET HOSPITAL 4N **99**
Huddersfield Road
Wyke
BRADFORD
BD12 8LR
Tel: 01274 605500

YORKSHIRE CLINIC, THE 8H **45**
Bradford Road
BINGLEY
BD16 1TW
Tel: 01274 550600

YORKSHIRE EYE HOSPITAL 8J **47**
937 Harrogate Road
Apperley Bridge
BRADFORD
BD10 0RD
Tel: 0800 3580825

SAFETY CAMERA INFORMATION

PocketGPSWorld.com's CamerAlert is a self-contained speed and red light camera warning system for
SatNavs and Android or Apple iOS smartphones/tablets. Visit www.cameralert.co.uk to download.

Safety camera locations are publicised by the Safer Roads Partnership which operates them in order to encourage drivers to comply
with speed limits at these sites. It is the driver's absolute responsibility to be aware of and to adhere to speed limits at all times.

By showing this safety camera information it is the intention of Geographers' A-Z Map Company Ltd., to encourage
safe driving and greater awareness of speed limits and vehicle speed. Data accurate at time of printing.

Printed and bound in the United Kingdom by Polestar Wheatons Ltd., Exeter.